The World Price of Oil
(2001 U.S. dollars per barrel)

First OPEC oil shock, 1974

Second OPEC oil shock, 1979–80

Collapse of OPEC, 1986

Iraq's invasion of Kuwait, 1990

U.S. invasion of Iraq, 2003

Dollars Per Barrel (2001 U.S. dollars)

Year

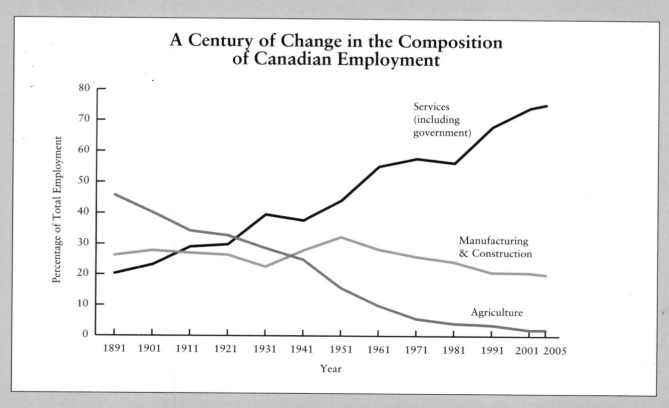

A Century of Change in the Composition
of Canadian Employment

Services (including government)

Manufacturing & Construction

Agriculture

Percentage of Total Employment

Year

Christopher T.S. Ragan | Richard G. Lipsey

McGill University

Professor Emeritus,
Simon Fraser University

**Twelfth
Canadian
Edition**

ECONOMICS

PEARSON

Addison
Wesley

Toronto

Library and Archives Canada Cataloguing in Publication

Ragan, Christopher
    Economics/Christopher T. S. Ragan, Richard G. Lipsey. —12th Canadian ed.

Includes index.

Authors' names in reverse order on Canadian 10th ed.
ISBN-13: 978-0-321-31489-5
ISBN-10: 0-321-31489-1

1. Economics—Textbooks. I. Lipsey, Richard G., 1928– . II. Title.

HB171.5.R35 2008   330   C2006-904886-X

ISBN-13: 978-0-321-31489-5
ISBN-10: 0-321-31489-1

Editor-in-Chief: Gary Bennett
Marketing Manager: Eileen Lasswell
Developmental Editor: Maurice Esses
Production Editor: Marisa D'Andrea
Copy Editor: Ann McInnis
Proofreader: Catharine Haggert
Production Coordinator: Andrea Falkenberg
Indexer: Belle Wong
Photo and Permissions Researcher: Mary Rose MacLachlan
Compositor: Nelson Gonzalez
Art Director: Julia Hall
Interior and Cover Design: Opus House Inc/Sonya Thursby
Cover Image: Getty Images/David Gould

2 3 4 5   12 11 10 09 08

Printed and bound in the United States.

PEARSON

Addison
Wesley

Brief Contents

Contents

List of Boxes

Additional Topics
on MyEconLab
(www.myeconlab.com)

To the Instructor

Economics is a living discipline, changing and evolving in response to developments in the world economy and in response to the research of many thousands of economists throughout the world. Through twelve editions, *Economics* has evolved with the discipline. Our purpose in this edition, as in the previous eleven, is to provide students with an introduction to the major issues facing the world's economies, to the methods that economists use to study those issues, and to the policy problems that those issues create. Our treatment is everywhere guided by three important principles:

1. Economics is *scientific,* in the sense that it progresses through the systematic confrontation of theory by evidence. Neither theory nor data alone can tell us much about the world, but combined they tell us a great deal.

2. Economics is *useful* and it should be seen by students to be so. An understanding of economic theory combined with knowledge about the economy produces many important insights about economic policy. Although we stress these insights, we are also careful to point out cases where too little is known to support strong statements about public policy. Appreciating what is not known is as important as learning what is known.

3. We strive always to be *honest* with our readers. Although we know that economics is not always easy, we do not approve of glossing over difficult bits of analysis without letting readers see what is happening and what has been assumed. We take whatever space is needed to explain why economists draw their conclusions, rather than just asserting the conclusions. We also take pains to avoid simplifying matters so much that students would have to unlearn what they have been taught if they continue their study beyond the introductory course. In short, we have tried to follow Albert Einstein's advice:

Everything should be made as simple as possible, but not simpler.

CURRENT ECONOMIC ISSUES

In writing the twelfth edition of *Economics*, we have tried to reflect the major economic issues that we face in the early twenty-first century.

Living Standards and Economic Growth

One of the most fundamental economic issues is the determination of overall living standards. Adam Smith wondered why some countries become wealthy while others remain poor. Though we have learned much about this topic in the past 230 years since Adam Smith's landmark work, economists recognize that there is still much we do not know.

The importance of technological change in determining increases in overall living standards is a theme that permeates both the microeconomics and macroeconomics halves of this book. Chapter 8 explores how firms deal with technological change at the micro level, and how changes in their economic environment lead them to create new products and new production processes. Chapters 11 and 12 discuss how imperfectly competitive firms often compete through their innovative practices, and the importance for policymakers of designing competition policy to keep these practices as energetic as possible.

Technological change also plays a central role in our discussions of long-run economic growth in Chapters 25 and 26. We explore the traditional channels of saving, investment, and population growth, but also the more recent economic theories that emphasize the importance of increasing returns and endogenous growth.

We are convinced that no other introductory economics textbook places as much emphasis on technological change and economic growth as we do in this book. Given the importance of continuing growth in living standards and understanding where that growth comes from, we believe this emphasis is appropriate. We hope you agree.

Globalization

Enormous changes have occurred throughout the world over the last few decades. Flows of trade and investment between countries have risen so dramatically that it is now common to speak of the "globalization" of the world economy. Today it is no longer possible to study any economy without taking into account developments in the rest of the world.

Throughout its history, Canada has been a trading nation, and our policies relating to international trade have often been at the centre of political debates. International trade shows up in many parts of this textbook, but it is the focus of two chapters. Chapter 33 discusses the theory of the gains from trade; Chapter 34 explores trade policy, with an emphasis on NAFTA and the WTO and its current Doha round of negotiations.

For some time, many Canadians have been worried about a possible "brain drain" to the United States. The fear is that Canada's "best and brightest" are leaving in increasing numbers, in pursuit of greater employment prospects, lower income taxes, and higher living standards available south of the border. How mobile is labour across international borders? Does such labour mobility imply that Canada's policies cannot diverge significantly from those in other countries? We explore these issues at various points throughout the book, especially in Chapters 13, 14, and 18.

With globalization and the international trade of goods and assets come fluctuations in exchange rates. In recent years there have been substantial changes in the Canada–U.S. exchange rate; a 15-percent depreciation followed the Asian economic crisis in 1997–1998, but an even greater appreciation occurred in the 2002–2006 period. Such volatility in exchange rates complicates the conduct of economic policy. In Chapters 28 and 29 we explore how the exchange rate fits into the design and operation of Canada's monetary policy. In Chapter 35 we examine the debate between fixed and flexible exchange rates.

The forces of globalization are with us to stay. In this twelfth edition of *Economics*, we have done our best to ensure that students are made aware of the world outside Canada and of how events elsewhere in the world affect the Canadian economy.

The Role of Government

The political winds appear to have shifted in Canada, the United States, and many other countries over the past two decades. Political parties that once advocated a greater role for government in the economy now argue the benefits of proscribed government. But has the fundamental role of government really changed? In order to understand the role of government in the economy, students must understand the benefits of free markets as well as the situations that cause markets to fail. They must also understand that governments often intervene in the economy for reasons related more to equity than to efficiency.

In this twelfth edition of *Economics*, we continue to incorporate the discussion of government policy as often as possible. Here are but a few of the many examples that we explore:

- tax incidence (in Chapter 4)
- the effects of minimum wages and rent controls (in Chapter 5)
- economic regulation and competition policy (in Chapter 12)
- pay equity policy (in Chapter 13)
- environmental policies (in Chapter 17)
- the disincentive effects of income taxes (in Chapter 18)
- fiscal policy (in Chapters 22 and 24)
- policies related to the economy's long-run growth rate (in Chapter 26)
- monetary policy (in Chapters 28, 29, and 30)
- policies that affect the economy's long-run unemployment rate (in Chapter 31)
- the importance of debt and deficits (in Chapter 32)
- trade policies (in Chapter 34)
- policies related to the exchange rate (in Chapter 35)

THE BOOK

Economic growth, globalization, and the role of government are pressing issues of the day. Much of our study of economic principles and the Canadian economy has been shaped by these issues. In addition to specific coverage of growth and internationally oriented topics, growth and globalization appear naturally throughout the book in the treatment of many topics once thought to be entirely "domestic."

Most chapters of *Economics* contain some discussion of economic policy. We have two main goals in mind when we present these discussions:

1. We aim to give students practice in using economic theory, because applying theory is both a wonderfully effective teaching method and a reliable test of students' grasp of theory.

2. We want to introduce students to the major policy issues of the day and to let them discover that few policy debates are as "black and white" as they often appear in the press.

Both goals reflect our view that students should see economics as useful in helping us to understand and deal with the world around us.

The choice of whether to study macro first or micro first is partly a personal one that cannot be decided solely by objective criteria. We believe that there are excellent reasons for preferring the micro–macro order, and we have organized the book accordingly. For those who prefer the macro–micro order, we have attempted to make reversibility easy. The first four chapters provide a solid foundation for first studying either microeconomics (Chapters 5–18) or macroeconomics (Chapters 19–35).

Microeconomics: Structure and Coverage

To open Part 1, Chapter 1 presents the market as an instrument of coordination. We introduce the issues of scarcity and choice and then briefly discuss alternative economic systems. The problems of converting command economies to market economies will be with us for some time, and comparisons with command economies help to establish what a market economy is *by showing what it is not*. Chapter 2 makes the important distinction between positive and normative inquiries and goes on to an introductory discussion of the construction and testing of economic theories. We also discuss graphing in detail.

Part 2 deals with demand and supply. After introducing price determination and elasticity in Chapters 3 and 4, we apply these tools in Chapter 5. The case studies are designed to provide practice in applying the tools rather than a full coverage of each case. Chapter 5 also has an intuitive and thorough treatment of economic value and market efficiency.

Part 3 presents the foundations of demand and supply. The theory of consumer behaviour is developed via marginal utility theory in Chapter 6, which also provides an introduction to consumer surplus and an intuitive discussion of income and substitution effects. The Appendix to Chapter 6 covers indifference curves, budget lines, and the derivation of demand curves using indifference theory. Chapter 7 introduces the firm as an institution and develops short-run costs. Chapter 8 covers long-run costs and the principle of substitution, and goes on to consider shifts in cost curves due to technological change. The latter topic is seldom, if ever, covered in the micro part of elementary textbooks, yet applied work on firms' responses to changing economic signals shows it to be extremely important.

The first two chapters of Part 4, Chapters 9 and 10, present the standard theories of perfect competition and monopoly with a thorough discussion of price discrimination and some treatment of international cartels. Chapter 11 deals with monopolistic competition and oligopoly, which are the market structures most commonly found in Canadian industries. Strategic behaviour plays a central part in the analysis of this chapter. The first half of Chapter 12 deals with the efficiency of competition and the inefficiency of monopoly. The last half of the chapter deals with regulation and competition policy.

Part 5 begins in Chapter 13 by discussing the general principles of factor pricing and how factor prices are influenced by factor mobility. Chapter 14 then examines the operation of labour markets, addressing issues such as wage differentials, discrimination, labour unions, and the "good jobs–bad jobs" debate. Chapter 15 discusses investment in physical capital, the role of the interest rate, and the overall functioning of capital markets.

The first chapter of Part 6 (Chapter 16) provides a general discussion of market success and market failure, and outlines the arguments for and against government intervention in a market economy. Chapter 17 deals with environmental regulation, with a detailed discussion of market-based policies. Chapter 18 analyzes taxes, public expenditure, and the main elements of Canadian social policy. These three chapters expand on the basics of microeconomic analysis by providing current illustrations of the relevance of economic theory to contemporary policy situations.

Macroeconomics: Structure and Coverage

Our treatment of macroeconomics is divided into six parts. We make a clear distinction between the economy in the short run and the economy in the long run, and we get quickly to the material on long-run economic growth. Students are confronted with issues of long-run economic growth *before* they are introduced to issues of money and banking. Given the importance of economic growth in driving overall living standards, we feel this is an appropriate ordering of the material; but for those who prefer to discuss money before thinking about economic growth, the ordering can be easily switched without any loss of continuity.

The first macro chapter, Chapter 19, introduces readers to the central macro variables, what they mean, and why they are important. The discussion of national income accounting in Chapter 20 provides a thorough treatment of the distinction between real and nominal GDP, the distinction between GDP and GNP, and a discussion of what measures of national income *do not measure*.

Part 8 develops the core short-run model of the macro economy, beginning with the fixed-price (Keynesian Cross) model in Chapters 21 and 22 and then moving on to the *AD/AS* model in Chapter 23. Chapter 21 uses a closed economy model with no government to explain the process of national-income determination and the nature of the multiplier. Chapter 22 extends the setting to include international trade and government spending and taxation. Chapter 23 rounds out our discussion of the short run with the *AD/AS* framework, discussing the importance of both aggregate demand and aggregate supply shocks. We place the Keynesian Cross before the *AD/AS* model to show that there is no mystery as to where the *AD* curve comes from and why it is downward sloping; the *AD* curve is derived directly from the Keynesian Cross model. In contrast, books that begin their analysis with the *AD/AS* model are inevitably less clear about where the model comes from. We lament the growing tendency to omit the Keynesian Cross from introductory macroeconomics textbooks; we believe the model has much to offer students in terms of economic insights.

Part 9 begins in Chapter 24 by showing how the short-run model evolves toward the long run through the adjustment of factor prices—what we often call the Phillips curve. We introduce potential output as an "anchor" to which real GDP returns following *AD* or *AS* shocks. This chapter also addresses issues in fiscal policy, including the important distinction between automatic stabilizers and discretionary fiscal stabilization policy. Chapter 25 is a short chapter that contrasts short-run with long-run macroeconomics, emphasizing the different typical causes of output changes over the two time spans. Using Canadian data, we show that long-run changes in GDP have their root causes in changes in factor supplies and productivity, whereas short-run changes in GDP are more closely associated with changes in the factor utilization rate. With this short-run/long-run distinction firmly in place, we are well positioned for the detailed discussion of long-run economic growth that appears in Chapter 26. Our treatment of long-run growth, which we regard as one of the most important issues facing Canada and the world today, goes well beyond the treatment in most introductory texts.

Part 10 focuses on the role of money and financial systems. Chapter 27 discusses the nature of money, various components of the money supply, the commercial banking system, and the Bank of Canada. In Chapter 28 we review the determinants of the demand for money. We then turn to a detailed discussion of the link between the money supply and other economic variables such as interest rates, the exchange rate, national income, and the price level. This chapter builds directly on the material in Chapters 23 and 24, with an emphasis on the distinction between short-run and long-run effects. In Chapter 29 we discuss the Bank of Canada's monetary policy, including a detailed discussion of inflation targeting. The chapter ends with a review of Canadian monetary policy over the past 30 years. This provides some important historical context for policy discussions later in the book, as well as an opportunity to draw some general conclusions about the operation of monetary policy.

Part 11 deals with some of today's most pressing macroeconomic policy issues. It contains separate chapters on inflation, unemployment, and government budget deficits. Chapter 30 on inflation examines the central role of expectations in determining inflation, and the importance of credibility on the part of the central bank. Chapter 31 on unemployment examines the determinants of frictional and structural unemployment and discusses likely reasons for increases in the NAIRU over the past few decades. Chapter 32 on budget deficits stresses the effect of deficits on long-term economic growth.

Virtually every macroeconomic chapter contains at least some discussion of international issues. However, the final part of *Economics* focuses primarily on international economics. Chapter 33 gives the basic treatment of international trade, developing both the traditional theory of static comparative advantage and newer theories based on imperfect competition and dynamic comparative advantage. Chapter 34 discusses both the positive and normative aspects of trade policy, as well as the WTO and NAFTA. Chapter 35 introduces the balance of payments and examines exchange-rate determination. Here we also discuss three important policy issues: the desirability of current-account deficits or surpluses, whether there is a "right" value for the Canadian exchange rate, and the costs and benefits of Canada's adopting a fixed exchange rate.

We hope you find this menu both attractive and challenging; we hope students find the material stimulating and enlightening. Many of the messages of economics are complex—if economic understanding were only a matter of common sense and simple observation, there would be no need for professional economists and no need for textbooks like this one. To understand economics, one must work hard. Working at this book should help readers gain a better understanding of the world around them and of the policy problems faced by all levels of government. Furthermore, in today's globalized world, the return to education is large. We like to think that we have contributed in some small part to the understanding that increased investment in human capital by the next generation is necessary to restore incomes to the rapid growth paths that so benefited our parents and our peers. Perhaps we may even contribute to some income-enhancing accumulation of human capital by some of our readers.

▌SUBSTANTIVE CHANGES TO THIS EDITION

We have done a major revision and update of the entire text with guidance from an extensive series of formal reviews and other feedback from both users and nonusers of the previous editions of this book. As always, we have strived very hard to improve the teachability and readability of the book. We have focused the discussions so that the major point is emphasized as clearly as possible, without the reader being distracted by non-essential points. We have removed some material from the textbook and placed it in the *Additional Topics* section of the book's MyEconLab (www.myeconlab.com), which also includes new material that has been written especially for this edition. (A complete listing of the *Additional Topics* on MyEconLab is provided following the List of Boxes.) As in recent editions, we have kept all core material in the main part of the text. The three boxes (Applying Economic Concepts, Lessons From History, and Extensions in Theory) are used to show examples or extensions that can be skipped without fear of missing an essential concept. But we think it would be a shame to skip too many of them, as there are many interesting examples and policy discussions in these boxes.

What follows is a brief listing of the main changes that we have made to the textbook.

Microeconomics

The structure of our microeconomics treatment has not changed from the previous edition because we feel that the current structure is more logical than any alternative. Following an introductory part, we first examine the basic theory of demand, supply, equilibrium, and elasticity, together with a chapter illustrating several applications of basic price theory. We then turn to the details of consumer and producer theory. Once production and costs are in hand, we turn to an examination of the four main market structures as well as a discussion of economic efficiency.

The next part of the book examines factor markets in detail, including separate chapters on labour markets and capital markets. The final part of the microeconomics treatment provides a detailed discussion of the role of government in the economy. We begin with a discussion of market failures, then provide a separate chapter on the economics of environmental protection, and finish off with an examination of taxation and public expenditure in Canada.

Though the overall structure of our micro treatment has not changed, we have tried to anticipate in earlier chapters the important issues of market failures and deadweight loss that do not get fully explained until later in the book. In this way, readers obtain a glimpse of some important and interesting economic issues early on, even though they must wait a while to see the full treatment.

Part 1: What Is Economics?
Chapter 1 introduces the central ideas of scarcity, choice, and opportunity cost. It also examines the idea behind the "invisible hand." We have combined the former discussions on central planning and alternative economic systems, and they now appear as the final major section.

Chapter 2 explores how economists build and test their theories. It discusses different kinds of data, what index numbers mean and how they are constructed, and the basics of graphing. We have clarified the discussion of correlation and causation, and also clarified the discussion of slopes of lines.

Part 2: An Introduction to Demand and Supply
The basics of demand, supply, and market price are developed in Chapter 3. In the box showing the algebra of market equilibrium, we have added a numerical example that should make the box more accessible to students. To the box examining weather shocks, we have added a discussion of the effects of Hurricane Katrina on the world price of oil.

Chapter 4 examines elasticity. We have changed the hypothetical data in Tables 4-1 and 4-2 to simplify the computations of elasticity. The former Appendix examining details about elasticity now appears as an *Additional Topic* on MyEconLab. We have added more examples to illustrate the relationship between elasticity and total expenditure. The box on payroll taxes has been moved to MyEconLab, and the section on income elasticity has been rewritten.

Chapter 5 offers many examples of markets in action, and helps the students to use the principles they have learned in the previous two chapters. We have removed the long section on agriculture and it now appears as a full-length *Additional Topic* on MyEconLab. In its place, we have created an entirely new discussion that introduces the reader to economic value and market efficiency. We begin by interpreting demand as "value" and supply as "cost," and go on to discuss the surplus generated through transactions. We then review the basics of price floors and price ceilings, highlighting the effects on total surplus and market efficiency. We have made this important change to this chapter in response to many reviewers' comments that revealed a desire to introduce the issue of market efficiency early on in the micro half of the book.

Part 3: Consumers and Producers
Chapter 6 examines marginal utility theory and uses it to motivate the discussion of consumer surplus. We have streamlined the discussion of income and substitution effects of price changes. The box on taxes and work effort has been moved to MyEconLab, where it is expanded to include the effects of taxes on saving. The discussion on consumer surplus has been shortened, as it now relates back to the new discussion in Chapter 5. The material on indifference curves remains in the Appendix.

Production and costs are the focus of Chapter 7. Our opening discussion of the organization of firms now leads to a new box on corporate social responsibility, a popular and important current topic. We have clarified the discussion of fixed and variable costs, and how these costs change when the firm's plant size increases. The former box on Ronald Coase's view of why firms exist has been removed, and the Appendix on whether firms really do maximize profits now appears as an *Additional Topic* on MyEconLab.

Chapter 8 examines firms' choices in the long run, when there are no fixed factors, and in the very long run, when technology changes. We have clarified our discussion of the condition for cost minimization, and used the rise in the use of ATMs to illustrate the principle of substitution. The material on isocost and isoquant analysis remains in the Appendix.

Part 4: Market Structure and Efficiency
The theory of perfectly competitive markets is developed in Chapter 9. We have used recent data on wheat production to improve the discussion of firm-level versus industry-level demand elasticity. We have added a new table to illustrate a situation where a firm makes losses but nonetheless chooses to produce positive output; we also illustrate the shut-down decision. The former discussion of long-run industry supply curves now appears as an *Additional Topic* on MyEconLab.

Chapter 10 examines monopoly, price discrimination, and cartels. We have rewritten the discussion of the inefficiency of monopoly, referring back to the new material in Chapter 5. In the discussion of price discrimination, we have added a numerical example and figure illustrating the greater profitability of charging different prices across segmented markets.

Imperfect competition and strategic behaviour are examined in Chapter 11. The former box on globalization now appears as an *Additional Topic* on

MyEconLab, where it is expanded to include data on the ongoing reductions in transportation and communications costs. We have shortened the discussion of why firms are (often) so large, and have added several examples of firm innovation to maintain entry barriers.

Chapter 12 examines in more detail the concepts of efficiency that were first introduced in Chapter 5. We begin by making the distinction between productive and allocative efficiency, and relating both concepts to the production possibilities boundary. We have streamlined the discussion of marginal-cost and average-cost pricing for natural monopolies, and have added a discussion about the recent CRTC ruling outlining the conditions under which the telecommunications industry would be deregulated. In the section on Canadian competition policy, we have added a new box outlining the cases for and against bank mergers.

Part 5: Factor Markets
Chapter 13 offers a general discussion of factor mobility and the operation of factor markets. We have streamlined the discussion of the demand for factors, and the former box on the possible "brain drain" has been moved to MyEconLab. In our treatment of economic rent, we have added a discussion of Alberta's oil royalties.

Several aspects of labour markets are examined in Chapter 14. We have enriched the discussion of labour-market discrimination, and have clarified the nature of the service sector in the discussion of "good" jobs and "bad" jobs. We now make the point that the service sector has many high-income jobs that are excellent in many respects. But it also has many low-paying jobs that are the source of concern in this debate.

Capital markets and the interest rate are examined in Chapter 15. We have modified the discussion of the demand for and supply of capital by expressing both demand and supply in terms of *flow* concepts. Thus, the model becomes one of an ordinary loanable-funds model in which the interaction of investment demand and saving supply determines the equilibrium interest rate.

Part 6: Government in the Market Economy
Chapter 16 offers a detailed treatment of market failures and the role of government in the economy. The section on the Coase theorem now appears as an *Additional Topic* on MyEconLab, where it is expanded to include a numerical example. The former box on elephants and buffaloes has been

removed. We have updated the discussion of declining fish stocks and have added some recent FAO data on the state of the world's fish stocks. The short discussion of missing markets has been removed.

Policies for environmental protection are the topic of Chapter 17. We have clarified the explanation for the inefficiency of direct pollution controls, and have added some relevant examples. The box on charging for garbage by the bag has been completely rewritten with up-to-date data drawn from recent Canadian experience. The former box on the Kyoto Protocol has been moved to MyEconLab where it provides an expanded discussion of the economic and social consequences of global warming, and the relationship between economic growth, energy use, and greenhouse-gas emissions.

Taxation and public expenditure are the central topics of Chapter 18. In our discussion of the tax system, we have clarified the message that an evaluation of the *system* is preferable to an evaluation of any individual tax. Several parts of the discussion of public expenditure have been rewritten to reflect recent developments in federal–provincial transfers, the alleged fiscal imbalance, and developments in the health-care debate.

Macroeconomics

Part 7: An Introduction to Macroeconomics
Throughout the macroeconomics half of the book, we have worked hard in this edition to clarify which of our statements are assumptions, which are predictions from the model, and which are observations about the actual economy. This clarification is crucial in order for students to recognize the difference between what we actually know and what our theory leads us to predict.

Chapter 19 provides an introduction to the main macroeconomic variables, how they are measured, and why they matter. We begin with a new discussion describing the two current competing approaches to macroeconomic research—models based on micro foundations and explicit optimizing behaviour, and models built explicitly on aggregate relationships. The extent of price flexibility also plays an important role in distinguishing these approaches. We clearly state that this textbook adopts the second approach and emphasizes the role of wage and price flexibility in several policy debates. In our discussion of the key macro variables, we have added a section on productivity, one of the most important current economic issues.

The measurement of national income is the focus of Chapter 20. We have written a new section on GDP and living standards in which we make the distinction between material living standards and a broader concept of well-being. This discussion leads to a new *Additional Topic* on how well GDP measures our overall well-being. Some of the motivation for this addition is the new research across many disciplines about happiness and well-being.

Part 8: The Economy in the Short Run

Chapter 21 presents the simplest possible macroeconomic model, in which the only components of aggregate expenditure are consumption and investment. The price level, interest rate, and exchange rate are fixed, and output is demand determined. In discussing the consumption function, we have added some data illustrating the close time-series relationship between consumption and income. Before introducing the equilibrium concept, we clarify our assumption that output is demand determined. The section on the saving/investment approach to equilibrium has been moved to MyEconLab, as this tended to complicate what is already a challenging chapter for students.

In Chapter 22, we add international trade and a government sector to the simple macro model. We have rewritten and streamlined our discussion of government purchases and net tax revenues, and the diagram of the public saving function has been removed. We have clarified the relationship between desired consumption and national income, and the saving/investment approach to equilibrium has been moved to MyEconLab. We have a new box on a realistic value of the simple multiplier for Canada where we connect the idea of the multiplier to the sort of public pronouncements often made by our political leaders. The result of our changes is a much leaner chapter, one that quickly gets to the central points and has minimal distractions.

The supply side of the economy and a variable price level are introduced in Chapter 23. This is the first chapter with aggregate demand (*AD*) and aggregate supply (*AS*) curves. We have clarified the discussion of the *AS* curve, and what causes it to shift. We have removed the diagram showing the special case of a vertical *AS* curve, as the central analysis is already provided with an upward-sloping *AS* curve. Our final discussion of shocks that affect both demand and supply has been reworked, with the recent oil-price increase used as an example. This dis-

cussion leads to a new *Additional Topic* on MyEconLab which examines in detail how changes in the world price of oil affect the Canadian economy.

Part 9: The Economy in the Long Run

Chapter 24 examines the adjustment process that takes the economy from a short-run equilibrium to a long-run equilibrium with real GDP equal to potential output. We have brought forward the discussion of the Phillips curve which relates the level of the output gap with the rate at which the *AS* curve is shifting (due to wage changes). We have removed the short discussion of shocks as *the* driving force of cycles, and we have shortened the discussion of changes in the long-run equilibrium, as this is more fully addressed in later chapters. In our discussion of fiscal policy, we have an improved discussion of how changes in government spending are likely to affect the composition of GDP, and thus affect long-run growth. This discussion provides an obvious segue into the next two chapters.

The different causes of short-run and long-run changes in real GDP are highlighted in Chapter 25. We make the simple point, supported by some Canadian data, that short-run changes in GDP are mostly caused by changes in the utilization of factors, whereas long-run changes are mostly caused by changes in productivity and factor supplies.

Chapter 26 examines the process of long-run economic growth in detail. We begin by discussing three different aspects of growth—growth in real GDP, real per capita GDP, and real GDP per hour worked. We have rewritten the discussion of how we use our short-run macro model in a different way to examine the determination of the real interest rate in the long run. The section on saving, investment, and growth now leads to a new *Additional Topic* on the relationship between saving and investment in open economies with mobile financial capital. We have emphasized the fact that the Neoclassical growth model takes technological change as given, thus providing solid motivation for the new growth theories. We have enriched our discussion of the limits to growth from resource exhaustion and environmental degradation.

Part 10: Money, Banking, and Monetary Policy

Chapter 27 explores the nature of money, the Canadian banking system, and the process of deposit creation. The box on globalization has been streamlined, while the box on deposit insurance has been moved to MyEconLab where it offers a more thorough treatment of the debate over deposit insurance. We have rewritten the section on target and excess reserves. In the discussion of deposit creation, we draw the parallel between the effects of a cash drain on the deposit multiplier and the effects of income taxes and imports on the simple (expenditure) multiplier from Chapter 21.

The role of money and interest rates in the *AD/AS* model is developed in Chapter 28. In the opening section, we have clarified the relationship between the market price of a bond and the bond's present value. The Appendix on the role of interest rates in determining the slope of the *AD* curve has been moved to MyEconLab. In our discussion of long-run money neutrality, we have made it clear that our macro model assumes the conditions that give rise to neutrality; this is one place where it is crucial to be clear about what is known fact and what is a prediction from a model.

Chapter 29 examines the actual practice of monetary policy in Canada. We have completely rewritten the first part of this chapter. We begin by outlining that central banks have two general approaches for implementing monetary policy: they can set the money supply or they can set the interest rate. We explain the disadvantages of setting the money supply, including imperfect control over deposit creation and uncertainty about the money demand curve. We then turn to how the Bank of Canada influences the overnight interest rate, and how, as a result, the money supply is endogenous. We have a new box on how the Bank passively uses open-market operations to accommodate the changing demand for money. We have also rewritten the introductory section on inflation targeting, and emphasized that high inflation is costly and that monetary policy is best able to influence inflation in the long run. We have clarified the discussion of CPI and core inflation, and have also simplified the discussion of the lags in monetary policy. The section on the past 30 years of monetary policy has been updated, with some emphasis on the challenges created by the recent sharp appreciation of the Canadian dollar. The section on whether inflation can be too low has been moved to MyEconLab where it is supplemented with a discussion of the zero lower bound for nominal interest rates.

Part 11: Macroeconomic Problems and Policies

Chapter 30 discusses sustained inflation in our macroeconomic model, and also provides a detailed analysis of disinflation. We have clarified the two distinct pressures operating on wages: excess demand or supply emanating from an output gap, and the expectations of future inflation. In the discussion of disinflation, we have clarified the competing forces acting on wages during the "stagflationary" phase. The box on the death of inflation has been revised.

Short-term fluctuations in unemployment and longer-term changes in the NAIRU are the focus of Chapter 31. The former box on the Canada–U.S. unemployment gap has been moved to MyEconLab and provides an example of how differences in definitions and measurements of unemployment can have a significant impact on data. We have rewritten the opening section on unemployment fluctuations, where we more clearly outline the competing New Classical and New Keynesian theories. We reserve the term "cyclical" unemployment for a New Keynesian perspective; for New Classical economists, all unemployment is either frictional or structural. In the section on the NAIRU, we have added a discussion of hiring and firing costs, especially in the EU, which reduce turnover and increase long-term unemployment.

Chapter 32 examines the economic effects of government budget deficits and debt. We have trimmed several pages out of this chapter, with the result that it is better focused than in the previous edition. We have significantly streamlined the opening section on facts and definitions. The section on Ricardian Equivalence has been moved to MyEconLab. The section on the effects of budget deficits now makes it clear that we *assume* that an increase in the budget deficit leads to a reduction in national saving. We have also streamlined the discussion of the cyclically adjusted deficit and changes in the debt-to-GDP ratio, and have added recent data to better illustrate both concepts. We have also improved and clarified the discussion of the long-term burden of the public debt.

Part 12: Canada in the Global Economy

Chapter 33 explores the gains from trade, and emphasizes that the gains arising from trade between individuals are the same as the gains that arise from trade between countries. We have sharpened the discussion of the importance of economies of scale and learning by doing, and have also put a little more emphasis on the idea that comparative advantages can be acquired as well as lost. This is the important idea that comparative advantage is a *dynamic* concept.

Trade policy is the topic of Chapter 34. In restating the case for free trade, we have argued that protection may have the effect of reducing the amount of innovation by protected firms, thus leading to an eventual loss of relative living standards. We have improved the discussion of the protection of infant industries, due either to scale economies or learning by doing, and we have also sharpened the discussion of strategic trade policy. We have updated the discussion of the WTO negotiations, and added a new box that outlines the debate about the success or failure of the WTO. The former box on headline trade disputes has been removed, but there is now a full-length item on MyEconLab about the history, politics, and economics of the softwood lumber dispute.

Chapter 35 examines exchange rates and the balance of payments. We have entirely rewritten the section explaining why the balance of payments must balance. We now explain at the *aggregate* level why a current account surplus must be matched by a capital outflow—a capital account deficit. Our box explaining an individual's balance of payments with the world remains, as students can easily identify with the story being told. We have expanded our discussion of fixed exchange rates slightly by describing China's current pegging of the yuan–dollar exchange rate above its free-market value. We have updated the discussion of exchange-rate changes by discussing the recent sharp appreciation of the Canadian dollar. Finally, in the discussion of fixed versus flexible exchange rates, we now mention that fixed rates imply that the central bank must give up control over inflation, as it has but a single instrument for its monetary policy.

If you are moved to write to us (and we hope that you will be!), please do. You can send any comments or questions regarding the text (or any of the supplementary material, such as the *Instructor's Manual,* the *Study Guide,* the *TestGen,* or the web-based *Additional Topics*) to:

Christopher Ragan
Department of Economics
McGill University
855 Sherbrooke St. West
Montreal, Quebec H3A 2T7
e-mail: christopher.ragan@mcgill.ca

To the Student

Welcome to what is most likely your first book about economics! You are about to encounter what is for most people a new way of thinking, which often causes people to see things differently than they did before. But learning a new way of thinking is not always easy, and you should expect some hard work ahead. We do our best to be as clear and logical as possible, and to illustrate our arguments whenever possible with current and interesting examples.

You must develop your own technique for studying, but the following suggestions may prove helpful. Begin by carefully considering the Learning Objectives at the beginning of a chapter. Read the chapter itself relatively quickly in order to get the general run of the argument. At this first reading, you may want to skip the boxes and any footnotes. Then, after reading the Summary and the Key Concepts (at the end of each chapter), reread the chapter more slowly, making sure that you understand each step of the argument.

With respect to the figures and tables, be sure you understand how the conclusions that are stated in boldface at the beginning of each caption have been reached. You should be prepared to spend time on difficult sections; occasionally, you may spend an hour on only a few pages. Paper and pencil are indispensable equipment in your reading. It is best to follow a difficult argument by building your own diagram while the argument unfolds rather than by relying on the finished diagram as it appears in the book.

The end-of-chapter Study Exercises require you to practise using some of the concepts that you learned in the chapter. These will be excellent preparation for your exams. To provide you with immediate feedback, we have posted Solutions to Selected Study Exercises on MyEconLab (www.myeconlab. com). The end-of-chapter Discussion Questions require you to apply what you have studied. We advise you to outline answers to some of the questions. In short, you should seek to understand economics, not to memorize it.

The bracketed boldface numbers in the text refer to a series of mathematical notes that are found starting on page M-1 at the end of the book. For those of you who like mathematics or prefer mathematical argument to verbal or geometric exposition, these may prove useful. Others may disregard them.

In this edition of the book, we have incorporated many elements to help you review material and prepare for examinations. A brief description of all the features in this book is given in the separate section that follows.

We encourage you to make use of the brand new MyEconLab for the book (www.myeconlab.com) at the outset of your studies. MyEconLab contains a wealth of valuable resources to help you. MyEconLab provides Solutions to Selected Study Exercises. It also includes many additional practice questions, some of which are modelled on Study Exercises in the book. The MyEconLab icon [myeconlab] identifies those Study Exercises that are reformulated online for you. In the book, the MyEconLab icon also directs you to online discussions of *Additional Topics*—these represent material written especially for this textbook, and include many interesting theoretical, empirical, and policy discussions. For more details about the resources provided on the MyEconLab, please see the description in the section on Supplements.

We strongly suggest you make use of the excellent *Study Guide* written expressly for this text. The *Study Guide* is closely integrated with the book. In fact, special references in the margins of the textbook will direct you to appropriate practice questions and exercises in the *Study Guide*. They will test and reinforce your understanding of the concepts and analytical techniques stressed in each chapter of the text and will help you prepare for your examinations. Explanations are provided for the answers to some of the Multiple-Choice Questions to facilitate your independent study. The ability to solve problems and to communicate and interpret your results are important goals in an introductory course in economics. The *Study Guide* can play a crucial role in your acquisition of these skills.

Over the years, the book has benefited greatly from comments and suggestions we have received from students. Please feel free to send your comments to christopher.ragan@mcgill.ca. Good luck, and we hope you enjoy your course in economics!

Features of This Edition

We have made a careful effort with this edition to incorporate features that will facilitate the teaching and learning of economics.

- A set of **Learning Objectives** at the beginning of each chapter clarifies the skills and knowledge to be learned in each chapter. These same learning objectives are used in the chapter summaries, as well as in the *Study Guide.*

- **Major ideas** are highlighted in red in the text.
- **Key terms** are boldfaced where they are defined in the body of the text and they are restated with their definitions in the margins. In the index at the back of the book, each key term and its page reference to its definition are boldfaced.
- **Weblinks** to useful Internet addresses are given in the margins. Each weblink presents a URL address, along with a brief description of the material available there. Some links are to government home pages where much data can be obtained. Other links are to organizations such as OPEC, the UN, and the WTO.
- **Study Guide** references in the margin direct students to appropriate questions in the *Study Guide* that reinforce the topic being discussed in the text.

- **A caption for each Figure and Table** summarizes the underlying economic reasoning. Each caption begins with a boldfaced statement of the relevant economic conclusion.
- The **colour scheme for Figures** consistently uses the same colour for each type of curve. For example, all demand curves are blue, whereas all supply curves are red.

- **Additional Topics on MyEconLab (www.myeconlab.com)** are referenced in special boxes inserted at the appropriate place in the body of the relevant chapter. The *Additional Topics* include the entire online Chapter 36W, Challenges Facing the Developing Countries.

- **Applying Economic Concepts** boxes demonstrate economics in action, providing examples of how theoretical material relates to issues of current interest.
- **Extensions in Theory** boxes provide a deeper treatment of a theoretical topic that is discussed in the text.

- **Lessons From History** boxes contain discussions of a particular policy debate or empirical finding that takes place in a historical context.
- **Photographs with short captions** are interspersed throughout the chapters to illustrate some of the arguments.

- **Chapter Summaries** are organized using the same numbered heading as found in the body of the chapter. The relevant learning objectives (LO) numbers are given in orange next to each heading in the summary.
- **Key Concepts** are listed near the end of each chapter.
- A set of **Study Exercises** is provided for each chapter. These often quantitative exercises require the student to analyze problems by means of computations, graphs, or explanations.
- **MyEconLab icons** tie certain Study Exercises in the book to exercises on MyEconLab (www.myeconlab.com).

- A set of **Discussion Questions** is also provided for each chapter. These questions require the student to synthesize and generalize. They are designed especially for discussion in class.

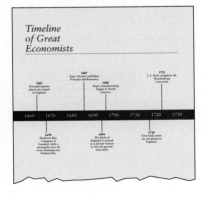

- A set of **Mathematical Notes** is presented in a separate section near the end of the book. Because mathematical notation and derivations are not necessary to understand the principles of economics but are more helpful in advanced work, this seems to be a sensible arrangement. References in the text to these mathematical notes are given by means of boldfaced numbers in square brackets.

- A **Timeline of Great Economists,** running from the mid-seventeenth century to the late-twentieth century, is presented near the end of the book. Along this timeline we have placed brief descriptions of the life and works of some great economists, most of whom the reader will encounter in the textbook. Along this timeline we have also listed some major world events in order to give readers an appreciation for when these economists did their work.

- **Economists on Record,** given on the inside of the back cover, quotes some classic excerpts that are relevant to the study and practice of economics.
- For convenience, a list of the **Common Abbreviations Used in the Text** is given on the inside of the front cover.

Supplements

A comprehensive set of supplements has been carefully prepared to assist students and instructors in using this new edition.

A thoroughly revised and expanded **Study Guide**, written by Paul T. Dickinson and Gustavo Indart, is designed for use either in the classroom or by students on their own. The *Study Guide* offers additional study support and reinforcement for each text chapter. It is closely integrated with the textbook. Special notes in the margins of the textbook direct students to appropriate practice exercises in the *Study Guide*. For this edition, we have increased the number of questions and exercises. And to facilitate independent study, we have provided explanations for more of the solutions to the Additional Multiple-Choice Questions. For each chapter, the *Study Guide* provides the following helpful material:

- Learning Objectives matching those in the textbook
- Chapter Overview
- Hints and Tips
- Chapter Review consisting of Multiple-Choice Questions, organized into sections matching the numbered sections in the textbook
- Short-Answer Questions
- Exercises
- Extension Exercises
- Additional Multiple-Choice Questions
- Solutions to all of the Questions and Exercises above
- Explanations for the solutions to at least 50 percent of the Additional Multiple-Choice Questions

The *Study Guide* is available as a cumulative volume or as split volumes for microeconomics and macroeconomics.

An **Instructor's Resource CD-ROM** has been specially prepared for this new edition. It contains the following items:

- An *Instructor's Manual* (in both Word and PDF format) written by Christopher Ragan. It includes full solutions to all the Study Exercises and suggested answers to all the Discussion Questions.
- *PowerPoint Slides* prepared by Christopher Ragan. Instructors can readily adapt these slides for lecture presentations.
- A thoroughly revised *TestGen*, written by Ingrid Kristjanson and Christopher Ragan, with contributions from Bogdan Buduru and Burc Kayahan. The testbank has been substantially expanded and now consists of more than 3600 multiple-choice questions. For the new edition, more emphasis has been placed on applied questions (as opposed to recall questions), quantitative questions (as opposed to qualitative questions), and questions with graphs or tables. Approximately 60 percent of the questions now test applied skills, about 20 percent of the questions are quantitative, and about 20 percent of the questions have a graph or table. All the questions have been carefully checked for accuracy. For each question, the authors have provided the correct answer, identified the relevant section number in the textbook chapter, specified the concept being tested, assigned a level of difficulty (easy, moderate, or challenging), identified the skill tested (recall or applied), noted whether the question is qualitative or quantitative, and noted whether the question involves a graph or table. *TestGen* enables instructors to search for questions according to any of these attributes and to sort questions into any order desired. With *TestGen*, instructors can easily edit existing questions, add questions, generate tests, and print the tests in a variety of formats. *TestGen* also allows instructors to administer tests on a local area network, have the tests graded electronically, and have the results prepared in electronic or printed reports.

MYECONLAB

myeconlab MyEconLab—the online homework and tutorial system packaged with every new copy of the text—puts you in control of your own learning with study and practice tools directly correlated to the textbook content. Within MyEconLab's structured environment, you can practise what you learn, test your understanding, and pursue a personalized study plan that MyEconLab generates for you based on your performance on practice tests.

To register your access code, or to get more information about MyEconLab, visit the MyEconLab website at **www.myeconlab.com**.

If you do not have an access code, you can purchase one from your bookstore:

Economics MyEconLab Student Access Kit:
   ISBN 978-0-321-46880-2
Microeconomics MyEconLab Student Access
   Kit: ISBN 978-0-321-46881-9
Macroeconomics MyEconLab Student Access
   Kit: ISBN 978-0-321-46882-6

MyEconLab is also available in CourseCompass. If your instructor is teaching with CourseCompass, he or she will provide you with the Course ID you will need to access your course.

MyEconLab: Problem Solving for Students

MyEconLab gives you the tools you need to learn from your mistakes whenever you might be struggling.

Personalized Study Plan A Study Plan is generated from each student's results on Sample Tests and instructor assignments. Students can clearly see which topics they have mastered and, more importantly, which they need to work on. The Study Plan links to additional practice problems and tutorial exercises to help with those topics.

Unlimited Practice Most Sample Test and Study Plan exercises contain algorithmically generated values, ensuring students get as much practice as they need. Every problem links students to learning resources that further reinforce concepts they need to master.

Learning Resources In the lower left-hand corner of each practice problem is a link to the eText page, which discusses the very concept being applied. Students also have access to guided solutions that take them step by step through many of the more complex problems. MyEconLab has a suite of graphing tools for practice and current news articles that tie chapter topics to everyday issues.

Tests and Other Assignments MyEconLab comes with two pre-loaded Sample Tests for each chapter so students can assess their understanding of the material themselves. Instructors can assign these Sample Tests or create assignments using a mix of publisher-supplied content and their own custom exercises.

MyEconLab: Solving Problems for Instructors

You decide the level of your own participation. Students benefit from full access to MyEconLab regardless of your choice. Full faculty involvement is possible in MyEconLab, and also in MyEconLab in CourseCompass, which is available to you if you choose.

Tutorial Help No instructor setup is needed at all for students to get two pre-loaded assessments per chapter, Study Plans, tutorial help, and more.

Ready-to-Use Assignments Use pre-loaded Sample Tests or create your own assignments using a mix of MyEconLab problems, the book's Testbank, and questions written using the Econ Exercise Builder. Assign problems as tests, quizzes, or homework, and student results will be captured in MyEconLab's powerful online Gradebook.

Automatic Grading MyEconLab grades every homework and quiz question—even those with graphing. Students get unlimited graphing practice and immediate feedback with links to specific learning tools for each question. At any time, instructors can check on students' progress in their online Gradebook.

Individual Student Settings Instructors can modify assignment settings for individual students, without other students seeing the changes or being affected by them. From either the Homework and Test Manager or a student's results page in the Gradebook, instructors can change any of the following assignment settings for individual students: due dates and times, number of attempts, time limit, whether to show remaining time during a test, whether a password is required (and what it is), whether a homework assignment is available to be worked on past its due date, and whether the work is assigned or unassigned.

MyEconLab can also be made available on request through Blackboard and WebCT. Contact your Pearson Education Canada sales representative for more information about these two course-management systems.

Acknowledgments

It would be impossible to acknowledge here by name all the teachers, colleagues, and students who contributed to the development and improvement of this book over its previous eleven editions. Hundreds of users have written to us with specific suggestions, and much of the credit for the improvement of the book over the years belongs to them. We can no longer list them individually but we thank them all sincerely.

For the development of this twelfth edition, we are grateful to the many people who offered informal suggestions. We would also like to thank the following instructors who provided us with formal reviews of the textbook. Their observations and recommendations were extremely helpful.

- Morris Altman (University of Saskatchewan)
- Soham Baksi (University of Winnipeg)
- Michael Benarroch (University of Winnipeg)
- Ugurhan G. Berkok (Queen's University)
- Ryan Compton (University of Manitoba)
- Yolina Denchev (Camosun College)
- Livio Di Matteo (Lakehead University)
- Oliver Franke (Athabasca University)
- Shahidul Islam (Grant MacEwan College)
- Alok Johri (McMaster University)
- Rafal Kosztirko (Mount Royal College)
- Carol Chui Ha Lau (Concordia University)
- Stephen Law (Mount Allison University)
- Ambrose Leung (Bishop's University)
- A. Gyasi Nimarko (Vanier College)
- Derek Pyne (Memorial University)
- Neil Roberts (Kwantlen University College)
- Francisco J. Santos-Arteaga (York University)
- Rob Scharff (Kwantlen University College)
- Jim Sentance (University of Prince Edward Island)
- Prakash Sharma (University of Ottawa)
- Maurice Tugwell (Acadia University)
- Jane Waples (Memorial University)

We would like to express our thanks to the many people at Pearson Education Canada involved in the production of this textbook. Through several editions, we have been privileged to work closely with Gary Bennett (Editor-in-Chief), Maurice Esses (Developmental Editor), and Marisa D'Andrea (Production Editor), and are grateful for their experience, professionalism, and diligence and care in guiding this book through the publication process. Eileen Lasswell joined the team on this edition as the Marketing Manager and has brought a great deal of energy, enthusiasm, and creativity to this project. These individuals have been a pleasure to work with each step along the way and we are deeply grateful for their presence and their participation, and delighted to consider them friends as well as professional colleagues.

Our thanks also to the many people at Pearson with whom we work less closely but who nonetheless toil behind the scenes to produce this book, including Matthew Christian, Andrea Falkenberg, Julia Hall, Nelson Gonzalez, and Mary Rose MacLachlan.

Thanks also to Ann McInnis for copyediting, Kit Pasula for the technical review, and to Catharine Haggert and Hallie Benjamin for proofreading, all of whom provided an invaluable service with their attention to detail.

In short, we realize that there is a great deal more involved in producing a book than *just* the writing. Without the efforts from all of these dedicated professionals, this textbook simply would not exist. Our sincere thanks to all of you.

Finally, we would like to express our appreciation to Ingrid Kristjanson, who is deeply involved in all of the detailed work of the revision of the textbook. She discusses the revision ideas, reads first and second drafts, does her fair share of rewriting, and carefully handles the often-complex transcription process. In addition, for this edition she has played a central role in our complete rewriting and expansion of the *TestGen*. Without her, the revision of the textbook would be far less pleasant and efficient than it now is.

Christopher Ragan
Richard Lipsey

CHAPTER 1

Economic Issues and Concepts

LO LEARNING OBJECTIVES

In this chapter you will learn

1. to view the market economy as a self-organizing entity in which order emerges from a large number of decentralized decisions.
2. the importance of scarcity, choice, and opportunity cost, and how all three concepts are illustrated by the production possibilities boundary.
3. about the circular flow of income and expenditure.
4. that all actual economies are mixed economies, having elements of free markets, tradition, and government intervention.

If you want a litre of milk, you go to your local grocery store and buy it. When the grocer needs more milk, he orders it from the distributor, who in turn gets it from the dairy, which in its turn gets it from the dairy farmer. The dairy farmer buys cattle feed and electric milking machines, and gets power to run all his equipment by putting a plug into a wall outlet where the electricity is supplied as he needs it. The milking machines are made from parts manufactured in several different places in Canada, the United States, and overseas. The parts themselves are made from materials mined and smelted in a dozen or more different countries.

As it is with the milk you drink, so it is with everything else that you buy. When you go to the appropriate store, what you want is normally on the shelf. Those who make these products find that all the required components and materials are available when they need them—even though these things typically come from many different parts of the world and are made by people who have no direct dealings with each other.

1.1 THE COMPLEXITY OF THE MODERN ECONOMY

Your own transactions are only a small part of the remarkably complex set of transactions that takes place every day in a modern society. Shipments arrive daily at our ports, railway terminals, and airports. These shipments include: raw materials, such as iron ore, logs, and oil; parts, such as automobile engines, transistors, and circuit boards; tools, such as screwdrivers, lathes, and digging equipment; perishables, such as fresh flowers, coffee beans, and fruit; and all kinds of manufactured goods, such as washing machines, computers, and personal DVD players. Railways and trucking lines move these goods among thousands of different destinations within Canada. Some go directly to consumers. Others are used by local firms to manufacture their products—some of which will be sold domestically and some exported to other countries.

Most people who want to work can find work. They spend their working days engaging in the activities just described. In doing so, they earn incomes that they then spend on goods and services produced by others. Other people own firms that employ workers to assist in the many activities described above, such as importing, making, transporting, and selling things. They earn their incomes as profits from these enterprises.

An **economy** is a system, typically a very complex one, in which scarce resources—such as labour, land, and machines—are allocated among competing uses. Decisions must be made about: which goods are produced, and which are not; who works where and at what wage; and who consumes which goods at what times. While each of these individual decisions may seem simple, the entire combination is remarkably complex, especially in modern societies.

economy A system in which scarce resources are allocated among competing uses.

The Self-Organizing Economy

Early in the development of modern economics, thoughtful observers wondered how such a complex set of dealings gets organized. Who coordinates the whole set of efforts? Who makes sure that all the activities fit together, providing jobs to produce the things that people want and delivering those things to where they are wanted? The answer is, surprisingly, no one!

The great insight of economists is that an economy based on free-market transactions is *self-organizing*.

By following their own self-interest, doing what seems best and most profitable for themselves, and responding to the incentives of prices determined in open markets, people produce a spontaneous economic order. In that order, literally thousands of millions of transactions and activities fit together to produce the things that people want within the constraints set by the resources that are available to the nation.

The great Scottish economist and political philosopher Adam Smith (1723–1790),[1] who was the first to develop this insight fully, put it this way:

> *It is not from the benevolence of the butcher, the brewer, or the baker, that we expect our dinner, but from their regard to their own interest. We address ourselves, not to their humanity but to their self-love, and never talk to them of our own necessities but of their advantages.*

Smith is not saying that benevolence is unimportant. Indeed, he praises it in many passages. He is saying, however, that the massive number of economic interactions that characterize a modern economy cannot all be motivated by benevolence. Although benevolence does motivate some of our actions, often the very dramatic ones, the vast majority of our everyday actions are motivated by self-interest. Self-interest, not benevolence, is therefore the foundation of economic order.

Adam Smith wrote An Inquiry into the Nature and Causes of the Wealth of Nations *in 1776. Now referred to by most people simply as* The Wealth of Nations, *it is considered to be the beginning of modern economics.*

---

1 Throughout this book, we encounter many great economists from the past whose ideas shaped the discipline of economics. At the back of the book you will find a timeline, beginning in the 1600s, that contains brief discussions of many of these thinkers and places them in their historical context.

Efficient Organization

Another great insight, which was hinted at by Smith and fully developed over the next century and a half, was that this spontaneously generated economic order is relatively *efficient.* Loosely speaking, efficiency means that the resources available to the nation are organized so as to produce the largest possible amount of the goods and services that people want to purchase, and to produce them with the least possible amount of resources.

An economy organized by free markets behaves almost as if it were guided by "an invisible hand," in Smith's now-famous words. This does not literally mean that a supernatural presence runs a market economy. Instead it refers to the relatively efficient order that emerges spontaneously out of the many independent decisions made by those who produce, sell, and buy goods and services. The key to explaining this market behaviour is that these decision makers all respond to the same set of prices, which are determined in markets that respond to overall conditions of national scarcity or plenty. Much of economics is devoted to a detailed elaboration of how this market order is generated, and to how efficiently that job is done.

Main Characteristics of Market Economies

What, then, are the main characteristics of market economies that produce this spontaneous self-organization?

Self-Interest. Individuals pursue their own self-interest, buying and selling what seems best for themselves and their families.

Incentives. People respond to incentives. Sellers usually want to sell more when prices are high; buyers usually want to buy more when prices are low.

Market Prices and Quantities. Prices and quantities are determined in free markets in which would-be sellers compete to sell their products to would-be buyers.

Institutions. All of these activities are governed by a set of institutions largely created by government. The most important are private property, freedom of contract, and the rule of law. The natures of private property and contractual obligations are defined by laws passed by legislatures and enforced by the police and the courts.

1.2 SCARCITY, CHOICE, AND OPPORTUNITY COST

All of the issues discussed so far would not matter much if we lived in an economy of such plenty that there was enough to satisfy all of everyone's wants. But such an economy is impossible. Why?

The short answer is, because we live in a world of *scarcity.* Compared to the known desires of individuals for such products as better food, clothing, housing, education, holidays, health care, and entertainment, the existing supplies of resources are clearly inadequate. They are sufficient to produce only a small fraction of the goods and services that people desire. This gives rise to the basic economic problem of choice under conditions of scarcity. If we cannot have everything we want, we must choose what we will and will not have.

One definition of *economics* comes from the great economist Alfred Marshall (1842–1924), whom we will encounter at several points in this book: "Economics is a study of mankind in the ordinary business of life." A more penetrating definition is the following:

Economics is the study of the use of scarce resources to satisfy unlimited human wants.

Scarcity is inevitable and is central to economic problems. What are society's resources? Why is scarcity inevitable? What are the consequences of scarcity?

Resources

A society's resources are often divided into the three broad categories of land, labour, and capital. *Land* includes all natural endowments such as arable land, forests, lakes, crude oil, and minerals. *Labour* includes all mental and physical human resources, including entrepreneurial capacity and management skills. *Capital* includes all manufactured aids to production such as tools, machinery, and buildings. Economists call such resources **factors of production** because they are used to produce the things that people desire. We divide what is produced into goods and services. **Goods** are tangible (e.g., cars and shoes), and **services** are intangible (e.g., haircuts and education).

People use goods and services to satisfy many of their wants. The act of making them is called **production,** and the act of using them to satisfy wants is called **consumption.** Goods are valued for the services they provide. An automobile, for example, helps to satisfy its owner's desires for transportation, mobility, and possibly status.

Scarcity and Choice

For almost all of the world's six billion people, scarcity is real and ever present. As we said above, relative to people's desires, existing resources are inadequate; there are enough to produce only a fraction of the goods and services that are wanted.

But are not the advanced industrialized nations rich enough that scarcity is nearly banished? After all, they have been characterized as affluent societies. Whatever affluence may mean, however, it does not mean the end of the problem of scarcity. Canadian households that earn $64 000 per year, the average Canadian household income in 2004 but a princely amount by *world* standards, have no trouble spending it on things that seem useful to them and they would certainly have no trouble convincing you that their resources are scarce relative to their desires.

Because resources are scarce, all societies face the problem of deciding what to produce and how much each person will consume. Societies differ in who makes the choices and how they are made, but the need to choose is common to all. Just as scarcity implies the need for choice, so choice implies the existence of cost. A decision to have more of something requires a decision to have less of something else. The less of "something else" can be thought of as the cost of having the more of "something."

Scarcity implies that choices must be made, and making choices implies the existence of costs.

Opportunity Cost   To see how choice implies cost, we look first at a trivial example and then at one that affects all of us; both examples involve precisely the same fundamental principles.

---

factors of production
Resources used to produce goods and services; frequently divided into the basic categories of land, labour, and capital.

goods Tangible commodities, such as cars or shoes.

services Intangible commodities, such as haircuts or medical care.

production The act of making goods or services.

consumption The act of using goods or services to satisfy wants.

Consider the choice David faces on a Saturday night when he goes out for pizza and beer with his friends. Suppose that he has only $16 for the night and that each beer costs $4 and each slice of pizza costs $2. Since David is both hungry and thirsty, he would like to have four slices of pizza and three beers, but this would cost $20 and is therefore unattainable given David's scarce resources of $16. There are several combinations, however, that are attainable: 8 slices of pizza and 0 beers; 6 slices of pizza and 1 beer; 4 slices of pizza and 2 beers; 2 slices of pizza and 3 beers; and 0 slices of pizza and 4 beers.

David's choices are illustrated in Figure 1-1, which graphs the combinations of beers and slices of pizza that David considers buying. The numbers of pieces of pizza are shown on the horizontal axis; the numbers of beers are shown on the vertical axis. The downward-sloping line connects the five possible combinations of beer and pizza that use up all of David's resources—$16. Notice that point *A* shows a combination—4 slices of pizza and 3 beers—that lies outside the line because its total cost is more than $16. Point *A* is *unattainable* to David. If David could buy fractions of a beer and of a piece of pizza, *all* points that lie on or inside the line would be *attainable* combinations.

In this setting David can ask himself, "What is the cost of one beer?" One answer is that the cost is $4. An equivalent answer, assuming that he wished to spend all of this $16 on these two items, is that the cost of one beer is the two slices of pizza he must give up to get it. In fact, we say in this case that two slices of pizza is the *opportunity cost* of one beer since it is the opportunity David must give up to get one extra beer.

Every time a choice is made, opportunity costs are incurred.

The idea of opportunity cost is one of the central insights of economics. Here is a precise definition. The **opportunity cost** of using resources for a certain purpose is defined to be *the benefit given up by not using them in the best alternative way.* That is, it is the cost measured in terms of other goods and services that could have been obtained instead. If, for example, resources that could have produced 20 km of road are best used instead to produce one hospital, the opportunity cost of a hospital is 20 km of road; looked at the other way round, the opportunity cost of 1 km of road is one-twentieth of a hospital.

See *Applying Economic Concepts 1-1* for an example of opportunity cost that should seem quite familiar to you—the opportunity cost of getting a university degree.

Production Possibilities Boundary Although David's choice between pizza and beer may seem to be a trivial consumption decision, the nature of the decision is the same whatever the choice being made. Consider, for example, the choice that any country must face between producing military and civilian goods.

FIGURE 1-1   Choosing Between Pizza and Beer

Limited resources force a choice among competing alternatives. Given a total of $16 to spend on $2 slices of pizza and $4 beers, some choices are unattainable, such as point *A*. The five points on the green line show all combinations that are attainable by spending the $16. If it were possible to buy parts of a beer and parts of a slice of pizza, then *all* combinations on the line and in the green area would be attainable. If the entire $16 is to be spent, the choice between more pizza and more beer involves an opportunity cost. The *slope* of the green line reflects opportunity costs. The opportunity cost of one extra slice of pizza is half of a beer; the opportunity cost of one extra beer is two slices of pizza.

Practise with Study Guide Chapter 1, Exercise 3.

opportunity cost The cost of using resources for a certain purpose, measured by the benefit given up by not using them in their best alternative use.

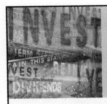

APPLYING ECONOMIC CONCEPTS 1-1

The Opportunity Cost of Your University Degree

As discussed in the text, the opportunity cost of choosing one thing is what must be given up as the best alternative. Computing the opportunity cost of a college or university education is a good example to illustrate which factors are included in the computation of opportunity cost. You may also be surprised to learn how expensive your university degree really is!*

Suppose that a bachelor's degree requires four years of study and that each year you spend $6000 for tuition fees—approximately the average at Canadian universities in 2007—and a further $1500 per year for books and materials. Does this mean that the cost of a university education is only $30 000? Unfortunately not; the true cost of a university degree is much higher.

The key point is that the opportunity cost of a university education does not just include the out-of-pocket expenses on tuition and books. You must also take into consideration *what you are forced to give up* by choosing to attend university. Of course, if you were not studying you could have been doing any one of a number of things, but the relevant one is *the one you would have chosen instead*—your best alternative to attending university.

Suppose that your best alternative to attending university was to get a job. In this case, the opportunity cost of your university degree must include the earnings that you would have received had you taken that job. Suppose that your (after-tax) annual earnings would have been $20 000 per year, for a total of $80 000 if you had stayed at that job for four years. To the direct expenses of $30 000, we must therefore add $80 000 for the earnings that you gave up by not taking a job. This brings the true cost of your university degree—the opportunity cost—up to $110 000!

---

*This box considers only the cost *to the student* of a university degree. For reasons that will be discussed in detail in Part Six of this book, provincial governments heavily subsidize post-secondary education in Canada. Because of this subsidy, the cost *to society* of a university degree is generally much higher than the cost to an individual student.

Notice that the cost of food, lodging, clothing, and other living expenses did not enter the calculation of the opportunity cost in this example. The living expenses must be incurred in either case—whether you attend university or get a job.

If the opportunity cost of a degree is so high, why do students choose to go to university? The simple answer is that they believe that they are better off by going to university than by not going (otherwise they would not go). Maybe the students simply enjoy learning, and thus are prepared to incur the high cost to be in the university environment. Or maybe they believe that a university degree will significantly increase their future earning potential. (In Chapter 14 we will see that this is true.) In this case, they are giving up four years of earnings at one salary so that they can invest in their own skills in the hope of enjoying many more years in the future at a considerably higher salary.

Whatever the reason for attending college or university, the recognition that a post-secondary degree is very expensive should convince students to make the best use of their time while they are there. Read on!

The opportunity cost to an individual completing a university degree in Canada is large. It includes the direct cost of tuition and books as well as the earnings forgone while attending university.

Practise with Study Guide Chapter 1,
Exercise 4.

If resources are fully and efficiently employed, it is not possible to have more of both. However, as the government cuts defence expenditures, resources needed to produce civilian goods will be freed up. The opportunity cost of increased civilian goods is therefore the forgone military output. Or, if we were considering an increase in military output, the opportunity cost of increased military output would be the forgone civilian goods.

The choice is illustrated in Figure 1-2. Because resources are scarce, some combinations—those that would require more than the total available supply of resources for their production—cannot be attained. The negatively sloped curve on the graph divides the combinations that can be attained from those that cannot. Points above and to the right of this curve cannot be attained because there are not enough resources; points below and to the left of the curve can be attained without using all of the available resources; and points on the curve can just be attained if all the available resources are used efficiently. The curve is called the **production possibilities boundary.** (Sometimes the word "boundary" is replaced with "curve" or "frontier.") It has a negative slope because when all resources are being used efficiently, producing more of one kind of good requires producing less of the other kind.

A production possibilities boundary illustrates three concepts: scarcity, choice, and opportunity cost. Scarcity is indicated by the unattainable combinations outside the boundary; choice, by the need to choose among the alternative attainable points along the boundary; and opportunity cost, by the negative slope of the boundary.

The shape of the production possibilities boundary in Figure 1-2 implies that an increasing amount of civilian production must be given up to achieve equal successive increases in military production. This shape, referred to as *concave* to the origin, indicates that the opportunity cost of either good increases as we increase the amount of it that is produced. A straight-line boundary, as in Figure 1-1, indicates that the opportunity cost of one good in terms of the other stays constant, no matter how much of it is produced.

The concave shape in Figure 1-2 is the way in which economists usually draw a country's production possibilities boundary. The shape occurs because each factor of production is not equally useful in producing all

production possibilities boundary A curve showing which alternative combinations of commodities can just be attained if all available resources are used efficiently; it is the boundary between attainable and unattainable output combinations.

FIGURE 1-2   A Production Possibilities Boundary

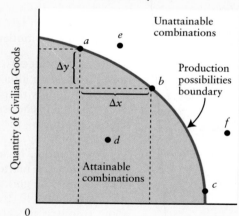

The negatively sloped boundary shows the combinations that are attainable when all resources are efficiently used. The production possibilities boundary separates the attainable combinations of goods, such as *a*, *b*, *c*, and *d*, from unattainable combinations, such as *e* and *f*. Points *a*, *b*, and *c* represent full and efficient use of society's resources. Point *d* represents either inefficient use of resources or failure to use all the available resources. If production moves from point *a* to point *b*, an opportunity cost is involved. The opportunity cost of producing Δ*x* more military goods is the necessary reduction in the production of civilian goods equal to Δ*y*.

Practise with Study Guide Chapter 1, Exercise 2.

goods. To see why differences among factors of production are so important, suppose we begin at point *c* in Figure 1-2, where most resources are devoted to the production of military goods, and then consider gradually shifting more and more resources toward the production of civilian goods. We might begin by shifting nutrient-rich land that is particularly well suited to growing wheat. This land may not be very useful for making military equipment, but it is very useful for making certain civilian goods (like bread). This shift of resources will therefore lead to a small reduction in military output but a substantial increase in civilian output. Thus, the opportunity cost of producing a few more units of civilian goods, which is equal to the forgone military output, is small. But as we shift more and more resources toward the production of civilian goods, and therefore move along the production possibilities boundary toward point *a*, we must shift more and more resources that are actually quite well suited to the production of military output, like aerospace engineers or the minerals needed to make gunpowder. As we produce more and more civilian goods (by having more and more resources devoted to producing them), the amount of military output that must be forgone to produce one *extra* unit of civilian goods rises. That is, the opportunity cost of producing one good rises as more of that good is produced.

Four Key Economic Problems

Modern economies involve thousands of complex production and consumption activities. Although this complexity is important, many of the basic kinds of decisions that must be made are not very different from those made in primitive economies in which people work with few tools and barter with their neighbours. Whatever the economic system, whether modern or primitive, there are four key economic questions.

Practise with Study Guide Chapter 1, Exercise 1.

resource allocation The allocation of an economy's scarce resources of land, labour, and capital among alternative uses.

What Is Produced and How?   This question concerns the *allocation* of scarce resources among alternative uses. Such **resource allocation** determines the quantities of various goods that are produced. Choosing to produce a particular combination of goods means choosing a particular allocation of resources among the industries or regions producing the goods. What determines which goods get produced and which ones do not?

Furthermore, because resources are scarce, it is desirable that they be used efficiently. Hence, it matters which of the available methods of production is used to produce each of the goods. What determines which methods of production get used and which ones do not? Any economy must have some mechanism by which these decisions about resource allocation are made.

What Is Consumed and By Whom?   What is the relationship between an economy's production of goods and the consumption enjoyed by its citizens? Economists seek to understand what determines the distribution of a nation's total output among its people. Who gets a lot, who gets a little, and why?

If production takes place on the production possibilities boundary, then how about consumption? Will the economy consume exactly the same goods that it produces? Or will the country's ability to trade with other countries permit the economy to consume a different combination of goods?

microeconomics The study of the causes and consequences of the allocation of resources as it is affected by the workings of the price system.

Questions relating to what is produced and how, and what is consumed and by whom, fall within the realm of microeconomics. **Microeconomics** is the study of the causes and consequences of the allocation of resources as it is affected by the workings of the price system and government policies that seek to influence it.

Why Are Resources Sometimes Idle? Sometimes many workers who would like to have jobs are unable to find employers to hire them. At the same time, the managers and owners of offices and factories could operate at a higher level of activity—that is, they could produce more goods and services. For some reason, however, these resources—labour, factories, and equipment—lie idle. Thus, in terms of Figure 1-2, the economy is operating inside its production possibilities boundary.

Why are resources sometimes idle? Should governments worry about such idle resources, or is there some reason to believe that such occasional idleness is appropriate in a well-functioning economy? Is there anything that the government can do to reduce such idleness?

Is Productive Capacity Growing? The capacity to produce goods and services grows rapidly in some countries, grows slowly in others, and actually declines in others. Growth in productive capacity can be represented by an outward shift of the production possibilities boundary, as shown in Figure 1-3. If an economy's capacity to produce goods and services is growing, some combinations that are unattainable today will become attainable in the future. Growth makes it possible to have more of all goods. What are the determinants of growth? Are there some undesirable side-effects of growth? Can governments do anything to influence economic growth?

Questions relating to the idleness of resources and the growth of productive capacity fall within the realm of macroeconomics. **Macroeconomics** is the study of the determination of economic aggregates such as total output, total employment, the price level, and the rate of economic growth.

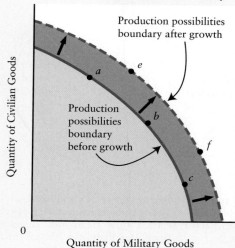

FIGURE 1-3   The Effect of Economic Growth on the Production Possibilities Boundary

Economic growth shifts the boundary outward and makes it possible to produce more of all products. Before growth in productive capacity, points *a*, *b*, and *c* were on the production possibilities boundary and points *e* and *f* were unattainable. After growth, as shown by the dark shaded band, points *e* and *f* and many other previously unattainable combinations are attainable.

macroeconomics The study of the determination of economic aggregates such as total output, the price level, employment, and growth.

1.3 WHO MAKES THE CHOICES AND HOW?

So choices have to be made, but who makes them and how are they made?

The Flow of Income and Expenditure

Figure 1-4 shows the basic decision makers and the flows of income and expenditure that they set up. Individuals own factors of production. They sell the services of these factors to producers and receive payments in return. These are their incomes. Producers use the factor services that they buy to make goods and services. They sell these to individuals, receiving payments in return. These are the incomes of producers. These basic flows of income and expenditure pass through markets. Individuals sell the services of the factor that they own in what are collectively called *factor markets*.

FIGURE 1-4 The Circular Flow of Income and Expenditure

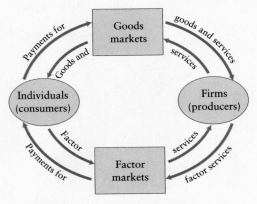

The red line shows the flows of goods and services; the blue line shows the payments made to purchase these. Factor services flow from individuals who own the factors (including their own labour) through factor markets to firms that use them to make goods and services. These goods and services then flow through goods markets to those who consume them. Money payments flow from firms to individuals through factor markets. These payments become the income of individuals. When they spend this income buying goods and services, money flows through goods markets back to producers.

When you get a part-time job during university, you are participating in the factor market. Producers sell their outputs of goods and services in what are collectively called *goods markets*. When you purchase a haircut or a new pair of shoes, for example, you are participating in the goods market.

The prices that are determined in these markets determine the incomes that are earned and the purchasing power of those incomes. People who get high prices for their factor services earn high incomes; those who get low prices earn low incomes. The income each person earns expressed as a fraction of all incomes that are earned in the nation shows the share of total income that each person can command. The *distribution of income* refers to how the nation's total income is distributed among its citizens. This is largely determined by the price that each type of factor service receives in factor markets.

Maximizing Decisions The basic decision makers in a market economy are individual consumers and producers. To these two groups we will shortly add a third, the government. The important assumption that economists usually make about how these two groups make their decisions is that everyone tries to do as well as possible for himself or herself. In the jargon of economics, people are assumed to be *maximizers*. When individuals decide how many factor services to sell to producers and how many products to buy from them, we assume that they make choices designed to maximize their well-being, or *utility*. When producers decide how many factor services to buy from individuals and how many goods to produce and sell to them, we assume that they make choices designed to maximize their *profits*.

Marginal Decisions Firms and consumers who are trying to maximize usually need to weigh the costs and benefits of their decisions *at the margin*. For example, when you consider buying an additional CD, you know the *marginal cost* of the CD—that is, how much you must pay to get one extra CD—and you need to weigh it against the *marginal benefit* that you will derive from that CD. If you are trying to maximize your utility, you will only buy that CD if you think that the benefit to you in terms of extra utility exceeds the marginal cost.

Similarly, a producer attempting to maximize its profits and considering whether to hire an extra worker must evaluate the *marginal cost* of the worker—the extra wages and benefits that must be paid—and weigh it against the *marginal benefit* of the worker—the increase in revenues that will be generated by the extra worker. A producer interested in maximizing its profit will only hire the extra worker if the benefit in terms of extra revenue exceeds the cost in terms of higher wages.

Consumers and producers who are maximizers are constantly making marginal decisions, whether to buy or sell a little bit more or less of the many things that they buy and sell.

Voting in an election is an example where decisions are *not* made on a marginal basis. When you vote in a Canadian federal election, you have only one vote and you must support one party over the others. When you do, you vote for everything that party stands for, even though you may prefer to pick and choose elements from each party's political platform. You cannot say "I vote for the Liberals on issue A and for the Conservatives on issue B." You must make a total, rather than a marginal, decision.

The Complexity of Production

Producers decide what to produce and how to produce it. Production is a very complex process in any modern economy. A typical car manufacturer assembles a product out of thousands of individual parts. It makes some of these parts itself. Most are subcontracted to parts manufacturers, and many of the major parts manufacturers subcontract some of their work out to smaller firms. This kind of production displays two characteristics noted long ago by Adam Smith—*specialization* and the *division of labour.*

Specialization In ancient hunter–gatherer societies, and in modern subsistence economies, most people make most of the things they need for themselves. However, from the time that people first engaged in settled agriculture and some of them began to live in towns, people have specialized in doing particular jobs. Artisan, soldier, priest, and government official were some of the earliest specialized occupations. Economists call this allocation of different jobs to different people the **specialization of labour.** There are two fundamental reasons why specialization is extraordinarily efficient compared with universal self-sufficiency.

> **specialization of labour** The specialization of individual workers in the production of particular goods or services.

First, individual abilities differ, and specialization allows each person to do what he or she can do relatively well while leaving everything else to be done by others. Even when people's abilities are unaffected by the act of specializing, the economy's total production is greater when people specialize than when they all try to be self-sufficient. This is true for individuals but it is also true for entire countries, and it is one of the most fundamental principles in economics: the principle of *comparative advantage.* A much fuller discussion of comparative advantage is found in Chapter 33, in which we discuss the gains from international trade.

The second reason that specialization is more efficient than self-sufficiency concerns changes in people's abilities that occur *because* they specialize. A person who concentrates on one activity becomes better at it than could a jack-of-all-trades. This is called *learning by doing,* and was a factor much stressed by early economists; modern research shows that it is important in many modern industries.

The Division of Labour Throughout most of history each artisan who specialized in making some product made the whole of that product. Over the last several hundred years, many technical advances have made it efficient to organize production methods into large-scale firms organized around what is called the **division of labour.** This term refers to specialization *within* the production process of a particular product.

> **division of labour** The breaking up of a production process into a series of specialized tasks, each done by a different worker.

Mass Production. In a mass-production factory, work is divided into highly specialized tasks using specialized machinery. Each individual repeatedly does one small task that is a small fraction of those necessary to produce any one product. This is an extreme case of the division of labour.

Artisans and Flexible Manufacturing. Two recent changes have significantly altered the degree of specialization found in many modern production processes. First, individual artisans have recently reappeared in some lines of production. They are responding to a revival in the demand for individually crafted, rather than mass-produced, products. Second, many manufacturing operations are being reorganized along new lines called "lean production" or "flexible manufacturing," which was pioneered by Japanese car manufacturers in the mid-1950s. It has led back to a more craft-based form of organization within the factory. In this technique, employees work as a team; each employee is able to do every team member's job rather than only one very specialized task at one point on the assembly line.

Globalization

Market economies constantly change, largely as a result of the development of new technologies. Many of the recent changes are referred to as *globalization,* a term often used loosely to mean the increased importance of international trade. International trade is, however, a very old phenomenon. The usual pattern over most of the last 200 years was manufactured goods being sent from Europe and North America to the rest of the world, with raw materials and primary products being sent in return. What is new in the last few decades is the globalization of manufacturing. Assembly of a product may take place in the most industrialized countries, but the hundreds of component parts are manufactured in dozens of different countries and delivered to the assembly plant "just in time" for assembly.

A major cause of globalization is the rapid reduction in transportation costs and the revolution in information technology that has occurred in the past 50 years. The cost of moving products around the world has fallen greatly over the last half of the twentieth century because of containerization and the increasing size of ships. Our ability to transmit and analyze data has been increasing even more dramatically, while the costs of doing so have been decreasing, equally dramatically. For example, today $1500 buys an ultra-slim laptop computer that has the same computing power as one that in 1970 cost $10 million and filled a large room. This revolution in information and communication technology has made it possible to coordinate economic transactions around the world in ways that were difficult and costly 50 years ago and quite impossible 100 years ago.

transnational corporations (TNCs) Firms that have operations in more than one country. Also called *multinational enterprises (MNEs).*

Globalization is as important for consumers as it is for producers. For example, as some tastes become universal to young people, spread by ever-increasing access to foreign television stations and global Internet chat lines, we can see the same clothes and hear the same music in virtually all big cities. And as tastes become more universal, many *corporations* are globalizing, as they become what economists call **transnational corporations (TNCs)**. McDonald's restaurants are as visible in Moscow or Beijing as in London, New York, Vancouver, or Montreal. Many other brands are also known around the world, such as Calvin Klein, Nike, Coca-Cola, Kellogg's, Heinz, Nestlé, Molson, Toyota, Rolls-Royce, Sony, and Mitsubishi.

Through the ongoing process of globalization, national economies are ever more linked to the global economy, in which an increasing share of jobs and incomes is created.

The word *globalization* has recently become a focal point for an important and contentious set of policy debates and public protests. These debates are often very confusing to the observer. See *Applying Economic Concepts 1-2* for a brief outline of the key issues.

The revolution in shipping and in computer technology has drastically reduced communication and transportation costs. This reduction in costs lies at the heart of globalization.

APPLYING ECONOMIC CONCEPTS 1-2

The Globalization Debate

Over the past several years, large public "globalization protests" have occurred in many cities around the world. These protests often occur when political leaders from many countries gather to discuss and negotiate agreements regarding international trade or finance. For example, in December 1999, the trade ministers from member countries of the World Trade Organization (WTO) met in Seattle to set the agenda for a new round of talks at which they would negotiate rules governing international trade. Thousands of angry protesters lined the streets of Seattle, throwing rocks and shouting slogans about the dangers of globalization and the undemocratic nature of the WTO talks. Thus, the "Battle of Seattle" was joined. Over the next few years, similar protests took place in Quebec City, Genoa, and several times in Washington, D.C. What are these protests about? What are the key issues?

The protesters, who generally refer to themselves as "anti-globalization activists," have two main arguments. First, they argue that increases in the flow of international trade and investment have been responsible for increasing global income inequality and worsening poverty in developing countries. Second, they argue that organizations such as the WTO, the World Bank, and the International Monetary Fund (IMF) operate in an undemocratic fashion and hold their meetings behind closed doors, out of view of and without critical input from the people whose lives their policies are so dramatically influencing. A related concern is that global economic agreements appear to give power to transnational corporations, taking power out of the hands of citizens. The anti-globalization activists are in favour of slowing down the process of globalization and reforming (if not eliminating) these international organizations.

On the other side of the barricades are the defenders of globalization and a rules-based approach to international trade. They argue that the process of globalization, far from being the cause of poverty in developing countries, is the best bet for *reducing* such poverty. They claim that freer trade between countries has been responsible for enormous advances in living standards over the past century, and that the developing countries of today will be much better off if trade is fur-

ther liberalized. Indeed, some defenders of globalization argue that one of the problems has been the developed countries' unwillingness to permit genuinely free international trade with the developing countries—especially for products such as agricultural commodities and textiles in which the developing countries have a competitive advantage. According to this view, the biggest contributor to poverty in developing countries is too *little* trade, not too much.

Defenders of globalization also point out that the meetings held by the WTO and other international organizations are voluntary meetings held between the democratically elected leaders of the member countries, and that no agreements are legal until each of the member countries ratifies them in its parliament. Thus, the process is democratic.

Is there a middle ground in this debate? On the democratic issue, the defenders of globalization are probably correct, at least literally. The agreements do not come into force until they are passed by the respective parliaments. The political challenge for all countries involved is to improve communications so that these complicated international agreements—which often run to thousands of pages in length—are made clear enough that they can be effectively debated in the respective parliaments. With effective political debates within each member country, citizens will be more involved in the policy-making process.

The more subtle issue is the relationship between globalization and poverty. Most economists would argue, for reasons that we will explore in Chapters 33 and 34, that freer trade will lead to increases in *average* living standards within both developed and developing countries. A typical empirical finding is that an economy whose trade share increases from 20 percent to 40 percent of its GDP can expect to experience a 10-percent increase in per capita income. But there is no guarantee that, within any particular country, these gains in living standards will be shared among the various segments of society in a socially just way. One of the crucial challenges faced by governments negotiating international economic agreements is to ensure that the benefits from such agreements are spread throughout the population, thus increasing their public acceptability.

Markets and Money

People who specialize in doing only one thing must satisfy most of their wants by consuming things made by other people. In early societies the exchange of goods and services took place by simple mutual agreement among neighbours. In the course of time, however, trading became centred on particular gathering places called *markets*. For example, the French markets or trade fairs of Champagne were well-known throughout Europe as early as the eleventh century. Even now, many small towns in Canada have regular market days. Today, however, the term *market* has a much broader meaning. We use the term *market economy* to refer to a society in which people specialize in productive activities and meet most of their material wants through voluntary exchanges with other people.

Specialization must be accompanied by trade. People who produce only one thing must trade most of it to obtain all of the other things they desire.

barter An economic system in which goods and services are traded directly for other goods and services.

Early trading was by means of **barter**, the trading of goods directly for other goods. But barter is costly in terms of time spent searching out satisfactory exchanges. If a farmer has wheat but wants a hammer, he must find someone who has a hammer and wants wheat. A successful barter transaction thus requires what is called a *double coincidence of wants*.

Money eliminates the cumbersome system of barter by separating the transactions involved in the exchange of products. If a farmer has wheat and wants a hammer, he merely has to find someone who wants wheat. The farmer takes money in exchange. Then he finds a person who wishes to sell a hammer and gives up the money for the hammer.

Money greatly facilitates specialization and trade.

▌ 1.4 IS THERE AN ALTERNATIVE TO THE MARKET ECONOMY?

In this chapter we have discussed the elements of an economy based on free-market transactions—what we call a *market economy*. But are there any alternatives to this type of economy? The answer is no in one sense and yes in another. We answer no because the modern economy has no *practical* alternative to reliance on market determination. We answer yes because it is possible to identify other types of economic systems.

Types of Economic Systems

It is helpful to distinguish three pure types of economies, called *traditional*, *command*, and *market* economies. These economies differ in the way in which economic decisions are coordinated. But no actual economy fits neatly into one of these three categories—all real economies contain some elements of each type.

traditional economy An economy in which behaviour is based mostly on tradition.

Traditional Economies   A **traditional economy** is one in which behaviour is based primarily on tradition, custom, and habit. Young men follow their fathers' occupations. Women do what their mothers did. There is little change in the pattern of goods produced from year to year, other than those imposed by the vagaries of nature. The techniques of production also follow traditional patterns, except when the effects of an occasional new invention are felt. Finally, production is allocated among the members according to long-established traditions.

Such a system works best in an unchanging environment. Under such static conditions, a system that does not continually require people to make choices can prove effective in meeting economic and social needs.

Traditional systems were common in earlier times. The feudal system, under which most people in medieval Europe lived, was a largely traditional society. Peasants, artisans, and most others living in villages inherited their positions in that society. They also usually inherited their specific jobs, which they handled in traditional ways.

Command Economies

In command economies, economic behaviour is determined by some central authority, usually the government, which makes most of the necessary decisions on what to produce, how to produce it, and who gets it. Such economies are characterized by the *centralization* of decision making. Because centralized decision makers usually lay down elaborate and complex plans for the behaviour that they wish to impose, the terms **command economy** and *centrally planned economy* are usually used synonymously.

command economy An economy in which most economic decisions are made by a central planning authority.

The sheer quantity of data required for the central planning of an entire economy is enormous, and the task of analyzing it to produce a fully integrated plan can hardly be exaggerated. Moreover, the plan must be continually modified to take account not only of current data but also of future trends in labour supplies, technological developments, and people's tastes for various goods and services. This is a notoriously difficult exercise, not least because of the unavailability of all essential, accurate, and up-to-date information.

Thirty years ago, more than one-third of the world's population lived in countries that relied heavily on central planning. Today, the number of such countries is small. Even in countries where central planning is the proclaimed system, as in Cuba, increasing amounts of market determination are being quietly permitted.

Free-Market Economies

In the third type of economic system, the decisions about resource allocation are made without any central direction. Instead, they result from innumerable independent decisions made by individual producers and consumers. Such a system is known as a **free-market economy** or, more simply, a *market economy*. In such an economy, decisions relating to the basic economic issues are *decentralized*. Despite the absence of a central plan, these many decentralized decisions are nonetheless coordinated. As we discussed earlier in the chapter, the main coordinating device is the set of market-determined prices—which is why free-market systems are often called *price systems*.

free-market economy An economy in which most economic decisions are made by private households and firms.

In a pure market economy, all of these decisions are made by buyers and sellers acting through unhindered markets. The state provides the background of defining property and protecting rights against foreign and domestic enemies but, beyond that, markets determine all resource allocation and income distribution.

Mixed Economies

Economies that are fully traditional or fully centrally planned or wholly free-market are pure types that are useful for studying basic principles. When we look in detail at any real economy, however, we discover that its economic behaviour is the result of some mixture of central control and market determination, with a certain amount of traditional behaviour as well.

In practice, every economy is a **mixed economy** in the sense that it combines significant elements of all three systems in determining economic behaviour.

mixed economy An economy in which some economic decisions are made by firms and households and some by the government.

Furthermore, within any economy, the degree of the mix varies from sector to sector. For example, in some planned economies, the command principle was used more often to determine behaviour in heavy-goods industries, such as steel, than in agriculture. Farmers were often given substantial freedom to produce and sell what they wished in response to varying market prices.

When economists speak of a particular economy as being centrally planned, we mean only that the degree of the mix is weighted heavily toward the command principle. When we speak of one as being a market economy, we mean only that the degree of the mix is weighted heavily toward decentralized decision making.

Although no country offers an example of either system working alone, some economies, such as those of Canada, the United States, France, and Hong Kong, rely much more heavily on market decisions than others, such as the economies of China, North Korea, and Cuba. Yet even in Canada, the command principle has some sway. Crown corporations, legislated minimum wages, rules and regulations for environmental protection, quotas on some agricultural outputs, and restrictions on the import of some items are just a few examples.

The Great Debate

As we saw earlier, in 1776 Adam Smith was one of the first people to analyze the operation of markets, and he stressed the relative efficiency of free-market economies. A century later, another great economist and political philosopher, Karl Marx (1818–1883), argued that although free-market economies would indeed be successful in producing high levels of output, they could not be relied on to ensure that this output would be justly distributed among citizens. He argued the benefits of a centrally planned system in which the government could ensure a more equitable distribution of output.

Beginning with the Soviet Union in the early 1920s, many nations followed Marx's thinking and adopted systems in which conscious government central planning replaced the operation of the free market. For almost a century, a great debate then raged on the relative merits of command economies versus market economies. Along with the Soviet Union, the countries of Eastern Europe and China were command economies for much of the twentieth century. Canada, the United States, and most of the countries of Western Europe were, and still are, primarily market economies. The apparent successes of the Soviet Union and China in the 1950s and 1960s, including the ability to mobilize considerable resources into heavy industries, suggested to many observers that the command principle was at least as good for organizing economic behaviour as the market principle. Over the long run, however, planned economies proved to be a failure of such disastrous proportions that they seriously depressed the living standards of their citizens. Within the last two decades of the twentieth century, these countries abandoned their central planning apparatus and began the difficult transition back toward market economies.

Lessons From History 1-1 discusses in more detail why the centrally planned economies failed. This failure suggests the superiority of decentralized markets over centrally planned ones as mechanisms for allocating an economy's scarce resources. Put another way, it demonstrates the superiority of mixed economies with substantial elements of market determination over fully planned command economies. However, it does *not* demonstrate, as some observers have asserted, the superiority of completely free-market economies over mixed economies.

There is no guarantee that completely free markets will, on their own, handle such urgent matters as controlling pollution or providing public goods (like national defence). Indeed, as we shall see in later chapters, much economic theory is devoted to explaining why free markets often *fail* to do these things. Mixed economies, with significant elements of government intervention, are needed to do these jobs.

Furthermore, acceptance of the free market over central planning does not provide an excuse to ignore a country's pressing social issues. Acceptance of the benefits of the free market still leaves plenty of scope to debate the most appropriate levels and types of government policies directed at achieving specific social goals. It follows that there is still considerable room for disagreement about the degree of the mix of market and government determination in any modern mixed economy—room enough to accommodate such divergent views as could be expressed by conservative, liberal, and modern social democratic parties.

So, the first answer to the question about the existence of an alternative to the market economy is no: There is no practical alternative to a mixed system with major reliance on markets but some government presence in most aspects of the economy. The second answer is yes: Within the framework of a mixed economy there are substantial alternatives among many different and complex mixes of free-market and government determination of economic life.

The debate regarding the appropriate roles of governments and free markets figures prominently in discussions of how today's developing countries can best bring about improvements in their citizens' living standards. For a detailed discussion of the "Challenges Facing the Developing Countries," see the *Additional Topics* section of this book's MyEconLab.

www.myeconlab.com

Government in the Modern Mixed Economy

Market economies in today's advanced industrial countries are based primarily on voluntary transactions between individual buyers and sellers. Private individuals have the right to buy and sell what they wish, to accept or refuse work that is offered to them, and to move where they want when they want.

Key institutions are private property and freedom of contract, both of which must be maintained by active government policies. The government creates laws of ownership and contract and then provides the institutions to enforce these laws.

In modern mixed economies, governments go well beyond these important basic functions. They intervene in market transactions to correct what economists call *market failures*. These are well-defined situations in which free markets do not work well. Some products, called *public goods*, are usually not provided at all by markets because their use cannot usually be restricted to those who pay for them. Defence and police protection are examples of public goods. In other cases, private transactors impose costs called *externalities* on those who have no say in the transaction. This is the case when factories pollute the air and rivers. The public is harmed but plays no part in the transaction. These market failures explain why governments sometimes intervene to alter the allocation of resources.

Also, important equity issues arise from letting free markets determine people's incomes. Some people lose their jobs because firms are reorganizing to become more

LESSONS FROM HISTORY 1-1

The Failure of Central Planning

The fall of the Berlin Wall in November 1989 was the beginning of the end of the Soviet system of central planning.

The Bolshevik Revolution in 1917 in Russia brought the world its first example of a large-scale communist society. With the rise to power of Joseph Stalin and the creation of the Soviet Union in 1922, communism and central economic planning began their spread throughout Eastern and Central Europe. This spread of central planning was accelerated by the Soviet Union's role following the Second World War in "liberating" several countries from Nazi domination, thus creating the group of countries that became known as the Eastern Bloc or the Soviet Bloc.

Despite the successful geographic spread of communism, the Soviet system of central economic planning had many difficulties. By 1989, communism had collapsed throughout Central and Eastern Europe, and the economic systems of formerly communist countries began the difficult transition from centrally planned to market economies. Although political issues surely played a role in these events, the economic changes generally confirmed the superiority of a market-oriented price system over central planning as a method of organizing economic activity. The failure of central planning had many causes, but four were particularly significant.

Failure of Coordination

In the centrally planned economies, a body of planners attempted to coordinate all the economic decisions about production, investment, trade, and consumption that were likely to be made by producers and consumers throughout the country. Without the use of prices to signal relative scarcity and abundance, central planning generally proved impossible to do with any reasonable degree of success. Bottlenecks in production, shortages of some goods, and gluts of others plagued the Soviet economy for decades.

efficient in the face of new technologies. Others keep their jobs, but the market places so little value on their services that they face economic deprivation. The old and the chronically ill may suffer if their past circumstances did not allow them to save enough to support themselves. For many reasons of this sort, almost everyone accepts some government intervention to redistribute income. Care must be taken, however, not to kill the goose that lays the golden egg. By taking too much from higher-income people, we risk eliminating their incentive to work hard and produce income, some of which is to be redistributed to those in need.

Failure of Quality Control

Central planners could monitor the number of units produced by any factory and reward plants that exceeded their production targets and punish those that fell short. Factory managers operating under these conditions would meet their quotas by whatever means were available, and once the goods passed out of their factory, what happened to them was someone else's headache.

In market economies, poor quality is punished by low sales, and retailers soon give a signal to factory managers by shifting their purchases to other suppliers. The incentives that obviously flow from such private-sector purchasing discretion were generally absent from centrally planned economies, where purchases and sales were organized by the body of planners and prices and profits were not used to signal customer satisfaction or dissatisfaction.

Misplaced Incentives

In market economies, relative wages and salaries provide incentives for labour to move from place to place, and the possibility of losing one's job provides an incentive to work diligently. This is a harsh mechanism that punishes job losers with loss of income (although social programs provide floors to the amount of economic punishment that can be suffered). In centrally planned economies, workers usually had complete job security.

Industrial unemployment was rare, and even when it did occur, new jobs were usually found for all who lost theirs. Although the high level of security was attractive to many people, it proved impossible to provide sufficient incentives for reasonably hard and efficient work under such conditions.

Environmental Degradation

Fulfilling production plans became the all-embracing goal in centrally planned economies, to the exclusion of most other considerations, including the environment. As a result, environmental degradation occurred in the Soviet Union and the countries of Eastern Europe on a scale unknown in advanced Western nations. A particularly disturbing example (only one of many) occurred in central Asia where high quotas for cotton output led to indiscriminate use of pesticides and irrigation. Birth defects became very common, and the vast Aral Sea has been half-drained, causing major environmental effects.

This failure to protect the environment stemmed from the pressure to fulfill production plans and the absence of a "political marketplace" where citizens could express their preferences for the environment. Imperfect though the system may be in democratic market economies—and in some particular cases it has been quite poor—their record of environmental protection has been vastly better than that of the centrally planned economies.

These are some of the reasons all modern economies are mixed economies. Throughout most of the twentieth century in advanced industrial societies, the mix had been altering towards more and more government participation in decisions about the allocation of resources and the distribution of income. In the past three decades, however, there has been a worldwide movement to reduce the degree of government participation. The details of this shift in the market/government mix, and the reasons for it, are some of the major issues that will be studied in this book.

S U M M A R Y

1.1 THE COMPLEXITY OF THE MODERN ECONOMY   LO 1

- A market economy is self-organizing in the sense that when individual consumers and producers act independently to pursue their own self-interest, responding to prices determined in open markets, the collective outcome is coordinated.

1.2 SCARCITY, CHOICE, AND OPPORTUNITY COST   LO 2

- Scarcity is a fundamental problem faced by all economies. Not enough resources are available to produce all the goods and services that people would like to consume. Scarcity makes it necessary to choose. All societies must have a mechanism for choosing what goods and services will be produced and in what quantities.
- The concept of opportunity cost emphasizes the problem of scarcity and choice by measuring the cost of obtaining a unit of one product in terms of the number of units of other products that could have been obtained instead.

- A production possibilities boundary shows all of the combinations of goods that can be produced by an economy whose resources are fully and efficiently employed. Movement from one point to another along the boundary requires a reallocation of resources.
- Four basic questions must be answered in all economies: What is produced and how? What is consumed and by whom? Why are resources sometimes idle? Is productive capacity growing?

1.3 WHO MAKES THE CHOICES AND HOW?   LO 3

- The interaction of consumers and producers through goods and factor markets is illustrated by the circular flow of income and expenditure. Individual consumers sell factor services to producers and thereby earn their income. Similarly, producers earn their income by selling goods and services to individual consumers.
- Individual consumers are assumed to make their decisions in an effort to maximize their well-being or utility. Producers' decisions are assumed to be designed to maximize their profits.

- Modern economies are based on the specialization and division of labour, which necessitate the exchange (trading) of goods and services. Exchange takes place in markets and is facilitated by the use of money.
- Driven by the ongoing revolution in transportation and communications technology, the world economy is rapidly globalizing.

1.4 IS THERE AN ALTERNATIVE TO THE MARKET ECONOMY?   LO 4

- There are three pure types of economies: traditional, command, and free-market. In practice, all economies are mixed economies in that their economic behaviour responds to mixes of tradition, government command, and price incentives.
- In the late 1980s, events in Eastern Europe and the Soviet Union led to the general acceptance that the system of fully centrally planned economies had failed to produce minimally acceptable living standards for its citizens. All of these countries are now moving toward greater market determination and less state command in their economies.
- Governments play an important role in modern mixed economies. They create and enforce important background institutions such as private property and freedom of contract. They intervene to correct market failures. They also redistribute income in the interests of equity.

KEY CONCEPTS

The self-organizing economy
Scarcity and the need for choice
Choice and opportunity cost
Production possibilities boundary

Resource allocation
Specialization
The division of labour
Globalization

Traditional economies
Command economies
Free-market economies
Mixed economies

STUDY EXERCISES

1. What is the difference between microeconomics and macroeconomics?

2. List the four main types of economic systems and their main attributes.

3. Explain the three economic concepts illustrated by the production possibilities boundary.

4. **myeconlab** Consider an economy that produces only food and clothing. Its production possibilities boundary is shown below.

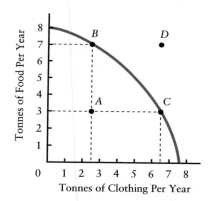

a. If the economy is at point *A*, how many tonnes of clothing and how many tonnes of food are being produced? At point *B*? At point *C*?

b. What do we know about the use of resources when the economy is at point *A*? At point *B*? At point *C*?

c. If the economy is at point *B*, what is the opportunity cost of producing one more tonne of food? What is the opportunity cost of producing one more tonne of clothing?

d. What do we know about the use of resources at point *D*? How would it be possible for the economy to produce at point *D*?

5. State and explain two reasons why the specialization of labour is more efficient than universal self-sufficiency.

6. Choiceland has 250 workers and produces only two goods, *X* and *Y*. Labour is the only factor of production, but some workers are better suited to producing

X than *Y* (and vice versa). The table below shows the maximum levels of output of each good possible from various levels of labour input.

Number of Workers Producing *X*	Annual Production of *X*	Number of Workers Producing *Y*	Annual Production of *Y*
0	0	250	1300
50	20	200	1200
100	45	150	900
150	60	100	600
200	70	50	350
250	75	0	0

a. Draw the production possibilities boundary for Choiceland on a scale diagram.

b. Compute the opportunity cost of producing an extra 10 units of *X* if the economy is initially producing 60 units of *X* and 600 units of *Y*. How does this compare to the opportunity cost if the economy were initially producing 70 units of *X*?

c. Suppose now that the technology associated with producing good *Y* improves, so that the maximum level of *Y* that can be produced from any given level of labour input increases by 10 percent. Explain (or show in a diagram) what happens to the production possibilities curve.

7. **myeconlab** Explain why a technological improvement in the production of one good means that a country can now produce more of *other* goods than it did previously. Hint: Draw a country's production possibilities boundary to help answer this question.

8. Consider your decision whether to go skiing for the weekend. Suppose transportation, lift tickets, and accommodation for the weekend costs $300. Suppose also that restaurant food for the weekend will cost $75. Finally, suppose you have a weekend job that you will have to miss if you go skiing, which pays you $120 (after tax) for the one weekend day that you work. What is the opportunity cost of going skiing? Do you need any other information before computing the opportunity cost?

9. Suppose you and a friend go wilderness camping for a week and must find your own food to survive. From past experience, you know that you and your friend have different abilities in fishing and hunting. If each of you were to work for one day either catching fish or trapping rabbits, the number of fish and rabbits that you could catch is given in the following table:

	Fish	Rabbits
You	6	3
Your friend	8	2

You and your friend decide that you should allocate the duties so that you get the most food for the least amount of effort. For simplicity, assume that one fish represents the same amount of food as one rabbit.

a. What is the opportunity cost for you to catch an additional rabbit? What is your friend's opportunity cost of catching an extra rabbit?

b. What allocation of tasks maximizes total output for the least amount of effort?

c. Suppose you both decide to work for two days according to the allocation in part (b). What is the total amount of output? What would it have been had you chosen the reverse allocation of tasks?

DISCUSSION QUESTIONS

1. What is the difference between scarcity and poverty? If everyone in the world had enough to eat, could we say that food was no longer scarce?

2. Evidence accumulates that the use of chemical fertilizers, which increases agricultural production greatly, damages water quality. Analyze the choice between more food and cleaner water involved in using such fertilizers. Use a production possibilities curve with agricultural output on the vertical axis and water quality on the horizontal axis. In what ways does this production possibilities curve reflect scarcity, choice, and opportunity cost? How would an improved fertilizer that increased agricultural output without further worsening water quality affect the curve? Suppose a pollution-free fertilizer were developed; would this mean that there would no longer be any opportunity cost in using it?

3. Discuss the following statement by a leading economist: "One of the mysteries of semantics is why the government-managed economies ever came to be called planned and the market economies unplanned. It is the former that are in chronic chaos, in which buyers stand in line hoping to buy some toilet paper or soap. It is the latter that are in reasonable equilibrium—where if you want a cake of soap or a steak or a shirt or a car, you can go to the store and find that the item is magically there for you to buy. It is the liberal economies that reflect a highly sophisticated planning system, and the government-managed economies that are primitive and unplanned."

4. Consider the market for doctors' services. In what way has this market taken advantage of the specialization of labour?

5. "It is not from the benevolence of the butcher, the brewer, or the baker, that we expect our dinner, but from their regard to their own interest. We address ourselves, not to their humanity but to their self-love, and never talk to them of our own necessities but of their advantages." Do you agree with this quotation from Adam Smith's classic, *The Wealth of Nations*? How are "our dinner" and "their self-interest" related to the price system? What does Smith assume to be the motives of firms and households?

6. In the chapter we used a simple idea of a production possibilities boundary to illustrate the concepts of scarcity, choice, and opportunity cost. We assumed there were only two goods—call them *X* and *Y*. But we all know that any economy produces many more than just two goods. Explain why the insights illustrated in Figure 1-2 are more general, and why the assumption of only two goods is a useful one.

CHAPTER 2

How Economists Work

LO LEARNING OBJECTIVES

In this chapter you will learn

1. to distinguish between positive and normative statements.
2. how economists use models to help them think about the economy.
3. about the interaction between economic theories and empirical observation.
4. to identify several types of economic data, including index numbers, time-series and cross-sectional data, and scatter diagrams.
5. that the slope of a relation between two variables, X and Y, is interpreted as the marginal response in Y to a unit change in X.

If you read the newspaper, watch television, listen to the radio, or surf Internet news sites you will often see or hear some economist's opinions being reported, perhaps about: unemployment, the exchange rate, or interest rates; some new tax; the case for privatization or regulation of an industry; or the possible reforms to Canada's health-care system. Where do economists' opinions come from? Are they supported by hard evidence, and if so, why do economists sometimes disagree with each other over important issues?

Economics is a social science, and in this chapter we explore what it means to be "scientific" in the study of economics. Along the way we will learn much about theories, hypotheses, data, testing, and graphing. We begin with the important distinction between positive and normative statements.

2.1 POSITIVE AND NORMATIVE ADVICE

Economists give two broad types of advice, called *normative* and *positive*. For example, they sometimes advise that the government ought to try harder to reduce unemployment. When they say such things they are giving normative advice; in this case, they are making judgements about the value of the various things that the government could do with its limited resources and about the costs and benefits of reducing unemployment. Advice that depends on a value judgement is normative—it tells others what they *ought* to do.

Another type of advice is illustrated by the statement, "If the government wants to reduce unemployment, reducing unemployment insurance benefits is an effective way of doing so." This is positive advice. It does not rely on a judgement about the value of reducing unemployment. Instead, the expert is saying, "If this is what you want to do, here is a way to do it."

normative statement A statement about what ought to be as opposed to what actually is.

positive statement A statement about what actually is (was or will be), as opposed to what ought to be.

Practise with Study Guide Chapter 2, Short-Answer Question 1.

Normative statements depend on value judgements and cannot be settled by recourse to facts. In contrast, **positive statements** do not involve value judgements. They are statements about matters of fact. The distinction between positive and normative is fundamental to scientific progress. Much of the success of modern science depends on the ability of scientists to separate their views on *what does happen* in the world from their views on *what they would like to happen*. For example, until the eighteenth century almost everyone believed that the Earth was only a few thousand years old. Evidence then began to accumulate that the Earth was billions of years old. This evidence was hard for most people to accept since it ran counter to a literal reading of many religious texts. Many did not want to believe the evidence. Nevertheless, scientists, many of whom were religious, continued their research because they refused to allow their feelings about what they wanted to believe to affect their scientific search for the truth. Eventually, all scientists came to accept that the Earth is about 4 billion years old.

Distinguishing what is actually true from what we would like to be requires distinguishing between positive and normative statements.

Examples of both types of statements are given in Table 2-1. All four positive statements in the table are assertions about the nature of the world in which we live. In contrast, the four normative statements involve value judgements. Notice two things about the positive/normative distinction. First, positive statements need not be true. Statement C is almost certainly false. Yet it is positive, not normative. Second, the inclusion of a value judgement in a statement does not necessarily make the statement normative. Statement D is a positive statement about the value judgements that people hold. We could conduct a survey to check if people really do prefer low unemployment to low inflation. We could ask them and we could observe how they voted. There is no need for the economist to rely on a value judgement in order to check the validity of the statement itself.

We leave you to analyze the remaining six statements to decide precisely why each is either positive or normative. Remember to apply the two tests. First, is the statement only about actual or alleged facts? If so, it is a positive one. Second, are value judgements necessary to assess the truth of the statement? If so, it is normative.

TABLE 2-1   Positive and Normative Statements

Positive	Normative
A Raising interest rates encourages people to save.	E People should be encouraged to save.
B High rates of income tax encourage people to evade paying taxes.	F Governments should arrange taxes so that people cannot avoid paying them.
C Lowering the price of tobacco leads people to smoke less.	G The government should raise the tax on tobacco to discourage people from smoking.
D The majority of the population would prefer a policy that reduced unemployment to one that reduced inflation.	H The government ought to be more concerned with reducing unemployment than inflation.

Disagreements Among Economists

Economists often disagree with each other in public discussions, frequently because of poor communication. The adversaries fail to define their terms or their points of reference clearly, and so they end up "arguing past" each other, with the only certain result being that the audience is left confused.

Another source of disagreement stems from some economists' failure to acknowledge the full state of their ignorance. There are many things on which the evidence is far from conclusive. Informed judgements are then required in order to take a position on even a purely positive question. In such cases, a responsible economist will make clear the extent to which his or her view is based on judgements about the relevant facts.

Economists often disagree with each other in the press or at conferences, but their debates are more often about normative issues than positive ones.

Perhaps the biggest source of public disagreement between economists is based on the positive/normative distinction. Different economists have different values, and these normative views play a large part in most discussions of public policy. Many economists stress the importance of individual responsibility and argue, for example, that lower employment insurance benefits would be desirable because people would have a greater incentive to search for a job. Other economists stress the need for a generous "social safety net" and argue that higher employment insurance benefits would be desirable because human hardship would be reduced. In such debates, and there are many in economics, it is the responsibility of the economist to state clearly what part of the proffered advice is normative and what part is positive.

Because the world is complex and because no issue can be settled beyond any doubt, economists rarely agree unanimously on an issue. Nevertheless, there is an impressive amount of agreement on many aspects of how the economy works and what happens when governments intervene to alter its workings. A survey published in the *American Economic Review*, perhaps the most influential economics journal, showed strong agreement among economists on many propositions, including: "Rent control leads to a housing shortage" (85 percent yes), "Tariffs usually reduce economic welfare" (93 percent yes), "Large government budget deficits have adverse effects on the economy" (83 percent yes), and "A minimum wage increases unemployment among young workers" (79 percent yes). Other examples of these areas of agreement will be found in many places throughout this book.

2.2 ECONOMIC THEORIES

Economists seek to understand the world by developing *theories* and *models* that explain some of the things that have been seen and to predict some of the things that will be seen. What is a theory and what is a model?

Theories

Theories are constructed to explain things. For example, what determines the number of eggs sold in Winnipeg on a particular day, and the price at which they are sold? As part of the answer to questions such as these, economists have developed theories of demand and supply—theories that we will study in detail in the next three chapters. Any theory is distinguished by its variables, assumptions, and predictions.

Variables The basic elements of any theory are its variables. A **variable** is a magnitude that can take on different possible values.

In our theory of the egg market, the variable *quantity of eggs* might be defined as the number of cartons of 12 Grade A large eggs. The variable *price of eggs* is the amount of money that must be given up to purchase each carton of eggs. The particular values taken on by those two variables might be: 2000 cartons at a price of $1.80 on July 1, 2006; 1800 cartons at a price of $1.95 on July 1, 2007; and 1950 cartons at a price of $1.85 on July 1, 2008.

There are two broad categories of variables that are important in any theory. An **endogenous variable** is one whose value is determined within the theory. An **exogenous variable** influences the endogenous variables but is itself determined outside the theory. To illustrate the difference, the price of eggs and the quantity of eggs are endogenous variables in our theory of the egg market—our theory is designed to explain them. The state of the weather, however, is an exogenous variable. It may well affect the number of eggs consumers demand or producers supply but we can safely assume that the state of the weather is not influenced by the market for eggs.

Assumptions A theory's assumptions concern motives, physical relations, directions of causation, and the conditions under which the theory is meant to apply.

Motives. The theories we study in this book make the fundamental assumption that everyone pursues his or her own self-interest when making economic decisions. People are assumed to know what they want, and to know how to go about getting it within the constraints set by the resources at their command.

Physical Relations. If egg producers buy more chicks and use more labour, land, and chicken feed, they will probably produce more eggs. This is an example of one of the most important physical relations in economics. It concerns assumptions about how the amount of output is related to the quantities of factors of production used to produce it. This relation is called a *production function*.

Direction of Causation. When economists assume that one variable is related to another, they are assuming some causal link between the two. For example, when the amount of eggs that producers want to supply is assumed to increase when the cost of their chicken feed falls, the causation runs from the price of chicken feed to the supply of eggs. Producers supply more eggs because the price of chicken feed has fallen; they are not assumed to get cheaper chicken feed because of their decision to supply more eggs.

Conditions of Application. Assumptions are often used to specify the conditions under which a theory is meant to hold. For example, a theory that assumes

variable Any well-defined item, such as the price or quantity of a commodity, that can take on various specific values.

endogenous variable A variable that is explained within a theory. Sometimes called an *induced variable* or a *dependent variable*.

exogenous variable A variable that is determined outside the theory. Sometimes called an *autonomous variable* or an *independent variable*.

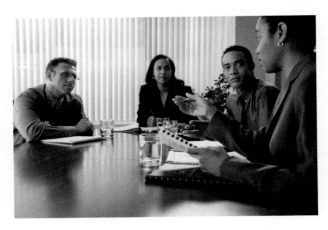

A key assumption in economics is that firms make decisions with the goal of maximizing their profits.

there is "no government" usually does not mean literally the absence of government, but only that the theory is meant to apply when governments are not significantly affecting the situation being studied.

Although assumptions are an essential part of all theories, students are often concerned about those that seem unrealistic. An example will illustrate some of the issues involved. Much of the theory that we are going to study in this book uses the assumption that owners of firms attempt to maximize their profits. The assumption of profit maximization allows economists to make predictions about the behaviour of firms, such as, "firms will supply more output if the market price increases."

Profit maximization may seem like a rather crude assumption. Surely, for example, the managers of firms sometimes choose to protect the environment rather than pursue certain highly polluting but profitable opportunities. Does this not discredit the assumption of profit maximization by showing it to be unrealistic?

The answer is no; to make successful predictions, the theory does not require that managers be solely and unwaveringly motivated by the desire to maximize profits at all times. All that is required is that profits be a sufficiently important consideration that a theory based on the assumption of profit maximization will lead to explanations and predictions that are substantially correct. It is not always appropriate to criticize a theory because its assumptions seem unrealistic. A good theory abstracts in a useful way; a poor theory does not. If a theory has ignored some genuinely important factors, its predictions will usually be contradicted by the evidence.

All theory is an abstraction from reality. If it were not, it would merely duplicate the world in all its complexity and would add little to our understanding of it.

Predictions   A theory's predictions are the propositions that can be deduced from it. They are often called *hypotheses*. For example, a prediction from our theory of the egg market is that, "if the price of chicken feed falls, producers will want to sell more eggs." Another prediction from the same theory is that "if the price of eggs declines, consumers will want to purchase more eggs."

Models

Economists use the term **economic model** in two different but related ways.

First, a model may be an illustrative abstraction, not meant to be elaborate enough to generate testable hypotheses. The circular flow of income and expenditure in Chapter 1 is a model of this sort, as is the production possibilities boundary. Both models help us to organize our thinking and gain crucial economic insights, even though the real world is much more complex than the model. In some ways, a model of this sort is like a political caricature. Its value is in the insights it provides that help us to understand key features of a complex world.

Second, the term *model* is used as a synonym for a theory, as when economists speak of the Keynesian model of the determination of national income, or the demand-and-supply model of the Winnipeg egg market that we discussed earlier. In both cases, the word *model* could easily be replaced by the word *theory*. Sometimes economists use *model* to refer to a specific quantitative version of a theory. In this case, specific numbers are attached to the mathematical relationships embodied in the theory. The result is that the predictions are more precise. For example, rather than a prediction such as "a decrease in the price of chicken feed will lead to an increase in the quantity of eggs supplied," the prediction from the more specific model might be "a 10-percent reduction in the price of chicken feed will lead to an 8-percent increase in the number of eggs supplied."

economic model A term used in several related ways: sometimes for an abstraction designed to illustrate some point but not designed to generate testable hypotheses, and sometimes as a synonym for theory.

2.3 **TESTING THEORIES**

A theory is tested by confronting its predictions with evidence. For example, is a decrease in the price of chicken feed *actually* followed by an increase in the amount of eggs producers want to sell? Generally, theories tend to be abandoned when they are no longer useful. A theory ceases to be useful when it cannot predict better than an alternative theory. When a theory consistently fails to predict better than an available alternative, it is either modified or replaced.

The old question "Which came first: the chicken or the egg?" is often raised when discussing economic theories. In the first instance, it was observation that preceded economic theories; people were not born with economic theories embedded in their minds. However, once economics was established as a scientific line of inquiry, theories and evidence interacted with each other. It has now become impossible to say that one precedes the other. In some cases, empirical evidence may suggest inadequacies that require the development of better theories. In other cases, an inspired guess may lead to a theory that has little current empirical support but is subsequently found to explain many observations. This interaction between theory and empirical observation is illustrated in Figure 2-1.

The scientific approach is central to the study of economics: Empirical observation leads to the construction of theories, theories generate specific hypotheses, and the hypotheses are tested by more detailed empirical observation.

Economists sometimes disagree about the usefulness of a theory or model. For a glimpse of one such debate between two Nobel Laureates, Milton Friedman and Ronald Coase, look for "How Economists Choose Their Theories" in the *Additional Topics* section of this book's MyEconLab.

w w w . m y e c o n l a b . c o m

Rejection Versus Confirmation

An important part of the scientific approach consists of setting up a theory that will explain some observation. A theory designed to explain observation X will typically generate a hypothesis about some other observable variables, Y and Z. The hypothesis about Y and Z can be tested and may be *rejected* by the data. If the hypothesis is rejected, the value of the theory is brought into question.

The alternative to this approach is to set up a theory and then look for *confirming* evidence. Such an approach is hazardous because the world is sufficiently complex that some confirming evidence can be found for any theory, no matter how unlikely the theory may be. For example, flying saucers, the Loch Ness monster, fortune-telling, and astrology all have their devotees who can quote confirming evidence in spite of the failure of many attempts to discover systematic, objective evidence of these things.

FIGURE 2-1   The Interaction Between Theory and Empirical
Observation

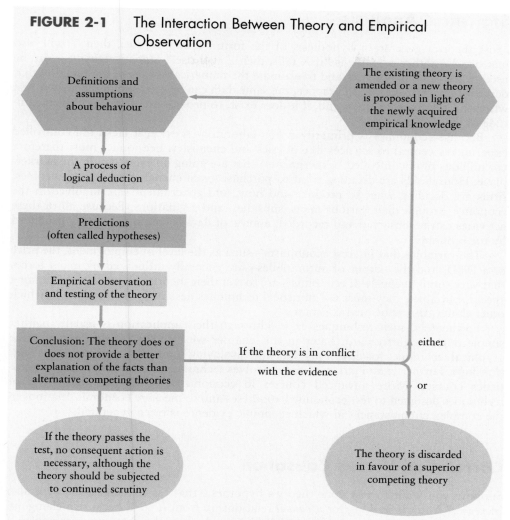

Theory and observation are in continuous interaction. Starting (at the top left) with the assumptions of a theory and the definitions of relevant terms, the theorist deduces by logical analysis everything that is implied by the assumptions. These implications are the predictions or the hypotheses of the theory. The theory is then tested by confronting its predictions with evidence. If the theory is in conflict with facts, it will usually be amended to make it consistent with those facts (thereby making it a better theory), or it will be discarded, to be replaced by a superior theory. The process then begins again: The new or amended theory is subjected first to logical analysis and then to empirical testing.

Statistical Analysis

Most theories generate a hypothesis of the form "if X increases, then Y will also increase." Another example is "if X falls, then Z will rise." Statistical analysis can be used to test such hypotheses and to estimate the numerical values of the function that describes the relationship. In practice, the same data can be used simultaneously to test whether a relationship exists and, if it does exist, to provide an estimate of the magnitude of that relationship.

Because economics is primarily a non-laboratory science, it lacks the controlled experiments central to sciences like physics and chemistry. Economics must therefore use millions of uncontrolled "experiments" that are going on every day in the marketplace. Households are deciding what to purchase given changing prices and incomes, firms are deciding what to produce and how, and governments are involved in the economy through their various taxes, subsidies, and regulations. Because all of these activities can be observed and recorded, a mass of data is continually being produced by the economy.

The variables that interest economists—such as the level of employment, the price of a DVD, and the output of automobiles—are generally influenced by many forces that vary simultaneously. If economists are to test their theories about relations among specific variables, they must use statistical techniques designed for situations in which other things *cannot* be held constant.

Fortunately, such techniques exist, although their application is usually neither simple nor straightforward. Later in this chapter we provide a discussion of some graphical techniques for describing data and displaying some of the more obvious relationships. Further examination of data involves techniques studied in elementary statistics courses. More advanced courses in econometrics deal with the array of techniques designed to test economic hypotheses and to measure economic relations in the complex circumstances in which economic evidence is often generated.

Correlation Versus Causation

Practise with Study Guide Chapter 2, Short-Answer Question 3.

Suppose you want to test your theory's hypothesis that "if X increases, Y will also increase." You are looking for a *causal* relationship from X to Y, because a change in X is predicted to *cause* a change in Y. When you look at the data, suppose you find that X and Y are positively correlated—that is, when X rises, Y also tends to rise. Is your theory supported? It might appear that way, but there is a potential problem.

A finding that X and Y are positively correlated means only that X and Y tend to move together. This correlation is *consistent* with the theory that X causes Y, but it is *not* direct evidence of this causal relationship. The causality may be in the opposite direction—from Y to X. Or X and Y may have no direct causal connection but may instead be jointly caused by some third variable, Z.

Here is a concrete example. Suppose your theory predicts that individuals who get more education will earn higher incomes as a result—the causality in this theory runs from education to income. In the data, suppose we find that education and income are positively correlated. This should not, however, be taken as direct evidence for the (causal) prediction. The data is certainly consistent with that theory, but it is also consistent with others. For example, individuals who grow up in higher-income households may "buy" more education, just as they buy more clothes or entertainment. This is a case of "reverse causality": income causes education, rather than the other way around. Another possibility is that education and income are positively correlated because the personal characteristics that lead people to become more educated—ability and motivation—are the same characteristics that lead to high incomes. In this case, the *causal* relationship runs from personal characteristics to both income and education.

Most economic predictions involve causality. Economists must take care when testing predictions to distinguish between correlation and causality. Correlation can establish that the data are consistent with the theory; establishing causality usually requires advanced statistical techniques.

2.4 ECONOMIC DATA

Economists seek to explain events that they see in the world. Why, for example, did the price of wheat rise last year even though the wheat crop increased? Explaining such observations typically requires an understanding of how the economy works, an understanding based in part on the insights economists derive from their theoretical models.

Economists also use real-world observations to test their theories. For example, did the amount that people saved last year rise—as the theory predicts it should have—when a large tax cut increased their after-tax incomes? To test this prediction we need reliable data for people's incomes and their savings.

Political scientists, sociologists, anthropologists, and psychologists often collect for themselves the data they use to formulate and test their theories. Economists are unusual among social scientists in mainly using data collected by others, often government statisticians. In economics there is a division of labour between collecting data and using it to test theories. The advantage is that economists do not need to spend much of their scarce research time collecting the data they use. The disadvantage is that they are often not as well informed about the limitations of the data collected by others as they would be if they had collected the data themselves.

Once data are collected they can be displayed in various ways, many of which we will see later in this chapter. They can be laid out in tables. They can be displayed in various types of graphs. And where we are interested in relative movements rather than absolute ones, the data can be expressed in *index numbers*. We begin with a discussion of index numbers.

For data on the Canadian economy and many other quantifiable aspects of Canadian life, see Statistics Canada's website:
www.statcan.ca

Index Numbers

Economists frequently look at data on prices or quantities and explore how specific variables change over time. For example, they may be interested in comparing the time paths of output in two industries: steel and newsprint. The problem is that it may be difficult to compare the time paths of the two different variables if we just look at the "raw" data.

Table 2-2 shows some hypothetical data for the volume of output in the steel and newsprint industries, and reveals that because the two variables are measured in different units, it is not immediately clear which of the two variables is more volatile or which, if either, has an upward or downward trend.

It is easier to compare the two paths if we focus on *relative* rather than *absolute* changes. One way to do this is to construct some **index numbers**.

index number An average that measures change over time of such variables as the price level and industrial production; conventionally expressed as a percentage relative to a base period, which is assigned the value 100.

TABLE 2-2   Volume of Steel and Newsprint Output

Year	Volume of Steel (thousands of tonnes)	Volume of Newsprint (thousands of rolls)
1998	200	3200
1999	210	3100
2000	225	3000
2001	215	3200
2002	250	3100
2003	220	3300
2004	265	3100
2005	225	3300
2006	255	3100
2007	230	3200
2008	245	3000

Comparing the time paths of two data series is difficult when absolute numbers are used. Since steel output and newsprint output are measured in different units and have quite different absolute numbers, it is difficult to detect which time series is more volatile.

How to Build an Index Number   We start by taking the value of the variable at some point in time as the "base" to which the values of the variable in other periods will be compared. We call this the *base period*. In the present example, we choose 1998 as the base year for both series. We then take the output in each subsequent year, called the given year, and divide it by the output in the base year, and then multiply the result by 100. This gives us an index number for the output of steel and a separate index number for the output of newsprint. For each index number, the value of output in the base year is equal to 100. The details of the calculations are shown in Table 2-3.

An index number simply expresses the value of some series in any given year as a percentage of its value in the base year. For example, the 2008 index of steel output of 122.5 tells us that steel output in 2008 was 22.5 percent greater than in 1998. In contrast, the 2008 index for newsprint output of 93.8 tells us that newsprint output in 2008 was only 93.8 percent of the output in 1998—that is, output was 6.2 percent lower in 2008 than in 1998. The results in Table 2-3 allow us to compare the relative fluctuations in the two series. It is apparent from the values in the table that the output of steel has shown significantly more percentage variability than has the output of newsprint. This is also clear in Figure 2-2.

TABLE 2-3   Constructing Index Numbers

Year	Steel Procedure		Index	Newsprint Procedure		Index
1998	(200/200) × 100	=	100.0	(3200/3200) × 100	=	100.0
1999	(210/200) × 100	=	105.0	(3100/3200) × 100	=	96.9
2000	(225/200) × 100	=	112.5	(3000/3200) × 100	=	93.8
2001	(215/200) × 100	=	107.5	(3200/3200) × 100	=	100.0
2002	(250/200) × 100	=	125.0	(3100/3200) × 100	=	96.9
2003	(220/200) × 100	=	110.0	(3300/3200) × 100	=	103.1
2004	(265/200) × 100	=	132.5	(3100/3200) × 100	=	96.9
2005	(225/200) × 100	=	112.5	(3300/3200) × 100	=	103.1
2006	(255/200) × 100	=	127.5	(3100/3200) × 100	=	96.9
2007	(230/200) × 100	=	115.0	(3200/3200) × 100	=	100.0
2008	(245/200) × 100	=	122.5	(3000/3200) × 100	=	93.8

Index numbers are calculated by dividing the value in the given year by the value in the base year, and multiplying the result by 100. The 2008 index number for steel tells us that steel output in 2008 was 22.5 percent greater than in the base year, 1998. The 2008 index number for newsprint tells us that newsprint output in 2008 was 93.8 percent of the output in the base year, 1998.

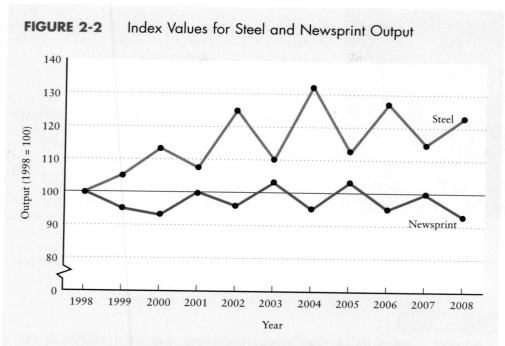

FIGURE 2-2   Index Values for Steel and Newsprint Output

Comparing the time paths of two variables is much easier when index numbers are used. Since both index numbers are equal to 100 in the base year, relative volatility and trends become clear. Steel output is clearly more volatile in percentage terms than newsprint output. Steel output also has an upward trend, whereas newsprint output appears to have little or no trend.

The formula of any index number is:

$$\text{Value of index in any given period} = \frac{\text{Absolute value in given period}}{\text{Absolute value in base period}} \times 100$$

Care must be taken, however, when using index numbers. The index number always tells you the percentage change compared with the base year, but when comparing an index number across non-base years, the percentage change in the index number is *not* given by the absolute difference in the values of the index number. For example, if you want to know how much steel output changed from 2002 to 2004, we know from Table 2-3 that the index number for steel output increased from 125.0 to 132.5. But this is not an increase of 7.5 percent. The *percentage* increase in steel output is computed as (132.5 − 125.0)/125.0 = 7.5/125.0 = 0.06, or 6 percent.

More Complex Index Numbers   Perhaps the most famous index number used by economists is the index of average prices—the consumer price index (CPI). This is a price index of the *average* price paid by consumers for the typical basket of goods that they buy. The inclusion of the word "average," however, makes the CPI a more complex index number than the ones we have constructed here.

With what you have just learned, you could construct separate index numbers for the price of beef, the price of coffee, and the price of orange juice. But in order to get the consumer price index we need to take the *average* of these separate price indexes (plus thousands of others for the goods and services we have ignored here). But it

Practise with Study Guide Chapter 2, Exercise 1.

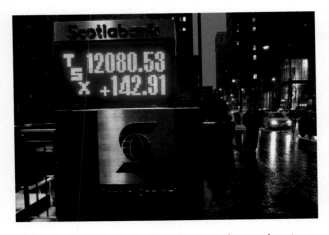

The S&P/TSX is one of the best-known index numbers in Canada. Its fluctuations reflect changes in the market value of the largest publicly traded companies in Canada.

cannot be a simple average. Instead, it must be a *weighted* average where the weight on each price index reflects the relative importance of that good in the typical consumer's basket of goods and services. For example, since the typical consumer spends a tiny fraction of income on sardines but a much larger fraction of income on housing, the weight on the "sardines" price index in the CPI will be very small and the weight on the "housing" price index will be very large. The result is that even huge swings in the price of sardines will have negligible effects on the CPI, whereas much more modest changes in the price of housing will have noticeable effects on the CPI.

We will spend much more time discussing the consumer price index when we study macroeconomics beginning in Chapter 19. For now, keep in mind the usefulness of the simple index numbers we have constructed here. They allow us to compare the time paths of different variables.

> ## myeconlab
> Another famous index that is reported every day on the news is the S&P/TSX, an index number showing the average market value of a specific set of companies traded on the Toronto Stock Exchange. For more information about the S&P/TSX index, look for "What the S&P/TSX Really Measures" in the *Additional Topics* section of this book's MyEconLab.
>
> w w w . m y e c o n l a b . c o m

Graphing Economic Data

cross-sectional data A set of observations made at the same time across several different units (such as households, firms, or countries).

time-series data A set of observations made at successive periods of time.

scatter diagram A graph of statistical observations of paired values of two variables, one measured on the horizontal and the other on the vertical axis. Each point on the coordinate grid represents the values of the variables for a particular unit of observation.

A single economic variable such as unemployment, GDP, or the average price of a house can come in two basic forms.

Cross-Sectional and Time-Series Data   The first is called **cross-sectional data**, which means a number of different observations on one variable all taken in different places at the same point in time. Figure 2-3 shows an example. The variable in the figure is the average selling price of a house. It is shown for each of the ten Canadian provinces in 2006.

The second type of data is called **time-series data**. It refers to observations of one variable at successive points in time. The data in Figure 2-4 show the unemployment rate for Canada from 1978 to 2006. (Note that the Canadian unemployment rate is simply a weighted average of the ten provincial unemployment rates, where the weight for each province is the size of that province's labour force expressed as a fraction of the total Canadian labour force.) Time-series graphs are quite useful in economics because we often want to know how specific economic numbers are changing over time. As is clear in Figure 2-4, the Canadian unemployment rate is relatively volatile over long periods of time, but in recent years has been low by historical standards.

Scatter Diagrams   Another way in which data can be presented is in a **scatter diagram**. This type of chart is more analytical than those above. It is designed to show the relation between two different variables, such as the price of eggs and the quantity of eggs purchased. To plot a scatter diagram, values of one variable are measured on the horizontal axis and values of the second variable are measured on the vertical axis. Any point on the diagram relates a specific value of one variable to a corresponding specific value of the other.

The data plotted on a scatter diagram may be either cross-sectional data or time-series data. An example of a cross-sectional scatter diagram is a scatter of the price of eggs and the quantity sold in July 2007 at two dozen different places in Canada. Each dot refers to a price–quantity combination observed in a different place at the same time. An example of a scatter diagram using time-series data is the price and quantity of eggs sold in Thunder Bay for each month over the last ten years. Each of the 120 dots refers to a price–quantity combination observed at the same place in one particular month.

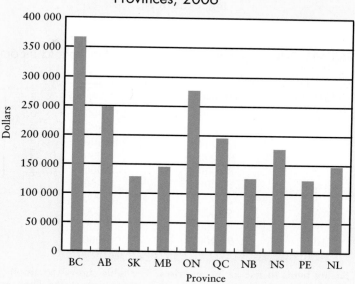

FIGURE 2-3   A Cross-Sectional Graph of Average Housing Prices for Ten Canadian Provinces, 2006

(*Source:* © 2007 The Canadian Real Estate Association. All Rights Reserved. These data are available at www.crea.ca/public/news_stats.)

FIGURE 2-4   A Time-Series Graph of the Canadian Unemployment Rate, 1978–2006

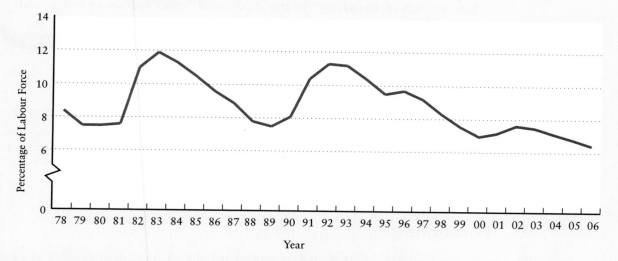

(*Source:* Annual average of monthly, seasonally adjusted data from Statistics Canada, CANSIM database, V2091177–282-0001 Canada; unemployment rate; both sexes; 15 years and over (monthly, 1978-01-01 to 2006-12-01). Reprinted with permission of Statistics Canada.)

The table in Figure 2-5 shows data for the income and saving of ten households in one particular year and these data are plotted on a scatter diagram. Each point in the figure represents one household, showing its income and its saving. The positive relation between the two stands out. The higher the household's income, the higher its saving tends to be.

FIGURE 2-5 A Scatter Diagram of Household Income and Saving

Household	Annual Income	Annual Saving
1	$ 70 000	$10 000
2	30 000	2 500
3	100 000	12 000
4	60 000	3 000
5	80 000	8 000
6	10 000	500
7	20 000	2 000
8	50 000	2 000
9	40 000	4 200
10	90 000	8 000

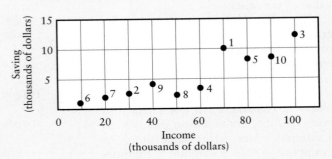

Saving tends to rise as income rises. The table shows the amount of income earned by ten selected households together with the amount they saved during the same year. The scatter diagram plots the income and saving for the ten households listed in the table. The number on each dot refers to the household in the corresponding row of the table.

 myeconlab

If you need a quick refresher course on graphing, look for "A Brief Introduction to Graphing" in the *Additional Topics* section of this book's MyEconLab.

www.myeconlab.com

2.5 GRAPHING ECONOMIC THEORIES

Theories are built on assumptions about relationships between variables. For example, the quantity of eggs demanded is assumed to fall as the price of eggs rises. Or, the total amount an individual saves is assumed to rise as his or her income rises. How can such relations be expressed?

Functions

When one variable, X, is related to another variable, Y, in such a way that to every value of X there is only one possible value of Y, we say that Y is a *function* of X. When we write this relation down, we are expressing a *functional relation* between the two variables.

Here is a specific example. Consider the relation between an individual's annual income, which we denote by the symbol Y, and the amount that person spends on goods and services during the year, which we denote by the symbol C (for consumption). Any particular example of the relation between C and Y can be expressed several ways—in words, in a table or schedule, in a mathematical equation, or in a graph.

Verbal Statement. When income is zero, the person will spend $800 a year (either by borrowing the money or by consuming past savings), and for every extra $1 of income the person will increase expenditure by 80 cents.

Schedule. This table shows selected values of the person's income and consumption.

Annual Income	Consumption	Reference Letter
$ 0	$ 800	p
2 500	2 800	q
5 000	4 800	r
7 500	6 800	s
10 000	8 800	t

Mathematical Equation. $C = \$800 + 0.8Y$ is the equation of the relation just described in words. As a check, you can first see that when Y is zero, C is $800. Further, you can see that every time Y increases by $1, the level of C increases by 0.8($1), which is 80 cents.

Graph. Figure 2-6 shows the points from the preceding schedule and the line representing the equation given in the previous paragraph.

Comparison of the values on the graph with the values in the schedule, and with the values derived from the equation just stated, shows that these are alternative expressions of the same relation between C and Y. All four of these modes of expression refer to the same relation between the person's consumption expenditure and income.

More Detail About Functions

Let us look in a little more detail at the mathematical expression of this relation between income and consumption. To state the expression in general form, detached from the specific numerical example above, we use a symbol to express the dependence of one variable on another. Using "f" for this purpose, we write

FIGURE 2-6   Income and Consumption

$$C = 800 + 0.8Y$$

Consumption expenditure rises as income rises. The figure graphs the schedule and the equation for the functional relation discussed in the text.

$$C = f(Y) \tag{2-1}$$

This is read, "C is a function of Y." Spelling this out more fully, we would say, "The amount of consumption expenditure depends upon the person's income."

The variable on the left-hand side is the dependent variable, since its value depends on the value of the variable on the right-hand side. The variable on the right-hand side is the independent variable, since it can take on any value. The letter "f" tells us that a functional relation is involved. This means that a knowledge of the value of the variable (or variables) within the parentheses on the right-hand side allows us to determine the value of the variable on the left-hand side. Although in this case we have used "f"

(as a memory-aid for "function"), any convenient symbol can be used to denote the existence of a functional relation.

Functional notation can seem intimidating to those who are unfamiliar with it. But it is helpful. Since the functional concept is basic to all science, the notation is worth mastering.

Functional Forms   The equation $C = f(Y)$ states that C is a function of Y. It says nothing about the *form* of this function. The term *functional form* refers to the specific nature of the relation between the variables in the function. The example above gave one specific functional form for this relation:

$$C = \$800 + 0.8Y \tag{2-2}$$

Equation 2-1 expresses the general assumption that consumption expenditure depends on the consumer's income. Equation 2-2 expresses the more specific assumption that C is equal to $800 when Y is zero and rises by 80 cents for every $1 that Y rises. An alternative assumption would be $C = \$600 + 0.9Y$. You should be able to say in words the behaviour implied in this relation. There is no reason why either of these assumptions must be true; indeed, neither may be consistent with the facts. But that is a matter for testing. What we do have in each equation is a precise statement of a particular assumption.

Notice that Equation 2-2 also specifies a *linear* consumption function—the relationship between C and Y is shown as a straight line in Figure 2-6. This is a very special case. Another possibility is that the relationship between C and Y is *non-linear*—so that the consumption function when graphed is not a straight line. This possibility takes us to our next discussion, of linear and non-linear functions, and of how to measure and interpret the *slopes* of functions.

Graphing Functional Relations

Different functional forms have different graphs, and we will meet many of these in subsequent chapters. Figure 2-6 is an example of a relation in which the two variables move together. When income goes up, consumption goes up. In such a relation the two variables are *positively related* to each other.

Figure 2-7 gives an example of variables that move in opposite directions. As the amount spent on reducing pollution goes up, the amount of remaining pollution goes down. In such a relation the two variables are *negatively related* to each other.

Both of these graphs are straight lines. In such cases the variables are *linearly related* to each other (either positively or negatively).

The Slope of a Straight Line   Slopes are important in economics. They show you how much one variable changes as the other changes. The slope is defined as the amount of change in the variable measured on the vertical axis per unit change in the variable measured on the horizontal axis. In the case of Figure 2-7 it tells us

FIGURE 2-7   Linear Pollution Reduction

Pollution as a linear function of clean-up expenditure. Between points A and B it costs $2000 to reduce pollution by 1000 tonnes. The cost of pollution reduction is the same elsewhere on the line. The slope of the line, –0.5, indicates that any $2000 expenditure on pollution clean-up reduces the amount of pollution by 1000 tonnes. The slope of the line is constant, indicating that *every* $1 spent on clean-up leads to a reduction of pollution of 0.5 tonnes.

how many tonnes of pollution, symbolized by P, are removed per dollar spent on reducing pollution, symbolized by E. Consider moving from point A to point B in the figure. If we spend $2000 more on clean-up, we reduce pollution by 1000 tonnes. This is 0.5 tonnes per dollar spent. On the graph the extra $2000 is indicated by ΔE, the arrow indicating that E rises by 2000. The 1000 tonnes of pollution reduction is indicated by ΔP, the arrow showing that pollution falls by 1000. (The Greek uppercase letter delta, Δ, stands for "the change in.") To get the amount of pollution reduction per dollar of expenditure we merely divide one by the other. In symbols this is $\Delta P / \Delta E$.

If we let X stand for whatever variable is measured on the horizontal axis and Y for whatever variable is measured on the vertical axis, the slope of a straight line is $\Delta Y / \Delta X$. [1][1]

Practise with Study Guide Chapter 2, Exercise 2.

The equation of the line in Figure 2-7 can be computed in two steps. First, note that when $E = 0$, the amount of remaining pollution, P, is equal to 6 (thousand tonnes). Thus, the line meets the vertical axis ($E = 0$) when P equals 6. Second, we have already seen that the slope of the line, $\Delta P / \Delta E$, is equal to -0.5, which means that for every one-unit increase in E, P falls by 0.5 unit. We can thus state the equation of the line as

$$P = 6 - (0.5) \, E$$

where both P and E are expressed as thousands of units (tonnes and dollars, respectively).

Non-Linear Functions   Although it is sometimes convenient to simplify a real relation between two variables by assuming them to be linearly related, this is seldom the case over their whole range. Non-linear relations are much more common than linear ones. In the case of reducing pollution, it is usually quite cheap to eliminate the first units of pollution. Then, as the environment gets cleaner and cleaner, the cost of further clean-up tends to increase because more and more sophisticated and expensive methods need to be used. As a result, Figure 2-8 is more realistic than Figure 2-7. Inspection of Figure 2-8 shows that as more and more is spent, the amount of pollution reduction for an additional $1 of clean-up expenditure gets smaller and smaller. This is shown by the diminishing slope of the curve as we move rightward along it. For example, as we move from point A to point B, an increase in expenditure of $1000 is required to reduce pollution by 1000 tonnes. Thus, each tonne of pollution reduction costs $1. But as we move from point C (where we have already reduced pollution considerably) to point D, an extra $6000 must be spent in order to reduce pollution by 1000 tonnes. Each tonne of pollution reduction therefore costs $6.

Economists call the change in pollution when a bit more or a bit less is spent on clean-up the *marginal* change. The figure shows that the slope of the curve at each point measures this marginal change. It also shows that, in the type of curve illustrated, the marginal change per dollar spent is diminishing as we spend more on reducing pollution. There is always a payoff to more expenditure over the range shown in the figure, but the payoff diminishes as more is spent. This relation can be described as *diminishing marginal response*. We will meet such relations many times in what follows, so we emphasize now that diminishing marginal response does not mean that the *total* response is diminishing. In Figure 2-8, the total amount of pollution continues to fall as more and more is spent on clean-up. But diminishing marginal response does

---

[1] Numbers in square brackets indicate mathematical notes that are found in a separate section at the back of the book.

FIGURE 2-8   Non-Linear Pollution Reduction

Pollution as a non-linear function of clean-up expenditure. The slope of the curve changes as we move along it. Between points *A* and *B*, it costs $1000 to reduce pollution by 1000 tonnes. Between points *C* and *D*, it costs $6000 to reduce pollution by 1000 tonnes. At point *Z*, the slope of the curve is equal to the slope of the straight line tangent to the curve at point *Z*. The slope of the tangent line is −0.75/1.75 = −0.43.

mean that the amount of pollution reduced per dollar of expenditure gets less and less as the total expenditure rises.

Figure 2-9 shows a graph where the marginal response is increasing. The graph shows the relationship between annual production costs and annual output for a firm that makes hockey sticks. Notice that the more hockey sticks produced annually, the higher the firm's costs. This is shown by the positive slope of the line. Notice also that as more and more hockey sticks are produced, the extra amount that the firm must pay to produce each extra hockey stick rises. For example, as the firm moves from point *A* to point *B*, annual costs rise by $30 000 in order to increase its annual output by 10 000 hockey sticks. Each extra hockey stick costs $3 ($30 000/10 000 = $3). But when the firm is producing many more hockey sticks, such as at point *C*, its factory is closer to its capacity and it becomes more costly to increase production. Moving from point *C* to point *D*, the firm's annual costs increase by $150 000 in order to increase its annual output by 10 000 hockey sticks. Each extra hockey stick then costs $15 ($150 000/10 000 = $15). This figure illustrates a case of *increasing marginal cost*, a characteristic of production that we will see often and learn more about later in this book.

Figures 2-8 and 2-9 show that with non-linear functions the slope of the curve changes as we move along the curve. For example, in Figure 2-8, the slope of the curve falls as the expenditure on pollution clean-up increases. In Figure 2-9, the slope of the curve increases as the volume of production increases.

How, exactly, do we measure the slope of a curved line? The answer is that we use the slope of a straight line *tangent to that curve* at the point that interests us. For example, in Figure 2-8, if we want to know the slope of the curve at point *Z*, we draw a straight line that touches the curve *only* at point Z; this is a tangent line. The slope of this line is −0.75/1.75 = −0.43. Similarly, in Figure 2-9, the slope of the curve at point Z is given by the slope of the straight line tangent to the curve at point Z.

For non-linear functions, the slope of the curve changes as X changes. Therefore, the marginal response of Y to a change in X depends on the value of X.

Functions with a Minimum or a Maximum

So far, all the graphs we have shown have had either a positive or negative slope over their entire range. But many relations change directions as the independent variable increases. For example, consider a firm that is attempting to maximize its profits and is trying to determine how much output to produce. The firm may find that its unit production costs are lower than the market price of the good, and so it can increase its profit by producing more. But as it increases its level of production, the firm's unit costs may be driven up because the capacity of the factory is being approached. Eventually, the firm may find that extra output will actually cost so much that its profits will be *reduced*. This is a relationship that we will study in detail in later chapters, and it is illustrated in Figure 2-10. Notice that when profits are maximized at point A, the slope of the curve is zero (because a tangent to the curve at point A is horizontal) and so the *marginal response* of profits to output is zero.

Now consider an example of a function with a minimum. You probably know that

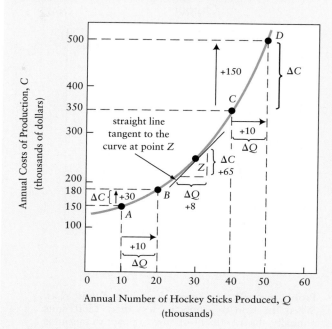

FIGURE 2-9   Increasing Production Costs

Production costs increase at an increasing rate as annual output rises. From point A to point B, an extra annual output of 10 000 hockey sticks increases annual costs by $30 000. Each extra hockey stick costs $3. From point C to point D, an extra output of 10 000 hockey sticks increases annual costs by $150 000. Each extra hockey stick then costs $15. This is a case of increasing marginal cost. At point Z, the slope of the curve is equal to the slope of the straight line tangent to the curve at point Z. The slope of the tangent line is 65/8 = 8.1.

when you drive a car the fuel consumption per kilometre depends on your speed. Driving very slowly uses a lot of fuel per kilometre travelled. Driving very fast also uses a lot of fuel per kilometre travelled. The best fuel efficiency—the lowest fuel consumption per kilometre travelled—occurs at a speed of approximately 95 kilometres per hour. The relationship between speed and fuel consumption is shown in Figure 2-11 and illustrates a function with a minimum. Note that at point A the slope of the curve is zero (because a tangent to the curve at point A is horizontal) and so the *marginal response* of fuel consumption to speed is zero.

At either a minimum or a maximum of a function, the slope of the curve is zero. Therefore, at the minimum or maximum, the marginal response of Y to a change in X is zero.

FIGURE 2-10   Profits as a Function of Output

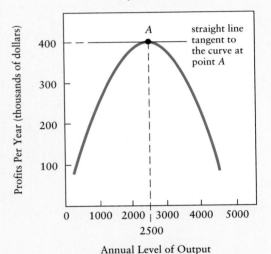

Profits rise and then eventually fall as output rises. When the firm is producing less than 2500 units annually, the marginal response of profit to output is positive—that is, an increase in output leads to an increase in profit. Beyond 2500 units annually, the marginal response is negative—an increase in output leads to a reduction in profit. At point *A*, profits are maximized and the marginal response of profit to output is zero. Because the tangent at point *A* is horizontal, the slope of the curve is zero at that point.

FIGURE 2-11   Average Fuel Consumption as a Function of Speed

Average fuel consumption falls and then eventually rises as speed increases. Average fuel consumption in litres per kilometre travelled is minimized at point *A* at a speed of approximately 95 kilometres per hour (km/h). At speeds less than 95 km/h, the marginal response is negative—that is, an increase in speed reduces fuel consumption per kilometre. At speeds above 95 km/h, the marginal response is positive—an increase in speed increases fuel consumption per kilometre. At 95 km/h, the marginal response is zero and fuel consumption per kilometre is minimized.

A Final Word

We have done much in this chapter. We have discussed why economists use theory and how they build economic models. We have discussed how they test their theories and how there is a continual back-and-forth process between empirical testing of predictions and refining the theoretical model. Finally, we have devoted considerable time and space to exploring the many ways that data can be displayed in graphs and how economists use graphs to illustrate their theories.

Many students find themselves intimidated when they are first confronted with all of the details about graphing. But try not to worry. You may not yet be a master of all the graphing techniques that we have discussed in this chapter, but you will be surprised at how quickly it all falls into place. And, as is true for most skills, there is no substitute for practice. In the next three chapters we will encounter many graphs. But we will start simply and then slowly attempt more complicated cases. We are confident that in the process of learning some basic economic theories you will get enough practice in graphing that you will very soon look back at this chapter and realize how straightforward it all is.

S U M M A R Y

2.1 **POSITIVE AND NORMATIVE ADVICE**

- A key to the success of scientific inquiry lies in separating positive questions about the way the world works from normative questions about how one would like the world to work.

2.2 **ECONOMIC THEORIES**

- Theories are designed to explain and predict what we see. A theory consists of a set of definitions of the variables to be employed, a set of assumptions about how things behave, and the conditions under which the theory is meant to apply.
- A theory provides conditional predictions of the type "if one event occurs, then another event will also occur."

- The term "model" is often used as a synonym for theory. It is also used to describe an illustrative abstraction that is used to organize our thinking even though it may not generate testable hypotheses.

2.3 **TESTING THEORIES**

- Theories are tested by checking their predictions against evidence. In some sciences, these tests can be conducted under laboratory conditions in which only one thing changes at a time. In economics, testing is almost always done using the data produced by the world of ordinary events.
- Economists make use of statistical analysis when testing their theories. They must take care to make the distinction between correlation and causation.

- The progress of any science lies in finding better explanations of events than are now available. Thus, in any developing science, one must expect to discard some existing theories and replace them with demonstrably superior alternatives.

2.4 **ECONOMIC DATA**

- Index numbers express economic series in relative form. Values in each period are expressed in relation to the value in the base period, which is given a value of 100.
- Economic data may be graphed in three different ways. Cross-sectional graphs show observations taken at the same time. Time-series graphs show observations on one variable taken over time. Scatter diagrams show many points, each one of which refers to specific observations on two different variables.

2.5 **GRAPHING ECONOMIC THEORIES**

- A functional relation can be expressed in words, in a schedule giving specific values, in a mathematical equation, or in a graph.
- A graph of two variables has a positive slope when they both increase or decrease together and a negative slope when they move in opposite directions.

- The marginal response of a variable gives the amount it changes in response to a change in a second variable. When the variable is measured on the vertical axis of a diagram, its marginal response at a specific point on the curve is measured by the slope of the line at that point.
- Some functions have a maximum or minimum point. At such points, the marginal response is zero.

KEY CONCEPTS

Positive and normative statements
Endogenous and exogenous variables
Theories and models
Variables, assumptions, and
  predictions

Correlation versus causation
Functional relations
Positive and negative relations between
  variables

Positively and negatively sloped curves
Marginal responses
Maximum and minimum values

STUDY EXERCISES

1. In the following examples, identify the exogenous (or independent) variable and the endogenous (or dependent) variable.

   a. The amount of rainfall on the Canadian prairies determines the amount of wheat produced in Canada.
   b. When the world price of coffee increases, there is a change in the price of your cup of coffee at Tim Hortons.
   c. If student loans were no longer available, there would be fewer students attending university.
   d. An increase in the tax on gasoline leads people to drive more fuel-efficient vehicles.

2. Use the appropriate graph—time-series, cross-sectional, or scatter diagram—to illustrate the economic data provided in each part below.

   a. Canada's prime interest rate in 2005:

January	4.25	July	4.25
February	4.25	August	4.25
March	4.25	September	4.50
April	4.25	October	4.75
May	4.25	November	4.75
June	4.25	December	5.00

   b. A comparison of average household expenditures across provinces in 2004:

British Columbia	64 266
Alberta	71 256
Saskatchewan	53 314
Manitoba	56 317
Ontario	71 583
Quebec	54 494
New Brunswick	51 531
Nova Scotia	54 559
Prince Edward Island	50 849
Newfoundland and Labrador	49 867

   c. Per capita growth rates of real GDP and investment rates for various countries, averaged over the period 1970–1990:

Country	Average Growth Rate (% per year)	Average Investment Rate (% of GDP)
Canada	2.6	22.0
Austria	2.6	25.5
Japan	3.6	31.0
United States	1.7	18.7
United Kingdom	2.1	18.2
Spain	2.5	23.0
Norway	3.2	28.2

3. **myeconlab** Use the following figure to answer the questions below.

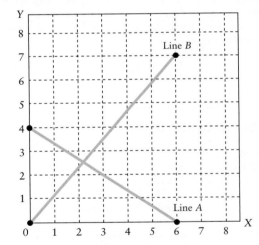

   a. Is the slope of Line *A* positive or negative? Line *B*?
   b. Calculate the slope of Line *A*. Write the equation describing the line in the form $Y = mX + b$ where *m* is the slope of the line and *b* is a constant term.
   c. Calculate the slope of Line *B*. Write the equation describing the line in the form $Y = mX + b$ where *m* is the slope of the line and *b* is a constant term.

4. (Ⓧ myeconlab) Suppose the relationship between the government's tax revenue (T) and national income (Y) is represented by the following equation: $T = 10 + 0.25Y$. Plot this relationship on a scale diagram, with Y on the horizontal axis and T on the vertical axis. Interpret the equation.

5. Consider the following three specific functional forms for a functional relation between X and Y:

   i) $Y = 50 + 2X$
   ii) $Y = 50 + 2X + 0.05X^2$
   iii) $Y = 50 + 2X - 0.05X^2$

   a. For the values of X of 0, 10, 20, 30, 40, and 50, plot X and Y on a scale diagram for each specific functional form. Connect these points with a smooth line.
   b. For each functional form, state whether the slope of the line is constant, increasing, or decreasing as the value of X increases.
   c. Describe for each functional form how the marginal change in Y depends on the value of X.

6. Suppose you want to create a price index for the price of pizza across several Canadian university campuses, as of March 1, 2007. The data are as follows:

University	Price Per Pizza
Dalhousie	$6.50
Laval	5.95
McGill	6.00
Queen's	8.00
Waterloo	7.50
Manitoba	5.50
Saskatchewan	5.75
Calgary	6.25
UBC	7.25
Victoria	7.00

   a. Using Calgary as the "base university," construct the Canadian university pizza price index.
   b. At which university is pizza the most expensive, and by what percentage is the price higher than in Calgary?
   c. At which university is pizza the least expensive, and by what percentage is the price lower than in Calgary?
   d. Are the data listed above time-series or cross-sectional data? Explain why.

7. For each of the functional relations listed below, plot the relations on a scale diagram (with X on the horizontal axis and Y on the vertical axis) and compute the slope of the line.

   i) $Y = 10 + 3X$
   ii) $Y = 20 + 4X$
   iii) $Y = 30 + 5X$
   iv) $Y = 10 + 5X$

8. Suppose we divide Canada into three regions—the West, the Centre, and the East. Each region has an unemployment rate, defined as the number of people unemployed, expressed as a fraction of that region's labour force. The table that follows shows each region's unemployment rate and the size of its labour force.

Region	Unemployment Rate	Labour Force
West	5.5%	5.3 million
Centre	7.2%	8.4 million
East	12.5%	3.5 million

   a. Compute an unemployment rate for Canada using a simple average of the rates in the three regions. Is this the "right" unemployment rate for Canada as a whole? Explain why or why not.
   b. Now compute an unemployment rate for Canada using weights that reflect the size of that region's labour force as a proportion of the overall Canadian labour force. Explain the difference in this unemployment rate from the one in part (a). Is this a "better" measure of Canadian unemployment? Explain why.

9. Draw three graphs in which the dependent variable increases at an increasing rate, at a constant rate, and at a diminishing rate. Then draw three graphs in which it decreases at an increasing, constant, and diminishing rate. For each of these graphs state a real relation that might be described by it—other than the ones given in the text of this chapter.

DISCUSSION QUESTIONS

1. What are some of the positive and normative issues that lie behind the disagreements in the following cases?

   a. Economists disagree on whether the government of Canada should try to stimulate the economy in the next six months.
   b. European and North American negotiators disagree over the desirability of reducing European farm subsidies.
   c. Economists argue about the merits of a voucher system that allows parents to choose the schools their children will attend.
   d. Economists debate the use of a two-tier medical system in Canada (whereby health care continues to be publicly provided, but individuals are permitted to be treated by doctors who bill the patient directly—"extra billing").

2. Much recent public debate has centred on the pros and cons of permitting continued unrestricted sale of cigarettes. Proposals for the control of cigarettes range from increasing excise taxes to the mandatory use of plain packaging to an outright ban on their sale. Discuss the positive and normative assumptions that underlie the national mood to reduce the consumption of tobacco products.

3. Economists sometimes make each of the following assumptions when they construct models. Discuss some situations in which each of these assumptions might be a useful simplification in order to think about some aspect of the real world.

   a. The earth is flat.
   b. There are no differences between men and women.
   c. There is no tomorrow.
   d. There are only two periods—this year and next year.
   e. A country produces only two types of goods.
   f. People are wholly selfish.

4. Untestable statements can often be reworded so that they can be tested by an appeal to evidence. How might you do this for each of the following assertions?

   a. Free-market economic systems are the best in the world.
   b. Unemployment insurance is eroding the work ethic and encouraging people to become wards of the state rather than productive workers.
   c. Robotics ought to be outlawed because it will destroy the future of working people.
   d. Laws requiring equal pay for work of equal value will make women better off.
   e. Free trade improves the welfare of a country's citizens.

5. There are hundreds of eyewitnesses to the existence of flying saucers and other UFOs. There are films and eyewitness accounts of Nessie, the Loch Ness monster. Are you convinced of their existence? If not, what would it take to persuade you? If you are already convinced, what would it take to make you change your mind?

CHAPTER 3

Demand, Supply, and Price

LO LEARNING OBJECTIVES

In this chapter you will learn

1. what determines "quantity demanded," the amount of some product that consumers want to purchase.
2. to distinguish between a shift in a demand curve and a movement along a demand curve.
3. what determines "quantity supplied," the amount of some product that producers want to sell.
4. to distinguish between a shift in a supply curve and a movement along a supply curve.
5. about the forces that drive market price to equilibrium, and how equilibrium price is affected by changes in demand and supply.

How do individual markets work? We are now ready to study this important question. The answer leads us to what are called the laws of supply and demand. And though there is much more to economics than just demand and supply (as many following chapters will illustrate), this is an essential starting point for understanding how a market, and thus a market economy, functions.

As a first step, we need to understand what determines the demand for and the supply of particular products. Then we can see how demand and supply together determine the prices of products and the quantities that are bought and sold. Finally, we examine how the price system allows the economy to respond to the many changes that impinge on it. Demand and supply help us to understand the price system's successes and failures, and the consequences of many government policies.

This chapter deals with the basic elements of demand, supply, and price. In the next two chapters we use the demand-and-supply apparatus to discuss such issues as cigarette taxes, legislated minimum wages, price controls on rental housing, and the burden of payroll taxes.

3.1 DEMAND

What determines the demand for any given product? How have Canadian consumers responded to the recent declines in the prices of personal computers and cellular telephones? How will they respond to the next sudden change in the world price of oil or coffee? We start by developing a theory designed to explain the demand for some typical product.

What Is "Quantity Demanded"?

The total amount of any particular good or service that consumers wish to purchase in some time period is called the **quantity demanded** of that product. It is important to notice two things about this concept.

First, quantity demanded is a *desired* quantity. It is the amount that consumers wish to purchase when faced with a particular price of the product, other products' prices, their incomes, their tastes, and everything else that might matter. It may be different from the amount that consumers actually succeed in purchasing. If sufficient quantities are not available, the amount that consumers wish to purchase may exceed the amount that they actually purchase. (For example, think of standing in line to purchase tickets to a show, only to find out that the show is sold out before you get to the head of the line.) To distinguish these two concepts, the term *quantity demanded* is used to refer to desired purchases, and a phrase such as *quantity actually bought* or *quantity exchanged* is used to refer to actual purchases.

Second, quantity demanded refers to a *flow* of purchases. It must therefore be expressed as so much per period of time: 1 million units per day, 7 million per week, or 365 million per year. For example, being told that the quantity of new television sets demanded (at current prices) in Canada is 50 000 means nothing unless you are also told the period of time involved. Fifty thousand TVs demanded per day would be an enormous rate of demand; 50 000 per year would be a very small rate for a country as large as Canada. The important distinction between *stocks* and *flows* is discussed in *Extensions in Theory 3-1*.

The total amount of some product that consumers in the relevant market wish to buy in a given time period is influenced by the following important variables: [2]

- Product's own price
- Average income
- Prices of other products
- Tastes
- Distribution of income
- Population
- Expectations about the future

We will discuss the separate effects of each of these variables later in the chapter. For now, we focus on the effects of changes in the product's own price. But how do we analyze the distinct effect of changes in one variable when all are likely to be changing at once? Since this is difficult to do, we manage it in two stages. First, we consider the influence of the variables one at a time. To do this, we hold all but one of them constant. Then we let the selected variable vary and study how its change affects quantity demanded. We can do the same for each of the other variables in turn, and in this way we can come to understand the importance of each. Second, we then combine the separate influences of the variables to discover what happens when several things change at the same time—as they often do.

Holding all other variables constant is often described by the expressions "other things being equal," "other things given," or the equivalent Latin phrase, *ceteris paribus*. When economists speak of the influence of the price of eggs on the quantity

EXTENSIONS IN THEORY 3-1

The Distinction Between Stocks and Flows

An important conceptual issue that arises frequently in economics is the distinction between *stock* and *flow* variables. Economic theories use both, and it takes a little practice to keep them straight.

As noted in the text, a flow variable has a time dimension—it is so much *per unit of time*. For example, the quantity of Grade A large eggs purchased in Edmonton is a flow variable. No useful information is conveyed if we are told that the number purchased was 2000 dozen eggs unless we are also told the period of time over which these purchases occurred. Two thousand dozen eggs per hour would indicate a much more active market in eggs than would 2000 dozen eggs per month.

In contrast, a stock variable is a variable whose value has meaning *at a point in time*. Thus, the number of eggs in the egg producer's warehouse on a particular day—for example, 20 000 dozen eggs on September 3, 2007—is a stock variable. All those eggs are there at one time, and they remain there until something happens to change the stock held in the warehouse. The stock variable is just a number at a point in time, not a rate of flow of so much per unit of time.

The terminology of stocks and flows can be understood in terms of an analogy to a bathtub. At any moment, the tub holds so much water. This is the *stock,* and it can be measured in terms of the volume of water, say, 100 litres. There might also be water flowing into the tub from the tap; this *flow* is measured as so much water per unit time, say, 10 litres per minute.

The distinction between stocks and flows is important. Failure to keep them straight is a common source of confusion and even error. Note, for example, that a stock variable and a flow variable cannot be added together without specifying some time period for which the flow persists. We cannot add the stock of 100 litres

of water in the tub to the flow of 10 litres per minute to get 110 litres. The new stock of water will depend on how long the flow persists; if it lasts for 20 minutes, the new stock will be 300 litres; if the flow persists for 60 minutes, the new stock will be 700 litres (or the tub will overflow!).

The amount of income earned is a flow; there is so much per year or per month or per hour. The amount of a consumer's expenditure is also a flow—so much spent per week or per month or per year. The amount of money in a bank account or a miser's hoard (earned, perhaps, in the past but unspent) is a stock—just so many thousands of dollars. The key test is always whether a time dimension is required to give the variable meaning.

The amount of water behind the dam at any time is the stock of water; the amount moving through the gate is the flow, which is measured per unit of time.

of eggs demanded, *ceteris paribus,* they refer to what a change in the price of eggs would do to the quantity of eggs demanded *if all other variables that influence the demand for eggs did not change.*

Quantity Demanded and Price[1]

We are interested in studying the relationship between the quantity demanded of a product and that product's price. This requires that we hold all other influences constant and ask, "How will the quantity demanded of a product change as its price changes?"

A basic economic hypothesis is that the price of a product and the quantity demanded are related *negatively*, other things being equal. That is, the lower the price, the higher the quantity demanded; the higher the price, the lower the quantity demanded.

The British economist Alfred Marshall (1842–1924) called this fundamental relation the "law of demand." In Chapter 6, we will derive the law of demand as a prediction that follows from more basic assumptions about individual consumer behaviour. For now, let's simply explore why this relationship seems reasonable. Products are used to satisfy desires and needs, and there is almost always more than one product that will satisfy any desire or need. Hunger may be alleviated by meat or vegetables; a desire for green vegetables can be satisfied by broccoli or spinach. The desire for a vacation may be satisfied by a trip to the ocean or to the mountains; the need to get there may be satisfied by different airlines, a bus, a car, or a train. For any general desire or need, there are many different products that will satisfy it.

Now consider what happens if income, tastes, population, and the prices of all other products remain constant and the price of only one product changes. As the price goes up, that product becomes an increasingly expensive means of satisfying a desire. Some consumers will stop buying it altogether; others will buy smaller amounts; still others may continue to buy the same quantity. Because many consumers will switch wholly or partly to other products to satisfy the same desire, less will be demanded of the product whose price has risen. As meat becomes more expensive, for example, some consumers will switch to meat substitutes; others may forgo meat at some meals and eat less meat at others. Taken together as a group, consumers will want to buy less meat when its price rises.

Conversely, as the price goes down, the product becomes a cheaper method of satisfying a desire. Households will demand more of it. Consequently, they will buy less of similar products whose prices have not fallen and as a result have become expensive *relative* to the product in question. When the price of tomatoes falls, shoppers switch to tomatoes and cut their purchases of many other vegetables that now look relatively more expensive.

Demand Schedules and Demand Curves

demand schedule A table showing the relationship between quantity demanded and the price of a commodity, other things being equal.

A **demand schedule** is one way of showing the relationship between quantity demanded and the price of a product, other things being equal. It is a table showing the quantity demanded at various prices.

The table in Figure 3-1 shows a hypothetical demand schedule for carrots. It lists the quantity of carrots that would be demanded at various prices, given the assumption that all other variables are held constant. We should note in particular that aver-

---

1 In this chapter we explore the demand curve for some product for the market as a whole—what we often call the *market demand curve*. In Chapter 6 we discuss how this market demand curve is derived by aggregating the demands of different individuals.

FIGURE 3-1   The Demand for Carrots

A Demand Schedule for Carrots

Reference Point	Price Per Tonne ($)	Quantity Demanded When Average Household Income Is $50 000 Per Year (tonnes per year)
U	20	110
V	40	85
W	60	65
X	80	50
Y	100	40

A Demand Curve for Carrots

Both the table and the graph show the total quantity of carrots that would be demanded at various prices, *ceteris paribus*. For example, row W indicates that if the price of carrots were $60 per tonne, consumers would desire to purchase 65 tonnes of carrots per year, holding constant the values of the other variables that affect quantity demanded. The demand curve, labelled D, relates quantity of carrots demanded to the price of carrots; its negative slope indicates that quantity demanded increases as price falls.

age household income is assumed to be $50 000 per year because later we will want to see what happens when income changes. The table gives the quantities demanded for five selected prices, but in fact a separate quantity would be demanded at each possible price from 1 cent to several hundreds of dollars.

A second method of showing the relationship between quantity demanded and price is to draw a graph. The five price–quantity combinations shown in the table are plotted in Figure 3-1. Price is plotted on the vertical axis, and the quantity demanded is plotted on the horizontal axis.

The curve drawn through these points is called a **demand curve**. It shows the quantity that consumers would like to buy at each price. The negative slope of the curve indicates that the quantity demanded increases as the price falls. Each point on the demand curve indicates a single price–quantity combination. The demand curve as a whole shows something more.

The demand curve represents the relationship between quantity demanded and price, other things being equal.

When economists speak of demand in a particular market, they are referring not just to the particular quantity being demanded at the moment (i.e., not just to one point on the demand curve) but to the entire demand curve—to the relationship between desired purchases and all the possible prices of the product.

The term **demand** therefore refers to the entire relationship between the quantity demanded of a product and the price of that product. In contrast, a single point on a demand schedule or curve is the quantity demanded at that point. This distinction between "demand" and "quantity demanded" is an extremely important one and we will examine it more closely later in this chapter.

demand curve The graphical representation of the relationship between quantity demanded and the price of a commodity, other things being equal.

demand The entire relationship between the quantity of a commodity that buyers wish to purchase and the price of that commodity, other things being equal.

Shifts in the Demand Curve   The demand curve is drawn with the assumption that everything except the product's own price is being held constant. But what if other things change, as they often do? For example, consider an increase in average household income while price remains constant. If consumers increase their purchases of the product, the new quantity demanded cannot be represented by a point on the original demand curve. It must be represented on a new demand curve that is to the right of the old curve. Thus, a rise in income that causes more to be demanded *at each price* shifts the demand curve to the right, as shown in Figure 3-2. This shift illustrates the operation of an important general rule.

A demand curve is drawn with the assumption that everything except the product's own price is held constant. A change in any of the variables previously held constant will shift the demand curve to a new position.

A demand curve can shift in two important ways. In the first case, more is desired at each price—the demand curve shifts rightward so that each price corresponds to a higher quantity than it did before. In the second case, less is desired at each price—the demand curve shifts leftward so that each price corresponds to a lower quantity than it did before.

We can assess the influence of changes in variables other than price by determining how changes in each variable shift the demand curve. Any change will shift the demand curve to the right if it increases the amount that households wish to buy at each price, other things remaining equal. It will shift the demand curve to the left if it decreases the amount that households wish to buy at each price, other things remaining equal.

FIGURE 3-2   An Increase in the Demand for Carrots

Demand Schedules

Price Per Tonne ($) p	Quantity Demanded When Average Household Income Is $50 000 Per Year (tonnes per year) D_0		Quantity Demanded When Average Household Income Is $60 000 Per Year (tonnes per year) D_1	
20	110	U	140	U'
40	85	V	115	V'
60	65	W	95	W'
80	50	X	80	X'
100	40	Y	70	Y'

An increase in average household income increases the quantity demanded at each price (for all normal goods). This is shown by the rightward shift in the demand curve, from D_0 to D_1. When average income rises from $50 000 to $60 000 per year, quantity demanded at a price of $60 per tonne rises from 65 tonnes per year to 95 tonnes per year. A similar rise occurs at every other price.

1. Average Income. If average income rises, consumers as a group can be expected to desire more of most products even if prices don't change at all. Goods for which the quantity demanded increases when income rises are called *normal goods;* goods for which the quantity demanded falls when income rises are called *inferior goods.* The term *normal goods* reflects economists' empirical finding that the demand for most goods rises when income rises. We therefore expect that a rise in average consumer income shifts the demand curve for most products to the right, indicating that more will be demanded at any given price. Such a shift is illustrated in Figure 3-2.

2. Prices of Other Goods. We saw that the negative slope of a product's demand curve occurs because the lower its price, the cheaper the product becomes relative to other products that can satisfy the same needs or desires. These other products are called **substitutes.** Another way for the same change to come about is that the price of the substitute product rises. For example, carrots can become cheap relative to broccoli either because the price of carrots falls or because the price of broccoli rises. Either change will increase the amount of carrots that consumers wish to buy as some consumers substitute away from broccoli and toward carrots. Thus, a rise in the price of a substitute for a product shifts the demand curve for the product to the right. More will be demanded at each price. For example, Coke and Pepsi are substitutes. If the price of Pepsi increases, the demand curve for Coke will shift to the right.

substitutes Goods that can be used in place of another good to satisfy similar needs or desires.

    Complements are products that tend to be used jointly. Cars and gasoline are complements; so are CD players and speakers, golf clubs and golf balls, electric stoves and electricity, and airplane flights to Calgary and ski-lift tickets in Banff. Because complements tend to be consumed together, a fall in the price of one will increase the quantity demanded of *both* products. Thus, a fall in the price of a complement for a product will shift that product's demand curve to the right. More will be demanded at each price. For example, a fall in the price of airplane trips to Calgary will lead to a rise in the demand for ski-lift tickets in Banff, even though the price of those lift tickets is unchanged. (So the demand curve for ski-lift tickets will shift to the right.)

complements Goods that tend to be consumed together.

3. Tastes. Tastes have an effect on people's desired purchases. A change in tastes may be long-lasting, such as the shift from fountain pens to ballpoint pens or from typewriters to computers, or it may be a short-lived fad as is common with many toys such as Pokémon cards and Beanie Babies. In either case, a change in tastes in favour of a product shifts the demand curve to the right. More will be demanded at each price. Of course, a change in tastes against some product has the opposite effect and shifts the demand curve to the left. The gradual but persistent reduction in demand for Camaro and Firebird cars eventually led General Motors in the late 1990s to close the plant at which those specific models were manufactured.

4. Distribution of Income. A change in the distribution of income will cause an increase in the demand for products bought most by consumers whose incomes increase and a decrease in the demand for products bought most by consumers whose incomes decrease. If, for example, the government increases the child tax credit and at the same time raises basic tax rates, income will be transferred from households without children to households with children. Demands for products more heavily bought by childless persons will decline, while demands for products more heavily bought by households with children will increase.

5. Population. Population growth does not create new demand unless the additional people have the means to purchase goods—that is, unless they have purchasing power. If there is an increase in population with purchasing power, the demands for all the products purchased by the new people will rise. Thus, we expect that an increase in

FIGURE 3-3 Shifts in the Demand Curve

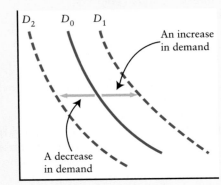

A rightward shift in the demand curve from D_0 to D_1 indicates an increase in demand; a leftward shift from D_0 to D_2 indicates a decrease in demand. An increase in demand means that more is demanded at each price. Such a rightward shift can be caused by a rise in income, a rise in the price of a substitute, a fall in the price of a complement, a change in tastes that favours that product, an increase in population, a redistribution of income toward groups that favour the product, or the anticipation of a future event that will increase the price.

A decrease in demand means that less is demanded at each price. Such a leftward shift can be caused by a fall in income, a fall in the price of a substitute, a rise in the price of a complement, a change in tastes that disfavours the product, a decrease in population, a redistribution of income away from groups that favour the product, or the anticipation of a future event that will decrease the price.

population will shift the demand curves for most products to the right, indicating that more will be demanded at each price.

6. Expectations About the Future. Our discussion has so far focused on how changes in the current value of variables may change demand. But it is also true that changes in people's *expectations about future values* of variables may change demand. For example, suppose you are thinking about buying a house in a small town in Nova Scotia, and you have learned that in the near future a large high-tech firm will be moving its head office and several hundred employees to this same small town. Since their future movement into your town will probably increase the demand for housing and drive up the *future* price of houses, this expectation will lead you (and others like you) to increase your demand *today* so as to make the purchase before the price rises. Thus, the demand curve for houses will shift to the right today in anticipation of a future event.

Figure 3-3 summarizes the reasons why demand curves shift.

Movements Along the Curve Versus Shifts of the Whole Curve

Suppose you read in today's newspaper that a sharp increase in the world price of coffee beans has been caused by an increased worldwide demand for coffee. Then tomorrow you read that the rising price of coffee is reducing the typical consumer's purchases of coffee, as shoppers switch to other beverages. The two stories appear to contradict each other. The first associates a rising price with rising demand; the second associates a rising price with declining demand. Can both statements be true? The answer is yes—because the two statements actually refer to different things. The first describes a shift in the demand curve; the second describes a movement along the demand curve in response to a change in price.

Consider first the statement that the increase in the price of coffee has been caused by an increased demand for coffee. This statement refers to a shift in the demand curve for coffee—in this case, a shift to the right, indicating more coffee demanded at each price. This shift, as we will see later in this chapter, will increase the price of coffee.

Now consider the second statement—that less coffee is being bought because of its rise in price. This refers to a movement along the *new* demand curve and reflects a change between two specific quantities demanded, one before the price increased and one afterward.

Possible explanations for the two stories are:

1. A rise in population and income in coffee-drinking countries shifts the demand curve for coffee to the right. This, in turn, raises the price of coffee (for reasons we will soon study in detail). This was the first newspaper story.

2. The rising price of coffee is causing each individual household to cut back on its coffee purchases. The cutback is represented by an upward movement to the left along the new demand curve for coffee. This was the second newspaper story.

To prevent the type of confusion caused by our two newspaper stories, economists use a specialized vocabulary to distinguish between shifts of demand curves and movements along demand curves.

We have seen that demand refers to the *entire* demand curve, whereas quantity demanded refers to the quantity that is demanded at a specific price, as indicated by a particular *point* on the demand curve. Economists reserve the term **change in demand** to describe a change in the quantity demanded at *every* price. That is, a change in demand refers to a shift of the entire demand curve. The term **change in quantity demanded** refers to a movement from one point on a demand curve to another point, either on the same demand curve or on a new one.

> **change in demand** A change in the quantity demanded at each possible price of the commodity, represented by a shift in the whole demand curve.
>
> **change in quantity demanded** A change in the specific quantity of the good demanded, represented by a change from one point on a demand curve to another point, either on the original demand curve or on a new one.

A change in quantity demanded can result from a shift in the demand curve with the price constant; from a movement along a given demand curve due to a change in the price; or from a combination of the two. [3]

We consider these three possibilities in turn.

An increase in demand means that the whole demand curve shifts to the right; a decrease in demand means that the whole demand curve shifts to the left. At any given price, an increase in demand causes an increase in quantity demanded, whereas a decrease in demand causes a decrease in quantity demanded. For example, in Figure 3-2, the shift in the demand curve for carrots from D_0 to D_1 represents an increase in demand, and at a price of $40 per tonne, quantity demanded increases from 85 tonnes to 115 tonnes, as indicated by the move from V to V'.

A movement down and to the right along a demand curve represents an increase in quantity demanded; a movement up and to the left along a demand curve represents a decrease in quantity demanded. For example, in Figure 3-2, with the demand for carrots given by the curve D_1, an increase in price from $40 to $60 per tonne causes a movement along D_1 from V' to W', and quantity demanded decreases from 115 tonnes to 95 tonnes.

When there is a change in demand *and* a change in the price, the overall change in quantity demanded is the net effect of the shift in the demand curve and the movement along the new demand curve. Figure 3-4 shows the combined effect of an increase in demand, shown by a rightward shift in the whole demand curve, and an upward movement to the left along the new demand curve due to an increase in price. The increase in demand causes an increase in quantity demanded at the initial price, whereas the movement along the new demand curve causes a decrease in the quantity demanded. Whether quantity demanded rises or falls overall depends on the relative magnitudes of these two changes.

FIGURE 3-4 Shifts Of and Movements Along the Demand Curve

An increase in demand means that the demand curve shifts to the right, and hence quantity demanded will be higher at each price. A rise in price causes a movement upward and to the left along the demand curve, and hence quantity demanded will fall. The demand curve is originally D_0 and price is p_0, which means that quantity demanded is Q_0. Suppose demand increases to D_1, which means that at any particular price, there is a larger quantity demanded; for example, at p_0, quantity demanded is now Q_1. Now suppose the price rises above p_0. This causes a movement up and to the left along D_1, and quantity demanded falls below Q_1. As the figure is drawn, the quantity demanded at the new price p_2 is less than Q_1 but greater than Q_0. So in this case the combined effect of the increase in demand and the rise in price is an increase in quantity demanded from Q_0 to Q_2.

3.2 SUPPLY

What determines the supply of any given product? Why do Canadian oil producers extract and sell more oil when the price of oil is high? Why do Canadian cattle ranchers sell more beef when the price of cattle-feed falls? We start by developing a theory designed to explain the supply of some typical product.

What Is "Quantity Supplied"?

quantity supplied The amount of a commodity that producers wish to sell during some time period.

The amount of some good or service that producers wish to sell in some time period is called the **quantity supplied** of that product. Quantity supplied is a flow; it is so much per unit of time. Note also that quantity supplied is the amount that producers are willing to offer for sale; it is not necessarily the amount that they succeed in selling, which is expressed by *quantity actually sold* or *quantity exchanged*.

The quantity supplied of a product is influenced by the following variables: [4]

- Product's own price
- Prices of inputs
- Technology
- Government taxes or subsidies
- Prices of other products
- Expectations about the future
- Number of suppliers

The situation with supply is the same as that with demand: There are several influencing variables, and we will not get far if we try to discover what happens when they all change at the same time. Again, we use the convenient *ceteris paribus* assumption to study the influence of the variables one at a time.

Quantity Supplied and Price

We begin by holding all other influences constant and ask, "How do we expect the total quantity of a product supplied to vary with its own price?"

A basic hypothesis of economics is that the price of the product and the quantity supplied are related *positively*, other things being equal. That is, the higher the product's own price, the more its producers will supply; the lower the price, the less its producers will supply.

In later chapters we will derive this hypothesis as a prediction from more basic assumptions about the behaviour of individual profit-maximizing firms. For now we simply note that as the product's price rises, producing and selling this product becomes a more profitable activity. Firms interested in increasing their profit will therefore choose to increase their production.

A rise in the price of wheat, other things being equal, will lead farmers to plant less of other crops and plant more wheat.

Supply Schedules and Supply Curves

The general relationship just discussed can be illustrated by a **supply schedule**, which shows the relationship between quantity supplied of a product and the price of the product, other things being equal. The table in Figure 3-5 presents a hypothetical supply schedule for carrots.

A **supply curve**, the graphical representation of the supply schedule, is illustrated in Figure 3-5. Each point on the supply curve represents a specific price–quantity combination; however, the whole curve shows something more.

The supply curve represents the relationship between quantity supplied and price, other things being equal; its positive slope indicates that quantity supplied increases when price increases.

When economists make statements about the conditions of supply, they are not referring just to the particular quantity being supplied at the moment—that is, not to just one point on the supply curve. Instead, they are referring to the entire supply curve, to the complete relationship between desired sales and all possible prices of the product.

Supply refers to the entire relationship between the quantity supplied of a product and the price of that product, other things being equal. A single point on the supply curve refers to the *quantity supplied* at that price.

Shifts in the Supply Curve
A shift in the supply curve means that at each price there is a change in the quantity supplied. An increase in the quantity supplied at each price is shown in Figure 3-6. This change appears as a rightward shift in the supply curve.

supply schedule A table showing the relationship between quantity supplied and the price of a commodity, other things being equal.

supply curve The graphical representation of the relationship between quantity supplied and the price of a commodity, other things being equal.

supply The entire relationship between the quantity of some commodity that producers wish to sell and the price of that commodity, other things being equal.

FIGURE 3-5   The Supply of Carrots

A Supply Schedule for Carrots

Reference Point	Price Per Tonne ($)	Quantity Supplied (tonnes per year)
u	20	20
v	40	45
w	60	65
x	80	80
y	100	95

A Supply Curve for Carrots

Both the table and the graph show the quantities that producers wish to sell at various prices, *ceteris paribus*. For example, row *w* indicates that if the price of carrots were $60 per tonne, producers would want to sell 65 tonnes per year. The supply curve, labelled *S*, relates quantity of carrots supplied to the price of carrots; its positive slope indicates that quantity supplied increases as price increases.

FIGURE 3-6   An Increase in the Supply of Carrots

Supply Schedules

Supply Curves

Price Per Tonne ($) p	Quantity Supplied Before Cost-Saving Innovation (tonnes per year) S_0	Quantity Supplied After Innovation (tonnes per year) S_1
20	20 u	50 u'
40	45 v	75 v'
60	65 w	95 w'
80	80 x	110 x'
100	95 y	125 y'

A cost-saving innovation increases the quantity supplied at each price. This is shown by the rightward shift in the supply curve, from S_0 to S_1. As a result of a cost-saving innovation, the quantity that is supplied at a price of $100 per tonne rises from 95 to 125 tonnes per year. A similar rise occurs at every price.

In contrast, a decrease in the quantity supplied at each price would appear as a leftward shift. For supply, as for demand, there is an important general rule:

A change in any of the variables (other than the product's own price) that affects the quantity supplied will shift the supply curve to a new position.

Let's now consider the possible causes of shifts in supply curves.

1. Prices of Inputs. All things that a firm uses to produce its outputs, such as materials, labour, and machines, are called the firm's *inputs.* Other things being equal, the higher the price of any input used to make a product, the less will be the profit from making that product. We expect, therefore, that the higher the price of any input used by a firm, the less the firm will produce and offer for sale at any given price of the product. A rise in the price of inputs therefore shifts the supply curve to the left, indicating that less will be supplied at any given price; a fall in the cost of inputs makes production more profitable and therefore shifts the supply curve to the right.

2. Technology. At any time, what is produced and how it is produced depend on what is known. Over time, knowledge changes. The enormous increase in production per worker that has been going on in industrial societies for about 200 years is due largely to improved methods of production. The Industrial Revolution is more than a historical event; it is a present reality. Discoveries in chemistry have led to lower costs of production for well-established products, such as paints, and to a large variety of new products made of plastics and synthetic fibres. Such inventions as silicon chips have radically changed products such as computers, televisions, and telephones, and the consequent development of smaller computers has revolutionized the production of countless other non-electronic products.

Any technological innovation that decreases the amount of inputs needed per unit of output reduces production costs and hence will increase the profits that can be earned at any given price of the product. Because increased profitability leads to increased willingness to produce, this change shifts the supply curve to the right.

3. Government Taxes or Subsidies. We have just seen that anything increasing firms' costs will shift the supply curve to the left, and anything decreasing firms' costs will shift the supply curve to the right. As we will see in later chapters, governments often levy special taxes on the production of specific goods, such as gasoline, cigarettes, and alcohol. These taxes make the production and sale of these goods less profitable. The result is that the supply curve shifts to the left.

For other goods, governments often subsidize producers—that is, they pay producers a specific amount for each unit of the good produced. This often occurs for agricultural products, especially in the United States and the European Union. In such situations, the subsidy increases the profitability of production and shifts the supply curve to the right.

4. Prices of Other Products. Changes in the price of one product may lead to changes in the supply of some other product because the two products are either *substitutes* or *complements* in the production process.

A prairie farmer, for example, can plant his field in wheat or oats. If the market price of oats falls, thus making oat production less profitable, the farmer will be more inclined to plant wheat. In this case, wheat and oats are said to be *substitutes* in production—for every extra acre planted in one crop, one fewer acre can be planted in the other. In this example, a reduction in the price of oats leads to an increase in the supply of wheat.

An excellent example in which two products are *complements* in production is oil and natural gas, which are often found together below the earth's surface. If the market price of natural gas rises, producers will do more drilling and increase their production of natural gas. But as more wells are drilled, the usual outcome is that more of *both* natural gas and oil are produced. Thus, the rise in the price of natural gas leads to an increase in the supply of the complementary product—oil.

5. Expectations About the Future. As in our discussion of shifts in demand curves, expectations about the future can play a role in shifting supply curves. This is especially important in agricultural markets in which farmers must make planting and production decisions several months ahead of when the output will actually be sold. In such cases, it is the expectation of the future price, and not just the current price, which guides farmers' decisions. A canola farmer who expects prices to be high in the fall will plant a large crop, even though actual prices in the spring may be low. Thus, other things being equal, an increase in the expected future price of a product leads to an increase in the supply of the product.

6. Number of Suppliers. For given prices and technology, the total amount of any product supplied depends on the number of firms producing that product and offering it for sale. If profits are being earned by current firms, then more firms will choose to enter this industry and begin producing. The effect of this increase in the number of suppliers is to shift the supply curve to the right. Similarly, if the existing firms are losing money, they will eventually leave the industry; such a reduction in the number of suppliers shifts the supply curve to the left.

Movements Along the Curve Versus Shifts of the Whole Curve
As with demand, it is important to distinguish movements along supply curves from shifts of the whole curve. Economists reserve the term **change in supply** to describe a shift of the whole supply curve—that is, a change in the quantity that will be supplied at every price. The

change in supply A change in the quantity supplied at each possible price of the commodity, represented by a shift in the whole supply curve.

change in quantity supplied
A change in the specific quantity supplied, represented by a change from one point on a supply curve to another point, either on the original supply curve or on a new one.

term **change in quantity supplied** refers to a movement from one point on a supply curve to another point, either on the same supply curve or a new one. In other words, an increase in supply means that the whole supply curve has shifted to the right, so that the quantity supplied at any given price has increased; a movement up and to the right along a supply curve indicates an increase in the quantity supplied in response to an increase in the price of the product.

A change in quantity supplied can result from: a change in supply, with the price constant; a movement along a given supply curve due to a change in the price; or a combination of the two.

An exercise you might find useful is to construct a diagram similar to Figure 3-4, emphasizing the difference between a shift of the supply curve and a movement along the supply curve.

Practise with Study Guide Chapter 3, Exercise 4.

3.3 **THE DETERMINATION OF PRICE**

So far we have considered demand and supply separately. We now come to a key question: How do the two forces of demand and supply interact to determine price?

The Concept of a Market

market Any situation in which buyers and sellers can negotiate the exchange of goods or services.

Originally the term *market* designated a physical place where products were bought and sold. We still use the term this way to describe places such as Granville Island Market in Vancouver, Kensington Market in Toronto, or Jean Talon Market in Montreal. Once developed, however, theories of market behaviour were easily extended to cover products such as wheat or oil, which can be purchased anywhere in the world at a price that tends to be uniform the world over. Today we can also buy and sell items in markets that exist in cyberspace—consider the online auction services provided by eBay—thus extending our viewpoint well beyond the idea of a single place to which consumers go to buy something.

For present purposes, a **market** may be defined as existing in any situation (a physical place or an electronic medium) in which buyers and sellers negotiate the exchange of some product or related group of products.

Individual markets differ in the degree of *competition* among the various buyers and sellers. In the next few chapters we will confine ourselves to examining markets in which the number of buyers and sellers is sufficiently large that no one of them has any appreciable influence on the market price. This is a very rough definition of what economists call *perfectly competitive markets*. Starting in Chapter 10, we will consider the behaviour of markets in which there are small numbers of either sellers or buyers. But our initial theory of markets will actually be a very good description of the markets for such things as wheat, pork, newsprint, coffee, copper, oil, and many other commodities.

eBay brings together buyers and sellers of thousands of different goods and services. It thus creates markets that exist only on the Internet.

Graphical Analysis of a Market

The table in Figure 3-7 brings together the demand and supply schedules from Figures 3-1 and 3-5. The quantities of carrots demanded and supplied at each price may now be compared.

There is only one price, $60 per tonne, at which the quantity of carrots demanded equals the quantity supplied. At prices less than $60 per tonne, there is a shortage of carrots because the quantity demanded exceeds the quantity supplied. This is a situation of **excess demand**. At prices greater than $60 per tonne, there is a surplus of carrots because the quantity supplied exceeds the quantity demanded. This is a situation of **excess supply**. This same story can also be told in graphical terms. The quantities demanded and supplied at any price can be read off the two curves; the excess supply or excess demand is shown by the horizontal distance between the curves at each price.

To examine the determination of market price, let's suppose first that the price is $100 per tonne. At this price, 95 tonnes are offered for sale, but only 40 tonnes are demanded. There is an excess supply of 55 tonnes per year. Sellers are then likely to cut their prices to get rid of this surplus. And purchasers, observing the stock of unsold carrots, will begin to offer less money for the product. In other words, *excess supply causes downward pressure on price.*

Now consider the price of $20 per tonne. At this price, there is excess demand. The 20 tonnes produced each year are snapped up quickly, and 90 tonnes of desired purchases cannot be made. Rivalry between would-be purchasers may lead them to offer more than the prevailing price to outbid other purchasers. Also, sellers may begin to ask a higher price for the quantities that they do have to sell. In other words, *excess demand causes upward pressure on price.*

excess demand A situation in which, at the given price, quantity demanded exceeds quantity supplied.

excess supply A situation in which, at the given price, quantity supplied exceeds quantity demanded.

FIGURE 3-7   Determination of the Equilibrium Price of Carrots

Demand and Supply Schedules

Price Per Tonne ($) p	Quantity Demanded (tonnes per year) D	Quantity Supplied (tonnes per year) S	Excess Demand (+) or Excess Supply (−) (tonnes per year) D − S
20	110	20	+90
40	85	45	+40
60	65	65	0
80	50	80	−30
100	40	95	−55

Demand and Supply Curves

The equilibrium price corresponds to the intersection of the demand and supply curves. At any price above $60, there is excess supply and thus downward pressure on price. At any price below $60, there is excess demand and thus upward pressure on price. Only at a price of $60 is there no pressure for price to change. Equilibrium occurs at point E, at a price of $60.

Finally, consider the price of $60. At this price, producers wish to sell 65 tonnes per year, and purchasers wish to buy that same quantity. There is neither a shortage nor a surplus of carrots. There are no unsatisfied buyers to bid the price up, nor are there unsatisfied sellers to force the price down. Once the price of $60 has been reached, therefore, there will be no tendency for it to change.

Equilibrium implies a state of rest, or balance, between opposing forces. The **equilibrium price** is the one toward which the actual market price will tend. Once established, it will persist until it is disturbed by some change in market conditions which shifts the demand curve, the supply curve, or both.

The price at which the quantity demanded equals the quantity supplied is called the equilibrium price, or the market-clearing price. [5]

Any price at which the market does not "clear"—that is, quantity demanded does not equal quantity supplied—is called a **disequilibrium price**. Whenever there is either excess demand or excess supply in a market, that market is said to be in a state of **disequilibrium**, and the market price will be changing.

Figure 3-7 makes it clear that the equilibrium price occurs where the demand and supply curves intersect. Below that price, there is excess demand and hence upward pressure on the existing price. Above that price, there is excess supply and hence downward pressure on the existing price.[2]

Changes in Market Prices

Changes in any of the variables, other than price, that influence quantity demanded or supplied will cause a shift in the demand curve, the supply curve, or both. There are four possible shifts: an increase in demand (a rightward shift in the demand curve), a decrease in demand (a leftward shift in the demand curve), an increase in supply (a rightward shift in the supply curve), and a decrease in supply (a leftward shift in the supply curve).

To discover the effects of each of the possible curve shifts, we use the method known as **comparative statics**.[3] With this method, we derive predictions about how the *endogenous* variables (equilibrium price and quantity) will change following a change in some *exogenous* variable. We start from a position of equilibrium and then introduce the change to be studied. We then determine the new equilibrium position and compare it with the original one. The difference between the two positions of equilibrium must result from the change that was introduced because everything else has been held constant.

equilibrium price The price at which quantity demanded equals quantity supplied. Also called the market-clearing price.

disequilibrium price A price at which quantity demanded does not equal quantity supplied.

disequilibrium A situation in a market in which there is excess demand or excess supply.

comparative statics The derivation of predictions by analyzing the effect of a change in some exogenous variable on the equilibrium.

---

[2] When economists graph a demand (or supply) curve, they put the variable to be explained (the dependent variable) on the horizontal axis and the explanatory variable (the independent variable) on the vertical axis. This is "backwards" to what is usually done in mathematics. The rational explanation of what is now economists' odd practice is buried in the history of economics and dates back to Alfred Marshall's *Principles of Economics* (1890) [6]. For better or worse, Marshall's scheme is now used by all economists, although mathematicians never fail to wonder at this example of the odd ways of economists.

[3] The term *static* is used because we are not concerned with the actual path by which the market goes from the first equilibrium position to the second or with the time taken to reach the second equilibrium. Analysis of these movements would be described as *dynamic analysis*.

Each of the four possible curve shifts causes changes that are described by one of the four "laws" of demand and supply. Each of the laws summarizes what happens when an initial position of equilibrium is disturbed by a shift in either the demand curve or the supply curve. By using the term "law" to describe what happens, economists do not mean that they are absolutely certain of the outcome. The term "law" in science is used to describe a theory that has stood up to substantial testing. The laws of demand and supply are thus hypotheses that predict certain kinds of behaviour in certain situations, and the predicted behaviour occurs sufficiently often that economists continue to have confidence in the underlying theory.

The four laws of demand and supply are illustrated in Figure 3-8. Study the figure carefully. Previously, we had given the axes specific labels, but because it is now intended to apply to any product, the horizontal axis is simply labelled "Quantity." This means quantity per period in whatever units output is measured. "Price," the vertical axis, means the price measured as dollars per unit of quantity for the same product.

The four laws of demand and supply are as follows:

1. An increase in demand causes an increase in both the equilibrium price and the equilibrium quantity exchanged.

2. A decrease in demand causes a decrease in both the equilibrium price and the equilibrium quantity exchanged.

3. An increase in supply causes a decrease in the equilibrium price and an increase in the equilibrium quantity exchanged.

FIGURE 3-8   The Four "Laws" of Demand and Supply

(i) The effect of shifts in the demand curve

(ii) The effect of shifts in the supply curve

The effects on equilibrium price and quantity of shifts in either demand or supply are known as the laws of demand and supply. In part (i), suppose the original demand and supply curves are D_0 and S, which intersect to produce equilibrium at E_0, with a price of p_0 and a quantity of Q_0. An increase in demand shifts the demand curve to D_1, taking the new equilibrium to E_1. Price rises to p_1 and quantity rises to Q_1. Starting at E_0, a decrease in demand shifts the demand curve to D_0, taking the new equilibrium to E_2. Price falls to p_2 and quantity falls to Q_2.

In part (ii), the original demand and supply curves are D and S_0, which intersect to produce equilibrium at E_0, with a price of p_0 and a quantity of Q_0. An increase in supply shifts the supply curve to S_1, taking the new equilibrium to E_1. Price falls to p_1, and quantity rises to Q_1. Starting at E_0, a decrease in supply shifts the supply curve from S_0 to S_2, taking the new equilibrium to E_2. Price rises to p_2 and quantity falls to Q_2.

EXTENSIONS IN THEORY 3-2

The Algebra of Market Equilibrium

This box presents a specific model of demand and supply and the algebraic method for determining the equilibrium price and quantity. For simplicity, we assume that the demand and supply curves are linear relationships between price and quantity.

Consider the following demand and supply curves:

Demand: $Q^D = a - bp$
Supply: $Q^S = c + dp$

where p is the price, Q^D is quantity demanded, Q^S is quantity supplied, and a, b, c, and d are positive constants. Both relationships are plotted in the accompanying figure.

What is the interpretation of the demand curve and how do we plot it? First, at a price of zero, consumers will buy a units—this is the horizontal intercept of the demand curve. Second, if the price rises to a/b, consumers will buy zero units, so a/b is the vertical intercept of the demand curve. Finally, the slope of the demand curve is $-1/b$; the quantity demanded increases by b units for every \$1 that price falls.

What is the interpretation of the supply curve, and how do we plot it? First, if the price is zero, suppliers will sell c units—this is the horizontal intercept of the supply curve. Second, for every \$1 increase in price, the quantity supplied increases by d units. Thus, the slope of the supply curve is $1/d$.

Given these demand and supply curves, the market equilibrium can be determined in two ways. The first is to construct a scale diagram and plot the two curves accurately. If you do this carefully, you will be able to read the equilibrium price and quantity off the diagram.

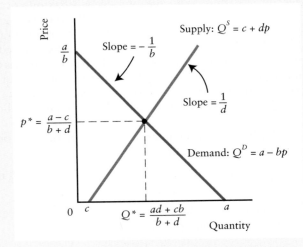

But your diagram will have to be very accurate for this to work!

A more precise method is to use algebra to solve for the equilibrium price and quantity. Here is how we do it. We know that in equilibrium quantity demanded equals quantity supplied, or $Q^D = Q^S$. We call the equilibrium quantity Q^*. But we also know that in equilibrium the price paid by the consumers will equal the price received by the producers—that is, there is only one equilibrium price, which we call p^*. Putting these two facts together we know that in equilibrium

Demand: $Q^* = a - bp^*$
Supply: $Q^* = c + dp^*$

4. A decrease in supply causes an increase in the equilibrium price and a decrease in the equilibrium quantity exchanged.

Demonstrations of these laws are given in the caption to Figure 3-8. The intuitive reasoning behind each is as follows:

1. **An increase in demand (the demand curve shifts to the right).** An increase in demand creates a shortage at the initial equilibrium price, and the unsatisfied buyers bid up the price. This rise in price causes a larger quantity to be supplied with the result that at the new equilibrium more is exchanged at a higher price.

We now have two equations and two unknown variables (p^* and Q^*) and can proceed to solve the system of equations. Since Q^* from the demand curve equals Q^* from the supply curve, it follows that

$$a - bp^* = c + dp^*$$

This implies

$$a - c = (b + d)p^*$$

which can be solved for p^* to get

$$p^* = \frac{a - c}{b + d}$$

This is the solution for the equilibrium market price. By substituting this value of p^* back into *either* the demand curve or the supply curve (it doesn't matter which) we get the solution for Q^*:

$$Q^* = a - bp^* = a - b[(a - c)/(b + d)]$$

which can be simplified to be

$$Q^* = \frac{(ad + bc)}{b+d}$$

We now have the precise solutions for the equilibrium price and quantity in this market. Notice that the solutions for p^* and Q^* naturally depend on those (exogenous) variables that shift the demand and supply curves. For example, an increase in demand for the product would be reflected by an increase in a. This would shift the demand curve to the right, increasing both p^* and Q^*. A decrease in supply would have a different effect. It would be reflected by a decrease in c that would shift the supply curve to the left, leading to an increase in p^* and a reduction in Q^*.

Now let's do the same thing but with even more specific demand and supply curves. Suppose we have the following relationships:

$$Q^D = 18 - 3p$$
$$Q^S = 2 + 5p$$

The equilibrium condition is that $Q^D = Q^S = Q^*$. And when quantity is equal to Q^*, price will be equal to p^*. Thus, in equilibrium we will have

$$Q^* = 18 - 3p^*$$
$$Q^* = 2 + 5p^*$$

Since Q^* from the demand curve obviously equals Q^* from the supply curve, we have

$$18 - 3p^* = 2 + 5p^*$$

which can be solved for p^* to get

$$8p^* = 16$$
$$p^* = 2$$

Putting this value of p^* back into the demand curve we get

$$Q^* = 18 - 3(2)$$
$$Q^* = 12$$

We have therefore solved for the equilibrium price and quantity in this specific numerical model of demand and supply.

Mastering the algebra of demand and supply takes a little practice, but is worth the effort. If you would like to practise, try the Study Exercises at the end of the chapter (and Chapters 4 and 5) that deal with the algebra of demand and supply.

2. **A decrease in demand (the demand curve shifts to the left).** A decrease in demand creates a surplus at the initial equilibrium price, and the unsuccessful sellers bid the price down. As a result, less of the product is supplied and offered for sale. At the new equilibrium, both price and quantity exchanged are lower than they were originally.

3. **An increase in supply (the supply curve shifts to the right).** An increase in supply creates a surplus at the initial equilibrium price, and the unsuccessful suppliers force the price down. This drop in price increases the quantity demanded, and the new equilibrium is at a lower price and a higher quantity exchanged.

4. **A decrease in supply (the supply curve shifts to the left).** A decrease in supply creates a shortage at the initial equilibrium price that causes the price to be bid up.

Practise with Study Guide Chapter 3, Exercise 3 and Short-Answer Question 4.

LESSONS FROM HISTORY 3-1

Ice Storms, Hurricanes, and Economics

Here are two simple examples of the demand and supply apparatus in action. Both examples show how the weather—something that changes in unpredictable and often dramatic ways—can have significant effects on either the demand or the supply of various products, with obvious implications for the observed market price.

The Weather and a Demand Shock

In January of 1998, Quebec, Eastern Ontario, and parts of the Northeastern United States were hit by a massive ice storm. So unprecedented was this storm in its magnitude that many electric power systems were devastated. Homes and businesses in the Montreal area went without power for as long as four weeks.

This electric power shortage had many economic effects, including lost factory production, damage to many businesses, the death of farm livestock, and the displacement of thousands of people into shelters. Another effect of the power shortage, as soon as it became clear that it would last for more than just a few hours, was a sudden and substantial increase in the demand for portable gas-powered electric generators. Within just a few days, all stores in the greater Montreal

area were sold out of such generators, and the prices for newly ordered units had increased.

Furthermore, the shortages and price increases for electric generators were not confined to the area directly hit by the ice storm. As it became clear that there was an excess demand for generators in Quebec, sellers in other parts of the country began to divert their supply toward Quebec. This reduction in supply caused shortages, and thus price increases, in other parts of the country, as far away as Edmonton.

The Weather and a Supply Shock

In late August of 2005, Hurricane Katrina emerged from the Caribbean, gathered strength as it crossed the Gulf of Mexico, and unleashed its fury on New Orleans, Louisiana. The damage to New Orleans was massive, especially after the levee holding back Lake Pontchartrain broke and much of the city was flooded. Katrina was the worst natural disaster in U.S. history; the cost of the damage to buildings, bridges, houses, and other infrastructure was estimated to be close to 200 billion U.S. dollars.

Hurricane Katrina had an instant effect on the world market for oil. Over short periods of time, the

This rise in price reduces the quantity demanded, and the new equilibrium is at a higher price and a lower quantity exchanged.

In this chapter, we have studied many forces that can cause demand or supply curves to shift. By combining this analysis with the four laws of demand and supply, we can link many real-world events that cause demand or supply curves to shift with changes in market prices and quantities. *Lessons From History 3-1* shows how we can use demand-and-supply analysis to examine the effects of two real-world weather shocks: Quebec's 1998 ice storm and the effects of Hurricane Katrina in 2005.

Our discussion of demand, supply, and equilibrium has explained why equilibrium price and quantity are found at the intersection of the demand and supply curves. And we have shown diagrams (Figures 3-7 and 3-8) illustrating this in the general case. But we have not presented a specific example of demand and supply and "solved" precisely for the equilibrium price and quantity. This is a useful exercise but requires some algebra. See *Extensions in Theory 3-2* for an algebraic solution to a specific model of demand and supply.

Practise with Study Guide Chapter 3, Exercise 5 and Extension Exercise E1.

world demand curve for oil is relatively steep, reflecting the fact that users of oil reduce their purchases only slightly when the price rises. For the two years prior to Katrina, strong economic growth around the world had been shifting this relatively steep demand curve to the right. At the same time, the supply curve was also quite steep because most producers were operating close to their production capacity. Growing demand combined with a steep supply curve thus led to significant price increases—from just over U.S.$30 per barrel in June 2004 to about U.S.$60 per barrel in August 2005.

Hurricane Katrina interrupted the local production and distribution of oil, thereby causing a temporary reduction in world supply. Several large oil rigs in the Gulf of Mexico were damaged and were shut down or operating well below their capacity for several weeks. In addition, the major pipelines that transport this oil from the Gulf ports to the inland refineries were also seriously damaged. For both reasons, the supply curve for oil shifted to the left. And given the relatively steep demand curve, this reduction in supply caused a sharp increase in the equilibrium price. The price per barrel of oil reached U.S.$70.35 on August 29, 2005, and stayed above U.S.$65 for about a month. As the rigs and pipelines were repaired, and Gulf-area oil production began to approach its pre-Katrina levels, the supply curve shifted back to the right and the price returned to levels between U.S.$55 and U.S.$60 per barrel.

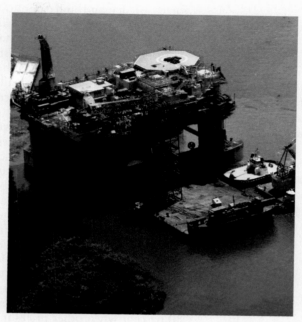

Hurricane Katrina in August 2005 damaged several oil platforms operating in the Gulf of Mexico and thus caused a temporary reduction in the supply of oil.

Relative Prices and Inflation

The theory we have developed explains how individual prices are determined by the forces of demand and supply. To facilitate matters, we have made *ceteris paribus* assumptions. Specifically, we have assumed the constancy of all prices except the one we are studying. Does this mean that our theory is inapplicable to an inflationary world in which all prices are rising at the same time? Fortunately, the answer is no.

The price of a product is the amount of money that must be spent to acquire one unit of that product. This is called the **absolute price** or *money price*. A **relative price** is the ratio of two absolute prices; it expresses the price of one good in terms of (relative to) another.

absolute price The amount of money that must be spent to acquire one unit of a commodity. Also called *money price*.

relative price The ratio of the money price of one commodity to the money price of another commodity; that is, a ratio of two absolute prices.

We have been reminded several times that what matters for demand and supply is the price of the product in question *relative to the prices of other products*; that is, what matters is the relative price. For example, if the price of carrots rises while the prices of other vegetables are constant, we expect consumers to reduce their quantity demanded of carrots as they substitute toward the consumption of other vegetables. In this case, the *relative* price of carrots has increased. But if the prices of carrots and all other vegetables are rising at the same rate, the relative price of carrots is constant. In this case we expect no substitution to take place between carrots and other vegetables.

In an inflationary world, we are often interested in the price of a given product as it relates to the average price of all other products. If, during a period when all prices were increasing by an average of 5 percent, the price of coffee increased by 30 percent, then the price of coffee increased relative to the prices of other goods as a whole. Coffee became *relatively* expensive. However, if coffee had increased in price by 30 percent when other prices increased by 40 percent, then the relative price of coffee would have fallen. Although the money price of coffee increased substantially, coffee became *relatively* cheap.

In this chapter we have been assuming that changes in a particular price occur when all other prices are constant. We can easily extend the analysis to an inflationary setting by remembering that any force that raises the price of one product when other prices remain constant will, given general inflation, raise the price of that product faster than the price level is rising. For example, consider a change in tastes in favour of carrots that raises their price by 5 percent when other prices are constant. The same change would raise their price by 8 percent if, at the same time, the general price level were rising by 3 percent. In each case, the price of carrots rises 5 percent *relative to the average of all prices*.

In microeconomics, whenever we refer to a change in the price of one product, we mean a change in that product's relative price; that is, a change in the price of that product relative to the prices of all other goods.

myeconlab

The world price of oil increased from about U.S.$15 per barrel in 1998 to over U.S.$75 during 2006. For more details on the many recent developments in the world oil market, including the role of various geopolitical tensions, look for "A Primer on the Market for Crude Oil" in the *Additional Topics* section of this book's MyEconLab.

www.myeconlab.com

SUMMARY

3.1 DEMAND

- The amount of a product that consumers wish to purchase is called *quantity demanded*. It is a flow expressed as so much per period of time. It is determined by tastes, average household income, the product's own price, the prices of other products, the size of the population, the distribution of income among consumers, and expectations about the future.
- The relationship between quantity demanded and price is represented graphically by a demand curve that shows how much will be demanded at each market price. Quantity demanded is assumed to increase as the price of the product falls, other things held constant. Thus, demand curves are negatively sloped.
- A shift in a demand curve represents a change in the quantity demanded at each price and is referred to as a *change in demand*.

- The demand curve shifts if:
  - average income changes
  - prices of other products change
  - consumers' tastes change
  - the distribution of income changes
  - population changes
  - expectations about the future are revised
- It is important to make the distinction between a movement along a demand curve (caused by a change in the product's price) and a shift of a demand curve (caused by a change in any of the other determinants of demand).

3.2 SUPPLY

- The amount of a good that producers wish to sell is called *quantity supplied*. It is a flow expressed as so much per period of time. It depends on the product's own price, the costs of inputs, the number of suppliers, government taxes or subsidies, the state of technology, prices of other products, and expectations about the future.
- The relationship between quantity supplied and price is represented graphically by a supply curve that shows how much will be supplied at each market price. Quantity supplied is assumed to increase as the price of the product increases, other things held constant. Thus, supply curves are positively sloped.

- A shift in the supply curve indicates a change in the quantity supplied at each price and is referred to as a *change in supply*.
- The supply curve shifts if:
  - the prices of inputs change
  - technology changes
  - the government imposes taxes or subsidies
  - the prices of other products change
  - expectations about the future are revised
  - the number of suppliers changes
- It is important to make the distinction between a movement along a supply curve (caused by a change in the product's price) and a shift of a supply curve (caused by a change in any of the other determinants of supply).

3.3 THE DETERMINATION OF PRICE

- The *equilibrium price* is the price at which the quantity demanded equals the quantity supplied. At any price below equilibrium, there will be excess demand; at any price above equilibrium, there will be excess supply. Graphically, equilibrium occurs where the demand and supply curves intersect.
- Price rises when there is excess demand and falls when there is excess supply. Thus, the actual market price will be pushed toward the equilibrium price. When it is reached, there will be neither excess demand nor excess supply, and the price will not change until either the supply curve or the demand curve shifts.
- Using the method of *comparative statics*, we can determine the effects of a shift in either demand or supply. An increase in demand raises both equilibrium price and equilibrium quantity; a decrease in demand lowers both. An increase in supply raises equilibrium quantity but lowers equilibrium price; a decrease in supply lowers equilibrium quantity but raises equilibrium price. These are called the laws of demand and supply.

- The absolute price of a product is its price in terms of money; its relative price is its price in relation to other products. In an inflationary period, a rise in the *relative price* of one product means that its absolute price rises by more than the average of all prices; a fall in its relative price means that its absolute price rises by less than the average of all prices.

KEY CONCEPTS

Ceteris paribus or "other things being equal"

Quantity demanded and quantity actually bought

Demand schedule and demand curve

Change in quantity demanded versus change in demand

Quantity supplied and quantity actually sold

Supply schedule and supply curve

Change in quantity supplied versus change in supply

Equilibrium, equilibrium price, and disequilibrium

Comparative statics

Laws of supply and demand

Relative price

STUDY EXERCISES

1. The following table shows hypothetical demand schedules for sugar for three separate months. To help make the distinction between changes in demand and changes in quantity demanded, choose the wording to make each of the following statements correct.

Quantity Demanded for Sugar (in kilograms)			
Price/kg	October	November	December
$1.50	11 000	10 500	13 000
1.75	10 000	9 500	12 000
2.00	9 000	8 500	11 000
2.25	8 000	7 500	10 000
2.50	7 000	6 500	9 000
2.75	6 000	5 500	8 000
3.00	5 000	4 500	7 000
3.25	4 000	3 500	6 000
3.50	3 000	2 500	5 000

a. When the price of sugar rises from $2.50 to $3.00 in the month of October there is a(n) (*increase/decrease*) in (*demand for/quantity demanded of*) sugar of 2000 kg.

b. We can say that the demand curve for sugar in December shifted (*to the right/to the left*) of November's demand curve. This represents a(n) (*increase/decrease*) in demand for sugar.

c. An increase in the demand for sugar means that quantity demanded at each price has (*increased/decreased*), while a decrease in demand for sugar means that quantity demanded at each price has (*increased/decreased*).

d. In the month of December, a price change for sugar from $3.50 to $2.75 per kilogram would mean a change in (*demand for/quantity demanded of*) sugar of 3000 kg.

e. Plot the three demand schedules on a graph and label each demand curve to indicate whether it is the demand for October, November, or December.

2. **myeconlab** For each of the following statements, determine whether there has been a change in supply or a change in quantity supplied. Draw a demand and supply diagram for each situation to show either a movement along the supply curve or a shift of the supply curve.

a. The price of Canadian-grown peaches skyrockets during an unusually cold summer that reduces the size of the peach harvest.

b. An increase in income leads to an increase in the price of beef and also to an increase in beef sales.

c. Technological improvements in the microchip lead to price reductions for personal computers and an increase in computer sales.

d. Greater awareness of the health risks from smoking lead to a reduction in the price of cigarettes and to fewer cigarettes being sold.

3. **myeconlab** The following diagram describes the hypothetical demand and supply for tuna in Canada in 2004.

a. Suppose the price of a can of tuna is $4.00. What is the quantity demanded? What is the quantity supplied? At this price, is there a shortage or a surplus? By what amount?

b. Suppose the price of a can of tuna is $1.50. What is the quantity demanded? What is the quantity supplied? At this price, is there a shortage or a surplus? By what amount?

c. What is the equilibrium price and quantity in this market?

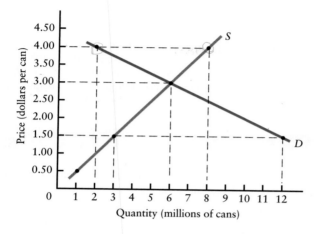

4. Consider households' demand for chicken meat. For each of the events listed below, state and explain the likely effect on the demand for chicken. How would each event be illustrated in a diagram?

   a. A medical study reports that eating chicken reduces the likelihood of suffering from particular types of heart problems.
   b. A widespread bovine disease leads to an increase in the price of beef.
   c. An increase in average household income.

5. **myeconlab** Consider the world market for a particular quality of coffee beans. The following table shows the demand and supply schedules for this market.

Price (per kilogram)	Quantity Demanded (millions of kilograms per year)	Quantity Supplied (millions of kilograms per year)
$2.00	28	10
$2.40	26	12
$3.10	22	13.5
$3.50	19.5	19.5
$3.90	17	22
$4.30	14.5	23.5

   a. Plot the demand and supply schedules on a diagram.
   b. Identify the amount of excess demand or supply associated with each price.
   c. Identify the equilibrium price in this market.
   d. Suppose that a collection of national governments were somehow able to set a minimum price for coffee equal to $3.90 per kilogram. Explain the outcome in the world coffee market.

6. Consider the supply for Grade A beef. As the price of beef rises, ranchers will tend to sell more cattle to the slaughterhouses. Yet a central prediction from the supply-and-demand model of this chapter is that an

increase in the supply of beef reduces the equilibrium price. Reconcile the apparent contradiction. Use a diagram to do so.

7. Consider the world market for wheat. Suppose there is a major failure in Russia's wheat crop due to a severe drought. Explain the likely effect on the equilibrium price and quantity in the world wheat market. Also explain why Canadian wheat farmers certainly benefit from Russia's drought. The diagrams below provide a starting point for your analysis.

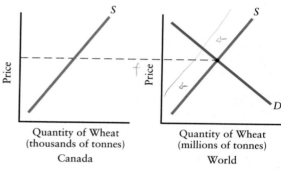

Canada   World

8. The *New York Times* recently stated:

   While the world's appetite for chocolate grows more voracious each year, cocoa farms around the globe are failing, under siege from fungal and viral diseases and insects . . . .Researchers predict a shortfall in beans from the cacao tree, the raw material from which chocolate is made, in as little as five to ten years.

   Describe in terms of the supply-and-demand apparatus what is described in the quote. What is the implied prediction for the equilibrium price of chocolate? What is the implied prediction for the equilibrium quantity of chocolate?

9. This is a challenging question and is similar to the example shown in *Extensions in Theory 3-2*. It requires you to solve a supply-and-demand model as a system of *simultaneous equations* (meaning simply that both equations apply at the same time). Letting p be the price of the product, suppose the demand and supply functions for some product are given by

$$Q^D = 100 - 3p$$

$$Q^S = 10 + 2p$$

   a. Plot both the demand curve and the supply curve.
   b. What is the condition for equilibrium in this market?
   c. By imposing the condition for equilibrium, solve for the equilibrium price.
   d. Substitute the equilibrium price into either the demand or supply function to solve for the equilibrium quantity. Check to make sure you get the

same answer whether you use the demand function or the supply function.

e. Now suppose there is an increase in demand so that the new demand function is given by

$$Q^D = 180 - 3p.$$

Compute the new equilibrium price and quantity. Is your result consistent with the "law" of demand?

f. Now suppose that, with the new demand curve in place, there is an increase in supply so that the new supply function is given by $Q^S = 90 + 2p$. Compute the new equilibrium price and quantity. Is your result consistent with the "law" of supply?

DISCUSSION QUESTIONS

1. Recently, a government economist predicted that this spring's excellent weather would result in larger crops of wheat and canola than farmers had expected. But the economist warned consumers not to expect prices to decrease because the cost of production was rising and foreign demand for Canadian crops was increasing. "The classic pattern of supply and demand won't work this time," the economist said. Discuss his observation.

2. What do you think would be the effect on the equilibrium price and quantity of marijuana if its sale and consumption were legalized?

3. Classify the effect of each of the following as (i) a decrease in the demand for fish or (ii) a decrease in the quantity of fish demanded. Illustrate each diagrammatically.

   a. The government of Canada closes the Atlantic cod fishery.
   b. People buy less fish because of a rise in fish prices.
   c. The Catholic Church relaxes its ban on eating meat on Fridays.
   d. The price of beef falls and, as a result, consumers buy more beef and less fish.
   e. Fears of mercury pollution lead locals to shun fish caught in nearby lakes.
   f. It is generally alleged that eating fish is better for one's health than eating meat.

4. Predict the effect on the price of at least one product of each of the following events:

   a. Winter snowfall is at a record high in the interior of British Columbia, but drought continues in Quebec ski areas.
   b. A recession decreases employment in Oshawa automobile factories.
   c. The French grape harvest is the smallest in 20 years.
   d. The province of Ontario cancels permission for campers to cut firewood in provincial campgrounds.

5. Are the following two observations inconsistent?

   a. Rising demand for housing causes prices of new homes to soar.
   b. Many families refuse to buy homes as prices become prohibitive for them.

6. Look back at the supply-and-demand figure inside *Extensions in Theory 3-2*. Notice that the supply curve has a positive horizontal intercept, suggesting that producers will wish to produce and sell a positive amount of this product when the price is zero. Is this reasonable? Under what conditions might this occur?

CHAPTER 4

Elasticity

LO **LEARNING OBJECTIVES**

In this chapter you will learn

1. the meaning of price elasticity of demand and how it is measured.
2. about the relationship between demand elasticity and total expenditure.
3. the meaning of price elasticity of supply and how it is measured.
4. why the effect of an excise tax on equilibrium price and quantity depends on demand and supply elasticity.
5. about normal and inferior goods, and how to measure the income elasticity of demand.
6. how to measure cross elasticity of demand, and the meaning of substitute and complement goods.

The laws of demand and supply predict the *direction* of changes in equilibrium price and quantity in response to various shifts in demand and supply. However, it usually is not enough to know merely whether price and quantity rise or fall; it is also important to know by *how much* each changes.

For example, in the previous chapter we described the effect of Hurricane Katrina on the world price of oil in 2005. The hurricane caused a temporary reduction in the supply of crude oil which led to a 20-percent increase in the world price. How can we explain why the increase in price was 20 percent rather than 50 percent or only 5 percent? As we will see in this chapter, the extent of price changes in response to shifts in demand or supply is largely determined by the *shapes* of the demand and supply curves. Specifically, it is the *elasticity* of demand and supply that we examine in this chapter.

4.1 PRICE ELASTICITY OF DEMAND

Suppose there is a decrease in the supply of some farm crop—that is, a leftward shift in the supply curve. We saw in Figure 3-8 when we examined the laws of supply and demand that such a decrease in supply will cause the equilibrium price to rise and the equilibrium quantity to fall. But by how much will each change? The answer depends on what is called the *price elasticity of demand*.

Loosely speaking, demand is said to be *elastic* when quantity demanded is quite responsive to changes in price. When quantity demanded is relatively unresponsive to changes in price, demand is said to be *inelastic*.

The importance of elasticity is illustrated in Figure 4-1. The two parts of the figure have the same initial equilibrium, and that equilibrium is disturbed by the same leftward shift in the supply curve. But the demand curves are different in the two parts of the figure, and so the sizes of the changes in equilibrium price and quantity are also different.

Part (i) of Figure 4-1 illustrates a case in which the quantity that consumers demand is relatively responsive to price changes—that is, demand is relatively *elastic*. The reduction in supply pushes up the price, but, because the quantity demanded is quite responsive, only a small change in price is necessary to restore equilibrium.

Part (ii) of Figure 4-1 shows a case in which the quantity demanded is relatively unresponsive to price changes—that is, demand is relatively *inelastic*. As in part (i), the decrease in supply at the original price causes a shortage that increases the price. However, in this case the quantity demanded by consumers does not fall much in response to the rise in price. The result is that equilibrium price rises more, and equilibrium quantity falls less, than in the first case.

In both cases shown in Figure 4-1, the shifts of the supply curve are identical. The sizes of the effects on the equilibrium price and quantity are different only because of the different elasticities of demand.

FIGURE 4-1   The Effects of a Supply Shift with Two Different Demand Curves

(i) Relatively elastic demand   (ii) Relatively inelastic demand

The more responsive the quantity demanded is to changes in price, the less the change in equilibrium price and the greater the change in equilibrium quantity resulting from any given shift in the supply curve. Both parts of the figure are drawn to the same scale. They show the same initial equilibrium, E_0, and the same shift in the supply curve, from S_0 to S_1. In each part, initial equilibrium is at price p_0 and output Q_0 and the new equilibrium, E_1, is at p_1 and Q_1. In part (i), the effect of the reduction in supply is a slight rise in the price and a large decrease in quantity. In part (ii), the effect of the identical reduction in supply is a large increase in the price and a relatively small decrease in quantity.

The Measurement of Price Elasticity

In Figure 4-1, we were able to say that the demand curve in part (i) showed more responsiveness to price changes than the demand curve in part (ii) because two conditions were fulfilled. First, both curves were drawn on the same scale. Second, the initial equilibrium prices and quantities were the same in both parts of the figure. Let's see why these conditions matter.

First, by drawing both figures on the same scale, we saw that the demand curve that *looked* steeper actually did have the larger absolute slope. (The slope of a demand curve tells us the amount by which price must change to cause a unit change in quantity demanded.) If we had drawn the two curves on different scales, we could have concluded nothing about which demand curve actually had the greater slope.

Second, because we started from the same price–quantity equilibrium in both parts of the figure, we did not need to distinguish between *percentage* changes and *absolute* changes. If the initial prices and quantities are the same in both cases, the larger absolute change is also the larger percentage change. However, when we wish to deal with different initial price–quantity equilibria, we need to decide whether we are interested in absolute or percentage changes.

To see why the difference between absolute and percentage change matters, consider the changes in price and quantity demanded for three different products: cheese, T-shirts, and CD players. The information is shown in Table 4-1. Should we conclude that the demand for CD players is not as responsive to price changes as the demand for cheese? After all, price cuts of $2 cause quite a large increase in the quantity of cheese demanded, but only a small increase in the quantity demanded of CD players. It should be obvious that a $2 price reduction is a large price cut for a low-priced product and an insignificant price cut for a high-priced product. In Table 4-1, each price reduction is $2, but they are clearly different proportions of the respective prices. It is usually more revealing to know the *percentage* change in the prices of the various products.

For similar reasons, knowing the quantity by which demand changes is not very revealing unless the initial level of demand is also known. An increase of 7500 kilograms is quite a significant change if the quantity formerly bought was 15 000 kilograms, but it is insignificant if the quantity formerly bought was 10 million kilograms.

Table 4-2 shows the original and new levels of price and quantity. Note that it also shows the *average* price and *average* quantity. These averages will be necessary for our computation of elasticity.

The **price elasticity of demand**, the measure of responsiveness of the quantity of a product demanded to a change in that product's price, is symbolized by the Greek letter eta, η. It is defined as follows:

$$\eta = \frac{\text{Percentage change in quantity demanded}}{\text{Percentage change in price}}$$

This measure is called the price elasticity of demand, or simply *demand elasticity*. Because the variable causing the change in quantity demanded is the product's own price, the term *own-price elasticity of demand* is also used.

price elasticity of demand (η) A measure of the responsiveness of quantity demanded to a change in the commodity's own price.

TABLE 4-1   Price Reductions and Corresponding Increases in Quantity Demanded for Three Products

Commodity	Reduction in Price	Increase in Quantity Demanded (per month)
Cheese	$2 per kilogram	7 500 kilograms
T-shirts	$2 per shirt	25 000 shirts
CD players	$2 per CD player	500 CD players

For each of the three products, the data show the change in quantity demanded resulting from the same absolute fall in price. The data are fairly uninformative about the responsiveness of quantity demanded to price because they do not tell us either the original price or the original quantity demanded.

TABLE 4-2 Price and Quantity Information Underlying Data of Table 4-1

Product	Unit	Original Price ($)	New Price ($)	Average Price ($)	Original Quantity	New Quantity	Average Quantity
Cheese	kilogram	5.00	3.00	4.00	116 250	123 750	120 000
T-shirts	shirt	17.00	15.00	16.00	187 500	212 500	200 000
CD players	player	81.00	79.00	80.00	9 750	10 250	10 000

These data provide the appropriate context for the data given in Table 4-1. The table relates the $2-per-unit price reduction of each product to the actual prices and quantities demanded.

The Use of Average Price and Quantity in Computing Elasticity Table 4-3 shows the percentage changes for price and quantity using the data from Table 4-2. The caption in Table 4-3 stresses that the demand elasticities are computed using changes in price and quantity measured in terms of the *average* values of each. Averages are used to avoid the ambiguity caused by the fact that when a price or quantity changes, the change is a different percentage of the original value than it is of the new value. For example, the $2.00 change in the price of cheese shown in Table 4-2 represents a 40 percent change in the original price of $5.00 but a 66.7 percent change in the new price of $3.00.

Using average values for price and quantity means that the measured elasticity of demand between any two points on the demand curve, call them A and B, is independent of whether the movement is from A to B or from B to A. In the example of cheese in Tables 4-2 and 4-3, the $2.00 change in the price of cheese is unambiguously 50 percent of the average price of $4.00, and that percentage applies to a price increase from $3.00 to $5.00 or to a price decrease from $5.00 to $3.00.

Once we have computed the average prices and quantities as in Table 4-2, the algebraic formula for price elasticity is straightforward. Suppose we have an initial price of p_0 and an initial quantity of Q_0. We then consider a new price of p_1 and a new quantity of Q_1 (both price-quantity combinations lie on the demand curve for the product). The formula for price elasticity is then

$$\eta = \frac{\Delta Q / \overline{Q}}{\Delta p / \overline{p}} = \frac{(Q_1 - Q_0)/\overline{Q}}{(p_1 - p_0)/\overline{p}}$$

where $\overline{p}$ is the average price and $\overline{Q}$ is the average quantity. In the case of cheese from Table 4-2, we have

$$\eta = \frac{7500/120\ 000}{2.0/4.0} = \frac{0.0625}{0.5} = 0.125$$

as shown in Table 4-3. Notice that elasticity is *unit free*—even though prices are measured in dollars and quantity of cheese is measured in kilograms, the elasticity of demand has no units.

We leave it to you to use this formula to confirm the price elasticities for T-shirts and CD players shown in Table 4-3. [7]

Practise with Study Guide Chapter 4, Exercise 4.

TABLE 4-3 Calculation of Demand Elasticities

Product	(1) Percentage Decrease in Price	(2) Percentage Increase in Quantity	(3) Elasticity of Demand (2) ÷ (1)
Cheese	50.0	6.25	0.125
T-shirts	12.5	12.5	1.0
CD players	2.5	5.0	2.0

Elasticity of demand is the percentage change in quantity demanded divided by the percentage change in price. The percentage changes are based on average prices and quantities shown in Table 4-2. For example, the $2.00-per-kilogram decrease in the price of cheese is 50 percent of $4.00. A $2.00 change in the price of CD players is only 2.5 percent of the average price per CD player of $80.00.

For more details about demand elasticity, including the use of calculus to measure elasticity along a non-linear demand curve, look for "Some Further Details About Demand Elasticity" in the *Additional Topics* section of this book's MyEconLab.

w w w . m y e c o n l a b . c o m

Interpreting Numerical Elasticities   Because demand curves have negative slopes, an increase in price is associated with a decrease in quantity demanded, and vice versa. Because the percentage changes in price and quantity have opposite signs, demand elasticity is a negative number. However, we will follow the usual practice of ignoring the negative sign and speak of the measure as a positive number, as we have done in the illustrative calculations in Table 4-3. Thus, the more responsive the quantity demanded to a change in price, the greater the elasticity and the larger is η.

The numerical value of demand elasticity can vary from zero to infinity. First consider the extreme cases. Elasticity is zero when a change in price leads to *no change* in quantity demanded. This is the case of a vertical demand curve, and is quite rare because it indicates that consumers do not alter their consumption at all when price changes. At the other extreme, elasticity is very large when even a very small change in price leads to an enormous change in quantity demanded. In these situations, which are also rare in the case of demands for individual commodities, the demand curve is very flat, almost horizontal. (In the limiting case, the demand curve is perfectly horizontal and elasticity is infinite.) Most of reality lies between the extremes of vertical and horizontal demand curves. We divide this "realistic" range of elasticities into two regions.

When the percentage change in quantity demanded is less than the percentage change in price (elasticity less than 1), there is said to be **inelastic demand**. When the percentage change in quantity is greater than the percentage change in price (elasticity greater than 1), there is said to be **elastic demand**. The dividing line between these two cases occurs when the percentage change in quantity demanded is exactly equal to the percentage change in price and so elasticity is equal to 1. Here we say that demand is *unit elastic*. This important terminology is summarized in part A of *Extensions in Theory 4-2*, which is found toward the end of the chapter.

A demand curve need not, and usually does not, have the same elasticity over its whole length. Figure 4-2 shows that a negatively sloped linear demand curve does not have a constant elasticity, even though it does have a constant slope. A linear demand curve has constant elasticity only when it is vertical or horizontal. Figure 4-3 illustrates these two cases, in addition to a third case of a particular *nonlinear* demand curve that also has a constant elasticity. (These are only three examples of many demand curves with constant elasticities.)

Practise with Study Guide Chapter 4, Exercise 1.

inelastic demand Following a given percentage change in price, there is a smaller percentage change in quantity demanded; elasticity less than 1.

elastic demand Following a given percentage change in price, there is a greater percentage change in quantity demanded; elasticity greater than 1.

What Determines Elasticity of Demand?

One of the main determinants of demand elasticity is the availability of substitutes. Some products, such as margarine, broccoli, lamb, and Toyota cars, have quite close substitutes—butter, other green vegetables, beef, and Mazda cars. A change in the prices of these products, *with the prices of the substitutes remaining constant*, can be expected to cause much substitution. A fall in price leads consumers to buy more of

Practise with Study Guide Chapter 4,
Exercises 3 and 6.

FIGURE 4-2 Elasticity Along a Linear Demand Curve

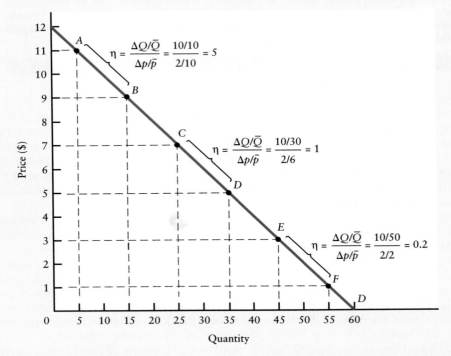

Moving down a linear demand curve, price elasticity falls continuously, even though the slope is constant. In the interval between points A and B, the percentage change in quantity is 100 ($\Delta Q = 10$ and $\overline{Q} = 10$) and the percentage change in price is 20 ($\Delta p = 2$ and $\overline{p} = 10$). The price elasticity over this interval of the demand curve is then $100/20 = 5$.

The same *absolute* changes in price and quantity occur over the intervals CD and EF, but elasticity differs because these absolute changes represent different *percentage* changes. Between points C and D, price elasticity is equal to 1. Between points E and F, price elasticity is equal to 0.2. Note that elasticity approaches infinity as we get closer to where the demand curve intersects the vertical axis; elasticity approaches zero as we get closer to where the demand curve intersects the horizontal axis.

the product and less of the substitutes, and a rise in price leads consumers to buy less of the product and more of the substitutes. Products defined more broadly, such as *all* foods or *all* clothing or *all* methods of transportation, have many fewer satisfactory substitutes. A rise in their prices can be expected to cause a smaller fall in quantities demanded than would be the case if close substitutes were available.

Products with close substitutes tend to have elastic demands; products with no close substitutes tend to have inelastic demands.

Demand elasticity depends to a great extent on the availability of substitutes. The availability of substitutes, in turn, depends on how the product is defined and on the time period being considered. We explore these aspects next.

Definition of the Product For food taken as a whole, demand is inelastic over a large price range. It does not follow, however, that any specific food, such as white bread or peanut butter, also has inelastic demand. Individual foods can have quite elastic demands, and they frequently do.

Clothing provides a similar example. Clothing as a whole has a less elastic demand than do individual kinds of clothes. For example, when the price of wool sweaters rises, many households may substitute away from wool sweaters and buy cotton sweaters or fleece jackets instead. Thus, although purchases of wool sweaters fall, total purchases of clothing do not.

Any one of a group of related products will have a more elastic demand than the group as a whole.

Short Run and Long Run Because it takes time to develop satisfactory substitutes, a demand that is inelastic in the short run may prove to be elastic when enough time has passed. A dramatic example of this principle occurred in 1973 when the Organization of Petroleum Exporting Countries (OPEC) shocked the world with its sudden and large increase in the price of oil. At that time, the short-run demand for oil proved to be highly inelastic. Large price increases were met in the short run by very small reductions in quantity demanded. In this case, the short run lasted for several years. Gradually, however, the high price of petroleum products led to such adjustments as the development of smaller, more fuel-efficient cars, economizing on heating oil by installing more efficient insulation, and replacement of fuel oil in many industrial processes with other power sources such as coal and hydroelectricity. The long-run elasticity of demand, relating the change in price to the change in quantity demanded after all adjustments were made, turned out to have an elasticity of well over 1, although the long-run adjustments took as much as a decade to work out.

The response to a price change, and thus the measured price elasticity of demand, will tend to be greater the longer the time span.

For such products as cornflakes and pillowcases, the full response to a price change occurs quickly, and there is little reason to make the distinction between short-run and long-run effects. But other products are typically used in connection with highly durable appliances or machines. A change in the price of, say, electricity and gasoline may not have its major effect until the stock of appliances and machines using these products has been adjusted. This adjustment may take several years to occur.

For products for which substitutes are developed over a period of time, it is helpful to identify two kinds of demand curves. A *short-run demand curve* shows the immediate response of quantity demanded to a change in price given the current stock of durable

FIGURE 4-3   Three Demand Curves with Constant Elasticity

Each of these demand curves has a constant elasticity. D_1 has zero elasticity: The quantity demanded is equal to Q_0, independent of the price. D_2 has infinite elasticity at the price p_0: A small price increase from p_0 decreases quantity demanded from an indefinitely large amount to zero. D_3 has unit elasticity: A given percentage increase in price brings an equal percentage decrease in quantity demanded at all points on the curve; it is a rectangular hyperbola for which price times quantity demanded is a constant.

Because most people cannot easily or quickly change the size of car they drive or their method of transportation, the demand for gasoline is much less elastic in the short run than in the long run.

FIGURE 4-4   Short-Run and Long-Run Equilibrium Following an Increase in Supply

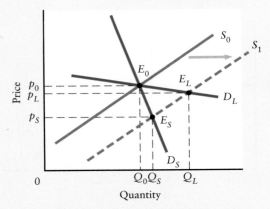

The magnitude of the changes in the equilibrium price and quantity following a shift in supply depends on the time allowed for demand to adjust. The initial equilibrium is at E_0, with price p_0 and quantity Q_0. Supply then increases and the supply curve shifts from S_0 to S_1.

Immediately following the increase in supply, the relevant demand curve is the short-run curve D_S, and the new equilibrium immediately following the supply shock is E_S. Price falls sharply to p_S, and quantity rises only to Q_S. In the long run, the demand curve is the more elastic one given by D_L, and equilibrium is at E_L. The long-run equilibrium price is p_L (greater than p_S), and quantity is Q_L (greater than Q_S).

Practise with Study Guide Chapter 4, Exercise 2 and Short-Answer Question 7.

For information on OPEC and its activities, see **www.opec.org**.

goods. The *long-run demand curve* shows the response of quantity demanded to a change in price after enough time has passed to change the stock of durable goods.

The long-run demand for a product is more elastic than the short-run demand.

Figure 4-4 shows the short-run and long-run effects of an increase in supply. In the short run, the supply increase leads to a movement down the relatively inelastic short-run demand curve; it thus causes a large fall in price but only a small increase in quantity. In the long run, demand is more elastic; thus long-run equilibrium has price and quantity above those that prevailed in short-run equilibrium.

Elasticity and Total Expenditure

We know that quantity demanded increases as price falls, but what happens to the total expenditure on that product? It turns out that the response of total expenditure depends on the price elasticity of demand.

To see the relationship between the elasticity of demand and total expenditure, we begin by noting that total expenditure at any point on the demand curve is equal to price times quantity:

$$\text{Total expenditure} = \text{Price} \times \text{Quantity}$$

Because price and quantity move in opposite directions along a demand curve, one falling when the other rises, the change in total expenditure is ambiguous if all we know about the demand curve is that it has a negative slope. The change in total expenditure depends on the relative percentage changes in the price and quantity. If the percentage change in price exceeds the percentage change in quantity (elasticity less than 1), the price change will dominate, and total expenditure will change in the same direction as the price changes. If the percentage change in the price is less than the percentage change in the quantity demanded (elasticity greater than 1), the quantity change will dominate, and total expenditure will change in the same direction as quantity changes. If the two percentage changes are equal, total expenditure is unchanged—this is the case of unit elasticity.

Figure 4-5 illustrates the relationship between price elasticity and total expenditure; it is based on the linear demand curve in Figure 4-2. Total expenditure at each of a number of points on the demand curve is calculated in the table, and the general relationship between total expenditure and quantity demanded is shown by the plotted curve. In the figure we see that expenditure reaches its maximum when price elasticity is equal to 1. [8]

Our earlier example of the 1973 OPEC-induced increase in the world price of oil can be used to illustrate this relationship between elasticity, price, and total expenditure. As the OPEC countries acted together to restrict supply and push up the world

FIGURE 4-5   Total Expenditure and Quantity Demanded

Price ($)	Quantity Demanded	Expenditure ($)
12	0	0
10	10	100
8	20	160
6	30	180
4	40	160
2	50	100
0	60	0

The change in total expenditure on a product in response to a change in price depends on the elasticity of demand. The table and graph are based on the demand curve shown in Figure 4-2. For quantities demanded that are less than 30, elasticity of demand is greater than 1, and hence any increase in quantity demanded will be proportionately larger than the fall in price that caused it. In that range, total expenditure increases as price falls. For quantities greater than 30, elasticity of demand is less than 1, and hence any increase in quantity demanded will be proportionately smaller than the fall in price that caused it. In that range, total expenditure decreases as price falls. The maximum of total expenditure occurs where the elasticity of demand equals 1.

price of oil, quantity demanded fell, but only by a small percentage—much smaller than the percentage increase in price. World demand for oil (at least in the short run) was very inelastic, and the result was that total expenditure on oil *increased* dramatically. The OPEC oil producers, therefore, experienced an enormous increase in income.

Another example relates to the world market for wheat, a market naturally influenced by weather conditions in the major wheat-producing countries. If one major wheat-producing country, like Russia, suffers a significant failure in its wheat crop, the world supply curve for wheat shifts to the left and the equilibrium world price rises. Because the world demand for wheat is inelastic, the world's total expenditure on wheat will rise. In this case, even though many individual Russian wheat producers will be worse off because their crop failed, the total income of the world's wheat producers will increase. One other observation is relevant: Wheat producers in other countries, like Canada, benefit by selling their (unchanged) crop at a higher world price. And the less elastic is the world demand for wheat, the more the price will rise as a result of the Russian crop failure, and thus the *more* Canadian wheat farmers will benefit.

4.2 PRICE ELASTICITY OF SUPPLY

The concept of elasticity can be applied to supply as well as to demand. **Price elasticity of supply** measures the responsiveness of the quantity supplied to a change in the product's price. It is denoted η_S and defined as follows:

$$\eta_S = \frac{\text{Percentage change in quantity supplied}}{\text{Percentage change in price}}$$

This is often called *supply elasticity*. The supply curves considered in this chapter all have positive slopes: An increase in price causes an increase in quantity supplied. Such supply curves all have positive elasticities because price and quantity change in the same direction.

Figure 4-6 shows a simple linear supply curve to illustrate the measurement of supply elasticity. Between points A and B, the change in price is $1.50 and the average price is $4.25. Between the same two points, the change in quantity supplied is 20 units and the average quantity is 40 units. The value of supply elasticity between points A and B is therefore

$$\eta_S = \frac{\Delta Q/\overline{Q}}{\Delta p/\overline{p}} = \frac{20/40}{1.50/4.25} = \frac{0.5}{0.353} = 1.42$$

As was the case with demand, care must be taken when computing supply elasticity. Keep in mind that even though the supply curve may have a constant slope, the measure of supply elasticity may be different at different places on the curve.

There are also important special cases of supply curves that should be noted. If the supply curve is vertical—the quantity supplied does not change as price changes—then elasticity of supply is zero. A horizontal supply curve has an infinite elasticity of supply: A small drop in price will reduce the quantity that producers are willing to supply from an indefinitely large amount to zero. Between these two extremes, elasticity of supply varies with the shape of the supply curve. Loosely speaking, steeper supply curves imply a smaller quantity response for a given change in price, and thus a lower elasticity.[1]

FIGURE 4-6   Computing Price Elasticity of Supply

Supply elasticity is computed using average price and average quantity supplied. Between points A and B, the elasticity of supply is 1.42. The same approach shown here can be used to compute elasticity between any two points on the supply curve.

Determinants of Supply Elasticity

Because much of the treatment of demand elasticity carries over to supply elasticity, we can cover the main points quickly.

---

[1] Here is another special case that is often puzzling at first glance. Consider a linear supply curve that begins at the origin. It is easy to show that the elasticity of supply along such a curve is always 1—no matter how steep the supply curve is! See Study Exercise #8 to explore this further.

Substitution and Production Costs   The ease of substitution can vary in production as well as in consumption. If the price of a product rises, how much more can be produced profitably? This depends in part on how easy it is for producers to shift from the production of other products to the one whose price has risen. If agricultural land and labour can be readily shifted from one crop to another, the supply of any one crop will be more elastic than if they cannot. Or, if machines used to produce coats can be easily modified to produce pants (and vice versa), then the supply of both pants and coats will be more elastic than if the machines cannot be so easily modified.

Supply elasticity also depends on how costs behave as output is varied. If the costs of producing a unit of output rise rapidly as output rises, then the stimulus to expand production in response to a rise in price will quickly be choked off by increases in costs. In this case, supply will tend to be rather inelastic. If, however, the costs of producing a unit of output rise only slowly as production increases, a rise in price that raises profits will elicit a large increase in quantity supplied before the rise in costs puts a halt to the expansion in output. In this case, supply will tend to be rather elastic.

Short Run and Long Run   As with demand, length of time for response is important. It may be difficult to change quantities supplied in response to a price increase in a matter of weeks or months, but easy to do so over a period of years. An obvious example is the planting cycle of crops. An increase in the price of wheat that occurs in mid-summer may lead wheat farmers to be more careful (and less wasteful) in their harvesting in the fall, but it occurs too late to influence how much wheat gets planted for this year's crop. If the high price persists, however, it will surely influence how much wheat gets planted the following spring. Another example relates to oil production. New oil fields can be discovered, wells drilled, and pipelines built over a period of years but not in just a few months. Thus, the elasticity of oil supply is much greater over five years than over one year.

As with demand, it is useful to make the distinction between the short-run and the long-run supply curves. The *short-run supply curve* shows the immediate response of quantity supplied to a change in price given producers' current capacity to produce the good. The *long-run supply curve* shows the response of quantity supplied to a change in price after enough time has passed to allow producers to adjust their productive capacity.

The long-run supply for a product is more elastic than the short-run supply.

Figure 4-7 illustrates the short-run and long-run effects of an increase in demand. The immediate effect of the shift in demand is a sharp increase in price (p_0 to p_S) and only a modest increase in quantity (Q_0 to Q_S). The inability of firms to change their output in the short run in response to the increase in demand means that the market-clearing response is mostly an increase in

FIGURE 4-7   Short-Run and Long-Run Equilibrium Following an Increase in Demand

The size of the changes in the equilibrium price and quantity following a shift in demand depends on the time frame of the analysis. The initial equilibrium is at E_0, with price p_0 and quantity Q_0. Demand then increases such that the demand curve shifts from D_0 to D_1.

Immediately following the demand shift, the relevant supply curve is the short-run curve S_S, so that the new equilibrium immediately following the demand shock is at E_S. Price rises sharply to p_S, and quantity rises only to Q_S. In the long run, the supply curve is the more elastic one given by S_L. The long-run equilibrium is at E_L; price is p_L (less than p_S) and quantity is Q_L (greater than Q_S).

price. Over time, however, as firms are more able to increase their output of the product, the consequences of the demand shift fall more on quantity and less on price.

A recent example of this price and quantity behaviour is found in the world oil market in the years between 1998 and 2006. Due to relatively rapid rates of economic growth in many countries, and especially in the large emerging markets of China and India, the world demand for oil was growing significantly. During this period, however, most oil producers were at or close to their production limits: The number of oil-producing wells could only increase with costly new exploration and drilling, and each active well delivered a daily flow of oil that was difficult to increase. Producers' inability to easily expand oil production in the short term means that the short-run supply of oil is quite inelastic. As a result, the increase in demand led to sharp price increases—from about U.S.$15 per barrel in 1998 to over U.S.$75 per barrel in mid 2006 (well after the effects of the supply disruptions caused by Hurricane Katrina in the fall of 2005 had disappeared).

Over time, however, to the extent that oil producers are able to increase their exploration and drilling activities, the high price should induce a larger increase in quantity supplied. In other words, the long-run supply of oil can be expected to be more elastic than the short-run supply. If no other significant changes occur in the world oil market, the effect of this new oil production should be to reduce oil prices from the very high levels observed in 2006.

4.3 AN IMPORTANT EXAMPLE WHERE ELASTICITY MATTERS

So far, this chapter has been fairly tough going. We have spent much time examining price elasticity (of both demand and supply) and how to measure it. But why should we care about this? In this section, we explore the important concept of *tax incidence* and show that elasticity is crucial to determining whether consumers or producers (or both) end up bearing the burden of (or paying) excise taxes.

The federal and provincial governments levy special sales taxes called **excise taxes** on many goods such as cigarettes, alcohol, and gasoline. At the point of sale of the product, the sellers collect the tax on behalf of the government and then periodically remit the tax collections.

When the sellers write their cheques to the government, these firms feel that they are the ones paying the tax. Consumers, however, argue that *they* are the ones who are shouldering the burden of the tax because the tax causes the price of the product to rise. Who actually bears the burden of the tax?

The question of who *bears the burden* of a tax is called the question of **tax incidence**. A straightforward application of demand-and-supply analysis will show that tax incidence has nothing to do with whether the government collects the tax directly from consumers or from firms.

The burden of an excise tax is distributed between consumers and sellers in a manner that depends on the relative elasticities of supply and demand.

Let's consider a case where the government imposes an excise tax on cigarettes. The analysis begins in Figure 4-8. To simplify the problem, we analyze the case where there is initially no tax. The equilibrium without taxes is illustrated by the solid supply and demand curves. What happens when a tax of $t per pack of cigarettes is introduced? With an excise tax, the price paid by the consumer, called the *consumer price,*

excise tax A tax on the sale of a particular commodity.

tax incidence The location of the burden of a tax; that is, the identity of the ultimate bearer of the tax.

and the price received by the seller, called the *seller price*, must differ by the amount of the tax, *t*.

In terms of the figure, we can analyze the effect of the tax by considering a new supply curve S' that is above the original supply curve S by the amount of the tax, *t*. To understand this new curve, consider the situation faced by firms at the original equilibrium quantity Q_0. To supply that quantity, producers must receive p_0 per pack of cigarettes sold. However, for producers to receive p_0 when there is a tax on cigarettes, the consumer must pay a total price of $p_0 + t$: whether the consumer "pays the tax directly" by giving p_0 to the firm and t to the government, or whether the consumer pays the total $p_0 + t$ to the firm and the firm then remits the tax t to the government. Either way, the total amount that consumers must pay to obtain a given quantity from firms has increased by the amount of the tax, *t*.

This upward shift in the supply curve for cigarettes is depicted in Figure 4-8 as the dashed curve, S'. This shift in the supply curve, caused by the imposition of the excise tax, will cause a movement *along* the demand curve, reducing the equilibrium quantity. At this new equilibrium, E_1, the consumer price rises to p_c (greater than p_0), the seller price falls to p_s (less than p_0), and the equilibrium quantity falls to Q_1.

Note that the quantity demanded *at the consumer price* is equal to the quantity supplied *at the seller price*, a condition that is required for equilibrium. As shown in the figure, compared to the original equilibrium, the consumer price is higher and the seller price is lower, although in each case the change in price is less than the full extent of the excise tax. The difference between p_0 and p_c is the amount of the

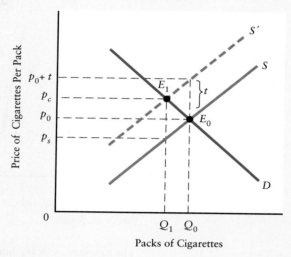

FIGURE 4-8   The Effect of a Cigarette Excise Tax

The burden of an excise tax is shared by consumers and producers. The original supply and demand curves for cigarettes are given by the solid lines S and D; equilibrium is at E_0 with price p_0 and quantity Q_0. When an excise tax of t per pack is imposed, the supply curve shifts up to the dashed line S', which lies above the original supply curve by the amount of the tax t. The new equilibrium is at E_1. The tax increases the consumer price, but by less than the full amount of the tax, and reduces the seller price, also by less than the full amount of the tax. It also reduces the equilibrium quantity exchanged.

tax that the consumer ends up paying; the difference between p_0 and p_s is the amount of the tax the seller ends up paying. The burden of the excise tax is shared between consumers and sellers in proportion to the rise in price to consumers relative to the fall in price received by sellers.

After the imposition of an excise tax, the difference between the consumer and seller prices is equal to the tax. In the new equilibrium, the quantity exchanged is less than that exchanged prior to the imposition of the tax.

The role of the relative elasticities of supply and demand in determining the incidence of the excise tax is illustrated in Figure 4-9. In part (i), demand is inelastic relative to supply; as a result, the fall in quantity is quite small, whereas the price paid by consumers rises by almost the full extent of the tax. Because neither the price received by sellers nor the quantity sold changes very much, sellers bear little of the burden of the tax. In part (ii), supply is inelastic relative to demand; in this case, consumers can more easily substitute away from cigarettes. There is little change in the price, and hence they bear little of the burden of the tax, which falls mostly on suppliers. Notice in Figure 4-9 that the size of the upward shift in supply is the same in the two cases, indicating the same tax in both cases.

FIGURE 4-9   Elasticity and the Incidence of an Excise Tax

(i) Inelastic demand

(ii) Inelastic supply

The distribution of the burden of an excise tax between consumers and producers depends on the relative elasticities of supply and demand. In both parts of the figure, the initial supply and demand curves are given by S and D; the initial equilibrium is at E_0 with equilibrium price p_0 and quantity Q_0. A tax of t per pack of cigarettes is imposed, causing the supply curve to shift up by the amount of the tax to S'. The new equilibrium is at E_1. The consumer price rises to p_c, the seller price falls to p_s, and the quantity falls to Q_1. Sellers bear little of the burden of the tax in the first case (and consumers bear a lot), whereas consumers bear little of the burden in the second case (and sellers bear a lot).

Practise with Study Guide Chapter 4, Exercise 8.

When demand is inelastic relative to supply, consumers bear most of the burden of excise taxes. When supply is inelastic relative to demand, producers bear most of the burden.

Now we can examine who really pays for cigarette tax increases (or tax increases on gasoline and alcohol). The demand for cigarettes is inelastic both overall and relative to supply, suggesting that the burden of a cigarette tax is borne more by consumers than by producers. The demand for gasoline is also inelastic, but much more so in the short run than in the long run. (In the long run, drivers can change their driving habits and improve the efficiency of their vehicles, but in the short run such changes are very costly.) The supply of gasoline, given world trade in petroleum and petroleum products, is elastic relative to demand. The relatively inelastic demand and elastic supply imply that the burden of gasoline taxes falls mostly on consumers.

Extensions in Theory 4-1 shows how to work through the algebra of demand and supply in the presence of an excise tax.

EXTENSIONS IN THEORY 4-1

The Algebra of Tax Incidence

It is straightforward to show the burden of an excise tax using algebra to solve for the equilibrium price and quantity. Suppose the demand-and-supply model of the market is given by the following two linear equations.

(1) $Q^D = a - bp_c$ Demand curve

(2) $Q^S = c + dp_s$ Supply curve

where Q^D is quantity demanded at the consumer price, p_c, and Q^S is quantity supplied at the seller price, p_s. The presence of an excise tax of t dollars per unit implies that the price received by the seller, p_s, must be t dollars less than the price paid by the consumer, p_c:

(3) $p_s = p_c - t$

We can substitute equation (3) into (2) to express the supply curve in terms of the consumer price:

(4) $Q^S = c + d(p_c - t)$

or

(5) $Q^S = c - dt + dp_c$

When the market is in equilibrium, $Q^D = Q^S$, and so we can equate Q^D from equation (1) with Q^S from equation (5). This gives us

$a - bp_c = c - dt + dp_c$

This equation allows us to solve for the equilibrium consumer price, p_c^*.

$$p_c^* = \frac{a - c}{b + d} + \frac{d}{b + d} t$$

This solution for p_c^* can now be substituted back into the demand curve, equation (1), to solve for the equilibrium quantity, Q^*.

$$Q^* = a - bp_c^* = a - \frac{b(a - c + dt)}{b + d}$$

Now consider these solutions for p_c^* and Q^* in the case where there is no tax, $t = 0$. This exercise reveals what we already know from Figures 4-8 and 4-9—that the excise tax increases the equilibrium consumer price and reduces the equilibrium quantity from the levels that we would observe in the absence of the excise tax.

Who bears the burden of the excise tax? To answer this question, we must examine both the equilibrium consumer and seller prices, p_c^* and p_s^*. We saw above that

(6) $$p_c^* = \frac{a - c}{b + d} + \frac{d}{b + d} t$$

and we also know that $p_c^* - t = p_s^*$. It follows that

(7) $$p_s^* = \frac{a - c}{b + d} + \frac{d}{b + d} t - t$$

$$= \frac{a - c}{b + d} - \frac{b}{b + d} t$$

Note that when $t = 0$, the equilibrium price in this model, for both consumers and sellers, is

$$p^* = \frac{a - c}{b + d}$$

We can therefore express the equilibrium consumer and seller prices in the presence of an excise tax in terms of p^*:

(8) $$p_c^* = p^* + \frac{d}{b + d} t$$

(9) $$p_s^* = p^* - \frac{b}{b + d} t$$

These solutions for p_c^* and p_s^* show how the burden of the excise tax depends on the slopes of the demand and supply curves. For example, consider a small value of d which reflects a relatively steep supply curve. The small value of d means that p_c^* is only a little above p^*, whereas p_s^* is considerably below p^*; thus, when the supply curve is relatively steep, sellers bear more of the burden of the tax. In contrast, consider a small value of b, which reflects a relatively steep demand curve. The small value of b means that p_s^* is only a little below p^*, but p_c^* is considerably above p^*; thus, consumers bear more of the burden of the tax when the demand curve is relatively steep.

Practise with *Study Guide* Chapter 4, Extension Exercise E3.

▌ 4.4 **OTHER DEMAND ELASTICITIES**

The price of the product is not the only important variable determining demand for that product. Changes in income and changes in the prices of other products also lead to changes in demand, and elasticity is a useful concept in measuring their effects.

Income Elasticity of Demand

income elasticity of demand (η_Y) A measure of the responsiveness of quantity demanded to a change in income.

One important determinant of demand is the income of the customers. The responsiveness of demand to changes in income is termed the **income elasticity of demand** and is symbolized η_Y.

$$\eta_Y = \frac{\text{Percentage change in quantity demanded}}{\text{Percentage change in income}}$$

normal good A good for which quantity demanded rises as income rises — its income elasticity is positive.

For most goods, increases in income lead to increases in demand—their income elasticity is positive. These are called **normal goods**. Goods for which demand decreases in response to a rise in income have negative income elasticities and are called **inferior goods.**

inferior good A good for which quantity demanded falls as income rises — its income elasticity is negative.

The income elasticity of normal goods can be greater than 1 (elastic) or less than 1 (inelastic), depending on whether the percentage change in quantity demanded is greater or less than the percentage change in income that brought it about. It is also common to use the terms *income-elastic* and *income-inelastic* to refer to income elasticities of greater or less than 1. (See *Extensions in Theory 4-2* for a summary of the different elasticity concepts.)

How the demand for goods and services reacts to changes in income has important economic effects. In most Western countries during the twentieth century, economic growth caused the level of income to double every 20 to 30 years. This rise in income was shared to some extent by almost all citizens. As they found their incomes increasing, they increased their demands for most products. In the first part of that century, however, the demands for some products (such as food and basic clothing) were income-inelastic whereas the demands for other products (such as durable goods) were income-elastic. As a result, the demand for food and clothing grew less rapidly than did the demand for durable goods. Later in the century, as incomes rose still further, the income elasticity of demand for manufactured durables (such as cars, TV sets, and refrigerators) fell while that for services (such as restaurant meals and movies) increased. During this period the ongoing income growth led the demand for services to grow more rapidly than the demand for durable goods.

In some developing countries today, where per capita incomes are close to those of the Western nations at the beginning of the twentieth century, it is the demands for durable manufactured goods that are increasing most rapidly as income rises. In future years (assuming that the current growth of income continues) these same countries will likely experience the same shift in demand toward services that was experienced by the Western countries in the last part of the twentieth century.

The uneven impact of the growth of income on the demands for different products has important effects on the pattern of employment. For example, in Western countries, employment in agriculture fell during the first part of the twentieth century, while employment in manufacturing rose. In the last half of the century, employment in manufacturing fell gradually whereas employment in services increased rapidly (and employment in agriculture continued its gradual decline). We shall see many other consequences of these demand shifts later in this book.

Luxuries Versus Necessities   Different products typically have different income elasticities of demand. For example, empirical studies find that basic food items—such as vegetables, bread, and cereals—usually have positive income elasticities less than 1 (so an increase in income of 10 percent leads to an increase in quantity demanded of less than 10 percent). Such goods are often called *necessities*. In contrast, more expensive foods—such as high-quality cuts of meat, prepared meals, and wine—usually have positive income elasticities greater than 1 (so an increase in income of 10 percent leads to an increase in quantity demanded of more than 10 percent). These products are often called *luxuries.*

The more necessary is an item in the consumption pattern of consumers, the lower is its income elasticity.

Income elasticities for any one product also vary with the level of a consumer's income. When incomes are low, consumers may eat almost no green vegetables and consume lots of starchy foods such as bread and potatoes; when incomes are higher, they may eat cheap cuts of meat and more green vegetables along with their bread and potatoes; when incomes are higher still, they are likely to eat higher quality and prepared foods of a wide variety.

The distinction between luxuries and necessities helps to explain differences in income elasticities. The case of restaurant meals is one example. Such meals are almost always more expensive, calorie for calorie, than meals prepared at home. It would thus be expected that at lower incomes, restaurant meals would be regarded as an expensive luxury but that the demand for them would expand substantially as consumers became richer. This is actually what happens.

Cross Elasticity of Demand

The responsiveness of demand to changes in the price of *another* product is called the **cross elasticity of demand**. It is denoted η_{XY} and defined as follows:

$$\eta_{XY} = \frac{\text{Percentage change in quantity demanded of good } X}{\text{Percentage change in price of good } Y}$$

cross elasticity of demand (η_{XY}) A measure of the responsiveness of the quantity of one commodity demanded to changes in the price of another commodity.

The change in the price of good Y causes the *demand curve* for good X to shift. If X and Y are substitutes, an increase in the price of Y leads to an increase in the demand for X. If X and Y are complements, an increase in the price of Y leads to a reduction in demand for X. In either case, we are holding the price of X constant. We therefore measure the change in the quantity demanded of X (at its unchanged price) by measuring the shift of the demand curve for X.

Cross elasticity can vary from minus infinity to plus infinity. Complementary products, such as cars and gasoline, have negative cross elasticities. A large rise in the price of gasoline will lead to a decline in the demand for cars, as some people decide to do without a car and others decide not to buy an additional car. Substitute products, such as cars and public transport, have positive cross elasticities. A large rise in the price of cars (relative to public transport) will lead to a rise in the demand for public transport as some people shift from cars to public transport. (See *Extensions in Theory 4-2* for a summary of elasticity terminology.)

Practise with Study Guide Chapter 4, Extension Exercise E1.

EXTENSIONS IN THEORY 4-2

The Terminology of Elasticity

Term	Numerical Measure of Elasticity	Verbal Description
A. Price elasticity of demand (supply)		
Perfectly or completely inelastic	Zero	Quantity demanded (supplied) does not change as price changes.
Inelastic	Between zero and 1	Quantity demanded (supplied) changes by a smaller percentage than does price.
Unit elastic	One	Quantity demanded (supplied) changes by exactly the same percentage as does price.
Elastic	Greater than 1, but less than infinity	Quantity demanded (supplied) changes by a larger percentage than does price.
Perfectly, completely, or infinitely elastic	Infinity	Purchasers (sellers) are prepared to buy (sell) all they can at some price and none at all at a higher (lower) price.
B. Income elasticity of demand		
Inferior good	Negative	Quantity demanded decreases as income increases.
Normal good	Positive	Quantity demanded increases as income increases:
Income-inelastic	Less than 1	Less than in proportion to income increase
Income-elastic	Greater than 1	More than in proportion to income increase
C. Cross elasticity of demand		
Substitute	Positive	Price increase of a substitute leads to an increase in quantity demanded of this good.
Complement	Negative	Price increase of a complement leads to a decrease in quantity demanded of this good.

Substitute products have a positive cross elasticity; an increase in the price of one leads to an increase in demand for the other.

The positive or negative signs of cross elasticities tell us whether goods are substitutes or complements.

Measures of cross elasticity sometimes prove helpful in defining whether producers of similar products are in competition with each other. For example, glass bottles and tin cans have a high cross elasticity of demand. The producer of bottles is thus in competition with the producer of cans. If the bottle company raises its price, it will lose substantial sales to the can producer. In contrast, men's shoes and women's shoes have a low cross elasticity and thus a producer of men's shoes is not in close competition with a producer of women's shoes. If the former raises its price, it will not lose many sales to the latter. Knowledge of cross elasticity can be important in matters of *competition policy* in which the issue is whether a firm in one industry is or is not competing with firms in another industry. We discuss competition policy in more detail in Chapter 12.

S U M M A R Y

4.1 **PRICE ELASTICITY OF DEMAND**

- *Price elasticity of demand* is a measure of the extent to which the quantity demanded of a product responds to a change in its price. Represented by the symbol η, it is defined as

$$\eta = \frac{\text{Percentage change in quantity demanded}}{\text{Percentage change in price}}$$

- The percentage changes are usually calculated as the change divided by the *average* value. Elasticity is defined to be a positive number, and it can vary from zero to infinity.
- When elasticity is less than 1, demand is *inelastic*—the percentage change in quantity demanded is less than the percentage change in price. When elasticity exceeds 1, demand is *elastic*—the percentage change in quantity

demanded is greater than the percentage change in price.
- The main determinant of price elasticity of demand is the availability of substitutes for the product. Any one of a group of close substitutes will have a more elastic demand than will the group as a whole.
- Items that have few substitutes in the short run tend to develop many substitutes when consumers and producers have time to adapt. Therefore, demand is more elastic in the long run than in the short run.
- Elasticity and total expenditure are related in the following way: If elasticity is less than 1, total expenditure is positively related with price; if elasticity is greater than 1, total expenditure is negatively related with price; and if elasticity is 1, total expenditure does not change as price changes.

4.2 **PRICE ELASTICITY OF SUPPLY**

- *Elasticity of supply* measures the extent to which the quantity supplied of some product changes when the price of that product changes. Represented by the symbol η_S, it is defined as

$$\eta_S = \frac{\text{Percentage change in quantity supplied}}{\text{Percentage change in price}}$$

- Supply tends to be more elastic in the long run than in the short run because it usually takes time for producers to alter their productive capacity in response to price changes.

4.3 **AN IMPORTANT EXAMPLE WHERE ELASTICITY MATTERS**

- The distribution of the burden of an excise tax between consumers and producers depends on the relative elasticities of supply and demand for the product.

- The less elastic demand is relative to supply, the more of the burden of an excise tax falls on the consumers. The more elastic demand is relative to supply, the more of the burden of an excise tax falls on producers.

4.4 **OTHER DEMAND ELASTICITIES**

- *Income elasticity of demand* is a measure of the extent to which the quantity demanded of some product changes as income changes. Represented by the symbol η_Y, it is defined as

$$\eta_Y = \frac{\text{Percentage change in quantity demanded}}{\text{Percentage change in income}}$$

- The income elasticity of demand for a product will usually change as income varies. A product that has a high income elasticity at a low income may have a low or negative income elasticity at higher incomes.

- *Cross elasticity of demand* is a measure of the extent to which the quantity demanded of one product changes when the price of a different product changes. Represented by the symbol η_{XY}, it is defined as

$$\eta_{XY} = \frac{\text{Percentage change in quantity demanded of good } X}{\text{Percentage change in price of good } Y}$$

It is used to define products that are substitutes for one another (positive cross elasticity) and products that are complements for one another (negative cross elasticity).

KEY CONCEPTS

Price elasticity of demand
Inelastic and perfectly inelastic demand
Elastic and infinitely elastic demand
Relationship between demand elasticity and total expenditure

Elasticity of supply
Short-run and long-run responses to shifts in demand and supply
The burden of an excise tax
Consumer price and seller price
Income elasticity of demand

Income-elastic and income-inelastic demands
Normal goods and inferior goods
Cross elasticity of demand
Substitutes and complements

STUDY EXERCISES

1. Fill in the blanks to make the following statements correct.

   a. When a 10-percent change in the price of a good brings about a 20-percent change in its quantity demanded, the price elasticity of demand is _____. We can say that demand for this good is _____.

   b. When a 10-percent change in the price of a good brings about a 4-percent change in its quantity demanded, the price elasticity of demand is _____. We can say that demand for this good is _____.

   c. When a 10-percent change in the price of a good brings about a 10-percent change in its quantity demanded, the price elasticity of demand is _____. We can say that demand for this good is _____.

2. A hypothetical demand schedule for comic books in a small town is provided below.

Demand Schedule for Comic Books

Price	Quantity Demanded	Total Expenditure	Percent Change in Price	Percent Change in Quantity Demanded	Elasticity of Demand
$11	1	11			
9	3	27	9-11/10		
7	5	35			
5	7	35			
3	9	27			
1	11	11			

   a. Fill in the table and calculate the price elasticity of demand over each price range. Be sure to use *average* prices and quantities when computing the percentage changes.

   b. Plot the demand curve and show the elasticities over the different ranges of the curve.

   c. Explain why demand is more elastic at the higher prices.

3. Suppose the market for frozen orange juice is in equilibrium at a price of $1.00 per can and a quantity of 4200 cans per month. Now suppose that at a price of $1.50 per can, quantity demanded falls to 3000 cans per month and quantity supplied increases to 4500 cans per month.

   a. Draw the appropriate diagram for this market.

   b. Calculate the price elasticity of demand for frozen orange juice between the prices of $1.00 and $1.50. Is the demand elastic or inelastic?

   c. Calculate the elasticity of supply for frozen orange juice between the prices of $1.00 and $1.50. Is the supply elastic or inelastic?

   d. Explain in general what factors would affect the elasticity of demand for frozen orange juice.

   e. Explain in general what factors would affect the elasticity of supply of frozen orange juice.

4. What would you predict about the *relative* price elasticity of demand for each of the following items? Explain your reasoning.

   a. food
   b. vegetables
   c. leafy vegetables
   d. leafy vegetables sold at your local supermarket
   e. leafy vegetables sold at your local supermarket on Wednesdays

5. Suppose a stamp dealer buys the only two existing copies of a stamp at an auction. After the purchase, the dealer goes to the front of the room and burns one of the stamps in front of the shocked audience. What must the dealer believe in order for this to be a wealth-maximizing action? Explain with a demand-and-supply diagram.

6. [myeconlab] For each of the following events, state the relevant elasticity concept. Then compute the measure of elasticity, using average prices and quantities in your calculations. In all cases, assume that these are *ceteris paribus* changes.

S, 7, 9

a. When the price of theatre tickets is reduced from $14.00 to $11.00, ticket sales increase from 1200 to 1350.
b. As average household income in Canada increases by 10 percent, annual sales of Toyota Camrys increase from 56 000 to 67 000.
c. After a major failure of Brazil's coffee crop sent coffee prices up from $3.00 per kilogram to $4.80 per kilogram, sales of tea in Canada increased from 7500 kg per month to 8000 kg per month.
d. An increase in the world demand for pulp (used in producing newsprint) increases the price by 14 percent. Annual Canadian production increases from 8 million tonnes to 11 million tonnes.

7. **myeconlab** The following table shows the demand schedule for denim jeans.

	Price (per unit)	Quantity Demanded (per year)	Total Expenditure
A	$30	400 000	
B	35	380 000	
C	40	350 000	
D	45	320 000	
E	50	300 000	
F	55	260 000	
G	60	230 000	
H	65	190 000	

a. Compute total expenditure for each row in the table.
b. Plot the demand curve and the total expenditure curve.
c. Compute the price elasticities of demand between points A and B, B and C, C and D, and so on.
d. Over what range of prices is the demand for denim jeans elastic? Explain.
e. Over what range of prices is the demand for denim jeans inelastic? Explain.

8. Consider the following straight-line supply curves. In each case, p is the price (measured in dollars per unit) and Q^S is the quantity supplied of the product (measured in thousands of units per month).

i) $p = 2Q^S$
ii) $p = 4Q^S$
iii) $p = 5Q^S$
iv) $p = 10Q^S$

a. Plot each supply curve on a scale diagram. In each case, plot point A (which corresponds to price equal to $20) and point B (which corresponds to price equal to $40).
b. For each supply curve, compute the price elasticity of supply between points A and B.
c. Explain why the *slope* of a supply curve is not the same as the *elasticity* of supply.

9. **myeconlab** This is a challenging question intended for those students who like mathematics. It will help you work through the issue of tax incidence. (See *Extensions in Theory 4-1* if you get stuck!)

Consider the market for gasoline. Suppose the market demand and supply curves are as given below. In each case, quantity refers to millions of litres of gasoline per month; price is the price per litre (in cents).

$$\text{Demand: } p = 80 - 5Q^D$$
$$\text{Supply: } p = 24 + 2Q^S$$

a. Plot the demand and supply curves on a scale diagram.
b. Compute the equilibrium price and quantity.
c. Now suppose the government imposes a tax of 14 cents per litre. Show how this affects the market equilibrium. What is the new "consumer price" and what is the new "producer price"?
d. Compute the total revenue raised by the gasoline tax. What share of this tax revenue is "paid" by consumers, and what share is "paid" by producers? (Hint: if the consumer price were unchanged from the pre-tax equilibrium, we would say that consumers pay none of the tax.)

DISCUSSION QUESTIONS

1. From the following quotations, what, if anything, can you conclude about elasticity of demand?

   a. "Good weather resulted in record wheat harvests and sent wheat prices tumbling. The result has been disastrous for many wheat farmers."

   b. "Ridership always went up when bus fares came down, but the increased patronage never was enough to prevent a decrease in overall revenue."

   c. "As the price of CD players fell, producers found their revenues soaring."

   d. "Coffee to me is an essential good—I've just gotta have it no matter what the price."

   e. "The soaring price of condominiums does little to curb the strong demand in Vancouver."

2. Home computers were a leader in sales appeal through much of the 1990s. But per capita sales are much lower in Mexico than in Canada, and lower in Newfoundland and Labrador than in Alberta. Manufacturers are puzzled by the big differences. Can you offer an explanation in terms of elasticity?

3. What elasticity measure or measures would be useful in answering the following questions?

   a. Will cheaper transport into the central city help to keep downtown shopping centres profitable?

   b. Will raising the bulk postage rate increase or decrease the revenues for Canada Post?

   c. Are producers of toothpaste and mouthwash in competition with each other?

   d. What effect will rising gasoline prices have on the sale of cars that use propane gas?

4. Interpret the following statements in terms of the relevant elasticity concept.

   a. "As fuel for tractors has become more expensive, many farmers have shifted from plowing their fields to no-till farming. No-till acreage increased dramatically in the past 20 years."

   b. "Fertilizer makers brace for dismal year as fertilizer prices soar."

   c. "When farmers are hurting, small towns feel the pain."

   d. "The development of the Hibernia oil field may bring temporary prosperity to Newfoundland and Labrador merchants."

5. When the New York City Opera faced a growing deficit, it cut its ticket prices by 20 percent, hoping to attract more customers. At the same time, the New York Transit Authority raised subway fares to reduce its growing deficit. Was one of these two opposite approaches to reducing a deficit necessarily wrong?

CHAPTER 5

Markets in Action

LO LEARNING OBJECTIVES

In this chapter you will learn

1. that individual markets do not exist in isolation, and that changes in one market typically have repercussions in other markets.
2. how a market works in the presence of price ceilings or price floors.
3. about the different short-run and long-run effects of legislated rent controls.
4. why government interventions that cause prices to deviate from their market-clearing levels are inefficient for society as a whole.

Over the past two chapters, we have developed the model of demand and supply that you can now use to analyze individual markets. A full understanding of the basic theory, however, comes only with practice. This chapter will provide some practice by analyzing several examples including minimum wages and rent controls.

Before examining these cases, however, we begin the chapter by discussing how various markets are related to each other. In Chapters 3 and 4, we used the simple demand-and-supply model to describe a single market, ignoring what was going on in other markets. For example, when we examined the market for carrots, we made no mention of the markets for broccoli, milk, or labour services. In other words, we viewed the market for carrots in isolation from all other markets. But this was only a simplification. In this chapter's opening section we note that the economy should *not* be viewed as a series of isolated markets. Rather, the economy is a complex system of inter-related markets. The implication of this complex structure is that events that lead to changes in one market typically lead to changes in other markets as well.

5.1 THE INTERACTION AMONG MARKETS

Suppose an advance is made that reduces the cost of extracting natural gas. This technological improvement would be represented as a rightward shift in the supply curve for natural gas. The equilibrium price of natural gas would fall and there would be an increase in the equilibrium quantity exchanged.

How would other markets be affected? As natural-gas firms expanded their production, they would increase their demand for the entire range of goods and services used for the extraction, processing, pumping, and distribution of natural gas. This increase in demand would raise the prices of those items, and lead the producers of those goods to devote more resources to their production. The natural-gas firms would also increase their demand for labour, since more workers would be required to drill for and extract more natural gas. The increase in demand for labour would tend to push wages up. Firms that hire similar workers in other industries would have to pay higher wages to retain their workers. The profits of those firms would fall and they would employ fewer workers, thus freeing up the extra workers needed in the natural-gas industry.

There would also be a direct effect on consumers. The reduction in the equilibrium price of natural gas would generate some substitution away from other fuels, such as oil or propane, and toward the now-lower-priced natural gas. Such reductions in demand would tend to push down the price of oil and propane, and producers of those fuels would devote fewer resources to their production.

In short, a technological improvement in the natural-gas industry would have effects in many other markets. But there is nothing special about the natural-gas industry. The same would be true about a change in almost any market you can think of.

No market or industry exists in isolation from the economy's many other markets.

Practise with Study Guide Chapter 5, Exercise 1.

A change in one market will lead to changes in many other markets. The induced changes in these other markets will, in turn, lead to changes in the first market. This is what economists call *feedback*. In the example of the natural-gas industry, the reduction in the price of natural gas leads consumers to reduce their demand for oil and propane, thus driving down the prices of these other fuels. But when we consider the demand and supply curves for natural gas, we assume that the *prices of all other goods are constant*. So, when the prices of oil and propane fall, the feedback effect on the natural-gas market is to shift the demand curve for natural gas to the left (because natural gas is a substitute for both oil and propane).

Predicting the precise size of this feedback effect is difficult, and the analysis of the natural-gas industry—or any other industry—would certainly be much easier if we could ignore it. But we cannot always ignore such feedback effects. Economists make a distinction between cases where the feedback effects are small enough that they can safely be ignored, and cases where the feedback effects are large enough that ignoring them would significantly change the analysis.

Partial-equilibrium analysis is the analysis of a single market in situations where the feedback effects from other markets are ignored. This is the type of analysis that we have used so far in this book, and it is the most common type of analysis in microeconomics. For example, when we examined the market for cigarettes at the end of Chapter 4, we ignored any potential feedback effects that could have come from the market for alcohol, coffee, or many other goods or services. In this case, we used partial-equilibrium analysis, focusing only on the market for cigarettes, because we assumed that the changes in the cigarette market would produce small enough changes on the other markets that the feedback effects from the other markets would, in turn, be sufficiently diffused that we could safely ignore them. This suggests the general rule telling us when partial-equilibrium analysis is a legitimate method of analysis.

If a specific market is quite small relative to the entire economy, changes in the market will have relatively small effects on other markets. The feedback effects on the original market will, in turn, be even smaller. In such cases, partial-equilibrium analysis can successfully be used to analyze the original market.

When economists study all markets together, rather than a single market in isolation, they use what is called **general-equilibrium analysis**. This is more complicated than partial-equilibrium analysis because the economist not only must consider what is happening in each individual market but also must take into account how events in each market affect all the other markets.

partial-equilibrium analysis The analysis of a single market in isolation, ignoring any feedbacks that may come from induced changes in other markets.

general-equilibrium analysis The analysis of all the economy's markets simultaneously, recognizing the interactions among the various markets.

General-equilibrium analysis is the study of how all markets function together, taking into account the various relationships and feedback effects between individual markets.

> ## myeconlab
>
> **For a detailed discussion and several examples of the various ways that seemingly unrelated markets may be linked, look for "Linkages Between Markets" in the *Additional Topics* section of this book's MyEconLab.**
>
> w w w . m y e c o n l a b . c o m

As you go on to learn more microeconomics in this and later chapters, you will encounter mostly partial-equilibrium analysis. The book is written this way intentionally—it is easier to learn about the basic ideas of monopoly, competition policy, labour unions, and environmental policy (as well as many other topics) by restricting our attention to single markets. But keep in mind that there are always many other markets "behind the scenes" that are linked to the individual markets we choose to study.

We now go on to examine the effects of government-controlled prices. These appear prominently in labour markets and rental housing markets.

5.2 GOVERNMENT-CONTROLLED PRICES

In a number of important cases, governments fix the price at which a product must be bought and sold in the domestic market. Here we examine the general consequences of such policies. Later, we look at some specific examples.

In a free market the equilibrium price equates the quantity demanded with the quantity supplied. Government *price controls* are policies that attempt to hold the price at some disequilibrium value. Some controls hold the market price below its equilibrium value, thus creating a shortage at the controlled price. Other controls hold price above its equilibrium value, thus creating a surplus at the controlled price.

Disequilibrium Prices

When controls hold price at some disequilibrium value, what determines the quantity *actually traded* on the market? This is not a question we have to ask when examining a free market because the price adjusts to equate quantity demanded with quantity supplied. But this adjustment cannot take place if the government is controlling the price. So, in this case, what determines the quantity actually exchanged?

The key to the answer is the fact that any *voluntary* market transaction requires both a willing buyer and a willing seller. So, if quantity demanded is less than quantity supplied, demand will determine the amount actually exchanged, while the rest of the quantity supplied will remain in the hands of the unsuccessful sellers. Conversely, if quantity demanded exceeds quantity supplied, supply will determine the amount actually exchanged, while the rest of the quantity demanded will represent unsatisfied demand of would-be buyers. Figure 5-1 illustrates the general conclusion:

At any disequilibrium price, quantity exchanged is determined by the *lesser* of quantity demanded or quantity supplied.

FIGURE 5-1   The Determination of Quantity Exchanged in Disequilibrium

In disequilibrium, quantity exchanged is determined by the lesser of quantity demanded and quantity supplied. At E, the market is in equilibrium, with quantity demanded equal to quantity supplied. For any price below p_0, the quantity exchanged will be determined by the supply curve. For any price above p_0, the quantity exchanged will be determined by the demand curve. Thus, the solid portions of the S and D curves show the actual quantities exchanged at different disequilibrium prices.

FIGURE 5-2   A Binding Price Floor

A binding price floor leads to excess supply. The free-market equilibrium is at E, with price p_0 and quantity Q_0. The government now establishes a binding price floor at p_1. The result is excess supply equal to Q_1Q_2.

Price Floors

Governments sometimes establish a *price floor*, which is the minimum permissible price that can be charged for a particular good or service. A price floor that is set at or below the equilibrium price has no effect because the free-market equilibrium remains attainable. If, however, the price floor is set above the equilibrium, it will raise the price, in which case it is said to be *binding*.

Price floors may be established by rules that make it illegal to sell the product below the prescribed price, as in the case of a legislated minimum wage. Or the government may establish a price floor by announcing that it will guarantee a certain price by buying any excess supply. Such guarantees are a feature of many agricultural support policies.

The effects of a binding price floor are illustrated in Figure 5-2, which establishes the following key result:

Binding price floors lead to excess supply. Either an unsold surplus will exist, or someone (usually the government) must enter the market and buy the excess supply.

The consequences of excess supply differ from product to product. If the product is labour, subject to a minimum wage, excess supply translates into people without jobs (unemployment). If the product is wheat, and more is produced than can be sold to consumers, the surplus wheat will accumulate in grain elevators or government warehouses. These consequences may or may not be worthwhile in terms of the other goals achieved. But worthwhile or not, these consequences are inevitable in a competitive market whenever a price floor is set above the market-clearing equilibrium price.

Why might the government wish to incur these consequences? One reason is that the people who succeed in selling their products at the price floor are better off than if they had to accept the lower equilibrium price. Workers and farmers are among the politically active, organized groups who have gained much by persuading the government to establish price floors that enable them to sell their goods or services at prices above free-market levels. If the demand is inelastic, as it often is for agricultural products, producers sell a lower quantity than they would at the equilibrium price (even though their total income is raised by the price floor). The losses are spread across the large and diverse set of purchasers, each of whom suffers only a small loss (although the *total* loss can be considerable).

Applying Economic Concepts 5-1 examines the case of a legislated minimum wage in more detail, and explains the basis of the often-heard claim that minimum wages increase unemployment. We discuss the effects of minimum wages in greater detail in Chapter 14 when we examine various labour-market issues.

For information on various labour-market policies in Canada, see HRSDC's website: **www.hrsdc.gc.ca**. Then click on "Labour and Workplace."

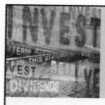

APPLYING ECONOMIC CONCEPTS 5-1

Minimum Wages and Unemployment

All Canadian governments, provincial and federal, have legislated minimum wages. For those industries covered by provincial legislation (which includes most industries except banking, airlines, trucking, and railways), the minimum wage in 2006 ranged from a low of $6.50 per hour in New Brunswick to a high of $8.50 per hour in Nunavut. This box examines the effects of implementing a minimum wage in a competitive labour market, and provides a basis for understanding the often-heard claim that minimum wages lead to an increase in unemployment.

The accompanying figure shows the demand and supply curves for labour services, with "Employment" on the horizontal axis and "Hourly Wage Rate" on the vertical axis. In the absence of any legislated minimum wage, the equilibrium in the labour market would be a wage equal to w_0 and a level of employment equal to E_0.

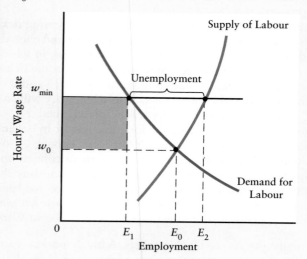

Now suppose the government introduces a minimum wage equal to w_{min} that is greater than w_0. The increased wage has two effects. First, by increasing the cost of labour services to firms, the minimum wage reduces the level of employment to E_1. The second effect is to increase the quantity supplied of labour services to E_2. Thus, the clear effect of the binding minimum wage, as seen in the figure, is to generate unemployment—workers that want a job but are unable to get one—equal to the amount E_1E_2.

Whom does this policy benefit? And whom does it harm? Firms are clearly made worse off since they are now required to pay a higher wage than before the minimum wage was imposed. They respond to this increase in costs by reducing their use of labour. Some (but not all) workers are made better off. The workers who are lucky enough to keep their jobs—E_1 workers in the figure—get a higher wage than before. The shaded area shows the redistribution of income away from firms and toward these fortunate workers. Some workers are harmed by the policy—the ones who lose their jobs as a result of the wage increase, shown in the figure as the quantity E_1E_0.

We have discussed here the effects of minimum wages in a *competitive* labour market—one in which there are many firms and many workers, none of whom have the power to influence the market wage. In Chapter 14 we will examine non-competitive labour markets and we will then see that minimum wages may have a different effect on the market. This different behaviour of competitive and non-competitive markets in the presence of minimum wages probably accounts for the disagreements among economists and policy-makers regarding the desirability of minimum-wage legislation. Until we proceed to that more advanced discussion, however, the analysis of a competitive labour market in this box provides an excellent example of the economic effects of a binding price floor in specific circumstances.

FIGURE 5-3   A Price Ceiling and Black-Market Pricing

A binding price ceiling causes excess demand and invites a black market. The equilibrium point, E, is at a price of p_0 and a quantity of Q_0. If a price ceiling is set at p_1, the quantity demanded will rise to Q_1 and the quantity supplied will fall to Q_2. Quantity actually exchanged will be Q_2. But if all the available supply of Q_2 were sold on a black market, the price to consumers would rise to p_2. Because black marketeers buy at the ceiling price of p_1 and sell at the black-market price of p_2, their profits are represented by the shaded area.

sellers' preferences Allocation of commodities in excess demand by decisions of the sellers.

black market A situation in which goods are sold illegally at prices that violate a legal price control.

Price Ceilings

A *price ceiling* is the maximum price at which certain goods and services may be exchanged. Price controls on oil, natural gas, and rental housing have been frequently imposed by federal and provincial governments. If the price ceiling is set above the equilibrium price, it has no effect because the free-market equilibrium remains attainable. If, however, the price ceiling is set below the free-market equilibrium price, the price ceiling lowers the price and is said to be *binding*. The effects of binding price ceilings are shown in Figure 5-3, which establishes the following conclusion:

Binding price ceilings lead to excess demand, with the quantity exchanged being less than in the free-market equilibrium.

Allocating a Product in Excess Demand   Free markets eliminate excess demand by allowing prices to rise, thereby allocating the available supply among would-be purchasers. Because this adjustment cannot happen in the presence of a binding price ceiling, some other method of allocation must be adopted. Experience suggests what we can expect.

If stores sell their available supplies on a *first-come, first-served* basis, people will rush to stores that are said to have stocks of the product. Buyers may wait hours to get into the store, only to find that supplies are exhausted before they can be served. This is why standing in lines became a way of life in the centrally planned economies of the Soviet Union and Eastern Europe in which price controls were pervasive.

In market economies, "first-come, first-served" is often the basis for allocating tickets to concerts and sporting events when promoters set a price at which demand exceeds the supply of available seats. In these cases, an illegal market often develops, in which ticket "scalpers" resell tickets at market-clearing prices. Storekeepers (and some ticket sellers) often respond to excess demand by keeping goods "under the counter" and selling only to customers of their own choosing. When sellers decide to whom they will and will not sell their scarce supplies, allocation is said to be by **sellers' preferences.**

If the government dislikes the allocation of products by long line-ups or by sellers' preferences, it can choose to *ration* the product. To do so, it prints only enough ration coupons to match the quantity supplied at the price ceiling and then distributes the coupons to would-be purchasers, who then need both money and coupons to buy the product. The coupons may be distributed equally among the population or on the basis of some criterion such as age, family status, or occupation. Rationing of this sort was used by Canada and many other countries during both the First and Second World Wars.

Black Markets   Price ceilings usually give rise to black markets. A **black market** is any market in which goods are sold illegally at prices that violate a legal price control.

Binding price ceilings always create the potential for a black market because a profit can be made by buying at the controlled price and selling at the black-market price.

Figure 5-3 illustrates the extreme case in which all the available supply is sold on a black market. We say this case is extreme because there are law-abiding people in every society and because governments ordinarily have at least *some* power to enforce their price ceilings. Although some units of a product subject to a binding price ceiling will be sold on the black market, it is unlikely that all of that product will be.

Does the existence of a black market mean that the goals sought by imposing price ceilings have been thwarted? The answer depends on what the goals are. A government might have three main goals for imposing a price ceiling.

1. To restrict production (perhaps to release resources for other uses, such as wartime military production)

2. To keep specific prices down

3. To satisfy notions of equity in the consumption of a product that is temporarily in short supply

When price ceilings are accompanied by a black market, it is not clear that any of these objectives are achieved. First, if producers are willing to sell (illegally) at prices above the price ceiling, there is nothing restricting them to the level of output of Q_2 in Figure 5-3. As long as they can receive more than a price of p_1, they have an incentive to increase their production. Second, black markets clearly frustrate the second objective since the *actual* prices are not kept down; if quantity supplied remains below Q_0, then the black-market price will be *higher* than the free-market equilibrium price, p_0. The third objective may also be thwarted since with an active black market it is likely that much of the product will be sold only to those who can afford the black-market price, which will often be well above the free-market equilibrium price.

To the extent that binding price ceilings give rise to a black market, it is likely that the government's objectives motivating the imposition of the price ceiling will be thwarted.

5.3 RENT CONTROLS: A CASE STUDY OF PRICE CEILINGS

For long periods over the past hundred years, rent controls existed in London, Paris, New York, and many other large cities. In Sweden and Britain, where rent controls on apartments existed for decades, shortages of rental accommodations were chronic. When rent controls were initiated in Toronto and Rome, severe housing shortages developed, especially in those areas where demand was rising.

Rent controls provide a vivid illustration of the short- and long-term effects of this type of market intervention. Note, however, that the specifics of rent-control laws vary greatly and have changed significantly since they were first imposed many decades ago. In particular, current laws often permit exemptions for new buildings and allowances for maintenance costs and inflation. Moreover, in many countries rent controls have evolved into a "second generation" of legislation that focuses more on *regulating* the rental housing market than simply *controlling the price* of rental accommodation.

In this section, we confine ourselves to an analysis of rent controls that are aimed primarily at holding the price of rental housing below the free-market equilibrium value. It is this "first generation" of rent controls that produced dramatic results in cities like London, Paris, New York, and Toronto.

The Predicted Effects of Rent Controls

Binding rent controls are a specific case of price ceilings and therefore Figure 5-3 can be used to predict some of their effects:

Practise with Study Guide Chapter 5, Exercise 3.

1. There will be a housing shortage in the sense that quantity demanded will exceed quantity supplied. Since rents are held below their free-market levels, the available quantity of rental housing will be less than if free-market rents had been charged.

2. The shortage will lead to alternative allocation schemes. Landlords may allocate by sellers' preferences, or the government may intervene, often through security-of-tenure laws, which protect tenants from eviction and thereby give them priority over prospective new tenants.

3. Black markets will appear. For example, landlords may (illegally) require tenants to pay "key money" equal to the difference in value between the free-market and the controlled rents. In the absence of security-of-tenure laws, landlords may force tenants out when their leases expire in order to extract a large entrance fee from new tenants.

The unique feature of rent controls, however, as compared to price controls in general, is that they are applied to a highly *durable good* that provides services to consumers for long periods of time. Once built, an apartment can be used for decades. As a result, the immediate effects of rent control are typically quite different from the long-term effects.

The short-run supply response to the imposition of rent controls is usually quite limited. Some conversions of apartment units to condominiums (that are not covered by the rent-control legislation) may occur but the quantity of apartments does not change much. The short-run supply curve for rental housing is quite *inelastic*.

In the long run, however, the supply response to rent controls can be quite dramatic. If the expected rate of return from building new rental housing falls significantly below what can be earned on comparable investments, funds will go elsewhere. New construction will be halted, and old buildings will be converted to other uses, or will simply be left to deteriorate. The long-run supply curve of rental accommodations is highly *elastic*.

Figure 5-4 illustrates the housing shortage that worsens as time passes under rent control. Because the short-run supply of housing is inelastic, the controlled rent causes only a moderate housing shortage in the short run. Indeed, most of the shortage comes from an increase in the quantity demanded rather than from a reduction in quantity supplied. As time passes, however, fewer new apartments are built, more conversions take place, and older buildings are not replaced (and not repaired) as they wear out. As a result, the quantity supplied shrinks steadily and the extent of the housing shortage worsens.

FIGURE 5-4 The Short-Run and Long-Run Effects of Rent Controls

Quantity of Rental Accommodations

Rent control causes housing shortages that worsen as time passes. The free-market equilibrium is at point E. The controlled rent of r_c forces rents below their free-market equilibrium value of r_1. The short-run supply of housing is shown by the perfectly inelastic curve S_S. Thus quantity supplied remains at Q_1 in the short run, and the housing shortage is Q_1Q_2. Over time, the quantity supplied shrinks, as shown by the long-run supply curve S_L. In the long run, there are only Q_3 units of rental accommodations supplied, fewer than when controls were instituted. The long-run housing shortage of Q_3Q_2 is larger than the initial shortage of Q_1Q_2.

Along with the growing housing shortage comes an increasingly inefficient use of rental accommodation space. Existing tenants will have an incentive to stay where they are even though their family size, location of employment, or economic circumstances may change. Since they cannot move without giving up their low-rent accommodation, some may accept lower-paying jobs nearby to avoid the necessity of moving. Thus, a situation will arise in which existing tenants will hang on to accommodation even if it is poorly suited to their needs while individuals and families who are newly entering the housing market will be unable to find any rental accommodation except at black-market prices.

The province of Ontario instituted rent controls in 1975 and tightened them on at least two subsequent occasions. The controls permitted significant increases in rents only where these were needed to pass cost increases on. As a result, the restrictive effects of rent controls were felt mainly in areas where demand was increasing rapidly (as opposed to areas where only costs were increasing rapidly).

During the mid- and late-1990s, the population of Ontario grew substantially but the stock of rental housing did not keep pace. A shortage developed in the rental-housing market, and was especially acute in Metro Toronto. This growing housing shortage led the Conservative Ontario government in 1997 to loosen rent controls, in particular by allowing landlords to increase the rent as much as they saw fit *but only as tenants vacated the apartment.* Not surprisingly, this policy had both critics and supporters. Supporters argued that a loosening of controls would encourage the construction of apartments and thus help to reduce the housing shortage. Critics argued that landlords would harass existing tenants, forcing them to move out so that rents could be increased for incoming tenants. (Indeed, this exact behaviour happened in rent-controlled New York City, where a landlord pleaded guilty in January 1999 to hiring a "hit man" to kill tenants and set fires to scare them out so that rents could be increased!)

In 2004, the newly elected Liberal government in Ontario revised the 1997 rent-control legislation and reduced the maximum rate of increase for rents on occupied apartments. The 2005 maximum was set at 1.5 percent, down from 3.9 percent three years earlier. Not surprisingly, the policy was heralded by tenants who saw the policy as increasing the affordability of rental housing, but decried by landlords who argued that a 1.5 percent increase was insufficient to cover their rising costs.

Who Gains and Who Loses?

Existing tenants in rent-controlled accommodations are the principal gainers from a policy of rent control. As the gap between the controlled and the free-market rents grows, and as the stock of available housing falls, those who are still lucky enough to live in rent-controlled housing gain more and more.

Landlords suffer because they do not get the rate of return they expected on their investments. Some landlords are large companies, and others are wealthy individuals. Neither of these groups attracts great public sympathy, even though the rental companies' shareholders are not all rich. But some landlords are people of modest means who may have put their retirement savings into a small apartment block or a house or two. They find that the value of their savings is diminished, and sometimes they find themselves in the ironic position of subsidizing tenants who are far better off than they are.

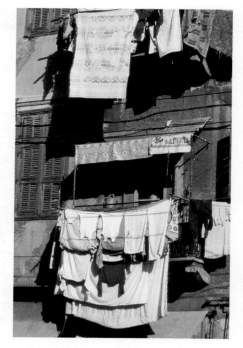

Perhaps the most striking effect of rent control is the long-term decline in the amount and quality of rental housing.

The other important group of people who suffer from rent controls are *potential future* tenants. The housing shortage hurts them because the rental housing they will require will not exist in the future. These people, who wind up living elsewhere, farther from their places of employment and study, are invisible in debates over rent control because they cannot obtain housing in the rent-controlled jurisdiction. Thus, rent control is often stable politically even when it causes a long-run housing shortage. The current tenants benefit, and they outnumber the current landlords, while the potential tenants, who are harmed, are nowhere to be seen or heard.

In some situations, legislated rent controls may impose relatively small costs. For a fuller explanation, look for "When Rent Controls Work and When They Don't" in the *Additional Topics* section of this book's MyEconLab.

www.myeconlab.com

Policy Alternatives

Most rent controls today are meant to protect lower-income tenants, not only against "profiteering" by landlords in the face of severe local shortages but also against the steadily rising cost of housing. The market solution is to let rents rise sufficiently to cover the rising costs. If people decide that they cannot afford the market price of apartments and will not rent them, construction will cease. Given what we know about consumer behaviour, however, it is more likely that people will make agonizing choices, both to economize on housing and to spend a higher proportion of total income on it, which mean consuming less housing and less of other things as well.

If governments do not wish to accept this market solution, there are many things they can do, but they cannot avoid the fundamental fact that the opportunity cost of good housing is high. Binding rent controls create housing shortages. The shortages can be removed only if the government, at taxpayer expense, either subsidizes housing production or produces public housing directly.

Alternatively, the government can make housing more affordable to lower-income households by providing income assistance to these households, allowing them access to higher-quality housing than they could otherwise afford. Whatever policy is adopted, it is important to recognize that providing greater access to rental accommodations has a resource cost. The costs of providing additional housing cannot be voted out of existence; all that can be done is to transfer the costs from one set of persons to another.

5.4 **AN INTRODUCTION TO MARKET EFFICIENCY**

In this chapter we have seen the effects of government intervening in competitive markets by setting price floors and price ceilings. In both cases, we noted that the imposition of a controlled price generates benefits for some individuals and costs for others. For example, in the case of the legislated minimum wage (a price floor), firms are made worse off by the minimum wage, but workers who retain their jobs are made better off. Other workers, those unable to retain their jobs at the higher wage, are made worse off. In the example of legislated rent controls (a price ceiling), landlords are made worse off by the rent controls, but some tenants are made better off. Those tenants who are no longer able to find an apartment when rents fall are made worse off.

Is it possible to determine the *overall* effects of such policies, rather than just the effects on specific groups? For example, can we say that a policy of legislated minimum wages, while harming firms, nonetheless makes *society as a whole* better off because it helps workers more than it harms firms? Or can we conclude that the imposition of rent controls makes society as a whole better off because it helps tenants more than it harms landlords?

To answer such questions, economists use the concept of *market efficiency*. We will explore this concept in more detail in later chapters, but for now we simply introduce the idea and see how it helps us understand the overall effects of price controls. We begin by taking a slightly different look at market demand and supply curves.

Demand as "Value" and Supply as "Cost"

In Chapter 3 we saw that the market demand curve for any product shows, for each possible price, how much of that product consumers want to purchase. Similarly, we saw that the market supply curve shows how much producers want to sell at each possible price. But we can turn things around and view these curves in a slightly different way—by starting with any given quantity and asking about the price. Specifically, we can consider the highest price that consumers are *willing to pay* and the lowest price that producers are *willing to accept* for any given unit of the product. As we will see, viewing demand and supply curves in this manner helps us think about how society as a whole benefits by producing and consuming any given amount of some product.

Let's begin by considering the market demand curve for pizza, as shown in part (i) of Figure 5-5. Each point on the demand curve shows the highest price consumers are willing to pay for a given pizza. At point *A* we see that consumers are willing to pay up to $20 for the 100th pizza, and at point *B* consumers are willing to pay up to $15 for the 200th pizza. In both cases, these maximum prices reflect the *value* consumers place on that particular pizza. If consumers valued the 100th pizza by more than $20, they would be willing to pay more to get that pizza, and the price as shown on the demand curve would be higher than $20. If they valued the 100th pizza less than $20, they would not be willing to pay as much as $20, and the price as shown on the demand curve would then be less than $20. Thus, for each pizza, the price on the demand curve shows the value to consumers from consuming that pizza.

There is nothing special about pizza, however. What is true for the demand for pizza is true for the demand for any other product.

For each unit of a product, the price on the market demand curve shows the value to consumers from consuming that unit.

Now let's consider the market supply curve for pizza, shown in part (ii) of Figure 5-5. Each point on the market supply curve shows the lowest price firms are willing to accept to produce and sell a given pizza. At point *E* firms are willing to accept a price no lower than $5 for the 100th pizza, and at point *F* firms are willing to accept a price no lower than $10 for the 200th pizza. The lowest acceptable price as shown on the supply curve reflects the *additional cost* firms incur to produce each given pizza. To see this, consider the production of the 200th pizza at point *F*. If the firm's total costs increase by $10 when this pizza is produced, the firm will be able to increase its profits as long as it can sell that pizza at a price greater than $10. If it sells the pizza at any price below $10, its profits will decline. If it sells the pizza at a price

FIGURE 5-5 Reinterpreting the Demand and Supply Curves in the Pizza Market

For each pizza, the price on the demand curve shows the value consumers receive from consuming that pizza; the price on the supply curve shows the additional cost to firms of producing that pizza. Each point on the demand curve shows the maximum price consumers are willing to pay to consume that unit. This maximum price reflects the value that consumers get from that unit of the product. Each point on the supply curve shows the minimum price firms are willing to accept for producing and selling that unit. This minimum price reflects the additional costs incurred by producing that unit.

of exactly $10, its profits will neither rise nor fall. Thus, for a profit-maximizing firm, the *lowest acceptable price* for the 200th pizza is $10.

Again, what is true for the supply of pizza is true for the supply of other products.

For each unit of a product, the price on the market supply curve shows the lowest acceptable price to firms for selling that unit. This lowest acceptable price reflects the additional cost to firms from producing that unit.

Economic Surplus and Market Efficiency

Practise with Study Guide Chapter 5, Short-Answer Question 3.

Once the demand and supply curves are put together, the equilibrium price and quantity can be determined. This brings us to the important concept of *economic surplus*. We continue with our pizza example in Figure 5-6, which shows the demand and supply curves together. Consider a quantity of 100 pizzas. For each one of those 100 pizzas, the value to consumers is given by the price on the demand curve. The additional cost to firms from producing each of these 100 pizzas is shown by the price on the supply curve. For the entire 100 pizzas, the difference between the value to consumers and the additional costs to firms is called *economic surplus* and is shown by the shaded area ① in the figure.

For any given quantity of a product, the area below the demand curve and above the supply curve shows the economic surplus associated with the production and consumption of that product.

What does this "economic surplus" represent? The economic surplus is the net value that *society as a whole* receives by producing and consuming these 100 pizzas. It arises because firms and consumers have taken resources that have a lower value (as shown by the height of the supply curve) and transformed them into something valued more highly (as shown by the height of the demand curve). To put it differently, the value from consuming the 100 pizzas is greater than the cost of the resources necessary to produce those 100 pizzas—flour, yeast, tomato sauce, cheese, and labour. Thus, the act of producing and consuming those 100 pizzas "adds value" and thus generates benefits for society as a whole.

We are now ready to introduce the concept of market efficiency. In later chapters, after we have explored consumer and firm behaviour in greater detail, we will have a more detailed discussion of efficiency. For now, we simply introduce the concept and see how it relates to the imposition of government price controls. Loosely speaking, a market for a specific product is said to be efficient if the quantity of the product produced and consumed is such that the *economic surplus* in the market is maximized.

Let's continue with the pizza example in Figure 5-6 and ask: What level of pizza production and consumption is efficient? Consider the quantity of 100 pizzas. At this quantity, the shaded area ① shows the total economic surplus that society receives from producing and consuming 100 pizzas. But if output were to increase beyond 100 pizzas, more economic surplus would be generated because the value placed by consumers on additional pizzas is greater than the additional costs associated with their production. Specifically, if production and consumption were to increase to 200 pizzas, additional economic surplus would be generated, as shown by

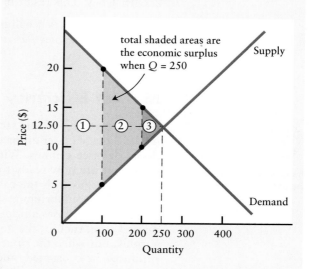

FIGURE 5-6   Economic Surplus in the Pizza Market

For any quantity of pizzas, the area below the demand curve and above the supply curve shows the economic surplus generated by the production and consumption of those pizzas. The demand curve shows the value consumers place on each additional pizza; the supply curve shows the additional cost associated with producing each pizza. For example, consumers value the 100th pizza at $20, whereas the additional cost to firms of producing that 100th pizza is $5. The economic surplus generated by producing and consuming this 100th pizza is therefore $15 ($20 − $5). For any range of quantity, the shaded area between the curves over that range shows the economic surplus generated by producing and consuming those pizzas.

Economic surplus in the pizza market is maximized—and thus market efficiency is achieved—at the free-market equilibrium quantity of 250 pizzas and price of $12.50. At this point, total economic surplus is the sum of the three shaded areas.

shaded area ②. Continuing this logic, we see that the amount of economic surplus is maximized when the quantity is 250 units, and at that quantity the total economic surplus is equal to the sum of areas ①, ②, and ③.

What would happen if the quantity of pizzas were to rise further, say to 300 units? For any pizzas beyond 250, the value placed on these pizzas by consumers is *less than* the additional costs associated with their production. In this case, producing the last 50 pizzas would actually *decrease* the amount of economic surplus in this market because society would be taking highly valued resources (flour, cheese, etc.) and transforming them into pizzas which are valued less.

In our example of the pizza market, as long as the price is free to adjust to excess demands or supplies, the equilibrium price and quantity will be determined where the demand and supply curves for pizza intersect. In Figure 5-6, the equilibrium quantity is 250 pizzas, the quantity that maximizes the amount of economic surplus in the pizza market. In other words, the free interaction of demand and supply will result in market efficiency. This result in the pizza market suggests a more general rule:

A competitive market will maximize economic surplus and therefore be efficient when price is free to achieve its market-clearing equilibrium level.[1]

Market Efficiency and Price Controls

Practise with Study Guide Chapter 5, Exercise 4.

At the beginning of this section we asked whether we could determine if *society as a whole* is made better off or worse off as a result of the government's imposition of price floors or price ceilings. With an understanding of economic surplus and market efficiency, we are now ready to answer these questions.

Let's begin with the case of a price floor, as shown in part (i) of Figure 5-7. The free-market equilibrium is shown by point E, with price p_0 and quantity Q_0. When the government imposes a price floor at p_1, the quantity exchanged falls to Q_1. In the free-market case, each of the units of output between Q_0 and Q_1 generate some economic surplus. But when the price floor is put in place, these units of the good are no longer produced or consumed, and thus they no longer generate any economic surplus. The purple shaded area is called the *deadweight loss* caused by the binding price floor and

FIGURE 5-7   Market Inefficiency with Price Controls

(i) Binding price floor

(ii) Binding price ceiling

Binding price floors and price ceilings in competitive markets lead to a reduction in overall economic surplus and thus to market inefficiency. In both parts of the figure, the free-market equilibrium is at point E with price p_0 and quantity Q_0. In part (i), the introduction of a price floor at p_1 reduces quantity to Q_1. In part (ii), the introduction of a price ceiling at p_2 reduces quantity to Q_2. In both parts, the purple shaded area shows the reduction in overall economic surplus—the deadweight loss—created by the price floor (or ceiling). Both outcomes display market inefficiency.

---

1 In Part 6 of this book, we will see some important exceptions to this rule when we discuss "market failures."

it represents the overall loss of economic surplus to society. The size of the deadweight loss reflects the extent of market *inefficiency*.

The imposition of a binding price floor in an otherwise free and competitive market leads to a loss of economic surplus, and thus to market inefficiency.

A price floor does more than make sellers better off at the expense of buyers. It also leads to an overall reduction in economic surplus. Society as a whole therefore suffers by having less economic surplus generated in this market than could be achieved when price is free to achieve its market-clearing level.

Now let's consider the case of a price ceiling, as shown in part (ii) of Figure 5-7. The free-market equilibrium is again shown by point E, with price p_0 and quantity Q_0. When the government imposes a price ceiling at p_2, the quantity exchanged falls to Q_2. In the free-market case, each of the units of output between Q_0 and Q_2 generate some economic surplus. But when the price ceiling is imposed, these units of the good are no longer produced or consumed and so they no longer generate any economic surplus. The purple shaded area is the *deadweight loss* and represents the overall loss to society caused by the policy. The size of the deadweight loss reflects the extent of market *inefficiency*.

The imposition of a binding price ceiling in an otherwise free and competitive market leads to a loss of economic surplus, and thus to market inefficiency.

As with the case of the binding price floor, a binding price ceiling leads to an overall reduction in economic surplus. Society as a whole therefore suffers by having less economic surplus generated in this market than would be the case if the price were free to achieve its market-clearing level.

One Final Application: Output Quotas

Before ending this chapter, it is useful to consider one final application of government intervention in a competitive market, and to examine the effects on overall economic surplus and market efficiency. Figure 5-8 illustrates the effects of introducing a system of *output quotas* in a competitive market. Output quotas are commonly used in Canadian agriculture, especially in the markets for milk, butter, and cheese. Output quotas are sometimes used in other industries as well; for example, they are often used in large cities to regulate the number of taxi drivers.

The equilibrium in the free-market case is at point E, with price p_0 and quantity Q_0. When the government introduces an output quota, it restricts total output of this product to Q_1 units and then distributes quotas—"licences to produce"—among the producers. With output restricted to Q_1 units, the market price rises to p_1, the price that consumers are willing to pay for this quantity of the product. The purple shaded area—the deadweight loss of the

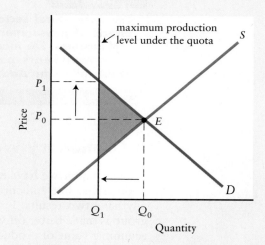

FIGURE 5-8   The Inefficiency of Output Quotas

Binding output quotas lead to a reduction in output and a reduction in overall economic surplus. The free-market equilibrium is at point E with price p_0 and quantity Q_0. Suppose the government then restricts total quantity to Q_1 by issuing output quotas to firms. The market price rises to p_1. The purple shaded area shows the reduction in overall economic surplus—the deadweight loss—created by the quota system.

output quota—shows the overall loss of economic surplus as a result of the quota-induced output restriction.

One interesting consequence of the use of output quotas relates to the market value of the quotas themselves. When quota systems are used, firms initially issued quotas by the government are usually permitted to buy or sell quotas to each other or to new firms interested in entering the industry. The quota itself simply provides the holder permission to produce and sell in that industry, but the market value of the quota reflects the profitability of that production.

As you can see from Figure 5-8, the output restriction created by the quota leads to an increase in the product's price. If demand for the product is inelastic, as is the case in the dairy markets where quotas are commonly used, total income to producers rises as a result of the reduction in output. But since their output falls, firms' production costs also are reduced. The introduction of a quota system therefore leads to a rise in revenues and a fall in production costs—a clear benefit for producers! Not surprisingly, producers are often prepared to pay a high price to purchase new quota because having more quota gives them the ability to produce more output.

There is a catch, however: Producers must incur a very high cost in order to purchase the quotas. For example, an average dairy farm in Manitoba has about 90 cows and produces about 2300 litres of milk per day. The market value of the quota required to produce this amount of milk is approximately $1.8 million. The ownership of quota therefore represents a considerable asset for those producers who were lucky enough to receive it (for free) when it was initially issued by the government. But for new producers wanting to get into the industry, the need to purchase expensive quota represents a considerable obstacle. These large costs from purchasing the quota offset the benefits from selling the product at the (quota-induced) high price.

myeconlab

The agricultural sector offers an excellent setting in which to analyze the effects of government policies designed to support and stabilize producers' incomes. For more details about the challenges faced by farmers and the government's policy responses, look for "Agriculture and the Farm Problem" in the *Additional Topics* section of this book's MyEconLab.

w w w . m y e c o n l a b . c o m

A Cautionary Word

In this chapter we have examined the effects of government policies to control prices in otherwise free and competitive markets, and we have shown that such policies usually have two results. First, there is a redistribution between buyers and sellers; one group is made better off while the other group is made worse off—at least as far as the economic value of production is concerned. Second, there is a reduction in the overall amount of economic surplus generated in the market; the result is that the outcome is inefficient and society as a whole is made worse off.

The finding that government intervention in otherwise free markets leads to inefficiency should lead one to ask why government would ever intervene in such ways. The answer in many situations is that the government policy is motivated largely by the desire to help a specific group of people, and that the overall costs to society are deemed to be a worthwhile price to pay in order to achieve the desired effect. For example, legislated minimum wages are often viewed by politicians as an effective means of reducing poverty—by increasing the wages received by low-wage workers.

The costs such a policy imposes on firms, and on society overall, may be viewed as costs worth incurring in order to redistribute economic surplus toward low-wage workers. Similarly, the use of output quotas in certain agricultural markets is sometimes viewed by politicians as an effective means of increasing income to specific farmers. The costs that such quota systems impose on consumers, and on society as a whole, may be viewed as acceptable costs in achieving a redistribution of economic surplus toward these farmers.

In advocating these kinds of policies, ones that redistribute economic surplus but also reduce the total amount of economic surplus available, policy-makers are making *normative* judgements regarding which groups in society deserve to be helped at the expense of others. These judgements may be informed by a careful study of which groups are most genuinely in need, and they may also be driven by political considerations that the current government deems important to its prospects for re-election. In either case, there is nothing necessarily "wrong" about the government's decision to intervene in these markets, even if these interventions lead to inefficiency.

The job of the economist is to carefully analyze the effects of such policies, taking care to identify both the distributional effects as well as the implications for the overall amount of economic surplus generated in the market. This is *positive* analysis, emphasizing the *actual* effects of the policy rather than what might be *desirable*. These analytical results can then be used as "inputs" to the decision-making process, where they will be combined with normative and political considerations before a final policy decision is reached. In many parts of this textbook, we will encounter policies that governments implement (or consider implementing) to alter market outcomes, and we will examine the effects of those policies. A full understanding of why specific policies are implemented requires paying attention to the effects of such policies on both the overall amount of economic surplus and the distribution of that surplus.

S U M M A R Y

5.1 THE INTERACTION AMONG MARKETS   LO 1

- Partial-equilibrium analysis is appropriate when the market being examined is small relative to the entire economy.

- Partial-equilibrium analysis is the study of a single market in isolation, ignoring events in other markets. General-equilibrium analysis is the study of all markets together.

5.2 GOVERNMENT-CONTROLLED PRICES   LO 2

- Government price controls are policies that attempt to hold the price of some good or service at some disequilibrium value—a value that could not be maintained in the absence of the government's intervention.
- A binding price floor is set above the equilibrium price; a binding price ceiling is set below the equilibrium price.
- Binding price floors lead to excess supply. Either the potential seller is left with quantities that cannot be

sold, or the government must step in and buy the surplus.
- Binding price ceilings lead to excess demand and provide a strong incentive for black marketeers to buy at the controlled price and sell at the higher free-market (illegal) price.

5.3 **RENT CONTROLS: A CASE STUDY OF PRICE CEILINGS**

- Rent controls are a widespread form of price ceiling. The major consequence of binding rent controls is a shortage of rental accommodations and the allocation of rental housing by sellers' preferences.

- Because the supply of rental housing is much more elastic in the long run than in the short run, the extent of the housing shortage caused by rent controls worsens over time.

5.4 **AN INTRODUCTION TO MARKET EFFICIENCY**   LO 4

- Demand curves show consumers' willingness to pay for each unit of the product. For any given quantity, the area below the demand curve shows the overall value that consumers place on that quantity of the product.
- Supply curves show the lowest price producers are prepared to accept in order to produce and sell each unit of the product. This lowest acceptable price for each additional unit reflects the firm's costs required to produce each additional unit.
- For any given quantity exchanged of a product, the area below the demand curve and above the supply curve (up to that quantity) shows the economic surplus generated by the production and consumption of those units.

- Economic surplus in a market is maximized when the quantity exchanged is determined by the intersection of the demand and supply curves. This outcome is said to be efficient.
- Policies that intervene in otherwise free and competitive markets—such as price floors, price ceilings, and production quotas—generally lead to a reduction in the total amount of economic surplus generated in the market. For this reason such policies are inefficient for society overall.

KEY CONCEPTS

Partial-equilibrium analysis
General-equilibrium analysis
Price controls: floors and ceilings
Allocation by sellers' preferences and
  by black markets

Rent controls
Short-run and long-run supply curves
  of rental accommodations
Economic surplus

Market efficiency
Inefficiency of price controls and
  production quotas

STUDY EXERCISES

1. Consider the market for straw hats on a tropical island. The demand and supply schedules are given below.

Price ($)	Quantity Demanded	Quantity Supplied
1	1000	200
2	900	300
3	800	400
4	700	500
5	600	600
6	500	700
7	400	800
8	300	900

a. The equilibrium price for straw hats is _____. The equilibrium quantity demanded and quantity supplied is _____.
b. Suppose the government believes that no islander should have to pay more than $3 for a hat. The government can achieve this by imposing a _____.
c. At the government-controlled price of $3 there will be a _____ of _____ hats.
d. Suppose now that the government believes the island's hat makers are not paid enough for their hats and that islanders should pay no less than $6 for a hat. They can achieve this by imposing a _____.
e. At the new government-controlled price of $6 there will be a _____ of _____ hats.

2. The following questions are about resource allocation in the presence of price ceilings and price floors.

   a. A binding price ceiling leads to excess demand. What are some methods, other than price, of allocating the available supply?
   b. A binding price floor leads to excess supply. How might the government deal with this excess supply?
   c. Why might the government choose to implement a price ceiling?
   d. Why might the government choose to implement a price floor?

3. **X myeconlab** Consider the market for some product X that is represented below in the demand-and-supply diagram.

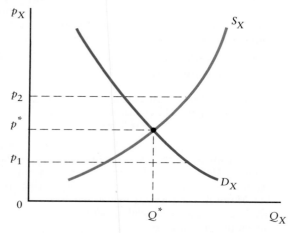

   a. Suppose the government decides to impose a price floor at p_1. Describe how this affects price, quantity, and market efficiency.
   b. Suppose the government decides to impose a price floor at p_2. Describe how this affects price, quantity, and market efficiency.
   c. Suppose the government decides to impose a price ceiling at p_1. Describe how this affects price, quantity, and market efficiency.
   d. Suppose the government decides to impose a price ceiling at p_2. Describe how this affects price, quantity, and market efficiency.

4. Consider the market for rental housing in Yourtown. The demand and supply schedules for rental housing are given in the table.

Price ($ per month)	Quantity Demanded (thousands of units)	Quantity Supplied (thousands of units)
1100	40	80
1000	50	77
900	60	73
800	70	70
700	80	67
600	90	65
500	100	60

   a. In a free market for rental housing, what is the equilibrium price and quantity?
   b. Now suppose the government in Yourtown decides to impose a ceiling on the monthly rental price. What is the highest level at which such a ceiling could be set, in order to have any effect on the market? Explain your answer.
   c. Suppose the maximum rental price is set equal to $500 per month. Describe the effect on the rental-housing market.
   d. Suppose a black market develops in the presence of the rent controls in (c). What is the black-market price that would exist if all of the quantity supplied were sold on the black market?

5. Explain and show in a diagram why the short-run effects of rent control are likely to be less significant than the long-run effects.

6. Consider the situation of Canadian barley farmers, who face weather conditions largely independent of those faced by barley growers in other countries. The incomes earned by the Canadian farmers, however, are affected by what happens to barley farmers in other countries. The key point is that Canadian barley farmers sell their barley on the same *world market* as all other barley farmers.

   a. Show in a diagram of the world barley market how a bumper crop of European barley will push down the world barley price.
   b. Show in a diagram of Canadian barley supply how a reduction in the world price of barley, *ceteris paribus,* will reduce the incomes of Canadian barley farmers.
   c. Explain why Canadian barley farmers are made better off when there are crop failures in other parts of the world.

7. Consider the market for burritos in a hypothetical Canadian city, blessed with thousands of students and dozens of small burrito stands. The demand and supply schedules are shown below.

Price ($)	Quantity Demanded	Quantity Supplied
	(thousands of burritos per day)	
0	500	125
1.00	400	175
1.50	350	200
2.00	300	225
2.50	250	250
3.00	200	275
3.50	150	300
4.00	100	325
5.00	0	375

a. Graph the demand and supply curves. What is the free-market equilibrium in this market?
b. What is the total economic surplus in this market in the free-market equilibrium? What area in the diagram represents this economic surplus?
c. Suppose the local government, out of concern for the students' welfare, enforces a price ceiling on burritos at a price of $1.50. Show in your diagram the effect on price and quantity exchanged.
d. Are students better off as a result of this policy? Explain.
e. What happens to overall economic surplus in this market as a result of the price ceiling? Show this in the diagram.

8. **myeconlab** Consider the market for milk in Saskatchewan. If p is the price of milk (cents per litre) and Q is the quantity of litres (in millions per month), suppose that the demand and supply curves for milk are given by:

Demand: $p = 225 - 15Q^D$
Supply: $p = 25 + 35Q^S$

a. Assuming there is no government intervention in this market, what is the equilibrium price and quantity?
b. Now suppose the government guarantees milk producers a price of $2 per litre and promises to buy any amount of milk that the producers cannot sell. What are the quantity demanded and quantity supplied at this guaranteed price?
c. How much milk would the government be buying (per month) with this system of price supports?
d. Who pays for the milk that the government buys? Who is helped by this policy and who is harmed?

9. **myeconlab** This question is related to the use of output quotas in the milk market in the previous question. Suppose the government used a quota system instead of direct price supports to assist milk producers. In particular, it issued quotas to existing milk producers for 1.67 million litres of milk per month.

a. If milk production is exactly equal to the amount of quotas issued, what price do consumers pay for milk?
b. Compared to the direct price controls in the previous question, whose income is higher under the quota system? Whose is lower?

10. This question relates to the section *Linkages Between Markets* found on the MyEconLab (www.myeconlab.com). In 1994, the Quebec and Ontario governments significantly reduced their excise taxes on cigarettes, but Manitoba and Saskatchewan left theirs in place. This led to cigarette smuggling between provinces that linked the provincial markets.

a. Draw a simple demand-and-supply diagram for the "Eastern" market and a separate one for the "Western" market.
b. Suppose that cigarette taxes are reduced in the Eastern market. Show the immediate effects.
c. Now suppose that the supply of cigarettes is (illegally) mobile. Explain and show what happens.
d. What limits the extent of smuggling that will take place in this situation?

DISCUSSION QUESTIONS

1. "When an item is vital to everyone, it is easier to start controlling the price than to stop controlling it. Such controls are popular with consumers, regardless of their harmful consequences." Explain why it may be inefficient to have such controls, why they may be popular, and why, if they are popular, the government might nevertheless choose to decontrol these prices.

2. It is sometimes asserted that the rising costs of construction are putting housing out of the reach of ordinary citizens. Who bears the heaviest cost when rentals are kept down by (a) rent controls, (b) a subsidy to tenants equal to some fraction of their rent payments, and (c) low-cost public housing?

3. "This year the weather smiled on us, and we made a crop," says a wheat farmer near Minnedosa in Manitoba. "But just as we made a crop, the economic situation changed." This quotation brings to mind the old saying, "If you are a farmer, the weather is always bad." Discuss the sense in which this saying might be true.

4. During the summer of 1993, severe floods swept through the American Midwest. Although many homes that flooded that year do not typically flood, for many people this was only one in a long string of floods. However, after the waters receded, most people rebuilt their homes, generally with low-interest loans and disaster relief grants from the federal government. Discuss how the policy of subsidizing the reconstruction of property following floods affects the market for real estate in flood-prone areas. Is the outcome more or less efficient in the long run with such government intervention?

5. Gary Storey, a professor of agricultural economics at the University of Saskatchewan, made the following statement: "One of the sad truths of the agricultural policies in Europe and the United States is that they do very little for the future generations of farmers. Most of the subsidies get capitalized into higher land prices, creating windfall gains for current landowners (i.e., gains that they did not expect). It creates a situation where the next generation of farmers require, and ask for, increased government support."

   a. Explain why subsidies to farmers increase land values and generate windfall gains to current landowners.

   b. Some Canadian agricultural policies are based on the use of production quotas. Do such quota systems avoid the problem described by Professor Storey?

6. This question relates to the section *Linkages Between Markets* found on the MyEconLab (www.myeconlab.com). Soon after the Liberal government was elected in 1993, an "infrastructure" program was implemented that involved spending several billion dollars on bridges, highways, sewer systems, and so on. One of the alleged benefits of this program was to create thousands of jobs, not only in the construction industry but also elsewhere in the economy as construction workers spent their now-higher income on cars, clothing, entertainment, and so on. Discuss how such spending would create jobs in the construction industry. Why would you expect some jobs to be *lost* in other industries as a result of this program?

CHAPTER 6

Consumer Behaviour

LO LEARNING OBJECTIVES

In this chapter you will learn

1. the difference between marginal and total utility.
2. that utility-maximizing consumers adjust their expenditure until the marginal utility per dollar spent is equalized across products.
3. how any change in price generates both an income and a substitution effect on quantity demanded.
4. that consumer surplus is the "bargain" the consumer gets by paying less for the product than the maximum price he or she is willing to pay.
5. the difference between total value and marginal value.

Imagine that you are walking down the aisle of a supermarket looking for a late-night snack to have while you are studying. With only a $5 bill in your pocket, you must choose how to divide this $5 between frozen burritos and cans of Coke. How do you make this decision? In this chapter we look at how economists think about such problems—the theory of consumer behaviour. Not surprisingly, economists (being consumers themselves) think about consumers as caring both about the prices of the goods and the satisfaction they get from the goods.

The first two sections of the chapter explore the underpinnings of consumer behaviour and explain in some detail why demand curves are negatively sloped—and also discuss the rare situations in which demand curves might be positively sloped. The third and final section examines an important implication of having negatively sloped demand curves and introduces the concept of *consumer surplus,* which is part of the economic surplus that we discussed in Chapter 5. As you will see in later chapters, consumer surplus is useful in showing that free and competitive markets often generate socially efficient outcomes.

6.1 MARGINAL UTILITY AND CONSUMER CHOICE

utility The satisfaction or well-being that a consumer receives from consuming some good or service.

Consumers make all kinds of decisions—they choose to drink coffee or tea (or neither), to go to the movies, to dine out, and to buy excellent (or not so good) computer equipment. As we discussed in Chapter 1, economists assume that in making their choices, consumers are motivated to maximize their **utility**, the total satisfaction that they derive from the goods and services that they consume.

Utility cannot be measured directly. But our inability to measure it does not mean it is not a useful concept. You know that you derive satisfaction—or utility—from a good meal, listening to a CD, or taking a walk through a park. And we need some way to think about how you as a consumer make your decisions. As we will see in this chapter, it is possible to construct a useful theory of consumer behaviour based on the idea of *utility maximization*.

In developing our theory of consumer behaviour, we begin by considering the consumption of a single product. It is useful to distinguish between the consumer's **total utility**, which is the full satisfaction resulting from the consumption of that product by a consumer, and the consumer's **marginal utility**, which is the *additional* satisfaction resulting from consuming one more unit of that product. For example, the total utility of consuming five Cokes per day is the total satisfaction that those five Cokes provide. The marginal utility of the fifth Coke consumed is the additional satisfaction provided by the consumption of that Coke.[1]

total utility The total satisfaction resulting from the consumption of a given commodity by a consumer.

marginal utility The additional satisfaction obtained by a consumer from consuming one additional unit of a commodity.

Diminishing Marginal Utility

The central hypothesis of utility theory, often called the *law of diminishing marginal utility*, is as follows:

The utility that any consumer derives from *successive* units of a particular product consumed over some period of time diminishes as total consumption of the product increases (if the consumption of all other products is unchanged).

Consider your utility from using clean water, either for drinking, bathing, washing your dishes or clothes, or some other purpose. Some minimum quantity is very important and you would, if necessary, give up a considerable sum of money to obtain that quantity of water. Thus, your marginal utility of that basic quantity of water is very high. You will, of course, consume more than this bare minimum, but your marginal utility of successive litres of water used over a period of time will decline steadily.

We will consider evidence for this hypothesis later, but you can convince yourself that it is at least reasonable by asking a few questions. How much money would be needed to induce you to reduce your consumption of water by one litre per week? The answer is: very little. How much would induce you to reduce it by a second litre? By a third litre? To only one litre consumed per week? The answer to the last question is: quite a bit. The fewer litres you are already using, the higher the marginal utility of one more litre of water.

Utility Schedules and Graphs

In Figure 6-1 we make the assumption that utility can be measured, and thus the different amount of utility received from consuming different units can be compared. Although this is an unrealistic assumption, it is a very helpful one in allowing us to see the important difference between total and marginal utility. The figure illustrates the assumptions that have been made about utility, using Alison's daily consumption of Coke as an example. The table shows that Alison's total utility rises as she drinks more

---

[1] Technically, *incremental* utility is measured over a discrete interval, such as from four Cokes to five Cokes, whereas *marginal* utility is a rate of change measured over an infinitesimal interval. However, common usage applies the word *marginal* when the last unit is involved, even if a one-unit change is not infinitesimal. [9]

FIGURE 6-1   Alison's Total and Marginal Utility from Drinking Coke

Number of Cokes Alison Drinks Per Day	Alison's Total Utility	Alison's Marginal Utility
0	0	
		30
1	30	
		20
2	50	
		15
3	65	
		10
4	75	
		8
5	83	
		6
6	89	
		4
7	93	
		3
8	96	
		2
9	98	
		1
10	99	

Total utility rises, but marginal utility declines, as consumption increases. The marginal utility of 20, shown as the second entry in the third column, arises because Alison's total utility increases from 30 to 50—a difference of 20—with consumption of the second Coke. To indicate that the marginal utility is associated with the *change* from one level of consumption to another, the figures in the third column are recorded between the rows of the figures in the second column.

Coke per day. However, the utility that she gets from each *additional* Coke per day is less than that of the previous one—that is, her marginal utility declines as the quantity she consumes rises. [10] The data are graphed in the two parts of Figure 6-1.

Maximizing Utility

Economists assume that consumers try to make themselves as well off as they possibly can in the circumstances in which they find themselves. In other words, consumers seek to maximize their total utility subject to the constraints they face—in particular, their income and the market prices of various products.

The Consumer's Decision   Now that we have examined the concepts of total utility and marginal utility, we are ready to answer the question posed at the beginning of the chapter: How should consumers decide to allocate their consumption of Cokes and burritos in such a way as to maximize their utility? Of course, we could ask the same question about any two goods, or any number of goods, but we will focus on Cokes and burritos to keep the example simple.

A simple answer to the question is that any utility-maximizing consumer should consume Cokes and burritos until the marginal utility from the last Coke consumed is equal to the marginal utility from the last burrito consumed. But this would be sensible only if the price of a Coke and the price of a burrito were the same. The correct answer is that the consumer should consume Cokes and burritos to the point where the marginal utility *per dollar spent* on the last Coke is just equal to the marginal utility *per dollar spent* on the last burrito. In this way, the consumer's utility will be maximized.

Let's consider a specific example. Suppose Alison is buying burritos for $3 each and Cokes for $1 each. Buying burritos represents a poor use of her money if the marginal utility from the last burrito equals the marginal utility from the last Coke. Why? Because Alison would be spending $3 on a burrito to get additional utility equal to what she could have acquired for only $1 by buying a Coke.

A utility-maximizing consumer allocates expenditures so that the utility obtained from the last dollar spent on each product is equal.

Imagine that Alison's utility from the last dollar spent on Coke is three times her utility from the last dollar spent on burritos. In this case, Alison can increase her total utility by switching a dollar of expenditure from burritos to Coke and by gaining the difference between the utilities of a dollar spent on each.

Alison will continue to switch her expenditure from burritos to Coke as long as her last dollar spent on Coke yields more utility than her last dollar spent on burritos. This switching, however, reduces the quantity of burritos consumed and, given the law of diminishing marginal utility, raises the marginal utility of burritos. At the same time, switching increases the quantity of Coke consumed and thereby lowers the marginal utility of Coke.

Eventually, the marginal utilities will have changed enough so that the utility received from the last dollar spent on Coke is just equal to the utility received from the last dollar spent on burritos. At this point, Alison gains nothing from further switches. (In fact, switching further would *reduce* her total utility.)

So much for the simple example. What can we say more generally about utility maximization? Suppose we denote the marginal utility of the last unit of product X by MU_X and its price by p_X. Let MU_Y and p_Y refer, respectively, to the marginal utility of a second product Y and its price. The marginal utility per dollar spent on X will be MU_X/p_X. For example, if the last unit of X increases utility by 30 and costs $3, its marginal utility per dollar is 30/3 = 10. If the last unit of Y increases utility by 10 and costs $1, its marginal utility per dollar is 10/1 = 10. With these numbers, the marginal utilities from the last dollar spent on X and Y are equal.

The condition required for a consumer to be maximizing utility, for any pair of products, is

$$\frac{MU_X}{p_X} = \frac{MU_Y}{p_Y} \tag{6-1}$$

Practise with Study Guide Chapter 6, Exercise 1 and Short-Answer Question 1.

This equation says that a utility-maximizing consumer will allocate expenditure so that the utility gained from the last dollar spent on one product is equal to the utility gained from the last dollar spent on any other product.

This is the fundamental equation of marginal utility theory. A consumer demands each good up to the point at which the marginal utility per dollar spent on it is the same as the marginal utility per dollar spent on every other good. When this condition is met for all goods, the consumer cannot increase utility further by reallocating expenditure. That is, utility will be maximized.

Notice from our example that when Alison is deciding how much of a given product to purchase, she compares the utility from that product to the utility she could derive from spending the same money on other things. Thus, the idea of *opportunity cost* is central to our theory of consumer behaviour.

When expenditure is adjusted to maximize utility, the value to the consumer of consuming the marginal unit of some good is just equal to the opportunity cost—the value to the consumer of the money used to make the purchase.

An Alternative Interpretation If we rearrange the terms in Equation 6-1, we can gain additional insight into consumer behaviour.

$$\frac{MU_X}{MU_Y} = \frac{p_X}{p_Y} \tag{6-2}$$

The right side of this equation is the *relative* price of the two goods. It is determined by the market and is beyond Alison's control. She reacts to these market prices but is powerless to change them. The left side is the *relative* ability of the two goods to add to Alison's utility. This is within her control because in determining the quantities of different goods to buy, she also determines their marginal utilities. (If you have difficulty seeing why, look again at Figure 6-1.)

If the two sides of Equation 6-2 are not equal, Alison can increase her total utility by rearranging her purchases of X and Y. Suppose that the price of X is $4 and the price of Y is $2. The right-hand side of Equation 6-2 is then $p_X/p_Y = 4/2 = 2$. Remember that Alison can do nothing to change the right-hand side of this equation—the prices are determined in the market and are beyond her control. Suppose also that Alison is currently purchasing X and Y such that the marginal utility for X is 12 and the marginal utility for Y is 4. The left-hand side of Equation 6-2 is then $MU_X/MU_Y = 12/4 = 3$. In this case $MU_X/MU_Y > p_X/p_Y$. Alison can increase her total utility by increasing her purchases of X and reducing her purchases of Y until the ratio MU_X/MU_Y is equal to 2, the same as the ratio of the prices. If she reduces her purchases of Y by 2 units (at $2 each) she frees up $4 and is able to buy one more unit of X (at $4 each). Because that one extra unit of X had a marginal utility of 12, whereas the two units of Y that she gave up had a marginal utility of only 4 each, Alison's total utility has increased as a result of this switch. In this case, she will continue to switch until the ratio of MU_X/MU_Y is equal to p_X/p_Y. At this point Alison cannot increase her total utility any further by rearranging her purchases between the two products.

Consider what Alison is doing. She is faced with a set of prices that she cannot change. She responds to these prices and maximizes her utility by adjusting the things that she *can* change—the quantities of the various goods that she purchases—until Equation 6-2 is satisfied for all pairs of products.

It may seem unrealistic to argue that consumers maximize utility in the precise way we have described. After all, who stands in the grocery store and computes ratios of marginal utilities and prices? Keep in mind, though, that utility theory is used by economists to predict how consumers will behave when faced with such events as changing prices and incomes. As long as consumers seek to do the best they can for themselves with their limited resources, the consumer's actual thought process does not concern us. The theory is not meant to be a description of *how* they reach their decisions but is rather a convenient way of discovering the *implications* of their maximizing behaviour. Like many theories, utility-maximization theory leads to predictions that can be tested empirically. Economists continue to use the theory of utility maximization because its predictions are rarely rejected by the data. One of the most important of these predictions is that consumers who act as if they are following a rule like Equation 6-2 have negatively sloped demand curves for goods and services. In the next section we derive this result.

The Consumer's Demand Curve

To derive the consumer's demand curve for a product, we need to ask what happens when there is a change in the price of that product. As an example, let us derive Alison's demand curve for Coke. Consider Equation 6-2 and let X represent Coke and Y represent *all other products taken together*. In this case, the price of Y is interpreted as the average price of all other products. What will Alison do if, with all other prices remaining constant, there is an increase in the price of Coke? When the price of Coke rises, the right side of Equation 6-2 increases. But, until Alison adjusts consumption, the left side is unchanged. Thus, after the price changes but before Alison reacts, she will be in a position in which the following circumstance prevails:

$$\frac{MU \text{ of Coke}}{MU \text{ of } Y} < \frac{\text{price of Coke}}{\text{price of } Y}$$

What does Alison do to restore the equality? The hypothesis of diminishing marginal utility tells us that as she buys fewer Cokes, the *marginal* utility of Coke will rise and thereby increase the ratio on the left side. Thus, in response to an increase in the price of Coke, with all other prices constant, Alison reduces her consumption of Coke until the marginal utility of Coke rises sufficiently that Equation 6-2 is restored.

This analysis leads to the basic prediction of demand theory:

A rise in the price of a product (with all other determinants of demand held constant) leads each consumer to reduce the quantity demanded of the product.

If this is what each consumer does, it is also what all consumers taken together do. Thus, the theory of consumer behaviour that we have considered here predicts a negatively sloped market demand curve in addition to a negatively sloped demand curve for each individual consumer. *Extensions in Theory 6-1* shows how we can obtain a market demand curve by adding up the demand curves of individual consumers.

Practise with Study Guide Chapter 6, Exercise 2.

6.2 INCOME AND SUBSTITUTION EFFECTS OF PRICE CHANGES

We have just seen the relationship between the *law of diminishing marginal utility* and the slope of the consumer's demand curve for some product. Here we consider an alternative method for thinking about the slope of an individual's demand curve. From the discussion in *Extensions in Theory 6-1*, this alternative method can also be used to think about the slope of a market demand curve.

Let's consider Tony, a student who loves to eat—and especially loves to eat ice cream. A fall in the price of ice cream affects Tony in two ways. First, it provides an incentive to buy more ice cream (and less of other things) because eating ice cream is now a cheaper way to satisfy some of his cravings. Thus, a reduction in the price of ice cream—which, with all other prices constant means a fall in the *relative* price of ice cream—leads Tony to *substitute* away from other products toward ice cream.

EXTENSIONS IN THEORY 6-1

Market and Individual Demand Curves

Market demand curves show how much is demanded by all purchasers. For example, in Figure 3-1, the market demand for carrots is 85 tonnes when the price is $40 per tonne. This 85 tonnes is the sum of the quantities demanded by millions of different consumers. The demand curve in Figure 3-1 also tells us that when the price rises to $60, the total quantity demanded falls to 65 tonnes per year. This quantity, too, can be traced back to individual consumers.

The market demand curve is the horizontal sum of the demand curves of individual consumers. It is the horizontal sum because we wish to add quantities

demanded at a given price, and quantities are measured in the horizontal direction on a conventional demand curve.

The figure below illustrates a market made up of only two consumers, Alison and Brenda. At a price of $3, Alison purchases 2 units and Brenda purchases 4 units; thus together they purchase 6 units, yielding one point on the market demand curve. No matter how many consumers are involved, the process is the same: Add the quantities demanded by all consumers at each price, and the result is the market demand curve.

Second, because the price of ice cream has fallen, Tony has more *purchasing power* or **real income** available to spend on all products. Suppose the price of premium ice cream fell from $5.00 to $4.00 per litre and Tony was in the habit of eating half a litre of ice cream a day. In the course of a 30-day month, Tony could keep his ice cream habit unchanged but save $15.00, money that would be available for any purpose—more ice cream, video rentals, or photocopies of your economics notes.

Let's now explore these two separate effects in a little more detail.

real income Income expressed in terms of the purchasing power of money income, that is, the quantity of goods and services that can be purchased with the money income.

The Substitution Effect

To isolate the effect of the change in relative price when the price of ice cream falls, we can consider what would happen if we also reduce Tony's money income to restore the original purchasing power. Suppose Tony's uncle sends him a monthly allowance for ice cream, and when the price of ice cream falls, the allowance is reduced so that Tony can buy just as much ice cream—and everything else—as he could before. Tony's purchasing power will be unchanged. If his behaviour remains unchanged, however, he will no longer be maximizing his utility. Recall that utility maximization requires that the ratio of marginal utility to price be the same for all goods. In our example, with no change in behaviour, the quantities (and hence marginal utilities) and the prices of all goods other than ice cream are unchanged. The quantity of ice cream is also unchanged, but the price has fallen. To maximize his utility after the price of ice cream falls, Tony must therefore increase his consumption (reduce his marginal utility) of ice cream and reduce his consumption of other goods.

When purchasing power is held constant, the change in the quantity demanded of a good whose relative price has changed is called the **substitution effect** of the price change.[2]

The substitution effect increases the quantity demanded of a good whose price has fallen and reduces the quantity demanded of a good whose price has risen.

substitution effect The change in the quantity of a good demanded resulting from a change in its relative price (holding real income constant).

The Income Effect

To examine the substitution effect, we reduced Tony's *money* income following the price reduction so that we could see the effect of the relative price change, holding purchasing power constant. Now we want to see the effect of the change in purchasing power, *holding relative prices constant at their new value.* To do this, suppose that after Tony has adjusted his purchases to the new price and his reduced income, he then calls his uncle and pleads to have his allowance restored to its original (higher) amount. Tony's uncle agrees, and Tony's money income is returned to its original level. If we assume that ice cream is a normal good, Tony will increase his consumption of ice cream (even beyond the increase we have already seen as a result of the substitution effect). The change in the quantity of ice cream demanded as a result of Tony's reaction to increased real income is called the **income effect**.

The income effect leads consumers to buy more of a product whose price has fallen, provided that the product is a normal good.

income effect The change in the quantity of a good demanded resulting from a change in real income (holding relative prices constant).

---

2 This measure, which isolates the substitution effect by holding the consumer's purchasing power constant, is known as the *Slutsky Effect.* A related but slightly different measure that holds the consumer's level of utility constant is discussed in the appendix to this chapter.

Notice that the size of the income effect depends on the amount of income spent on the good whose price changes and on the amount by which the price changes. In our example, if Tony were initially spending half of his income on ice cream, a reduction in the price of ice cream from $5 to $4 would be equivalent to a 10-percent increase in real income (20 percent of 50 percent). Now consider a different case: The price of gasoline falls by 20 percent. For a consumer who was spending only 5 percent of income on gas, this is equivalent to only a 1-percent increase in real income (20 percent of 5 percent).

The Slope of the Demand Curve

We have now divided Tony's reaction to a change in the price of ice cream into a substitution effect and an income effect. Of course, when the price changes, Tony moves directly from the initial consumption pattern to the final one; we do not observe any "halfway" consumption pattern. However, by breaking this movement into two parts for analytical purposes, we are able to study Tony's total change in quantity demanded as a response to a change in relative prices plus a response to a change in real income.

What is true for Tony is also true, in general terms, for all consumers. The substitution effect leads consumers to increase their demand for goods whose prices fall. The income effect leads consumers to buy more of all normal goods whose prices fall.

Putting the income and substitution effects together gives the following statement of the law of demand:

Because of the combined operation of the income and substitution effects, the demand curve for any normal commodity will be negatively sloped. Thus, a fall in price will increase the quantity demanded.

Practise with Study Guide Chapter 6, Exercise 3.

Figure 6-2 illustrates how the combination of the substitution effect and the income effect determines the slope of any demand curve. In each part of the figure, we begin at point A with the price p_0. We then consider a reduction in the price to p_1. In each case, the substitution effect (shown by the green arrow) increases the quantity demanded. In each case there is also an income effect (the red arrow), but the size and sign of the income effect differs in each case. The sum of the income and substitution effects determines how overall quantity demanded responds to the price reduction. Note that all normal goods have negatively shaped demand curves. The same is true for *most* inferior goods. The figure illustrates why in the case of an inferior good the income effect must be very strong in order to generate a positively sloped demand curve. This is a very rare case in economics, but there is some interesting history behind it.

Giffen Goods   Great interest was generated by the apparent refutation of the law of demand by the English economist Sir Robert Giffen (1837–1910). He is alleged to have observed that when a rise in the price of imported wheat led to an increase in the price of bread, members of the British working class *increased* their consumption of bread, suggesting that their demand curve for bread was positively sloped.

As is clear in Figure 6-2, two things must be true in order for a good to have a positively sloped demand curve—a so-called **Giffen good**. First, the good must be an inferior good, meaning that a reduction in real income leads households to purchase *more* of that good. Second, the good must take a large proportion of total household expenditure and therefore have a large income effect. Bread was indeed a dietary staple of the British working classes during the nineteenth century. A rise in the price of bread would therefore cause a large reduction in people's real income. This could lead people to eat more bread (and less meat) in order to consume enough calories to stay alive.

Giffen good An inferior good for which the income effect outweighs the substitution effect so that the demand curve is positively sloped.

FIGURE 6-2   Income and Substitution Effects of a Price Change

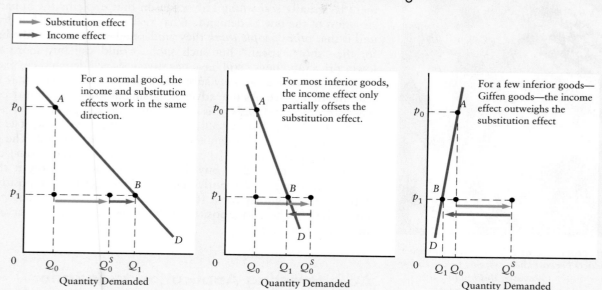

Demand curves for inferior goods are negatively sloped unless the income effect outweighs the substitution effect. In each of the diagrams, the initial price is p_0 and the initial quantity demanded is Q_0. Thus, A is a point on all three demand curves. For all three goods, a price reduction to p_1 creates a substitution effect that increases quantity demanded to Q_0^S.

For normal goods in part (i), the reduction in price increases real income and leads to a further increase in quantity demanded. The income effect is shown as the increase from Q_0^S to Q_1. The total increase in quantity demanded is therefore from Q_0 to Q_1, and point B is on the negatively sloped demand curve.

For inferior goods, the price reduction causes an increase in real income that leads to a *reduction* in quantity demanded. If the good makes up a small fraction of the consumer's total expenditure, which is the case for most goods, then this income effect will be small. In part (ii), the income effect reduces quantity demanded from Q_0^S to Q_1 and the overall change is therefore from Q_0 to Q_1. In this case, the income effect does not fully offset the substitution effect and so the demand curve is still negatively sloped through point B. In part (iii), the income effect is very large, reducing quantity demanded from Q_0^S to Q_1 and the overall change is therefore a *reduction* in quantity demanded from Q_0 to Q_1. In this case the demand curve is positively sloped through point B. This is the case of a Giffen good.

Though possible, such cases are all but unknown in the modern world, for in all but the poorest societies, typical households do not spend large proportions of their incomes on any single inferior good.

Conspicuous Consumption Goods Thorstein Veblen (1857–1929), in *The Theory of the Leisure Class,* noted that some products were consumed not for their intrinsic qualities but because they had "snob appeal." He suggested that the more expensive such a commodity became, the greater might be its ability to confer status on its purchaser.

Consumers might value diamonds, for example, precisely because everyone knows they are expensive. Thus, a fall in price might lead them to stop buying diamonds and to switch to a more satisfactory object of conspicuous consumption. They may behave in the same way with respect to luxury cars, buying them *because* they are expensive. Does this sort of behaviour violate our basic theory of utility maximization?

Some people are attracted to very expensive products because their extreme prices confer status on the purchaser. But holding the amount of this status constant, people would still probably buy more at lower prices, suggesting a downward-sloping demand curve.

Two comments are in order. First, in a case where individuals appear to buy more goods at a higher price *because of the high price*, there is actually something else going on that explains the apparent violation of the law of demand. What really appeals to such individuals is that *other people think* they paid a high price—this is the basis for the "snob appeal." But such snobs would still buy more at a lower price (and hence still have negatively sloped demand curves) as long as they were absolutely sure that other people *thought* they had paid the high price. As one advertising slogan for a discount department store puts it: "Only you know how little you paid."

Second, even if such conspicuous consumers do exist, it is still unlikely that the *market* demand curve is positively sloped. The reason is easy to discover. The fact that countless lower-income consumers would be glad to buy diamonds or Cadillacs only if these commodities were sufficiently inexpensive suggests that positively sloped demand curves for a few individual wealthy households are much more likely than a positively sloped *market* demand curve for the same commodity.

An Interesting Application to Taxation

Finally, note that the logic of breaking down a price change into the separate income and substitution effects is not limited to the analysis of demand. The same logic applies to two things that most individuals supply—their work effort (to labour markets) and their saving (to financial markets). For example, for a given pre-tax wage, a change in the income-tax rate will change the after-tax wage that workers earn. It will also change the after-tax interest rate that savers (lenders) receive. Using the same analysis as we used above with Tony and the change in the price of ice cream, we can analyze the effects of tax changes on the supply of work effort and the supply of saving. In both cases, in order to understand the overall effect of the change in tax rates, we need to make the important distinction between the income effects and the substitution effects.

---

myeconlab

For a detailed discussion of the income and substitution effects of tax changes, on both the supply of work effort and the supply of saving, look for "Do Taxes Discourage Work Effort and Saving?" in the *Additional Topics* section of this book's MyEconLab.

www.myeconlab.com

6.3 CONSUMER SURPLUS

Our discussion of consumer behaviour has led us to a better understanding of demand curves and how they are derived. At the heart of our discussion has been the concept of utility, and the law of diminishing marginal utility.

In this section we introduce the important concept of *consumer surplus,* which requires that we make a clear distinction between *marginal* and *total* utility. Understanding this difference will help us to resolve a famous paradox in the history of economic theory.

The Concept

Imagine yourself facing an either/or choice concerning some particular product, say, ice cream: You can have the amount you are now consuming, or you can have none of it. Suppose you would be willing to pay as much as $100 per month for the eight litres of gourmet ice cream that you now consume, rather than do without it. Further suppose you actually buy those eight litres for only $40 instead of $100. What a bargain! You have paid $60 less than the most you were willing to pay. Actually this sort of bargain occurs every day in the economy. Indeed, it is so common that the $60 "saved" in this example has been given a name: *consumer surplus.* **Consumer surplus** is the difference between the total value that consumers place on all the units consumed of some product and the payment they actually make to purchase that amount of the product.

Consumer surplus is a direct consequence of negatively sloped demand curves. This is easiest to understand if you think of an individual's demand curve as showing his or her willingness to pay for successive units of the product. (You may recall our discussion of this point in the final section of Chapter 5.) To illustrate the concept, suppose we have interviewed your classmate Moira and displayed the information from the interview in the table in Figure 6-3. Our first question to Moira is, "If you were drinking no milk at all, how much would you be willing to pay for one litre per week?" With no hesitation she replies, "$6.00." We then ask, "If you had already consumed that one litre, how much would you be willing to pay for a second litre per week?" After a bit of thought, she answers, "$3.00." Adding one litre per week with each question, we discover that she would be willing to pay $2.00 to get a third litre per week and $1.60, $1.20, $1.00, $0.80, $0.60, $0.50, and $0.40 for successive litres from the fourth to the tenth litre per week.

The sum of the values that she places on each litre of milk gives us the *total value* that she places on all ten litres. In this case, Moira values the ten litres of milk per week at $17.10. This is the amount that she would be willing to pay if she faced the either/or choice of 10 litres or none. This is also the amount she would be willing to pay if she were offered the milk one litre at a time and charged the maximum she was willing to pay for each litre.

However, Moira does not have to pay a different price for each litre of milk she consumes each week; she can buy all she wants at the prevailing market price. Suppose the price is $1.00 per litre. She will buy six litres per week because she values the sixth litre just at the market price but all earlier litres at higher amounts. She does not buy a seventh litre because she values it at less than the market price.

Because Moira values the first litre at $6.00 but gets it for $1.00, she makes a "profit" of $5.00 on that litre. Between her $3.00 valuation of the second litre and what she has to pay for it, she clears a "profit" of $2.00. She clears a "profit" of $1.00 on the third litre and so on. This "profit," which is shown in the third column of the table, is Moira's consumer surplus on each litre of milk.

We can calculate Moira's total consumer surplus of $8.80 per week by summing her surplus on each litre; we can calculate the same total by first summing what she would be willing to pay for all six litres, which is $14.80, and then subtracting the $6.00 that she actually does pay.

consumer surplus The difference between the total value that consumers place on all units consumed of a commodity and the payment that they actually make to purchase that amount of the commodity.

Practise with Study Guide Chapter 6, Short-Answer Question 5.

FIGURE 6-3   Moira's Consumer Surplus on Milk Consumption

Litres of Milk Moira Consumes Per Week	Amount Moira Is Willing to Pay to Obtain This Litre	Moira's Consumer Surplus on Each Litre If Milk Costs $1.00 Per Litre
First	$6.00	$5.00
Second	3.00	2.00
Third	2.00	1.00
Fourth	1.60	0.60
Fifth	1.20	0.20
Sixth	1.00	0.00
Seventh	0.80	—
Eighth	0.60	—
Ninth	0.50	—
Tenth	0.40	—

Consumer surplus on each unit consumed is the difference between the market price and the maximum price that the consumer is willing to pay to obtain that unit. The table shows the value that Moira puts on successive litres of milk consumed each week. Her negatively sloped demand curve shows that she would be willing to pay progressively smaller amounts for each additional unit consumed. If the market price is $1.00 per litre, Moira will buy six litres of milk per week and pay the amount in the dark shaded area. The total value she places on these six litres is the entire shaded area. Her consumer surplus is the light shaded area.

For any unit consumed, consumer surplus is the difference between the maximum amount the consumer is prepared to pay for that unit and the price the consumer actually pays.

Practise with Study Guide Chapter 6, Exercises 4 and 5.

For each unit of a product consumed, consumer surplus is the difference between what the consumer is willing to pay for that unit and what the consumer actually pays.

The data in the first two columns of the table give Moira's demand curve for milk. It is her demand curve because she will go on buying litres of milk as long as she values each litre at least as much as the market price she must pay for it. When the market price is $6.00 per litre, she will buy only one litre; when it is $3.00, she will buy two litres; and so on. The total valuation is the area below her demand curve, and consumer surplus is the part of the area that lies above the price line. These areas are shown in Figure 6-3.

Figure 6-4 shows that the same relationship holds for the smooth market demand curve that indicates the total amount that all consumers would buy at each price. Figure 6-3 is a bar chart because we only allowed Moira to vary her consumption in discrete units of one litre at a time. Had we allowed her to vary her consumption of milk one drop at a time, we could have traced out a continuous curve similar to the one shown in Figure 6-4.

The market demand curve shows the valuation that consumers place on each unit of the product. For any given quantity, the area under the demand curve and above the price line shows the consumer surplus received from consuming those units.

Applications

Consumer surplus is an important concept. It will prove useful in later chapters when we evaluate the performance of the market system.[3] For now, however, we discuss two examples where the concept of consumer surplus helps us to understand apparently paradoxical market outcomes. Central to both examples is the distinction between total value and marginal value.

The Paradox of Value Early economists, struggling with the problem of what determines the relative prices of products, encountered what they called the *paradox of value*. Many necessary products, such as water, have prices that are low compared to the prices of luxury products, such as diamonds. Water is necessary to our existence, whereas diamonds are used mostly for luxury purposes and are not in any way essential to life. Does it not seem odd, then, that water is so cheap and diamonds are so expensive? As it took a long time to resolve this apparent paradox, it is not surprising that even today, similar confusions cloud many policy discussions.

The first step in resolving this paradox is to use the distinction between the total and marginal values of any product. We have seen already that the area under the demand curve is a measure of the *total value* placed on all of the units that the consumer consumes. For example, for all consumers together, the total value of consuming Q_0 units is the entire shaded area (light and dark) under the demand curve in Figure 6-4.

What about the *marginal value* that consumers place on one additional unit? This is given by the product's market price, which is p_0 in Figure 6-4. Facing a market price of p_0, each consumer buys all the units that he or she values at p_0 or greater but does not purchase any units valued at less than p_0. Therefore, each consumer values the last unit consumed of any product at that product's price.

The second step in resolving the paradox is to recognize that supply plays just as important a role in determining market price as does demand. Early economists thought the price or "value" of a product depended only on its use by consumers—that is, by demand. But we now know that supply aspects are just as important—including the costs of production, the number of producers, and so on.

Given this joint importance of supply and demand, it is easy to imagine a situation in which two products, such as water and diamonds, have very different market prices (and hence *marginal* values) even if their respective prices do not reflect the *total* value consumers place on the two goods. Figure 6-5 resolves the diamond–water paradox.

FIGURE 6-4 Consumer Surplus for the Market

Total consumer surplus is the area under the demand curve and above the price line. The area under the demand curve shows the total valuation that consumers place on all units consumed. For example, the total value that consumers place on Q_0 units is the entire shaded area under the demand curve up to Q_0. At a market price of p_0, the amount paid for Q_0 units is the dark shaded area. Hence consumer surplus is the light shaded area.

---

[3] Indeed, consumer surplus is part of what in Chapter 5 we called *economic surplus* when we discussed market efficiency. We will return to a discussion of market efficiency in Chapter 12.

FIGURE 6-5   Resolving the Paradox of Value

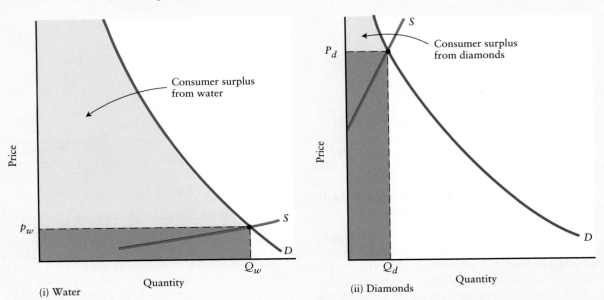

The market price of a product bears no necessary relationship to the total value that consumers place on that amount. The graph presents hypothetical demand curves for water and diamonds. The total value that consumers place on Q_w units of water, as shown by the total shaded area under the demand curve, is great. The total value that consumers place on Q_d units of diamonds is shown by the total shaded area under the demand curve for diamonds. This is clearly less than the total value placed on water.

The large supply of water makes water plentiful and makes water low in price, as shown by p_w in part (i) of the figure. The relatively low supply of diamonds makes diamonds scarce and keeps diamonds high in price, as shown by p_d in part (ii) of the figure. The high total value for water, combined with its low price, leads to a large consumer surplus for water. For diamonds, the low total value and high price lead to a small consumer surplus.

The resolution of the paradox of value is that a good that is very plentiful, such as water, will have a low price and will thus be consumed to the point where all consumers place a low value on the last unit consumed, whether or not they place a high value on their *total* consumption of the product. By contrast, a product that is relatively scarce in the marketplace will have a high market price, and consumption will therefore stop at a point where consumers place a high value on the last unit consumed, regardless of the value that they place on their total consumption of the good.

Because the market price of a product depends on both demand and supply, there is nothing paradoxical in there being a product on which consumers place a high *total* value (such as water) selling for a low price and hence having a low *marginal* value.

Attitude Surveys   Attitude surveys often ask people which of several alternatives they prefer. Such questions reveal *total* rather than *marginal* utilities. Where the behaviour being predicted involves an either/or decision, such as whether to vote for the Liberal or Conservative or NDP or any other candidate, the total utility that is attached to each party or candidate will indeed be what matters, because the voter must choose one and reject the others. However, where the decision is a marginal one regarding a little more or a little less, total utility is not what will determine behaviour. If one attempts to predict behaviour in these cases from knowledge of total utilities, even if the information is correct, one will make serious errors.

Here are two examples of how surveys can be misinterpreted. A Canadian market research survey recently asked people to name the household device they thought was most important. Though many appliances ranked highly, vacuum cleaners were judged by the most households as being the most important device. Suppliers of a new version of vacuum cleaner used the survey to predict demand but subsequently found that it had failed to do so accurately. A post-mortem revealed that most people did not respond to the sales promotion because they already had a vacuum cleaner and were unwilling to pay the advertised price for a second one. In other words, although the *total* utility they got from their vacuum cleaner was high, the utility they would get from an additional one—their *marginal* utility—was low.

For a second example, a political party in the United Kingdom conducted a survey to determine what types of public expenditure people thought most valuable. Unemployment benefits rated very highly. The party was subsequently surprised when it aroused great voter hostility by advocating an increase in unemployment benefits. Although the party was surprised, there was nothing inconsistent or irrational in the voters' feeling that protection of the unemployed was a very good thing, providing a high total utility, but that *additional* payments were unnecessary, and therefore had a low marginal utility.

S U M M A R Y

6.1 MARGINAL UTILITY AND CONSUMER CHOICE

- Marginal utility theory distinguishes between the total utility from the consumption of *all units* of some product and the incremental (or marginal) utility derived from consuming *one more unit* of the product.
- The basic assumption in marginal utility theory is that the utility consumers derive (over some given time period) from the consumption of successive units of a product diminishes as the number of units consumed increases.
- Consumers are assumed to make their decisions in a way that maximizes their utility. Utility-maximizing consumers make their choices such that the utilities derived from the last dollar spent on each product are equal. For two goods X and Y, utility will be maximized when

$$\frac{MU_X}{p_X} = \frac{MU_Y}{p_Y}$$

- Demand curves have negative slopes because when the price of one product falls, each consumer responds by increasing purchases of that product sufficiently to restore the ratio of that product's marginal utility to its now lower price (MU/p) to the same level achieved for all other products.

6.2 INCOME AND SUBSTITUTION EFFECTS OF PRICE CHANGES

- A change in the price of a product generates both an income effect and a substitution effect. The substitution effect is the reaction of the consumer to the change in relative prices, with purchasing power (real income) held constant. The substitution effect leads the consumer to increase purchases of the product whose relative price has fallen.
- The income effect is the reaction of the consumer to the change in purchasing power (real income) that is caused by the price change, holding relative prices constant at their new level. A fall in one price will lead to an increase in the consumer's real income and thus to an increase in purchases of all normal goods.
- The combined income and substitution effects ensure that the quantity demanded of any normal good will increase when its price falls, other things being equal. Normal goods, therefore, have negatively sloped demand curves.
- An inferior good will have a negatively sloped demand curve unless the income effect is strong enough to outweigh the substitution effect. This situation is very rare and is called a Giffen good.

6.3 CONSUMER SURPLUS

- For each unit of a product, consumer surplus is the difference between what consumers would be *willing to pay* for that unit and what consumers *actually pay* for that unit.
- Consumer surplus arises because demand curves are negatively sloped and consumers purchase units of a product up to the point where the value of the marginal unit consumed—the *marginal value*—equals the market price. On all units before the marginal unit, consumers value the product more than the price and hence they earn consumer surplus.

- It is important to distinguish between total and marginal values because choices concerning a bit more and a bit less cannot be predicted from a knowledge of total values. The paradox of value involves a confusion between total value and marginal value.
- Price is related to the *marginal* value that consumers place on having a bit more or a bit less of some product; it bears no necessary relationship to the *total* value that consumers place on all of the units consumed of that product.

KEY CONCEPTS

Total utility and marginal utility
Utility maximization
Equality of *MU/p* across different
  goods

Slope of the demand curve
Income effect and substitution effect
Giffen goods and conspicuous
  consumption goods

Consumer surplus
The paradox of value

STUDY EXERCISES

1. Fill in the blanks to make the following statements correct.

   a. Utility theory is based on the hypothesis that the _____ received from each additional unit of the good _____ as total consumption of the good increases.

   b. A utility-maximizing consumer will allocate expenditure such that the _____ per dollar spent on each product is _____ for all products.

   c. An equation that represents a utility-maximizing pattern of consumption of two goods, *A* and *B*, is _____.

   d. Marginal utility analysis tells us that a rise in the price of a good, *ceteris paribus*, leads each consumer to reduce the _____ of the good. This, in turn, predicts a _____ demand curve.

2. (X myeconlab) The table below shows how Brett's utility increases as the number of avocados he consumes (per month) increases. Brett's utility is measured in *utils,* a name that economists invented to describe units of utility.

Avocados	Total Utility (in utils)	Marginal Utility (in utils)
Zero	0	____
First	100	____
Second	185	____
Third	245	____
Fourth	285	____
Fifth	315	____
Sixth	335	____
Seventh	345	____
Eighth	350	

   a. Plot Brett's total utility on a scale diagram, with utils on the vertical axis and the number of avocados (per month) on the horizontal axis.

   b. Compute the marginal utility for each avocado and fill in the table.

   c. Plot the marginal utility on a scale diagram, with utils on the vertical axis and the number of avocados (per month) on the horizontal axis. (Make sure to plot marginal utility at the midpoints between units.)

   d. Explain why it is reasonable that Brett's utility increases by smaller and smaller amounts for each successive avocado consumed.

3. **myeconlab** In each of the cases listed below, identify whether Claudia's expenditure on each product should rise or fall in order to maximize her utility.

Case	Price of X ($)	Marginal Utility of X (units of utility)	Price of Y ($)	Marginal Utility of Y (units of utility)
A	10	2	5	3
B	12	4	4	2
C	3	1	6	2
D	4	2	4	2
E	8	4	4	3

4. **myeconlab** Rupert really loves pizza, but he eventually tires of it. The table below shows the highest price that Rupert is willing to pay for each successive pizza per week.

Pizza	Rupert's Willingness to Pay
First	$18
Second	$16
Third	$13
Fourth	$9
Fifth	$4
Sixth	$0

a. Suppose Rupert were to eat five pizzas per week. What is the total value Rupert would place on his five weekly pizzas?

b. If the market price is $10 per pizza, how many pizzas will Rupert eat per week?

c. If the market price is $10 per pizza, what is the weekly consumer surplus that Rupert gets from eating pizza?

5. Suppose there is a 10-percent increase in the prices of the following products. Explain whether you think the income effect in each case would be small or large, and why.

a. salt
b. blue jeans
c. canned vegetables
d. gasoline
e. mini-vans
f. rental apartments
g. luxury cars

6. Use the following diagram of a market for potted plants to answer the questions below about consumer surplus.

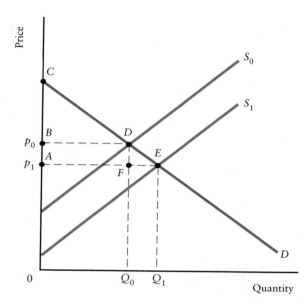

a. With demand curve D and supply curve S_0 the equilibrium price and quantity in this market are p_0 and Q_0. At the price p_0, what is the area that represents total consumer surplus in this market? (Use the letter point labels to describe the area.)

b. Now suppose supply increases to S_1. Determine the new equilibrium price and quantity. What is the area that now represents total consumer surplus?

c. At the new lower price, what is the area that represents the *increased* consumer surplus earned on the *original* units purchased?

d. At the new lower price, what is the area that represents consumer surplus earned on the *new* units purchased?

7. In what situations do the substitution effect and the income effect each predict a downward sloping demand curve? In what situations do they have opposing effects?

8. Consider the following supply-and-demand diagrams depicting the markets for X and Y, respectively. In the market for good X, supply is perfectly elastic, indicating that producers are prepared to supply any amount of X at price p_0.

a. In the market for X, demand increases from D_0 to D_1. Explain what happens to the *total* value that consumers place on X.

b. Explain how the increase in demand for X alters the *marginal* value that consumers place on X.

c. In the market for Y, a technological improvement causes supply to increase from S_0 to S_1, causing price to fall from p_0 to p_1. Explain what happens to the total value that consumers place *on a given quantity* of Y.

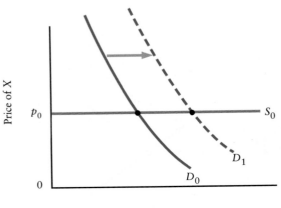

d. Explain why the increase in supply leads consumers to reduce their *marginal* value of Y even though there has been no change in their preferences regarding Y (and thus no shift in the demand curve).

9. Consider the market for some product. The demand and supply curves are given by:

Demand: $p = 30 - 4Q^D$
Supply: $p = 6 + 2Q^S$

a. Plot the demand and supply curves on a scale diagram. Compute the equilibrium price (p^*) and quantity (Q^*).

b. Show in the diagram the total value that consumers place on Q^* units of the good.
c. What is the value that consumers place on an *additional* unit of the good?
d. Now suppose that production costs fall and so the market supply curve shifts to a new position given by $p = 2 + 2Q^S$. How do consumers now value an additional unit of the good?
e. Explain why consumers' marginal value has fallen even though there has been no change in their preferences (and thus no change in the demand curve).

DISCUSSION QUESTIONS

1. Describe the difference in behaviour at a party at which drinks are free between someone who imbibes up to the point where the *marginal* value of more alcohol consumed is zero and someone who imbibes up to the point where the *average* value of alcohol consumed is zero.

2. Compare the consequences of the income effect of a drastic fall in food prices with the consequences of a rise in incomes when prices are constant.

3. Two U.S. economics professors, Jeff Biddle and Daniel Hamermesh, recently estimated that a 25-percent increase in wages will cause the average individual to reduce the time that he or she spends sleeping by about 1 percent. Interpret this finding in terms of the income and substitution effects of a wage change.

4. Consider the following common scenario. An economist is attending a conference in an unfamiliar city. She is in the mood for a high-quality dinner and wanders through the centre of the city looking for a restaurant. After narrowing her search to two establishments, she ultimately selects the restaurant with the higher prices. What might account for this behaviour?

5. Many medical and hospital services in Canada are provided at zero cost to all Canadians and are financed out of general government revenues. What would be the *marginal value* of such services consumed by each Canadian if the government provided the necessary resources to satisfy *all* demand? How does this relate to the *total* value that Canadians probably place on medical services?

Indifference Curves

In Chapter 6, we covered some basic material concerning the theory of demand; here we extend the treatment of demand theory by considering in more detail the assumptions about consumer behaviour that underlie the theory of demand.

The history of demand theory has seen two major breakthroughs. The first was *marginal utility theory*, which we used in Chapter 6. By distinguishing total and marginal values, this theory helped to explain the so-called paradox of value. The second breakthrough came with *indifference theory*, which showed that the stringent assumption of measurable utility (required for marginal utility theory) could be dispensed with. Indifference theory is based on the much weaker assumption that consumers can always say which of two consumption bundles they prefer without having to say *by how much* they prefer it.

6A.1 INDIFFERENCE CURVES

Suppose Hugh currently has available some specific bundle of goods, say, 18 units of clothing and 10 units of food. Now offer him an alternative bundle of, say, 13 units of clothing and 15 units of food. This alternative combination of goods has 5 fewer units of clothing and 5 more units of food than the first one. Whether Hugh prefers this new bundle depends on the relative valuation that he places on 5 more units of food and 5 fewer units of clothing. If he values the extra food more than the forgone clothing, he will prefer the new bundle to the original one. If he values the extra food less than the forgone clothing, he will prefer the original bundle. If Hugh values the extra food the same as the forgone clothing, he is said to be *indifferent* between the two bundles.

Suppose that after much trial and error, we have identified several bundles between which Hugh is indifferent. In other words, all bundles give him equal satisfaction or utility. They are shown in the table in Figure 6A-1.

Of course, there are combinations of the two products other than those enumerated in the table that will give Hugh the same level of utility. All of these combinations are shown in Figure 6A-1 by the smooth curve that passes through the points plotted from the table. This curve, called an *indifference curve*, shows all combinations of products that yield Hugh the same utility.

The consumer is indifferent between the combinations indicated by any two points on one indifference curve.

Any points above the curve show combinations of food and clothing that Hugh prefers to points on the curve. Consider, for example, the combination of 20 units of food and 18 units of clothing, represented by point *g* in Figure 6A-1. Although it may not be obvious that this bundle must be preferred to bundle *a* (which has more clothing but less food), it is obvious that it will be preferred to bundle *c* because both less clothing and less food are represented at *c* than at *g*. Inspection of the graph shows that any point above the curve will be superior to some points on the curve in the sense that it will contain both more food and more clothing than those points on the curve. However, because all points on the curve are equal in Hugh's eyes, any point above the curve must be superior to all points on the curve. By a similar argument, all points below and to the left of the curve represent bundles that are inferior to bundles represented by points on the curve.

Any point above an indifference curve is preferred to any point along that same indifference curve; any point on the curve is preferred to any point below it.

Diminishing Marginal Rate of Substitution

How much clothing would Hugh be willing to give up to get one more unit of food but to keep his utility unchanged? The answer to this question measures what is called Hugh's marginal rate of substitution of

FIGURE 6A-1   Hugh's Indifference Curve

Alternative Bundles Giving Hugh Equal Utility

Bundle	Clothing	Food
a	30	5
b	18	10
c	13	15
d	10	20
e	8	25
f	7	30

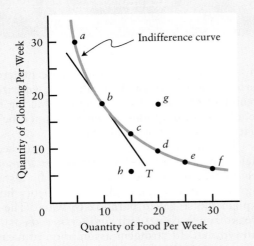

This indifference curve shows combinations of food and clothing that yield equal utility and between which Hugh is indifferent. The smooth curve through the points is an indifference curve; all combinations on it give Hugh equal utility. Point *g* above the line is a preferred combination to any point on the line; point *h* below the line is an inferior combination to any point on the line. The slope of the line *T* gives the marginal rate of substitution at point *b*. Moving down the indifference curve from *b* to *f*, the slope flattens, showing that the more food and the less clothing Hugh has, the less willing he is to sacrifice further clothing to get more food.

clothing for food. The *marginal rate of substitution (MRS)* is the amount of one product that a consumer is willing to give up to get one more unit of another product.

The first basic assumption of indifference theory is that the algebraic value of the *MRS* between two goods is always negative.

A negative *MRS* means that to increase consumption of one product, Hugh is prepared to decrease consumption of a second product. The negative value of the marginal rate of substitution is indicated graphically by the negative slope of indifference curves.

Consider a case in which Hugh has a lot of clothing and only a little food. Common sense suggests that he might be willing to give up quite a bit of plentiful clothing to get one more unit of scarce food. It suggests as well that if Hugh had little clothing and a lot of food he would be willing to give up only a little scarce clothing to get one more unit of already plentiful food.

This example illustrates the hypothesis of *diminishing marginal rate of substitution*. The less of one product, A, and the more of a second product, B,

that the consumer has already, the smaller the amount of A that the consumer will be willing to give up to get one additional unit of B. The hypothesis says that the marginal rate of substitution changes when the amounts of two products consumed change. The graphical expression of this hypothesis is that any indifference curve becomes flatter as the consumer moves downward and to the right along the curve. In Figure 6A-1, a movement downward and to the right means that Hugh is consuming less clothing and more food. The decreasing steepness of the curve means that Hugh is willing to sacrifice less and less clothing to get each additional unit of food. [11]

Diminishing marginal rate of substitution (MRS) is the second basic assumption of indifference theory.

The hypothesis of diminishing marginal rate of substitution is illustrated in Table 6A-1, which is based on the example in Figure 6A-1. The last column of the table shows the rate at which Hugh is prepared to sacrifice units of clothing per unit of food obtained. At first, Hugh will sacrifice 2.4 units of clothing to get 1 unit more of food, but as his consumption of clothing diminishes and his consump-

TABLE 6A-1	Hugh's Marginal Rate of Substitution Between Clothing and Food		
	(1)	(2)	(3)
			Marginal
	Change	Change	Rate of
	in	in	Substitution
Movement	Clothing	Food	(1) ÷ (2)
From *a* to *b*	−12	5	−2.4
From *b* to *c*	−5	5	−1.0
From *c* to *d*	−3	5	−0.6
From *d* to *e*	−2	5	−0.4
From *e* to *f*	−1	5	−0.2

The marginal rate of substitution of clothing for food declines (in absolute value) as the quantity of food increases. This table is based on Figure 6A-1. When Hugh moves from *a* to *b*, he gives up 12 units of clothing and gains 5 units of food; he remains at the same level of overall utility. At point *a*, Hugh is prepared to sacrifice 12 units of clothing for 5 units of food (i.e., 12/5 = 2.4 units of clothing per unit of food obtained). When he moves from *b* to *c*, he sacrifices 5 units of clothing for 5 units of food (a rate of substitution of 1 unit of clothing for each unit of food).

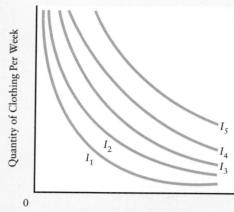

FIGURE 6A-2 Hugh's Indifference Map

An indifference map consists of a set of indifference curves. All points on a particular curve indicate alternative combinations of food and clothing that give Hugh equal utility. The farther the curve is from the origin, the higher is the level of utility it represents. For example, I_5 is a higher indifference curve than I_4, which means that all the points on I_5 give Hugh a higher level of utility than do the points on I_4.

tion of food increases, Hugh becomes less and less willing to sacrifice further clothing for more food.

The Indifference Map

So far, we have constructed only a single indifference curve for Hugh. However, starting at any other point in Figure 6A-1, such as *g*, there will be other combinations that will give Hugh equal utility. If the points indicating all of these combinations are connected, they will form another indifference curve. This exercise can be repeated many times, and we can thereby generate many indifference curves for Hugh. The farther any indifference curve is from the origin, the higher will be the level of Hugh's utility given by any of the points on the curve.

A set of indifference curves is called an *indifference map*, an example of which is shown in Figure 6A-2. It specifies the consumer's tastes by showing his rate of substitution between the two products for every possible level of current consumption of these products.

When economists say that a consumer's tastes are given, they do not mean that the consumer's current consumption pattern is given; rather, they mean that the consumer's entire indifference map is given.

6A.2 THE BUDGET LINE

Indifference curves illustrate consumers' tastes. To develop a complete theory of their choices, we must also illustrate the available alternatives. These are shown as the solid line *ab* in Figure 6A-3. That line, called a *budget line*, shows all the combinations of food and clothing that Hugh can buy if he spends a fixed amount of money, in this case his entire money income of $720 per week, at fixed prices of the products (in this case, $12 per unit for clothing and $24 per unit for food).

FIGURE 6A-3   Hugh's Budget Line

The budget line shows the quantities of goods available to a consumer given money income and the prices of goods. Any point in this diagram indicates a combination (or bundle) of so much food and so much clothing. Point x_1, for example, indicates 40 units of clothing and 10 units of food per week.

With an income of $720 a week and prices of $24 per unit for food and $12 per unit for clothing, Hugh's budget line is ab. This line shows all the combinations of F and C available to him if he spends the entire $720 per week. He could spend all of this money income on clothing and obtain 60 units of clothing and zero food each week. Or he could go to the other extreme and purchase only food, buying 30 units of F and zero units of C. Hugh could also choose an intermediate position and consume some of both goods—for example, spending $240 to buy 10 units of F and $480 to buy 40 units of C (point x_1). Points above the budget line, such as x_2, are not attainable.

Properties of the Budget Line

The budget line has several important properties:

1. Points on the budget line indicate bundles of products that use up the consumer's entire income. (Try, for example, the point 20C, 20F.)

2. Points between the budget line and the origin indicate bundles of products that cost less than the consumer's income. (Try, for example, the point 20C, 10F.)

3. Points above the budget line indicate combinations of products that cost more than the consumer's income. (Try, for example, the point 30C, 40F.)

The budget line shows all combinations of products that are available to the consumer given his money income and the prices of the goods that he purchases.

We can also show Hugh's alternatives with an equation that uses symbols to express the information contained in the budget line. Let E stand for Hugh's money income, which must be equal to his total expenditure on food and clothing. If p_F and p_C represent the money prices of food and clothing, respectively, and F and C represent the quantities of food and clothing that Hugh chooses, then his spending on food is equal to p_F times F, and his spending on clothing is equal to p_C times C. Thus the equation for the budget line is

$$E = p_F \times F + p_C \times C$$

The Slope of the Budget Line

Look again at Hugh's budget line in Figure 6A-3. The vertical intercept is 60 units of clothing, and the horizontal intercept is 30 units of food. Thus the slope is equal to -2. The minus sign means that increases in Hugh's purchases of one of the goods must be accompanied by decreases in his purchases of the other. The numerical value of the slope indicates how much of one good must be given up to obtain an additional unit of the other; in our example, the slope of -2 means that Hugh must forgo the purchase of 2 units of clothing to acquire 1 extra unit of food.

Recall that in Chapter 3 we contrasted the *absolute*, or *money*, price of a product with its *relative* price, which is the ratio of its absolute price to that of some other product or group of products. One important point is that the relative price determines the slope of the budget line. In terms of our example of food and clothing, the slope of the budget line is determined by the relative price of food in terms of clothing, p_F/p_C; with the price of food (p_F) at $24 per unit and the price of clothing (p_C) at $12 per unit, the slope of the budget line (in absolute value) is 2. [12]

The significance of the slope of Hugh's budget line for food and clothing is that it reflects his *oppor-*

tunity cost of food in terms of clothing. To increase food consumption while maintaining expenditure constant, Hugh must move along the budget line and therefore consume less clothing; the slope of the budget line determines how much clothing he must give up to obtain an additional unit of food.

The opportunity cost of food in terms of clothing is measured by the (absolute value of the) slope of the budget line, which is equal to the relative price ratio, p_F/p_C.

In the example, with fixed income and with the relative price of food in terms of clothing (p_F/p_C) equal to 2, Hugh must forgo the purchase of 2 units of clothing to acquire 1 extra unit of food. The opportunity cost of a unit of food is thus 2 units of clothing. Notice that the relative price (in our example, $p_F/p_C = 2$) is consistent with an infinite number of absolute prices. If $p_F = \$40$ and $p_C = \$20$, it is still necessary to sacrifice 2 units of clothing to acquire 1 unit of food.[4] Thus relative, not absolute, prices determine opportunity cost.

6A.3 THE CONSUMER'S UTILITY-MAXIMIZING CHOICES

An indifference map describes the preferences of a consumer, and a budget line describes the possibilities available to a consumer. To predict what a consumer will actually do, both sets of information must be combined, as is done in Figure 6A-4. Hugh's budget line is shown by the straight line, and the curves from the indifference map are also shown. Any point on the budget line is attainable, but which point will Hugh actually choose?

Because Hugh wishes to maximize utility, he wishes to reach the highest attainable indifference curve. Inspection of Figure 6A-4 shows that if Hugh purchases any bundle on the budget line at a point cut by an indifference curve, he can reach a higher indifference curve. Only when the bundle purchased is such that the indifference curve is tangent to the budget line is it impossible for Hugh to reach a higher curve by altering his purchases.

---

[4] Of course, with a given income, Hugh can afford much less of each at these higher money prices, but the opportunity cost of food in terms of clothing remains unchanged.

FIGURE 6A-4 Hugh's Utility-Maximizing Choice

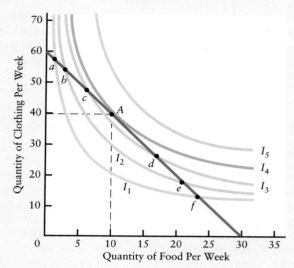

The consumer's utility is maximized at *A*, where an indifference curve is tangent to the budget line. Hugh has a money income of $720 per week and faces money prices of $12 per unit for clothing and $24 per unit for food. A combination of units of clothing and food indicated by point *a* on I_1 is attainable but, by moving along the budget line, Hugh can reach higher indifference curves. The same is true at *b* on I_2 and at *c* on I_3. At *A*, however, where an indifference curve (I_4) is tangent to the budget line, Hugh cannot reach a higher curve by moving along the budget line.

The consumer's utility is maximized at the point where an indifference curve is tangent to the budget line. At that point, the consumer's marginal rate of substitution for the two goods is equal to the relative prices of the two goods.

The intuitive explanation for this result is that if Hugh values goods differently from the way the market does, there is room for profitable exchange. Hugh can give up some of the good that he values relatively less than the market does and take in return some of the good that he values relatively more than the market does. When he is prepared to exchange goods at the same rate as they can be traded on the market, there is no further opportunity for him to raise utility by substituting one product for the other.

The theory thus proceeds by supposing that Hugh is presented with market prices that he cannot change and then analyzing how he adjusts to these prices by choosing a bundle of goods such that, at the margin, his own subjective evaluation of the goods coincides with the valuations given by market prices.

We will now use this theory to predict the typical consumer's response to a change in income and in prices.

The Consumer's Reaction to a Change in Income

A change in Hugh's money income will, *ceteris paribus*, shift his budget line. For example, if Hugh's income doubles, he will be able to buy twice as much of both food and clothing compared with any combination on his previous budget line. His budget line will therefore shift out parallel to itself to indicate this expansion in his consumption possibilities. (The fact that it will be a parallel shift is established by the previous demonstration that the slope of the budget line depends only on the relative prices of the two products.)

For each level of Hugh's income, there will be a utility-maximizing point at which an indifference curve is tangent to the relevant budget line. Each such utility-maximizing position means that Hugh is doing as well as possible at that level of income. If we move the budget line through all possible levels of income and if we join up all the utility-maximizing points, we will trace out what is called an *income–consumption line,* an example of which is shown in Figure 6A-5. This line shows how Hugh's consumption bundle changes as his income changes, with relative prices being held constant.

The Consumer's Reaction to a Change in Price

We already know that a change in the relative prices of the two goods changes the slope of the budget line. Given the price of clothing, for each possible price of food there is a different utility-maximizing consumption bundle for Hugh. If we connect these bundles, at a given money income, we will trace out a *price–consumption line,* as shown in Figure 6A-6. Notice that in this example, as the relative prices of food and clothing change, the quantities of food and clothing

FIGURE 6A-5 Hugh's Income–Consumption Line

The income–consumption line shows how the consumer's purchases react to a change in money income with relative prices being held constant. Increases in Hugh's money income cause a parallel outward shift of his budget line, moving his utility-maximizing point from *A* to *B* to *C*. By joining all the utility-maximizing points, Hugh's income–consumption line is traced out.

that Hugh purchases also change. In particular, as the price of food falls, Hugh buys more food and less clothing.

6A.4 DERIVING THE DEMAND CURVE

What happens to the consumer's demand for some product, say, gasoline, as the price of that product changes, *holding constant the prices of all other goods?*

If there were only two products purchased by consumers, we could derive a demand curve for one of the products from the price–consumption line like the one we showed for Hugh in Figure 6A-6. When there are many products, however, a change in the price of one product generally causes substitution toward (or away from) *all other goods.* Thus we would like to have a simple way of representing the individual's tastes in a world of many products.

In part (i) of Figure 6A-7, a new type of indifference map is plotted in which litres of gasoline per

FIGURE 6A-6 Hugh's Price–Consumption Line

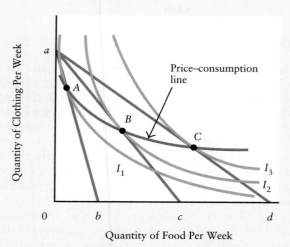

The price–consumption line shows how the consumer's purchases react to a change in one price with money income and other prices being held constant. Decreases in the price of food (with money income and the price of clothing held constant) pivot Hugh's budget line from *ab* to *ac* to *ad*. Hugh's utility-maximizing bundle moves from *A* to *B* to *C*. By joining all the utility-maximizing points, a price–consumption line is traced out, showing that Hugh purchases more food and less clothing as the price of food falls.

FIGURE 6A-7 Derivation of a Consumer's Demand Curve

(i) Price–consumption line

(ii) Demand curve

Every point on the price–consumption line corresponds to both a price of the product and a quantity demanded; this is the information required for a demand curve. In part (i), the consumer has a money income of $4000 and alternatively faces prices of $1.50, $1.00, and $0.50 per litre of gasoline, choosing positions *A*, *B*, and *C* at each price. The information for litres of gasoline demanded at each price is then plotted in part (ii) to yield the consumer's demand curve. The three points *a*, *b*, and *c* in part (ii) correspond to the points *A*, *B*, and *C* in part (i).

month are measured on the horizontal axis and the *value* of all other goods consumed per month is plotted on the vertical axis. We have in effect used "everything but gasoline" as the second product. The indifference curves in this figure then show the rate at which the consumer is prepared to substitute gasoline for money (which allows him to buy all other goods) at each level of consumption of gasoline and of all other goods.

To illustrate the derivation of demand curves, we use the numerical example shown in Figure 6A-7. The consumer is assumed to have an after-tax money income of $4000 per month. This level of money income is plotted on the vertical axis, showing that if the consumer consumes no gasoline, he can consume $4000 worth of other goods each month. When gasoline costs $1.50 per litre, the consumer could buy a maximum of 2667 litres per month. This set of choices gives rise to the innermost budget line. Given the consumer's tastes, utility is maximized at point *A*, consuming 600 litres of gasoline and $3100 worth of other products.

Next, let the price of gasoline fall to $1.00 per litre. Now the maximum possible consumption of gasoline is 4000 litres per month, giving rise to the middle budget line in the figure. The consumer's utility is maximized, as always, at the point where the new budget line is tangent to an indifference curve. At this point, B, the consumer is consuming 1200 litres of gasoline per month and spending $2800 on all other goods. Finally, let the price fall to 50 cents per litre. The consumer can now buy a maximum of 8000 litres per month, giving rise to the outermost of the three budget lines. The consumer maximizes utility by consuming 2200 litres of gasoline per month and spending $2900 on other products.

If we let the price vary over all possible amounts, we will trace out a complete price–consumption line, as shown in Figure 6A-7. The points derived in the preceding paragraph are merely three points on this line.

We have now derived all that we need to plot the consumer's demand curve for gasoline, now that we know how much the consumer will purchase at each price. To draw the curve, we merely replot the data from part (i) of Figure 6A-7 onto a demand graph, as shown in part (ii) of Figure 6A-7.

Like part (i), part (ii) has quantity of gasoline on the horizontal axis. By placing one graph under the other, we can directly transcribe the quantity determined on the upper graph to the lower one. We first do this for the 600 litres consumed on the innermost budget line. We now note that the price of gasoline that gives rise to that budget line is $1.50 per litre. Plotting 600 litres against $1.50 in part (ii) produces the point a, derived from point A in part (i). This is one point on the consumer's demand curve. Next we consider the middle budget line, which occurs when the price of gasoline is $1.00 per litre. We take the figure of 1200 litres from point B in part (i) and transfer it to part (ii). We then plot this quantity against the price of $1.00 to get the point b on the demand curve. Doing the same thing for point C yields the point c in part (ii): price 50 cents, quantity 2200 litres.

Repeating the operation for all prices yields the demand curve in part (ii). Note that the two parts of Figure 6A-7 describe the same behaviour. Both parts measure the quantity of gasoline on the horizontal axes; the only difference is that in part (i) the price of gasoline determines the slope of the budget line, whereas in part (ii) the price of gasoline is plotted explicitly on the vertical axis.

Income and Substitution Effects

The price–consumption line in part (i) of Figure 6A-7 indicates that as price decreases, the quantity of gasoline demanded increases, thus giving rise to the negatively sloped demand curve in part (ii). As we saw in Chapter 6, the key to understanding the negative slope of the demand curve is to distinguish between the income effect and the substitution effect of a change in price. We can make this distinction more precisely, and somewhat differently, using indifference curves.

In Chapter 6, we examined the substitution effect of a reduction in price by eliminating the income effect. We did this by reducing money income until the consumer could just purchase the original bundle of goods. We then examined how the change in relative prices affected the consumer's choices. In indifference theory, however, the income effect is removed by changing money income until the *original level of utility*—the original indifference curve— can just be achieved. This method results in a slightly different measure of the income effect, but the principle involved in separating the total change into an income effect and a substitution effect is exactly the same as in Chapter 6.

The separation of the two effects according to indifference theory is shown in Figure 6A-8. The figure shows in greater detail part of the price–consumption line first drawn in Figure 6A-7. Points A_0 and A_2 are on the price–consumption line for gasoline; A_0 is the consumer's utility-maximizing point at the initial price, whereas A_2 is the consumer's utility-maximizing point at the new price.

We can think of the separation of the income and substitution effects as occurring in the following way. After the price of the good has fallen, we reduce money income *until the original indifference curve can just be obtained*. The consumer moves from point A_0 to an intermediate point A_1, and this response is defined as the substitution effect. Then, to measure the income effect, we restore money income. The consumer moves from the point A_1 to the final point A_2, and this response is defined as the income effect.

FIGURE 6A-8   The Income and Substitution Effects of a Price Change

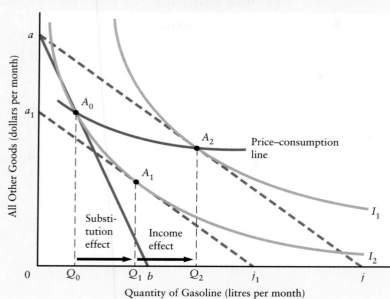

Quantity of Gasoline (litres per month)

The substitution effect is defined by sliding the budget line around a fixed indifference curve; the income effect is defined by a parallel shift of the budget line. The original budget line is at *ab*, and a fall in the price of gasoline takes it to *aj*. The original utility-maximizing point is at A_0 with Q_0 of gasoline being consumed, and the new utility-maximizing point is at A_2 with Q_2 of gasoline being consumed. To remove the income effect, imagine reducing the consumer's money income until the original indifference curve is just attainable. We do this by shifting the line *aj* to a parallel line nearer the origin $a_1 j_1$ that just touches the indifference curve that passes through A_0. The intermediate point A_1 divides the quantity change into a substitution effect $Q_0 Q_1$ and an income effect $Q_1 Q_2$.

<hr>

STUDY EXERCISES

1. Consider Katie's preferences for videos and ice cream cones. Several "consumption bundles" are shown in the table below.

Bundle	Ice Cream Cones	Videos
a	9	0
b	7	2
c	6	2
d	5	3
e	4	4
f	4	3
g	3	4
h	2	6
i	0	6

   a. On a scale diagram with the quantity of ice cream cones on the vertical axis and the quantity of videos on the horizontal axis, plot the various bundles.
   b. Suppose that Katie is indifferent between bundles *c* and *i*. She is also indifferent between bundles *d*, *g*, and *h*, but all three of these are preferred to *c* or *i*. Finally, suppose that, of the bundles shown in the

table, bundle *e* is Katie's favourite. Draw three indifference curves showing this information.
   c. Consider bundles *e*, *f*, and *g*. What can you conclude about how Katie would rank these bundles?

2. Continue with Katie from the previous question. Katie has a monthly allowance of $18 that she chooses to divide between video rentals and ice cream cones. Videos rent for $3 each and ice cream cones cost $2 each.

   a. For each of the consumption bundles shown in the table, compute the total expenditure. Which ones can Katie afford, and which ones can't she afford?
   b. Draw Katie's budget line. What is the slope of the line?
   c. Given Katie's monthly budget constraint, which bundle does she choose to maximize her utility?

3. Debra travels to Mexico and enjoys both burritos and Coronas. The diagram shows her utility-maximizing choices.

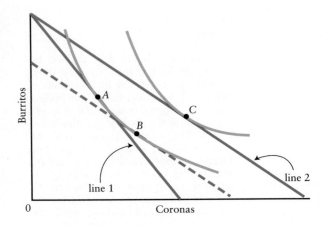

a. If the budget line is line 1, describe why point *A* is Debra's utility-maximizing choice.
b. What event can explain why the budget line moves to line 2?

c. What is the meaning of point *B* in the figure?
d. Suppose Coronas are a normal good for Debra. What does this restriction imply about the location of point *C*? Is this restriction satisfied in the diagram?
e. Suppose Coronas were an inferior good for Debra. How would this information be reflected in her choice following the move of the budget line to line 2?

4. Consider your sets of indifference curves for

i) Coke and chips
ii) Coke and Pepsi

Explain why these sets of indifference curves are likely to look different. Illustrate with a diagram. What does this difference imply about the magnitude of the substitution effects in response to changes in the price of Coke?

Producers in the Short Run

LO LEARNING OBJECTIVES

In this chapter you will learn

1. the various forms of business organization and the different ways that firms can be financed.
2. the difference between accounting profits and economic profits.
3. about the relationships between total product, average product, and marginal product, and the law of diminishing marginal returns.
4. the difference between fixed and variable costs, and the relationships between total costs, average costs, and marginal costs.

In Chapter 6, we went behind the demand curve to understand how it is determined by the behaviour of consumers. In this chapter and the next, we go behind the supply curve to understand how it is determined by the behaviour of firms.

We begin by comparing the firms that we see in the real world with those that appear in economic theory. Next we introduce the concepts of costs, revenues, and profits and outline the key role that profits play in determining the allocation of the nation's resources. To determine the most profitable quantity for a firm to produce and supply to the market, we need to see how its costs vary with its output.

When examining the relationship between output and cost, *time* plays an important role. In this chapter, we focus on the short run, where a firm can change only some of its inputs, and output is governed by the famous "law of diminishing returns." In the next chapter we examine the firm's behaviour in the long run—when all the firm's factors are variable—and in the very long run—when the state of technology changes. There we encounter scale economies and firms' incentives for research and development.

7.1 WHAT ARE FIRMS?

We start by taking a brief look at the basic unit of production, the firm. How are firms organized? How are firms financed? What are their goals?

Organization of Firms

A firm can be organized in any one of six different ways.

single proprietorship A firm which has one owner who is personally responsible for the firm's actions and debts.

ordinary partnership A firm which has two or more joint owners, each of whom is personally responsible for the firm's actions and debts.

limited partnership A firm which has two classes of owners: general partners, who take part in managing the firm and are personally liable for the firm's actions and debts, and limited partners, who take no part in the management of the firm and risk only the money that they have invested.

corporation A firm which has a legal existence separate from that of the owners.

state-owned enterprise A firm that is owned by the government. In Canada, these are called *Crown corporations.*

non-profit organizations Firms that provide goods and services with the objective of just covering their costs.

multinational enterprises (MNEs) Firms that have operations in more than one country.

1. A **single proprietorship** has one owner–manager who is personally responsible for all aspects of the business, including its debts.

2. An **ordinary partnership** has two or more joint owners, each of whom is personally responsible for all of the partnership's debts.

3. The **limited partnership**, which is less common than ordinary partnerships, provides for two types of partners. *General partners* take part in the running of the business and are liable for all the firm's debts. *Limited partners* take no part in the running of the business, and their liability is limited to the amount they actually invest in the enterprise.

4. A **corporation** is a firm regarded in law as having an identity of its own; its owners are not personally responsible for anything that is done in the name of the firm, though its directors may be. The shares of a *private* corporation are not traded on any stock exchange (such as the Toronto or New York Stock Exchanges) whereas the shares of a *public* corporation are.

5. A **state-owned enterprise** is owned by the government but is usually under the direction of a more or less independent, state-appointed board. Although its ownership differs, the organization and legal status of a state-owned enterprise are similar to those of a corporation. In Canada, such state-owned enterprises are called *Crown corporations.*

6. **Non-profit organizations** are established with the explicit objective of providing goods or services to customers, but any profits that are generated remain with the organization and are not claimed by individuals. In many cases, some goods or services are sold to consumers while others are provided free of charge. Non-profit firms therefore earn their revenues from a combination of sales and donations. An example is your local YMCA—it sells memberships to consumers for use of the health facilities, but it also provides free services to needy individuals in the community.

Not all production in the economy takes place within firms. Many government agencies provide goods and services, such as defence, roads, primary and secondary education, and health-care services. In most of these cases, goods and services are provided to citizens without charging directly for their use; costs are financed through the government's general tax revenues.

Firms that have locations in more than one country are often called **multinational enterprises (MNEs)**. Their numbers and importance have increased greatly over the last few decades. A large amount of international trade represents business transactions of MNEs—between different corporations as well as between different regional operations of the same corporation. The growing number of MNEs thus reveals an increasing role for these corporations in the ongoing process of globalization.

---

myeconlab

For a more detailed discussion of multinational enterprises, and especially their role in determining flows of foreign investment, look for "Multinational Enterprises and Foreign Direct Investment" in the *Additional Topics* section of this book's MyEconLab.

www.myeconlab.com

Financing of Firms

The money a firm raises for carrying on its business is sometimes called its financial capital, as distinct from its real capital, which is the firm's physical assets such as factories, machinery, offices, and stocks of materials and finished goods. Although the use of the term "capital" to refer to both an amount of money and a quantity of goods can be confusing, it will usually be clear from the context which sense is being used.

The basic types of financial capital used by firms are *equity* and *debt*. Equity is the funds provided by the owners of the firm. Debt is the funds borrowed from creditors outside the firm.

Equity   In individual proprietorships and partnerships, one or more owners provide much of the required funds. A corporation acquires funds from its owners in return for stocks, shares, or equities (as they are variously called). These are basically ownership certificates. The money goes to the company and the shareholders become owners of the firm, risking the loss of their money, and gaining the right to share in the firm's profits. Profits that are paid out to shareholders are called **dividends.**

One easy way for an established firm to raise money is to retain current profits rather than paying them out to shareholders. Financing investment from such *undistributed profits* has become an important source of funding in modern times. Reinvested profits add to the value of the firm, and hence raise the market value of existing shares; they are funds provided by owners.

Debt   The firm's creditors are not owners; they have lent money in return for some form of loan agreement, or IOU. There is a bewildering array of such agreements, which are collectively called *debt instruments* in the business world and **bonds** in economic theory. Each has its own set of characteristics and its own name. Two characteristics are, however, common to all debt instruments issued by firms. First, they carry an obligation to repay the amount borrowed, called the *principal* of the loan. Second, they carry an obligation to make some form of payment to the lender called *interest*. The time at which the principal is to be repaid is called the *redemption date* of the debt. The amount of time between the issue of the debt and its redemption date is called its *term*. See *Applying Economic Concepts 7-1* for more details about debt instruments.

dividends Profits paid out to shareholders of a corporation. Sometimes called distributed profits.

bond A debt instrument carrying a specified amount and schedule of interest payments and (usually) a date for redemption of its face value.

Goals of Firms

The theory of the firm that we study in this book is based on two key assumptions. First, all firms are assumed to be profit-maximizers, seeking to make as much profit for their owners as possible. Second, each firm is assumed to be a single, consistent decision-making unit.

The desire to maximize profits is assumed to motivate all decisions made within a firm, and such decisions are assumed to be unaffected by the peculiarities of the persons making the decisions and by the organizational structure in which they work.

These assumptions allow the theory to ignore the firm's internal organization and its financial structure. Using these assumptions, economists can predict the behaviour of firms. To do this, they first study the choices open to the firm, establishing the effect that each choice would have on the firm's profits. They then predict that the firm will select the alternative that produces the largest profits.

Is maximizing profit the only thing firms should care about? In recent years there has been much public discussion of the need for firms to be "socially responsible" in

To see what the Canadian Council of Chief Executives thinks about "corporate citizenship," go to **www.ceocouncil.ca** and click on "Corporate and Public Governance."

APPLYING ECONOMIC CONCEPTS 7-1

Kinds of Debt Instruments

Most debt instruments can be grouped into three broad classes. First, some debt is in the form of *loans* from financial institutions such as chartered banks. These are private agreements between the firm and the bank usually calling for the periodic payment of interest and repayment of the principal, either at a stipulated future date or "on demand," meaning whenever the bank requests repayment.

Second, *bills* and *notes* are commonly used for short-term loans of up to a year. They carry no fixed interest payments, only a principal value and a redemption date. Interest arises because the borrowing firm sells the new bills that it issues at a price below their redemption value. If, for example, a bill promising to pay $1000 in one year's time is sold to a lender for $950, this gives the lender an interest payment of $50 in one year's time when the bill that he bought for $950 is redeemed for $1000. This makes an interest rate of 5.26 percent per year ($(50/950) \times 100$). Bills are *negotiable,* which means they can be bought and sold in financial markets. So if you buy a 90-day bill from some firm and want your money back 30 days later, you can sell the bill on the open market. The purchaser must be prepared to assume the loan to the firm for the 60 days that it still has to run.

The third type of instrument carries a fixed redemption date, as does a bill, and the obligation to make periodic interest payments, as do most loans. These instruments have many different details and cor-respondingly many different names, such as *bonds* and *debentures.* They are commonly used for long-term loans—up to 20 or 30 years. A firm that issues a 7-percent 30-year bond of this sort with redemption value of $1000 is borrowing money now and promising to pay $70 a year for 30 years and then to pay $1000 on the redemption date. All such bonds are negotiable. This is important, because few people would be willing to lend money for such long periods of time if there were no way to get it back before the redemption date.

Many large firms borrow money by issuing long-term bonds, like this one issued by Alcan Aluminium Limited.

A relatively new Canadian magazine is devoted entirely to discussing and identifying socially responsible corporate behaviour. See **www.corporateknights.ca**.

addition to being motivated by the pursuit of profits. Some people argue that every firm has a responsibility to society that goes well beyond the responsibility to its shareholders. Others disagree, and argue that by maximizing profits, firms *are* providing a valuable service to society. For a discussion of both sides of this interesting debate, see *Applying Economic Concepts 7-2.*

myeconlab

Firms that choose objectives other than maximizing profits may become a "takeover" target in the market for corporate control. For a more detailed discussion of whether firms actually maximize profits, and the possible consequences of not doing so, look for "Do Firms Really Maximize Profits?" in the *Additional Topics* section of this book's MyEconLab.

www.myeconlab.com

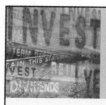

APPLYING ECONOMIC CONCEPTS 7-2

Is It Socially Responsible to Maximize Profits?

In recent years there has been growing public discussion of the need for firms, especially large ones, to behave in a socially responsible manner. Advocates of this view start from the position that unadorned capitalism, and the associated goal of profit maximization, does not serve the broader public interest: Corporate profits clearly help firms' shareholders, but the public interest is not being served. In this view, corporate social responsibility must involve more than simply maximizing profits.

Others argue that firms should indeed focus on the goal of maximizing profits and that, by doing so, they are providing significant benefits to their customers and their employees, not just their shareholders. In addition, it is the pursuit of profits that leads firms to develop new products and production methods, innovations which lie at the heart of ongoing improvements in overall living standards. This opposing view is grounded in the same insight of Adam Smith's that we saw in Chapter 1—that the pursuit of private gain creates benefits for society as a whole.

But what about corporate profits generated through a production process that damages the environment? Surely there are costs imposed on society when firms, through their profit-maximizing decisions, are led to emit poisonous effluents into the air or into local waterways. Or how about firms making unethical business decisions and thereby earning profits at the expense of other parties? Isn't simple profit maximization in these cases socially irresponsible?

One response to these arguments is that it is the duty of governments to set rules in the public interest and then leave firms free to maximize their profits within the constraints set by those rules. For example, the government can design and enforce environmental, labour, accounting, and tax regulations deemed to be in the public interest. Faced with these laws and regulations, private firms are then free to take whatever action is expected to maximize their profits; violations of the established laws or regulations will be met with appropriate penalties. Such a division of responsibilities—the government setting the rules and the firms maximizing profits within the implied constraints—recognizes that although private firms are usually not good judges of the public interest, they are quite good at making decisions about how best to use scarce resources in order to satisfy consumers' desires. Government policymakers, through a process that involves consultation with various groups in society, and the trading off of competing demands, are usually better placed to judge what is and is not in the public interest.

The adoption of this position still recognizes two methods for modifying corporate behaviour. Those who believe that certain corporate actions are not in the public interest can try to convince policymakers to design new rules that will make it costly for firms to continue such actions. Various non-governmental organizations (NGOs), ranging from environmental organizations to consumer-advocacy groups, can play an important role in identifying and publicizing poor corporate behaviour, and also in lobbying the government for change. If the case is persuasive, and sufficient public pressure can be brought to bear on the policymakers, policies will eventually be changed. An example is the relatively recent design of environmental protection policies. Many years ago, Canadian firms could pollute the environment with impunity, whereas today many types of pollution are illegal and some emissions are closely monitored by government agencies.

A second way that firms can be encouraged to change their behaviour is by the expression of consumers' preferences in the marketplace. If enough consumers dislike a certain activity by a specific firm, and these views can be expressed clearly enough in terms of consumers' demand for the firm's products, the firm may be convinced to change its behaviour. In this case, new laws or regulations may not be required; the firm decides, on the basis of the possible decline in sales it will suffer if it continues its unpopular activities, that a change in its behaviour is required for profit maximization. An example occurred in the mid-1990s when Nike was heavily criticized for contracting its production to Asian "sweatshops" where workers were treated poorly and paid very low wages. A widespread boycott of Nike products began and Nike eventually responded by raising wages, improving working conditions, and allowing independent monitors into its factories. The threat of a loss of sales was so powerful that competing companies Reebok and Adidas, who had not yet attracted any negative publicity, began making improvements in their factories just to prevent being tarred by the Nike brush.

What is the bottom line? Corporations *do* change their behaviour over time—in response to changes in laws and regulations, and also in response to changes in consumer attitudes. If governments can be relied upon to establish and enforce rules and regulations in the public interest, and consumers continue to actively express their preferences through their decisions in the marketplace, then firms may be able to be socially responsible and profit-maximizing at the same time.

▌ 7.2 **PRODUCTION, COSTS, AND PROFITS**

We must now specify a little more precisely the concepts of production, costs, and profits that are used by economists.

Production

In order to produce the goods or services that it sells, each firm needs inputs. Hundreds of inputs enter into the production of any specific output. Among the many inputs entering into car production, for example, are steel, rubber, spark plugs, electricity, the site of the factory, machinists, accountants, spray-painting machines, forklift trucks, painters, and managers. These can be grouped into four broad categories:

- inputs to the car firm that are outputs from some other firm, such as spark plugs, electricity, and steel;
- inputs that are provided directly by nature, such as land;
- inputs that are provided directly by people, such as the services of workers and managers; and
- inputs that are provided by the factories and machines used for manufacturing cars.

intermediate products All outputs that are used as inputs by other producers in a further stage of production.

The items that make up the first group of inputs are called **intermediate products**. For example, one firm mines iron ore and sells it to a steel manufacturer. Iron ore is an intermediate product: an output of the mining firm and an input for the steel plant. These appear as inputs only because the stages of production are divided among different firms. If these intermediate products are traced back to their sources, all production can be accounted for by the services of the other three kinds of input, which we first discussed in Chapter 1 and which are called *factors of production*. These are: the gifts of nature, such as soil and raw materials called *land*; physical and mental efforts provided by people, called *labour*; and factories, machines, and other manmade aids to production, called *capital*.

production function A functional relation showing the maximum output that can be produced by each and every combination of inputs.

The **production function** describes the technological relationship between the inputs that a firm uses and the output that it produces. In terms of functional notation, a simplified production function (in which we ignore the role of land) is written as

$$Q = f(L,K)$$

where Q is the flow of output, K is the flow of capital services, and L is the flow of labour services.[1] "f" is the production function itself. Changes in the firm's technology, which alter the relationship between inputs and output, are reflected by changes in the function f.

Costs and Profits

The production function specifies the amount of output that can be obtained from any given amounts of inputs. Firms arrive at what they call profits by taking the revenues

---

1 Remember that production is a flow: It is so many units per period of time. For example, when we say that production rises from 100 to 101 units, we mean that the rate of production has risen from 100 units each period to 101 units each period.

they obtain from selling their output and deducting all the costs associated with their inputs. When all costs have been correctly deducted, the resulting profits are the return to the owners' capital.

Economic Versus Accounting Profits   Compared with accountants, economists use somewhat different concepts of costs and profits. When accountants measure profits, they begin with the firm's revenues and then subtract all of the *explicit* costs incurred by the firm. By explicit costs, we mean the costs that actually involve a purchase of goods or services by the firm. The obvious explicit costs include the hiring of workers, the rental of equipment, interest payments on debt, and the purchase of intermediate inputs.[2]

Practise with Study Guide Chapter 7, Exercise 2 and Short-Answer Question 2.

Accounting profits = Revenues − Explicit costs

Like accountants, economists subtract from revenues all explicit costs, but they also subtract some *implicit* costs that accountants ignore. These are items for which there is no market transaction but for which there is still an opportunity cost for the firm that should be included in the complete measure of costs. The two most important implicit costs are the opportunity cost of the owner's time (over and above his or her salary) and the opportunity cost of the owner's capital (including a possible risk premium). When this more complete set of costs is subtracted from the firm's revenues, the result is called **economic profit** and is sometimes called *pure profit*.

Economic profits = Revenues − (Explicit costs + Implicit costs)
= Accounting profits − Implicit costs

economic profits The difference between the revenues received from the sale of output and the opportunity cost of the inputs used to make the output. Negative economic profits are called economic losses.

Opportunity Cost of Owner's Time. Especially in small and relatively new firms, owners spend a tremendous amount of their time developing the business. Often they pay themselves far less than they could earn if they were instead to offer their labour services to other firms. For example, an entrepreneur who opens a restaurant may pay herself only $1000 per month while she is building her business, even though she could earn $4000 per month in her next best alternative job. In this case, there is an *implicit* cost to her firm of $3000 per month that would be missed by the accountant who measures only the explicit cost of her wage at $1000 per month.[3]

Opportunity Cost of Owner's Capital. What is the opportunity cost of the financial capital that the owner has tied up in a firm? The answer is best broken into two parts. First, ask what could be earned by lending this amount to someone else in a *riskless* loan. The owners could have purchased a government bond, which has no significant risk of default. Suppose the return on this is 6 percent per year. This amount is the risk-free rate of return on capital. It is clearly an opportunity cost, since the firm could close down operations, lend out its money, and earn a 6-percent return. Next, ask what the firm could earn in addition to this amount by lending its money to another firm where risk of default was equal to the firm's own risk of loss. Suppose this is an additional 4 percent. This is the risk premium and it is clearly also a cost. If the firm does not expect to earn this much in its own operations, it could close down and lend its money out to some equally risky firm and earn 10 percent (6-percent pure return plus 4-percent risk premium).

---

[2] *Depreciation* is also among the firm's explicit costs, even though it does not involve a market transaction. Depreciation is a cost to the firm that arises due to the wearing out of its physical capital.

[3] For larger firms that are not operated by their owners, this element of implicit costs is not relevant because the owners usually do not work at the firm. In these cases, the salaries to the firm's managers appear in the firm's accounts as explicit costs.

TABLE 7-1 Accounting Versus Economic Profit for Ruthie's Gourmet Soup Company

Total Revenues ($)		2000
Explicit Costs ($)		
Wages and Salaries	500	
Intermediate Inputs	400	
Rent	80	
Interest on Loan	100	
Depreciation	80	
Total Explicit Costs	1160	
Accounting Profit		840
Implicit Costs ($)		
Opportunity Cost of Owner's Time	160	
Opportunity Cost of Owner's $1500 Capital		
(a) risk-free return of 6%	90	
(b) risk premium of 4%	60	
Total Implicit Costs	310	
Economic Profit		530

Economic profits are less than accounting profits because of implicit costs. The table shows a simplified version of a real profit-and-loss statement. Accounting profits are computed as revenues minus explicit costs (including depreciation), and in the table are equal to $840 for the period being examined. When the correct opportunity cost of the owner's time (in excess of what is recorded in wages and salaries) and capital are recognized as implicit costs, the firm appears less profitable. Economic profits are still positive but equal only $530.

Implicit costs are just as important as explicit costs. Economists include both implicit and explicit costs in their measurement of profits, whereas accounting profits include only explicit costs. Economic profits are therefore less than accounting profits.

Table 7-1 compares economic and accounting profits for a hypothetical owner-operated firm that produces gourmet soups. In that example, both accounting profits and economic profits are positive (though accounting profits are larger). Another possibility, however, is that a firm has positive *accounting* profits even though it has zero *economic* profits. If a firm's accounting profits represent a return just equal to what is available if the owner's capital and time were used elsewhere, then opportunity costs are just being covered. In this case, there are zero *economic* profits, even though the firm's accountant will record positive profits.

Is one of these concepts better than the other? No. Firms are interested in the return to their owners, which is what they call profits. They must also conform with tax laws which define profits in the same way. In contrast, economists are interested in how profits affect resource allocation and their definition is best for that purpose and is the definition used throughout this book. Let's see why economic profit is a useful concept when thinking about resource allocation.

Profits and Resource Allocation When resources are valued by the opportunity-cost principle, their costs show how much these resources would earn if used in their best alternative uses. If the revenues of all the firms in some industry exceed opportunity cost, the firms in that industry will be earning pure or economic profits. Hence, the owners of factors of production will want to move resources into the industry, because the earnings potentially available to them are greater there than in alternative uses. If, in some other industry, firms are incurring economic losses, some or all of this industry's resources are more highly valued in other uses, and owners of the resources will want to move them to those other uses.

Economic profits and losses play a crucial signalling role in the workings of a free-market system.

Economic profits in an industry are the signal that resources can profitably be moved into the industry. Losses are the signal that the resources can profitably be moved elsewhere. Only if there are zero economic profits is there no incentive for resources to move into or out of an industry.

Profit-Maximizing Output

To develop a theory of supply, we need to determine the level of output that will maximize a firm's profit, to which we give the symbol π (the lowercase Greek letter pi). This is the difference between the total revenue (TR) each firm derives from the sale of its output and the total cost (TC) of producing that output:

$$\pi = TR - TC$$

Thus, what happens to profits as output varies depends on what happens to both revenues and costs.[4] In the rest of this chapter, we develop a theory of how costs vary with output when the firm has some inputs that are fixed. In the next chapter, we allow all inputs to be variable. The theory that we develop about costs and output is common to all firms. In the chapters that follow, we consider how revenue varies with output. Costs and revenues are then combined to determine the profit-maximizing choices for firms in various market situations. The resulting theory can then be used to predict the outcome of changes in such things as demand, costs, taxes, and subsidies. This may seem like quite a long route to get to a theory of supply, and it is, but the payoff when we get there is in being able to understand and evaluate a great deal of economic behaviour.

We start with inputs. Suppose that a firm wishes to increase its rate of output. To do so, it must increase the inputs of one or more factors of production. For the rest of this chapter, we consider a very simple example relating to the production of some industrial product such as newsprint or aluminum. We can best focus on essentials by dealing with only two inputs. The first is labour, to which we give the symbol L. The second is capital, to which we give the symbol K. Thus, we are ignoring land and all intermediate inputs and dealing with the simplified production function introduced earlier in this chapter:

$$Q = f(L,K)$$

where Q is quantity of output per period of time, L is the flow of labour services employed in production, and K is the flow of capital services used. The letter f again stands for the relation that links the inputs to the output.

Time Horizons for Decision Making

Economists classify the decisions that firms make into three types: (1) how best to use existing plant and equipment—the *short run*; (2) what new plant and equipment and production processes to select, given known technical possibilities—the *long run*; and (3) how to encourage, or adapt to, the development of new techniques—the *very long run*.

The Short Run   The **short run** is a time period in which the quantity of some inputs, called **fixed factors**, cannot be changed. A fixed factor is usually an element of capital (such as plant and equipment), but it might be land, the services of management, or even the supply of skilled labour. Inputs that are not fixed but instead can be varied in the short run are called **variable factors.**

The short run does not correspond to a specific number of months or years. In some industries, it may extend over many years; in others, it may be a matter of months or even weeks. In the electric power industry, for example, it takes three or more years to acquire and install a steam turbine generator. An unforeseen increase in demand will involve a long period during which the extra demand must be met with

short run A period of time in which the quantity of some inputs cannot be increased beyond the fixed amount that is available.

fixed factor An input whose quantity cannot be changed in the short run.

variable factor An input whose quantity can be changed over the time period under consideration.

---

[4] From this point on, all costs include both explicit and implicit costs, and thus profits are economic rather than accounting profits.

the existing capital equipment. In contrast, a machine shop can acquire new equipment in a few weeks. An increase in demand will have to be met with the existing stock of capital for only a brief time, after which it can be adjusted to the level made desirable by the higher demand.

The short run is the length of time over which some of the firm's factors of production are fixed.

long run A period of time in which all inputs may be varied, but the existing technology of production cannot be changed.

The Long Run

The **long run** is a time period in which all inputs may be varied but in which the basic technology of production cannot be changed. Like the short run, the long run does not correspond to a specific length of time.

The long run corresponds to the situation the firm faces when it is planning to go into business, to expand the scale of its operations, to branch out into new products or new areas, or to change its method of production. The firm's *planning decisions* are long-run decisions because they are made from given technological possibilities but with freedom to choose from a variety of production processes that will use factor inputs in different proportions.

The long run is the length of time over which all of the firm's factors of production can be varied, but its technology is fixed.

very long run A period of time that is long enough for the technological possibilities available to a firm to change.

The Very Long Run

Unlike the short run and the long run, the **very long run** is a period of time in which the technological possibilities available to a firm will change. Modern industrial societies are characterized by continuously changing technologies that lead to new and improved products and production methods.

The very long run is the length of time over which all the firm's factors of production and its technology can be varied.

For the remainder of this chapter, we consider costs and production in the short run. We continue with our simplified situation in which there are only two factors of production—labour and capital. We will assume that capital is the fixed factor whereas labour is the variable factor. In the next chapter, we explore the firm's decisions in the long run and the very long run.

7.3 PRODUCTION IN THE SHORT RUN

Consider a Winnipeg-based company producing hockey sticks. The firm owns a small factory with the necessary machinery and equipment—this is the firm's stock of capital, and we will assume that it is fixed in quantity. We call these the *fixed* factors of production. The firm also purchases intermediate inputs such as wood, glue, and electricity and, of course, hires workers. The intermediate inputs and the labour services are the firm's *variable* inputs.

In the following discussion, we will focus on the relationship between the firm's use of labour and the firm's production of output. In particular, we want to know—with a fixed amount of capital—how output changes as the firm varies its amount of labour. The table in Figure 7-1 shows three different ways of looking at how output varies with the quantity of labour services.

FIGURE 7-1   Total, Average, and Marginal Products in the Short Run

Quantity of Labour (L)	Total Product (TP)	Average Product $\left(AP = \dfrac{TP}{L}\right)$	Marginal Product $\left(MP = \dfrac{\Delta TP}{\Delta L}\right)$
(1)	(2)	(3)	(4)
0	0		
1	3	3	3
2	7	3.5	4
3	13	4.3	6
4	22	5.5	9
5	35	7.0	13
6	55	9.2	20
7	80	11.4	25
8	98	12.3	18
9	107	11.9	9
10	113	11.3	6
11	117	10.6	4
12	119	9.9	2
13	120	9.2	1

(i) Total product

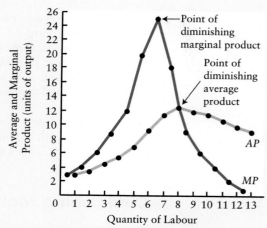

(ii) Average and marginal product

The relation of output to changes in the quantity of the variable factor can be looked at in three different ways. As the quantity of labour increases, total output increases, as shown in column 2. The average product in column 3 is found by dividing the total product in column 2 by the quantity of labour shown in the corresponding row of column 1. The marginal product is shown between the rows because it refers to the change in output from one level of labour input to another. The curves are plotted from the data in the table. In part (i), the *TP* curve shows the total product steadily rising, first at an increasing rate, then at a decreasing rate. This causes both the average and the marginal product curves in part (ii) to rise at first and then decline. Where *AP* reaches its maximum, *MP* = *AP*.

Total, Average, and Marginal Products

Total product (*TP*) is the total amount that is produced during a given period of time. Total product will change as more or less of the variable factor is used in conjunction with the given amount of the fixed factor. This variation is shown in columns 1 and 2 of the table in Figure 7-1. Part (i) of Figure 7-1 plots the schedule from the table. (The shape of the curve will be discussed shortly.)

Average product (*AP*) is the total product divided by the number of units of the variable factor used to produce it. If we let the number of units of labour be denoted by *L*, the average product is given by

$$AP = \frac{TP}{L}$$

total product (*TP*) Total amount produced by a firm during some time period.

average product (*AP*) Total product divided by the number of units of the variable factor used in its production.

marginal product (*MP*) The change in total output that results from using one more unit of a variable factor.

Practise with Study Guide Chapter 7, Exercise 3.

Notice in column 3 of the table that as more labour is used, average product first rises and then falls. The level of labour input at which average product reaches a maximum (8 units of labour in the example) is called the *point of diminishing average productivity*. Up to that point, average product is increasing; beyond that point, average product is decreasing.

Marginal product (*MP*) is the change in total product resulting from the use of one additional unit of labour. [13] Recalling that the Greek letter Δ (delta) means "the change in," marginal product is given by:

$$MP = \frac{\Delta TP}{\Delta L}$$

Computed values of marginal product are shown in column 4 of the table in Figure 7-1. The values in this column are placed between the other rows of the table to stress that the concept refers to the *change* in output caused by the *change* in quantity of the variable factor. For example, the increase in labour from 3 to 4 units ($\Delta L = 1$) increases output from 13 to 22 ($\Delta TP = 9$). Thus the *MP* equals 9, and it is recorded between 3 and 4 units of labour. Note that *MP* in the table first rises and then falls as output increases. The level of labour input at which marginal product reaches a maximum (between 6 and 7 units of labour in this example) is called the *point of diminishing marginal productivity*.

Part (ii) of Figure 7-1 plots the average product and marginal product curves from the table. Although three different curves are shown in Figure 7-1, they are all aspects of the same single relationship described by the production function. As we vary the quantity of labour, with capital being fixed, output changes. Sometimes it is interesting to look at total product, sometimes at average product, and sometimes at the marginal product.

We will see later in this chapter that understanding firms' costs requires understanding how total, average, and marginal products are related to each other. We now turn to examining two aspects of this relationship.

Diminishing Marginal Product

The variations in output that result from applying more or less of a variable factor to a given quantity of a fixed factor are the subject of a famous economic hypothesis, referred to as the **law of diminishing returns**.

law of diminishing returns The hypothesis that if increasing quantities of a variable factor are applied to a given quantity of fixed factors, the marginal product of the variable factor will eventually decrease.

The law of diminishing returns states that if increasing amounts of a variable factor are applied to a given quantity of a fixed factor (holding the level of technology constant), eventually a situation will be reached in which the marginal product of the variable factor declines.

Notice in Figure 7-1 that the marginal product curve rises at first and then begins to fall with each successive increase in the quantity of labour.

The common sense explanation of the law of diminishing returns is that as output is increased in the short run, more and more of the variable factor is combined with a given amount of the fixed factor. As a result, each unit of the variable factor has less and less of the fixed factor to work with. When the fixed factor is capital and the variable factor is labour, each unit of labour gets a declining amount of capital to assist it as the total output grows. It is not surprising, therefore, that sooner or later, equal increases in labour eventually begin to add less and less to total output.

To illustrate the concept, consider the number of workers in our hockey-stick manufacturing firm. If there is only one worker, that worker must do all the tasks, shifting from one to another and becoming competent at each. As a second, third, and subsequent workers are added, each can specialize in one task, becoming expert at it. One can cut the wood into the required pieces, the second can glue the pieces together, and the third worker can do the necessary planing and sanding. This process, as we noted in Chapter 1, is called the *division of labour*. If additional workers allow more efficient divisions of labour, marginal product will rise: Each newly hired worker will add more to total output than each previous worker did. However, according to the law of diminishing returns, the scope for such increases must eventually disappear, and sooner or later the marginal products of additional workers must decline. When the decline takes place, each additional worker will increase total output by less than did the previous worker.

Eventually, as more and more of the variable factor is employed, marginal product may reach zero and even become negative. It is not hard to see why if you consider the extreme case, in which there would be so many workers in a limited space that additional workers would simply get in the way, thus reducing the total output.

Empirical confirmation of diminishing marginal returns occurs frequently. Some examples are illustrated in *Applying Economic Concepts 7-3*. But one might wish that it were not so. There would then be no reason to fear a food crisis caused by the population explosion in developing countries. If the marginal product of additional workers applied to a fixed quantity of land were constant, food production could be expanded in proportion to population growth merely by keeping a constant fraction of the population on farms. With fixed techniques, however, diminishing returns dictate an inexorable decline in the marginal product of each additional worker because an expanding population must work with a fixed supply of agricultural land.

Thus, except where it is offset by sufficiently powerful improvements in the techniques of production, continuous population growth would bring with it, according to the law of diminishing returns, declining living standards and eventually widespread famine. Because he did not appreciate the extent to which agricultural technologies would be improved over time, the English economist Thomas Malthus (1766–1834) predicted that the increase in the world's population would be accompanied by such a fall in living standards. His gloomy (and incorrect) forecast is discussed further in the next chapter.

The Average–Marginal Relationship

We have so far examined the concept of diminishing *marginal* returns; but *average* returns are also expected to diminish. If increasing quantities of a variable factor are applied to a given quantity of fixed factors, the average product of the variable factor will eventually decrease. [14]

Notice that in part (ii) of Figure 7-1, the *MP* curve cuts the *AP* curve at the *AP*'s maximum point. This is not a matter of luck or the way the artist just happened to draw the figure. Rather, it illustrates a fundamental property of the relationship between average and marginal product curves, one that is important to understand.

If you have a portfolio of financial assets that earns 10 percent per year, adding a new asset will only increase the portfolio's average rate of return if the return on the new (marginal) asset exceeds 10 percent.

APPLYING ECONOMIC CONCEPTS 7-3

Three Examples of Diminishing Returns

Sport Fishing

British Columbia's Campbell River, a noted sport-fishing area, has long been the centre of a thriving, well-promoted tourist trade. As sport fishing has increased over the years, the total number of fish caught has steadily increased, but the number of fish *per person fishing* has decreased and the average hours fished for each fish caught has increased.*

Pollution Control

When Southern California Edison was required to modify its Mojave power plant to reduce the amount of pollutants emitted into the atmosphere, it discovered that a series of filters applied to the smokestacks could do the job. A single filter eliminated one-half of the discharge. Five filters in series reduced the discharge to the 3 percent allowed by law. When a state senator proposed a

---

*For a *given stock of fish* and increasing numbers of boats, this example is a good illustration of the law of diminishing returns. But in recent years the story has become more complicated as overfishing has depleted the stock of fish. We examine the reasons for overfishing in Chapter 16.

new standard that would permit no more than 1 percent of the pollutant to be emitted, the company brought in experts who testified that this would require at least 15 filters per stack and would triple the cost. In other words, increasing the number of filters leads to diminishing marginal returns in pollution reduction.

Wartime Protection

During the early days of the Second World War, so few naval ships were available that each North Atlantic convoy had only a few escort vessels to protect it from German submarines. The inadequate number of escorts sank very few submarines. As the construction program made more ships available, the escorts could protect the whole convoy more effectively: Some could close in on the various flanks; others could hunt farther afield. Not only did the total number of submarines sunk per convoy rise, but also the number of submarines sunk per escort vessel rose. Still later in the war, as each successive convoy was provided with more and more escort vessels, the number of submarines sunk per convoy continued to rise, but the number of submarines sunk *per escort vessel* began to fall sharply. Total output (submarines sunk) increased, but marginal output per escort vessel fell.

The average product curve slopes upward as long as the marginal product curve is *above* it; whether the marginal product curve is itself sloping upward or downward is irrelevant. For example, if an additional worker is to raise the average product of all workers, that additional worker's output must be greater than the average output of the other workers. In other words, in order for the average product to rise, the marginal product must exceed the average product. [15]

The relationship between marginal and average measures is very general. If the marginal is greater than the average, the average must be rising; if the marginal is less than the average, the average must be falling. For example, if you had a 3.6 cumulative grade point average (GPA) through last semester and in this (marginal) semester you get only a 3.0 GPA, your cumulative GPA will fall. To increase your cumulative GPA, you must score better in this (marginal) semester than you have on average in the past—that is, to increase the average, the marginal must be greater than the average.

7.4 COSTS IN THE SHORT RUN

We now shift our attention from production to costs. The majority of firms cannot influence the prices of the inputs that they employ; instead they must pay the going market price for their inputs. For example, a shoe factory in Montreal, a metals manufacturer in Sarnia, a rancher in Red Deer, and a boat builder in Prince Rupert are each too small a part of the total demand for the factors that they use to be able to influence their prices significantly. The firms must pay the going rent for the land that they need, the going wage rate for the labour that they employ, and the going interest rate that banks charge for loans; so it is with most other firms. Given these prices and the physical returns summarized by the product curves, the costs of different levels of output can be calculated.

Defining Short-Run Costs

There are several different types of costs that are relevant in the short run, and we must be careful to get them straight. They are all related to the product concepts that we have just discussed.

Total Cost (TC). Total costs are the sum of all costs that the firm incurs to produce a given level of output. **Total cost** is divided into two parts: total fixed cost and total variable cost.

$$TC = TFC + TVC$$

total cost (*TC*) The total cost of producing any given level of output; it can be divided into *total fixed cost* and *total variable cost*.

Total Fixed Cost (TFC). Total fixed cost is the cost of the fixed factor(s). This does not vary with the level of output; it is the same whether output is one unit or 1000 units. **Total fixed cost** is also referred to as *overhead cost.* An example of a fixed cost is the annual cost associated with renting a factory (or servicing the debt incurred to build a factory). Whether the level of output increases or decreases, this annual cost does not change.

total fixed cost (*TFC*) All costs of production that do not vary with the level of output.

Total Variable Cost (TVC). **Total variable cost** is the cost of the variable factors. It varies directly with the level of output—that is, it rises when output rises and it falls when output falls. Examples of variable costs are the cost of labour and intermediate inputs that are used to produce output. As the level of output increases or decreases, the amount of labour and intermediate inputs required for production will typically change in the same direction.

total variable cost (*TVC*) Total costs of production that vary directly with the level of output.

Average Total Cost (ATC). The total cost of producing any given number of units of output divided by that number of units tells us the **average total cost** per unit of output. We let *Q* be the total units of output (what we earlier referred to as total product, *TP*). Since total cost is divided into fixed and variable costs, we can also divide average total cost into its fixed and variable components:

$$ATC = TC/Q$$

$$ATC = AFC + AVC$$

average total cost (*ATC*) Total cost of producing a given output divided by the number of units of output; it can also be calculated as the sum of average fixed costs and average variable costs. Also called *unit cost* or *average cost.*

Average Fixed Cost (AFC). Total fixed cost divided by the number of units of output tells us the average fixed cost per unit of output. **Average fixed cost** declines continuously as output increases because the amount of the fixed cost attributed to each unit of output falls. This is known as *spreading overhead.*

$$AFC = TFC/Q$$

average fixed cost (*AFC*) Total fixed costs divided by the number of units of output.

average variable cost (AVC) Total variable costs divided by the number of units of output.

Average Variable Cost (AVC). Total variable cost divided by the number of units of output tells us the average variable cost per unit of output. For reasons that we will soon see, **average variable cost** first declines as output rises, reaches a minimum, and then increases as output continues to rise.

$$AVC = TVC/Q$$

marginal cost (MC) The increase in total cost resulting from increasing output by one unit.

Marginal Cost (MC). The increase in total cost resulting from a one-unit increase in the level of output is called **marginal cost**. (Marginal costs are always marginal *variable* costs because fixed costs do not change as output varies.) Marginal cost is calculated as the change in total cost divided by the change in output that brought it about: [16]

$$MC = \Delta TC/\Delta Q$$

Short-Run Cost Curves

Practise with Study Guide Chapter 7, Exercise 6.

Using the firm's production relationships from Figure 7-1, suppose the price of labour is $20 per unit and the price of capital is $10 per unit. Also suppose the firm has 10 units of capital (the fixed factor). The firm's resulting costs are shown in Table 7-2.

Columns 4 through 6 in Table 7-2 show the firm's total costs. *TFC* is simply $10 per unit of capital times 10 units of capital. *TVC* is $20 per unit of labour times the increasing amount of labour shown in column 2. *TC* is the sum of *TFC* and *TVC*. Columns 7 through 9 show the average costs. For each average cost concept, the number is computed as the total cost from columns 4, 5, or 6 divided by the number of units of output shown in column 3.

TABLE 7-2   Short-Run Costs: Fixed Capital and Variable Labour

Inputs		Output	Total Costs			Average Costs			Marginal Cost
Capital (K) (1)	Labour (L) (2)	(Q) (3)	Fixed (TFC) (4)	Variable (TVC) (5)	Total (TC) (6)	Fixed (AFC) (7)	Variable (AVC) (8)	Total (ATC) (9)	(MC) (10)
10	0	0	$100	$0	$100	—	—	—	
10	1	3	100	20	120	$33.33	$6.67	$40.00	$6.67
10	2	7	100	40	140	14.29	5.71	20.00	5.00
10	3	13	100	60	160	7.69	4.62	12.31	3.33
10	4	22	100	80	180	4.55	3.64	8.18	2.22
10	5	35	100	100	200	2.86	2.86	5.71	1.54
10	6	55	100	120	220	1.82	2.18	4.00	1.00
10	7	80	100	140	240	1.25	1.75	3.00	0.80
10	8	98	100	160	260	1.02	1.63	2.65	1.11
10	9	107	100	180	280	0.93	1.68	2.62	2.22
10	10	113	100	200	300	0.88	1.77	2.65	3.33
10	11	117	100	220	320	0.85	1.88	2.74	5.00
10	12	119	100	240	340	0.84	2.02	2.86	10.00
10	13	120	100	260	360	0.83	2.17	3.00	20.00

These cost schedules are computed from the product curves of Figure 7-1, given the price of capital of $10 per unit and the price of labour of $20 per unit.

Column 10 shows the marginal cost. For each *change* in the level of output, MC is equal to the change in TC divided by the change in output. For example, as output increases from 22 to 35 units, total costs rise from $180 to $200. Thus, marginal cost over this range of output is equal to $20/13 = $1.54.

The graphs in Figure 7-2 plot the cost curves from the data in Table 7-2. Part (i) plots the various total cost curves and shows that TVC rises at a decreasing rate until output is approximately 60 units. For output levels above 60, TVC rises at an increasing rate. Total fixed costs (TFC), of course, do not vary as the level of output changes. Since TFC is horizontal, the shape of TC comes from the shape of TVC.

Part (ii) of Figure 7-2 plots the average cost curves and the marginal cost curve. Notice that the MC curve cuts the ATC curve and the AVC curve at their lowest points. This is another example of the relationship between a marginal and an average curve. The ATC curve slopes downward whenever the MC curve is below it; it slopes upward whenever the MC curve is above it. Now let's consider the various curves in a little more detail.

The AFC, AVC, and ATC Curves

In part (ii) of Figure 7-2, the average fixed cost (AFC) curve is steadily declining as output rises. Since there is a given amount of capital with a total fixed cost of $100, increases in the level of output lead to a steadily declining fixed cost per unit of output. This is the phenomenon of *spreading overhead*.

The average variable cost (AVC) curve shows the variable cost per unit of output. It declines as output rises, reaching a minimum at approximately 100 units of output. As output increases above this level, AVC rises.

Since average total cost (ATC) is simply the sum of AFC and AVC, it follows that the ATC curve is derived geometrically by vertically adding the AFC and AVC curves. That is, for each level of output, the point on the ATC curve is derived by adding together the values of AFC and AVC. The result is an ATC curve that declines initially as output increases, reaches a minimum, and then rises as output increases further. Economists usually refer to this as a "U-shaped" ATC curve.

The MC Curve

Figure 7-2 also shows the marginal cost (MC) curve. Notice that the points on the curve are plotted at the *midpoint* of the output interval shown in the table (because marginal cost refers to the *change* in cost as output rises from one level to another). For example, when we plot the marginal cost of $1.54 as output increases from 22 to 35 units, the point is plotted at an output level of 28.5 units (the midpoint between 22 and 35). The MC curve declines steadily as output initially increases, reaches a minimum somewhere near 70 units of output, and then rises as output increases further.

Why U-Shaped Cost Curves?

It is clear from Figure 7-2 that the AVC, ATC, and MC curves are all U-shaped. What explains this shape?

Recall that the MP and AP curves in Figure 7-1 are both "hill-shaped" (an inverted "U") whereas the AVC and MC curves are both U-shaped. Is this just a coincidence, or is there some relationship between the two sets of curves? The answer is that this is no coincidence. Since labour input adds directly to cost, it should not surprise you that the relationship between labour input and output—the AP and MP curves—is closely linked to the relationship between output and cost—the AVC and MC curves.

Consider first the relationship between the AP and AVC curves. The AP curve shows that as the amount of labour input increases, the average product of labour rises, reaches a maximum, and then eventually falls. But each unit of labour adds the same amount to total variable cost ($20 in this example). Thus, each additional worker adds the same amount to cost but a different amount to output. When output per worker (AP) is rising, the variable cost per unit of output (AVC) is falling, and when

Practise with Study Guide Chapter 7, Exercises 4 and 5.

FIGURE 7-2   Total, Average, and Marginal Cost Curves

(i) Total cost curves

(ii) Marginal and average cost curves

These curves are plotted from the data in Table 7-2. Total fixed cost does not vary with output. Total variable cost and the total of all costs ($TC = TVC + TFC$) rise with output, first at a decreasing rate, then at an increasing rate. The total cost curves in (i) give rise to the average and marginal curves in (ii). Average fixed cost (AFC) declines as output increases. Average variable cost (AVC) and average total cost (ATC) fall and then rise as output increases. Marginal cost (MC) does the same, intersecting the ATC and AVC curves at their minimum points. Capacity output is at the minimum point of the ATC curve, which is an output of about 105 in this example.

output per worker (AP) is falling, average variable cost (AVC) is rising. AVC is at its minimum when AP reaches its maximum. [17]

Eventually diminishing average product of the variable factor implies eventually increasing average variable cost.

Exactly the same logic applies to the relationship between the *MP* and *MC* curves. Since each unit of labour adds the same amount to cost but has a different marginal product, it follows that when *MP* is rising *MC* is falling, and when *MP* is falling *MC* is rising. The *MC* curve reaches its minimum when the *MP* curve reaches its maximum. [18]

Eventually diminishing marginal product of the variable factor implies eventually increasing marginal costs.

Finally, we can return to the *ATC* curve to consider its shape. Since *ATC* = *AFC* + *AVC*, the *ATC* curve gets its shape from both the *AFC* and *AVC* curves. The *AFC* curve is steadily declining as a given amount of overhead (fixed factor) is spread over an increasing number of units of output. And the *AVC* curve is U-shaped for the reasons we have just seen regarding the relationship between *AP* and *AVC*. It follows that the *ATC* curve only begins to rise (after reaching its minimum) when the effect of the increasing *AVC* dominates the effect of the declining *AFC*. We therefore see the *ATC* curve reaching its minimum at a level of output above where *AVC* reaches its minimum.

Capacity

The level of output that corresponds to the minimum short-run average total cost is often called the *capacity* of the firm. In this sense, capacity is the largest output that can be produced without encountering rising average costs per unit. In part (ii) of Figure 7-2, capacity output is about 105 units, but higher outputs can be achieved, provided that the firm is willing to accept the higher per-unit costs that accompany any level of output that is "above capacity." A firm that is producing at an output less than the point of minimum average total cost is said to have *excess capacity*.

The technical definition gives the word *capacity* a meaning that is different from the one used in everyday speech, in which it often means an upper limit that cannot be exceeded. The technical definition is, however, a useful concept in economic and business discussions.

Shifts in Short-Run Cost Curves

Remember that a firm's short-run cost curves are drawn holding two things constant. First, the amount of the fixed factor used by the firm is held constant (indeed, it is the existence of such a fixed factor that ensures we are in the short run). Second, factor prices—the price per unit of labour and the price per unit of capital—are held constant. How would changes in factor prices and in the amount of the fixed factor affect the firm's short-run cost curves?

Changes in Factor Prices Factor prices change frequently, sometimes dramatically, and such changes naturally affect firms' costs. Consider a change in the wage, the price of a unit of labour services. An increase in the wage increases variable costs, leaves fixed costs unaffected, and therefore increases the firm's total costs. Since marginal costs are always marginal *variable* costs, such a change will also increase the firm's marginal costs. An increase in the price of the variable factor will therefore cause an upward shift in the firm's *ATC* and *MC* curves, as shown in Figure 7-3.

Now consider an increase in the price of a unit of the fixed factor. The firm's total *fixed* costs will rise, but its variable costs will be unaffected. Thus, in a diagram like Figure 7-3, the *ATC* curve will shift up but the *MC* curve will not move.

FIGURE 7-3   An Increase in Variable Input Prices

A change in the price of a variable input shifts the average total cost curve and the marginal cost curve. The original average total cost and marginal cost curves are shown by ATC_0 and MC_0. A rise in the price of a variable input—for example, the wage rate—raises the cost of producing each level of output. As a result, the average total cost curve and the marginal cost curve shift upward to ATC_1 and MC_1.

Changes in the Amount of the Fixed Factor   In the short run, the firm has a fixed amount of some factor of production. Economists usually think of physical capital as the fixed factor in the short run, especially the physical capital embodied in a plant or factory. What happens to the firm's production costs if it increases the size of its factory?

There are two effects from such a change. First, once the larger factory is in place, the firm's total fixed costs have increased. Second, the increase in the size of the factory means that labour and other variable factors now have more physical capital with which to work, and this generally increases their average and marginal product, and thus reduces marginal and average costs (at any given level of output). What is the combined effect of these two forces?

The overall effect on the ATC curve is difficult to predict without having more information about the firm's technology. It depends on how much the firm's output rises when it increases its use of *all* factors. In other words, we need to have more detailed information about the firm's production function before we know how a change in the firm's plant size will affect its ATC curve.

Changing from one plant size to another is considered by economists to be a long-run decision by the firm. This brings us to the next chapter, in which we explore how firms make decisions in a setting in which all factors of production are variable.

SUMMARY

7.1 WHAT ARE FIRMS?

LO 1

- Production is organized either by private-sector firms, which take four main forms—single proprietorships, ordinary partnerships, limited partnerships, and corporations—or by state-owned enterprises and non-profit organizations.
- Modern firms finance themselves by selling shares, re-investing their profits, or borrowing from lenders such as banks.

- A firm's profit is the difference between its total revenue and its total costs.
- Economists usually assume that firms attempt to maximize profits.

7.2 PRODUCTION, COSTS, AND PROFITS

LO 2

- The production function relates inputs of factor services to output.

- Accounting profit is the difference between the firm's revenues and its explicit costs, including labour costs, capital costs, and the costs of intermediate inputs.

- Economic profit is the difference between the firm's revenues and total costs, including both explicit and implicit costs. Implicit costs include the opportunity cost of the owner's time (for owner-managed firms) and capital.
- Economic profits play a key role in resource allocation. Positive economic profits attract resources into an industry; negative economic profits induce resources to move elsewhere.

- Economists divide the firm's production decisions into three time frames. The short run involves decisions in which one or more factors of production are fixed. The long run involves decisions in which all factors are variable but technology is unchanging. The very long run involves decisions in which technology can change.

7.3 PRODUCTION IN THE SHORT RUN

- The theory of short-run costs is concerned with how output varies as different amounts of the variable factors are combined with given amounts of the fixed factors. Total, average, and marginal product describe relationships between output and the quantity of the variable factors of production.

- The law of diminishing returns asserts that if increasing quantities of a variable factor are combined with given quantities of fixed factors, the marginal and the average products of the variable factor will eventually decrease. For given factor prices, this hypothesis implies that marginal and average costs will eventually rise.

7.4 COSTS IN THE SHORT RUN

- Short-run average total cost curves are often U-shaped because average productivity increases at low levels of outputs but eventually declines sufficiently to offset advantages of spreading overheads. The output corresponding to the minimum point of a short-run average total cost curve is called the plant's capacity.

- Changes in factor prices shift the short-run cost curves—upward when prices rise and downward when prices fall.

KEY CONCEPTS

Forms of business organization
Methods of financing modern firms
Profit maximization
Inputs and factors of production
Accounting versus economic profits

Economic profits and resource allocation
Short run, long run, and very long run
Total product, average product, and marginal product
The law of diminishing returns

Total cost, marginal cost, and average cost
The relationship between productivity and cost
Short-run cost curves
Capacity

STUDY EXERCISES

1. Fill in the blanks to make the following statements correct.

   a. The relationship between the inputs of factor services and output is called the _____.
   b. A firm earning positive accounting profits could have zero _____ if the owner's capital is earning exactly its _____.

   c. A firm's planning decisions made when some inputs are variable but others are fixed are made in the time period known as the _____.
   The time period over which all factors are variable but technology is fixed is known as the _____.

2. Fill in the blanks to make the following statements correct.

   a. The _____ tells us that as more of a variable factor is used in combination with given quantities of fixed factors, the marginal product of the variable factor will eventually decrease.

   b. The _____ is the change in total output resulting from the use of one additional unit of the variable factor.

   c. If average product and marginal product curves are plotted on a graph, the *AP* curve is rising as long as the *MP* curve lies _____ the *AP* curve. The *AP* curve is falling when the *MP* curve lies _____ the *AP* curve.

3. Fill in the blanks to make the following statements correct.

   a. For given factor prices, when average product per worker is at a maximum, average variable cost is at a __minimum__.

   b. If marginal costs are above average costs, then producing one more unit of output will __increase__ the average cost.

   c. The level of output that corresponds to a firm's minimum short-run average total cost is called the _____ of the firm.

4. Wacky Wintersports Inc. can produce snowboards according to the following schedule. Complete the table by calculating the marginal and average products.

Inputs of Labour (per week)	Number of Snowboards (per week)	Average Product	Marginal Product
0	0	—	
1	2	—	—
2	5	—	—
3	9	—	—
4	14	—	—
5	18	—	—
6	21	—	—
7	23	—	—
8	24	—	—

5. Consider the revenues and costs in 2007 for Spruce Decor Inc., an Alberta-based furniture company entirely owned by Mr. Harold Buford.

Furniture Sales	$645 000
Catalogue Sales	$ 12 000
Labour Costs	$325 000
Materials Costs	$157 000
Advertising Costs	$ 28 000
Debt-Service Costs	$ 32 000

a. What would accountants determine Spruce Decor's profits to be in 2007?

b. Suppose Mr. Buford has $400 000 of capital invested in Spruce Decor. Also suppose that equally risky enterprises earn a 16-percent rate of return on capital. What is the opportunity cost for Mr. Buford's capital?

c. What are the *economic* profits for Spruce Decor in 2007?

d. If Spruce Decor's economic profits were typical of furniture makers in 2007, what would you expect to happen in this industry? Explain.

6. Consider an example of a production function that relates the monthly production of widgets to the monthly use of capital and labour services. Suppose the production function takes the following specific algebraic form:

$$Q = KL - (0.1) L^2$$

where *Q* is the output of widgets, *K* is the input of capital services, and *L* is the input of labour services.

a. Suppose that, in the short run, *K* is constant and equal to 10. Fill in the following table.

K	L	Q
10	5	—
10	10	—
10	15	—
10	20	—
10	25	—
10	30	—
10	40	—
10	50	—

b. Using the values from the table, plot the values of *Q* and *L* on a scale diagram, with *Q* on the vertical axis and *L* on the horizontal axis.

c. Now suppose that *K* increases to 20 because the firm increases the size of its widget factory. Recompute the value of *Q* for each of the alternative values of *L*. Plot the values of *Q* and *L* on the same diagram as in (b).

d. Explain why an increase in *K* increases the level of *Q* (for any given level of *L*).

7. The following table shows how the total output of skates (per month) changes when the quantity of the variable input (labour) changes. The firm's amount of capital is fixed.

Hours of Labour (per month)	Pairs of Skates (per month)	Average Product	Marginal Product
100	200	—	
120	260	—	—
140	350	—	—
160	580	—	—
180	720	—	—
200	780	—	—
220	800	—	—
240	810	—	—

a. Compute the average product of labour for each level of output and fill in the table. Plot the *AP* curve on a scale diagram.

b. Compute the marginal product of labour for each interval (that is, between 100 and 120 hours, between 120 and 140 hours, and so on). Fill in the table and plot the *MP* curve on the same diagram. Remember to plot the value for *MP* at the midpoint of the intervals.

c. Is the "law of diminishing marginal returns" satisfied?

d. Explain the relationship between the marginal product of labour and the average product of labour.

8. Consider the table below, which shows the total fixed costs (*TFC*) and total variable costs (*TVC*) for producing specialty bicycles in a small factory with a fixed amount of capital.

Output Per Year (thousands of bicycles)	TFC	TVC	AFC	AVC	ATC
		(thousands of dollars)			
1	200	40	—	—	—
2	200	70	—	—	—
3	200	105	—	—	—
4	200	120	—	—	—
5	200	135	—	—	—
6	200	155	—	—	—
7	200	185	—	—	—
8	200	230	—	—	—
9	200	290	—	—	—
10	200	350	—	—	—
11	200	425	—	—	—

a. Compute average fixed costs (*AFC*) for each level of output.

b. Compute average variable costs (*AVC*) for each level of output.

c. Compute average total cost (*ATC*) for each level of output. What level of output (per year) is the firm's "capacity"?

d. Plot the *AFC*, *AVC*, and *ATC* curves on a scale diagram with dollars on the vertical axis and the level of output on the horizontal axis.

9. **myeconlab** This question requires you to understand the relationship between total product, average product, and marginal product. Each of the diagrams below shows how total product (*TP*) changes as the quantity of the variable input (which we call *L*) changes. These reflect four *different* production functions.

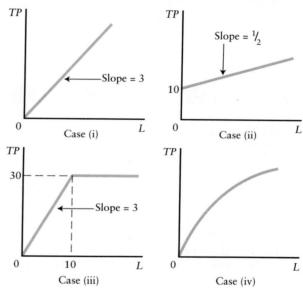

a. In each case, describe in words how total output depends on the amount of variable input.

b. For each production function, draw a diagram showing the average product (*AP*) curve. (Recall that *AP* is given by total output divided by total variable input. The value of *AP* is also equal to the slope of a straight line from the origin to the *TP* curve.)

c. On the same diagram, draw the marginal product (*MP*) curve. (Recall that *MP* is given by the *change* in total output divided by the *change* in the variable input. The value of *MP* is also equal to the slope of a tangent line to the *TP* curve.)

d. Is the relationship between *AP* and *MP* discussed in the text satisfied by each of the production functions?

10. In 1921, a classic set of experiments with chemical fertilizers was performed at the Rothampsted Experimental Station, an agricultural research institute in Hertfordshire, England. Researchers applied different amounts of a particular fertilizer to 10 apparently identical plots of land. The results for one test, using identical seed grain, are listed in the following table. Compute the average and marginal product of fertilizer, and identify the (approximate) points of diminishing average and marginal productivity.

Plot	Fertilizer Dose	Yield Index*
1	15	104.2
2	30	110.4
3	45	118.0
4	60	125.3
5	75	130.2
6	90	131.4
7	105	131.9
8	120	132.3
9	135	132.5
10	150	132.8

* Yield without fertilizer = 100.

DISCUSSION QUESTIONS

1. Which concept of profits—accounting or economic—is implied in the following quotations?

   a. "Profits are necessary if firms are to stay in business."
   b. "Profits are signals for firms to expand production and investment."
   c. "Accelerated depreciation allowances reduce profits and thus benefit the company's owners."

2. Does the short run consist of the same number of months for increasing output as for decreasing it? Must the short run in an industry be the same length for all firms in the industry? Under what circumstances might the short run actually involve a longer time span than the very long run for one particular firm?

3. Indicate whether each of the following conforms to the hypothesis of diminishing returns and, if so, whether it refers to marginal returns, average returns, or both.

   a. "The bigger they are, the harder they fall."
   b. "As more and more of the population receives chicken pox vaccinations, the reduction in the chicken pox disease rate for each additional 100 000 vaccinations becomes smaller."
   c. "Five workers produce twice as much today as 10 workers did 40 years ago."
   d. "Diminishing returns set in last year when the rising rural population actually caused agricultural output to fall."

4. Consider the education of a person as a process of production. Regard years of schooling as one variable factor of production. What are the other factors? What factors are fixed? At what point would you expect diminishing returns to set in? For an Einstein, would diminishing returns set in during his lifetime?

5. A carpenter quits his job at a furniture factory to open his own cabinetmaking business. In his first two years of operation, his sales average $100 000 and his operating costs for wood, workshop and tool rental, utilities, and miscellaneous expenses average $70 000. Now his old job at the furniture factory is again available. Should he take it or remain in business for himself? How would you make this decision?

6. The point of minimum average cost is referred to as the capacity of the firm. Yet we draw the average cost curve extending both to the left and to the right of this point. Obviously, a firm can operate below capacity, but how can a firm operate above capacity? Are there any types of firms for which it may be desirable to have a capacity below the level at which the firm may have to produce occasionally or even relatively frequently? Explain.

CHAPTER 8

Producers in the Long Run

LO LEARNING OBJECTIVES

In this chapter you will learn

1. why profit maximization requires firms to equate the marginal product per dollar spent for all factors.
2. why profit-maximizing firms will use more of the factors whose prices have fallen, and less of the factors whose prices have increased.
3. about the relationship between short-run and long-run cost curves.
4. the importance of technological change and why firms are often motivated to improve their production methods.

In the first part of this chapter, we look at the long run, in which firms are free to vary all factors of production. Recall from the last chapter that different amounts of the fixed factor lead to different short-run cost curves. The choice faced by a firm in the long run is to determine how much of the fixed factor to use—that is, to decide *which* of the several short-run cost curves to be using. Some firms use a great deal of capital and only a small amount of labour. Others use less capital and more labour. Here we examine the effects these choices have on firms' costs, and we look at the conditions that influence these choices.

In the second part of the chapter, we examine the very long run, a period of analysis over which technology changes. The discussion concerns the improvements in technology and productivity that have dramatically increased output and incomes in all industrial countries over centuries. Firms are among the most important economic actors that cause technological advances to take place. Evidence shows that the hypothesis of profit maximization can help us to understand technological changes. Here, as in the short and long run, firms respond to events such as changes in factor prices. But in the very long run, firms often respond by innovating—that is, by developing *new* technologies.

Throughout this chapter, we should remember that the lengths of the various "runs" under consideration are defined by the kinds of changes that can take place, not by calendar time. Thus, we would expect actual firms in any given time period: to be on their short-run cost curves, as described in Chapter 7; to choose among alternative short-run cost curves in the long run, as described in the first part of this chapter; and to change technologies in the very long run as described in the latter part of this chapter.

8.1 THE LONG RUN: NO FIXED FACTORS

In the short run, in which at least one factor is fixed, the only way to produce a given output is to adjust the input of the variable factors. In the long run, in which all factors can be varied, there are numerous ways to produce any given output. For example, the firm could use many machines and few workers, or few machines and many workers. Thus, firms in the long run must choose the type and amount of plant and equipment and the size of their labour force.

In making these choices, the profit-maximizing firm will try to be **technically efficient** by using no more of all inputs than necessary—that is, the firm does not want to waste any of its valuable inputs. For example, consider the situation faced by a crate-manufacturing firm. If the firm is *able* to produce 100 crates per day using two machines and eight workers, the firm would be technically *inefficient* if it decided instead to produce only 90 crates while still employing the same amount of (expensive) labour and capital. If the firm decided that it wished to produce only 90 crates per day, technical efficiency requires that it use fewer workers, fewer machines, or both.

Technical efficiency is not enough, however. In order to maximize its profit, the firm must choose from among the many technically efficient options the one that produces a given level of output at the lowest cost. For example, if the firm decides to produce 100 crates per day, it still must decide whether to use two machines and eight workers, or perhaps three machines and six workers. It should choose the combination that minimizes its total costs.

Such choices about how much capital and labour to use are *long-run* choices because all factors of production are assumed to be variable. These long-run planning decisions are important. A firm that decides to build a new steel mill and invest in the required machinery will choose among many alternatives. Once installed, that equipment is fixed for a long time. If the firm makes a wrong choice, its survival may be threatened; if it estimates correctly, it may be rewarded with large profits.

technical efficiency When a given number of inputs are combined in such a way as to maximize the level of output.

Practise with Study Guide Chapter 8, Exercise 1 and Short-Answer Question 1.

> **myeconlab**
>
> **Concepts of efficiency used by economists differ from those used by other professionals, especially engineers. For a detailed explanation of the differences, look for "Explaining Different Concepts of Efficiency" in the *Additional Topics* section of this book's MyEconLab.**
>
> w w w . m y e c o n l a b . c o m

Profit Maximization and Cost Minimization

Any firm that is trying to maximize its profits in the long run should select the production method that produces its output at the lowest possible cost. This implication of the hypothesis of profit maximization is called **cost minimization**: From among the many technically efficient methods of production available to it, the profit-maximizing firm will choose the least costly means of producing whatever level of output it chooses.

cost minimization An implication of profit maximization that firms choose the production method that produces any given level of output at the lowest possible cost.

Long-Run Cost Minimization   If it is possible to substitute one factor for another to keep output constant while reducing total cost, the firm is currently not minimizing its costs. In such a situation, the firm should substitute one factor for another factor as long as the marginal product of the one factor *per dollar spent on it* is greater than the marginal product of the other factor *per dollar spent on it*. The firm is not minimizing its costs whenever these two magnitudes are unequal. For example, if an extra dollar spent on labour produces more output than an extra dollar spent on capital, the firm can reduce costs by spending less on capital and more on labour.

Suppose we use K to represent capital, L to represent labour, and p_L and p_K to represent the prices per unit of the two factors. The necessary condition for cost minimization is then:

$$\frac{MP_K}{p_K} = \frac{MP_L}{p_L} \qquad (8\text{-}1)$$

Whenever the ratio of the marginal product of each factor to its price is not equal for all factors, there are possibilities for factor substitutions that will reduce costs (for a given level of output).

To see why Equation 8-1 must be satisfied when costs are being minimized, consider an example where the equation is *not* satisfied. Suppose the marginal product of capital is 40 units of output and the price of one unit of capital is \$10. Also suppose the marginal product of labour is 20 units of output and the price of one unit of labour is \$2. Then we have:

$$\frac{MP_K}{p_K} = \frac{40}{10} = 4 < \frac{MP_L}{p_L} = \frac{20}{2} = 10$$

Thus, the last dollar spent on capital adds only 4 units to output, whereas the last dollar spent on labour adds 10 units to output. In this case, the firm can reduce the cost of producing its current level of output by using more labour and less capital. Specifically, suppose the firm used two more units of labour and one fewer unit of capital. The two more units of labour would cause output to rise by 40 units and costs to increase by \$4; the one fewer unit of capital would cause output to fall back by 40 units and costs to decline by \$10. After this substitution of labour for capital, output would be unchanged but costs would be lower by \$6. Thus, the original combination of factors was not a cost-minimizing one.

Oil is a very important input in many industries. Increases in the price of oil will lead profit-maximizing firms to substitute away from oil toward other factors of production, whenever that is technically possible.

Of course, as the firm substitutes between labour and capital, the marginal products of both factors, MP_L and MP_K, will change. Specifically, the law of diminishing marginal returns says that, with other inputs held constant, an increase in the amount of one factor used will decrease that factor's marginal product. So as the firm in the previous example reduces its use of K and increases its use of L, MP_K will rise and MP_L will fall. These changes help to restore the equality in Equation 8-1.

By rearranging the terms in Equation 8-1, we can look at the cost-minimizing condition a bit differently.

$$\frac{MP_K}{MP_L} = \frac{p_K}{p_L} \qquad (8\text{-}2)$$

Practise with Study Guide Chapter 8, Exercise 1 and Short-Answer Question 2.

The ratio of the marginal products on the left side compares the contribution to output of the last unit of capital and the last unit of labour. The right side shows how the cost of an additional unit of capital compares to the cost of an additional unit of labour. If the two sides of Equation 8-2 are the same, then the firm cannot make any substitutions between labour and capital to reduce costs (if output is held constant). However, with the marginal products and factor prices used in the example above, the left side of the equation equals 2 but the right side equals 5; the last unit of capital is twice as productive as the last unit of labour but it is five times as expensive. It will thus pay the firm to switch to a method of production that uses less capital and more labour. If, however, the ratio on the right side were less than the ratio on the left, then it would pay the firm to switch to a method of production that used less labour and more capital. Only when the ratio of marginal products is exactly equal to the ratio of factor prices is the firm using the cost-minimizing production method.[1]

Profit-maximizing firms adjust the quantities of factors they use to the prices of the factors given by the market.

The Principle of Substitution

principle of substitution The principle that methods of production will change if relative prices of inputs change, with relatively more of the cheaper input and relatively less of the more expensive input being used.

The Principle of Substitution   The preceding discussion suggests that profit-maximizing (and therefore cost-minimizing) firms will react to changes in factor prices by changing their methods of production. This is referred to as the **principle of substitution.**

Suppose the firm's use of capital and labour currently satisfies Equation 8-1. Then consider a decrease in the price of capital while the price of labour remains unchanged. The least-cost method of producing any output will now use less labour and more capital than was required to produce the same output before the factor prices changed.

Methods of production will change if the relative prices of factors change. Relatively more of the cheaper factor and relatively less of the more expensive factor will be used.

The principle of substitution plays a central role in resource allocation because it relates to the way in which individual firms respond to changes in relative factor prices that are caused by the changing relative scarcities of factors in the economy as a whole. Individual firms are motivated to use less of factors that become scarcer to the economy and more of factors that become more plentiful. Here are two examples of the principle of substitution in action.

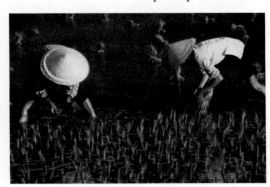

In many developing countries, labour is used much more intensively in agriculture than is the case in richer, developed countries. This does not mean methods are somehow "backward" in the developing countries; the intensive use of labour simply reflects a cost-minimizing response to low wages.

Over the past three decades, the improvements in computing equipment have led to many changes in everyday life. One change involves customers' transactions with their commercial banks—especially cash deposits and withdrawals. Banks used to employ large numbers of tellers to deal with the hundreds of customers that needed to be serviced each day. Now most retail banking transactions are facilitated with computers and are dealt with either by automated teller machines (ATMs), automated telephone banking, or Internet banking. The dramatic reduction in the price of computers over the past three decades (and also the more modest increase in wages) has encouraged banks to make this substitution of capital for labour.

The principle of substitution can also explain why methods of producing the same product often differ across countries. In Canada, where labour is generally highly skilled and expensive, farmers use elaborate machinery to economize on labour. In China, however, where labour is abundant and

---

1 The appendix to this chapter provides a graphical analysis of this condition, which is similar to the analysis of consumer behaviour that we developed in the appendix to Chapter 6.

capital is scarce, a much less mechanized method of production is appropriate. The Western engineer who believes that the Chinese are inefficient because they are using methods long ago discarded in the West is missing the truth about efficiency in the use of resources: Where factor scarcities differ across nations, so will the cost-minimizing methods of production.

Long-Run Cost Curves

We have been discussing a typical firm's cost-minimizing choices between capital and labour. Remember that these are *long-run* decisions because we are assuming that the firm is free to alter the amounts of all factors of production. As we have seen, when all factors can be varied, there exists a least-cost method of producing any given level of output. Thus, with given factor prices, there is a minimum achievable cost for each level of output; if this cost is expressed in terms of dollars per unit of output, we obtain the long-run average cost of producing each level of output. When this minimum cost of producing each level of output is plotted on a graph, the result is called a **long-run average cost (*LRAC*) curve**. Figure 8-1 shows one such curve.

The *LRAC* curve is determined by the firm's current technology and by the prices of the factors of production. It is a "boundary" in the sense that points below it are unattainable; points on the curve, however, are attainable if sufficient time elapses for all inputs to be adjusted. To move from one point on the *LRAC* curve to another requires an adjustment in *all* factor inputs, which may, for example, require building a larger, more elaborate factory.

The *LRAC* curve is the boundary between cost levels that are attainable, with known technology and given factor prices, and those that are unattainable.

Just as the short-run cost curves discussed in Chapter 7 relate to the production function describing the physical relationship between factor inputs and output, so does the *LRAC* curve. The difference is that in deriving the *LRAC* curve, there are no fixed factors of production. Thus, since all costs are variable in the long run, we do not need to distinguish between *AVC, AFC,* and *ATC,* as we did in the short run; in the long run, there is only one *LRAC* for any given set of input prices.

The Shape of the Long-Run Average Cost Curve   The *LRAC* curve shown in Figure 8-1 first falls and then rises. Like the short-run cost curves we saw in Chapter 7, this curve is often described as U-shaped, although empirical studies suggest it is often "saucer-shaped." Consider the three portions of any such saucer-shaped *LRAC* curve.

Decreasing Costs. Over the range of output from zero to Q_m, the firm has falling long-run average costs: An expansion of output permits a reduction of average costs. When long-run average costs fall as output rises, the firm is said to have **economies of scale**. Because the *LRAC* curve is drawn under the assumption of constant factor prices, the decline in long-run average cost occurs because output is increasing *more than* in proportion to inputs as the scale of the firm's production expands. Over this range of output, the decreasing-cost firm is often said to enjoy long-run **increasing returns**.[2]

Increasing returns may occur as a result of increased opportunities for specialization of tasks made possible by the division of labour. Even the most casual observation of the differences in production techniques used in large and small plants shows that

long-run average cost (*LRAC*) curve The curve showing the lowest possible cost of producing each level of output when all inputs can be varied.

economies of scale Reduction of long-run average costs resulting from an expansion in the scale of a firm's operations so that more of all inputs is being used.

increasing returns (to scale) A situation in which output increases more than in proportion to inputs as the scale of a firm's production increases. A firm in this situation is a decreasing-cost firm.

---

[2] Economists shift back and forth between speaking in physical terms ("increasing returns") and cost terms ("decreasing costs"). As the text explains, the same relationship can be expressed either way.

FIGURE 8-1   A "Saucer-Shaped" Long-Run Average Cost Curve

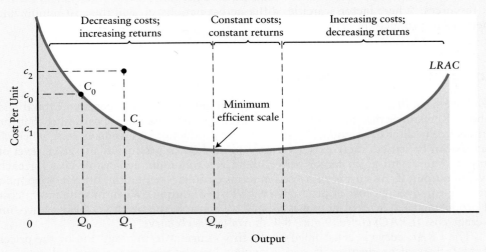

The long-run average cost ($LRAC$) curve is the boundary between attainable and unattainable levels of costs. If the firm wishes to produce output Q_0, the lowest attainable cost is c_0 per unit. Thus, point C_0 is on the $LRAC$ curve. At point C_1, the firm has achieved the lowest possible average cost of producing Q_1. Suppose a firm is producing at Q_0 and desires to increase output to Q_1. In the long run, a larger plant can be built and the average cost of c_1 can be attained. However, in the short run, it will not be able to vary all factors, and thus costs per unit will be above c_1, say, c_2. For a range of output beginning at Q_m, the firm attains its lowest possible average cost of production for the given technology and factor prices.

larger plants use greater specialization. These differences arise because large, specialized equipment is useful only when the volume of output that the firm can sell justifies employment of that equipment. For example, assembly lines and body-stamping machinery are cost-minimizing techniques for automobile production only when individual operations are repeated thousands of times. Use of elaborate and very expensive harvesting equipment provides the least-cost method of production on a big farm but not on one of only a few acres.

Constant Costs. In Figure 8-1, the firm's long-run average costs fall until output reaches Q_m, which is known as the firm's **minimum efficient scale**. It is the smallest level of output at which $LRAC$ reaches its minimum. The $LRAC$ curve is then flat over some range of output. With such a flat portion, the firm would be encountering constant costs over the relevant range of output, meaning that the firm's long-run average costs do not change as its output changes. Because factor prices are assumed to be fixed, the firm's output must be increasing *exactly in proportion to* the increase in inputs. When this happens, the constant-cost firm is said to be exhibiting **constant returns.**

Increasing Costs. When the $LRAC$ curve is rising, a long-run expansion in production is accompanied by a rise in average costs. If factor prices are constant, the firm's output must be increasing *less than* in proportion to the increase in inputs. When this happens,

minimum efficient scale (MES) The smallest output at which *LRAC* reaches its minimum. All available economies of scale have been realized at this point.

constant returns (to scale) A situation in which output increases in proportion to inputs as the scale of production is increased. A firm in this situation is a constant-cost firm.

the increasing-cost firm is said to encounter long-run **decreasing returns**. Decreasing returns imply that the firm suffers some *diseconomies of scale*.

Such diseconomies may be associated with the difficulties of managing and controlling an enterprise as its size increases. For example, planning problems do not necessarily vary in direct proportion to size. At first, there may be scale economies as the firm grows and benefits from greater specialization. But, sooner or later, planning and coordination problems may multiply more than in proportion to the growth in size. If so, management costs per unit of output will rise.

Other diseconomies are the possible alienation of the labour force as size increases; it becomes more difficult to provide appropriate supervision as more layers of supervisors and middle managers come between the person at the top and the workers on the shop floor. Control of middle-range managers may also become more difficult. As the firm becomes larger, managers may begin to pursue their own goals rather than devote all of their efforts to making profits for the firm. Much of the "re-engineering" of large firms in the 1990s has been aimed at reducing the extent to which management difficulties increase with firm size, but the problem has not been, and probably cannot be, eliminated entirely.

Note that long-run decreasing returns differ from short-run diminishing returns. In the short run, at least one factor is fixed, and the law of diminishing returns ensures that returns to the variable factor will eventually diminish. In the long run, all factors are variable, and it is possible that physically diminishing returns will never be encountered—at least as long as it is genuinely possible to increase inputs of all factors.

The Relationship Between Long-Run and Short-Run Costs   The short-run cost curves from the previous chapter and the long-run cost curve studied in this chapter are all derived from the same production function. Each curve assumes given prices for all factor inputs. The long-run average cost ($LRAC$) curve shows the lowest cost of producing any output when all factors are variable. Each short-run average total cost ($SRATC$) curve shows the lowest cost of producing any output when one or more factors are fixed.

No short-run cost curve can fall below the long-run cost curve because the $LRAC$ curve represents the lowest attainable cost for each possible output.

As the level of output is changed, a different-size plant is normally required to achieve the lowest attainable cost. Figure 8-2 shows the $SRATC$ curve above the $LRAC$ curve at all levels of output except Q_0.

As we saw in the last chapter, any individual $SRATC$ curve is just one of many such curves. The $SRATC$ curve in Figure 8-2 shows how costs vary as output is varied, holding the plant size constant. Figure 8-3 shows a family of $SRATC$ curves, along with a single $LRAC$ curve. The $LRAC$ curve is sometimes called an *envelope curve* because it encloses a series of $SRATC$ cost curves by being tangent to them.

Each $SRATC$ curve is tangent to the $LRAC$ curve at the level of output for which the quantity of the fixed factor is optimal and lies above it for all other levels of output.

decreasing returns (to scale) A situation in which output increases less than in proportion to inputs as the scale of a firm's production increases. A firm in this situation is an increasing-cost firm.

Practise with Study Guide Chapter 8, Exercise 3.

FIGURE 8-2   *LRAC and SRATC Curves*

Each $SRATC$ curve is tangent at some point to the $LRAC$ curve. With given technology, each plant size gives rise to a different $SRATC$ curve. The $SRATC$ curve shown corresponds to the optimal plant size for producing Q_0 units of output because the average cost, c_0, is the lowest attainable. For output levels less than or greater than Q_0, such as Q_1 or Q_2, the plant size embodied in $SRATC_0$ is not optimal because the cost given by the $SRATC_0$ curve is greater than the minimum possible cost, given by the $LRAC$ curve.

FIGURE 8-3   The Relationship Between the *LRAC* Curve and the *SRATC* Curves

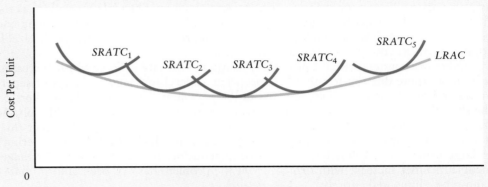

To every point on the **LRAC** curve, there is an associated **SRATC** curve tangent at that point. Each short-run curve is drawn for a given plant size, and shows how costs vary if output varies (holding constant the size of the plant). The level of output at the tangency between each *SRATC* curve and the *LRAC* curve shows the level of output for which the plant size is optimal.

The relationship between the *LRAC* curve and the many different *SRATC* curves has a famous history in economics. The economist who is credited with first working out this relationship, Jacob Viner, initially made a serious mistake that ended up being published; *Lessons From History 8-1* explains his mistake and shows how it illustrates an important difference between short-run and long-run costs.

Shifts in *LRAC* Curves

We saw in Chapter 7 how changes in either technological knowledge or factor prices will cause the entire family of short-run cost curves to shift. The same is true for long-run cost curves. Because loss of existing technological knowledge is rare, we focus on the effects of technological improvement. Improved ways of producing existing products make lower-cost methods of production available, thereby shifting *LRAC* curves downward.

Changes in factor prices can exert an influence in either direction. If a firm has to pay more for any factor that it uses, the cost of producing each level of output will rise; if the firm has to pay less for any factor that it uses, the cost of producing each level of output will fall.

A rise in factor prices shifts *LRAC* curves upward. A fall in factor prices or a technological improvement shifts *LRAC* curves downward.

LESSONS FROM HISTORY 8-1

Jacob Viner and the Clever Draftsman

Jacob Viner (1892–1970) was born in Montreal and studied economics at McGill University under Stephen Leacock (1869–1944). Viner was clearly an outstanding student and, according to some of his McGill class-mates, knew much more about economics than did Leacock, who was actually better known as a humorist than an economist. Viner was such a good economist that he was the first person to work out the relationship between a firm's long-run average costs and its short-run average costs. He went on to teach economics at the University of Chicago and at Princeton University and became one of the world's leading economic theorists.

The student who finds the relationship between *SRATC* and *LRAC* hard to understand may take some comfort from the fact that when Jacob Viner first worked out this relationship, and published it in 1931, he made a crucial mistake. In preparing a diagram like Figure 8-3, he instructed his draftsman to draw the *LRAC* curve through the *minimum points* of all the *SRATC* curves, "but so as to never lie above" the *SRATC* curves. Viner later said of the draftsman: "He is a mathematician, however, not an economist, and he saw some mathemat-ical objection to this procedure which I could not succeed in understanding. I could not persuade him to disregard his scruples as a craftsman and to follow my instructions, absurd though they might be."

Viner's mistake was to require that the draftsman connect all of the *minimum* points of the *SRATC* curves rather than to construct the curve that would be the *lower envelope* of all the *SRATC* curves. The former curve can of course be drawn, but it *is not* the *LRAC* curve. The latter curve *is* the *LRAC* curve, and is tan-gent to each *SRATC* curve.

Since Viner's article was published in 1931, gener-ations of economics students have experienced great satisfaction when they finally figured out his crucial mistake. Viner's famous article was often reprinted, for its fame was justly deserved, despite the importance of

the mistake. But Viner always rejected suggestions that he correct the error because he did not wish to deprive other students of the pleasure of feeling one up on him.

The economic sense of the fact that tangency is *not* at the minimum points of *SRATC* rests on the subtle distinction between the least-cost method of utilizing *a given plant* and the least-cost method of producing *a given level of output*. The first concept defines the minimum of any given *SRATC* curve, whereas the sec-ond defines a point on the *LRAC* curve for any given level of output. It is the second concept that interests us in the long run. If bigger plants can achieve lower aver-age costs, there will be a gain in building a bigger plant *and underutilizing it* whenever the gains from using the bigger plant are enough to offset the costs of being inef-ficient in the use of the plant. If there are gains from building bigger plants (i.e., if *LRAC* is declining), some underutilization is always justified.

Montreal-born Jacob Viner taught at Princeton and Chicago and was one of the world's leading economic theorists.

8.2 **THE VERY LONG RUN: CHANGES IN TECHNOLOGY**

In the long run, profit-maximizing firms faced with given technologies choose the cost-minimizing mix of factors to produce their desired level of output. Firms are therefore on, rather than above, their long-run cost curves. In the very long run, however, there are changes in the available techniques and resources. Such changes cause *shifts* in long-run cost curves.

The decrease in costs that can be achieved by choosing from among available factors of production, known techniques, and alternative levels of output is necessarily limited by the existing state of knowledge. Improvements by invention and innovation are potentially limitless, however, and hence sustained growth in living standards is critically linked to technological change.

Technological change refers to all changes in the available techniques of production. To measure its extent, economists usually use the notion of **productivity**, defined as a measure of output produced per unit of input used. Two widely used measures of productivity are output per worker and output per hour of work. The rate of increase in productivity provides one measure of technological change. The significance of productivity growth is explored in *Applying Economic Concepts 8-1*.

technological change Any change in the available techniques of production.

productivity Output produced per unit of some input; frequently used to refer to labour productivity, measured by total output divided by the amount of labour used.

myeconlab

In recent years, many economists and policymakers have expressed concern about Canada's low rate of productivity growth, especially as compared with that in the United States. But there is little agreement on how best to address the issue. For more details, look for "Understanding and Addressing Canada's Productivity Challenges" in the *Additional Topics* section of this book's MyEconLab.

www.myeconlab.com

Technological Change

Practise with Study Guide Chapter 8, Exercise 4.

Technological change was once thought to be mainly a random process, brought about by inventions made by crackpots and eccentric scientists working in garages and scientific laboratories. As a result of recent research by economists, we now know better.

Changes in technology are often *endogenous responses* to changing economic signals; that is, they result from responses by firms to the same things that induce the substitution of one factor for another within the confines of a given technology.

In our discussion of long-run demand curves in Chapter 4, we looked at just such technological changes in response to rising relative prices when we spoke of the development, in the 1970s, of smaller, more fuel-efficient cars in the wake of dramatic increases in the price of gasoline. From the mid-1980s to the mid-1990s, declines in the price of gasoline led to the re-emergence of large cars and the development of fuel-inefficient "sport utility vehicles," or SUVs. More recently, however, we have once again seen consumers respond to higher gasoline prices by reducing their demand for such large vehicles, returning to smaller, more fuel-efficient cars.

Production methods in many parts of the economy have responded to changes in relative factor prices. For example, much of the move to substitute capital for labour in manufacturing, transportation, communications, mining, and agriculture in

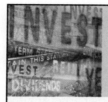

APPLYING ECONOMIC CONCEPTS 8-1

The Significance of Productivity Growth

Economics used to be known as the "dismal science" because some of its predictions were grim. Thomas Malthus (1766–1834) and other Classical economists predicted that the pressure of more and more people on the world's limited resources would cause a decline in output per person due to the law of diminishing returns. Human history would see more and more people living less and less well and the surplus population, which could not be supported, dying off from hunger and disease.

This prediction has proven wrong for industrialized countries for two main reasons. First, their populations have not expanded as rapidly as predicted by early economists, who were writing before birth-control techniques were widely used. Second, technological advances have been so important during the past 150 years that output has increased much faster than the population. We have experienced sustained growth in productivity

that has permitted significant increases in output per person. As the accompanying figure shows, real output per worker in Canada increased by 318 percent between 1926 and 2005, an average annually compounded growth rate of 1.8 percent.

Even such small annual productivity increases are a powerful force for increasing living standards over many years. Our great-grandparents would have regarded today's standard of living in most industrialized countries as unattainable. An apparently modest rate of increase in productivity of 2 percent per year leads to a doubling of per capita output every 35 years.

Due to the importance of productivity growth in raising long-run living standards, it is not surprising that explaining the sources of technological progress has become a very active area of research, among both academic and government economists.

(*Source:* Statistics Canada, CANSIM database (Real GDP: Series V3862685. Employment: Series V2091072) and authors' calculations.)

response to rising wage rates has taken the form of inventing new labour-saving methods of production.

Consider three kinds of change that influence production and cost in the very long run—*new techniques, improved inputs,* and *new products.*

New Techniques Throughout the nineteenth and twentieth centuries, changes in the techniques available for producing existing products have been dramatic; this is called *process innovation*. A century ago, roads and railways were built by gangs of workers who used buckets, shovels, and draft horses. Today, bulldozers, giant trucks, and other specialized equipment have banished the workhorse completely from construction sites and to a great extent have displaced the pick-and-shovel worker. Prior to the Second World War, electricity was generated either by burning fossil fuels or by harnessing the power of flowing water. With the rise of the atomic age immediately following the war, many countries developed large-scale nuclear generating capacity. Economies of scale in electricity production were significant. In recent years, however, the development of small-scale, gas-combustion and wind-powered turbines has permitted inexpensive construction of small generating stations that can produce electricity at a lower average cost than the much larger nuclear, hydro, or fossil fuel-burning generating stations. The product—electricity—is absolutely unchanged, but the techniques of production have changed markedly over the past several decades.

Improved Inputs Improvements in health and education raise the quality of labour services. Today's workers and managers are healthier and better educated than their grandparents. Many of today's unskilled workers are literate and competent in arithmetic, and their managers are apt to be trained in methods of business management and computer science.

Similarly, improvements in material inputs are constantly occurring. For example, the type and quality of metals have changed. Steel has replaced iron, and aluminum substitutes for steel in a process of change that makes a statistical category such as "primary metals" seem unsatisfactory. Even for a given category, say, steel, today's product is lighter, stronger, and more flexible than the "same" product manufactured only 20 years ago. Furthermore, the modern "materials revolution" allows new materials to be tailor-made for the specific purposes for which they are required.

The invention of new production techniques and the development of new and better inputs are important aspects of technological improvement. They lead to reductions in firms' costs and a downward shift in *LRAC* curves.

New Products New goods and services are constantly being invented and marketed; this is called *product innovation*. VCRs, personal computers, Palm Pilots, CD players, DVDs, cellular phones, and many other current consumer products did not exist thirty years ago. Other products have changed so dramatically that the only connection they have with the "same" product from the past is the name. Today's Ford automobile is very different from a 1920 Ford, and it is even different from a 1980 Ford in size, safety, and gasoline consumption. Modern jet airliners are revolutionary compared with the first passenger jet aircraft, which were in turn many times larger and faster than the DC–3, the workhorse of the airlines during the 1930s and 1940s. Beyond having wings and engines, the DC–3 itself bore little resemblance to the Wright brothers' original flying machine.

The development of new products is a crucial part of the steady increase in living standards.

Applying Economic Concepts 8-2 discusses an everyday example of technological change in banking: the creation and adoption of the automated teller machine (ATM). The adoption of ATMs by commercial banks involves both long-run decisions—substitutions between capital and labour—and very-long-run decisions involving innovation and the creation of new products.

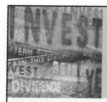

APPLYING ECONOMIC CONCEPTS 8-2

Substitution and Innovation with Automated Teller Machines (ATMs)

Before the relatively recent invention of automated teller machines (ATMs), all personal banking required a visit to the bank. For many working individuals, banking could only take place on the lunch hour with the result that long line-ups were commonplace. Banks were then faced with a difficult choice: Have unhappy customers in long line-ups, or hire more tellers.

The development of ATMs, made possible by the declining cost and increasing efficiency of computing equipment, revolutionized banking and presented banks with a new set of choices. As you know, ATMs are now located on street corners, in shopping malls and universities, and inside many large stores and even some small ones. As a result, individuals do not have to go to a bank to gain access to their money. And ATMs are very efficient: They take no time at all to "learn" their job and they can handle thousands of transactions per week—all with no direct labour cost per transaction. There is, of course, a significant capital cost for each ATM as well as some labour cost for servicing the equipment.

Since the early 1980s, the use of ATMs has sky-rocketed in Canada. Whereas in 1982 there were only a handful in the downtown core of even the major Canadian cities, today it is virtually impossible to walk even a few blocks anywhere in any Canadian city without seeing one. Over the same period, there has been a decline in the number of bank tellers (although because of ATMs we typically go to the bank so seldom that we don't notice this!). In the language of this chapter, the rise of ATMs and decline of bank tellers has been a long-run substitution of capital for labour.

There are also some very-long-run changes involved in this story. The creation of ATMs—and the related developments in telephone and online banking—has truly revolutionized personal banking. Not only are traditional types of transactions made easier,

but new banking services have been created. One example is the creation of online accounts for buying and selling stocks and bonds in the global financial markets. Whereas even a few years ago individuals could only make such transactions by employing the services of a registered stock broker (at considerable expense), it is now very simple to create a trading account at your bank—linked to your other accounts and accessible by the ATMs—and make trades whenever you want and at a much lower cost per transaction. In the language of this chapter, such creation of new banking services is an example of very-long-run innovation.

The development and widespread provision of ATMs by commercial banks represents both a long-run substitution of capital for labour and a very-long-run innovation.

Firms' Choices in the Very Long Run

Firms respond to signals that indicate changes in the economic environment. For example, consider the situation faced by Stelco—a major Canadian steel producer—when the price of coal (a major input) increases and is expected to remain at the higher level for some time. How can Stelco respond to this change in the economic environment?

One option for Stelco is to make a long-run response by substituting away from the use of coal by changing its production techniques within the confines of existing technology. This might involve switching to other fuels (whose prices have not increased) to operate Stelco's enormous blast furnaces. Another option is to invest in research in order to develop new production techniques that innovate away from coal (and other fuels as well), such as the design of blast furnaces that require less fuel to process each unit of iron ore.

Faced with increases in the price of an input, firms may either *substitute away* or *innovate away* from the input—or do both over different time horizons.

It is important to recognize that the two options can involve quite different actions and can ultimately have quite different implications for productivity.

For example, consider three different responses to an increase in Canadian labour costs. One firm reallocates its production activities to Mexico or Southeast Asia, where labour costs are relatively low and hence labour-intensive production techniques remain quite profitable. A second firm chooses to reduce its use of labour but increase its use of capital equipment. These two firms have, in different ways, chosen to *substitute away* from the higher-priced Canadian labour. A third firm devotes resources to developing new production techniques, perhaps using robotics or other new equipment. This firm has *innovated away* from higher-priced Canadian labour.

All three are possible reactions to the changed circumstances. The first two are largely well understood in advance and will lead to reduced costs relative to continued reliance on the original production methods. The third response, depending on the often unpredictable results of the innovation, may reduce costs sufficiently to warrant the investment in research and development and may even lead to substantially more effective production techniques that allow the firm to maintain an advantage over its competitors for a number of years.

S U M M A R Y

8.1 **THE LONG RUN: NO FIXED FACTORS**

- There are no fixed factors in the long run. Profit-maximizing firms choose from the available alternatives the least-cost method of producing any specific output. A long-run cost curve represents the boundary between attainable and unattainable costs for the given technology and given factor prices.
- The principle of substitution states that, in response to changes in factor prices, profit-maximizing firms will substitute toward the cheaper factors and substitute away from the more expensive factors.
- The shape of the *LRAC* curve depends on the relationship of inputs to outputs as the whole scale of a firm's operations changes. Increasing, constant, and decreasing returns lead, respectively, to decreasing, constant, and increasing long-run average costs.
- The *LRAC* and *SRATC* curves are related. Each *SRATC* curve represents a specific plant size and is tangent to the *LRAC* curve at the level of output for which that plant size is optimal.
- *LRAC* curves shift upward or downward in response to changes in the prices of factors or changes in technology. Increases in factor prices shift *LRAC* curves upward. Decreases in factor prices and technological advances shift *LRAC* curves downward.

8.2 THE VERY LONG RUN: CHANGES IN TECHNOLOGY   Ⓛⓞ ④

- Over the very long run, the most important influence on costs of production and on standards of living has been increases in output made possible by technological improvements.
- Changes in technology are often *endogenous responses* to changing economic signals; that is, they result from the firms' responses to changes in the economic environment.

- There are three important kinds of technological change—developments of new production techniques, improved inputs, and new products. All three play an important role in increasing living standards.
- To understand any industry's response to changes in its operating environment, it is important to consider the effects of endogenous innovations in technology as well as substitution based on changes in the use of existing technologies.

KEY CONCEPTS

The implication of cost minimization
The interpretation of
  $MP_K/MP_L = p_K/p_L$
The principle of substitution

Increasing, constant, and decreasing returns
Economies of scale
LRAC curve as an envelope of *SRATC* curves

Technological change and productivity growth
Changes in technology as endogenous responses

STUDY EXERCISES

1. Explain why a profit-maximizing firm must also minimize costs.

2. Ⓧ **myeconlab** Industrial Footwear Inc. uses capital and labour to produce workboots. Suppose this firm is using capital and labour such that the MP_K is equal to 80 and the MP_L is equal to 20.

   a. If the prices per unit of capital and labour are $2 and $10, respectively, is this firm minimizing its costs? If not, what factor substitution should be made to minimize costs?

   b. If the prices per unit of capital and labour are $20 and $5, respectively, is this firm minimizing its costs? If not, what factor substitution should be made to minimize costs?

   c. If the prices per unit of capital and labour are $40 and $5, respectively, is this firm minimizing its costs? What factor substitution should be made to minimize costs?

3. Use the principle of substitution to predict the effect in each of the following situations.

   a. During the past 10 years, technological advances in the computer industry have led to dramatic reductions in the prices of personal and business computers. At the same time, real wages have increased slowly.

   b. The ratio of land costs to building costs is much higher in big cities than in small cities.

   c. Wages of textile workers and shoe machinery operators are higher in Canada than in the Southern United States, but the price of capital equipment is approximately the same.

   d. A new collective agreement results in a significant increase in wages for pulp and paper workers.

4. The following table shows the marginal product of capital and labour for each of several methods of producing 1000 kilograms of flour per day.

Production Method	MP_K	MP_L
A	14	3
B	12	6
C	10	9
D	8	12
E	6	15
F	4	18
G	2	21

   a. As we move from *A* to *G*, are the production methods becoming more or less *capital intensive*? Explain.

   b. If capital costs $8 per unit and labour costs $4 per unit, which production method minimizes the cost of producing 1000 kg of flour?

c. For each of the methods that are not cost minimizing (with the factor prices from part (b), describe how the firm would have to adjust its use of capital and labour to minimize costs.

d. Now suppose the price of capital falls to \$4 per unit and the price of labour rises to \$6 per unit. Which method now minimizes costs?

5. Consider the following diagram of *SRATC* and *LRAC* curves.

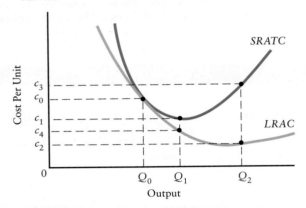

a. The *SRATC* curve is drawn for a given plant size. Given this plant size, what is the level of output that minimizes short-run average costs? What are unit costs in the short run at this level of output?

b. What is the level of output for which this plant size is optimal in the long run? What are unit costs in the short run at this level of output?

c. Explain the economics of why c_1 is greater than c_4.

d. Suppose the firm wants to increase output to Q_2 in the short run. How is this accomplished, and what would unit costs be?

e. Suppose the firm wants to increase output to Q_2 in the long run. How is this accomplished, and what would unit costs be?

6. The following diagram shows three possible *SRATC* curves and an *LRAC* curve for a single firm producing light bulbs, where each *SRATC* curve is associated with a different-sized plant.

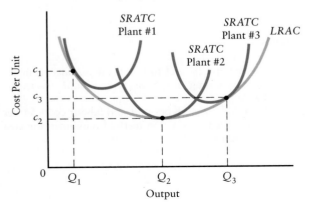

a. If the firm is producing Q_1 light bulbs with Plant #1, what are the firm's average costs?

b. At Q_1, does the firm display decreasing, constant, or increasing costs?

c. How does your answer in (b) relate to the concept of *economies of scale*?

d. Repeat parts (a), (b), and (c) for output level Q_2 with Plant #2 and output level Q_3 with Plant #3.

7. In the text, we stated that the *LRAC* curve eventually slopes upward because of *diseconomies of scale*. In the previous chapter we saw that the *SRATC* curve eventually slopes upward because of *diminishing marginal product of the variable factor*.

a. Explain the difference between *diseconomies of scale* and *diminishing marginal product of the variable factor*. Why is one a short-run concept and the other a long-run concept?

b. Draw a diagram with short-run and long-run average cost curves that illustrates *for the same level of output* both diseconomies of scale and diminishing marginal product of the variable factor.

8. In the text, we stated that the *LRAC* curve initially slopes downward because of *economies of scale*. In the previous chapter we saw that the *SRATC* curve can initially slope downward because of *spreading overhead*.

a. Explain the difference between *economies of scale* and *spreading overhead*. Why is one a short-run concept and the other a long-run concept?

b. Draw a diagram with short-run and long-run average cost curves that illustrates *for the same level of output* both economies of scale and spreading overhead.

9. This question combines the various concepts from Questions 7 and 8.

a. Draw a diagram with short-run and long-run average cost curves that illustrates *for the same level of output* economies of scale in the long run but diminishing marginal product for the variable factor in the short run.

b. Draw a diagram with short-run and long-run average cost curves that illustrates *for the same level of output* diseconomies of scale in the long run but falling average total costs in the short run.

10. This question relates to the material in the Appendix. The following table shows several methods of producing 500 rubber tires per day. There are two factors, labour and capital, with prices per unit of \$3 and \$6, respectively.

Production Method	Units of Labour	Units of Capital	Total Cost
A	110	20	—
B	90	25	—
C	70	33	—
D	50	43	—
E	30	55	—
F	10	70	—

a. Compute the total cost for each production method and fill in the table.
b. Which production method minimizes costs for producing 500 tires?
c. Plot the isoquant for 500 tires.
d. Given the factor prices, draw the isocost line that corresponds to the cost-minimizing production method.
e. Now suppose the price of labour rises to $5 per unit but the firm still wants to produce 500 tires per day. Explain how a cost-minimizing firm adjusts to this change (with no change in technology).

DISCUSSION QUESTIONS

1. In *The Competitive Advantage of Nations,* Michael Porter of Harvard University claimed: "Faced with high relative labor cost,... American consumer electronics firms moved to locate labor-intensive activities in ... Asian countries, leaving the product and production process essentially the same.... Japanese rivals ... set out instead to eliminate labor through automation. Doing so involved reducing the number of components which further lowered cost and improved quality. Japanese firms were soon building assembly plants in the United States, the place American firms had sought to avoid." Discuss these reactions in terms of changes over the long run and the very long run.

2. Why must a profit-maximizing firm choose the least-cost method of producing any given output? Might a non-profit-maximizing organization such as a university, church, or government intentionally choose a method of production other than the least-cost one?

3. What is the interpretation of a move from one point on a long-run average cost curve to another point on the same curve? Contrast this with a movement along a short-run average total cost curve.

4. Each of the following is a means of increasing productivity. Discuss which groups in a society might oppose each one.

a. A labour-saving invention that permits all goods to be manufactured with less labour than before
b. The removal of all government production safety rules
c. A reduction in corporate income taxes

5. Policymakers and commentators often argue that the Canadian health-care system is "more efficient" than the U.S. health-care system. What do they mean by "more efficient"?

6. In December 1998, after a year in which Asian demand for B.C. lumber had fallen dramatically, an article in *The Globe and Mail* had the following headline: "Drastic Cost Reductions Needed to Save 13 B.C. Sawmills."

a. Does the headline suggest that the B.C. lumber companies are not profit maximizers?
b. If long-run unit costs are "too high," what is stopping the lumber companies from simply moving down their *LRAC* curves?

7. "Necessity is the mother of invention." Explain why this statement captures the essence of the view that firms often innovate their way around unfavourable changes in their economic environment.

Isoquant Analysis

The production function gives the relationship between the factor inputs that the firm uses and the output that it obtains. In the long run, the firm can choose among many different combinations of inputs that yield the same output. The production function and the long-run choices open to the firm can be represented graphically by using *isoquants*.

8A.1 ISOQUANTS

The table in Figure 8A-1 illustrates a hypothetical example in which several combinations of two inputs, labour and capital, can produce a given quantity of output. The data from the table are plotted graphically in Figure 8A-1. A smooth curve is drawn through the points to indicate that there are additional ways, which are not listed in the table, of producing the same output.

This curve is called an *isoquant*. It shows the whole set of technically efficient factor combinations for producing a given level of output. This is an example of graphing a relationship among three variables in two dimensions. It is analogous to the contour line on a map, which shows all points of equal altitude, and to an indifference curve (discussed in the Appendix to Chapter 6), which shows all combinations of products that yield the consumer equal utility.

As we move from one point on an isoquant to another, we are *substituting one factor for another* while holding output constant. If we move from point *b* to point *c*, we are substituting 1 unit of labour for 3 units of capital.

The marginal rate of substitution measures the rate at which one factor is substituted for another with output being held constant.

Sometimes the term *marginal rate of technical substitution* is used to distinguish this concept from the analogous one for consumer theory (the marginal rate of substitution) that we examined in Chapter 6.

Graphically, the marginal rate of substitution is measured by the slope of the isoquant at a particular point. We adopt the standard practice of defining the marginal rate of substitution as the negative of the slope of the isoquant so that it is a positive number. The table in Figure 8A-1 shows the calculation of some marginal rates of substitution between various points on an isoquant. [19]

The marginal rate of substitution is related to the marginal products of the factors of production. To see how, consider an example. Suppose at the present level of inputs of labour and capital, the marginal product of labour is 2 units of output and the marginal product of capital is 1 unit of output. If the firm reduces its use of capital and increases its use of labour to keep output constant, it needs to add only one-half unit of labour for 1 unit of capital given up. If, at another point on the isoquant with more labour and less capital, the marginal products are 2 for capital and 1 for labour, the firm will have to add 2 units of labour for every unit of capital it gives up. The general proposition is this:

The marginal rate of (technical) substitution between two factors of production is equal to the ratio of their marginal products.

Economists assume that isoquants satisfy two important conditions: They are downward sloping, and they are convex when viewed from the origin. What is the economic meaning of these conditions?

The downward slope indicates that each factor input has a positive marginal product. If the input of one factor is reduced and that of the other is held constant, output will be reduced. Thus, if one input is decreased, production can be held constant only if the other factor input is increased.

To understand the convexity of the isoquant, consider what happens as the firm moves along the isoquant of Figure 8A-1 downward and to the right. Labour is being added and capital reduced to keep output constant. If labour is added in increments of exactly 1 unit, how much capital can be dispensed with each time? The key to the answer is that both factors are assumed to be subject to the law of diminishing returns. Thus, the gain in output associated

FIGURE 8A-1 An Isoquant

Alternative Methods of Producing a Given Level of Output

Method	K	L	ΔK	ΔL	Marginal Rate of Substitution (absolute value of ΔK/ΔL)
a	18	2			
b	12	3	−6	1	6.00
c	9	4	−3	1	3.00
d	6	6	−3	2	1.50
e	4	9	−2	3	0.67
f	3	12	−1	3	0.33
g	2	18	−1	6	0.17

An isoquant describes the firm's alternative methods for producing a given level of output. Method *a* uses a great deal of capital (K) and very little labour (L). As we move down the table, labour is substituted for capital in such a way as to keep output constant. Finally, at the bottom, most of the capital has been replaced by labour. The marginal rate of substitution between the two factors is calculated in the last three columns of the table. Note that as we move down the table, the marginal rate of substitution declines.

When the isoquant is plotted it is downward sloping and convex. The downward slope reflects the requirement of technical efficiency: Keeping the level of output constant, a reduction in the use of one factor requires an increase in the use of the other factor. The convex shape of the isoquant reflects a diminishing marginal rate of (technical) substitution.

with each additional unit of labour added is *diminishing,* whereas the loss of output associated with each additional unit of capital forgone is *increasing.* Therefore, it takes ever-smaller reductions in capital to compensate for equal increases in labour. Viewed from the origin, therefore, the isoquant is convex.

An Isoquant Map

The isoquant of Figure 8A-1 is for a given level of output. Suppose it is for 6 units. In this case, there is another isoquant for 7 units, another for 7000 units, and a different one for every other level of output. Each isoquant refers to a specific level of output and connects combinations of factors that are technically efficient methods of producing that output. If we plot a representative set of these isoquants from the same production function on a single graph, we get an *isoquant map* like that in Figure 8A-2. The higher the level of output along a particular isoquant, the farther the isoquant is from the origin.

FIGURE 8A-2 An Isoquant Map

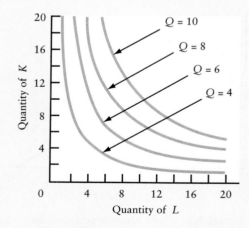

An isoquant map shows a set of isoquants, one for each level of output. Each isoquant corresponds to a specific level of output and shows factor combinations that are technically efficient methods of producing that output.

8A.2 COST MINIMIZATION

Finding the cost-minimizing method of producing any output requires knowledge of the factor prices. Suppose capital is priced at $4 per unit and labour at $1 per unit. An *isocost line* shows alternative combinations of factors that a firm can buy for a given total cost. Four different isocost lines appear in Figure 8A-3. The slope of each isocost line reflects *relative* factor prices. For given factor prices, a series of parallel isocost lines will reflect the alternative levels of expenditure on factor purchases that are available to the firm. The higher the level of expenditure, the farther the isocost line is from the origin.

In Figure 8A-4, the isoquant and isocost maps are brought together. The cost-minimizing method of production must be a point on an isoquant that just touches (is tangent to) an isocost line. If the isoquant cuts the isocost line, it is possible to move along the isoquant and reach a lower level of cost. Only at a point of tangency is a movement in either direction along the isoquant a movement to a higher cost level.

As shown in Figure 8A-4, the lowest attainable cost of producing 6 units is $24 and this requires using 12 units of labour and 3 units of capital.

The least-cost position is given graphically by the tangency point between the isoquant and the isocost lines.

The slope of the isocost line is given by the ratio of the prices of the two factors of production. The slope of the isoquant is given by the ratio of their marginal products. When the firm reaches its cost-minimizing position, it has equated the price ratio (which is given to it by the market) with the ratio of the marginal products (which it can adjust by changing its usage of the factors). In symbols,

$$\frac{MP_L}{MP_K} = \frac{p_L}{p_K}$$

This is the same condition that we derived in the text (see Equation 8-2), but here we have derived it by using the isoquant analysis of the firm's decisions. [20]

Note the similarity of this condition for a cost-minimizing firm to Equation 6-2 where we saw how utility maximization for a consumer requires that the ratio of marginal utilities of consuming two products must equal the ratio of the two product prices. Both conditions reveal the basic principle that the decision makers (consumers or producers) face market prices beyond their control and so adjust quantities (consumption or factor inputs) until they are achieving their objective (utility maximization or cost minimization).

The Principle of Substitution

Suppose with technology unchanged (that is, for a given isoquant map), the price of one factor changes. In particular, suppose with the price of capital unchanged at $4 per unit, the price of labour rises from $1 to $4 per unit. Originally, the cost-minimizing factor combination for producing 6 units of output was 12 units of labour and 3 units of capital. Total cost was $24. To produce that same output in the same way would now cost $60 at the new factor prices. Figure 8A-5 shows why this production method is no longer the cost-minimizing one. The slope of the isocost line has changed, which makes it efficient to substitute the now relatively cheaper capital for the relatively more expensive labour. The change in slope of the isocost line illustrates the principle of substitution.

FIGURE 8A-3   Isocost Lines

Each isocost line shows alternative factor combinations that require the same expenditure. The graph shows the four isocost lines that result when labour costs $1 per unit and capital $4 per unit and when expenditure (total cost, *TC*) is held constant at $12, $24, $36, and $48, respectively.

FIGURE 8A-4   Cost Minimization

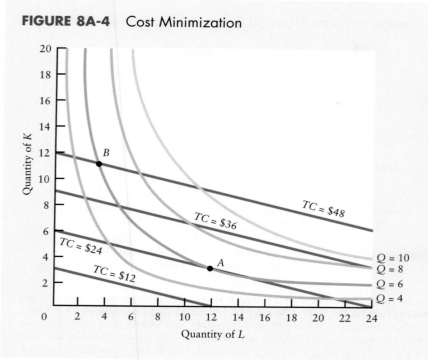

Cost minimization occurs at points of tangency between isoquant and isocost lines. The isoquant map of Figure 8A-2 and the isocost lines of Figure 8A-3 are brought together. Consider point A. It is on the 6-unit isoquant and the $24 isocost line. Thus, it is possible to achieve the output Q = 6 for a total cost of $24. There are other ways to achieve this output, for example, at point B, where TC = $48. Moving along the isoquant from point A in either direction increases cost. Similarly, moving along the isocost line from point A in either direction lowers output. Thus, either move would raise cost per unit.

Changes in relative factor prices will cause a partial replacement of factors that have become relatively more expensive by factors that have become relatively cheaper.

Of course, substitution of capital for labour cannot fully offset the effects of a rise in the cost of labour, as Figure 8A-5(i) shows. Consider the output attainable for $24. In the figure, there are two isocost lines representing $24 of outlay—at the old and new prices of labour. The new isocost line for $24 lies inside the old one (except where no labour is used). The $24 isocost line must therefore be tangent to a lower isoquant. Thus, if production is to be held constant, higher costs must be accepted. However, because of substitution, it is not necessary to accept

costs as high as those that would accompany an unchanged factor proportion. In the example, 6 units can be produced for $48 rather than the $60 that would be required if no change in factor proportions were made.

This analysis leads to the following predictions:

A rise in the price of one factor with all other factor prices held constant will (1) shift the cost curves of products that use that factor upward and (2) lead to a substitution of factors that are now relatively cheaper for the factor whose price has risen.

Both of these predictions were stated in Chapter 8; now they have been derived formally by the use of isoquants and isocost lines.

FIGURE 8A-5   The Effects of a Change in Factor Prices on Costs and Factor Proportions

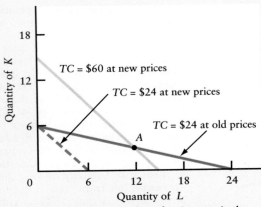

(i) The effect on the isocost line of an increase in the price of labour

(ii) Substitution of capital for labour resulting from an increase in the price of labour

An increase in the price of labour pivots the isocost line inward, increasing its slope. This changes the cost-minimizing method of producing any level of output. In part (i), the rise in the price of L from \$1 to \$4 per unit (with the price of K being held constant at \$4) pivots the \$24 isocost line inward to the dashed line. Any output previously produced for \$24 will cost more at the new prices if it uses any labour. The new cost of using the factor combination at A rises from \$24 to \$60. In part (ii), the steeper isocost line is tangent to the $Q = 6$ isoquant at C, not A, so that more capital and less labour is used. Costs at C are \$48, higher than they were before the price increase but not as high as they would be if the factor substitution had not occurred.

CHAPTER 9

Competitive Markets

LO LEARNING OBJECTIVES

In this chapter you will learn

1. the key assumptions of the theory of perfect competition.
2. how to derive a competitive firm's supply curve.
3. to determine whether competitive firms are making profits or losses in the short run.
4. the role played by profits, entry, and exit in a competitive industry's long-run equilibrium.

Does American Express compete with Visa? Does a wheat farmer from Biggar, Saskatchewan, compete with a wheat farmer from Brandon, Manitoba? If we use the ordinary meaning of the word compete, the answer to the first question is plainly yes, and the answer to the second question is no.

American Express and Visa both advertise extensively to persuade consumers to use their credit cards. A host of world travellers in various tight spots attest on television or in magazines to the virtues of American Express, while other happy faces advise us that only with a Visa card can their pleasures be ours.

When we shift our attention to wheat farmers, however, we see the Saskatchewan farmer can do nothing to affect either the sales or the profits of the Manitoba farmer. Even if the Saskatchewan farmer could do something to influence the profits of the Manitoba farmer, there would be no point in doing so, since changes in the profits of the Manitoba farmer would not affect the Saskatchewan farmer.

To sort out the questions of who is competing with whom and in what sense, it is useful to distinguish between the behaviour of individual firms and the type of market in which they operate. Economists are interested in two different concepts—*competitive market structure* and *competitive behaviour*.

market structure All features of a market that affect the behaviour and performance of firms in that market, such as the number and size of sellers, the extent of knowledge about one another's actions, the degree of freedom of entry, and the degree of product differentiation.

9.1 MARKET STRUCTURE AND FIRM BEHAVIOUR

The term **market structure** refers to all the features that may affect the behaviour and performance of the firms in a market, such as the number of firms in the market or the type of product that they sell. In this chapter, we focus on a *competitive* market structure.

Competitive Market Structure

market power The ability of a firm to influence the price of a product or the terms under which it is sold.

Economists say that firms have **market power** when they can influence the price of their product or the terms under which their product is sold. The *competitiveness* of the market is the extent to which individual firms *lack* such market power.

A market is said to have a competitive structure when its firms have little or no market power. The more market power the firms have, the less competitive is the market structure.

The extreme form of competitive market structure occurs when each firm has zero market power. In such a case, there are so many firms in the market that each must accept the price set by the forces of market demand and market supply. The firms perceive themselves as being able to sell as much as they choose at the prevailing market price and as having no power to influence that price. If the firm charged a higher price, it would make no sales; so many other firms would be selling at the market price that buyers would take their business elsewhere.

This extreme is called a *perfectly competitive market structure* or, more simply, a *perfectly competitive market*. In such a market there is no need for individual firms to compete actively with one another because none has any power over the market. One firm's ability to sell its product does not depend on the behaviour of any other firm. For example, the Saskatchewan and Manitoba wheat farms operate in a perfectly competitive market over which they have no power. Neither can change the market price for its wheat by altering its own behaviour.

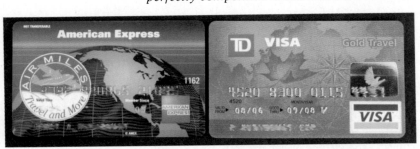

American Express and VISA "compete" very actively against each other in the credit-card market, but economists nonetheless refer to the structure of this market as imperfectly competitive.

Competitive Behaviour

In everyday language, the term *competitive behaviour* refers to the degree to which individual firms actively vie with one another for business. For example, American Express and Visa clearly engage in competitive behaviour. It is also true, however, that both companies have some real power over their market. Each has the power to decide the fees that people will pay for the use of their credit cards, within limits set by buyers' tastes and the fees of competing cards. Either firm could raise its fees and still continue to attract some customers. Even though they actively compete with each other, they do so in a market that does not have a perfectly competitive structure.

In contrast, the Saskatchewan and Manitoba wheat farmers do not engage in competitive behaviour because the only way they can affect their profits is by changing their own outputs of wheat or their own production costs.

The distinction that we have just made between behaviour and structure explains why firms in perfectly competitive markets (e.g., the Saskatchewan and Manitoba wheat producers) do not compete actively with each other, whereas firms that do compete actively with each other (e.g., American Express and Visa) do not operate in perfectly competitive markets.

The Significance of Market Structure

When a firm decides how much output to produce in order to maximize its profit, it needs to know the demand for its product and also the costs of production. We examined the various costs in detail in Chapters 7 and 8. Now we need to think about the demand for the firm's product. This is where market structure enters the picture because the details of market structure determine how we get from the *industry* demand curve to the demand curve facing any individual *firm* in that industry.

We will see in the next few chapters that market structure plays a central role in determining the behaviour of individual firms and also in the overall *efficiency* of the market outcomes. In this chapter, we focus only on *competitive* market structures. In later chapters, we explore non-competitive market structures.

A wheat farmer in Saskatchewan does not "compete" in any real way with a wheat farmer elsewhere in the world. However, both exist in what economists call a highly "competitive" market.

9.2 THE THEORY OF PERFECT COMPETITION

The perfectly competitive market structure—usually referred to simply as **perfect competition**—applies directly to a number of markets, especially many agricultural and raw-materials markets. It also provides an important benchmark for comparison with other market structures.

perfect competition A market structure in which all firms in an industry are price takers and in which there is freedom of entry into and exit from the industry.

The Assumptions of Perfect Competition

In addition to the fundamental assumption that firms seek to maximize their profits, the theory of perfect competition is built on a number of assumptions relating to each firm and to the industry as a whole.

1. All the firms in the industry sell an identical product. Economists say that the firms sell a **homogeneous product.**

2. Consumers know the nature of the product being sold and the prices charged by each firm.

3. The level of a firm's output at which its long-run average cost reaches a minimum is small relative to the *industry's* total output. (This is a precise way of saying that the firm is small relative to the size of the industry.)

4. The industry is characterized by *freedom of entry and exit*; that is, any new firm is free to enter the industry and start producing if it so wishes, and any existing firm is free to cease production and leave the industry. Existing firms cannot block the entry of new firms, and there are no legal prohibitions or other barriers to entering or exiting the industry.

homogeneous product In the eyes of purchasers, every unit of the product is identical to every other unit.

The first three assumptions imply that each firm in a perfectly competitive industry is a **price taker,** meaning that the firm can alter its rate of production and sales

price taker A firm that can alter its rate of production and sales without affecting the market price of its product.

without affecting the market price of its product. Thus, a firm operating in a perfectly competitive market has no market power. It must passively accept whatever happens to be the market price, but it can sell as much as it wants at that price.

The Saskatchewan and Manitoba wheat farmers we considered earlier provide us with good illustrations of firms that are operating in a perfectly competitive market. Because each individual wheat farmer is just one of a very large number of producers who are all growing the same product, one firm's contribution to the industry's total production is a tiny drop in an extremely large bucket. Each firm will correctly assume that variations in its output have no effect on the price of wheat. Thus, each firm, knowing that it can sell as much or as little as it chooses at that price, adapts its behaviour to a given market price of wheat. Furthermore, there is nothing that any one farmer can do to stop another farmer from growing wheat, and there are no legal deterrents to becoming a wheat farmer. Anyone who has enough money to buy or rent the necessary land, labour, and equipment can become a wheat farmer.

The difference between the wheat farmers and American Express is the *degree of market power*. Each firm that is producing wheat is an insignificant part of the whole market and thus has no power to influence the price of wheat. American Express does have power to influence the credit-card market because its own sales represent a significant part of the total sales of credit-card services.

The Demand Curve for a Perfectly Competitive Firm

Practise with Study Guide Chapter 9, Short-Answer Question 4.

A major distinction between firms in perfectly competitive markets and firms in any other type of market is the shape of the demand curve facing the firm.

Even though the demand curve for the entire industry may be negatively sloped, each firm in a perfectly competitive market faces a horizontal demand curve because variations in the firm's output have no effect on price.

The horizontal (perfectly elastic) demand curve does not indicate that the firm could actually sell an infinite amount at the going price. It indicates, rather, that the variations in production *that it will normally be possible for the firm to make* will leave price unchanged because their effect on total industry output will be negligible.

Figure 9-1 contrasts the market demand curve for the product of a competitive industry with the demand curve that a single firm in that industry faces. *Applying Economic Concepts 9-1* provides an example of the important difference between the firm's demand curve and the market demand curve. It uses a numerical example to show why the demand curve facing any individual wheat farmer is very nearly perfectly elastic, even though the *market* demand for wheat is quite inelastic.

Total, Average, and Marginal Revenue

total revenue (*TR*) Total receipts from the sale of a product; price times quantity.

To study the revenues that firms receive from the sale of their products, economists define three concepts called *total, average,* and *marginal revenue*.

Total revenue (*TR*) is the total amount received by the firm from the sale of a product. If Q units are sold at p dollars each:

$$TR = p \times Q$$

FIGURE 9-1   The Demand Curve for a Competitive Industry and for One Firm in the Industry

(i) Competitive industry's demand curve

(ii) Competitive firm's demand curve

The industry's demand curve is negatively sloped; the competitive firm's demand curve is horizontal. Notice the difference in the quantities shown on the horizontal scale in each part of the figure. The competitive industry has an output of 200 million units when the price is $3. The individual firm takes that market price as given and considers producing up to, say, 6000 units. The firm's demand curve in part (ii) is horizontal because any change in output that this single firm could manage would leave price virtually unchanged at $3. The firm's output variation has an imperceptible effect on industry output.

Average revenue (AR) is the amount of revenue per unit sold. It is equal to total revenue divided by the number of units sold, and is thus equal to the price at which the product is sold:

$$AR = \frac{TR}{Q} = \frac{(p \times Q)}{Q} = p$$

average revenue (AR) Total revenue divided by quantity sold; this is the market price when all units are sold at the same price.

Marginal revenue (MR) is the change in a firm's total revenue resulting from a change in its sales by 1 unit. Whenever output changes by more than 1 unit, the change in revenue must be divided by the change in output to calculate marginal revenue. For example, if an increase in output of 3 units is accompanied by an increase in revenue of $1500, the marginal revenue is $1500/3, or $500. [21]

marginal revenue (MR) The change in a firm's total revenue resulting from a change in its sales by one unit.

$$MR = \frac{\Delta TR}{\Delta Q}$$

To illustrate each of these revenue concepts, consider a farmer who is selling barley in a perfectly competitive market at a price of $3 per bushel. Total revenue rises by $3 for every bushel sold. Because every bushel brings in $3, the average revenue per bushel sold is clearly $3. Furthermore, because each *additional* bushel sold brings in $3, the marginal revenue of an extra bushel sold is also $3. The table in Figure 9-2 shows calculations of these revenue concepts for a range of outputs between 10 and 13 bushels. The figure plots the various revenue curves.

The important point illustrated in the table is that as long as the firm's own level of output cannot affect the price of the product it sells, then the firm's marginal revenue is equal to its average revenue. Thus, for a price-taking firm, $AR = MR$ = price. Graphically, as shown in part (i) of Figure 9-2, average revenue and marginal revenue are the same horizontal line drawn at the level of market price. Because the firm can sell any quantity it chooses at this price, the horizontal line is also the firm's demand curve; it shows that any quantity the firm chooses to sell will be associated with this same market price.

APPLYING ECONOMIC CONCEPTS 9-1

Demand Under Perfect Competition: Firm and Industry

Consider an individual wheat farmer and the world market for wheat. Since products have negatively sloped market demand curves, any increase in the industry's output (caused by a shift in supply) will cause some fall in the market price. However, as the calculations here show, any conceivable increase that one wheat farm could make in its output has such a negligible effect on the industry's price that the farmer correctly ignores it—the individual wheat farmer is thus a price taker.

The *market* elasticity of demand for wheat is approximately 0.25. (Recall from Chapter 4 that an elasticity of 0.25 means that a 10 percent decline in market price is associated with only a 2.5 percent increase in quantity demanded.) Thus, if the quantity of wheat supplied in the world were to increase by 1 percent, the price of wheat would have to fall by roughly 4 percent to induce the world's wheat buyers to purchase the extra wheat.

The total world production of wheat in 2003 was approximately 550 million tonnes, of which 23.5 million tonnes were produced in Canada. In that year there were approximately 20 000 wheat farms in Canada. Thus, the average crop size for a Canadian wheat farmer in 2003 was about 1175 tonnes (= 23.5 million/20 000), only 0.0002 percent of the world wheat crop.

As a result of being such a small fraction of the overall market, individual wheat farmers face a horizontal demand curve. To see this, suppose an individual farmer on an average-sized farm decided in one year to produce nothing and in another year managed to produce twice the average output of 1175 tonnes. This is an extremely large variation in one farm's output. The increase in output from zero to 2350 tonnes represents a 200-percent variation measured around the farm's average output. Yet the percentage increase in world output is only (2350 / 550 million) × 100 = 0.0004 percent. Given the demand elasticity of 0.25, this increase in output would lead to a decrease in the world price of 0.0016 percent.

This very small decline in price, together with the 200-percent increase in the farm's *own* output, implies that the farm's own demand curve has an elasticity of 125 000 (= 200 / 0.0016). This enormous elasticity of demand means that the farm would have to increase its output by 125 000 percent to bring about a 1-percent decrease in the world price of wheat. Because the farm's output cannot be varied this much, it is not surprising that the farmer regards the price of wheat as unaffected by any change in output that he or she could conceivably make. For all intents and purposes, the individual farmer faces a perfectly elastic—horizontal—demand curve for the product and is thus a *price taker*.

If the market price is unaffected by variations in the firm's output, the firm's demand curve, its average revenue curve, and its marginal revenue curve all coincide in the same horizontal line.

This result can be stated in a slightly different way that turns out to be important for our later study:

For a firm in perfect competition, price equals marginal revenue.

FIGURE 9-2 Revenues for a Price-Taking Firm

Revenue Concepts

Price p	Output Q	$TR = p \times Q$	$AR = TR/Q$	$MR = \Delta TR/\Delta Q$
$3	10	$30	$3	
3	11	33	3	$3
3	12	36	3	3
3	13	39	3	3

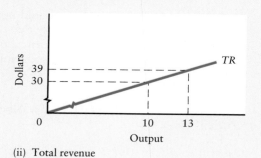

Revenue Curves

(i) Average and marginal revenue

(ii) Total revenue

When the firm is a price taker, $AR = MR = p$. Because price does not change as a result of the firm changing its output, neither marginal revenue nor average revenue varies with output. In the table, marginal revenue is shown between the rows because it represents the *change* in total revenues in response to a *change* in quantity. When price is constant, total revenue (which is price times quantity) is an upward-sloping straight line starting from the origin.

9.3 SHORT-RUN DECISIONS

We learned in Chapter 7 how each firm's costs vary with its output in the short run. Recall that in the short run, the firm has one or more fixed factors, and the only way it can change its output is by changing the amount of its variable factor inputs. In this chapter, we have seen how the firm's total, average, and marginal revenues vary as the firm changes its level of output. The next step is to put the cost and revenue information together to determine the level of output that will maximize the firm's profits.

Rules for All Profit-Maximizing Firms

Two rules apply to *all* profit-maximizing firms, whether or not they operate in perfectly competitive markets. The first rule determines whether the firm should produce at all, and the second determines how much it should produce.

Should the Firm Produce at All? The firm always has the option of producing nothing. If it produces nothing, it will have an operating loss that is equal to its fixed costs. If it decides to produce, it will add the variable cost of production to its costs and the receipts from the sale of its product to its revenue. Therefore, since it must pay its fixed costs in any event, it will be worthwhile for the firm to produce as long as it can find some level of output for which revenue exceeds *variable* cost. However, if its revenue is less than its variable cost at every level of output, the firm will actually lose more by producing any level of output than by not producing at all.

Table 9-1 shows an example of a profit-maximizing firm that decides to produce no output when facing a low market price. The table shows the firm's variable and fixed costs for each level of output. (If you were to graph the *TVC, TFC,* and *TC* curves from this table, you would find that they look very much like the curves we studied in Chapter 7.) The table also shows the firm's total revenues and profits at each level of output. When the market price is $2 per unit, the firm's profits are negative *at any level of output*—the firm's revenues *never* cover its costs. At this low market price, the firm's revenues don't even cover its variable costs and, in fact, the negative profits (losses) only grow larger as output increases. In this situation, the firm is better off to shut down and produce no output at all. (The table also presents a situation where the price is $5 per unit; for reasons that we will soon see, the firm's best option is then to produce output even though its profits are negative.)

Rule 1: A firm should not produce at all if, for all levels of output, the total variable cost of producing that output exceeds the total revenue derived from selling it. Equivalently, the firm should not produce at all if, for all levels of output, the average variable cost of producing the output exceeds the price at which it can be sold. [22]

TABLE 9-1   Negative Profits and the Firm's Shut-Down Decision

| | | | | Price = $2 | | Price = $5 | |
Q	TVC	TFC	TC	TR	Profit	TR	Profit
0	0	200	200	0	−200	0	−200
10	50	200	250	20	−230	50	−200
20	80	200	280	40	−240	100	−180
30	100	200	300	60	−240	150	−150
40	110	200	310	80	−230	200	−110
50	130	200	330	100	−230	250	−80
60	160	200	360	120	−240	300	−60
70	200	200	400	140	−260	350	−50
80	260	200	460	160	−300	400	−60
90	320	200	520	180	−340	450	−70
100	380	200	580	200	−380	500	−80

A competitive firm may maximize its profits (or minimize its losses) by shutting down and producing zero output. The data in the table show costs and revenues at various levels of output. The firm must pay its fixed costs even if it shuts down and earns no revenue. At a price of $2, there is *no* level of output at which the firm's revenues cover its variable costs. In this situation, the firm can minimize its losses by shutting down and producing zero output.

At a higher price of $5, the profit-maximizing firm should choose to produce 70 units of output even though its profits are negative. At this level of output, the firm's revenues more than cover its variable costs and help to pay some portion of the fixed costs. Since the firm must pay its fixed costs no matter what level of output is produced, it would be worse off if it chose to produce zero output.

The price at which the firm can just cover its average variable cost, and so is indifferent between producing and not producing, is called the **shut-down price**. Such a price is shown in part (i) of Figure 9-4. (We will return in a moment to Figure 9-3.) At the price of $20, the firm can just cover its average variable cost by producing Q_0 units. For any price below $20, there is no output at which variable costs can be covered, and thus the firm will shut down. The price of $20 in part (i) is therefore the shut-down price.

shut-down price The price that is equal to the minimum of a firm's average variable costs. At prices below this, a profit-maximizing firm will shut down and produce no output.

How Much Should the Firm Produce?

If a firm decides that, according to Rule 1, production is worth undertaking, it must then decide *how much* to produce. The key to understanding how much the firm should produce is to think about it on a unit-by-unit basis. If any unit of production adds more to revenue than it does to cost, producing and selling that unit will increase profits. According to the terminology introduced earlier, a unit of production raises profits if the *marginal* revenue obtained from selling it exceeds the *marginal* cost of producing it. The reverse is also true: An extra unit of production will reduce profits if the marginal revenue is less than the marginal cost.

Now let a firm with some existing rate of output consider increasing or decreasing that output. If a further unit of production will increase the firm's revenues by *more* than it increases costs ($MR > MC$), the firm should expand its output. However, if the last unit produced increases revenues by *less* than it increases costs ($MR < MC$), the firm should reduce its output. From this it follows that the only time the firm should leave its output unaltered is when the last unit produced adds the same amount to revenues as it does to costs ($MR = MC$).[1]

Rule 2: If it is worthwhile for the firm to produce at all, the firm should produce the output at which marginal revenue equals marginal cost. [23]

The two rules that we have stated refer to each firm's own costs and revenues, and they apply to all profit-maximizing firms, whatever the market structure in which they operate.

Rule 2 Applied to Price-Taking Firms

Rule 2 tells us that any profit-maximizing firm that produces at all will produce at the point where marginal cost equals marginal revenue. However, we have already seen that for price-taking firms, marginal revenue is equal to the market price. Combining these two results gives us an important conclusion:

A firm that is operating in a perfectly competitive market will produce the output that equates its marginal cost of production with the market price of its product (as long as price exceeds average variable cost).

In a perfectly competitive industry, the market determines the price at which the firm sells its product. The firm then picks the quantity of output that maximizes its profits. We have seen that this is the output for which price equals marginal cost. When the firm has reached a position where its profits are maximized, it has no incentive to change its output. Therefore, unless prices or costs change, the firm will continue to produce this output because it is doing as well as it can do, given the market situation. This profit-maximizing behaviour is illustrated in Figure 9-3.

The perfectly competitive firm adjusts its level of output in response to changes in the market-determined price.

Practise with Study Guide Chapter 9, Exercise 1.

---

[1] The equality of MR and MC is a *necessary* condition for profit maximization but it is not *sufficient*. If the MC curve cuts the MR curve from above, as it might if MC were *falling* as output increased, then the level of output where MR equals MC would actually *minimize* profits. Here, we restrict ourselves to the more realistic settings in which the MC curve is upward sloping over the relevant range of output. In such cases, the equality of MR and MC is both necessary and sufficient for profit maximization.

FIGURE 9-3 Profit Maximization for a Competitive Firm

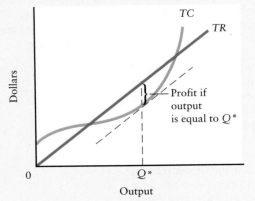

(i) Total costs and total revenues

(ii) Marginal cost and marginal revenue

The firm chooses the level of output at which profits are maximized. If it is profitable to produce at all (so that price exceeds the minimum of average variable cost), the firm chooses the level of output where marginal revenue equals marginal cost. In part (i), this is shown as the level of output where the vertical distance between TR and TC is largest (and thus where the slopes of the TR and TC curves are the same). In part (ii), price is equal to marginal revenue since the firm is a price taker, and so the profit-maximizing level of output is where price (marginal revenue) equals marginal cost. For each of the Q^* units sold, the firm earns revenue of p and the average total cost is c; therefore, total profit is $(p - c)Q^*$, which is the shaded area.

Figure 9-3 shows the profit-maximizing choice of the firm in two different ways. In part (i), the firm's total cost and total revenue curves are shown, and the profit-maximizing level of output, Q^*, is the level that shows the largest positive gap between total revenues and total costs. In part (ii), the firm's average and marginal cost curves are shown together with the market price (which for a price-taking firm equals average and marginal revenue) and the profit-maximizing level of output, Q^*, is the level at which price equals marginal cost. These are two different ways of viewing the same profit-maximization problem; the value of Q^* in part (i) must be the same as the value of Q^* in part (ii).

Short-Run Supply Curves

Now that we know how the perfectly competitive firm determines its profit-maximizing level of output, we can derive its supply curve that reflects these decisions. Once we have derived the individual firm's supply curve, we can derive the supply curve for the entire market.

The Supply Curve for One Firm   The competitive firm's supply curve is derived in part (i) of Figure 9-4, which shows a firm's marginal cost curve and four alternative prices. The horizontal line at each price is the firm's demand curve when the market price is at that level. The firm's marginal cost curve gives the marginal cost corresponding to each level of output. What we are trying to derive is a supply curve that shows the quantity of output that the firm will supply at each price. For prices below average variable cost, the firm will supply zero units (Rule 1). For prices above average variable cost, the competitive firm will choose its level of output to equate price and marginal cost (Rule 2). This behaviour leads to the following conclusion:

A competitive firm's supply curve is given by the portion of its marginal cost curve that is above its average variable cost curve.

The Supply Curve for an Industry   Figure 9-5 shows the derivation of an industry supply curve for an industry containing only two firms. The general result is as follows:

In perfect competition, the industry supply curve is the horizontal sum of the marginal cost curves (above the level of average variable cost) of all firms in the industry.

FIGURE 9-4   The Derivation of the Supply Curve for a Competitive Firm

(i) Marginal cost and average variable
     cost curves

(ii) Firm's supply curve

The supply curve of the competitive firm is the portion of its *MC* curve above the *AVC* curve. For prices below $20, output is zero because there is no output at which *AVC* can be covered. The point *A*, where the price of $20 is just equal to *AVC*, is the point at which the firm will shut down. As price rises to $30, $40, and $50, the profit-maximizing point changes to *B*, *C*, and *D*, taking output to Q_1, Q_2, and Q_3. At any of these prices, the firm's revenue exceeds its variable costs of production and thus can help to cover some part of its fixed costs.

FIGURE 9-5   The Derivation of a Competitive Industry's Supply Curve

(i) Firm A's supply curve

(ii) Firm B's supply curve

(iii) Industry supply curve

The industry's supply curve is the horizontal sum of the supply curves of each of the firms in the industry. At a price of $3, Firm A would supply 4 units and Firm B would supply 3 units. Together, as shown in part (iii), they would supply 7 units. If there are hundreds of firms, the process is the same. In this example, because Firm B does not enter the market at prices below $2, the supply curve $S_{A + B}$ is identical to S_A up to price $2 and is the horizontal sum of S_A and S_B above $2.

Each firm's marginal cost curve shows how much that firm will supply at each given market price, and the industry supply curve is the sum of what each firm will supply.

This supply curve, based on the short-run marginal cost curves of all the firms in the industry, is the industry's supply curve that we first encountered in Chapter 3. We have now established the profit-maximizing behaviour of individual firms that lies behind that curve. It is sometimes called a *short-run supply curve* because it is based on the short-run, profit-maximizing behaviour of all the firms in the industry.

Short-Run Equilibrium in a Competitive Market

The price of a product sold in a perfectly competitive market is determined by the inter-action of the industry's supply curve and the market demand curve. Although no single firm can influence the market price significantly, the collective actions of all firms in the industry (as shown by the industry supply curve) and the collective actions of households (as shown by the market demand curve) together determine the equilibrium price. This occurs at the point where the market demand and supply curves intersect.

short-run equilibrium For a competitive industry, the price and output at which industry demand equals short-run industry supply, and all firms are maximizing their profits. Either profits or losses for individual firms are possible.

When a perfectly competitive industry is in **short-run equilibrium**, each firm is producing and selling a quantity for which its marginal cost equals the market price. No firm is motivated to change its output in the short run. Because total quantity demanded equals total quantity supplied, there is no reason for market price to change in the short run.

When an industry is in short-run equilibrium, quantity demanded equals quantity supplied, and each firm is maximizing its profits given the market price.

Practise with Study Guide Chapter 9, Exercise 2.

Figure 9-6 shows the relationship between the market equilibrium, determined by the intersection of demand and supply, and a typical profit-maximizing firm within that market. The individual firm is shown to have positive (economic) profits in the short-run equilibrium. We know the firm's profits are positive because the market price exceeds average total costs when the firm is producing its profit-maximizing level of output, q^*. But such positive profits need not always be the case in the short run. In general, we do not know whether firms in the short-run competitive equilibrium will be earning positive, zero, or negative profits. We *do* know that each firm is maximizing its profits; we just don't know how large those profits are.

Figure 9-7 shows three possible positions for a firm when the industry is in short-run equilibrium. In all cases, the firm is maximizing its profits by producing where price equals marginal cost, but in part (i) the firm is suffering losses, in part (ii) it is just covering all of its costs (breaking even), and in part (iii) it is making profits because price exceeds average total cost. In all three cases, the firm is doing as well as it can, given its costs and the market price.

It is worth emphasizing that some firms will continue producing even though they are making losses. The firm shown in part (i) of Figure 9-7 is incurring losses every period that it remains in business, but it is still better for it to carry on producing than to temporarily halt production. If the firm produces nothing this period it still must pay its fixed costs, so it makes sense to continue producing as long as its revenues more than cover its variable costs or, equivalently, as long as price exceeds *AVC*. Any amount of money left over after the variable costs have been paid can then go toward paying some of the fixed costs. This is more than the firm would have if it simply produced nothing and hence earned no revenue whatsoever. (Look back to Table 9-1 to see an example of this situation, in the case where market price is $5 per unit.) *Applying*

FIGURE 9-6   A Typical Firm When the Competitive Market Is in Short-Run Equilibrium

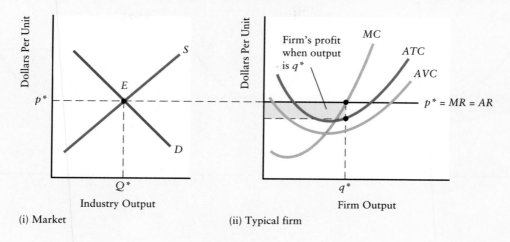

Short-run equilibrium in a competitive market has a market-clearing price and each firm is maximizing its profits. Part (i) shows the overall market. The equilibrium price and quantity (p^*, Q^*) are determined at the intersection of the market demand and supply curves at point E. Part (ii) shows a typical firm in the market. Notice that the horizontal scales are different in the two parts of the figure—total market output is designated by Q, whereas firm-level output is designated by q. The equilibrium price in part (i) becomes the MR curve for each firm in the market. Given its MC curve, the firm's profit-maximizing level of output is q^*. In the case shown, the firm is making positive profits equal to the shaded area.

Economic Concepts 9-2 on page 206 discusses an interesting example of a firm that remains in operation even though it is making losses. You have probably seen many firms like this one as you drive through small towns in any part of Canada.

A firm that is maximizing its profit but still making losses is actually *minimizing* its losses. To see a detailed numerical example of a firm in such a situation, look for "An Example of Loss Minimization as Profit Maximization" in the *Additional Topics* section of this book's MyEconLab.

w w w . m y e c o n l a b . c o m

9.4 **LONG-RUN DECISIONS**

In Chapters 7 and 8, we described the short run as the span of time for which individual firms have a fixed factor of production (typically capital), and the long run as the span of time for which individual firms have no fixed factors. When we look at the entire industry, the distinction is very similar. In the short run, there is a given number of firms and each has a given plant size. In the long run, both the number of firms and the size of each firm's plant are variable.

FIGURE 9-7   Alternative Short-Run Profits of a Competitive Firm

(i) Losses   (ii) Zero profit   (iii) Positive profit

When the industry is in short-run equilibrium, a competitive firm may be suffering losses, breaking even, or making profits. The diagrams show a firm with given costs that faces three alternative short-run equilibrium market prices: p_1, p_2, and p_3. In each part of the figure, $MC = MR$ = price. Because in all three cases price exceeds AVC, the firm produces positive output in each case.

In part (i), price is p_1 and the firm is suffering losses, shown by the red shaded area, because price is below average total cost. Because price exceeds average variable cost, it is worthwhile for the firm to keep producing, but it is not worthwhile for it to replace its capital equipment as it wears out. In part (ii), price is p_2 and the firm is just covering its total costs. It is worthwhile for the firm to replace its capital as it wears out, since it is covering the full opportunity cost of its capital. In part (iii), price is p_3 and the firm is earning profits, shown by the green shaded area.

We begin our discussion of the long run by assuming that all firms in the industry have the same technology and therefore have the same set of cost curves. Thus, the short-run equilibrium in the industry will have *all* firms in the industry being equally profitable (or making equal losses). Toward the end of the chapter we relax this assumption when we allow new firms to have better technologies and thus lower costs than older firms already in the industry.

Entry and Exit

The key difference between a perfectly competitive industry in the short run and in the long run is the entry or exit of firms. We have seen that all the firms in the industry may be making profits, suffering losses, or just breaking even when the industry is in short-run equilibrium. Because costs include the opportunity cost of capital, if the firms are just breaking even they are doing as well as they could do by investing their capital elsewhere. Hence, there will be no incentive for firms to leave the industry if profits are zero. Similarly, if new entrants expect just to break even, there will be no incentive for firms to enter the industry because capital can earn the same return elsewhere in the economy. If, however, the existing firms are earning revenues in excess of all costs, including the opportunity cost of capital, new capital will eventually enter the industry to share in these profits. Conversely, if the existing firms are suffering losses, capital will eventually leave the industry because a better return can be obtained elsewhere in the economy. Let us now consider this process in a little more detail.

An Entry-Attracting Price   First, suppose there are 100 firms in a competitive industry, all making positive profits like the firm shown in part (iii) of Figure 9-7. New firms, attracted by the profitability of existing firms, will enter the industry. Suppose that in response to the high profits, 20 new firms enter. The market supply curve that formerly added up the outputs of 100 firms must now add up the outputs of 120 firms. At any price, more will be supplied because there are more producers. This entry of new firms into the industry causes a rightward shift in the industry supply curve.

With an unchanged market demand curve, this rightward shift in the industry supply curve will reduce the equilibrium price. Both new and old firms will have to adjust their output to this new price. New firms will continue to enter, and the equilibrium price will continue to fall, until all firms in the industry are just covering their total costs. The industry has now reached what is called a *zero-profit equilibrium*. The entry of new firms then ceases. The effect of entry is shown in Figure 9-8.

Profits in a competitive industry are a signal for the entry of new firms; the industry will expand, pushing price down until profits fall to zero.

An Exit-Inducing Price   We saw in Figure 9-4 that the firm's supply curve is the section of its marginal cost curve above the average variable cost curve. If the market price falls below the minimum of average variable cost, the firm will simply shut down its

FIGURE 9-8   The Effect of New Entrants Attracted by Positive Profits

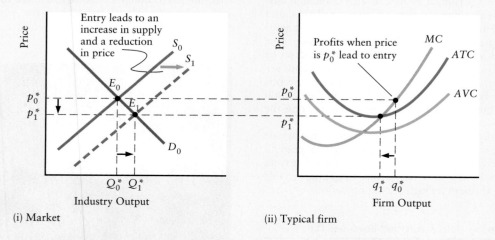

(i) Market   (ii) Typical firm

Positive profits lead to the entry of new firms; this entry reduces the equilibrium market price and reduces the profits of all firms. The initial short-run equilibrium is E_0 in part (i) with equilibrium price p_0^*. At this price, a typical firm in the industry is producing q_0^* units of output and is earning positive profits (since $p_0^* > ATC$ at q_0^*). These positive profits attract other firms who then enter the industry, causing the supply curve to shift to the right and reducing the market price. The process of entry will continue until profits are driven to zero. S_1 is the final supply curve and the equilibrium market price has fallen to p_1^*. At the new market price, firms have each reduced their output to q_1^* and are now just covering their total costs. Notice that each of the original firms is producing less than before, but because of the new entrants total industry output has increased from Q_0^* to Q_1^*.

APPLYING ECONOMIC CONCEPTS 9-2

The Parable of the Seaside Inn

Why do some resort hotels stay open during the off-season, even though to do so they must offer bargain rates that do not even cover their "full costs"? Why do the managers of other hotels allow them to fall into disrepair even though they are able to attract enough customers to stay in business? Are the former being overly generous, and are the latter being irrational penny-pinchers?

To illustrate what is involved, consider an imaginary resort hotel called the Seaside Inn. Its revenues and costs of operating during the four months of the high-season and during the eight months of the off-season are shown in the accompanying table. When the profit-maximizing price for its rooms is charged in the high-season, the hotel earns revenues of $58 000 and incurs variable costs equal to $36 000. Thus, there is an "operating profit" of $22 000 during the high-season. This surplus goes toward meeting the hotel's annual fixed costs of $24 000. Thus, $2000 of the fixed costs are not yet paid.

If the Seaside Inn were to charge the same rates during the off-season, it could not attract enough customers even to cover its costs of maids, bellhops, and managers. However, the hotel discovers that by charging lower rates during the off-season, it can rent some of its rooms and earn revenues of $20 000. Its costs of operating (variable costs) during the off-season are $18 000. So, by operating at reduced rates in the off-season, the hotel is able to contribute another $2000 toward its annual fixed costs, thereby eliminating the shortfall.

Therefore, the hotel stays open during the whole year by offering off-season bargain rates to grateful guests. Indeed, if it were to close during the off-season, it would not be able to cover its total fixed and variable costs solely through its high-season operations.

We have not yet discussed firms' long-run decisions in the chapter, but you can get a feel for the issues by considering the following situation. Suppose the off-season revenues fall to $19 000 (everything else remaining the same). The short-run condition for staying open, that total revenue (*TR*) must exceed total variable cost (*TVC*), is met both for the high-season and for the off-season. However, since the *TR* over the whole year of $77 000 is less than the total costs of $78 000, the hotel is now making losses for the year as a whole. The hotel will remain open as long as it can do so with its present capital—it will produce in the short run. However, it will not be worthwhile for the owners to replace the capital as it wears out.

If the reduction in revenues persists, the hotel will become one of those run-down hotels about which guests ask, "Why don't they do something about this place?"—but the owners are behaving quite sensibly. They are operating the hotel as long as it covers its variable costs, but they are not putting any more investment into it because it cannot cover its fixed costs. Sooner or later, the fixed capital will become too old to be run, or at least to attract customers, and the hotel will be closed.

The Seaside Inn: Total Costs and Revenues ($)

Season	Total Revenue (*TR*)	Total Variable Cost (*TVC*)	Contribution to Fixed Costs (*TR-TVC*)	Total Fixed Costs
High-Season	58 000	36 000	22 000	
Off-Season	20 000	18 000	2 000	
Total	78 000	54 000	24 000	24 000

Hotels and other resorts often charge low prices in the off-season, low enough that they do not cover their total costs. But as long as the price more than covers the variable costs, it is better than shutting down during the off-season.

production. Indeed, the firm's *shut-down price* is defined to be the minimum of the firm's average variable costs because, at any price lower than this, the firm is better off producing nothing than producing any positive amount.

If market price declines below the minimum of a competitive firm's *AVC* curve, the firm will shut down immediately and exit the industry.

If firms are making losses but the market price is *above* the shut-down point, there will still be exit from the industry, but it will be more gradual. Suppose the firms in a competitive industry are making losses, like the firm shown in part (i) of Figure 9-7. Although the firms are covering their variable costs, the return on their capital is less than the opportunity cost of capital. They are not covering their total costs. This is a signal for the gradual exit of firms. Old plants and equipment will not be replaced as they wear out. As a result, the industry's supply curve eventually shifts leftward, and the market price rises. Firms will continue to exit, and the market price will continue to rise, until the remaining firms can cover their total costs. Once again the market reaches a zero-profit equilibrium. The exit of firms then ceases. This gradual process of exit is shown in Figure 9-9.

Losses in a competitive industry are a signal for the exit of firms; the industry will contract, driving the market price up until the remaining firms are just covering their total costs.

FIGURE 9-9   The Effect of Exit Caused by Losses

(i) Market   (ii) Typical firm

Negative profits lead to the eventual exit of some firms as their capital becomes obsolete or becomes too costly to operate; this exit increases the equilibrium price and increases profits for those firms remaining in the market. The initial market equilibrium is E_0 in part (i), with equilibrium price p_0^*. At this market price, a typical firm is producing q_0^* units and is making *negative* profits but, because price exceeds *AVC*, the firm remains in business. Since firms are earning less than the opportunity cost on their capital, they do not replace their capital as it becomes obsolete. Eventually, some firms close down. As firms exit the industry, the industry supply curve shifts to the left and the market price increases to p_1^*. For the remaining firms, this price increase leads them to increase their output from q_0^* to q_1^*, the level of output at which they are just covering their total costs. Notice that the remaining firms are producing more than before, but because of the exit of firms total industry output has fallen from Q_0^* to Q_1^*.

Sunk Costs and the Speed of Exit   The process of exit is not always quick and is sometimes painfully slow for the loss-making firms in the industry. The rate at which firms leave unprofitable industries depends on how quickly their capital becomes obsolete or becomes too costly to operate due to rising maintenance costs as it ages. In many professional service industries, such as graphic design or consulting, the physical capital is mostly office equipment such as computers, printers, and so on. This equipment becomes obsolete in just a few years, and thus loss-making firms will tend to exit the industry very quickly. In other industries, such as railways or shipping, the physical capital takes much longer to become obsolete. The result is that loss-making firms in these industries will remain in operation for many years.

The longer it takes for firms' capital to become obsolete or too costly to operate, the longer firms will remain in the industry while they are earning economic losses.

Another important factor in the speed of exit from an industry is the nature of firms' fixed costs. Economists divide a firm's fixed costs into *sunk costs*—costs that could never be recovered—and *non-sunk costs*—costs that could be recovered by the firm selling its capital or terminating its rental agreement.

As an example, consider a competitive firm in the machine-tools industry. It builds a factory and equips it for a total cost of $30 million. This $30 million is an important fixed cost for the firm. If the factory and machines are useful only for producing in this industry, it might be very difficult to sell the factory if the firm ever wanted to exit the industry. If the firm is unable to sell the plant at all, the $30 million is a sunk cost. On the other hand, if the factory and equipment can be used to produce other products, as is often the case, then the firm could sell the factory if it ever wanted to exit the industry. If the firm could sell its factory for the full $30 million, the factory would be a fixed, but non-sunk, cost.

Not all fixed costs are associated with the capital cost of building or renting a factory. Other costs that are fixed while the firm is operating include the rental or leasing costs of office equipment and furniture. Such fixed costs are often non-sunk costs for the firm, however, because if the firm shuts down it can terminate these rental or lease agreements, thus avoiding the costs altogether.

This distinction between sunk and non-sunk costs affects the speed of exit for loss-making firms. To see why, suppose our machine-tools firm is making losses in the short-run market equilibrium (as in Figure 9-9). If the $30 million factory is a sunk cost, then the firm cannot recover the cost by selling the factory. In this case, the firm will remain in business as long as the market price of its product exceeds its *AVC*; the alternative of closing down and earning no revenue is less profitable. If all firms are like this, the adjustment shown in Figure 9-9 will be slow and gradual. On the other hand, if the firm is able to sell the factory, it can shut down its production and *avoid* paying the fixed costs. In this case, it makes no sense to remain in business making losses just because price is greater than average variable cost. It would be better to sell the factory, recover the fixed costs, and exit the industry. If all firms are like this, the adjustment shown in Figure 9-9 will be relatively quick.

If firms' fixed costs are mostly sunk costs, the process of exit in loss-making industries will be slow. If firms' fixed costs are mostly non-sunk costs, the process of exit will be faster.

Long-Run Equilibrium

Because sooner or later firms exit when they are making losses and enter in pursuit of profits, we get the following conclusion:

Practise with Study Guide Chapter 9, Exercises 3 and 4.

The long-run equilibrium of a competitive industry occurs when firms are earning zero profits.

When a perfectly competitive industry is in long-run equilibrium, each firm will be like the firm in part (ii) of Figure 9-7, earning zero economic profit. For such firms, the price p_2 is sometimes called the **break-even price**. It is the price at which all costs, including the opportunity cost of capital, are being covered. Any firm that is just breaking even is willing to stay in the industry. It has no incentive to leave, nor do other firms have an incentive to enter.

break-even price The price at which a firm is just able to cover all of its costs, including the opportunity cost of capital.

Conditions for Long-Run Equilibrium   The previous discussion suggests four conditions for a competitive industry to be in long-run equilibrium.

1. Existing firms must be maximizing their profits, given their existing capital. Thus, short-run marginal costs of production must be equal to market price.

2. Existing firms must not be suffering losses. If they are suffering losses, they will not replace their capital and the size of the industry will decline over time.

3. Existing firms must not be earning profits. If they are earning profits, then new firms will enter the industry and the size of the industry will increase over time.

4. Existing firms must not be able to increase their profits by changing the size of their production facilities. Thus, each existing firm must be at the minimum point of its *long-run* average cost (*LRAC*) curve.

This last condition is new to our discussion. Figure 9-10 shows that if the condition does not hold—that is, if the firm is *not* at the minimum of its *LRAC* curve—a firm can increase its profits. In the case shown, although the firm is maximizing its profits with its existing production facilities, there are unexploited economies of scale. By building a larger plant, the firm can move down its *LRAC* curve and reduce its average cost. Alternatively, if the firm were producing at an output that put it beyond the lowest point on its *LRAC* curve, it could raise its profits by reducing its plant size. Because in either situation average cost is just equal to the market price, any reduction in average cost must yield profits.

FIGURE 9-10   Short-Run Versus Long-Run Profit Maximization for a Competitive Firm

A competitive firm that is not at the minimum point on its *LRAC* curve is not maximizing its long-run profits. A competitive firm with short-run cost curves *SRATC* and *MC* faces a market price of p_0. The firm produces Q_0, where *MC* equals price and total costs are just being covered. However, the firm's long-run average cost curve lies below its short-run curve at output Q_0. The firm could produce output Q_0 at cost c_0 by building a larger plant so as to take advantage of economies of scale. Profits would rise, because average total costs of c_0 would then be less than price p_0. The firm cannot be maximizing its long-run profits at any output below Q_m because, with any such output, average total costs can be reduced by building a larger plant. The output Q_m is the *minimum efficient scale* of the firm.

FIGURE 9-11 A Typical Competitive Firm When the Industry Is in Long-Run Equilibrium

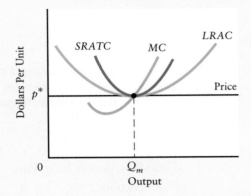

In **long-run competitive equilibrium, each firm is operating at the minimum point on its** *LRAC* **curve.** In long-run equilibrium, each firm must be (1) maximizing short-run profits, *MC* = *p*; (2) earning profits of zero on its existing plant, *SRATC* = *p*; and (3) unable to increase its profits by altering the scale of its operations. These three conditions can be met only when the firm is at the minimum point on its *LRAC* curve, with price *p** and output Q_m.

For a competitive firm to be maximizing its long-run profits, it must be producing at the minimum point on its *LRAC* curve.

As we saw in Chapter 8, the level of output at which *LRAC* reaches a minimum is known as the firm's *minimum efficient scale (MES)*.

When each firm in the industry is producing at the minimum point of its long-run average cost curve and just covering its costs, as in Figure 9-11, the industry is in long-run equilibrium. Because marginal cost equals price, no firm can improve its profits by varying its output in the short run. Because each firm is at the minimum point on its *LRAC* curve, there is no incentive for any existing firm to alter the scale of its operations. Because there are neither profits nor losses, there is no incentive for entry into or exit from the industry.

In long-run competitive equilibrium, each firm's average cost of production is the lowest attainable, given the limits of known technology and factor prices.

Changes in Technology

Our discussion of firms' long-run decisions has assumed that all firms in the industry have the same technology and thus the same cost curves. We now relax that assumption and consider how a competitive industry responds to technological improvements *by new firms*.

Consider a competitive industry in long-run equilibrium. Because the industry is in long-run equilibrium, each firm must be earning zero profits. Now suppose that some technological development lowers the cost curves of *newly built plants*. Because price is just equal to the average total cost for the *existing plants*, new plants will be able to earn profits, and some of them will now be built. The resulting expansion in capacity shifts the short-run supply curve to the right and drives price down.

The expansion in industry output and the fall in price will continue until price is equal to the short-run average total cost of the *new* plants. At this price, old plants will not be covering their long-run costs. As long as price exceeds their average variable cost, however, such plants will continue in production. As the outmoded plants wear out or become too costly to operate, they will gradually be closed. Eventually, a new long-run equilibrium will be established in which all plants will use the new technology; market price will be lower and output higher than under the old technology.

New plants are usually built with the latest technology. This often results in new plants having lower unit costs (and thus higher profits) than the existing plants built with older technology.

What happens in a competitive industry in which technological change does not occur as a single isolated event but instead happens more or less continuously? Plants built in any one year will tend to have lower costs than plants built in any previous year. This common occurrence is illustrated in Figure 9-12.

Industries that are subject to continuous technological change have three common characteristics. The first is that plants of different ages and with different costs exist side by side. In the steel and newsprint industries, for example, there are ongoing and gradual technological improvements, and thus it is common for new plants to have considerably lower costs than the plants built several years earlier. Most of us do not see these differences, however, because we rarely if ever visit production facilities in these industries. But the same characteristic is dramatically displayed in an industry that most of us observe casually through our car windows—agriculture. You will probably have noticed different farms with different vintages of agricultural machinery; some farms have much newer and better equipment than others. Indeed, even any individual farm that has been in operation for a long time will have various vintages of equipment, all of which are in use. Older models are not discarded as soon as a better model comes on the market.

Critics who observe the continued use of older, higher-cost plants and equipment often urge that something be done to "eliminate these wasteful practices." These critics miss an important aspect of profit maximization. If the plant or piece of equipment is already there, it can be profitably operated as long as its revenues more than cover its *variable* costs. As long as a plant or some equipment can produce goods that are valued by consumers at an amount above the value of the resources currently used up for their production (variable costs), the value of society's total output is increased by using it.

FIGURE 9-12 Plants of Different Vintages in an Industry with Continuous Technological Progress

(i) Plant 1: High costs   (ii) Plant 2: Medium costs   (iii) Plant 3: Low costs

Entry of progressively lower-cost firms forces price down, but older plants with higher costs remain in the industry as long as price covers their average variable costs. Plant 3 is the newest plant with the lowest costs. Long-run equilibrium price will be determined by the average total costs of plants of this type because entry will continue as long as the owners of the newest plants expect to earn profits from them. Plant 1 is the oldest plant in operation. It is just covering its AVC, and if the price falls any further, it will be closed down. Plant 2 is a plant of intermediate age. It is covering its variable costs and earning some contribution toward its fixed costs. Losses at all but the newest plants, in parts (i) and (ii), are shown by the shaded areas.

Practise with Study Guide Chapter 9, Exercise 5.

In industries with continuous technological improvement, low-cost firms will exist side by side with older high-cost firms. The older firms will continue operating as long as their revenues cover their variable costs.

A second characteristic of a competitive industry that is subject to continuous technological improvement is that price is eventually governed by the minimum *ATC* of the *lowest-cost* plants. New firms using the latest technologies will enter the industry until their plants are just expected to earn normal profits over their lifetimes. The benefits of the new technology are passed on to consumers because all of the units of the product, whether produced by new or old plants, are sold at a price that is related solely to the *ATCs* of the new plants. Owners of older plants find that their returns over variable costs fall steadily as newer plants drive the price of the product down.

A third characteristic is that old plants are discarded (or "mothballed") when the price falls below their *AVCs*. This may occur well before the plants are physically worn out. In industries with continuous technological progress, capital is usually discarded because it is *economically obsolete*, not because it is physically worn out. Old capital is obsolete when the market price of output does not even cover its average variable cost of production. Thus, a steel mill that is still fully capable of producing top-quality steel may be shut down for perfectly sensible reasons; if the price of steel cannot cover the average variable cost of the steel produced, then profit-maximizing firms will shut down the plant.

Declining Industries

What happens when a competitive industry in long-run equilibrium experiences a continual decrease in the demand for its product? One example of this might be a long-term change in tastes that leads households to substitute away from red meat and toward fish and poultry. Another example is the ongoing substitution away from glass beverage containers to plastic ones. As market demand for these products declines, market price falls, and firms that were previously covering average total costs are no longer able to do so. They find themselves suffering losses instead of breaking even; the signal for the exit of capital is given, but exit takes time.

The Response of Firms The profit-maximizing response to a steadily declining demand is to continue to operate with existing equipment as long as its variable costs of production can be covered. As equipment becomes obsolete because the firm cannot cover even its variable cost, it will not be replaced unless the new equipment can cover its total cost. As a result, the capacity of the industry will shrink. If demand keeps declining, capacity will continue shrinking.

Declining industries typically present a sorry sight to the observer. Revenues are below long-run total costs and, as a result, new equipment is not brought in to replace old equipment as it wears out. The average age of equipment in use rises steadily. The untrained observer, seeing the industry's plight, is likely to blame it on the old equipment.

The antiquated equipment in a declining industry is often the effect rather than the cause of the industry's decline.

The Response of Governments Governments are often tempted to support declining industries because they are worried about the resulting job losses. Experience suggests, however, that propping up genuinely declining industries only delays their demise—at significant national cost. When the government finally withdraws its support, the decline is usually more abrupt and, hence, the required adjustment is more difficult than it would have been had the industry been allowed to decline gradually under the natural market forces.

Once governments recognize the decay of certain industries and the collapse of certain firms as an inevitable aspect of a changing and evolving economy, a more effective response is to provide retraining and income-support schemes that cushion the impacts of change. These can moderate the effects on the incomes of workers who lose their jobs and make it easier for them to transfer to expanding industries. Intervention that is intended to increase mobility while reducing the social and personal costs of mobility is a viable long-run policy; trying to freeze the existing industrial structure by shoring up an inevitably declining industry is not.

---

myeconlab

Demand shocks in competitive industries naturally lead to price changes. As prices change, firms' profits rise or fall, and these adjustments cause entry to or exit from the industry. After a new long-run equilibrium is reached, will the market price be at its initial level? The answer depends on the nature of costs within the industry. For more details, look for "The Long-Run Industry Supply Curve" in the *Additional Topics* section of this book's MyEconLab.

w w w . m y e c o n l a b . c o m

S U M M A R Y

9.1 MARKET STRUCTURE AND FIRM BEHAVIOUR

- A competitive market structure is one in which individual firms have no market power—that is, they have no power to influence the market in which they sell their product.
- Competitive behaviour exists when firms actively compete against one another, responding directly to other firms' actions.

- Perfectly competitive firms *do not* have competitive behaviour because the actions of any one firm would have no effect on any other firm.

9.2 THE THEORY OF PERFECT COMPETITION

- Four key assumptions of the theory of perfect competition are as follows:

  1. All firms produce a homogeneous product.
  2. Consumers know the nature of the product and the price charged for it.
  3. Each firm's minimum efficient scale occurs at a level of output that is small relative to the industry's total output.

  4. The industry displays freedom of entry and exit.

- Each firm in perfect competition is a price taker. It follows that each firm faces a horizontal demand curve at the market price (even though the market demand curve is downward sloping).

9.3 SHORT-RUN DECISIONS

- Any profit-maximizing firm will produce at a level of output at which (a) price is at least as great as average variable cost and (b) marginal cost equals marginal revenue. In perfect competition, firms are price takers, so marginal revenue is equal to price. Thus, a profit-maximizing competitive firm chooses its output so that its marginal cost equals the market price.
- Under perfect competition, each firm's short-run supply curve is identical to its marginal cost curve above average variable cost. The perfectly competitive industry's short-run supply curve is the horizontal sum of the supply curves of the individual firms.
- In short-run equilibrium, each firm is maximizing its profits. However, any firm may be suffering losses (price is less than average total cost), making profits (price is greater than average total cost), or just breaking even (price is equal to average total cost).

9.4 LONG-RUN DECISIONS

- In the long run, profits or losses will lead to firms' entry into or exit out of the industry. This pushes any competitive industry to a long-run, zero-profit equilibrium and moves production to the level that minimizes average cost.
- The long-run response of an industry to steadily changing technology is the gradual replacement of less efficient plants by more efficient ones. Older plants will be discarded and replaced by more modern ones only when price falls below average variable cost.
- The long-run response of a declining industry will be to continue to satisfy demand by employing its existing plants as long as price exceeds short-run average variable cost.

KEY CONCEPTS

Competitive behaviour and competitive market structure
Perfect competition
Price taking and a horizontal demand curve

Average revenue, marginal revenue, and price under perfect competition
Rules for maximizing profits
The relationship of supply curves to marginal cost curves

Short-run and long-run equilibrium of competitive industries
Entry and exit in achieving long-run equilibrium

STUDY EXERCISES

1. Fill in the blanks to make the following statements correct.
   a. The demand curve faced by a single firm in a perfectly competitive market is _horizontal_.
   b. The demand curve faced by a single firm in a perfectly competitive industry coincides with the firm's _____ curve and its _____ curve.
   c. Total revenue is calculated by multiplying _____ and _____. Average revenue is calculated by dividing ___TR___ by ___Q___. Marginal revenue is calculated by dividing _____ by _____.
   d. A firm's loss when it produces *no* output is equal to its _____.

2. Fill in the blanks to make the following statements correct.
   a. The shut-down price is the price at which the firm can just cover its _AVC_.
   b. If the average variable cost of producing any given level of output exceeds the price at which it can be sold, then the firm should _shut down → exit_.
   c. If a firm is producing a level of output such that $MC > MR$, that firm should _decrease_ output.
   d. The profit-maximizing level of output for a price-taking firm is the output at which MR and MC are _____ and the gap between TR and TC is _____.
   e. If a perfectly competitive firm is producing its profit-maximizing level of output and the price of its output rises, then MR will be _larger_ MC and the firm should _____ output.

3. Fill in the blanks to make the following statements correct.

   a. The short-run supply curve for a perfectly competitive firm is that firm's marginal cost curve for levels of output where marginal cost exceeds _____.

   b. If a firm is producing a level of output where MR = MC but is suffering losses, we know that price is below _____. This firm should continue to produce as long as price exceeds _____.

   c. If a firm is earning profits, we know that price is above its _____. There is an incentive for other firms to _____ this industry.

4. In Figure 9-1 in the chapter, we explain the difference between the demand curve for a competitive industry and the demand curve facing an individual firm in that industry. Review that figure and answer the following questions.

   a. Explain what would happen if the individual firm tried to charge a higher price for its product.

   b. Explain why the individual firm has no incentive to charge a lower price for its product.

   c. Explain why the demand curve for an individual firm is horizontal at the current market price.

5. **myeconlab** Consider the following table showing the various revenue concepts for DairyTreat Inc., a perfectly competitive firm that sells milk by the litre. Suppose the firm faces a constant market price of $2 per litre.

Price (p)	Quantity	Total Revenue (TR)	Average Revenue (AR)	Marginal Revenue (MR)
$2	150	—	—	
2	175	—	—	—
2	200	—	—	—
2	225	—	—	—
2	250	—	—	—

   a. Compute total revenue for each level of output. Fill in the table.

   b. Compute average and marginal revenue for each level of output. Fill in the table. (Remember to compute marginal revenue *between* successive levels of output.)

   c. Explain why for a perfectly competitive firm, AR = MR = p.

   d. Plot the TR, MR, and AR curves on a scale diagram. What is the slope of the TR curve?

6. The diagram below shows the various short-run cost curves for a perfectly competitive firm.

   a. Based on the diagram above, and the assumption that the firm is maximizing its profit, fill in the following table. The last three columns require only a "yes" or "no."

Market Price ($)	Firm's Output	Is price >ATC?	Is price >AVC?	Are Profits Positive?
$3	—	—	—	—
4	—	—	—	—
5	—	—	—	—
6	—	—	—	—
7	—	—	—	—
8	—	—	—	—
9	—	—	—	—
10	—	—	—	—

   b. What is this firm's shut-down price? Explain.

   c. What is this firm's supply curve? Explain.

7. **myeconlab** Consider the table below showing the supply schedules for three competitive firms, each producing honey. These three firms make up the entire industry.

Market Price ($/kg)	Output (kg)			
	Firm A	Firm B	Firm C	Industry
2.50	100	0	0	—
3.00	125	0	0	—
3.50	150	100	0	—
4.00	175	150	0	—
4.50	200	200	100	—
5.00	225	250	175	—
5.50	250	300	250	—
6.00	275	350	325	—

a. Compute the total industry supply at each price and fill in the table.
b. On a scale diagram similar to Figure 9-5, plot the supply curve for each firm and for the industry as a whole.
c. Explain why Firm B produces no output at prices $3 and lower, and why Firm C produces no output at prices $4 and lower.

8. Consider the perfectly competitive barley industry. It is initially in long-run equilibrium at quantity Q_0 and price p_0.

a. Draw a supply-and-demand diagram for the barley market, showing the initial long-run equilibrium.

b. Draw a diagram for a typical firm when the industry is in its initial long-run equilibrium, showing its *MC*, *ATC*, and *LRAC* curves. Are any profits being earned by the typical barley farmer?
c. Now suppose there is an increase in demand (caused by an increase in demand for beer, which uses barley as an input). Price rises to p_1. In your diagram, show the typical firm's response to the increase in market price from p_0 to p_1. Show the typical firm's profits at this new price.
d. Explain how this industry adjusts to its new long-run equilibrium. Illustrate this adjustment both in the demand-and-supply diagram and in the diagram of the typical firm. (You may assume that costs for barley firms are unaffected by this change.)

9. This question is based on the section "The Long-Run Industry Supply Curve" found on this book's MyEconLab (www.myeconlab.com). A major theme of this chapter is the role that *free entry and exit* play in determining a competitive industry's long-run equilibrium. Keeping this theme in mind, think of the following statement:

In Industry X, demand and supply do determine price in the short run, but in the long run, only supply matters.

a. Assuming that Industry X is a constant-cost industry, use a demand-and-supply diagram to illustrate why the statement is exactly correct.
b. Now, assuming that Industry X is an increasing-cost industry, show in a demand-and-supply diagram why the statement is not quite correct.

DISCUSSION QUESTIONS

1. Discuss the common allegation that when all firms in an industry are charging the same price, this indicates the absence of competition and the presence of some form of price-setting agreement.

2. Which of the following observed facts about an industry are inconsistent with its being a perfectly competitive industry?

a. Different firms use different methods of production.
b. The industry's product is extensively advertised by a trade association.
c. Individual firms devote a large fraction of their sales receipts to advertising their own product brands.
d. There are 24 firms in the industry.

e. The largest firm in the industry makes 40 percent of the sales, and the next largest firm makes 20 percent of the sales, but the products are identical, and there are 61 other firms.
f. All firms made large profits last year.

3. In which of the following sectors of the Canadian economy might you expect to find competitive *behaviour*? In which might you expect to find industries that are classified as operating under perfectly competitive market *structures*?

a. Manufacturing
b. Agriculture
c. Transportation and public utilities
d. Wholesale and retail trade
e. Illegal drugs

4. Today's typical office contains personal computers of various vintages, with the newest machines having the largest output per unit of cost. There are also old machines that, though still able to function, are not in use at all. What determines the secondhand price of the older machines? What is the economic value of the machines that are no longer used?

5. What, if anything, does each one of the following tell you about ease of entry into or exit from an industry?

   a. Profits have been very high for two decades.
   b. No new firms have entered the industry for 20 years.
   c. The average age of the firms in the 40-year-old industry is less than 7 years.
   d. Most existing firms are using old-technology equipment alongside newer, more modern equipment.
   e. Profits are low or negative; many firms are still producing, but from steadily aging equipment.

6. This question refers to "The Long-Run Industry Supply Curve" in the *Additional Topics* section of the MyEconLab. Explain why perfectly competitive agricultural industries may have external economies of scale—and thus may be declining-cost industries—arising from the behaviour of the farm machinery industry. Is it relevant that the farm machinery industry is dominated by a small number of very large firms?

CHAPTER 10

Monopoly, Cartels, and Price Discrimination

LEARNING OBJECTIVES

In this chapter you will learn

1. why marginal revenue is less than price for a profit-maximizing monopolist.
2. how entry barriers allow monopolists to maintain positive profits in the long run.
3. how firms can form a cartel to restrict industry output and increase their profits.
4. why firms can increase their profits through price discrimination.

monopoly A market containing a single firm.

monopolist A firm that is the only seller in a market.

Perfect competition is at one end of the spectrum of market structures. At the other end is **monopoly**. Economists say that a monopoly occurs when the output of an entire industry is produced and sold by a single firm, called a **monopolist** or a *monopoly firm*. Examples of monopoly are rare at the national level but are more common for smaller geographical areas. The company that supplies electric power to your home is almost certainly a monopoly, as are the firms that provide local (but not long-distance) telephone service and cable television. Because monopoly is the market structure that allows for the maximum possible exercise of market power on the part of the firm, monopoly markets and perfectly competitive markets provide two extremes of behaviour that are useful for economists in their study of market structure.

In this chapter we examine how a profit-maximizing monopolist determines its price and quantity. We begin by considering a monopolist that sells all of its output at a single price. We then consider *cartels* that are formed when several firms band together in order to behave more like a monopolist. We end the chapter by examining situations in which firms with market power are able to charge different prices to different customers—something you have probably observed with airlines, movie theatres, and even your local grocery store.

10.1 A SINGLE-PRICE MONOPOLIST

We look first at a monopolist that charges a single price for its product. This firm's profits, like those of all firms, will depend on the relationship between its costs and its revenues.

Cost and Revenue in the Short Run

We saw in Chapter 7 that U-shaped short-run cost curves are a consequence of the law of diminishing returns. Because this law applies to the conditions under which goods are produced rather than to the market structure in which they are sold, monopolists have U-shaped short-run cost curves for the same reasons as do perfectly competitive firms. Therefore we do not need to introduce any new cost concepts to analyze a monopoly firm—everything that we saw in Chapter 7 applies equally to firms in *all* market structures. We can therefore focus our attention on a monopolist's revenues.

Because a monopolist is the sole producer of the product that it sells, the demand curve it faces is simply the market demand curve for that product. The market demand curve, which shows the total quantity that buyers want to purchase at each price, also shows the quantity that the monopolist will be able to sell at each price.

Unlike a perfectly competitive firm, a monopolist faces a negatively sloped demand curve.

A monopolist therefore faces a tradeoff between the price it charges and the quantity it can sell at that price. For a monopolist, sales can be increased only if price is reduced, and price can be increased only if sales are reduced.

Average Revenue   Starting with the market demand curve, we can readily derive the monopolist's average and marginal revenue curves. When the monopolist charges the same price for all units sold, its total revenue (*TR*) is simply equal to the single price times the quantity sold,

$$TR = p \times Q$$

Since average revenue is total revenue divided by quantity, it follows that average revenue is equal to the price,

$$AR = \frac{TR}{Q} = \frac{p \times Q}{Q} = p$$

And since the price is given by the position of the demand curve, it follows that the demand curve is also the monopolist's average revenue curve.

Marginal Revenue   Now let's consider the monopolist's *marginal revenue*—the revenue resulting from the sale of one more unit of the product. Because its demand curve is negatively sloped, the monopolist must reduce the price that it charges on *all* units in order to sell an extra unit. But this implies that the price received for the extra unit sold is *not* the firm's marginal revenue because, by reducing the price on all previous units, the firm lost some revenue. Marginal revenue is therefore equal to the price *minus* this lost revenue. It follows that the marginal revenue resulting from the sale of an extra unit is less than the price that the monopolist receives for that unit.

The monopolist's marginal revenue is less than the price at which it sells its output. Thus the monopolist's *MR* curve is below its demand curve. [24]

The relationship between marginal revenue and price for an example is shown in detail in Figure 10-1. Consider the table first. Notice that the numbers in columns 4 and 5 are plotted between the rows that refer to specific prices, because the numbers refer to what happens when the price changes from one row to the next. As price declines and quantity sold increases, marginal revenue is calculated as the change in total revenue divided by the change in quantity:

$$MR = \frac{\Delta TR}{\Delta Q}$$

FIGURE 10-1   A Monopolist's Average and Marginal Revenue

Computing Average and Marginal Revenue

Price (Average Revenue) (1)	Quantity Sold Q (2)	Total Revenue $(p \times Q)$ (3)	Change in Total Revenue (ΔTR) (4)	Marginal Revenue $(\Delta TR/\Delta Q)$ (5)
10	0	0		
			90	9
9	10	90		
			70	7
8	20	160		
			50	5
7	30	210		
			30	3
6	40	240		
			10	1
5	50	250		
			−10	−1
4	60	240		
			−30	−3
3	70	210		
			−50	−5
2	80	160		
			−70	−7
1	90	90		
			−90	−9
0	100	0		

Average and Marginal Revenue Curves

Marginal revenue is less than price because the price must be reduced in order to sell more units. The data show that every time the firm lowers its price by $1, its sales increase by 10 units. At a price of $6, the firm sells 40 units for a total revenue of $240. If it lowers its price to $5 *on all units,* total sales rise to 50 units and total revenue rises to $250. The purple rectangle shows the $50 gain in revenue associated with the 10 extra units sold at $5 each. The green rectangle shows the $40 *loss* in revenue associated with reducing the price by $1 on the original 40 units sold. Thus, the firm's marginal revenue when it reduces its price from $6 to $5 is the change in total revenue ($250 – $240 = $10) divided by the change in quantity (50 – 40 = 10). MR = $10/10 = $1.

Now look at the figure. It plots the demand curve described by the price and quantity values shown in the table. It also plots the marginal revenue curve and locates the specific points on it that were calculated in the table. For purposes of illustration, a straight-line demand curve has been chosen.[1]

Notice that marginal revenue is positive up to 50 units of sales, indicating that reductions in price between $10 and $5 increase total revenue. Notice also that marginal revenue is *negative* for sales greater than 50 units, indicating that reductions in price below $5 cause total revenue to fall.

---

1 When drawing these curves, note that if the demand curve is a negatively sloped straight line, the *MR* curve is also a negatively sloped straight line but is exactly twice as steep as the demand curve. The *MR* curve's price intercept (where $Q = 0$) is the same as that of the demand curve, and its quantity intercept (where $p = 0$) is one-half that of the demand curve. [25]

The figure also illustrates the two opposing forces that are present whenever the price is changed. As an example, consider the reduction in price from $6 to $5. First, the 40 units that the firm was already selling bring in less money at the new lower price than at the original higher price. This loss in revenue is the amount of the price reduction multiplied by the number of units already being sold (40 units × $1 per unit = $40). This is shown as the green shaded area in the figure. The second force, operating in the opposite direction, is that new units are sold, which adds to revenue. This gain in revenue is given by the number of new units sold multiplied by the price at which they are sold (10 units × $5 = $50). This is shown as the purple shaded area. The *net change* in total revenue is the *difference* between these two amounts. In the example shown in the figure, the increase resulting from the sale of new units exceeds the decrease resulting from existing sales now being made at a lower price. Marginal revenue is thus positive. Furthermore, the change in total revenue is $10, whereas the change in the number of units sold is 10 units. Thus, marginal revenue, given by $\Delta TR/\Delta Q$, is equal to $10/10 = $1.

The proposition that marginal revenue is always less than price for a monopolist provides an important contrast with perfect competition. Recall that in perfect competition, the firm's marginal revenue from selling an extra unit of output is equal to the price at which that unit is sold. The reason for the difference is not difficult to understand. The perfectly competitive firm is a price taker; it can sell all it wants at the given market price. In contrast, the monopolist faces a negatively sloped demand curve; it must reduce the market price to increase its sales.

If you plot the data on *TR* from Figure 10-1, you will notice that *TR* rises (*MR* is positive) as price falls, reaching a maximum where $p = $5 and $MR = 0$. Then, as price continues to fall, *TR* falls (*MR* is negative). Using the relationship between elasticity and total revenue that we first saw in Chapter 4, it follows that demand is elastic ($\eta > 1$) when *MR* is positive and demand is inelastic ($\eta < 1$) when *MR* is negative. The value of η declines steadily as we move down the demand curve. As we will see shortly, a profit-maximizing monopolist will always produce on the elastic portion of its demand curve (that is, where *MR* is positive).

Short-Run Profit Maximization

We began this chapter by noting that the cost concepts from Chapter 7 apply equally to a monopolist as to a competitive firm. We have now examined a monopolist's average and marginal revenues and are therefore ready to combine the cost and revenue information to determine the monopolist's profit-maximizing price and level of output.

Recall the two general rules about profit maximization from Chapter 9:

Rule 1: The firm should not produce at all unless its average revenue exceeds its average variable cost.

Rule 2: If the firm does produce, it should produce a level of output such that its marginal revenue equals its marginal cost.

Figure 10-2 illustrates a monopolist's choice of output to equate its marginal cost with its marginal revenue. At this profit-maximizing level of output, the monopolist's price is then read off the demand curve. With the firm's costs given by the *ATC* curve shown in the figure, the monopolist is making positive profits, as shown by the red shaded area.

Practise with Study Guide Chapter 10, Exercises 1 and 2.

FIGURE 10-2   Short-Run Profit Maximization for a Monopolist

The profit-maximizing output is Q^*, where $MR = MC$; price is p^*. The rules for profit maximization require $MR = MC$ and $p > AVC$. (AVC is not shown in the graph, but it must be below ATC.) With average costs given by ATC, unit costs at Q^* are given by c and the monopolist makes positive profits shown by the red shaded area.

In general, however, a profit-maximizing monopolist need not be making *positive* profits. Even when the firm is choosing its quantity to maximize its profits, the *size* of those profits depends on the position of the ATC curve. In Figure 10-2 the monopolist is earning positive profits. But you can easily imagine other possibilities. If the firm's ATC curve was higher (perhaps because of higher fixed costs) the firm with the same level of output and charging the same price could be breaking even (zero profits) or even making negative profits (losses). (Readers can create their own diagrams like Figure 10-2 and draw in the appropriate ATC curves to illustrate these two possibilities.)

Nothing guarantees that a monopolist will make positive profits in the short run, but if it suffers persistent losses, it will eventually go out of business.

No Supply Curve for a Monopolist   In describing the monopolist's profit-maximizing behaviour, we did not introduce the concept of a supply curve, as we did in the discussion of perfect competition. In perfect competition, each firm's supply curve is given by its own MC curve. It follows that in perfect competition there is a unique relationship between market price and quantity supplied by any single firm: An increase in the market price leads to an increase in quantity supplied. But there is no such unique relationship in monopoly.

For a monopolist, there is no unique relationship between market price and the quantity of output supplied. A monopolist therefore does not have a supply curve.

The simple explanation is that the price set by a monopolist depends on the *shape* of the demand curve, and therefore the monopolist's profit-maximizing quantity is not necessarily higher when it sets its price higher.

To prove this point to yourself, draw a monopolist's marginal cost curve and any marginal revenue curve to intersect the MC curve at some output that you call Q^*. Now draw as many other different MR curves as you like, all of which intersect MC at Q^*. All of these curves give rise to profit-maximizing output of Q^*, but because each MR curve is different, each must be associated with a different demand curve and hence a different price at which Q^* is sold. This exercise shows that a given quantity may be associated with many different prices, depending on the slope of the demand curve that the monopolist faces.

Firm and Industry   Because the monopolist is the only producer in an industry, there is no need for a separate discussion about the firm and the industry, as is necessary with perfect competition. The monopolist *is* the industry. Thus, the short-run, profit-maximizing position of the firm, as shown in Figure 10-2, is also the short-run equilibrium of the industry.

Competition and Monopoly Compared The comparison of monopoly with perfect competition is important. For a perfectly competitive industry, the equilibrium is determined by the intersection of the industry demand and supply curves. Since the industry supply curve is simply the sum of the individual firms' marginal cost curves, the equilibrium output in a perfectly competitive industry is such that price equals marginal cost. For the monopolist, in contrast, equilibrium output is such that price is greater than marginal cost. And since demand curves are downward sloping and MC curves are typically upward sloping, the gap between price and marginal cost implies one thing: The level of output in a monopolized industry is less than the level of output that would be produced if the industry were instead made up of many price-taking firms. This comparison is illustrated in Figure 10-3.

A perfectly competitive industry produces a level of output such that price equals marginal cost. A monopolist produces a lower level of output, with price exceeding marginal cost.

In Chapter 5 we briefly discussed the meaning of *market efficiency* and how it relates to the amount of *economic surplus* generated in the market. We will examine these concepts in more detail in Chapter 12. For now we can observe why the decisions of the monopolist—though perhaps very profitable for the firm—lead to an inefficient outcome for society as a whole.

Since price exceeds marginal cost for a monopolist, society as a whole would benefit if more units of the good were produced—because the marginal value to society of extra units, as reflected by the price, exceeds the marginal cost of producing the extra units. In the terminology we introduced in Chapter 5, more *economic surplus* would be generated for society if the monopolist increased its level of output. The monopolist's profit-maximizing decision to restrict output below the competitive level creates a loss of economic surplus for society—a deadweight loss—and thus leads to market *inefficiency*.

FIGURE 10-3   The Inefficiency of Monopoly

The level of output in a monopolized industry is less than the level of output that would be produced if the industry were perfectly competitive. If the industry is made up of many price-taking firms, the industry supply curve S is the horizontal sum of the many individual marginal cost curves. Given the market demand curve D, the competitive equilibrium quantity is Q_c and the price is p_c. Now suppose the industry has a monopolist with marginal costs given by the MC curve shown. In this case, MR is the monopolist's marginal revenue curve. The profit-maximizing monopolist produces Q_m units of output and charges a price of p_m.

Notice in the monopoly outcome that for the units of output between Q_m and Q_c, the marginal value to society of extra units of the good (as shown by the demand curve) exceeds the marginal cost of producing extra units, and thus society would benefit from having these units produced. The monopolist's restriction of output below Q_c creates a deadweight loss for society shown by the purple area. The monopoly outcome is *inefficient*.

A monopolist restricts output below the competitive level and thus reduces the amount of economic surplus generated in the market. The monopolist therefore creates an inefficient market outcome.

Entry Barriers and Long-Run Equilibrium

In a monopolized industry, as in a perfectly competitive one, losses and profits provide incentives for exit and entry. If the monopoly is suffering losses in the short run, it will continue to operate as long as it can cover its variable costs. In the long run, however, it will leave the industry unless it can find a scale of operations at which its full opportunity costs can be covered.

If the monopoly is making profits, other firms will wish to enter the industry in order to earn more than the opportunity cost of their capital. If such entry occurs, the firm will cease to be a monopoly. Instead of facing the entire market demand curve, the (former) monopolist will have to compete with the new firms and thus will capture only part of the overall market demand.

If monopoly profits are to persist in the long run, the entry of new firms into the industry must be prevented.

entry barrier Any barrier to the entry of new firms into an industry. An entry barrier may be natural or created.

Anything that prevents the entry of new firms is called an **entry barrier**. They may be natural or created.

Practise with Study Guide Chapter 10, Exercise 3.

natural monopoly An industry characterized by economies of scale sufficiently large that only one firm can cover its costs while producing at its minimum efficient scale.

Natural Entry Barriers Natural barriers most commonly arise as a result of economies of scale. When the long-run average cost curve is negatively sloped over a large range of output, big firms have significantly lower average total costs than small firms. Recall from Chapter 8 that the *minimum efficient scale (MES)* is the smallest-size firm that can reap all of the economies of large-scale production. It occurs at the level of output where the firm's long-run average cost curve reaches a minimum.

To see how economies of scale can act as an entry barrier, consider the production of hockey sticks. Suppose the technology of hockey-stick production is such that a firm's *MES* is 10 000 sticks per week at an average total cost of $20 per stick. Further suppose that at a price of $20, the quantity demanded in the entire market is 11 000 sticks per week. Under these circumstances, only one firm can operate at or near its *MES*. Any potential entrant would have unit costs higher than those of the existing firm and so could not compete successfully.

A **natural monopoly** occurs when the industry's demand conditions allow no more than one firm to cover its costs while producing at its minimum efficient scale. Electrical power transmission is a natural monopoly—with current technology it is cheaper to have only one set of power lines (rather than two or more) serving a given region.

Another type of natural entry barrier is *setup cost*. If a firm could be catapulted fully grown into the market, it might be able to compete effectively with the existing monopolist. However, the cost to the new firm of entering the market, developing its products, and establishing such things as its brand image and its dealer network may be so large that entry would be unprofitable.

Created Entry Barriers Many entry barriers are created by conscious government action. Patent laws, for instance, may prevent entry by conferring on the patent holder the sole legal right to produce a particular product for a specific period of time. A firm may also be granted a charter or a franchise that prohibits competition by law. Canada Post, for example, has a government-sanctioned monopoly on the delivery of

Many industries have considerable economies of scale. These scale economies can provide an entry barrier and allow existing firms to sustain high profits.

first-class mail. In other cases the regulation and/or licensing of firms severely restricts entry. Professional organizations for dentists or engineers, for example, might restrict the number of places in accredited dental or engineering schools, and thus restrict entry into those industries.

Other barriers can be created by the firm or firms already in the market. In extreme cases, the threat of force or sabotage can deter entry. The most obvious entry barriers of this type are encountered in organized crime, where operation outside the law makes available an array of illegal but potent barriers to new entrants. But law-abiding firms must use legal tactics in an attempt to increase a new entrant's setup costs. Such tactics range from the threat of price cutting—designed to impose unsustainable losses on a new entrant—to heavy brand-name advertising. (These and other created entry barriers will be discussed in more detail in Chapter 11.)

The Significance of Entry Barriers Because there is freedom of entry and exit in perfect competition, and thus no entry barriers, profits cannot persist in the long run. In monopolized industries, however, profits can persist in the long run whenever there are effective barriers to entry.

In competitive industries, profits attract entry, and entry erodes profits. In monopolized industries, positive profits can persist as long as there are effective entry barriers.

Applying Economic Concepts 10-1 discusses an interesting example from Ireland where government regulations, by restricting entry, have led local pubs to have considerable monopoly power. At a time when Irish pubs are becoming a popular trend in many countries, it is ironic to see how a booming Irish economy combined with government regulation has caused a shortage of Irish pubs in Ireland itself!

The Very Long Run and Creative Destruction

In the very long run, technology changes. New ways of producing old products are invented, and new products are created to satisfy both familiar and new wants. These are related to the concept of entry barriers; a monopoly that succeeds in preventing the entry of new firms capable of producing its product will sooner or later find its barriers circumvented by innovations. Here are three examples.

First, a firm may be able to develop a new production process that avoids a patent upon which a monopolist relies to bar the entry of competing firms.

Second, a firm may compete by producing a somewhat different product satisfying the same need as the monopolist's product. An example is the courier services provided by United Parcel Service or Federal Express that compete with the package delivery of Canada Post. Canada Post still has a government-granted monopoly on the delivery of first-class mail, but it has no monopoly on the delivery of "packages," whatever their size.

Finally, a firm may get around a natural monopoly by inventing a technology that produces at a low minimum efficient scale (*MES*) and allows it to enter the industry and still cover its full costs. The creation of cellular-phone technology, for example, allows the provider of cell-phone services to compete with the provider of local "land line" telephone services without having to establish an expensive network of wires, thus allowing successful competition at a much smaller scale of operations.

A monopolist's entry barriers are often circumvented by the innovation of production processes and the development of new goods and services. Such innovation explains why monopolies rarely persist, except those that are protected through government charter or regulation.

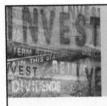

APPLYING ECONOMIC CONCEPTS 10-1

Entry Barriers for Irish Pubs

In recent years, the Irish economy has been booming—so much so that many economists refer to it as the "Celtic Tiger," putting it in the same category as the Asian tigers of Taiwan, Singapore, Hong Kong, and South Korea. As the Irish economy has boomed, however, line-ups and prices in many Irish pubs have skyrocketed. The shortage of pubs has been so severe that some pub operators have implemented their own rationing schemes by turning away young people, bachelor parties, and sloppy dressers. In some cases, publicans have even threatened to expel anyone who starts to sing, a long-standing tradition in Irish pubs.

So what is going on in the pub industry in Ireland? Ordinarily, as demand increases and profits rise, new pubs would be established. This entry of new pubs would keep the existing pubs from earning high profits.

The problem in Ireland is that the issuance of pub licences is governed by a 1902 law that froze the number of licences at the level in place at that time. As incomes grew over time and the demand for pubs increased, the entry of new pubs was prevented. It is therefore no surprise that prices in pubs have been rising and that existing pubs are extremely profitable. This profitability is reflected in the high purchase prices of the pub licences, which are freely tradable (although in fixed total supply). If pubs earned zero economic profit, these licences would have no market value. The Irish Competition Authority estimated the total value of existing licences at between 1 billion and 2 billion euros. The market value of these licences is a rough measure of the cost imposed on society by the regulations limiting the entry of new pubs.

Another aspect of the 1902 legislation that has caused local pub shortages is that pub owners are prevented from transferring licences across county lines. As the population has increasingly moved from small towns to larger cities over the past several decades, small towns are left with too many pubs while neighbourhoods in the larger cities have far too few. This distortion is seen clearly in Dublin, where approximately 35 percent of the Irish population is served by only 12 percent of the country's pubs. Though new pubs cannot be built in urban areas, the legislation does allow existing urban pubs to expand. This enables more consumers to be served, but some complain that it has led to the rise of the "super pubs"—larger establishments that lack the social atmosphere that made Irish pubs famous the world over.

Who gains from this legislation, and who loses? The clear losers are the pubs' customers (especially in growing towns and cities) who are faced with higher prices and longer line-ups. The clear gainers are the current owners of the pubs in areas where demand is strong. It is no surprise, therefore, that Ireland's powerful pub lobby continues to fight efforts by the government to review pub legislation.

Government legislation in Ireland has restricted the entry of new pubs and has therefore permitted existing pubs to earn high profits without the threat of competition.

(For the Irish Competition Authority's submission to the Liquor Licensing Commission (October 2001), see www.tca.ie and click on "Authority Documents.")

The distinguished economist Joseph Schumpeter (1883–1950) took the view that entry barriers were not a serious problem in the very long run. He argued that the short-run profits of a monopoly provide a strong incentive for others, through their own innovations and product development, to try to usurp some of these profits for themselves. If a frontal attack on the monopolist's entry barriers is not possible, the barriers will be circumvented by such means as the development of similar products against which the monopolist will not have entry protection.

LESSONS FROM HISTORY 10-1

Creative Destruction Through History

Creative destruction, the elimination of one product by a superior product, is a major characteristic of all advanced countries. It eliminates the strong market position of the firms and workers who make the threatened product.

The steel-nibbed pen eliminated the quill pen with its sharpened bird's feather nib. The fountain pen eliminated the steel pen and its accompanying inkwell. The ballpoint pen virtually eliminated the fountain pen. Who knows what will come next in writing implements?

The silent films eliminated vaudeville. The talkies eliminated silent films and colour films have all but eliminated black and white. Television seriously reduced the demand for films (and radio) while not eliminating either of them. Cable greatly reduced the demand for direct TV reception by offering a better picture and a more varied selection. Satellite TV is now threatening to eliminate cable by offering much more selection, and access to programs on the Internet is now challenging the dominance of television networks.

For long-distance passenger travel by sea, the steamship eliminated the sailing vessel around the beginning of the twentieth century. The airplane eliminated the ocean liner in the 1950s and 1960s. For passenger travel on land, the train eliminated the stage coach while the bus competed with the train without eliminating it. The airplane wiped out the passenger train in most of North America while leaving the bus still in a low-cost niche used mainly for short and medium distances.

These examples all involve the elimination of a product by the development of a new, preferred product. But creative destruction also occurs with the development of better *processes*. The laborious hand-setting of metal type for printing was replaced by the linotype that allowed the type to be set by a keyboard operator, but that still involved a costly procedure for making corrections. The linotype was swept away by computer typesetting and much of the established printing shop operations have now been replaced by desktop publishing.

A century ago, automobiles were produced with skilled craftsmen operating relatively unsophisticated equipment. When Henry Ford perfected the techniques of mass production in the early 1920s, masses of less-skilled workers operated specialized and inflexible equipment. Now, far fewer workers, but more highly skilled ones, operate even more sophisticated robotics equipment to produce today's vehicles.

These cases all illustrate the same general message. Technological change transforms the products we consume, how we make those products, and how we work. It continually sweeps away positions of high income and economic power established by firms that were in the previous wave of technological change and by those who work for them. It is an agent of dynamism in our economy, an agent of change and economic growth, but it is not without its dark side in terms of the periodic loss of privileged positions on the part of the replaced firms and their workers.

Schumpeter called the replacement of one product by another the *process of creative destruction*. "Creative" referred to the rise of new products; "destruction" referred to the demise of the existing products and perhaps the firms that produced them. Some examples of creative destruction are presented in *Lessons From History 10-1*.

Schumpeter argued that this process of creative destruction reflects new firms' abilities to circumvent entry barriers that would otherwise permit monopolists to earn profits in the long run. He also argued that because creative destruction thrives on innovation, the existence of monopoly profits is a major incentive to economic growth. Schumpeter was writing at a time when the two dominant market structures studied by economists were perfect competition and monopoly. His argument easily extends, however, to any market structure that allows profits to exist in the long run. Today, pure monopolies are few, but there are many industries in which profits can be earned for long periods of time. Such industries, which are called *oligopolies,* are candidates for the operation of the process of creative destruction. We study these industries in detail in Chapter 11.

10.2 **CARTELS AS MONOPOLIES**

cartel An organization of producers who agree to act as a single seller in order to maximize joint profits.

So far in our discussion, a monopoly has meant that there is only one firm in an industry. A second way a monopoly can arise is for many firms in an industry to agree to cooperate with one another, eliminating competition among themselves. In this case, they would band together and behave as if they were a single seller with the objective of maximizing their *joint profits*. Such a group of firms is called a **cartel**. The firms can agree among themselves to restrict their total output to the level that maximizes their *joint profits*.

Some of the best examples of cartels come from history. In the United States in the last half of the nineteenth century, cartels existed in the steel and oil industries. These cartels were so successful in restricting output and elevating prices that much of current U.S. anti-trust policy dates from that time. As we will see in Chapter 12, U.S. and Canadian policy has been quite effective at preventing the creation of large cartels that would otherwise possess considerable market power.

To learn more about OPEC, see its website at **www.opec.org**.

As a result of successful policies aimed at preventing the creation of *domestic* cartels, the best current examples of cartels are ones that operate in global markets and are supported by national governments. The Organization of Petroleum Exporting Countries (OPEC) is perhaps the best-known cartel in the world. This cartel first came to prominence when, in 1973, its members collectively agreed to restrict their output of crude oil and thereby increased the world price of oil by nearly 200 percent. In 1979, further output restrictions led the price to increase by another 120 percent. During the 1980s and 1990s, as oil production by non-OPEC countries increased significantly, OPEC found it difficult to maintain such a controlling influence on the oil market. OPEC also ran into problems enforcing the agreements among its members. As we will see in this section, these are typical challenges that all cartels face.

A less well-known example, but one that has been successful over many years, is the diamond cartel, controlled by the South African company DeBeers. DeBeers produces roughly 40 percent of the world's annual production of rough diamonds but also purchases diamonds from smaller producers worldwide. The result is that about half of the world's annual diamond supply is marketed through the DeBeers-controlled Diamond Trading Company (DTC). In years when demand is slack, DeBeers restricts the output of diamonds through the DTC to keep prices from falling.

Notice in both examples that there are firms *outside* the cartel. There are many oil producers (including Canada) that are not part of OPEC; similarly, there are many diamond mines that are not owned or controlled by DeBeers (two of which are the Ekati and Diavik mines in the Northwest Territories that together make up approximately 14 percent of total world diamond production). Indeed, this type of cartel is much more common than one in which *all* firms in the industry successfully band together.

DeBeers controls approximately half of the world's supply of diamonds through its Diamond Trading Company.

In this chapter, however, we simplify the analysis by considering the case in which *all* firms in the industry form a cartel. This is the easiest setting in which to see the central point—that cartels are inherently unstable.

The Effects of Cartelization

If all firms in a competitive industry come together to form a cartel, they must recognize the effect their *joint* output has on price. That is, like a monopolist they must recognize that an increase in the volume of their sales requires a reduction in price. They can agree to restrict industry output to the level that maximizes their joint profits (where the industry's marginal cost is equal to the industry's marginal revenue). The incentive for firms to form a cartel lies in the cartel's ability to restrict output, thereby raising price and increasing profits. This is shown in Figure 10-4.

The profit-maximizing cartelization of a competitive industry will reduce output and raise price from the perfectly competitive levels.

Problems That Cartels Face

Cartels encounter two characteristic problems. The first is ensuring that members follow the behaviour that will maximize the cartel members' *joint* profits. The second is preventing these profits from being eroded by the entry of new firms.

Enforcement of Output Restrictions The managers of any cartel want the industry to produce its profit-maximizing output. Their job is made more difficult if individual firms either stay out of the cartel or join the cartel and then "cheat" by producing too much output. Any one firm, however, has an incentive to do just this—to be either the one that stays out of the organization or the one that enters and then cheats. For the sake of simplicity, assume that all firms enter the cartel; thus enforcement problems are concerned strictly with cheating by its members.

If Firm X is the only firm to cheat, it is then in the best of all possible situations. All other firms restrict output and hold the industry price up near its monopoly level. They earn profits but only by restricting output. Firm X can then reap the full benefit of the other firms' output restraint and sell some additional output at the high price that has been set by the cartel's actions. However, if all of the firms cheat, the price will be pushed back to the competitive level, and all of the firms will return to their competitive position.

This conflict between the interests of the group as a whole and the interests of each individual firm is the cartel's main dilemma. Provided that enough firms cooperate in restricting output, all firms are better off than they would be if the industry remained perfectly competitive. Any one firm, however, is even better off if it remains outside or if it enters and cheats. However, if all firms act on this incentive, all will be worse off than if they had joined the cartel and restricted output.

Cartels tend to be unstable because of the incentives for individual firms to violate the output restrictions needed to sustain the joint-profit-maximizing (monopoly) price.

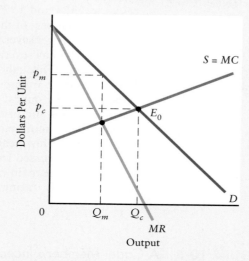

FIGURE 10-4 The Effect of Cartelizing a Competitive Industry

Cartelization of a competitive industry can always increase that industry's profits. Equilibrium for a competitive industry occurs at E_0. Equilibrium price and output are p_c and Q_c.

If the industry is cartelized, profits can be increased by reducing output. All units between Q_m and Q_c add less to revenue than to cost—the MR curve lies below the MC curve—and therefore will not be produced by a profit-maximizing cartel. The cartel maximizes its joint profits by producing output of Q_m and setting price equal to p_m.

Practise with Study Guide Chapter 10, Exercise 4.

The conflict between the motives for cooperation and for independent action is analyzed in more detail in Figure 10-5. In Chapter 11, we will consider an explicit theory, called *game theory*, that economists use to analyze conflicts of this kind.

The predicted instability of cartels is evident in the data. After the tremendous successes in 1973 and 1979 in restricting the output of crude oil and elevating its world price, the members of the OPEC cartel began to encounter difficulties in enforcing their agreements. After several years of sluggish world demand for oil, the cartel almost collapsed in 1986 as several OPEC members increased their output in efforts to generate more income. Throughout the 1990s, however, OPEC members learned the important lesson that their attempts to push oil prices very high attract alternative oil supplies and undermine their output restrictions. As a result, OPEC members avoided the large output restrictions and price increases of the 1970s, instead trying to keep oil prices relatively stable at more moderate levels.

In the last few years, however, OPEC's market power has increased. The world price of oil increased from about U.S.$15 per barrel in 1998 to over U.S.$75 per barrel in 2006. The main cause of the price increase (in addition to some geopolitical tensions, especially during 2006) was growing world demand in a market in which most

FIGURE 10-5 A Cartel Member's Incentive to Cheat

(i) Market equilibrium

(ii) Firm incentives

Cooperation leads to the monopoly price, but individual self-interest leads to production in excess of the monopoly output. Market conditions are shown in part (i), and the situation of a typical firm is shown in part (ii). (The change of scale between the two graphs is reflected by the upper case Q in part (i) and the lower case q in part (ii).) Initially, the market is in competitive equilibrium with price p_0 and quantity Q_0. The individual firm is producing output q_0 and is just covering its total costs.

A successful cartel reduces total output to Q_1 and elevates price to p_1. Q_1 is the joint profit-maximizing level of output because industry MR equals industry MC. A typical firm in the cartel then produces output of q_1 in part (ii). The firm's profits rise from zero to the amount shown by the grey shaded area in part (ii). Once price is raised to p_1, however, the individual firm would like to increase output to q_2, where marginal cost is equal to the price set by the cartel. This would allow the firm to earn much larger profits, shown by the diagonally striped area. However, if all firms increase their output, industry output will increase beyond Q_1, and the resulting fall in price will reduce the joint profits of the cartel.

producers had a limited ability to increase production. In other words, the world demand curve was shifting to the right while the world supply curve was quite steep. In this environment, a decision by OPEC to considerably restrict output, even though OPEC represents only about a third of total world production, would have a significant effect on the market price.

Another example of a cartel's instability involves the world coffee market. In 2000, the Association of Coffee Producing Countries (ACPC), a cartel of 15 countries that produced approximately 75 percent of the world's coffee, agreed to restrict coffee output to keep coffee prices between U.S.$0.95 and U.S.$1.05 per pound. Within two years, however, a bumper crop in Brazil, the world's largest coffee producer, led to the inevitable pressure to cheat. Brazil had the incentive to sell its new production rather than incur storage costs. Other countries, facing low prices, had the incentive to increase their sales to bolster their incomes. By January of 2003, the ACPC planned to close down its operations. Perhaps the cartel will be re-established at some point in the future when it has improved its ability to enforce its members' behaviour.

For interesting information about coffee and the world coffee market, go to **www.ico.org**.

Restricting Entry   A successful cartel not only must police the behaviour of its members but also must be able to prevent the entry of new producers. An industry that is able to support a number of individual firms presumably has no overriding natural entry barriers. Thus, if it is to maintain its profits in the long run, a cartel of many separate firms must create barriers that prevent the entry of new firms that are attracted by the cartel's profits. Successful cartels are often able to license the firms in the industry and to control entry by restricting the number of licences. This practice is often used by professionals, from physicians to beauticians. At other times, the government has operated a quota system and has given it the force of law. If no one can produce without a quota and the quotas are allocated among existing producers, entry is successfully prevented. This approach is used to limit the number of taxicabs in many cities.

As we mentioned earlier, for many years DeBeers was successful at preventing the entry of new diamond producers and was able to control a large fraction of the world's annual sales of rough diamonds. But recently, restricting entry into the diamond industry has been more challenging. In the diamond industry, of course, "entry" means the development of new diamond mines. In 2004, two new mines in the Northwest Territories reached full-scale production. The combined annual output of rough diamonds from the Ekati and Diavik mines is about U.S.$1.65 billion, roughly 14 percent of total world production. The owners of the Ekati and Diavik mines, however, will market the diamonds independently rather than going through DeBeers. With entries such as this, combined with some Russian and Australian producers also choosing to sell their diamonds independently, DeBeers is faced with the challenge of keeping diamond prices supported above competitive levels. Time and further developments will determine how successful DeBeers will be in maintaining its dominant position in the industry.

For more information on the diamond industry in the Northwest Territories, see **www.iti.gov.nt.ca/ diamond/development.htm**.

10.3 PRICE DISCRIMINATION

So far in this chapter, we have assumed that the monopolist charges the same price for every unit of its product, no matter where or to whom it sells that product. But as we shall soon see, a monopolist always finds it profitable to sell different units of the same product at different prices whenever it gets the opportunity. Because this practice is prevalent both for monopoly and for markets in which there are a few large sellers, the range of examples we will discuss covers both types of market structure.

Airlines often charge less to people who stay over a Saturday night than to those who come and go within the week. In countries where medical services are provided by the market, physicians in private practice often charge for their services according to the incomes of their patients. Movie theatres often have lower admission prices for seniors. Electric companies sell electricity at one rate to homes and at a different rate to firms.

price discrimination The sale by one firm of different units of a commodity at two or more different prices for reasons not associated with differences in cost.

Price discrimination occurs when a producer charges different prices for different units of the same product *for reasons not associated with differences in cost*. Not all price differences represent price discrimination. Quantity discounts, differences between wholesale and retail prices, and prices that vary with the time of day or the season of the year may not represent price discrimination because the same product sold at a different time, in a different place, or in different quantities may have different costs. An excellent example is electricity. If an electric power company has unused capacity at certain times of the day, it may cost less for the company to provide service at those hours than at peak demand hours.

If price differences reflect cost differences, they are not discriminatory. When a price difference is based on different buyers' valuations of the same product, it is discriminatory.

It does not cost a movie-theatre operator less to fill seats with senior citizens than with non-seniors, but it is worthwhile for the movie theatre to let the seniors in at a discriminatory low price if few of them would attend at the full adult fare and if they take up seats that would otherwise be empty. Similarly, it does not cost an airline any less to sell a ticket to a student than to a non-student. But since few students may be inclined to buy airline tickets at the full price, it is profitable for the airline to attract more students with a lower price and, in that manner, fill up seats that would otherwise be empty.

Why do firms price discriminate? It may seem odd that they sell some units of output at a low price and other units at a high price. The simple answer is that firms price discriminate because they find it profitable to do so. As we will see shortly, price discrimination is profitable for two reasons. First, even if firms do not alter their level of output, price discrimination allows them to "capture" some consumer surplus that would otherwise go to the buyer. Second, price discrimination allows firms to sell extra units of output without reducing the price on their existing sales.

Any firm that faces a downward-sloping demand curve can increase its profits if it is able to charge different prices for different units of its product.

Practise with Study Guide Chapter 10, Exercise 5.

Note two important points. First, only firms facing downward-sloping demand curves—that is, firms with market power—are able to price discriminate. Perfectly competitive firms are price takers and therefore have no ability to set one price, let alone set multiple prices. Second, firms will price discriminate *if they are able* to. Before we explore the various types of price discrimination, let's lay out the conditions under which it is possible.

When Price Discrimination Is Possible

Three conditions must be satisfied before a firm can successfully price discriminate.

1. Market Power   As we said above, any firm that is a price taker cannot discriminate because it has no power to influence the price at which it sells its product. Our entire discussion about price discrimination therefore applies only to firms with some amount of market power. For simplicity, we will consider the case of a monopoly firm, although *any* firm with market power will, in general, be interested in the greater profits that are possible through price discrimination.

2. Consumers with Different Valuations of the Product Price discrimination is only possible when consumers value different units of the product differently. This could occur in two situations. First, the same consumer might be prepared to pay a different price for each unit of the good. Second, consumers of one particular type (or in one geographic region) may be prepared to pay more for the good than consumers of a different type (or in a different region). We will see some examples shortly.

In the situation where price discrimination occurs between groups of consumers, the firm must somehow be able to determine which group of consumers is prepared to pay a high price and which group is prepared to pay only a low price. This is referred to as *segmenting* the market. Sometimes this market segmentation is relatively easy, as when the market is divided into geographic regions. Other times the firm must create innovative pricing strategies that will lead consumers to segment themselves. We will see examples of both below.

3. No Arbitrage Whenever the same product is being sold at different prices, there is an incentive for buyers to purchase the product at the lower price and re-sell it at the higher price, thereby making a profit on the transaction. This is called *arbitrage*. A price-discriminating firm must be able to prevent people from conducting such transactions. Otherwise the firm will end up selling only at the low price and all of the profits that the strategy of price discrimination was designed to produce will accrue to those who do the arbitrage. As we will soon see, the successful prevention of this arbitrage depends crucially on the nature of the product being sold.

Different Forms of Price Discrimination

Now that we have seen the conditions that make price discrimination possible, let's examine the two general forms that it can take: price discrimination among *units of output* and price discrimination among *market segments*.

Price Discrimination Among Units of Output
Recall our discussion in Chapter 6 where we noted that the demand curve can be viewed as a *willingness to pay* curve. We also discussed the concept of *consumer surplus,* the difference between the price the consumer is *willing* to pay and the price that the consumer *actually* pays.

A firm that charges different prices for different units of a product is trying to capture this consumer surplus. Figure 10-6 shows a monopolist's profits in two situations. In the first, the monopolist is only able to charge a single price per unit. In the second, the monopolist is able to charge different prices on different units of output and it increases its profits by doing so. Notice that even in the case where the firm charges several prices, consumers still earn some consumer surplus. In principle, however, a firm could charge a different price for each different unit of the product and thereby extract all of the consumer surplus. This situation is referred to as *perfect price discrimination* and is very rare because it is very difficult for the firm to ascertain the consumers' willingness to pay for each individual unit. However, in some countries where local doctors know their patients very well and thus can make informed judgements about the consumers' willingness to pay, this type of price discrimination is observed.

Price discrimination among units of output sold to the same consumer requires that the firm be able to keep track of the units that a buyer consumes in each period. Thus, the tenth unit purchased by a given consumer in a given month can be sold at a

Practise with Study Guide Chapter 10, Exercise 6.

FIGURE 10-6 Price Discrimination Among Units of Output

Profits can be increased by price discriminating. A single-price monopolist produces where $MR = MC$; output is Q_m and price is p_m. In this case, profits are the light shaded area, and consumers receive consumer surplus given by the entire area above p_m and below the demand curve.

Price discrimination is designed to transfer some of this consumer surplus to the firm. Suppose the firm keeps output constant at Q_m but is able to charge different prices for different blocks of units. For example, it might charge p_1 for the first Q_1 units, p_2 for the next block of units up to Q_2, p_3 for the next block of units up to Q_3, and p_m for the remaining units up to Q_m. (The firm would expand output beyond Q_m if it could offer even more prices, but we simplify here to focus on the transfer of surplus with unchanged output.) In this case, the firm's costs have not changed but its revenues have increased by the dark shaded area. Since costs have not changed, the increase in revenue earned by price discrimination also represents an increase in profits for the firm. Consumer surplus has been reduced to the unshaded triangles just below the demand curve.

price that is different from the fifth unit *only* if the firm can keep track of that consumer's purchases. This can be done, for example, by an electric company through its meter readings or by a magazine publisher by distinguishing between renewals and new subscriptions. Another way in which some sellers keep track of the consumer's purchases is to offer quantity discounts that take the form "buy two and get the third at half-price."

Price Discrimination Among Market Segments It is often easier for firms to distinguish between different groups of consumers of a product—different market segments—than it is to detect an individual consumer's willingness to pay for different units of that product. As a result, price discrimination among market segments is more common than price discrimination among units.

Suppose a monopolist faces a market demand curve that is made up of distinct market segments. These market segments may correspond to the age of consumers, such as children, adults, and seniors. Or the segments may correspond to different regions in which the consumers live, such as the North American automobile market being segmented into the Canadian and U.S. market segments. Whatever the nature of the market segmentation, suppose the monopolist recognizes the distinct market segments and is able to prevent any purchase-and-resale between them. What is the firm's profit-maximizing pricing policy?

The answer is for the firm to charge a higher price in the market segment with the *less elastic demand,* as shown in the numerical example in Figure 10-7. To understand this result, recall our discussion from Chapter 4 regarding elasticity. The elasticity of demand reflects consumers' ability or willingness to substitute between this product and other products. The market segment with less elastic demand therefore contains consumers that are more "committed" to this product than are the consumers in the market segment with more elastic demand. To put it differently, the consumers with less elastic demand represent a more "captive" market for the firm. It should not be surprising, therefore, that the profit-maximizing firm will charge a higher price to the more captive consumers and a lower price to those consumers who can more easily substitute away to other products.

Practise with Study Guide Chapter 10, Exercise 7.

A firm with market power that can identify distinct market segments will maximize its profits by charging higher prices in those segments with less elastic demand.

Price discrimination among market segments is very common. When the different segments occur in different regions or countries, distance and transport costs or government regulation help to keep the markets separate. For example, Levi Strauss, the manufacturer of jeans, actively discriminates in its pricing of Levi's 501s (and other products). The price in France is more than twice that in the United States. Ordinarily we would expect importers in France to import inexpensive 501s from the United States and sell them in France, thus pushing down the price. In this case, however, the price discrimination is made possible by European Union legislation barring the import of less expensive brand-name goods from outside the European Union. French consumers understandably don't like this price discrimination, but their less elastic demand combined with the EU legal barriers leads Levi Strauss to maximize its profits by charging much more in France than in the United States.

A more familiar example of price discrimination among market segments is the different prices charged by movie theatres for adults and seniors. The cost to the theatre of providing a seat to any customer is independent of the customer's age. But the two market segments contain consumers who are thought to have different elasticities of demand, the adults with the less elastic demand than seniors. The profit-maximizing pricing policy by the theatre is therefore to charge a higher price to adults than to seniors. This same logic applies to many goods and services for which there are "seniors' discounts."

The example of seniors' discounts at theatres also illustrates an important point about how the firm prevents arbitrage when price discriminating. When you buy a ticket to see a movie, you are buying a *service* rather than a tangible good. You don't take anything away with you after the movie—you are really just paying for the right to see the movie. This aspect of the product makes price discrimination easier to enforce. A young adult trying to circumvent the price discrimination could buy a senior's ticket, but upon entry to the theatre that person would be stopped and easily recognized as ineligible for the seniors' discount.

Price discrimination is easier for services than for tangible goods because for most services the firms transact directly with the customer, and thus can more easily prevent arbitrage.

That price discrimination is easier to sustain with services than with goods explains another familiar observation. As we noted above, seniors' discounts are quite common, even for tangible goods such as groceries. What prevents entrepreneurial seniors in these situations from buying a large number of units at the special price and re-selling them to non-seniors at a higher price? The answer is that firms usually place quantity limits on special deals, thus preventing any large-scale arbitrage that would undermine their pricing policy.

FIGURE 10-7 A Numerical Example of Profitable Price Discrimination

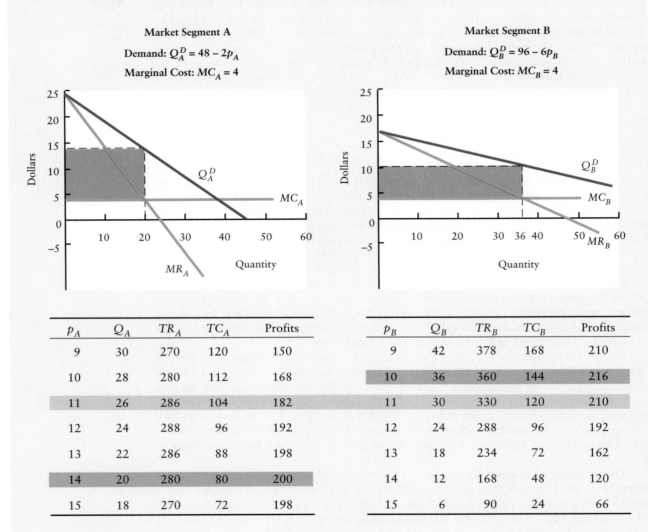

p_A	Q_A	TR_A	TC_A	Profits		p_B	Q_B	TR_B	TC_B	Profits
9	30	270	120	150		9	42	378	168	210
10	28	280	112	168		10	36	360	144	216
11	26	286	104	182		11	30	330	120	210
12	24	288	96	192		12	24	288	96	192
13	22	286	88	198		13	18	234	72	162
14	20	280	80	200		14	12	168	48	120
15	18	270	72	198		15	6	90	24	66

Profit-maximizing price discrimination results in higher prices in those market segments with less elastic demand. The figure shows two market segments, each with a different demand curve. At any given price, demand in segment A is less elastic than demand in segment B. Profit-maximizing price discrimination requires that $MC = MR$ in each market segment.

For each market segment, the table shows different possible prices, and the associated quantities, revenues, costs, and profits. Marginal costs are assumed to be $4 for each unit produced. If the firm is unable to price discriminate, and therefore must charge the same price in both market segments, the single profit-maximizing price is $11, total output is 56 units, and the resulting total profit is $392, as shown by the green shaded row. The firm can increase its profits, however, if it can price discriminate across the two market segments. By charging $14 in segment A and only $10 in segment B, the firm's total output is unchanged at 56 units, but the allocation of that output across the market segments is changed, and the firm's total profit increases to $416, as shown by the two red shaded rows.

myeconlab

In recent years, Canadian entrepreneurs have taken advantage of international price discrimination in prescription drugs by creating on-line businesses to sell inexpensive drugs from Canada to U.S. consumers. For a detailed discussion, look for "The Growing Battle Over On-line Prescription Drugs" in the *Additional Topics* section of this book's MyEconLab.

www.myeconlab.com

Hurdle Pricing Often there are market segments that are well defined but very difficult to detect by the firm. For example, we all know people who are sufficiently impatient that they *must* buy new electronic equipment—such as personal DVD players or cellular phones—when they first come out, whereas many other people are prepared to wait several months until they are no longer such hot items and buy them at considerably lower prices. This pricing strategy is intentional and is referred to as *hurdle pricing*. The firms producing these goods know that some people are patient and others are impatient. By setting a high initial price and a lower price only after several months, the firms are setting a "hurdle" that consumers must "jump over" in order to get the low price. In this case, the hurdle is that consumers must wait a few months. This same type of hurdle exists in the pricing of high-priced hardcover books and lower-priced paperback books that are released a few months later. In this case, the slightly altered products do have different costs, although the cost differences are considerably smaller than the differences in prices.

Hurdle pricing exists when firms create an obstacle that consumers must overcome in order to get a lower price. Consumers then assign themselves to the various market segments—those who don't want to jump the hurdle and are willing to pay the high price, and those who choose to jump the hurdle in order to benefit from the low price.

Another familiar example of hurdle pricing involves coupons for discounts at grocery stores. Most of us receive grocery-store flyers in the mail every week. Many people ignore them because they can't be bothered to look through them. Others carefully scan the coupons and clip the ones they will use, and it is common to see someone in a grocery-store line-up with a dozen or more coupons to apply to the purchase. In this case, the price discrimination is between those people who can't be bothered to deal with the coupons, and those people who care enough about the discounts to clip the coupons. Everyone is presented with the option between higher prices and lower prices, and the hurdle of clipping coupons is designed to have people assign themselves to the two market segments.

The Consequences of Price Discrimination

What are the consequences of price discrimination? We can examine the consequences for firm profits, output, and consumer welfare.

Price Discrimination and Firm Profits Our first proposition is about the consequences of price discrimination for firm profits:

For any given level of output, the most profitable system of discriminatory prices will always provide higher profits to the firm than the profit-maximizing single price.

This proposition, which was illustrated in Figure 10-6, requires only that the demand curve have a negative slope. To see that the proposition is correct, remember that a monopolist with the power to discriminate could produce exactly the same quantity as a single-price monopolist and charge everyone the same price. Therefore, it need never receive less revenue, and it can do better if it can raise the price on even one unit sold, so long as the price need not be reduced on any other.

Price Discrimination and Output   Our second proposition relates to how price discrimination affects the level of output.

A monopolist that price discriminates among units will produce more output than will a single-price monopolist.

To understand this second proposition, remember that a single-price monopolist will produce less than would all the firms in a perfectly competitive industry (recall Figure 10-3). It produces less because it knows that selling more depresses the price. Price discrimination allows it to reduce this disincentive. To the extent that the firm can sell its output in separate blocks, it can sell another block without spoiling the market for blocks that are already sold. In the case of perfect price discrimination, in which every unit of output is sold at a different price, the profit-maximizing monopolist will produce every unit for which the price charged is greater than or equal to its marginal cost. A perfect-price-discriminating monopolist will therefore produce the same quantity of output as would all firms combined in a perfectly competitive industry.

This second proposition has implications for *market efficiency,* a concept we introduced in Chapter 5 and reviewed earlier in this chapter. Recall that a single-price monopolist produces at a level of output where price exceeds marginal cost. Thus, society would benefit from having more of the good produced because the marginal value of the good to society (as reflected by its price) exceeds the marginal cost of the good. Put differently, a higher level of output would lead to more economic surplus being generated in the market, and thus a more efficient outcome for society as a whole.

For a monopolist that price discriminates among units, however, there are several prices rather than just a single price. As you can see in Figure 10-6, if the firm sold another block of output beyond Q_m at a price below p_m it would increase its profits further (because the new price would still be above MC). And the more output it produces, the more economic surplus is generated in the market.

If price discrimination leads the firm to increase total output, the total economic surplus generated in the market will increase, and the outcome will be more efficient.

Price Discrimination and Consumer Welfare   The final aspect of price discrimination is its effect on consumers, and here is where we often witness strong emotional reactions to price discrimination. But one's view will depend on who benefits and who loses.

For instance, when railways discriminate against small farmers, the results arouse public anger. It seems acceptable to many people, however, that doctors practise price discrimination in countries where medical services are provided by the market, charging lower prices to poor patients than to wealthy ones. Not everyone disapproves when airlines discriminate by giving senior citizens and vacationers lower fares than business travellers.

By increasing the seller's profits, price discrimination transfers income from buyers to sellers. When buyers are poor and sellers are rich, this transfer may seem undesirable. However, as in the case of doctor's fees and senior citizens' discounts, discrimination sometimes allows lower-income people to buy a product that they would otherwise be unable to afford if it were sold at the single price that maximized the producer's profits. In this case some consumers are made better off by the firm's decision to price discriminate.

There is no general relationship between price discrimination and consumer welfare. Price discrimination makes some consumers better off and other consumers worse off.

SUMMARY

10.1 **A SINGLE-PRICE MONOPOLIST**

- Monopoly is a market structure in which an entire industry is supplied by a single firm. The monopolist's own demand curve is identical to the market demand curve for the product. The market demand curve is the monopolist's average revenue curve, and its marginal revenue curve always lies below its demand curve.
- A single-price monopolist is maximizing its profits when its marginal revenue is equal to marginal costs. Since marginal costs are positive, profit maximization means that marginal revenue is positive. Thus, in turn, elasticity of demand is greater than 1 at the monopolist's profit-maximizing level of output.
- A monopolist produces such that price exceeds marginal cost, whereas in a perfectly competitive industry price equals marginal cost. By restricting output below the competitive level, the monopolist imposes a dead-

weight loss on society; this is the inefficiency of monopoly.
- The profits that a monopoly earns may be positive, zero, or negative in the short run, depending on the relationship between demand and cost.
- For monopoly profits to persist in the long run, there must be effective barriers to the entry of other firms. Entry barriers can be natural or created.
- Monopoly power is limited by the presence of substitute products, the development of new products, and the entry of new firms. In the very long run, it is difficult to maintain entry barriers in the face of the process of creative destruction—the invention of new processes and new products to attack the entrenched position of existing firms.

10.2 **CARTELS AS MONOPOLIES**

- A group of firms may form a cartel by agreeing to restrict their joint output to the monopoly level. Cartels tend to be unstable because of the strong incentives for

each individual firm to cheat by producing more than its agreed-upon level of output.

10.3 **PRICE DISCRIMINATION**

- A price-discriminating monopolist can capture some of the consumer surplus that exists when all of the units of a product are sold at a single price.
- Successful price discrimination requires that the firm be able to control the supply of the product offered to particular buyers and to prevent the resale of the product.
- A firm that price discriminates among units will produce more output than if it sets only a single price. Price discrimination of this type is possible only if it can monitor use of the product by consumers.
- A firm that discriminates between different market segments will equate MC and MR in each market. The market with the less elastic demand will have the higher price.

- Hurdle pricing is a common form of price discrimination that requires customers to overcome some obstacle in order to benefit from a lower price. This method of price discrimination leads customers to reveal which market segment they are in.
- If price discrimination leads the firm to increase output, market efficiency is improved. In general, some consumers will benefit and others will be made worse off by the firm's ability to price discriminate.

KEY CONCEPTS

The relationship between price and marginal revenue for a monopolist
Short-run monopoly profits
Natural and created entry barriers
The process of creative destruction

Cartels as monopolies
The instability of cartels
Arbitrage
Price discrimination among units

Perfect price discrimination
Price discrimination among market segments
Hurdle pricing

STUDY EXERCISES

1. Fill in the blanks to make the following statements correct.

   a. A perfectly competitive firm faces a _____ demand curve, whereas a single-price monopolist faces a _____ demand curve.

   b. A single-price monopolist that maximizes profits will produce at the output where _____ equals _____. A perfectly competitive firm (and industry) produces a level of output such that price _____ marginal cost. The monopolist produces a level of output such that price _____ marginal cost.

   c. A monopolist will be earning profits as long as price is _____ average total cost.

   d. At its profit-maximizing level of output, marginal cost for a single-price monopolist is always _____ the price it charges for its output.

2. **myeconlab** The following table shows data for a monopolist. The first two columns provide all the data necessary to plot the monopolist's demand curve.

Price	Quantity Demanded	Total Revenue (*TR*)	Average Revenue (*AR*)	Marginal Revenue (*MR*)
$20	100	—	—	—
18	125	—	—	—
16	150	—	—	—
14	175	—	—	—
12	200	—	—	—
10	225	—	—	—
8	250	—	—	—
6	275	—	—	—
4	300	—	—	—

   a. Compute total and average revenue for each level of output and fill in the third and fourth columns in the table. Explain why average revenue is equal to price.

   b. Compute marginal revenue for each successive *change* in output and fill in the last column. Explain why *MR* is less than price.

   c. On a scale diagram, plot the demand (average revenue) curve and the marginal revenue curve.

   d. On a second scale diagram, with dollars on the vertical axis and output on the horizontal axis, plot the *TR* curve. What is the value of *MR* when *TR* reaches its maximum?

3. **myeconlab** The diagram below shows the demand curve, marginal revenue curve, and cost curves for a monopolist that owns all the golf courses on Golf Island. The monopolist's product is 18-hole golf games.

   a. What is the profit-maximizing price and output (number of rounds of golf per week) for the monopolist on Golf Island?

   b. What is the average total cost per round of golf at the profit-maximizing level of output?

   c. Calculate the profit, in dollars per week, to this monopolist.

4. The diagram below shows a monopolist's *MC* and *ATC* curves as well as the industry demand and *MR* curves.

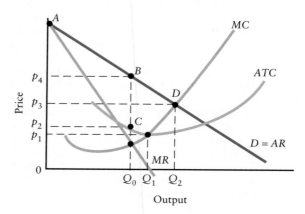

Output

a. What is the profit-maximizing price and level of output for the monopolist?
b. What area in the figure shows the level of profits for the monopolist? Are profits positive or negative?
c. What area shows the deadweight loss to society resulting from the monopolist's output decision?
d. Now suppose the industry is made up of many small, price-taking firms (with the same technology). What are the equilibrium price and level of output in this case?

5. Imagine a monopolist that has fixed costs but no variable costs (thus there are no marginal costs, so $MC = 0$). For example, consider a firm that owns a spring of water that can produce indefinitely once it installs certain pipes, in an area where no other source of water is available.

a. Draw a downward-sloping demand curve for water, its associated *MR* curve, and the monopolist's *MC* curve.
b. On your diagram, show the monopolist's profit-maximizing price and level of output.
c. What is the marginal value of this good to society, and how does it compare to the marginal cost?

6. Consider the market for corn. Suppose this is a competitive industry, made up of many price-taking farmers. We begin in a situation where market price is p_0, industry output is Q_0, and the typical farm is earning zero profit.

a. Draw two diagrams like the ones at the bottom of this page.
b. Now suppose that the farmers in this industry form a cartel and collectively agree to restrict the industry output of corn to the level that a monopolist would produce. Call this level of output Q^m and call the new price p^m. Each firm now produces output of $q^m < q_0$. Show this outcome in the two diagrams.
c. Show how the cartel raises the profits for the typical farmer.
d. Now consider the incentives for an individual farm to cheat on its fellow cartel members. Would it be profitable to produce an extra unit and sell it at the cartel price? How is this incentive illustrated in your diagram?
e. Show how the typical farm's profits would rise if it were the only farm to cheat. What level of output would the cheating farm produce?
f. Explain what would happen if *all* farms tried to cheat in this way.

7. Consider each of the following examples where a firm sells the same product to different customers at different prices. Identify in each case whether price discrimination is likely to be taking place. If there is unlikely

Corn Industry

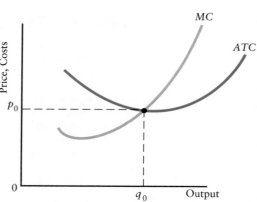

Typical Corn Farmer

to be price discrimination occurring, what explains the different prices?

a. Weekend airline fares that are less than mid-week fares.

b. Business-class airline fares that are 50% higher than economy-class fares. (Recognize that two business-class seats take the same space inside the plane as three economy-class seats.)

c. Discounts on furniture negotiated from "suggested retail price" for which sales personnel are authorized to bargain and to get as much in each transaction as the customer is prepared to pay.

d. Higher tuition for law students than for graduate students in economics.

8. Look back to the diagram of the monopolist on Golf Island in Question 3.

a. Suppose the monopolist is able to practise *perfect* price discrimination. What would be the total number of rounds of golf sold per week? What would be the price on the last round sold?

b. What is the area representing consumer surplus in the absence of any price discrimination?

c. What is the area representing consumer surplus when the monopolist is practising perfect price discrimination?

d. Could this monopolist realistically engage in perfect price discrimination? Describe a more likely form of price discrimination that this monopolist could achieve on Golf Island.

9. In the text we mentioned how Levi Strauss price discriminates between the European and American markets. This question is designed to help you analyze this situation. The following equations are hypothetical demand curves for Levi's 501s in Europe and in America. We have expressed the price in dollars in both markets, and quantity is thousands of units per year.

European Demand: $Q^D_E = 150 - p$
American Demand: $Q^D_A = 250 - 4p$

a. On two separate scale diagrams, one for Europe and one for America, plot the two demand curves.

b. Recalling that a straight-line demand curve has an associated *MR* curve that has twice its slope, plot the two *MR* curves.

c. Suppose Levi Strauss has a constant marginal cost of $15 per unit. Plot the *MC* curve in both diagrams.

d. What is the profit-maximizing price in each market? Explain why profit maximization requires that *MC* be equated to *MR in each market segment*.

e. Compute the price elasticity of demand (at the profit-maximizing points) in each market segment. (You may want to review Chapter 4 on elasticity at this point.) Does the market segment with less elastic demand have the higher price?

10. Consider each of the following examples of price discrimination. For each case, explain how the price discrimination works. Also explain which consumers would be worse off and which consumers would be better off if the firm were *unable* to price discriminate in this way.

a. Seniors pay lower prices for theatre tickets than do other adults.

b. Consumers pay less for paperback books than for hardcover books, but must wait six to twelve months before the paperbacks are made available.

c. Customers at garage sales often pay a lower price if they ask for one—that is, if they reveal that they are prepared to haggle.

d. Airline customers get a discount fare if they are prepared to stay over a Saturday night at their destination.

DISCUSSION QUESTIONS

1. Suppose only one professor teaches economics at your university. Would you say that this professor is a monopolist who can exact any "price" from students in the form of readings assigned, tests given, and material covered? Suppose now that two additional professors have been hired. Has the original professor's market power been decreased? What if the three professors form a cartel agreeing on common reading lists, workloads, and the like?

2. Which of these industries—licorice candy, copper wire, outboard motors, coal, or the local newspaper—would it be most profitable to monopolize? Why?

Does your answer depend on several factors or on just one or two? Which would you as a consumer least like to have monopolized by someone else? If your answers to the two questions are different, explain why.

3. Aristotle Murphy owns movie theatres in two towns of roughly the same size, 100 kilometres apart. In Monopolia, he owns the only chain of theatres; in Competitia, there is no theatre chain, and he is only one of a number of independent theatre operators. Would you expect movie prices to be higher in Monopolia or in Competitia in the short run? In the

long run? If differences occur in his prices, would Murphy be discriminating in price?

4. Airline fares to Europe are higher in summer than in winter. Some railways charge lower fares during the week than on weekends. Electric companies charge consumers lower rates the more electricity they use. Are these all examples of price discrimination? What additional information would you like to have before answering this question?

5. Acme Department Store has a sale on luggage. It is offering $30 off any new set of luggage to customers who trade in an old suitcase. Acme has no use for the old luggage and throws it away at the end of each day. Is this price discrimination? Why or why not? Which of the conditions necessary for price discrimination are or are not met?

6. The world price of coffee has declined in real terms over the past 40 years. In 1950, coffee was priced at just under U.S.$3 per pound (in 1994 dollars), whereas by 1995 the world price had fallen to just over U.S.$1 per pound. On July 29, 1995, *The Economist* magazine reported that

> *On July 26 the Association of Coffee Producing Countries agreed in New York to limit exports to 60m bags for 12 months. The current level is 70m bags.... Coffee prices rallied a bit on the news, but few expect the pact to last: some big coffee producers such as Mexico have not signed up, and even those who have will probably cheat.*

a. Explain why "few expect the pact to last" in situations like this when producers form a cartel.
b. Early in 2006, the price of coffee was approximately U.S.$1.25 per pound. Was the cartel successful?

CHAPTER 11

Imperfect Competition and Strategic Behaviour

The two market structures that we have studied so far—perfect competition and monopoly—are polar cases; they define the two extremes of a firm's market power within an industry. Under perfect competition, firms are price takers, price is equal to marginal cost, and economic profits in the long run are zero. Under monopoly, the firm is a price setter, it sets price above marginal cost, and it can earn positive profits in the long run if there are sufficient entry barriers.

Although they provide important insights, these two polar cases are insufficient for understanding the behaviour of *all* firms. Indeed, most of the products that we easily recognize—computers, breakfast cereals, automobiles, cameras, and fast food, to name a few—are produced by firms that have some market power yet are not monopolists.

This chapter discusses market structures that lie between these two polar cases of perfect competition and monopoly. Before discussing the theory, however, we turn to a brief discussion of the prevalence of these "intermediate" market structures in the Canadian economy.

11.1 **THE STRUCTURE OF THE CANADIAN ECONOMY**

We can divide Canadian industries into two broad groups—those with a large number of relatively small firms and those with a small number of relatively large firms.

Industries with Many Small Firms

About two-thirds of Canada's total annual output is produced by industries made up of firms that are small relative to the size of the market in which they sell.

The perfectly competitive model does quite well in explaining the behaviour of some of these industries. These are the ones in which individual firms produce more-or-less identical products and so are price takers. Forest and fish products are two broad examples. Agriculture also fits fairly well in most ways since individual farmers are clearly price takers. Many basic raw materials, such as iron ore, tin, and copper, are sold on world markets where most individual firms lack significant market power.

Other industries, however, are not well described by the perfectly competitive model, even though they contain many small firms. In retail trade and in services, for example, most firms have some influence over prices. Your local grocery stores, clothing shops, night clubs, and restaurants spend a good deal of money advertising on television and in newspapers—something they would not have to do if they were price takers. Moreover, each store in these industries has a unique location that may give it some local market power over nearby customers.

The theory of *monopolistic competition,* which we will examine in this chapter, was originally developed to help explain economic behaviour and outcomes in industries in which there are many small firms, each with some market power.

Industries with a Few Large Firms

About one-third of Canada's total annual output is produced by industries that are dominated by either a single firm or a few large ones.

The most striking cases of monopolies in today's economy are the electric utilities (which are typically owned by provincial governments) and the firms that provide local telephone and cable or digital TV and Internet services (which are subject to government regulation and which we examine in Chapter 12). Other than these and a few other similar cases in which government ownership or regulation play an important role, cases of monopoly are rare in Canada today. However, there are some notable examples of monopoly (or near monopoly) from many years ago. For example, the Eddy Match Company was virtually the sole producer of wooden matches in Canada between 1927 and 1940, and Canada Cement Limited produced nearly all of the output of cement until the 1950s.

This type of market dominance by a single large firm is now a thing of the past. Today, most modern industries that are dominated by large firms contain several firms. Their names are part of the average Canadian's vocabulary: Canadian National and Canadian Pacific; Bank of Montreal, Royal Bank, and Scotiabank; Imperial Oil, Petro-Canada, and Irving; Stelco, Dofasco, and Algoma; Alcan, Barrick, and Teck Cominco; Loblaws, Safeway, and Sobey's; Ford, Toyota, and GM; Sony, Mitsubishi, and Toshiba; Great West Life, Sun Life, and Manulife; and General Foods, Nabisco, and Kellogg. Many service industries that used to be dominated by small independent producers have in recent decades seen the development of large firms operating on a world-wide basis. SNC-Lavalin and Acres are two examples of very large engineering firms that have business contracts all over the world. In management consulting, McKinsey & Co., Boston Consulting Group, and Monitor are also very large firms with market power.

The theory of *oligopoly,* which we will examine later in this chapter, helps us understand industries in which there are small numbers of large firms, each with market power, that compete actively with each other.

Industrial Concentration

For data on many aspects of Canadian industries, see Industry Canada's web-site: **www.strategis.ic.gc.ca**.

An industry with a small number of relatively large firms is said to be highly *concentrated*. An industry with a large number of relatively small firms is less concentrated. A formal measure of such industrial concentration is given by the *concentration ratio*.

Concentration Ratios   When we measure whether an industry has power concentrated in the hands of only a few firms or dispersed over many, it is not sufficient to count the firms. For example, an industry with one enormous firm and 29 very small ones is more concentrated in any meaningful sense than an industry with only five equal-sized firms. One approach to this problem is to calculate what is called a **concentration ratio**, which shows the fraction of total market sales controlled by the largest sellers. Common types of concentration ratios cite the share of total market sales made by the largest four or eight firms.

concentration ratio The fraction of total market sales (or some other measure of market activity) controlled by a specified number of the industry's largest firms.

Figure 11-1 shows the four-firm concentration ratios in several Canadian manufacturing industries. As is clear, the degree of concentration is quite varied across these industries. In the tobacco industry, for example, the largest four firms account for almost 100 percent of total sales, and in the petroleum and transportation equipment industries the largest four firms account for over 70 percent of sales. At the other extreme, the largest four firms in the furniture and clothing industries account for less than 10 percent of sales. These largest firms may be large in some absolute sense, but the low concentration ratios suggest that they have quite limited market power.

Defining the Market   The main problem associated with using concentration ratios is to *define the market* with reasonable accuracy. On the one hand, the market may be much smaller than the whole country. For example, concentration ratios in national cement sales are low, but they understate the market power of cement companies because high transportation costs divide the cement *industry* into a series of regional *markets*, with each having relatively few firms. On the other hand, the market may be larger than one country, as is the case for most internationally traded commodities. This is particularly important for Canada.

The globalization of competition brought about by the falling costs of transportation and communication has been one of the most significant developments in the world economy in recent decades. As the world has "become smaller" through the advances in transportation and com-

FIGURE 11-1   Concentration Ratios in Selected Canadian Industries

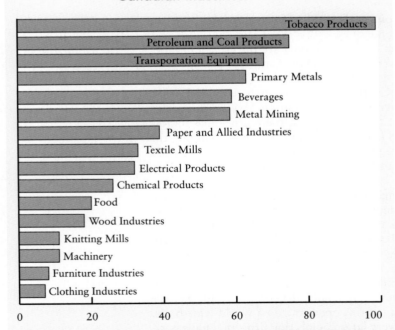

Concentration ratios vary greatly among manufacturing industries. These data show the share of total annual shipments (in dollar terms) accounted for by the four largest firms in the industry.

(*Source:* Based on Douglas West, *Modern Canadian Industrial Organization*, HarperCollins 1994, p. 37.)

munication technologies, the nature of domestic markets has changed dramatically. For example, the presence of only a single firm in one industry in Canada in no way implies monopoly power when it is in competition with several foreign firms that can easily sell in the Canadian market. This is the situation faced by many Canadian companies producing raw materials, such as Petro-Canada, Canfor, Alcan, and Barrick. These companies may be large relative to the *Canadian* market, but the relevant market in each case (oil, forest products, aluminum, and gold) is the *global* one in which these firms have no significant market power.

However, concentration ratios, adjusted to define the relevant market correctly, can still be used to provide valuable information about the degree to which production in a given market is concentrated in the hands of a few firms.

⟨X⟩ myeconlab

The ongoing forces of globalization have been changing the world economy for centuries. For more information on how relatively recent advances in transportation and communications technologies have led to changes in the location of production and the nature of competition, look for "The Nature of Globalization" in the *Additional Topics* section of this book's MyEconLab.

w w w . m y e c o n l a b . c o m

11.2 WHAT IS IMPERFECT COMPETITION?

We have identified two types of industries that are not well described by the theories of perfect competition or monopoly. In one type, there is a large number of small firms, but the theory of perfect competition is not appropriate because each of the many firms has some market power. In the other type, there is a small number of large firms, each with considerable market power. That these industries have more than a single firm makes the theory of monopoly inappropriate. We need theories to understand these market structures *between* the polar cases of perfect competition and monopoly.

The market structures that we are now going to study are called *imperfectly competitive*. The word *competitive* emphasizes that we are not dealing with monopoly, and the word *imperfect* emphasizes that we are not dealing with perfect competition (in which firms are price takers). Let's begin by noting a number of characteristics that are typical of imperfectly competitive firms. To help organize our thoughts, we classify these under two main headings. First, firms choose the *variety* of the product that they produce and sell. Second, firms choose the *price* at which they will sell that product.

Firms Choose Their Products

If a new farmer enters the wheat industry, the full range of products that the farmer can produce is already in existence. In contrast, if a new firm enters the snack food industry, that firm must decide on the characteristics of the new snacks that it is to produce. It will not produce snacks that are identical to those already in production. Rather, it will develop variations on existing snack foods or even a totally new food. Each of these will have its own distinctive characteristics. As a result, firms in the snack food industry sell an array of differentiated products, no two of which are identical.

differentiated product A group of commodities that are similar enough to be called the same product but dissimilar enough that all of them do not have to be sold at the same price.

The term **differentiated product** refers to a group of commodities that are similar enough to be called the same product but dissimilar enough that they can be sold at different prices. For example, although one brand of shampoo is similar to most others, shampoos differ from each other in chemical composition, colour, smell, brand name, packaging, reputation, and a host of other characteristics that matter to customers. All shampoos taken together can be regarded as one differentiated product.

Most firms in imperfectly competitive markets sell differentiated products. In such industries, the firm itself must choose which characteristics to give the products that it will sell.

Firms Choose Their Prices

Because firms in perfect competition sell an identical product, they face a market price that they are unable to influence. In all other market structures, firms face negatively sloped demand curves and thus face a tradeoff between the price that they charge and the quantity that they sell.

Whenever different firms' products are not identical, each firm must decide on a price to set. For example, no market sets a single price for cars or TVs or jeans by equating overall demand with overall supply. What is true for cars and TVs is true for virtually all consumer goods. Any one manufacturer will typically have several product lines that differ from each other and from the competing product lines of other firms. Each product has a price that must be set by its producer.

administered price A price set by the conscious decision of the seller rather than by impersonal market forces.

price setter A firm that faces a downward sloping demand curve for its product. It chooses which price to set.

In such circumstances, economists say that firms *administer* their price. An **administered price** is a price set by the conscious decision of an individual firm rather than by impersonal market forces. Firms that administer their prices are said to be **price setters.** Each firm has expectations about the quantity it can sell at each price that it might set. Unexpected demand fluctuations then cause unexpected variations in the quantities that are sold at the administered prices.

In market structures other than perfect competition, firms set their prices and then let demand determine sales. Changes in market conditions are signalled to the firm by changes in the firm's sales.

One striking contrast between perfectly competitive markets and markets for differentiated products concerns the behaviour of prices. In perfect competition, prices change continually in response to changes in demand and supply. In markets where differentiated products are sold, prices change less frequently.

Modern firms that sell differentiated products typically have hundreds of distinct products on their price lists. Changing such a long list of administered prices is often costly enough that it is done only infrequently—although improved computer technology has made rapid price changes increasingly possible, as when airlines post prices on their websites that change hourly. The costs of changing the prices include the costs of printing new list prices and notifying all customers, the difficulty of keeping track of frequently changing prices for purposes of accounting and billing, and the loss of customer and retailer goodwill due to the uncertainty caused by frequent changes in prices. As a result, imperfectly competitive firms often respond to fluctuations in demand by changing output and holding prices constant. Only after changes in demand are expected to persist will firms incur the expense of adjusting their entire list of prices.

These breakfast cereals are different enough that each can have its own price, but they are similar enough to be called the same product—they are a differentiated product.

Non-Price Competition

Firms in imperfect competition behave in other ways that are not observed under either perfect competition or monopoly.

First, many firms spend large sums of money on advertising. They do so in an attempt both to shift the demand curves for the industry's products and to attract customers from competing firms. A firm in a perfectly competitive market would not engage in advertising because the firm faces a perfectly elastic (horizontal) demand curve at the market price and so advertising would involve costs but would not increase the firm's revenues. A monopolist has no competitors in the industry and so will not advertise to attract customers away from other brands. However, in some cases a monopolist will still advertise in an attempt to convince consumers to shift their spending away from other types of products and toward the monopolist's product.

Second, many firms engage in a variety of other forms of non-price competition, such as offering competing standards of quality and product guarantees. In the automobile industry, for example, Toyota and GM compete actively in terms of the duration of their "bumper-to-bumper" warranties. Many firms also compete through the services they offer along with their products. The automobile industry is again a good example, with manufacturers and dealers competing in their "after-sales" services provided to the customer, ranging from oil changes and car washes to emergency on-road assistance.

Third, firms in many industries engage in activities that appear to be designed to hinder the entry of new firms, thereby preventing existing pure profits from being eroded by entry. For example, the public commitment to match any price offered by a competitor may convince potential entrants not to enter the industry.

Two Market Structures

Our discussion in this section has been a general one concerning firms in imperfectly competitive market structures. We now go into a little more detail, and make a distinction between industries with a large number of small firms and industries with a small number of large firms.

Behaviour in the first group of industries can be understood with the theory of *monopolistic competition*. To understand behaviour in the second group we use the theory of *oligopoly*, in which *game theory* plays a central role. As you will see in the remainder of this chapter, a key difference between these two market structures is the amount of *strategic behaviour* displayed by firms.

11.3 MONOPOLISTIC COMPETITION

The theory of **monopolistic competition** was originally developed to deal with the phenomenon of product differentiation. This theory was first developed by the U.S. economist Edward Chamberlin in his pioneering 1933 book, *The Theory of Monopolistic Competition*.

This market structure is similar to perfect competition in that the industry contains many firms and exhibits freedom of entry and exit. It differs, however, in one important respect: Whereas firms in perfect competition sell an identical product and are price takers, firms in monopolistic competition sell a differentiated product and thus have some power over setting price.

monopolistic competition
Market structure of an industry in which there are many firms and freedom of entry and exit but in which each firm has a product somewhat differentiated from the others, giving it some control over its price.

Familiar retail stores like these ones compete in industries in which there are many firms. Such industries are said to be monopolistically competitive.

Product differentiation leads to the establishment of brand names and advertising, and it gives each firm a degree of market power over its own product. Each firm can raise its price, even if its competitors do not, without losing all its sales. This is the *monopolistic* part of the theory. However, each firm's market power is severely restricted in both the short run and the long run. The short-run restriction comes from the presence of similar products sold by many competing firms; this causes the demand curve faced by each firm to be very elastic. The long-run restriction comes from free entry into the industry, which permits new firms to compete away the profits being earned by existing firms. These restrictions comprise the *competition* part of the theory.

The Assumptions of Monopolistic Competition

The theory of monopolistic competition is based on three key simplifying assumptions.

1. Each firm produces one specific brand of the industry's differentiated product. Each firm thus faces a demand curve that, although negatively sloped, is highly elastic because competing firms produce many close substitutes.

2. The industry contains so many firms that each one ignores the possible reactions of its many competitors when it makes its own price and output decisions. In this respect, firms in monopolistic competition are similar to firms in perfect competition.

3. There is freedom of entry and exit in the industry. If profits are being earned by existing firms, new firms have an incentive to enter. When they do, the demand for the industry's product must be shared among more brands.

Predictions of the Theory

Product differentiation, which is the *only* thing that makes monopolistic competition different from perfect competition, has important consequences for behaviour in both the short and the long run.

The Short-Run Decision of the Firm   In the short run, a firm that is operating in a monopolistically competitive market structure is similar to a monopoly. It faces a negatively sloped demand curve and maximizes its profits by equating marginal cost with marginal revenue. The firm shown in part (i) of Figure 11-2 makes positive profits.

The Long-Run Equilibrium of the Industry   Profits, as shown in part (i) of Figure 11-2, provide an incentive for new firms to enter the industry. As they do so, the total demand for the industry's product must be shared among this larger number of firms; thus, each firm gets a smaller share of the total market. Such entry shifts the demand curve for each existing firm's product to the left. Entry continues until profits are eliminated. When this has occurred, each firm is in the position shown in part (ii) of Figure 11-2. Its demand curve has shifted to the left until the curve is *tangent* to the

Practise with Study Guide Chapter 11, Exercises 1 and 2.

FIGURE 11-2   Profit Maximization for a Firm in Monopolistic Competition

(i) A typical firm in the short run

(ii) A typical firm when the industry is in long-run equilibrium

The short-run position for a monopolistically competitive firm is similar to that of a monopolist. In the long run, firms in a monopolistically competitive industry have zero profits and excess capacity. Note the very elastic demand curve—this reflects the fact that each firm produces a good for which there are many close (but not perfect) substitutes. Short-run profit maximization occurs in part (i) at E_s, the output for which $MR = MC$. Price is p_S and quantity is Q_S. Profits may exist; in this example they are shown by the shaded area. Starting from the short-run position shown in part (i), entry of new firms shifts each firm's demand curve to the left and eliminates profits. In part (ii), point E_L, where demand is tangent to $LRAC$, is the position of each firm when the industry is in long-run equilibrium. Price is p_L and quantity is Q_L. Price is greater and quantity is less than would exist in the long run if the industry were perfectly competitive (p_C and Q_C). When the industry is in long-run equilibrium, each monopolistically competitive firm has excess capacity of $Q_L Q_C$.

long-run average cost ($LRAC$) curve. Each firm is maximizing its profit, but its profit is equal to zero.[1]

To see why this "tangency solution" provides the only possible long-run equilibrium for an industry that fulfills all of the theory's assumptions, consider the two possible alternatives. First, suppose the firm's demand curve *nowhere touched* the $LRAC$ curve. There would then be no output at which costs could be covered, and exit would occur. The exit of firms from the industry would then lead each *remaining* firm's demand curve to shift to the right, until it eventually touched the $LRAC$ curve. Second, suppose the demand curve *cut* the $LRAC$ curve. There would then be a range of output over which profits could be earned. These profits would lead firms to enter the industry, and this entry would shift each *remaining* firm's demand curve to the left until it was just tangent to the $LRAC$ curve.

The Excess-Capacity Theorem   Part (ii) of Figure 11-2 makes it clear that monopolistic competition results in a long-run equilibrium of zero profits, even though each individual firm faces a negatively sloped demand curve. It does this by forcing each

---

[1] A standard assumption in this theory is that the industry is *symmetric* in the sense that when a new firm enters the industry, it takes demand away *equally* from all existing firms, thus ensuring that all industry profits are eliminated in the long run. The asymmetric case, in which long-run profits are possible, is discussed in advanced courses in industrial organization.

firm into a position in which it has *excess capacity;* that is, each firm is producing an output less than that corresponding to the lowest point on its long-run average cost (*LRAC*) curve. If the firm were to increase its output, it would reduce its cost per unit, but it does not do so because selling more would reduce revenue by more than it would reduce cost. This result is often called the **excess-capacity theorem.**

In long-run equilibrium in monopolistic competition, goods are produced at a point where average total costs are not at their minimum, in contrast to perfect competition, where they are produced at their lowest possible cost.

excess-capacity theorem
The property of long-run equilibrium in monopolistic competition that firms produce on the falling portion of their long-run average cost curves. This results in excess capacity, measured by the gap between present output and the output that coincides with minimum average cost.

The excess-capacity theorem once aroused passionate debate among economists because it seemed to show that all industries selling differentiated products would produce them at a higher cost than was necessary. Because product differentiation is a characteristic of virtually all modern consumer goods industries, this theorem suggested that modern market economies were systematically inefficient.

Subsequent analysis by economists has shown that the charge of inefficiency has not been proven. The excess capacity of monopolistic competition does not necessarily indicate a waste of resources because some benefits accrue to consumers from the greater choice and variety of products.

Saying that consumers value variety is not saying that *each* consumer necessarily values variety. You might like only one of the many brands of toothpaste and be better off if only that one brand were produced and the price were lower. But other consumers would prefer one of the other brands. Thus, it is the differences in tastes *across many consumers* that gives rise to the social value of variety, and the price of that greater variety is the higher price per unit.

From society's point of view, there is a tradeoff between producing more brands to satisfy diverse tastes and producing fewer brands at a lower cost per unit.

Monopolistic competition produces a wider range of products but at a somewhat higher cost per unit than perfect competition. As consumers clearly value variety, the benefits of variety must be matched against the extra cost that variety imposes in order to find the *socially optimal* amount of product differentiation. Product differentiation is wasteful only if the costs of providing variety exceed the benefits conferred by providing that variety. Depending on consumers' tastes and firms' costs, monopolistic competition may result in too much, too little, or the optimal amount of product variety.

The Canadian wine-making industry contains many firms producing similar but differentiated products. It is a monopolistically competitive industry.

Empirical Relevance of Monopolistic Competition

A controversy raged for several decades as to the empirical relevance of monopolistic competition. Of course, product differentiation is pervasive in many industries. Nonetheless, many economists maintained that the monopolistically competitive market structure was almost never found in practice.

To see why, we need to distinguish between products and firms. Single-product firms are extremely rare in manufacturing industries. Typically, a vast array of differentiated products is produced by each of the few firms in the industry. Most of the vast variety of breakfast cereals, for example, is produced by only three firms

(Kellogg, Nabisco, and General Foods). Similar circumstances exist in soap, chemicals, cigarettes, and numerous other industries where many competing products are produced by a few very large firms. These industries are clearly not perfectly competitive and neither are they monopolies. Are they monopolistically competitive? The answer is no because they contain few enough firms for each to take account of the others' reactions when determining its own behaviour. Furthermore, these firms often earn large profits without attracting new entry (thereby violating the third assumption of monopolistic competition). In fact, they operate under the market structure called *oligopoly*, which we consider in the next section.

Although monopolistic competition is not applicable to differentiated products produced in industries with high concentration, many economists think that the theory is useful for analyzing industries where concentration ratios are low and products are differentiated, as in the cases of restaurants, clothing and furniture stores, gas stations, dry cleaners, hair salons, and landscaping services. Indeed, many of the small stores and services that are located in or near your neighbourhood are monopolistically competitive firms.

11.4 **OLIGOPOLY AND GAME THEORY**

Industries that are made up of a small number of large firms have a market structure called *oligopoly*, from the Greek words *oligos polein*, meaning "few to sell." An **oligopoly** is an industry that contains two or more firms, at least one of which produces a significant portion of the industry's total output. Whenever there is a high concentration ratio for the firms that are serving one particular market, that market is oligopolistic. The market structures of oligopoly, monopoly, and monopolistic competition are similar in that firms in all of these markets face negatively sloped demand curves.

> **oligopoly** An industry that contains two or more firms, at least one of which produces a significant portion of the industry's total output.

In contrast to a monopoly (which has no competitors) and to a monopolistically competitive firm (which has many competitors), an oligopolistic firm faces only a few competitors. The number of competitors is small enough for each firm to realize that its competitors may respond to anything that it does and that it should take such possible responses into account. In other words, *oligopolists are aware of the interdependence among the decisions made by the various firms in the industry.*

Economists say that oligopolists exhibit **strategic behaviour**, which means that they take explicit account of the impact of their decisions on competing firms and of the reactions they expect competing firms to make. In contrast, firms in perfect competition or monopolistic competition are assumed to engage in *non-strategic behaviour*, which means they make decisions based on their own costs and their own demand curves without considering any possible reactions from their large number of competitors. Monopolists also do not engage in strategic behaviour—simply because they have no competitors to worry about.

> **strategic behaviour** Behaviour designed to take account of the reactions of one's rivals to one's own behaviour.

The Basic Dilemma of Oligopoly

The basic dilemma faced by oligopolistic firms is very similar to the dilemma faced by the members of a cartel, which we studied in Chapter 10. There we saw that the cartel as a whole had an incentive to form an agreement to restrict total output, but each individual member of the cartel had the incentive to cheat on the agreement and increase its own level of output.

For the small number of firms in an oligopoly, the incentives are the same. We say that firms can either *cooperate* (or *collude*) in an attempt to maximize joint profits, or they can *compete* in an effort to maximize their individual profits. Not surprisingly, the decision by one firm to cooperate or to compete will depend on how it thinks its rivals will respond to its decision.

Oligopolistic firms often make strategic choices; they consider how their rivals are likely to respond to their own actions.

When thinking about how firm behaviour leads to market outcomes, we distinguish between *cooperative* and *non-cooperative* behaviour. If the firms cooperate to produce among themselves the monopoly output, they can maximize their joint profits. If they do this, they will reach what is called a **cooperative (or collusive) outcome,** which is the position that a single monopoly firm would reach if it owned all the firms in the industry.

If the firms are at the cooperative outcome, it will usually be worthwhile for any one of them to cut its price or to raise its output, so long as the others do not do so. However, if every firm does the same thing, they will be worse off as a group and may all be worse off individually. An industry outcome that is reached when firms proceed by calculating only their own gains without cooperating with other firms is called a **non-cooperative outcome.**

The behaviour of firms in an oligopoly is complex, and studying it requires much attention to detail. As in other market structures, it is necessary to think about how individual firm behaviour affects the overall market outcome. Unlike other market structures, however, in oligopoly each firm typically thinks about how the other firms in the industry will react to its own decisions. Then, of course, the other firms may respond to what the first firm does, and so on. To help us keep our thoughts organized, we will use *game theory.*

Some Simple Game Theory

Game theory is used to study decision making in situations in which there are a number of players, each knowing that others may react to their actions and each taking account of others' expected reactions when making moves. For example, suppose a firm is deciding whether to raise, lower, or maintain its price. Before arriving at an answer, it asks: "What will the other firms do in each of these cases, and how will their actions affect the profitability of whatever decision I make?"

When game theory is applied to oligopoly, the players are firms, their game is played in the market, their strategies are their price or output decisions, and the payoffs are their profits.

An illustration of the basic dilemma of oligopolists, to cooperate or to compete, is shown in Figure 11-3 for the case of a two-firm oligopoly, called a **duopoly**. In this simplified game, we assume that both firms are producing the same product, and so there is a single market price. The only choice for each firm is how much output to produce. If the two firms "cooperate" to jointly act as a monopolist, each firm produces one-half of the monopoly output and each earns large profits. If the two firms "compete," they each produce more than half (say two-thirds) of the monopoly output, and in this case both firms earn low profits. As we will see, even this very simple example is sufficient to illustrate several key ideas in the modern theory of oligopoly.

A Payoff Matrix Figure 11-3 shows a *payoff matrix* for this simple game. It shows the profits that each firm earns in each possible combination of the two firms' actions. The upper-left cell in this example shows that if each firm produces one-half of the monopoly output, each firm will earn profits of 20. The lower-right cell shows that if each firm produces two-thirds of the monopoly output, each firm will earn a profit of 17. Since *joint* profits must be maximized at the monopoly output, the total profit in the upper-left cell (40) is greater than the total profit in the lower-right cell (34).

The upper-right and lower-left cells show the profits in the case where one firm produces one-half of the monopoly output and the other firm produces two-thirds of the monopoly output. Note that in these cells, the firm that produces more earns the greater profit. The firm that produces one-half of the monopoly output is helping to restrict output and keep prices high. The firm that produces two-thirds of the monopoly output then benefits from the first firm's output restrictions.

Strategic Behaviour The payoff matrix shows the profit each player earns with each combination of the two players' moves. But what will actually happen? To answer this question, we must first know what type of game is being played. Specifically, can the players *cooperate* or is the game a *non-cooperative* one?

Cooperative Outcome. If the two firms in this duopoly can cooperate, the payoff matrix shows that their highest *joint* profits will be earned if each firm produces one-half of the monopoly output. This is the cooperative outcome. The payoff matrix also shows, however, that if each firm thinks the other will cooperate (by producing half of the monopoly output), then it has an incentive to cheat and produce two-thirds of the monopoly output. Thus, the cooperative outcome can only be achieved if the firms have some effective way to enforce their output-restricting agreement. As we will see in Chapter 12, overt output-restricting agreements are usually illegal.

Non-Cooperative Outcome. Now suppose that firms believe that cooperation is not possible because they have no way of enforcing an agreement. What will be the non-cooperative outcome in this duopoly game? To answer this question, we must examine each player's incentives, given the possible actions of the other player.

Firm A reasons as follows: "If B produces one-half of the monopoly output (upper row of the matrix), then my profit will be higher if I produce two-thirds of the monopoly output. Moreover, if B produces two-thirds of the monopoly output (bottom row of the matrix), my profit will be higher if I also produce two-thirds of the monopoly

FIGURE 11-3 The Oligopolist's Dilemma: To Cooperate or to Compete?

Cooperation to determine the overall level of output can maximize joint profits, but it leaves each firm with an incentive to cheat. The figure shows a payoff matrix for a two-firm game. Firm A's production is indicated across the top, and its payoffs (profits in millions of dollars) are shown in the green circles within each cell. Firm B's production is indicated down the left side, and its payoffs are shown in the red circles within each cell.

If A and B cooperate, each produces one-half the monopoly output and receives a payoff of 20, as shown in the upper-left cell. But at this position, each firm has an incentive to cheat and produce the larger amount, so the cooperative outcome is only achievable if the firms can somehow enforce their agreement.

Now suppose that A and B make their decisions non-cooperatively. A reasons that whether B produces either one-half or two-thirds of the monopoly output, A's best output is two-thirds. B reasons similarly. In this case, they reach the non-cooperative outcome, where each produces two-thirds of the monopoly output, and each makes less than it would if the two firms cooperated. In this example, the non-cooperative outcome is a Nash equilibrium.

output. Therefore, no matter what B does, I will earn more profit if I produce two-thirds of the monopoly output." A quick look at the payoff matrix in Figure 11-3 reveals that this game is *symmetric,* and so Firm B's reasoning will be identical to A's: it will conclude that its profit will be higher if it produces two-thirds of the monopoly output no matter what A does.

The final result is clear. Each firm will end up producing two-thirds of the monopoly output and each firm will receive a profit of 17. This is the non-cooperative outcome. Note that each firm will be worse off than it would have been had they been able to achieve the cooperative outcome. This type of game, in which the non-cooperative outcome makes *both* players worse off than if they had been able to cooperate, is called a *prisoners' dilemma.* The reason for this curious name is discussed in *Extensions in Theory 11-1.*

myeconlab

Our discussion of game theory has used examples of *simultaneous* games in which both players make their decisions at the same time. But often one firm is in a position to make its decision before its competitors. To see an example of a *sequential* game, look for "A Sequential Game in Fibre Optics" in the *Additional Topics* section of this book's MyEconLab.

www.myeconlab.com

Nash Equilibrium   The non-cooperative outcome shown in Figure 11-3 is called a **Nash equilibrium,** after the U.S. mathematician John Nash, who developed the concept in the 1950s and received the Nobel Prize in Economics in 1994 for this work. (The 2002 movie *A Beautiful Mind* is about John Nash's life and contains a few fascinating bits of game theory!) In a Nash equilibrium, each player's best strategy is to maintain its present behaviour *given the present behaviour of the other players.*

> **Nash equilibrium** An equilibrium that results when each firm in an industry is currently doing the best that it can, given the current behaviour of the other firms in the industry.

It is easy to see that there is only one Nash equilibrium in Figure 11-3. In the bottom-right cell, the best decision for each firm, given that the other firm is producing two-thirds of the monopoly output, is to produce two-thirds of the monopoly output itself. Between them, they produce a joint output of 1⅓ times the monopoly output. Neither firm has an incentive to depart from this position (except through enforceable cooperation with the other). In any other cell, each firm has an incentive to change its output *given the output of the other firm.*

The basis of a Nash equilibrium is rational decision making in the absence of co-operation. Its particular importance in oligopoly theory is that it is the only type of self-policing equilibrium. It is self-policing in the sense that there is no need for group behaviour to enforce it. Each firm has a self-interest to maintain it because no move will improve its profits, given what other firms are currently doing.

If a Nash equilibrium is established by any means whatsoever, no firm has an incentive to depart from it by altering its own behaviour.

11.5 OLIGOPOLY IN PRACTICE

We have examined the incentives for firms in an oligopoly to cooperate, and also the incentives for firms to cheat on any cooperative agreement. We can now look at the behaviour that we actually observe among oligopolists. How do they cooperate? How do they compete?

EXTENSIONS IN THEORY 11-1

The Prisoners' Dilemma

The game shown in Figure 11-3 is often known as a prisoners' dilemma game. This is the story that lies behind the name:

Two men, John and William, are arrested for jointly committing a crime and are interrogated separately. They know that if they both plead innocence, they will get only a light sentence, and if they both admit guilt they will both receive a medium sentence. Each is told, however, that if either protests innocence while the other admits guilt, the one who claims innocence will get a severe sentence while the other will be released with no sentence at all.

Here is the payoff matrix for that game:

		John's Plea	
		Innocent	Guilty
William's Plea	Innocent	J light sentence / W light sentence	J no sentence / W severe sentence
	Guilty	J severe sentence / W no sentence	J medium sentence / W medium sentence

John reasons as follows: William will plead either guilty or innocent. If he pleads innocent, I will get a light sentence if I also plead innocent but no sentence at all if I plead guilty, so guilty is my better plea. If he pleads guilty, I will get a severe sentence if I plead innocent and a medium sentence if I plead guilty. So once again guilty is my preferred plea. William reasons in the same way and, as a result, they both plead guilty and get a medium sentence. Note, however, that if they had been able to communicate and coordinate their pleas, they could both have agreed to plead innocent and get off with a light sentence.

The prisoners' dilemma arises in many economic situations. We have already seen an example of a two-firm oligopoly. Economists use the basic structure of this simple game to think about how firms compete in their decisions to build new factories, launch advertising campaigns, and adjust the prices of their differentiated products.

Simple game theory and the prisoner's dilemma also figure prominently in the study of political science. Robert Axelrod's 1984 book *The Evolution of Cooperation* discusses how the key insights from the prisoners' dilemma have been used in the analysis of elections (where candidates' choices are their electoral platforms) and the nuclear arms race (in which national governments' choices are their decisions to build and stockpile weapons).*

---

* For those interested in a very readable treatment of game theory applied to many aspects of life, see *Thinking Strategically* (Norton, 1993), written by Avinash Dixit and Barry Nalebuff, two leading economists.

Types of Cooperative Behaviour

When firms agree to cooperate in order to restrict output and raise prices, their behaviour is called **collusion**. Collusive behaviour may occur with or without an explicit agreement to collude. Where explicit agreement occurs, economists speak of *overt* or *covert collusion,* depending on whether the agreement is open or secret. Where no explicit agreement actually occurs, economists speak of *tacit collusion.* In this case, all firms behave cooperatively without an explicit agreement to do so. They merely understand that it is in their mutual interest to restrict output and to raise prices.

collusion An agreement among sellers to act jointly in their common interest. Collusion may be overt or covert, explicit or tacit.

Explicit Collusion   The easiest way for firms to ensure that they will all maintain their joint profit-maximizing output is to make an explicit agreement to do so. Such collusive agreements have occurred in the past, although they have been illegal among privately owned firms in Canada for a long time. When they are discovered today, they are rigorously prosecuted. We shall see, however, that such agreements are not illegal everywhere in the world, particularly when they are supported by national governments.

We saw in Chapter 10 that when several firms get together to act in this way, they create a *cartel*. Cartels show in stark form the basic conflict between cooperation and competition that we just discussed. Cooperation among cartel members allows them to restrict output and raise prices, thereby increasing the cartel members' profits. But it also presents each cartel member with the incentive to cheat. The larger the number of firms, the greater the temptation for any one of them to cheat. After all, cheating by one small firm may not be noticed because it will have a small effect on price. Conversely, a cartel made up of a small number of firms is more likely to persist because cheating by any one member is more difficult to conceal from the other members.

As we mentioned in Chapter 10, DeBeers is an example of a firm that has been able to assemble a cartel in the world's diamond industry. Through its own Diamond Trading Company (DTC), DeBeers markets almost 50 percent of the world's annual diamond production. With such influence over the market, it is able to manage the flow of output, in response to changes in world demand, to keep prices high. In recent years, however, the discovery of large diamond mines by firms that wished to remain independent of DeBeers has led to a reduction in DeBeers' ability to set the market price. In fact, the independent producers—in particular, Canadian—have been successful at establishing their own "brand" of diamonds. This has led DeBeers to reduce its efforts through the DTC to manage market prices and instead focus more of its efforts on creating its own brand of diamonds and other luxury products. Only time will tell how this brand competition in the diamond industry will develop.

The most famous example of a cartel—and the one that has had the most dramatic effect on the world economy—is the Organization of Petroleum Exporting Countries (OPEC). OPEC's explicit cooperation over the past three decades is discussed in *Lessons From History 11-1*.

Tacit Collusion   Although collusive behaviour that affects prices is illegal, a small group of firms that recognize the influence that each has on the others may act without any explicit agreement to achieve the cooperative outcome. In such tacit agreements, the two forces that push toward cooperation and competition are still evident. First, firms have a common interest in cooperating to maximize their joint profits at the cooperative solution. Second, each firm is interested in its own profits, and any one of them can usually increase its profits by behaving competitively.

In many industries there is suggestive evidence of tacit collusion, although it is very difficult to prove rigorously. For example, when one large steel company announces that it is raising its price for a specific quality of steel, other steel producers will often announce similar price increases within a day or two. This seemingly coordinated price increase may be the result of a secret explicit agreement or of tacit collusion. On the other hand, the firms that followed the first firm's price increase could easily argue (and usually do in such cases) that with their competitor raising prices, and driving some customers toward them, the natural response is to raise their own prices.

Practise with Study Guide Chapter 11, Exercise 4.

For more information on OPEC, check out its website: **www.opec.org**.

Types of Competitive Behaviour

Although the most obvious way for a firm to violate the cooperative solution is to produce more than its share of the joint profit-maximizing output, there are other ways in which rivalrous behaviour can occur.

Competition for Market Share Even if *joint* profits are maximized, there is still a question of how the profit-maximizing level of sales is to be divided among the colluding firms. Competition for market share may upset the tacit agreement to hold to joint profit-maximizing behaviour. Firms often compete for market share through various forms of non-price competition, such as advertising and variations in the quality of their product. Such costly competition may be largely a zero-sum activity among the firms, and thus may reduce industry profits.

In an industry with many differentiated products and in which sales are often by contract between buyers and sellers, covert rather than overt cheating may seem attractive. Secret discounts and rebates can allow a firm to increase its sales at the expense of its competitors while appearing to hold to the tacitly agreed price.

Innovation A firm may find that by innovating it can behave competitively, keeping ahead of its rivals, and thereby maintain a larger market share. In this way, it will earn larger profits than it would if it cooperated with the other firms in the industry, even though all the firms' joint profits are lower. As Joseph Schumpeter argued about the process of "creative destruction," such competition through innovation contributes to the long-run growth of living standards and may provide social benefits over time that outweigh any losses due to the restriction of output at any one point in time.

Oligopolistic firms typically compete by innovating. A firm can rectify a mistake in its price-setting decisions easily, but falling behind its competitors in developing new products and new production processes can spell disaster. A reading of the business pages of any newspaper shows firms in continuous competition to outdo each other in innovations.

Oligopolistic firms producing differentiated products often compete very little through prices. Sometimes the most aggressive competition takes place through their continual processes of innovation, as well as the introduction of new products.

There are strong incentives for oligopolistic firms to compete rather than to maintain the cooperative outcome, even when they understand the inherent risks to their joint profits.

A good example is the continuous process of innovation by the relatively small number of firms producing cellular phones, such as Nokia, Ericsson, NEC, and Panasonic. As one firm introduces a new feature, such as text messaging, video screens, or full audio/video capability, the competing firms quickly follow suit. In this market, the introduction of new product features is an important part of competitive behaviour.

The Importance of Entry Barriers

Suppose firms in an oligopolistic industry succeed in raising prices above long-run average costs and earn substantial profits that are not completely eliminated by non-price competition. In the absence of significant entry barriers, new firms will enter the

LESSONS FROM HISTORY 11-1

Explicit Cooperation in OPEC

The experience of the Organization of Petroleum Exporting Countries (OPEC) in the 1970s and 1980s illustrates the power of cooperative behaviour to create short-run profits, as well as the problems of trying to exercise long-run market power in an industry without substantial entry barriers.

OPEC did not attract worldwide attention until 1973, when its members voluntarily restricted their output by negotiating quotas among themselves. In that year, OPEC countries accounted for about 70 percent of the world's supply of crude oil. Although it was not a complete monopoly, the cartel came close to being one. By reducing output, the OPEC countries were able to reduce the world supply of oil and thereby increase its world price by almost 300 percent. Their actions resulted in massive profits both for themselves and for non-OPEC producers, who obtained the high prices without having to limit their output. After several years of success, however, OPEC began to experience the typical problems of cartels.

Entry

Entry became a problem for the OPEC countries. The high price of oil encouraged the development of new supplies, and within a few years, new productive capacity was coming into use at a rapid rate in non-OPEC countries. The development of North Sea oil by the United Kingdom and the development of the Athabasca Tar Sands in Alberta are two examples of this new productive capacity.

Long-Run Adjustment of Demand

The short-run demand for oil proved to be highly inelastic. Over time, however, adaptations to reduce the demand for oil were made within the confines of existing technology. Homes and offices were insulated more efficiently, and smaller, more fuel-efficient cars became popular. This is an example of the distinction between the short-run and long-run demand for a commodity first introduced in Chapter 4.

Innovation further reduced the demand for oil in the very long run. Over time, technologies that were more efficient in their use of oil were developed, as were alternative energy sources. Had the oil prices stayed up longer than they did, major breakthroughs in solar and geothermal energy would surely have occurred in the 1970s or early 1980s.

This experience in both the long run and the very long run shows the price system at work, signalling the need for adaptation and providing the incentives for that adaptation. It also provides an illustration of Joseph Schumpeter's concept of creative destruction, which we first discussed in Chapter 10. To share in the profits generated by high energy prices, new technologies and new substitute products were developed, and these reduced much of the market power of the original cartel.

Cheating

At first, there was little incentive for OPEC countries to violate quotas. Member countries found themselves with such undreamed-of increases in incomes that they found it difficult to use all of their money productively. As the output of non-OPEC oil grew, however, OPEC's output had to be reduced to maintain the high prices. Furthermore, as the long-run adjustments in demand occurred, even larger output restrictions by OPEC were required to prop up the price of oil. Incomes in OPEC countries declined as a result.

Many OPEC countries had become used to their enormous incomes, and their attempts to maintain them in the face of falling output quotas brought to the surface the instabilities inherent in all cartels. In 1981, oil prices reached U.S.$35 per barrel. In real terms, this was about five times as high as the 1972 price, but production quotas were less than one-half of OPEC's capacity. Eager to increase their oil revenues, many individual OPEC members gave in to the pressure to cheat and produced in excess of their production quotas. In 1984, Saudi Arabia indicated that it would not tolerate further cheating by its partners and demanded that others share equally in reducing their quotas yet further. However, agreement proved impossible. In December 1985, OPEC decided to eliminate production quotas and let each member make its own decisions about output.

After the Collapse

OPEC's collapse as an output-restricting cartel led to a major reduction in world oil prices. Early in 1986, the downward slide took the price to U.S.$20 per barrel, and it fell to U.S.$11 per barrel later in the year. Allowing for inflation, this was still double the price that had prevailed just before OPEC introduced its output restrictions in 1973. Following the 1986 collapse, and for the next decade or so, the world price of oil fluctuated between U.S.$15 per barrel and U.S.$25 per barrel. With the continuing expansion of output from non-OPEC producers, OPEC's share of world output steadily fell, reaching approximately 35 percent by the mid-1990s, where it remains today.

Beginning in the late 1990s, the world price of oil began to rise again, as the accompanying figure shows. Measured in 2001 dollars, the price increased sharply from a low of about U.S.$13 per barrel in 1998 to over U.S.$55 per barrel in 2006. This price increase was *not* caused by OPEC output restrictions. In addition to some growing political tensions in the Middle East, especially in 2006, the main cause of the price increase was a steadily growing world demand for oil, driven by relatively rapid economic growth, especially in the large emerging markets of China and India. The sharp price increase reflected an increase in demand at a time when the world supply curve was relatively inelastic. This supply inelasticity, in turn, reflected the fact that most oil producers—both inside and outside OPEC—were producing at or close to their capacity, and thus were unable to easily respond to higher prices by increasing their output. In this setting of low global excess capacity, OPEC's ability to increase prices through output restrictions was partially restored, even though their share of world output was much less than in the 1970s. By late in 2006, however, the OPEC producers had not appeared to take advantage of their renewed market power.

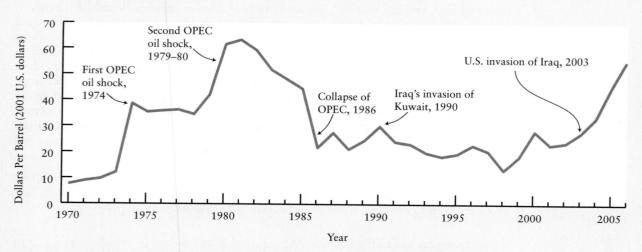

(*Source:* Nominal U.S.-dollar price of OPEC's reference basket: www.opec.org. U.S. CPI (all items): www.bls.gov.)

Many beer-producing firms produce several brands. Such brand proliferation by individual firms is an effective way to deter other firms from entering the market.

industry and erode the profits of existing firms, as they do in monopolistic competition. Natural barriers to entry were discussed in Chapter 10. They are an important part of the explanation of the persistence of profits in many oligopolistic industries.

Where such natural entry barriers do not exist, however, oligopolistic firms can earn profits in the long run only if they can *create* entry barriers. To the extent this is done, existing firms can move toward joint profit maximization without fear that new firms will enter the industry. We now discuss some types of *firm-created* entry barriers.

Brand Proliferation as an Entry Barrier   By altering the characteristics of a differentiated product, it is possible to produce a vast array of variations on the general theme of that product, each with its unique identifying brand. Think, for example, of the many different brands of soap or shampoo, breakfast cereals or cookies, and even automobiles or motorcycles. In these cases, each firm in the industry produces *several* brands of the differentiated product.

Although such brand proliferation is no doubt partly a response to consumers' tastes, it can have the effect of discouraging the entry of new firms. To see why, suppose the product is the type for which there is a substantial amount of brand switching by consumers. In this case, the larger the number of brands sold by existing firms, the smaller the expected sales of a new entrant.

Suppose, for example, that an industry contains three large firms, each selling one brand of beer, and say that 30 percent of all beer drinkers change brands in a random fashion each year. If a new firm enters the industry, it can expect to pick up one-third of the customers who change brands (a customer who switches brands now has three *other* brands among which to choose). The new firm would get 10 percent (one-third of 30 percent) of the total market the first year merely as a result of picking up its share of the random switchers, and it would keep increasing its share for some time thereafter. If, however, the existing three firms have five brands each, there would be 15 brands already available, and a new firm selling one new brand could expect to pick up only one-fifteenth of the brand switchers, giving it only 2 percent of the total market the first year, with smaller gains also in subsequent years. This is an extreme case, but it illustrates a general result.

The larger the number of differentiated products that are sold by existing oligopolists, the smaller the market share available to a new firm that is entering with a single new product. Brand proliferation therefore can be an effective entry barrier.

Advertising as an Entry Barrier   Advertising is one means by which existing firms can impose heavy costs on new entrants. Advertising, of course, serves purposes other than that of creating barriers to entry. Among them, it performs the useful function of informing buyers about their alternatives. Indeed, a new firm may find that advertising is essential, even when existing firms do not advertise at all, simply to call attention to its entry into an industry in which it is currently unknown.

Nonetheless, advertising can also operate as a potent entry barrier by increasing the costs of new entrants. Where heavy advertising has established strong brand images for existing products, a new firm may have to spend heavily on advertising to create its own brand images in consumers' minds. If the firm's sales are small, advertising costs *per unit* will be large, and price will have to be correspondingly high to cover those costs. Consider Nike, Reebok, and their competitors. They advertise not so much the quality of their athletic shoes as images that they wish consumers to associate with the shoes. The same is true for cosmetics, beer, cars, hamburgers, and many more consumer goods. The ads are lavishly produced and photographed. They constitute a formidable entry barrier for a new producer.

A new entrant with small sales but large required advertising costs finds itself at a substantial cost disadvantage relative to its established rivals.

Advertising can be very informative for consumers. But by raising the costs of new entrants, advertising can also act as a potent entry barrier.

The combined use of brand proliferation and advertising as an entry barrier helps to explain one apparent paradox of everyday life—that one firm often sells multiple brands of the same product, which compete actively against one another as well as against the products of other firms. The soap and beer industries provide classic examples of this behaviour. Because all available scale economies can be realized by quite small plants, both industries have few natural barriers to entry. Both contain a few large firms, each of which produces an array of heavily advertised products. The numerous existing products make it harder for a new entrant to obtain a large market niche with a single new product. The heavy advertising, although directed against existing products, creates an entry barrier by increasing the average costs of a new product that seeks to gain the attention of consumers and to establish its own brand image.

Predatory Pricing as an Entry Barrier A firm will not enter a market if it expects continued losses after entry. An existing firm can create such an expectation by cutting prices below costs whenever entry occurs and keeping them there until the entrant goes bankrupt. The existing firm sacrifices profits while doing this, but it sends a discouraging message to potential future rivals, as well as to present ones. Even if this strategy is costly in terms of lost profits in the short run, it may pay for itself in the long run by creating *reputation effects* that deter the entry of new firms at other times or in other markets that the firm controls.

Predatory pricing is controversial. Some economists argue that pricing policies that appear to be predatory can be explained by other motives and that existing firms only hurt themselves when they engage in such practices instead of accommodating new entrants. Others argue that predatory pricing has been observed and that it is in the long-run interests of existing firms to punish the occasional new entrant even when it is costly to do so in the short run.

Canadian courts have taken the position that predatory pricing does indeed occur and a number of firms have been convicted of using it as a method of restricting entry. The airline industry provides an interesting example.

Soon after Air Canada merged with Canadian Airlines in 1999, it was accused of charging prices below its average costs in an attempt to drive its young competitors out of the market. Air Canada argued that it was simply responding to the competitive pressures introduced by WestJet and other small, but growing, airlines that had recently entered the industry. The federal government argued that the short-term benefits to consumers from low airfares were unlikely to offset the long-term costs from much higher airfares that would occur if Air Canada was successful at driving WestJet and others out of business.

See Industry Canada's website at **www.strategis.gc.ca** for a discussion of predatory pricing in Canada.

Over the next few years, it was Air Canada that experienced severe financial difficulties. In 2004, Air Canada emerged from bankruptcy protection as a restructured company with a modified corporate strategy. It increased its use of small regional jets and introduced several different categories to its pricing of airline tickets. Meanwhile, WestJet expanded out of its base in Western Canada and began servicing all major cities across the country. As both firms appear to become more firmly established, the main strategic decisions—for both firms—will likely be whether they choose to cooperate or compete.

> ## myeconlab
>
> **We have been discussing how the entry of firms to an industry can reduce oligopoly profits toward the competitive level. But sometimes it is only the *threat* of entry that is necessary to achieve this outcome. For a detailed discussion of this point, look for "Oligopoly and Contestable Markets" in the *Additional Topics* section of this book's MyEconLab.**
>
> www.myeconlab.com

Oligopoly and the Economy

Oligopoly is found in many industries and in all advanced economies. It typically occurs in industries where both perfect and monopolistic competition are made impossible by the existence of major economies of scale. In such industries, there is simply not enough room for a large number of firms all operating at or near their minimum efficient scales.

Three questions are important for the evaluation of oligopoly. First, do oligopolistic firms respond to changes in market conditions very differently than perfectly competitive firms? Second, in their short-run and long-run outcomes, where do oligopolistic firms typically settle between the extreme outcomes of earning zero profits and earning monopoly profits? Third, how much do oligopolists contribute to economic growth by encouraging innovative activity in the very long run? We consider each of these questions in turn.

Market Adjustment Under Oligopoly   We have seen that under perfect competition, prices are set by the impersonal forces of demand and supply, whereas firms in oligopolistic markets administer their prices. The market signalling system works slightly differently when prices are administered rather than being determined by the market. Changes in market conditions are signalled to the perfectly competitive firm by changes in the price of its product. For example, an increase in demand will lead to an increase in market price; as the market price rises, the competitive firm will choose to increase its output.

For an oligopolist, however, the order of events is a little different. An increase in demand will cause the sales of oligopolistic firms to rise. Firms will then respond by increasing output. Only after the increase in demand is expected to persist will oligopolistic firms increase their prices.

Temporary changes in demand lead to more price volatility in perfectly competitive markets than in oligopoly markets. Permanent changes in demand, however, lead to similar adjustments in both market structures.

Profits Under Oligopoly   Some firms in some oligopolistic industries succeed in coming close to joint profit maximization in the short run. In other oligopolistic industries, firms compete so intensely among themselves that they come close to achieving competitive prices and outputs.

In the long run, those profits that do survive competitive behaviour among existing firms will tend to attract entry. Profits will persist only insofar as entry is restricted either by natural barriers, such as large minimum efficient scales for potential entrants, or by barriers created, and successfully defended, by the existing firms.

Innovation   Which market structure—oligopoly or perfect competition—is most conducive to innovation? As we discussed in Chapter 8, innovation and productivity improvements are the driving force of the economic growth that has so greatly raised living standards over the past two centuries. They are intimately related to Schumpeter's concept of creative destruction, which we first encountered in our discussion of entry barriers in Chapter 10.

Examples of creative destruction abound. In the nineteenth century, railways began to compete with wagons and barges for the carriage of freight. In the twentieth century, trucks operating on newly constructed highways began competing with trains. During the 1950s and 1960s, airplanes began to compete seriously with both trucks and trains. In recent years, fax machines and e-mail have eliminated the monopoly of the postal service in delivering hard-copy (printed) communications. Cellular phones have significantly weakened the monopoly power that telephone companies had for the provision of local phone service. And the Internet has allowed consumers to download music easily, thereby reducing the market power of the music production companies that sell CDs.

An important defence of oligopoly is based on Schumpeter's idea of creative destruction. Some economists argue that oligopoly leads to more innovation than would occur in either perfect competition or monopoly. They argue that the oligopolist faces strong competition from existing rivals and cannot afford the more relaxed life of the monopolist. Moreover, oligopolistic firms expect to keep a good share of the profits that they earn from their innovative activity and thus have considerable incentive to innovate.

Everyday observation provides support for this view. Leading North American firms that operate in highly concentrated industries, such as Abitibi-Consolidated, DuPont, Kodak, General Electric, Alcan, Canadian National, Xerox, and Boeing, have been highly innovative over many years.

This observation is not meant to suggest that *only* oligopolistic industries are innovative. Much innovation is also done by very small new firms (although most of these are in monopolistically competitive rather than perfectly competitive markets). If today's small firms are successful in their innovation, they may become tomorrow's corporate giants. For example, Hewlett-Packard, Microsoft, and Intel, which are enormous firms today, barely existed 30 years ago; their rise from new start-up firms to corporate giants reflects their powers of innovation.

Oligopoly is an important market structure in modern economies because there are many industries in which the minimum efficient scale is simply too large to support many competing firms. The challenge to public policy is to keep oligopolists competing, rather than colluding, and using their competitive energies to improve products and to reduce costs, rather than merely to erect entry barriers.

SUMMARY

11.1 THE STRUCTURE OF THE CANADIAN ECONOMY

- Most industries in the Canadian economy lie between the two extremes of monopoly and perfect competition. Within this spectrum of market structure we can divide Canadian industries into two broad groups—those with a large number of relatively small firms and those with a small number of relatively large firms. Such intermediate market structures are called imperfectly competitive.
- When measuring whether an industry has power concentrated in the hands of only a few firms or dispersed over many, it is not sufficient to count the firms.

Instead, economists consider the concentration ratio, which shows the fraction of total market sales controlled by a group of the largest sellers.
- One important problem associated with using concentration ratios is to define the market with reasonable accuracy. Since many goods produced in Canada compete with foreign-produced goods, the national concentration ratios overstate the degree of industrial concentration.

11.2 WHAT IS IMPERFECT COMPETITION?

- Most firms operating in imperfectly competitive market structures sell differentiated products whose characteristics they choose themselves.

- Imperfectly competitive firms usually administer their prices and engage in non-price competition.

11.3 MONOPOLISTIC COMPETITION

- Monopolistic competition is a market structure that has the same characteristics as perfect competition except that the many firms each sell a differentiated product rather than all selling a single homogeneous product. Firms face negatively sloped demand curves and may earn profits in the short run.
- As in a perfectly competitive industry, the long run in the theory of monopolistic competition sees new firms enter the industry whenever profits can be made. Long-

run equilibrium in the industry requires that each firm earn zero profits.
- In long-run equilibrium in the theory of monopolistic competition, each firm produces less than its minimum-cost level of output. This is the excess-capacity theorem associated with monopolistic competition.
- Even though each firm produces at a cost that is higher than the minimum attainable cost, the resulting product choice is valued by consumers and so may be worth the extra cost.

11.4 OLIGOPOLY AND GAME THEORY

- Oligopolies are dominated by a few large firms that usually sell differentiated products and have significant market power. They can maximize their joint profits if they cooperate to produce the monopoly output. By acting individually, each firm has an incentive to depart from this cooperative outcome.
- Oligopolists have difficulty cooperating to maximize joint profits unless they have a way of enforcing their output-restricting agreement.

- Economists use game theory to think about the strategic behaviour of oligopolists—that is, how each firm will behave when it recognizes that other firms may respond to its actions.
- A possible non-cooperative outcome is a Nash equilibrium in which each player is doing the best it can, given the actions of all other players.

11.5 **OLIGOPOLY IN PRACTICE**   LO 5

- Explicit collusion between oligopolists is illegal in domestic markets. But it can take place in situations where firms in global markets are supported by national governments, as is the case for OPEC.
- Tacit collusion is possible but may break down as firms struggle for market share, indulge in non-price competition, and seek advantages through the introduction of new technology.
- Oligopolistic industries will exhibit profits in the long run only if there are significant barriers to entry. Natural barriers relate to the economies of scale in pro-

duction, finance, and marketing, and also to large entry costs. Firm-created barriers can be created by proliferation of competing brands, heavy brand-image advertising, and the threat of predatory pricing when new entry occurs.

- In the presence of major scale economies, oligopoly may be the best of the feasible alternative market structures. Evaluation of oligopoly depends on how much interfirm competition (a) drives the firms away from the cooperative, profit-maximizing solution and (b) leads to innovations in the very long run.

KEY CONCEPTS

Concentration ratios
Administered prices
Product differentiation
Monopolistic competition
The excess-capacity theorem

Oligopoly
Strategic behaviour
Game theory
Cooperative and non-cooperative
  outcomes

Nash equilibrium
Explicit and tacit collusion
Natural and firm-created entry
  barriers
Oligopoly and creative destruction

STUDY EXERCISES

1. Fill in the blanks to make the following statements correct.

   a. Suppose the four largest steel producers in Canada among them control 85 percent of total market sales. We would say that this industry is highly _____. We say that 85 percent is the _____ in this industry.

   b. A firm that has the ability to set prices faces a _____ demand curve.

   c. The theory of monopolistic competition helps explain industries with a _____ number of _____ firms. The theory of oligopoly helps explain industries with a _____ number of _____ firms.

   d. A firm operating in a monopolistically competitive market structure maximizes profits by equating _____ and _____. A firm that is operating in an oligopolistic market structure maximizes profit by equating _____ and _____.

   e. In long-run equilibrium, and in comparison to perfect competition, monopolistic competition produces a _____ range of products but at a _____ cost per unit.

2. Fill in the blanks to make the following statements correct.

   a. Economists say that oligopolistic firms exhibit _____ behaviour. These firms are aware of and take account of the decisions of _____.

   b. The firms in an oligopoly have a collective incentive to _____ in order to maximize joint _____; individually, each firm has an incentive to _____ in order to maximize individual _____.

   c. Oligopolistic firms exhibit profits in the long run only if there are significant _____.

   d. Three examples of non-competitive behaviour practised by firms with market power are: _____, _____, and _____.

   e. An important defence of oligopoly is the idea that it leads to more _____ than would occur in either perfect competition or monopoly. The oligopolistic firm has an incentive to _____ because it can expect to keep a good share of the resulting profit.

3. Each of the statements below describes a characteristic of the following market structures: perfect competition, monopolistic competition, oligopoly, and monopoly. Identify which market structure displays each of the characteristics. (There may be more than one.)

- each firm faces a downward-sloping demand curve
- price is greater than marginal revenue
- each firm produces at MES in long-run equilibrium
- firms earn profit in long-run equilibrium
- firms produce a homogeneous product
- firms advertise their product
- each firm produces output where $MC = MR$
- each firm produces output where $P = MC$
- there is free entry to the industry
- firms produce a differentiated product

4. (X myeconlab) The following table provides annual sales for the four largest firms in four industries in Canada. Also provided are total Canadian and total world sales for the industry. (All figures are hypothetical and are in millions of dollars.)

	Firm 1	Firm 2	Firm 3	Firm 4	Total Sales (Canada)	Total Sales (World)
Forestry products	185	167	98	47	550	1368
Chemicals	27	24	9	4	172	2452
Women's clothing	6	5	4	2	94	3688
Pharmaceuticals	44	37	22	19	297	2135

a. Suppose Canada does not trade internationally any of the goods produced in these industries. Compute the four-firm Canadian concentration ratio for each industry.
b. Rank the industries in order from the most concentrated to the least concentrated.
c. Now suppose goods in these industries are freely traded around the world. Are the concentration ratios from (a) still relevant? Explain.

5. The table below provides price, revenue, and cost information for a monopolistically competitive firm selling drive-through car washes in a large city.

Quantity (number of car washes per month)	Price	Total Revenue	Marginal Revenue	Total Cost	Average Total Cost	Marginal Cost	Profit (per car wash)
1000	30	____		25 000	____		____
1100	29	____	____	26 000	____	____	____
1200	28	____	____	27 200	____	____	____
1300	27	____	____	28 500	____	____	____
1400	26	____	____	30 000	____	____	____
1500	25	____	____	32 200	____	____	____
1600	24	____	____	35 000	____	____	____
1700	23	____	____	38 500	____	____	____
1800	22	____	____	43 000	____	____	____

a. Complete the table.
b. Plot the demand, marginal revenue, marginal cost, and average cost curves for the firm. (Be sure to plot *MR* and *MC* at the midpoint of the output intervals.)
c. What is the profit-maximizing number of car washes (per month)?
d. What is the profit-maximizing price?
e. Calculate the total maximum profit (per month).
f. How can this firm differentiate its product from other car washes?

6. Draw two diagrams of a monopolistically competitive firm. In the first, show the firm earning profits in the short run. In the second, show the firm in long-run equilibrium earning zero profits. What changed for this firm between the short run and the long run?

7. The following figure shows the revenue and cost curves for a typical monopolistically competitive firm in the short run.

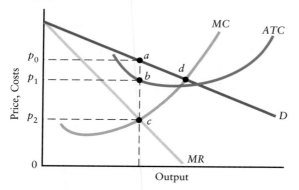

a. Note that the firm's demand curve is shown to be quite flat. Explain which assumption of monopolistic competition suggests a relatively elastic demand curve for each firm.
b. Show the profit-maximizing level of output for the firm on the diagram.
c. At the profit-maximizing level of output, are profits positive or negative? What area in the diagram represents the firm's profits?
d. Will firms enter or exit the industry? Explain.

8. The diagram below shows a typical monopolistically competitive firm when the industry is in long-run equilibrium.

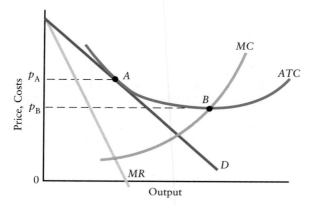

a. Explain why free entry and exit implies that the long-run equilibrium is at point A.
b. What is the significance of point B and price p_B?

c. Explain the sense in which long-run equilibrium in monopolistic competition is less efficient than in perfect competition.

9. In the text we argued that a key difference between monopolistic competition and oligopoly is that in the former firms do not behave *strategically* whereas in the latter they do. For each of the goods or services listed below, state whether the industries are likely to be best described by monopolistic competition or oligopoly. Explain your reasoning.

a. Car repair
b. Haircuts
c. Dry cleaning
d. Soft drinks
e. Breakfast cereals
f. Restaurant meals
g. Automobiles

10. **myeconlab** The table below is the payoff matrix for a simple two-firm game. Firms A and B are bidding on a government contract, and each firm's bid is not known by the other firm. Each firm can bid either $10 000 or $5000. The cost of completing the project for each firm is $4000. The low-bid firm will win the contract at its stated price; the high-bid firm will get nothing. If the two bids are equal, the two firms will split the price and costs evenly. The payoffs for each firm under each situation are shown in the matrix.

	A bids $10 000	**A bids $5000**
B bids $10 000	Firms share the contract	A wins the contract
	Payoff to A = $3000	Payoff to A = $1000
	Payoff to B = $3000	Payoff to B = $0
B bids $5000	B wins the contract	Firms share the contract
	Payoff to A = $0	Payoff to A = $500
	Payoff to B = $1000	Payoff to B = $500

a. Recall from the text that a Nash equilibrium is an outcome in which each player is maximizing his or her own payoff *given the actions of the other players*. Is there a Nash equilibrium in this game?
b. Is there more than one Nash equilibrium? Explain.
c. If the two firms could cooperate, what outcome would you predict in this game? Explain.

11. The table below shows the payoff matrix for a game between Toyota and Honda, each of which is contemplating building a factory in a new market. Each firm can either build a small factory (and produce a small number of cars) or build a large factory (and produce

a large number of cars). Suppose no other car manufacturers are selling in this market.

		Toyota's Decision	
		Small Factory	Large Factory
Honda's Decision	Small Factory	High Industry Price Honda profits: $20 million Toyota profits: $20 million	Medium Industry Price Honda profits: $12 million Toyota profits: $25 million
	Large Factory	Medium Industry Price Honda profits: $25 million Toyota profits: $12 million	Low Industry Price Honda profits: $14 million Toyota profits: $14 million

a. Assuming that the demand curve for cars in this new market is negatively sloped and unchanging, explain the economic reasoning behind the prices and profits shown in each cell in the payoff matrix.

b. What is the cooperative outcome in this game? Is it likely to be achievable? Explain.

c. What is Honda's best action? Does it depend on Toyota's action?

d. What is Toyota's best action? Does it depend on Honda's action?

e. What is the non-cooperative outcome in this game? Is it a Nash equilibrium?

DISCUSSION QUESTIONS

1. It is sometimes said that there are more drugstores and gasoline stations than are needed. In what sense might this be correct? Does the consumer gain anything from this plethora of retail outlets?

2. Do you think any of the following industries might be monopolistically competitive? Why or why not?

   a. Textbook publishing (more than 12 introductory economics textbooks are in use on campuses in Canada this year)
   b. Post-secondary education
   c. Cigarette manufacturing
   d. Restaurant operation
   e. Automobile retailing

3. "The periods following each of the major OPEC price shocks proved to the world that there were many available substitutes for gasoline, among them bicycles, car pools, moving closer to work, cable TV, and Japanese cars." Discuss how each of these may be a substitute for gasoline.

4. Evidence suggests that the profits earned by all the firms in many oligopolistic industries are less than the profits that would be earned if the industry were monopolized. What are some reasons why this might be so?

5. What is the key difference between monopolistic competition and oligopoly? Assume that you are in an industry that is monopolistically competitive. What actual steps might you take to transform your industry into a more oligopolistic form?

6. Consider the following industries in Canada that have traditionally been oligopolistic.

   - Brewing
   - Airlines
   - Railways
   - Banking

   a. What are the barriers to entry in each of these industries that might explain persistently high profits?
   b. Explain in each case how technology is changing in ways that circumvent these entry barriers.

CHAPTER 12

Economic Efficiency and Public Policy

LEARNING OBJECTIVES

In this chapter you will learn

1. the distinction between productive and allocative efficiency.
2. why perfect competition is allocatively efficient, whereas monopoly is allocatively inefficient.
3. alternative methods for regulating a natural monopoly.
4. some details about Canadian competition policy.

In the previous three chapters we examined various market structures, from perfect competition at one end of the spectrum to monopoly at the other end. In the middle were two forms of imperfect competition: monopolistic competition and oligopoly. We have considered how firms behave in these various market structures, and we are now able to evaluate the *efficiency* of the market structures. Then we will see why economists are suspicious of monopolistic practices and seek to encourage competitive behaviour. Table 12-1 provides a review of the four market structures and the industry characteristics relevant to each.

We begin our discussion in this chapter by examining the various concepts of efficiency used by economists. This discussion will develop more fully the concept of efficiency we first saw at the end of Chapter 5. We then discuss how public policy deals with the challenges of monopoly and oligopoly in an effort to improve the efficiency of the economy.

12.1 PRODUCTIVE AND ALLOCATIVE EFFICIENCY

Efficiency requires that factors of production are fully employed. However, full employment of resources is not enough to prevent the *waste* of resources. Even when resources are fully employed, they may be used inefficiently. Here are three examples of inefficiency in the use of fully employed resources.

1. If firms do not use the least-cost method of producing their chosen outputs, they are being inefficient. For example, a firm that produces 30 000 pairs of shoes at a resource cost of $400 000 when it could have been done at a cost of only $350 000 is using resources inefficiently. The lower-cost method would allow $50 000 worth of resources to be transferred to other productive uses.

TABLE 12-1   Review of Four Market Structures

Market Structure	Industry Characteristics
Perfect competition	• Many small firms • Firms sell identical products • All firms are price takers • Free entry and exit • Zero profits in long-run equilibrium • Price = MC
Monopolistic competition	• Many small firms • Firms sell differentiated products • Each firm has some power to set price • Free entry and exit • Zero profits in long-run equilibrium • Price > MC; less output than in perfect competition; excess capacity
Oligopoly	• Few firms, usually large • Strategic behaviour among firms • Firms usually sell differentiated products and are price setters • Often significant entry barriers • Usually economies of scale • Profits depend on the nature of firm rivalry and on entry barriers
Monopoly	• Single firm faces the entire market demand • Firm is a price setter • Profits persist if sufficient entry barriers • Price > MC; less output than perfect competition

2. If the marginal cost of production is not the same for every firm in an industry, the industry is being inefficient. For example, if the cost of producing the last tonne of steel is higher for some firms than for others, the industry's overall cost of producing a given amount of steel is higher than necessary. The same amount of steel could be produced at lower total cost if the total output were distributed differently among the various producers.

3. If too much of one product and too little of another product are produced, the economy's resources are being used inefficiently. To take an extreme example, suppose so many shoes are produced that every consumer has all the shoes he or she could possibly want and thus places a zero value on obtaining an additional pair of shoes. Suppose also that so few coats are produced that consumers place a high value on obtaining an additional coat. In these circumstances, consumers can be made better off if resources are reallocated from shoe production, where the last shoe produced has a low value in the eyes of each consumer, to coat production, where one more coat produced would have a higher value to each consumer.

These three examples illustrate inefficiency in the use of resources. But the *type* of inefficiency is different in each case. The first example considers the cost for a single firm producing some level of output. The second example is closely related, but the focus is on the total cost for all of the firms in an industry. The third example relates to the level of output of one product compared to another. Let's explore these three types of efficiency in more detail.

Productive Efficiency

Productive efficiency has two aspects, one concerning production within each firm and one concerning the allocation of production among the firms in an industry. The first two examples above relate to these two different aspects of productive efficiency.

productive efficiency for the firm When the firm chooses among all available production methods to produce a given level of output at the lowest possible cost.

Productive efficiency for the firm requires that the firm produce any given level of output at the lowest possible cost. In the short run, with only one variable factor, the firm merely uses enough of the variable factor to produce the desired level of output. In the long run, however, more than one method of production is available. Productive efficiency requires that the firm use the least costly of the available methods of producing any given output—that is, firms are located on, rather than above, their long-run average cost curves.

Productive efficiency for the firm requires the firm to be producing its output at the lowest possible cost.

Any firm that is not being productively efficient is producing at a higher cost than is necessary and thus will have lower profits than it could have. It follows that any profit-maximizing firm will seek to be productively efficient no matter the market structure within which it operates—perfect competition, monopoly, oligopoly, or monopolistic competition.

Productive efficiency for the industry requires that the industry's total output be allocated among its individual firms in such a way that the total cost in the industry is minimized. If an industry is productively *inefficient*, it is possible to reduce the industry's total cost of producing any given output by reallocating production among the industry's firms.

Productive efficiency for the industry requires that the marginal cost of production must be the same for each firm.

To see why marginal costs must be equated across firms, consider a simple example that is illustrated in Figure 12-1. Aslan Shoe Company has a marginal cost of $80 for the last shoe of some standard type it produces. Digory Shoes Inc. has a marginal cost of only $40 for its last shoe of the same type. If Aslan were to produce one fewer pair of shoes and Digory were to produce one more pair, total shoe production would be unchanged. Total industry costs, however, would be lower by $40.

Profit-maximizing firms will adopt the lowest-cost methods of production, and thus will be productively efficient. An industry will be productively efficient only when its firms all have the same marginal cost.

productive efficiency for the industry When the industry is producing a given level of output at the lowest possible cost. This requires that marginal cost be equated across all firms in the industry.

FIGURE 12-1   Production Efficiency for the Industry

Aslan Shoe Co.

Digory Shoes Inc.

Productive efficiency for the industry requires that marginal costs be equated for all firms. At the initial levels of output, Q_A and Q_D, marginal costs are $80 for Aslan and $40 for Digory. If Digory increases output by ΔQ to Q'_D and Aslan reduces output by the same amount, ΔQ, to Q'_A, total output is unchanged. Aslan's total costs have fallen by the green shaded area, whereas Digory's total costs have increased by the smaller purple shaded area. Total industry costs are therefore reduced when output is reallocated between the firms. When marginal costs are equalized, at $60 in this example, no further reallocation of output can reduce costs—productive efficiency will have been achieved.

FIGURE 12-2 Production Efficiency and the Production Possibilities Boundary

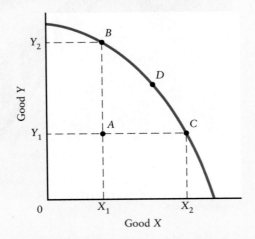

Any point on the production possibilities boundary is productively efficient. The boundary shows all combinations of two goods X and Y that can be produced when the economy's resources are fully employed and productively efficient.

Any point inside the curve, such as A, is productively inefficient. If the inefficiency exists in industry X, then either some producer of X is productively inefficient or industry X as a whole is productively inefficient. In either case, it is possible to increase total production of X without using more resources, and thus without reducing the output of Y. This would take the economy from point A to point C. Similarly, if the inefficiency exists in industry Y, production of Y could be increased, moving the economy from point A to point B.

Clearly, this cost saving can go on as long as the two firms have different marginal costs. However, as Aslan produces fewer shoes, its marginal cost falls, and as Digory produces more shoes, its marginal cost rises. Once marginal cost is equated across the two firms, at a marginal cost of $60 in the figure, there are no further cost savings to be obtained by reallocating production.

Over the next few pages we will see *how* such an efficient allocation of output across firms is achieved, but for now the point is simply that if marginal costs are not equated across firms, then a reallocation of output is necessary in order for the industry to become productively efficient.

Productive Efficiency and the Production Possibilities Boundary If firms are productively efficient, they are minimizing their costs; there is no way for them to increase output without using more resources. If an industry is productively efficient, the industry as a whole is producing its output at the lowest possible cost; the industry could not increase its output without using more resources.

Now think about the economy's production possibilities boundary (PPB), which we first saw in Chapter 1 and which is shown again in Figure 12-2. The PPB shows the combinations of output of two products that are possible when the economy is using its resources *efficiently*. An economy that is producing at a point inside the PPB is being productively inefficient—it could produce more of one good without producing less of the other. This may occur because individual firms are not minimizing their costs or because, within an industry, marginal costs are not equalized across the various firms. Either situation would lead the economy to be inside its production possibilities boundary.

If firms and industries are productively efficient, the economy will be on, rather than inside, the production possibilities boundary.

In Figure 12-2, every point on the PPB is productively efficient. Is there one point on the PPB that is "better" in some way than the others? The answer is yes, and this brings us to the concept of *allocative efficiency*.

Allocative Efficiency

allocative efficiency A situation in which the market price for each good is equal to that good's marginal cost.

Allocative efficiency concerns the quantities of the various products to be produced. When the combination of goods produced is allocatively efficient, economists say that the economy is *Pareto efficient*, in honour of the nineteenth-century Italian economist Vilfredo Pareto (1843–1923), who developed this concept of efficiency.

How do we find the allocatively efficient point on the production possibilities boundary? The answer is as follows:

The economy is allocatively efficient when, for each good produced, its marginal cost of production is equal to its price.

To understand this answer, recall our discussion in Chapters 5 and 6 about the marginal value that consumers place on the next unit of some good. When consumers face the market price for some good, they adjust their consumption of the good until their marginal value is just equal to the price. Thus, the market price reflects consumers' marginal value of the good. Since price reflects the marginal value of the good to consumers, we can restate the condition for allocative efficiency to be that, for each good produced, marginal cost must equal marginal value.[1]

If the level of output of some product is such that marginal cost to producers exceeds marginal value to consumers, too much of that product is being produced, because the cost to society of the last unit produced exceeds the benefits of consuming it. Conversely, if the level of output of some good is such that the marginal cost is less than the marginal value, too little of that good is being produced, because the cost to society of producing the next unit is less than the benefits that would be gained from consuming it.

Allocative Efficiency and the Production Possibilities Boundary Figure 12-3 shows a production possibilities boundary in an economy that can produce wheat and steel, and also shows the individual supply-and-demand diagrams for the two markets. Notice that the vertical axis in each of the supply-and-demand diagrams shows the *relative* price of the appropriate good. For example, in the market for wheat, the relevant price is the price of wheat *relative to the price of steel*. This is consistent with our initial treatment of supply and demand in Chapter 3, in which we held constant all other prices and then examined how the price of any specific product was determined.

Figure 12-3 illustrates how the allocation of resources in the economy changes as we move along the production possibilities boundary. For example, as the economy moves from point A to point B to point C along the PPB, resources are being transferred from the steel sector to the wheat sector. Thus, steel output is falling and wheat output is rising.

What is the allocatively efficient combination of steel and wheat output? Allocative efficiency will be achieved when in each market the marginal cost of producing the good equals the marginal value of consuming the good. In Figure 12-3, allocative efficiency is achieved at point B, with S_B steel being produced and W_B wheat being produced.[2]

---

[1] Allocative efficiency is exactly the same concept as *market efficiency* that we discussed in Chapter 5. Now that we have introduced the distinction between productive and allocative efficiency, we will continue to use these two terms only.

[2] Note that allocative efficiency requires that price equal marginal cost in *all* industries simultaneously. Based on what economists call the "theory of the second best," there is no guarantee that achieving $p = MC$ in one industry will improve overall welfare when price does not equal marginal cost in all other industries. For the purposes of this introductory textbook, however, we assume that the concept of allocative efficiency is useful for examining welfare improvements within individual industries.

FIGURE 12-3   Allocative Efficiency and the Production Possibilities Boundary

Allocative efficiency requires that all goods be produced to the point where the marginal cost to producers equals the marginal value to consumers. The production possibilities boundary shows the combinations of wheat and steel that are possible if firms and industries are productively efficient. The lower diagrams show the marginal cost (supply) and marginal value (demand) curves in each industry.

At point A, steel output is S_A and wheat output is W_A. As the lower figures show, however, at W_A, the marginal value of wheat consumption exceeds its marginal cost of production. Thus, society would be better off if more wheat were produced. Similarly, at S_A, the marginal cost of steel production exceeds its marginal value to consumers, and thus society would be better off with less steel being produced.

Point A is therefore not allocatively efficient; there is too little wheat and too much steel being produced. Resources should be reallocated to move the economy toward point B. The argument is similar at point C, at which there is too much wheat and too little steel being produced. Only at point B is each good produced to the point where the marginal cost to producers is equal to the marginal value to consumers. Only point B is allocatively efficient.

Which Market Structures Are Efficient?

We now know that for productive efficiency, all firms must be minimizing their costs and marginal cost should be the same for all firms in any one industry. For allocative efficiency, marginal cost should be equal to price in each industry. Do the market structures that we have studied in earlier chapters lead to productive and allocative efficiency?

Perfect Competition   We saw in Chapter 9 that in the long run under perfect competition, each firm produces at the lowest point on its long-run average cost curve. Therefore, no one firm could reduce its costs by altering its own production. Every firm in perfect competition is therefore productively efficient.

We also know that in perfect competition, all firms in an industry face the same price of their product and they equate marginal cost to that price. It follows immediately that marginal cost will be the same for all firms. (Suppose, for example, that Aslan and Digory faced the same market price in Figure 12-1. Aslan would produce where $MC_A = p$ and Digory would produce where $MC_D = p$. It follows that $MC_A = MC_D$.) Thus, in perfectly competitive industries, the industry as a whole is productively efficient.

We have already seen that perfectly competitive firms maximize their profits by choosing an output level such that marginal cost equals market price. Thus, when perfect competition is the market structure for the whole economy, price is equal to marginal cost in each industry, resulting in allocative efficiency.

Perfectly competitive industries are productively efficient. If an economy could be made up entirely of perfectly competitive industries, the economy would be allocatively efficient.

Note, however, that perfect competition exists only in some industries in modern economies. So, while specific industries may be perfectly competitive and therefore allocatively efficient, entire modern economies are neither perfectly competitive nor allocatively efficient.

Monopoly   Monopolists have an incentive to be productively efficient because their profits will be maximized when they adopt the lowest-cost production method. Hence, profit-maximizing monopolists will operate on their *LRAC* curves and thus be productively efficient.

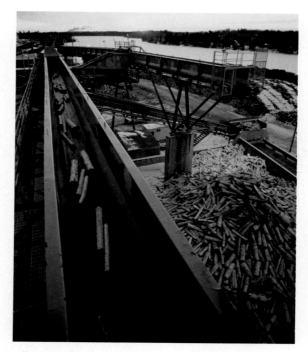

Although a monopolist will be productively efficient, it will choose a level of output that is too low to achieve allocative efficiency. This result follows from what we saw in Chapter 10—that the monopolist chooses an output at which the price charged is *greater than* marginal cost. Such a choice violates the conditions for allocative efficiency because the price, and hence the marginal value to consumers, exceeds the marginal cost of production. From this result follows the classic efficiency-based preference for competition over monopoly:

Monopoly is not allocatively efficient because the monopolist's price always exceeds its marginal cost.

This result has important policy implications for economists and for policymakers, as we shall see later in this chapter.

Other Market Structures   The allocative inefficiency of monopoly extends to other imperfectly competitive market structures. Whenever a firm has any market power, in the sense that it faces a negatively sloped demand curve, its marginal revenue will be less than its price. When it equates marginal cost to marginal revenue, as

Allocative efficiency is a property of the entire economy. The economy is allocatively efficient only when the quantity of each product is such that its marginal cost equals its price.

all profit-maximizing firms do, marginal cost will also be less than price. This inequality implies allocative inefficiency. Thus, oligopoly and monopolistic competition are also allocatively inefficient.

Oligopoly is an important market structure in today's economy because in many industries the minimum efficient scale is simply too high to support a large number of competing firms. Monopolistic competition is also important, especially in the many manufactured-goods industries in which economies of scale are not so extreme but product differentiation is an important market characteristic. Although neither oligopoly nor monopolistic competition achieves the conditions for allocative efficiency, they may nevertheless produce more satisfactory results than monopoly.

We observed one reason why oligopoly may be preferable to monopoly in Chapter 11: Competition among oligopolists encourages innovations that result in both new products and cost-reducing methods of producing old ones. An important defence of oligopoly as an acceptable market structure is that it may be the best of the available alternatives when minimum efficient scale is large. As we observed at the end of Chapter 11, the challenge to public policy is to keep oligopolists competing and using their competitive energies to improve products and to reduce costs rather than to restrict interfirm competition and to erect entry barriers. As we shall see later in this chapter, much public policy has just this purpose. What economic policymakers call *monopolistic practices* include not only output restrictions operated by firms with complete monopoly power but also anticompetitive behaviour among firms that are operating in oligopolistic industries.

producer surplus The price of a good minus the marginal cost of producing it, summed over the quantity produced.

FIGURE 12-4   Consumer and Producer Surplus in a Competitive Market

Consumer surplus is the area under the demand curve and above the market price line. Producer surplus is the area above the supply curve and below the market price line. The total value that consumers place on Q_0 of the commodity is given by the area under the demand curve up to Q_0. The amount they pay is the rectangle $p_0 Q_0$. The difference, shown as the blue shaded area, is consumer surplus.

The revenue to producers from the sale of Q_0 units is $p_0 Q_0$. The area under the supply curve is the minimum amount producers require to supply the output. The difference, shown as the red shaded area, is producer surplus.

Allocative Efficiency and Total Surplus

By using the concepts of marginal value to consumers and the marginal cost of production, we have established the basic points of productive and allocative efficiency. A different way of thinking about allocative efficiency—though completely consistent with the first approach—is to use the concepts of consumer and producer surplus, both of which are part of the economic surplus that we first introduced in Chapter 5.

Consumer and Producer Surplus Recall from Chapter 6 that consumer surplus is the difference between the value that consumers place on a product and the payment that they actually make to buy that product. In Figure 12-4, if the competitive market price is p_0 and consumers buy Q_0 units of the product, consumer surplus is the blue shaded area.

Producer surplus is an analogous concept to consumer surplus. **Producer surplus** is the difference between the actual price that the producer receives for a product and the lowest price that the producer would be willing to accept for the sale of that product. By producing one more unit, the producer's costs increase by the marginal cost, and this is the lowest amount that the producer will accept for the product. To accept any amount less than the marginal cost would *reduce* the firm's profits.

For each unit sold, producer surplus is the difference between price and marginal cost.

For a producer that sells many units of the product, total producer surplus is the difference between price and marginal cost summed over all the units sold. So, for an individual producer, total producer surplus is the area above the marginal cost curve and below the price line.

For the industry as a whole, we need to know the industry supply curve in order to compute overall producer surplus. Since in perfect competition the industry supply curve is simply the horizontal sum of all firms' *MC* curves, producer surplus in a perfectly competitive market is the area above the supply curve and below the price line, as shown in Figure 12-4.

The Allocative Efficiency of Perfect Competition Revisited In Chapter 5 we said that market (allocative) efficiency exists in a market if the total economic surplus is maximized. At that point, we did not make the distinction between the component parts of total surplus—consumer surplus and producer surplus. Now that we have identified these different parts of total surplus, we can restate the conditions for allocative efficiency in a slightly different way.

Allocative efficiency occurs where the sum of consumer and producer surplus is maximized.

The allocatively efficient output occurs under perfect competition where the demand curve intersects the supply curve—that is, the point of equilibrium in a competitive market. This is shown as the output Q^* in Figure 12-5. For any level of output below Q^*, such as Q_1, the demand curve lies above the supply curve, showing that consumers value the product more than it costs to produce it. Thus, society would be better off if more than Q_1 units were produced. Notice that if output is only Q_1 there is no consumer or producer surplus earned on the units between Q_1 and Q^*. Thus, the areas 1 and 2 in Figure 12-5 represent a loss to the economy. Total surplus—consumer plus producer surplus—is lower at Q_1 than at Q^*.

For any level of output above Q^*, such as Q_2, the demand curve lies below the supply curve, showing that consumers value the product less than the cost of producing it. Society would be better off if less than Q_2 units were produced. If output is Q_2, total surplus is less than it is at Q^*. To see this, suppose that the price is p^*. Producers would earn *negative* producer surplus on the units above Q^* because the

Practise with Study Guide Chapter 12, Exercise 1.

FIGURE 12-5 The Allocative Efficiency of Perfect Competition

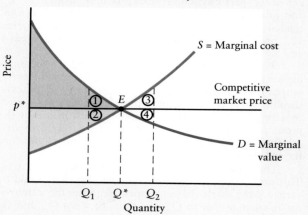

Competitive equilibrium is allocatively efficient because it maximizes the sum of consumer and producer surplus. The competitive equilibrium occurs at the price–output combination of p^* and Q^*. At this equilibrium, consumer surplus is the blue area above the price line, while producer surplus is the red area below the price line.

For any output that is less than Q^*, the sum of the two surpluses is less than at Q^*. For example, reducing the output to Q_1 but keeping price at p^* lowers consumer surplus by area 1 and lowers producer surplus by area 2.

For any output that is greater than Q^*, the sum of the surpluses is also less than at Q^*. For example, if producers are forced to produce output Q_2 and to sell it to consumers, who are in turn forced to buy it at price p^*, producer surplus is reduced by area 3 while the amount of consumer surplus is reduced by area 4.

FIGURE 12-6   The Deadweight Loss of Monopoly

Monopoly restricts output and reduces total surplus, thereby imposing a deadweight loss on society. If this market were perfectly competitive, output would be Q_c and price would be p^*. Total surplus would be the total shaded area. Consumer surplus would be the sum of areas 1, 2, and 3. Producer surplus would be the sum of areas 4 and 5.

When the industry is monopolized, and the monopolist has the same marginal costs as the competitive industry, output is restricted to Q_m and price rises to p_m. Consumer surplus is reduced to the blue area. Producer surplus rises by area 2 but falls by area 5. (Since p_m must maximize the producer's profit, we know that area 2 is larger than area 5.) Total producer surplus for the monopolist is therefore the red area.

The deadweight loss of monopoly is the purple area. This area represents the additional surplus that would be earned if the market were competitive. Since the monopolist restricts output to Q_m, the units between Q_m and Q_c are not produced and therefore they generate neither consumer nor producer surplus.

marginal cost on those units exceeds p^*. Similarly, consumers would earn *negative* consumer surplus on the units above Q^* because their marginal value of the product is less than p^*. (You should be able to convince yourself that for *any* price, the total surplus earned on the units above Q^* is negative.) From the figure, we conclude that at any level of output above Q^*, total surplus is less than it is at Q^*.

The sum of producer and consumer surplus is maximized only at the perfectly competitive level of output. This is the only level of output that is allocatively efficient.

The Allocative Inefficiency of Monopoly Revisited   We have just seen in Figure 12-5 that the output in perfectly competitive equilibrium maximizes the sum of consumer and producer surplus. It follows that the lower monopoly output must result in a smaller total of consumer and producer surplus.

The monopoly equilibrium is not the outcome of a voluntary agreement between the one producer and the many consumers. Instead, it is imposed by the monopolist by virtue of the power it has over the market. When the monopolist chooses an output below the competitive level, market price is higher than it would be under perfect competition. As a result, consumer surplus is diminished, and producer surplus is increased. In this way, the monopolist gains at the expense of consumers. This is not the whole story, however.

When output is below the competitive level, there is always a *net loss* of total surplus: More surplus is lost by consumers than is gained by the monopolist. Some surplus is lost because output between the monopolistic and the competitive levels is not produced. This loss of surplus is called the *deadweight loss of monopoly*. It is illustrated in Figure 12-6.

It follows that there is a conflict between the private interest of the monopolist and the public interest of all the nation's consumers. This creates grounds for government intervention to prevent the formation of monopolies or at least to control their behaviour.

Allocative Efficiency and Market Failure

Practise with Study Guide Chapter 12, Exercise 2.

We have seen that perfect competition is allocatively efficient and that monopoly, in general, is not. Most of the remainder of this chapter presents ways in which public policy has attempted to deal with problems raised by monopoly. Before we go on, however, it is important to re-emphasize that perfect competition is a theoretical ideal that exists in a small number of industries, is at best only approximated in some others, and is not even closely resembled in most. Hence, to say that perfect competition is allocatively efficient is not to say that real-world market economies are ever allocatively efficient.

In Chapter 16, we discuss the most important ways (other than monopoly) in which market economies may fail to produce efficient outcomes. In Chapters 17 and 18, we discuss and evaluate the most important public policies that have been used to try to correct for these *market failures*. One of the most important problems arises when market transactions—production and consumption—impose costs or confer benefits on economic agents who are not involved in the transaction. Cases like these, which are called *externalities* because they involve economic effects that are "external" to the transaction, generally raise the possibility that market outcomes will be allocatively inefficient.

A simple example illustrates the problem. We know that markets for most agricultural commodities are highly competitive, with many small producers who are unable to affect the price of the goods they are producing. At the same time, the technology of agricultural production involves the extensive use of fertilizers that pollute nearby streams and rivers. This pollution imposes costs on downstream households who use the water for drinking. Because these costs are not taken into account in the market for the agricultural products, they will be external to transactions in those markets. Generally, when production of a good or service causes pollution, the quantity produced in a perfectly competitive industry will exceed the efficient amount.

One of the most important issues in public policy is whether, and under what circumstances, government action can increase the allocative efficiency of market outcomes.

As we will see later in this book, there are many circumstances in which there is room to increase the efficiency of market outcomes, but there are also many cases in which the cure is worse than the disease. In the remainder of this chapter we examine economic regulation and competition policy, both of which are designed to promote allocative efficiency.

12.2 ECONOMIC REGULATION TO PROMOTE EFFICIENCY

Monopolies, cartels, and price-fixing agreements among oligopolists, whether explicit or tacit, have met with public suspicion and official hostility for over a century. These and other non-competitive practices are collectively referred to as *monopoly practices*. The laws and other instruments that are used to encourage competition and discourage monopoly practices make up *competition policy*. By and large, Canadian competition policy has sought to create more competitive market structures where possible, to discourage monopolistic practices, and to encourage competitive behaviour where competitive market structures cannot be established.

Pollution produced by one firm imposes costs on others. This "externality" is an example of what economists call a market failure because the unregulated market produces more than what is socially optimal. Carefully designed government intervention can, in principle, solve the problem.

To learn about the Canadian Radio-television and Telecommunications Commission (CRTC), see its website: **www.crtc.gc.ca**.

Federal, provincial, and local governments also employ *economic regulations,* which prescribe the rules under which firms can do business and in some cases determine the prices that businesses can charge for their output. For example, the Canadian Radio-television and Telecommunications Commission (CRTC) is a federal agency that regulates many aspects of the radio, television, and telecommunications industries. Provincial governments regulate the extraction of fossil fuels and the harvesting of forests within their provincial boundaries. Local governments regulate the zoning of land and thus have an important influence on where firms can and cannot operate their businesses.

The quest for allocative efficiency provides rationales both for competition policy and for economic regulation. Competition policy is used to promote allocative efficiency by increasing competition in the marketplace. Where effective competition is not possible (as in the case of natural monopolies such as natural gas or electricity distribution companies), public ownership or economic regulation of privately owned firms can be used as a substitute for competition. Consumers can then be protected from the high prices and restricted output that result from the use of monopoly power.[3]

In the remainder of this chapter, we look at a variety of ways in which policymakers have chosen to intervene in the workings of the market economy using economic regulation and competition policy.

Regulation of Natural Monopolies

natural monopoly An industry characterized by economies of scale sufficiently large that one firm can most efficiently supply the entire market demand.

The clearest case for public intervention arises with a **natural monopoly**—an industry in which economies of scale are so dominant that there is room for *at most* one firm to operate at the minimum efficient scale. (Indeed, economies of scale could be so important that even a single firm could satisfy the entire market demand before reaching its minimum efficient scale.) Natural monopolies are found mainly in public utilities, such as electricity transmission, natural gas distribution, cable television, and local telephone service. These industries require the establishment of large and expensive distribution networks (transmission lines, pipelines, or cable networks) and the size of the market is such that only a single firm can achieve its minimum efficient scale while still covering these fixed costs.

Crown corporations In Canada, business concerns owned by the federal or provincial government.

One response to natural monopoly is for government to assume ownership of the single firm. In Canada, such government-owned firms are called **Crown corporations**. In these cases, the government appoints managers and directors who are supposed to set prices in the national interest. Another response to the problem of natural monopoly is to allow private ownership but to *regulate* the monopolist's behaviour. In Canada, both government ownership (e.g., Canada Post and most of the provincial hydro authorities) and regulation (e.g., cable television, local Internet service providers, and local telephone) are used actively. In the United States, with a few notable exceptions, private ownership with regulation has been the preferred alternative.

Whether the government owns or merely regulates natural monopolies, the industry's pricing policy is determined by the government. The industry is typically required to follow some pricing policy that conflicts with the goal of profit maximization. We will see that such government intervention must deal with problems that arise in the short run, the long run, and the very long run.

---

[3] A second kind of regulation involves the legislated rules that require firms to consider the environmental and other consequences of their behaviour. Environmental regulation is discussed in Chapter 17.

Short-Run Price and Output   There are three general types of pricing policies for regulated natural monopolies: *marginal-cost pricing, two-part tariffs,* and *average-cost pricing.* We discuss each in turn.

Marginal-Cost Pricing.   Sometimes the government dictates that the natural monopoly set a price where the market demand curve and the firm's marginal cost curve intersect. This policy, called **marginal-cost pricing,** leads to the allocatively efficient level of output. This is not, however, the profit-maximizing output, which is where marginal cost equals marginal revenue. Thus, marginal-cost pricing sets up a tension between the regulator's desire to achieve the allocatively efficient level of output and the monopolist's desire to maximize profits.

Figure 12-7 illustrates a case where the natural monopoly is operating on the downward-sloping portion of its *ATC* curve. In this case, marginal cost will be less than average total cost. It follows that when price is set equal to marginal cost, price will be less than average cost, and marginal-cost pricing will lead to losses.

When a natural monopoly with falling average costs sets price equal to marginal cost, it will suffer losses.

If regulations impose marginal-cost pricing, and the firm ends up incurring economic losses, this situation cannot be sustained for long. This problem provides the motivation for two alternative pricing policies.

Two-Part Tariff.   One pricing policy that permits the natural monopoly to cover its costs is to allow it to charge a **two-part tariff** in which customers pay one price to gain access to the product and a second price for each unit consumed. Consider the case of a regulated cable TV company or Internet service provider (ISP). In principle, the hook-up fee covers fixed costs, and then each unit of output can be priced at marginal cost. Indeed, most new subscribers to cable TV or Internet service are surprised at how high the hook-up fee is—clearly much higher than the cost of the cable guy's half-hour to complete the job! Yet, if this fee also includes that household's share of the firm's fixed costs (spread over many thousands of households), then the large hook-up fee is more understandable.

Average-Cost Pricing.   Another method of regulating a natural monopoly is to set prices just high enough to cover total costs, thus generating neither profits nor losses. The firm produces the level of output where the demand curve cuts the *ATC* curve. Figure 12-7 shows that for a firm with declining average costs, this pricing policy requires producing at less than the allocatively

marginal-cost pricing Setting price equal to marginal cost so that buyers for the last unit are just willing to pay the amount that it cost to make that unit.

two-part tariff A method of charging for a good or a service in which the consumer pays a flat access fee and a specified amount per unit purchased.

FIGURE 12-7   Pricing Policies for Natural Monopolies with Falling Costs

For a natural monopoly with falling average costs, marginal-cost pricing leads to losses, whereas average-cost pricing leads to inefficiency. Average costs are falling as output rises, and thus the *MC* curve is below the *ATC* curve. If regulations insist on setting price equal to marginal cost, then output is Q_1 and price is p_1. In this case, allocative efficiency is achieved but the firm makes economic losses given by the shaded area.

If regulations instead permit price to equal average cost, then output is Q_2 and price is p_2. In this case, the firm just covers its costs (economic profits are zero) but because price exceeds marginal cost, the level of output is too low for allocative efficiency.

Practise with Study Guide Chapter 12, Exercise 3.

efficient output. The firm's financial losses that would occur under marginal-cost pricing are avoided by producing less output than what is socially optimal.

For a natural monopoly with falling average costs, a policy of average-cost pricing will not result in allocative efficiency because price will not equal marginal cost.

On what basis do we choose between marginal-cost pricing and average-cost pricing? Marginal-cost pricing generates allocative efficiency, but the firm may incur losses. In this case, the firm will eventually go out of business unless someone is prepared to cover the firm's losses. If the government is unwilling to do so, seeing no reason why taxpayers should subsidize the users of the product in question, then average-cost pricing may be preferable. It provides the lowest price that can be charged and the largest output that can be produced, given the requirement that revenue must cover the total cost of producing the product.

Long-Run Investment   So far, we have examined the implications of different pricing policies in the short run. Recall that in the short run the amount of the firm's capital is fixed, and that amount determines the position of the firm's marginal cost curve. What should determine the firm's long-run capital stock? In answering this question, we begin by assuming that the demand for the product is constant.

To determine the efficient level of capital, we need to compare the current (regulated) price with the *long-run* marginal cost of producing the product. The current price reflects the value consumers place on one additional unit of output. The long-run marginal cost reflects the full resource cost (including capital costs) of providing an extra unit of output. Thus, if the current price exceeds long-run marginal cost, allocative efficiency requires that more output be produced. In this case, the natural monopoly should increase its *capacity* (so that it can increase its output). If current price is less than long-run marginal cost, allocative efficiency requires that less output be produced. In this case, the natural monopoly should allow its capacity to decline as its capital wears out.

The previous paragraph assumed that demand was constant and so the *current* market price was relevant to the long-run investment decision. But what if demand is expected to increase in the future, and therefore consumers' marginal value of the product will rise? In this case, the appropriate comparison is between the *future* price and the long-run marginal cost, and so it may be efficient to increase capacity even if the current price is below the long-run marginal cost. Similarly, if demand is expected to fall in the future, then it may be efficient to decrease capacity even though the current price is above long-run marginal cost.

In the long run, allocative efficiency requires that capacity be chosen so that the expected market price is equal to the long-run marginal cost of production.

We have seen the practical reasons why regulators may choose average-cost pricing rather than marginal-cost pricing. What is the implication of this choice in the long run? Since marginal cost is generally different from average cost, average-cost pricing will generally lead to inefficient patterns of long-run investment. For example, consider the situation depicted in Figure 12-7—a natural monopoly operating on the downward-sloping portion of its *ATC* curve and required to set price equal to average cost. Since price equals average cost, the firm will be just breaking even and thus it will have no incentive to increase its amount of fixed capital. Note, however, that the price in this case must exceed the short-run marginal cost (because marginal cost must be below average cost if average cost is falling). If the price also exceeds the long-run marginal cost, society would benefit by having a larger amount of fixed capital allocated to producing this good. But the regulated utility will not undertake this socially desirable investment.

Average-cost pricing generally leads to inefficient long-run investment decisions.

Very-Long-Run Innovation

In many places in the last few chapters we have discussed the importance of innovation and technological change. In particular, we mentioned how innovation can lead to the erosion of market power through Schumpeter's process of "creative destruction." Technological changes have led to the evolution of many natural monopolies into more competitive industries.

A striking example is found in the telecommunications industry. Thirty years ago, hard-copy message transmission was close to a natural monopoly belonging to the post office. Today, technological developments such as efficient courier services, e-mail, fax machines, and the Internet have made this activity highly competitive.

Other examples of industries that used to be natural monopolies but are now much more competitive include airlines, long-distance telephone service, and the generation of electricity (the *distribution* of electricity continues to be a natural monopoly).

For many years, both the production and distribution of electricity was viewed as a natural monopoly. But in recent years, technological changes have allowed the production of smaller generating stations, and thus most economists no longer view electricity generation as a natural monopoly. Electricity distribution that requires massive networks of power lines, however, is still a natural monopoly.

The case of electricity is particularly interesting. The combined production and distribution of electricity was once viewed as a natural monopoly, and the policy response was either to establish publicly owned power authorities (as happened in Canadian provinces) or to regulate privately owned power companies (as occurred in the United States). The source of the natural monopoly was twofold. First, the generation of electricity at low unit cost required large and expensive generating stations. Second, the transmission of power required the establishment of power grids, with networks of wires running from the generating stations to the users.

In recent years, however, the technology of electricity generation has changed. Though nuclear and hydro stations are still very expensive to build, it is now possible to build small and relatively inexpensive natural-gas-powered generating stations that produce electricity at low unit costs. These technological changes have led to the realization that the generation of electricity is no longer a natural monopoly even though the distribution of electricity still is. In the past few years, this realization has led several jurisdictions in both Canada and the United States to embark on a path of privatization or deregulation of electricity markets. While this path has been rough in some areas—especially in California and Alberta, both of which experienced severe brownouts and price escalations on a temporary basis—the underlying technological change continues to suggest that the generation of electricity is no longer a natural monopoly.

Practical Problems

Many practical problems arise with regulations designed to prevent natural monopolies from charging profit-maximizing prices. These problems begin with the fact that regulators do not have enough data to determine demand and cost curves precisely. In the absence of accurate data, regulators have tended to judge prices according to the level of the regulated firm's profits. Regulatory agencies tend to permit price increases only when profits fall below "fair" levels and require price reductions if profits exceed such levels. What started as price regulation becomes instead profit regulation, which is often called *rate-of-return regulation*. Concepts of marginal cost and allocative efficiency are typically ignored in such regulatory decisions.

If average-cost regulation is successful, only a normal rate of return will be earned; that is, economic profits will be zero. Unfortunately, the reverse is not necessarily true. Profits can be zero for any of a number of reasons, including inefficient operation and misleading accounting. Thus, regulatory commissions that rely on rate of return as their guide to pricing must monitor a number of other aspects of the regulated firm's behaviour in order to limit the possibility of wasting resources. This monitoring itself requires a considerable expenditure of resources.

Reflecting some of these concerns with regulation, in 2006 a government-appointed commission recommended that the CRTC move toward full deregulation of the Canadian telecommunications industry—especially local telephone markets. The recommendations suggested that technological changes and the recent creation of new firms had made the industry much more competitive, thus reducing the need for regulation. The CRTC responded by setting two conditions under which it would deregulate the industry. First, the largest telephone companies—Bell Canada and Telus—would be required to reduce their market shares by 25 percent. Second, these large companies with well-established land-line networks would have to ensure that rivals continue to have well-functioning access to these networks. The CRTC argued that only once these conditions were met would the industry be competitive enough that regulation would be unnecessary.

Regulation of Oligopolies

Governments have from time to time intervened in industries that were oligopolies (rather than natural monopolies), seeking to enforce the type of price and entry behaviour that was thought to be in the public interest. Such intervention has typically taken two distinct forms. In the period following the Second World War, many European countries, including Britain, primarily used nationalization of whole oligopolistic industries such as railways, steel, and coal mining, which were then to be run by government-appointed boards. In the United States, firms such as airlines and railways were left in private hands, but their decisions were regulated by government-appointed bodies that set prices and regulated entry. As often happens, Canada followed a mixture of British and American practices. Many Canadian Crown corporations were established, and many firms that remained in private hands were regulated. For example, Canadian Pacific Railway was privately owned and regulated while Canadian National Railway, until it was privatized in 1995, was a Crown corporation.

Canadian National Railway was privatized in 1995, and both CNR and Canadian Pacific Railway have been partially deregulated in recent years.

Skepticism About Direct Control Policymakers have become increasingly skeptical of their ability to improve the behaviour of oligopolistic industries by having governments control the details of their behaviour through either ownership or regulation. Two main experiences have been important in developing this skepticism.

Oligopolies and Economic Growth. During the twentieth century and into the present, new products and production methods have followed each other in rapid succession, leading to higher living standards and higher productivity. Many of these innovations have been provided by firms in oligopolistic industries such as automobiles, agricultural machinery, petroleum refining, chemicals, electronics, computing, and telecommunications. As long as oligopolists continue to compete with each other, rather than cooperating to produce monopoly profits, most economists see no need to regulate such things as the prices at which oligopolists sell their products and the conditions of entry into oligopolistic industries.

Protection from Competition. The record of postwar government intervention into regulated industries seemed poorer in practice than its supporters had predicted. Research by the University of Chicago Nobel Laureate George Stigler (1911–1991) and others established that in many industries, regulatory bodies were "captured" by the very firms that they were supposed to be regulating. As a result, the regulatory bodies that were meant to ensure competition often acted to enforce monopoly practices that would have been illegal if instituted by the firms themselves.

Practise with Study Guide Chapter 12, Exercise 4.

Airline regulation in Canada and the United States provides a good example. When airline routes and fares were first regulated, it was possible to argue that demand was too low to permit effective competition among many firms. Whatever the validity of that argument in earlier times, by the 1960s and 1970s, the airline market had grown to the point where effective competition was possible. By that time, the regulation was plainly protecting the industry, allowing it to charge higher fares, earn higher profits, and pay higher wages than it would under more competitive conditions.

Why did regulatory bodies shift from protecting consumers to protecting firms? One reason is that the regulatory commissions were gradually captured by the firms they were supposed to regulate. In part, this capture was natural enough. When regulatory bodies were hiring staff, they needed people who were knowledgeable about the industries they were regulating. Where better to go than to people who had worked in these industries? Naturally, these people tended to be sympathetic to firms in their own industries. Also, because many of them aspired to go back to those industries once they had gained experience within the regulatory bodies, they were not inclined to arouse the wrath of industry officials by imposing policies that were against the firms' interests.

Deregulation and Privatization

The 1980s witnessed the beginning of a movement in many advanced industrial nations to reduce the level of government control over industry. Various experiences in these countries were pushing in this direction:

- The realization that regulatory bodies often sought to reduce, rather than increase, competition
- The dashing of the hopes that publicly owned firms would work better than privately owned firms in the areas of efficiency, productivity growth, and industrial relations
- The awareness that falling transportation costs and revolutions in data processing and communications exposed local industries to much more widespread international competition than they had previously experienced domestically

These revised views led to two policy responses. The first was deregulation—intended to leave prices and entry free to be determined by private decisions. The second was privatization of publicly owned firms.

For many years Air Canada was a Crown corporation, owned by the federal government. It is now privately owned and operated.

In the United States, where regulation rather than government ownership had been the adopted policy, many industries were deregulated. In the United Kingdom, virtually all of the formally nationalized industries were privatized. The level of public ownership in that country now compares with that in the United States. In Canada, hundreds of Crown corporations that the government had acquired for a variety of reasons (but were neither natural monopolies nor operating in highly concentrated industries) were sold off. Many large Crown corporations operating in oligopolistic industries, such as Air Canada, Petro-Canada, and Canadian National Railway, were privatized. Also, many industries, such as airlines and gas and oil, were deregulated. Prices were freed, to be set by the firms in the industries, and entry was no longer restricted by government policy.

> **myeconlab**
>
> **The recent case of privatization and deregulation in Ontario's electricity sector has been particularly interesting—and certainly not without some problems! For more on this topic, look for "Ontario's Troubled Electricity Sector" in the *Additional Topics* section of this book's MyEconLab.**
>
> w w w . m y e c o n l a b . c o m

12.3 **CANADIAN COMPETITION POLICY**

competition policy Policy designed to prohibit the acquisition and exercise of monopoly power by business firms.

The least stringent form of government intervention is designed neither to force firms to sell at particular prices nor to regulate the conditions of entry and exit; it is designed, instead, to create conditions of competition by preventing firms from merging unnecessarily or from engaging in anticompetitive practices such as colluding to set monopoly prices. This is referred to as **competition policy**.

The Evolution of Canadian Policy

Canadian competition policy began in the late 1890s and evolved gradually over the next half-century. By the 1950s, the following three broad classes of activity were illegal:

- Price-fixing agreements that unduly lessen competition
- Mergers or monopolies that operate to the detriment of the public interest
- "Unfair" trade practices

An alleged offence under any of these categories was handled by the criminal justice system, and conviction required the standard level of proof "beyond a reasonable doubt."

Many cases of unfair trade practices were successfully pursued under these laws, but few cases were brought against mergers, and none of those that were brought was successful. The reasons most often cited for this lack of success were the inability of criminal legislation to cope with complex economic issues and the inability to establish proof "beyond a reasonable doubt."

A major review of Canadian legislation was undertaken in the late 1960s and led to changes in policy that were implemented in stages. The revisions were completed with the *Competition Act* of 1986. This Act is currently in force and contains some important modifications to the earlier legislation. Perhaps most important is that the Act allows *civil* actions, rather than *criminal* actions, to be brought against firms for alleged offences in the three categories listed above. This change is important because in civil cases the standard of proof is less strict than in criminal cases.

In order to adjudicate such civil cases, the *Competition Act* created a Competition Tribunal. The Commissioner of the Competition Bureau now acts as a "watchdog" for the economy, looking out for mergers or trade practices that are likely to have detrimental effects on overall welfare. In such cases, the Commissioner sends the alleged violations to the Competition Tribunal for adjudication.

In the case of a large merger that might substantially lessen competition, the firms are required to notify the Competition Bureau of their intention to merge. The Bureau then reviews the proposed merger, evaluates its probable effect on the economy, and then allows or disallows it.

Another important aspect of the 1986 legislation is that economic effects are now considered to be directly relevant in judging the acceptability of a proposed merger. When reviewing a merger, the Competition Bureau is obliged to consider such things as effective competition after the merger, the degree of foreign competition, barriers to entry, the availability of substitutes, and the financial state of the merging firms.

A recent example that shows both the relevance of the economic issues and the flexibility of the legislation relates to the purchase of Réno-Dépôt home-improvement stores in Quebec by its Quebec-based rival RONA. When RONA purchased all of the shares in Réno-Dépôt in 2003, the Commissioner of the Competition Bureau argued that the merger was likely to lessen competition in the Sherbrooke region, since RONA would henceforth own the only two big-box home renovation stores in that region. RONA agreed to divest itself of (sell) its newly acquired Réno-Dépôt store in Sherbrooke. However, by early 2005 it had become apparent that Home Depot, a large competitor in this industry, would be opening a new store in Sherbrooke. On the grounds that the presence of Home Depot in the Sherbrooke region would ensure sufficient competition, the Competition Tribunal agreed that the economic conditions had changed sufficiently to eliminate the need for RONA to sell its Réno-Dépôt store in Sherbrooke.

The Competition Bureau also considers any reduction in costs that a merger might generate. Even in a situation where there are considerable entry barriers to an industry, a merger may bring benefits to consumers even though it raises the industry's measured concentration. If, by merging, two firms can achieve scale economies that were not achievable separately, reductions in average total costs may get passed on to consumers in the form of lower prices.

This possibility presents a significant challenge to competition policy. The challenge is to prevent those mergers that mostly lead to less competition, producing only small cost reductions, but to allow those mergers that mostly lead to cost reductions, with only small reductions in competition. The practical problem for the authorities is to identify the likely effects of each merger. An excellent example in the Canadian context is the possibility of mergers among the large chartered banks. *Applying Economic Concepts 12-1* describes this debate that has been ongoing for over a decade.

To read the Competition Bureau's assessment of various proposed mergers, go to its website: **www.competitionbureau.gc.ca**.

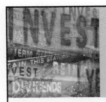

APPLYING ECONOMIC CONCEPTS 12-1

The Ongoing Debate Over Bank Mergers

As we said in the text, the 1986 *Competition Act* places considerable emphasis on the probable economic effects of proposed mergers. One challenge for the Competition Bureau is to weigh the possible benefits of a merger, resulting from cost reductions, against any lessening of competition when the merger reduces the number of actively competing firms.

A high-profile example is the possible mergers of some of Canada's largest chartered banks, an issue that has been debated on and off over the past decade. In the spring of 1998, the Royal Bank and the Bank of Montreal announced their intention to merge. Toronto Dominion and CIBC announced their intention to merge only a few days later. In the case of Canada's chartered banks, however, it is the federal Minister of Finance, and not the Competition Tribunal, that must ultimately approve the merger. Not surprisingly, the mergers became as much a political issue as an economic one. Considerable public hostility toward bank mergers created political pressure on the Minister of Finance, Paul Martin, and it did not take long before he disallowed the mergers. But the issue did not go away, and by 2006 the government was again being asked by the banks to re-open the issue and consider the possibility of bank mergers.

The Case Against Bank Mergers

When the four chartered banks first announced their intentions to merge in 1998, the Competition Bureau began to study the issue. After studying all relevant aspects of the financial-services industry, it concluded that bank mergers would substantially lessen competition in many local personal banking markets, especially in many of the small towns scattered across the

Canadian landscape. The Competition Bureau predicted that many small towns would be left with only a single bank after the mergers and that the reduction in competition would result in higher fees and poorer service. The Bureau also predicted a lessening of competition to occur in many banking markets for small and medium-sized businesses, with the result that such firms would find it more difficult to secure loans and expand their operations.

The existence of considerable entry barriers is an important part of the case against bank mergers. The large chartered banks currently have extensive networks of bank branches that reach into all parts of the country. Any potential entrant to this industry, in order to compete effectively with the established banks, would need to build a competing branch network; but this would be extremely difficult, if not impossible, to do in a short period of time. The existence of such entry barriers suggests that if mergers among some of the existing banks lead to reduced competition and higher profits, new firms would not be able to easily enter the market and compete those profits away. In this case, there may be little to prevent the abuse of the banks' increased market power. The Competition Bureau argued that even if the existing legislation barring foreign firms from operating banks in Canada were amended, the established network of branch banking would give the existing banks a stranglehold on the Canadian banking industry.

The Case For Bank Mergers

Since their 1998 merger announcement, the four chartered banks have consistently argued that in order to compete effectively in the *world* market for financial

Looking Forward

The 1986 *Competition Act* will not be the end of the evolution of Canadian competition policy, but it appears to have marked the end of a major chapter. Canadian legislation has for a long time provided substantial protection to consumers against the misuse of market power by large firms. For the first time, it now also seems to provide some substantial protection against the creation, through mergers, of market power that is not justified by gains to efficiency or international competitiveness.

services, they needed to achieve larger scale. They argue that their current small scale prevents them from participating in the financing of many large international projects, and therefore a ban on mergers would preclude them from competing in the global financial market. In addition, they argue that mergers would allow them to spread some of their enormous fixed costs (such as computing systems) over a much larger customer base, thereby achieving reductions in their average costs. Indeed, some recent empirical research by the Bank of Canada suggests that a doubling of output by a Canadian chartered bank (roughly what would happen if two of the banks merged and consolidated these large fixed costs) would reduce average total costs by between 6 and 20 percent.*

The banks also argue that their large branch banking networks are *not* the entry barrier they once were. With the rise of the Internet and telephone banking, companies based elsewhere in the world can easily offer an entire range of financial services—deposits, mortgages, credit cards, and asset management—to Canadians without having to establish a *physical* presence in the Canadian market. As a result, the Canadian market for financial services is much more competitive than would be suggested by the simple observation that the six largest banks have over 90 percent of the established branches.

An Added Twist

By 2006, a new issue was added to the debate. In addition to bank mergers, the chartered banks were pushing to be permitted to sell insurance inside their bank branches—an additional financial product that would fit naturally within the suite of financial services that banks already provide to their customers. The banks

argue that by allowing them to sell insurance, the level of competition in that market would rise and services to consumers would improve. Not surprisingly, independent insurance brokers are generally opposed to the possibility that firms as large and successful as Canadian chartered banks might suddenly appear as direct competitors. As of 2006, banks *can* own insurance companies but they are prohibited from selling insurance products inside their bank branches. In some cases, the chartered banks simply establish branches of their insurance companies right beside their bank branches, giving their banking customers easy access to the insurance products being sold next door. Many observers think this is merely the first step toward new legislation that will allow chartered banks to openly compete with the insurance companies.

A Resolution on the Merger Issue?

At the time this book went to print (late fall 2006), the issue of bank mergers had not yet been resolved. In 2006, the newly elected Conservative government under Prime Minister Stephen Harper was showing no sign that this issue was a priority. But many people think it is only a matter of time before the government again closely reviews the issue. When that time comes, the difficulty for the Minister of Finance (aside from the political issues involved) will be to determine the relative merits of the two arguments above. A final decision will require weighing the magnitude of the possible cost reductions against the importance of the potential lessening in competition.

---

*See J. Allen and Y. Liu, "Efficiency and Economies of Scale of Large Canadian Banks," Bank of Canada Working Paper 2005-13.

What type of reforms might we expect in the years ahead? The ongoing process of globalization poses two challenges for Canadian competition policy. First, as the flow of goods and services across national boundaries increases, it becomes more important to define markets on an international rather than a national basis. For example, consider the Canadian banking industry. With the continuing development of the Internet, it becomes possible for foreign-based banks to sell some financial services to Canadians without establishing a costly *physical* presence in Canada—such as a network of branches. In this case, the appropriate definition of the market (for the case of assessing the impact of a merger) is larger than just the one defined by Canada's borders.

The second challenge posed by globalization is the desirability of standardizing competition policy across countries. Firms that are mobile and have considerable market power may tend to locate their firms where competition policy is the most lax, exporting into other countries. To avoid such socially inefficient locational choices, countries have an incentive to standardize their competition policy—in this case, firms would choose their locations on the basis of economic rather than legal forces.

These are challenges for the near future. Time will tell how Canadian competition authorities respond.

SUMMARY

12.1 PRODUCTIVE AND ALLOCATIVE EFFICIENCY

- Economists distinguish two main kinds of efficiency: productive and allocative.
- Productive efficiency for the firm requires that the firm be producing its output at the lowest possible cost. Productive efficiency for the industry requires that all firms in the industry have the same marginal cost.
- Allocative efficiency in an individual industry exists when the level of output is such that the marginal cost

of production equals the market price. The overall economy is allocatively efficient when price equals marginal cost in all industries simultaneously.
- Productive efficiency and allocative efficiency are both achieved in perfect competition.
- Monopoly is allocatively inefficient because price exceeds marginal cost. Monopoly leads to a deadweight loss for the economy.

12.2 ECONOMIC REGULATION TO PROMOTE EFFICIENCY

- Two broad types of policies are designed to promote allocative efficiency in imperfectly competitive markets. These can be divided into *economic regulations* and *competition policy*. Economic regulation is used both in the case of a natural monopoly and in the case of an oligopolistic industry. Competition policy applies more to the latter.
- Marginal-cost pricing is allocatively efficient but will lead the firm to make economic losses if it is on the declining portion of the *ATC* curve.

- Average-cost pricing allows the firm to break even but leads to allocative inefficiency (because price is not equal to marginal cost).
- Two-part tariffs can allow the firm with falling long-run costs to break even and also be consistent with allocative efficiency.
- The deregulation of oligopolistic industries has been based on the observations that: (1) oligopolistic industries are major engines of growth, and (2) direct control of such industries has produced disappointing results in the past.

12.3 CANADIAN COMPETITION POLICY

- Canadian competition policy is designed to restrict mergers and trade practices that unduly lessen competition.
- In the past, mergers were criminal offences and difficult to prosecute. The current legislation allows civil cases to be brought against firms, making prosecution less difficult.

- The *Competition Act* of 1986 established a Competition Tribunal to adjudicate cases brought to it by the Competition Bureau.
- In the case of mergers, the Competition Bureau and Tribunal must consider whether the merger will generate cost reductions that will offset the effects of any lessening of competition.

KEY CONCEPTS

Productive and allocative efficiency
Consumer and producer surplus
The allocative efficiency of
   competition

The allocative inefficiency of
   monopoly
Regulation of natural monopolies
Marginal- and average-cost pricing

Two-part tariffs
Regulation of oligopolies
Deregulation and privatization
Canadian competition policy

STUDY EXERCISES

1. **myeconlab** Summer Tees and Fancy Tees are two firms producing T-shirts. The table below shows the average cost of producing T-shirts for the two companies.

Summer Tees				Fancy Tees			
Quantity	ATC	TC	MC	Quantity	ATC	TC	MC
5	$ 8	—		5	$ 9	—	
10	7	—	—	10	7	—	—
15	6	—	—	15	6	—	—
20	6	—	—	20	5	—	—
25	7	—	—	25	5.50	—	—
30	9	—	—	30	6.50	—	—
35	11	—	—	35	8	—	—

a. Calculate *TC* and *MC* for both companies and fill in the table.
b. Draw, in two separate diagrams, the *ATC* and *MC* curves for each firm.
c. Summer Tees is initially producing 30 shirts; Fancy Tees is initially producing 15 shirts. What is the total industry production cost?
d. Now suppose that Summer Tees produces 10 fewer shirts. By how much do its costs fall?
e. Suppose that Fancy Tees produces 10 more shirts. By how much do its costs rise?
f. If the two firms are to produce 45 shirts in total, what is the cost-minimizing way to allocate production between the two firms? (Assume that production must be changed by increments of five shirts, as shown in the table.)

2. Fill in the blanks to make the following statements correct.

a. If the marginal cost of producing the last unit of a product is the same for all firms in an industry, we can say that the industry is _____ efficient, but we do not know enough to say that the industry is _____ efficient.

b. If the marginal cost of some product is $12, and the market price of that product is $15, then to achieve allocative efficiency, the economy should produce _____ of this product and therefore _____ of other products.
c. The market structure that leads to both productive and allocative efficiency is _____.
d. A monopolistic industry may be productively efficient but will not be allocatively efficient because _____.
e. The sum of consumer surplus and producer surplus is _____ at the competitive equilibrium.
f. At the monopolist's profit-maximizing output there is _____ total surplus than at the competitive output. Some surplus is transferred from _____ to _____. The surplus lost because the output is not produced is called _____.

3. **myeconlab** Assume that the market for eggs is perfectly competitive. The diagram shows the demand and supply for eggs.

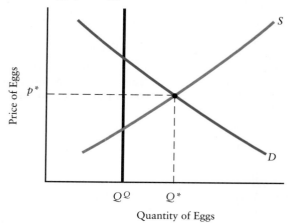

a. At the free-market equilibrium, *p** and *Q**, show what areas represent consumer and producer surplus.

b. Now suppose the egg producers organize themselves and establish a system of quotas. Each farmer's output is restricted by an amount to keep aggregate output at Q^Q. What happens to industry price?

c. In the quota system in part (b), what areas now represent consumer and producer surplus? Is the quota system allocatively efficient? Explain.

4. The diagram below shows supply and demand in the labour market.

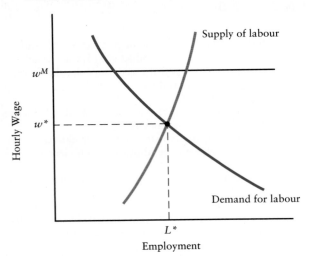

a. At the free-market equilibrium, w^* and L^*, show what areas represent consumer and producer surplus.

b. Now suppose the government establishes a minimum wage at w^M. What is the level of employment in this case?

c. In the situation of part (b), what areas now represent consumer and producer surplus? Is the outcome allocatively efficient? Explain.

5. The diagram below shows the demand, marginal cost, and marginal revenue curves for a monopolist. Redraw the diagram for yourself to be able to answer the following questions.

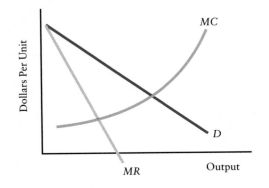

a. If the monopolist charges its single profit-maximizing price, show what areas are consumer surplus and producer surplus.

b. Now suppose the industry is perfectly competitive and the industry supply curve is given by the MC curve. What areas would be consumer and producer surplus in this case?

c. Use the concept of surplus to explain the economic argument against monopoly and in favour of competition.

d. Consider again the situation of monopoly, but now assume the firm can *perfectly* price discriminate—that is, it can charge a different price for every unit of the good. What areas now represent consumer and producer surplus?

e. Does the possibility of perfect price discrimination lead you to change your argument from part (c)? Are there considerations other than allocative efficiency that might be important here?

6. The diagram below shows the production possibilities boundary for a country that produces only two goods, limes and coconuts. Assume that resources are fully employed at points A, B, C, and D.

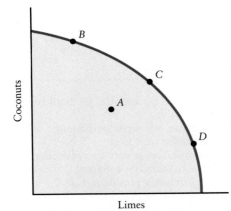

a. Suppose individual firms in the lime industry are not producing at their minimum possible cost. Which point(s) could represent this situation?

b. Suppose all firms and both industries are productively efficient. Which points could represent this situation?

c. Suppose point B occurs when the lime industry is monopolized but the coconut industry is perfectly competitive. Is point B allocatively efficient? Is it productively efficient?

d. Suppose point D occurs when the coconut industry is monopolized but the lime industry is perfectly competitive. Is point D allocatively efficient? Is it productively efficient?

e. Suppose point C is allocatively efficient. What do we know about each industry in this case?

7. Fill in the blanks to make the following statements correct.

   a. The term *natural monopoly* refers to an industry where only a single firm can operate at its _____.

   b. A regulated natural monopoly that is forced to set its price equal to marginal cost will earn _____ if its average costs are falling.

   c. A regulated natural monopoly that is subject to average-cost pricing and operating on the downward-sloping portion of its average cost curve will earn _____ profits. Since price _____ marginal cost, this outcome will not be allocatively efficient.

   d. Marginal-cost pricing for a natural monopoly is an efficient pricing system, but it leads to _____ for the firm if average costs are falling.

8. The following diagram shows the *ATC* and *MC* curves for a natural monopoly—average costs are falling over the entire range of the demand curve.

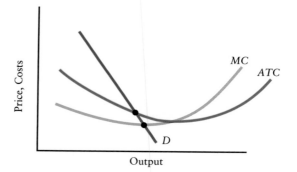

   a. Identify what price and quantity would exist if the firm were required by regulators to set price equal to average cost.

   b. In the diagram, show the profits (or losses) in this case.

   c. Would the outcome be allocatively efficient? Explain why or why not.

   d. Suppose now that the firm were required by regulators to set price equal to marginal cost. What would be the price and quantity in this case?

   e. In the diagram, show the profits (or losses) in this case.

   f. Would the outcome be allocatively efficient? Explain why or why not.

9. One important factor that the Canadian Competition Bureau must consider when assessing the likely effects of a merger is the definition of the market. Discuss how geography is likely to affect the definition of the market for the following products:

   a. Fresh-baked breads and cakes
   b. Cement
   c. Gold jewellery
   d. Computer hardware

DISCUSSION QUESTIONS

1. Suppose allocative inefficiency of some economy amounts to 5 percent of the value of production. What does this statement mean? If it is true, would consumers *as a whole* be better off if policy measures were successful in moving the economy to an allocatively efficient outcome? Would *every* consumer be better off if the economy moved to an allocatively efficient outcome?

2. Evaluate the wisdom of having the Competition Bureau use profits as a measure of monopoly power in deciding whether to prosecute a case. Would such a rule be expected to affect the behaviour of firms with high profits? In what ways might any changes induced by such a rule be socially beneficial, and in what ways might they be socially harmful?

3. It is often asserted that whenever a regulatory agency is established, ultimately it will become controlled by the people whom it was intended to regulate. (This argument raises the question of who regulates the regulators.) Can you identify why this phenomenon might happen? How might the integrity of regulatory boards be protected?

4. This chapter has identified several strategies for dealing with natural monopolies and their associated inefficiencies. Alternatively, assume that you are a regulator and that the monopoly you face is able to price discriminate—perhaps perfectly. Does this ability change the options you have for encouraging the efficient level of production? Would you choose to use this additional option? Why or why not?

5. "Canadian air travellers opting for U.S. carriers were [partly] responsible for Canadian airlines deregulation."

—C. D. Howe Institute

"Canadian consumers crossing the border to buy cheap U.S. agricultural products may be responsible for the end of supply management in Canada."

—Canadian economist

What market forces lie behind each of these quotations? What difficulties do they reveal for the regulation of particular industries?

6. "Allocative efficiency is really about whether the economy 'has the quantities right'—it is not really about prices at all. Prices are important only in a discussion about allocative efficiency because *in a free market* changes in prices bring about the efficient allocation of resources."

Comment.

CHAPTER 13

How Factor Markets Work

LO **LEARNING OBJECTIVES**

In this chapter you will learn

1. about the size and functional distributions of income in Canada.
2. what determines a profit-maximizing firm's demand for a factor.
3. about the role of factor mobility in determining factor supply.
4. how to distinguish between temporary and equilibrium factor-price differentials.
5. how economic rent is related to factor mobility.

What determines the wages that individuals earn? What explains why neurosurgeons usually are paid more than family doctors, or why movie stars are paid more than the "extras"? Labour is not the only factor of production, of course. Physical capital and land are also important. What determines the payments that these factors earn? Why does an acre of farm land in Northern Saskatchewan rent for much less than an acre of land in downtown Toronto? Not surprisingly, understanding why different factors of production earn different payments requires us to understand both demand-side and supply-side aspects of the relevant factor markets.

In this chapter we examine the issue of factor pricing and the closely related issue of factor mobility. Understanding what determines the payments to different factors of production will help us to understand the overall distribution of income in the economy, which is where we begin.

13.1 INCOME DISTRIBUTION

The founders of Classical economics, Adam Smith (1723–1790) and David Ricardo (1772–1823), were concerned with the distribution of income among what were then the three great social classes: workers, capitalists, and landowners. They defined three factors of production as labour, capital, and land. The payment to each factor was treated as the income of the respective social class.

Smith and Ricardo were interested in what determined the share of total income that each class received. Their theories predicted that as society progressed, landlords would become relatively better off and capitalists would become relatively worse off. Karl Marx (1818–1883) had a different theory, which predicted that as growth occurred, capitalists would become relatively better off and workers would become relatively worse off (until the whole capitalist system collapsed).

functional distribution of income The distribution of national income among the major factors of production: labour, capital, and land.

size distribution of income The distribution of income among individuals, without regard to source of income.

These nineteenth-century debates focused on what is now called the **functional distribution of income**, defined as the distribution of national income among the major factors of production. Modern economists, however, emphasize the **size distribution of income**. This refers to the distribution of income among different individuals without reference to the source of the income or the "social class" of the individual.

If we want to measure and understand the income inequality between individuals, the size distribution of income is a better indicator than is the functional distribution of income. The reason is that income classes no longer coincide closely with "social" classes. Many capitalists, such as the owners of small retail stores, are in the lower part of the income scale. Conversely, many wage earners, such as professional athletes, are in the upper income scale. Furthermore, it is becoming increasingly difficult to distinguish "workers" from "capitalists." Through employer-sponsored pension plans, workers now own much more of the country's capital than do the richer "non-working" capitalists.

Figure 13-1 shows that even among full-time, full-year workers, there was substantial inequality in the distribution of (pre-tax) income across individuals in 2000, the most recent year for which Census data are available. Another way to show the size

FIGURE 13-1 Earnings of Full-Time, Full-Year Workers

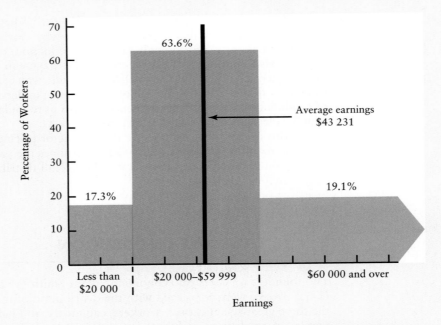

There is considerable inequality in the distribution of (pre-tax) earned income, even among full-time workers. At the time of Canada's most recent Census, just over 19 percent of full-time workers earned more than $60 000 per year; 17.3 percent earned less than $20 000. Nearly two-thirds of full-time workers earned between $20 000 and $60 000 per year. With perfect equality of income, all individuals would have the same earnings. In this case, the figure would show a single bar of height 100 percent at the average income level—$43 231 in the year 2000.

(*Source*: These data are from the 2001 Census and are available on Statistics Canada's website: www.statcan.ca. Click on "Census" and go to "Data and Analysis." Then click on "Search by Topic" and go to "Earnings of Canadians." Reprinted with permission of Statistics Canada.)

distribution of income is found in Figure 13-2. The curve in the figure is a **Lorenz curve,** showing how much of total income goes to different proportions of the nation's families. If every family had the same income, 20 percent of total income would go to 20 percent of families, 40 percent of total income would go to 40 percent of families, and so on. In this case, the Lorenz curve would lie exactly along the diagonal. The farther the curve bends away from the diagonal, the less equal the distribution of income. The curve in Figure 13-2 shows that at the time of Canada's most recent Census in 2001, the bottom 20 percent of all Canadian families received 5.2 percent of all pretax income, whereas the highest-income 20 percent of families received 43.6 percent of all pre-tax income.

To understand the size distribution of income, we must first study how individual incomes are determined. Superficial explanations of differences in income, such as "People earn according to their ability," are inadequate. Incomes are distributed much more unequally than any *measured* index of ability, be it IQ, physical strength, or typing skill. The best professional sports players may only score twice as many points as the average players, but their salary is many times more than the average salary. Something other than simple ability is at work here. However, if answers that are couched in terms of ability are easily refuted, so are answers such as "It's all a matter of luck" or "It's just the system." In this chapter, we look beyond such superficial explanations.

Lorenz curve A graph showing the extent of inequality of income distribution.

FIGURE 13-2   The Lorenz Curve for Family Income

	Families		Income	
	Percentage	Cumulative Percentage	Percentage	Cumulative Percentage
A	Lowest 20	20	5.2	5.2
B	Second-lowest 20	40	11.3	16.5
C	Middle 20	60	16.7	33.2
D	Second-highest 20	80	23.3	56.5
E	Highest 20	100	43.6	100.0

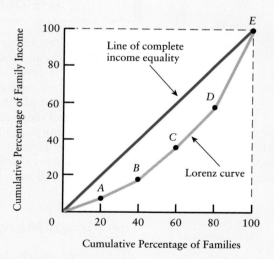

The size of the area between the Lorenz curve and the diagonal is a measure of the inequality of income distribution. If there were complete income equality, the bottom 20 percent of income receivers would receive 20 percent of total income, and so forth, and the Lorenz curve would coincide with the diagonal line.

(*Source:* These data are from the 2001 Census and are available on Statistics Canada's website: www.statcan.ca. Click on "Census" and go to "Analysis Series." Then go to "Income of Canadian Families." Reprinted with permission of Statistics Canada.)

A Glimpse of the Theory Ahead

In this chapter, we confine ourselves to factor markets that are perfectly competitive. As a result, the firms we study face a given price of each factor that they buy. Similarly, owners of factors face a given price for the factor services that they sell.

Dealing first with competitive factor markets allows us to study the principles of factor-price determination in the simplest context. Once these principles are understood, it is relatively easy to extend the theory to more complicated settings. This is done for labour markets in Chapter 14.

Goods markets and factor markets are closely related. Firms' production decisions imply specific demands for the various factors of production. These demands, together with the supplies of the factors of production (which are determined by the owners of the factors), come together in factor markets. Together they determine the quantities of the various factors of production that are employed, their prices, and the incomes earned by their owners. This relationship between goods markets and factor markets leads to one of the great insights about economics:

When demand and supply interact to determine the prices and quantities of various goods, they also determine the incomes of the factors that are used in producing the goods.

The rest of this chapter is an elaboration of this important theme. We first study the demand for factors, then their supply, and finally how demand and supply come together to determine equilibrium factor prices and quantities.

13.2 THE DEMAND FOR FACTORS

Firms require the services of land, labour, and capital to be used as inputs. Firms also use as inputs the products of other firms, such as steel, legal services, computer software, and electricity.

Firms require inputs not for their own sake but as a means to produce goods and services. For example, the demand for computer programmers and technicians is growing as more and more computers and software are produced. The demand for carpenters and building materials rises and falls as the amount of housing construction rises and falls. The demand for any input is therefore *derived from the demand* for the goods and services that it helps to produce; for this reason, the demand for a factor of production is said to be a **derived demand**.

> **derived demand** The demand for a factor of production that results from the demand for the products that it is used to make.

The Firm's Marginal Decision on Factor Use

What determines whether an individual firm will choose to hire one extra worker, or whether the same firm will decide to use one extra machine, or an extra kilowatt-hour of electricity? Since we are considering whether the firm will use *one extra unit* of some factor, we refer to this as the firm's *marginal* decision on factor use.

As we have seen in earlier chapters, any profit-maximizing firm increases its output until its marginal cost equals its marginal revenue. Since producing more output requires hiring more factors of production, we can describe this decision another way—the firm will increase its use of any factor of production until the last unit of the factor adds as much to revenue as it does to costs.

When a firm hires one more unit of a factor, the firm's total costs rise. This increase in total cost is the factor's marginal cost. For example, if the going wage in a competitive labour market is $10 per hour, then labour's marginal cost is $10.

Hiring an extra unit of the factor also leads to an increase in the firm's output and revenue. The increase in the firm's revenue attributed to this extra unit of the factor is called the factor's **marginal revenue product (MRP)**. The factor's *MRP* has two components—a *physical* component and a *dollar* component. The physical component is how much one unit of the factor adds to total output. This is the factor's *marginal product*, a concept discussed in detail in Chapter 7. The dollar component is the amount that total revenue rises per extra unit of output. This is the firm's *marginal revenue*, a concept discussed in both Chapters 9 and 10.

A railway's demand for locomotives—a factor input—is derived from the demand for the product it provides—transportation services.

The factor's marginal revenue product is simply the combination of this physical component and this dollar component—it is the marginal product (*MP*) times the firm's marginal revenue (*MR*). [26] For example, if the factor's marginal product is 2 units and the firm's marginal revenue is $7.50, the factor's *MRP* is $15 ($7.50 × 2).

marginal revenue product (MRP) The extra revenue that results from using one unit more of a variable factor.

We can now restate the condition for a firm to be maximizing its profits:

$$\frac{\text{Marginal cost}}{\text{of the factor}} = \frac{\text{Marginal revenue product}}{\text{of the factor}} \qquad (13\text{-}1)$$

This condition applies to *any* firm and any factor, in any market structure. In the special case of competitive goods and factor markets, however, we can simplify the equation. In competitive factor markets the marginal cost of the factor is simply the factor's price, since the firm can hire any amount of the factor at a given price. Call this factor price *w*. Also, we know that in competitive goods markets, the firm's *MR* is just the market price of the product, *p*. It follows that *MRP* is equal to *MP* × *p*. Thus, the condition for profit maximization becomes

$$w = MP \times p \qquad (13\text{-}2)$$

To check your understanding of Equation 13-2, consider an example. Suppose labour is available to the firm at a cost of $10 per hour (*w* = $10). Suppose also that employing another hour of labour adds 3 units to output (*MP* = 3). Suppose further that any amount of output can be sold for $5 per unit (*p* = $5). Thus, the additional hour of labour adds $15 to the firm's revenue but only $10 to its costs. In this case, the firm will increase profits by hiring more hours of labour.

Now suppose, however, that the last hour of labour hired by the firm has a marginal product of 1 unit of output and so adds only $5 to revenue. In this case, the firm can increase profits by reducing its use of labour.

Finally, suppose another hour of labour adds to revenue by $10. Now the firm cannot increase its profits by altering its use of labour in either direction.

To maximize its profits, any firm must hire each factor of production to the point where the factor's marginal revenue product equals the factor's price.

In Chapters 9 and 10, we saw the firm varying its output until the marginal cost of producing another unit was equal to the marginal revenue derived from selling that unit. Now we see the same profit-maximizing behaviour in terms of the firm's varying its inputs until the marginal cost of another unit of input is just equal to the extra revenue derived from selling that unit's marginal product.

The Firm's Demand Curve for a Factor

Practise with Study Guide Chapter 13, Exercise 1.

We now know what determines the quantity of a variable factor a profit-maximizing firm will buy when facing some specific price of the factor and some specific price of its output. Next, we wish to derive the firm's *entire* demand curve for a factor, which tells us how much of the factor the firm will buy at *each* price.

To derive a firm's demand curve for a factor, we start by considering the right-hand side of Equation 13-1, which tells us that the factor's marginal revenue product is composed of a physical component and a dollar component. We examine these two components in turn.

The Physical Component: MP As the quantity of the variable factor changes, output will change. The hypothesis of diminishing marginal returns, first discussed in Chapter 7, predicts what will happen: As the firm adds further units of the variable factor to a given quantity of the fixed factor, the additions to output will eventually get smaller and smaller. In other words, the factor's marginal product declines, as shown in part (i) of Figure 13-3.

The Dollar Component: MR To convert the marginal product curve of Figure 13-3(i) into a curve showing the marginal revenue product of the factor, we need to know the dollar value of the extra output. Part (ii) of Figure 13-3 shows a marginal revenue product curve in the case where the firm sells its product in a competitive market at a price (and *MR*) of $5 per unit. The *MRP* curve represents *MP* × *MR* for each additional unit of the factor. Since the *MR* for a firm in perfect competition is simply equal to the price of the product, the *MRP* curve has the same shape as the *MP* curve.

From MRP to the Demand Curve Equation 13-2 states that a profit-maximizing competitive firm will employ additional units of the factor up to the point at which the *MRP* equals the price of the factor. For example, in Figure 13-3, if the price of hiring one unit of the factor were $2000 per month, the profit-maximizing firm would employ 60 units of the factor. However, if hiring an extra unit of the factor cost $3000 per month, the firm would only choose to hire 45 units. It should be clear that since the *MRP* curve shows how many units of the factor will be hired at different factor prices, the factor's *MRP* curve is the firm's demand curve for the factor.

A competitive firm's demand curve for a factor is given by that factor's *MRP* curve.

This logic applies equally to any factor of production. A profit-maximizing farmer will rent land up to the point where the marginal revenue product from an extra acre of land is just equal to the rental price for that acre of land. A profit-maximizing machine-tools manufacturer will use extra machines (capital) until the marginal revenue product from an extra machine just equals the price of using that machine. And a profit-maximizing paper mill will hire workers up to the point where the marginal revenue product of an extra worker is just equal to that worker's wage.

FIGURE 13-3   From Marginal Product to Demand Curve

(i) The *MP* curve

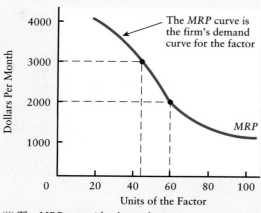

(ii) The *MRP* curve (the demand curve)

The law of diminishing marginal returns implies that firms have a negatively sloped demand curve for factors of production. In part (i), the *MP* curve for a factor is downward sloping because of the law of diminishing marginal returns. If the firm uses 60 units of the factor per month, the factor's *MP* will be 400 units of output per month. In part (ii), it is assumed that each unit of the firm's output can be sold at $5. If the firm uses 60 units of the factor per month, the factor's *MRP* is $2000 (400 units per month × $5 per unit). Since the *MRP* curve shows, for each separate factor price, how many units of the factor will be hired by a profit-maximizing firm, the *MRP* curve is the firm's demand curve for the factor.

Note that if the firm is not perfectly competitive in its product market, each additional unit of output produced leads to a decline in the product's price. In this case, the firm's *MR* decreases as output increases and so the factor's *MRP* curve is steeper than the one shown here.

Elasticity of Factor Demand

The elasticity of demand for a factor measures the *degree* of the response of the quantity demanded to a change in its price. The preceding sections have explained the *direction* of the response; that is, that quantity demanded is negatively related to price. But you should not be surprised to learn that the magnitude of the response depends on the strength of various effects. For example, the extent of diminishing returns to labour and the ability of the firm to substitute between labour and other factors of production will both affect the firm's elasticity of demand for labour.

Diminishing Returns The first influence on the slope of the demand curve for a factor is the diminishing marginal product of that factor. If marginal product declines rapidly as more of a factor is employed, a fall in the factor's price will not induce many more units to be employed. This is the case of a relatively steep *MP* curve, and thus *MRP* curve, in Figure 13-3. Conversely, if marginal product falls only slowly as more of a factor is employed, there will be a large increase in quantity demanded as price falls. This is the case of a relatively flat *MP* curve, and thus *MRP* curve, in Figure 13-3.

Substitution Between Factors In the long run, all factors are variable. If one factor's price rises, profit-maximizing firms will substitute relatively cheaper factors for it. (This is the *principle of substitution,* which we first encountered in Chapter 8.) For this reason, the slope of the demand curve for a factor is influenced by the ease with which other factors can be substituted for the factor whose price has changed.

The ease of substitution depends on the substitutes that are available and on the technical conditions of production. It is often possible to vary factor proportions in surprising ways. For example, in automobile manufacturing and in building construction, glass and steel can be substituted for each other simply by varying the dimensions of the windows.

Importance of the Factor Other things being equal, the more important is a factor in producing some good, the greater the elasticity of demand for that factor.

To see this, suppose that for some particular firm wages account for 50 percent of the marginal costs of producing a good and raw materials account for 10 percent. A 20-percent rise in the price of labour raises the firm's marginal costs by 10 percent (20 percent of 50 percent), but a 20-percent rise in the price of raw materials raises the firm's marginal costs by only 2 percent (20-percent of 10 percent). The larger the increase in marginal costs, the more the firm reduces its level of output and hence reduces its demand for factors of production. So, in this case, a 20-percent rise in the price of labour leads to a large decline in the amount of labour used; in contrast, the same 20-percent increase in the price of raw materials leads to only a small reduction in the amount of raw materials used. In other words, the firm's demand for labour (the more important factor) is more elastic than its demand for raw materials (the less important factor).

Elasticity of Demand for the Output Other things being equal, the more elastic is the demand for the product that the factor is used to produce, the more elastic is the demand for the factor.

If an increase in the price of the product causes a large decrease in the quantity demanded—that is, if the demand for the product is highly elastic—there will be a large decrease in the quantity of a factor needed to produce it in response to a rise in the factor's price. However, if an increase in the price of a product causes only a small decrease in the quantity demanded—that is, if the demand for the product is inelastic—there will be only a small decrease in the quantity of the factor required in response to a rise in its price. Figure 13-4 illustrates this principle in the case where the price of the factor falls and hence each firm's marginal cost curve—and thus the industry supply curve—shifts to the right.

We have discussed a firm's demand curve for any specific factor of production and have examined what influences the elasticity of demand for that factor. Two issues remain to be discussed. First, how do

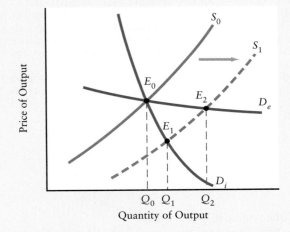

FIGURE 13-4 More Elastic Product Demand Leads to More Elastic Factor Demand

The more elastic the demand for the product, the more elastic the demand for the factors that are used to make it. The original demand and supply curves for the industry's product intersect at E_0 to produce an industry output of Q_0. A fall in the price of a factor reduces firms' costs and causes the industry supply curve to shift to S_1.

When demand for the product is relatively inelastic, as shown by the curve D_i, industry output increases by only a small amount, to Q_1. The quantity of the factor demanded increases by a correspondingly small amount.

When demand for the product is relatively elastic, as shown by the curve D_e, industry output increases by a large amount to Q_2. The quantity of the factor demanded then increases by a correspondingly large amount.

we get from a firm's demand for a factor to the overall market demand? Second, what causes a shift in the market demand curve for various factors of production?

The Market Demand Curve for a Factor

We saw in Chapter 6 that the market demand curve for any good or service is simply the horizontal summation of all the individual consumers' demand curves. With factor demand curves, the same basic logic applies except for one important complication. As all firms hire more of any specific factor of production, the supplies of the goods produced by that factor increase and the prices of these products fall. This decline in product prices leads firms to increase their hiring of the factors by less than would otherwise occur. The result is that the *market* demand curve for any specific factor of production is *less elastic* than would be the case if we took a simple horizontal summation of the individual firms' factor demand curves.

An example will clarify this point. Consider a competitive furniture-building industry and the individual firms' demand for carpenters. Any one firm's production of furniture will have no significant effect on the equilibrium price of furniture, and so its hiring of carpenters similarly has no effect on the market price of furniture. But all furniture-building firms taken together *do* have an effect on the equilibrium price of furniture. As *all* such firms increase their hiring of carpenters, the total supply of furniture increases and the equilibrium price of furniture declines. As the price falls, each firm will reduce its hiring of carpenters, offsetting to some extent the initial increase in hiring.

The market demand curve for any factor of production is less elastic than what would result from a simple horizontal summation of all the firms' demand curves for that factor.

Practise with Study Guide Chapter 13, Short-Answer Question 2.

Shifts of the Market Factor Demand Curve

Why might the market demand curve for a factor shift? To answer this question, let's go back and think about what is happening at the level of the individual firms. If we know why individual firms' factor demand curves shift, we will also know why the *market* factor demand curve shifts.

Figure. 13-3 illustrated a firm's demand curve for a factor of production and showed that the factor's *MRP* curve was also the firm's demand curve for that factor. Since *MRP* is equal to *MP* times *MR*, there are two reasons why the demand curve for a factor can shift—because of a shift in the factor's *MP* curve or because of a change in firms' *MR*.

Practise with Study Guide Chapter 13, Short-Answer Question 3.

A Change in the Factor's Marginal Product Anything that changes the marginal product of a factor will change the *MP* curve and therefore the *MRP* curve in Figure 13-3. Improvements in technology often increase the marginal product of factors of production, and thus lead to a rightward shift of the *MP* curve. For example, if better education increases the marginal product of labour, the *MP* curve for labour will shift to the right, firms' demand for labour will increase, and firms will hire more labour at any given wage.

A second way in which the marginal product of a factor can increase is if there are more units of other factors with which to work. An increase in the amount of capital, for example, will generally increase the marginal product of any given amount of labour. Suppose that Figure 13-3 shows the marginal product (and *MRP*) for labour under the assumption that the firm has a given stock of capital. If the firm now expands its capital stock by building a larger factory, the marginal product of any given amount of labour will increase, thus shifting the *MP* curve in part (i) to the right. The result will be that the *MRP* curve in part (ii) also shifts to the right, thus increasing the firm's demand for labour.

Any increase in a factor's marginal product will lead to an increase in demand for that factor. Such an increase can come about through improvements in the quality of the factor or an increase in the amount of other factors of production.

A Change in Firms' Marginal Revenue Anything that increases firms' marginal revenue will increase the *MRP* of a factor and thus lead to an increase in demand for that factor. For firms that operate in a competitive product market, an increase in marginal revenue is simply an increase in the market price of the product. In Figure 13-3, if the product price rises from $5 to $10, the *MRP* curve shifts to the right (even though the *MP* curve does not move). For imperfectly competitive firms, an increase in *MR* occurs if the demand curve faced by those firms shifts to the right. In both cases, the increase in *MR* leads to an increase in the demand for the factor.

Anything that leads to an increase in demand for a product will lead to an increase in demand for the factors used to produce that product.

13.3 THE SUPPLY OF FACTORS

When we consider the supply of any factor of production, we can consider supply at three different levels of aggregation:

- the amount supplied to the economy as a whole
- the amount supplied to a particular industry
- the amount supplied to a particular firm

This individual seeking employment has decided to supply her labour services to the economy's labour market. But she must still decide to which industry and to which firm she will supply her services.

To illustrate, consider your decision to seek employment—to supply your labour services to the labour market. You must make three general decisions. First, you must decide whether to supply your labour services at all, the alternative being not to seek employment. Your decision will influence the overall supply of labour to the economy (though only by a tiny amount). Second, once you have decided to supply your labour services, you must choose an industry and occupation. Your decision to seek employment in the telecommunications industry rather than the automobile manufacturing industry influences the economy's allocation of labour across industries. Third, once you have decided to seek employment in a particular industry, you must choose which firms in that industry appeal to you. Your decision influences the allocation of labour across firms.

The elasticity of supply of a factor will normally be different at each of these levels of aggregation because the amount of *factor mobility* is different at these different levels of aggregation. A given factor of production is often very mobile between firms within a given industry, less mobile between different industries, and even less mobile from the perspective of the entire economy. For example, an electrician may be very mobile between industries within a given city, and reasonably mobile between provinces, but it may be very difficult for that electrician to move to another country to find a job. In this section, we examine the relationship between factor mobility and the supply of factors of production. We start with the highest level of aggregation, the supply of each factor to the economy as a whole.

The Supply of Factors to the Economy

At any one time, the total supply of each factor of production is given. For example, in each country, the labour force is of a certain size, so much arable land is available, and there is a given supply of discovered petroleum. However, these supplies can and do change. Sometimes the change is very gradual, as when climate change slowly turns arable land into desert or when medical advances reduce the rate of infant mortality and increase the rate of population growth, thereby eventually increasing the supply of adult labour. Sometimes the changes can be quite rapid, as when a boom in business activity brings retired persons back into the labour force.

Physical Capital   The capital stock in a country is the existing machines, factories, and equipment. Capital is a manufactured factor of production, and its total supply changes only slowly. Each year, the stock of capital goods is diminished by the amount that becomes physically or economically obsolete and is increased by the amount that is newly produced. On balance, the trend has been for the capital stock to grow from decade to decade over the past few centuries. We will consider the determinants of investment in capital in Chapter 15.

Land   The total area of dry land in a country is almost completely fixed, but the supply of *fertile* land is not. Considerable care and effort are required to sustain the productive power of land. If farmers earn low incomes, they may not provide the necessary care, and the land's fertility may be destroyed within a short time. In contrast, high earnings from farming may provide the incentive to increase the supply of arable land by irrigation and other forms of reclamation.

Labour   The number of people willing to work is called the labour force; the total number of hours they are willing to work is called the *supply of labour*. The supply of labour depends on three influences: the size of the population, the proportion of the population willing to work, and the number of hours that each individual wishes to work. Each of these is partly influenced by economic forces.

Population.   The population of a country varies over time, and these variations are influenced to some extent by economic forces. There is some evidence, for example, that the birthrate and the net immigration rate (immigration minus emigration) are higher in good times than in bad.

Labour-Force Participation.   The proportion of the total population that is willing to work is called the *labour-force participation rate*. Economists also define participation rates for subgroups, such as women or youths. Participation rates vary in response to many influences, including changes in attitudes and tastes. The enormous rise in female participation rates in the past four decades, for example, has had a significant effect on the Canadian labour force.

The significant increase in female labour-force participation that occurred between the 1960s and the 1990s had a significant effect on the growth of Canada's aggregate labour supply.

Changes in real wages also play a role in determining the labour-force participation rate. A rise in the demand for labour, and an accompanying rise in the wage, will lead to an increase in the proportion of the population willing to work. For example, in Alberta in 2006, a booming economy driven by high energy prices increased wages up to the point that there was a notable increase in high-school drop-out rates as some students chose instead to pursue employment in the labour market.

Hours Per Person. The wage rate not only influences the number of people that want to work, but also the number of hours that each person wants to work. When workers sell their labour services to employers, they are giving up leisure in order to gain income with which to buy goods. They can therefore be thought of as trading leisure for goods. A rise in the wage implies a change in the relative price of goods and leisure. An increase in the wage means that leisure becomes more expensive relative to goods, because each hour of leisure consumed is at the cost of more goods forgone.

It is not necessarily the case, however, that an increase in the wage increases the amount of hours worked. In fact, an increase in the wage generates both income and substitution effects (see Chapter 6). As the wage rises, the substitution effect leads the individual to work more hours (consume less leisure) because leisure is now relatively more expensive. The income effect of a higher wage, however, leads the individual to work fewer hours (consume more leisure). Because the two effects work in the opposite direction we are, in general, unsure how a rise in the wage will affect the number of hours an individual chooses to work.

The total supplies of land, labour, and capital each respond to economic forces, but tend to change only gradually.

The Supply of Factors to a Particular Industry

Most factors have many uses. A given piece of land can be used to grow any one of several crops, or it can be subdivided for a housing development. A computer programmer living in the Ottawa Valley can work for one of many firms, for the government, or for Carleton University. A lathe can be used to make many different products, and it requires no adaptation when it is turned for one use or another.

One industry can attract a factor away from another industry, even though the economy's total supply of that factor may be fixed. Thus, a factor's elasticity of supply to a particular industry is larger than its elasticity of supply to the entire economy.

factor mobility The ease with which a factor of production can move between firms, industries, occupations, or regions.

When we consider the supply of a factor for a particular use, the most important concept is **factor mobility**. A factor that shifts easily between uses in response to small changes in incentives is said to be *mobile*. Its supply to any one use will be elastic because a small increase in the price offered will attract many units of the factor from other uses. A factor that does not shift easily from one use to another, even in response to large changes in remuneration, is said to be *immobile*. It will be in inelastic supply in any one use because even a large increase in the price offered will attract only a small inflow from other uses. Generally, a factor is less mobile in the short run than in the long run.

An important determinant of factor mobility is time: The longer the time interval, the easier it is for a factor to convert from one use to another.

Consider the factor mobility among particular uses of each of the three key factors of production.

The Mobility of Capital Some kinds of capital equipment—lathes, trucks, and computers, for example—can be shifted readily among firms, among industries, and even across different regions of the country. These are considered *mobile* capital. Other kinds of capital are quite immobile. For example, some plants and machinery are built for a specific purpose, and are difficult if not impossible to modify for other purposes. Equipment of this type is immobile across uses, although it might be mobile in the sense that one firm could sell it to another. Factories designed for a specific purpose are immobile both across uses and across regions, though they could still be transferred from one owner to another.

The Mobility of Land Land, which is physically the least mobile of factors, is one of the *most* mobile in an economic sense. Consider agricultural land. In a given year, one crop can be harvested and a totally different crop can be planted. A farm on the outskirts of a growing city can be sold for subdivision and development on short notice. Once land is built on, however, its mobility is much reduced.

Although land is highly mobile among alternative uses, it is completely immobile as far as location is concerned. There is only so much land within a given distance of the centre of any city, and no increase in the price paid can induce further land to be located within that distance. This locational immobility has important consequences, including high prices for desirable locations and the tendency to build tall buildings to economize on the use of scarce land. It is no accident that the downtown cores of New York, Hong Kong, Toronto, Chicago, and many other large cities are populated by so many tall buildings.

The Mobility of Labour The supply of labour services often requires the physical presence of the person who supplies it. Absentee landlords, while continuing to live in the place of their choice, can obtain income from land that is located in remote parts of the world. Similarly, investment can be shifted from iron mines in South Africa to mines in Labrador while the mine owners commute between Calgary and Hawaii. The same is true for some workers, such as designers or bookkeepers, who can work in one location and submit their work to clients in other locations. But almost all workers involved in manufacturing and most of those involved in serving the public in stores, restaurants, and so on, must actually be present to supply their labour services to an employer. When a worker who is employed by a firm producing men's ties in Montreal decides instead to supply his or her labour services to a firm producing women's shoes in Winnipeg, the worker must physically travel to Winnipeg. This has an important consequence.

Because of the need for labour's physical presence when its services are provided for the production of many goods, non-monetary considerations are much more important for the supply of labour than for other factors of production.

People may be satisfied with or frustrated by the kind of work that they do, where they do it, the people with whom they do it, and the social status of their occupations. Because these considerations influence their decisions about what they will do with their labour services, they will not always move just because they could earn a higher wage.

Nevertheless, labour is mobile among industries, occupations, and regions in response to changes in the signals provided by wages and opportunities for employment. The ease with which such mobility occurs depends on many forces. For example, it is not difficult for a secretary to shift from one company to another in order to

A cruise ship like this one is very mobile between firms, but almost completely immobile between industries—it is very difficult to convert a cruise ship into any other kind of capital equipment.

take a job in Edmonton instead of Regina, but it can be difficult for a secretary to become an editor, a model, a machinist, or a doctor within a short period of time. Workers who lack ability, training, or inclination find certain kinds of mobility difficult or impossible.

Some barriers to movement may be virtually insurmountable once a person's training has been completed. For example, it may be impossible for a farmer to become a surgeon or for a truck driver to become a professional athlete, even if the relative wage rates change greatly. However, the children of farmers, doctors, truck drivers, and athletes, when they are deciding how much education or training to obtain, are not nearly as limited in their choices as their parents, who have already completed their education and are settled in their occupations.

The labour force as a whole is mobile, even though many individual members in it are not.

One particular case of labour mobility has been actively debated in Canada over the past few years—Canada's alleged "brain drain" to the United States. For more details, look for "Is Canada Suffering a Brain Drain?" in the *Additional Topics* section of this book's MyEconLab.

www.myeconlab.com

The Supply of Factors to a Particular Firm

Most firms usually employ only a very small proportion of the economy's total supply of each factor. As a result, they can usually obtain their factors at the going market price. This is true for labour, capital, and land. For example, a commercial bank that is hoping to expand its economics department can hire an extra economist and it will need to pay the going wage (or salary) to attract that economist. An automotive manufacturer can purchase new robotics equipment and will pay the market price to get it. And a rancher can buy more land at the going market price. In each case the firm's actions will have no effect on the market price for the factors of production.

Individual firms generally face perfectly elastic supply curves for factors, even though the supply for the economy as a whole may be quite inelastic.

▌ 13.4 **THE OPERATION OF FACTOR MARKETS**

Once you have mastered the basic analysis of demand and supply in Chapters 3 through 5, the determination of the price, quantity, and income of a factor in a single market poses no new problems. Figure 13-5 shows a competitive market for a factor. In both parts of the figure, the intersection of the demand and supply curves determines

FIGURE 13-5   Demand and Supply Shifts in a Competitive Factor Market

(i) An increase in factor demand

(ii) An increase in factor supply

Equilibrium factor prices and quantities are determined by the demand for and supply of factors. In both parts of the figure, the initial equilibrium is determined by D_0 and S_0. The equilibrium factor price is w_0 and the equilibrium quantity of the factor is Q_0.

In part (i), an increase in demand for the factor shifts the demand curve to D_1. The equilibrium factor price rises to w_1 and quantity increases to Q_1. Since both price and quantity have increased, the total income earned by the factor clearly increases.

In part (ii), an increase in the supply of the factor shifts the supply curve to S_1. The equilibrium factor price falls to w_1 but the quantity increases to Q_1. Since price falls but quantity rises, the effect on total factor income is unclear. If demand for the factor is inelastic, total factor income will fall; if demand is elastic, total factor income will rise.

the factor's price and the quantity of the factor employed. The total income earned by the factor is given by the equilibrium price times the equilibrium quantity.

Changes in factor markets can occur either because of a change in demand for the factor or because of a change in the supply of the factor, or both. Part (i) of Figure 13-5 illustrates a case in which an increase in demand for a factor leads to a rise in that factor's price and an increase in total income earned by that factor. What could cause such a change? Recall that the market demand curve for any factor comes from the many firms' *MRP* curves for that factor. An increase in the productivity of that factor would lead to a rightward shift in the *MRP* curves and thus to an increase in the market demand for the factor. Indeed, increases in productivity account for a gradual but ongoing increase in the demand for most factors of production.

Part (ii) of Figure 13-5 shows that an increase in the supply of some factor of production leads to a decline in that factor's equilibrium price and an increase in the quantity of the factor employed. (The total income earned by the factor may rise or fall, depending on the elasticity of demand for the factor.) Though the supply of any factor to a specific firm may change suddenly, the supply to the economy as a whole tends to change very gradually. The labour force grows slowly, physical capital accumulates gradually as firms build more capital equipment, and the amount of arable land changes slowly as new land is cleared or reclaimed.

We now go on to explore three issues relating to factor pricing. First, what explains the differences in payments received by different units of the same factor? For example, why do some workers get paid more than others? Second, what is the effectiveness of government policies designed to reduce these differences? Finally, we explore the important concept of *economic rent*.

Differentials in Factor Prices

Airline pilots typically get paid more than auto mechanics. And a hectare of land in downtown Calgary rents for much more than a hectare of land 150 kilometres away in the Crowsnest Pass. Are such *factor-price differentials* to be expected in well-functioning factor markets?

If all workers were the same, if the attractiveness of all jobs were the same, and if workers moved freely among markets, all workers would earn the same wage. Imagine what would happen if wages were different across jobs that were very similar. Workers would move from low-wage to high-wage jobs. The supply of labour would fall in low-wage occupations and the resulting labour shortage would tend to force those wages up. Conversely, the supply of labour would increase in high-wage occupations and would force those wages down. The movement would continue until there were no further incentives to change occupations—that is, until wages were equalized in all uses.

In fact, however, wage differentials commonly occur, as is clear from even the most cursory examination of the help-wanted ads in any newspaper. As it is with labour, so it is with other factors of production. If all units of any factor of production were identical and moved freely among markets, all units would receive the same remuneration in equilibrium. In fact, however, different units of any one factor receive different payments.

Factor-price differentials can be divided into two types: those that exist only temporarily and those that exist in long-run equilibrium.

Temporary factor-price differentials lead to, and are eroded by, factor mobility. Equilibrium differentials in factor prices are not eliminated by factor mobility.

Temporary Differentials   Some factor-price differentials reflect temporary disturbances such as the growth of one industry or the decline of another. The differentials themselves lead to the movement of factors, and such movements in turn act to eliminate the differentials.

Consider the effect on factor prices of a rise in the demand for air transport when there is no change in the demand for rail transport. The airline industry's demand for factors increases while there is no change in demand for factors in the railway industry. Factor prices will rise in the airline industry and create a factor-price differential. The differential in factor prices causes a net movement of factors away from the railway industry and toward the airline industry, and this movement causes the differentials to lessen and eventually to disappear. This adjustment process is illustrated in Figure 13-6. How long this process takes depends on how easily factors can be reallocated from one industry to the other—that is, on the degree of factor mobility.

The behaviour that causes the erosion of temporary differentials is summarized in the hypothesis of the *maximization of net advantage*: The owners of factors of production will allocate those factors to uses that maximize the net advantages to themselves, taking both monetary and non-monetary rewards into consideration. If net advantages were higher in occupation *A* than in occupation *B*, factors would move from *B* to *A*. The increased supply in *A* and the reduced supply in *B* would drive fac-

Practise with Study Guide Chapter 13, Exercise 6.

FIGURE 13-6   The Creation and Erosion of Temporary Factor-Price Differentials

(i) Airline industry

(ii) Railway industry

The mobility of factors leads to the erosion of temporary differentials in factor prices. The two figures show the markets for some factor of production (land, labour, or capital) in the airline and railway industries. Suppose the initial equilibrium has the factor receiving the same price in both industries ($w_A = w_R$). Q_A units are employed in the airline industry, and Q_R units are employed in the railway industry.

An increase in demand for air travel leads to an increase in demand for factors in the airline industry. The demand curve shifts to D_A' and factor prices in that industry rise to w_A'. As factor prices in the airline industry rise, factors leave the railway industry and enter the airline industry. This flow of factors is a leftward shift of S_R to S_R' and a movement upward along S_A. There is a reduction of factors employed in the railway industry and an increase in the airline industry. The flow of factors stops when factor prices are again equalized, $w_A' = w_R'$.

tor earnings down in *A* and up in *B* until net advantages would be equalized, after which no further movement would occur. This analysis gives rise to the prediction of *equal net advantage*: In equilibrium, units of each kind of factor of production will be allocated among alternative possible uses in such a way that the net advantages in all uses are equalized.

A change in the relative price of a factor between two uses will change the net advantages of the uses. It will lead to a shift of some units of that factor to the use for which relative price has increased.

Equilibrium Differentials   Some factor-price differentials persist without generating any forces that eliminate them. These equilibrium differentials can be explained by intrinsic differences in the factors themselves and, for labour, by differences in the cost of acquiring skills and by different non-monetary advantages of different occupations.

The long and costly training required to become a surgeon reduces the supply of surgeons relative to many other occupations. As a result, surgeons typically earn very high incomes. This is an equilibrium wage differential.

Intrinsic Differences. If various units of a factor have different characteristics, the price that is paid may differ among these units. If dexterity is required to accomplish a task, manually dexterous workers will earn more than less dexterous workers. If land is to be used for agricultural purposes, highly fertile land will earn more than poor land. These differences will persist even in long-run equilibrium.

Acquired Differences. If the fertility of land can be increased only by costly methods, then more fertile land must command a higher price than less fertile land. If it did not, landowners would not incur the costs of improving fertility. The same principle holds true for labour since it is costly to acquire most skills. For example, an engineer must train for some time, and unless the earnings of engineers remain sufficiently above what can be earned in less skilled occupations, people will not incur the cost of training.

Compensating Differentials. Whenever working conditions differ across jobs, workers will earn different equilibrium wages. The difference between a test pilot's wage and a chauffeur's wage is only partly a matter of skill; the rest is compensation to the worker for facing the higher risk of testing new planes as compared to driving a car. If both were paid the same, there would be an excess supply of chauffeurs and a shortage of test pilots. Because such factor-price differentials *compensate* for non-monetary aspects of the job, they are commonly called **compensating differentials**; they were introduced into economics more than 200 years ago by Adam Smith.

Academic researchers commonly earn less than they could earn in the world of commerce and industry because of the substantial non-monetary advantages of academic employment. If chemists were paid the same in both sectors, many chemists would prefer academic to industrial jobs. Excess demand for industrial chemists and excess supply of academic chemists would then force chemists' wages up in industry and down in academia until the two types of jobs seemed equally attractive on balance.

Compensating differentials also exist in the regional earnings of otherwise identical factors. People who work in remote logging or mining areas are paid more than are people who do jobs requiring similar skills in large cities. Without higher pay, not enough people would be willing to work at sometimes dangerous jobs in unattractive or remote locations.

compensating differential
A difference in the financial payment to a factor of production (usually labour) across two jobs to compensate the factor for differences in non-monetary aspects of the two jobs.

Practise with Study Guide Chapter 13, Short-Answer Question 4.

Policies to Promote "Pay Equity"

The distinction between temporary and equilibrium factor-price differentials raises an important consideration for policy. Trade unions and governments often have explicit policies about earnings differentials, sometimes seeking to eliminate them in the name of equity. The success of such policies depends to a great extent on the kind of differential that is being attacked. An important general lesson from this experience is the following: Policies that attempt to eliminate *temporary* differentials may be successful in speeding up what may otherwise be a slow adjustment process. But policies aimed at eliminating *equilibrium* differentials will encounter several difficulties.

In recent years, Canadian governments have introduced legislation to redress male–female wage differentials that appear to exist *only* because of discrimination in the labour market. We will discuss labour-market discrimination in more detail in Chapter 14, but for now think of discrimination between men and women who have the same qualifications and are in the same jobs. As the social norms that sustain these discriminatory forces change, so too will the wage differentials. But the adjustment may be very gradual, as the norms themselves will change only gradually. Canadian *pay-equity* legislation has been designed to speed this adjustment and, in the process, reduce the underlying discriminatory forces. These policies have been successful in reducing male–female wage differentials in situations where the men and women concerned are equally qualified and are in the same jobs.

Other government pay-equity legislation is less successful because it attempts to reduce or eliminate *equilibrium* wage differentials. Some pay-equity legislation is based on the principle of *equal pay for work of equal value,* an idea that is very difficult to implement in practice. Such policy is designed to eliminate the wage differentials that exist between workers *in different jobs* but who are deemed to have approximately the same skills and responsibilities. For example, the policy might require that a nurse with 10 years of experience receive the

Jobs with unpleasant working conditions usually pay higher wages than more pleasant jobs requiring the same skills. Such differences in wages are called "compensating differentials." Any policy that attempts to eliminate these differentials is likely to be ineffective.

same salary as a teacher with 10 years of experience. Whatever the social value of such laws, they run into trouble whenever they require equal pay for jobs that have different non-monetary advantages.

To illustrate the nature of the problem encountered by such legislation, consider the example of two types of construction workers—those who work mostly indoors doing home and building renovations, and those who work mostly outdoors on bridges or the exteriors of buildings. Suppose these two jobs demand equal skills, training, and everything else that is taken into account in a decision about what constitutes work of equal value. But in a city with a harsh climate, the outside construction job is less pleasant than the inside construction job. If legislation requires equal pay for both jobs, there will be a shortage of people who are willing to work outside and an excess of people who want to work inside. Employers will seek ways to attract outside workers. Higher pensions, shorter hours, and longer holidays may be offered. If these are allowed, they will achieve the desired result but will defeat the original purpose of equalizing the monetary benefits of the inside and outside jobs; they will also cut down on the number of outside workers that employers will hire because the total cost of an outside worker to an employer will have risen. If the jobs are unionized or if the government prevents such "cheating," the shortage of workers for outside jobs will remain.

In Chapter 14, we discuss the effects of race and sex discrimination on wage differentials. Although these effects can be important, it remains true that many factor-price differentials are a natural market consequence of supply and demand conditions that have nothing to do with inequitable treatment of different groups in the society.

Policies that seek to eliminate equilibrium factor-price differentials without consideration of what causes them or how they affect the supply of the factor often have perverse results.

Economic Rent

One of the most important concepts in economics is that of *economic rent*.

A factor must earn a certain amount in its present use to prevent it from moving to another use—the great nineteenth-century economist Alfred Marshall called this amount the factor's **transfer earnings**. If there were no non-monetary advantages in alternative uses, as is typically the case for land and capital, the factor would have to earn its opportunity cost (what it could earn elsewhere) to prevent it from moving elsewhere.

For labour, however, the non-monetary advantages of various jobs are very important. Labour must earn enough in each use to equate the total advantages—both monetary and non-monetary—among various jobs. For example, in order to remain in a job that is dirty or unsafe, workers will require a higher wage so that the total advantage of the unsafe job equals the total advantage of some alternative job.

A factor's transfer earnings are the amount it needs in order to remain in its current use. Any amount that the factor earns *above* this is called **economic rent**. Economic rent is analogous to economic profit as a surplus over the opportunity cost of capital. Here are three examples:

1. Consider a farmer who grows wheat and earns $1000 per hectare. She has calculated that if her earnings fall to $900 per hectare, she will switch to growing barley instead, her next best alternative. In this case, each hectare of land growing wheat is earning $100 of economic rent.

2. A famous actor earns $15 million per year. He decides that his next best alternative to acting is to promote automobiles in television commercials, in which case he would earn $2.5 million per year. He is earning $12.5 million per year of economic rent.

3. An individual has invested $300 000 of capital into a restaurant, and currently earns a 20-percent annual return—investment income of $60 000 annually. The next best alternative investment (with similar risk) can earn a 15-percent return, or $45 000 annually. The $300 000 of capital is thus earning economic rent equal to $15 000 per year. In this case, rent is just another name for profit in the economist's sense of the term.

The concept of economic rent is crucial in predicting the effects that changes in earnings have on the movement of factors among alternative uses. However, the terminology is confusing because economic rent is often simply called *rent*, which can of course also mean the price paid to hire something, such as a machine, a piece of land, or an apartment. How the same term came to be used for these two different concepts is explained in *Lessons From History 13-1*.

How Much of Factor Earnings Is Rent?

In most cases, as in the three previous examples, economic rent makes up part of the factor's total earnings. From the definitions above, however, note that total earnings for any factor are the sum of its transfer earnings and its economic rent.

A factor's transfer earnings plus its economic rent equals its total earnings.

But *how much* of total earnings is economic rent? A different but related question is: How much would the factor price have to fall before the factor left its current use?

The possibilities are illustrated in Figure 13-7. When supply is perfectly elastic, as in part (i), the factor is extremely mobile between various uses. In this case, all of the

---

transfer earnings The minimum payment required by a factor in order to prevent it from leaving to other uses.

economic rent The excess of total earnings over the minimum necessary to prevent a factor from moving to another use.

Practise with Study Guide Chapter 13, Exercises 3 and 5.

LESSONS FROM HISTORY 13-1

David Ricardo and "Economic Rent"

In the early nineteenth century, there was a public debate about the high price of wheat in England. The high price was causing great hardship because bread was a primary source of food for the working class. Some people argued that wheat had a high price because landlords were charging high rents to tenant farmers. In short, it was argued that the price of wheat was high because the rents of agricultural land were high. Some of those who held this view advocated restricting the rents that landlords could charge.

David Ricardo (1772–1823), a great British economist who was one of the originators of Classical economics, argued that the situation was exactly the reverse. The price of wheat was high, he said, because there was a shortage, caused by the Napoleonic Wars. Because wheat was profitable to produce, there was keen competition among farmers to obtain land on which to grow wheat. This competition in turn forced up the rental price of wheat land. Ricardo advocated removing the existing tariff on wheat so that imported wheat could come into the country. The increase in imports would then increase the supply of wheat in England and lower its price. This would then reduce the rent on land.

The essentials of Ricardo's argument were these: The supply of land was fixed. Land was regarded as

having only one use, the growing of wheat. Nothing had to be paid to prevent land from transferring to a use other than growing wheat because it had no other use. No landowner would leave land idle as long as some return could be obtained by renting it out. Therefore, all the payment to land, that is, rent in the ordinary sense of the word, was a surplus over and above what was necessary to keep it in its present use.

Given a fixed supply of land, the price of land depended on the demand for land, which depended in turn on the demand for wheat (i.e., the demand for land was *derived from* the demand for wheat). Rent, the term for the payment for the use of land, thus became the term for a surplus payment to a factor over and above what was necessary to keep it in its present use.

Later, two facts were realized. First, land often had alternative uses, and, from the point of view of any one use, part of the payment made to land would necessarily have to be paid to keep it in that use. Second, factors of production other than land also often earned a surplus over and above what was necessary to keep them in their present use. This surplus is now called *economic rent*, whether the factor is land, labour, or a piece of capital equipment.

factor's income is transfer earnings and so none of it is economic rent. If any lower price is offered, nothing whatsoever will be supplied since all units of the factor will transfer to some other use.

When supply is perfectly inelastic, as in part (iii), the same quantity is supplied whatever the price. Evidently, the quantity supplied does not decrease, no matter how low the price goes. This inelasticity indicates that the factor has no alternative use, and thus requires no minimum payment to keep it in its present use. In this case, there are no transfer earnings and so the whole of the payment is economic rent.

The more usual situation is that of an upward-sloping supply curve, as shown in part (ii) of Figure 13-7. A rise in the factor's price serves the allocative function of attracting more units of the factor into the market in question, but the same rise provides additional economic rent to all units of the factor that are *already employed*. We know that the extra pay that is going to the units

Increases in the price of oil that are not needed to increase the quantity supplied generate economic rents for producers. For example, if the owner of this well is only willing to operate it when the price of oil is $35 per barrel or higher, then any price above that level generates some economic rent for the producer.

FIGURE 13-7   The Determination of Rent in Factor Markets

(i) Perfectly elastic supply

(ii) Positively sloped supply

(iii) Perfectly inelastic supply

The amount of a factor's earnings that is economic rent depends on the mobility (and thus on the elasticity of supply) of the factor. In each case, the equilibrium is determined by the intersection of the demand and supply curves, and total factor earnings are given by factor price times quantity, wQ.

In part (i), supply is perfectly elastic, indicating that even a slightly lower factor price would cause the factor to leave. None of the earnings are economic rent; all are the factor's transfer earnings.

In part (ii), supply is positively sloped, indicating that more units of the factor will be supplied at a higher price. The area below the supply curve is the amount needed to keep Q_2 units of the factor in its current use—this area is the factor's transfer earnings. The red shaded area above the supply curve is economic rent.

In part (iii), supply is perfectly inelastic, indicating that the factor has no other uses. In this case, transfer earnings are zero and all of the factor's earnings are economic rent.

already employed is economic rent because the owners of these units were willing to supply them at the lower price.

The production and sale of oil (and natural gas) in Alberta in the past few years provides a good example of economic rent and market prices. In Canada, natural resources are owned by the province, and oil producers must pay a share of their revenues as *royalties* to the provincial government. Alberta's supply curve for oil is upward-sloping, as in part (ii) of Figure 13-7. As the market price for oil rises, production from wells that were not profitable at lower prices comes on-line and producers therefore increase the quantity of barrels supplied. For these *marginal* barrels of oil, the market price is just equal to the transfer earnings; there are no economic rents earned on these units. But the increase in market price does generate pure economic rent for those output levels that were already being produced at lower prices; these units were being produced anyway (at lower prices), and the rise in market price simply increases the rents earned by the producer. These economic rents in Alberta's oil industry account for a considerable fraction of that province's increase in income in recent years.

Various Perspectives on Economic Rent   The proportion of a given factor payment that is economic rent varies from situation to situation. We cannot point to a factor of production and assert that some fixed fraction of its income is always its economic rent. The proportion of its earnings that is rent depends on its alternatives.

Consider first a narrowly defined use of a given factor—say, its use by a particular firm. From that firm's point of view, the factor will be highly mobile, as it could readily move to another firm in the same industry. The firm must pay the going wage or risk losing that factor. From the perspective of the single firm, a large proportion of the payment made to a factor is needed to prevent it from transferring to another use. Thus, only a small portion of its payment is rent.

Now consider a more broadly defined use—for example, the factor's use in an entire industry. From the industry's point of view, the factor is less mobile because it would be more difficult for it to gain employment quickly outside the industry. From the perspective of the particular *industry* (rather than the specific *firm* within the industry), a larger proportion of the payment to a factor is economic rent.

From the even more general perspective of a particular *occupation,* mobility is likely to be even less, and the proportion of the factor payment that is economic rent is likely to be more. It may be easier, for example, for a carpenter to move from the construction industry to the furniture industry than to retrain to be a computer programmer.

As the perspective moves from a narrowly defined use of a factor to a broadly defined use of a factor, the mobility of the factor decreases; as mobility decreases, the share of the factor payment that is economic rent increases.

Consider how this relationship applies to the often controversial large salaries that are received by some highly specialized types of labourers, such as movie stars and professional athletes. These performers have a unique style and a talent that cannot be duplicated, whatever the training. The earnings that they receive are mostly economic rent from the viewpoint of the occupation: These performers generally enjoy their occupations and would pursue them for much less than the high remuneration that they actually receive.

For example, Sidney Crosby would probably have chosen hockey over other alternatives even at a much lower salary. However, because of Crosby's amazing skills as a hockey player, most hockey teams would pay handsomely to have him on their rosters, and he is able to command a high salary from the team for which he does play. From the perspective of the individual firm, the Pittsburgh Penguins, most of Crosby's salary is required to keep him from switching to another team and hence is not economic rent. From the point of view of the hockey "industry," however, much of his salary is economic rent.

Notice also that Sidney Crosby's salary is largely determined by the demand for his services. The supply is perfectly inelastic—no one else has his particular combination of skills. So the market-clearing price is determined by the position of the demand curve.

A Final Word

This chapter has examined the operation of factor markets. You should now be able to answer the questions that we posed in the opening paragraph. Here are some of the key points for two of those questions.

What explains why neurosurgoens usually get paid more than family doctors? Part of the answer surely lies in the fact that to be a neurosurgeon requires more years of costly specialized training than that needed to be a family doctor. Since that extra training is costly

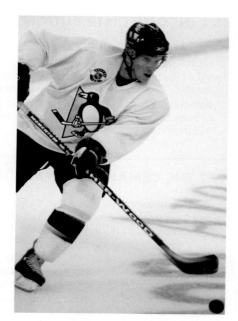

Whether Sidney Crosby's salary with the Pittsburgh Penguins is economic rent depends on the perspective. From the perspective of the entire NHL, most of his salary is economic rent.

and time-consuming, it is not surprising that fewer people are willing to become neurosurgeons than family doctors. This lower supply for neurosurgeons, other things being equal, leads to a higher wage.

Why does a hectare of farm land in Northern Saskatchewan rent for far less than a hectare of land in downtown Toronto? To answer this, just think about the alternative uses for the farm land, and compare them to the alternative uses for the hectare in downtown Toronto. The hectare of farm land has very few alternative uses. Or, more correctly, it has many alternative uses, but there is little demand to use that particular piece of land to build a skyscraper, shopping mall, or baseball stadium. But one hectare of land in downtown Toronto has many alternative uses—there always seems to be demand for additional space for parking garages, office buildings, retail stores, and many other things. Since the piece of farm land in Saskatchewan must stay where it is, its rental price is determined by demand. Since there is little demand for the land, its rental price is low. Similarly, the land in downtown Toronto cannot move anywhere, and so its rental price is determined by demand. And since there is lots of demand for a hectare in downtown Toronto, its rental price is high.

Having learned about factor markets in general, we are now ready to examine some specific factor markets. In Chapter 14, we examine some details about labour markets, such as minimum wages, discrimination, and labour unions. In Chapter 15, we examine physical capital and the interest rate.

S U M M A R Y

13.1 INCOME DISTRIBUTION

- The functional distribution of income refers to the shares of total national income going to each of the major factors of production; it focuses on sources of income. The size distribution of income refers to the shares of total national income going to various groups of households; it focuses only on the amount of income, not its source.

- Canada has considerable inequality in the distribution of income. The poorest fifth of families currently receives 5.2 percent of aggregate pre-tax income; the richest fifth receives 43.6 percent.

13.2 THE DEMAND FOR FACTORS

- A firm's decisions on how much to produce and how to produce it imply demands for factors of production, which are said to be derived from the demand for goods they are used to produce.
- A profit-maximizing firm will hire units of a factor until the last unit adds as much to cost as it does to revenue. Thus, the marginal cost of the factor will be equated with that factor's marginal revenue product.
- When the firm is a price taker in factor markets, the marginal cost of the factor is its price per unit. When the firm sells its output in a competitive market, the marginal revenue product is the factor's marginal product multiplied by the market price of the output.

- A price-taking firm's demand for a factor is negatively sloped because the law of diminishing returns implies that the marginal product of a factor declines as more of that factor is employed (with other inputs held constant).
- The industry's demand for a factor will be more elastic (a) the less the marginal product of the factor declines as more of the factor is used, (b) the larger the proportion of costs accounted for by the factor in question, and (c) the more elastic the demand for the good that the factor is used to produce.

13.3 **THE SUPPLY OF FACTORS**

LO 3

- The total supply of each factor is fixed at any moment but varies over time. The supply of labour depends on the size of the population, the participation rate, and the number of hours that people want to work.
- A rise in the wage rate has a substitution effect, which tends to induce more work, and an income effect, which tends to induce less work (more leisure consumed).

- The supply of a factor to a particular industry or occupation is more elastic than its supply to the whole economy because one industry can bid units away from other industries. The elasticity of supply to a particular use depends on factor mobility, which tends to be greater the longer the time allowed for a reaction to take place.

13.4 **THE OPERATION OF FACTOR MARKETS**

LO 4 5

- Factor-price differentials often occur in competitive markets. Temporary differentials in the earnings of different units of factors of production induce factor movements that eventually remove the differentials. Equilibrium differentials reflect differences among units of factors as well as non-monetary benefits of different jobs; they can persist indefinitely.
- Factors will be allocated between uses to generate the greatest net advantage to their owners, allowing for both the monetary and non-monetary advantages of a particular employment.

- Some amount must be paid to a factor to prevent it from transferring to another use. This amount is the factor's transfer earnings. Economic rent is the difference between that amount and a factor's actual earnings.
- Whenever the supply curve is positively sloped, part of the total payment going to a factor is needed to prevent it from transferring to another use, and part of it is economic rent. The more narrowly defined the use, the larger the fraction that is transfer earnings and the smaller the fraction that is economic rent.

KEY CONCEPTS

Functional distribution and size distribution of income
Derived demand for a factor
Marginal product (*MP*)
Marginal revenue product (*MRP*)

The determinants of elasticity of factor demand
Factor mobility
Temporary versus equilibrium factor-price differentials

Equal net advantage
Transfer earnings
Economic rent

STUDY EXERCISES

1. **myeconlab** The table below shows the size distribution of income for Fantasyland.

Household Income Rank	Percentage of Aggregate Income	Cumulative Total
Lowest fifth	6.8	—
Second fifth	14.1	—
Third fifth	21.5	—
Fourth fifth	26.2	—
Highest fifth	31.4	—

a. Compute the cumulative percentage of total income. Fill in the table.

b. On a scale diagram, with the percentage of households on the vertical axis and the percentage of aggregate income on the horizontal axis, plot the Lorenz curve for Fantasyland.
c. How does the diagram show the extent of income inequality in Fantasyland?
d. Now suppose Fantasyland introduces a system that redistributes income from higher-income households to lower-income households. How would this affect the Lorenz curve?

2. Demands for the following goods and services are increasing rapidly. In each case, list two derived demands that you predict will be increasing as a result.

a. Demand for natural gas
b. Demand for medical services

c. Demand for international travel
d. Demand for children's computer games

3. Fill in the blanks to make the following statements correct.

   a. Marginal revenue product is calculated by multiplying _____ and _____.
   b. Marginal revenue product represents the addition to a firm's total revenue as a result of _____.
   c. To maximize its profits, a firm will hire all units of a factor that have an _____ greater than or equal to their _____.
   d. To maximize its profits, any firm will hire each factor of production to the point where the factor's _____ equals the _____.

4. Fill in the blanks to make the following statements correct.

   a. The *MRP* curve for a factor is the same as the firm's _____ for that factor.
   b. Demand for a factor will be relatively _____ if the marginal product declines rapidly as more of that factor is used.
   c. Other things being equal, if the demand for a product that a factor is used to produce is relatively inelastic, the demand for that factor will be relatively _____.
   d. An increase in the price at which a competitive firm sells its product leads the firm's demand curve for its factor to _____.
   e. If a technological improvement leads every unit of a given factor to produce 10 percent more output than previously, the _____ curve will _____ and thus the firm's demand curve for the factor will _____.

5. The Apple Pie Factory produces apple pies. The firm sells its product and hires its workers in competitive markets. The market price (*p*) for a pie is $4 and the wage rate (*w*) is $10 per hour. The table at the bottom of the page shows the total hourly production for varying amounts of workers. (Remember that for a price-taking firm, *p* = *MR*.)

   a. Fill in the *p* and *w* columns.
   b. Calculate the *MP* and the *MRP* for each amount of labour employed. Put the numbers *between* the rows.
   c. What is the logic of the firm's profit-maximizing condition for hiring labour?
   d. How many workers should this profit-maximizing firm hire?

6. Refer back to the production schedule for the Apple Pie Factory in Question 5. In this question we will derive the firm's demand curve for labour.

   a. On a diagram, with *MRP* on the vertical axis and the number of workers on the horizontal axis, plot the *MRP* curve.
   b. If the wage is $10 per hour, how many workers will be hired? Why?
   c. If the wage is $5 per hour, how many workers will be hired? Why?
   d. If the wage is $20 per hour, how many workers will be hired? Why?
   e. Explain why the *MRP* curve is the firm's factor demand curve.

Number of Workers	Output	Wage Rate (*w*) ($ per hour)	Price of a Pie (*p*)	*MP*	*MRP*
4	40	———	———		
5	48	———	———	———	———
6	55	———	———	———	———
7	61	———	———	———	———
8	66	———	———	———	———
9	70	———	———	———	———
10	73	———	———	———	———
11	75	———	———	———	———
12	76	———	———	———	———

7. The diagram below shows the market for fast-food workers in British Columbia.

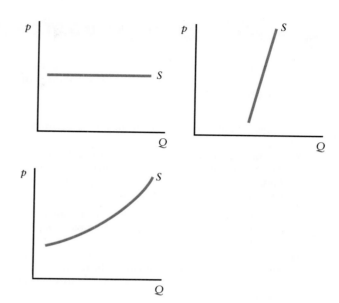

a. The supply curve is upward sloping. If the wage in this industry rises, from where do the extra workers come?

b. Suppose there is a significant decrease in demand for fast food. How is this likely to affect fast-food workers' earnings? Show this in the diagram.

c. Now suppose new legislation bans high school students from doing any homework. As a result, more students look for jobs in the fast-food industry. How will this affect the labour market for fast-food workers? Show this in the diagram.

d. What will be the effect on total earnings in the fast-food industry from the change in part (c)? On what does the answer depend?

8. The three following diagrams show the supply of luxury ocean liners at three different levels of aggregation—the entire world, a particular country, and a particular firm.

a. Which diagram shows the supply of ocean liners to the world as whole? Explain its elasticity.

b. Which diagram shows the supply of ocean liners to Canada? Explain its elasticity.

c. Which diagram shows the supply of ocean liners to an individual Canadian firm? Explain its elasticity.

d. What is the general relationship between factor mobility and the elasticity of factor supply?

9. In the text we argued that temporary factor-price differentials tend to be eroded by factor mobility. This question requires you to think about this process. Consider the two markets for sheet-iron workers and steel-pipe workers in the same region. Suppose both markets are competitive. We begin in a situation in which both sheet-iron workers and steel-pipe workers earn $20 per hour. Assume that workers can switch easily between the two jobs.

a. Draw diagrams showing the supply and demand for labour in each market.

b. Now suppose there is a sharp increase in the demand for steel pipe. Explain what happens in the market for steel-pipe workers.

c. If the employment of steel-pipe workers increased in part (b), explain where the extra workers came from.

d. What effect does the event in part (b) have on the market for sheet-iron workers?

e. What is the long-run effect of the shock on the relative wages in the two types of jobs?

10. How much of the following payments for factor services is likely to be economic rent?

a. The $750 per month that a landlord receives for an apartment rented to students

b. The salary of the Canadian prime minister

c. The annual income of Tiger Woods or Shania Twain

d. The salary of a window cleaner who says, "It's dangerous work, but it beats driving a truck."

DISCUSSION QUESTIONS

1. Other things being equal, how would you expect each of the following events to affect the size distribution of after-tax income?

   a. An increase in unemployment
   b. Rapid population growth in an already crowded city
   c. An increase in food prices relative to other prices
   d. An increase in social insurance benefits and taxes
   e. Elimination of the personal income-tax exemption for interest earned within an RRSP.

2. A labour dispute has broken out at a university between the faculty and the university's board of governors. One of the issues is the faculty's complaint that summer school teaching salaries are below the regional average and hence too low. The trustees argue that considering that they have more professors asking to teach summer school at the current pay than they have courses for these faculty to teach, the pay is adequate. Comment.

3. This chapter introduced the Lorenz curve, which gives a graphical representation of the equality of income distribution. Many observers criticize Canadian policy because Canada's Lorenz curve is bent significantly off the diagonal. Can you provide an economically valid defence of this criticism? If you could pick a shape for the nation's Lorenz curve, what would it be? Defend your choice using positive economic tools.

4. A recent *Wall Street Journal* article asks, "Why do baseball players earn millions of dollars a year for their negligible contribution to society while major contributors—such as schoolteachers, police officers, firefighters, and ambulance drivers—earn barely enough to survive?" Can you offer an answer based on what was discussed in this chapter?

5. For most of the years in the past two decades, the unemployment rate in the province of Quebec has been higher than the Canadian average. It has also been higher than the unemployment rate in next-door Ontario. Given that there are few legal restrictions on the flow of labour across Canadian provincial boundaries, provide an explanation for how such a gap in unemployment rates can persist for so long.

6. Using the concepts of transfer earnings and economic rent, can you derive a form of taxation—of the earnings by oil companies, for example—that would generate tax revenue but *not* influence the companies' supply decisions? Is your approach consistent with that followed by Canada's provincial governments when they collect royalties on natural-resource revenues?

CHAPTER 14

Labour Markets

LO LEARNING OBJECTIVES

In this chapter you will learn

1. how to explain wage differentials in both competitive and non-competitive labour markets.
2. the effects of legislated minimum wages.
3. about the tradeoff that unions face between wages and employment.
4. why the trend away from manufacturing jobs and toward service jobs is not necessarily a problem for the economy as a whole.

The competitive theory of factor-price determination, presented in Chapter 13, tells us a great deal about the determinants of factor prices, factor movements, and the distribution of income. In this chapter, we look specifically at labour markets. We begin by discussing why some workers get high wages and others get low wages. We then look beyond our theory of competitive labour markets to examine situations where either firms or workers have some market power. We also discuss the effects of legislated minimum wages, as well as the debate surrounding this contentious policy. The chapter then discusses labour unions, and the tradeoff they face between increasing their membership and increasing their members' wages. Finally, we examine an often-heard claim that Canada and other developed economies are gaining "bad jobs" in the service sector at the expense of "good jobs" in the manufacturing sector.

14.1 WAGE DIFFERENTIALS

We argued in the last chapter that if all workers were identical, all jobs had the same working conditions, and labour markets were perfectly competitive, all workers would earn the same wage. In reality, however, wages vary enormously across such dimensions as occupations, skills, amounts of education, and geographical areas. Generally, the more education and experience a worker has, the higher are his or her wages. Given equal education and experience, women on average earn less than men. Workers in highly unionized industries tend to get paid more than workers with similar skills and experience in non-unionized industries. Such differentials arise because workers are not all identical, jobs are not all identical, and because many important non-competitive forces operate in labour markets. We now look more systematically at some of the main reasons why different types of labour earn different wages.

Wage Differentials in Competitive Markets

Many jobs involve dangerous or unpleasant working conditions. Wages in such jobs are generally higher than in other jobs requiring comparable skills. These are called compensating wage differentials.

Where there are many employers (buyers) and many workers (sellers), there is a competitive labour market of the kind discussed in Chapter 13. Under competitive conditions, the wage rate and level of employment are set by supply and demand. No worker or group of workers, and no firm or group of firms, is able to affect the market wage. In practice, however, there are many kinds of workers and many kinds of jobs. We can therefore think of a series of related labour markets rather than a single national market. Among these various labour markets, there are several reasons for wage differentials.

Working Conditions Given identical skills, those working under relatively onerous or risky conditions earn more than those working in pleasant or safe conditions. For example, construction workers who work the "high iron," assembling the frames for skyscrapers, are paid more than workers who do similar work at ground level. The reason is simple: Risk and unpleasantness reduce the supply of labour, thus raising the wage above what it would otherwise be. Different working conditions in different jobs thus lead to *compensating differentials* as we discussed in Chapter 13. These wage differentials are not temporary—they are *equilibrium* wage differentials.

In competitive labour markets, supply and demand set the equilibrium wage, but the wage will differ according to the non-monetary aspects of the job.

Inherited Skills Large incomes will be earned by people who have scarce skills that cannot be taught and that are in high demand—for example, an NBA basketball player, an opera singer, or a movie star. In these cases, the combination of a small and inelastic supply and a large enough demand of the relevant kind of labour cause the market-clearing wage to be high. Wage differentials of this kind are also equilibrium wage differentials.

Inherited skills, which are mostly beyond the individual's control, can have important effects on wages.

Human Capital A machine is physical capital. It requires an investment of time and money to create it, and once created, it yields valuable services over a long time. In the same way, labour skills require an investment of time and money to acquire, and once acquired, they may yield an increased income to their owner over a long time. Since investment in labour skills is similar to investment in physical capital, acquired skills are called **human capital**. The more costly it is to acquire the skill required for a particular job, the higher its pay must be to attract people to train for it.

human capital The acquired skills that individuals have; usually from formal education or on-the-job training.

Investment in human capital is costly, and the return is usually in terms of higher future wages.

The two main ways in which human capital is acquired are through formal education and on-the-job training.

Formal Education. Compulsory primary and secondary education provides some minimum human capital for all citizens. People who decide to stay in school beyond the years of compulsory education, such as those of you who are reading this book, are deciding to invest voluntarily in acquiring further human capital. The opportunity cost is measured by the income that you could have earned if you had entered the labour force immediately, in addition to any out-of-pocket costs for such items as tuition fees and equipment. The return is measured by the higher income earned when a better job is obtained.

How large is the payoff to higher education? Figure 14-1 shows how average employment income varies with years of schooling. In 2001, the year of Canada's most recent Census, the average employment income for Canadians with a university degree was over $48 500; in contrast, someone who failed to complete high school had an average employment income of less than half this amount.

Evidence suggests that in recent years the demand for workers with more skills and education has been rising relative to the demand for those with less. As we would expect, this change in relative demand raises the relative wages of more-educated people, thereby increasing the payoff to their investment in education. Not surprisingly, students today find the further investment in human capital much more important than did students a generation ago.

Changes in demand and supply change the costs and benefits of acquiring human capital. Individuals respond according to their personal assessment of these costs and benefits.

On-the-Job Training. Wage differentials according to experience are readily observable in most firms and occupations. To a significant extent, these differentials are a response to human capital acquired on the job. For example, a civil engineer with 20 years' experience in bridge design will generally earn more than a newly graduated civil engineer, even though they both have the same formal education.

On-the-job training is important in creating rising wages for employees and for making firms competitive. Evidence suggests that people who miss on-the-job training early in life are handicapped relative to others throughout much of their later working careers.

Temporary or Equilibrium Differentials? Wage differentials due to differences in human capital are partly temporary and partly equilibrium differentials. If university graduates earn much more than high school graduates, more people will decide to attend university in pursuit of the higher earnings. This increase in the supply of university-trained individuals will reduce their wage relative to high school graduates, thus diminishing the observed differentials such as those shown in Figure 14-1. As long as it is costly to acquire human capital—and as you know, attending university *is* costly—then in equilibrium there will still be wage differentials in favour of university graduates. In equilibrium, the higher wages of university graduates will just compensate them for the higher costs associated with acquiring their greater stock of human capital.

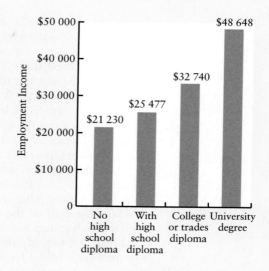

FIGURE 14-1 Education and Employment Income

There is a financial payoff to formal education, especially a university degree. The increase in employment income that can be expected from extra education is modest for levels of education below a university degree. But the payoff for completing a university degree is very substantial.

(*Source:* These data are available on Statistics Canada's website, www.statcan.ca, by searching for "Earnings.")

Practise with Study Guide Chapter 14, Short-Answer Question 1.

Wage differentials due to differences in human capital acquisition lead to changes in the pattern of human-capital acquisition, and to an erosion of the differentials. As long as human capital is costly to acquire, however, some wage differentials will persist in equilibrium.

Discrimination Crude statistics show that incomes vary by race and gender. For example, in 2006 the average female worker in Canada earned about 83 percent of the wage of the average full-time male worker. More detailed studies suggest that a significant part of these differences can be explained by such considerations as the nature of the job and the amount of human capital acquired through both formal education and on-the-job experience. When all such explanations are taken into account, however, there still appears to be some discrimination on the basis of both gender and race.

To understand the effects of labour-market discrimination, we begin by building a simplified picture of a non-discriminating labour market and then introduce discrimination between two sets of equally qualified workers. The discussion here is phrased in terms of males and females but the analysis applies equally well to any situation in which workers are distinguished on grounds *other than* their ability, such as race or skin colour, citizenship, religion, sexual preference, or political beliefs.

Suppose half of the people in the labour force are male and the other half are female. Each group has the same proportion who are educated to various levels, identical distributions of talent, and so on. Suppose also that there are two occupations. Occupation E (*elite*) requires people of above-average education and skills, and occupation O (*ordinary*) can use anyone. Finally, suppose the non-monetary aspects of the two occupations are the same.

In the absence of discrimination, the theory of competitive factor markets that we have developed suggests that the wages in E occupations will be bid up above those in O occupations in order that the E jobs attract the workers of above-average skills. Men and women of above-average skill will take the E jobs, while the others, both men and women, will have no choice but to seek O jobs. Because skills are equally distributed between both sexes, each occupation will employ one-half men and one-half women.

Now suppose discrimination enters in an extreme form. All E occupations are hereafter open only to men, but O occupations are open to either men or women. The immediate effect is to reduce by 50 percent the supply of job candidates for E occupations; all previously qualified female candidates are no longer eligible because candidates must now be *both* men and above average. The discrimination also increases the supply of applicants for O jobs because the women who cannot be employed in E jobs move instead to get O jobs. The new group of O-job candidates now includes all women and the below-average men.

As shown in Figure 14-2, wages rise in E occupations and fall in O occupations.

Labour-market discrimination, by changing equilibrium supply, decreases the wages of a group that is discriminated against and increases the wages of the "favoured" group.

In the longer run, further changes may occur. Employers that continue to discriminate against women may find ways to attract the slightly-below-average male workers away from the O occupations. Although this will raise O wages slightly, it will also make these occupations increasingly "female occupations." If discrimination has been in place for a sufficient length of time, women will learn that it does not pay to acquire above-average skills. Regardless of ability, women are forced by discrimination to work in unskilled jobs.

The final point to address regarding labour-market discrimination is whether discriminatory wage differentials are equilibrium or temporary differentials. The simple

FIGURE 14-2   The Effect of Discrimination on Wages

(i) Elite market (E)   (ii) Ordinary market (O)

If market E discriminates against one group and market O does not, wages will rise in E and fall in O. Market E requires above-average skills, while market O requires only ordinary skills. When there is no discrimination, demand and supply are D_E and S_E in market E and D_O and S_O in market O. Initially, the wage rate is w_0 and employment is L_0 in each market. (w_0 in market E is higher than w_0 in market O because the workers in E have higher skills than those in O. This is an equilibrium wage differential.) When discrimination excludes women from E occupations, the supply curve shifts to S'_E, and the wage earned by the remaining workers, all of whom are men, rises to w_1. Women put out of work in the E occupations now seek work in the O occupations. The resulting shift in the supply curve to S'_O reduces the wage to w_2 in the O occupations. Because all women are in O occupations, they have a lower wage rate than many men. The average male wage in the economy is higher than the average female wage.

answer is that the differentials will persist as long as the discrimination itself persists. Consider three general cases.

In the first case, the discrimination is supported by government policy, as in the South African apartheid system in which blacks were prohibited by law from holding prestigious and high-paying jobs. In such cases, as long as the law remains in place, so too will the discriminating wage differentials. If political pressure forces a change in the law, as happened in South Africa in the 1980s and 1990s, the effects of the discrimination will be reversed, but it may take some time. In particular, it will take time for the once-discriminated-against individuals, who had little incentive to invest in their own human capital, to acquire the human capital necessary for them to qualify for the prestigious jobs. The effects of the legislated discrimination will linger beyond the policy itself.

In the second case, discrimination is not supported by official government policy but instead reflects the views of the firms' managers. In this case, there are economic pressures opposing the discrimination. For example, if some firms discriminate against even well-qualified women, our analysis in Figure 14-2 suggests there will be well-qualified women who can only find low-wage jobs. There is an incentive for other, non-discriminating, firms to hire these well-qualified women and thereby benefit from lower costs. If enough firms see this advantage, there will be an increase in demand for

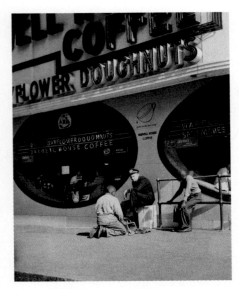

The attitudes of many white customers were responsible for much discrimination against black people in the United States in the first few decades of the past century. As long as these attitudes persist, so will the discrimination, unless legislation forces a change.

well-qualified women, eventually reversing the effects of the initial discrimination.

In the third case, the cause of the discrimination is the preferences of the *customers*. Unlike the second case where the discrimination reflects the views of the firms' managers, there are no economic forces working to offset this customer-driven discrimination. As long as such discriminatory views persist, the discriminatory wage differentials will be sustained—only legislation or fundamental changes in customers' attitudes will reverse the situation. For many years, this was an important aspect of racial discrimination in the southern U.S. states, where many white customers were not prepared to have some services, such as haircuts, provided to them by blacks.

If discrimination is supported by governments or reflects the views of consumers, the discriminatory wage differentials will persist as long as the discrimination itself persists. If the discrimination only reflects the views of the firms' managers, the pursuit of profits generates economic forces that tend to reduce the discriminatory wage differentials.

myeconlab

Public officials often announce how their assistance to particular firms or industries will "create jobs." An understanding of wage differentials and the mobility of labour, however, suggests that governments may create fewer jobs than they think. For more details, look for "Do Government Job-Creation Programs Really Create Jobs?" in the *Additional Topics* section of this book's MyEconLab.

www.myeconlab.com

Wage Differentials in Non-Competitive Markets

We have examined several explanations for why wage differentials exist in competitive labour markets. Another explanation for wage differentials is that the labour market may *not* be competitive. In Chapters 9 through 11, we distinguished different *structures* for the markets in which firms sell their outputs. The inputs that firms use are also bought in markets that can have different structures. Although many factor markets are perfectly competitive, some show elements of market power on either the demand or the supply side.

To study the influence of different labour-market structures on wages, consider the case of an industry that employs identical workers for only one kind of job. In this way, we eliminate the possibility that any wage differentials are caused by differences between workers or differences between jobs—we thus highlight the role of market structure.

Let's examine two general cases. The first is one in which workers form a group and exercise some market power over setting the wage. This is a case in which a labour union acts as a monopoly seller of labour services. The second case is one in which a single firm is the only purchaser of labour—a *monopsony* firm in the labour market.

A Union in a Competitive Labour Market For the purposes of our discussion of labour markets, a **union** (or *labour union*) is an association that is authorized to represent workers in negotiations with their employers. We examine unions in greater detail later in this chapter. For now we take the simple view that when workers are represented by a labour union, there is only a single supplier of labour.

As the single seller of labour for many buyers, the union is a monopolist, and it can establish a wage below which no one will work, thus changing the supply curve of labour. Firms can hire as many units of labour as are prepared to work at the union wage but no one at a lower wage. Thus, the industry as a whole (and each firm in the industry) faces a supply curve that is horizontal at the level of the union wage up to the maximum quantity of labour that is willing to work at that wage.

If the union uses its monopoly power, it will negotiate a wage above the competitive level. This situation is shown in Figure 14-3, in which the intersection of this horizontal supply curve and the demand curve establishes a higher wage rate and a lower level of employment than the competitive equilibrium. In this case, there will be some workers who would like to work in the unionized industry or occupation but cannot. A conflict of interest has been created between serving the interests of the union's employed and unemployed members.

An alternative way to achieve the higher wage is to shift the supply curve to the left. The union may do this by restricting entry into the occupation by methods such as lengthening the required period of apprenticeship and reducing openings for trainees. The union could also shift the supply curve to the left by persuading the government to impose restrictive licensing or certification requirements on people who wish to work in certain occupations. The union might even lobby the government to implement restrictive immigration policies in an attempt to reduce the supply of labour to specific industries.

By restricting entry into the occupation or industry, unions can drive the wage above the competitive level. As a result, the level of employment will fall.

Raising wages by restricting entry is not limited to unions. It occurs, for example, with many professional groups, including doctors, architects, engineers, and lawyers. By limiting enrollments in professional programs at universities, the restricted supply of labour drives wages in these occupations higher than they would otherwise be.

A Monopsony Firm in the Labour Market A **monopsony** is a market in which there is only one buyer; monopsony is to the buying side of the market what monopoly is to the selling side. Although monopsony is not very common, it sometimes occurs in small towns that contain only one industry and often only one large plant or mine. For example, Iroquois Falls in Ontario and Pine Falls in Manitoba are small towns where the principal employer is a single firm that operates a newsprint plant. Although

union An association authorized to represent workers in bargaining with employers. Also called a *labour union.*

monopsony A market structure in which there is a single buyer.

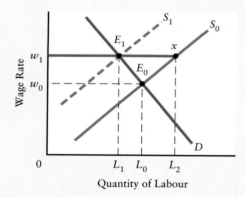

FIGURE 14-3   A Union in a Competitive Labour Market

A union can raise the wages of people who continue to be employed but only by reducing the number of people employed. The competitive equilibrium is at E_0, the wage is w_0, and employment is L_0. If a monopoly union enters this market and sets a wage of w_1, a new equilibrium will be established at E_1. The supply curve has become $w_1 x S_0$. At the new wage w_1, employment will be L_1, and there will be $L_1 L_2$ workers who would like to work but whom the industry will not hire.

The wage w_1 can be achieved without generating a pool of unemployed persons. To do so, the union must restrict entry into the occupation and thus shift the supply curve to the left to S_1. Employment will again be L_1.

Practise with Study Guide Chapter 14, Exercise 2 and Extension Exercise E1.

both towns provide alternative sources of employment in retailing and service establishments, the large industrial employer has some monopsony power over the local labour market. In other cases, local labour markets may contain only a few large industrial employers. Individually, each has substantial market power, and if they act together, either explicitly or tacitly, they can behave as if they were a single monopsonist. Our analysis applies whenever employers have substantial monopsony power, but for concreteness, we consider a case in which the few firms operating in one labour market form an employers' hiring association in order to act as a single buying unit. We therefore refer to a single monopsonist.

Monopsony Without a Union. Suppose there are many potential workers and they are not members of a union. The monopsonist can offer any wage rate that it chooses, and the workers must either accept employment at that rate or find a different job.

Suppose the monopsonist decides to hire some specific quantity of labour. The labour supply curve shows the wage that it must offer. To the monopsonist, this wage is the *average cost* of labour. In deciding how much labour to hire, however, the monopsonist trying to maximize its profits is interested in the *marginal cost* of hiring additional workers. The monopsonist wants to know how much its total costs will increase as it takes on additional units of labour.

Whenever the supply curve of labour slopes upward, the marginal cost of employing extra units will exceed the average cost.

The marginal cost exceeds the wage paid (the average cost) because the increased wage rate necessary to attract an extra worker must also be paid to *everyone already employed.* [27] For example, assume that 100 workers are employed at $15.00 per hour and that to attract an extra worker, the wage must be raised to $15.25 per hour. The marginal cost of the 101st worker is not the $15.25 per hour paid to the worker but $40.25 per hour—made up of the extra 25 cents per hour paid to the 100 existing workers and $15.25 paid to the new worker. Thus, the marginal cost is $40.25, whereas the average cost is $15.25.

The profit-maximizing monopsonist will hire labour up to the point at which the marginal cost of labour just equals the amount that the firm is willing to pay for an additional unit of labour. That amount is determined by labour's marginal revenue product (*MRP*) and is shown by the demand curve illustrated in Figure 14-4.

The full exercise of monopsony power in a labour market will result in a lower level of employment and lower wages than would exist in a competitive labour market.

The intuitive explanation is that the monopsonistic employer is aware that by trying to purchase more, it is responsible for driving up the wage. If it wishes to maximize its profits it will therefore stop short of the point that is reached when workers are hired by many competitive firms, no one of which can exert a significant influence on the wage rate.

FIGURE 14-4 Monopsony in a Labour Market

A profit-maximizing monopsonist lowers both the wage rate and employment below their competitive levels. *MRP* and *S* are the competitive demand and supply curves, respectively. The competitive equilibrium is E_0. The marginal cost of labour (*MC*) to the monopsonist is above the average cost. The monopsonistic firm maximizes profits at E_1. It hires only L_1 units of labour. At L_1, the marginal cost of the last worker is just equal to the amount that the worker adds to the firm's revenue, as shown by the demand curve. The wage that must be paid to get L_1 workers is only w_1.

Monopsony with a Union. In situations where there is a single large firm in the labour market, workers often create or join a labour union so their collective market power can better match that of the firm. This situation is often referred to as *bilateral monopoly* since both sides of the market have considerable market power. In this case, the two sides will settle the wage through a process known as *collective bargaining*. The outcome of this bargaining process will depend on each side's objective and on the skill that each has in bargaining for its objective. We have seen that, left to itself, the profit-maximizing employer's organization will set the monopsonistic wage shown in Figure 14-4. To understand the possible outcomes for the wage after the monopoly union enters the market, let us ask what the union would do if it had the power to set the wage unilaterally. The result will give us insight into the union's objectives in the actual collective bargaining that does occur.

Suppose the union can set a wage below which its members will not work. Here, just as in the case of a wage-setting union in a competitive market, the union presents the employer with a horizontal supply curve (up to the maximum number of workers who will accept work at the union wage). As shown in Figure 14-5, if the union sets the wage above the monopsony wage but below the competitive wage, the union can raise *both* wages and employment above the monopsonistic level.

However, the union may not be content merely to neutralize the monopsonist's market power. It may choose to raise wages further above the competitive level. If it does, the outcome will be similar to that shown in Figure 14-3. If the wage is raised above the competitive level, the employer will no longer wish to hire all the labour that is offered at that wage. The amount of employment will fall, and unemployment will develop. These changes are also shown in Figure 14-5.

We now know that the profit-maximizing employer would like to set the monopsonistic wage (w_1) while the union would like a wage *no less than* the competitive wage (w_0). (Any wage below w_0 will reduce *both* wages and employment.) The union may target a still higher wage, depending on how it trades off employment losses against wage gains. If the union is content with an amount of employment as low as would occur at the monopsonistic wage, it could target a wage substantially higher than the competitive wage.

Simple demand and supply analysis can take us no further. The actual outcome will depend on such other things as what target wage the two sides actually set for themselves, their relative bargaining skills, and how each side assesses the costs of concessions. We discuss unions in more detail in the next section of this chapter.

Practise with Study Guide Chapter 14, Exercise 3.

FIGURE 14-5 Bilateral Monopoly in the Labour Market

By presenting a monopsonistic employer with a fixed wage, the union can raise both wages and employment over the monopsonistic level. The monopsony position before the union enters is at E_1 (from Figure 14-4), with a wage rate of w_1 and L_1 workers hired. A union now enters and sets the wage at w_0. The supply curve of labour becomes w_0E_0S, and wages and employment rise to their competitive levels of w_0 and L_0 without creating a pool of unemployed workers. If the wage is raised further, say, to w_2, the supply curve will become w_2xS, the quantity of employment will fall below the competitive level to L_2, and a pool of unsuccessful job applicants of L_2L_3 will develop.

Legislated Minimum Wages

We have examined wage differentials arising in competitive and non-competitive labour markets. Government policy can also affect observed wage differentials by legislating minimum wages. Governments in Canada and many other countries legislate specific **minimum wages**, which define the lowest wage rates that may legally be paid. In 2006, minimum wages ranged from $6.50 per hour in New Brunswick and Newfoundland and Labrador to $8.50 per hour in Nunavut.

For a large proportion of all employment covered by the law, the minimum wage is below the actual market wage, and thus in such cases the minimum wage is *not binding*. Some workers, however, are employed in industries in which the free-market wage would be below the legal minimum, and thus the legislated minimum wage is *binding*. It is only in these cases where the effects of minimum wages are of interest.

Although legislated minimum wages are now an accepted part of the labour scene in Canada and many other industrialized countries, many economists are skeptical about the benefits from such a policy. As our analysis in Chapter 5 indicated, a binding price floor in a competitive market leads to a market surplus of the product—in this case, an excess supply of labour, or unemployment. Thus, theory predicts that a policy that legislates minimum wages in an otherwise competitive market will benefit some workers only by hurting others. In the cases of non-competitive labour markets, however, the analysis is a little more complicated.

Theoretical Effects of a Minimum Wage   Minimum-wage laws usually apply uniformly to almost all occupations, but they will be *binding* only in the lowest-paid occupations and industries, which often involve unskilled or semi-skilled workers. These workers are usually not members of labour unions. Thus, the situations in which minimum wages are likely to be binding include competitive labour markets and those in which employers exercise some monopsony power. The effects on employment are different in the two cases.

Competitive Labour Markets. The predicted consequences for employment of a binding minimum wage are unambiguous when the labour market is competitive. By raising the wage that employers must pay, minimum-wage legislation leads to a reduction in the quantity of labour that is demanded and an increase in the quantity of labour that is supplied. As a result, the actual level of employment falls, and unemployment rises. The excess supply of labour at the minimum wage also creates incentives for people to evade the law by working "under the table" at wages below the legal minimum wage. The predicted effect of a minimum wage in a competitive labour market is shown in part (i) of Figure 14-6.

Firms with Monopsony Power. Our theory predicts that the minimum-wage law can simultaneously increase both wages and employment in markets in which firms have monopsony power. In part (ii) of Figure 14-6, the monopsony wage is w_1. If the minimum wage pushes the wage up only slightly, to w_2, both employment and wages will rise. But beyond the competitive wage (w^*), further increases in the minimum wage will begin to decrease employment and create a pool of unemployed workers.

Many workers in the fast-food industry are young and earn the legislated minimum wage. To the extent that the minimum wage is effective, they get more than they would in its absence, while there is mixed evidence regarding the effects on the overall level of employment.

FIGURE 14-6   The Effects of Legislated Minimum Wages

(i) Competitive labour market   (ii) Firms have monopsony power

Minimum wages are predicted to reduce employment in competitive labour markets; the predicted effects on employment in monopsonistic labour markets are less clear. Part (i) shows a competitive labour market with the competitive equilibrium at w^* and L^*. A binding minimum wage raises the wage to w_{min}. Firms respond by reducing employment to L_1. The quantity of labour supplied by workers increases to L_2. Unemployment is equal to L_1L_2 workers.

Part (ii) shows a labour market in which firms behave as a monopsonist. The monopsony equilibrium is w_1 and L_1. If the minimum wage is set at w_2, employment will rise to L_2. If the minimum wage is set as high as the competitive wage w^*, employment rises to the competitive level L^*. But if the minimum wage rises above w^*, employment will fall below L^*. If the minimum wage were set above w_3, employment would fall below the monopsony level, L_1.

Evidence on the Effects of Minimum Wages
Empirical research on the effects of minimum-wage laws reflects these mixed theoretical predictions. There is some evidence that people who keep their jobs gain when the minimum wage is raised. There is some evidence that some groups suffer a decline in employment consistent with raising the wage in a fairly competitive market. At other times and places, there is evidence that both wages and employment rise when the minimum wage rises, consistent with labour markets in which employers have monopsony power.

Some widely discussed research in the United States has produced hotly debated results. David Card, from Berkeley, and Alan Krueger, from Princeton University, traced the effects of minimum-wage increases in California during 1988 and New Jersey during 1992 and found that substantial rises in these states' minimum wages not only increased wages but also were associated with small employment *gains* for teenagers. Card and Krueger argue that these findings are inconsistent with a competitive labour market and thus take the results as evidence in support of the view that firms have some monopsony power in the labour market.

The Card and Krueger results have been criticized by many economists in the last few years. One criticism is that some of the data used by Card and Krueger are faulty, and that their conclusions are therefore suspect. Another relates to the short span of time covered by their study. The argument is that firms will not immediately reduce the

APPLYING ECONOMIC CONCEPTS 14-1

The Puzzle of Interindustry Wage Differentials in Canada

Differences in wages across industries have been observed for as long as information on wages has been collected. But only recently have economists examined carefully whether they can be explained by differences in skills, jobs, or market structure. In Canada, a study published by Surendra Gera and Gilles Grenier shows the extent of these wage differentials in 1986.*

The table shows results from their study for selected industries; for each industry, the number in the table shows the industry's *wage premium*—that is, the amount by which wages in each industry exceed the average after controlling for such factors as the worker's education, age, gender, occupation, union status, and so on. The challenge is to explain such wage premia.

Competitive Wage Differentials?

Following our discussion in the text, three possible explanations of these wage differentials are consistent with the labour market being competitive.

The first possibility is that these observed wage differentials for 1986 may reflect temporary shifts in the pattern of labour demand or supply across industries. For example, a large increase in demand in the forestry industry that occurs together with a large decline in demand in the textiles industry could account for some of the data in the table. To address this possible explanation, Gera and Grenier examine Canadian Census data for 1970, 1980, and 1985. They find that the pattern of interindustry wage differentials is very similar across these three periods, suggesting that the observed wage differentials are not simply temporary phenomena.

The second possibility is that the wage differentials can be explained by differences in the quality of the workers that are not observable to economists when conducting such a study. For example, they are not able

to observe whether a worker is "highly motivated," "innovative," or "a good problem solver." But many of these characteristics *are* observable to potential employers, either by watching the individual work for a short period of time or by asking previous employers who know the worker. To examine this explanation, Gera and Grenier examine the group of individuals in their sample that move from a job in one industry to a job in a different industry. For example, if high wages to a particular worker in the tobacco industry are due to that worker's unobserved skills, then when that worker switches to the clothing industry, the high wage should persist. But Gera and Grenier find the opposite. A worker who moves from a high-wage industry to a low-

Selected Industry Wage Premia in Canada (percentage above average wage)	
Tobacco Products	33.4
Mineral Fuels	25.5
Forestry	18.9
Electric Power, Gas, and Water Utilities	14.4
Paper and Allied Products	12.0
Communications	10.5
Transportation Equipment	7.0
Wholesale Trade	3.8
Electrical Products	2.6
Education and Related Services	−1.0
Food and Beverages	−3.5
Insurance and Real Estate Agencies	−4.1
Clothing	−8.1
Fishing and Trapping	−9.5
Personal Services	−16.7
Retail Trade	−11.1
Textiles	−19.0
Accommodation and Food Services	−20.3

*S. Gera and G. Grenier, "Interindustry Wage Differentials and Efficiency Wages: Some Canadian Evidence," *Canadian Journal of Economics,* 1994. © 2002–2007 Canadian Economics Association.

wage industry tends to suffer a fall in wage; similarly, a worker who moves from a low-wage industry to a high-wage industry tends to experience a rise in the wage. This finding suggests that the observed wage differentials are not due mainly to unobserved labour quality.

The final possible explanation consistent with a competitive labour market is that the observed wage differentials reflect different characteristics of the *jobs*. Maybe the jobs in the high-wage industries are less pleasant jobs—longer hours, less job security, less safe—than those in the low-wage industries. Gera and Grenier offer two pieces of evidence against this explanation. First, they note that workers in *similar occupations* receive very different wages in different industries, and it is difficult to believe that working conditions for, say, a clerk are very different in the tobacco industry than in the textiles industry. Second, if the observed wage differentials reflect just different job characteristics, then in competitive equilibrium workers are indifferent between (pleasant) jobs in the low-wage industries and (unpleasant) jobs in the high-wage industries. Yet workers appear to quit jobs in the high-wage industries much less frequently than they quit jobs in the low-wage industries. In other words, workers *appear* to view the high-wage jobs as valuable relative to the low-wage jobs. This phenomenon suggests that the observed wage differentials are reflecting more than just differences in working conditions.

Other Explanations?

Maybe the explanation for these observed wage differentials lies in a non-competitive market structure. Perhaps unions have a large presence in some industries and little or no presence in others. When Gera and Grenier examine this possibility, they find that the interindustry wage differentials are just as marked among unionized workers as they are among non-unionized workers.

If the observed wage differentials across Canadian industries cannot be explained by considering different characteristics of the workers, jobs, or market structures, what is the explanation? One possible explanation is based on the theory of *efficiency wages*. According to this theory, firms in even a competitive labour market may find it profitable to pay *more* than the competitive wage to their workers. Firms do this because they perceive that a higher wage will make their workers more productive. Since workers are receiving more than is required to attract their services, they are earning *economic rents* (a concept that we examined in Chapter 13). The fact that workers are receiving rents, in turn, explains why they are reluctant to leave these good jobs—and thus their quit rates from such jobs are low.

Though the efficiency-wage theory offers one possible explanation for why some workers might earn rents, it does not directly offer an explanation for why these rents might be different across industries. In order for the efficiency-wage theory to explain the observed interindustry wage differentials, it must explain why firms' incentives to pay higher wages are greater in some industries than in others. So far, proponents of the theory have not come up with convincing reasons.

The efficiency-wage theory generates considerable disagreement among economists. But there is little debate that there exist significant wage differentials across industries, even after taking account of observable characteristics of workers and jobs. As more data become available, perhaps economists will find better explanations for the observed interindustry wage differentials.

Workers in the forestry industry receive wages roughly 20 percent higher than workers of similar ages and skills in the average industry.

level of employment in response to an increase in the minimum wage—they will instead choose *not to replace* workers who leave their jobs in the natural turnover process that occurs in labour markets. But workers who are receiving the minimum wage may be more reluctant to leave their job after an increase in their wage, thereby reducing this natural turnover. Thus, it is not surprising to see few employment losses (or slight gains) when one examines the labour market immediately before and immediately after the change in legislation. Proponents of this view argue that the total employment effects of minimum wages can be detected only by examining the data over longer periods of time.

Several Canadian studies have examined the relationship between minimum wages and employment (or unemployment). Though the studies differ in their approaches and data used, there is a broad consensus that minimum wages decrease the level of employment (and raise unemployment), particularly for low-skilled workers. Since workers with few skills often earn only low wages, a binding minimum wage has a larger impact on the employment prospects of these workers than it does for higher-skilled, higher-wage workers. In this sense, the Canadian results confirm the theoretical predictions of the effects of minimum wages in competitive labour markets. In these cases, the wage gains by the majority of workers who retain their jobs must be set against the loss of employment by a smaller group of workers.

A Final Word

We have examined several explanations for why some workers get paid more than others. The explanations include differences in workers' educations and skills, differences in job characteristics, discrimination, and differences in the structure of the various labour markets. But this apparent abundance of explanations should not lead you to believe that economists understand *all* wage differentials observed in the labour market. Recent studies, both in Canada and in the United States, have revealed significant differences in wages across industries that appear to defy explanations based on the sorts of arguments we have examined. *Applying Economic Concepts 14-1* discusses the continuing puzzle of interindustry wage differentials in Canada.

FIGURE 14-7   Union Membership in Canada, 1921–2002

As a share of the labour force, the number of union members has increased significantly over the past century, but has declined since the 1980s. The large increases in Canadian unionization occurred during and after the Second World War, and during the 1960s.

(*Source:* Most recent data are available at the website for Human Resources and Social Development Canada: www.hrsdc.gc.ca. © Public Works and Government Services Canada.)

14.2 **LABOUR UNIONS**

Unions currently represent about 25 percent of the labour force in Canada. Of those workers employed in the public sector, however, approximately two-thirds are unionized. Figure 14-7 shows how union membership has changed in Canada over the past several decades. Table 14-1 shows unionization rates by industry. As is clear from the table, unionization is most common in the public and educational sectors and least common in agriculture, finance, and trade.

Despite the relatively low degree of unionization among Canada's private-sector workers, unions have a considerable influence in the private sector. One reason is the impact that union wage contracts have on other labour markets. When, for example, the Canadian Auto Workers negotiates a new contract with an automobile producer in Oshawa, its provisions set a pattern that directly or indirectly affects other labour markets, both in Ontario and in other provinces. A second reason is the major leadership role that unions have played in the past 50 years in the development of labour market practices and in lobbying for legislation that applies to all workers.

In this section, we discuss the process of *collective bargaining* and, in particular, examine the inherent conflict that unions face between striving for higher wages and for increasing employment. *Lessons From History 14-1* examines the historical development of labour unions in Canada.

Collective Bargaining

The process by which unions and employers reach an agreement is known as **collective bargaining**. This process has an important difference from the theoretical models that we discussed in the previous section. In those models, we assumed that the union had the power to set the wage unilaterally; the employer then decided how much labour to hire. In actual collective bargaining, however, the firm and union typically bargain over the wage (as well as other aspects of the employment relationship such as fringe benefits, working conditions, overtime conditions, and flexibility in scheduling). There is usually a substantial range over which an agreement can be reached, and the actual result in particular cases will depend on the strengths of the two bargaining parties and on the skill of their negotiators.

To see the possible outcomes, refer back to Figure 14-5. It may be that the firm wants the wage to be w_1 and the union wants the wage to be w_2. Depending on each side's market power, and on their bargaining tactics, the final agreed-upon wage may be anywhere in between. Note that while actual collective bargaining has the firm and union bargaining over the wage, it is typically the case that the firm retains the "right to manage"—meaning that the firm can decide how much labour it wants to employ at the negotiated wage.

Wages Versus Employment Unions seek many goals when they bargain with management. They may push for higher wages, higher fringe benefits, or less onerous working conditions. Many unions in Canada also emphasize the importance of "job security," meaning a commitment by the firm not to lay workers off in the event of a downturn in business conditions. Firms, however, are understandably reluctant to promise such security since reducing their workforce is an effective way to reduce costs when business conditions deteriorate.

TABLE 14-1 Unionization Rates by Industry, 2005

Industry	Union Density (membership as percentage of paid workers)
Goods Producing	29.6
Agriculture	6.8
Natural Resources	21.5
Utilities	66.8
Construction	29.9
Manufacturing	29.6
Services Producing	30.1
Trade	13.1
Transportation and Warehousing	41.3
Finance, Insurance, and Real Estate	8.3
Management and Administrative	12.5
Education	68.2
Health Care	53.0
Public Administration	68.1
Total Canadian Economy	30.0

There is considerable variation across Canadian industries in the extent of unionization. The public sector and the educational services sector are the most unionized; agriculture, finance, and trade are the least unionized.

(*Source:* Statistics Canada, *Perspectives on Labour and Income,* Catalogue no. 75-001. Reprinted with permission of Statistics Canada.)

collective bargaining The process by which unions and employers arrive at and enforce agreements.

LESSONS FROM HISTORY 14-1

The Development of Unions in Canada

Early Canadian unionization was strongly dominated by the influence of international unions, which had their headquarters and an overwhelming proportion of their membership outside Canada. The creation of Canadian locals of American unions began in the 1860s. By 1911, 90 percent of Canadian workers who were union members belonged to international unions.

During the first half of the twentieth century, there was strong pressure: first, toward a single national federation; and second, to achieve autonomy from American unions. The issues became intertwined when conflicts in the United States arose between craft and industrial unions. Until the 1930s, *craft unions*—which cover persons in a particular occupation—were the characteristic form of collective action in the United States. In Canada, meanwhile, trade unionists were attracted to *industrial unions* that embraced unskilled workers as well as skilled craftsmen in one industry such as steel making, forest products, or railways.

Because of the impossibility of establishing bargaining strength by controlling the supply of unskilled workers, the rise of industrial unionism in Canada was associated with political action as an alternative means of improving the lot of the membership. In general, social and political reform were given much more emphasis by Canadian unionists than by their American counterparts. Political action here extended to the support for social democratic political parties: first, the Co-operative Commonwealth Federation (CCF), established in 1932, and later its successor, the New Democratic Party (NDP), formed in 1961.

The late senator Eugene Forsey, a former director of research for the Canadian Labour Congress (CLC), viewed the unification of the bulk of Canadian unions under the CLC in 1956 as the beginning of virtual autonomy for Canadian locals from their U.S. head offices. Throughout the postwar period, the percentage of total Canadian union membership represented by international unions fell: In the mid-1950s, it was about 70 percent, and by the mid-1990s, it was just over 30 percent.

One factor in the increased share of national unions is the growth of membership in the two unions representing government workers: the Canadian Union of Public Employees and the Public Service Alliance. Another major component of non-international union membership has arisen out of the distinct aspirations of French-Canadian workers. More recently, the formation of the Canadian Auto Workers, independent of the American Auto Workers, represented a significant further reduction of membership in international unions.

Rapid gains in union membership in Canada occurred in the years during the Second World War. This led to pressure for the rights of workers to organize and to elect an exclusive bargaining agent. These rights were established by provisions of the *Wartime Labour Relations Regulations Act* of 1944.

The Winnipeg General Strike of 1919 began a wave of increased unionism and militancy across Canada.

Whatever unions' specific goals, unless they face a monopsonist across the bargaining table, they must deal with a fundamental dilemma.

There is an inherent conflict between the level of wages and the size of the union itself.

The more successful a union is in raising wages, the more management will reduce the size of its workforce, substituting capital for labour. This will lead to lower union membership. However, if the union does not provide some wage improvement for its members, they will have little incentive to stay around.

The Union Wage Premium Despite the costs to unions (i.e., reduced membership) of pushing for higher wages, there is clear evidence in Canada of a *union wage premium*—that is, a higher wage attributed only to the union status of the job. It is not easy to measure this wage premium, however, because it is not appropriate simply to compare the average wage of unionized workers with the average wage of non-unionized workers. After all, unions may occur mainly in industries where workers have higher skills or where working conditions are less pleasant. And we know from the first section of this chapter that differences in skills or working conditions can lead to wage differentials. Economists have therefore been forced to use complicated statistical techniques to identify this union wage premium. The consensus appears to be that the union wage premium in Canada is somewhere between 10 and 15 percent—that is, unionized workers with a particular set of skills in particular types of jobs get paid 10 to 15 percent more than *otherwise identical workers* who are not members of unions.

Unionized workers earn, on average, between 10 and 15 percent higher wages than non-unionized workers with similar characteristics.

There is also evidence that the size of this union wage premium differs across industries. Given that workers in different industries and with different occupations are often represented by different unions, this cross-industry difference in the union wage premium may simply reflect the differences in unions' preferences for higher wages versus higher employment.

Employment Effects of Unions We said earlier that unions face an inherent conflict between the level of wages and the level of employment. This conflict simply reflects the firm's profit-maximizing behaviour as embodied in its downward-sloping demand curve for labour. As the union pushes for higher wages, the firm naturally chooses to hire fewer workers.

What continues to puzzle economists, however, is how the clear evidence of a 10- to 15-percent union wage premium can be consistent with a second empirical result—the absence of any clear effect on employment. One possible explanation for the absence of an employment effect is that unions use the collective bargaining process to pressure firms to hire more workers than they otherwise would. This practice is known as *featherbedding,* and for years was infamous in the railways where union contracts required the railways to hire firemen (whose job was to keep the coal fires burning) long after the widespread adoption of diesel locomotives.

If such featherbedding is pervasive in unionized firms, it may be the explanation for the absence of an observable union effect on employment. The employment reduction caused by the higher wage may be offset by the employment increase due to featherbedding.

Another possible explanation for the absence of a union employment effect is union campaigns to increase the demand for the goods produced by their members. We sometimes see labels on products that proclaim them to be "union made" or "made with union labour." Unions also spend considerably on magazine and television advertising stressing the value of union labour. Some unions also lobby the government to restrict the import of foreign-made products in an attempt to increase Canadian consumers' demand for the domestic goods made with union labour. To the extent that these campaigns convince consumers to buy more union-made products than they otherwise would, the result will be an increase in demand for union labour.

Figure 14-8 shows how the combination of the union wage premium and the increases in demand for union labour (either through featherbedding or advertising) can explain the *absence* of an observed union employment effect.

For information on the Canadian labour movement, see the website for the Canadian Labour Congress: **www.clc.org**.

FIGURE 14-8   The Union Employment Effect

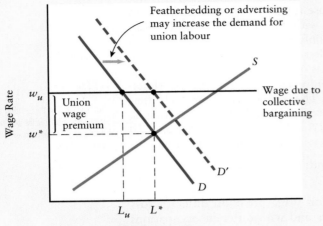

Quantity of Labour

Featherbedding and advertising may explain the absence of a union employment effect even though there is a clear union wage effect. If the labour market is competitive, wages and employment will be given by w^* and L^*. The collective bargaining between firms and unions results in a wage of w_u, showing a clear premium above the competitive wage. If the demand for labour remains at D, employment would fall to L_u and there would be a reduction in employment caused by the union. If the collective agreement requires firms to use more labour, however, or if the union successfully promotes union-made products, the demand for labour shifts to D'. In this case, the combination of the higher wage and the greater demand for labour results in the competitive level of employment.

Unanswered Questions

Labour unions have played a significant role in the economies of Canada, the United States, and Europe for many years. It is therefore surprising how little economists actually know about how unions influence economic outcomes and, in particular, how unions affect long-run productivity.

Unions may reduce long-run productivity through a process known as the *hold-up* of capital. Much physical capital, once it is installed, is very difficult to move or resell. For this reason, *installed* capital has a very inelastic supply and, following the discussion from Chapter 13, a large part of its factor payment takes the form of economic rent. The union may be able to extract these rents from the firm in the form of higher wages. That is, once the firm has already installed its capital equipment the union may be able to *hold up* the firm by forcing it to pay higher wages; the firm is stuck with its installed capital and thus pays the higher wages and, in turn, receives lower profits. If firms are forward-looking, however, they can anticipate this sort of behaviour from unions *before* making such investments in physical capital. The possibility of being held up by union wage demands reduces the expected profitability of investment and may result in a reduction in investment. This decision to invest less would likely have negative implications for productivity growth in the industry.

There is some empirical evidence that the presence of a union does reduce investment by firms. It is not yet clear, however, whether such reduced investment has long-term effects on productivity. This issue is currently unresolved.

14.3 THE "GOOD JOBS–BAD JOBS" DEBATE

Figure 14-9 shows how the composition of Canadian employment has changed over the past century. The share of total employment in agriculture fell from 45 percent in 1891 to just over 2 percent today, while the share of total employment in services (including government) increased from 20 percent in 1891 to just over 75 percent today. The combined share for manufacturing and construction has been more variable over the last century, but has been on a clear downward trend for the past 50 years, falling from about 35 percent in 1951 to about 20 percent today.

The rise of service-sector employment, and the decline in the relative importance of the agriculture and manufacturing sectors as providers of jobs, is not just a

FIGURE 14-9 A Century of Change in the Composition of Canadian Employment

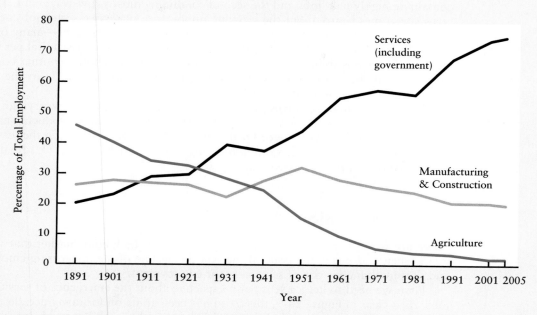

Over the past century, major shifts in employment have taken place between sectors of the economy. In 1891, over 45 percent of Canadian employment was in agriculture, and only 20 percent in services (including government). By 2005, agriculture accounted for only 2.1 percent of employment, while services had increased to over 75 percent. The share of employment in manufacturing and construction increased from 26 percent in 1891 to 32 percent just after the Second World War, and then declined back to 20 percent by 2005.

(*Source: Canadian Census,* various years, and authors' calculations. The most recent data are available on the Statistics Canada website at www.statcan.ca. Search for "Employment," and then choose "Employment by industry." Reprinted with permission of Statistics Canada.)

Canadian phenomenon—it has happened in all developed economies. Table 14-2 shows the percentage of total employment provided by the service sector in several developed countries in 2004.

The service sector contains an enormous variety of occupations. Many jobs in the service sector require considerable education and training and thus the workers in these jobs are highly paid. Obvious examples include lawyers, doctors, architects, design engineers, accountants, management consultants, and professors. On the other hand, the service sector also contains many jobs that require much less training and whose workers therefore receive much lower wages. Examples of these occupations include many

TABLE 14-2 The Importance of Service-Sector Employment, 2004

Country	Percentage of Employment in Services
Australia	74.9
Belgium	73.1
Canada	75.0
France	72.6
Japan	67.1
Sweden	75.2
United Kingdom	76.4
United States	78.4

(*Source: OECD in Figures,* 2005 Edition, www.oecd.org. © OECD. All rights reserved.)

restaurant waiters, fast-food employees, store clerks, flight attendants, telephone solic-itors, janitors, and hotel maids.

In general, we can divide service-sector employment into two parts—the first part containing highly paid jobs and the second containing mostly low-wage jobs. The con-cerns sometimes heard about the growing importance of service-sector jobs are really concerns about this low-wage part of the service sector. In these jobs—many of which are in the retail sector—there are fewer possibilities for using more capital per worker, and thus fewer possibilities to increase the productivity of labour. Another concern is that many of these low-wage service-sector jobs offer workers little in the way of advancement or job security.

Are these dramatic changes in the composition of employment worrying? Is there something undesirable about the fact that fewer workers are now producing manufac-tured goods than forty years ago? Or that more workers are working in the service sec-tor than forty years ago? Are good jobs being replaced by bad jobs? This final section of the chapter addresses this contentious issue.

Five Observations

There are five observations about the economy and the labour market that we must make when addressing the issue of the relative decline of manufacturing employment and the simultaneous rise of service-sector employment.

First, we need to keep a sense of perspective about the emergence of service-sector jobs. As is clear in Figure 14-9, this trend has been going on for many decades, yet real income per hour worked has been rising throughout this period; as a nation, Canadians are getting richer, not poorer.

Second, keep in mind that even the lowest-paying service jobs play an important role in the Canadian economy. The fast-food industry is often held up as an example of an industry in which employers provide bad jobs—low wages and little job secu-rity—to their workers. It *is* true that wages are low in this industry and, due to the part-time nature of the jobs, there are often no benefits and no job security. But it is also true that the vast majority of workers in the fast-food industry have little formal training and are between the ages of 15 and 20. Firms in this industry often provide young workers with their first paid jobs, helping them get their "foot in the door" of the labour market. After this first job, in which they acquire some skills and demon-strate responsibility, many young workers move on to jobs that are more demanding and for which they would not have qualified before their experience in the fast-food industry. In other words, some low-paying service-sector jobs provide employment to young, untrained individuals who would otherwise find it difficult to find a job at all.

The reduction in manufacturing employment is partly the result of that sector's dynamism—more and more output can be produced with fewer and fewer workers.

Third, relating directly to the manufacturing sector, the decrease in the share of manufacturing in total employment is largely a result of that sector's dynamism. More and more manu-factured goods have been produced by fewer and fewer workers, leaving more workers to produce services. This movement is anal-ogous to the one out of agriculture in the twentieth century. At the turn of the twentieth century, nearly 45 percent of the Canadian labour force worked on farms. Today that number is just over 2 percent, yet they produce more total output than did the 45 per-cent in 1900. This movement away from agricultural employment freed workers to move into manufacturing, raising our living standards and transforming our way of life. In like manner, the movement away from manufacturing has been freeing workers to move into services, and by replacing the grimy blue-collar jobs of the smokestack industries with more pleasant white-collar jobs in the service industries, it has once again transformed our way of life.

Fourth, the decrease in the share of manufacturing in total employment also follows from consumers' tastes. Just as consumers in the first half of the century did not want to go on consuming more and more food products as their incomes rose, today's consumers do not wish to spend all of their additional income on manufactured products. Households have chosen to spend a high proportion of their increased incomes on services, thus creating employment opportunities in that sector. This simply reflects the fact that many products of the service sector—like restaurant meals, hotel stays, and airline flights—are products that have a high income elasticity of demand. Thus, as the income of the average Canadian household increases, so too does that household's demand for these products of the service sector.

Finally, it is easy to underestimate the scope for quality, quantity, and productivity increases in services. But these changes permit us to have a higher standard of living than we would otherwise have. As just one example of productivity increases, consider your ability to make an automatic cash withdrawal, at any time of the day or night, from your bank account in Nova Scotia, while you are on vacation in Brazil. Now compare that to the apprehension your parents faced 35 years ago when they had to get to their bank branch before 3:00 p.m. on a Friday afternoon to make sure they had enough cash for the weekend. It would have been simply impossible for them to cash a cheque in Brazil without having made elaborate prior arrangements.

Also, many quality improvements in services go unrecorded. Today's hotel room is vastly more comfortable than a hotel room of 40 years ago, yet this quality improvement does not show up in our national income statistics. Measuring such technological improvements is even more difficult when they take the form of entirely new products. Airline transportation, telecommunication, fast-food chains, and financial services are prominent examples. The resulting increase in output is not always properly captured in existing statistics.

A Mixed Blessing?

It is easy to become concerned when looking at the official statistics, which show low wages earned in some service jobs. Indeed, the shift in employment toward services is, like most changes that hit the economy, a mixed blessing. It entails a significant increase in the number of "bad" service-sector jobs with low pay or low job security. Further, such transitions often generate temporary unemployment as workers get laid off from a shrinking manufacturing sector and only slowly find jobs in the expanding service sector. Such transitions suggest a role for government policy to maintain the income of those workers temporarily unemployed (we will discuss employment insurance and other income-support programs in Chapter 18). However, if we focus on the *overall economy,* and consider the growth in the real living standards of the *average* Canadian household, we are reminded that average real income has continued to rise, not only throughout the shift from agriculture to manufacturing, but also throughout the shift from manufacturing to services. There is little reason to think that the continued growth of the service sector will stand in the way of this slow but steady improvement in Canadians' living standards.

S U M M A R Y

14.1 WAGE DIFFERENTIALS

- In a competitive labour market, wages are set by the forces of supply and demand. Differences in wages will arise because some skills are more valued than others, because some jobs are more onerous than others, because of varying amounts of human capital, and because of discrimination based on such factors as gender and race.
- A union entering a competitive market can act as a monopolist and can raise wages, but at a predicted cost of reducing employment.
- A profit-maximizing monopsonistic employer entering a competitive labour market will reduce both the wage and the level of employment.

- A union in a monopsonistic labour market—a case of bilateral monopoly—may increase both employment and wages relative to the pure monopsony outcome. If the union sets wages above the competitive level, however, the prediction is that it will create a pool of workers who are unable to get the jobs that they want at the going wage.
- Governments set some wages above their competitive levels by passing minimum-wage laws. In competitive labour markets, a minimum wage is predicted to reduce employment and create some unemployment. In monopsonistic labour markets, a legislated minimum wage (as long as it is not too high) can raise both wages and employment.

14.2 LABOUR UNIONS

- Labour unions seek many goals when they bargain with management. They may push for higher wages, higher fringe benefits, more stable employment, or less onerous working conditions. Whatever their specific goals, unless they face a monopsonist across the bargaining table, they must recognize the inherent conflict between the level of wages and the size of the union itself.

- There is clear evidence in Canada of a union wage premium: Unionized workers with a particular set of skills in particular types of jobs get paid 10 to 15 percent more than otherwise identical workers who are not union members.

14.3 THE "GOOD JOBS–BAD JOBS" DEBATE

- The past half-century has witnessed an increase in the share of total employment in the service sector and a decline in the share of employment in manufacturing. One part of the service sector requires considerable skills and pays high wages, another part requires few skills and pays low wages. Some people are concerned that some "good" manufacturing jobs are being replaced by "bad" service jobs.

- The decline in manufacturing employment is partly due to the technological improvements in that sector and partly due to shifts in consumers' tastes toward services.
- Though the shift away from manufacturing and toward services involves some costs during the transition period, the ongoing growth in average per capita income (plus the hard-to-measure quality improvements) suggests that the shift is not a problem for the economy as a whole.

KEY CONCEPTS

Wage differentials in competitive labour markets
Effects of discrimination on wages and employment

Labour unions as monopolists
Single employer as monopsonist
Bilateral monopoly
Effects of legislated minimum wages

Collective bargaining
Union goals: wages versus employment
Union wage premium
"Good jobs" vs. "bad jobs"

STUDY EXERCISES

1. Fill in the blanks to make the following statements correct.

   a. If all workers were identical, all jobs had identical working conditions, and labour markets were perfectly competitive, then all wages would be _____.

   b. In reality there is wide variation in wages. Four reasons for wage differentials are _____, _____, _____, and _____.

   c. A country that invests in its public education and public health systems is improving the _____ of its population.

   d. If there are two groups of workers in a competitive labour market, and one group becomes discriminated against, the labour supply curve for jobs that remain available for that group will shift to the _____ and the wages for these jobs will _____.

2. Suppose there are only two industries in the economy. All workers have the same skills and the same preferences. But the jobs in the two industries are different. In the Pleasant industry, working conditions are desirable (quiet, safe, clean, etc.). In the Grimy industry, working conditions are awful (noisy, unsafe, dirty, etc.).

   a. Draw supply-and-demand diagrams for the labour market in each industry.

   b. In which industry are wages higher? Why?

   c. Now suppose the Grimy industry made its working conditions just as pleasant as in the Pleasant industry. Explain what happens in *both* labour markets.

3. Suppose there are two types of basketball players—black and white. Suppose also that, on average, black players are no better and no worse than white players. Furthermore, suppose there are only two types of basketball teams—good and bad. Good teams hire only good players; bad teams will hire both good and bad players. The two diagrams that follow show the initial outcomes in the labour markets for good teams and bad teams. Assume there is *no discrimination based on race*.

   a. As shown in the figures, the wage paid by good teams is higher than the wage paid by bad teams. What explains this wage differential?

   b. Do black players earn more or less than white players, on average? Explain.

   c. Now suppose the good teams discriminate against white players—rightly or wrongly they *believe* that black players are better than white players. Show in your diagram what happens in both labour markets.

   d. In the situation in part (c), what happens to the wage differential between good and bad teams?

   e. In the situation in part (c), what happens to the average black–white wage differential?

(i) Good teams

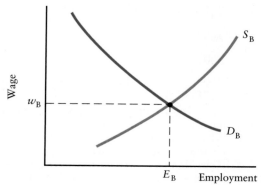

(ii) Bad teams

4. Suppose *in the real world* you observe that black basketball players get paid more than white basketball players. Do you conclude that discrimination is present? Explain why or why not.

5. Fill in the blanks to make the following statements correct.

   a. If workers in a competitive labour market join together to form a union, the effect will be a(n) _____ wage and _____ quantity of labour demanded.

   b. If firms in a competitive labour market form an employers' association and become a monopsonist, employment will be _____ and wages will be _____ than in the competitive outcome.

c. A legislated and binding minimum wage in a competitive labour market will lead to a(n) _____ in the quantity of labour demanded and a(n) _____ in the quantity of labour supplied. The actual number of workers employed will _____.

d. A legislated and binding minimum wage in a market where the employer has monopsony power and the wage is initially below the competitive level will lead to a(n) _____ in the number of workers employed.

6. (X myeconlab) The table below shows how many workers are prepared to work at various hourly wages in the forestry industry. It also shows the workers' marginal revenue product (*MRP*).

Number of Workers	Wage ($)	Marginal Cost of Labour ($)	MRP ($)
50	10	—	50
100	12	14	40
150	14	18	30
200	16	—	24
250	18	—	22
300	20	—	20
350	22	—	18

a. On a diagram, draw the supply of labour curve and the demand for labour curve.

b. What is the equilibrium wage and level of employment if the labour market is competitive?

c. Now suppose there is only a single buyer for labour—a *monopsonist*. Compute the marginal cost of labour for each level of employment and fill in the table. (Recall that the *MC* of labour is the change in labour cost divided by the change in employment. The first two rows have been completed for you.)

d. What wage and level of employment would the monopsonist choose? Explain.

7. (X myeconlab) The following diagram shows the market for labour in a particular industry. It shows both the supply of labour (the average cost of labour) and the marginal cost of labour.

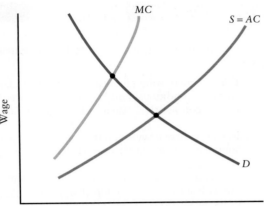

a. Suppose the labour market is competitive. What will be the equilibrium wage and level of employment (call them w^* and L^*)?

b. Now suppose the government imposes a minimum wage equal to $w^{min} > w^*$. Show what happens to wages and employment.

c. In the absence of a minimum wage, show the outcome if there is a monopsony buyer of labour services. Call this wage w^p.

d. Beginning with the monopsony outcome, show what happens if the government imposes a minimum wage above w^p but lower than w^*.

e. Do minimum wages always reduce employment? Explain.

8. Fill in the blanks to make the following statements correct.

a. In the case of labour unions, there is an inherent conflict between _____ and _____.

b. The union wage premium in Canada is estimated to be between _____ and _____ percent.

c. In Canada, the agricultural industry has a _____ rate of unionization and the public sector has a _____ rate of unionization.

d. The shift in employment from manufacturing jobs to service jobs in Canada has coincided with _____ real income per hour worked.

e. The decline in the share of total employment in the manufacturing sector in Canada is partly due to the _____ in the total output per worker in that sector.

9. The following diagram shows the market for labour in a particular industry. It shows both the supply of labour (the average cost of labour) and the marginal cost of labour. If the labour market were competitive, the outcome would be w^* and L^*.

    a. Suppose the workers in this industry form a union that is able to raise the wage above w^*. Show the expected outcome in the figure.

    b. Now suppose there is no union, but there is a monopsony buyer of labour. Show the expected outcome in this market.

    c. Now suppose there is both a union and a monopsony firm. What can you predict about the outcome in this case?

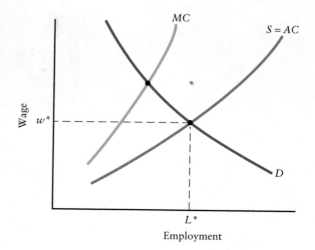

DISCUSSION QUESTIONS

1. "The great increase in the number of women entering the labour force for the first time means that relatively more women than men earn beginning salaries. It is therefore not evidence of discrimination that the average wage earned by females is less than that earned by males." Discuss.

2. Physicians are among the highest-paid of workers. However, in addition to a bachelor's degree, would-be physicians must attend four years of medical school, three years of residency, and up to seven additional years of residency to be specialists. How does this lengthy training change your perception with respect to how much physicians are paid? What additional information would you need to determine whether physicians' real pay is higher than that of other professionals?

3. In trying to measure the extent to which labour unions are responsible for increasing wages, economists use sophisticated statistical methods to compare the wages of unionized workers with those of non-unionized workers. Explain why it is not legitimate simply to compare the average wage across the two groups and attribute the difference to the effects of unionization.

4. "One can judge the presence or absence of discrimination by looking at the proportion of the population in different occupations." Does such information help?

Does it suffice? Consider each of the following examples. Relative to their numbers in the total population, there are

    a. Too many blacks and too few Jews among professional athletes
    b. Too few male secretaries
    c. Too few female judges
    d. Too few female prison guards
    e. Too few male schoolteachers
    f. Too few female graduate students in economics

5. "Equal pay for work of equal value" is a commonly held goal, but "equal value" is hard to define. What would be the consequences of legislation that enforces equal pay for what turns out to be work of unequal value?

6. There is clear evidence of a union wage premium of between 10 and 15 percent. There is also clear evidence that firms' demand curves are downward sloping. Reconcile these two "facts" with the third fact that there is *no* clear evidence that unions lead to employment reductions.

7. One concern often expressed about the ongoing rise of services and decline of manufacturing is that the production of "things" is somehow better for wealth generation than the production of intangible services. Can you provide an argument in support of this view?

Interest Rates and the Capital Market

In this chapter you will learn

1. how to compute the present value of an asset that delivers a stream of future benefits.
2. why the demand for investment is negatively related to the interest rate.
3. why the supply of saving is positively related to the interest rate.
4. how the equilibrium interest rate is determined and how it is affected by various economic events.

Economists use the word *capital* in three different ways. *Human capital,* which we discussed in Chapter 14, is the set of skills that workers acquire through education and on-the-job training. *Physical capital* is a produced factor of production, such as a machine, a factory, or a bridge. *Financial capital* refers to financial assets in the form of *loans, bonds,* or *stocks.* In this chapter, we focus on what economists call the "capital market," which involves both physical and financial capital, and the role played by the interest rate in this market.

15.1 A BRIEF OVERVIEW OF THE CAPITAL MARKET

Firms require physical capital to produce their goods and services. Their purchase of new capital equipment is called *investment* in physical capital. We saw in Chapter 7 that firms can finance their investment in one of four ways. First, they can use profits that are not remitted to shareholders—these are called *retained earnings*. Second, they can borrow from commercial banks or other financial intermediaries, such as credit unions and trust companies. Third, they can issue *bonds* (an IOU) and thereby borrow directly from lenders. Fourth, they can issue and sell *stock* (a share of the company) directly to shareholders. However firms choose to finance their investments, their demand for financial capital comes mostly from their demand for physical capital.

Firms' demand for financial capital is derived from their demand for physical capital.

The supply of financial capital comes mostly from households' saving decisions. Every year, millions of households decide how much of their income to save. These funds are often deposited into various types of accounts at commercial banks, each of which is a loan from the household to the bank. Sometimes the funds are used to buy bonds so that the household is lending directly to a nonbank borrower. The household may also decide to purchase stock, and thereby acquire a share of some firm. Whatever form households choose for their saving, their saving decisions determine their total supply of financial capital.

Households' supply of financial capital is derived from their supply of saving.

Figure 15-1 illustrates the interaction of firms and households in the market for financial capital. Note that some funds flow directly between firms and households (bond and stock purchases) whereas other funds flow through financial intermediaries (bank deposits and loans). Financial intermediaries play an important role in the economy for two reasons. First, they are specialists in assessing the *riskiness* of potential borrowers and thus are

FIGURE 15-1 The Interaction of Firms and Households in the Capital Market

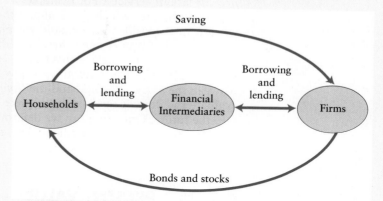

The capital market connects households' saving decisions with firms' borrowing decisions. Households save some part of their income. They can lend (make a deposit) to a commercial bank or other financial intermediary. They can lend directly to a firm by buying a bond. Or they can purchase stock and thereby become a part owner in a firm. Firms finance their investment (purchases of new capital equipment) either by using their retained earnings, borrowing from a bank, issuing a bond and borrowing directly from a lender, or issuing and selling stock.

better suited than most households to making loans to firms. Second, they have the ability to *pool* the savings from a large number of households and thereby make large loans to firms. Despite the importance of financial intermediaries to the economy, in this chapter we will focus our attention on households and firms, thus focusing on the fundamental determinants of the demand for and supply of capital.

In this chapter, we look first at firms' demand for physical capital, which leads us to an understanding of their demand for financial capital. As we will see, the interest rate plays an important role in determining how much capital is demanded by firms. We then examine households' saving decisions and thus their supply of financial capital. The interest rate also plays an important role in determining how much financial capital households want to supply. Once we understand the demand and supply for financial capital, we will be ready to put the two sides of the capital market together to determine the equilibrium "price" of financial capital—the interest rate. Finally, we will look at how economic events or policies can affect the equilibrium levels of investment, saving, and the interest rate.

Before beginning our analysis of the demand for capital, it is necessary to clarify one important difference between labour and physical capital as factors of production. When economists speak of the demand and supply for labour, they are referring to the *flow* of labour services. For example, a firm considers hiring the services of a worker for a month, after which the firm and the worker go their separate ways. In contrast, when a firm considers its demand for physical capital, it is considering purchasing a new piece of equipment and thereby adding to its *stock* of capital. This piece of capital equipment will usually deliver services to the firm over many years before it eventually wears out. The durability of physical capital means that we must distinguish between the *stock* of capital and the *flow* of services that it delivers. We need a way to evaluate the flow of services that a piece of capital equipment delivers for many years into the future. Only then can we determine how much a firm would be willing to pay for the piece of capital equipment. This takes us to the concept of *present value*.

15.2 **PRESENT VALUE**

Suppose a firm buys a piece of capital equipment and thereby obtains the use of that equipment until it wears out. The capital equipment delivers a flow of benefits over its lifetime—that is, it delivers some benefit every year for many years. The benefit to the firm in any given year is the marginal revenue product (*MRP*) of that unit of capital. A given piece of capital may deliver different *MRP*s in different years—the *MRP* may change because of changes in market conditions or simply because the capital wears out slowly over time. In reality, the stream of future *MRP*s is uncertain. No firm can predict with certainty how its market will evolve, how consumers will respond to the product, or even how long the capital equipment will last.

How much would a firm be willing to pay today to purchase a piece of capital equipment that will deliver an uncertain stream of benefits into the future? In order to answer this question we introduce the concept of *present value*. The **present value** of a future amount is the most that someone would be prepared to pay today to get that amount in the future. The concept of present value is used extensively in financial analysis as well as in the analysis of economic policies where costs and benefits occur at different points in time.

In what follows, we simplify our discussion by assuming that the future benefits from a piece of capital equipment are known with certainty. This allows us to develop the central insights about present value and the interest rate without dealing with complications arising from uncertainty.

present value The value today of a future stream of payments discounted using the market interest rate.

The Present Value of a Single Future Payment

To begin our analysis, consider a very simple setting in which the piece of capital equipment produces an *MRP* only in one future period. Since most physical capital is durable and thus generates a *stream* of benefits, this assumption is quite unrealistic, but is only our starting point. In the first case, the *MRP* occurs one period from now. In the second, the *MRP* occurs several periods from now.

One Period in the Future   How much would a firm be prepared to pay now to purchase a capital good that produces an *MRP* of $100 in one year's time, after which time the capital good will be useless? One way to answer this question is to ask a somewhat *opposite* question: How much would the firm have to *lend* now in order to be repaid

$100 a year from now? Suppose for the moment that the interest rate is 5 percent per year, which means that $1.00 loaned today will lead to a repayment of $1.05 in one year's time.

If we use PV to stand for this unknown amount, we can write $PV \times (1.05) =$ $100. Thus, $PV = \$100/1.05 = \$95.24$. This tells us that the present value of $100 receivable in one year's time is $95.24 when the interest rate is 5 percent. Anyone who lends out $95.24 for one year at 5-percent interest will receive $95.24 back plus $4.76 in interest, or $100 in total. When we calculate this present value, the interest rate is used to *discount* (reduce to its present value) the $100 to be received in one year's time.

The actual present value that we have calculated depended on our assumption that the interest rate was 5 percent. What if the interest rate is 7 percent? At that interest rate, the present value of the $100 receivable in one year's time would be $100/1.07 = $93.46.

These examples are easy to generalize. In both cases, we have found the present value by dividing the sum that is receivable in the future by 1 plus the rate of interest.[1] In general, if the interest rate is i per year, then the present value of the MRP (in dollars) received one year hence is

$$PV = MRP/(1 + i)$$

Table 15-1 computes the present value of an MRP of $500, received one year from now, under alternative assumptions of the interest rate. There is a negative relationship between present value and the interest rate.

Several Periods in the Future   Now we know how to calculate the present value of a single sum that is receivable one year in the future. The next step is to ask what would happen if the sum were receivable at a later date. For example, what is the present value of $100 to be received *two* years hence when the interest rate is 5 percent? The answer is $100/[(1.05)(1.05)] = $90.70. We can check this by seeing what would happen if $90.70 were lent out for two years. In the first year, the loan would earn interest of $(0.05)(\$90.70)$ = $4.54, and hence after one year, the outstanding loan would be worth $95.24. If we assume that interest is compounded annually, then in the second year the interest earned would equal $(0.05)(\$95.24) =$ $4.76. Hence, after two years the firm would be repaid $100.

In general, the present value of MRP dollars received t years in the future when the interest rate is i per year is

$$PV = MRP/(1 + i)^t$$

TABLE 15-1	The Present Value of a Single Sum One Year in the Future		

	MRP	Interest Rate Per Year	Present Value
1.	$500	4% = 0.04	$500/(1.04) = $480.77
2.	$500	5% = 0.05	$500/(1.05) = $476.19
3.	$500	6% = 0.06	$500/(1.06) = $471.70
4.	$500	7% = 0.07	$500/(1.07) = $467.29
5.	$500	8% = 0.08	$500/(1.08) = $462.96

For any given sum at a given point in the future, the present value of the sum is negatively related to the interest rate. The firm earns an MRP of $500 in one year's time. Using the formula developed in the text, it is clear that present value is lower when the interest rate is higher.

---

[1] In this type of formula, the interest rate i is expressed as a decimal fraction where, for example, a 7-percent annual interest rate is expressed as 0.07, so that $1 + i$ equals 1.07. We also assume throughout our analysis that discounting by the interest rate occurs annually rather than semi-annually, monthly, or continuously.

This formula simply discounts the *MRP* by the interest rate, repeatedly, once for each of the *t* periods that must pass until the *MRP* becomes available. If we look at the formula, we see that the higher is *i* or *t*, the higher is the whole term $(1 + i)^t$. This term, however, appears in the denominator, so *PV* is *negatively* related to both *i* and *t*.

Table 15-2 computes the present value of an *MRP* of $500 received several years in the future. The table has two parts. In Part A, we keep the date of the *MRP* fixed and vary the interest rate. In Part B, we keep the interest rate fixed and vary the date of the *MRP*. This allows us to see the separate effects of varying *i* and *t*, and leads to the following conclusion.

Other things being equal, the present value of a given sum payable in the future will be smaller the more distant the payment date and it will be smaller the higher the rate of interest.

The Present Value of a Stream of Future Payments

Now consider the present value of a stream of payments that continues for many periods into the future. As we said earlier, the future benefits that a firm receives from a piece of capital equipment may not be constant. Changes in market conditions, technology, or the quality of the capital itself may result in different *MRP*s in different periods. For example, one new lathe may generate a marginal revenue product equal to $200 one year from now, $180 two years from now, and $210 in the third year—before it wears out and ceases to generate any further benefits.

TABLE 15-2   The Present Value of a Single Sum Several Years in the Future

Part A: Date Fixed; Interest Rate Variable

	MRP	Date	Interest Rate Per Year	Present Value
1.	$500	3 years	4% = 0.04	$500/(1.04)^3 = $444.50
2.	$500	3 years	5% = 0.05	$500/(1.05)^3 = $431.92
3.	$500	3 years	6% = 0.06	$500/(1.06)^3 = $419.81
4.	$500	3 years	7% = 0.07	$500/(1.07)^3 = $408.15

Part B: Date Variable; Interest Rate Fixed

	MRP	Date	Interest Rate Per Year	Present Value
1.	$500	2 years	6% = 0.06	$500/(1.06)^2 = $445.00
2.	$500	3 years	6% = 0.06	$500/(1.06)^3 = $419.81
3.	$500	4 years	6% = 0.06	$500/(1.06)^4 = $396.05
4.	$500	5 years	6% = 0.06	$500/(1.06)^5 = $373.63

The present value of a future sum is negatively related to the interest rate and negatively related to the length of time before the sum occurs. In all the rows in Part A, the firm receives an *MRP* of $500 in three years' time, but the interest rate varies. Using the formula from the text, we see that the higher is the interest rate, the lower is the present value of the future *MRP*. In all the rows in Part B, the interest rate is 6 percent per year, but the future date of the *MRP* varies. The computations show that the more distant in time is the *MRP*, the lower is the present value.

How do we compute the present value of such an uneven stream of MRPs? The answer is surprisingly simple. We just treat each future MRP as a single MRP that occurs at some point in the future. We then apply our earlier formula to each MRP and add them up. For example, suppose the interest rate is 6 percent per year and the capital generates MRPs equal to $200 in one year, $180 in two years, $210 in three years, and nothing thereafter. The present value of this stream of MRPs is

$$PV = \frac{\$200}{1.06} + \frac{\$180}{(1.06)^2} + \frac{\$210}{(1.06)^3}$$
$$= \$188.68 + \$160.20 + \$176.32$$
$$= \$525.20$$

In general, if MRP_t is the MRP that occurs t years from now, if i is the interest rate, and if the stream of MRPs lasts for N years, the present value of the stream of MRPs is

$$PV = \frac{MRP_1}{1+i} + \frac{MRP_2}{(1+i)^2} + \cdots + \frac{MRP_N}{(1+i)^N}$$

Table 15-3 computes the present value of several streams of MRPs. It confirms the relationships we observed earlier. First, other things being equal, a higher interest rate leads to a lower present value. Second, for a given interest rate, a larger MRP leads to a larger present value. But now that we have a stream of MRPs that lasts for several periods, rather than just a single period, we can add a third general result: The longer a stream of MRPs lasts into the future, the greater is the present value.

Conclusions

The concept of present value can at first be confusing, but you should now see the straightforward way to evaluate a stream of benefits into the distant future. Let's summarize our findings.

1. A piece of capital is valuable because it generates a *stream* of benefits into the future. These benefits are the capital's marginal revenue product (MRP). The value to the firm of owning this capital now is what we have called its *present value.*

2. The larger is each future MRP, or the longer the stream of MRPs lasts, the greater is the present value of the capital.

3. For a given stream of future MRPs, the present value of the capital is negatively related to the interest rate. That is, when interest rates are higher, a given piece of capital is valued less. When interest rates are lower, the capital is valued more highly.

4. Capital that delivers its MRPs in the more distant future has a lower present value than capital that delivers the same stream of MRPs sooner.

We now go on to examine an individual firm's demand for capital goods. We will then consider the economy's overall demand for capital. Present value and the interest rate play a central role in our analysis.

Practise with Study Guide Chapter 15, Exercises 1 and 4.

TABLE 15-3 The Present Value of a Stream of Future Payments

Part A: Alternative Interest Rates

	MRP_1	MRP_2	MRP_3	Interest Rate Per Year	Present Value
1.	$500	$400	$300	8% = 0.08	$\dfrac{500}{1.08} + \dfrac{400}{(1.08)^2} + \dfrac{300}{(1.08)^3} = \$1044.05$
2.	$500	$400	$300	5% = 0.05	$\dfrac{500}{1.05} + \dfrac{400}{(1.05)^2} + \dfrac{300}{(1.05)^3} = \$1098.15$

Part B: Alternative MRPs

	MRP_1	MRP_2	MRP_3	Interest Rate Per Year	Present Value
3.	$300	$300	$300	5% = 0.05	$\dfrac{300}{1.05} + \dfrac{300}{(1.05)^2} + \dfrac{300}{(1.05)^3} = \$816.97$
4.	$400	$400	$400	5% = 0.05	$\dfrac{400}{1.05} + \dfrac{400}{(1.05)^2} + \dfrac{400}{(1.05)^3} = \$1089.30$

Part C: Alternative Lengths of Stream

	MRP_1	MRP_2	MRP_3	Interest Rate Per Year	Present Value
5.	$500	$500	$0	5% = 0.05	$\dfrac{500}{1.05} + \dfrac{500}{(1.05)^2} + 0 = \$929.70$
6.	$500	$500	$500	5% = 0.05	$\dfrac{500}{1.05} + \dfrac{500}{(1.05)^2} + \dfrac{500}{(1.05)^3} = \$1361.62$

The present value of a future stream of sums is negatively related to the interest rate, positively related to the size of each payment, and positively related to the length of time the stream continues. Part A presents a given stream of MRPs over three years but considers two different interest rates. The PV of the stream of MRPs is higher when the interest rate is lower.

Part B uses only a single interest rate of 5 percent but considers two different streams of MRPs. One is a stream of $300 that lasts for three years; the other is a higher stream of $400 that also lasts for three years. The stream with the higher MRPs has the higher present value.

Part C uses an interest rate of 5 percent and a constant stream of MRPs of $500 per year. One stream lasts for two years, whereas the other lasts for three years. The longer-lasting stream of MRPs has the higher present value.

15.3 INVESTMENT DEMAND

As we said earlier, a firm's demand for financial capital comes from its demand for physical capital. Economists assume that the amount of physical capital the firm chooses to use comes from its objective of maximizing profit. We now examine this decision in detail.

The Firm's Demand for Capital

An individual firm faces a given interest rate and a given purchase price of capital goods. The firm can vary the quantity of capital that it employs, and as a result, the marginal revenue product of its capital varies. The hypothesis of diminishing marginal returns (see Chapter 7) predicts that the more capital the firm uses, the lower its *MRP*.

The Decision to Purchase a Unit of Capital

Consider a profit-maximizing firm that is deciding whether or not to add to its capital stock and is facing an interest rate of *i* at which it can borrow or lend money. The first thing the firm has to do is to estimate the expected stream of *MRP*s from the new piece of capital over its lifetime. Then it discounts this stream at the interest rate of *i* per year to find the present value of the stream of receipts the machine will gener-

A profit-maximizing firm will purchase units of physical capital up to the point where the present value of the future stream of output produced by the last unit of capital equals its purchase price.

ate. Having computed the *PV* of the stream of *MRP*s, the firm can then compare this *PV* with the purchase price of the capital good. The decision rule for a profit-maximizing firm is simple: If the *PV* is greater than or equal to the purchase price, the firm should buy the capital good; if the *PV* is less than the purchase price, the firm should not buy it.

Consider the following simple example. Suppose a computer has an *MRP* of $1000 each year—that is, by buying this computer the firm can produce more output and thereby achieve a net addition to its revenues of $1000 each year. Suppose further that the computer delivers benefits this year (now) and for two more years—after that, the computer is completely obsolete and worth nothing. Finally, suppose the interest rate is 6 percent per year. The *PV* of this stream of *MRP*s is then equal to

$$PV = \$1000 + \$1000/(1 + 0.06) + \$1000/(1 + 0.06)^2$$
$$= \$2833.40$$

The present value tells us how much any flow of future receipts is worth now. If the firm can buy the computer for less than its *PV*—that is, for any amount less than $2833.40—then this computer is a good buy. If it must pay more, the computer is not worth its price.

If a firm wants to maximize its profits, it is worthwhile to buy another unit of capital whenever the present value of the stream of future *MRP*s generated by that unit equals or exceeds its purchase price.

The Firm's Optimal Capital Stock

Because of the law of diminishing marginal returns, the *MRP* of each unit of capital declines as the firm buys more capital. The profit-maximizing firm will thus go on adding to its stock of capital until the present value of the stream of *MRP*s generated by the *last unit* added is equal to the purchase price of that unit.

Practise with Study Guide Chapter 15, Exercises 2 and 3.

The profit-maximizing capital stock of the firm is such that the present value of the flow of *MRP*s that is provided by the last unit of capital is equal to its purchase price.

Figure 15-2 continues our earlier example of a firm considering the purchase of a computer. In this case, however, the firm is determining *how many* computers it wants to own, and so must compare the purchase price and the present value of the stream of *MRP*s produced by each successive computer. Because the *MRP* of each computer declines as the firm uses more of them, Figure 15-2 shows a negative relationship between the purchase price of the computer and the quantity the firm chooses to own.

What economic events, other than a change in the price of capital, might lead the firm to change its optimal capital stock? In terms of the example shown in Figure 15-2, anything that increases the *PV* of the future *MRP*s of computers will increase the height of the bars in the figure and, for a given purchase price of computers, lead the firm to purchase more computers. More generally, anything that increases the *PV* of the future *MRP*s of capital will lead firms to increase their desired capital stock. The future *MRP*s can increase in two ways.

Technological Improvement. If capital becomes more productive so that the stream of future *MRP*s increases, firms will choose to own more capital even if the purchase price of capital is unchanged. For example, in Figure 15-2, if a technological improvement increases the annual *MRP* for each computer by 20 percent, each computer's *PV* will also increase by 20 percent. The bars in the figure will increase in height and, for any given purchase price, the firm will increase its desired stock of computers.

Reduction in the Interest Rate. A second way in which the *PV* of the stream of *MRP*s will increase is if the interest rate falls. A lower interest rate means that future *MRP*s get discounted at a lower rate—and therefore have greater present value. Thus, as the interest rate declines, the firm's optimal capital stock increases. In Figure 15-2, imagine that the interest rate is 3 percent per year instead of 6 percent. In this case, the *PV*

FIGURE 15-2   The Firm's Optimal Capital Stock

	Annual *MRP*	Present Value
1st computer	$1000	$1000 + \dfrac{1000}{1.06} + \dfrac{1000}{(1.06)^2} = \$2833.40$
2nd computer	$ 900	$900 + \dfrac{900}{1.06} + \dfrac{900}{(1.06)^2} = \$2550.06$
3rd computer	$ 800	$800 + \dfrac{800}{1.06} + \dfrac{800}{(1.06)^2} = \$2266.72$
4th computer	$ 700	$700 + \dfrac{700}{1.06} + \dfrac{700}{(1.06)^2} = \$1983.38$
5th computer	$ 600	$600 + \dfrac{600}{1.06} + \dfrac{600}{(1.06)^2} = \$1700.04$

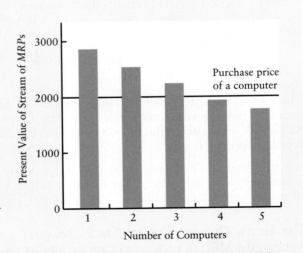

The firm's optimal capital stock is chosen so that the present value of the future *MRP*s on the last unit of capital is just equal to its purchase price. In this example, each computer delivers a stream of *MRP*s that begins now and lasts for two years, and the interest rate is 6 percent per year. The second column in the table shows the diminishing marginal product of capital—the annual *MRP* generated by each computer is less than for the previous one. The third column computes the *PV* of the stream of *MRP*s for each computer, and these are plotted in the accompanying figure. If the purchase price of a computer is $2000, the firm will choose to own only three computers; any additional computer delivers a *PV* of *MRP*s that is less than the purchase price and thus is not profitable to the firm. An increase in the purchase price of a computer to $2400 leads the firm to reduce its desired stock of computers to two.

of each computer's stream of future *MRP*s will rise, and each bar in the figure will increase in height. For a given purchase price of computers, the firm will therefore increase its desired stock of computers.

Anything that causes the present value of future *MRP*s of capital to increase—technological improvement or a reduction in the interest rate—leads firms to increase their desired capital stock.

From Capital Stock to Investment Demand   We have just examined how a profit-maximizing firm determines its optimal stock of physical capital. It is important to emphasize again the distinction between *stocks* and *flows*—in this case the distinction between the firm's optimal *stock* of capital and its optimal *flow* of investment. In any given period, a firm can determine its optimal stock of capital. But if the economic environment changes either because of a change in technology or a change in interest rates, the firm's optimal capital stock will also change. In order for the firm to adjust its capital stock appropriately, it needs to carry out *investment*. A positive flow of investment—buying new capital—leads to an increase in the capital stock; a negative flow of investment—selling existing capital—leads to a decline in the capital stock.[2]

    How do we get from the firm's optimal capital stock to its demand for investment? For any period, the firm's investment demand is determined by the *change* in the firm's optimal capital stock, which in turn is determined by changes in the economic environment. To illustrate, continue with our example of a firm with an optimal capital stock of 100 computers at the beginning of 2007. During the year 2007, suppose interest rates decline, thereby increasing the firm's optimal capital stock to 110 computers. For the year 2007, the firm would therefore have a demand for investment equal to the *change* in this optimal stock—in this case, 10 computers. After the firm carries out this investment (after it buys 10 new computers), it would again possess its optimal capital stock.

In any given period, the profit-maximizing firm's investment demand is given by the *change* in the firm's optimal capital stock.

Emphasis on the Interest Rate   In Figure 15-2, there is a negative relationship between the purchase price of a computer and the desired stock of computers the firm wants to own. Firms use many types of physical capital, however, including buildings, furniture, computer equipment, and various types of tools and machines. Each different type of physical capital has a different price and therefore it is impossible to think of any individual firm's desired capital stock in terms of any single price. For this reason, economists focus on the negative relationship between the firm's desired capital stock and the interest rate. Indeed, since firms use financial capital to purchase their physical capital, it is natural to think of the interest rate as the "price" of financial capital.

    We saw above that when the interest rate falls, the *PV* of the future stream of *MRP*s will rise. This increase in the present value of capital will lead firms to increase their desired capital stock, and thus the quantity of investment demanded. The opposite happens when the interest rate rises. We thus get a general prediction about firms' investment behaviour:

Other things being equal, firms' demand for investment (additions to physical capital) is negatively related to the interest rate.

Practise with Study Guide Chapter 15, Short-Answer Question 5.

----

[2] Positive investment may not add to the firm's capital stock if it is replacing obsolete capital. In this discussion, however, we make the simplifying assumption that all investment increases the firm's capital stock.

FIGURE 15-3   The Interest Rate and the Firm's Investment Demand

Flow of Investment
(additions to physical capital)

The lower the rate of interest, the larger is the firm's demand for investment. The lower the interest rate, the higher is the present value of any given stream of *MRPs* and hence the more capital that the firm will wish to use.

Anything that increases the future stream of *MRPs* produced by the capital leads the firm to demand more units of capital at any interest rate—the investment demand curve shifts to *I'*.

This relationship is shown in Figure 15-3. The negative relationship between the interest rate and the quantity of investment demanded can be thought of as the firm's demand curve for additional physical capital where the relevant "price" is the interest rate.

What would cause a firm's investment demand curve to shift? First, suppose the firm's expectations about future demand for its product improve. This optimism leads the firm to expect an increase in the future stream of *MRPs* produced by capital. With higher expected *MRPs*, the firm is prepared to purchase more units of capital (at any interest rate). Thus, the firm's investment demand curve shifts to the right. Second, suppose an improvement in technology increases the future stream of *MRPs*. Again, the higher future *MRPs* lead the firm to purchase more units of capital at any interest rate—a rightward shift in the firm's investment demand curve.

Any event that increases the expected future stream of *MRPs* leads to an increase in the firm's investment demand.

The Economy's Demand for Investment

The economy's overall demand for investment is determined from the demands of individual firms. Thus, there is a negative relationship between the interest rate and the desired *aggregate* investment for the same reasons that the negative relationship exists for any individual firm. The economy's demand for investment can therefore be represented by a downward-sloping curve just as in Figure 15-3.

The economy's investment demand curve shifts for the same reasons that individual firms' demand curves shift. Anything that increases the future stream of *MRPs* of capital leads to a rightward shift in the investment demand curve. Technological improvements are a key reason for such increases in the demand for investment. (We will say more about this later.)

15.4 THE SUPPLY OF SAVING

The supply of financial capital is determined by households' saving decisions. Saving is the difference between income and current spending. At any given time, households have a stock of *assets* that represents the accumulation of their past saving. During any given year, households modify their accumulated stock of assets by either saving or borrowing. (Saving leads to an increase in the accumulated stock of assets; borrowing leads to a reduction in the accumulated stock of assets.) Thus, the annual *flow* of saving by households leads to a change in the total *stock* of assets.

Households save because it allows them to spend in the future some of the income they earned today. They do this for several reasons. First, most people work for only part of their lives and, during their retirement, must live off their accumulated assets. Saving in the current year is a way of building up this retirement "nest egg." A second reason people save is that the future is uncertain. Next year they might become unemployed and thus lose their source of income, or they may have to provide for a relative who has lost a job or become incapacitated. In any case, uncertainty about the future provides a good reason to save. Finally, many households save in anticipation of specific large future expenditures. Young couples, for example, save in order to accumulate enough funds for a down payment on a house. Couples with young children save to help finance their children's university education.

Despite the many and varied reasons why any individual household chooses to save a lot or a little, to understand the economy's overall supply of financial capital, economists focus on three key determinants of saving—current income, expected future income, and the interest rate.

Saving and Current Income

Most people try to *smooth* their spending across time. Instead of spending a lot when income is high and spending only a little when income is low, most people prefer to spend a relatively constant amount from year to year. The result is that in high-income years people tend to save a lot, and in low-income years people tend to save only a little. (In years when income is very low, people may save a negative amount, meaning that they spend partially out of their accumulated assets.) When economists examine statistics across many households in the economy, they find that the positive relationship between total income and total saving is quite stable.

Household saving is positively related to current income. An increase in current income increases the supply of financial capital.

Saving and Expected Future Income

For any given level of current income, households tend to save less when their expected future income is higher. If people anticipate that their income will be higher in the near future, their desire to smooth their spending (between now and the future) means that they will want to spend some of that higher income now. An increase in their current spending, however, combined with an unchanged level of *current* income, means that their current saving must fall.

The best example of this behaviour is shown by many of you who are reading this book. Students are busy acquiring human capital and are usually earning little or no income. As we discussed in Chapter 14, people with university degrees earn more on average than people with only a high school diploma. Thus, students are examples of people whose expected future income is considerably higher than their current income. The result is that many students are spending at levels that would be unaffordable (and quite imprudent!) if they were to earn their current incomes permanently. These students are spending at relatively high levels precisely because they expect to have much higher incomes in the near future. They are borrowing now (from parents or through student loans) because their future income will be high enough to pay back these debts.

An increase in expected future income leads to a decline in current saving, and thus to a reduction in the supply of financial capital.

Saving and the Interest Rate

How does an increase in the interest rate affect households' desire to save, and thus their supply of financial capital?

The interest rate is the "price" of financial capital. Like any price, the interest rate represents an opportunity cost—it is the opportunity cost of spending now rather than in the future. For example, suppose the interest rate is 5 percent per year. Your decision to spend $100 now "costs" you $105 in forgone spending one year from now. An increase in the interest rate increases the "price"—or opportunity cost—of current spending. Households respond to an increase in the interest rate by substituting away from (relatively expensive) current spending and toward (relatively inexpensive) future spending.

An increase in the interest rate causes households to reduce their spending and increase their saving, thus increasing the quantity of financial capital supplied.[3]

FIGURE 15-4   The Economy's Supply of Saving

An increase in current income leads to an increase in the supply of saving.

Interest Rate

Flow of Saving

There is a positive relationship between the interest rate and the flow of saving supplied by households. An increase in the interest rate increases the opportunity cost of current spending and leads households to increase their desired saving.

The Economy's Supply of Saving

The economy's supply of saving is shown in Figure 15-4, and shows a positive relationship between the interest rate and the quantity of financial capital supplied by households. An increase in the interest rate leads the economy's households to increase their desired saving. This is a movement upward along the supply curve.

An increase in current income leads to an increase in households' desired saving *at any given interest rate* and thus causes the supply curve to shift to the right. An increase in expected future income (holding current income constant) leads to a decrease in households' desired saving *at any given interest rate* and thus causes the supply curve to shift to the left.

15.5 INVESTMENT, SAVING, AND THE INTEREST RATE

We have discussed how the economy's demand for financial capital is related to the interest rate; a rise in the interest rate leads firms to reduce their desired capital stock and thus reduce their need for financial capital. We have also discussed how the econ-

---

[3] This is the substitution effect of an increase in the interest rate and it works in the same direction for all individuals. There is also an income effect, which operates in one direction for households with negative net assets (debtors) and in the opposite direction for households with positive net assets (creditors). Economists usually assume that, when summed across all households in the economy, some of which are debtors and others creditors, the overall effect of a change in the interest rate is usually in the direction of the substitution effect.

omy's supply of financial capital is related to the interest rate; a rise in the interest rate leads households to increase their desired saving and thus provide more financial capital. We are now ready to put these two sides of the capital market together to examine market equilibrium.

There is an important difference between the analysis of individual firms and households, on the one hand, and the analysis of the overall capital market, on the other. Individual firms and households take the interest rate as given because they are so small relative to the entire economy that their own actions have no effect on the interest rate. For firms and households, the interest rate is *exogenous*. In the overall capital market, however, the interest rate is determined by the interaction of demand and supply—that is, the interest rate is *endogenous*. This important distinction is analogous to the one that exists in any competitive market; firms face a given market price for the product they sell, but the price is determined in equilibrium through the interaction of demand and supply.

One thing should be mentioned before we go on. In this chapter we have spent much time discussing the role of the interest rate in determining how firms and households behave. But we have ignored an important distinction between the *nominal* interest rate and the *real* interest rate. The *nominal* interest rate is the rate stated in the loan agreement. The *real* interest rate adjusts the nominal interest rate for the effects of inflation, and better represents the true cost of borrowing. (The real interest rate is approximately equal to the nominal interest rate minus the rate of inflation. The quality of this approximation is better, the lower are interest and inflation rates.) *Extensions in Theory 15-1* examines this distinction in more detail. In the discussion that follows, we restrict our attention to the real interest rate.

Figure 15-5 shows how the interest rate is determined in the market for financial capital. The intersection of the investment demand curve and the saving supply curve determines the equilibrium interest rate, i^*. If the interest rate were above i^*, there would be an excess supply of capital; households' desired saving would exceed firms' desired borrowing. This excess supply of financial capital would cause the interest rate—the price of financial capital—to fall. Conversely, if the interest rate were below i^*, there would be an excess demand for capital; firms' desired borrowing would exceed households' desired saving. This excess demand for capital would cause the interest rate to rise. Only at i^* is the market in equilibrium—the quantity of investment demanded by firms is just equal to the quantity of saving supplied by households.

FIGURE 15-5   The Market for Financial Capital

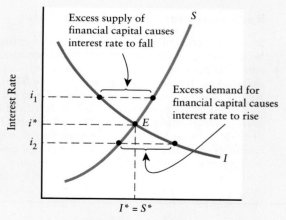

At the equilibrium interest rate, the quantity of investment demanded equals the quantity of saving supplied. The equilibrium interest rate is i^* where the quantity of investment demanded by firms equals the quantity of saving supplied by households (point E). At any interest rate above i^*, the excess supply of financial capital causes the interest rate to fall. At any interest rate below i^*, the excess demand for financial capital causes the interest rate to rise.

EXTENSIONS IN THEORY 15-1

Inflation and Interest Rates

Inflation means the prices of all goods in the economy are rising. More correctly, it means that the prices of goods are rising on *average*—some prices may be rising and others may be falling, but if there is inflation then the price of the average good is rising. Economists refer to the average price of all goods as the *price level*. When the price level is rising, inflation is positive; if prices are rising at a rate of 5 percent per year, the rate of inflation is 5 percent. When the price level is falling, inflation is negative. If prices are falling at a rate of 2 percent per year, the rate of inflation is −2 percent.

Real and Nominal Interest Rates

In the presence of inflation, we need to distinguish between the *real interest rate* and the *nominal interest rate*. The nominal interest rate is measured simply in dollars paid. If you pay me $7 interest for a $100 loan for one year, the nominal interest rate is 7 percent.

Consider further my one-year loan to you of $100 at the nominal rate of 7 percent. The real rate that I earn depends on what happens to the price level during the course of the year. If the price level remains constant over the year, then the real rate that I earn is also 7 percent—because I can buy 7 percent more real goods and

services with the $107 that you repay me than with the $100 that I lent you. However, if the price level were to rise by 7 percent during the year, the real rate would be zero because the $107 you repay me will buy exactly the same quantity of real goods as did the $100 I gave up. If I were unlucky enough to have lent money at a nominal rate of 7 percent in a year in which prices rose by 10 percent, the real rate would be −3 percent. The real rate of interest concerns the ratio of the purchasing power of the money repaid to the purchasing power of the money initially borrowed, and it will be different from the nominal rate whenever inflation is not zero. *The real interest rate is the difference between the nominal interest rate and the rate of inflation.*

If lenders and borrowers are concerned with the real costs measured in terms of purchasing power, the nominal interest rate will be set at the real rate they require plus an amount to cover any expected rate of inflation. Consider a one-year loan that is meant to earn a real return to the lender of 3 percent. If the expected rate of inflation is zero, the nominal interest rate for the loan will also be 3 percent. If, however, a 10-percent inflation is expected, the nominal interest rate will have to be set at 13 percent in order that the real return be 3 percent.

Changes in the Capital-Market Equilibrium

Practise with Study Guide Chapter 15, Exercise 6.

We are now ready to examine some of the changes that occur in the market for financial capital, and how these changes affect the equilibrium interest rate and levels of investment and saving.

Increases in the Supply of Financial Capital Anything that increases the flow of households' desired saving *at the given interest rate* will shift the supply curve for saving to the right. At the initial interest rate, this increase in desired saving will lead to an excess supply of financial capital and thus to a decline in the equilibrium interest rate. As the equilibrium interest rate falls, firms will find it profitable to expand their capital stock and will therefore increase their quantity of investment demanded. The rightward shift in the saving supply curve will therefore lead to a movement downward along the investment demand curve. The effect of an increase in the supply of saving is illustrated in part (i) of Figure 15-6. Three possible causes of such an increase in the supply of saving are provided below.

This point is often overlooked, and as a result people are surprised at the high nominal interest rates that exist during periods of high inflation. But it is the real interest rate that matters more to borrowers and lenders. For example, as the accompanying figure shows, in 1981 the nominal interest rate on 3-month Treasury bills was almost 18 percent, but the high inflation rate at the time meant that the real interest rate was just over 5 percent. In contrast, a decade later in 1990, nominal rates had fallen to just below 13 percent but inflation had fallen further so that the real interest rate had actually *increased* to almost 8 percent. Thus, the period of lower nominal interest rates was actually a period of higher real interest rates.

Back to Capital

In this chapter we have examined investment demand by firms and the supply of saving by households. In both cases, the interest rate plays an important role. For firms, the interest rate reflects the cost of financial capital required to purchase physical capital. For households, the interest rate reflects the benefit of delaying their spending until the future and thus increasing their current saving. In both cases, though we did not say it, we were referring to the *real* interest rate.

When you go on to study *macroeconomics*, you will learn more about what causes inflation, and thus what forces us to make the distinction between real and nominal interest rates. For now, however, we assume in this chapter that there is no inflation; thus, real and nominal interest rates are the same.

(*Source:* Nominal interest rate: 3-month treasury bill rate, CANSIM Series V122541. Real interest rate is based on authors' calculations of CPI inflation, Series PCPISA from www.bankofcanada.ca.)

Income Growth. As income increases, households desire to consume more, both now and in the future. The greater income leads to an increase in households' desired saving and thus to an increase in the supply of financial capital. Gradual but ongoing income growth over a period of many years is an important reason why the economy's supply of saving continues to increase.

Population Growth. An increase in the population—either through higher birth rates or greater immigration—leads to an increase in the supply of financial capital. The simple reason is that most households save, and so an increase in the number of households leads to an increase in the total amount of desired saving. For the effects on the capital market, there is little difference between an increase in the supply of capital due to an increase in the number of households, and an increase in the supply of capital due to higher income for an unchanged number of households. Both events will increase the economy's total income and thus total desired saving; both events will increase the economy's supply of financial capital.

FIGURE 15-6   Changes in Demand and Supply in the Market for Financial Capital

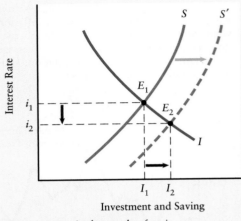

(i) An increase in the supply of saving

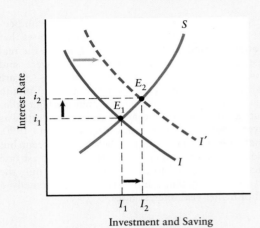

(ii) An increase in investment demand

Changes in the demand for or the supply of financial capital lead to changes in the equilibrium interest rate and levels of investment and saving. Part (i) illustrates an increase in the supply of saving. As households decide to increase the amount of their saving (at any given interest rate), the excess supply of capital leads to a reduction in the interest rate, from i_1 to i_2. As the interest rate falls, firms increase their quantity of investment demanded. The equilibrium level of investment (and saving) increases from I_1 to I_2.

Part (ii) illustrates an increase in investment demand. As firms decide to increase their desired investment, they require more financial capital (at any given interest rate). This leads to an excess demand for capital and to an increase in the interest rate, from i_1 to i_2. As the interest rate rises, households decide to increase their desired saving. The equilibrium level of investment (and saving) increases from I_1 to I_2.

Policies to Increase Desired Saving. Some Canadian government policies may increase households' desired saving. Registered Retirement Savings Plans (RRSPs), for example, offer tax benefits to households who contribute to special "registered" savings accounts. For every dollar contributed to an RRSP (up to a limit), the household reduces its taxable income by a dollar, and thus benefits by paying less income tax. While the funds remain in the registered account, the household does not pay any tax on the interest income earned. When the funds are eventually removed from the account at some point in the future, the full amount of the withdrawal gets added to the household's taxable income at that point. The scheme makes saving more attractive by offering the household a tax benefit for saving.

There is some debate about whether RRSPs actually increase the *total* amount of household saving. Many households have taken advantage of these plans and have a large stock of accumulated assets inside their registered accounts. The debate, however, centres on whether the funds inside these registered accounts would have been saved anyway through ordinary, non-registered savings accounts. Current economic research suggests that there is much substitution away from such "normal" saving and toward RRSP saving, but that the total amount of saving by households has also increased.

If RRSPs are successful in increasing the flow of total saving by households, the result is an increase in the economy's supply of financial capital and a reduction in the equilibrium interest rate. As the interest rate falls, firms will increase their planned investment. In the new equilibrium, the levels of both investment and saving will be higher.

Increases in the Demand for Financial Capital Anything that increases firms' desired investment *at the given interest rate* will shift the investment demand curve to the right. At the initial interest rate, this increase in the need for financial capital will lead to an excess demand for capital and thus to a rise in the equilibrium interest rate. As the equilibrium interest rate increases, households will find it desirable to reduce their current spending and increase their saving. The rightward shift in the investment demand curve will therefore lead to a movement upward along the saving supply curve. This case is illustrated in part (ii) of Figure 15-6. Let's briefly review some possible causes of an increase in the demand for financial capital.

Population and Income Growth. As the economy's total income grows, either through growth in population or in per capita income, the demand for goods and services increases. This increase in the demand for firms' products leads to an increase in the marginal revenue product (*MRP*) of capital. As we saw earlier in the chapter, an increase in capital's *MRP* leads to an increase in the economy's investment demand. The gradual but ongoing growth in the economy's total income is an important explanation for the gradual increase in the economy's investment demand.

Technological Improvement. Over time, there are technological improvements in the quality of factors of production. This is especially true for physical capital. Many of these improvements occur when worn-out capital is replaced by new and better capital. For example, dramatic improvements in computer and information technology have occurred over the past two decades. New desktop computers are hundreds of times faster and more powerful than two decades ago, and access to the Internet makes large quantities of information more readily available than it has ever been. Such improvements in computing power imply a large increase in the marginal product of capital, and thus to an increase in the economy's investment demand.

Policies to Encourage Investment. Over the years, Canadian federal and provincial governments have designed policies to encourage firms to increase their investment in physical capital. One effect of such policies is to increase firms' demand for financial capital. Reductions in corporate income-tax rates, special investment tax credits, and loans guaranteed by governments are three different policies that increase the profitability of investment to firms and lead to an increase in their demand for financial capital.

---

myeconlab

Our simple model of the capital market is based on the assumption that the economy is closed to international trade in financial capital. To see how the mobility of financial capital across international borders affects the analysis of investment, saving, and interest rates, look for "Investment and Saving in Globalized Financial Markets" in the *Additional Topics* section of this book's MyEconLab.

Long-Run Trends in the Capital Market Part (i) of Figure 15-7 shows the annual flow of non-residential investment from 1965 to 2005. It is quite volatile over time, though always positive. Part (ii) shows how this volatile flow of investment has led to an ever-increasing non-residential capital stock; it grew at an average annual rate of 3.2 percent over the period shown. Even in years when the flow of investment is relatively large, the growth rate of the overall capital stock rises only slightly, reflecting the small size of the investment *flow* relative to the large accumulated capital *stock*. Part (iii) of the figure shows the path of the real interest rate, which is quite volatile and displays no clear trend over the 40-year period. How can we use our model of the capital market to understand these data?

Over long periods of time, technological change and population growth can explain both a rising capital stock and an interest rate with no clear long-run trend. We have already stated that population growth leads to an increase in both the demand for and the supply of financial capital. A larger population implies more demand for goods and services, and thus greater investment demand by firms. A larger population, even

FIGURE 15-7 Investment, the Capital Stock, and the Real Interest Rate in Canada, 1965–2005

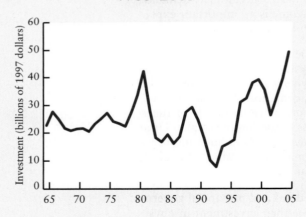

(i) Annual flow of non-residential investment

(ii) Non-residential capital stock

The annual flow of investment is quite volatile, although the accumulated capital stock grows more steadily; the real interest rate is quite volatile and has no clear trend. Canada's non-residential capital stock has increased by over three times since 1965, an average annual growth rate of 3.2 percent. The real interest rate (here measured as the nominal interest rate on 3-month Treasury bills minus the annual rate of inflation) is much more volatile.

(*Source:* The capital stock is from Statistics Canada, series V1078482; the nominal interest rate is series V122541 and the rate of inflation is the rate of change of the CPI (all items), both from the Bank of Canada.)

(iii) Real interest rate

with an unchanged level of income per person, leads to more income and greater saving by households. With both the demand and supply curves for financial capital shifting to the right due to population growth, there will be ongoing growth in the flow of investment, and an ever-rising capital stock; the effect on the interest rate will depend on the relative size of the demand and supply shifts.

Technological change also affects both sides of the capital market. Improvements in technology that increase capital's *MRP* lead firms to increase their investment demand. As we have said several times already in this book, technological change also lies at the heart of increasing productivity and growing per capita income. As income grows, so too does the supply of saving. Thus, through its effect on income, technological improvements that stimulate investment demand also lead to an increase in the supply of financial capital. With both the demand and supply curves shifting to the right due to technological improvements, there will be growth in the flow of investment and an ever-rising capital stock; the effect on the interest rate will again depend on the relative size of the demand and supply shifts.

Ongoing technological improvement and population growth, by increasing both the demand for and the supply of financial capital, explain a rising capital stock with no clear trend in the interest rate.

Our model of the capital market and the equilibrium interest rate can also be used to shed light on some *macroeconomic* issues—in particular, the nature of aggregate economic fluctuations. *Applying Economic Concepts 15-1* examines why during *recessions* and *booms* the demand for capital and the supply of capital often move in opposite directions, and why this helps to explain the volatility of the equilibrium interest rate.

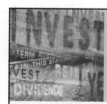

APPLYING ECONOMIC CONCEPTS 15-1

The Capital Market and Macroeconomics

In the text we said that ongoing technological improvement and population growth can explain an upward trend in the capital stock with no clear trend in the interest rate. If this is the case, what explains fluctuations in the interest rate? The answer is that the demand and supply shifts in the market for financial capital are not happening at exactly the same time or in the same magnitude. In particular, firms' demand for investment can be quite volatile over relatively short periods of time.

In periods when the demand for financial capital is falling, the interest rate falls. An example is periods in which there is a slowdown in aggregate economic activity—what economists call a *recession*. The recession generates uncertainty for firms, which are then reluctant to embark on investment projects, thus reducing the demand for capital. During periods of slow economic activity, therefore, the demand for financial capital tends to decrease. The result is that the equilibrium interest rate falls and the flow of investment (and saving) declines.

The opposite is true during periods in which economic activity is growing quickly—what economists call *booms*. During booms, the level of production is high and growing in many industries, and there is growing demand for many factors of production. Firms are actively engaged in planning investment projects. These are times when the economy's demand for financial capital is growing. The result is that the equilibrium interest rate rises and the flow of investment (and saving) increases.

The topic of this box gets us into *macroeconomics*—the study of aggregate economic activity, including such things as unemployment, inflation, and business cycles. The study of macroeconomics is well beyond the scope of this chapter, but we will discuss it in detail in the second half of this textbook, beginning in Chapter 19. At this point, however, it is worth noting that when you go on to study macroeconomics, you will learn that the central bank (in Canada, it is called the Bank of Canada) also plays an important role in influencing the interest rate, at least over the short run.

S U M M A R Y

15.1 A BRIEF OVERVIEW OF THE CAPITAL MARKET

- The demand for financial capital comes from firms' need to finance their investment in new physical capital. The supply of financial capital comes from households' saving decisions.

- The capital market connects households' saving decisions with firms' financing requirements.
- Financial intermediaries—such as commercial banks—play an important role in bringing the two sides of the capital market together.

15.2 PRESENT VALUE

- Since physical capital is durable, it delivers benefits to its owners over many years. As a result, firms need to evaluate the stream of future benefits produced by capital.
- *Present value* is the value today of any stream of future sums; it is computed by discounting the future sums

using the rate of interest. The present value of X receivable in t years' time when the interest rate is i per year is:

$$PV = \frac{X}{(1 + i)^t}$$

15.3 INVESTMENT DEMAND

- Profit-maximizing firms will purchase capital up to the point where the present value of the future stream of *MRP*s generated by the last unit of capital equals its purchase price.
- Economists focus on the relationship between the interest rate and firms' desired capital stock; an increase in the interest rate reduces the present value of any given stream of future *MRP*s and thus reduces firms' desired capital stock.

- Since firms require financial capital to finance their investment in additional capital equipment, the economy's demand for financial capital comes from the many individual firms' demand for investment. An increase in the interest rate leads to a decline in firms' quantity of investment demanded.
- An increase in the marginal product of capital increases firms' desired capital stock at any given interest rate and therefore leads to an increase in the economy's demand for financial capital. This is represented by a rightward shift in the economy's investment demand curve.

15.4 **THE SUPPLY OF SAVING**

- The economy's supply of capital comes from households' flow of desired saving.
- An increase in the interest rate increases the opportunity cost of current spending and thus leads households to increase their desired saving. This is a movement upward along the economy's supply of saving curve.

- An increase in aggregate income—either through population growth or growth in per capita income—leads to an increase in total household saving at any given interest rate. The result is a rightward shift in the economy's supply of saving curve.

15.5 **INVESTMENT, SAVING, AND THE INTEREST RATE**

- Equilibrium in the market for financial capital is determined where the quantity of capital supplied by households equals the quantity of capital demanded by firms.
- Changes in the demand for capital or the supply of capital lead to changes in the equilibrium interest rate and equilibrium levels of investment and saving.

- Technological improvement and population growth lead to increases in both the demand for and the supply of capital. Continual technological improvement and population growth can therefore explain the ongoing growth in the capital stock with little or no trend in the interest rate.

KEY CONCEPTS

Physical capital and financial capital
Present value and the interest rate
A firm's optimal capital stock
The economy's demand for financial capital

Households' saving decisions
The economy's supply of financial capital

Equilibrium interest rate
Technological change and a rising capital stock

STUDY EXERCISES

1. Fill in the blanks to make the following statements correct.

   a. A firm's demand for financial capital is derived from its demand for _____.
   b. A firm that decides to invest in additional machinery will _____ its requirement for financial capital.
   c. An increase in the marginal product of capital will lead firms to _____ their desired capital stock and therefore _____ their demand for financial capital.
   d. An increase in the interest rate will _____ the present value of capital's *MRP* and therefore _____ firms' desired capital stock. The result will be a _____ in the quantity of financial capital demanded by firms.
   e. An increase in capital's *MRP* results in a _____ in the economy's investment demand curve, whereas an increase in the interest rate results in a _____ the economy's investment demand curve.

2. Fill in the blanks to make the following statements correct.

   a. An increase in the interest rate leads households to _____ their current spending and _____ their current saving. The result is an _____ in the quantity of financial capital supplied.
   b. An increase in current income leads to an _____ in household saving at any given interest rate. This results in a _____ in the economy's supply curve for capital.
   c. An increase in expected future income leads to an _____ in current household spending. The result is a _____ in household saving and therefore a _____ in the quantity of capital supplied at any given interest rate. This is represented by a _____ in the economy's supply curve for financial capital.

3. Fill in the blanks to make the following statements correct.

   a. The economy's equilibrium interest rate is determined where _____. At an interest rate above the equilibrium interest rate, the quantity of capital supplied _____ the quantity of capital demanded, and the result is a _____ in the interest rate.

   b. At an interest rate below the equilibrium interest rate, the quantity of capital demanded _____ the quantity of capital supplied, and the result is a _____ in the interest rate.

   c. Beginning in equilibrium in the capital market, an increase in the supply of financial capital leads to a _____ in the equilibrium interest rate, a _____ in borrowing by firms, and an _____ in the equilibrium level of investment and saving.

   d. Beginning in equilibrium in the capital market, an increase in the demand for financial capital leads to an _____ in the equilibrium interest rate, an _____ in desired saving by households, and an _____ in the equilibrium level of investment and saving.

   e. Technological improvements lead to an _____ in both the demand for and supply of financial capital. As a result, technological improvements can explain a _____ capital stock and _____ in the interest rate.

4. **myeconlab** The following table shows the stream of income produced by several different assets. In each case, P_1, P_2, and P_3 are the payments made by the asset in years 1, 2, and 3.

Asset	i	P_1	P_2	P_3	Present Value
A	8%	$1000	$0	$0	—
B	7%	0	0	5000	—
C	9%	200	0	200	—
D	10%	50	40	60	—

   a. For each asset, compute the asset's present value. (Note that the market interest rate, i, is not the same in each situation.)

   b. In each case, what is the most a firm would be prepared to pay to acquire the asset?

   c. Suppose the listed purchase price for an asset were less than its present value. What would you expect to observe?

5. The following table shows how the present value of the future MRPs produced by each unit of capital changes as the firm's total capital stock increases.

Units of Capital	PV of future MRPs
100	$10 000
101	9 000
102	8 000
103	7 000
104	6 000
105	5 000
106	4 000
107	3 000

   a. Notice that the present value of the MRP declines as more capital is used. What economic principle accounts for this?

   b. If a unit of capital can be purchased for $5000, how many will the firm purchase? Explain.

   c. Suppose the market interest rate falls. Explain what happens to the PV of the stream of future MRPs. What happens to the firm's profit-maximizing level of capital?

6. The diagram below shows an individual firm's investment demand curve. The market interest rate is i_0.

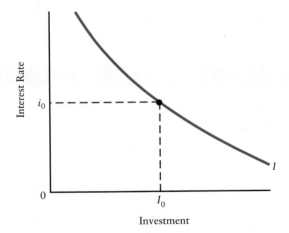

   a. Explain why the firm's investment demand curve is downward sloping.

   b. Suppose the firm now expects the market for its product to be especially good in the future. Explain what happens to its investment demand curve.

   c. Now suppose some technical problem leads to a reduction in the future stream of MRPs produced by capital. How does this affect the firm's investment demand curve?

7. 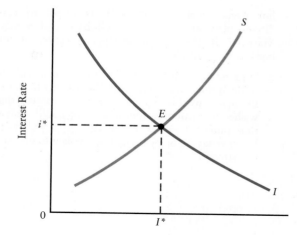 myeconlab For each interest rate below, compute the opportunity cost (in terms of forgone spending next year) to a household of spending $1000 this year:

   a. The interest rate is 5 percent per year
   b. The interest rate is 7 percent per year
   c. The interest rate is 9 percent per year
   d. Explain why, other things being equal, households save more when the interest rate is higher.

8. The accompanying figure shows the economy's capital market, with the initial equilibrium at point E, with an interest rate of i^* and investment (and saving) equal to I^*.

   a. Suppose the government introduces a program of tax credits to firms that increase their desired investment in new physical capital. What is the effect on the equilibrium interest rate, investment, and saving of this policy? Show the effect of this policy in the diagram.
   b. In part (a), the policy has led to a higher interest rate *and* higher investment by firms. Does this contradict our discussion in this chapter about how changes in the interest rate affect firms' investment behaviour? Explain.
   c. Now suppose the government introduces a program of tax credits to households who save. What is the effect on the equilibrium interest rate, investment, and saving of this policy? Show the effect of this policy in the diagram.

   d. In part (c), the policy has led to a lower interest rate *and* higher saving by households. Does this contradict our discussion in this chapter about how changes in the interest rate affect households' saving behaviour? Explain.

Investment and Saving

DISCUSSION QUESTIONS

1. How would you go about evaluating the present value of each of the following?

   a. The existing reserves of a relatively small oil company
   b. The total world reserves of an exhaustible natural resource with a known completely fixed supply
   c. A long-term bond, issued by a very unstable third-world government, that promises to pay the bearer $1000 per year forever
   d. A lottery ticket that your neighbour bought for $10, which was one of 1 million tickets sold for a drawing which will be held in one year's time paying $2 million to the single winner

2. Your parents argue that it makes more sense for you to take taxis and, on occasion, to rent a car while you are at university because you will be spending most of your time in the library and your need for a car should be minimal. Make an argument based on the rental price of transportation (not on the other advantages of having the car) that it may be cheaper for you to buy a car for use while you are at university.

3. "Profit-maximizing firms will reduce their desired investment when the interest rate rises, other things being equal. As a result, empirical economists should always expect to see a negative correlation between actual investment and the interest rate." Comment.

4. Since the interest rate is the price of financial capital, a change in the interest rate generates both an income effect and a substitution effect.

   a. Explain how the substitution effect of an increase in the interest rate influences households' desired saving.
   b. Explain how the income effect of an increase in the interest rate influences households' desired saving. Why does the direction of the income effect depend on whether the household is a net debtor or a net creditor?
   c. Explain why, for the economy as a whole, the substitution effect is likely to dominate the income effect.
   d. What is the importance of the result in part (c) for the economy's supply of financial capital?

5. For parts of this question, it is useful to read "Investment and Saving in Globalized Financial Markets" in the *Additional Topics* section of this book's MyEconLab.

   a. Suppose Canada were a closed economy, with no trade in financial capital with the rest of the world. In such a world, explain why a government that wished to encourage domestic saving could achieve this outcome *either* by designing a policy to increase saving or by designing a policy to increase investment.

   b. Now suppose financial capital is easily tradable between countries. What determines the Canadian real interest rate in such a setting?

   c. Explain why the government objective to increase saving now requires a policy aimed directly at increasing saving (and not investment).

CHAPTER 16

Market Failures and Government Intervention

LO LEARNING OBJECTIVES

In this chapter you will learn

1. about the "informal" defence of free markets.
2. about externalities and why they lead to allocative inefficiency.
3. why public goods are underprovided by private markets.
4. why free markets may not achieve some desirable social goals.
5. the direct and indirect costs of government intervention, and some of the important causes of government failure.

Many aspects of Canadian economic life are determined in free markets. Most of the goods and services that you buy are produced by privately owned profit-making firms, and the prices of those goods and services are determined in free markets. The incomes of most Canadian workers are also determined by free-market forces.

But government intervention and regulation are also pervasive. Canadian governments regulate the pricing of cable TV, land-line and cellular telephone service, and electricity. The Canadian government owns Canada Post, and dozens of other Crown corporations that sell goods or services to firms and households. Canadian governments also have extensive regulations regarding many aspects of our lives, including waste disposal, workplace safety, building codes, minimum wages, taxi service, and so on. And governments take a substantial portion of our incomes in the form of taxes, with which they finance their provision of services to us.

Which elements of the economy can be left to free markets and which elements require government intervention? Governments are clearly necessary to provide law and order and to define and enforce property rights. But beyond these basic functions—ones that we all too often take for granted—what is the case for government intervention in otherwise free markets?

The general case for some reliance on free markets is that allowing decentralized decision making is more desirable than having all economic decisions made by a centralized planning body. The general case for some government intervention is that almost no one wants to let markets decide *everything* about our economic affairs. Most people believe that there are areas in which markets do not function well and in which government intervention can improve the general social good.

The operative choice is not between an unhampered free-market economy and a fully centralized command economy. It is rather the choice of *which mix* of markets and government intervention best suits people's hopes and needs.

In this chapter, we discuss the role of the government in market-based economies, identifying why markets sometimes fail and why government policies sometimes fail. We begin by examining the basic functions of government.

16.1 BASIC FUNCTIONS OF GOVERNMENT

Governments are very old institutions. They arose shortly after the Neolithic Agricultural Revolution turned people from hunter–gatherers into settled farmers about 10 000 years ago. An institution that has survived that long must be doing something right! Over the intervening 100 centuries the functions undertaken by governments have varied enormously. But through all that time the function that has not changed is to provide what is called a *monopoly of violence*. Violent acts can be conducted by the military and the civilian police arms of government, and through its judicial system the government can deprive people of their liberty by incarcerating them or, in extreme cases, by executing them. This is a dangerous monopoly that is easily abused. For this reason satisfactory societies have systems of checks and balances designed to keep the government's monopoly directed to the general good rather than to the good of a narrow government circle.

The importance of having a monopoly of violence can be seen in those countries whose governments do not have it. Somalia in recent decades and China in the 1920s provide examples of countries in which individual warlords commanded armies that could not vanquish each other. Colombia and, to some extent, Russia provide examples of organized crime having substantial power to commit violence that the government cannot control. In extreme cases where many groups have almost equal ability to exert military violence, power struggles can create havoc with normal economic and social life. Life then becomes "nasty, brutish, and short"—to use the words of the seventeenth-century English political philosopher Thomas Hobbes (1588–1679).

The importance of having checks on the government's arbitrary use of its monopoly is seen in the disasters that ensue in the many dictatorships that misuse their power. The USSR under Stalin, Uganda under Idi Amin, Nigeria under Sanni Abacha, Cambodia under Pol Pot, Iraq under Saddam Hussein, and Liberia under Charles Taylor are a few of many examples from the past 75 years.

When the government's monopoly of violence is secure and functions with effective restrictions against its arbitrary use, citizens can safely carry on their ordinary economic and social activities.

A related government activity is to provide security of property. Governments define and enforce property rights that give people a secure claim to the fruits of their own labour. These property rights include clear definition and enforcement of the rights and obligations of institutions such as corporations, religious organizations, and non-profit enterprises.

As the founder of British classical economics, Adam Smith, put it a long time ago:

The first duty of the sovereign [is] that of protecting the society from the violence and invasion of other independent societies.... The second duty of the sovereign [is] that of protecting, as far as possible, every member of the society from the injustice or oppression of every other member of it.[1]

---

1 Adam Smith, *The Wealth of Nations* (1776; New York: Random House, 1937 ed., pp. 653, 669).

In a modern complex economy, providing these "minimal" government services is no simple task. Countries whose governments are not good at doing these things have seldom prospered economically.

The importance of these basic functions of government should not be underestimated. In recent years, economists and policymakers in rich, developed countries have come to a greater understanding of the challenges in developing countries that stem from their ineffective political structures. Local corruption, powerful warlords, and a lack of basic political infrastructure combine to make official development aid less effective than it would be in countries with more stable and representative political structures. As a result, a growing share of official assistance to developing countries is taking the form of *political* rather than *economic* assistance—a process often referred to as *institution building*.

16.2 **THE CASE FOR FREE MARKETS**

Within a secure framework of law and order, and well-defined and enforced property rights, a modern economy can function at least moderately well without further government assistance. In this section we review the case for free markets. In subsequent sections we study government functions that arise when free markets fail to produce acceptable results.

Free markets are impressive institutions. Consumers' tastes and producers' costs help to generate price signals. These signals coordinate separate decisions taken by millions of independent agents, all pursuing their own self-interest. In doing so, they allocate the nation's resources without conscious central direction. Markets also determine the distribution of income by establishing prices of factors of production, which provide incomes for their owners. Furthermore, modern market economies, where firms compete to get ahead of each other by producing better goods more cheaply, generate the technological changes that have raised average living standards fairly steadily over the past two centuries.

In presenting the case for free markets, economists have used two quite different approaches. The first of these may be characterized as the "formal defence," and is based on the concept of allocative efficiency, discussed in Chapters 5 and 12. The essence of the formal defence of free-market economies is that if all markets were perfectly competitive, and if governments allowed all prices to be determined by demand and supply, then price would equal marginal cost for all products and the economy would be allocatively efficient. Allocative efficiency is a worthy goal because it means resources are used in such a way that total surplus to society—consumer surplus plus producer surplus—is maximized. Since we discussed allocative efficiency extensively in earlier chapters, we will say no more about it at this point.

The other defence of free markets—what might be called the "informal defence"—is at least as old as Adam Smith and is meant to apply to market economies whether or not they are perfectly competitive. It is based on the theme that markets are a very effective mechanism for coordinating the decisions of decentralized decision makers. The informal defence is intuitive in that it is not laid out in a formal model of an economy, but it does follow from some hard reasoning, and over the years it has been subjected to much intellectual probing.

This informal defence of free markets is based on three central arguments.

1. Free markets provide automatic coordination of the actions of decentralized decision makers.

2. The pursuit of profits in free markets provides a stimulus to innovation and rising material living standards.

3. Free markets permit a decentralization of economic power.

Automatic Coordination

Defenders of the market economy argue that, compared with the alternatives, the decentralized market system is more flexible and adjusts more quickly to changes.

Suppose, for example, that the world price of oil rises. One household might prefer to respond by maintaining a high temperature in its house and economizing on its driving; another household might do the reverse. A third household might give up air-conditioning instead. This flexibility can be contrasted with centralized control, which would force the same pattern on everyone, say, by fixing the price, by rationing heating oil and gasoline, by regulating permitted temperatures, and by limiting air-conditioning to days when the temperature exceeded 27°C.

Furthermore, as conditions continue to change, prices in a market economy will also change, and decentralized decision makers can react continually. In contrast, government quotas, allocations, and rationing schemes are much more difficult to adjust. As a result, there are likely to be shortages and surpluses before adjustments are made. One great value of the market is that it provides automatic signals *as a situation develops* so that not all of the consequences of an economic change have to be anticipated and allowed for by a group of central planners. Millions of responses to millions of changes in thousands of markets are required every year, and it would be a Herculean task to anticipate and plan for them all.

A market system allows for coordination *without anyone needing to understand how the whole system works*. As Professor Thomas Schelling, who was awarded the Nobel Prize in economics in 2005, illustrated this idea:

> *The dairy farmer doesn't need to know how many people eat butter and how far away they are, how many other people raise cows, how many babies drink milk, or whether more money is spent on beer or milk. What he needs to know is the prices of different feeds, the characteristics of different cows, the different prices... for milk..., the relative cost of hired labor and electrical machinery, and what his net earnings might be if he sold his cows and raised pigs instead.*[2]

It is, of course, an enormous advantage that all the producers and consumers of a country collectively can make the system operate—yet not one of them, much less all of them, has to understand how it works.

Innovation and Growth

Technology, tastes, and resource availability are changing all the time, in all economies. Thirty years ago there was no such thing as a DVD player or a digital camera. Hybrid cars did not exist. Manuscripts existed only as hardcopy, not as electronic files in an ultralight, wireless, laptop computer. The Internet did not exist—nor did MP3 players, BlackBerrys, cellular phones, electronic airline tickets, cost-effective solar panels and wind turbines, income-tax software packages, computer-assisted design (CAD)

---

2 T.C. Schelling, *Micro Motives and Macro Behavior* (New York: Norton, 1978).

programs, regional jets, standardized containers for transoceanic shipping, and a whole host of other goods and services that we now take for granted.

Digital cameras, personal computers, hybrid cars, and regional jets are all products that were invented or developed by individuals or firms in pursuit of profits. An entrepreneur who correctly "reads" the market and perceives that a demand for some product may exist or be created will be inclined to develop it.

The next 20 years will also surely see changes great and small. Changes in technology may make an idea that is not practical today practical five years from now. New products and techniques will be devised to adapt to shortages, gluts, and changes in consumer demands and to exploit new opportunities made available by new technologies.

In a market economy, individuals risk their time and money in the hope of earning profits. Though many fail, some succeed. New products and processes appear and disappear. Some are fads or

Producers in market economies have the incentive to provide the goods and services that customers value, and the result is that line-ups like these rarely exist in these economies. In the former Soviet Union, however, the central planning system was very slow to respond, and line-ups like this were very common.

have little impact; others become items of major significance. The market system works by trial and error to sort them out and allocates resources to what prove to be successful innovations.

In contrast, planners in more centralized systems have to guess which innovations will be productive and which goods will be strongly demanded. Central planning may achieve wonders by permitting a massive effort in a chosen direction, but central planners also may guess incorrectly about the direction and put too many eggs in the wrong basket or reject as unpromising something that will turn out to be vital. Perhaps the biggest failure of centrally planned economies was their inability to encourage the experimentation and innovation that have proven to be the driving forces behind long-run growth in advanced market economies. It is striking that since the early 1990s most centrally planned economies abandoned their system in favour of a price system in one fell swoop while the only remaining large planned economy, China, is increasing the role of markets in most aspects of its economy.

Decentralization of Power

Another important part of the case for a free-market economy is that it tends to decentralize power and thus requires less coercion of individuals than any other type of economy. Of course, even though markets tend to diffuse power, they do not do so completely; large firms and large labour unions clearly have and exercise substantial economic power.

Though the market power of large corporations is not negligible, it tends to be constrained both by the competition of other large entities and by the emergence of new products and firms. This is the process of creative destruction that was described by Joseph Schumpeter and that we examined in Chapter 10. In any case, say defenders of the free market, even such concentrations of private power are far less substantial than government power.

Governments must coerce if markets are not allowed to allocate people to jobs and goods to consumers. Not only will such coercion be regarded as arbitrary (especially by those who do not like the results), but the power creates major opportunities for bribery, corruption, and allocation according to the tastes of the central administrators. If, at the going prices and wages, there are not enough apartments or coveted jobs to go around, the bureaucrats can allocate some to those who pay the largest bribe, some to those with religious beliefs or political views that they like, and only the rest to those whose names come up on the waiting list.

This line of reasoning has been articulated forcefully by the late Nobel laureate Milton Friedman (1912–2006), who was for many years a professor of economics at the University of Chicago. Friedman argued that economic freedom—the ability to allocate resources through private markets—is essential to the maintenance of political freedom.[3] Other economists and social theorists have challenged this proposition.

16.3 MARKET FAILURES

Free markets do all of the good things that we have just discussed in the informal defence; yet there are many circumstances in which the free market does not produce the allocatively efficient outcome. In these cases, economists say that markets have *failed*. The case for intervening in free markets turns in large part on identifying the conditions that lead to market failure. Much of the following discussion is devoted to this task.

We must be careful when using the expression *market failure* because the word *failure* may convey the wrong impression. Market failure does not mean that nothing good has happened. It means, instead, that the *best attainable outcome* has not been achieved. More precisely, **market failure** refers to a situation in which private markets, in the absence of government intervention, fail to achieve allocative efficiency. In other words, in some market or markets, the marginal benefit of the product differs from its marginal cost.

> Market failure describes a situation in which the free market, in the absence of government intervention, fails to achieve allocative efficiency.

It is useful to recall the distinction between normative and positive statements that we first encountered in Chapter 2. The statement that the economy is allocatively efficient (or not) is a *positive* statement. We can say that the economy has or has not achieved allocative efficiency without making any value judgement—the statement uses only an observation about the economy and the definition of allocative efficiency. It is important to note, however, that the allocatively efficient outcome may not be the most desirable outcome in a normative sense. For example, the economy may be allocatively efficient even though the distribution of income is judged by some to be undesirable. As we see later in the chapter, such concerns provide another motivation for government intervention.

We now examine four situations in which the free market fails to achieve allocative efficiency—*market power, externalities, non-rivalrous* and *non-excludable goods,* and *asymmetric information.* All of these market failures provide a justification, at least in principle, for government intervention in markets. We then discuss other reasons for government intervention that are not based on market failure—chief among these is intervention to achieve a more desirable distribution of income.

market failure Failure of the unregulated market system to achieve allocative efficiency.

---

3 Milton Friedman, *Capitalism and Freedom* (Chicago: The University of Chicago Press, 1982).

Market Power

Market power is inevitable in any modern market economy for at least two reasons. First, in many industries economies of scale are such that there is room for only a few firms to operate efficiently, each having some ability to influence market conditions. Second, in most manufacturing and service industries, firms sell differentiated products and thus have some ability to set price. As we saw in Chapters 10, 11, and 12, firms that have market power will maximize their profit at a level of output where price exceeds marginal cost. The result is allocative inefficiency.

Government policy is not aimed at *eliminating* firms' market power, however. Not only would this be impossible, given the pervasiveness of oligopoly and monopolistic competition, but it would also be undesirable since much of the innovation and productivity growth that our economy produces comes from firms with market power. Instead, the goal of government policy is to prevent firms from abusing their market power in a way that unduly harms consumers and reduces the amount of innovation. As we saw in Chapter 12, the government's standard approaches for this problem include regulation and competition policy.

Externalities

Recall from Chapter 12 that in order for the economy to be allocatively efficient, marginal benefit must equal marginal cost for all products. But whose benefits and costs are relevant? Firms that are maximizing their *own* profits are interested only in their own costs of production—they may not care about any benefits or costs their actions might create for others. Similarly, insofar as individual consumers are interested in the benefits *they* receive from any given product, they ignore any costs or benefits that may accrue to others. An **externality** occurs whenever actions taken by firms or consumers directly impose costs or confer benefits on others. When you smoke a cigarette in a restaurant, you might impose costs on others present; when you renovate your home, you might confer benefits on your neighbours by improving the general look of the neighbourhood. Externalities are also called *third-party effects* because parties other than the two primary participants in the transaction (the buyer and the seller) are affected.

externality An effect on parties not directly involved in the production or use of a commodity. Also called *third-party effects*.

The foregoing discussion suggests the importance of the distinction between *private cost* and *social cost*. **Private cost** measures the cost faced by the private decision maker, including production costs, advertising costs, and so on. **Social cost** includes the private cost (since the decision maker is a member of society) but also includes any other costs imposed on third parties. There is a similar distinction between *private benefit* and *social benefit*. To simplify things, however, we will discuss all externalities in terms of the distinction between private and social cost. But this does not limit our discussion in any way. If we want to consider a situation in which your listening to good music confers benefits to your nearby friends, we can think of your action as either increasing their benefits or, equivalently, as decreasing their costs. Similarly, your smoking of cigarettes can be viewed either as reducing their benefits or, equivalently, as increasing their costs. By expressing everything in terms of costs (rather than benefits), we merely simplify the discussion.

private cost The value of the best alternative use of resources used in production as valued by the producer.

social cost The value of the best alternative use of resources used in production as valued by society.

Discrepancies between private cost and social cost occur when there are externalities. The presence of externalities, even when all markets are perfectly competitive, leads to allocatively inefficient outcomes.

Practise with Study Guide Chapter 16, Exercise 1.

FIGURE 16-1 An Externality Leads to Allocative Inefficiency

When there is an externality, either too much or too little of the good is produced. If the market for this good is perfectly competitive and there is no government intervention, the equilibrium is shown by p^C and Q^C. If there is no externality, social and private marginal cost are the same and so the outcome is allocatively efficient.

Now suppose the production or the consumption of the good imposes costs on third parties. This is a *negative* externality—social marginal costs are MC_S^1, above MC_P. The vertical distance between MC_P and MC_S^1 reflects the per-unit external cost. The allocatively efficient quantity is now Q^1 where MB equals MC_S^1. But the free market will produce Q^C, too much of the good.

If the production or consumption of the good instead confers benefits on third parties, this is a positive externality—social marginal costs are MC_S^2, below MC_P. The vertical distance between MC_P and MC_S^2 reflects the per-unit external benefit. The allocatively efficient quantity is now Q^2 where MB equals MC_S^2. But the free market will produce Q^C, too little of the good.

Externalities arise in many different ways, and they may be harmful or beneficial to the third parties. When they are harmful they are called *negative externalities*; when they are beneficial, they are called *positive externalities*. Figure 16-1 shows why an externality leads to allocative inefficiency, even though the market is perfectly competitive. Here are two examples.

Consider the case of a firm whose production process for steel generates harmful smoke as a byproduct. Individuals who live and work near the firm bear real costs as they cope with breathing (or trying to avoid breathing) the harmful smoke. When the firm makes its decision concerning how much steel to produce, it ignores the costs that it imposes on other people. This is a negative externality. In this case, because the firm ignores those parts of social cost that are not its own private cost, the firm will produce too much steel relative to what is allocatively efficient.

A second example involves an individual who renovates her home and thus improves its external appearance. Such improvements enhance the neighbours' view and the value of their property. Yet the individual renovator ignores the benefits that her actions have on the neighbours. This is a positive externality. In this case, because the renovator ignores those parts of social benefits that are not her own private benefits, there will be too little home renovation done relative to what is allocatively efficient.

With a positive externality, a competitive free market will produce too little of the good. With a negative externality, a competitive free market will produce too much of the good.

myeconlab

Ronald Coase, a Nobel-Prize–winning economist, presented the famous argument that as long as property rights are clearly assigned, externalities need not lead to allocative inefficiency. For more details and a numerical example, look for "Externalities and the Coase Theorem" in the *Additional Topics* section of this book's MyEconLab.

www.myeconlab.com

Non-Rivalrous and Non-Excludable Goods

Economists classify goods and services into four broad categories depending on the *rivalry* for the good and the *excludability* of the good. Table 16-1 shows these four types of goods.

A good or service is said to be **rivalrous** if one person's consumption of the good means that no one else can also consume it. For example, a chocolate bar is rivalrous because if you eat the entire bar, it cannot also be eaten by your friend. In contrast, a television signal is not rivalrous. You and your friend can sit in your separate living rooms and both receive the same signal, neither of you diminishing the amount available to the other.

A good is said to be **excludable** if people can be prevented from consuming it. A chocolate bar is excludable because you cannot eat it unless you buy it first. A regular TV signal is not excludable, but some speciality channels are because only those who pay for the special receivers can view them. Your use of the light produced by street lights is non-excludable, as is your access to the air you breathe.

The airborne emissions from coal-fired power plants are one important example of a negative externality. In this case, the social costs associated with the sulphur-dioxide emissions exceed the private costs.

Private Goods   Most goods and services that you consume are both rivalrous and excludable. Your consumption of food, clothing, a rental apartment, a car, gasoline, CDs, airline tickets, and textbooks are only possible because you pay the seller for the right to own those goods or services. Furthermore, your consumption of those goods reduces the amount available for others. In Table 16-1 we simply refer to these goods as **private goods**.

Goods that are both rivalrous and excludable—private goods—pose no particular problem for public policy.

Common-Property Resources   Goods that are rivalrous but non-excludable pose an interesting challenge for public policy. Note in Table 16-1 that the examples of these goods include such things as fisheries, common grazing land, wildlife, rivers and streams, and so on. These are called **common-property resources**. My use of river water reduces the amount available for you, but there is no practical way that my access to the water can be controlled. And since my access to the water cannot be controlled, there is no practical way to make me pay for it. The result is that there is a zero price. The zero price leads to the obvious result that, in the absence of government intervention, private users will tend to *overuse* common-property resources. In other words, private users will use these resources to the point where the marginal cost to society will exceed the marginal benefit to society. Society would be better off if less of these resources were used.

Goods that are rivalrous and non-excludable are called common-property resources. They tend to be overused by private firms and consumers.

The overuse of common-property resources is especially noticeable in such cases as the Atlantic cod and Pacific salmon fisheries where individual fishermen have a natural incentive to overfish. After all, if they don't catch a particular fish, they will merely be leaving it to be caught by the next fisherman who comes along. It is this natural inclination to overuse the fisheries that has led the Canadian government over the years to develop a system of licences and quotas whereby individual fishermen must pay to have access to the common-property resource. *Applying Economic Concepts 16-1* examines the depletion of the world's fisheries.

rivalrous A good or service is rivalrous if, when one person consumes one unit of it, there is one less unit available for others to consume.

excludable A good or service is excludable if its owner can prevent others from consuming it.

private goods Goods or services that are both rivalrous and excludable.

common-property resource A product that is rivalrous but not excludable.

TABLE 16-1   Four Types of Products

	Excludable	Non-Excludable
Rivalrous	*Private Goods* DVDs A seat on an airplane An hour of legal advice	*Common-Property Resources* Fisheries Rivers and streams Wildlife Clean air
Non-Rivalrous (up to capacity)	Art galleries Roads Bridges Cable or satellite TV signal	*Public Goods* National defence Public information Public protection Regular TV signal

Free markets cope best with rivalrous and excludable goods—what we here call "private" goods. The table gives examples of goods in each of four categories, depending on whether consumption of the good is rivalrous and whether one can be excluded from consuming the good.

Overfishing is a serious problem in Canada and many other countries, to the point where most of the world's fisheries have become significantly depleted and some have little chance of recovering. Recovery will require enforceable international agreements as well as difficult national political decisions.

Excludable But Non-Rivalrous Goods Goods that are excludable but not rivalrous are also interesting, and many of the obvious examples of these—art galleries, roads, and bridges—are typically provided by government. The non-rivalry for these goods means that the marginal cost of providing the good to one extra person is zero. As an example, just ask yourself what it costs for an extra person to walk through the Canadian Museum of Civilization in Hull, given that it is already open but not many people are there. Or, what is the cost for one more person to drive on an uncrowded road? The answer in both cases is zero. But if the marginal cost to society of providing one more unit of the good is zero, then allocative efficiency requires that the price also be zero. Any positive price would prevent some people from using it, but this would be inefficient. As long as their marginal benefit exceeds the social marginal cost of providing the good (zero in this case), it is efficient for these people to use the good.

To avoid inefficient exclusion, the government often provides non-rivalrous but excludable goods and services.

For this reason, art galleries, museums, libraries, roads, bridges, and national parks are often provided by various levels of government. In some cases, like libraries and roads, the price to consumers is usually zero. In others, like national parks and art galleries, there is usually some positive price.

The positive price in some of these cases can be explained by another feature of these goods. What happens in the Canadian Museum of Civilization on a summer Saturday morning? What happens on Highway 401 outside Toronto at rush hour? The answer is *congestion*. When congestion occurs on roads and bridges, or in art galleries and museums, it is no longer true that the marginal cost of providing the good to one more user is zero. By increasing the amount of congestion, providing the good to one more person imposes costs on those already using the good. If I enter an already-busy highway, I slow down all the existing traffic. If you visit an already-crowded museum, you make it less pleasant for everybody else. In these cases, a good that is non-rivalrous when uncongested becomes rivalrous when congested. At this point it becomes (in economic terms) a private good, and a positive price is appropriate.

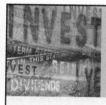

APPLYING ECONOMIC CONCEPTS 16-1

The World's Endangered Fish

The fish in the ocean are a common-property resource, and theory predicts that such a resource will be over-exploited if there is a high enough demand for the product and suppliers are able to meet that demand. In the past centuries there were neither enough people eating fish nor efficient enough fishing technologies to endanger stocks. Over the last 50 years, however, the population explosion has added to the demand for fish and advances in technology have vastly increased the ability to catch fish. Large boats, radar detection, and more murderous nets have tipped the balance in favour of the predator and against the prey. As a result, the overfishing prediction of common property theory has been amply borne out. Today, fish are a common-property resource; tomorrow, they could become no one's resource.

Since 1950 the world's annual capture of fish has increased by over four times, from 20 million tonnes in 1950 to over 80 million tonnes today (not including the "catch" from farmed fish, which raises the current annual haul to over 130 million tonnes). The increase was sustained only by substituting smaller, less desirable fish for the diminishing stocks of the more desirable fish and by penetrating ever further into remote oceans. Today, all available stocks are being exploited, and now even the total tonnage of captured fish is beginning to fall. The UN estimates that the total value of the world's catch could be increased by nearly $30 billion if fish stocks were properly managed by governments interested in the total catch, rather than exploited by individuals interested in their own catch.

The developed countries have so overfished their own stocks that Iceland and the European Union could cut their fleets by 40 percent and catch as much fish as they do today. This is because more fish would survive to spawn, allowing each boat in a smaller fleet to catch about 40 percent more than does each boat in today's large fishing fleet.

The problem has become so acute that Canada shut down its entire Atlantic cod fishing industry in 1992 and its Pacific salmon industry in 1998. Tens of thousands of Newfoundland and Labrador residents lost their livelihoods in an industry that had flourished for five centuries.

Canada and the European Union have since been in conflict over what Canada claims is predatory overfishing by EU boats just outside Canadian territorial waters. These tensions heightened in March 1995 when the Spanish fishing trawler *Estai* was fired at and forced into St. John's harbour by a Canadian fisheries-protection vessel for fishing turbot just outside Canada's 200-nautical-mile "economic zone." The EU (on behalf of Spain) accused Canada of piracy. Canada accused Spain of overfishing and depleting the value of Canada's turbot fishery.

Some developing countries are taking action to conserve their fish stocks but the majority are encouraging rapid expansion of their own fishing fleets with the all-too-predictable results that their domestic waters will soon be seriously overfished.

Worldwide action saved most species of whales. It remains to be seen how many types of fish will be caught to extinction and how many will recover as individual nations slowly learn the lesson of economic theory. Common-property resources need central management if they are not to be overexploited to an extent that risks extinction.

State of the World's Fish Stocks, 2004

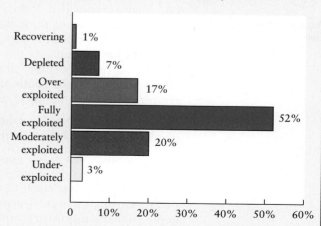

(*Source: Review of the State of World Marine Fishery Resources,* p. 10, FAO Fisheries Technical Paper #457, 2005. See: www.fao.org. © Food and Agriculture Organization of the United Nations (FAO), 2007.)

A near-empty road or highway has little rivalry in use, and is much like a public good. But once the crowds appear, there is considerable rivalry for space on the road and it therefore becomes more like a private good. Some jurisdictions have introduced financial charges to drivers to better allocate the scarce resource during peak hours.

public goods Goods or services that can simultaneously provide benefits to a large group of people. Also called *collective consumption goods.*

Practise with Study Guide Chapter 16, Exercise 2.

Governments who provide such goods often charge a price to help ration the good when rivalry becomes significant. An excellent example of this is some toll highways that, with the aid of powerful cameras and computers, charge motorists a different amount per kilometre driven depending on the congestion of the highway. As the traffic slows down due to congestion, the price per kilometre increases to reflect the higher marginal cost. This higher price is indicated on electronic highway signs posted regularly along the highway. Drivers can then choose either to remain on the highway and pay the higher price, or exit the highway and take another (less expensive) route to their destination.

Public Goods   Finally, there are some goods that are neither excludable nor rivalrous. These are called **public goods** or sometimes *collective consumption goods.* The classic case of a public good is national defence. All Canadians are equally protected and defended by the Canadian Forces. It is not possible to provide national defence to some Canadians and not to others.

Information is also often a public good. Suppose a certain food additive causes cancer. The cost of discovering this fact needs to be borne only once. The information is then of value to everyone who might have used the additive, and the cost of making the information available to one more consumer is approximately zero. Furthermore, once the information about the newly discovered carcinogen is available, it is impossible to prevent people from using that information. Other public goods include street lighting, weather forecasts (a type of information), and some forms of environmental protection.

All of these examples raise what is called the *free-rider problem.* Since public goods are (by definition) not excludable, it is impossible to prevent anyone from using them once they are provided. If the provider charged a price, non-payers would take a *free-ride* at the expense of those individuals with a social conscience that do pay. But the existence of free riders, in turn, implies that the private market will generally not produce efficient amounts of the public good because once the good is produced, it is impractical (or impossible) to make people pay for its use. Indeed, free markets may fail to produce public goods at all. The obvious remedy in these cases is for the government to provide the good, financed from its tax revenues.

Because of the free-rider problem, private markets will not always provide public goods. Public goods must therefore be provided by government.

How much of a public good should the government provide? It should provide the public good up to the point where the *sum* of everyone's individual marginal benefit from the good is just equal to the marginal cost of providing the good. We add everyone's individual marginal benefit to get the total marginal benefit because a public good—unlike an ordinary private good—can be used simultaneously by everyone. It therefore generates value to more than one person at a time. Figure 16-2 shows the optimal provision of a public good in the simple case of only two individuals.

The optimal quantity of a public good is such that the marginal cost of the good equals the *sum* of all users' marginal benefits of the good.

Asymmetric Information

Information is, of course, a valuable commodity, and markets for information and expertise are well developed, as every student is aware. Markets for expertise are conceptually identical to markets for any other valuable service. They can pose special problems, however. One of these we have already discussed: Information is often a public good and when it is it tends to be underproduced by a free market.

Even where information is not a public good, markets for expertise are prone to market failure. The reason is that one party to a transaction can often take advantage of special knowledge in ways that change the nature of the transaction itself. Situations where one party to a transaction has special knowledge are called situations of **asymmetric information.**

The importance of asymmetric information to the operation of the economy has received considerable attention in recent years. In 2001, Professors George Akerlof, Michael Spence, and Joseph Stiglitz shared the Nobel Prize in economics for their insights about how asymmetric information can lead to market failures. The two important sources of market failure that arise from situations of asymmetric information are *moral hazard* and *adverse selection*.

Moral Hazard In general, **moral hazard** exists when one party to a transaction has both the *incentive* and the *ability* to shift costs onto the other party. Moral hazard problems often arise from insurance contracts. The classic example is the homeowner who does not bother to shovel snow from his sidewalk because he knows that his insurance will cover the cost if the mail carrier should fall and break a leg. The costs of the homeowner's lax behaviour will be borne largely by others, including the mail carrier and the insurance company.

Individuals and firms who are insured against loss will often take less care to prevent that loss than they would in the absence of insurance. They do so because they do not bear all of the marginal cost imposed by the risk, whereas they do bear all of the marginal cost of taking action to reduce the risk.

With moral hazard, the market failure arises because the action by the insured individual or firm raises total costs for society. In the first example above, the decision not to shovel the sidewalk reduces costs for the individual but, in the event of an accident, increases by much more the costs to other individuals and firms.

Insurance is not the only context in which moral hazard problems arise. Another example is professional services. Suppose you ask a dentist whether your teeth are healthy or a lawyer whether you need legal assistance. The dentist and the lawyer both face moral hazard in that they both have a financial interest in giving you answers that will encourage you to buy their services, and it is difficult for you to find out if their advice is good. In both cases, one party to the transaction has special knowledge that he or she could use to change the nature of the transaction in his or her favour. Codes of professional ethics and licensing and certification practices, both governmental and private, are reactions to concerns about this kind of moral hazard.

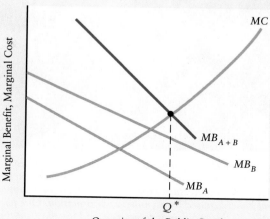

FIGURE 16-2   The Optimal Provision of a Public Good

Determining the optimal provision of a public good requires adding together the marginal benefits for each individual. The figure shows marginal benefit curves for a public good for two individuals, Andrew and Brenda. By adding MB_A and MB_B *vertically* we derive society's marginal benefit curve, MB_{A+B}. The marginal cost of providing the public good is shown by MC. The allocatively efficient level of the public good is Q^*, where the marginal cost to society is just equal to the marginal benefit to society.

asymmetric information A situation in which one party to a transaction has more or better relevant information about the transaction than the other party.

moral hazard A situation in which an individual or a firm takes advantage of special knowledge while engaging in socially inefficient behaviour.

Your auto mechanic probably knows far more about cars than you do, and is therefore able to benefit by convincing you to make unnecessary expenditures. This is an example of moral hazard caused by asymmetric information. One partial solution to this problem is to get a second (or third!) estimate before you spend any money.

adverse selection Self-selection, within a single risk category, of persons of above-average risk.

Adverse Selection   **Adverse selection** refers to the tendency for people who are more at risk than the average to purchase insurance and for those who are less at risk than the average to reject insurance. A person who has a heart condition may seek to increase his life insurance coverage by purchasing as much additional coverage as is available without a medical examination. People who buy insurance almost always know more about themselves as individual insurance risks than do their insurance companies. The company can try to limit the variation in risk by requiring physical examinations (for life or health insurance) and by setting up broad categories based on variables, such as age and occupation, over which actuarial risk is known to vary. The rate charged is then different across categories and is based on the average risk in each category, but there will always be much variability of risk *within* any one category.

People who know that they are well above the average risk for their category are offered a bargain and will be led to take out more car, health, life, or fire insurance than they otherwise would. Their insurance premiums will also not cover the full expected cost of the risk against which they are insuring. Once again, their private cost is less than the social cost. On the other side, someone who knows that she is at low risk and pays a higher price than the amount warranted by her risk is motivated to take out less insurance than she otherwise would. In this case, her private cost is more than the social cost. In both cases, resources are allocated inefficiently because the marginal private benefit of the action (taking out insurance) is not equal to the marginal social cost.

An excellent and familiar example of market failure due to asymmetric information and adverse selection is the apparent overdiscounting of the prices of used cars because of the buyer's risk of acquiring a "lemon." See the discussion of this problem in *Applying Economic Concepts 16-2.*

Summary

Our discussion about market failures has covered a lot of ground. Before we move on to explore some details of government intervention, it is worthwhile to summarize briefly what we have learned. The following four situations result in market failures and, at least in principle, provide a rationale for government intervention.

1. Firms with market power will charge a price greater than marginal cost. The level of output in these cases is less than the allocatively efficient level.

2. When there are externalities, social and private marginal costs are not equal. If there is a negative externality, output will be greater than the allocatively efficient level. If there is a positive externality, output will be less than the allocatively efficient level.

3. Common-property resources will be overused by private firms and consumers. Public goods will be underprovided by private markets.

APPLYING ECONOMIC CONCEPTS 16-2

Used Cars and the Market for "Lemons"

It is common for people to regard the large loss of value of a new car in the first year of its life as a sign that consumers are overly style-conscious and will always pay a big premium for the latest in anything. Professor George Akerlof of the University of California at Berkeley suggests a different explanation. His theory, contained in his now-famous paper "The Market for Lemons," is based on the proposition that the flow of services expected from a one-year-old car that is *purchased on the used-car market* will be lower than that expected from an *average* one-year-old car on the road. Consider his theory.

Any particular model year of automobile will include a certain proportion of "lemons"—cars that have one or more serious defects. Purchasers of new cars of a certain year and model take a chance on their car turning out to be a lemon. Those who are unlucky and get a lemon are more likely to resell their car than those who are lucky and get a high-quality car. Hence, in the used-car market, there will be a disproportionately large number of lemons for sale. For example, maybe only 1 percent of all 2006 Toyota Corollas have a significant defect and are thus lemons. But, in the market for *used* 2006 Toyota Corollas, 20 percent of them may be lemons.

Buyers of used cars are therefore right to be on the lookout for lemons, while salespeople are quick to invent reasons for the high quality of the cars they are selling. Because it is difficult to identify a lemon or a badly treated used car before buying it, the purchaser is prepared to buy a used car only at a price that is low enough to offset the increased probability that it is a lemon.

The market failure in this situation arises because of the asymmetric information between the buyers and the sellers. If there were perfect information, prices would better reflect the quality of the used car. Good used cars would command higher prices than used cars known to be lemons. Buyers and sellers would then conduct more transactions, for two reasons. First, sellers of good used cars would be more likely to sell them since they know they will get a good price. In contrast, when information is poor, owners of good used cars are less inclined to sell their cars because the prices of used cars reflect the average quality, which of course is diminished by the presence of the lemons. Second, when information is good, consumers know precisely what it is they are buying. Consumers who wish to spend more on a good used car can do so; other consumers who want the bargain price on a car known to be a lemon can also be satisfied. A larger number of successful transactions between buyers and sellers means more surplus on both sides of the market—that is, a more efficient outcome.

Owners have an incentive to keep good-quality used cars because it is difficult to convince buyers that a used car is not a "lemon." As a result, lemons represent a larger proportion of used-car sales than of the total car population.

4. Situations in which there is asymmetric information—both moral hazard and adverse selection—can lead to allocative inefficiency.

These situations of market failure justify a role for government in a market economy. We now explore some reasons for government intervention that are *not* based on market failures.

16.4 **BROADER SOCIAL GOALS**

Suppose the market *did* generate the allocatively efficient outcome. That is, suppose all markets were perfectly competitive and there were no problems of market power, externalities, public goods, or asymmetric information. In such an extreme world, does the achievement of allocative efficiency mean that the government would have no reason to intervene in free markets? The answer, in general, is no.

Even if there are no market failures, the government may choose to intervene in markets to achieve broader social goals.

It should not be surprising that even if the free-market system were to generate an allocatively efficient outcome, it would be unlikely to achieve broader social goals. Some of these goals (for example, the desire for an "equitable" income distribution) are basically economic. Some, especially notions that people in a given society should have shared values, such as patriotism or a belief in basic human rights, are clearly not economic. In either set of cases, however, markets are not very effective, precisely because the "goods" in question are not of the kind that can be exchanged in decentralized transactions.

Practise with Study Guide Chapter 16, Exercise 3.

Income Distribution

As we saw in Chapter 13, an important characteristic of a market economy is the *distribution of income* that it determines. People whose services are in heavy demand relative to supply, such as good television news anchors, corporate CEOs, and outstanding hockey players, earn large incomes, whereas people whose services are not in heavy demand relative to supply, such as high school graduates without work experience, earn much less.

Such differentials in income, as we discussed in Chapter 13, can be either temporary or equilibrium phenomena. The temporary differentials, caused by changes in demand or supply in specific industries or regions, will eventually be eliminated by the mobility of workers. Equilibrium differentials will persist, whether they are created by differences in non-monetary aspects of the job or by differences in human capital or acquired or inherited skills.

Even equilibrium differences in income may seem unfair. A free-market system rewards certain groups and penalizes others. Because the workings of the market may be stern, even cruel, society often chooses to intervene. Should heads of households be forced to bear the full burden of their misfortune if, through no fault of their own, they lose their jobs? Even if they lose their jobs through their own fault, should they and their families have to bear the whole burden, which may include starvation? Should the ill and the aged be thrown on the mercy of their families? What if they have no families? Both private charities and a great many government policies are concerned with modifying the distribution of income that results from such things as where one starts, how able one is, how lucky one is, and how one fares in the labour market.

We might all agree that it is desirable to have a more equal distribution of income than the one generated by the free market. We would probably also agree that the pursuit of allocative efficiency is a good thing. It is important to understand, however, that the goal of a more equitable distribution of income often conflicts with the goal of allocative efficiency. To understand why this is so, see *Extensions in Theory 16-1*, which discusses Arthur Okun's famous analogy of the "leaky bucket."

EXTENSIONS IN THEORY 16-1

Arthur Okun's "Leaky Bucket"

Economists recognize that government actions can affect both the allocation of resources and the distribution of income. Resource allocation is easier to talk about simply because economists have developed precise definitions of *efficient* and *inefficient* allocations. Distribution is more difficult because we cannot talk about *better* or *worse* distributions of income without introducing value judgements.

To the extent that society chooses to redistribute income, allocative efficiency will often be reduced. Arthur Okun (1928–1980), who was a noted economist at Yale University, developed the image of a "leaky bucket" to illustrate this problem. Suppose we have a well-supplied reservoir of water and we wish to get some water to a household that is not able to come to the reservoir. The only vessel available for transporting the water is a leaky bucket; it works, in that water is deliverable to the intended location, but it works at a cost, in that some of the water is lost on the trip. Thus, to get a litre of water to its destination, more than a litre of water has to be removed from the reservoir. It may be possible to design better or worse buckets, but all of them will leak somewhat.

The analogy to an economy is this: The act of redistribution (carrying the water) reduces the total value of goods and services available to the economy (by the amount of water that leaks on the trip). Getting a dollar to the poor reduces the resources available to everyone else by more than a dollar. Thus, pursuing social goals—like the redistribution of income—conflicts with the goal of allocative efficiency.

Why is the bucket always leaky? Because there is no way to redistribute income without changing the incentives that private households and firms face. For example, a tax-and-transfer system that takes from the rich and gives to the poor will reduce the incentives of both the rich and the poor to produce income. This redistribution of income will often lead to less total income being generated. As another example, a policy of subsidizing goods that are deemed to be important, such as post-secondary education or daycare services, will cause the market prices of those goods to be lower than marginal costs, a result implying that resources used to produce those goods could be used to produce goods of higher value elsewhere in the economy.

Measuring the efficiency costs of redistribution is an important area of economic research. One result from this research is that some methods of redistribution are more efficient than others. For example, most economists agree that programs that directly redistribute income are more efficient (per dollar of resources made available to a given income group) than programs that subsidize the prices of specific goods. One reason for this is that price subsidies apply even when high-income households purchase the goods in question. These high-income households therefore benefit from the subsidy—an unintended (and perhaps undesirable) consequence of the program.

Redistribution often entails some efficiency cost. However, this inefficiency does *not* imply that such programs should not be undertaken. (That buckets leak surely does not imply that they should not be used to transport water, given that we want to transport water and that the buckets we have are the best available tools.) Whatever the social policy regarding redistribution of income, economics has an important role to play in measuring the efficiency costs and distributional consequences of different programs of redistribution. Put another way, it has useful things to say about the design and deployment of buckets.

Preferences for Public Provision

Police protection and justice could in principle be provided by private-market mechanisms. Security guards, private detectives, and bodyguards all provide policelike protection. Privately hired arbitrators, "hired guns," and vigilantes of the Old West represent private ways of obtaining "justice." Yet the members of society may believe that a public police force is *preferable* to a private one and that public justice is preferable to justice for hire. The question of the boundary between public and private provision of any number of goods and services became an important topic of debate during the late 1980s and early 1990s, and the debate shows no sign of waning. In Canada, the United States, and Western Europe, the issue is framed as *privatization*. In the formerly socialist countries of Eastern Europe, the disposition of much of the productive capacity of entire countries is currently under dispute. In all of these cases, part of the debate is about the magnitude of the efficiency gains that could be realized by private organization, and part is about less tangible issues, such as changes in the nature and distribution of goods and services that may take place when production is shifted from one sector to the other.

Protecting Individuals from Others

People can use and even abuse other people for economic gain in ways that the members of society find offensive. Child labour laws, minimum standards of working conditions, and laws against physical abuse and sexual harassment are responses to such actions. Yet direct abuse is not the only example of this kind of undesirable outcome. In an unhindered free market, the adults in a household would usually decide how much education to buy for their children. Selfish parents might buy no education, while egalitarian parents might buy the same education for all of their children, regardless of their abilities. The rest of society may want to interfere in these choices, both to protect the child of the selfish parent and to ensure that some of the scarce educational resources are distributed according to the ability and the willingness to use them rather than according to a family's wealth. The government requires all households to provide a minimum of education for their children, and a number of inducements are offered—through public universities, scholarships, and other means—for talented children to consume more education than they or their parents might choose if they had to pay the entire cost themselves.

A judicial system could be provided privately, with the judges levying charges to plaintiffs and defendants in order to hear their cases. But most people believe that for reasons of fairness and objectivity, it is better for the government to provide the judicial system, using money raised through general taxation.

Paternalism

Members of society, acting through government, often seek to protect adult (and presumably responsible) individuals, not from others, but from themselves. Laws prohibiting the use of addictive drugs and laws prescribing the installation and use of seat belts are intended primarily to protect individuals from their own ignorance or shortsightedness. Other laws restrict the sale of medicinal drugs in Canada until they are approved by a government body, thus protecting individuals who are unlikely to be well-informed about the chemical composition of the drugs. These kinds of interference in the free choices of individuals are examples of **paternalism**. Whether such actions reflect the wishes of the majority in the society or whether they reflect the actions of overbearing governments, there is no doubt that the market will not provide this kind of protection. Buyers do not buy what they do not want, and sellers have no motive to provide it.

paternalism Intervention in the free choices of individuals by others (including governments) to protect them against what is presumed to be their own ignorance or folly.

Social Responsibility

In a free-market system, if you can pay another person to do things for you, you may do so. If you persuade someone else to clean your house in return for $75, presumably both parties to the transaction are better off (otherwise neither of you would have voluntarily conducted the transaction). Normally, society does not interfere with people's ability to negotiate mutually advantageous contracts.

Most people do not feel this way, however, about activities that are regarded as social responsibilities. For example, in countries where military service is compulsory, contracts similar to the one between you and a housekeeper could also be negotiated. Some persons faced with the obligation to do military service could no doubt pay enough to persuade others to do their military service for them. Indeed, during the U.S. Civil War, it was common practice for a man to avoid the draft by hiring a substitute to serve in his place. Yet such contracts are usually prohibited by law. They are prohibited because there are values to be considered other than those that can be expressed in a market. In times when it is necessary, military service is usually held to be a duty that is independent of an individual's tastes, wealth, influence, or social position. It is felt that everyone *ought* to do this service, and exchanges between willing traders are prohibited.

Military service is not the only example of a social obligation. Citizens cannot buy their way out of jury duty or legally sell their voting rights to others, even though in many cases they could find willing trading partners.

Economic Growth

Over the long haul economic growth is the most powerful determinant of material living standards. Whatever their policies concerning efficiency and equity, people who live in economies with rapid rates of growth find their real per capita incomes rising (on average) faster than those of people who live in countries with low rates of growth. Over a few decades these growth-induced changes tend to have much larger effects on living standards than any policy-induced changes in the efficiency of resource allocation or the distribution of income.

For the last half of the twentieth century most economists viewed growth mainly as a macroeconomic phenomenon related to total saving and total investment. Reflecting this view, many textbooks do not even mention growth in the chapters on microeconomic policy.

More recently there has been a shift back to the perspective of earlier economists, who saw technological change as the engine of growth, with the individual entrepreneurs and firms as the agents of innovation. This is a microeconomic perspective, which is meant to add to, not replace, the macroeconomic emphasis on total saving and total investment.

Over the last decade or so, governments have placed considerable emphasis on this new microeconomic perspective on economic growth. Today few microeconomic policies escape being exposed to the question, "Even if this policy achieves its main goal, will it have unfavourable effects on growth?" Answering yes is not a sufficient reason to abandon a specific policy. But it is a sufficient reason to think again. Is it possible to redesign the policy so that it can still achieve its main micro objectives, while removing its undesirable side-effects on economic growth?

A General Principle

We have discussed how the free market may fail to achieve social goals that members of society deem to be desirable. This discussion suggests the following general principle:

Even if free markets generated allocatively efficient outcomes, they would be unlikely to generate outcomes consistent with most people's social goals. Furthermore, there is often a tradeoff between achieving these social goals and increasing allocative efficiency.

16.5 GOVERNMENT INTERVENTION

Private collective action can sometimes remedy the failures of private individual action. For example, volunteer fire departments can fight fires, firms in shopping centres can hire their own security staff, and insurance companies can guard against adverse selection by more careful classification of clients. However, by far the most common remedy for market failure is some form of government intervention.

Since markets sometimes *do* fail, there is a potential scope for governments to intervene in beneficial ways. Whether government intervention is warranted in any particular case depends both on the magnitude of the market failure that the intervention is designed to correct and on the costs of the government action itself.

The benefits of some types of government intervention—such as a publicly provided justice system—are both difficult to quantify and potentially very large. Further, government intervention often imposes difficulties of its own. For many types of government activity, however, *cost–benefit analysis* can be helpful in considering the general question of when and to what extent governments can successfully intervene.

cost–benefit analysis An approach for evaluating the desirability of a given policy, based on comparing total (opportunity) costs with total benefits.

The idea behind **cost–benefit analysis** is simple: Add up the (opportunity) costs of a given policy, then add up the benefits, and implement the policy only if the benefits outweigh the costs. In practice, however, cost–benefit analysis is usually quite difficult for three reasons. First, it may be difficult to ascertain what will happen when an action is undertaken. Second, many government actions involve costs and benefits that will occur only in the distant future; thus, they will be more complicated to assess. Third, some benefits and costs—such as the benefits of prohibiting actions that would harm members of an endangered animal species—are difficult to quantify. Indeed, some people argue that they cannot be and should not be quantified, as they involve values that are not commensurate with money. The practice then is to use cost–benefit analysis to measure the things that can be measured and to be sure that the things that cannot be measured are not ignored when collective decisions are made. By narrowing the range of things that must be determined by informal judgement, cost–benefit analysis can still play a useful role.

In this chapter, we have been working toward a cost–benefit analysis of government intervention. We have made a general case against government intervention, stressing that free markets are great economizers on information and coordination costs. We have also made a general case for government intervention, emphasizing that free markets fail to produce allocative efficiency when there are firms with market power, public goods, externalities, or information asymmetries, and may also fail to achieve broader social goals. We now turn to the more specific issues of how governments intervene, the costs of government intervention, and why government intervention sometimes fails to improve on imperfect market outcomes.

The Tools of Government Intervention

The legal power of governments to intervene in the workings of the economy is limited by the Charter of Rights (as interpreted by the courts), the willingness of Parliament and provincial legislatures to pass laws, and the willingness and ability of governments to enforce them. There are numerous ways in which one or another level of government can prevent, alter, complement, or replace the workings of the unrestricted market economy.

1. Public Provision National defence, the criminal justice system, public schools, universities, the highway system, and national parks are all examples of goods or services that are provided by governments in Canada. Public provision is the most obvious remedy for market failure to provide public goods, but it is also often used in the interest of redistribution (e.g., hospitals) and other social goals (e.g., public schools). We will consider public spending in detail in Chapter 18.

See the Government of Canada's web page to see how many federal government departments and Crown corporations exist: **www.gc.ca**.

2. Redistribution Programs Taxes and spending are often used to provide a distribution of income that is different from that generated by the free market. Government transfer programs affect the distribution of income in this way. We examine the distributive effects of the Canadian tax system in Chapter 18.

3. Regulation Government regulations are public rules that apply to private behaviour. In Chapter 12, we saw that governments regulate private markets to limit monopoly power. In Chapter 17, we will focus on regulations designed to deal with environmental degradation. Among other things, government regulations prohibit minors from consuming alcohol, require that children attend school, penalize racial discrimination in housing and labour markets, and require that new automobiles have seat belts. Government regulation is used to deal with all of the sources of market failure that we have discussed in this chapter; it applies at some level to virtually all spheres of modern economic life.

Almost all government actions, including the kinds we have discussed here, change the incentives that consumers and firms face. If the government provides a park, people will have a weakened incentive to own large plots of land of their own. Fixing minimum or maximum prices (as we saw in Chapter 5) affects privately chosen levels of output. If the government taxes income, people may have a reduced incentive to work.

The government can adjust the tax system to provide subsidies for some kinds of behaviour and penalties for others. For example, taxes on gasoline raise the price to consumers and may lead them to reduce the quantity used, especially over the long run. Tax exemptions for contributions to Registered Retirement Savings Plans (RRSPs) increase the rate of return to saving and may lead individuals to increase their total amount of saving. In both cases, the government policy alters prices and sends the household different signals from those sent by the free market.

The Costs of Government Intervention

Consider the following argument: The market system produces some particular outcome that is deemed to be undesirable; government has the legal means to improve the situation; therefore, the public interest will be served by government intervention.

At first glance the argument is appealing. But it is deficient because it neglects three important considerations. First, government intervention is itself costly since it uses

Practise with Study Guide Chapter 16, Exercise 4.

scarce resources; for this reason alone, not every undesirable outcome is worth correcting because the cost of doing so may exceed the perceived benefits. Second, government intervention is generally imperfect. Just as markets sometimes succeed and sometimes fail, so government interventions sometimes succeed and sometimes fail. Third, deciding what governments are to do and how they are to do it is also costly and intrinsically imperfect.

Large potential benefits do not necessarily justify government intervention, nor do large potential costs necessarily make it unwise. What matters is the balance between benefits and costs.

There are several different costs of government intervention. Economists divide these costs into two categories—*direct costs* and *indirect costs*.

Direct Costs   Government intervention uses real resources that could be used elsewhere. Civil servants must be paid and computer systems need to be purchased. Paper, photocopying, and other trappings of bureaucracy—the steel in the navy's ships, the fuel for the army's tanks, and the pilot of the prime minister's jet—all have valuable alternative uses. The same is true of the accountants who administer the Canada Pension Plan, the economists who are employed by the Competition Bureau, and the educators who retrain displaced workers.

Similarly, when government inspectors visit plants to monitor compliance with federally imposed standards of health, industrial safety, or environmental protection, they are imposing costs on the public in the form of their salaries and expenses. When regulatory bodies develop rules, hold hearings, write opinions, or have their staff prepare research reports, they are incurring costs. The costs of the judges, clerks, and court reporters who hear, transcribe, and review the evidence are also imposed by government regulation. All these activities use valuable resources that could have provided very different goods and services.

All forms of government intervention use real resources and hence impose direct costs.

The direct costs of government intervention are fairly easy to identify, as they almost always involve well-documented expenditures. In the 2004–2005 fiscal year, the total expenditures by all levels of governments (excluding transfer payments) in Canada were $304 billion, just over 21 percent of total national income.

Indirect Costs   Most government interventions in the economy impose costs on firms and households over and above the taxes that must be paid to the government to finance its policies. The nature and the size of the extra costs borne by firms and households vary with the type of intervention. A few examples will illustrate what is involved.

1. Changes in Costs of Production. Government safety and emissions standards for automobiles have raised the costs of both producing and operating cars. Environmental policies that require firms to treat their waste products and emissions also increase the overall costs. In both cases, these costs are much greater than the direct budgetary costs of administering the regulations.

2. Costs of Compliance. Government regulation and supervision generate a flood of reporting and related activities that are often referred to collectively as *red tape*. The number of hours of business time devoted to understanding, reporting, and contesting regulatory provisions is enormous. Regulations dealing with occupational safety and environmental control have all increased the size of non-production payrolls. The legal costs alone of a major corporation sometimes can run into tens or hundreds of millions of dollars per year. While all this provides lots of employment for lawyers and economic experts, it is costly because there are other tasks these professionals could do that would add more to the production of consumer goods and services.

Households also bear compliance costs directly. A recent study found that the time and money cost of filling out individual income-tax returns was about 8 percent of the total revenue that is collected. In addition to costs of compliance, there are costs borne as firms and households try to avoid regulation. There is a substantial incentive to find loopholes in regulations. Resources that could be used elsewhere are devoted to the search for such loopholes and then, in turn, by the regulators to counteracting such evasion.

Farmers in Canada often request government assistance to offset the effects of low crop prices or bad weather. This is one example of "rent seeking."

Red tape is a problem in advanced, industrialized economies, but it is even more serious in some developing economies. For examples of how red tape can stand in the way of economic development, look for "How Excessive Regulation Hobbles Development" in the *Additional Topics* section of this book's MyEconLab.

w w w . m y e c o n l a b . c o m

3. Rent Seeking. A different kind of problem arises from the mere existence of government and its potential to use its tools in ways that affect the distribution of economic resources. This phenomenon has been dubbed **rent seeking** by economists because private firms, households, and business groups will use their political influence to seek *economic rents* from the government in ways that do not advance the public interest. These valuable rents can come in the form of favourable regulations, direct subsidies, and profitable contracts that do not use public funds in a prudent manner. Democratic governments are especially vulnerable to manipulation of this kind because they respond to well-articulated interests of all sorts.

rent seeking Behaviour whereby private firms and individuals try to use the powers of the government to enhance their own economic well-being in ways that are not in the social interest.

Rent seeking is endemic to mixed economies. Because of the many things that governments are called on to do, they have the power to act in ways that transfer resources among private entities. Because they are democratic, they are responsive to public pressures of various kinds. If a government's behaviour can be influenced, whether by voting, campaign contributions, lobbying, or bribes, real resources will be used in trying to do so.

In the aggregate, the indirect costs of government intervention are substantial. But they are difficult to measure and are usually dispersed across a large number of firms and households.

Government Failure

Even in the cases where the benefits and costs of government intervention can be easily identified and measured, governments, like private markets, are imperfect. Often they will fail, in the same sense that markets do, to achieve their potential.

The reason for government failure is not that public-sector employees are less able, honest, or virtuous than people who work in the private sector. Rather, the causes of government failure are inherent in government institutions, just as the causes of market failure stem from the nature of markets. Importantly, some government failure is an inescapable cost of democratic decision making.

Decision Makers' Objectives   By far the most important cause of government failure arises from the nature of the government's own objectives. Traditionally, economists did not concern themselves greatly with the motivation of government. The theory of economic policy implicitly assumed that governments had no objectives of their own. As a result, economists only needed to identify places where the market functioned well on its own, and places where government intervention could improve the market's functioning. Governments would then stay out of the former markets and intervene as necessary in the latter.

This model of government behaviour never fitted reality, and economists were gradually forced to think more deeply about the motivation of governments. Today economists no longer assume that governments are faceless robots doing whatever economic analysis suggests is in the social interest. Instead they are modelled just as are producers and consumers—as units with their own objectives, which they seek to maximize.

Governments undoubtedly do care about the social good to some extent, but public officials have their careers, their families, and their prejudices as well. As a result, public officials' own needs are seldom wholly absent from their consideration of the actions they will take. Similarly, their definition of the public interest is likely to be influenced heavily by their personal views of what policies are best. It is therefore often the case that the policies supported by the public are different from the policies advocated by policymakers.

Modelling governments as maximizers of their own welfare, and then incorporating them into theoretical models of the working of the economy, was a major intellectual breakthrough. One of the pioneers of this development was the American economist James Buchanan, who was awarded the 1986 Nobel Prize in economics for his work in this field. The theory that he helped to develop is called *public choice theory*. The key breakthrough was to view the government as just another economic agent engaging in its own maximizing behaviour.

Public Choice Theory   Full-blown public choice theory deals with three maximizing groups. Elected officials seek to maximize their votes. Civil servants seek to maximize their salaries and their influence. Voters seek to maximize their own utility. To this end, voters look to the government to provide them with goods and services and income transfers that raise their personal utility. No one cares about the general interest!

On the one hand, this surely is not a completely accurate characterization of motives. Elected statesmen have acted in what they perceive to be the public interest, hoping to be vindicated by history even if they know they risk losing the next election. Some civil servants expose inside corruption—so-called whistleblowers—even though it can cost them their jobs. Some high-income individuals vote for the political party that advocates the most, not the least, income redistribution, and some poorer taxpayers vote for a party that advocates lower taxes on the rich and lower transfers to the poor.

On the other hand, the characterization is close to the mark in many cases. Most of us have read of politicians whose only principle is, "What will get me the most votes?" And many voters ask only, "What is in it for me?" This is why the theory can take us a long way in understanding what we see, even though real behaviour is more complex.

Here is one example relevant to Canada and many other developed economies. Why, in spite of strong advice from economists, have governments persisted in assisting agriculture for decades, until many governments now have major farm crises on their hands? Public choice theory looks at the winners and the losers among the voters.

The winners from agricultural supports are farmers. They are a politically powerful group, and are aware of what they will lose if farm supports are reduced. They would show their disapproval of such action by voting against any government that even suggests it. The losers are the entire group of consumers or taxpayers. Although they are more numerous than farmers, and although their total loss is large, each individual suffers only a small loss. Citizens have more important things to worry about, and so do not vote against the government just because it supports farmers. As long as the average voters are unconcerned about, and often unaware of, the losses they suffer, the vote-maximizing government will ignore the interests of the many and support the interests of the few. The vote-maximizing government will consider changing the agricultural policy only when the cost of agricultural support becomes so large that ordinary taxpayers begin to be concerned by the cost. What is required for a policy change, according to this theory, is that those who lose become sufficiently aware of their losses for this awareness to affect their voting behaviour.

Public choice theory seeks to explain how public officials make their decisions. They are assumed to act not in the best interests of their constituents but according to their own agendas that often conflict with the public interest.

Another example that we will see in Chapter 34 is the use of tariffs. When a tariff is imposed on an imported good, it increases the domestic price of the good. Tariffs therefore provide protection to the domestic firms producing competing products. This protection typically raises prices, profits, and wages in those firms. The costs of such tariffs are borne by a much larger number of consumers, each of whom is hurt a relatively small amount by the higher price. This concentration of benefits and the dispersion of costs explains to a large extent why tariffs, once in place, are so politically difficult to remove.

The ability of elected officials and civil servants to ignore the public interest is strengthened by a phenomenon called **rational ignorance**. Many policy issues are extremely complex. For example, even the experts are divided when assessing the pros and cons of Canada's maintaining a flexible exchange rate rather than pegging the value of the Canadian dollar to the U.S. dollar. Much time and effort is required for a layperson even to attempt to understand the issue. Similar comments apply to the evidence for and against capital punishment or lowering the age of criminal liability. Yet one person's vote has little influence on which party gets elected or on what they will really do about the issue in question once elected. So the costs of informing oneself are large, while the benefits of acting on that information are small. Thus, a majority of rational, self-interested voters will choose to remain innocent of the complexities involved in most policy issues.

Who will be the informed minority? The answer is those who stand to gain or lose a lot from the policy, those with a strong sense of moral obligation, and those policy junkies who just like thinking about these kinds of issues.

rational ignorance When agents have no incentive to become informed about some government policy because the costs of becoming informed exceed the benefits of any well-informed action the agent might take.

Democracy and Inefficient Public Choices At the core of most people's idea of democracy is the notion that all citizens' votes should have the same weight. One of the insights of the theory of public choice is that resource allocation, based on the principle of one vote per person, will generally be inefficient because it fails to take into account the *intensity of preferences.* Consider three farmers, Albert, Bob, and Charlene, who are contemplating building access roads to their farms. Suppose the road to Albert's farm is worth $7000 to him and that the road to Bob's farm is worth $7000 to him. Charlene's farm is on the main road, which already exists, and so an extra road is of no value to her. Suppose also that the cost of building each access road is $6000 and that under the current tax rules each of the three farmers would have to pay $2000 per road built.

The data for this example are summarized in Table 16-2, which shows each farmer's net benefits (benefits minus costs) from the construction of each road, and also the total net benefits for each road. For example, building the road to Albert's farm, and financing it by taxing each farmer $2000, generates net benefits of $5000 for Albert, and –$2000 each for Bob and Charlene. Total net benefits for this road are therefore $1000, revealing that the total benefits from building the road exceed the total costs. It is therefore efficient to build this road.

As the data in the table show, it is efficient to build roads to both Albert's and Bob's farms, but it is not efficient to build an (additional) road to Charlene's farm since it generates no benefits but costs $6000. The problem, however, is that both of the roads that should be built on the grounds of efficiency would be defeated 2–1 in a simple majority vote. Bob and Charlene would each vote against the road to Albert's farm, and Albert and Charlene would each vote against the road to Bob's farm. In this case, the democratic process leads to an inefficient outcome.

Now suppose we allow Albert and Bob to make a deal: "I will vote for your road if you will vote for mine." Although such deals are often decried by political commentators, the deal enhances efficiency: Both roads now get 2–1 majorities, and both roads get built. However, such deals can just as easily reduce efficiency. If the gross value of each road were $5000 instead of $7000, and Albert and Bob again make their deal, each road will still command a 2–1 majority, but building the roads will now be inefficient. (The gross value of each road is now only $5000, but the cost is still $6000.) Albert and Bob will be using democracy to appropriate resources from Charlene (the taxes she would have to pay) while reducing economic efficiency.

The possibility of inefficient public choices stems in large part from the problems inherent to a democratic system. *Extensions in Theory 16-2* discusses Kenneth Arrow's famous result in the theory of public choice. Arrow's somewhat unsettling theorem is that there is very often a tradeoff between democracy and efficiency.

Practise with Study Guide Chapter 16, Extension Exercise E1.

Governments as Monopolists Governments face the same problems of cost minimization that private firms do but often operate in an environment where they are

TABLE 16-2	Net Benefits from Road Construction			
Build Road to	Net Benefits to Albert	Net Benefits to Bob	Net Benefits to Charlene	Total Net Benefits
Albert's Farm	$7000 – $2000 = $5000	$0 – $2000 = –$2000	$0 – $2000 = –$2000	$1000
Bob's Farm	$0 – $2000 = –$2000	$7000 – $2000 = $5000	$0 – $2000 = –$2000	$1000
Charlene's Farm	$0 – $2000 = –$2000	$0 – $2000 = –$2000	$0 – $2000 = –$2000	–$6000

EXTENSIONS IN THEORY 16-2

A Problem with Democracy

Nobel laureate Kenneth Arrow from Stanford University has shown that it is generally impossible to construct a set of rules for making public choices that is at once comprehensive, democratic, efficient, and consistent. This striking idea—called Arrow's Impossibility Theorem—has led to decades of work on the part of economists, philosophers, and political scientists, who have tried to find conditions under which democracy can be expected to yield efficient allocations of resources. The news is generally not good. Unless individual preferences or their distribution in the population meet fairly unlikely criteria, either democracy or efficiency must be sacrificed in the design of public-choice mechanisms.

The Arrow theorem can be illustrated by a simple case, depicted in the following table.

Density of Trees	Voter		
	A	B	C
Sparse (1)	3	1	2
Medium (2)	1	2	3
Dense (3)	2	3	1

Imagine we have a society that consists of three voters who are choosing how many trees to plant in the local park. The three possibilities are as follows: (1) Plant very few trees, in one corner. This would make the park suitable for playing Frisbee and soccer but not for walks in the woods. (2) Plant trees in moderate density throughout the park. In this case, the park would be nice for jogging but not usable for most sports. (3) Plant trees densely everywhere. This would make the park a pleasant place to get away from it all (for whatever reasons) but not a good place to jog. Voter A loves jogging, hates Frisbee, and likes walking in the woods. His ranking of the alternatives is 3–1–2. Voter B likes the wide open spaces. His ranking is 1–2–3. Voter C likes to play Frisbee, likes solitude even more, and has little taste for a park that provides neither. Her ranking is 2–3–1.

Now suppose the electorate gets to choose between alternatives that are presented two at a time. What does majority rule do? Unfortunately, there is no unique democratic outcome; the result of such voting depends on which two alternatives are presented. In a choice of 1 versus 2, 1 wins, getting votes from B and C. When the choice is between 2 and 3, 2 wins, getting votes from A and B. When 3 is pitted against 1, 3 wins with the support of A and C. Thus, the public-choice mechanism of majority rule is *inconsistent*. It tells us that 1 is preferred to 2, 2 is preferred to 3, and 3 is preferred to 1. There is no way to make a choice without arbitrarily—that is, undemocratically—choosing which set of alternatives to offer the electorate. This is the essence of Arrow's famous argument that, in general, democracy and efficiency cannot both be achieved in issues of public choice.

monopoly producers without shareholders. Large governments (provinces, big cities, the federal government) face all of the organizational problems faced by large corporations. They tend to use relatively rigid rules and hence respond slowly to change. Building codes are an example of this type of problem. Most local governments have detailed requirements regarding the materials that must go into a new house, factory, or office. When technology changes, the codes often lag behind. For example, plastic pipe, which is cheaper and easier to use than copper pipe, was prohibited by building codes for decades after its use became efficient. Changes in technology may make a regulation inefficient, but the regulation may stay in place for a long time.

In the private sector, market forces often push firms into revising their view of the problem at hand, whereas there is ordinarily no market mechanism to force governments to adopt relatively efficient regulations. Put another way, much government failure arises precisely because governments do not have competitors and are not constrained by the "bottom line."

How Much Should Government Intervene?

Do governments intervene too little, or too much, in response to market failure? This question reflects one aspect of the continuing debate over the role of government in the economy. While many economists might agree on the theoretical principles that should guide government intervention in selected cases, there is more disagreement about the broader role of government in the economy. Unfortunately, the issue is often framed ideologically. Those on the "right wing" tend to compare heavy-handed government with a hypothetical and perfectly operating competitive market. In contrast, those on the "left wing" tend to compare hypothetical and ideal government intervention with a laissez-faire economy rife with market failures. Both perspectives are in danger of missing the more relevant debate.

Evaluating the costs and benefits of government intervention requires a comparison of the private economic system as it actually works (not as it might work ideally) with the pattern of government intervention as it actually performs (not as it might perform ideally).

Over the last three decades in most of the advanced industrial countries, the mix of free-market determination and government ownership and regulation has been shifting toward more market determination. No reasonable person believes that government intervention can, or should, be reduced to zero. Do we still have a long way to go in reversing the tide of big intrusive government that flowed through most of the twentieth century? Or perhaps we have gone too far and have given some things to the market that governments could do better? This will be one of the great social debates of the early decades of the twenty-first century.

The cases we have made for the costs and benefits of government intervention are both valid, depending on time, place, and the values that are brought to bear. At this point, we turn to the issue of what government actually does, something that will perhaps illuminate the question of what it could do better. In Chapter 12, we discussed government action that is designed to affect monopoly and competition. In the next two chapters, we discuss in some detail three other important types of intervention in the Canadian economy today: environmental regulation, taxation, and public spending.

SUMMARY

16.1 BASIC FUNCTIONS OF GOVERNMENT

- The government's monopoly of violence gives it the ability to enforce laws and protect its citizens. But restrictions on the government's power are required to ensure that individuals' rights are not unnecessarily violated.

16.2 THE CASE FOR FREE MARKETS

- The case for free markets can be made in two different ways. The "formal defence" is based on the concept of allocative efficiency. This was the basis for the appeal of competitive markets as discussed in Chapters 5 and 12.

- The "informal defence" of free markets is not specifically based on the idea of allocative efficiency, and thus applies to market structures other than just perfect competition. The informal defence of free markets is based on three central arguments:

1. Free markets provide automatic coordination of the actions of decentralized decision makers.
2. The pursuit of profits, which is central to free markets, provides a stimulus to innovation and economic growth.
3. Free markets permit a decentralization of economic power.

16.3 MARKET FAILURES

- Market failure refers to situations in which the free market does not achieve allocative efficiency. Four main sources of market failure are

  1. market power
  2. externalities
  3. public goods
  4. information asymmetries

- Pollution is an example of an externality. A producer who pollutes the air or water does not pay the social cost of the pollution and is therefore not motivated to avoid the costs. Private producers will therefore produce too much pollution relative to what is allocatively efficient.
- National defence is an example of a public good. Markets fail to produce public goods because the benefits of such goods are available to people whether they pay for them or not.
- Information asymmetries cause market failure when one party to a transaction is able to use personal expertise to manipulate the transaction in his or her own favour. Moral hazard and adverse selection are consequences of information asymmetries.

16.4 BROADER SOCIAL GOALS

- Changing the distribution of income is one of the roles for government intervention that members of a society may desire. Others include values that are placed on public provision for its own sake, on protection of individuals from themselves or from others, on recognition of social responsibilities, and on the promotion of economic growth.

16.5 GOVERNMENT INTERVENTION

- Major tools of microeconomic policy include (a) public provision, (b) redistribution, and (c) regulation.
- Most government actions—especially taxes or subsidies—change incentives that consumers and firms face.
- The costs and benefits of government intervention must be considered in deciding whether, when, and how much intervention is appropriate. Among the costs are the direct costs that are incurred by the government, the costs that are imposed on the parties who are regulated, directly and indirectly, and the costs that are imposed on third parties. These costs are seldom negligible and are often large.
- The possibility of government failure, as well as the costs of successful intervention, must be balanced against the potential benefits of removing market failure. It is neither possible nor efficient to correct all market failure; neither is it always efficient to do nothing.

KEY CONCEPTS

Market failure
Externalities
Private and social cost
Excludable and non-excludable goods
Rivalrous and non-rivalrous goods

Private goods
Common-property resource
Public goods
Information asymmetries
Moral hazard and adverse selection

Cost–benefit analysis
Rent seeking
Government failure
Public choice theory

STUDY EXERCISES

1. Fill in the blanks to make the following statements correct.

    a. The "formal defence" of free markets is that, if all markets were perfectly competitive, then prices would equal _____ for all products and the economy would be _____.

    b. The "informal defence" of free markets is based on the following three central arguments:

    ● _____
    ● _____
    ● _____

    c. A situation in which the free market, in the absence of government intervention, fails to achieve allocative efficiency is called _____.

    d. There are four major market failures that, in principle, justify government intervention in markets. They are:

    ● _____
    ● _____
    ● _____
    ● _____

2. Fill in the blanks to make the following statements correct.

    a. The marginal cost faced by the private decision maker is known as _____. The marginal cost faced by the private decision maker *plus* any other costs imposed on third parties is known as _____. If there is a divergence between these two marginal costs then we can say that _____ are present.

    b. An economic outcome is allocatively efficient when marginal social cost and marginal social benefit are _____.

    c. Suppose a potato chip plant is operating beside a residential neighbourhood and produces noise and an unpleasant odour. We can say that there is a _____ externality because the marginal social cost of producing potato chips is _____ the private cost of producing potato chips. As a result, the free market is producing too _____ potato chips.

    d. Suppose an apple orchard is operating beside a residential neighbourhood and provides beautiful blossoms and a pleasant fragrance. We can say that there is a _____ externality because the marginal social cost of apples is _____ the marginal private cost of apples. As a result, the free market is producing too _____ apples.

3. Fill in the blanks to make the following statements correct.

    a. A good or service that is rivalrous and excludable (e.g., a restaurant meal or a sofa) is known as a _____ good and is most efficiently provided by the _____.

    b. A good that is rivalrous and non-excludable (e.g., fish in the ocean, or common grazing land) is known as a _____ and tends to be overused by _____.

    c. Goods that are non-rivalrous and excludable (e.g., roads, museums, and parks) are often provided by government because the marginal cost of provision to society is _____ and so the allocatively efficient price is _____.

    d. Goods and services that are non-rivalrous and non-excludable (e.g., national defence, a lighthouse) are known as _____. Private markets will not provide these goods or services because of the _____ problem.

    e. If an auto mechanic tells you that your car needs a new transmission, there is the possibility of market failure in the form of _____.

    f. If you take up cliff diving as a new hobby and increase your life insurance, just in case, there is a possible market failure in the form of _____.

4. For each of the situations in the table below, indicate whether there is a positive or a negative externality. Indicate in each case whether social marginal cost (MC_S) is greater than or less than private marginal cost (MC_P).

	Positive or Negative Externality?	MC_S greater than or less than MC_P?
You smoke a cigarette and blow the smoke into others' faces.		
You cut your lawn early on a Sunday morning.		
A firm conducts R&D and generates useful "basic" knowledge that is freely available.		
A firm produces aluminum, but also produces toxic waste as a byproduct.		

5. **myeconlab** Consider the following diagram showing the perfectly competitive market for newsprint. The demand curve shows the marginal benefit to society of consuming an extra unit of newsprint. The supply curve shows the firms' marginal costs of producing an extra unit of newsprint.

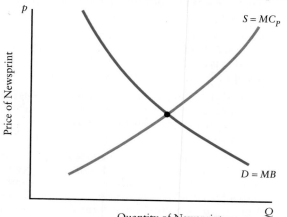

a. Describe the equilibrium in this competitive market.
b. Now suppose that, as a byproduct to producing newsprint, some toxic chemicals are also produced that get dumped in public streams and rivers. Suppose that for each unit of newsprint produced, one unit of toxic chemicals is also produced, imposing an external cost of $100. Show the social marginal cost curve in the diagram.
c. What is the allocatively efficient quantity of newsprint?

6. For each of the listed goods indicate whether they are rivalrous or non-rivalrous, and also indicate whether the use of them is excludable or non-excludable.

	Rivalrous?	Excludable?
CD player		
Clothing		
Library		
Lighthouse		
Medical services		
Published product safety information		
Pacific salmon		

a. Which of the goods in the table are public goods? Explain.
b. Which are common-property resources? Explain.

7. Art galleries, museums, roads, and bridges are usually provided by the government.

a. Explain why uncrowded goods of this sort should have a price of zero if allocative efficiency is to be achieved.
b. Would allocative efficiency be achieved if private firms provided these goods? Explain.
c. What happens when access to these goods becomes congested? Does efficiency still require a zero price? Explain.

8. **myeconlab** Consider a small town deciding whether to build a public park. The town council conducts a survey of its 100 residents and asks them how much they would each value the park. The survey results are as follows:

Number of people	Value of park per person	Total
10	$1000	$10 000
30	500	15 000
30	200	6 000
20	50	1 000
10	0	0
100		$32 000

a. Suppose it costs $35 000 to build the park. Should the town do it?
b. Suppose the park costs only $20 000 to build. Should the town build the park? If so, how should the town pay for building the park?
c. Suppose the town builds the park but charges people $50 for an annual pass. Does this present a problem for efficiency? Explain.

9. In the text we discussed how rent seeking is one of the costs of government intervention. Consider a group of pig farmers who are lobbying the federal government for some form of financial assistance (as they did in 1998 when the world price of pork declined steeply).

a. Explain why economists call such lobbying "rent seeking."
b. Suppose the farmers spend $500 000 in their lobbying efforts but have no effect on government policy. What is the cost to society of the rent seeking? Explain.
c. Suppose the $500 000 of lobbying *does* lead to a change in government policy. Now what is the social cost of the rent seeking?

DISCUSSION QUESTIONS

1. In each case, identify any divergence between social and private costs.

   a. Cigarette smoking
   b. Getting a university education
   c. Private ownership of guns
   d. Drilling for offshore oil

2. Consider the possible beneficial and adverse effects of each of the following forms of government intervention.

   a. Charging motorists a tax for driving in the downtown areas of large cities and using the revenues to provide peripheral parking and shuttle buses
   b. Prohibiting juries from awarding large malpractice judgements against doctors
   c. Mandating no-fault automobile insurance, in which the automobile owner's insurance company is responsible for damage to his or her vehicle no matter who causes the accident

3. The president of Goodyear Tire and Rubber Company complained that government regulation had imposed $30 million per year in "unproductive costs" on his company, as listed here. How would one determine whether these costs were "productive" or "unproductive"?

   a. Environmental regulation, $17 million
   b. Occupational safety and health, $7 million
   c. Motor vehicle safety, $3 million
   d. Personnel and administration, $3 million

4. Your local government almost certainly provides a police department, a fire department, and a public library. What are the market imperfections, if any, that each of these seeks to correct? Which of these are closest to being public goods? Which are furthest?

5. Suppose that for $100, a laboratory can accurately assess a person's probability of developing a fairly rare disease that is costly to treat. What would be the likely effects of such a test on health-insurance markets?

6. What market failures does public support of higher education seek to remedy? How would you go about evaluating whether the benefits of this support outweigh the costs?

7. This question is based on "Externalities and the Coase Theorem" on the book's MyEconLab at www.myeconlab.com. Consider a steel producer that dumps one litre of toxic waste into a river for every tonne of steel produced. A fishing camp located downstream bears the cost of cleaning up this toxic waste: $10 for every litre. Discuss how negotiations between the steel producer and the fishing camp may result in an allocatively efficient level of steel output even without direct government involvement. Does the nature of the negotiations depend on who owns the river?

CHAPTER 17

The Economics of Environmental Protection

LO LEARNING OBJECTIVES

In this chapter you will learn

1. how an externality can be internalized, and how this can lead to allocative efficiency.
2. why direct pollution controls are often inefficient.
3. how market-based policies such as emissions taxes and tradable pollution permits can improve economic efficiency.
4. about some of the most common arguments against market-based environmental policies.

For information about the *Canadian Environmental Protection Act,* see Environment Canada's website: **www.ec.gc.ca**.

In almost everything we do, we are subject to some form of government regulation. The system of criminal law regulates our interactions with people and property. Local zoning laws regulate the ways in which the land that we own or occupy may be used. Regulatory commissions set rates for electricity, natural gas, local telephone service, and a host of other goods and services. Seat belts, brake lights, turn signals, air bags, internal door panels, bumpers, and catalytic converters are compulsory and regulated in quality—all in a single industry. The list goes on and on. A good case can be made that various governments in Canada have more effect on the economy through regulation than through taxing and spending.

The focus in this chapter is on a specific type of government regulation, one that has become increasingly important in recent years. In particular, we examine the negative externalities that lead to environmental degradation and the various government policies designed to address them. As we will see, policies intended to protect the environment do not always do so in an efficient manner. One of the central themes in this chapter is that the information available to the regulatory agencies, especially regarding firms' technologies for reducing pollution, is generally incomplete. This lack of good information leads to the result that *market-based* environmental regulations are usually more successful than methods based on the government's *direct control.*

17.1 THE ECONOMIC RATIONALE FOR REGULATING POLLUTION

Pollution is a negative externality. As a consequence of producing or consuming goods and services, "bads" are produced as well. Steel plants produce smoke in addition to steel. Farms produce chemical runoff as well as food. Logging leads to soil erosion that contaminates fish-breeding grounds. Cars, trucks, and factories, by burning carbon-rich fossil fuels such as coal, oil, and natural gas, produce carbon dioxide and other "greenhouse" gases that contribute to global climate change. Households produce human waste and garbage as they consume goods and services. In all of these cases, the technology of production and consumption automatically generates pollution. Indeed, there are few human endeavours that do not have negative pollution externalities.

FIGURE 17-1   A Pollution Externality in a Competitive Market

A negative externality implies that a competitive free market will produce more output than the allocatively efficient level. If the externality can be internalized, allocative efficiency can be achieved. A competitive free market will produce where the demand and supply curves intersect—that is, at Q^c and p^c. If each unit of output of this good also generates an external cost of MEC, then social marginal cost is greater than private marginal cost by this amount. The allocatively efficient level of output is where marginal benefit equals *social* marginal cost—that is, at Q^*. The competitive free market therefore produces too much output.

If firms in this industry are now required to pay a tax of $\$MEC$ per unit of output, the private marginal cost curve, MC_P, shifts up to MC_S. The externality will thus be *internalized* because firms will now be forced to pay the full social cost of their production. The new competitive equilibrium will be p^*, Q^*, and allocative efficiency will be achieved.

Pollution as an Externality

Polluting firms do not regard a clean environment as a scarce resource and therefore fail to consider the full costs of using this resource when producing their product. When a paper mill produces newsprint for the world's newspapers, more people are affected than just its suppliers, employees, and customers. Its water-discharged effluent hurts the fishing boats that ply nearby waters, and its smog makes many resort areas less attractive, thereby reducing the tourist revenues that local motel operators and boat renters can expect. The profit-maximizing paper mill neglects these external effects of its actions because its profits are not directly affected by them.

As shown in Figure 17-1, allocative efficiency requires that the price (the value that consumers place on the marginal unit of output) be just equal to the marginal social cost (the value of the resources that society gives up to produce the marginal unit of output). When there are negative externalities, *social* marginal cost exceeds *private* marginal cost because the act of production generates costs for society that are not faced by the producer.

By producing where price equals private marginal cost and thereby ignoring the externality, the firms are maximizing profits but producing too much output. The price that consumers pay just covers the private marginal cost but does not pay for the external damage. The *social benefit* of the last unit of output (the market price) is less than the social cost (private marginal cost plus the extra cost to society from the externality). Reducing output by one unit would increase allocative efficiency and thus make society as a whole better off.

Making polluting firms bear the entire social cost of their production is called **internalizing the externality**. This leads them to produce a lower level of output, as shown in Figure 17-1. Indeed, at the optimal level of output, where the externality is completely internalized, consumer prices would just cover all of the *social* marginal cost of production. We would have the familiar condition for allocative efficiency that marginal benefits to consumers are just equal to the marginal (social) cost of producing these benefits.

The socially optimal level of output is at the quantity where all marginal costs, private plus external, equal the marginal benefit to society.

In order to internalize the externality successfully, it is necessary to measure its size accurately. Looking at Figure 17-1, we must be able to measure the magnitude of the marginal external cost, *MEC*. In practice, however, external costs are quite difficult to measure. This measurement is especially difficult in the case of air pollution, where the damage is often spread over hundreds of thousands of square kilometres and can affect millions of people.

internalizing the externality
A process that results in a producer or consumer taking account of a previously external effect.

Practise with Study Guide Chapter 17, Exercise 1.

The Optimal Amount of Pollution Abatement

Notice from Figure 17-1 that the allocatively efficient outcome still has some pollution being generated. This is because the production of each unit of output in Figure 17-1 generates some pollution. It is simply impossible to produce goods and services without generating *some* environmental damage. The economic problem is then to determine how much environmental damage to allow or, equivalently, how much pollution abatement (reduction) to implement. In general it is not optimal to eliminate all pollution.

Zero environmental damage is generally not allocatively efficient.

The economics of determining how much pollution to prohibit, and therefore how much to allow, is summarized in Figure 17-2, which depicts the marginal benefits and marginal costs of pollution abatement. The analysis might be thought of as applying, for example, to water pollution in a specific watershed. It is drawn from the perspective of a public authority whose mandate is to maximize social welfare.

Note that the figure is drawn in terms of the amount of pollution that is prevented (or abated) rather than in terms of the total amount of pollution produced. We do this because pollution abatement (rather than pollution itself) is a "good" of economic value, and we are more familiar with applying the concepts of supply and demand for

FIGURE 17-2   The Optimal Amount of Pollution Abatement

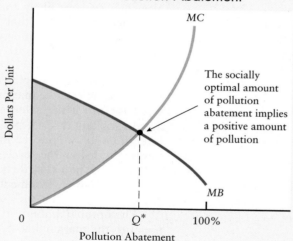

The socially optimal amount of pollution abatement implies a positive amount of pollution

The optimal amount of pollution abatement occurs where the marginal cost of reducing pollution is just equal to the marginal benefits from doing so. *MB* represents the marginal benefit of reducing pollution by one unit. *MC* represents the marginal cost of reducing pollution by one unit. The optimal level of pollution abatement is Q^*, where *MB = MC*. *Notice that not all pollution is eliminated.* For each unit up to Q^*, the marginal benefit derived from pollution abatement exceeds the marginal cost. The total net benefit from the optimal amount of pollution abatement is given by the shaded area—the sum of the difference between marginal benefit and marginal cost at each level of abatement. Any further efforts to reduce pollution beyond Q^* would add more to social costs than to social benefits.

Pollution is an externality. Unless they are required by law to do so, most firms do not take the social costs of their pollution into account when they make their private profit-maximizing decisions.

goods with positive values. If no pollution is abated, the watershed will be subjected to the amount of pollution that would occur in an unregulated market. The greater the amount of pollution abated, the smaller the amount of pollution that remains. Thus, as we move to the right along the horizontal axis, there is more pollution abatement and therefore less remaining pollution. On the vertical axis, measured in dollars per unit, we show the marginal benefit and marginal cost of pollution abatement.

The marginal cost of abating pollution is likely to be small at low levels of abatement but to rise steeply after some point. This is the upward-sloping line shown in Figure 17-2. There are two reasons for believing that this shape is generally accurate. First is the familiar logic behind increasing marginal costs. Because some antipollution measures can be taken fairly easily, the first units of pollution abatement will be cheap relative to later units. In addition, it is likely that pollution prevention of any degree will be easier for some firms than for others. New facilities are likely to run more cleanly than old ones, for example. Pollution abatement in a factory that was designed in the era of environmental concern may be much easier than obtaining similar abatement in an older factory. After some point, however, the easy fixes are exhausted, and the marginal cost of preventing pollution further rises steeply.

The downward-sloping curve in Figure 17-2 is the "demand" for pollution abatement, and reflects the marginal benefit of pollution reduction. The curve slopes downward for much the same reason that the typical demand curve slopes downward. Starting at any level of pollution, people will derive some benefit from reducing the level of pollution, but the marginal benefit from a given amount of abatement will be lower, the lower the level of pollution (or the higher the level of abatement). Put another way, in a very dirty environment, a little cleanliness will be much prized, but in a very clean environment, a little more cleanliness will be of only small additional value.

The optimal amount of pollution abatement occurs where the marginal benefit is equal to the marginal cost—where "supply" and "demand" in Figure 17-2 intersect. In trying to reach this optimum, the pollution-control authority faces three serious problems.

First, although Figure 17-2 looks like a supply–demand diagram, we have already seen that the private sector will not by itself create a market in pollution control. Hence, the government must intervene in private-sector markets if the optimal level of control shown in Figure 17-2 is to be attained.

The second problem is that the optimal level of pollution abatement is not easily known because the marginal benefit and the marginal cost curves shown in Figure 17-2 are not usually observable. In practice, the government can only estimate these curves, and accurate estimates are often difficult to obtain, especially when the technology of pollution abatement is changing rapidly and the health consequences of various pollutants are not known. An excellent recent example of our ignorance regarding the marginal costs and benefits of pollution abatement is related to the debate on greenhouse-gas emissions and global warming. Though there is now a broad consensus among scientists that humankind's emissions of greenhouse gases are contributing to global warming, the estimates of the *magnitude* of the effects of the earth's warming vary considerably.

The third problem is that the available techniques for regulating pollution are themselves imperfect. Even if the optimal level of pollution abatement were known with precision, there are both technical and legal impediments to achieving that level through regulation.

▌ 17.2 **POLLUTION-CONTROL POLICIES**

We examine three different types of policies designed to bring about the optimal amount of pollution abatement (or the optimal amount of pollution). These are *direct controls, emissions taxes,* and *tradable pollution permits.*

Direct Controls

Direct control is the form of environmental regulation that is used most often in Canada and the United States, although it is often invisible to consumers. (Policies of direct control are sometimes referred to as *command-and-control* policies.) Automobile emissions standards are one example. The standards must be met by all new cars that are sold in Canada. They require that emissions per kilometre of a number of pollutants be less than certain specified amounts. The standards are the same no matter where the car is driven. The marginal benefit of reducing carbon monoxide emissions in rural Saskatchewan, where there is relatively little air pollution, is certainly much less than the marginal benefit in Montreal, where there is already a good deal of air pollution. Yet the standard is the same in both places.

Practise with Study Guide Chapter 17, Exercise 4.

Direct controls often require that specific *techniques* be used to reduce pollution. For example, coal-fired electric plants were sometimes required to use devices called "scrubbers" to reduce sulphur dioxide emissions, even in cases where other techniques could have achieved the same level of pollution abatement at lower cost.

Another form of direct control is the simple prohibition of certain polluting behaviours. For example, many cities and towns prohibit the private burning of leaves and other trash because of the air pollution problem (as well as the fire dangers) that the burning would cause. A number of communities have banned the use of wood-burning stoves for the same reason. Similarly, the Canadian federal government gradually reduced the amount of lead allowed in leaded gasoline and then eliminated leaded gasoline altogether.

Problems with Direct Controls The government can legislate a certain amount of pollution abatement through direct controls, and assuming that the legislation can be enforced, this amount of abatement will be achieved. An important problem with direct controls, however, is not with the amount of pollution abated, but rather with the total cost of achieving the given amount of abatement. In the terminology of Chapter 12, direct pollution controls are not *productively efficient* because the total cost of achieving a given amount of pollution abatement is not minimized.

Pollution is being abated efficiently when the marginal cost of pollution abatement is the same for all firms.

When firms are required to abide by direct pollution controls, however, the marginal cost of pollution abatement is usually *not* equated across firms. To see this, consider two firms that have different technologies and thus face different marginal costs of pollution abatement, as shown in Figure 17-3. These firms may be in the same

FIGURE 17-3   The Inefficiency of Direct Pollution Controls

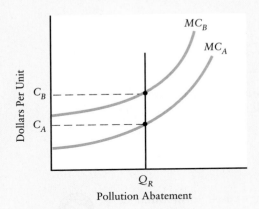

Pollution Abatement

Requiring equal amounts of pollution abatement from different polluters is inefficient when the different polluters have different technologies of pollution abatement. Firm A is able to reduce its emissions according to the marginal cost curve MC_A. Firm B has a different abatement technology and has a higher marginal cost of abatement, MC_B. Suppose a regulatory authority requires that the two firms reduce pollution by the same amount, Q_R. Firm A will have a marginal cost of pollution abatement of C_A, whereas Firm B's marginal cost will be C_B, which is larger than C_A.

To see that this outcome is inefficient, consider what happens if Firm A increases its pollution abatement by one unit while Firm B decreases its abatement by one unit. Total pollution remains the same, but total costs fall.

industry, producing similar products, or they may be in different industries altogether. In either case, they are assumed to have different abilities to abate pollution. Suppose that, for any level of pollution abatement, Firm A's marginal costs of abatement are lower than those for Firm B.

In this situation, consider a system of direct pollution controls that requires Firm A and Firm B each to reduce pollution by a given amount, say Q_R. As shown in Figure 17-3, Firm A's marginal cost at Q_R (C_A) is less than Firm B's marginal cost (C_B). As long as C_A is less than C_B, it is possible to reduce the *total* cost of this amount of pollution abatement by reallocating it between the two firms. For example, suppose C_A is $10 and C_B is $18. If Firm A abated one more unit of pollution, its costs would rise by $10; if Firm B abated one *less* unit of pollution, its costs would fall by $18. By reallocating one unit of pollution abatement from Firm B to Firm A, total pollution abatement would be unaffected, but the total cost of the abatement would be reduced by $8. As long as the two firms' marginal costs of abatement are not equal, it is possible to reduce total costs further by further redistributing the abatement between the firms. Only when marginal costs are equal across the two firms is the given level of pollution abatement being achieved at the lowest possible cost.

Direct pollution controls are inefficient because they do not minimize the cost of a given amount of pollution abatement.

Direct controls are also expensive to monitor and to enforce. The regulatory agency has to check—factory by factory, farm by farm—how many pollutants of what kinds are being emitted. It then also needs a mechanism for penalizing offenders. Accurate monitoring of all potential sources of pollution requires a level of resources that is much greater than has ever been made available to the relevant regulatory agencies. Moreover, the existing system of fines and penalties, in the view of many critics, is not nearly harsh enough to have much effect. A potential polluter, required to limit emissions of a pollutant to so many kilograms or litres per day, will take into account the cost of meeting the standard, the probability of being caught, and the severity of the penalty before deciding how to behave. If the chances of being caught and the penalties for being caught are small, the direct controls may have little effect.

Monitoring and enforcement of direct pollution controls are costly, and this costliness reduces the effectiveness of the controls.

Finally, some direct controls can have undesirable effects. For example, automobile manufacturers in the United States are required to achieve an average level of fuel efficiency on the entire fleet of cars they produce. Cars that could burn either ethanol or gasoline were first produced in 1997, and because fuel-efficiency is so much greater when burning ethanol, the production of these cars was much celebrated. However, because very few service stations sold ethanol, owners of these new cars soon turned to fuelling their cars with ordinary gasoline. But the regulations still counted these vehicles as fuel-efficient ethanol-burning cars even though they were, in practice, no more efficient than "normal" gasoline-burning cars. As a result, the manufacturers were able to produce *more* gasoline-guzzling SUVs and still achieve, at least on paper, their overall fuel-efficiency standards. Thus, the mere existence of cars that were able to (but didn't actually) burn ethanol contributed to an *increase* in the average per-vehicle consumption of gasoline.

Emissions Taxes

An alternative method of pollution control is to levy a tax on emissions at the source. The advantage of such a procedure is that it internalizes the pollution externality so that decentralized decisions can lead to allocatively efficient outcomes. Again, suppose Firm A can reduce emissions cheaply, while it is more expensive for Firm B to reduce emissions. And further suppose that all firms are required to pay a tax equal to $t per unit of pollution emitted. Since firms must pay $t for every unit of pollution they produce, they will save $t for every unit of pollution they *do not produce*. It follows that the emissions tax of $t is each firm's marginal benefit of pollution abatement. The goal of profit maximization will then lead firms to reduce emissions to the point where the marginal cost of further reduction is just equal to $t. Firm A will reduce emissions much more than Firm B and both will then have the same marginal cost of further abatement, which is required in order to minimize the cost of a given total amount of pollution abatement. Such a situation is illustrated in Figure 17-4.

Note that if the regulatory agency is able to obtain a good estimate of the marginal damage done by pollution, it could set the tax rate just equal to that amount. In such a case, polluters would be forced by the tax to internalize the full pollution externality and allocative efficiency would be achieved. In terms of Figure 17-1, each firm's private marginal cost curve would shift up by the full amount of the tax (set to equal the marginal external cost, *MEC*) and thus the allocatively efficient level of output (and pollution) would be produced.

A second advantage of using emissions taxes is that regulators are not required to specify anything about *how* polluters should abate pollution, and thus are not required to have expertise about the firms' technologies. Rather, polluters themselves can be left to find the most efficient abatement techniques. The profit motive will lead them to do so because they will want to avoid paying the tax.

Practise with Study Guide Chapter 17, Exercise 2 and Extension Exercise E1.

FIGURE 17-4 The Efficiency of Emissions Taxes

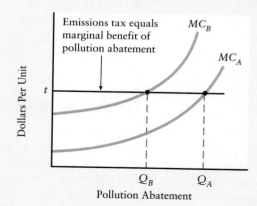

Emission taxes can lead to efficient pollution abatement. As in Figure 17-3, Firm A faces a lower marginal cost of pollution abatement than does Firm B. Suppose the regulatory authority imposes a tax of t dollars per unit of pollution. Since each firm must then pay t dollars for each unit of pollution it produces, t can be viewed as each firm's marginal benefit of pollution abatement.

Firm A chooses to reduce its pollution by Q_A. Up to this point, the tax saved (marginal benefit) from reducing pollution exceeds the marginal cost of reducing pollution. Firm B chooses to abate only a small amount of pollution, Q_B. Since the marginal cost of abatement is equated across firms, the total amount of pollution abatement $(Q_A + Q_B)$ is achieved at minimum cost. This is efficient pollution abatement.

Emissions taxes can internalize pollution externalities so that profit-maximizing firms will produce the allocatively efficient amount of pollution abatement.

Applying Economic Concepts 17-1 discusses a simple type of pollution tax that is becoming more common in Canadian cities—charging for household garbage by the bag.

Problems with Emissions Taxes Emissions taxes can work only if it is possible to measure emissions with reasonable accuracy. For some kinds of pollution-creating activities, this does not pose much of a problem, but for many other types of pollution, good measuring devices that can be installed at reasonable cost do not exist. Obviously, in these cases, emissions taxes cannot work, and direct controls are the only feasible approach.

When there is good reason to prohibit a pollutant completely, direct controls are obviously better than taxes. Municipal bans on the burning of leaves fall in this category, as do the occasional emergency bans on some kinds of pollution that are invoked during an air pollution crisis in cities such as Los Angeles, Toronto, and Vancouver.

Another problem with emissions taxes involves setting the tax rate. Ideally, the regulatory agency would obtain an estimate of the marginal social damage caused per unit of each pollutant and set the tax equal to this amount. This ideal tax rate would perfectly internalize the pollution externality. However, the information that is needed to determine the marginal external cost (*MEC*) shown in Figure 17-1 is often difficult to obtain. If the regulatory agency sets the tax rate too high, too many resources will be devoted to pollution control. If the tax is set too low, there will be too little pollution abatement and thus too much pollution.

A disadvantage with emissions taxes is that information necessary to determine the optimal tax rate is often unavailable.

Tradable Pollution Permits

tradable pollution permits
Government-granted rights to emit specific amounts of specified pollutants that private firms may buy and sell among themselves.

Practise with Study Guide Chapter 17, Exercise 3.

Like emissions taxes, tradable pollution permits can minimize the cost of a given amount of pollution abatement. **Tradable pollution permits** are permits that allow firms to emit a specified amount and type of pollution and which can be traded among firms at prices determined in a free market. For example, the government might issue permits for a total of 10 000 megatonnes of annual sulphur dioxide emissions and distribute to each of 20 firms a permit for 500 megatonnes. In any given year, a firm is restricted to emitting an amount of sulphur dioxide no greater than the amount allowed by the permits its holds. Firms can then trade the permits freely among themselves and a market-determined price will be established.

To see the efficiency of tradable pollution permits, consider starting from a situation similar to that with direct pollution controls. In Figure 17-5, both firms are abating pollution by Q_R units. (The inefficiency of this initial situation is reflected by the differential in marginal costs of the two firms.) Now suppose the government issues permits for a total amount of emissions consistent with the same total amount of pollution abatement (= $2 \times Q_R$ in the figure). What should each of the firms do? Should they abate more pollution, or less?

Note that at Q_R units of pollution abatement, the marginal costs for Firm B exceed the marginal costs for Firm A—pollution abatement is more difficult for Firm B than for Firm A. Suppose the two firms could agree on a price p^* at which to buy and sell permits. Who would buy, and who would sell? Firm B, the high-abatement-cost firm, would rather buy permits at p^* and avoid having to reduce pollution at high marginal

APPLYING ECONOMIC CONCEPTS 17-1

Charging for Garbage by the Bag

One of the most common forms of pollution is house-hold garbage. In bags or cans or just "bunches," it is typically removed from the curb by a municipally owned (or hired) garbage truck and transported to a landfill site outside the city. But landfills eventually become full, and new sites must be found. As a result, appropriate landfill sites are becoming scarce—and expensive. In some of the more populated regions of Canada and the United States, the garbage is transported for several hundred kilometres before it is dumped!

The cost of garbage removal and dumping is usually borne by the city, and financed through property taxes. The typical annual payment for this service is between $150 and $250 per Canadian household. But since individual households do not face a *direct* cost associated with each bag of garbage they put out, economic theory suggests this service will be overused, and the outcome will be allocatively inefficient. Too much garbage will be produced.

The externality in this case is the use of scarce landfill sites, which have a considerable, and rising, opportunity cost. When households throw out their garbage, they bear no direct cost associated with the use of these landfills. If households were charged directly for each bag of garbage they put out, economic theory suggests they would take more account of the value of this scarce resource (i.e., the externality would be internalized). As a result, households would reduce their production of garbage and come up with alternative means of dealing with their waste, including a greater emphasis on composting and recycling.

U.S. cities began introducing per-bag garbage-pricing policies in the late 1970s, and now over 6000 U.S. cities have them. Canadian cities have been much slower to adopt these policies, perhaps reflecting the greater availability and lower price of landfill sites. The first Canadian per-bag garbage-pricing policies appeared in 1991. Today, they exist in over 200 cities, mostly in Ontario and in the B.C. Lower Mainland.

The details of these programs differ from city to city. Some require households to purchase special stickers from the municipalities for between $1 and $2 each, and to affix these stickers to any garbage bags to be picked up. Other programs allow the household to pay a fee, such as $150 per year, giving the household the right to have one garbage bag picked up per week. In this case, a household that wants a second bag picked up on a regular basis must pay an additional $150 annual fee.

The theoretical proposition that charging for garbage by the bag leads to more recycling and less garbage being picked up is supported by recent evidence in both Canada and the United States. For example, in Peterborough, Ontario, a garbage-pricing program was introduced in 1993. By 2000, the annual amount of waste being collected had fallen by 21 percent and the annual amount of waste being recycled had increased by 49 percent. Similar results were observed in Markham, Barrie, and Orillia, all in Ontario, and in St. Albert, near Edmonton, Alberta.*

There are some difficulties with such garbage-pricing policies, however. First, it is difficult to determine the optimal price per bag of garbage. As long as landfill sites have some opportunity cost, however, it is obvious that the optimal price is greater than zero. Perhaps a more important problem relates to enforcement. Faced with the requirement to pay for each bag of garbage disposed, some households will choose the (privately) cheaper option of dumping their garbage in a park, in public garbage cans, or under a nearby bridge. In these cases, the households are simply *shifting* costs from themselves to society.

---

* These results do not control for changes in the amount of garbage and recycling that might have occurred even without the new pricing policies, such as what would be expected from the introduction of the free "blue box" programs designed to encourage recycling. For more details, see "Taking Out the Trash: How to Allocate the Costs Fairly," by M. Kelleher, J. Robins, and J. Dixie, C. D. Howe Institute *Commentary*, July 2005.

If a price is charged for every bag of garbage picked up from the curb, individuals have a strong incentive to reduce their garbage. This is one way to deal with the growing scarcity of landfill sites.

FIGURE 17-5   The Efficiency of Tradable Pollution Permits

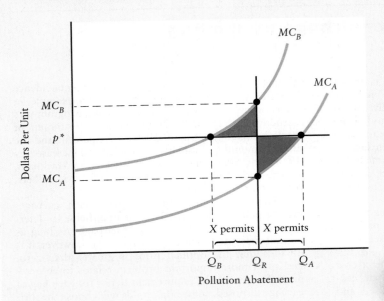

Tradable pollution permits are an efficient way to achieve a given amount of pollution abatement. As in Figure 17-3 and Figure 17-4, Firm A has lower marginal costs of pollution abatement than does Firm B. If each firm abates pollution by Q_R units, the firms' marginal costs are not equated and the pollution abatement is inefficient.

All firms can be better off if they are issued tradable pollution permits even though total pollution abatement remains unchanged. The price of the permits reflects firms' marginal benefit of pollution abatement. If the price is p^*, Firm A would sell X permits to Firm B. Firm B would reduce its abatement to Q_B and reduce its costs by the red area, while Firm A would increase its abatement to Q_A and increase its earnings by the blue area. Since the marginal costs of abatement are equated across firms, this is efficient pollution abatement.

costs. By buying X pollution permits from Firm A, Firm B ends up abating Q_B units of pollution and reduces its costs by the red shaded area. Firm A, the low-abatement-cost firm, would rather sell its permits at p^* and abate more pollution at low marginal cost. By selling X permits to Firm B, Firm A ends up abating Q_A units of pollution and increases its profits by the blue shaded area.

Therefore, with low-abatement-cost firms selling pollution permits to high-abatement-cost firms, both types of firms are better off than when they are subject to direct pollution controls even though the total amount of pollution abatement is unchanged. Since the marginal cost of abatement is now equal across firms, we know that the given amount of pollution abatement is being achieved at the lowest possible cost.

With tradable pollution permits, profit-maximizing firms will reduce pollution until their marginal abatement costs equal the price of pollution permits. The costs of a given amount of pollution abatement will be minimized.

What determines the equilibrium market price for pollution permits? The total supply of pollution permits is determined by the government policy. Let this amount be Q^S—it is represented by a vertical supply curve in Figure 17-6. The demand for pollution permits comes from firms and depends on their costs of pollution abatement.

For every unit of pollution that a firm abates, the firm requires one fewer pollution permit. The price of the pollution permit is therefore firms' marginal benefit of abatement. As the price of the permit increases, each firm decides to abate more pollution and therefore demand fewer pollution permits. Thus, the demand curve for pollution permits is downward sloping, as shown in Figure 17-6. At the equilibrium price for pollution permits, p^*, the number of permits demanded by firms will exactly equal the number of permits issued by the government.

In the market for pollution permits, the quantity is set by government policy. Given that quantity, the equilibrium price is determined by firms' demand for pollution permits.

Technological Change We said earlier that one problem with direct pollution controls is that they tend, like much government regulation, to respond only slowly to changes in technology or market conditions. In contrast, tradable pollution permits, because they are a market-based method of pollution control, maintain their efficiency even in the midst of frequent and substantial changes in technology. As technological advances occur that reduce firms' costs of pollution abatement, firms' demands for pollution permits will fall. The result will be a reduction in the equilibrium price of pollution permits. Whatever the market price for permits, profit-maximizing firms will equate the price to their marginal abatement costs, thus minimizing the total cost of a given amount of pollution abatement.

Improvements in abatement technology will lead to a reduction in the demand for emissions permits and thus a reduction in their equilibrium price. The total cost of a given amount of pollution abatement will still be minimized.

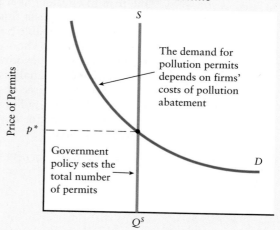

FIGURE 17-6 The Market for Tradable Pollution Permits

The equilibrium price in the market for pollution permits is determined by government policy and by firms' technology of pollution abatement. The government sets the total quantity of pollution permits at Q^S. This is the vertical supply curve. At a lower price for permits (the marginal benefit of abatement) firms decide to abate less pollution and they therefore require more pollution permits. The demand curve for permits is therefore downward sloping. At the equilibrium price, the quantity of permits demanded by firms is equal to the number issued by the government.

myeconlab

The U.S. *Clean Air Act* of 1990 created a national market for tradable permits for sulphur dioxide, the major cause of acid rain. For more details, look for "A Market for SO$_2$ Emissions in the United States" in the *Additional Topics* section of this book's MyEconLab.

www.myeconlab.com

Problems with Tradable Pollution Permits Tradable permits pose some problems of implementation. Some of these involve technical difficulties in measuring pollution and in designing mechanisms to ensure that firms and households comply with regulations (some of these problems also exist for direct controls and emissions taxes). Furthermore, the potential efficiency gains arising from tradable permits cannot be realized if regulatory agencies are prone to change the rules under which trades may take place. Such changes have been a problem in the past, but they are a problem that can be corrected.

One problem with tradable permits is more political than economic, but it is certainly important in explaining why such policies are relatively rare. Opponents of tradable permits often argue that by providing permits, rather than simply outlawing pollution above some amount, the government is condoning crimes against society.

Direct controls, according to this argument, have much greater normative force because they say that violating the standards is simply wrong. Emissions taxes and markets for pollution make violating the standards just one more element of cost for the firm to consider as it pursues its private goals.

Most economists find arguments of this kind unpersuasive. An absolute ban on pollution is impossible because any production of goods and services generates at least some pollution. In choosing how much pollution to allow, society must recognize the tradeoff between devoting resources toward pollution abatement and other valuable things. Economic analysis has a good deal to say about how a society might minimize the cost of *any* degree of pollution abatement. By taking the moral attitude that pollution is wrong and pollution permits should not be allowed, the result is that *less* pollution gets abated for any given amount of society's scarce resources that are allocated toward this goal.

The creation of markets for pollution emissions may become one of the most promising strategies for efficiently overcoming the market failure that leads to environmental pollution.

17.3 **THE POLITICS OF POLLUTION CONTROL**

To see a copy of the Kyoto Protocol, go to the website for the United Nations Framework Convention on Climate Change: **www.unfccc.de**.

Tradable pollution permits increased in prominence after the 1997 conference on global warming held in Kyoto, Japan. At this conference, representatives for 166 countries met to discuss the need for reducing the emissions of greenhouse gases—gases that most scientists now believe are responsible for trapping the earth's heat and raising the earth's average surface temperature significantly. Thirty-eight countries initially signed the "Kyoto Protocol" and many more have signed since then. Canada signed the Protocol in 1997 and the Canadian Parliament ratified Canada's participation in the international agreement in 2002. By adopting the Kyoto standards, individual countries agree to reduce their emissions of carbon dioxide and other greenhouse gases by a specified amount by 2012. An important part of the Kyoto Protocol is its advocacy of tradable pollution permits, in particular between the participating countries.

There is considerable debate about whether the reduction of greenhouse-gas emissions as outlined in the Kyoto Protocol will have a significant effect in the overall effort to combat global climate change. Even among strong supporters of the Kyoto Protocol, and of environmental protection more generally, there is skepticism about the use of market-based pollution control policies—especially tradable pollution permits. To better understand this skepticism, we consider the respective views of producers, the public, and the environmentalists.

myeconlab

The social and economic implications of global warming are potentially disastrous. For a detailed discussion of the relationship between energy use and global climate change, as well as the technological challenges we face in limiting the emission of greenhouse gases, look for "Climate Change, Energy Use, and the Kyoto Emissions Targets" in the *Additional Topics* section of this book's MyEconLab.

w w w . m y e c o n l a b . c o m

Producers

Some firms object to the costs they are asked to pay in terms of emissions taxes or the purchase prices of emissions permits. However, there is no reason why payments to government (to purchase permits) under any market-based scheme need to be an unjustified "tax grab." Emissions taxes need not be in excess of the costs imposed on society by the industry's activities. If government uses the introduction of a market-based scheme to raise general revenue—and thus levies emissions taxes in excess of the costs generated by the pollution—firms can oppose the extra tax burden without opposing the market-based scheme itself.

The introduction of market-based measures may signal the end of a free ride that producers have been taking at society's expense. If the firms in an industry were bearing none of the cost of their pollution, any efficient antipollution scheme would impose a burden on them—but only to the extent of forcing them to bear the costs of their own activities. The difference between direct controls and the market-based solution, however, is that the former will cost the average firm in the industry more than the market solution. (This difference just reflects the fact that direct controls are generally less efficient than emissions taxes or tradable pollution permits.)

Under market-based schemes (rather than direct controls), many firms feel a sense of unfairness because their competitors continue polluting while they must clean up. Such complaints ignore the fact that those firms that continue to pollute have paid for the right to do so, either by paying effluent taxes or by buying pollution rights, and that the complaining firm could do the same if it wished (it does not do so because cleaning up is cheaper for it than paying to pollute, as the competitors are doing).

These points make clear a key issue in assessing market-based solutions: Such solutions must not be judged relative to a "no action" policy. Given a government's decision to reduce pollution, the market solution must be compared with other alternatives that reduce pollution by the same amount. When such a comparison is made, much of the opposition from producers fades away.

Some firms argue that environmental protection reduces overall welfare because output and employment will fall if firms are required to pay emissions taxes or the price of pollution permits. This argument is misleading. It is surely true, as is clear in Figure 17-1, that firms required to pay for the external cost of the pollution they create will experience an increase in marginal cost—this is precisely how the externality gets internalized. It is also true that the level of output and employment in such firms will fall. But there is no tradeoff here between the environment and overall welfare. The environment is part of overall welfare. When we say that one unit of pollution generates an external cost of $100, we are measuring the cost imposed on the environment (or, equivalently, the amount of resources required to clean up that environmental damage).

If steel-producing firms are required to pay the external cost of their pollution, the reduction in output and employment in those firms will indeed cause some pain. Profits will be lower, and some workers will be laid off. But this reduction in the amount of total resources devoted to the steel industry is part of the *solution* to the pollution externality. A negative externality in the steel industry means that too much steel is being produced. Thus, it will improve overall welfare—not reduce it—to reduce the amount of resources in the steel industry. The resources that are no longer used in the steel industry are now free to be used in other industries, producing goods and services that society values more at the margin, and that cause less environmental damage, than an extra unit of steel.

The General Public

Some members of the general public have a moral opposition to selling anyone the right to pollute. Since it involves human survival, dealing in the right to pollute seems evil to many people. As we said earlier, however, it is not possible simply to ban pollution outright since all production invariably generates some pollution. The relevant question then becomes: How best can society reduce pollution by a given amount? Economic analysis suggests that tradable pollution permits are an efficient way of reducing pollution, and are more efficient than direct pollution controls.

Opposition to the outcome where those who have the highest costs of cleaning up continue to pollute while those with the lowest costs do the cleaning up. Morality may dictate to many observers that the biggest polluters should do the cleaning up. Economists cannot show this reaction to be wrong; they can only point out the costs in terms of unnecessary resource use and less overall pollution abatement that follow from adopting such a position.

Environmentalists

Over the past decade or so, many environmental groups have accepted the logic of economists' argument that market-based schemes to reduce environmental damage are efficient and therefore desirable. These environmentalists continue to devote their energies to convincing governments as well as the rest of society that the problem of environmental damage must be seriously addressed. Other environmentalists, however, do not accept the efficiency arguments that we have developed in this chapter. What are some of the arguments commonly heard from these groups?

Many environmentalists are skeptical about the efficiency and desirability of markets. Some do not understand economists' reasoning as to why markets can be, and often are, efficient mechanisms for allocating scarce resources. Others understand the economists' case but reject it, although few complete their argument by trying to demonstrate that direct government controls will be more effective.

Many environmentalists do not like the use of self-interest incentives to solve what they regard as "social" rather than "economic" issues. Economists who point to the voluminous evidence of the importance of self-interest incentives are often accused of ignoring higher motives such as social responsibility, self-sacrifice, and compassion. Although such motives are absent from the simple theories that try to explain the everyday behaviour of buyers and sellers, economists since Adam Smith have been aware that these higher motives do exert strong influences on human behaviour.

Such higher motives are very powerful at some times and in some situations, but they do not govern many people's behaviour in the course of day-to-day living. If we want to understand how people behave in the aftermath of a flood, or an earthquake, or a war, we need motives in addition to self-interest; if we want to understand how people behave day after day in their buying and selling, we need little other than a theory of the self-interested responses to market incentives. Since control of the environment requires influencing the mass of small decisions, as well as a few large ones, the appeal to self-interest is the only currently known way to induce the required behaviour through voluntary actions.

Some environmentalists have the view that resources such as clean air and pure water are above mere monetary calculation and should thus be treated in special ways. The economist can point out that almost

Many environmentalists do not recognize that markets can be an efficient tool for protecting the environment.

all human activity has an impact on the environment and that we all face tradeoffs between our environmental concerns and other wants and needs. To put clean air and water in a special category prevents us from seeking a socially desirable outcome through cost-benefit analysis. Moreover, attaching a monetary value to environmental quality may be the most convincing way to demonstrate that environmental factors can be valued more highly than material goods.

Summary

This chapter has examined the main economic issues, and some of the political issues, associated with pollution control. The fact that pollution is a byproduct of some other production process means that pollution is a negative externality. Producers think about their own private costs but ignore the pollution costs that their production imposes on the rest of society. The efficient solution to this problem involves *internalizing the externality*—that is, making sure that the producers of the pollution are made to bear its full external cost. In the chapter we reviewed two efficient ways of internalizing pollution externalities: emissions taxes and tradable pollution permits.

If properly designed, such market-based environmental policies can reverse the effects of the pollution externality. In terms of Figure 17-1, these policies have the effect of shifting the private marginal cost curve up by the full amount of the marginal external cost, thus equating private marginal cost with social marginal cost. When this occurs, firms will reduce the output of the goods that produce pollution as a byproduct, and the amount of pollution produced will also decline.

There is considerable opposition among some environmentalists and some of the general public to market-based environmental policies. Tradable pollution permits, especially, appear to generate much skepticism among non-economists. Much of this skepticism has the same source as skepticism toward other policies that advocate the use of markets: *the lack of understanding of how markets work to allocate resources efficiently.* In response, economists can only continue to explain how markets work, illustrate what happens when markets are not permitted to operate, and present the costs and benefits of various environmental policies. Eventually the message will get through.

S U M M A R Y

17.1 **THE ECONOMIC RATIONALE FOR REGULATING POLLUTION**   LO 1

- Pollution can be analyzed as a negative externality. Polluting firms and households going about their daily business do harm to the environment and fail to take account of the costs that they impose on others.
- In a market that produces pollution as a byproduct, the external cost of the pollution implies that too much of the good is produced compared with what is allocatively efficient. Social marginal cost exceeds private marginal cost.

- The allocatively efficient level of pollution is generally not zero; it is the level where the marginal cost of further pollution reduction is just equal to the marginal benefit of pollution reduction.
- If a firm or a household faces incentives that cause it to internalize fully the costs that pollution imposes, it will choose the allocatively efficient level of pollution.

17.2 POLLUTION-CONTROL POLICIES

- Pollution can be regulated either directly or indirectly. Direct controls are used most often. They are often inefficient because they require that all polluters meet the same standard regardless of the benefits and costs of doing so.
- Efficient pollution abatement requires that the marginal cost of abatement is equated across firms. This can be achieved with market-based policies, such as emissions taxes or tradable pollution permits.
- Emission taxes work by requiring polluters to pay a tax per unit of pollution produced. The tax becomes the marginal benefit of pollution abatement to the firms.

Since all firms face the same tax per unit of pollution, their profit-maximizing behaviour will bring about efficiency in pollution abatement.
- Tradable pollution permits work by the government issuing permits to firms and then allowing those permits to be freely traded. The market price of the permit then represents firms' marginal benefit of pollution abatement. Efficiency in pollution abatement is achieved because firms' profit-maximizing behaviour leads their marginal abatement costs to be equated.

17.3 THE POLITICS OF POLLUTION CONTROL

- There is considerable opposition by some of the public to the use of market-based environmental policies—especially the use of tradable pollution permits.
- Many firms oppose having to pay for pollution permits. But if the quantity of permits is chosen appropriately, the permit price will equal the marginal external cost of pollution, and thus firms will only pay the external cost that their production imposes on society.

- Some environmentalists and other members of the public oppose on moral grounds that firms should be able to pay for the "right to pollute." These criticisms ignore the fact that pollution is an important economic problem, and a strong case can be made for wanting to minimize the total cost of any given level of pollution abatement.

KEY CONCEPTS

Negative pollution externalities
Marginal external cost

Costs and benefits of pollution
   abatement
The efficient level of pollution

Direct pollution controls
Emissions taxes
Tradable pollution permits

STUDY EXERCISES

1. Consider the following costs and benefits associated with cleaning up a polluted city lake.

Cleanliness of Water (%)	Marginal Cost ($)	Marginal Benefit ($)
0	50 000	550 000
20	100 000	400 000
40	160 000	300 000
60	230 000	230 000
80	350 000	180 000
100	infinite	150 000

a. Explain why the marginal cost of pollution reduction increases as the cleanliness of the water increases. Plot the MC curve in a diagram.
b. Explain why the marginal benefit of pollution reduction falls as the cleanliness of the water increases. Plot the MB curve in the same diagram.
c. What is the optimal level of water cleanliness?
d. Explain why the efficient level of pollution is greater than zero.

2. Fill in the blanks to make the following statements correct.

a. When there are pollution externalities associated with the production of steel, _____ marginal costs of steel production exceed _____ marginal costs of steel production.

b. By imposing a _____ on the production of steel, the externality can be _____.

c. If the tax is chosen to be exactly equal to the _____, the externality can be completely internalized. The result will be that private firms produce the _____ level of steel (and pollution).

3. Fill in the blanks to make the following statements correct.

a. Suppose the Canadian government announced that all homeowners must insulate their homes with R-40 insulation. As a pollution-control policy, this is an example of _____.

b. Suppose the Canadian government announced a tax of $2.50 per litre of home heating oil consumed. As a pollution-control policy, this is an example of _____.

c. Suppose the Canadian government distributed coupons to all homeowners allowing them to burn specified amounts of fossil fuels for home heating, and allowed homeowners to buy and sell these coupons. As a pollution-control policy, this is an example of _____. A _____ would develop for these coupons.

4. **myeconlab** Consider the market for lumber, which we assume here to be perfectly competitive.

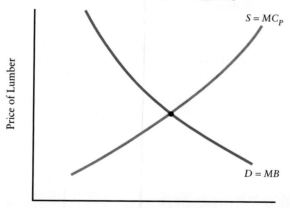

Quantity of Lumber

a. Suppose that for each unit of lumber produced, the firm also generates $10 of damage to the environment. Draw the social marginal cost curve in the diagram.

b. What is the allocatively efficient level of lumber output? Explain.

c. Describe and show the new market outcome if lumber producers are required to pay a tax of $10 per unit of lumber produced. Explain.

d. In part (c), does the equilibrium price of lumber rise by the full $10 of the tax? Explain.

5. The following diagram shows society's marginal benefit and marginal cost for abating a particular type of pollution—say greenhouse-gas emissions.

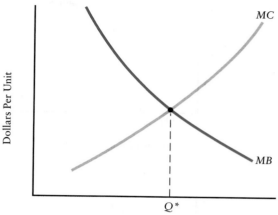

Amount of Pollution Abatement

a. Explain why the marginal cost curve is upward sloping.

b. Explain why the marginal benefit curve is downward sloping.

c. At Q^*, are all greenhouse-gas emissions eliminated? Explain.

d. Is there an "optimal" level of greenhouse-gas emissions? Explain.

6. **myeconlab** Suppose there are only two firms— Softies Inc. and Cuddlies Inc.—producing disposable diapers. Both firms are releasing dioxins into the same river. To reduce the pollution, the regulatory agency must choose between using direct controls and emissions taxes. The diagrams on the next page show each firm's marginal cost of pollution abatement.

a. Suppose the regulatory agency requires that the two firms each abate Q_3 units of pollution. What is each firm's marginal abatement cost at Q_3?

b. Could the total cost of this amount of pollution abatement be reduced? Explain how.

c. Now suppose the regulatory agency instead imposes an emissions tax of $40 per unit of emissions. Explain why this tax can be thought of as each firm's "marginal benefit of abatement."

d. In part (c), how much pollution will each firm choose to abate?

e. Is it possible to reduce the total cost of the amount of abatement being done in part (d)?

CHAPTER 18

Taxation and Public Expenditure

LO LEARNING OBJECTIVES

In this chapter you will learn

1. about the main taxes used in Canada.
2. why a tax can lead to allocative inefficiency.
3. about the concept of fiscal federalism in Canada.
4. how Canada's major social programs are financed.
5. some common pitfalls in evaluating government's role in the economy.

In Chapter 16, we saw some of the reasons why the scope of government is so extensive. Taxation is needed to raise money for public spending, and it can also play a policy role in its own right. Taxes and government expenditure both affect the distribution of income—some people get taxed more than others and some people benefit more from government spending programs than others. Moreover, taxation and public expenditure influence the allocation of resources. In some cases, government policy is carefully designed with such effects in mind; in other cases, the effects are unintentional byproducts of policies pursued for other purposes.

In this chapter, we examine the various sources of government tax revenues and the various types of government expenditures. We ask how taxation and public expenditure affect the allocation of resources and the distribution of income, and to what extent they are effective tools of public policy. We examine the basis on which to evaluate a tax system, emphasizing the distinction between equity and efficiency. The types of public expenditures in Canada are examined along with the important concept of fiscal federalism. Finally, we briefly discuss Canada's main social programs, which account for approximately 60 percent of combined government spending.

18.1 TAXATION IN CANADA

There is a bewildering array of taxes in Canada today. These are levied at the federal, provincial, and local levels. Some are highly visible, such as income taxes and the Goods and Services Tax (GST). Others are all but invisible because they do not show up on income-tax forms or on receipts for purchases. For example, there are special taxes levied on the sales of alcohol, cigarettes, and gasoline, but these taxes are levied directly on the producers (rather than the retailers) of these goods. People and firms are taxed on what they earn, on what they spend, and on what they own. Not only are taxes numerous, but taken together they raise a large amount of revenue. Table 18-1

For detailed information about the Canadian tax system, go to the website of the independent Canadian Tax Foundation: **www.ctf.ca**.

shows, for the federal, provincial, and local governments combined, the amount of revenue raised by the different types of taxes in 2005.

Canada lies roughly in the middle of other developed countries in terms of tax revenues as a share of GDP. Among the major industrialized countries, Denmark and Sweden collect roughly 50 percent of GDP in taxes. The lowest-tax industrialized country is Japan, which collects about 27 percent of GDP in taxes. Canada is in the middle of the pack, collecting taxes equal to approximately 38 percent of GDP.

Progressive Taxes

Before discussing details about the Canadian tax system, we examine the concept of *progressivity* of taxes.

When the government taxes one income group in society more heavily than it taxes another, it influences the distribution of income. The effect of taxes on the distribution of income can be summarized in terms of *progressivity*. A **progressive tax** takes a larger percentage of income from high-income people than it does from low-income people. A **proportional tax** takes amounts of money from people in direct proportion to their incomes—for example, every individual might pay 10 percent of his or her income in taxes. A **regressive tax** takes a larger percentage of income from low-income people than it does from high-income people.

Note that the progressivity or regressivity of a tax is expressed in terms of *shares* of income rather than absolute dollar amounts. Thus, a tax that collects $1000 from each individual clearly collects the same dollar amount from everybody, though it collects a higher share of income from low-income people than from higher-income people. A tax of this type is therefore a regressive tax. It is often called a *lump-sum tax*, one that is the same at all levels of income.

Since a progressive tax takes a larger share of income from high-income people than it does from low-income people, progressive taxes reduce the inequality of income. A regressive tax increases the inequality of income.

The progressivity of a tax involves an important distinction between the average tax rate and the marginal tax rate. The **average tax rate** is the percentage of income that the individual pays in taxes. The **marginal tax rate** is the percentage *of the next dollar* earned that the individual pays in taxes. Progressivity of a tax requires an *average* tax rate that rises with income; we will see in this chapter that such progressivity can be achieved with either rising or constant marginal tax rates.

TABLE 18-1   Tax Revenues of Canadian Governments, 2005

	Billions of Dollars	Percent of GDP
Income taxes	$205.1	14.5
Consumption taxes (GST, provincial sales taxes, and excise taxes)	104.1	7.4
Property and related taxes	46.8	3.3
Other taxes	17.7	1.3
Health and social insurance premiums	70.7	5.0
Total tax revenues	**$444.4**	**31.5**
Non-tax revenues (sales of goods and services, investment income)	86.2	6.1
Total government revenues	**$530.6**	**37.6**

Canadian governments (at all levels) collect over $530 billion in various taxes, over 37 percent of GDP. These data show total tax revenues for all levels of government combined. Notice that Canadian governments have considerable revenue, over $86 billion in 2005, from non-tax sources.

(*Source:* These data are available on Statistics Canada's website: www.statcan.ca. Search for "government" and then look for "consolidated government revenue and expenditure." Reprinted with permission of Statistics Canada.)

progressive tax A tax that takes a larger percentage of income the higher the level of income.

proportional tax A tax that takes a constant percentage of income at all levels of income.

regressive tax A tax that takes a lower percentage of income the higher the level of income.

average tax rate The ratio of total taxes paid to total income earned.

marginal tax rate The fraction of an additional dollar of income that is paid in taxes.

EXTENSIONS IN THEORY 18-1

Who Really Pays the Corporate Income Tax?

As we saw in Chapter 7, there are two different measures of a firm's profit—*accounting* profit and *economic* profit. Accounting profit is the difference between the firm's revenues and its explicit costs such as labour, materials, overhead, and depreciation. The same firm's economic profit would also take into account the opportunity costs of the owner's time and financial capital. Since there are additional costs included, economic profits are less than accounting profits. As it turns out, the burden of the corporate income tax depends crucially on which measure of profit is used as the basis for the tax.

Let's examine two alternative taxes: one that applies to economic profits, and another that applies to accounting profits. To illustrate the two taxes, we consider an imaginary firm that produces hockey equipment—Canada Hockey Inc. (CHI), located in Brampton, Ontario. Suppose in 2007 CHI earns accounting profits of $1.5 million. Also suppose the opportunity cost of the owner's capital and time is $1.1 million. Once these opportunity costs are considered, CHI's economic profits are equal to $400 000.

A Tax on Economic Profits

Recall that *economic* profits are the return to the owner's capital over and above what could be earned elsewhere. In other words, CHI's $400 000 of economic profits represents the firm's return to its capital in excess of what that capital could earn in the (equally risky) next-best alternative investment. If CHI faces a 30-percent corporate tax that applies to its economic profits, it will pay $120 000 in corporate taxes, and it will still have after-tax economic profits equal to $280 000. Since CHI is still earning positive economic profits—that is, it is still earning more than it could earn elsewhere—it has no incentive to leave this industry.

In fact, the firm has no incentive to do anything differently than it was doing previously—the tax on the firm's economic profit has *no effect* on the firm's output, prices, employment, or long-run investment choices. Before the tax, CHI was making output, employment, price, and investment decisions to maximize its (economic) profits. With the tax, some fraction of these economic profits must be paid to the government, but CHI still chooses to maximize its profits by doing whatever it was doing before the tax.

The implication is that if the corporate income tax applies to *economic* profits, firms and their owners bear the entire burden of the tax. But the tax will have no effect on the allocation of resources, and in this sense the tax would be efficient.

A Tax on Accounting Profits

Now consider the alternative case in which the corporate income tax applies not to economic profit but to *accounting* profit. CHI's accounting profits are

---

when they were sold to consumers. Figure 18-1 shows how the GST is calculated at each stage from the mining of iron ore to the final retail sale of a washing machine.

Like sales and excise taxes, the GST is applied to expenditure rather than income. The GST taken alone would therefore be mildly regressive, because the proportion of income saved, and hence not taxed, rises with income. This regressivity is reduced by exempting food and, more importantly, by giving low- and middle-income households a refundable tax credit. For the lowest-income households, the GST is a progressive tax because the refundable tax credit exceeds the value of GST that they would pay even if they spent all of their incomes on taxable commodities.

Property Taxes   The property tax is the most important Canadian tax that is based on wealth and is an important source of revenue for municipalities. It is different from any other important tax because it is not related directly to a current transaction. In contrast, income taxes are levied on the current payment to a factor of production (income) and sales taxes are levied on the value of a currently purchased good or service.

$1.5 million, which are greater than (and include) its economic profits. If CHI faces a 30-percent corporate tax on accounting profits, it will pay $450 000 in corporate taxes. CHI's after-tax accounting profits will now be $1.05 million. But the presence of the corporate tax does not change the opportunity cost of the owner's capital and time; when including these costs ($1.1 million), CHI's *economic* profits are –$50 000. Negative economic profits indicate that the owner's capital is now earning less than could be available in the (equally risky) next-best alternative investment. In this situation, CHI may soon leave this industry.

Negative economic profits and the exit from the industry will obviously have implications for its output and employment decisions. In particular, as CHI scales down its operations, its workers will be laid off or have their wages reduced. And as supply in this industry falls, product prices will rise until the remaining firms earn enough profits to keep them in the industry.

The bottom line is that if the corporate income tax applies to *accounting* profits (and results in negative economic profits), some of the burden of the tax falls on consumers and workers. Only part of the burden of the tax falls on firms and their owners. Because the tax leads to changes in the allocation of resources, it also generates some inefficiency (we will see this idea in more detail later in this chapter when we discuss what economists call the "excess burden" of taxation).

Perhaps the biggest burden of the corporate income tax in this case is on the economy's long-run growth. By taxing accounting profits rather than economic profits, investment in physical capital is made less attractive. The result will be lower investment in new machinery and equipment, and thus less adoption of many of the

latest technologies that are usually embodied in such physical capital. The overall result for the economy is lower productivity growth and, eventually, slower growth in average living standards.

Which Tax Do We Use?

In Canada and other countries, corporations are taxed on the basis of their *accounting* profits, not their economic profits, despite the greater efficiency of the latter. Why do we use such a tax, given its inefficiency? The explanation comes down to simplicity: Accounting profits are easy to measure, whereas economic profits require an identification and measurement of the opportunity cost of the owner's time and capital. The precise identification of such opportunity costs, for each and every firm and group of owners, would be technically impossible for the tax authorities.*

The end result is that the burden of the corporate tax in Canada is not borne only by firms and their owners—consumers and workers share the burden through higher product prices and lower wages. These effects are subtle, but nonetheless important. Equally subtle, and probably more important, are the longer-term effects on the growth rate of the economy and Canadians' average standard of living.

---

* Economic profit is not an entirely impractical concept, however. Business managers and financial analysts use the concept of Economic Value Added (EVA) to measure economic profits as a means of pricing companies' stocks.

Taxing the value of existing property creates two problems. First, someone has to assess the current market value of the property that may not have changed hands in many years. Because the assessment is only an estimate, it is always subject to challenge. Second, sometimes owners of valuable property have low *incomes* (though considerable wealth) and thus have difficulty paying the tax.

The progressivity of the property tax has been studied extensively. It is obvious that the rich typically live in more expensive houses than the poor, and thus pay more in property taxes. But this does not mean that the rich pay more property taxes *as a fraction of their total income* than the poor. Thus, it is not readily apparent that property taxes are progressive. Indeed, most studies have shown that the property tax is mildly regressive.

FIGURE 18-1   The Operation of the GST

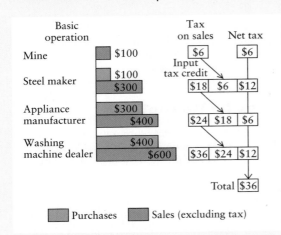

A tax on value added is the same as a tax on the value of final goods with a credit allowed for the tax paid for purchased inputs. The example is for the stages involved as iron ore is mined and then sold to a steel maker, the steel then sold to an appliance manufacturer, and the washing machine sold to a retailer and then to a consumer. The example makes the simplifying assumption that no produced inputs are used in the mining operation (so that the value of the iron ore is all value added); at all further stages, however, the use of produced inputs makes the firm's value added less than the value of final output at that stage. The steel maker's value added is $200, and its tax is thus $12; $18 on the total value of its output less the $6 credit on the taxes already paid to the mine on the value of the iron ore. Total taxes paid equal $36, which is 6 percent of the $600 value of the final product; each firm pays 6 percent of its share in creating that $600 value.

The value of residential property forms the base of the property tax, an important source of revenue for Canada's cities and towns. The property tax is the most important tax in Canada based on wealth.

18.2 EVALUATING THE TAX SYSTEM

We have so far described several individual taxes in Canada, and in each case noted the tax's effects on behaviour as well as its progressivity. The overall tax *system*, however, is a complex combination of these various taxes. More important than evaluating each individual tax is evaluating the system as a whole. What makes one tax system better or worse than another? Economists deal with this question by considering two aspects of taxation—equity and efficiency. We deal with equity first.

Taxation and Equity

Debate about income distribution and tax policy usually involves the important but hard-to-define concept of *equity.*

What Do We Mean By Equity? *Equity* (or fairness) is a normative concept; what one group thinks is fair may seem outrageous to another. Two principles can be helpful in assessing equity in taxation: equity according to *ability to pay,* and equity according to *benefits received.*

The Ability-to-Pay Principle. Most people view an equitable tax system as being based on people's ability to pay taxes. In considering equity that is based on ability to pay, two concepts need to be distinguished.

Vertical equity concerns equity *across* income groups; it focuses on comparisons between individuals or families with different levels of income. The concept of vertical equity is central to discussions of the progressivity of taxation. Proponents of progressive taxation argue as follows. First, taxes should be based on ability to pay. Second, the greater one's income, the greater the percentage of income that is available for goods and services beyond the bare necessities. It follows, therefore, that the greater one's income, the greater the proportion of income that is available to pay taxes. Thus, an ability-to-pay standard of vertical equity requires progressive taxation.

Horizontal equity concerns equity *within* a given income group; it is concerned with establishing just who should be considered equal to whom in terms of ability to pay taxes. Two households with the same income may have different numbers of children to support. One of the households may have greater expenses for the care of an aging parent, leaving less for life's necessities and for taxes. One of the households may incur expenses that are necessary for earning income (e.g., requirements to buy uniforms or to pay union dues). There is no objective way to decide how much these and similar factors affect the ability to pay taxes. In practice, the income-tax law makes some allowance for factors that create differences in ability to pay by permitting taxpayers to exempt some of their income from tax. However, the corrections are rough at best.

For information about the Canadian tax system, see the website for the Canada Revenue Agency: **www.cra-arc.gc.ca**.

The Benefit Principle. According to the benefit principle, taxes should be paid in proportion to the benefits that taxpayers derive from public expenditure. From this perspective, the ideal taxes are *user charges,* such as those that would be charged if private firms provided the government services.

The benefit principle is the basis for the gasoline tax, since gasoline usage is closely related to the services obtained from using public roads. The benefit principle may also explain high taxes on cigarettes, since smokers tend to require more health-care services that, in Canada, are mostly provided by government. Although there are other examples, especially at the local level, the benefit principle has historically played only a minor role in the design of the Canadian tax system. But its use is growing in Canada and elsewhere as governments seek new ways to finance many of their expenditures. For example, a decade ago Statistics Canada supplied data for free to anybody who wanted it. Now, Statistics Canada charges on a "cost recovery basis" for any data other than the most general data, which it makes available on its website.

The benefit principle can be easily applied to some government-provided goods and services. But it is difficult to see how the benefit principle could be applied to many of the most important categories of government spending. Who gets how much benefit from national defence or from interest on the public debt? It is even more difficult to imagine applying the benefit principle to government programs that redistribute income.

How Progressive Is the Canadian Tax System?

For a modern government to raise sufficient funds, many taxes must be used. We have already discussed personal and corporate income taxes, excise and provincial sales taxes, the Canada-wide GST, and municipal property taxes. Not all of them are equally progressive in design and each one has its own loopholes and anomalies. So, how high-, middle-, and low-income households are taxed relative to each other depends on how the entire tax system impacts on each group.

Assessing how the entire tax system affects the distribution of income is complicated by two factors. First, the progressivity of the system depends on the mix of the different taxes. Federal taxes tend to be somewhat progressive; the progressivity of the income-tax system and the use of a low-income GST tax credit more than offset the regressivity of the federal GST. Provincial and municipal governments rely heavily on property and sales taxes and thus have tax systems that are probably slightly regressive.

Second, income from different sources is taxed at different rates. For example, in the federal personal income tax, income from royalties on oil wells is taxed less than income from royalties on books, and profits from sales of assets (capital gains) are taxed less than wages and salaries. To evaluate progressivity, therefore, one needs to know the way in which different *levels* of income are related with different *sources* of income.

Many economists have concluded that the overall Canadian tax system is roughly proportional for middle-income classes and mildly progressive for low- and high-income persons. Thus, the overall tax system is redistributing some income from high-income households to low-income households, and doing little redistribution among the middle-income households.

Taxation and Efficiency

The tax system influences the allocation of resources by altering such things as the relative prices of various goods and factors and the relative profitability of various industries. Individual taxes shift consumption and production toward goods and services that are taxed relatively lightly and away from those that are taxed more heavily. This alteration of free-market outcomes often causes allocative inefficiency.

Of course, if we were to live in a world without any taxes we would face other problems. For example, it would be impossible to pay for any government programs or public goods desired by society. In practice, then, the relevant objective for tax policy is to design a tax system that minimizes inefficiency, *holding constant the amount of revenue to be raised*. In designing such a tax system, a natural place to start would be with taxes that both raise revenue and enhance efficiency. An example of such a tax is the emissions tax that we discussed in Chapter 17. Unfortunately, such taxes cannot raise nearly enough revenue to finance all of government expenditure.

In the following discussion we examine how taxes affect the economy's allocation of resources. We focus on the effects of excise taxes and income taxes since these are the main taxes used by Canadian governments to raise revenues.

The Two Burdens of Taxation   A tax normally does two things. It takes money from the taxpayers, and it changes their behaviour. The money taken away from taxpayers is given to the government and is thus available to finance government policies of various kinds. So, while the money taken from taxpayers, called the **direct burden** of the tax, is clearly a cost to taxpayers, it is *not* a cost to society overall; it is merely a transfer of resources within the economy.

When a tax changes behaviour, however, there are costs to taxpayers as well as to society overall. The cost that results from the induced changes in behaviour is called the **excess burden** and reflects the allocative inefficiency or *deadweight loss* of the tax.

> The direct burden of a tax is the amount paid by taxpayers. The excess burden reflects the allocative inefficiency of the tax.

Figure 18-2 shows an example that illustrates this important distinction. Suppose your provincial government imposes a $2 excise tax on the purchase of compact discs. Suppose further that you are a serious music lover and that this tax does not change your quantity demanded of CDs—that is, your demand for them is perfectly inelastic and hence you continue to buy your usual five CDs per month. In this case, you pay $10 in excise taxes per month, and you therefore have to reduce your consumption of other goods (or your saving) by $10 per month.

The direct burden to you of this excise tax is $10 because that is what you pay to the government in taxes. There is no excess burden to you because the tax does not cause you to reduce your purchases of CDs. Thus, the total burden on you is equal to the direct burden, $10 a month; there is no excess burden of this tax. The absence of any excess burden from this tax is just another way of saying that there is no allocative inefficiency; the cost of raising $10 a month for the province is just the $10 a month that you pay in taxes. In this case, the tax is *purely* a redistribution of resources from you to the government.

Now suppose a friend of yours is also a music lover but is not quite so dedicated—she has a downward-sloping demand curve for CDs. The tax leads her to cut back on her consumption of CDs from two per month to none. In this case, your friend pays no taxes and therefore experiences no reduction in her overall purchasing power. The direct burden of the tax is therefore zero. However, your friend is still worse off as a

direct burden For an individual tax, the amount of money that is collected from taxpayers.

excess burden The allocative inefficiency or deadweight loss generated by a tax.

FIGURE 18-2   Direct and Excess Burdens of an Excise Tax

(i) You   (ii) Your friend   (iii) Entire market

The allocative inefficiency of a tax is measured by its excess burden. The excess burden is greater the more elastic is demand. Part (i) shows your demand for CDs. It is perfectly inelastic at five CDs per month. When the government imposes an excise tax of $2 per CD, the price rises from $15 to $17. Your quantity demanded is unchanged, and so you pay $10 per month in taxes ($2 tax per CD $\times$ 5 CDs). The direct burden of the tax is $10; but because your quantity of CDs demanded is unchanged, there is no excess burden.

Part (ii) shows your friend's demand. Her quantity demanded falls from two CDs per month to zero as a result of the tax. Since she pays no tax (because she buys no CDs), she bears no direct burden of the tax. But because she has lost consumer surplus, she bears an excess burden from the tax.

Part (iii) shows the entire market demand. There is both a direct burden, the red shaded area, and an excess burden, the purple shaded area. The more elastic is the demand curve, the larger is the excess burden of the tax.

result of this tax. She is worse off by the amount of consumer surplus that she would have received had she made her usual purchases of two CDs per month. In this case, the direct burden is zero (because no tax is paid) but there *is* an excess burden. The excess burden is equal to her loss in consumer surplus from the two CDs per month that she no longer enjoys.

When an excise tax is imposed, some people behave like the music buff and do not change their consumption of the taxed good at all, others cease consuming the taxed good altogether, and most simply reduce their consumption. There will be an excess burden for those in the latter two groups. Thus, the revenue collected will understate the total cost to taxpayers of generating that revenue.

The same basic analysis applies to income taxes. Figure 18-3 shows the effect of levying a tax on workers' incomes. The income tax shifts the labour supply upwards because workers will only be prepared to supply any given amount of labour services if the pre-tax wage is increased to offset the effect of the tax.

The income tax generates both a direct burden and an excess burden. The tax raises revenue by collecting some percentage of workers' wages. This is a cost borne by both workers and firms. By reducing the equilibrium level of employment and creating a deadweight loss, the income tax also creates an excess burden. As with the case of excise taxes, the revenue collected by the tax understates the total cost of the tax.

Excise taxes and income taxes impose costs in two ways. By taking resources from market participants (consumers, firms, workers), they impose a direct burden. By reducing the volume of market transactions, they also generate a deadweight loss—this is the excess burden of the tax.

Practise with Study Guide Chapter 18, Exercise 2.

FIGURE 18-3   Direct and Excess Burdens of an Income Tax

An income tax generates both a direct and an excess **burden.** Without an income tax, the labour-market equilibrium has employment of L_0 and a wage of w_0. A tax on workers' incomes shifts the supply of labour curve upward. The result is an increase in the pre-tax wage to w_1 and a reduction in the level of employment to L_1. The tax revenue generated is the red area; this is the direct burden of the income tax. The tax also generates a deadweight loss, as shown by the purple area; this is the excess burden of the income tax. (As our discussion of tax incidence in Chapter 4 showed, the less elastic is labour demand and supply, the lower will be the deadweight loss of the tax.)

Recall that our exercise in judging the efficiency of a tax is to hold constant the amount of revenue raised, and therefore to hold constant the direct burden of the tax. This leads us to the following important conclusion:

An efficient tax system is one that minimizes the amount of excess burden (deadweight loss) for any given amount of tax revenue generated.

As Figure 18-2 shows, the excess burden of an excise tax is smaller when the demand for the product is less elastic. In the extreme case of a perfectly inelastic demand, the excess burden of an excise tax is zero; the tax raises revenue but leads to no reduction in consumption of the product. Unfortunately, because the demand for many of life's necessities (such as food) is very inelastic, a tax system that was based only on imposing excise taxes on goods with inelastic demands would prove to be very regressive.

Many economists argue that taxing income is more efficient and more equitable than imposing large numbers of excise taxes on products. The greater efficiency of the income tax comes from the fact that the supply of labour is relatively inelastic with respect to the real wage. Figure 18-3 shows that an income tax does generate an excess burden. But if the labour supply curve is very steep—as most empirical evidence suggests—the excess burden is small, and the income tax is therefore relatively efficient. The greater equity of the income tax comes from the fact that the income tax can be designed to be either proportional or progressive, thus permitting some redistribution from high-income households to low-income households. The regressive effects of excise taxes can be reduced by greater reliance on income taxes.

Disincentive Effects of Income Taxes   Our discussion of income taxes, and the illustration in Figure 18-3, shows how an income tax affects workers' incentives. If an increase in the income-tax rate leads to a reduction in the amount of work effort, it is possible that total tax revenue might actually *fall* as a result. This possibility is illustrated in Figure 18-4, which shows what economists call a *Laffer curve*.

The reasoning behind the general shape of the Laffer curve is as follows. At a zero tax rate, no revenue would be collected. As rates are raised above zero, some revenue will be gained. But as rates continue to rise, revenue will eventually fall because the very high tax rates will lead people to work less and less. At a tax rate of 100 percent, they will not bother to work at all (because all of their income would go to the government) and so tax revenue will be zero. It follows that there must be *some* tax rate, greater than zero and less than 100 percent, at which tax revenue reaches a maximum.

Figure 18-4 is drawn under the assumption that there is a steady increase in tax revenue as tax rates rise to t_0, and a steady decrease in tax revenues as tax rates continue to rise toward 100 percent. This particular shape—with a single peak in tax revenues—is not necessary. But the precise shape is beside the point. The key point is that there is *some* tax rate like t_0 that maximizes total tax revenue. And therefore tax rates above or below t_0 will raise less tax revenue than the amount raised at t_0.

Just where this maximum occurs—whether at average tax rates closer to 40 or to 70 percent—is currently unknown for either corporate or personal income taxes. Also, there will be a separate Laffer curve for each type of tax. The curve does, however, provide an important warning: Governments cannot increase their tax revenues to any desired level simply by increasing their tax rates. Sooner or later, further increases in the rates will reduce work incentives so much that total tax revenues will fall.

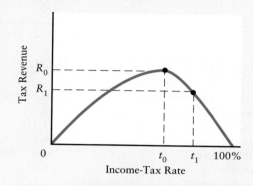

FIGURE 18-4   A Laffer Curve

Increases in income-tax rates beyond some level will decrease rather than increase tax revenues. The curve relates the government's tax revenue to the tax rate. As drawn, revenue reaches a maximum level of R_0 at the tax rate t_0. If the tax rate were t_1, then *reducing* it to t_0 would increase the government's tax revenue.

18.3 PUBLIC EXPENDITURE IN CANADA

Spending by the consolidated public sector—which includes federal, provincial, and municipal governments—currently equals about 37 percent of Canadian GDP. Table 18-2 gives the distribution of consolidated government spending across a number of major *functions* for 2005. As can be seen, health care, education, and social services are very large items; collectively, they make up over 63 percent of the total spending of $519 billion. Interest on the public debt makes up about 9 percent of total spending. The remaining quarter covers everything else, from police protection and sanitation to general administration of government, environmental protection, and foreign aid.

Table 18-2 does not show which of the three levels of government actually do the spending. For example, of the $76.5 billion spent on education in 2005, the vast majority was spent by provincial and municipal governments. In contrast, expenditures on foreign affairs and foreign aid are made exclusively by the federal government. Expenditures on social services are about equally divided between the federal and provincial governments with only a small role played by the municipalities. Another thing that Table 18-2 does not show is the important distinction between the purchase of goods and services by government, and transfers that are made to individuals or firms.

Government Purchases of Goods and Services   The government spends to provide goods and services to the public, as when the government pays for physicians' services, highway repair, primary and secondary education, and so on. Included in this category of expenditures are the salaries that the government pays to its employees. Also included is the interest that governments pay on their outstanding stock of debt. A government's stock of debt is equal to the accumulation of its past budget deficits, where the deficit is the excess of spending over revenues.

TABLE 18-2 Expenditures by Canadian Governments, 2005

Category of Spending	Billions of Dollars	Percent of GDP
General government services	16.7	1.2
Protection of persons and property	42.0	3.0
Transportation and communication	21.4	1.5
Health	96.2	6.8
Social services	154.8	11.0
Education	76.5	5.4
Resource conservation, environment, and industrial development	32.7	2.3
Recreation and culture	13.5	1.0
Housing	3.9	0.3
Labour, employment, and immigration	3.4	0.2
Foreign affairs and international aid	5.1	0.4
Debt charges	46.5	3.3
Other expenditures	5.9	0.4
Total spending	518.6	36.7

Expenditures on health, social services, and education together make up over 63 percent of total government expenditure. These data show the various categories of spending by all levels of government combined.

(*Source:* These data are available on the Statistics Canada website: www.statcan.ca. Search for "government" and then look for "consolidated government revenue and expenditures." Reprinted with permission of Statistics Canada.)

transfer payment A payment to an individual, firm, or organization that is not made in exchange for a good or service.

Transfer Payments The government also makes **transfer payments**. These are payments to individuals, firms, organizations, or other levels of government that are *not* made in exchange for a good or a service. For example, when the federal government pays employment insurance benefits to an unemployed individual, the government is not getting any good or service in return. Similarly, when the federal government transfers money to the provincial governments, it is not getting any good or service in return. Table 18-3 shows total government transfers to individuals, which totalled $125 billion in 2003, about 26 percent of total government spending.

Fiscal Federalism

Canada is a federal state with governing powers divided between the central authority and the ten provinces and three territories. Municipalities provide a level of government, whose powers are determined by the provincial legislatures. Understanding the fiscal interaction of the various levels of government is central to understanding the nature of government expenditure in Canada. In this section, we examine the concept of *fiscal federalism*; in the next section we examine how fiscal federalism affects the operation of Canada's social programs.

The Logic of Fiscal Federalism The essence of fiscal federalism is the recognition that Canada is a country with many different fiscal authorities (federal, provincial, and municipal governments) that need a certain amount of coordination to be responsive to the needs and desires of the citizens—who are free to move from one area to another. Four main considerations are important in understanding Canada's system of fiscal federalism.

1. Differences in Tax Bases. Canadian provinces vary considerably in terms of their average levels of prosperity. Newfoundland and Labrador and Quebec have for many years lagged the national average in terms of per capita real incomes, whereas Alberta and Ontario have for many years exceeded the national average. In order to provide services as varied as medical care, highways, and judicial systems, the provincial governments must levy various types of provincial taxes. Provinces that are more prosperous, and thus have larger tax bases, are able to provide a given amount of services while having relatively low tax rates. In contrast, less affluent provinces with smaller tax bases will be able to provide the same amount of services only by having higher tax rates.

One of the guiding principles in Canada's system of fiscal federalism is that individuals, no matter where they live, should have approximately the same access to what is regarded as a reasonable level and quality of public services and should face approximately the same tax rates to finance those services. Since revenue sources do not always match revenue needs at each level, *intergovernmental transfers* are required. This is the underlying motivation behind Canada's system of *equalization payments*, which transfers resources from the richer provinces to the poorer ones. We examine this shortly.

2. Geographic Scope of Services. Because the government of a province or a municipality is unlikely to be responsive to the needs of citizens outside its jurisdiction, some public services may not be provided adequately unless responsibility for them is delegated to the level of government appropriate to the scope of the service provided. For example, national defence is normally delegated to the central government because it provides benefits to all residents of the country. At the other extreme is fire protection. If fire protection is to be effective, it is necessary that there be fire stations serving small geographic areas. Accordingly, responsibility for fire stations lies with municipal governments.

3. Regional Differences in Preferences. The delegation of some functions to lower levels of government may provide a political process that is more responsive to regional differences in preferences for public versus private goods. Some people may want to live in communities with higher-quality schools and police protection, and they may be prepared to pay the high taxes required. Others may prefer lower taxes and lower levels of services. The differences in provincial tax rates that we noted earlier presumably reflect each provincial government's own view of the appropriate level of taxation.

4. Administrative Efficiency. Administrative efficiency requires that duplication of the services provided at different levels of government be minimized and that related programs be coordinated. For this reason, in all provinces except Quebec and Alberta, income taxes are reported on a single form and paid to the federal government, which then remits the appropriate share of those taxes to the relevant provincial government. This coordination avoids the administrative burden that would exist if each province had its own tax-collection system.

Intergovernmental Transfers Canada's system of fiscal federalism requires transfers between various levels of government. For example, since income taxes are paid to the federal government (except in Quebec) but spending on hospitals, education, and highways is undertaken by provincial governments, federal–provincial transfers must be made. In addition, if some provinces have large tax bases, while others have much smaller tax bases, there is a role for transferring resources between provinces. Canada has two major programs in which cash is transferred from the federal to the provincial governments.

1. Canada Health and Social Transfers. The federal government makes two block grants to each provincial and territorial government every year—one to help finance expenditures on health care and the other to help finance expenditures on post-secondary education, social assistance, and early learning and childcare. Though the Canada Health Transfer (CHT) and the Canada Social Transfer (CST) are each described as being

TABLE 18-3 Government Transfer Payments to Individuals, 2003

	Billions of Dollars
Federal Government	62.5
Child Tax Benefit	8.1
War pensions and veterans' allowances	1.7
Employment Insurance benefits	13.4
Old Age Security payments	26.9
Grants to aboriginal persons	5.0
GST tax credit	3.3
Other transfers	4.1
Provincial Governments	29.9
Income maintenance	6.7
Other social assistance	3.1
Workers' Compensation benefits	5.2
Grants to benevolent associations	8.3
Other transfers	6.6
Local Governments	3.8
Canada/Quebec Pension Plan	29.0
Total Transfers	125.2

(*Source:* These data are available on the Statistics Canada website: www.statcan.ca. Search for "transfers" and then look for "government transfer payments to persons." Reprinted with permission of Statistics Canada.)

directed at these specific categories of expenditure, there is no practical way to prevent provincial governments from spending this money on whatever they deem to be appropriate. These block grants are therefore financial support with "no strings attached."

Until recently, the CHT and CST block grants were allocated to provinces on a per capita basis. In the last few years, however, wealthier provinces have received less in per capita terms than less wealthy provinces. For the fiscal year 2005–2006, the federal transfers to provinces under the CHT totalled $20.3 billion, and those under the CST totalled $8.4 billion. Both block transfers are scheduled to increase significantly over the next several years.

2. Equalization Payments. With the object of ensuring that citizens in all regions of the country have access to a reasonable level of public services, **equalization payments** are made out of federal government general revenues to provinces with below-average tax capacity. Since the federal government collects revenues from economic activity generated in *all* provinces, and uses this revenue to support only the lower-income ones, the equalization program is effectively a redistribution program from high-income to low-income provinces. In recent years, typically only Alberta and Ontario have *not* received equalization payments; the other provinces do receive equalization payments and are thus sometimes referred to as the "have not" provinces. Equalization payments are calculated by a complicated formula that involves 30 different revenue sources. From their inception in 1957, equalization payments have increased significantly. In the 2005–2006 fiscal year, total equalization payments were $10.9 billion.

equalization payments
Transfers of tax revenues from the federal government to the low-income provinces.

A Fiscal Imbalance?

In recent years, many observers of Canadian fiscal federalism have noted a growing "fiscal imbalance" between the federal and the provincial governments. They point specifically to the large federal budget surpluses since 1998, indicating that the federal government is collecting more money than what is necessary to finance its program spending. During the same period, the provinces struggled to balance their books, partly because the fastest-growing categories of public spending have been health care, education, and other social services—all within provincial jurisdiction. Thus, tax revenue being collected at the federal level is increasingly necessary for public expenditures at the provincial level.

Some economists argue that this fiscal imbalance is indeed a problem and that it must be corrected through a change in *federal* policy. Specifically, they argue that the federal government should amend its CHT and CST block transfers (and perhaps its equalization formula as well) in ways that transfer more funds to the provinces. Alternatively, the federal government could reduce its personal and corporate income-tax rates, thereby creating more "tax room" within which the provinces would be free to raise their tax rates.

Other economists, while recognizing the basic facts of federal surpluses and growing provincial spending on health and social services, deny that the fiscal imbalance requires a significant change in federal policy. First, these economists note that the federal budget surpluses since 1998 are not simply "unnecessary money" being collected; on the contrary, these surpluses represent the gradual paying down of Canada's public debt that had become so large in the mid-1990s that merely making the interest payments on the debt threatened to crowd out other categories of government spending. They also note that in recent years the federal government has lowered both personal and corporate income-tax rates, and therefore the provinces could have increased their tax rates if they had chosen to do so. In their view, the correction of the fiscal imbalance requires provinces to make some difficult political decisions regarding their own spending and taxing policies.

Conservative Prime Minister Stephen Harper, elected early in 2006, campaigned partly on the promise to correct the fiscal imbalance between the federal and provincial governments. At the time this book went to press (late fall 2006), his precise policy approach to this issue was yet to be outlined.

Canadian Social Programs

Table 18-2 shows that government spending on health, education, and other social services represents over 63 percent of total government spending in Canada. Given their obvious fiscal importance, it is worth briefly reviewing Canada's major social programs.

Some social programs are universal, in the sense that they pay benefits to anyone meeting only such minimal requirements as age or residence. These are referred to as **demogrants**. Other programs are selective, in the sense that they pay benefits only to people who qualify by meeting specific conditions, such as by having young children or being unemployed. When these conditions are related to the individual's income, the term **income-tested benefits** is used. Some benefits are expenditure programs (including direct transfers to persons), while others are delivered through the tax system. Some programs are administered by the federal government, some by the provincial governments, and still others by the municipalities.

In this section we examine the five pillars of Canadian social policy: education, health care, income support, employment insurance, and retirement benefits. Each of these pillars, at various points in recent years, has been the focus of attention as financially strapped governments have explored new ways to provide these vital social services in a cost-effective manner.

demogrants Social benefits paid to anyone meeting only minimal requirements such as age or residence; in particular, *not* income-tested.

income-tested benefits Social benefits paid to recipients who qualify because their income is less than some critical level.

Education Public education, one of the earliest types of social expenditure in Canada, remains one of the most important. It has been supplemented over the years by numerous other public programs aimed at developing human capital.

Basic Education. Primary and secondary schools are funded by provincial governments in Canada, but are managed by local school boards. Basic education is publicly financed for both efficiency and equity reasons. In terms of efficiency, a literate and numerate population is necessary for an informed electorate that can participate in democratic society. Society as a whole is therefore better off when all of its citizens have at least a basic level of education. The equity argument is based on the fact that basic skills acquired in primary and secondary schools are usually necessary in order for individuals to secure careers that can provide reasonable incomes. If basic education were not financed by the government, many low-income households could not afford to send their children to school. The result in many cases would be a vicious circle of poverty in which children from low-income families would lack basic education and thus secure only poor jobs, thus earning only low incomes themselves.

Post-secondary Education. Post-secondary education is a provincial responsibility in Canada. As discussed earlier in this chapter, however, the federal government makes large

More than half of the operating revenues of Canadian universities come from provincial governments. Only 20 percent of revenues come from students' tuition fees. There is an active debate in Canada about how much students should be paying toward the full costs of their post-secondary education.

For data on the financial position of Canadian universities, see Statistics Canada's website: **www.statcan.ca**. Click on "Canadian Statistics" and then type in "universities."

payments to the provinces to support post-secondary education as part of the Canada Social Transfer (CST).

In Canada, universities are public institutions, and university education is heavily subsidized by government. In 2005, total revenues for universities and colleges were $27.7 billion, with 57 percent coming from various levels of government. Only 20 percent came from student tuition fees. (The remaining 23 percent comes from various other sources—including those overpriced shirts that you can't afford to buy from your campus bookstore!) In addition, many students receive student loans from commercial banks where the loans are guaranteed by the federal government. In cases where students default on their loans, the repayment by the government amounts to a subsidy to the student.

Two arguments can be advanced for subsidizing higher education; one is an efficiency argument, and the other an equity argument. The efficiency argument is based on the claim that there are positive externalities from higher education—that is, that the country as a whole benefits when a student receives higher education. In many cases these externalities cannot be internalized by the students receiving the education, so, left to their own maximizing decisions, students who had to pay the full cost of their education would choose less than what is socially optimal. The equity argument is that if students were forced to pay anything like the full cost of the services they receive, a university education would become prohibitively expensive to low- and even middle-income families. Government subsidies help provide education according to ability rather than according to income.

Arguments that rely on higher tuition to finance a larger fraction of the costs of running universities start with the observation that the value of many kinds of post-secondary education is internalized and recaptured in higher incomes earned by the recipients later in their life. This is particularly true of professional training in such fields as law, medicine, dentistry, management, and computer science. Yet students in these fields typically pay a smaller part of their real education costs than students in the arts, where the argument for externalities is greatest. Also, subsidized education does represent a significant income transfer from taxpayers to students, even though the average taxpayer may have a lower income than the average post-secondary student can expect to earn in the future.

Health Care In Canada, basic health care is financed mainly by the provincial governments, with significant transfers from the federal government under the Canada Health Transfer (CHT). In most provinces, residents pay nothing to receive medical attention—health care is free to users and is financed out of the government's general tax revenues. Though health care is publicly financed, physicians and private (non-profit) hospitals working on a "fee for service" basis form the core of Canada's health-care delivery system. Thus, the Canadian health-care system is based on public *financing* but private *delivery*.

Health care is financed by government for reasons of both efficiency and equity. The efficiency argument is much the same as for basic education—a healthy population is as important to the smooth functioning of a democratic country as is an educated one. The equity argument is even more powerful: Most people believe that basic health care is so important that denying it to people who cannot afford it would be unacceptable.

Cost Containment. Taking federal and provincial payments into account, Canada's public health-care system is the country's single most expensive social program. In 2005, government expenditure on health care was $96.2 billion, about 19 percent of total government expenditure and 6.8 percent of GDP. Private spending on health care brought total spending up to over 10 percent of GDP. In other words, one out of every ten dollars in income produced in the Canadian economy gets spent on health care.

"Cost containment" in the health-care sector has become a priority for most provincial governments and the debate currently rages over what reforms would be practicable and acceptable. Most observers agree that some type of expenditure-controlling reform is urgently needed. Unfortunately, agreement stops there.

The Role of the Private Sector. Much of the debate over the reform of Canada's health-care system rests on the appropriate role of the private sector in what is a publicly financed system. Some provincial governments, notably Alberta, have suggested that allowing a greater role for private, for-profit hospitals and clinics can reduce waiting lists and therefore improve the overall quality of health care that citizens receive.

The main concern with allowing a greater role for private clinics and hospitals is that private hospitals may begin "extra billing" their patients. In this case there would develop a "two-tiered" health-care system in which individuals with higher incomes have faster access to health care than do individuals with lower incomes. If extra billing becomes a feature of private hospitals, then only those individuals who can afford to pay the extra fees will be able to use the private hospitals. Furthermore, many nurses and doctors that are currently within the financially strapped public health-care system may move to the private hospitals if salaries or working conditions are better there. The overall concern, therefore, is that the introduction of private hospitals into the existing public health-care system, even while reducing waiting lists and providing more health-care services overall, may create a high-quality system for the wealthy and a low-quality system for lower-income people. Many people think that such a two-tiered health-care system would destroy the equity that the public system was initially designed to promote.

Advocates of allowing a greater role for private hospitals and clinics, on the other hand, argue that to a significant extent, Canada already has a two-tiered system. For example, for services such as laser eye surgery and diagnosis with MRIs, private clinics have existed for several years; people have a choice between waiting in line for service in the public hospitals, sometimes for many months, or going to a private clinic immediately and paying for treatment. Even for more serious surgery, some Canadians, frustrated by the long waiting lists in the Canadian public health-care system, travel to the United States for medical treatment. Advocates of private for-profit hospitals also argue that the lack of public funding in the Canadian health-care system has already caused many doctors and nurses to leave Canada and move to the United States and that the introduction of private hospitals would help stem the flow of nurses and doctors out of Canada, thereby *improving* Canada's overall health-care system. Furthermore, they argue that two-tier systems do not seem to lead to major health-care inequalities in the countries of Western Europe, all of whom operate some form of two-tier system.

myeconlab

The debate over reforming Canada's health-care system continues to rage. For a more detailed discussion, including the recommendations of a recent Royal Commission, a Senate Report, and a Supreme Court decision, look for "Debate More Healthy than Health Care" in the *Additional Topics* section of this book's MyEconLab.

www.myeconlab.com

Income-Support Programs   Canada has various programs that provide assistance for people in financial need—these programs constitute what is often called the "social safety net." The overriding objectives of this safety net are to reduce poverty and increase individuals' sense of economic security. Though nothing like the serious problem it was in Canada's past and still is in many other countries, poverty remains a matter of real concern to Canadian policymakers.

poverty line An estimate of the annual family income that is required to maintain a minimum adequate standard of living.

Statistics Canada defines the **poverty line** or *low-income cutoff* as the level of income below which the typical household spends more than 55 percent of its income on the three necessities of food, shelter, and clothing. Not surprisingly, this poverty line varies depending on the size of the family and where it lives. In 2004, Statistics Canada's estimated poverty line for a family of four living in a major urban centre was $37 253. Thus, a family of four with income less than this amount would be defined to be living in poverty. In 2004, 7.8 percent of Canadian families had incomes below Statistics Canada's estimated poverty line. This percentage includes some of the working poor, whether stuck in low-paying jobs or doing their first job; some whom were not working at all; and some whose incomes were only temporarily below the poverty line, such as students or other trainees.

There is considerable debate, however, about the methods used to estimate poverty. Central to this debate is whether poverty is best viewed as an *absolute* or a *relative* concept. If poverty is viewed as an absolute concept, then anybody without enough income to purchase a certain amount of food, shelter, and clothing is said to be in poverty. With such an absolute definition of poverty, sufficient growth in the economy could, at least in principle, eliminate poverty entirely as low-income households eventually see their income rise above the threshold level.

With a *relative* definition of poverty, however, there will *always* be some families defined to be impoverished. For example, suppose households are defined to be impoverished whenever their income is less than 25 percent of the economy's average household income. Since any realistic distribution of income will contain *some* households whose income is 25 percent of the average, there will always be some poverty when it is defined this way. Advocates of a relative measure of poverty argue that poverty is more than just the absence of enough food and clothing—it is also the social exclusion from mainstream society that typically comes from having much lower income than most households.

myeconlab

There is continuing debate in Canada about how best to measure poverty, and thus debate about how much poverty really exists. For a more detailed discussion of poverty in Canada, look for "Who Are Canada's Poor?" in the *Additional Topics* section of this book's MyEconLab.

www.myeconlab.com

Whatever the precise definition, all experts agree that many Canadians live in poverty. Canada has several income-support programs designed to address this important problem. They can be divided into three types. The first is designed to provide income assistance to those individuals whose incomes are deemed to be too low to provide an adequate standard of living. The second is designed to assist specifically those individuals who are in financial need because of temporary job loss—employment insurance. The third is designed to provide income assistance specifically to the elderly. In this subsection, we examine the first type. The next two subsections discuss employment insurance and elderly benefits, respectively.

Welfare. Social assistance for individuals below retirement age, usually called *welfare*, is mainly a provincial responsibility in Canada. The details of the programs vary considerably across the provinces even though they are partly financed by transfers received from the federal government under the Canada Social Transfer (CST).

One important problem with welfare occurs with what are called *poverty traps.* **Poverty traps** occur whenever the tax-and-transfer system results in individuals having very little incentive to increase their pre-tax income (by accepting a job, for example) because such an increase in their pre-tax income would make them ineligible for some benefits (such as welfare) and might even make them worse off overall. The presence of such poverty traps reflects a tax-and-transfer system that has been modified in many small steps over many years, the result of which is a plethora of programs often working at cross purposes. The elimination of such poverty traps requires that the tax-and-transfer system be examined in its entirety rather than on a piecemeal basis. *Applying Economic Concepts 18-1* discusses one possible reform of the tax-and-transfer system that maintains progressivity of the system while eliminating poverty traps. This is the idea of the negative income tax.

Poverty and homelessness exist in Canada, though there is disagreement about how widespread these problems are.

poverty trap Occurs whenever individuals have little incentive to increase their pre-tax income because the resulting loss of benefits makes them worse off.

Child Benefits. The support system for families with children has been evolving quite rapidly over the years. Prior to 1993 the system was a combination of universal family allowance payments and tax credits. In 1993, universality was eliminated. A Child Tax Benefit is now paid according to the number of children in the family and varies according to family income. For families with net incomes below about $23 000, the Child Tax Benefit pays approximately $200 per child per month. The amount declines as family income increases, finally reaching zero at an annual income of $79 000.

In 2006, the newly elected Conservative government implemented the Universal Child Care Benefit, a program which pays parents $100 per month for each child under the age of six. The payments are taxed in the hands of the lower-earning parent.

Employment Insurance

Employment insurance (EI) is a federal program designed to provide temporary income support to workers who lose their jobs. Employers and employees remit EI premiums to the government equal to a small percentage of wages and salaries. These premiums then finance the EI payments to unemployed workers who qualify for the benefits. In boom times, when there is little unemployment, the total amount of EI premiums collected exceeds the total amount dispersed as EI benefits; in times of high unemployment, the benefits exceed the premiums. As a result, the EI program is approximately self-financing over the duration of the average business cycle (six to seven years).

EI gives incentives to remain in seasonal jobs and in areas with poor employment prospects and to take EI-financed holidays. Saying that the EI system encourages behaviour that increases unemployment and reduces regional mobility does not say that the unemployed themselves are responsible for the "abuses" of the system that lead to these results. The responsibility lies with the people who designed the incentives and those who strive to preserve them. It is they who can alter the system to make it deliver the intended benefits with fewer incentives for undesired behaviour.

Retirement Benefits

There are three components of the system of retirement benefits. These are the Canada Pension Plan (CPP), retirement income-support programs such as Old Age Security (OAS) and Guaranteed Income Supplement (GIS), and tax-assisted saving plans.

For details on Canada's Employment Insurance program, go to the website for Human Resources and Social Development Canada: **www.hrsdc.gc.ca**. Then click on "financial benefits."

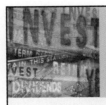

APPLYING ECONOMIC CONCEPTS 18-1

Poverty Traps and the Negative Income Tax

A tax is negative when the government pays the tax-payer rather than the other way around. The *negative income tax (NIT)* is designed to combat poverty by making taxes negative at very low incomes. Furthermore, the NIT potentially avoids some of the extreme disincentive effects that are caused by very high marginal tax rates. Finally, by combining taxes and transfers into a single system, the negative income tax also avoids the occurrence of poverty traps.

The underlying principle of the NIT is that a family of a given size should be *guaranteed* a minimum annual income. The tax system must be designed, however, to guarantee this income without eliminating the household's incentive to be self-supporting.

As an example, consider a system in which each household is guaranteed a minimum annual income of $10 000 and the marginal tax rate is 40 percent. Money can be thought of as flowing in two directions; the government gives every household $10 000, and then every household remits 40 percent of any *earned* income back to the government. The *break-even* level of income in this example is $25 000. All households earning less than $25 000 pay negative taxes overall; they receive more money from the government than they remit in

taxes. Households earning exactly $25 000 pay no net taxes—their $10 000 from the government exactly equals the taxes they remit to the government on their earned income. All households earning more than $25 000 pay more than $10 000 in taxes and so they are paying *positive* taxes overall.

The figure shows the operation of this scheme by relating earned income on the horizontal axis to after-tax income on the vertical axis. The red 45° line shows what after-tax income would be if there were no taxes.

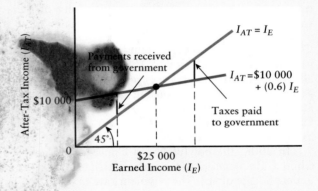

The Canada Pension Plan (CPP). The CPP provides a basic level of retirement income for all Canadians who have contributed to it over their working lives. A separate but similar scheme exists in Quebec—the Quebec Pension Plan or QPP. Unlike some private programs, the pension provided by the CPP is *portable*—changing jobs does not cause any loss of eligibility. Crucial to understanding the problems faced by the CPP is recognizing that the payments to current retirees are financed by the contributions made by those currently working.

Given the "pay-as-you-go" nature of the Canada Pension Plan, it is inevitable that the CPP will encounter financing problems as the population ages. As the oldest members of the baby boom begin to retire around 2010, the ratio of retirees to contributors will rise rapidly. As this ratio rises, working people must contribute more to the CPP in order to maintain a given level of benefits for the retirees. In 1996, the CPP was judged to be in a crisis situation—either contributions had to increase or retirement benefits had to fall in order to keep the CPP financially sound. In 1998, the Canadian government reformed the CPP by increasing the required level of contributions by both employers and employees. The system is now less vulnerable to demographic shifts than it was earlier.

The blue line shows after-tax income with a NIT. It starts at the guaranteed annual income of $10 000, rises by 60 cents for every one dollar increase in earned income, and crosses the 45° line at the break-even level of income, $25 000. The vertical distance between the two lines shows the net transfers between the household and the government.

Note that the NIT is a progressive tax, despite the *constant* marginal income-tax rate. To see this, note that a household's *average* tax rate is equal to the total taxes paid divided by total earned income. If I_E is earned income, then

$$\text{Average tax rate} = \frac{(0.40) \times I_E - \$10\,000}{I_E}$$

$$= (0.40) - \frac{\$10\,000}{I_E}$$

Thus, the average tax rate for the household rises as earned income rises, but the average tax rate is *always less* than the marginal tax rate (40 percent). That the average tax rate rises with earned income means that higher-income households pay a larger fraction of their income in taxes than is paid by lower-income households—that is, the NIT is progressive.

Supporters of the NIT believe that it would be an effective tool for reducing poverty. The NIT provides a minimum level of income as a matter of right, not of charity, and it does so without removing the work incentives for people who are eligible for payments; every dollar earned adds to the after-tax income of the family. Poverty traps are avoided.

One step toward the NIT was taken in 1987 when the personal income-tax system was substantially reformed. In those reforms, many personal exemptions were replaced with tax credits. An exemption reduces an individual's taxable income and hence is more valuable the higher the tax bracket. In contrast, a tax credit reduces taxes payable by the amount of the credit and hence is equally valuable at all levels of income. At present, however, the tax credit is not refundable—the credit can be used to reduce taxes payable to zero, but cannot be used to reduce taxes payable to a negative number. Thus, if an individual has taxes payable equal to $5000 and then receives a tax credit, total taxes payable fall only to zero—the unused credit ($1000) cannot be claimed back from the government. If the tax credit were fully refundable, however, someone whose taxes on earned income were less than the tax credit would receive the difference from the government. This would be a negative income tax.

Retirement Income-Support Programs. The existing public benefits system for the elderly is in many ways analogous to the child benefits system. There are two major parts to the system. First, a universal benefit called the Old Age Security (OAS) program acts much like the family allowance. Under the OAS program, the government sends out monthly benefit cheques to each Canadian over the qualifying age of 65. OAS payments to relatively wealthy individuals are fully recaptured by means of a tax "clawback."

Second, an income-tested program, called the Guaranteed Income Supplement (GIS), provides benefits targeted to the low-income elderly. (In some provinces this is supplemented by further targeted assistance.) The GIS provides for most of the progressivity that arises in the elderly benefits system.

Tax-Assisted Saving Plans. The CPP, OAS, and GIS are programs that involve direct spending on the part of the government. The government has also introduced programs that require no direct government spending but instead rely on *tax expenditures* (i.e., beneficial tax treatment). These tax expenditures are designed to provide incentives for individuals to save more for their retirement. There are two types of programs. The first is through Registered Retirement Savings Plans (RRSPs) and the second is through employer-sponsored Registered Pension Plans (RPPs).

RRSPs provide an incentive for individuals to provide for their own retirement, either because they are not covered by a company plan or because they wish to supplement their company plan. Funds contributed are deductible from taxable income (and accumulate year by year without any tax being paid) but they become fully taxable when they are withdrawn. It is thus a tax deferral plan, and as such it is more valuable the higher one's current taxable income and the lower one's expected future income.

Individuals without RRSPs may still receive some tax assistance for saving if their employer has a Registered Pension Plan. In this case, contributions to the company pension plan (which are often mandatory and are withdrawn directly from the regular paycheque) are tax deductible in a manner similar to an RRSP contribution.

18.4 EVALUATING THE ROLE OF GOVERNMENT

Earlier we pointed out that it is more informative to assess the progressivity of the overall tax system than any individual tax. It is even more informative to assess the progressivity of the combination of taxes and expenditures—that is, the entire tax-expenditure system. For example, a tax-expenditure system could be highly progressive even if taxes were proportional, as long as government expenditures (including . . . accounted for a higher portion of real incomes of the poor than of the rich. . . . that the overall Canadian tax-expenditure system is progressive and . . . the inequalities of income generated by the market.

Even . . . there . . . that the Canadian tax-expenditure system is progressive, and . . . the redistribution is desirable, there is still considerable disagree . . . appropriate level of government activity in the economy.

Public Versus Private Sector

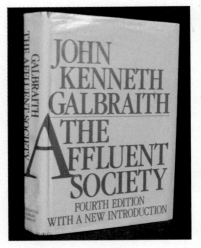

In this classic book, Galbraith argued that western democracies often undervalue public goods and place too much value on private consumption. He lamented the resulting contrast between "private affluence" and "public squalor."

When the government raises money by taxation and spends it on an activity, it increases the spending of the public sector and decreases that of the private sector. Since the public sector and the private sector spend on different things, the government is changing the allocation of resources. Is this change good or bad? Should there be more schools and fewer houses or more houses and fewer schools?

For all goods that are produced and sold on the market, consumers' demand has a significant influence on the relative prices and quantities produced and thus on the allocation of the nation's resources. But no market provides relative prices for private houses versus public schools; thus, the choice between allowing money to be spent in the private sector and allowing it to be spent for public goods is a matter to be decided by Parliament and other legislative bodies.

John Kenneth Galbraith's 1958 bestseller, *The Affluent Society*, proclaimed that a correct assignment of marginal utilities would show them to be higher for an extra dollar's worth of public parks, clean water, and education than for an extra dollar's worth of television sets, shampoo, or automobiles. In Galbraith's view, the political process often fails to translate preferences for public goods into effective action; thus more resources are devoted to the private sector and fewer to the public sector than would be the case if the political mechanism were as effective as the market. He lamented the resulting "private affluence and public squalor."

An alternative view has many supporters, who agree with Nobel laureate James Buchanan that society has reached a point where the value of the *marginal* dollar spent by government is less than the value of that dollar left in the hands of households or firms. These people argue that because bureaucrats are spending other people's money, they care very little about a few million or billion dollars here or there. They have only a weak sense of the opportunity cost of public expenditure and, thus, tend to spend beyond the point where marginal benefits equal marginal costs.

Scope of Government Activity

One of the most difficult problems for the student of the Canadian economic system is to maintain the appropriate perspective about the scope of government activity in the market economy. On the one hand, there are thousands of laws, regulations, and policies that affect firms and households. Many people believe that a general reduction in the role of government is both possible and desirable. On the other hand, policy decision makers still have an enormous amount of discretion about what they do and how they do it.

One pitfall is to become so impressed (or obsessed) with the many ways in which government activity impinges on the individual that one fails to see that these activities make changes—sometimes large, but often small—in market signals in a system that basically leaves individuals free to make their own decisions. It is in the private sector that most individuals choose their occupations, earn their incomes, spend their incomes, and live their lives. In this sector too, firms are formed, choose products, live, grow, and sometimes die.

A different pitfall is to fail to see that a significant share of the taxes paid by the private sector is used to buy goods and services that add to the welfare of individuals. By and large, the public sector complements the private sector, doing things the private sector would leave undone or would do differently. For example, Canadians pay taxes that are used to finance expenditures on health and education. But certainly Canadians would continue to use hospitals and attend schools even if the various levels of government did not provide these goods, and instead left more money in people's pockets. Thus, in many cases, the government is levying taxes to raise money to finance goods that people would have purchased anyway. To recognize that we often benefit directly from government spending, however, in no way denies that it is often wasteful, and sometimes worse.

Evolution of Policy

Public policies in operation at any time are not the result of a single master plan that specifies precisely where and how the public sector shall seek to complement or interfere with the workings of the market mechanism. Rather, as individual problems arise, governments attempt to meet them by passing appropriate legislation to deal with the problem. These laws stay on the books, and some become obsolete and unenforceable. This pattern is generally true of systems of law.

Many anomalies exist in our economic policies; for example, laws designed to support the incomes of small farmers have created some agricultural millionaires, and commissions created to ensure competition between firms often end up creating and protecting monopolies. Neither individual policies nor whole programs are above criticism.

In a society that elects its policymakers at regular intervals, however, the majority view on the amount of government intervention that is desirable will have some considerable influence on the amount of intervention that actually occurs. Fundamentally, a free-market system is retained because it is valued for its lack of coercion and its ability to do much of the allocating of society's resources better than any known alternative. But we are not mesmerized by it; we feel free to intervene in pursuit of a better world in which to live. We also recognize, however, that sometimes government intervention has proved ineffective or even counterproductive.

S U M M A R Y

18.1 TAXATION IN CANADA

- Although the main purpose of the tax system is to raise revenue, tax policy is potentially a powerful device for income redistribution because the progressivity of different kinds of taxes varies greatly.
- The most important taxes in Canada are the personal income tax, the corporate income tax, excise and sales taxes (including the nationwide GST), and property taxes.

- The progressivity of a tax is determined by how the average tax rate (taxes paid divided by income) changes as income changes. If the average tax rate rises as income rises, the tax is progressive. If the average tax rate falls as income rises, the tax is regressive.

18.2 EVALUATING THE TAX SYSTEM

- Evaluating the tax system involves evaluating the efficiency and progressivity of the entire system, rather than of individual taxes within the system. For a given amount of revenue to be raised, efficiency and progressivity can be altered by changing the mix of the various taxes used.
- The total Canadian tax structure is roughly proportional, except for very low-income and very high-income groups (where it is mildly progressive).
- Taxes often generate allocative inefficiency. The allocative inefficiency of a tax is measured by the excess

burden. Because of the excess burden, a tax is more costly than just the amount paid by the taxpayers (the direct burden).
- There are potentially important disincentive effects of taxation, as represented by a Laffer curve. A rise in the tax rate initially raises total tax revenue; after some point, however, further increases in the tax rate reduce the incentive to produce taxable income, and so total tax revenue falls. Thus, governments cannot always raise tax revenues by raising tax rates.

18.3 PUBLIC EXPENDITURE IN CANADA

- A large part of public expenditure is for the provision of goods and services. Other types of expenditures including subsidies, transfer payments to individuals, and intergovernmental transfers are also important.
- Fiscal federalism is the idea that the various fiscal authorities should be coordinated in their spending plans and should have a mechanism for transfers between the various levels of government.

Understanding the relationship between the federal government and the various provincial governments is of utmost importance in understanding many of Canada's most important government spending programs.
- The five pillars of Canadian social policy are:

  1. Education
  2. Health care

3. Income support programs (welfare and child benefits)
4. Employment insurance

5. Retirement benefits (CPP, GIS, OAS, and tax-assisted saving plans)

18.4 EVALUATING THE ROLE OF GOVERNMENT

- Government taxation and expenditure have a major effect on the allocation of resources. The government determines how much of society's total output is devoted to education, health care, highways, the armed forces, and so on.
- The overall Canadian tax-expenditure system is progressive in that it reduces income inequalities produced by the market.
- When evaluating the overall role of government in the economy, we should keep three basic issues in mind:

1. What is the appropriate mix between public goods and private goods?
2. Much government activity is directed to providing goods and services that add directly to the welfare of the private sector.
3. We should continually re-evaluate existing programs; some that were needed in the past may no longer be needed; others may have unintended and undesirable side effects.

KEY CONCEPTS

Progressive, proportional, and regressive taxes
The benefit principle and the ability-to-pay principle

Vertical and horizontal equity
Direct and excess burdens of a tax
Disincentive effects of taxation
Transfer payments to individuals

Fiscal federalism
Intergovernmental transfers
Canadian social programs

STUDY EXERCISES

1. Fill in the blanks to make the following statements correct.

   a. Suppose you earn an annual income of $22 500 and you paid a total of $3600 in taxes. Your average tax rate is _____.

   b. Suppose you earn an annual income of $22 500 and each dollar earned is taxed at the same rate. Your marginal tax rate is the same as _____.

   c. Suppose the marginal tax rate on the first $25 000 of income is 20 percent, and on any income above that, the rate rises to 30 percent. If your annual income is $42 000, you will pay total income tax of _____.

   d. Lower-income groups typically spend a higher proportion of their income than do higher-income groups. For this reason, excise and sales taxes are considered to be somewhat _____.

   e. The most important source of revenue for municipalities is the _____ tax. Rather than being a tax on income or expenditure, it is a tax on _____.

2. Fill in the blanks to make the following statements correct.

   a. Evaluating a tax system requires consideration of the following two aspects of taxation: _____ and _____.

   b. Taxation usually causes allocative inefficiency because it distorts the equality between marginal _____ and marginal _____ of a given activity.

   c. Economists refer to the revenue collected as a result of a tax as the _____ burden of taxation. Economists refer to other costs imposed on society because of the tax as the _____ burden of taxation.

   d. An efficient tax system is one that collects a given amount of revenue while minimizing the amount of _____.

   e. The Laffer curve suggests that above some tax rate, further increases in the tax rate will _____ tax revenue.

3. Consider an income-tax system that has four tax brackets. The following table shows the marginal tax rate that applies to the income in each tax bracket.

Earned Income	Tax Rate in Bracket
Up to $20 000	0%
$20 001–$40 000	15%
$40 001–$80 000	30%
$80 001 and higher	35%

a. Compute the average income-tax rate at income levels $10 000, $20 000, and each increment of $10 000 up to $120 000.
b. Compute the marginal income-tax rate for each level of income in part (a).
c. On a graph with the tax rates on the vertical axis and income on the horizontal axis, plot the average and marginal tax rates for each level of income.
d. Is this tax system progressive? Explain.

4. **myeconlab** The diagrams below show the market for gasoline in two countries, Midas and Neptune. In Midas, demand is perfectly inelastic; in Neptune, demand is relatively elastic. In both countries, supply is identical and upward sloping. The government in each country imposes an excise tax of t per litre on the producers of gasoline. This tax shifts the supply curve up by t.

Midas

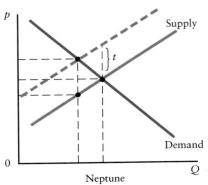

Neptune

a. In each case, shade the area that is the direct burden of the tax.
b. In each case, shade the area that is the excess burden of the tax.
c. In which country does the tax cause the greater allocative inefficiency? Explain.

5. Rank the following taxes according to which has the highest excess burden relative to the direct burden. Start with the highest. Recall that the direct burden of the tax is equal to the revenue that the tax raises.

a. An excise tax on one brand of breakfast cereal
b. An excise tax on all breakfast cereals
c. An excise tax on all food
d. An excise tax on everything (which is basically what the GST is)

6. Classify each of the following government expenditures as either a transfer payment or a purchase of goods and services. Which ones clearly tend to decrease the inequality of income distribution?

a. Payments of wages and family living allowances to Canadian soldiers overseas
b. Employment insurance payments to unemployed workers
c. Payments to provinces for support of highway construction
d. Pensions of retired Supreme Court justices
e. Salaries paid to government workers

7. Governments in Canada, at all levels, make considerable transfer payments to individuals and to businesses. This question will show you how significant these transfer payments are. Go to Statistics Canada's website (www.statcan.ca), click on "Canadian Statistics" and then type in "transfers." Then answer the following questions.

a. For the years 2001–2005, what were the federal transfers for (un)employment insurance benefits?
b. Have total government transfers been growing faster or slower than GDP?
c. For the years 2001–2005, what were the total federal and provincial government transfers to universities and colleges?

8. **myeconlab** The Negative Income Tax has been proposed as a means of increasing both the efficiency and equity of Canada's tax system (see *Applying Economic Concepts 18-1*). The most basic NIT can be described by two variables: the guaranteed annual income and the marginal tax rate. Suppose the guaranteed annual income is $8000 and the marginal tax rate on *every dollar earned* is 35 percent. With this NIT, after-tax income is given by:

After-tax income = $8000 + (1 − 0.35) × (Earned income)

a. On a scale diagram with after-tax income on the vertical axis and earned income on the horizontal axis, draw the NIT relationship between earned income and after-tax income.

b. What is the level of income at which taxes paid on earned income exactly equal the guaranteed annual income?

c. The average tax rate is equal to total *net* taxes paid divided by earned income. Provide an algebraic expression for the average tax rate.

d. On a scale diagram with earned income on the horizontal axis and tax rates on the vertical axis, plot the average and marginal tax rates for the NIT. Is the NIT progressive?

DISCUSSION QUESTIONS

1. In Canada, capital gains are taxed at half the rates applicable to other income. Who are the likely beneficiaries of this policy? What are the likely effects on the distribution of income and the allocation of resources? Can you think of both equity and efficiency arguments supporting the special treatment of capital gains?

2. "Taxes on tobacco and alcohol are nearly perfect taxes. They raise lots of revenue and discourage smoking and drinking." In this statement, to what extent are the two effects inconsistent? How is the incidence of an excise tax related to the extent to which it discourages use of the product?

3. Suppose the government spends $1 billion on a new program to provide the poor with housing, better clothing, more food, and better health services.

   a. Argue the case for and against assistance of this kind rather than giving the money to the poor to spend as they think best.

   b. Should federal transfers to the provinces be conditional grants or grants with no strings attached? Is this issue the same as that raised in part (a) or is it a different one?

4. Is the tax deduction allowed for RRSPs progressive or regressive (or neither)?

5. In 1998, CPP contribution rates were increased to help secure the solvency of the system. An alternative proposal at the time was to reduce benefit rates. Who stood to lose and benefit from each proposal?

6. It is common to read articles in the newspapers by people who think Canadians pay too much in taxes. One popular concept is "tax freedom day," the day in the year beyond which you get to keep your income rather than pay it to the government as taxes. For example, if the government collects 33 percent of GDP in taxes, then "tax freedom day" is the 122nd day of the year, May 2.

   a. Does everyone in the economy have the same tax freedom day, no matter what their income?

   b. How sensible is the concept of "tax freedom day" in a country where the government provides some goods and services to the people that they would otherwise purchase on their own, such as primary education?

7. In 2001, the Alberta government permitted private, for-profit hospitals to exist within the public health-care system. Explain how private hospitals can make a profit if they receive the same payments for services that public hospitals receive.

CHAPTER 19

What Macroeconomics
Is All About

LEARNING OBJECTIVES

In this chapter you will learn

1 the meaning and importance of the key macroeconomic variables, including national income, unemployment, inflation, interest rates, exchange rates, and trade flows.

2 that most macroeconomic issues are about either long-run trends or short-run fluctuations, and that government policy is relevant for both.

Turn on the evening news or read your local newspaper, and you will likely hear talk of unemployment, inflation, exchange rates, and productivity growth. Almost everyone cares about economic issues. Workers are anxious to avoid the unemployment that comes with recessions and to share in the rising income that is brought about by productivity growth. Firms are concerned about how interest rates, changes in exchange rates, and foreign competition affect their profits. Consumers want to know how changes in interest rates affect mortgage payments and how changes in exchange rates affect the prices of the goods they purchase. Pensioners worry that inflation may erode the purchasing power of their fixed dollar incomes.

Macroeconomics is the study of how the economy behaves in broad outline without dwelling on much of the detail that occurs in markets for individual products. **Macroeconomics** is concerned with the behaviour of economic *aggregates,* such as total output, total investment, total exports, and the price level, and with how government policy may influence these aggregates. These aggregates result from activities in many different markets and from the combined behaviour of millions of different decision makers.

We know perfectly well that an economy producing a lot of wheat and few computers is different from one producing many computers but little wheat. We also know that an economy with cheap wheat and expensive computers is different from one with cheap computers and expensive wheat. Studying aggregates may cause us to miss these important differences, but it focuses our attention on some important issues for the economy as a whole.

In return for suppressing some valuable detail, studying economic aggregates allows us to view the big picture. When aggregate output rises, the output of many commodities and the incomes of many people rise with it. When the price level rises, many people in the economy are forced to make adjustments. When the unemployment

macroeconomics The study of the determination of economic aggregates, such as total output, total employment, the price level, and the rate of economic growth.

rate rises, many workers suffer reductions in their incomes. Such movements in economic aggregates matter for most individuals because they influence the health of the industries in which they work and the prices of the goods that they purchase. This is why macroeconomic issues get airtime on the evening news, and it is one of the important reasons why we study macroeconomics.

It will become clear as we proceed through this chapter (and later ones) that macroeconomists consider two different aspects of the economy. They think about the *short-run* behaviour of macroeconomic variables, such as output, employment, and inflation, and about how government policy can influence these variables. This concerns, among other things, the study of *business cycles*. They also examine the *long-run* behaviour of the same variables, especially the long-run path of aggregate output. This is the study of *economic growth* and is concerned with explaining how technological change occurs and how our material living standards continue to increase over long periods of time.

A full understanding of macroeconomics requires understanding the nature of short-run fluctuations as well as the nature of long-run economic growth.

Before we examine some key macroeconomic variables, it is worth pointing out that there are two different streams of research in macroeconomics, even though the researchers in the two groups are generally interested in understanding the same macroeconomic phenomena. The first group of researchers takes an approach to macroeconomics that is based explicitly on *microeconomic foundations*. These economists build models of the economy that are populated by workers, consumers, and firms, all of whom are assumed to be *optimizers*. Having explicitly modelled these agents' optimization problems, and their resulting choices for work effort, consumption, and investment, the economists proceed to *aggregate* the choices of these agents to arrive at the model's values for aggregate employment, consumption, output and so on.

The second group of researchers builds macroeconomic models based only implicitly on these same micro foundations. They do not explicitly model the choices of optimizing agents. Instead, these economists construct their models using aggregate relationships for consumption, investment, and employment, each of which has been subjected to extensive empirical testing and is assumed to represent the behaviour of the many firms and consumers in the economy.

A second difference between these two approaches relates to the assumptions regarding the flexibility of prices. Economists using the first approach usually assume that wages and prices are perfectly flexible and thus adjust quickly to clear their respective markets. In contrast, economists using the second approach usually assume that due to the nature of well-established institutions in both labour and product markets, wages and prices are slow to adjust, and thus markets can be in disequilibrium for longer periods of time.

This textbook follows the second approach to macroeconomic analysis. The macro model we begin building in Chapter 21 is not explicitly based on optimizing firms and consumers, although the macro relationships we introduce are well-motivated by microeconomic behaviour. Moreover, the model begins in its simplest version by assuming *no* wage and price flexibility. But as we gradually make the model more complicated and also more realistic, we introduce more wage and price flexibility. In later chapters we will see that the degree of wage and price flexibility is crucial in determining how the economy responds to shocks of various kinds, including changes in government policy. We will also see that our macroeconomic model is sufficiently versatile that we can use it to illustrate the case of perfect wage/price flexibility as a special case.

19.1 KEY MACROECONOMIC VARIABLES

In this chapter, we discuss several important macroeconomic variables, with an emphasis on what they mean and why they matter for our well-being. Here and in Chapter 20 we also explain how the key macroeconomic variables are measured. The remainder of this book is about the causes and consequences of changes in each of these variables, the many ways in which they interact, and the effects they have on our well-being.

Output and Income

The most comprehensive measure of a nation's overall level of economic activity is the value of its total production of goods and services, called *national product*.

One of the most important ideas in economics is that the production of output generates income.

As a matter of convention, economists define their terms so that, for the nation as a whole, all of the value that is produced ultimately belongs to someone in the form of an income claim on that value. For example, if a firm produces $100 worth of ice cream, that $100 ultimately represents income for the firm's workers, the firm's suppliers of material inputs, and the firm's owners. Thus, the national product is *by definition* equal to national income.

There are several related measures of a nation's total output and total income. Their various definitions, and the relationships among them, are discussed in detail in the next chapter. In this chapter, we use the generic term *national income* to refer to both the value of total output and the value of the income claims generated by the production of that output.

Aggregating Total Output   To measure total output, quantities of many different goods are *aggregated*. To construct such totals, we add up the *values* of the different products. We cannot add tonnes of steel to loaves of bread, but we can add the money value of steel production to the money value of bread production. We begin by multiplying the number of units of each good produced by the price at which each unit is sold. This yields a dollar value of production for each good. We then sum these values across all the different goods produced in the economy to give us the quantity of total output *measured in dollars*.

This value of total output gives the money value of national output, usually called **nominal national income**. A change in this measure can be caused by a change in either the physical quantities or the prices on which it is based. To determine the extent to which any change is due to quantities or to prices, economists calculate **real national income**. This measures the value of individual outputs, not at current prices, but at a set of prices that prevailed in some base period.

Nominal national income is often referred to as *current-dollar national income*. Real national income is often called *constant-dollar national income*. Denoted by the symbol Y, real national income tells us the value of current output measured at constant prices—the sum of the quantities valued at prices that prevailed in the base period. Since prices are held constant when computing real national income, changes in real national income reflect *only* changes in quantities. Comparing real national incomes of different years therefore provides a measure of the change in real output that has occurred during the intervening period.

nominal national income Total national income measured in current dollars. Also called current-dollar national income.

real national income National income measured in constant (base-period) dollars. It changes only when quantities change.

National Income: Recent History   One of the most commonly used measures of national income is called *gross domestic product (GDP)*. GDP can be measured in either real or nominal terms; we focus here on real GDP. The details of its calculation will be discussed in Chapter 20.

Part (i) of Figure 19-1 shows real national income produced by the Canadian economy since 1962; part (ii) shows its annual percentage change for the same period. The GDP series in part (i) shows two kinds of movement. The major movement is a positive trend that increased real output by approximately four times since 1962. This is what economists refer to as *long-term economic growth*.

A second feature of the real GDP series is *short-term fluctuations* around the trend. Overall growth so dominates the real GDP series that the fluctuations are hardly visible in part (i) of Figure 19-1. However, as can be seen in part (ii), the growth of GDP has never been smooth. In most years, GDP increases, but in 1982 and 1991 GDP actually decreased, as shown by the negative rate of growth in the figure.

The **business cycle** refers to this continual ebb and flow of business activity that occurs around the long-term trend. For example, a single cycle will usually include an interval of quickly growing output, followed by an interval of slowly growing or even falling output. The entire cycle may last for several years. No two business cycles are exactly the same—variations occur in duration and magnitude. Some expansions are long and drawn out. Others come to an end before high employment and industrial capacity are reached. Nonetheless, fluctuations are systematic enough that it is useful to identify common factors, as is done in *Applying Economic Concepts 19-1*.

To see the most recent values for most of the macroeconomic variables discussed in this chapter, go to Statistics Canada's website: **www.statcan.ca** and search for "Latest Indicators."

business cycle Fluctuations of national income around its trend value that follow a more or less wavelike pattern.

FIGURE 19-1   Growth and Fluctuations in Real GDP, 1962–2005

(i) The level of real GDP

(ii) Annual growth rate of real GDP

Real GDP measures the quantity of total output produced by the nation's economy over the period of a year. Real GDP is plotted in part (i). With only a few interruptions, it has risen steadily since 1962, demonstrating the long-term growth of the Canadian economy. Short-term fluctuations are obscured by the long-term trend in part (i) but are highlighted in part (ii). The growth rate fluctuates considerably from year to year. The long-term upward trend in part (i) reflects the positive average growth rate in part (ii), shown by the dashed line.

(*Source:* These data are from Statistics Canada's CANSIM database, Series V3862685–380-0017 Gross Domestic Product. Reprinted with permission of Statistics Canada. Current data are available at www.statcan.ca by searching for "GDP.")

APPLYING ECONOMIC CONCEPTS 19-1

The Terminology of Business Cycles

The accompanying figure shows a stylized business cycle, with real GDP fluctuating around a steadily rising level of potential GDP—the economy's normal capacity to produce output. We begin our discussion of terminology with a trough.

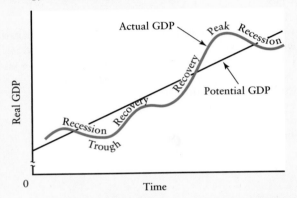

A *trough* is characterized by unemployed resources and a level of output that is low in relation to the economy's capacity to produce. There is thus a substantial amount of unused productive capacity. Business profits are low; for some individual companies, they are negative. Confidence about economic prospects in the immediate future is lacking, and, as a result, many firms are unwilling to risk making new investments.

The process of *recovery* moves the economy out of a trough. The characteristics of a recovery are many: run-down equipment is replaced; employment, income, and consumer spending all begin to rise; and expecta-

tions become more favourable. Investments that once seemed risky may be undertaken as firms become more optimistic about future business prospects. Production can be increased with relative ease merely by re-employing the existing unused capacity and unemployed labour.

Eventually the recovery comes to a *peak* at the top of the cycle. At the peak, existing capacity is used to a high degree; labour shortages may develop, particularly in categories of key skills, and shortages of essential raw materials are likely. As shortages develop, costs begin to rise, but because prices rise also, business remains profitable.

Peaks are eventually followed by *recessions*. A **recession**, or contraction, is a downturn in economic activity. Common usage defines a recession as a fall in real GDP for two successive quarters. As output falls, so do employment and households' incomes. Profits drop, and some firms encounter financial difficulties. Investments that looked profitable with the expectation of continually rising income now appear unprofitable. It may not even be worth replacing capital goods as they wear out because unused capacity is increasing steadily. In historical discussions, a recession that is deep and long-lasting is often called a *depression,* such as the Great Depression in the early 1930s during which the level of economic activity fell so much that output fell by 30 percent and the unemployment rate increased to 20 percent!

These terms are non-technical but descriptive. The entire falling half of the cycle is often called a *slump,* and the entire rising half is often called a *boom.*

recession A downturn in the level of economic activity. Often defined precisely as two consecutive quarters in which real GDP falls.

potential output (Y*) The real GDP that the economy would produce if its productive resources were employed at their normal levels of utilization. Also called *potential GDP.*

Potential Output and the Output Gap   National output represents what the economy *actually* produces. An important related concept is *potential* output, which measures what the economy would produce if all resources—land, labour, and productive capacity—were employed at their normal levels of utilization. This concept is usually referred to as **potential output** (but is sometimes called *full-employment output*).[1] Its symbol, Y*, distinguishes it from actual output, indicated by Y.

1 The words *real* and *actual* have similar meanings in everyday usage. When national income is measured, however, their meanings are different. *Real* national income is distinguished from *nominal* national income; and *actual* national income is distinguished from *potential* national income. The latter both refer to *real* measures of national income.

The **output gap** measures the difference between potential output and actual output, and is computed as $Y - Y^*$. When actual output is less than potential output $(Y < Y^*)$, the gap measures the market value of goods and services that are not produced because the economy's resources are not fully employed. When Y is less than Y^*, the output gap is called a **recessionary gap**. When actual output exceeds potential output $(Y > Y^*)$, the gap measures the market value of production in excess of what the economy can produce on a sustained basis. Y can exceed Y^* because the latter is defined for a *normal* rate of utilization of factors of production, and there are many ways in which these normal rates can be exceeded temporarily. Labour may work longer hours than normal or factories may operate an extra shift. When Y exceeds Y^* there is often upward pressure on prices, and thus we say the output gap is an **inflationary gap**.

Figure 19-2 shows the path of potential GDP since 1971. The upward trend reflects the growth in the productive capacity of the Canadian economy over this period, caused by increases in the labour force, capital stock, and the level of technological knowledge. The figure also shows actual GDP (reproduced from Figure 19-1), which has kept approximately in step with potential GDP. The distance between the two, which is the output gap, is plotted in part (ii) of Figure 19-2. Fluctuations in economic activity are apparent from fluctuations in the size of the output gap.

output gap Actual national income minus potential national income, $Y - Y^*$.

recessionary gap A situation in which actual output is less than potential output, $Y < Y^*$.

inflationary gap A situation in which actual output exceeds potential output, $Y > Y^*$.

Practise with Study Guide Chapter 19, Exercise 2.

FIGURE 19-2 Potential GDP and the Output Gap, 1971–2005

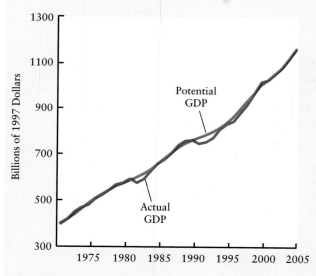

(i) Potential and actual GDP

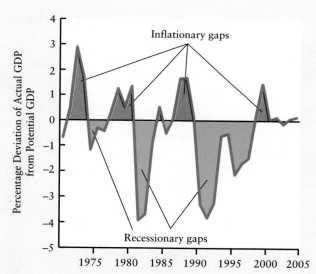

(ii) The output gap

Potential and actual GDP both display an upward trend. The output gap measures the difference between an economy's potential output and its actual output; the gap is expressed here as a percentage of potential output. Since 1971, potential and actual GDP have increased by almost three times. The output gap in part (ii) shows clear fluctuations. Shaded areas show inflationary and recessionary gaps.

(*Source:* Actual GDP: Statistics Canada, CANSIM database, Series V3862685–380-0017 Gross Domestic Product. Output gap: www.bankofcanada.ca. Potential output is based on authors' calculations.)

Why National Income Matters   National income is an important measure of economic performance. Short-run movements in the business cycle receive the most attention in politics and in the press, but most economists agree that long-term growth—as reflected by the growth of *potential GDP*—is in many ways the more important of the two.

Recessions are associated with unemployment and lost output. When actual GDP is below potential GDP, economic waste and human suffering result from the failure to use the economy's resources at their normal intensity of use. Booms, although associated with high employment and high output, can bring problems of their own. When actual GDP exceeds potential GDP, inflationary pressure usually ensues, causing concern for any government that is committed to keeping the inflation rate low.

The long-run trend in real per capita national income is an important determinant of improvements in a society's overall standard of living. When income per person grows, each generation can expect, on average, to be better off than preceding ones. For example, if real per capita income grows at the relatively modest rate of 1.5 percent per year, the average person's lifetime income will be about *twice* that of his or her grandparents.

Although economic growth makes people materially better off *on average*, it does not necessarily make *every* individual better off—the benefits of growth do not typically fall evenly on all members of the population. For example, if growth involves significant changes in the structure of the economy, such as a shift away from agriculture and toward manufacturing (as happened in the first part of this century), then these changes will reduce some people's material living standards for extended periods of time.

Employment, Unemployment, and the Labour Force

Practise with Study Guide Chapter 19, Exercise 3.

employment The number of persons 15 years of age and older who have jobs.

unemployment The number of persons 15 years of age and older who are not employed and are actively searching for a job.

labour force The number of persons employed plus the number of persons unemployed.

unemployment rate Unemployment expressed as a percentage of the labour force, denoted *U*.

National income and employment are closely related. If more is to be produced, either more workers must be used in production, or existing workers must produce more. The first change means a rise in employment; the second means a rise in output per person employed, which, as we have seen, is a rise in productivity. In the short run, changes in productivity tend to be very small; most short-run changes in output are accomplished by changes in employment. Over the long run, however, changes in both productivity and employment are significant.

Employment denotes the number of adult workers (defined in Canada as workers aged 15 and over) who have jobs. **Unemployment** denotes the number of adult workers who are not employed but who are actively searching for a job. The **labour force** is the total number of people who are either employed or unemployed. The **unemployment rate** is the number of unemployed people expressed as a fraction of the labour force.

$$\text{Unemployment rate} = \frac{\text{Number of people unemployed}}{\text{Number of people in the labour force}} \times 100 \text{ percent}$$

The level of unemployment in Canada is estimated from the Labour Force Survey conducted each month by Statistics Canada. Persons who are currently without a job but who say they have searched actively for one during the sample period are recorded as unemployed.

Frictional, Structural, and Cyclical Unemployment   When the economy is at potential GDP, economists say there is *full employment*. But for two reasons there will still be some unemployment even when the economy is at potential GDP.

First, there is a constant turnover of individuals in given jobs and a constant change in job opportunities. New people enter the workforce; some people quit their jobs; others are fired. It may take some time for these people to find jobs. So at any point in time, there is unemployment due to the normal turnover of labour. Such unemployment is called *frictional unemployment*.

Second, because the economy is constantly changing and adapting, at any moment there will always be some mismatch between the characteristics of the labour force and the characteristics of the available jobs. The mismatch may occur, for example, because labour does not currently have the skills that are in demand or because labour is not in the part of the country where the demand is located. This is a mismatch between the *structure* of the supplies of labour and the *structure* of the demands for labour. Such unemployment is called *structural unemployment*.

Even when the economy is said to be at full employment, some unemployment exists due to natural turnover in the labour market and to mismatch between jobs and workers.

Full employment is said to occur when the *only* unemployment is frictional and structural. At full employment, factors of production are being used at their normal intensity, and the economy is at potential GDP. When GDP is below potential GDP, unemployment rises above its full-employment level; when GDP is above potential GDP, unemployment falls below its full-employment level. Unemployment that is neither structural nor frictional is called *cyclical unemployment* because it changes with the ebb and flow of the business cycle.

Unemployment also has *seasonal* fluctuations. For example, workers employed in the fishing industry are often unemployed during the winter and ski instructors may be unemployed in the summer. Because these seasonal fluctuations are relatively regular and therefore easy to predict, Statistics Canada *seasonally adjusts* the unemployment statistics to remove these fluctuations, thus revealing more clearly the cyclical and trend movements in the data. For example, suppose that, on average, the Canadian unemployment rate increases by 0.3 percentage points in December. Statistics Canada would then adjust the December unemployment rate so that it shows an increase only if the increase in the *unadjusted* rate exceeds 0.3 percentage points. In this way, the (seasonally adjusted) December unemployment rate is reported to increase only if unemployment rises by more than its normal seasonal increase. All of the unemployment data shown in this book are seasonally adjusted.

Employment and Unemployment: Recent History

Figure 19-3 shows the trends in the labour force, employment, and unemployment since 1960. Despite booms and slumps, employment has grown roughly in line with the growth in the labour force. Although the long-term trend dominates the employment data, the figure also shows that the short-term fluctuations in the unemployment rate have been substantial. The unemployment rate has been as low as 3.4 percent in 1966 and as high as 12 percent in 1982. By 2006, after the economy had been growing steadily for several years, the unemployment rate was 6.3 percent, the lowest it had been in 30 years. Part (ii) of Figure 19-3 also shows that there has been a slight upward trend in the unemployment rate over the past 40 years. In Chapter 31 we discuss how some structural changes in the economy can help explain this trend.

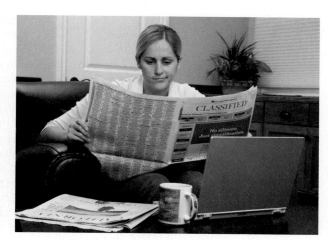

Economists make the distinction between frictional, structural, and cyclical unemployment. But this distinction matters little to the individual who has difficulty finding an appropriate job.

FIGURE 19-3   Labour Force, Employment, and Unemployment, 1960–2006

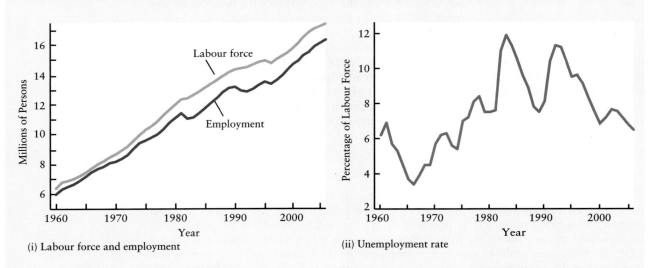

(i) Labour force and employment

(ii) Unemployment rate

The labour force and employment have grown since 1960 with only a few interruptions. The unemployment rate responds to the cyclical behaviour of the economy. The labour force and the level of employment in Canada have both almost tripled since 1960. Booms are associated with a low unemployment rate and slumps with a high unemployment rate.

(*Source:* These data are from Statistics Canada's CANSIM database. Labour force: Series V2091051. Employment: Series V2091072. Unemployment rate: Series V2091177. Current labour-force statistics are available on Statistics Canada's website at www.statcan.ca by searching for "unemployment." Reprinted with permission of Statistics Canada.)

Why Unemployment Matters The social significance of unemployment is enormous because it involves economic waste and human suffering. Human effort is the least durable of economic commodities. If a fully employed economy has 17 million people who are willing to work, their services must either be used this year or wasted. When only 16 million people are actually employed, one year's potential output of one million workers is lost forever. In an economy in which there is not enough output to meet everyone's needs, such a waste of potential output is cause for concern.

The loss of income associated with unemployment is clearly harmful to individuals. In some cases, the loss of income pushes people into poverty. But this lost income does not capture the full cost of unemployment. A person's spirit can be broken by a long period of desiring work but being unable to find it. Research has shown that crime, mental illness, and general social unrest tend to be associated with long-term unemployment.

In the not-so-distant past, only personal savings, private charity, or help from friends and relatives stood between the unemployed and starvation. Today, welfare and employment insurance have created a safety net, particularly when unemployment is for short periods, as is most often the case in Canada. However, when an economic slump lasts long enough, as in the early 1980s and the early 1990s, some unfortunate people exhaust their employment insurance and lose part of that safety net.

Productivity

Figure 19-1 shows that Canadian real GDP has increased relatively steadily for many years, reflecting steady growth in the country's productive capacity. This long-run growth has had three general sources. First, as shown in Figure 19-3, the level of employment has increased significantly. Rising employment generally results from a rising population, but at times is also explained by an increase in the proportion of the population that chooses to participate in the labour force. Second, Canada's stock of physical capital—the buildings, factories, and machines used to produce output—has increased more or less steadily over time. Third, productivity in Canada has increased in almost every year since 1960.

Productivity is a measure of the amount of output that the economy produces per unit of input. Since there are many inputs to production—land, labour, and capital—we can have several different measures of productivity. The measure most commonly used is **labour productivity**, which is the amount of real GDP produced per unit of labour employed. (The amount of labour employed can be measured either as the number of employed workers or by the number of hours worked.)

Productivity: Recent History

Figure 19-4 shows two measures of Canadian labour productivity since 1976. The first is the amount of real GDP per employed worker (expressed in thousands of 1997 dollars). In 2005, real GDP per employed worker was $72 300. The second measure shows the amount of real GDP per *hour worked* (expressed in 1997 dollars). In 2001, the most recent year the data on hours are available, real GDP per hour worked was $38.95.

The second measure is more accurate because the average number of hours worked per employed worker changes over time. In addition to fluctuating over the business cycle, it has shown a long-term decline, from just over 1850 hours per year in 1976 to just under 1780 hours per year in 2001. The second measure of productivity takes account of these changes in hours worked, whereas the first measure does not.

One pattern is immediately apparent for both measures of productivity. There has been a significant increase in labour productivity over the past three decades. Real GDP per employed worker increased by 39.1 percent from 1976 to 2005, an annual average growth rate of 1.1 percent. Real GDP per hour worked increased by 39.0 percent over the slightly shorter period ending in 2001, an annual average growth rate of 1.3 percent.

Why Productivity Matters

Productivity growth is the single largest cause of rising material living standards over long periods of time. Over periods of a few years, changes in average real incomes may have more to do with the ebb and flow of the business cycle than with changes in productivity; increases in employment during an economic recovery and

Practise with Study Guide Chapter 19, Short-Answer Question 3 and Exercise 4.

labour productivity The level of real GDP divided by the level of employment (or total hours worked).

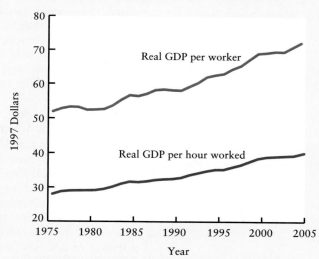

FIGURE 19-4   Canadian Labour Productivity, 1976–2005

Rising labour productivity is an important contributor to rising material living standards. The figure shows two measures of labour productivity: real GDP per employed worker, and real GDP per hour worked. The first is expressed in thousands of 1997 dollars per worker, and has increased at an average annual rate of 1.1 percent. The second is expressed in 1997 dollars per hour, and has grown at the annual rate of 1.3 percent.

(*Source:* All data are from Statistics Canada's CANSIM database. Real GDP: Series V3862685. Average hours worked per worker: Series V716596. Employment: annual averages of Series V2091072. Reprinted with permission of Statistics Canada.)

reductions in employment during recessions explain much of the short-run movements in average real incomes. As is clear from Figure 19-1, however, these short-run fluctuations are dwarfed over many years by the steady upward trend in real GDP—an upward trend that comes in large part from rising productivity.

Why is the real income for an average Canadian this year so much greater than it was for the average Canadian 50 or 100 years ago? Most of the answer lies in the fact that the Canadian worker today is vastly more productive than was his or her counterpart in the distant past. This greater productivity comes partly from the better physical capital with which Canadians now work, and partly from their greater skills. The higher productivity for today's workers explains why their *real wages* (the purchasing power of their earnings) are so much higher than for workers in the past.

The close connection between productivity growth and rising material living standards explains the importance that is now placed on understanding the determinants of productivity growth. It is a very active area of economic research, but there are still many unanswered questions. In Chapter 26 we address the process of long-run growth in real GDP and explore the determinants of productivity growth.

Inflation and the Price Level

Practise with Study Guide Chapter 19, Exercise 5.

price level The average level of all prices in the economy, expressed as an index number.

inflation A rise in the average level of all prices (the price level).

Consumer Price Index (CPI) An index of the average prices of goods and services commonly bought by households.

To compute the rate of inflation from any point in your lifetime to today, check out the "inflation calculator" at the Bank of Canada's website: **www.bankofcanada.ca/ english/inflation_calc.htm.**

Inflation means that prices of goods and services are going up, *on average*. If you are a typical reader of this book, inflation has not been very noticeable during your lifetime. When your parents were your age, however, high inflation was a major economic problem. (Some countries have had their economies almost ruined by very high inflation, called *hyperinflation*. We will say more about this in Chapter 27.)

For studying inflation, there are two related but different concepts that are sometimes confused, and it is important to get them straight. The first is the **price level**, which refers to the average level of all prices in the economy and is given by the symbol *P*. The second is the rate of **inflation**, which is the rate at which the price level is rising.

To measure the price level, the economic statisticians at Statistics Canada construct a *price index*, which averages the prices of various commodities according to how important they are. The best-known price index in Canada is the **Consumer Price Index (CPI)**, which measures the average price of the goods and services that are bought by the typical Canadian household. *Applying Economic Concepts 19-2* shows how a price index such as the CPI is constructed.

As we saw in Chapter 2, a price index is a pure number—it does not have any units. Yet as we all know, prices in Canada are expressed in dollars. When we construct a price index, the units (dollars) are eliminated because the price index shows the price of a basket of goods at some specific time *relative to the price of the same basket of goods in some base period*. Currently, the base year for Statistics Canada's calculation of the CPI is 1992, which means that the price of the basket of goods is set to be 100 in 1992. If the CPI in 2006 is computed to be 130, the meaning is that the price of the basket of goods is 30 percent higher in 2006 than in 1992.

Since the price level is measured with an index number, its value at any specific time only has meaning when it is compared to its value at some other time.

By allowing us to compare the general price level at different times, a price index such as the CPI also allows us to measure the rate of inflation. For example, the value of the CPI in March 2006 was 129.3 and in March 2005 was 126.5. The *rate of*

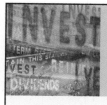

APPLYING ECONOMIC CONCEPTS 19-2

How the CPI Is Constructed

Although the details are somewhat more complicated, the basic idea behind the Consumer Price Index is straightforward, as is illustrated by the following hypothetical example.

Suppose we wish to discover what has happened to the overall cost of living for typical university students. A survey of student behaviour in 1997 shows that the average university student consumed only three goods—pizza, coffee, and photocopying—and spent a total of $200 a month on these items, as shown in Table 1.

TABLE 1	Expenditure Behaviour in 1997		
Product	Price	Quantity per Month	Expenditure per Month
Photocopies	$0.10 per sheet	140 sheets	$14.00
Pizza	8.00 per pizza	15 pizzas	120.00
Coffee	0.75 per cup	88 cups	66.00
Total expenditure			$200.00

By 2007, the price of photocopying has fallen to 5 cents per copy, the price of pizza has increased to $9.00, and the price of coffee has increased to $1.00. What has happened to the cost of living over this 10-year period? In order to find out, we calculate the cost of purchasing the 1997 bundle of goods at the prices that prevailed in 2007, as shown in Table 2.

The total expenditure required to purchase the bundle of goods that cost $200.00 in 1997 has risen to $230.00. The increase in required expenditure is $30.00, which is a 15-percent increase over the original $200.00.

If we define 1997 as the *base year* for the "student price index" and assign an index value of 100 to the cost of the average student's expenditure in that year, the value of the index in 2007 is 115. Thus, goods and

TABLE 2	1997 Expenditure Behaviour at 2007 Prices		
Product	Price	Quantity per Month	Expenditure per Month
Photocopies	$0.05 per sheet	140 sheets	$7.00
Pizza	9.00 per pizza	15 pizzas	135.00
Coffee	1.00 per cup	88 cups	88.00
Total expenditure			$230.00

services that cost $100.00 in the base year cost $115.00 in 2007, exactly what is implied by Table 2.

The Consumer Price Index, as constructed by Statistics Canada, is built on exactly the same principles as the preceding example. In the case of the CPI, many thousands of consumers are surveyed, and the prices of thousands of products are monitored, but the basic method is the same:

1. Survey the consumption behaviour of consumers.
2. Calculate the cost of the goods and services purchased by the average consumer in the year in which the original survey was done. Define this as the base period of the index.
3. Calculate the cost of purchasing the same bundle of goods and services in other years.
4. Divide the result of Step 3 (in each year) by the result of Step 2, and multiply by 100. The result is the value of the CPI for each year.

The CPI is not a perfect measure of the cost of living because it does not automatically account for ongoing quality improvements or for changes in consumers' expenditure patterns. Changes of this type require the underlying survey of consumer expenditure to be updated from time to time to make sure that the expenditure patterns in the survey approximately match consumers' actual expenditure patterns.

inflation during that one-year period, expressed in percentage terms, is equal to the change in the price level divided by the initial price level, times 100:

$$\text{Rate of inflation} = \frac{129.3 - 126.5}{126.5} \times 100 \text{ percent}$$

$$= 2.21 \text{ percent}$$

Inflation: Recent History   The rate of inflation in Canada is currently around 2 percent per year, and has been at that level for over a decade. But it has not always been so. There was a time—not so long ago—when inflation in Canada was both high and unpredictable from year to year.

Figure 19-5 shows the CPI and the inflation rate (measured by the annual rate of change in the CPI) from 1960 to 2006. What can we learn from this figure? First, we learn that the price level has not fallen at all since 1960 (in fact, the last time it fell was in 1953, and even then it fell only briefly). The cumulative effect of this sequence of repeated increases in the price level is quite dramatic: By 2006, the price level was over six times higher than it was in 1960. In other words, you now pay over $6 for what cost $1 in 1960. The second thing we learn is that, although the price level appears in the figure to be smoothly increasing, the rate of inflation is actually quite volatile. The increases in the inflation rate into double-digit levels in 1974 and 1979 were associated with major increases in the world prices of oil and foodstuffs and with loose monetary policy. The declines in inflation that followed were delayed responses to major recessions.

Why Inflation Matters   Money is the universal yardstick in our economy. This does not mean that we care only about money—it means simply that we measure *economic values* in terms of money, and we use money to conduct our economic affairs. Things as diverse as wages, bank balances, the value of a house, and a university's endowment are all stated in terms of money. We value money, however, not for itself but for what we can purchase with it. The terms **purchasing power of money** and *real value of money* refer to the amount of goods and services that can be purchased with a given amount of money. The purchasing power of money is negatively related to the price level. For example, if the price level doubles, a dollar will buy only half as much, whereas if the price level halves, a dollar will buy twice as much. Inflation reduces the real value of anything whose price is *fixed* in money terms. Thus, the real value of a money wage, a savings account, or the balance that is owed on a student loan is reduced by inflation.

Inflation reduces the purchasing power of money. It also reduces the real value of any sum fixed in nominal terms.

When analyzing the effects of inflation, economists usually make the distinction between *anticipated* and *unanticipated* inflation. If households and firms fully anticipate inflation over the coming year, they will be able to adjust many nominal prices and wages so as to maintain their real values. In this case, inflation will have fewer real effects on the economy than if it comes unexpectedly. For example, if workers and firms expect 5-percent inflation over the coming year, they can agree to increase nominal wages by 5 percent, thus leaving wages constant in real terms.

Unanticipated inflation, on the other hand, generally leads to changes in the real value of prices and wages. Suppose workers and firms expect 5-percent inflation and they increase nominal wages accordingly. If actual inflation ends up being 10 percent, real wages will be reduced and the quantities of labour demanded by firms and supplied by workers will therefore be altered. As a result, the economy's allocation of resources will be affected.

purchasing power of money The amount of goods and services that can be purchased with a unit of money.

interest The payment for the use of borrowed money.

interest rate The price paid per dollar borrowed per period of time, expressed either as a proportion (e.g., 0.06) or as a percentage (e.g., 6 percent).

Most economists agree that anticipated inflation has a smaller effect on the economy than unanticipated inflation.

In reality, inflation is rarely fully anticipated or fully unanticipated. Usually there is some inflation that is expected but also some that comes as a surprise. As a result, some adjustments in wages and prices get made by firms and workers and consumers, but not all the adjustments that would be required to leave the economy's allocation of resources unaffected. We will see later, in our discussions of monetary policy and inflation in Chapters 29 and 30, how the distinction between anticipated and unanticipated inflation helps us to understand the cost of *reducing* inflation.

Interest Rates

If a bank lends you money, it will charge you **interest** for the privilege of borrowing the money. If, for example, you borrow $1000 today, repayable in one year's time, you may also be asked to pay $6.67 per month in interest. This makes $80 in interest over the year, which can be expressed as an interest rate of 8 percent per annum.

The **interest rate** is the price that is paid to borrow money for a stated period of time. It is expressed as a percentage amount per year per dollar borrowed. For example, an interest rate of 8 percent per year means that the borrower must pay 8 cents per year for every dollar that is borrowed.

There are many interest rates. A bank will lend money to an industrial customer at a lower rate than it will lend money to you—there is a lower risk of not being repaid. The rate charged on a loan that is not to be repaid for a long time will usually differ from the rate on a loan that is to be repaid quickly.

When economists speak of "the" interest rate, they mean a rate that is typical of all the various interest rates in the economy. Dealing with only one interest rate suppresses much interesting detail. However, because interest rates usually rise and fall together, at least for major changes, following the movement of one rate allows us to consider changes in the general level of interest rates. The *prime interest rate,* the rate that banks charge to their best business customers, is noteworthy

FIGURE 19-5 The Price Level and the Inflation Rate, 1960–2006

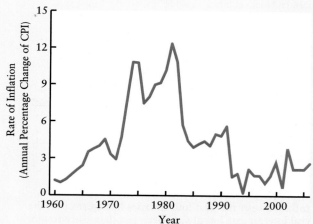

The rate of inflation measures the annual rate of increase in the price level. The trend in the price level has been upward over the past half-century. The rate of inflation has varied from almost 0 to over 12 percent since 1960.

(*Source:* These data are available on the Bank of Canada's website: www.bankofcanada.ca. The price level used is the seasonally adjusted consumer price index, PCPISA. Current data are also available from Statistics Canada, www.statcan.ca. Search for "consumer price index.")

Practise with Study Guide Chapter 19, Exercise 6.

nominal interest rate The price paid per dollar borrowed per period of time.

real interest rate The nominal rate of interest adjusted for the change in the purchasing power of money. Equal to the nominal interest rate minus the rate of inflation.

because when the prime rate changes, most other rates change in the same direction. Another high-profile interest rate is the *bank rate*, the interest rate that the Bank of Canada (Canada's central bank) charges on short-term loans to commercial banks. The interest rate that the Canadian government pays on its short-term borrowing is also a rate that garners some attention.

Interest Rates and Inflation How does inflation affect interest rates? To begin developing an answer, imagine that your friend lends you $100 and that the loan is repayable in one year. The amount that you pay her for making this loan, measured in money terms, is determined by the **nominal interest rate**. If you pay her $108 in one year's time, $100 will be repayment of the amount of the loan (which is called the *principal*) and $8 will be payment of the interest. In this case, the nominal interest rate is 8 percent.

How much purchasing power has your friend gained or lost by making this loan? The answer depends on what happens to the price level during the year. The more the price level rises, the worse off your friend will be and the better the transaction will be for you. This result occurs because the more the price level rises, the less valuable are the dollars that you use to repay the loan. The **real interest rate** measures the return on a loan in terms of purchasing power.

If the price level remains constant over the year, the real rate of interest that your friend earns would also be 8 percent, because she can buy 8 percent more goods and services with the $108 that you repay her than with the $100 that she lent you. However, if the price level rises by 8 percent, the real rate of interest would be zero because the $108 that you repay her buys the same quantity of goods as the $100 that she originally gave up. If she is unlucky enough to lend money at 8 percent in a year in which prices rise by 10 percent, the real rate of interest that she earns is −2 percent. The repayment of $108 will purchase 2 percent fewer goods and services than the original loan of $100.

The burden of borrowing depends on the real, not the nominal, rate of interest.

For example, a nominal interest rate of 8 percent combined with a 2-percent rate of inflation is a much greater real burden on borrowers than a nominal rate of 16 percent combined with a 14-percent rate of inflation. Figure 19-6 shows the nominal and real interest rates paid on short-term government borrowing since 1960.

Why Interest Rates Matter Changes in real interest rates affect the standard of living of savers and borrowers. Many retirees, for example, rely on interest earnings from their stock of accumulated assets to provide much of their household income, and thus benefit when real interest rates rise. In contrast, borrowers are made better off with low

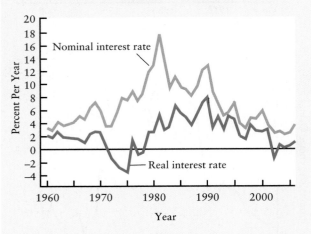

FIGURE 19-6   Real and Nominal Interest Rates, 1960–2006

Inflation over the past four decades has meant that the real interest rate has always been less than the nominal interest rate. The data for the nominal interest rate show the average rate on three-month Treasury bills in each year since 1960. The real interest rate is calculated as the nominal interest rate minus the actual rate of inflation over the same period. Through the early 1970s, the real interest rate was negative, indicating that the inflation rate exceeded the nominal interest rate. The 1980s saw real interest rates rise as high as 8 percent. Since then, real rates have declined again to levels that are closer to the long-term historical average.

(*Source:* Nominal interest rate: 3-month treasury bill rate, Statistics Canada, CANSIM database, Series V122541. Real interest rate is based on authors' calculation of CPI inflation, using Series PCPISA from the Bank of Canada.)

real interest rates. This point was dramatically illustrated during the 1970s when homeowners who had long-term fixed-rate mortgages benefited tremendously from several years of unanticipated inflation, which resulted in negative real interest rates.

Interest rates also matter for the economy as a whole. As we will see in Chapter 21, real interest rates are an important determinant of the level of investment by firms. Changes in real interest rates lead to changes in the cost of borrowing and thus to changes in firms' investment plans. Such changes in the level of desired investment have important consequences for the level of economic activity. We will see in Chapters 28 and 29 how the Bank of Canada influences interest rates as part of its objective of controlling inflation.

The International Economy

Two important variables that reflect the importance of the global economy to Canada are the *exchange rate* and *net exports*.

The Exchange Rate   If you are going on a holiday to France, you will need euros to pay for your purchases. Many of the larger banks, as well as any foreign-exchange office, will make the necessary exchange of currencies for you; they will sell you euros in return for your Canadian dollars. If you get 0.7 euros for each dollar that you give up, the two currencies are trading at a rate of 1 dollar = 0.7 euros or, expressed another way, 1 euro = 1.43 dollars.

As our example shows, the exchange rate can be defined either as dollars per euro or euros per dollar. In this book we adopt the convention of defining the **exchange rate** between the Canadian dollar and any foreign currency as the number of Canadian dollars required to purchase one unit of foreign currency. For example, on April 26, 2006, 1 Canadian dollar was worth 71.1 euro cents; expressed the other way, 1 euro was worth 1.41 Canadian dollars. The exchange rate on that day was therefore equal to 1.41, telling us that it took $1.41 (Canadian) to purchase 1 euro.

The exchange rate is the number of Canadian dollars required to purchase one unit of foreign currency.[2]

The term **foreign exchange** refers to foreign currencies or claims on foreign currencies, such as bank deposits, cheques, and promissory notes, that are payable in foreign money. The **foreign-exchange market** is the market where foreign exchange is traded—at a price expressed by the exchange rate.

Depreciation and Appreciation   A rise in the exchange rate means that it takes *more* Canadian dollars to purchase one unit of foreign currency—this is referred to as a **depreciation** of the Canadian dollar. Conversely, a fall in the exchange rate means that it takes *fewer* Canadian dollars to purchase one unit of foreign currency—this is referred to as an **appreciation** of the dollar.

Figure 19-7 shows the path of the Canadian–U.S. exchange rate since 1970. Since over 80 percent of Canada's trade is with the United States, this is the exchange rate

Practise with Study Guide Chapter 19, Exercise 7.

exchange rate The number of units of domestic currency required to purchase one unit of foreign currency.

foreign exchange Foreign currencies that are traded on the foreign-exchange market.

foreign-exchange market The market where different national currencies are traded.

depreciation A rise in the exchange rate—it takes more units of domestic currency to purchase one unit of foreign currency.

appreciation A fall in the exchange rate—it takes fewer units of domestic currency to purchase one unit of foreign currency.

---

2 Some economists use a reverse definition of the exchange rate—the number of units of foreign currency that can be purchased by one Canadian dollar. It is up to the student, then, to examine carefully the definition that is being used by a particular writer or speaker. In this book the exchange rate is defined as the number of Canadian dollars required to purchase one unit of foreign currency because this measure emphasizes that foreign currency, like any other good or service, has a price in terms of Canadian dollars. In this case, the price has a special name—the exchange rate.

FIGURE 19-7 Canadian–U.S. Dollar Exchange Rate, 1970–2006

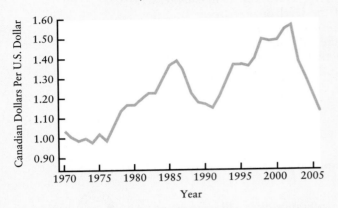

The Canadian–U.S. exchange rate has been quite volatile over the past 35 years. The Canadian-dollar price of one U.S. dollar increased from just over $1 in the early 1970s to over $1.55 in 2003 and then fell to about $1.10 in 2006.

(*Source:* Annual average of monthly data, Statistics Canada, CANSIM database, Series V37432, foreign exchange rates in Canadian dollars. Reprinted with permission of Statistics Canada.)

most often discussed and analyzed in Canada. In countries with trade more evenly spread across several trading partners, more attention is paid to what is called a *trade-weighted exchange rate*—this is a weighted-average exchange rate between the home country and its trading partners, where the weights reflect each partner's share in the home country's total trade. In Canada, the path of such a trade-weighted exchange rate is virtually identical to the Canadian–U.S. exchange rate shown in Figure 19-7, reflecting the very large proportion of total Canadian trade with the United States.

As we will see in later chapters, both domestic policy and external events have important effects on the Canadian exchange rate. For example, most economists believe that the appreciation of the Canadian dollar between 1986 and 1992 was caused in part by the Bank of Canada's efforts to reduce the rate of inflation. The Bank's policy was controversial at the time, not least because of the effect it had on the exchange rate and the many export-oriented firms that were harmed by Canada's strong dollar. We examine the link between monetary policy and exchange rates in detail in Chapters 28 and 29.

The depreciation of the Canadian dollar in the late 1990s is thought by most economists to have resulted from a nearly 30-percent decline in the world prices of commodities, many of which are important Canadian exports. The appreciation of the Canadian dollar during the 2002–2006 period was associated with sharp increases in commodity prices. In both cases, the commodity prices were being driven by changes in global economic growth, illustrating the important point that events in faraway lands can have dramatic effects on the Canadian exchange rate. We examine the link between world commodity prices and the Canadian exchange rate in Chapter 35.

Exports and Imports Canada has long been a trading nation, buying many goods and services from other countries—Canada's *imports*—and also selling many goods and services to other countries—Canada's *exports*. Figure 19-8 shows the dollar value of Canada's exports, imports, and *net exports* since 1970. Net exports is the difference between exports and imports and is often called the *trade balance*.

Canadian exports and imports have increased fairly closely in step with each other over the past 35 years. The trade balance has therefore fluctuated mildly over the years, but has stayed relatively small, especially when viewed as a proportion of total GDP.

Also apparent in Figure 19-8 is that Canadian trade flows (both imports and exports) began to grow more quickly after 1990. The increased importance of international trade is largely due to the Canada–U.S. Free Trade Agreement, which began in 1989, and to the North American Free Trade Agreement (which added Mexico), which began in 1994.

19.2 GROWTH VERSUS FLUCTUATIONS

This chapter has provided a quick tour through macroeconomics, and has introduced you to many important macroeconomic issues. If you take a few moments to flip again through the figures in this chapter, you will notice that most of the macroeconomic variables that we discussed are characterized by *long-run trends* and *short-run fluctuations*.

Figure 19-1, which shows the path of real GDP, provides an excellent example of both characteristics. The figure shows that real GDP has increased by over four times since 1962—this is substantial *economic growth*. The figure also shows considerable, and sometimes dramatic, year-to-year *fluctuations* in the growth rate of GDP.

An important theme in this book is that a full understanding of macroeconomics requires an understanding of both long-run growth and short-run fluctuations. As we proceed through this book, we will see that these two characteristics of modern economies have different sources and explanations. And broad macroeconomic policies have roles to play in both.

Long-Term Economic Growth

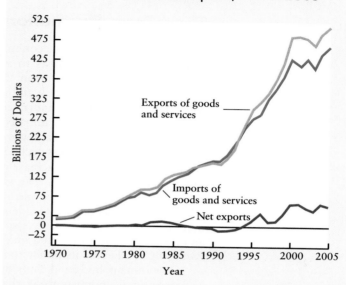

FIGURE 19-8   Canadian Imports, Exports, and Net Exports, 1970–2005

Though imports and exports have increased dramatically over the past 35 years, the trade balance has remained roughly in balance. The nominal values of imports and exports rose steadily over the past few decades, due to both price increases and quantity increases. The growth of trade increased sharply after the early 1990s. The trade balance—net exports—is usually close to zero.

(*Source:* Statistics Canada, CANSIM database. Exports: Series V499540. Imports: Series V499557. Reprinted with permission of Statistics Canada.)

Both total output and output per person have risen for many decades in most industrial countries. These long-term trends have meant rising average living standards. Although long-term growth gets less play on the evening news than current economic developments, it has considerably more importance for a society's living standards from decade to decade and from generation to generation.

There is considerable debate regarding the ability of government policy to influence the economy's long-run rate of growth. Most economists believe that a policy designed to keep inflation low and stable will contribute to the economy's growth. Some, however, believe there are dangers from having inflation too low—that a moderate inflation rate is more conducive to growth than a very low inflation rate.

Many economists also believe that when governments spend less than they raise in tax revenue—and thus have a budget surplus—the reduced need for borrowing drives down interest rates and stimulates investment by the private sector. Such increases in investment imply a higher stock of physical capital available for future production, and thus an increase in economic growth. Do government budget surpluses increase future growth? Or do budget surpluses have no effect

International trade is very important to the Canadian economy. Exports and imports of goods and services each represent over 40 percent of Canada's GDP.

at all on the economy's future ability to produce? We address this important debate in Chapter 32.

Short-Term Fluctuations

Short-run fluctuations in economic activity, like the ones shown in part (ii) of Figure 19-1, lead economists to wonder about the causes of *business cycles*. What caused the Great Depression in the 1930s, when almost one-fifth of the Canadian labour force was out of work and massive unemployment plagued all major industrial countries? Why did the Canadian economy begin a significant recession in 1990–1991, from which recovery was initially very gradual? What explains why, by 2006, the Canadian unemployment rate was lower than it had been in over 30 years?

Understanding business cycles requires an understanding of monetary policy. Most economists agree that the increase in inflation in the 1970s and early 1980s was related to monetary policy, though they also agree that other events were partly responsible. When the Bank of Canada implemented a policy in the early 1990s designed to reduce inflation, was it merely a coincidence that a significant recession followed? Most economists think not, though they also think that the slowdown in the U.S. economy was an important contributor to Canada's recession. Chapters 28 and 29 focus on how the Bank of Canada uses its policy to influence the level of economic activity.

Government budget deficits and surpluses also enter the discussion of business cycles. Some economists think that, in recessionary years, the government ought to increase spending (and reduce taxes) in an effort to stimulate economic activity. Similarly, they believe that taxes should be raised to slow down a booming economy. Indeed, several government policies, from income taxation to unemployment insurance, are designed to mitigate the short-term fluctuations in national income. Other economists believe that the government cannot successfully "fine-tune" the economy by spending and taxing because our knowledge of how the economy works is imperfect and because such policies tend to be imprecise. We address these issues in Chapters 22 to 24.

What Lies Ahead?

There is much work to be done before any of these interesting policy debates can be thoroughly understood. Like firms that invest now to increase their production in the future, the next few chapters of this book will be an investment for you—an investment in understanding basic macro theory. The payoff will come when you are able to use a coherent model of the economy to analyze and debate some of the key macro issues of the day.

We begin in Chapter 20 by discussing the measurement of GDP. National income accounting is not exciting but is essential to a complete understanding of the chapters that follow. We then proceed to build a simple model of the economy to highlight some key macroeconomic relationships. As we proceed through the book, we modify the model, step by step, making it ever more complete and realistic. With each step we take, more of today's controversial policy issues come within the grasp of our understanding. We hope that by the time you get to the end of the book, you will have developed some of the thrill for analyzing macroeconomic issues that we feel. Good luck, and enjoy the journey!

SUMMARY

19.1 KEY MACROECONOMIC VARIABLES

LO ❶

- The value of the total production of goods and services in a nation is called its national product. Because production of output generates income in the form of claims on that output, the total is also referred to as national income. One of the most commonly used measures of national income is gross domestic product (GDP).
- Potential output is the level of output produced when factors of production are employed at their normal intensity of use. The output gap is the difference between actual and potential output.
- The unemployment rate is the percentage of the labour force not employed and actively searching for a job. The labour force and employment have both grown steadily for the past half-century. The unemployment rate fluctuates considerably from year to year. Unemployment imposes serious costs on the economy in the form of economic waste and human suffering.
- Labour productivity is measured as real GDP per employed worker. It is an important determinant of material living standards.

- The price level is measured by a price index, which measures the price of a set of goods in one year relative to their price in a base year. The inflation rate measures the rate of change of the price level. Although it fluctuates considerably, the inflation rate has been consistently positive.
- The interest rate is the price that is paid to borrow money for a stated period and is expressed as a percentage amount per dollar borrowed. The nominal interest rate is this price expressed in money terms; the real interest rate is this price expressed in terms of goods or purchasing power.
- The exchange rate is the number of Canadian dollars needed to purchase one unit of foreign currency. A rise in the exchange rate is a depreciation of the Canadian dollar; a fall in the exchange rate is an appreciation of the Canadian dollar.

19.2 GROWTH VERSUS FLUCTUATIONS

LO ❷

- Most macroeconomic variables have both long-run trends and short-run fluctuations. The sources of the two types of movements are different.

- Important questions for macroeconomics involve the role of policy in influencing long-run growth as well as short-run fluctuations.

KEY CONCEPTS

National product and national income
Real and nominal national income
Potential and actual output
The output gap
Employment, unemployment, and the labour force

Full employment
Frictional, structural, and cyclical unemployment
Labour productivity
The price level and the rate of inflation

Real and nominal interest rates
The exchange rate
Depreciation and appreciation of the Canadian dollar
Exports, imports, and net exports

STUDY EXERCISES

1. Fill in the blanks to make the following statements correct.

   a. The value of total production of goods and services in Canada is called its _____. National _____ and national _____ are equal because all production generates a claim on its value in the form of income.

   b. In measuring Canada's total output, it would be meaningless to add together all goods and services produced during one year (i.e., 50 000 trucks plus 14 million dozen eggs plus 100 million haircuts, etc.). Instead, total output is measured in _____.

   c. The difference between nominal national income and real national income is that with the latter, _____ are held constant to enable us to see changes in _____.

   d. If all of Canada's resources—its land, labour, and capital—are being employed at normal levels of utilization, then we say that Canada is producing its _____.

   e. The output gap measures the difference between _____ and _____. During booms, _____ is greater than _____ and during recessions _____ is less than _____.

2. Fill in the blanks to make the following statements correct.

   a. The labour force includes people who are _____ and people who are _____. The unemployment rate is expressed as the number of people who are _____ as a percentage of people in the _____.

   b. At any point in time, some people are unemployed because of the normal turnover of labour (new entrants to the labour force, job leavers, and job seekers). This unemployment is referred to as _____. Some people are said to be _____ unemployed because their skills do not match the skills necessary for the available jobs.

   c. Suppose 1996 is the base year in which the price of a basket of goods is set to be 100. If the price of the same basket of goods in 2006 is 137, then we can say that the price level is _____ and that the price of the basket of goods has increased by _____ percent between 1996 and 2006.

   d. Suppose Canada's CPI in May 2002 was 112.7 and in May 2003 was 113.4. The rate of inflation during that one-year period was _____ percent.

   e. The price that is paid to borrow money for a stated period of time is known as the _____.

   f. The real interest rate is equal to the nominal interest rate _____ the rate of inflation.

   g. The number of Canadian dollars required to purchase one unit of foreign currency is the _____ between the Canadian dollar and that foreign currency.

   h. A _____ in the exchange rate reflects a depreciation of the Canadian dollar; a _____ in the exchange rate reflects an appreciation of the Canadian dollar.

3. (X myeconlab) Consider the macroeconomic data shown below for a hypothetical country's economy.

Year	Real GDP Actual (billions of $)	Real GDP Potential (billions of $)	Output Gap (% of potential)	Unemployment Rate (% of labour force)
2000	768	788	—	11.1
2001	784	796	—	10.2
2002	797	805	—	9.1
2003	811	815	—	8.3
2004	825	825	—	7.6
2005	840	836	—	7.3
2006	853	847	—	7.1
2007	862	858	—	7.3
2008	870	870	—	7.6

   a. Compute the output gap for each year.
   b. Explain how GDP can exceed potential GDP.
   c. Does real GDP ever fall in the time period shown? What do economists call such periods?
   d. What is the unemployment rate when this economy is at "full employment"? What kind of unemployment exists at this time?

4. Consider the data shown on the next page for the Canadian Consumer Price Index (CPI), drawn from the *Bank of Canada Review*.

   a. Compute the missing data in the table.
   b. Do average prices ever fall in the time period shown? In which year do prices come closest to being stable?
   c. Across which two consecutive years is the rate of inflation closest to being stable?
   d. In a diagram with the price level on the vertical axis and time on the horizontal axis, illustrate the difference between a situation in which the price level is stable and a situation in which the rate of inflation is stable.

Year	CPI (1992 = 100)	CPI Inflation (% change from previous year)
1990	93.3	4.83
1991	98.5	5.57
1992	100.0	——
1993	101.8	——
1994	102.0	0.20
1995	104.2	2.16
1996	105.9	——
1997	107.6	——
1998	108.9	1.21
1999	111.5	2.39
2000	115.1	——
2001	115.9	——
2002	120.4	——
2003	122.8	1.99
2004	125.4	——
2005	128.1	——

5. **myeconlab** The data below show the nominal interest rate and the inflation rate for several developed economies as reported in *The Economist* on May 27, 2006.

Country	Nominal Interest Rate (on 10-year government bonds)	Inflation Rate (% change in CPI from previous year)	Real Interest Rate
Australia	5.68	3.0	—
Canada	4.34	2.4	—
Euro area	3.83	2.4	—
Japan	1.85	0.3	—
Switzerland	2.68	1.1	—
U.K.	4.57	2.0	—
U.S.A.	5.05	3.5	—

a. Compute the real interest rate for each country, assuming that people expected the inflation rate at the time to persist.
b. If you were a lender, in which country would you have wanted to lend in May of 2006? Explain.
c. If you were a borrower, in which country would you have wanted to borrow in May of 2006? Explain.

6. **myeconlab** Consider the following data drawn from *The Economist*. Recall that the Canadian exchange rate is the number of Canadian dollars needed to purchase one unit of some foreign currency.

Currency	Cdn Dollar Exchange Rate	
	May 2006	May 2005
U.S. dollar	1.12	1.27
Japanese yen	0.0099	0.0117
British pound	2.07	2.31
Swedish krona	0.012	0.013
Euro	1.44	1.61

a. Which currencies appreciated relative to the Canadian dollar from May 2005 to May 2006?
b. Which currencies depreciated relative to the Canadian dollar from May 2005 to May 2006?
c. Using the information provided in the table, can you tell whether the Japanese yen depreciated or appreciated *against the U.S. dollar* from May 2005 to May 2006? Explain.

DISCUSSION QUESTIONS

1. Explain carefully what has happened to the CPI to justify each of the following newspaper headlines.

   a. "Prices on the rise again after a year of stability"
   b. "Inflation increases for three successive months"
   c. "Finance minister pleased at moderation in inflation rate"
   d. "Cost-of-living increases devastating pensioners"

2. Explain why during booms it is possible for the unemployment rate to increase even while total employment is rising.

3. Evaluate the following statements about unemployment.

   a. "Unemployment is a personal tragedy and a national waste."
   b. "No one needs to be unemployed these days; just look at the Help Wanted ads in the newspapers and the signs in the stores."
   c. Employment insurance is a boondoggle for the lazy and unnecessary for the industrious."

4. Consider a 10-year period over which output per worker falls, but GDP increases. How can this happen? Do you think this is likely to be good for the economy?

5. When the Canadian dollar depreciates in foreign-exchange markets, many people view this as "good" for the Canadian economy. Who is likely to be harmed by and who is likely to benefit from a depreciation of the Canadian dollar?

CHAPTER 20

The Measurement of National Income

LEARNING OBJECTIVES

In this chapter you will learn

1. how the concept of value added solves the problem of "double counting" when measuring national income.
2. the income approach and the expenditure approach to measuring national income.
3. the difference between real and nominal GDP and the meaning of the GDP deflator.
4. about the many important omissions from official measures of GDP.
5. why real per capita GDP is a good measure of average "material" living standards but an incomplete measure of overall "well-being."

This chapter provides a detailed look at the measurement of national income. Once we know more precisely what is being measured and how it is measured, we will be ready to build a macroeconomic model to explain the determination of national income. Understanding how national income is measured is an important part of understanding how and why it changes. Indeed, this is a general rule of all economics and all science: Before using any data, it is essential to understand how those data are developed and what they measure.

20.1 NATIONAL OUTPUT AND VALUE ADDED

The central topic of macroeconomics is the overall level of economic activity—aggregate output and the income that is generated by its production. We start by asking: What do we mean by output?

This question may seem odd. Surely your local bakery knows what it produces. And if Air Canada or Imperial Oil or Bombardier do not know their own outputs, what do they know? If each firm knows the value of its total output, the national income statisticians simply have to add up each separate output value to get the nation's output—or is it really that simple?

The reason that obtaining a total for the nation's output is not quite that simple is that one firm's output is often another firm's input. The local baker uses flour that is the output of the flour milling company, and the flour milling company, in turn, uses wheat that is the farmer's output. What is true for bread is true for most goods and services.

Production occurs in stages: Some firms produce outputs that are used as inputs by other firms, and these other firms, in turn, produce outputs that are used as inputs by yet other firms.

If we merely added up the market values of all outputs of all firms, we would obtain a total greatly in excess of the value of the economy's actual output. Consider the example of wheat, flour, and bread. If we added the total value of the output of the wheat farmer, the flour mill, and the baker, we would be counting the value of the wheat three times, the value of the milled flour twice, and the value of the bread once.

intermediate goods All outputs that are used as inputs by other producers in a further stage of production.

The error that would arise in estimating the nation's output by adding all sales of all firms is called *double counting*. "Multiple counting" would actually be a better term because if we added up the values of all sales, the same output would be counted every time that it was sold by one firm to another. The problem of double counting could in principle be solved by distinguishing between two types of output. **Intermediate goods** are outputs of some firms that are used as inputs by other firms. **Final goods** are products that are not used as inputs by other firms, at least not in the period of time under consideration.

final goods Goods that are not used as inputs by other firms but are produced to be sold for consumption, investment, government, or exports during the period under consideration.

If the sales of firms could be easily disaggregated into sales of final goods and sales of intermediate goods, then measuring total output would be straightforward. It would simply equal the value of all *final* goods produced by firms. However, when Stelco sells steel to the Ford Motor Company, it does not care, and usually does not know, whether the steel is for final use (say, construction of a warehouse that will not be sold by Ford) or for use as part of an automobile that will be sold again. Even in our earlier example of bread, a bakery cannot be sure that its sales are for final use, for the bread may be further "processed" by a restaurant prior to its final sale to a customer. In general, it is extremely difficult if not impossible to successfully distinguish final from intermediate goods. The problem of double counting must therefore be resolved in some other manner.

value added The value of a firm's output minus the value of the inputs that it purchases from other firms.

To avoid double counting, economists use the concept of **value added**, which is the amount of value that firms and workers add to their products over and above the costs of intermediate goods. An individual firm's value added is:

$$\text{Value added} = \text{Revenue} - \text{Cost of intermediate goods}$$

Consider an example of a steel mill. A steel mill's value added is the revenue it earns from selling the steel it produces minus the cost of the ore that it buys from the mining company, the cost of the electricity and fuel oil that it uses, and the costs of all other inputs that it buys from other firms.

Practise with Study Guide Chapter 20, Short-Answer Question 4, Exercises 1 and 2.

We have said that a firm's value added equals its revenue minus the cost of intermediate goods *purchased from other firms*. Earnings by factors of production, such as labour income or profits, are not purchases from other firms, and hence are not subtracted from the firm's revenue when computing value added. But since the firm's revenue must be equal to the cost of intermediate goods *plus* earnings by factors of production (including profits), it follows that value added is exactly equal to the sum of factor incomes.[1]

$$\text{Value added} = \text{Income to factors of production}$$

---

1 We are ignoring here the role of indirect taxes, such as provincial sales taxes or the Goods and Services Tax (GST). Such taxes are included in the market value of a firm's output, but these taxes are remitted to the government and do not represent a payment to factors of production.

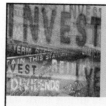

APPLYING ECONOMIC CONCEPTS 20-1

Value Added Through Stages of Production

Because the output of one firm often becomes the input of other firms, the total value of goods sold by all firms greatly exceeds the value of the output of final products. This general principle is illustrated by a simple example in which a mining company starts from scratch and produces iron ore valued at $1000; this firm's value added is $1000. The mining company then sells the iron ore to a different firm that produces steel valued at $1500. The steel producer's value added is $500 because the value of the goods is increased by $500 as a result of the firm's activities. Finally, the steel producer sells the steel to a metal fabricator who transforms the steel into folding chairs valued at $1800; the metal fabricator's value added is $300. We find the value of the final goods, $1800, either by counting only the sales of the last firm or by taking the sum of the values added by each firm. This value is much smaller than the $4300 that we would obtain if we merely added up the market value of the commodities sold by each firm.

	Mining Company (produces iron ore)	Steel Producer	Metal Fabricator (produces chairs)	All Firms	
Transactions at Three Different Stages of Production					
A. Purchases from other firms	$ 0	$1000	$1500	$2500	Total interfirm sales
B. Purchases of factors of production	1000	500	300	1800	Total value added
A + B = value of product	$1000	$1500	$1800	$4300	Total value of all sales

Value added is the correct measure of each firm's contribution to total output—the amount of market value that is produced by that firm.

The firm's value added is the *net value* of its output. It is this net value that is the firm's contribution to the nation's total output, representing the firm's own efforts that add to the value of what it takes in as inputs. The concept of value added is further illustrated in *Applying Economic Concepts 20-1*. In this simple example, as in all more complex cases, the value of the nation's total output is obtained by summing all the individual values added.

The sum of all values added in an economy is a measure of the economy's total output.

20.2 NATIONAL INCOME ACCOUNTING: THE BASICS

The measures of national income and national product that are used in Canada derive from an accounting system called the National Income and Expenditure Accounts (NIEA), which are produced by Statistics Canada. These accounts are not simply collections of economic data. They have a logical structure, based on the simple yet important idea of the circular flow of income, which you first saw in Chapter 1 and which is shown again in Figure 20-1. The figure shows the overall flows of national income and expenditure, and also how government, the financial system, and foreign countries enter the flows. The key point from the circular flow is:

The value of domestic output is equal to the value of the expenditure on that output, and is also equal to the total income claims generated by producing that output.

The circular flow of income suggests three different ways of measuring national income. The first is simply to add up the value of all goods and services produced in the economy. This requires the concept of value added, which we discussed in the previous section. The remaining two approaches correspond to the two "halves" of the circular flow of income. One approach is to add up the total flow of *expenditure* on domestic output; the other is to add up the total flow of *income* generated by the flow

FIGURE 20-1   The Circular Flow of Expenditure and Income

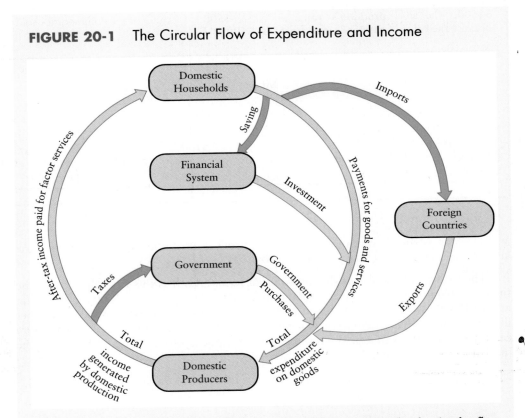

National income is equal to national product. Their flows are shown by the circular flow of income and expenditure. Consider first only the red lines. In this case, the flow would be a simple circle from households to producers and back to households. Now add the blue and green lines. The blue lines represent *injections* to the circular flow (exports, investment, and government purchases) while the green lines represent *withdrawals* from the circular flow (imports, saving, and taxes). Injections and withdrawals complicate the picture but do not change the basic relationship: Domestic production creates a claim on the value of that production. When all of the claims are correctly added up, they must equal the total value of production.

of domestic production. All three measures yield the same total, which is called **gross domestic product (GDP)**. When it is calculated by adding up the total value added in the economy, it is called *GDP by value added*. When it is calculated by adding up total expenditure for each of the main components of final output, the result is called *GDP on the expenditure side*. When it is calculated by adding up all the income claims generated by the act of production, it is called *GDP on the income side*.

The conventions of double-entry bookkeeping require that all value produced must be accounted for by a claim that someone has to that value. Thus, the two values calculated from the income and the expenditure sides are identical conceptually and differ in practical measurements only because of errors of measurement. Any discrepancy arising from such errors is then reconciled so that one common total is given as *the* measure of GDP. Both calculations are of interest, however, because each gives a different and useful breakdown. Also, having two independent ways of measuring the same quantity provides a useful check on statistical procedures and on errors in measurement.

GDP from the Expenditure Side

GDP for a given year is calculated from the expenditure side by adding up the expenditures needed to purchase the final output produced in that year. Total expenditure on final output is the sum of four broad categories of expenditure: consumption, investment, government purchases, and net exports. In the following chapters, we will discuss in considerable detail the causes and consequences of movements in each of these four expenditure categories. Here we define what they are and how they are measured. Throughout, it is important to remember that these four categories of expenditure are exhaustive—they are *defined* in such a way that all expenditure on final output falls into one of the four categories.

1. Consumption Expenditure   **Consumption expenditure** includes expenditure on all goods and services sold to their final users during the year. It includes: services, such as haircuts, dental care, and legal advice; non-durable goods, such as fresh vegetables, clothing, cut flowers, and fresh meat; and durable goods, such as cars, TVs, and air conditioners. *Actual* measured consumption expenditure is denoted by the symbol C_a.

2. Investment Expenditure   **Investment expenditure** is expenditure on goods not for present consumption, including inventories, capital goods such as factories, machines and warehouses, and residential housing. Such goods are called *investment goods*. Let's examine these three categories in a little more detail.

Inventories. Almost all firms hold stocks of their inputs and their own outputs. These stocks are called **inventories**. Inventories of inputs and unfinished materials allow firms to maintain a steady stream of production despite interruptions in the deliveries of inputs bought from other firms. Inventories of outputs allow firms to meet orders despite fluctuations in the rate of production.

The accumulation of inventories during any given year counts as current investment for that year because it represents goods produced but not used for current consumption. These goods are included in the national income accounts at market value, which includes the wages and other costs that the firm incurred in producing them as well as the profit that the firm will make when they are sold in the future. The drawing down of inventories, often called *decumulation*, counts as disinvestment (negative investment) because it represents a reduction in the stock of finished goods that are available to be sold.

gross domestic product (GDP) The total value of goods and services produced in the economy during a given period.

Practise with Study Guide Chapter 20, Short-Answer Questions 1 and 4, Exercise 6 (part a).

consumption expenditure Household expenditure on all goods and services. Represented by the symbol *C* as one of the four components of aggregate expenditure.

investment expenditure Expenditure on the production of goods not for present consumption. Represented by the symbol *I*.

inventories Stocks of raw materials, goods in process, and finished goods held by firms to mitigate the effect of short-term fluctuations in production or sales.

Unsold merchandise becomes part of firms' inventories. In national-income acounting, firms' expenditures on inventories are considered one part of investment expenditure.

Plant and Equipment. All production uses capital goods, which are manufactured aids to production, such as tools, machines, and factory buildings. The economy's total quantity of capital goods is called the **capital stock.** Creating new capital goods is an act of investment and is called *business fixed investment,* often shortened to **fixed investment.**

Residential Housing. A house or an apartment building is a durable asset that yields its utility over a long period of time. Because such an asset meets the definition of investment that we gave earlier, housing construction—the building of a *new* house—is counted as investment expenditure rather than as consumption expenditure. However, when an individual purchases a house from a builder or from another individual, an existing asset is simply transferred, and the transaction is not part of national income. Only when a new house is built does it appear as residential investment in the national accounts.

capital stock The aggregate quantity of capital goods.

fixed investment The creation of new plant and equipment.

depreciation The amount by which the capital stock is depleted through the production process.

Gross and Net Investment. The total investment that occurs in the economy is called gross investment. Gross investment is divided into two parts: replacement investment and net investment. Replacement investment is the amount of investment required to replace that part of the capital stock lost through the process of **depreciation.** Net investment is equal to gross investment minus depreciation.

$$\text{Net investment} = \text{Gross investment} - \text{Depreciation}$$

When net investment is positive, the economy's capital stock is growing. If net investment is negative—which rarely happens—the economy's capital stock is shrinking.

All investment goods are part of the nation's total current output, and their production creates income whether the goods produced are a part of net investment or are merely replacement investment. Thus, all of gross investment is included in the calculation of national income. *Actual* total investment expenditure is denoted by the symbol I_a.

3. Government Purchases

When governments provide goods and services that households want, such as street-cleaning and firefighting, they are adding to the sum total of valuable output in the economy. With other government activities, the case may not seem so clear. Should expenditures by the federal government to send peacekeepers overseas, or to pay a civil servant to refile papers from a now-defunct department, be regarded as contributions to national income?

National income statisticians do not speculate about such matters. Instead they include all **government purchases** of goods and services as part of national income (some of which is government expenditure on investment goods). *Actual* government purchases of goods and services are denoted G_a.

government purchases All government expenditure on currently produced goods and services, exclusive of government transfer payments. Represented by the symbol *G.*

Cost Versus Market Value. Government output is typically valued at cost rather than at market value. In many cases, there is really no choice. What, for example, is the market value of the law courts? No one knows. But, since we do know what it costs the government to provide these services, we value them at their cost of production.

Although valuing at cost is the only possible way to measure many government activities, it does have one curious consequence. If, because of an increase in productivity, one civil servant now does what two used to do, and the displaced worker shifts to the private sector, the government's measured contribution to national income will fall (but the private sector's contribution will rise). Conversely, if two workers now do what one worker used to do, the government's contribution will rise. Both changes could occur even though what the government actually produces has not changed. This is an inevitable but curious consequence of measuring the value of the government's output by the cost of producing it.

Government Purchases Versus Government Expenditure. Only government *purchases* of currently produced goods and services are included as part of GDP. A great deal of government expenditure does *not* count as part of GDP. For example, when the government makes payments to a retired person through the Canada Pension Plan, it is not purchasing any currently produced goods or services from the retiree. The payment itself does not add to total output. The same is true of payments for employment insurance, welfare, and interest on the national debt (which transfers income from taxpayers to holders of government bonds). These are examples of **transfer payments**, which are government expenditures that are not made in return for currently produced goods and services. They are not a part of expenditure on the nation's total output and are therefore not included in GDP. (Of course, the recipients of transfer payments often choose to spend their money on consumption goods. Such expenditure then counts in the same way as any other consumption expenditure.)

> **transfer payment** A payment to an individual or institution not made in exchange for a good or service.

4. Net Exports

The fourth category of aggregate expenditure arises from foreign trade. How do imports and exports influence national income? **Imports** are domestic expenditure on foreign-produced goods and services, whereas **exports** are foreign expenditure on domestically produced goods and services.

Imports. A country's national income is the total value of final goods produced in that country. If you buy a car that was made in Japan, only a small part of that value will represent expenditure on Canadian production. Some of it represents payment for the services of the Canadian dealers and for transportation; the rest is expenditure on Japanese products. If you take your next vacation in Italy, much of your expenditure will be on goods and services produced in Italy and thus will contribute to Italian GDP rather than to Canadian GDP.

Similarly, when a Canadian firm makes an investment expenditure on a machine that was made partly with imported raw materials, only part of the expenditure is on Canadian production; the rest is expenditure on foreign production. The same is true for government expenditure on such things as roads and dams; some of the expenditure is for imported materials, and only part of it is for domestically produced goods and services.

Consumption, investment, and government expenditures all have an import content. To arrive at total expenditure *on Canadian products,* we need to subtract from total Canadian expenditure any expenditure on imports. The value of actual imports is given the symbol IM_a.

> **imports** The value of all goods and services purchased from firms, households, or governments in other countries.
>
> **exports** The value of all goods and services sold to firms, households, and governments in other countries.

Exports. If Canadian firms sell goods to German households, the goods are part of German consumption expenditure but also constitute expenditure on Canadian output. Indeed, all goods and services that are produced in Canada and sold to foreigners must be counted as part of Canadian production and income; they are produced in Canada, and they create incomes for the Canadian residents who produce them. They are not purchased by Canadian residents, however, so they are not included as part of

net exports The value of total exports minus the value of total imports. Represented by the symbol *NX*.

C_a, I_a, or G_a. Therefore, to arrive at the total value of expenditure *on Canadian output*, it is necessary to add in the value of Canadian exports of goods and services. The value of actual exports is denoted X_a.

It is customary to group actual imports and actual exports together as **net exports**. Net exports are defined as total exports minus total imports ($X_a - IM_a$), which is also denoted NX_a. When the value of Canadian exports exceeds the value of Canadian imports, net exports are positive. When the value of imports exceeds the value of exports, net exports are negative.

Total Expenditures   Gross domestic product measured from the expenditure side is equal to the sum of the four major expenditure categories that we have just discussed. In terms of a simple equation, we have

$$GDP = C_a + I_a + G_a + (X_a - IM_a)$$

These data are shown in Table 20-1 for Canada in 2005, including some data on the expenditure in the various subcategories.

GDP from the Income Side

Practise with Study Guide Chapter 20, Exercises 3 and 6 (part b).

As we said earlier, the conventions of national income accounting ensure that the production of a nation's output generates income *exactly* equal to the value of that production. Labour must be employed, land must be rented, and capital must be used. The calculation of GDP from the income side involves adding up factor incomes and other claims on the value of output until all of that value is accounted for.

1. Factor Incomes   National income accountants distinguish three main components of factor incomes: wages and salaries, interest, and business profits.

Wages and Salaries. Wages and salaries are the payment for the services of labour and they include all pre-tax labour earnings: take-home pay, income taxes withheld, employment-insurance contributions, pension-fund contributions, and other fringe benefits. In total, wages and salaries represent the part of the value of production that is attributable to labour.

Interest. Interest includes interest that is earned on bank deposits, interest that is earned on loans to firms, and miscellaneous other investment income (but excludes interest income earned from loans to Canadian governments).[2]

Business Profits. Some profits are paid out as *dividends* to owners of firms; the rest are retained for use by firms and are called *retained earnings*. Both dividends and retained earnings are included in the calculation of GDP. For accounting purposes, total profits include corporate profits, incomes of unincorporated businesses (mainly small businesses, farmers, partnerships, and professionals), and profits of government business enterprises and Crown corporations (such as Canada Post and Export Development Canada).

---

2 The treatment of interest in the national accounts is a little odd. Interest paid by the government is considered a transfer payment, whereas interest paid by private households or firms is treated as expenditure (and its receipt is counted as a factor payment). This is only one example of arbitrary decisions in national income accounting. Others are discussed in *Extensions in Theory 20-1*.

Profits and interest together represent the payment for the use of capital—interest for borrowed capital and profits for capital contributed by the owners of firms.

Net Domestic Income. The sum of wages and salaries, interest, and profits is called *net domestic income at factor cost.* It is "net" because it excludes the value of output that is used as replacement investment. It is "domestic income" because it is the income accruing to domestic factors of production. It is "at factor cost" because it represents only that part of the value of final output that accrues to factors in the form of payments due to them for their services. As we will see immediately, some part of the value of final output does not accrue to the factors at all.

2. Non-Factor Payments

Every time a consumer spends $10 on some item, less than $10 is generated as income for factors of production. This shortfall is due to the presence of indirect taxes and depreciation.

Indirect Taxes and Subsidies. An important claim on the market value of output arises out of indirect taxes, which are taxes on the production and sale of goods and services. In Canada, the most important indirect taxes are provincial sales taxes, excise taxes on specific products, and the federal Goods and Services Tax (GST).

For example, if a good's market price of $10.00 includes 50 cents in provincial sales taxes and 60 cents in federal GST, only $8.90 is available as income to factors of production. Governments are claiming $1.10 of the $10.00 initial value of the good. Adding up income claims to determine GDP therefore necessitates including the portion of the total market value of output that is the governments' claims exercised through their taxes on goods and services.

It is also necessary to subtract government subsidies on goods and services, since these payments allow factor incomes to *exceed* the market value of output. Suppose a municipal bus company spends $150 000 producing bus rides and covers its costs by selling $140 000 in fares and obtaining a $10 000 subsidy from the local government. The total income that the company will generate from its production is $150 000, but the total market value of its output is only $140 000, with the difference made up by the subsidy. To get from total income to the market value of its total output, we must subtract the amount of the subsidy.

Depreciation. Another claim on the value of final output is depreciation. Depreciation is the value of capital that has been used up in the process of producing final output. It is part of gross profits, but because it is needed to compensate for capital used up in the process of production, it is not part of net profits. Hence, depreciation is not income earned by any factor of production.

TABLE 20-1 GDP from the Expenditure Side, 2005

Category	Billions of Dollars	Percent of GDP
Consumption		
Durable goods	100.3	
Semi-durable goods	64.5	
Non-durable goods	189.2	
Services	407.9	
	761.9	55.7
Investment		
Plant and equipment	155.3	
Residential structures	89.6	
Inventories	9.5	
	254.4	18.6
Government Purchases		
Current expenditure	262.4	
Investment	35.2	
	297.6	21.7
Net Exports		
Exports of goods and services	518.3	
Imports of goods and services	−464.0	
	54.3	4.0
Statistical Discrepancy	0.7	0.0
Total GDP	1368.9	100.0

GDP measured from the expenditure side of the national accounts gives the size of the major components of aggregate expenditure.

(*Source:* These data are available at the website for Statistics Canada: www.statcan.ca. Search for "GDP" and then choose "gross domestic product, expenditure-based." Reprinted with permission of Statistics Canada.)

TABLE 20-2   GDP from the Income Side, 2005

Category	Billions of Dollars	Percent of GDP
Factor Incomes		
Wages, salaries and supplementary income	$ 678.9	49.6
Interest and miscellaneous investment income	61.2	4.5
Business profits (including net income of farmers and unincorporated businesses)	293.1	21.4
Net domestic income at factor cost	1033.2	75.5
Non-Factor Payments		
Depreciation	181.4	13.3
Indirect taxes less subsidies	154.7	11.3
Statistical discrepancy	–0.4	–0.0
Total	$1368.9	100.0

GDP measured from the income side of the national accounts gives the sizes of the major components of the income generated by producing the nation's output.

(*Source:* These data are available at the website for Statistics Canada: www.statcan.ca. Search for "GDP" and then select "gross domestic product, income-based." Reprinted with permission of Statistics Canada.)

3. Total National Income

From the income side, GDP is the sum of factor incomes *plus* indirect taxes (net of subsidies) *plus* depreciation.

The various components of the income side of the GDP in the Canadian economy in 2005 are shown in Table 20-2. Note that one of the terms in the table is called *statistical discrepancy*. This is a "fudge factor" to make sure that the independent measures of income and expenditure come to the same total. Statistical discrepancy is a clear indication that national income accounting is not error-free. Although national income and national expenditure are conceptually identical, in practice both are measured with slight error.

We have now seen the two methods for computing a country's national income. Both are correct and give us the same measure of GDP, but each gives us some different additional information. For some questions, such as what the likely future path of the nation's capital stock will be, it is useful to know the relative importance of consumption and investment. In this case, the expenditure approach for computing GDP provides some of the necessary information (Table 20-1). For other questions, such as what is happening to the distribution of income between labour and capital, we need information about the composition of factor incomes. In this case, a useful starting point would be to examine GDP on the income side (Table 20-2).

Measuring national income is not problem-free. As in any accounting exercise, many arbitrary rules are used. Some of them seem odd, but the important thing is to use these rules consistently over time. That way, comparisons of GDP over time will reflect genuine changes in economic activity, which is what we desire for the measure. *Extensions in Theory 20-1* discusses the issue of arbitrariness in national income accounting.

myeconlab

Canada and six other countries together form what is called the "G7" group of advanced industrialized nations. For a comparison of GDP growth in the G7 countries over the past decade, look for "Growth in Canada and Other G7 Countries" in the *Additional Topics* section of this book's MyEconLab.

www.myeconlab.com

EXTENSIONS IN THEORY 20-1

Arbitrary Decisions in National Income Accounting

National income accounting practices contain many arbitrary decisions. For example, goods that are finished and held in inventories are valued at market value, thereby anticipating their sale, even though the actual selling price may not be known. In the case of a Ford in a dealer's showroom, this practice may be justified because the *value* of this Ford is perhaps virtually the same as that of an identical Ford that has just been sold to a customer. However, what is the correct market value of a half-finished house or an unfinished novel? Accountants arbitrarily treat goods in process at cost (rather than at market value) if the goods are being made by firms. They ignore completely the value of the unfinished novel. The arbitrary nature of these decisions is inevitable: Because people must arrive at some practical compromise between consistent definitions and measurable magnitudes, any decision will be somewhat arbitrary.

Such arbitrary decisions surely affect the size of measured GDP. But does it matter? The surprising answer, for many purposes, is no. It is wrong to think that just because a statistical measure is imperfect (as all statistical measures are), it is useless. Simple measures often give estimates to the right order of magnitude, and substantial improvements in sophistication may make only trivial improvements in these estimates.

In 2005, for example, Canadian GDP was measured as $1368.9 billion. It is certain that the market value of all production in Canada in that year was neither $500 billion nor $2000 billion, but it might well have been $1300 billion or $1400 billion had different measures been defined with different arbitrary decisions built in. Similarly, Canadian per capita GDP is about three times the Spanish per capita GDP and is about 20 percent less than U.S. per capita GDP. Other measures might differ, but it is unlikely that any measure would reveal the Spanish per capita GDP to be higher than Canada's, or Canada's to be significantly above that of the United States.

20.3 NATIONAL INCOME ACCOUNTING: SOME FURTHER ISSUES

Now that we have examined the basics of national income accounting, we are ready to explore some more detailed issues. We discuss the distinction between GDP and the related concept of gross national product (GNP), the important difference between real and nominal GDP, and some simple measures of productivity.

GDP and GNP

A measure of national output closely related to GDP is **gross national product (GNP)**. The difference between GDP and GNP is the difference between *income produced* and *income received*. GDP measures the value of total output *produced in Canada* and the total income generated as a result of that production. GNP measures the total amount of income *received by Canadian residents,* no matter where that income was generated. How can GDP differ from GNP? Let's consider two examples.

For the first example, consider a Toyota factory located in Cambridge, Ontario. Suppose in 2007 that the value added generated by that factory is $100 million. Canadian GDP is therefore higher by $100 million as a result of that production. But suppose $5 million of the profits (part of the value added) generated at that factory is

gross national product (GNP) The value of total incomes earned by domestic residents.

Toyota cars produced in Canada contribute to Canada's GDP. But the portion of profits that returns to foreign shareholders is not part of Canada's GNP.

remitted to foreign owners. Since only $95 million of the value added generates income *for Canadian residents,* Canadian GNP is higher by only $95 million.

The second example involves any Canadian-owned business located outside of Canada. The value added produced by that business contributes to the GDP in a foreign country, but not in Canada. But if there are profits remitted to the Canadian owners, those profits will be part of the income of Canadian residents and thus part of Canadian GNP.

GDP measures the value of all production located in Canada, no matter who receives the income from that production. GNP measures the income received by Canadian residents, no matter where the production occurred to generate that income.

The relative sizes of GDP and GNP depend on the balance between income earned by Canadian residents from Canadian investments located abroad, and income paid to foreign residents from foreign-owned investments located in Canada. For most of Canada's history, Canada has been a *net debtor* country. Thus, the value of foreign-located assets owned by Canadian residents has been less than the value of Canadian-located assets owned by foreigners. As a result, the foreign-generated income received by Canadian residents is less than the Canadian-generated income going to foreigners. This makes Canadian GNP less than Canadian GDP. But the difference is small. In most years, GNP is only 3 or 4 percent lower than GDP.

Which Measure Is Better?   Given the difference between GDP and GNP, we are naturally led to ask if one measure is better than the other. The answer depends on what we want to measure.

GDP is superior to GNP as a measure of domestic economic activity. GNP is superior to GDP as a measure of the income of domestic residents.

If you want to know how easy it will be to find a job or whether factories are working double shifts or whether new buildings are going up right and left, look to changes in the GDP. By its definition, it is the GDP that tells us how much is being produced within a nation's borders. To know how much income is available to the residents of a country, however, one should look at the GNP, which counts income earned abroad and subtracts out income generated at home that accrues to residents of other nations. Thus, the GNP is a better measure of the income of a country's residents.

Disposable Personal Income   Both GDP and GNP are important measures of overall economic activity and of national income. Most important to consumers, however, is **disposable personal income,** the part of national income that is available to households to spend or to save. The easiest way to calculate disposable personal income is to subtract from GNP the parts of the GNP that are not available to households. Hence, we must subtract all taxes (both income and sales taxes), depreciation, retained earnings, and interest paid to institutions. We then need to add in the transfer payments made to households. In recent years, disposable income has represented about 60 percent of GDP.

disposable personal income The part of national income that accrues to households and is available to spend or save.

Real and Nominal GDP

In Chapter 19, we distinguished between real and nominal measures of aggregate output. When we add up money values of outputs, expenditures, or incomes, we end up with what are called *nominal values.* Nominal GDP increased by 101.3 percent between 1990 and 2005. If we want to compare *real* GDP in 2005 to that in 1990, we need to determine how much of that nominal increase was due to increases in prices and how much was due to increases in quantities produced. Although there are many possible ways of doing this, the underlying principle is always the same: The value of output in each period is computed by using a common set of *base-period prices*. When this is done, economists say that real output is measured in *constant dollars*.

Total GDP valued at current prices is called *nominal national income*. GDP valued at base-period prices is called *real national income*.

Any change in nominal GDP reflects the combined effects of changes in quantities and changes in prices. However, when real income is measured over different periods by using a common set of base-period prices, changes in real income reflect only changes in quantities. Table 20-3 shows real and nominal GDP for selected years in Canada since 1980.

The GDP Deflator

If nominal and real GDP change by different amounts over a given time period, then prices must have changed over that period. For example, if nominal GDP has increased by 6 percent and real GDP has increased by only 4 percent over the same period, we know that average prices must have increased by 2 percent. Comparing what has happened to nominal and real GDP over the same period implies the existence of a price index measuring the change in prices over that period—"implies" because no explicit price index is used in calculating either real or nominal GDP. However, an index can be inferred by comparing these two values. The *GDP deflator* is defined as follows:

TABLE 20-3 Nominal and Real GDP in Canada: Selected Years (billions of dollars)

Year	Nominal GDP (current prices)	Real GDP (1997 prices)	GDP Deflator
1980	314.4	576.4	54.5
1985	485.7	660.3	73.6
1990	679.9	762.4	89.2
1995	810.4	832.1	97.4
1997	882.7	882.7	100.0
2000	1065.0	1013.1	105.1
2005	1368.9	1157.4	118.3

Nominal GDP tells us about the money value of output; real GDP tells us about the quantity of physical output. Nominal GDP gives the total value of output in any year, valued at the prices of that year. Real GDP gives the total value of output in any year, *valued at prices from some base year*, in this case 1997. The comparison of real and nominal GDP implicitly defines a price index, changes in which reveal changes in the (average) prices of goods produced domestically. Note that in 1997, nominal GDP equals real GDP (measured in 1997 prices) and thus the GDP deflator equals 100.

(*Source:* Statistics Canada, CANSIM database. Real GDP: Series V3862685. Nominal GDP: Series V646937. Reprinted with permission of Statistics Canada.)

$$\text{GDP deflator} = \frac{\text{GDP at current prices}}{\text{GDP at base-period prices}} \times 100 = \frac{\text{Nominal GDP}}{\text{Real GDP}} \times 100$$

Practise with Study Guide Chapter 20, Exercise 4 and Extension Exercise E1.

The **GDP deflator** is the most comprehensive available index of the price level because it includes all the goods and services that are produced by the entire economy. It uses the current year's basket of production to compare the current year's prices with those prevailing in the base period. (Because it uses the current basket of goods and services, it does not run into the CPI's problem of sometimes being based on an out-of-date basket.) The GDP deflator was 18.3 percent higher in 2005 than in 1997 (see Table 20-3). Thus, it cost 18.3 percent more in 2005 than it would have cost to produce the same goods and services in 1997. *Applying Economic Concepts 20-2* illustrates the calculation of real and nominal GDP and the GDP deflator for a simple hypothetical economy that produces only wheat and steel.

GDP deflator An index number derived by dividing nominal GDP by real GDP. Its change measures the average change in price of all the items in the GDP.

APPLYING ECONOMIC CONCEPTS 20-2

Calculating Nominal and Real GDP

To see what is involved in calculating nominal GDP, real GDP, and the GDP deflator, an example may be helpful. Consider a simple hypothetical economy that produces only two commodities, wheat and steel. Table 1 gives the basic data for output and prices in the economy for two years.

TABLE 1   Data for a Hypothetical Economy

	Quantity produced		Prices	
	Wheat (bushels)	Steel (tonnes)	Wheat ($/bushel)	Steel ($/tonne)
Year 1	100	20	10	50
Year 2	110	16	12	55

Table 2 shows nominal GDP, calculated by adding the money values of wheat output and of steel output

for each year. In year 1, the values of both wheat and steel production were $1000, so nominal GDP was $2000. In year 2, wheat output rose to $1320, and steel output fell to $880. Since the rise in the value of wheat was greater than the fall in the value of steel, nominal GDP rose by $200.

TABLE 2   Calculation of Nominal GDP

Year 1: (100 × $10) + (20 × $50) = $2000
Year 2: (110 × $12) + (16 × $55) = $2200

Table 3 shows real GDP, calculated by valuing output in each year *at year-2 prices*; that is, year 2 is used as the base year. In year 2, wheat output rose, but steel output fell. If we use year-2 prices, the fall in the value of steel output between years 1 and 2 exceeded the rise in the value of wheat output, and so real GDP fell.

As we said above, a change in nominal national income can be split into a change due to prices and a change due to quantities. For example, from the data in Table 20-3 we see that in 2005, Canadian nominal GDP was 101.3 percent higher than in 1990. This increase was due to a 32.6-percent increase in prices and a 51.8-percent increase in real GDP.[3]

GDP Deflator Versus the CPI   An important point about the GDP deflator is that it does not necessarily change in line with changes in the CPI. The two price indices are measuring different things. Movements in the CPI measure the change in the average price of *consumer* goods whereas movements in the GDP deflator reflect the change in the average price of goods *produced* in Canada. So changes in the world price of coffee, for example, would have a larger effect on the CPI than on the GDP deflator, since Canadians drink a lot of coffee but no coffee is produced here. Conversely, a change in the world price of wheat is likely to have a bigger effect on the GDP deflator than on the CPI since most of Canada's considerable production of wheat is exported to other countries, thus leaving a relatively small fraction to appear in the Canadian basket of consumer products.

---

[3] For large percentage changes in price and quantity, the nominal percentage change is not exactly equal to the sum of the price and the quantity changes; generally, the relationship is multiplicative. In this case, prices and quantities are respectively 1.326 and 1.518 times their original values. Thus, nominal GDP is (1.326) × (1.518) = 2.013 times its original value, which is an increase of 101.3 percent. For small percentage changes, the sum is a very good approximation of the multiplicative change. If prices grow by 2 percent and quantities by 3 percent, the nominal change is (1.02) × (1.03) = 1.0506, which is very close to 1.05.

TABLE 3   Calculation of Real GDP Using Year-2 Prices

Year 1: $(100 \times \$12) + (20 \times \$55) = \$2300$
Year 2: $(110 \times \$12) + (16 \times \$55) = \$2200$

In table 4, the ratio of nominal to real GDP is calculated for each year and multiplied by 100. This ratio implicitly measures the change in prices over the period in question and is called the *GDP deflator*. The deflator shows that the price level increased by 15 percent between year 1 and year 2.

TABLE 4   Calculation of the GDP Deflator

Year 1: $(2000/2300) \times 100 = 86.96$
Year 2: $(2200/2200) \times 100 = 100.00$

Throughout this box we have used year 2 as the base year. But we could just as easily have used year 1.

The changes we would have computed in real GDP and the deflator would have been very similar—but not identical—to the ones we did compute using year 2 as the base year. The choice of base year matters because of different *relative* prices in the different years (note that the price of steel relative to the price of wheat is lower in year 2 than in year 1). Put simply, with different relative prices in different years, the various output changes get weighted differently depending on which prices we use, and thus the *aggregate* measure of real GDP changes by different amounts. (If you want to understand this point in more detail, try doing Study Exercise #8 at the end of the chapter.)

How do we choose the "right" base year? As with many other elements of national income accounting, there is some arbitrariness in the choice. There is no "right" year. The important thing is not which year to use—the important thing is to be clear about which year you are using and then, for a given set of comparisons, to be sure that you are consistent in your choice.

The GDP deflator and Consumer Price Index (CPI) similarly reflect overall inflationary trends. But changes in relative prices may lead the two price indices to change in different ways.

Omissions from GDP

National income as measured in the National Income and Expenditure Accounts provides an excellent measure of the flow of economic activity in organized markets in a given year. But much economic activity takes place outside the markets that the national income accountants survey. Although these activities are not typically included in the measure of GDP, they nevertheless use real resources and satisfy real wants and needs.

Illegal Activities   GDP does not measure illegal activities, even though many of them are ordinary business activities that produce goods and services sold in markets and that generate factor incomes. Many forms of illegal gambling, prostitution, and drug trade come into this category. To gain an accurate measure of the total demand for factors of production, of total marketable output, or of total incomes generated, we should include these activities, whether or not they are legal. The omission of illegal activities is no trivial matter: The drug trade alone is a multibillion-dollar business.

Prostitution and other illegal activities involve genuine market transactions, but they are not included in official measures of national income.

Note that some illegal activities do get included in national income measures, although they are generally misclassified by industry. The income is included because people sometimes report their illegally earned income as part of their earnings from legal activities. They do this to avoid the fate of Al Capone, the famous Chicago gangster in the 1920s and 1930s, who, having avoided conviction on many counts, was finally caught for income-tax evasion.

The Underground Economy   A significant omission from GDP is the so-called underground economy. The transactions that occur in the underground economy are perfectly legal in themselves; the only illegality involved is that such transactions are not reported for tax purposes. One example of this is the carpenter who repairs a leak in your roof and takes payment in cash (and does not report it as income) to avoid taxation. Because such transactions go unreported, they are omitted from GDP.

The growth of the underground economy is facilitated by the rising importance of services in the nation's total output. It is much easier for a carpenter to pass unnoticed by government authorities than it is for a manufacturing establishment. Estimates of the value of income earned in the underground economy run from 2 percent to 15 percent of GDP. In some countries, the figures are even higher. The Italian underground economy, for example, has been estimated at close to 25 percent of that country's GDP.

Non-Market Activities   If a homeowner hires a firm to do some landscaping, the value of the landscaping enters into GDP (as long as the landscaper records the transaction and thus declares the income); if the homeowner does the landscaping herself, the value of the landscaping is omitted from GDP because there is no recorded market transaction. Such production of goods and services in the home is called *home production* and includes all of the "ordinary" work that is required to keep a household functioning. Other non-market activities include voluntary work such as canvassing for a political party or coaching a local hockey team. Both home production and volunteer activities clearly add to economic well-being, and both use economic resources. Yet neither is included in official measures of national income since they are non-market activities.

The extraction, refining, and transportation of oil are all included as goods and services in measures of GDP. But the environmental damage inflicted by an oil spill—an economic "bad"—is not included in any measure of GDP.

One extremely important non-market activity is *leisure*. If an attorney voluntarily chooses to reduce her time at work from 2400 hours to 2200 hours per year, measured national income will fall by the attorney's wage rate times 200 hours. Yet the value to the attorney of the 200 hours of new leisure enjoyed outside of the marketplace must exceed the lost wages (otherwise she would not have chosen to reduce her work effort by 200 hours), so total economic well-being has increased even though measured GDP has fallen. Until recently, one of the most important ways in which economic growth benefited people was by permitting increased amounts of leisure. Because the leisure time is not marketed, its value does not show up in measures of national income.

Economic "Bads"   When an electric power plant sends sulphur dioxide into the atmosphere, leading to acid rain and environmental damage, the value of the electricity sold is included as part of GDP, but the value of the damage done by the acid rain is not deducted. Similarly, the gasoline that we use in our cars is part of national income when it is produced, but the environmental damage done by burning that gasoline is not deducted. To the extent that economic growth brings with it increases in pollution, congestion, and other disamenities of modern living, measurements of national income will overstate the improvement in living standards. Such measures capture the increased output of goods and services, but they fail to account for the increased output of "bads" that generally accompany economic growth.

Do the Omissions Matter? GDP does a good job of measuring the flow of goods and services through the market sector of the economy. Usually, an increase in GDP implies greater opportunities for employment for households that sell their labour services in the market.

Unless the importance of unmeasured economic activity changes rapidly, *changes* in GDP will probably do a satisfactory job of measuring *changes* in economic opportunities.

However, when the task at hand is measurement of the overall flow of goods and services available to satisfy people's wants, regardless of the source of the goods and services, then the omissions that we have discussed become undesirable and potentially serious. Still, in the relatively short term, changes in GDP will usually be a good measure of the direction, if not the exact magnitude, of changes in material living standards.

GDP and Living Standards

We have said that GDP does a good job of measuring the flow of economic activity during a given time period. But we have also said that many things are omitted from this measure, some of which represent beneficial economic activity and some of which represent economic "bads." These observations lead to the obvious question: To what extent does GDP provide even a rough measure of our living standards?

The answer depends on what we mean by "living standards." For many people, this term refers to our *purchasing power* or *real income*. When GDP rises, do we experience a rise in our average real incomes? The answer is: not necessarily. As we will see in detail in Chapters 25 and 26, real GDP can rise for two general reasons. First, there may be an increase in the amounts of land, labour, and capital used as inputs to production. Second, these inputs may become more productive in the sense that there is an increase in the amount of output *per unit of input*. The *average* level of real income in the economy is best measured by real GDP *per person* but this does not necessarily rise whenever real GDP rises. If real GDP rises because more people become employed, real GDP per person may not rise. However, if real GDP rises because the existing labour force becomes more productive, then average real incomes will also rise. This explains why most economists believe that productivity growth is such an important determinant of living standards.

To many people, however, the term "living standards" is much broader than simply real per capita income—it includes such important but intangible things as religious and political freedom, the quality of local community life, environmental sustainability, the distribution of income, and our ability to prevent and treat illness and disease. And since measures of real GDP omit many of these intangible things that contribute positively to our overall well-being, it is not clear that changes in even real per capita GDP accurately reflect changes in this broader concept of living standards. For example, greater productivity may lead to an increase in real per capita income and thus to a rise in our average material living standards, but if this change also leads to greater environmental damage or greater inequality in the distribution of income, some people may argue that while our material living standards have increased, our overall well-being has declined.

Changes in real per capita income are a good measure of average material living standards. But material living standards are only part of what most people consider their overall well-being.

S U M M A R Y

20.1 NATIONAL OUTPUT AND VALUE ADDED

- Each firm's contribution to total output is equal to its value added, which is the value of the firm's output minus the values of all intermediate goods and services—that is, the outputs of other firms—that it uses.

The sum of all the values added produced in an economy is the economy's total output, which is called gross domestic product (GDP).

20.2 NATIONAL INCOME ACCOUNTING: THE BASICS

- From the circular flow of income, there are three ways to compute national income. One is to add up each firm's value added. The second is to add up total expenditure on domestic output. The third is to add up the total income generated by domestic production. By standard accounting conventions, these three aggregations define the same total.
- From the expenditure side of the national accounts,

$$GDP = C_a + I_a + G_a + (X_a - IM_a)$$

- C_a comprises consumption expenditures of households. I_a is investment in plant and equipment, residential construction, and inventory accumulation. G_a is government purchases of goods and services. $(X_a - IM_a)$ represents net exports of goods and services.
- GDP measured from the income side adds up all claims to the market value of production. Wages, interest, profits, depreciation, and indirect taxes net of subsidies are the major categories.

20.3 NATIONAL INCOME ACCOUNTING: SOME FURTHER ISSUES

- GDP measures the value of all production located in Canada, no matter who receives the income from that production. GNP measures the income received by Canadian residents, no matter where the production occurred to generate that income. Because Canada is a net debtor, its GNP is usually 3 to 4 percent less than its GDP.
- Real measures of national income reflect changes in real quantities. Nominal measures of national income reflect changes in both prices and quantities. Any change in nominal income can be split into a change in quantities and a change in prices.
- The comparison of nominal and real GDP yields the implicit GDP price deflator, an index of the average price of all goods and services produced in the economy.

- GDP and related measures of national income must be interpreted with their limitations in mind. GDP excludes production resulting from activities that are illegal, that take place in the underground economy, or that do not pass through markets.
- Notwithstanding its limitations, GDP remains a useful measure of the total economic activity that passes through the nation's markets. Recorded *changes* in GDP will generally do an accurate job of measuring *changes* in economic activity.
- Real per capita GDP is a good measure of average material living standards. But because GDP omits many intangible things that contribute positively to our quality of life, GDP-based measures miss important parts of our overall well-being.

KEY CONCEPTS

Intermediate and final goods
Value added
GDP as the sum of all values added
GDP from the expenditure side

GDP from the income side
GNP versus GDP
Disposable personal income
GDP deflator

Omissions from GDP
Per capita GDP and productivity
Living standards and GDP

STUDY EXERCISES

1. Fill in the blanks to make the following statements complete.

   a. If, when measuring Canada's national output, we add the market values of all firms' outputs in Canada, then we are committing the error of _____. Such an amount would greatly _____ the economy's actual output.

   b. Statisticians use the concept of _____ to avoid double counting in measuring national income. Each firm's _____ is the value of its output minus the costs of _____ that it purchases from other firms.

   c. If we measure GDP from the expenditure side, we are adding four broad categories of expenditure: _____, _____, _____, and _____. As an equation it is written as GDP = _____.

   d. If we measure GDP from the income side, we are adding three main components of factor incomes: _____, _____ and _____. To these items we must add non-factor payments of _____ and _____.

2. **myeconlab** Fill in the blanks to make the following statements correct.

   a. Comparing GDP and GNP, if we want the best measure of Canada's domestic economic activity, we should look at _____; if we want the best measure of the income of Canada's residents, then we should look at _____.

   b. If nominal GDP increases by 35 percent over a 10-year period, then it is unclear how much of this increase is due to increases in _____ and how much is due to increases in _____. To overcome this problem, we look at GDP valued at _____ prices and we refer to this measure as _____ national income.

   c. GDP divided by total population gives us a measure of _____.

   d. GDP divided by the number of employed persons in Canada gives us a measure of labour _____.

3. In measuring GDP from the expenditure side (GDP $= C_a + I_a + G_a + NX_a$), which of the following expenditures are included, and within which of the four categories?

   a. expenditures on automobiles by consumers
   b. expenditures on automobiles by firms
   c. expenditures on new machinery by Canadian-owned forest companies in Canada
   d. expenditures on new machinery by Canadian-owned forest companies in the United States
   e. expenditures on new machinery by U.S.-owned forest companies in Canada
   f. reductions in business inventories
   g. purchases of second-hand cars and trucks
   h. the hiring of economic consultants by the Manitoba government
   i. the purchase of Canadian-produced software by a firm in Japan

4. **myeconlab** The list below provides some national income figures for the country of Econoland. All figures are in millions of dollars.

Wages and salaries	5000
Interest income	200
Personal consumption	3900
Personal saving	1100
Personal income taxes	200
Business profits	465
Indirect taxes	175
Subsidies	30
Government purchases	1000
Exports	350
Imports	390
Net private investment	950
Depreciation	150

   a. Using the expenditure approach, what is the value of GDP for Econoland?
   b. Using the income approach, what is the value of GDP?
   c. What is the value of net domestic income at factor cost?

5. The table below shows data for real and nominal GDP for a hypothetical economy over several years.

Year	Nominal GDP (billions of $)	Real GDP (billions of 2005 $)	GDP Deflator
2003	775.3	798.4	—
2004	814.1	838.6	—
2005	862.9	862.9	—
2006	901.5	882.5	—
2007	951.3	920.6	—
2008	998.8	950.5	—

a. Compute the GDP deflator for each year.
b. Compute the total percentage change in nominal GDP from 2003 to 2008. How much of this change was due to increases in prices and how much was due to changes in quantities?

6. Would inflation, as measured by the rate of change in the GDP deflator, ever be different from inflation as measured by the rate of change in the Consumer Price Index? Would it ever be the same? Explain.

7. For each of the following events, describe the likely effect on real GDP.

a. The Quebec ice storm of 1998 increases the demand for building materials to repair damage to homes.
b. The Quebec ice storm of 1998 damages many factories.
c. The building of a larger arena in Vancouver increases the demand for Canucks tickets by Vancouverites.

d. The building of a larger arena in Vancouver increases the demand for Canucks tickets by residents of Washington.

8. (X myeconlab) Consider the following data for a hypothetical economy that produces two goods, milk and honey.

| | Quantity Produced | | Prices | |
	Milk (litres)	Honey (kg)	Milk ($/litre)	Honey ($/kg)
Year 1	100	40	2	6
Year 2	120	25	3	6

a. Compute nominal GDP for each year in this economy.
b. Using year 1 as the base year, compute real GDP for each year. What is the percentage change in real GDP from year 1 to year 2?
c. Using year 1 as the base year, compute the price deflator for each year. What is the percentage change in real GDP from year 1 to year 2?
d. Now compute the GDP deflator for each year, using year 1 as the base year.
e. Now compute the GDP deflator for each year, using year 2 as the base year.
f. Explain why the measures of real GDP growth (and growth in the deflator) depend on the choice of base year.

DISCUSSION QUESTIONS

1. Residents of some Canadian cities have recently become concerned about the growing proportion of their local real estate that is being bought up by foreign residents. What is the effect of this transfer of ownership on Canadian GDP and GNP?

2. What would be the effects of the following events on the measured value of Canada's real GDP? Speculate on the effects of each event on the true well-being of Canadians.

a. destruction of thousands of homes by flood water
b. destruction of hundreds of businesses by an ice storm
c. complete cessation of all imports from Europe
d. an increase in the amount of acid rain that falls
e. an increase in the amount of spending on devices that reduce pollution at a major hydroelectricity plant
f. reduction in the standard workweek from 37 hours to 30 hours
g. hiring of all welfare recipients as government employees

h. outbreak of hostilities in the Middle East in which Canadian troops became involved.

3. A recent United Nations study concluded that Canada's "quality of life" makes it among the very best countries in which to live. Explain why Canada's ranking for quality of life can be higher than its ranking of real per capita GDP.

4. One way of estimating the size of the underground economy is to see the amount of cash Canadians are carrying relative to the total value of GDP. Why would a rapid rise in the ratio of cash held by the public to GDP indicate a rise in the underground economy?

5. A company's wages and salaries are part of its value added. Suppose, however, that the cleaning and machinery maintenance that its own employees used to do are now contracted out to specialist firms who come in to do the same work more cheaply. What happens to the company's value added when a company follows this recent trend of "contracting out"? What happens to value added in the economy as a whole?

CHAPTER 21

The Simplest Short-Run Macro Model

LO LEARNING OBJECTIVES

In this chapter you will learn

1. the difference between desired expenditure and actual expenditure.
2. the determinants of desired consumption and desired investment expenditures.
3. how to define equilibrium national income.
4. how a change in desired expenditure affects equilibrium income, and how this change is reflected by the multiplier.

In Chapters 19 and 20, we encountered a number of important macroeconomic variables. We considered how they are measured and how they have behaved over the past several decades. We now turn to a more detailed study of what *causes* these variables to behave as they do. In particular, we study the forces that determine real national income and the price level over short periods of time, say up to a few years. In particular, in this chapter and the next two we examine how the level of real GDP is determined and how it fluctuates around the level of potential GDP. For simplicity, we assume that potential GDP is constant; in later chapters we explore the long-run forces that explain the growth of potential GDP.

Real national income and the price level are determined simultaneously. It is, however, easier to study them one at a time. So, in this chapter and the next, we simplify matters by seeing how real national income is determined *under the assumption that the price level is constant.* The simplified analysis is an important first step toward understanding how prices and incomes are determined together, which is the subject of Chapter 23.

Our ability to explain the behaviour of real national income depends on our understanding of what determines the amount that households and firms spend. So, we begin with an examination of their expenditure decisions.

21.1 DESIRED AGGREGATE EXPENDITURE

In Chapter 20, we discussed how national income statisticians divide *actual* GDP into its expenditure components: consumption, investment, government purchases, and net exports.

In this chapter and the next, we are concerned with a different concept. It is variously called *desired* or *planned* expenditure. Of course, all people would like to spend virtually unlimited amounts, if only they had the resources. Desired expenditure does not refer, however, to what people would like to do under imaginary circumstances; it refers to what people desire to spend out of the resources that they actually have. Recall from Chapter 20 that the *actual* values of the various categories of expenditure are indicated by C_a, I_a, G_a, and $(X_a - IM_a)$. Economists use the same letters without the subscript "a" to indicate the *desired* expenditure in the same categories: C, I, G, and $(X - IM)$.

Everyone makes expenditure decisions. Fortunately, it is unnecessary for our purposes to look at each of the millions of such individual decisions. Instead, it is sufficient to consider four main groups of decision makers: domestic households, firms, governments, and foreign purchasers of domestically produced commodities. The sum of their *desired* expenditures on domestically produced output is called **desired aggregate expenditure (*AE*)**:

$$AE = C + I + G + (X - IM)$$

Desired expenditure need not equal actual expenditure, either in total or in any individual category. For example, firms might not plan to invest in inventory accumulation this year but might do so unintentionally if sales are unexpectedly low—the unsold goods that pile up on their shelves are undesired inventory accumulation. In this case, actual investment expenditure, I_a, will exceed desired investment expenditure, I.

National income accounts measure *actual* expenditures in each of the four expenditure categories. National income theory deals with *desired* expenditures in each of these four categories.

You may be wondering why the distinction between desired and actual expenditure is so important. The answer will become clear in the next section where we discuss the concept of *equilibrium* national income, which involves the relationship between desired and actual expenditure. For now, however, the remainder of this section examines more fully the various components of desired expenditure.

Autonomous Versus Induced Expenditure. In what follows, it will be useful to distinguish between *autonomous* and *induced* expenditure. Components of aggregate expenditure that do *not* depend on national income are called **autonomous expenditures**. Autonomous expenditures can and do change, but such changes do not occur systematically in response to changes in national income. Components of aggregate expenditure that *do* change systematically in response to changes in national income are called **induced expenditures**. As we will see, the induced response of desired aggregate expenditure to a change in national income plays a key role in the determination of equilibrium national income.

Important Simplifications. Our goal in this chapter is to develop the simplest possible model of national-income determination. To do so, we focus on only two of the four components of desired aggregate expenditure—consumption and investment. Consumption is by far the largest component of aggregate expenditure; it also provides the most important link between desired aggregate expenditure and real national income. Investment includes the accumulation of inventories plus expenditure on new machines or factories which add to the stock of physical capital. Investment is smaller than consumption but also more volatile; understanding investment is therefore important for understanding fluctuations in real national income.

We begin by considering a **closed economy**—that is, one that does not trade with other countries. We also suppose there is no government and that the price level is con-

---

desired aggregate expenditure (*AE*) The sum of desired or planned spending on domestic output by households, firms, governments, and foreigners.

autonomous expenditure Elements of expenditure that do not change systematically with national income.

induced expenditure Any component of expenditure that is systematically related to national income.

closed economy An economy that has no foreign trade in goods, services, or assets.

stant. These extreme assumptions serve a vital purpose. As we will soon see, the presence of government and foreign trade is *not* essential to understanding the basic principles of national-income determination. By simplifying the model as much as possible, we are better able to understand its structure and therefore how more complex versions of the model work. In following chapters we will complicate our simple macro model by adding a government and international trade and then by removing the assumption of a fixed price level. The result will be a much more complete model of the macro economy.

Desired Consumption Expenditure

Recall from Chapter 20 that *disposable income* is the amount of income households receive after deducting what they pay in taxes. In our simple model with no government and no taxation, disposable income, Y_D, is equal to national income, Y. We define **saving** as all disposable income that is not spent on consumption.

By definition, there are only two possible uses of disposable income—consumption and saving. When the household decides how much to put to one use, it has automatically decided how much to put to the other use.

Figure 21-1 shows the time series for per capita consumption and disposable income in Canada over the past 25 years. It is clear that the two variables tend to move together over time, although the relationship is not exact. The vertical distance between the two lines is the amount of saving done by households, and the figure shows that household saving as a share of disposable income has been declining over this period. In the early 1980s, household saving was roughly 25 percent of disposable income whereas by 2005 it was less than 5 percent. What determines the amount of their disposable income that households decide to consume and the amount they decide to save? The factors that influence this decision are summarized in the *consumption function* and the *saving function*.

The Consumption Function The **consumption function** relates the total desired consumption expenditures of all households to the several factors that determine it. The key factors influencing desired consumption are assumed to be:

- disposable income
- wealth
- interest rates
- expectations about the future

In building our simple macro model, we emphasize the role of disposable income in influencing desired consumption; but as we will see, changes in the other variables are also important.

The assumption that desired consumption is related to disposable income is not surprising. As income rises, households naturally want to spend more, both now and in the future. For example, if a household's monthly disposable income permanently increases from $1000 to $1500, its monthly consumption will also increase, but probably by less than the full $500 increase. The remainder will be added to its monthly saving—money that will accumulate and help finance future vacations, education, home purchases, or even retirement.

Holding constant other determinants of desired consumption, an increase in disposable income is assumed to lead to an increase in desired consumption.

saving All disposable income that is not spent on consumption.

consumption function The relationship between desired consumption expenditure and all the variables that determine it; in the simplest case, the relationship between desired consumption expenditure and disposable income.

FIGURE 21-1 Consumption and Disposable Income in Canada, 1981–2005

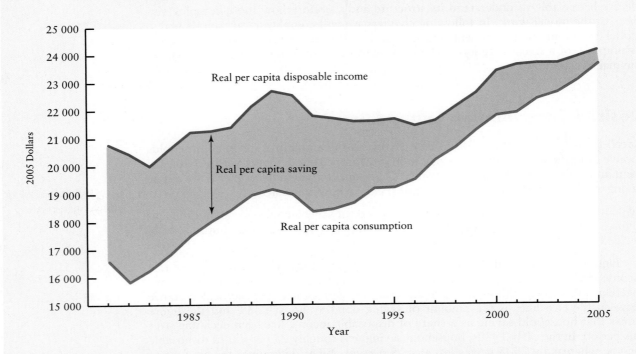

Per capita consumption and disposable income move broadly together over time. The relationship between consumption and disposable income is not exact, but they clearly move broadly together. The vertical distance between the lines is household saving, which as a share of income has been declining since 1981.

(*Source:* All data are from Statistics Canada, CANSIM database. Disposable income: Series V691566. Consumption expenditure: Series V691578. Population: Series V466668. Conversion from nominal to real values based on CPI: Series V737344. Reprinted with permission of Statistics Canada.)

The consumption function has an interesting history in economics. *Extensions in Theory 21-1* discusses consumption behaviour in two hypothetical households, and illustrates a debate regarding the importance of *current* disposable income in determining consumption. As the discussion shows, however, our simple assumption that desired consumption is positively related to disposable income is a good approximation of the behaviour of the *average* household, and therefore is suitable for explaining aggregate behaviour.

Part (i) of Figure 21-2 illustrates a hypothetical consumption function. The first two columns of the table show the value of desired consumption (C) associated with each value of disposable income (Y_D). There is clearly a positive relationship. The figure plots these points and connects them with a smooth line. In this hypothetical economy, the equation of the consumption function is

$$C = 30 + 0.8Y_D$$

In words, this equation says that if disposable income is zero, desired aggregate consumption will be $30 billion, and that for every one-dollar increase in Y_D, desired consumption rises by 80 cents.

Practise with Study Guide Chapter 21, Exercise 1.

FIGURE 21-2   The Consumption and Saving Functions

Disposable Income (Y_D)	Desired Consumption (C)	Desired Saving (S)	$APC = C/Y_D$	ΔY_D	ΔC	$MPC = \Delta C/\Delta Y_D$
0	30	−30	—			
				30	24	0.8
30	54	−24	1.80			
				120	96	0.8
150	150	0	1.00			
				150	120	0.8
300	270	30	0.90			
				150	120	0.8
450	390	60	0.87			
				75	60	0.8
525	450	75	0.86			
				75	60	0.8
600	510	90	0.85			

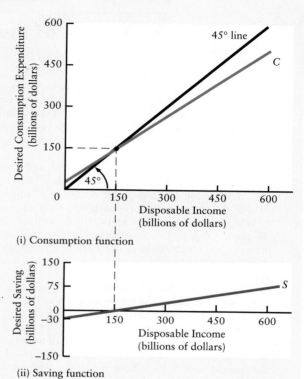

(i) Consumption function

(ii) Saving function

Both desired consumption and desired saving are assumed to rise as disposable income rises. Line C in part (i) of the figure relates desired consumption expenditure to disposable income by plotting the data from the second column of the accompanying table. The consumption function cuts the 45° line at the break-even level of disposable income. Note that the level of autonomous consumption is $30 billion. The slope of the consumption function is equal to the marginal propensity to consume, which is shown in the table to be 0.8.

The relationship between desired saving and disposable income is shown in part (ii) by line S, which plots the data from the third column of the table. The vertical distance between C and the 45° line in part (i) is by definition the height of S in part (ii); that is, any given level of disposable income must be either consumed or saved. Note that the level of autonomous saving is −$30 billion.

The $30 billion is said to be *autonomous* consumption because it is autonomous (or independent) of the level of income. The $0.8Y_D$ is called *induced* consumption because it is induced (or brought about) by a change in income. In part (i) of Figure 21-2, the autonomous part of desired consumption is the vertical intercept of the consumption function. The induced part of consumption occurs as disposable income changes and we move along the consumption function.

We now go on to examine the properties of the consumption function in more detail.

Average and Marginal Propensities to Consume. To discuss the consumption function concisely, economists use two technical expressions.

EXTENSIONS IN THEORY 21-1

The Theory of the Consumption Function

Though it may seem natural to assume that a household's current consumption depends largely on its current disposable income, much debate and research has surrounded the issue of how to model consumption behaviour. To see what is involved, consider two quite different households.

The first household is short-sighted and spends everything it receives and puts nothing aside for a rainy day. When some overtime work results in a large paycheque, the members of the household go out and spend it. When it is hard to find work, the household's paycheque is small and its members reduce their expenditures. This household's monthly expenditure is therefore exactly equal to its current monthly disposable income.

The second household is forward-looking. Its members think about the future as much as the present and make plans that stretch over their lifetimes. They put money aside for retirement and for the occasional rainy day when disposable income may fall temporarily. An unexpected windfall of income will be saved. An unexpected shortfall of income will be cushioned by spending some of the accumulated savings that were put

aside for just such a rainy day. In short, this household's monthly expenditure will be closely related to its *permanent* monthly disposable income—the average monthly income it expects over its lifetime. Fluctuations in its current monthly income will have little effect on its current consumption expenditure. Economists refer to this behaviour as *consumption smoothing*.

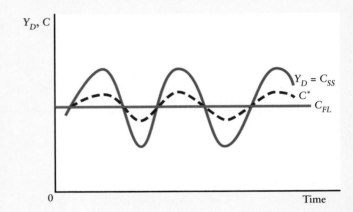

average propensity to consume (APC) Desired consumption divided by the level of disposable income.

The **average propensity to consume (APC)** is desired consumption expenditure divided by disposable income:

$$APC = C/Y_D$$

The fourth column of the table in Figure 21-2 shows the APC calculated from the data in the table. Note that APC falls as disposable income rises.

marginal propensity to consume (MPC) The change in desired consumption divided by the change in disposable income that brought it about.

The **marginal propensity to consume (MPC)** relates the *change* in desired consumption to the *change* in disposable income that brought it about. MPC is the change in desired consumption divided by the change in disposable income:

$$MPC = \Delta C/\Delta Y_D$$

where the Greek letter Δ, delta, means "a change in." The last column of the table in Figure 21-2 shows the MPC that corresponds to the data in the table. Note that in this simple example, the MPC is constant and equal to 0.8. [28]

The Slope of the Consumption Function. The consumption function shown in Figure 21-2 has a slope of $\Delta C/\Delta Y_D$, which is, by definition, the marginal propensity to consume.

The figure shows the difference between our two sample households, short-sighted and forward-looking, and how their respective consumption expenditure is related to their current disposable income. We assume that disposable income, Y_D, fluctuates over time, as shown by the solid blue line. C_{SS} is the consumption path of the short-sighted household and is the same as the path of disposable income. C_{FL} is the consumption path for the forward-looking household and is flat.

John Maynard Keynes (1883–1946), the famous English economist who developed much of the basic theory of macroeconomics, populated his theory with households whose current consumption expenditure depended mostly on their current income. But these households are not as extreme as the short-sighted households we discussed above. Keynes did not assume that households *never* saved. He simply assumed that their current level of expenditure and saving depended on their *current* level of income. To this day, a consumption function based on this assumption is called a *Keynesian consumption function*.

During the 1950s, two U.S. economists, Franco Modigliani and Milton Friedman, both of whom were subsequently awarded Nobel Prizes in economics, analyzed the behaviour of forward-looking households. Their theories, which Modigliani called the *life-cycle theory* and Friedman called the *permanent-income theory*, explain some observed consumer behaviour that cannot be explained by the Keynesian consumption function.

The differences between the theories of Keynes, on the one hand, and Friedman and Modigliani, on the other, are not as great as it might seem at first sight. To see why this is so, let us return to our two imaginary households.

Even the extremely short-sighted household may be able to do some consumption smoothing in the face of income fluctuations. Most households have some money in the bank and some ability to borrow, even if it is just from friends and relatives. As a result, every change in income need not be matched by an equal change in consumption expenditures.

In contrast, although the forward-looking household wants to smooth its pattern of consumption, it may not have the borrowing capacity to do so. Its bank may not be willing to lend money for consumption when the security consists of nothing more than the *expectation* that the household's income will be higher in later years. As a result, the household's consumption expenditure might fluctuate with its current income more than it would wish.

The foregoing discussion suggests that the consumption expenditure of both types of households will fluctuate to some extent with their current disposable incomes and to some extent with their expectations of future disposable income. Moreover, in any economy there will be households of both types, and aggregate consumption will be determined by a mix of the two types. The consumption behaviour for the *average* household in such an economy is shown in the figure as the path C^*. Consumption fluctuates in response to changes in disposable income, rising when income rises and falling when income falls.

The positive slope of the consumption function shows that the *MPC* is positive; increases in income lead to increases in desired consumption expenditure. The *constant* slope of the consumption function shows that the *MPC* is the same at any level of disposable income.

The 45° Line. Figure 21-2(i) contains a line that is constructed by connecting all points where desired consumption (measured on the vertical axis) equals disposable income (measured on the horizontal axis). Because both axes are given in the same units, this line has a positive slope equal to 1; that is, it forms an angle of 45° with the axes. The line is therefore called the *45° line*.

The 45° line is a useful reference line. In part (i) of Figure 21-2, the consumption function cuts the 45° line at what is called the "break-even" level of income—in this example, at $150 billion. When the consumption function is above the 45° line, desired consumption exceeds disposable income. In this case, desired saving must be negative; households are financing their consumption either by spending out of their accumulated saving or by borrowing funds. When the consumption function is below the 45° line, desired consumption is less than disposable income and so desired saving is positive; households are paying back debt or accumulating assets. At the break-even level of disposable income, desired consumption exactly equals disposable income and so desired saving is zero.

The Saving Function Households decide how much to consume and how much to save. As we have said, this is only a single decision—how to divide disposable income between consumption and saving. Therefore, once we know the relationship between desired consumption and disposable income, we automatically know the relationship between desired saving and disposable income.

There are two saving concepts that are exactly parallel to the consumption concepts of *APC* and *MPC*. The **average propensity to save (*APS*)** is the proportion of disposable income that households want to save, computed by dividing desired saving by disposable income:

$$APS = S/Y_D$$

The **marginal propensity to save (*MPS*)** relates the change in desired saving to the change in disposable income that brought it about:

$$MPS = \Delta S/\Delta Y_D$$

There is a simple relationship between the saving and the consumption propensities. *APC* and *APS* must sum to 1; and *MPC* and *MPS* must also sum to 1. Because all disposable income is either spent or saved, it follows that the fractions of income consumed and saved must account for all income (*APC* + *APS* = 1). It also follows that the fractions of any *increment* to income consumed and saved must account for all of that increment (*MPC* + *MPS* = 1). **[29]** .

Look back at the table in Figure 21-2 and calculate *APC* and *APS* for yourself by computing C/Y_D and S/Y_D for each row in the table. You will notice that the sum of *APC* and *APS* is *always* 1. Similarly, calculate *MPC* and *MPS* by computing $\Delta C/\Delta Y_D$ and $\Delta S/\Delta Y_D$ for each row in the table. You will also notice that *MPC* and *MPS* *always* add up to 1.

Part (ii) of Figure 21-2 shows the saving function in our simple model. Notice that it is positively sloped, indicating that increases in disposable income are assumed to lead to an increase in desired saving. Note also that the amount of desired saving is always equal to the vertical distance between the consumption function and the 45° line. When desired consumption exceeds income, desired saving is negative; when desired consumption is less than income, desired saving is positive.

Shifts of the Consumption Function Earlier we said that desired consumption is assumed to depend on four things—disposable income, wealth, interest rates, and households' expectations about the future. In Figure 21-2, we illustrate the most important relationship—between desired consumption and disposable income. In this diagram, changes in disposable income lead to *movements along* the consumption function. Changes in the other three factors will lead to *shifts of* the consumption function. Let's see why.

A Change in Wealth. Household wealth is the value of all accumulated assets minus accumulated debts. The most common types of household assets are savings accounts, mutual funds (portfolios of stocks or bonds), Registered Retirement Savings Plans (RRSPs), and the ownership of homes and cars. The most common household debts are home mortgages, car loans, and outstanding lines of credit from banks.

What happens to desired consumption if household wealth increases? Suppose, for example, that a rising stock market (often called a "bull" market) leads to an increase in aggregate household wealth. To the extent that this increase in wealth is expected to persist, less current income needs to be saved for the future, and households will therefore

---

average propensity to save (*APS*) Desired saving divided by disposable income.

marginal propensity to save (*MPS*) The change in desired saving divided by the change in disposable income that brought it about.

Practise with Study Guide Chapter 21, Extension Exercise E2.

tend to spend a larger fraction of their current income. The consumption function will shift up, and the saving function down, as shown in Figure 21-3. Current estimates suggest that an increase in aggregate wealth of $1 billion leads to an increase in desired aggregate consumption of approximately $50 million.

An increase in wealth shifts the consumption function up; a decrease in wealth shifts the consumption function down.

A Change in Interest Rates. Household consumption can be divided into consumption of *durable* and *non-durable* goods. Durable goods are goods that deliver benefits for several years, such as cars and household appliances. Non-durable goods are consumption goods that deliver benefits to households only for short periods of time, such as groceries, restaurant meals, and clothing. Since many durable goods are also expensive, many of them are purchased on credit—that is, households borrow in order to finance their purchases.

   The cost of borrowing, as we discussed in Chapter 19, is the interest rate. A fall in the interest rate reduces the cost of borrowing and leads to an increase in desired consumption expenditure, especially of durable goods. That is, for any given level of disposable income, a fall in the interest rate leads to an increase in desired consumption; the consumption function shifts up and the saving function shifts down, as shown in Figure 21-3.

A fall in interest rates leads to an increase in desired consumption at any level of disposable income; the consumption function shifts up. A rise in interest rates shifts the consumption function down.

A Change in Expectations. Households' expectations about the future are important in determining their desired consumption. Suppose, for example, that large numbers of households become pessimistic about the future state of the economy and about their own employment prospects. In many cases, these fears will lead households to increase their current saving in anticipation of rough economic times (possibly unemployment) ahead. But increasing their current saving implies a reduction in current consumption (at the given level of disposable income). The result will be a downward shift in the consumption function.

   The reverse also tends to be true. Favourable expectations about the future state of the economy will lead many households to increase their current desired consumption, and reduce their current desired saving. The result will be an upward shift in the consumption function and a downward shift in the saving function.

FIGURE 21-3   Shifts in the Consumption Function

(i) The consumption function shifts upward with an increase in wealth, a decrease in interest rates, or an increase in optimism about the future

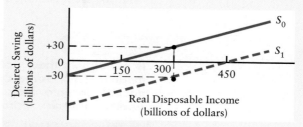

(ii) The saving function shifts downward with an increase in wealth, a decrease in interest rates, or an increase in optimism about the future

Changes in wealth, interest rates, or expectations about the future shift the consumption function. In part (i), line C_0 reproduces the consumption function from Figure 21-2(i). The consumption function then shifts up by $60 billion, so with disposable income of $300 billion, for example, desired consumption rises from $270 billion to $330 billion.

   The saving function in part (ii) shifts down by $60 billion, from S_0 to S_1. At a disposable income of $300 billion, for example, desired saving falls from $30 billion to –$30 billion.

Expectations about the future state of the economy influence desired consumption. Optimism leads to an upward shift in the consumption function; pessimism leads to a downward shift in the consumption function.

Summary   It is useful to summarize what we have learned so far about the consumption function. As you will soon see, it will play a crucial role in our simple model of national income determination. The main points are:

1. Desired consumption is assumed to be positively related to disposable income. In a graph, this relationship is shown by the positive slope of the consumption function, which is equal to the marginal propensity to consume (*MPC*).

2. There are both *autonomous* and *induced* components of desired consumption. A movement along the consumption function shows changes in consumption induced by changes in disposable income. A shift of the consumption function shows autonomous changes in consumption.

3. An increase in household wealth, a fall in interest rates, or greater optimism about the future are all assumed to lead to an increase in desired consumption and an upward shift of the consumption function.

4. By definition, all disposable income is either consumed or saved. Therefore, there is a saving function associated with the consumption function. Any event that causes the consumption function to shift must also cause the saving function to shift by an equal amount in the opposite direction.

> **ᴍ myeconlab**
>
> **Is our simple theory of the consumption function supported by empirical evidence? For some Canadian data on aggregate consumption and disposable income, look for "The Consumption Function in Canada" in the *Additional Topics* section of this book's MyEconLab.**
>
> w w w . m y e c o n l a b . c o m

Desired Investment Expenditure

Our simple macroeconomic model has only consumption and investment. Having spent considerable time discussing desired consumption expenditure, we are now ready to examine the determinants of desired investment. Recall from Chapter 20 the three categories of investment:

- inventory investment
- residential investment
- new plant and equipment

Investment expenditure is the most volatile component of GDP, and changes in investment are strongly associated with economic fluctuations. As shown in Figure 21-4, total investment in Canada fluctuates around an average of about 17 percent of GDP. In each of the last two recessions (1982 and 1991) investment as a share of GDP fell by over five percentage points. In contrast, consumption, government purchases, and net exports are much smoother over the business cycle, each typically changing by less than one percentage point. An important part of our understanding of business cycles will therefore rely on our understanding of the fluctuations in investment.

FIGURE 21-4   The Volatility of Investment, 1977–2005

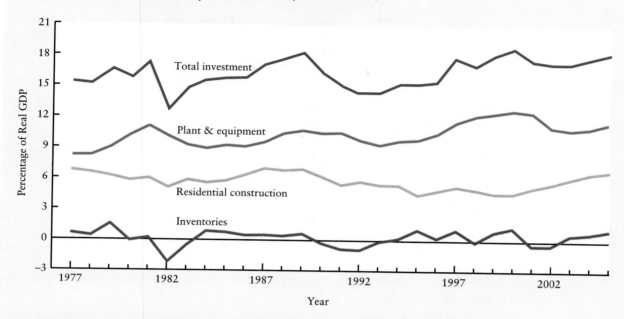

Total investment as a share of GDP fluctuates considerably. In percentage terms, changes in inventories are the most volatile component of investment.

(*Source: Bank of Canada Review,* various issues. The most recent data are also available at Statistics Canada's website, www. statcan.ca, by searching for "GDP.")

What explains such fluctuations in investment? Here we examine three important determinants of aggregate investment expenditure:

- the real interest rate
- changes in the level of sales
- business confidence

Let's now examine these in turn.

Desired Investment and the Real Interest Rate   The real interest rate represents the real opportunity cost of using money (either borrowed money or retained earnings) for investment purposes. A rise in the real interest rate therefore reduces the amount of desired investment expenditure. This relationship is most easily seen if we separate investment into three components: inventories, residential construction, and new plant and equipment.

Inventories. Changes in inventories represent only a small percentage of private investment in a typical year. As shown by the bottom line in Figure 21-4, inventory investment has always been between –2 percent and 2 percent of GDP over the past 20 years. (Inventory investment of –2 percent in a year means that inventories *fall* by 2 percent of GDP.) But the average size

The largest part of investment by firms is in new plants and equipment, such as this expansion of a pulp mill in British Columbia.

of such changes is not an adequate measure of their importance. Since they are one of the more volatile elements of total investment, they have an important influence on fluctuations in investment expenditure.

When a firm ties up funds in inventories, those same funds cannot be used elsewhere to earn income. As an alternative to holding inventories, the firm could lend the money out at the going rate of interest. Hence, the higher the real rate of interest, the higher the opportunity cost of holding an inventory of a given size; the higher the opportunity cost, the smaller the inventories that will be desired.

Residential Construction. Expenditure on residential housing is also volatile. Most houses are purchased with money that is borrowed by means of mortgages. Interest on the borrowed money typically accounts for over one-half of the purchaser's annual mortgage payments; the remainder is repayment of the original loan, called the *principal.* Because interest payments are such a large part of mortgage payments, variations in interest rates exert a substantial effect on the demand for housing.

New Plant and Equipment. The real interest rate is also a major determinant of investment in new plant and equipment. When interest rates are high, it is expensive for firms to borrow funds that can be used for fixed investment. Similarly, firms with cash on hand can earn high returns on interest-earning assets, again making investment in plant and equipment a less attractive alternative. Thus, high real interest rates lead to a reduction in desired investment in plant and equipment, whereas low real interest rates increase desired investment.

The real interest rate reflects the opportunity cost associated with investment, whether it is investment in inventories, residential construction, or plant and equipment. The higher the real interest rate, the higher the opportunity cost of investment, and thus the lower the amount of desired investment.

Figure 21-4 shows these three components of investment over the past 30 years. Inventory investment is clearly the smallest of the three but in relative terms is actually the most volatile. Note that the three components move broadly together. They all fell in the 1981–1982 recession, and again in the 1990–1991 recession. Since 2002, all three components of investment have increased.

Desired Investment and Changes in Sales

Firms hold inventories because of unexpected changes in sales and production, and they usually have a target level of inventories that depends on their normal level of sales. Because the size of inventories is related to the level of sales, the *change* in inventories (which is part of current investment) is related to the *change* in the level of sales.

For example, suppose a firm wants to hold inventories equal to 10 percent of its monthly sales. If normal monthly sales are $100 000, it will wish to hold inventories valued at $10 000. If monthly sales increase to $110 000, it will want to hold inventories of $11 000. Over the period during which its stock of inventories is being increased, there will be a total of $1000 of new inventory investment.

The higher the level of sales, the larger the desired stock of inventories. Changes in the rate of sales therefore cause temporary bouts of investment (or disinvestment) in inventories.

Changes in sales have similar effects on investment in plant and equipment. For example, if there is a general increase in consumers' demand for products that is expected to persist and that cannot be met by existing capacity, investment in new plant and equipment will be needed. Once the new plants have been built and put into operation, however, the rate of new investment will fall.

Desired Investment and Business Confidence   Investment takes time. When a firm invests, it increases its future capacity to produce output. If it can sell the new output profitably, the investment will prove to be a good one. If the new output does not generate profits, the investment will have been a bad one. When it undertakes an investment, the firm does not know if it will turn out well or badly—it is betting on a favourable future that cannot be known with certainty.

The Conference Board of Canada publishes regular surveys of business and consumer confidence. Visit its website: **www.conferenceboard.ca**.

When firms expect good times ahead, they will want to invest now so that they have a larger productive capacity in the future ready to satisfy the greater demand. When they expect bad times ahead, they will not invest because they expect no payoff from doing so.

Investment depends on firms' expectations about the future state of the economy. Optimism leads to more desired investment; pessimism leads to less desired investment.

Desired Investment as Autonomous Expenditure
We have seen that desired investment is influenced by many things, and a complete discussion of the determination of national income is not possible without including all of these factors.

For the moment, however, our goal is to build the *simplest* model of the aggregate economy in which we can examine the interaction of actual national income and desired aggregate expenditure. To build this simple model, we begin by treating desired investment as *autonomous*—that is, we assume it to be unaffected by changes in national income. Figure 21-5 shows the investment function as a horizontal line.

It is important not to confuse the assumption that desired investment is *autonomous* with respect to national income (which we are making) with the assumption that it is *constant* (which we are not making). As we have said, investment is the most volatile component of aggregate expenditure, and it will therefore be important in our model that investment be able to change; shocks to firms' investment behaviour will end up being an important explanation for fluctuations in national income. Our assumption that investment is autonomous with respect to national income (and hence the *I* function in Figure 21-5 is horizontal) is mainly a simplifying one. But the assumption does reflect the fact that investment is an act undertaken by firms for *future* benefit, and thus the *current* level of GDP is unlikely to have a significant effect on desired investment.

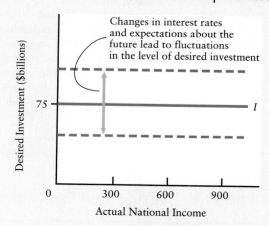

FIGURE 21-5   Desired Investment as Autonomous Expenditure

Desired investment is assumed to be autonomous with respect to current national income. In this example, the level of desired investment is $75 billion. However, changes in interest rates or business confidence will lead to upward or downward shifts in the investment function.

The Aggregate Expenditure Function

The **aggregate expenditure (AE) function** relates the level of desired aggregate expenditure to the level of actual income. (In both cases we mean *real* as opposed to *nominal* variables.) In the simplified economy of this chapter, in which there is no

aggregate expenditure (AE) function The function that relates desired aggregate expenditure to actual national income.

government and no international trade, desired aggregate expenditure is just equal to desired consumption plus desired investment, $C + I$.

$$AE = C + I$$

The table in Figure 21-6 shows how the AE function can be calculated, given the consumption function from Figure 21-2 and the investment function from Figure 21-4. In this specific case, all of desired investment expenditure is autonomous, as is the $30 billion of consumption that would be desired if national income were equal to zero. Total autonomous expenditure is therefore $105 billion—induced expenditure is just equal to induced consumption, which is equal to the MPC times disposable income $(0.8 \times Y_D)$. Furthermore, since our simple model has no government and no taxes, disposable income, Y_D, is equal to national income, Y. Hence, desired aggregate expenditure can be written as:

$$AE = \$105 \text{ billion} + (0.8)Y$$

The Marginal Propensity to Spend The fraction of any increment to national income that people spend on purchasing domestic output is called the economy's **marginal propensity to spend**. The marginal propensity to spend is measured by the change in desired aggregate expenditure divided by the change in national income, or $\Delta AE/\Delta Y$. This is the slope of the aggregate expenditure function. In this book, the marginal propensity to spend is denoted by the symbol z, which is a number greater than zero and less than 1. For the example given in Figure 21-6, the marginal propensity to spend is 0.8. If national income increases by a dollar, 80 cents will go into increased (consumption) expenditure; 20 cents will go into increased saving and will not be spent. The marginal propensity to spend should not be confused with the marginal propensity to consume.

The marginal propensity to spend is the amount of extra total expenditure induced when national income rises by $1, whereas the marginal propensity to consume is the

marginal propensity to spend The change in desired aggregate expenditure on domestic output divided by the change in national income that brought it about.

FIGURE 21-6   The Aggregate Expenditure Function

National Income (Y)	Desired Consumption Expenditure (C = 30 + 0.8 × Y)	Desired Investment Expenditure (I = 75)	Desired Aggregate Expenditure (AE = C + I)
30	54	75	129
150	150	75	225
300	270	75	345
450	390	75	465
525	450	75	525
600	510	75	585
900	750	75	825

The aggregate expenditure function relates desired aggregate expenditure to actual national income. The curve AE in the figure plots the data from the first and last columns of the accompanying table. Its intercept, which in this case is $105 billion, shows the sum of autonomous consumption and autonomous investment. The slope of AE is equal to the marginal propensity to spend, which in this simple economy is just the marginal propensity to consume.

amount of extra consumption expenditure induced when households' disposable income rises by $1.

In the simple model of this chapter, the marginal propensity to spend is equal to the marginal propensity to consume. In later chapters, however, when we add government and international trade to the model, the marginal propensity to spend differs from the marginal propensity to consume. Both here and in later chapters, it is the more general measure—the marginal propensity to spend—that is important for determining equilibrium national income.

Practise with Study Guide Chapter 21, Exercise 3.

21.2 EQUILIBRIUM NATIONAL INCOME

We have constructed an *AE* function that combines the spending plans of households and firms. The function shows, for any given level of *actual* national income, the level of *desired* aggregate spending. We are now ready to see what determines the *equilibrium* level of national income. When something is in equilibrium, there is no tendency for it to change. Any conditions that are required for something to be in equilibrium are called *equilibrium conditions*. We will see that the distinction between desired and actual expenditure is central to understanding the equilibrium conditions for national income.

In this chapter and the next, we make an important assumption that influences the nature of equilibrium. In particular, we assume that firms are able and willing to produce any amount of output that is demanded of them, and that changes in their production levels do not require a change in their product prices. In this setting, we say that output is *demand determined*. This is an extreme assumption, and we will relax it in Chapter 23 when we discuss the determination of the price level. Until then, however, it is a very useful assumption that allows us more easily to understand how our macro model works.

Table 21-1 illustrates the determination of equilibrium national income for our simple model economy. Suppose firms are producing a final output of $300 billion, and thus national income is $300 billion. According to the table, at this level of actual national income, desired aggregate expenditure is $345 billion. If firms persist in producing a current output of only $300 billion in the face of desired aggregate expenditure of $345 billion, one of two things will happen.

One possibility is that households and firms will be unable to spend the extra $45 billion that they would like to spend, so lines or waiting lists of unsatisfied customers will appear. These shortages will send a signal to firms that they could increase their sales if they increased their production. When the firms do increase their production, national income rises. Of course, the individual firms are interested only in their own sales and profits, but their individual actions have as their inevitable consequence an increase in GDP.

A more realistic possibility is that all spenders will spend everything that they wanted to spend. But since desired expenditure exceeds the actual amount of output, this is only possible if some sales come from the producers' accumulated inventories. In our example, the fulfillment of plans to purchase $345 billion worth of goods in the face of a current output of only $300 billion will reduce inventories by $45 billion. As long as inventories last, more goods can be sold than are currently being produced. But since firms want to maintain a certain level of inventories, they will eventually increase their production. Once again, the consequence of each individual firm's decision to increase production is an increase in national income. Thus, the final response to an

TABLE 21-1   Equilibrium National Income

Actual National Income (Y)	Desired Aggregate Expenditure (AE = C + I)	Effect
30	129	Inventories are falling; firms increase output
150	225	
300	345	
450	465	
525	525	Equilibrium income
600	585	Inventories are rising; firms reduce output
900	825	

National income is in equilibrium when desired aggregate expenditure equals actual national income. The data are from Figure 21-6.

FIGURE 21-7   Equilibrium National Income

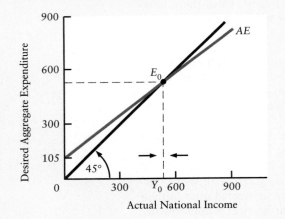

Equilibrium national income is that level of national income where desired aggregate expenditure equals actual national income. If actual national income is below Y_0, desired aggregate expenditure will exceed national income, and output will rise. If national income is above Y_0, desired aggregate expenditure will be less than national income, and production will fall. Only when national income is equal to Y_0 will the economy be in equilibrium, as shown at E_0.

excess of desired aggregate expenditure over actual output is a rise in national income.

For any level of national income at which desired aggregate expenditure exceeds actual income, there will be pressure for actual national income to rise.

Next consider the $900 billion level of actual national income in Table 21-1. At this level of output, desired expenditure on domestically produced goods is only $825 billion. If firms persist in producing $900 billion worth of goods, $75 billion worth must remain unsold. Therefore, inventories must rise. However, firms will not allow inventories of unsold goods to rise indefinitely; sooner or later, they will reduce the level of output to the level of sales. When they reduce their level of output, national income will fall.

For any level of income at which desired aggregate expenditure is less than actual income, there will be pressure for national income to fall.

Finally, look at the national income level of $525 billion in Table 21-1. At this level, and only at this level, desired aggregate expenditure is equal to actual national income. Purchasers can fulfill their spending plans without causing inventories to change. There is no incentive for firms to alter output. Because everyone wishes to purchase an amount equal to what is actually being produced, output and income will remain steady; they are in equilibrium.

The equilibrium level of national income occurs where desired aggregate expenditure equals actual national income.

In other words, the *equilibrium condition* for our simple model of national income determination is:

$$Y = AE$$

As we will now see, the combination of our *AE* function and this condition will determine the equilibrium level of national income.

Consider Figure 21-7. The line labelled *AE* graphs the specific aggregate expenditure function that we have been working with throughout this chapter. The 45° line (*AE = Y*) graphs the equilibrium condition that desired aggregate expenditure equals actual national income. Anywhere along the 45° line, the value of desired aggregate expenditure, which is measured on the vertical axis, is equal to the value of actual national income, which is measured on the horizontal axis.

Graphically, equilibrium occurs at the level of income at which the *AE* line intersects the 45° line. This is the level of income where desired aggregate expenditure is just equal to actual national income. In Figure 21-7, the equilibrium level of national income (real GDP) is Y_0.

To understand how Figure 21-7 illustrates economic behaviour, consider some level of real GDP below Y_0. At this level of income, the *AE* curve lies above the 45° line, indicating that desired spending exceeds actual output. The vertical distance between *AE* and the 45° line reflects the size of this excess demand. As we said earlier, this excess demand may lead to a *reduction* in inventories and eventually lead firms to increase their production. Conversely, at any level of GDP above Y_0, the *AE* curve is below the 45° line, indicating that desired spending is less than actual output. The vertical distance between the curves in this case shows the size of the excess supply, which may lead to an *accumulation* of inventories and an eventual decrease in firms' production. Only when real GDP equals Y_0 is desired spending equal to actual output, thus providing firms with no incentive to change their production.

Now that we have explained the meaning of equilibrium national income, we will go on to examine the various forces that can *change* this equilibrium. We will then be well on our way to understanding some of the sources of short-run fluctuations in real GDP.

(X) myeconlab

A different, but equivalent, way of thinking about the equilibrium level of national income involves comparing desired saving with desired investment. For more details, look for "Investment, Saving, and Equilibrium GDP" in the *Additional Topics* section of this book's MyEconLab.

w w w . m y e c o n l a b . c o m

▌ 21.3 **CHANGES IN EQUILIBRIUM NATIONAL INCOME**

A glance at Figure 21-7 shows that the equilibrium level of national income (Y_0) occurs where the *AE* function intersects the 45° line. Through the adjustment in firms' inventories and production levels, the level of actual national income will adjust until this equilibrium level is achieved. Because the *AE* function plays a central role in determining equilibrium national income, you should not be surprised to hear that *shifts* in the *AE* function are central to explaining why national income changes.

Practise with Study Guide Chapter 21, Short-Answer Question 2.

Shifts of the *AE* Function

The *AE* function shifts when one of its components shifts—that is, when there is a shift in the consumption function or in the investment function. As we have already mentioned, both the consumption function and the investment function will shift if there is a change in interest rates or expectations of the future state of the economy. A change in household wealth is an additional reason for the consumption function to shift. Let's now consider what happens when there is an upward shift in the *AE* function.

Upward Shifts in the *AE* Function Suppose households experience an increase in wealth and thus increase their desired levels of consumption spending at each level of disposable income. Or, suppose firms' expectations of higher future sales lead them to increase their planned investment. What is the effect of such events on national income?

Because any increase in autonomous expenditure shifts the entire *AE* function upward, the same analysis applies to each of the changes mentioned. Two types of shifts in *AE* can occur. First, if the same addition to expenditure occurs at all levels of income, the *AE* function shifts parallel to itself, as shown in part (i) of Figure 21-8. Second, if there is a change in the marginal propensity to spend, the slope of the *AE* function changes, as shown in part (ii) of Figure 21-8.

Figure 21-8 shows that an upward shift in the *AE* function increases equilibrium national income. After the shift in the *AE* curve, income is no longer in equilibrium at its original level because at that level desired aggregate expenditure exceeds actual national income. Given this excess demand, firms' inventories are being depleted and firms respond by increasing production. Equilibrium national income rises to the higher level indicated by the intersection of the *new AE* curve with the 45° line.

Downward Shifts in the *AE* Function   What happens to national income if there is a decrease in the amount of consumption or investment expenditure desired at each level of income? These changes shift the *AE* function downward, as shown in Figure 21-8 by the movement from the dashed *AE* curve to the solid *AE* curve. An equal reduction

FIGURE 21-8   Shifts in the Aggregate Expenditure Function

(i) A parallel shift in *AE*

(ii) A change in the slope of *AE*

Upward shifts in the *AE* function increase equilibrium income; downward shifts decrease equilibrium income. In parts (i) and (ii), the *AE* function is initially AE_0 with equilibrium national income equal to Y_0.

In part (i), a parallel upward shift in the *AE* curve from AE_0 to AE_1 reflects an increase in desired expenditure at each level of national income. For example, at Y_0, desired expenditure rises from e_0 to e_1' and therefore exceeds actual national income. Equilibrium is reached at E_1, where income is Y_1. The increase in desired expenditure from e_1' to e_1, represented by a movement along AE_1, is an induced response to the increase in income from Y_0 to Y_1.

In part (ii), a non-parallel upward shift in the *AE* curve from AE_0 to AE_2 reflects an increase in the marginal propensity to spend. This leads to an increase in equilibrium national income. Equilibrium is reached at E_2, where national income is equal to Y_2.

in desired expenditure at all levels of income shifts AE parallel to itself. A fall in the marginal propensity to spend out of national income reduces the slope of the AE function. In both cases, the equilibrium level of national income decreases; the new equilibrium is found at the intersection of the 45° line and the *new AE* curve.

The Results Restated We have derived two important general propositions from our simple model of national income determination.

1. A rise in the amount of desired aggregate expenditure at each level of national income will shift the AE curve upward and increase equilibrium national income.

2. A fall in the amount of desired aggregate expenditure at each level of national income will shift the AE curve downward and reduce equilibrium national income.

The Multiplier

We have learned whether specific changes in the AE function will cause equilibrium national income to rise or fall. We would now like to understand the *size* of these changes. A measure of the magnitude of such changes is provided by the *multiplier*. A change in autonomous expenditure increases equilibrium national income by a *multiple* of the initial change in autonomous expenditure. That is, the change in national income is *larger than* the initial change in desired expenditure.

The multiplier is the change in equilibrium national income divided by the change in autonomous expenditure that brought it about. In the simple macro model, the multiplier is greater than 1.[1]

To see why the multiplier is greater than 1 in this model, consider a simple example. Imagine what would happen to national income if Kimberley-Clark decided to spend an additional $500 million per year on the construction of new paper mills. Initially, the construction of the paper mills would create $500 million worth of new national income and a corresponding amount of income for households and firms on which the initial $500 million is spent. But this is not the end of the story. The increase in national income of $500 million would cause an induced increase in desired consumption.

Electricians, masons, and carpenters—who would gain new income directly from the building of the paper mills—would spend some of it on food, clothing, entertainment, cars, TVs, and other commodities. When output expanded to meet this demand, new incomes would be created for workers and firms in these industries. When they, in turn, spent their newly earned incomes, output would rise further. More income would be created, and more expenditure would be induced. Indeed, at this stage, we might wonder whether the increases in income would ever come to an end. To deal with this concern, we need to consider the multiplier in somewhat more precise terms.

Let autonomous expenditure be denoted by A. Now consider an increase in autonomous expenditure of ΔA, which in our example above was $500 million per year. Remember that ΔA stands for *any* increase in autonomous expenditure; this could

---

[1] In this chapter and the next we assume that firms can readily change their output in response to changes in demand (perhaps because there is some unemployed labour and capital). This assumption of *demand-determined* output is central to the result of a multiplier greater than one. We relax this assumption in later chapters.

be an increase in investment or in the autonomous component of consumption. The *AE* function shifts upward by Δ*A*. National income is no longer in equilibrium because desired aggregate expenditure now exceeds actual income. Equilibrium is restored by a *movement along* the new *AE* curve.

simple multiplier The ratio of the change in equilibrium national income to the change in autonomous expenditure that brought it about, calculated for a constant price level.

The **simple multiplier** measures the change in equilibrium national income that occurs in response to a change in autonomous expenditure *at a constant price level*. We refer to it as "simple" because we have simplified the situation by assuming that the price level is fixed (an assumption we will remove in Chapter 23). Figure 21-9 illustrates the simple multiplier and makes clear that it is greater than 1. *Applying Economic Concepts 21-1* provides a numerical example.

The Size of the Simple Multiplier The size of the simple multiplier depends on the slope of the *AE* function—that is, on the marginal propensity to spend, *z*.

As shown in Figure 21-10, a high marginal propensity to spend means a steep *AE* curve. The expenditure induced by any initial increase in income is large, with the result that the final rise in income is correspondingly large. By contrast, a low marginal propensity to spend means a relatively flat *AE* curve. The expenditure induced by the initial increase in income is small, and the final rise in income is not much larger than the initial rise in autonomous expenditure that brought it about.

Practise with Study Guide Chapter 21, Short-Answer Question 4.

The larger the marginal propensity to spend, the steeper the *AE* function and thus the larger the simple multiplier.

APPLYING ECONOMIC CONCEPTS 21-1

The Multiplier: A Numerical Example

Consider an economy that has a marginal propensity to spend out of national income of 0.80. Suppose an increase in business confidence leads many firms to increase their investment in new buildings and factories. Specifically, suppose desired investment increases by $1 billion per year. National income initially rises by $1 billion, but that is not the end of it. The factors of production that received the first $1 billion spend $800 million. This second round of spending generates $800 million of new income. This new income, in turn, induces $640 million of third-round spending, and so it continues, with each successive round of new income generating 80 percent as much in new expenditure. Each additional round of expenditure creates new income and yet another round of expenditure.

The table carries the process through 10 rounds. Students with sufficient patience (and no faith in mathematics) may compute as many rounds in the process as they wish; they will find that the sum of the rounds of expenditures approaches a limit of $5 billion, which is five times the initial increase in expenditure. [30]

Notice that most of the total change in national income occurs in the first few rounds. Of the total change of $5 billion, 68 percent ($3.4 billion) occurs after only five rounds of activity. By the end of the tenth round, 89 percent ($4.5 billion) of the total change has taken place.

Round of Spending	Increase in Expenditure (millions of dollars)	Cumulative Total (millions of dollars)
1 (initial increase)	1000.0	1000.0
2	800.0	1800.0
3	640.0	2440.0
4	512.0	2952.0
5	409.6	3361.6
6	327.7	3689.3
7	262.1	3951.4
8	209.7	4161.1
9	167.8	4328.9
10	134.2	4463.1
11 to 20 combined	479.3	4942.4
All others	57.6	5000.0

We can derive the precise value of the simple multiplier by using elementary algebra. (The formal derivation is given in *Extensions in Theory 21-2*.) The result is:

$$\text{Simple Multiplier} = \frac{\Delta Y}{\Delta A} = \frac{1}{1-z}$$

Recall that z is the marginal propensity to spend out of national income and is between zero and 1. The *smallest* simple multiplier occurs when z equals zero. In this case, $(1-z)$ equals 1 and so the multiplier equals 1. On the other hand, if z is very close to 1, $(1-z)$ is close to zero and so the multiplier becomes very large. The relationship between the slope of the AE function (z) and the size of the multiplier is shown in Figure 21-10.

A Realistic Estimate for the Simple Multiplier
To estimate the size of the simple multiplier in an actual economy, we need to estimate the value of the marginal propensity to spend out of national income in that economy. Evidence suggests that the Canadian value is much smaller than the 0.8 that we used in our example, in large part because our simple model currently has no taxation by government or spending on foreign goods and services. Both of these important elements (which we discuss in the next chapter) reduce the amount of each new dollar of income that gets spent on domestic output—that is, they reduce the value of z. For the current Canadian economy a realistic estimate of z is about 0.2. Hence, a realistic estimate of the simple multiplier in Canada is approximately $1/(1 - 0.2) = 1/0.8 = 1.25$.

FIGURE 21-9   The Simple Multiplier

An increase in autonomous aggregate expenditure increases equilibrium national income by a multiple of the initial increase. The initial equilibrium is at E_0, where AE_0 intersects the 45° line. At this point, desired aggregate expenditure, e_0, is equal to actual national income, Y_0. An increase in autonomous expenditure of ΔA then shifts the AE function upward to AE_1.

Equilibrium occurs when income rises to Y_1. Here desired expenditure, e_1, equals national income, Y_1. The increase in desired expenditure from e_1' to e_1 represents the induced increase in expenditure that occurs as national income rises. Because ΔY is greater than ΔA, the simple multiplier is greater than 1 ($\Delta Y/\Delta A > 1$).

Economic Fluctuations as Self-Fulfilling Prophecies

Expectations about the future play an important role in macroeconomics. We said earlier that households' and firms' expectations about the future state of the economy influence desired consumption and desired investment. But as we have just seen, changes in desired aggregate expenditure will, through the multiplier process, lead to changes in national income. This link between expectations and national income suggests that expectations about a healthy economy can actually produce a healthy economy—what economists call a self-fulfilling prophecy.

Imagine a situation in which many firms begin to feel optimistic about future economic prospects. This optimism may lead them to increase their desired investment, thus shifting up the economy's AE function. As we have seen, however, any upward shift in the AE function will lead to an increase in national income. Such "good" economic times will then be seen by firms to have justified their initial optimism. Many firms in such a situation may take pride in their ability to predict the future—but this would be misplaced pride. The truth of the matter is that if enough firms are optimistic

FIGURE 21-10 The Size of the Simple Multiplier

 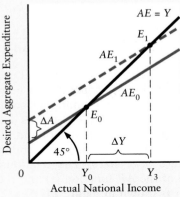

(i) Flat *AE*, multiplier equal to 1   (ii) Intermediate case   (iii) Steep *AE*, multiplier large

The larger the marginal propensity to spend out of national income (z), the steeper is the *AE* curve and the larger is the multiplier. In each part of the figure, the initial *AE* function is AE_0, equilibrium is at E_0, with income Y_0. The *AE* curve then shifts upward to AE_1 as a result of an increase in autonomous expenditure of ΔA. ΔA is the same in each part. The new equilibrium in each case is at E_1.

In part (i), the *AE* function is horizontal, indicating a marginal propensity to spend of zero ($z = 0$). The change in equilibrium income ΔY is only the increase in autonomous expenditure because there is no induced expenditure by the people who receive the initial increase in income. The simple multiplier is then equal to 1, its minimum possible value.

In part (ii), the *AE* curve slopes upward but is still relatively flat (z is low). The increase in equilibrium national income to Y_2 is only slightly greater than the increase in autonomous expenditure that brought it about. The simple multiplier is slightly greater than 1.

In part (iii), the *AE* function is quite steep (z is high). Now the increase in equilibrium income to Y_3 is much larger than the increase in autonomous expenditure that brought it about. The simple multiplier is much larger than 1.

and take actions based on that optimism, their actions will *create* the economic situation that they expected.

Now imagine the opposite situation in which many firms begin to feel pessimistic about future economic conditions. This pessimism may lead them to scale down or cancel planned investment projects. Such a decline in planned investment would shift the *AE* function down and lead to a decrease in national income. The "bad" economic times will then be seen by the firms as justification for their initial pessimism, and many will take pride in their predictive powers. But again their pride would be misplaced; the truth is that sufficient pessimism on the part of firms will tend to *create* the conditions that they expected.

Politicians in Canada and elsewhere are often heard "talking up" their national economies. This can be understood by examining the role that expectations play in booms and recessions. For more on this topic, look for "Recessions and Booms As Self-Fulfilling Prophecies" in the *Additional Topics* section of this book's MyEconLab.

EXTENSIONS IN THEORY 21-2

The Algebra of the Simple Multiplier

Basic algebra is all that is needed to derive the exact expression for the multiplier. Readers who feel at home with algebra may want to follow this derivation. Others can skip it and rely on the graphical and numerical arguments that have been given in the text.

First, we derive the equation for the AE curve. Desired aggregate expenditure comprises autonomous expenditure and induced expenditure. In the simple model of this chapter, autonomous expenditure is equal to investment plus autonomous consumption. Induced expenditure is equal to induced consumption.

Hence, we can write

$$AE = z Y + A \qquad [1]$$

where A is autonomous expenditure and $z Y$ is induced expenditure, z being the marginal propensity to spend out of national income. In the simple model of this chapter, with no government and no international trade, z is equal to the marginal propensity to consume.

Now we write the equation of the 45° line,

$$AE = Y \qquad [2]$$

which states the equilibrium condition that desired aggregate expenditure equals actual national income. Equations 1 and 2 are two equations with two unknowns, AE and Y. To solve them, we substitute Equation 1 into Equation 2 to obtain

$$Y = z Y + A \qquad [3]$$

Equation 3 can be easily solved to get Y expressed in terms of A and z. The solution is

$$Y = \frac{A}{1 - z} \qquad [4]$$

Equation 4 tells us the equilibrium value of Y in terms of autonomous expenditures and the marginal propensity to spend out of national income. Now consider a \$1 increase in A. The expression $Y = A/(1 - z)$ tells us that if A changes by one dollar, the resulting change in Y will be $1/(1 - z)$ dollars. Generally, for a change in autonomous spending of ΔA, the resulting change in Y will be

$$\Delta Y = \frac{\Delta A}{1 - z} \qquad [5]$$

Dividing through by ΔA gives the value of the multiplier:

$$\text{Simple Multiplier} = \frac{\Delta Y}{\Delta A} = \frac{1}{1 - z} \qquad [6]$$

SUMMARY

21.1 DESIRED AGGREGATE EXPENDITURE

- Desired aggregate expenditure (AE) is equal to desired consumption plus desired investment plus desired government purchases plus desired net exports. It is the amount that economic agents want to spend on purchasing the national product.

$$AE = C + I + G + (X - IM)$$

- The relationship between disposable income and consumption is called the consumption function. The constant term in the consumption function is autonomous expenditure. The part of consumption that responds to income is called induced expenditure.

- A change in disposable income leads to a change in desired consumption and desired saving. The responsiveness of these changes is measured by the marginal propensity to consume (MPC) and the marginal propensity to save (MPS), both of which are positive, and which sum to 1, indicating that all disposable income is either consumed or saved.

- Changes in wealth, interest rates, or expectations about the future lead to a change in autonomous consumption. As a result, the consumption function shifts.

- Firms' desired investment depends, among other things, on real interest rates, changes in sales, and business confidence. In our simplest model of the economy, investment is treated as autonomous with respect to changes in national income.

21.2 EQUILIBRIUM NATIONAL INCOME

- Equilibrium national income is defined as that level of national income where desired aggregate expenditure equals actual national income. At incomes above equilibrium, desired expenditure is less than national income. In this case, inventories accumulate and firms will eventually reduce output. At incomes below equilibrium, desired expenditure exceeds national income.

In this case, inventories are depleted and firms will eventually increase output.

- Equilibrium national income is represented graphically by the point at which the aggregate expenditure (*AE*) curve cuts the 45° line—that is, where desired aggregate expenditure equals actual national income.

21.3 CHANGES IN EQUILIBRIUM NATIONAL INCOME

- Equilibrium national income is increased by a rise in either autonomous consumption or autonomous investment expenditure. Equilibrium national income is reduced by a fall in these desired expenditures.
- The magnitude of the effect on national income of shifts in autonomous expenditure is given by the multiplier. It is defined as $\Delta Y/\Delta A$, where ΔA is the change in autonomous expenditure.
- The simple multiplier is the multiplier when the price level is constant. The simple multiplier $= \Delta Y/\Delta A = 1/(1 - z)$, where z is the marginal propensity to spend

out of national income. The larger is z, the larger is the multiplier.
- It is a basic prediction of our simple macro model that the simple multiplier is greater than 1.
- Expectations play an important role in the determination of national income. Optimism can lead households and firms to increase desired expenditure, which, through the multiplier process, leads to increases in national income. Pessimism can similarly lead to decreases in desired expenditure and national income.

KEY CONCEPTS

Desired versus actual expenditure
The consumption function
Average and marginal propensities to consume
Average and marginal propensities to save

The aggregate expenditure (*AE*) function
Marginal propensity to spend
Equilibrium national income

Effect on national income of shifts in the *AE* curve
The simple multiplier
The size of the multiplier and slope of the *AE* curve

STUDY EXERCISES

1. Fill in the blanks to make the following statements correct.

   a. The equation for *actual* national income from the expenditure side is written as: GDP = <u>C + I + G + Nx</u> .

   b. The equation for *desired* aggregate expenditure is written as: *AE* = <u>C + I + G + Nx</u> .

   c. National income accounts measure <u>actual</u> expenditures in four broad categories. National income theory deals with <u>desired</u> expenditure in the same four categories.

$y = mx + b$

d. The equation for a simple consumption function is written as $C = a + bY$. The letter a represents the _autonomous consumption_ part of consumption. The letters bY represent the _MPC_ part of consumption. When graphing a consumption function, the vertical intercept is given by the letter _a_, and the slope of the function is given by the letter _b_.

e. In the simple macro model of this chapter, all investment is treated as _autonomous_ expenditure, meaning that it is unaffected by changes in national income.

f. The aggregate expenditure function in the simple macro model of this chapter is written as $AE = $ _C + I_, and is graphed with _desired Aggregate Expenditure_ on the vertical axis and _national income_ on the horizontal axis.

g. An example of an aggregate expenditure function is $AE = \$47$ billion $+ 0.92Y$. Autonomous expenditure is _47 billion_ and the marginal propensity to spend out of national income is _0.92_. In the simple model in this chapter, the marginal propensity to spend is the same as the marginal propensity to consume because _____.

2. Fill in the blanks to make the following statements correct.

a. If actual national income is $200 billion and desired aggregate expenditure is $180 billion, inventories may begin to _____, firms will _____ the level of output, and national income will _____.

b. If actual national income is $200 billion and desired aggregate expenditure is $214 billion, inventories may begin to _____, firms will _____ the level of output, and national income will _____.

c. If households experience an increase in wealth that leads to an increase in desired consumption, the AE curve will shift _____. Equilibrium national income will _____ to the level indicated by the intersection of the AE curve with the _____ line.

d. When autonomous desired expenditure increases by $10 billion, national income will increase by _____ than $10 billion. The magnitude of the change in national income is measured by the _____.

e. The larger is the marginal propensity to spend, the _____ is the multiplier. Where z is the marginal propensity to spend, the multiplier is equal to _____.

3. Consider the following table for a household's consumption expenditures and disposable income. All values are expressed in real 1997 dollars.

Disposable Income (Y_D)	Desired Consumption (C)	$APC = C/Y_D$	$MPC = \Delta C/\Delta Y_D$
0	150	—	
100	225	—	—
200	300	—	—
300	375	—	—
400	450	—	—
500	525	—	—
600	600	—	—
700	675	—	—
800	750	—	—

a. Compute the average propensity to consume for each level of income and fill in the table.

b. Compute the marginal propensity to consume for each successive change in income and fill in the table.

c. Plot the consumption function on a scale diagram. What is its slope?

4. This question relates to desired saving, and is based on the table from Question 3.

a. Compute desired saving at each level of disposable income. Plot the saving function on a scale diagram. What is its slope?

b. Show that the average propensity to save plus the average propensity to consume must equal 1.

5. In the chapter we explained at length the difference between _desired_ expenditures and _actual_ expenditures.

a. Is national income accounting based on desired or actual expenditures? Explain.

b. Suppose there were a sudden decrease in desired consumption expenditure. Explain why this would lead to an equally sudden increase in _actual_ investment expenditure. Which type of investment would rise?

c. Illustrate the event from part (b) in a 45°-line diagram. Illustrate the increase in actual investment.

6. **myeconlab** Consider the following diagram of the AE function and the 45° line.

Actual National Income

a. Suppose the level of actual national income is Y_1. What is the level of desired aggregate expenditure? Is it greater or less than actual output? Are inventories being depleted or accumulated?

b. If actual income is Y_1, explain the process by which national income changes toward equilibrium.

c. Suppose the level of actual national income is Y_2. What is the level of desired aggregate expenditure? Is it greater or less than actual output? Are inventories being depleted or accumulated?

d. If actual income is Y_2, explain the process by which national income changes toward equilibrium.

7. **myeconlab** Consider a simple model like the one developed in this chapter. The following equations show the levels of desired consumption and investment:

$$C = 500 + 0.9Y$$
$$I = 100$$

Y	C	I	AE
0			
2 000			
4 000			
6 000			
8 000			
10 000			

a. Complete the table above.

b. What is the equilibrium level of national income in this model? Why?

8. **myeconlab** Suppose you are given the following information for an economy without government spending, exports, or imports. C is desired consumption, I is desired investment, and Y is income. C and I are given by:

$$C = 1400 + 0.8Y$$
$$I = 400$$

a. What is the equation for the aggregate expenditure (AE) function?

b. Applying the equilibrium condition that $Y = AE$, determine the level of equilibrium national income.

c. Using your answer from part (b), determine the values of consumption, saving, and investment when the economy is in equilibrium.

9. Consider an economy characterized by the following equations:

$$C = 500 + 0.75Y + 0.05W$$
$$I = 150$$

where C is desired consumption, I is desired investment, W is household wealth, and Y is national income.

a. Suppose $W = 10\ 000$. Draw the aggregate expenditure function on a scale diagram along with the 45° line. What is the equilibrium level of national income?

b. The marginal propensity to spend in this economy is 0.75. What is the value of the multiplier?

c. Using your answer from part (b), what would be the change in equilibrium national income if desired investment increased to 250? Can you show this in your diagram?

d. Now suppose household wealth increases from 10 000 to 15 000. What happens to the AE function and by how much does national income change?

10. The "Paradox of Thrift" is a famous idea in macroeconomics—one that we will discuss in later chapters. The basic idea is that if every household in the economy tries to increase its level of desired saving, the level of national income will fall and they will end up saving no more than they were initially. Use the model and diagrams of this chapter to show how an (autonomous) increase in desired saving would reduce equilibrium income and lead to no change in aggregate saving. (Though it is not essential, you may find it useful to see "Investment, Saving, and Equilibrium GDP" in the *Additional Topics* section of the MyEconLab.)

DISCUSSION QUESTIONS

1. Relate the following newspaper headlines to shifts in the C, S, I, and AE functions and to changes in equilibrium national income.

a. "Revival of consumer confidence leads to increased spending."

b. "High mortgage rates discourage new house purchases."

c. "Concern over future leads to a reduction in inventories."

d. "Accelerated depreciation allowances in the new federal budget set off boom on equipment purchases."

e. "Consumers spend as stock market soars."

2. Why might an individual's marginal propensity to consume be higher in the long run than in the short run? Why might it be lower? Is it possible for an individual's average propensity to consume to be greater than 1 in the short run? In the long run? Can a country's average propensity to consume be greater than 1 in the short run? In the long run?

3. Explain why a sudden, unexpected fall in consumer expenditure would initially cause an increase in actual investment expenditure by firms.

4. In the simple model of this chapter, aggregate investment was assumed to be autonomous. The simple multiplier was $1/(1 - z)$, where z was the marginal propensity to spend. With autonomous investment, the marginal propensity to spend is simply the marginal propensity to consume. Now suppose that investment is *not* completely autonomous. That is, suppose that $I = \bar{I} + mY$, where $\bar{I}$ is autonomous investment and m is the "marginal propensity to invest" ($m > 0$). Explain how this modification to the simple model changes the simple multiplier.

CHAPTER 22

Adding Government and Trade to the Simple Macro Model

LEARNING OBJECTIVES

In this chapter you will learn

1. how government purchases and tax revenues are related to national income.
2. how exports and imports are related to national income.
3. how to distinguish between the marginal propensity to consume and the marginal propensity to spend.
4. why the presence of government and foreign trade reduces the value of the simple multiplier.
5. how government can use fiscal policy to influence the level of national income.

In Chapter 21, we developed a simple short-run model of national income determination in a closed economy with fixed prices. In this chapter, we add a government and a foreign sector to that model. In Chapter 23, we will expand the model further to explain the determination of the price level.

Adding government to the model allows us to study *fiscal policy,* the government's use of its taxing and spending powers to affect the level of national income. Adding foreign trade allows us to examine some ways in which external events affect the Canadian economy. Fortunately, the key elements of the last chapter's theory of income determination are unchanged even after government and the foreign sector are incorporated.

22.1 INTRODUCING GOVERNMENT

fiscal policy The use of the government's tax and spending policies.

A government's **fiscal policy** is defined by its plans for taxes and spending. Government spending and taxation influence national income in both the short and the long run. Our discussion of fiscal policy begins in this chapter; we go into more detail in Chapter 24 and again in Chapter 32.

Government Purchases

In Chapter 20, we distinguished between government *purchases of goods and services* and government *transfer payments.* The distinction bears repeating here. When the government hires a bureaucrat, buys office supplies, or purchases fuel for the Canadian Forces, it is adding directly to the demands for the economy's current output of goods and services. Hence, desired government purchases, G, are part of aggregate desired expenditure.

The other part of government spending, transfer payments, also affects desired aggregate expenditure, but only indirectly. Consider welfare or employment-insurance benefits, for example. These government expenditures place no direct demand on the nation's production of goods and services since they merely transfer funds from taxpayers to the recipients. However, when recipients spend some of these payments on consumption, their expenditure is part of aggregate expenditure. Thus, government transfer payments do affect aggregate expenditure but only through the effect these transfers have on households' *disposable* income.

In this chapter we make the simple assumption that the level of government purchases, G, is autonomous with respect to the level of national income. As GDP rises or falls, the level of the government's transfer payments will generally change, but we assume that G does not automatically change just because GDP changes. We then view any change in G as a result of a government policy decision.

Net Tax Revenues

Taxes reduce households' disposable income relative to national income. In contrast, transfer payments raise disposable income relative to national income. For the purpose of calculating the effect of government policy on desired consumption expenditure, it is the net effect of the two that matters.

Net taxes are defined as total tax revenue received by the government minus total transfer payments made by the government, and it is denoted T. (For the remainder of this chapter, the term "taxes" means "net taxes" unless stated otherwise.) Because transfer payments are smaller than total tax revenues, net tax revenues are positive. Disposable income is therefore substantially less than national income. (It was about two-thirds of Canadian GDP in 2006.)

net taxes Total tax revenue minus transfer payments, denoted *T.*

In the model in this chapter, we assume that net tax revenues vary directly with the level of national income, but that the *tax rate* is an autonomous policy variable. As national income rises, a tax system with given tax rates will yield more revenue. For example, when income rises, people will pay more income tax in total even though the tax *rates* are unchanged. We will use the following simple form for government net tax revenues, T:

$$T = tY$$

where t is the **net tax rate** or the *marginal propensity to tax*—the increase in net tax revenue generated when national income increases by \$1.

net tax rate The increase in net tax revenue generated when national income rises by one dollar. Also called the *marginal propensity to tax.*

It may be tempting to think of t as the income tax rate, but note that we are trying to represent in a simple way what in reality is a complex tax structure that includes the taxation of personal income, corporate income, overall expenditures, the value of property, and expenditure on specific products. For that reason, we avoid associating t with any specific type of tax. Instead, in what follows we simply refer to t as the *net tax rate.*

The Budget Balance

The *budget balance* is the difference between total government revenue and total government expenditure; equivalently, it equals net tax revenue minus government purchases, $T - G$. When net revenues exceed purchases, the government has a **budget surplus.** When purchases exceed net revenues, the government has a **budget deficit.**[1] When the two amounts are equal, the government has a *balanced budget.*

In the simple model of Chapter 21, all saving was private since we had no government in the model. But now we must make a distinction between *private saving* and *public saving.* **Private saving** is the difference between disposable income and consumption expenditure, or the amount that households choose to save. **Public saving** is the difference between the government's tax revenues and its expenditures. Public saving is therefore equal to the budget surplus, $T - G$.

When government has a budget surplus, public saving is positive; when government has a budget deficit, public saving is negative.

budget surplus Any excess of current revenue over current expenditure.

budget deficit Any shortfall of current revenue below current expenditure.

private saving Saving on the part of households—the part of disposable income that is not spent on current consumption.

public saving Saving on the part of governments, equal to the government budget surplus.

The federal Department of Finance designs and implements Canada's fiscal policy. See its website: **www.fin.gc.ca**.

Practise with Study Guide Chapter 22, Exercise 1.

Provincial and Municipal Governments

Many people are surprised to learn that the Canadian provincial and municipal governments account for *more* purchases of goods and services than does the federal government. The federal government raises about the same amount of tax revenue as do the provincial and municipal governments combined, but transfers a considerable amount of its revenue to the provinces.

When measuring the overall contribution of government to desired aggregate expenditure, all levels of government must be included.

As we proceed through this chapter discussing the role of government in the determination of national income, think of "the government" as the combination of all levels of government—federal, provincial, territorial, and municipal.

Summary

Before introducing foreign trade, let's summarize how the presence of government affects our simple model.

1. All levels of government add directly to desired aggregate expenditure through their purchases of goods and services, G. Later in this chapter when we are constructing the aggregate expenditure (AE) function for our model, we will include G, and we will treat it as autonomous expenditure.

2. Governments also collect tax revenue and make transfer payments. Net tax revenues are denoted T and are positively related to national income. Since T does not represent any expenditure on goods and services, it is not included directly in the

---

[1] When the government runs a budget deficit, it must borrow the excess of spending over revenues. It does this by issuing additional *government debt* (bonds or treasury bills). When the government runs a surplus, it uses the excess revenue to buy back outstanding government debt. Deficits and debt are the principal topics of Chapter 32.

AE function. *T* will enter the *AE* function *indirectly,* however, through its effect on disposable income (Y_D) and consumption. Recall that $Y_D = Y - T$ and that desired consumption depends on Y_D.

22.2 INTRODUCING FOREIGN TRADE

Of all the goods and services produced in Canada in a given year, roughly 40 percent are exported. A similar value of goods and services is imported into Canada every year. Thus, while *net* exports may contribute only a few percent to Canada's GDP in a typical year, trade is tremendously important to Canada's economy.

Canada imports all kinds of goods and services, from French wine and Peruvian anchovies to Swiss financial and American architectural services. Canada also exports a variety of goods and services, including timber, nickel, automobiles, engineering services, computer software, flight simulators, and commuter jets. U.S.–Canadian trade is the largest two-way flow of trade between any two countries in the world today.

Practise with Study Guide Chapter 22, Short-Answer Question 1 and Exercise 3.

Net Exports

Exports depend on spending decisions made by foreign households and firms that purchase Canadian products. Typically, exports will not change as a result of changes in Canadian national income. We therefore treat exports as autonomous expenditure.

Imports, however, depend on the spending decisions of Canadian households and firms. Almost all consumption goods have an import content. Canadian-made cars, for example, use large quantities of imported components in their manufacture. Canadian-made clothes most often use imported cotton or wool. And most restaurant meals contain some imported fruits, vegetables, or meats. Hence, as consumption rises, imports will also increase. Because consumption rises with national income, we also get a positive relationship between imports and national income. In this chapter, we use the following simple form for imports:

marginal propensity to import The increase in import expenditures induced by a $1 increase in national income. Denoted by *m*.

$$IM = mY$$

where *m* is the **marginal propensity to import**, the amount that desired imports rise when national income rises by $1.

In our simple model, net exports can be described by the following simple equation:

$$NX = X - mY$$

Since exports are autonomous with respect to *Y* but imports are positively related to *Y*, we see that *net exports* are negatively related to national income. This negative relationship is called the *net export function.* Data for a hypothetical economy with autonomous exports and with imports that are 10 percent of national income (*m* = 0.1) are illustrated in Figure 22-1. In this example, exports form the autonomous component and imports the induced component of the desired net export function.

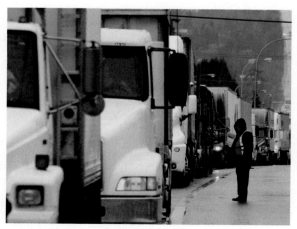

International trade is very important for the Canadian economy. Over $2.5 billion worth of goods and services flows across the Canada–U.S. border every day, much of it in trucks like these.

FIGURE 22-1   The Net Export Function

Actual National Income (Y)	Exports (X)	Imports ($IM = 0.1 \times Y$)	Net Exports ($NX = X - IM$)
0	72	0	72
300	72	30	42
600	72	60	12
720	72	72	0
900	72	90	−18

(i) Export and import functions

(ii) Net export function

Net exports fall as national income rises. The data are hypothetical. In part (i), exports are constant at $72 billion while imports rise with national income; the marginal propensity to import is assumed to be 0.10. Therefore, net exports, shown in part (ii), decline with national income. The slope of the import function in part (i) is equal to the marginal propensity to import. The slope of the net export function in part (ii) is the negative of the marginal propensity to import.

Shifts in the Net Export Function

The net export function is drawn under the assumption that everything affecting net exports, except domestic national income, remains constant. The major factors that must be held constant are foreign national income, domestic and foreign prices, and the exchange rate. A change in any of these factors will shift the net export function. Notice that anything affecting Canadian exports will shift the net export function parallel to itself, upward if exports increase and downward if exports decrease. Also notice that anything affecting the *proportion of income* that Canadian consumers wish to spend on imports will change the *slope* of the net export function. Let's now explore some of these changes in detail.

Changes in Foreign Income An increase in foreign income, other things being equal, will lead to an increase in the quantity of Canadian goods demanded by foreign countries—that is, to an increase in Canadian exports. This change causes the X curve to shift upward and therefore the NX function also to shift upward, parallel to its original position. A fall in foreign income leads to a reduction in Canadian exports and thus to a parallel downward shift in the net export function.

Changes in Relative International Prices Any change in the prices of Canadian goods *relative* to those of foreign goods will cause both imports and exports to change. These changes will shift the net export function.

Consider what happens with a rise in Canadian prices relative to those in foreign countries. The increase in Canadian prices means that foreigners now see Canadian goods as more expensive relative both to goods produced in their own country and to goods imported from countries other than Canada. As a result, the value of Canadian exports will fall.[2] The X curve

---

2 The rise in Canadian prices leads to a reduction in the quantity of Canadian goods demanded by foreigners. But in order for the *value* of Canadian exports to fall, the price elasticity of demand for Canadian exports must exceed 1 (so that the quantity reduction dominates the price increase). Throughout this book, we make this assumption, which is generally believed to be true.

shifts down in Figure 22-2. Similarly, Canadians will see imports from foreign countries become cheaper relative to the prices of Canadian-made goods. As a result, they will shift their expenditures toward foreign goods and away from Canadian goods. That is, Canadians will spend a higher fraction of national income on imports—the *IM* curve in Figure 22-2 will rotate up. The combination of these two effects is that the net export function shifts downward and becomes steeper. A fall in Canadian prices relative to foreign prices would have the opposite effect, shifting the *X* function up and the *IM* function down, and thus shifting the *NX* function up.

A rise in Canadian prices relative to those in other countries reduces Canadian net exports at any level of national income. A fall in Canadian prices increases net exports at any level of national income.

The most important cause of a change in international relative prices is a change in the exchange rate. A *depreciation* of the Canadian dollar means that foreigners must pay less of their money to buy one Canadian dollar, and Canadian residents must pay more Canadian dollars to buy a unit of any foreign currency. As a result, the price of foreign goods in terms of Canadian dollars rises, and the price of Canadian goods in terms of foreign currency falls. This reduction in the relative price of Canadian goods will cause a shift in expenditure away from foreign goods and toward Canadian goods. Canadian residents will import less at each level of Canadian national income, and foreigners will buy more Canadian exports. The net export function thus shifts upward.

An example may help to clarify the argument. Suppose something causes the Canadian dollar to depreciate relative to the euro (the common currency in the European Union). The depreciation of the Canadian dollar leads Canadians to switch away from French wines and German cars, purchasing instead more B.C. wine and Ontario-made cars. This reduction in imports is reflected by the downward rotation of the *IM* curve. The depreciation of the Canadian dollar relative to the euro also stimulates Canadian exports. Quebec furniture and Maritime vacations now appear cheaper to Europeans than previously, and so their expenditure on such Canadian goods increases. This increase in Canadian exports is reflected by an upward shift in the *X* curve. The overall effect is that the net export function shifts up and becomes flatter.

One final word of caution regarding prices, exchange rates, and net exports. It is important to keep in mind that the simple model in this chapter treats prices and exchange rates as *exogenous* variables. That is, though we can discuss what happens if they change, we do not yet *explain* where these changes come from. Of course, in the actual economy the price level and the exchange rate are key macroeconomic variables that we wish to understand. In the next chapter, the price level becomes *endogenous* in

FIGURE 22-2   Shifts in the Net Export Function

(i) Export and import functions

(ii) Net export function

Changes in relative international prices shift the NX function. A rise in Canadian prices relative to foreign prices lowers exports from *X* to *X'* and raises the import function from *IM* to *IM'*. This shifts the net export function downward from *NX* to *NX'*. A fall in Canadian prices has the opposite effect.

For lots of interesting information on Canada's international trade, go to the website for the Department of Foreign Affairs and International Trade: **www.dfait.gc.ca**.

our model and we therefore consider why it changes. In Chapter 35, the exchange rate becomes endogenous. For now, however, keep in mind that the price level and the exchange rate are exogenous variables—we can explain what happens in our model *if* they change but we cannot use our present model to explain *why* they change.

Summary

How does the presence of foreign trade modify our basic model? Let's summarize.

1. Foreign firms and households purchase Canadian-made goods. Changes in foreign income and relative prices (including exchange rates) will affect Canadian exports (X), but we assume that X is autonomous with respect to Canadian national income. When we construct the economy's aggregate expenditure (AE) function we will include X since it represents expenditure on domestic goods.

2. All components of domestic expenditure (C, I, and G) include some import content. Since C is positively related to national income, imports (IM) are also related positively to national income. When we construct the economy's AE function, which shows the desired aggregate expenditure on *domestic* products, we will *subtract IM* because these expenditures are on foreign goods.

22.3 EQUILIBRIUM NATIONAL INCOME

As in Chapter 21, equilibrium national income is the level of income where desired aggregate expenditure equals actual national income. The addition of government and net exports changes the calculations that we must make but does not alter the meaning of equilibrium or the basic workings of the model.

Desired Consumption and National Income

When there are taxes, disposable income (Y_D) is less than national income (Y). We take several steps to determine the relationship between consumption and national income in the presence of taxes.

1. First, we assume that the net tax rate, t, is 10 percent, so that net tax revenues are 10 percent of national income:

$$T = (0.1)Y$$

2. Disposable income must therefore be 90 percent of national income:

$$Y_D = Y - T = (0.9)Y$$

3. The consumption function we used last chapter is given as:

$$C = 30 + (0.8)Y_D$$

which tells us that the *MPC* out of disposable income is 0.8.

4. We can now substitute $(0.9)Y$ for Y_D in the consumption function. By doing so, we get:

$$C = 30 + (0.8)(0.9)Y$$

$$\Rightarrow C = 30 + (0.72)Y$$

We can therefore express desired consumption as a function of Y_D or as a *different* function of Y. In this example, 0.72 is equal to the *MPC* times $(1 - t)$, where t is the net tax rate. So, whereas 0.8 is the marginal propensity to consume out of *disposable* income, 0.72 is the marginal propensity to consume out of *national* income.

In the presence of taxes, the marginal propensity to consume out of national income is less than the marginal propensity to consume out of disposable income.

Practise with Study Guide Chapter 22, Exercise 2.

The *AE* Function

In Chapter 21, the only components of desired aggregate expenditure were consumption and investment. We now add government purchases and net exports. The separate components in their general form are:

$C = a + bY_D$	consumption
I	autonomous investment
G	autonomous government purchases
$T = tY$	net tax revenues
X	autonomous exports
$IM = mY$	imports

Our first step is to express desired consumption in terms of national income. Using the four steps from above, we write desired consumption as:

$$C = a + b(1 - t)Y$$

Now we sum up the four components of desired aggregate expenditure:

$$AE = C + I + G + (X - IM)$$

$$= a + b(1 - t)Y + I + G + (X - mY)$$

$$AE = \underbrace{[a + I + G + X]}_{\substack{\text{Autonomous} \\ \text{expenditure}}} + \underbrace{[b(1 - t) - m]Y}_{\substack{\text{Induced} \\ \text{expenditure}}}$$

In this last equation, we can see the distinction between autonomous aggregate expenditure and induced aggregate expenditure. The first set of square brackets brings together all of the autonomous parts of expenditure—consumption, investment, government purchases, and exports. The second set of square brackets brings together all of the induced parts of expenditure, those that change when national income changes—consumption and imports. This second term in square brackets shows how much total desired spending changes when national income changes by one dollar—the marginal propensity to spend out of national income.

Figure 22-3 graphs the *AE* function for our hypothetical economy in which we assume that desired investment is $75 billion and the level of government purchases is $51 billion. Notice that the slope of the *AE* function measures the change in desired aggregate expenditure (*AE*) that comes about from a $1 increase in national income (*Y*).

Practise with Study Guide Chapter 22, Exercises 4, 6, and 7.

FIGURE 22-3   The Aggregate Expenditure Function

The aggregate expenditure function is the sum of desired consumption, investment, government purchases, and net export expenditures. The autonomous components of desired aggregate expenditure are desired investment, desired government purchases, desired export expenditures, and the constant term in desired consumption expenditure. These sum to $228 billion in the given example and this sum is the vertical intercept of the AE curve. The induced component is $(b(1 - t) - m)Y$ which in our example is equal to $(0.8(0.9) - 0.1)Y = 0.62Y$.

The equation for the AE function is $AE = 228 + 0.62Y$. The slope of the AE function, $\Delta AE/\Delta Y$, is 0.62, indicating that a $1 increase in Y leads to a 62-cent increase in desired expenditure. This is the marginal propensity to spend on domestic output. The equilibrium level of national income is $600 billion, the level of Y where the AE function intersects the 45° line.

Point	Actual National Income (Y)	Desired Consumption Expenditure (C = 30 + 0.72 Y)	Desired Investment Expenditure (I = 75)	Desired Government Expenditure (G = 51)	Desired Net Export Expenditure (X − IM = 72 − 0.1 Y)	Desired Aggregate Expenditure (AE = C + I + G + X − IM)
A	0	30	75	51	72	228
B	150	138	75	51	57	321
C	300	246	75	51	42	414
D	600	462	75	51	12	600
E	900	678	75	51	−18	786

This is the marginal propensity to spend out of national income, and is equal to $b(1 - t) - m$.

Note that, unlike in Chapter 21, the marginal propensity to spend out of national income is not simply equal to the marginal propensity to consume. To understand why, suppose the economy produces $1 of extra national income and that the response to this is governed by the relationships in Figure 22-3. Because 10 cents is collected by the government as net taxes, 90 cents becomes disposable income, and 80 percent of this amount (72 cents) is spent on consumption. However, 10 cents of all expenditure goes to imports, so expenditure on domestic goods rises by only 62 cents (72 − 10). Hence, z, the marginal propensity to spend, is 0.62. In algebraic terms,

$$
\begin{aligned}
z &= b(1 - t) - m \\
  &= (0.8)(1 - 0.1) - 0.1 \\
  &= 0.72 - 0.1 \\
  &= 0.62
\end{aligned}
$$

Equilibrium National Income

As in Chapter 21, we are assuming (for now) that firms are able and willing to produce whatever level of output is demanded of them at a constant price level. When output is *demand determined* in this way, the equilibrium level of national income is that level of national income where desired aggregate expenditure (along the *AE* function) equals the actual level of national income. As also was true in Chapter 21, the 45° line shows the *equilibrium condition*—the collection of points where $Y = AE$. Thus, the equilibrium level of national income in Figure 22-3 is at point *D*, where the *AE* function intersects the 45° line.

Suppose national income is less than its equilibrium amount. The forces leading back to equilibrium are exactly the same as those described in Chapter 21. When households, firms, foreign demanders, and governments try to spend at their desired amounts, they will try to purchase more goods and services than the economy is currently producing. Hence, some of the desired expenditure must either be frustrated or take the form of purchases of inventories of goods that were produced in the past. As firms see their inventories being depleted, they will increase production, thereby increasing the level of national income.

The opposite sequence of events occurs when national income is greater than desired aggregate expenditure. Now the total of desired household consumption, business investment, government purchases, and net foreign demand on the economy's production is less than national output. Firms will notice that they are unable to sell all of their output. Their inventories will be rising, and sooner or later they will seek to reduce the level of output until it equals the level of sales. When they do, national income will fall.

Finally, when national income is equal to desired aggregate expenditure ($600 billion in Figure 22-3), there is no pressure for output to change. Desired consumption, investment, government purchases, and net exports just add up to national output.

---

myeconlab

An alternative (but equivalent) approach to determining the level of national income is based on the relationship between national saving and the accumulation of national assets. For more details, look for "The Saving–Investment Approach to Equilibrium in an Open Economy with Government" in the *Additional Topics* section of this book's MyEconLab.

www.myeconlab.com

22.4 CHANGES IN EQUILIBRIUM NATIONAL INCOME

Changes in any of the components of desired aggregate expenditure will cause changes in equilibrium national income. In Chapter 21, we investigated the consequences of shifts in the consumption function and in the investment function. Here we take a first look at fiscal policy—the effects of changes in government spending and taxation. We also consider shifts in the net export function. First, we explain why the simple multiplier is reduced by the presence of taxes and imports.

The Multiplier with Taxes and Imports

In Chapter 21, we saw that the *simple multiplier,* the amount by which equilibrium national income changes when autonomous expenditure changes by one dollar, was equal to $1/(1 - z)$, where z is the marginal propensity to spend out of national income. In the simple model of Chapter 21, with no government and no international trade, z was simply the marginal propensity to consume out of disposable income. But in the more complex model of this chapter, which contains both government and foreign trade, we have seen that the marginal propensity to spend out of national income is slightly more complicated.

The presence of imports and taxes reduces the marginal propensity to spend out of national income and thus reduces the value of the simple multiplier.

Let's be more specific. In Chapter 21, the marginal propensity to spend, z, was just equal to the marginal propensity to consume. That is,

Without Government and Foreign Trade:

$$z = MPC$$
$$\text{Simple multiplier} = 1/(1 - z)$$
$$= 1/(1 - MPC)$$

In our example, the MPC was 0.8 and so the simple multiplier was equal to 5.

$$\text{Simple multiplier}$$
$$= 1/(1 - 0.8) = 1/0.2 = 5$$

In our expanded model with government and foreign trade, the marginal propensity to spend out of national income must take account of the presence of net taxes and imports, both of which reduce the value of z.

With Government and Foreign Trade:

$$z = MPC(1 - t) - m$$
$$\text{Simple multiplier} = 1/(1 - z)$$
$$= 1/\{1 - [MPC(1 - t) - m]\}$$

In our example, $t = 0.1$ and $m = 0.1$. This makes the simple multiplier equal to 2.63.

$$\text{Simple multiplier} = 1/\{1 - [0.8(1 - 0.1) - 0.1]\} = 1/[1 - (0.72 - 0.1)\}$$
$$= 1/(1 - 0.62) = 2.63$$

What is the central point here? With taxes and imports both increasing in response to an increase in national income, every increase in national income induces a smaller increase in desired expenditure *on domestically produced goods* than would be the case in the simpler world with no taxes or imports. The result is that the overall change in equilibrium national income is lower.

The higher is the marginal propensity to import, the lower is the simple multiplier. The higher is the net tax rate, the lower is the simple multiplier.

Applying Economic Concepts 22-1 examines what the size of the simple multiplier is likely to be in the Canadian economy. You may be surprised at the result!

Net Exports

Earlier in this chapter, we discussed the determinants of net exports and of shifts in the net export function. As with the other elements of desired aggregate expenditure, if the net export function shifts upward, equilibrium national income will rise; if the net export function shifts downward, equilibrium national income will fall.

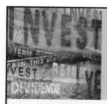

APPLYING ECONOMIC CONCEPTS 22-1

How Large Is the Simple Multiplier in Canada?

In our macro model, the "simple multiplier" expresses the overall change in equilibrium national income resulting from an increase in desired autonomous spending. But to the extent that increases in output are only possible in the short run by increasing the level of employment, the multiplier can also tell us something about the total change in employment that will result from an initial increase in spending. And this is the way we usually hear about the effects of the multiplier in the popular press.

Imagine you are listening to a news story on the radio or TV about a recent announcement by the government to increase its annual spending by $1 billion on the repairs of highways and bridges. Rather than claiming that the $1 billion increase in spending will lead to an overall increase in national income by several times this amount, the official making the announcement is likely to speak in terms of the number of jobs "created" in the economy as a result of the new government spending. For example, the official might claim that this new spending will *directly* create 5000 new jobs and that an additional 10 000 new jobs will be created *indirectly*. With such a claim, the government official appears to believe that the simple multiplier is equal to 3—the total increase in employment (and output) will be three times the direct increase. Is this a realistic estimate for Canada?

In the simple model we have developed in this chapter, we have used values for key parameters that are simple to work with but not necessarily realistic. In particular, we assumed values of t and m that are well below their actual values. To find a realistic estimate for the multiplier in Canada, we need to use more realistic values for the net tax rate (t) and the marginal propen-

sity to import (m). In Canada a reasonable value for t is 0.3, the approximate share of combined government net taxation in GDP. Imports into Canada are close to 40 percent of GDP and so $m = 0.40$ is a reasonable value. If we use these more realistic values for t and m, and continue the reasonable assumption that the marginal propensity to consume out of disposable income is 0.8, the implied value of z is

$$z = MPC(1 - t) - m$$
$$= 0.8(1 - 0.3) - 0.4 = 0.16$$

and so the implied value of the simple multiplier is

$$\text{Simple multiplier} = 1/(1 - z) = 1/0.84 = 1.19$$

Two main lessons emerge from this analysis:

1. Net taxes and imports reduce the size of the simple multiplier.

2. Realistic values of t and m in Canada suggest a simple multiplier that is much closer to 1 than to 2, and certainly far below the value of 5 that we used in the very simple model of Chapter 21.

So the next time you hear a government official make claims about how new spending plans are likely to have large effects on the level of employment and economic activity, think about what the implied value of the simple multiplier must be in order for the claims to be reasonable. The analysis here suggests that the simple multiplier in Canada is probably very close to 1.*

---

* In the next two chapters we will see that once we allow for a price level that can adjust to changes in demand, the multiplier gets even smaller.

Generally, exports themselves are autonomous with respect to domestic national income. Foreign demand for Canadian goods and services depends on foreign income, on foreign and Canadian prices, and on the exchange rate, but it does not depend on Canadian income. Export demand could also change because of a change in tastes. Suppose foreign consumers develop a taste for Canadian-made furniture and desire to consume $1 billion more per year of these goods than they had in the past. The net export function (and the aggregate expenditure function) will shift up by $1 billion, and equilibrium national income will increase by $1 billion times the simple multiplier.

Fiscal Policy

Fiscal policy involves the use of government spending and taxation, often motivated by the desire to alter the equilibrium level of national income. Because government purchases increase desired aggregate expenditure and taxation decreases it, the *directions* of the required changes in spending and taxation are generally easy to determine once we know the direction in which the government wishes to change national income. But the *timing* and *magnitude* of the changes are more difficult issues.

stabilization policy Any policy designed to reduce the economy's cyclical fluctuations and thereby stabilize national income.

Any policy that attempts to stabilize national income at or near any particular level (usually potential national income) is called **stabilization policy**. Here we introduce the idea of stabilization through fiscal policy. In Chapters 24 and 32, we examine various issues of fiscal policy in more detail, including why the practice of fiscal policy is more complicated than our simple theory suggests.

The basic idea of stabilization policy follows from what we have already learned. A reduction in tax rates or an increase in government purchases shifts the *AE* curve upward, setting in motion the multiplier process that tends to increase equilibrium national income. An increase in tax rates or a decrease in government purchases shifts the *AE* curve downward and tends to decrease equilibrium income.

If the government has some target level of national income, it can use its taxes and expenditures in an attempt to push the economy toward that target. First, suppose national income is well below the level of potential national income. In this case, the government would like to increase national income. The available fiscal tools are to raise government purchases or to lower tax rates (or both). Second, suppose the economy is "overheated," meaning that national income is above potential. What can the government do? The fiscal tools at its command are to reduce government purchases or to raise tax rates, both of which have a depressing effect on national income.

Figure 22-4 illustrates the two situations: one in which the government's objective is to increase the level of national income, and the other in which the government's objective is to reduce the level of national income. In both cases, the "target" level of national income is the level of potential national income, Y^*, at which there is full employment. Let's now examine these two fiscal tools—government purchases and taxation—in a little more detail.[3]

Changes in Government Purchases   Suppose the government decides to reduce its purchases of all economic consulting services, saving $100 million per year in spending. Planned government purchases (G) would fall by $100 million, shifting *AE* downward by the same amount. How much would equilibrium income change? This

---

[3] The government would rarely attempt to *reduce* the level of GDP. But in a situation where real GDP is above potential output and also growing more quickly, it may try to reduce the growth rate of GDP, thus closing the gap between real GDP and potential output.

FIGURE 22-4   The Objective of Stabilization Policy

(i) Equilibrium $Y < Y^*$

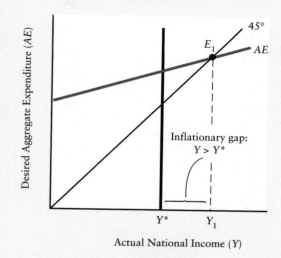

(ii) Equilibrium $Y > Y^*$

Stabilization policy is intended to bring national income closer to the level of potential national income, Y^*. In parts (i) and (ii), Y^* is the level of potential national income, where all factors of production are fully employed. In part (i), equilibrium is at E_0 where national income is Y_0, which is less than Y^*; this is a recessionary gap. The government could either increase G or reduce t to shift the AE function upwards and thus increase equilibrium national income. In part (ii), equilibrium is at E_1 where national income is Y_1, which is greater than Y^*; this is an inflationary gap. The government could either reduce G or increase t to shift the AE function downward and thus to reduce equilibrium national income.

amount can be calculated by using the simple multiplier. Government purchases are part of autonomous expenditure, so a *change* in government purchases of ΔG will lead to a *change* in equilibrium national income equal to the simple multiplier times ΔG. In this example, equilibrium income will fall by $100 million times the simple multiplier. Earlier we argued that a realistic value for the simple multiplier in Canada is about 1.2. Using this value in our example, the effect of the $100 million reduction in G is to reduce equilibrium national income by $120 million.

Increases in government purchases would have the opposite effect. If the government increases its spending by $1 billion on new highways, equilibrium national income will rise by $1 billion times the simple multiplier.

Changes in Tax Rates If tax rates change, the relationship between disposable income and national income changes. As a result, the relationship between desired consumption and national income also changes. Consequently, a

Changes in government purchases and tax rates can have significant effects on desired aggregate expenditure and thus on equilibrium national income.

FIGURE 22-5   The Effect of Changing the Tax Rate

Changing the tax rate changes equilibrium income by rotating the AE curve. A reduction in tax rates rotates the AE curve from AE_0 to AE_1. The new curve has a steeper slope because the lower tax rate withdraws a smaller amount of national income from the desired consumption flow. Equilibrium income rises from Y_0 to Y_1. An increase in the tax rate has the opposite effect.

change in tax rates will cause a change in z, the marginal propensity to spend out of national income.

Consider first a decrease in tax rates. If the government decreases its net tax rate so that it collects 5 cents less out of every dollar of national income, disposable income rises in relation to national income. Hence, consumption also rises at every level of national income. This increase in consumption results in a (non-parallel) upward shift of the AE curve, that is, an increase in the slope of the curve, as shown in Figure 22-5. The result of this shift will be an increase in equilibrium national income.

A rise in tax rates has the opposite effect. A rise in tax rates causes a decrease in disposable income, and hence consumption expenditure, at each level of national income. This results in a (non-parallel) downward shift of the AE curve and decreases the level of equilibrium national income.

Note that when the AE function shifts in a non-parallel manner, as happens if anything causes z to change, the simple multiplier is *not* used to tell us about the resulting change in equilibrium national income. The simple multiplier is only useful to tell us how much equilibrium national income changes in response to a change in *autonomous* desired spending—that is, in response to a *parallel* shift in the AE function.

> **myeconlab**
>
> **Governments can also combine an increase in government purchases with an increase in tax revenues in such a way that the budget is left unchanged. How do such *balanced budget changes* affect the level of national income? To see more details on this type of fiscal policy, look for "What Is the Balanced Budget Multiplier?" in the *Additional Topics* section of this book's MyEconLab.**
>
> w w w . m y e c o n l a b . c o m

22.5 DEMAND-DETERMINED OUTPUT

In this and the preceding chapter, we have discussed the determination of the four categories of aggregate expenditure and have seen how they simultaneously determine equilibrium national income in the short run. An algebraic exposition of the model is presented in the appendix to this chapter.

Our macro model is based on three central concepts, and it is worth reviewing them.

Equilibrium National Income The equilibrium level of national income is that level where *desired* aggregate expenditure equals *actual* national income. If actual national income exceeds desired expenditure, firms will eventually reduce production, causing national income to fall. If actual national income is less than desired expenditure, firms will eventually increase production, causing national income to rise.

The Simple Multiplier The simple multiplier measures the change in equilibrium national income that results from a simple change in the *autonomous* part of desired aggregate expenditure. The simple multiplier is equal to $1/(1 - z)$, where z is the marginal propensity to spend out of national income. In the model of Chapter 21, in which there is no government and no international trade, z is simply the marginal propensity to consume out of disposable income. In our expanded model that contains both government and foreign trade, z is reduced by the presence of net taxes and imports. To review:

$$\text{Simple multiplier} = 1/(1 - z)$$

Closed economy with no government: $z = MPC$

Open economy with government: $z = MPC(1 - t) - m$

Demand-Determined Output The model that we have examined is constructed *for a given price level*—that is, the price level is assumed to be constant. This assumption of a given price level is related to another assumption that we have been making. We have been assuming that firms are able and willing to produce any amount of output that is demanded without requiring any change in prices. When this is true, national income depends only on how much is demanded—that is, national income is *demand determined*. Things get more complicated if firms are either unable or unwilling to produce enough to meet all demands without requiring a change in prices. We deal with this possibility in Chapter 23 when we consider *supply-side* influences on national income.

There are two situations in which we might expect national income to be demand determined. First, when there are unemployed resources and firms have excess capacity, firms will often be prepared to provide whatever is demanded from them at unchanged prices. In contrast, if the economy's resources are fully employed and firms have no excess capacity, increases in output may only be possible with higher unit costs, and these cost increases may lead to price increases.

The second situation is where firms are *price setters*. Readers who have studied some microeconomics will recognize this term. It means that the firm has the ability to influence the price of its product, either because it is large relative to the market or, more usually, because it sells a product that is *differentiated* to some extent from the products of its competitors. Firms that are price setters often respond to changes in demand by altering their production and sales, at least initially, rather than by adjusting their prices. Only after some time has passed, and the change in demand has persisted, do such firms adjust their prices. This type of behaviour corresponds well to our short-run macro model in which changes in demand lead to changes in output (for a given price level).

Our simple model of national income determination assumes a constant price level. In this model, national income is demand determined.

In the following chapters, we expand the model by making the price level an *endogenous* variable—that is, movements in the price level get explained within the model. We do this by considering the *supply side* of the economy—that is, those things that influence firms' abilities to produce output, such as technology and factor prices. When we consider the demand side and the supply side of the economy simultaneously, we will see that changes in desired aggregate expenditure usually cause both prices and real national income to change.

S U M M A R Y

22.1 INTRODUCING GOVERNMENT

- Government desired purchases, G, are assumed to be part of autonomous aggregate expenditure. Taxes minus transfer payments are called net taxes and affect aggregate expenditure indirectly through households' disposable income. Taxes reduce disposable income, whereas transfers increase disposable income.

- The budget balance is defined as net tax revenues minus government purchases, $(T - G)$. When $(T - G)$ is positive, there is a budget surplus; when $(T - G)$ is negative, there is a budget deficit.
- When there is a budget surplus, there is positive public saving.

22.2 INTRODUCING FOREIGN TRADE

- Exports are foreign purchases of Canadian goods, and do not depend on Canadian national income. Desired imports are assumed to increase as national income increases. Hence, net exports decrease as national income increases.
- Changes in international relative prices lead to shifts in the net export function. A depreciation of the Canadian

dollar implies that Canadian goods are now cheaper relative to foreign goods. This leads to a rise in exports and a fall in imports, shifting the net export function up. An appreciation of the Canadian dollar has the opposite effect.

22.3 EQUILIBRIUM NATIONAL INCOME

- As in Chapter 21, national income is in equilibrium when desired aggregate expenditure equals actual national income. The equilibrium condition is

$$Y = AE, \text{ where } AE = C + I + G + (X - IM)$$

- The slope of the AE function in the model with government and foreign trade is $z = MPC\,(1 - t) - m$, where MPC is the marginal propensity to consume out of disposable income, t is the net tax rate, and m is the marginal propensity to import.

22.4 CHANGES IN EQUILIBRIUM NATIONAL INCOME

- The presence of taxes and net exports reduces the value of the simple multiplier. With taxes and imports, every increase in national income induces less new spending than in a model with no taxes or imports.
- An increase in government purchases shifts up the AE function and thus increases the equilibrium level of national income. A decrease in the net tax rate makes

the AE function rotate upward and increases the equilibrium level of national income.
- An increase in exports can be caused by an increase in foreign demand for Canadian goods, a fall in the Canadian price level, or a depreciation of the Canadian dollar. An increase in exports shifts the AE function up and increases the equilibrium level of national income.

22.5 **DEMAND-DETERMINED OUTPUT**

- Our simple model of national income determination is constructed for a given price level. That prices are assumed not to change in response to an increase in desired expenditure reflects a related assumption that output is demand determined.
- Output may be demand determined in two situations: if there are unemployed resources, or if firms are price setters.

- In later chapters when we consider the demand side and the supply side of the economy simultaneously, we will see that changes in desired aggregate expenditure usually cause both prices and real national income to change.

KEY CONCEPTS

Taxes, transfers, and net taxes
The budget balance
The net export function

Calculation of the simple multiplier in an open economy with government

Fiscal policy and equilibrium income
Demand-determined output

STUDY EXERCISES

1. Consider the following table showing national income and government net tax revenues in billions of dollars. Assume that the level of government purchases is $155 billion.

Actual National Income (Y)	Net Tax Revenues (T)	Public Saving ($T - G$)
100	45	—
200	70	—
300	95	—
400	120	—
500	145	—
600	170	—
700	195	—
800	220	—

a. Compute the level of public saving (the government budget surplus) for each level of national income and fill in the table.
b. What is the net tax rate? Explain.
c. Suppose the government decides to increase the level of its purchases of goods and services by $15 billion. What happens to the level of public saving for any level of national income?

2. Consider the following table showing national income and imports in billions of dollars. Assume that the level of exports is $300 billion.

Actual National Income (Y)	Imports (IM)	Net Exports ($X - IM$)
100	85	—
200	120	—
300	155	—
400	190	—
500	225	—
600	260	—
700	295	—
800	330	—

a. Compute the level of net exports for each level of national income and fill in the table.
b. Plot the net export function on a scale diagram. Explain why it is downward sloping.
c. What is the marginal propensity to import? Explain.
d. Suppose one of Canada's major trading partners experiences a significant recession. Explain how this affects the net export function in your diagram.

3. Each of the following headlines describes an event that will have an effect on desired aggregate expenditure. What will be the effect on equilibrium national income? In each case, describe how the event would be illustrated in the 45° line diagram.

a. "Minister takes an axe to the armed forces."
b. "Russia agrees to buy more Canadian wheat."
c. "High-tech firms to cut capital outlays."

d. "Finance minister pledges to cut income-tax rates."
e. "U.S. imposes import restrictions on Canadian lumber."
f. "Asian slump means smaller market for B.C. lumber."
g. "Weak dollar spurs exports from Ontario manufacturers."

4. **myeconlab** The following diagram shows desired aggregate expenditure for the economy of Sunset Island. The AE curve assumes a net tax rate (t) of 10 percent, autonomous exports of $25 billion, and a marginal propensity to import (m) of 15 percent.

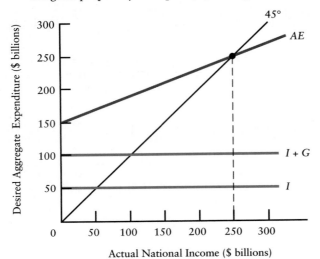

Actual National Income ($ billions)

a. What is the level of desired investment expenditure (I)?
b. What is the level of government purchases (G)?
c. What is the autonomous portion of consumption?
d. What is total autonomous expenditure?
e. Starting from equilibrium national income of $250 billion, suppose government purchases decreased by $25 billion. Describe the effect on the AE curve and on equilibrium national income.
f. Starting from equilibrium national income of $250 billion, suppose the net tax rate increased from 10 percent to 30 percent of national income. Describe the effect on the AE curve and on equilibrium national income.
g. Starting from equilibrium national income of $250 billion, suppose investment increased by $50 billion. Describe the effect on the AE curve and on equilibrium national income.
h. Starting from equilibrium national income of $250 billion, suppose the marginal propensity to import fell from 15 percent to 5 percent of national income. Describe the effect on the AE curve and on equilibrium national income.

5. **myeconlab** The economy of Sunrise Island has the following features:
- fixed price level
- no foreign trade
- autonomous desired investment (I) of $20 billion
- autonomous government purchases (G) of $30 billion
- autonomous desired consumption (C) of $15 billion
- marginal propensity to consume out of disposable income of 0.75
- net tax rate of 0.20 of national income

a. Write an equation expressing consumption as a function of disposable income.
b. Write an equation expressing net tax revenues as a function of national income.
c. Write an equation expressing disposable income as a function of national income.
d. Write an equation expressing consumption as a function of national income.
e. What is the marginal propensity to spend out of national income?
f. Calculate the simple multiplier for Sunrise Island.

6. The following table shows alternative hypothetical economies and the relevant values for the marginal propensity to consume out of disposable income (MPC), the net tax rate (t), and the marginal propensity to import, m.

Economy	MPC	t	m	z	Simple Multiplier $1/(1 - z)$
A	0.75	0.2	0.15	—	—
B	0.75	0.2	0.30	—	—
C	0.75	0.4	0.30	—	—
D	0.90	0.4	0.30	—	—

a. Recall that z, the marginal propensity to spend out of national income, is given by the simple expression $z = MPC(1 - t) - m$. Using this expression, compute z for each of the economies and fill in the table.
b. Compare Economies A and B (they differ only by the value of m). Which one has the larger multiplier? Explain why the size of the multiplier depends on m.
c. Compare Economies B and C (they differ only by the value of t). Which one has the larger multiplier? Explain why the size of the multiplier depends on t.
d. Compare Economies C and D (they differ only by the value of MPC). Which one has the larger multiplier? Explain why the size of the multiplier depends on MPC.

7. This question is based on the MyEconLab item "The Saving-Investment Approach to Equilibrium in an Open Economy with Government." Consider the diagram below showing the national saving function and the national asset formation function.

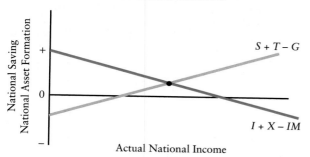

Actual National Income

a. Explain why the national asset formation function is downward sloping. What determines its slope?
b. Explain why the national saving function is upward sloping. What determines its slope?
c. Suppose the government decided to increase its level of purchases. How would this policy change be illustrated in the diagram? What would happen to national income?
d. Suppose domestic firms decided to increase their desired investment. How would this change be illustrated in the diagram? What would happen to national income?
e. Suppose the Canadian government reduced net-tax rates. How would this change be illustrated in the diagram? What would happen to national income?

8. This question requires you to solve a macro model algebraically. Reading the appendix to this chapter will help you to answer this question. But, just in case, we lead you through it step by step. The equations for the model are as follows:

i) $C = a + bY_D$ Consumption
ii) $I = I_0$ Investment (autonomous)
iii) $G = G_0$ Government purchases (autonomous)
iv) $T = tY$ Net tax revenue
v) $X = X_0$ Exports (autonomous)
vi) $IM = mY$ Imports

a. Step 1: Recall that $Y_D = Y - T$. Using this fact, substitute the tax function into the consumption function and derive the relationship between desired consumption and national income.
b. Step 2: Sum the four components of desired aggregate expenditure (C, I, G, NX). This is the aggregate expenditure (AE) function.
c. Step 3: Recall the equilibrium condition, $Y = AE$. Form the equation $Y = AE$, where AE is your expression for the AE function from part (b).
d. Step 4: Now collect terms and solve for Y. This is the equilibrium value of national income.
e. Step 5: Suppose the level of autonomous expenditure, which we could call A, rises by ΔA. What is the effect on the level of equilibrium national income?

9. **myeconlab** This question repeats the exercise of Question 8, but for specific numerical values. The equations of the model are:

$C = 50 + 0.7Y_D$ $T = (0.2)Y$
$I = 75$ $X = 50$
$G = 100$ $IM = (0.15)Y$

a. Compute the AE function and plot it in a diagram. What is total autonomous expenditure?
b. What is the slope of the AE function?
c. Compute the equilibrium level of national income.
d. Suppose X rises from 50 to 100. How does this affect the level of national income?
e. What is the simple multiplier in this model?

DISCUSSION QUESTIONS

1. The Canadian federal government embarked on a significant path of deficit reduction in the mid-1990s. What fiscal measures were at its disposal? Why might a reduction of 10 percent in government expenditure accomplish much less than a 10-percent decrease in the deficit, at least in the first instance?

2. For many years in Canada it was typical for the federal government's forecasts of its own budget deficit to be less than the forecasts made by private-sector economists. Much of the discrepancy seemed to be accounted for by assumptions about the state of the economy over the coming year. How do assumptions about the economy affect estimates of the budget deficit?

3. Classify each of the following government activities as either government purchases or transfers.

a. Welfare payments for the poor
b. Payments to teachers in public schools
c. Payments to teachers at a military college
d. Payments on account of hospital and medical care
e. Public Health Service vaccination programs

4. The trade deficit that the United States has with China has received much attention in recent years. Given an economy in equilibrium, what is the relationship

between saving and investment if the government budget remains balanced but there exists a trade deficit? What additional role must foreigners play in this situation? Can you explain why this situation is viewed by many Americans as troublesome? Do you agree with them?

5. In Chapter 20 we examined how national income was *measured*. Using the expenditure approach, we showed that GDP is always equal to the sum of consumption, investment, government purchases, and net exports. In Chapters 21 and 22 we examined the *determination* of national income. We showed that equilibrium national income occurs when actual national income equals the sum of desired consumption, investment, government purchases, and net exports. Does this mean that national income is always at its equilibrium level? Explain the important difference between "actual" and "desired" expenditures.

An Algebraic Exposition of the Simple Macro Model

We start with the definition of desired aggregate expenditure:

$$AE = C + I + G + (X - IM) \qquad [1]$$

For each component of *AE*, we write down a behavioural function.

$$C = a + bY_D \; (consumption\ function) \qquad [2]$$

$$I = I_0 \; (autonomous\ investment) \qquad [3]$$

$$G = G_0 \; (autonomous\ government\ purchases) \quad [4]$$

$$X = X_0 \; (autonomous\ exports) \qquad [5]$$

$$IM = mY \; (imports) \qquad [6]$$

where *a* is autonomous consumption spending, *b* is the marginal propensity to consume, and *m* is the marginal propensity to import. Obviously, the "behavioural" functions for investment, government purchases, and exports are very simple: These are all assumed to be independent of the level of national income.

Before deriving aggregate expenditure, we need to determine the relationship between national income (*Y*) and disposable income (Y_D), because it is Y_D that determines desired consumption expenditure. Y_D is defined as income after net taxes. In Chapter 22 we examined a very simple linear tax of the form

$$T = tY \qquad [7]$$

Taxes must be subtracted from national income to obtain disposable income:

$$Y_D = Y - tY = Y(1 - t) \qquad [8]$$

Substituting Equation 8 into the consumption function allows us to write consumption as a function of national income.

$$C = a + b(1 - t)Y \qquad [9]$$

Now we can add up all of the components of desired aggregate expenditure, substituting Equations 3, 4, 5, 6, and 9 into Equation 1:

$$AE = a + b(1 - t)Y + I_0 + G_0 + X_0 - mY \quad [10]$$

Equation 10 is the *AE* function, which shows desired aggregate expenditure as a function of actual national income.

In equilibrium, desired aggregate expenditure must equal actual national income:

$$AE = Y \qquad [11]$$

Equation 11 is the equilibrium condition for our model. It is the equation of the 45° line in the figures in this chapter.

To solve for the equilibrium level of national income, we want to solve for the level of *Y* that satisfies both Equations 10 and 11. That is, solve for the level of *Y* that is determined by the intersection of the *AE* curve and the 45° line. Substitute Equation 11 into Equation 10:

$$Y = a + b(1 - t)Y + I_0 + G_0 + X_0 - mY \quad [12]$$

Group all the terms in *Y* on the right-hand side, and subtract them from both sides:

$$Y = Y[b(1 - t) - m] + a + I_0 + G_0 + X_0 \quad [13]$$

$$Y - Y[b(1 - t) - m] = a + I_0 + G_0 + X_0 \quad [14]$$

Notice that $[b(1 - t) - m]$ is exactly the marginal propensity to spend out of national income, defined earlier as *z*. When national income goes up by one dollar, only $1 - t$ dollars go into disposable income, and only *b* of that gets spent on consumption. Additionally, *m* gets spent on imports, which are not expenditures on domestic national income. Hence $[b(1 - t) - m]$ gets spent on domestic output.

Substituting *z* for $[b(1 - t) - m]$ and solving Equation 14 for equilibrium *Y* yields

$$Y = \frac{a + I_0 + G_0 + X_0}{1 - z} \qquad [15]$$

Notice that the numerator of Equation 15 is total autonomous expenditure, which we call A. Hence, Equation 15 can be rewritten as

$$Y = \frac{A}{1 - z} \qquad [16]$$

Notice also that if autonomous expenditure rises by some amount ΔA, Y will rise by $\Delta A/(1 - z)$. So, the simple multiplier is $1/(1 - z)$.

The Algebra Illustrated

The numerical example that was carried through Chapters 21 and 22 can be used to illustrate the preceding exposition. In that example, the behavioural equations are:

$$C = 30 + 0.8Y_D \qquad [17]$$
$$I = 75 \qquad [18]$$
$$G = 51 \qquad [19]$$
$$X - IM = 72 - 0.1Y \qquad [20]$$
$$T = 0.1Y \qquad [21]$$

From Equation 8, disposable income is given by $Y(1 - t) = 0.9Y$. Substituting this into Equation 17 yields

$$C = 30 + 0.72Y$$

as in Equation 9.

Now, recalling that in equilibrium $AE = Y$, we add up all of the components of AE and set the sum equal to Y, as in Equation 12:

$$Y = 30 + 0.72Y + 75 + 51 + 72 - 0.1Y \qquad [22]$$

Collecting terms yields

$$Y = 228 + 0.62Y$$

Subtracting $0.62Y$ from both sides gives

$$0.38Y = 228$$

and dividing through by 0.38, we have

$$Y = \frac{228}{0.38} = 600$$

This can also be derived by using Equation 16. Autonomous expenditure is 228, and z, the marginal propensity to spend out of national income, is 0.62. Thus, from Equation 16, equilibrium income is $228/(1 - 0.62) = 600$, which is exactly the equilibrium we obtained in Figure 22-3.

CHAPTER 23

Output and Prices in the Short Run

In this chapter you will learn

1. why an exogenous change in the price level shifts the *AE* curve and changes the equilibrium level of real GDP.
2. how to derive the aggregate demand (*AD*) curve and what causes it to shift.
3. the meaning of the aggregate supply (*AS*) curve and why it shifts when technology or factor prices change.
4. how to define macroeconomic equilibrium.
5. how aggregate demand and aggregate supply shocks affect real GDP and the price level.

In Chapters 21 and 22, we developed a simple model of income determination. We saw that changes in wealth, interest rates, the government's fiscal policies, or expectations about the future lead to changes in desired aggregate expenditure. Through the multiplier process, such changes in desired expenditure caused equilibrium national income to change.

The simple model in Chapters 21 and 22 had a constant price level. We assumed that firms were prepared to provide more output when it was demanded without requiring an increase in prices. In this sense, we said that output was *demand determined*.

The actual economy, however, does not have a constant price level. Rather than assuming it is constant, we would like to understand what causes it to change. In other words, we would now like to expand our model to make the price level an *endogenous* variable—one that is explained within the model.

We make the transition to a variable price level in three steps. First, we study the consequences for national income of *exogenous* changes in the price level—changes that happen for reasons that are not explained by our model of the economy. We ask how changes in the price level affect desired aggregate expenditure. That is, we examine the *demand side* of the economy. Second, we examine the *supply side* by exploring the relationship between the price level, the prices of factor inputs, and the level of output producers would like to supply. Finally, we examine the concept of *macroeconomic equilibrium* that combines both the demand and supply sides to determine the price level and real national income simultaneously.

▮ 23.1 **THE DEMAND SIDE OF THE ECONOMY**

Consider the macro model in Chapter 22. What happens to equilibrium GDP in that model when the price level changes for some exogenous reason? To find out, we need to understand how the change affects desired aggregate expenditure.

Exogenous Changes in the Price Level

The *AE* curve shifts in response to a change in the price level. This shift occurs because a change in the price level affects desired consumption expenditures and desired net exports. These are the changes on which we will focus in this chapter. (In later chapters, we will see that changes in the price level will change interest rates and shift the *AE* curve for an additional reason.)

Changes in Consumption You might think it is obvious that a fall in the price level leads to an increase in desired consumption for the simple reason that the demand curves for most individual products are downward sloping. As we will see in a few pages, however, this logic is incorrect in the context of our aggregate model—our focus here is on the aggregate price level rather than on the prices of individual products. The relationship between the price level and desired consumption has to do with how changes in the price level lead to changes in household *wealth*, and thus to changes in desired spending.

Changes in the price level cause changes in the real value of cash held by households and firms. This change in wealth leads to changes in the amount of desired consumption expenditure.

Much of the private sector's total wealth is held in the form of assets with a fixed nominal value. The most obvious example is money itself. We will discuss money in considerable detail in Chapters 27 and 28, but for now just note that most individuals and businesses hold money in their wallets, in their cash registers, or in their chequing accounts. What this money can buy—its real value—depends on the price level. The higher the price level, the less a given amount of money can purchase. For this reason, a rise in the domestic price level lowers the real value of money holdings. Similarly, a reduction in the price level raises the real value of money holdings.

A rise in the price level lowers the real value of money held by the private sector. A fall in the price level raises the real value of money held by the private sector.

Other examples of assets that have fixed nominal values include government and corporate bonds. The bondholder has lent money to the issuer of the bond and receives a repayment from the issuer when the bond matures. What happens when there is a change in the price level in the intervening period? A rise in the price level means that the repayment to the bondholder is lower in real value than it otherwise would be. This is a decline in wealth for the bondholder. However, the issuer of the bond, having made a repayment of lower real value because of the increase in the price level, has experienced an increase in wealth. In dollar terms, the bondholder's reduction in wealth is exactly offset by the issuer's increase in wealth.

Changes in the price level change the wealth of bondholders and bond issuers, but because the changes offset each other there is no change in aggregate wealth.[1]

---

1 Some economists argue that in the case of *government* bonds, there *will* be a change in aggregate wealth when the price level changes. The argument relies on changes in the wealth of the bond issuers (governments) not being recognized by taxpayers, the individuals who are ultimately responsible to repay government debt. We will discuss this debate in Chapter 32.

In summary, a rise in the price level leads to a reduction in the real value of the private sector's wealth. And as we saw in Chapter 21, a reduction in wealth leads to a decrease in autonomous desired consumption and thus to a downward shift in the AE function.

A rise in the domestic price level reduces private-sector wealth; this leads to a fall in desired consumption, and thus a downward shift in the AE curve. A fall in the domestic price level leads to a rise in wealth and desired consumption and thus to an upward shift in the AE curve.

Changes in Net Exports When the domestic price level rises, Canadian goods become more expensive relative to foreign goods. As we saw in Chapter 22, this change in relative prices causes Canadian consumers to reduce their purchases of Canadian-made goods, which have now become relatively more expensive, and to increase their purchases of foreign goods, which have now become relatively less expensive. At the same time, consumers in other countries reduce their purchases of the now relatively more expensive Canadian-made goods. We saw in Chapter 22 that these changes cause a downward shift in the net export function.

A rise in the domestic price level shifts the net export function downward, which causes a downward shift in the AE curve. A fall in the domestic price level shifts the net export function and hence the AE curve upward.

Changes in Equilibrium GDP

Because it causes downward shifts in both the net export function and the consumption function, an exogenous rise in the price level causes a downward shift in the AE curve, as shown in Figure 23-1. When the AE curve shifts downward, the equilibrium level of real GDP falls.

Conversely, with a fall in the price level, Canadian goods become relatively cheaper internationally, so net exports rise. Also, the purchasing power of assets denominated in money terms is increased, so households spend more. The resulting increase in desired expenditure on Canadian goods causes the AE curve to shift upward. The equilibrium level of real GDP therefore rises.

A Change of Labels. In Chapters 21 and 22 the horizontal axis was labelled "Actual National Income." Notice in Figure 23-1, however, that we have labelled the horizontal axis "Real GDP." We use GDP rather than *national income* but these two words have the same meaning. It is still *actual,* as opposed to *desired,* but we leave that off, also for simplicity. Finally, we add *real* because from this chapter onward the price level will be changing and thus it is necessary to distinguish changes in nominal GDP from changes in real GDP.

FIGURE 23-1 Desired Aggregate Expenditure and the Price Level

An exogenous change in the price level causes the *AE* curve to shift and equilibrium GDP to change. At the initial price level, the *AE* curve is given by the solid line AE_0, and hence equilibrium is at E_0 with real GDP equal to Y_0. An increase in the price level causes the *AE* curve to shift downward to the dashed line, AE_1. As a result, equilibrium changes to E_1 and equilibrium GDP falls to Y_1.

The Aggregate Demand Curve

We have just seen, in the simple model from Chapters 21 and 22, that the price level and real equilibrium GDP are negatively related to each other. This negative relationship can be shown in an important new concept, the *aggregate demand curve*.

Recall that the *AE* curve is drawn with real GDP on the horizontal and desired aggregate expenditure on the vertical axis, and that it is plotted for a *given* price level. We are now going to let the price level vary and keep track of the various equilibrium points that occur as the *AE* function shifts. This will give us an **aggregate demand (AD) curve** that shows the relationship between the price level and the equilibrium level of real GDP. It will be plotted with the price level on the vertical axis and real GDP on the horizontal axis. Because the horizontal axes of both the *AE* and *AD* curves measure real GDP, the two curves can be placed one above the other so that the levels of GDP on both can be compared directly. This is shown in Figure 23-2.

Now let us see how the *AD* curve is derived. Given a value of the price level, P_0, equilibrium GDP is determined in part (i) of Figure 23-2 at the point where the AE_0 curve crosses the 45° line. The equilibrium level of real GDP is Y_0. Part (ii) of the figure shows the same equilibrium level of GDP, Y_0, plotted against the price level P_0. The equilibrium point in part (i), E_0, corresponds to point E_0 on the *AD* curve in part (ii).

As the price level rises to P_1, the *AE* curve shifts down to AE_1 and the equilibrium level of real GDP falls to Y_1. This determines a second point on the *AD* curve, E_1. By joining these points, we trace out the *AD* curve.

For any given price level, the *AD* curve shows the level of real GDP for which desired aggregate expenditure equals actual GDP.

Note that because the *AD* curve relates equilibrium GDP to the price level, changes in the price level that cause *shifts in* the *AE* curve cause *movements along* the *AD* curve. A movement along the *AD* curve thus traces out the response of equilibrium GDP to a change in the price level.

The Slope of the *AD* Curve Figure 23-2 provides us with sufficient information to establish that the *AD* curve is negatively sloped.

1. A rise in the price level causes the *AE* curve to shift downward and hence leads to a movement upward and to the left along the *AD* curve, reflecting a fall in the equilibrium level of GDP.

2. A fall in the price level causes the *AE* curve to shift upward and hence leads to a movement downward and to the right along the *AD* curve, reflecting a rise in the equilibrium level of GDP.

In Chapter 3, we saw that demand curves for individual goods such as coffee, Mp3 players, and automobiles are downward sloping. However, the reasons for the negative slope of the *AD* curve are different from the reasons for the negative slope of individual demand curves used in microeconomics. Why is this the case?

An individual demand curve describes a situation in which the price of one commodity changes *while the prices of all other commodities and consumers' money incomes are constant.* Such an individual demand curve is downward sloping for two reasons. First, as the price of the commodity falls, the purchasing power of each consumer's money income will rise, and this rise in real income will lead to more units of the good being purchased. Second, as the price of the commodity falls, consumers buy more of that commodity and fewer of the now relatively more expensive substitutes.

The first reason has no application to the *AD* curve, which relates the total demand for all output to the *price level* rather than to any particular (relative) price. All prices and total output are changing as we move along the *AD* curve. Because the value of output determines income, consumers' money incomes will also be changing along this curve.

The second reason does apply to the aggregate demand curve, but only in a limited way. A fall in the price level entails a fall in *all* domestic commodity prices. Hence, there is no incentive to substitute among domestic commodities whose prices do not change relative to each other. However, as we saw earlier in this chapter, it does lead to some substitution between domestic and foreign products. Domestic goods fall in price relative to imported goods, and the switch in expenditure will increase desired aggregate expenditure on domestic output and hence will increase equilibrium national income.

So, what is the central reason that the *AD* curve is downward sloping? As we saw earlier, the key relationship is that between the price level and private-sector wealth. A fall in the price level increases the real value of the private sector's holdings of money and therefore increases wealth. As wealth rises, desired aggregate expenditure also rises. The *AE* function shifts upward and equilibrium national income increases. A lower price level is therefore associated with a higher value of real GDP.

(In later chapters we will see another, more important reason for a negatively sloped *AD* curve that involves interest rates and investment, but we will have to wait a few chapters before we see this in detail.)

Shifts in the AD Curve

What can cause the *AD* curve to shift? For a given price level, any change in an *autonomous* component of aggregate expenditure will cause the *AD* curve to shift. The change in autonomous expenditure could be the result of a change in government policy, such as the level of government purchases or taxation (or, as we will see later, a policy-induced change in interest rates). Or the change in autonomous expenditure could be caused by something beyond the government's control, such as a change in households' consumption expenditure, firms' investment behaviour, or foreigners' demand for Canadian exports.

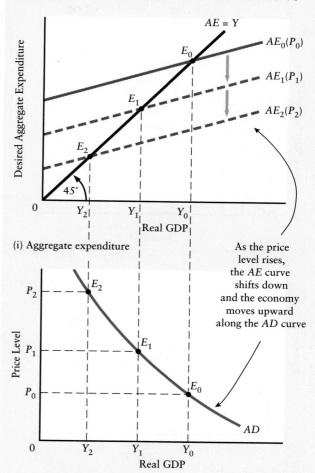

FIGURE 23-2 Derivation of the *AD* Curve

(i) Aggregate expenditure

(ii) Aggregate demand

As the price level rises, the *AE* curve shifts down and the economy moves upward along the *AD* curve

Equilibrium GDP is determined by the *AE* curve for each given price level; the level of equilibrium GDP and its associated price level are then plotted to yield a point on the *AD* curve. When the price level is P_0, the *AE* curve is AE_0, and hence equilibrium GDP is Y_0, as shown in part (i). Plotting Y_0 against P_0 yields the point E_0 on the *AD* curve in part (ii).

An increase in the price level to P_1 causes the *AE* curve to shift downward to AE_1 and causes equilibrium GDP to fall to Y_1. Plotting this new level of GDP against the higher price level yields a second point, E_1, on the *AD* curve. A further increase in the price level to P_2 causes the *AE* curve to shift downward to AE_2, and thus causes equilibrium GDP to fall to Y_2. Plotting P_2 and Y_2 yields a third point, E_2, on the *AD* curve.

A change in the price level causes a shift in the *AE* curve but a movement along the *AD* curve.

FIGURE 23-3 The Simple Multiplier and Shifts in the *AD* Curve

(i) Aggregate expenditure

(ii) Aggregate demand

A change in autonomous expenditure changes equilibrium GDP for any given price level. The simple multiplier measures the resulting horizontal shift in the *AD* curve. The original *AE* curve is AE_0 in part (i). Equilibrium is at E_0, with GDP of Y_0 at price level P_0. This yields point E_0 on the curve AD_0 in part (ii).

The *AE* curve in part (i) then shifts upward from AE_0 to AE_1, due to an increase in autonomous desired expenditure of ΔA. Equilibrium GDP now rises to Y_1, with the price level still constant at P_0. Thus, the *AD* curve in part (ii) shifts to the right to point E_1, indicating the higher equilibrium GDP of Y_1 associated with the same price level P_0. The size of the horizontal shift, ΔY, is equal to the simple multiplier times ΔA.

Figure 23-3 shows a shift in the *AD* curve. Because the *AD* curve plots equilibrium GDP as a function of the price level, anything that alters equilibrium GDP *at a given price level* must shift the *AD* curve. In other words, any change—other than a change in the price level—that causes the *AE* curve to shift will also cause the *AD* curve to shift. Such a shift is called an **aggregate demand shock**.

For example, in the 2002–2006 period, strong economic growth in the United States and elsewhere led to an increase in demand for Canadian-produced raw materials. This increase in demand caused an upward shift in Canada's net export function. This event, taken by itself, would shift Canada's *AE* function upward and thus would shift Canada's *AD* curve to the right.

For a given price level, an increase in autonomous aggregate expenditure shifts the *AE* curve upward and the *AD* curve to the right. A fall in autonomous aggregate expenditure shifts the *AE* curve downward and the *AD* curve to the left.

Remember the following important point. In order to shift the *AD* curve, the change in autonomous expenditure must be caused by something *other than* a change in the domestic price level. As we saw earlier in this chapter, a change in aggregate expenditure caused by a change in the domestic price level leads to a movement along (not a shift of) the *AD* curve.

The Simple Multiplier and the *AD* Curve   We saw in Chapters 21 and 22 that the simple multiplier measures the size of the change in equilibrium national income in response to a change in autonomous expenditure *when the price level is held constant*. It follows that this multiplier gives the size of the *horizontal shift* in the *AD* curve in response to a change in autonomous expenditure, as illustrated in Figure 23-3.

The simple multiplier measures the horizontal shift in the *AD* curve in response to a change in autonomous desired expenditure.

If the price level remains constant and producers are willing to supply everything that is demanded at that price level, the simple multiplier will also show the change in equilibrium income that will occur in response to a change in autonomous expenditure. This mention of producers' willingness to supply output brings us to a discussion of the *supply side* of the economy.

23.2 **THE SUPPLY SIDE OF THE ECONOMY**

So far, we have explained how the equilibrium level of GDP is determined *when the price level is taken as given* and how that equilibrium changes as the price level is changed exogenously. We are now ready to take the important next step: adding an *explanation* for changes in the price level. To do this, we need to take account of the supply decisions of firms.

The Aggregate Supply Curve

Aggregate supply refers to the total output of goods and services that firms would like to produce. The **aggregate supply (AS) curve** relates the price level to the quantity of output that firms would like to produce and sell *on the assumption that technology and the prices of all factors of production remain constant*. What does the *AS* curve look like?

aggregate supply (AS) curve A curve showing the relation between the price level and the quantity of aggregate output supplied, on the assumption that technology and all factor prices are held constant.

The Positive Slope of the AS Curve   To study the slope of the *AS* curve, we need to see how costs are related to output and then how prices are related to output.

Costs and Output. Suppose firms wish to increase their output above current levels. What will this do to their costs per unit of output—usually called their **unit costs**? The aggregate supply curve is drawn on the assumption that technology and the prices of all factors of production remain constant. This does not, however, mean that unit costs will be constant. As output increases, less efficient standby plants may have to be used, and less efficient workers may have to be hired, while existing workers may have to be paid overtime rates for additional work. For these and other similar reasons, unit costs will tend to rise as output rises, even when technology and input prices are constant. (Readers who have studied microeconomics will recognize the *law of diminishing returns* as one reason why costs rise in the short run as firms squeeze more output out of a fixed quantity of capital equipment.)

unit cost Cost per unit of output, equal to total cost divided by total output.

Prices and Output. To consider the relationship between price and output, we need to consider firms that sell in two distinct types of markets: those in which firms are *price takers* and those in which firms are *price setters*.

Some industries, especially those that produce raw materials, contain many individual firms. In these cases, each firm is too small to influence the market price, which is set by the overall forces of demand and supply. Each firm must accept whatever price is set by the market. Such firms are said to be *price takers*. When the market price changes, these firms will react by altering their level of production.

If their unit costs rise with output, price-taking firms will produce more only if price increases. They will produce less if the price falls.

Many other industries, including most of those that produce manufactured products, contain few enough firms that each can influence the market price of its product. Most firms in these industries sell products that differ from one another, although all are similar enough to be thought of as a single product produced by one industry. For example, no two kinds of automobiles are exactly the same, but all are sufficiently alike that we have no trouble talking about the automobile industry and its product, automobiles. In such cases, each firm must quote a price at which it is prepared to sell each of its products; that is, the firm is a *price setter*. If the demand for the output of price-setting firms increases sufficiently to take their outputs into the range in which

FIGURE 23-4 The Aggregate Supply Curve

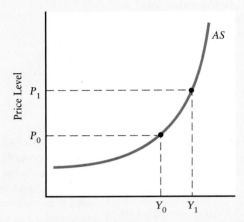

The *AS* curve is positively sloped, indicating that firms will provide more aggregate output only at a higher price level. The *AS* curve is drawn for a given level of technology and factor prices. At price level P_0, firms are prepared to produce and supply output equal to Y_0. An expansion of their output to Y_1 leads to an increase in unit costs, and thus firms are only prepared to supply Y_1 at a higher price level, P_1.

The higher is the level of output, the faster unit costs tend to rise with each extra increment to output. This explains why the *AS* curve becomes steeper as output rises.

their unit costs rise, these firms will not increase their outputs unless they can pass at least some of these extra costs on through higher prices. When demand falls, they will reduce output, and competition among them will tend to cause a reduction in prices whenever their unit costs fall.

Price-setting firms will increase their prices when they expand their output into the range where unit costs are rising. They will eventually decrease their prices if a reduction in their output leads to a reduction in unit costs.

This is the basic behaviour of firms in response to the changes in demand and prices when technology and factor prices are constant, and it explains the slope of the *AS* curve, such as the one shown in Figure 23-4.

The actions of both price-taking and price-setting firms cause the price level and the supply of output to be positively related—the aggregate supply (*AS*) curve is upward sloping.

The Increasing Slope of the AS Curve In Figure 23-4 we see that at low levels of GDP the *AS* curve is relatively flat, but as GDP rises the *AS* curve gets progressively steeper. What explains this shape?

When output is low (below potential output), firms typically have excess capacity—some plant and equipment are idle. When firms have excess capacity, only a small increase in the price of their output may be needed to induce them to expand production. Once output is pushed above normal capacity, however, unit costs tend to rise quite rapidly. Many higher-cost production methods may have to be adopted—such as standby capacity, overtime, and extra shifts. These higher-cost production methods will not be used unless the selling price of the output has risen enough to cover them. The more output is expanded beyond normal capacity, the more that unit costs rise and hence the larger is the rise in price that is necessary to induce firms to increase output. This increasing slope of the *AS* curve is sometimes called the *first asymmetry* in the behaviour of aggregate supply. (The second will be discussed in the next chapter.)

As we will see later in this chapter, the shape of the *AS* curve is crucial for determining how the effect of an aggregate demand shock is divided between a change in the price level and a change in real GDP.

Shifts in the Aggregate Supply Curve

aggregate supply shock Any shift in the aggregate supply (*AS*) curve.

For a given level of output, anything that changes firms' production costs will cause the *AS* curve to shift. Such shifts are called **aggregate supply shocks**. Two sources of aggregate supply shocks are of particular importance: changes in the prices of inputs and changes in productivity.

Changes in Input Prices Factor prices are held constant along the *AS* curve, and when they change, the curve shifts. If factor prices rise, firms will find the profitability of their current production reduced. For any given level of output to be produced, an increase in the price level will be required. If prices do not rise, firms will react by decreasing production. For the economy as a whole, there will be less output supplied at each price level than before the increase in factor prices. Or, to put it another way, there will be a higher price level for each level of output than before the increase in factor prices. Thus, if factor prices rise, the *AS* curve shifts upward (and to the left). This is a decrease in aggregate supply, and is shown in Figure 23-5.

Changes in the prices of raw materials—such as the lumber shown here—lead to changes in firms' production costs. Such changes cause shifts in the AS curve.

Similarly, a fall in factor prices causes the *AS* curve to shift downward (and to the right). There will be more output supplied at each price level. Or, to put the same point differently, the same amount of output will be supplied at a lower price level. This is an increase in aggregate supply. A dramatic example of such a reduction in factor prices occurred in 1997 and 1998 when the world prices of raw materials fell by an average of 30 percent. In the many countries that use raw materials as inputs in manufacturing, the *AS* curves shifted to the right. The opposite happened in 2002–2006 when energy and other commodity prices increased dramatically, thus shifting the *AS* curves to the left.

Changes in Productivity If labour productivity rises—that is, each worker can produce more with a given amount of effort and other resources—the unit costs of production will fall. Lower costs typically lead to lower prices, as competing firms cut prices in attempts to raise their market shares. That the same output is sold at a lower price causes a shift in the *AS* curve downward and to the right. This shift is an increase in aggregate supply, as illustrated in Figure 23-5.

A change in either factor prices or productivity will shift the *AS* curve because any given output will be supplied at a different price level than previously. An increase in factor prices or a decrease in productivity shifts the *AS* curve to the left; an increase in productivity or a decrease in factor prices shifts the *AS* curve to the right.

FIGURE 23-5   Shifts in the *AS* Curve

For any given level of output, anything that increases firms' costs will shift the *AS* curve upward (and to the left). Starting from (P_0, Y_0), a rise in input prices or a reduction in productivity would increase firms' unit costs. Firms would be prepared to continue supplying output of Y_0 only at the higher price level P_1. Or, at the initial price level P_0, firms would now be prepared to supply output of only Y_1. In either case, the *AS* curve has shifted up (or to the left) from AS_0 to AS_1. This is called a *reduction* in aggregate supply.

A fall in input prices or an increase in productivity would cause the *AS* curve to shift down (and to the right). This is an *increase* in aggregate supply.

23.3 **MACROECONOMIC EQUILIBRIUM**

FIGURE 23-6 Macroeconomic Equilibrium

Macroeconomic equilibrium occurs at the intersection of the *AD* and *AS* curves and determines the equilibrium values for real GDP and the price level. Given the *AD* and *AS* curves in the figure, macroeconomic equilibrium occurs at E_0.

If the price level were equal to P_1, the desired output of firms would be Y_1. However, at P_1, the level of output that is consistent with expenditure decisions would be Y_2. Hence, when the price level is less than P_0, the desired output of firms will be less than the level of real GDP that is consistent with expenditure decisions. Conversely, for any price level above P_0, the desired output of firms exceeds the level of output that is consistent with expenditure decisions.

The only price level where the supply decisions of firms are consistent with desired expenditure is P_0. At P_0, firms wish to produce Y_0. When they do so, they generate a real GDP of Y_0; when real GDP is Y_0, decision makers wish to spend exactly Y_0, thereby purchasing the nation's output. Hence, all decisions are consistent with each other.

We are now ready to see how both real GDP and the price level are simultaneously determined by the interaction of aggregate demand and aggregate supply. To begin, we assume that input prices and technology are constant.

The equilibrium values of real GDP and the price level occur at the intersection of the *AD* and *AS* curves, as shown by the pair Y_0 and P_0 that arises at point E_0 in Figure 23-6. The combination of real GDP and price level that is on both the *AD* and *AS* curves is called a *macroeconomic equilibrium*.

To see why the point (Y_0, P_0) is the only macroeconomic equilibrium, first consider what Figure 23-6 shows would happen if the price level were below P_0. At this lower price level, the desired output of firms, as given by the *AS* curve, is less than desired aggregate expenditure—there is an excess demand for goods. Conversely, at a price level above P_0, the desired output by firms exceeds desired aggregate expenditure—there is an excess supply of goods.

Only at the combination of real GDP and price level given by the intersection of the *AS* and *AD* curves are demand behaviour and supply behaviour consistent.

Macroeconomic equilibrium thus requires that two conditions be satisfied. The first is familiar to us because it comes from Chapters 21 and 22. At the prevailing price level, desired aggregate expenditure must be equal to actual GDP—that is, households are just willing to buy all that is produced. The *AD* curve is constructed in such a way that this condition holds everywhere along it. The second requirement for macroeconomic equilibrium is introduced by consideration of aggregate supply. At the prevailing price level, firms must wish to produce the prevailing level of GDP, no more and no less. This condition is fulfilled everywhere along the *AS* curve. Only where the two curves intersect are both conditions fulfilled simultaneously.

Changes in the Macroeconomic Equilibrium

Practise with Study Guide Chapter 23, Exercise 3.

The aggregate demand and aggregate supply curves can now be used to understand how various shocks to the economy change both real GDP and the price level.

As indicated earlier, a shift in the *AD* curve is called an aggregate demand shock. A rightward shift in the *AD* curve is an increase in aggregate demand; it means that at all price levels, expenditure decisions will now be consistent with a higher level of real GDP. This is called a *positive* shock. Similarly, a leftward shift in the *AD* curve is a decrease in aggregate demand—that is, at all price levels, expenditure decisions will now be consistent with a lower level of real GDP. This is called a *negative* shock.

Also as indicated earlier, a shift in the *AS* curve is called an aggregate supply shock. A rightward shift in the *AS* curve is an increase in aggregate supply; at any given price level, more real GDP will be supplied. This is a *positive* shock. A leftward shift in the *AS* curve is a decrease in aggregate supply; at any given price level, less real GDP will be supplied. This is a *negative* shock.

Aggregate demand and supply shocks are labelled according to their effect on real GDP. Positive shocks increase equilibrium GDP; negative shocks reduce equilibrium GDP.

Let's now examine aggregate demand and supply shocks in detail.

Aggregate Demand Shocks

Figure 23-7 shows the effects of an increase in aggregate demand—a positive *AD* shock. This increase could have occurred because of, say, increased investment or government purchases, an increase in foreigners' demand for Canadian goods, or an increase in household consumption resulting from a reduction in personal income taxes. (Remember that each of these events causes the *AE* curve to shift up, and therefore the *AD* curve to shift to the right.) Whatever the cause, the increase in aggregate demand means that more domestic output is demanded at any given price level. As is shown in the figure, the increase in aggregate demand causes both the price level and real GDP to rise in the new macroeconomic equilibrium. Conversely, a decrease in demand causes both the price level and real GDP to fall.

Aggregate demand shocks cause the price level and real GDP to change in the same direction; both rise with an increase in aggregate demand, and both fall with a decrease in aggregate demand.

The Multiplier When the Price Level Varies We saw earlier in this chapter that the simple multiplier gives the size of the horizontal shift in the *AD* curve in response to a change in autonomous expenditure. If the price level remains constant and firms supply all that is demanded at the existing price level (as would be the case with a horizontal *AS* curve), the simple multiplier gives the increase in equilibrium national income.

But what happens in the more usual case in which the *AS* curve slopes upward? As can be seen in Figure 23-7, when the *AS* curve is positively sloped, the change in real GDP caused by a change in autonomous expenditure is no longer equal to the size of the horizontal shift in the *AD* curve. Part of the expansionary impact of an increase in demand is dissipated by a rise in the price level, and only part is transmitted to a rise in real GDP. Of course, an increase in output does occur; thus, a multiplier may still be calculated, but its value is not the same as that of the *simple* multiplier.

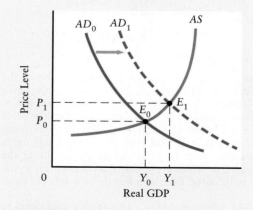

FIGURE 23-7 Aggregate Demand Shocks

Shifts in aggregate demand cause the price level and real GDP to move in the same direction. An increase in aggregate demand shifts the *AD* curve to the right, from AD_0 to AD_1. Macroeconomic equilibrium moves from E_0 to E_1. The price level rises from P_0 to P_1, and real GDP rises from Y_0 to Y_1, reflecting a movement along the *AS* curve.

FIGURE 23-8   The Multiplier When the Price Level Varies

(i) Aggregate expenditure

(ii) Aggregate demand and supply

An increase in autonomous expenditure causes the AE curve to shift upward, but the rise in the price level causes it to shift part of the way down again. Hence, the multiplier is smaller than when the price level is constant. Originally, equilibrium is at point E_0 in both part (i) and part (ii). Desired aggregate expenditure then shifts by ΔA to AE_1', shifting the AD curve to AD_1. These shifts are shown by arrow ① in both parts. But the adjustment is not yet complete.

The shift in the AD curve raises the price level to P_1 because the AS curve is positively sloped. The rise in the price level shifts the AE curve down to AE_1, as shown by arrow ② in part (i). This is shown as a *movement along* the new AD curve, as indicated by arrow ② in part (ii). The new equilibrium is thus at E_1. The amount Y_0Y_1 is ΔY, the actual increase in real GDP. The multiplier, adjusted for the effect of the price increase, is the ratio $\Delta Y/\Delta A$ in part (i).

When the AS curve is upward sloping, an aggregate demand shock leads to a change in the price level. As a result, the multiplier is smaller than the simple multiplier.

Why is the multiplier smaller when the AS curve is positively sloped? The answer lies in the behaviour that is summarized by the AE curve. To understand this, it is useful to think of the final change in real GDP as occurring in two stages, as shown in Figure 23-8.

First, with prices remaining constant, an increase in autonomous expenditure shifts the AE curve upward (from AE_0 to AE_1'). This increase in autonomous expenditure is shown in part (ii) by a shift to the right of the AD curve. The movement marked ① is the end of the first stage, but is not the end of the whole story.

In the second stage we must take account of the rise in the price level that occurs because of the positive slope of the AS curve. As we saw earlier in this chapter, a rise in the price level, via its effect on net exports and desired consumption, leads to a downward shift in the AE curve (from AE_1' to AE_1). This second shift of the AE curve partly counteracts the initial rise in real GDP and so reduces the size of the multiplier. The second stage shows up as a downward shift of the AE curve in part (i) of Figure 23-8 and a movement upward and to the left along the new AD curve, as shown by arrow ② in part (ii).

The Importance of the Shape of the AS Curve

We have now seen that the shape of the AS curve has important implications for how the effects of an aggregate demand shock are divided between changes in real GDP and changes in the price level. Figure 23-9 highlights the price level and GDP effects of aggregate demand shocks by considering AD shocks in the presence of an AS curve that exhibits three distinct ranges.

Over the *flat* range, any change in aggregate demand leads to no change in prices and, as seen earlier, a response of output equal to that predicted by the simple multiplier.

Over the *intermediate* range, along which the AS curve is positively sloped, a shift in the AD curve gives rise to appreciable changes in both real GDP and the price level. Because of the increase in the price level, the multiplier in this case is positive, but smaller than the simple multiplier.

Over the *steep* range, very little more can be produced, no matter how large the increase in demand. This range deals with an economy near its capacity constraints. Any change in aggregate demand leads to a sharp change in the price level and to little or no change in real GDP. The multiplier in this case is nearly zero.

The effect of any given shift in aggregate demand will be divided between a change in real output and a change in the price level, depending on the conditions of aggregate supply. The steeper the *AS* curve, the greater the price effect and the smaller the output effect.

Extensions in Theory 23-1 deals with the special case of a horizontal *AS* curve—sometimes called a *Keynesian AS* curve. In that case, the aggregate supply curve determines the price level, and the *AD* curve determines real GDP.

Reconciliation with Previous Analysis   One of the central points of this chapter is that aggregate demand shocks typically lead to changes in *both* the price level and the level of real GDP. Furthermore, with a steep enough *AS* curve, such aggregate demand shocks will result in no change in real GDP, but only a change in the price level. How do we reconcile this possibility with the analysis of Chapters 21 and 22, where shifts in *AE always* change real GDP? The answer is that each *AE* curve is drawn on the assumption that there is a constant price level. An upward shift in the *AE* curve shifts the *AD* curve to the right. However, a positively sloped *AS* curve means that the price level rises, and this rise shifts the *AE* curve back down, offsetting some of its initial rise. This process was explained in Figure 23-8.

It is instructive to consider an extreme version of Figure 23-8, one with a vertical *AS* curve. If you draw this diagram for yourself, you will note that an increase in autonomous expenditure shifts the *AE* curve upward, thus raising the amount demanded. However, a vertical *AS* curve means that output cannot be expanded to satisfy the increased demand. Instead, the extra demand merely forces prices up, and as prices rise, the *AE* curve shifts down again. The rise in prices continues until the *AE* curve is back to where it started. Thus, the rise in prices offsets the expansionary effect of the original shift and consequently leaves both real aggregate expenditure and equilibrium real GDP unchanged.

A vertical *AS* curve, however, is quite unrealistic. Most economists agree that the *AS* curve is shaped something like the one shown in Figure 23-9—that is, relatively flat for low levels of GDP and becoming steeper as GDP rises.

We now complete our discussion of changes in the macroeconomic equilibrium by discussing supply shocks.

FIGURE 23-9   The Effects of Increases in Aggregate Demand

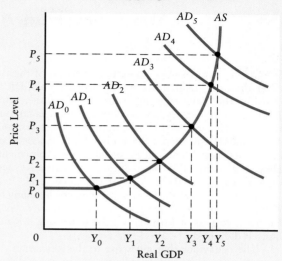

The effect of increases in aggregate demand is divided between increases in real GDP and increases in the price level, depending on the slope of the *AS* curve. Because of the increasing slope of the *AS* curve, increases in aggregate demand up to AD_0 have virtually no impact on the price level. Successive further increases bring larger price increases and relatively smaller output increases. By the time aggregate demand is at AD_4 or AD_5, virtually all of the effect is on the price level.

Practise with Study Guide Chapter 23, Extension Exercise E1.

EXTENSIONS IN THEORY 23-1

The Keynesian *AS* Curve

In this box, we consider an extreme version of the *AS* curve that is horizontal over some range of real GDP. It is called the *Keynesian aggregate supply curve*, after John Maynard Keynes (1883–1946), who in his famous book *The General Theory of Employment, Interest and Money* (1936) pioneered the study of the behaviour of economies under conditions of high unemployment. Despite its name, this curve does not describe Keynes' own views on the behaviour of the price level. It is instead the version of aggregate supply used by many of Keynes' followers in their early attempts to express Keynes' work in a formal model—something Keynes himself did not do.

The behaviour that gives rise to the Keynesian *AS* curve can be described as follows. When real GDP is below potential GDP, individual firms are operating with excess capacity. They then respond to changes in demand by altering output while keeping prices constant. In other words, they will supply whatever they can sell at their existing prices as long as they are producing below their normal capacity.*

Under these circumstances, the economy has a horizontal *AS* curve, indicating that any output up to potential output will be supplied at the going price level. The amount that is actually produced is then deter-

mined by the position of the *AD* curve, as shown in the figure. Thus, real GDP is said to be *demand determined*. If demand rises enough so that firms are trying to squeeze more than normal output out of their plants, their costs will rise, and so will their prices. Hence, the horizontal Keynesian *AS* curve applies only to levels of GDP below potential GDP.

This special case of a horizontal *AS* curve corresponds to the macro model that we developed in Chapters 21 and 22. Recall that in that simple model we assumed a constant price level. In other words, if the *AS* curve is horizontal, our macro model in this chapter is *exactly the same* as the simple version in Chapters 21 and 22. In this case, a change in autonomous expenditure, ΔA, will lead to increases in equilibrium GDP equal to ΔA times the simple multiplier. (In Figure 23-3 this is exactly the distance of the horizontal shift in the *AD* curve in response to any given ΔA.)

---

* There is considerable evidence that many firms do behave like this for short periods of time. One possible explanation for this behaviour is that changing prices frequently is too costly, so firms set the best possible (profit-maximizing) prices when output is at normal capacity and then do not change prices in the face of short-term fluctuations in demand.

Aggregate Supply Shocks

Practise with Study Guide Chapter 23, Exercises 4 and 5.

A negative aggregate supply shock, shown by a shift to the left in the *AS* curve, means that less real output will be supplied at any given price level. A positive aggregate supply shock, shown by a shift to the right in the *AS* curve, means that more real output will be supplied at any given price level.

Figure 23-10 illustrates the effects on the price level and real GDP of a negative aggregate supply shock. This could have occurred because of, say, an increase in the world price of important inputs, such as oil, copper, or iron ore. As can be seen from the figure, following the decrease in aggregate supply, the price level rises and real GDP falls. Conversely, an increase in aggregate supply leads to an increase in real GDP and a decrease in the price level.

Aggregate supply shocks cause the price level and real GDP to change in opposite directions. With an increase in supply, the price level falls and GDP rises; with a decrease in supply, the price level rises and GDP falls.

Oil-price increases provided two major examples of negative aggregate supply shocks in the 1970s. The economy is especially responsive to changes in the price for oil because, in addition to being used to produce energy, oil is an input into plastics and many other materials that are widely used in manufacturing. Massive increases in oil prices occurred during 1973–1974 and 1979–1980, caused by the successful efforts of the OPEC countries to form a cartel and restrict the output of oil. These increases in the price of oil caused leftward shifts in the *AS* curve in most countries. Real GDP fell while the price level rose. (We will discuss shortly the more recent oil-price increases that occurred in the 2002–2006 period.)

Commodity prices have provided an important recent example of a positive aggregate supply shock. The Southeast Asian countries of Indonesia, Malaysia, Thailand, and South Korea are all significant users of raw materials. When their economies plunged into a major recession in 1997 and 1998, the world demand for raw materials fell, and the prices of such goods fell as a result. From the summer of 1997 to the end of 1998, the average price of raw materials fell by approximately 30 percent.

Though these were clearly bad economic times for much of Southeast Asia, the reduction in raw materials prices was a *positive* aggregate supply shock for countries that used raw materials as inputs for production. In countries like Canada, the United States, and most of Western Europe, the *AS* curves shifted to the right. The effect was to increase real GDP and reduce the price level.[2]

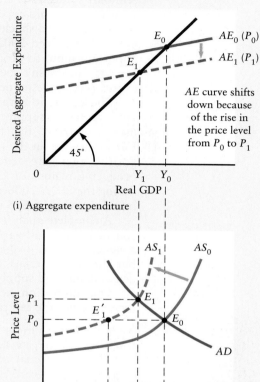

FIGURE 23-10 A Negative Aggregate Supply Shock

(i) Aggregate expenditure

(ii) Aggregate demand and supply

Aggregate supply shocks cause the price level and real GDP to move in opposite directions. The original equilibrium is at E_0, with GDP of Y_0 appearing in both parts of the figure. The price level is P_0 in part (ii), and at that price level, the desired aggregate expenditure curve is AE_0 in part (i).

A negative aggregate supply shock now shifts the *AS* curve in part (ii) to AS_1. At the original price level of P_0, firms are now only willing to supply Y_1'. The fall in supply causes a rise in the price level. The new equilibrium is reached at E_1, where the *AD* curve intersects AS_1. At the new and higher equilibrium price level of P_1, the *AE* curve has fallen to AE_1, as shown in part (i).

---

[2] Actually, it is more accurate to say that the shock reduced the price level *compared to what it otherwise would have been*. Due to ongoing inflation, the causes of which we will discuss in Chapters 29 and 30, the price level in Canada rarely falls. But we have been assuming throughout this chapter that there is no ongoing inflation, and in that setting a positive *AS* shock like the one described in the text would indeed cause the price level to fall.

For information on OPEC, see its website: **www.opec.org**.

A Word of Warning

We have discussed the effects of aggregate demand and aggregate supply shocks on the economy's price level and real GDP. Students are sometimes puzzled, however, because some events would appear to be *both* demand and supply shocks. How do we analyze such complicated shocks? For example, when the world price of oil rises, as it did significantly between 2002 and 2006, this is a *negative supply shock* because oil is an important input to production for many firms. But for Canada, which produces and exports oil, doesn't the increase in the world price of oil also imply an increase in export revenue? And doesn't this imply a *positive demand shock*?

The answer to both questions is yes. An increase in world oil prices is indeed a negative aggregate supply shock to any country that uses oil as an input (which means most countries). But for those countries that also produce and export oil—like Canada—a rise in the price of oil generates an increase in income to oil producers, a positive aggregate demand shock. (It is no surprise that the economies of the oil-producing regions of Canada, especially Alberta and Newfoundland, were booming during the 2002–2006 period, when the price of oil increased from about U.S.$30 per barrel to over U.S.$75 per barrel.)

A complete analysis of the macroeconomic effect of a rise in world oil prices must consider both a leftward shift of the *AS* curve and, for those countries that produce oil, a rightward shift of the *AD* curve. The equilibrium price level will certainly increase, but the overall effect on real GDP will depend on the relative importance of the demand-side and supply-side effects.

Our discussion here has been about the macroeconomic effects of oil-price increases, but the central message is more general:

Many economic events—especially changes in the world prices of raw materials—cause both aggregate demand and aggregate supply shocks in the same economy. The overall effect on real GDP in that economy depends on the relative importance of the two separate effects.

This general principle should be kept in mind whenever our *AD/AS* macro model is used to analyze the macroeconomy. *Lessons From History 23-1* uses our model to interpret the effects of the 1997–1998 Asian economic crisis on the Canadian economy. As you will see in that discussion, the Asian crisis generated both *AD* and *AS* shocks for Canada.

---

myeconlab

The increase in the world price of oil from 2002 to 2006 was dramatic, but many observers were surprised at its modest impact on the Canadian economy. For more information on how changes in oil prices affect Canada, and for why the negative *AS* effect is smaller now than in the 1970s, look for "Oil Prices and the Canadian Economy" in the *Additional Topics* section of this book's MyEconLab.

www.myeconlab.com

LESSONS FROM HISTORY 23-1

The Asian Crisis and the Canadian Economy

In the summer of 1997, the currencies of several countries in Southeast Asia plummeted (relative to the U.S. and Canadian dollars) as their central banks were no longer able to "peg" their exchange rates. We will discuss how such pegged exchange rates operate in Chapter 35. For now, the important point is that, for various reasons, banks, firms, and households in these countries had accumulated a large stock of debt denominated in foreign currencies, especially U.S. dollars. The sudden depreciations of their currencies—in some cases by 70 percent in just a few days—led to dramatic increases in the amount of domestic income required to pay the interest on this debt. Manufacturing firms and financial institutions went bankrupt, workers were laid off, and economic output fell sharply. By late in 1997, the economies of Malaysia, Indonesia, Thailand, South Korea, and the Philippines were suffering major recessions.

How did this Asian crisis affect Canada? It had offsetting positive and negative effects on the level of economic activity in Canada. The events in Asia generated both a *negative* aggregate demand shock and a *positive* aggregate supply shock for Canada.

To understand the demand side of the story, we must recognize that these Asian economies are important users of raw materials. When their level of economic activity declined sharply, so too did their demand for raw materials. Indeed, average raw materials prices fell by roughly 30 percent between 1997 and 1998. But raw materials are an important export for Canada. The decline in the world's demand for raw materials implied a reduction in demand for Canadian goods. As a result, Canadian producers of copper, pork, newsprint, lumber, iron ore, and many other raw materials suffered significantly. In terms of our macroeconomic model, the demand part of the Asian crisis is represented as a leftward shift of the Canadian AD curve.

But the story does not end there. Also important to Canada is the fact that many Canadian manufacturing firms use raw materials as inputs for their production of car parts, pre-fabricated houses and trailers, electrical equipment, and so on. A dramatic reduction in the

prices of raw materials implies a reduction in costs for manufacturing firms. This is a positive aggregate supply shock, and is illustrated by a rightward shift of the Canadian AS curve.

What is the overall effect on the Canadian economy? The effect of each shock taken separately is to reduce the price level—so the overall effect is unambiguously a lower price level.* In contrast, the effect on real GDP would appear to be ambiguous since the AD shock reduces GDP whereas the AS shock increases it. But this is not quite right. Since Canada is a net exporter of raw materials (it exports more raw materials than it imports), it must experience a decrease in national income when these prices fall. In other words, the net effect of the negative demand shock and the positive supply shock is to reduce Canadian GDP. The figure is therefore drawn with the AD shock being larger than the AS shock and so the new equilibrium level of GDP, Y_1, is lower than in the initial equilibrium, Y_0.

---

*Recall footnote 2 on page 561. We are assuming in this analysis that there is no ongoing inflation, so a positive AS shock or a negative AD shock reduces the price level. A more accurate description for the Canadian economy in 1998, with some ongoing inflation, is that the price level fell below what it otherwise would have been. This appears as a reduction in the rate of inflation.

S U M M A R Y

23.1 THE DEMAND SIDE OF THE ECONOMY

- The *AE* curve shows desired aggregate expenditure for each level of GDP at a particular price level. Its intersection with the 45° line determines equilibrium GDP for that price level. Equilibrium GDP thus occurs where desired aggregate expenditure equals actual GDP. A change in the price level changes private-sector wealth and thus causes a shift in the *AE* curve: upward when the price level falls, and downward when the price level rises. This leads to a new equilibrium level of real GDP.
- The *AD* curve plots the equilibrium level of GDP that corresponds to each possible price level. A change in equilibrium GDP following a change in the price level is shown by a movement along the *AD* curve.
- A rise in the price level lowers exports and lowers autonomous consumption expenditure (because it decreases wealth). Both of these changes reduce equilibrium GDP and cause the *AD* curve to have a negative slope.
- The *AD* curve shifts horizontally when any element of autonomous expenditure changes, and the simple multiplier measures the size of the shift.

23.2 THE SUPPLY SIDE OF THE ECONOMY

- Firms' unit costs usually rise when their output rises, and thus they are willing to supply more output only at higher prices. As a result, the *AS* curve is upward sloping.
- Each *AS* curve is drawn for given levels of factor (input) prices and productivity.
- An increase in productivity or a decrease in factor prices shifts the *AS* curve to the right. This is an increase in aggregate supply. A decrease in productivity or an increase in factor prices shifts the *AS* curve to the left. This is a decrease in aggregate supply.

23.3 MACROECONOMIC EQUILIBRIUM

- Macroeconomic equilibrium refers to equilibrium values of real GDP and the price level, as determined by the intersection of the *AD* and *AS* curves. Shifts in the *AD* and *AS* curves, called aggregate demand and aggregate supply shocks, change the equilibrium values of real GDP and the price level.
- When the *AS* curve is upward sloping, an aggregate demand shock causes the price level and real GDP to move in the same direction. When the *AS* curve is flat, shifts in the *AD* curve primarily affect real GDP. When the *AS* curve is steep, shifts in the *AD* curve primarily affect the price level.
- In the usual case with an upward sloping *AS* curve, a demand shock leads to a change in the price level. As a result, the multiplier is smaller than the simple multiplier in Chapter 22.
- An aggregate supply shock moves equilibrium GDP along the *AD* curve, causing the price level and real GDP to move in opposite directions. A leftward shift in the *AS* curve causes a reduction in real GDP and an increase in the price level. A rightward shift causes an increase in real GDP and a fall in the price level.
- Some events are both aggregate supply and aggregate demand shocks. Changes in the world prices of raw materials, for example, shift the *AS* curve. If the country (like Canada) is also a producer of such raw materials, there will also be a shift in the *AD* curve. The overall effect then depends on the relative sizes of the separate effects.

K E Y   C O N C E P T S

Effects of an exogenous change in the price level
Relationship between the *AE* and *AD* curves

Negative slope of the *AD* curve
Positive slope of the *AS* curve
Macroeconomic equilibrium
Aggregate demand shocks

The multiplier when the price level varies
Aggregate supply shocks

STUDY EXERCISES

1. Fill in the blanks to make the following statements correct.

   a. In the simple macro model of the previous two chapters, the price level was _____. In the macro model of this chapter, the price level is _____.

   b. A change in the price level shifts the *AE* curve because the price level change affects desired _____ and desired _____.

   c. A rise in the price level causes a(n) _____ in households' wealth, which leads to a _____ in desired consumption, which causes the *AE* curve to shift _____. A fall in the price level causes a(n) _____ in households' wealth, which leads to a _____ in desired consumption, which causes the *AE* curve to shift _____.

   d. A rise in the domestic price level causes net exports to _____, which causes the *AE* curve to shift _____. A fall in the domestic price level causes net exports to _____, which causes the *AE* curve to shift _____.

   e. Equilibrium GDP is determined by the position of the *AE* function for each given price level. An equilibrium point for a particular price level corresponds to one point on the _____ curve.

   f. A rise in the price level causes a downward shift of the _____ curve and a movement upward along the _____ curve.

   g. An increase in autonomous expenditure, with no change in the price level, causes the *AE* curve to _____ and causes the *AD* curve to _____.

2. Fill in the blanks to make the following statements correct.

   a. The ___A^s___ curve relates the price level to the quantity of output that firms would like to produce and sell.

   b. Each aggregate supply curve is drawn under the assumption that _technology_ and _factor prices_ remain constant.

   c. The aggregate supply curve is upward sloping because firms will produce more output only if price _rises_ to offset higher unit costs.

   d. The aggregate supply curve is relatively flat when GDP is below potential output because firms typically have _____ and are able to expand production without much increase in unit costs.

   e. The aggregate supply curve is relatively steep when GDP is above potential output because firms are operating above _capacity_ and _prices_ are rising rapidly.

   f. The aggregate supply curve shifts in response to changes in _productivity_ and changes in _factor prices_. These are known as supply _shocks_.

3. Fill in the blanks to make the following statements correct.

   a. Macroeconomic equilibrium occurs at the intersection of _____ and _____, and determines equilibrium levels of _____ and _____.

   b. A positive *AD* shock will cause the price level to _____ and real GDP to _____. A negative *AD* shock will cause the price level to _____ and real GDP to _____.

   c. A positive *AS* shock will cause the price level to _____ and real GDP to _____. A negative *AS* shock will cause the price level to _____ and real GDP to _____.

   d. In previous chapters, the simple multiplier measured the change in real GDP in response to a change in autonomous expenditure when the price level was constant. When the price level varies, the multiplier is _____ than the simple multiplier.

   e. An increase in autonomous government spending is a _____ *AD* shock, which will initially cause a(n) _____ shift of the *AE* curve and a(n) _____ shift of the *AD* curve. Given an upward-sloping aggregate supply curve, there will be a _____ in the price level, which leads to a partial _____ shift of the *AE* curve.

4. Consider the effects of an exogenous increase in the domestic price level. For each of the assets listed, explain how the change in the price level would affect the wealth of the asset holder. Then explain the effect on *aggregate* (private sector) wealth.

   a. Cash holdings
   b. Deposits in a bank account
   c. A household mortgage
   d. A corporate bond that promises to pay the bondholder $10 000 on January 1, 2011
   e. A government bond that promises to pay the holder $10 000 on January 1, 2011

5. Ⓧ myeconlab Consider the following simplified *AE* function:

   $$AE = 350 + 0.8Y + 0.1(M/P)$$

   where *AE* is desired aggregate expenditure, *Y* is real GDP, *M* is the private sector's *nominal wealth*, and *P* is the price level. Suppose that *M* is constant and equal to 6000.

   a. Explain why the expression for *AE* above makes sense. Why do *M* and *P* enter the *AE* function?

b. Fill in the table below:

P	M/P	AE
1	—	—
2	—	—
3	—	—
4	—	—
5	—	—
6	—	—

c. Plot each of the *AE* functions—one for each price level—on the same scale 45°-line diagram.
d. Compute the level of equilibrium national income for each of the values of *P*.
e. Plot the pairs of price level and equilibrium national income on a scale diagram with *P* on the vertical axis and *Y* on the horizontal axis.

6. **myeconlab** Consider the following diagram showing the *AD* curves in two different economies. One economy is Autarkland—it does not trade with the rest of the world (*autarky* is a situation in which a country does not trade with other countries). The other economy is Openland—it exports to and imports from the rest of the world.

a. Explain why an increase in the domestic price level (for a given exchange rate) reduces net exports in Openland. How would you illustrate this with the *AE* curve in the 45°-line diagram?
b. Explain why the *AD* curve is steeper in Autarkland than in Openland.
c. If there are never any net exports in Autarkland, why isn't the *AD* curve vertical? Explain what other aspect of the economy generates a downward-sloping *AD* curve.

7. **myeconlab** The economy of Neverland has the following *AD* and *AS* schedules. Denote Y_{AD} as the level of real GDP along the *AD* curve; let Y_{AS} be the level of real GDP along the *AS* curve. GDP is shown in billions of 1997 dollars.

Price Level	Y_{AD}	Y_{AS}
90	1100	750
100	1000	825
110	900	900
120	800	975
130	700	1050
140	600	1125

a. Plot the *AD* and *AS* curves on a scale diagram.
b. What is the price level and level of real GDP in Neverland's macroeconomic equilibrium?
c. Suppose the level of potential output in Neverland is $950 billion. Is the current equilibrium level of real GDP greater than or less than potential? How does one refer to this particular output gap?

8. Each of the following events is either a *cause* or a *consequence* of a shift in the *AD* or *AS* curve in Canada. Identify which it is and, if it is a cause, describe the effect on equilibrium real GDP and the price level.

a. OPEC's actions significantly increased the world price of oil in 1979–1980.
b. During 1996–2001, Canadian real GDP was growing at a healthy pace but inflation showed no signs of rising.
c. World commodity prices declined sharply in 1997–1998. Many of these commodities are both produced in Canada and used as important inputs for Canadian firms.
d. The end of the Cold War led to large declines in defence spending in many countries (including Canada).
e. Several provinces lowered their personal income tax rates in the late 1990s.
f. The federal government increased its level of government purchases (*G*) in the early 2000s.

9. The diagrams on the next page show the *AD* and *AS* curves in two different economies.

a. Explain what aspect of firms' behaviour might give rise to the horizontal *AS* curve in Economy A.
b. Explain what aspect of firms' behaviour gives rise to the upward-sloping *AS* curve in Economy B.
c. In which economy is output demand determined? Explain.
d. Consider the effects of an increase in autonomous expenditure. Which economy has the larger multiplier? Explain your reasoning.

Economy A

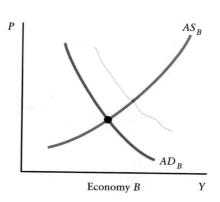

Economy B

10. This question involves algebraically solving the system of two equations given by the AD and AS curves. The equations for the curves are given by:

AD: $Y_{AD} = 710 - 30P + 5G$

AS: $Y_{AS} = 10 + 5P - 2P_{OIL}$

where Y is real GDP, P is the price level, G is the level of government purchases, and P_{OIL} is the world price of oil.

a. Explain the various terms in the AD curve. What is the value of the simple multiplier? (Hint: the simple multiplier is the change in equilibrium real GDP when some autonomous component of expenditure, like G, changes by $1 if the price level is held constant.)

b. Explain the various terms in the AS curve. Explain why the price of oil enters negatively.

c. Solve for the equilibrium value of real GDP and the price level.

d. Using your solution to part (c), what is the effect of a change in G on equilibrium Y and P?

e. Using your solution to part (c), what is the effect of a change in P_{OIL} on equilibrium Y and P?

DISCUSSION QUESTIONS

1. In 1979 and 1980, the British government greatly reduced income taxes but restored the lost government revenue by raising excise and sales taxes. These actions led to a sharp increase in the price level and a fall in output. Explain these events in terms of shifts in the aggregate demand or aggregate supply curves (or both).

2. This chapter discussed the meaning of aggregate demand and aggregate supply shocks, and several examples were given of each. But some shocks can be both demand-side shocks and supply-side shocks. Consider the prices of many commodities, such as lumber, newsprint, oil, copper, grains, and iron ore. The prices of such commodities are determined in world markets, and are subject to significant fluctuations from year to year. For example, in 2002–2006, there was a significant increase in the prices of many such commodities. Explain how such a rise in commodity prices can lead to both an increase in Canadian aggregate demand and a fall in Canadian aggregate supply. How would you determine the net effect on real GDP and the price level?

3. Show the effects on the price level and real GDP of a major union wage settlement that significantly increases wages. Is this a supply shock, a demand shock, or both?

4. On the next page are the combinations of output and price level given by real GDP and the CPI, respectively, for some recent years. Treat each pair as if it is the intersection of an AD and an AS curve. Plot these data. Then think about the possible shifts in the AD or AS curves that could have caused them. Is it possible to know what the underlying shifts are? Why or why not?

Year	CPI (1992 = 100)	GDP (billions of 1997 dollars)
1994	102.0	810.0
1995	104.2	832.1
1996	105.9	845.2
1997	107.6	882.7
1998	108.9	919.0
1999	110.5	967.6
2000	113.5	1013.1
2001	116.4	1026.9
2002	119.0	1062.0
2003	122.3	1088.8
2004	124.6	1124.7
2005	127.3	1157.7

5. Consider a government policy to reduce both personal and corporate income tax rates. Explain the effects of such a policy on the macroeconomic equilibrium. Is this a demand-side or a supply-side policy? Explain.

CHAPTER 24

From the Short Run to the Long Run: The Adjustment of Factor Prices

LO LEARNING OBJECTIVES

In this chapter you will learn

1. why output gaps cause wages and other factor prices to change.
2. how induced changes in factor prices affect firms' costs and shift the *AS* curve.
3. why real GDP gradually returns to potential output following an *AD* or *AS* shock.
4. why lags and uncertainty place limitations on the use of fiscal stabilization policy.

In the previous three chapters, we developed a model of the *short-run* determination of the equilibrium levels of real GDP and the price level. In this chapter, we discuss how this short-run macroeconomic equilibrium evolves, through an adjustment process where wages and other factor prices change, into a *long-run* equilibrium, in which real GDP is equal to potential output, Y^*. In the next two chapters we examine theories explaining why Y^* increases over many years—what we call *long-run economic growth*. Before we proceed, however, we will define carefully our assumptions regarding the short run, the adjustment process, and the long run.

The Short Run   The defining characteristics of the *short run* in our macroeconomic model are:

- factor prices are assumed to be exogenous; they may change, but any change is not explained within the model
- technology and factor supplies are assumed to be constant (and therefore Y^* is constant)

With these assumptions, the short-run macroeconomic equilibrium is determined by the intersection of the *AD* and *AS* curves, both of which are subject to shocks of various kinds. The level of real GDP therefore fluctuates around a *constant* level of potential output, Y^*. This version of our macroeconomic model is convenient to use when analyzing the economy over short periods. Even though factor prices, technology, and factor supplies are rarely constant, even over short periods of time, by making the simplifying assumption that they are constant in our short-run model we can focus on the most important changes over this time span: the fluctuations of real GDP relative to the level of potential output—what economists call *business cycles*.

The Adjustment of Factor Prices   As we will see in detail in this chapter, our theory of the *adjustment process* that takes the economy from the short run to the long run is based on the following assumptions:

- factor prices are assumed to be flexible and to adjust to output gaps
- technology and factor supplies are assumed to be constant (and therefore Y^* is constant)

This chapter will explain our model's prediction that deviations of real GDP from potential output cause wages and other factor prices to adjust. It will also explain how this adjustment is central to the economy's evolution from its short-run equilibrium to its long-run equilibrium. Note that, as in the short-run version of the model, the adjustment process is assumed to take place with a constant level of potential output.

Our theory of the macroeconomic adjustment process is useful for examining how the effects of shocks or policies differ in the short and long runs. As we will see, the assumption that potential output is constant leads to the prediction that *AD* or *AS* shocks have no long-run effect on real GDP; output eventually returns to Y^*.

In reality, neither technology nor factor supplies are constant over time; the level of potential output is continually changing. Our assumption throughout this chapter of a constant value for Y^* is a simplifying one, allowing us to focus on the *adjustment process* that brings the level of real GDP back to potential output.

The Long Run   As we will see in Chapters 25 and 26, the defining characteristics of the *long run* in our macro model are:

- factor prices are assumed to have fully adjusted to any output gap
- technology and factor supplies are assumed to be changing

A central prediction of our model is that, after factor prices have fully adjusted, real GDP will return to the level of potential output. The second assumption above implies that the level of potential output is changing (and typically growing). Thus, in the long-run version of our macroeconomic model, our focus is not on the nature of business cycles but rather on the nature of *economic growth*—where technological change and the growth of factor supplies play key roles.

The economy is probably never "in" the long run in the sense that *AD* or *AS* shocks would not cause real GDP to deviate from Y^*. But the long-run version of our model is still useful for examining some issues. For example, if we want to understand why our children's material standard of living will be significantly greater than our grandparents', we should not focus on short-run issues of *AD* or *AS* shocks and stabilization policies; the effects of particular shocks will disappear after a few years. Instead, we will gain more understanding if we abstract from short-run issues and focus on why Y^* increases dramatically over periods of several decades.

Summary   The three time spans that are central to macroeconomic analysis are summarized in Table 24-1. Note for each time span the assumptions made regarding factor prices and the level of potential output, and also the implied causes of output changes. As we proceed through this chapter and the next two, you may find it useful to refer back to this table.

You already know from Chapter 23 how the short-run version of our macro model works. And now that you have a sketch of what is meant by the adjustment process and the long run, we are ready to fill in the details. In this chapter we will see how this adjustment process takes the economy from its short-run equilibrium to its long-run equilibrium. To repeat, we make the following important assumptions for our theory of the macroeconomic adjustment process:

TABLE 24-1 Time Spans in Macroeconomic Analysis

Variables	Assumptions Regarding:		
	The Short Run	**The Adjustment Process**	**The Long Run**
Factor prices	Exogenous	Flexible (endogenous)	Fully adjusted (endogenous)
Technology and factor supplies (and therefore Y*)	Constant (exogenous)	Constant (exogenous)	Changing (endogenous)
	Implied Causes of Output Changes:		
	AD/AS shocks cause Y to fluctuate around constant Y*	Following AD or AS shocks, Y returns to Y*	Changes in Y* determine changes in Y

- factor prices are assumed to be flexible and to adjust to output gaps
- technology and factor supplies are assumed to be constant (and therefore Y* is constant)

24.1 THE ADJUSTMENT PROCESS

We develop our theory of the adjustment process by examining the relationship between output gaps, factor markets, and factor prices.

Potential Output and the Output Gap

Recall that *potential output* is the total output that can be produced when all productive resources—land, labour, and capital—are being used at their *normal rates of utilization*. When a nation's actual output diverges from its potential output, the difference is called the output gap.

Although growth in potential output has powerful effects from one decade to the next, its change from one *year* to the next is small enough that we ignore it when studying the year-to-year behaviour of real GDP and the price level. In this chapter, therefore, we view variations in the output gap as determined solely by variations in *actual* GDP around a constant level of *potential* GDP. (In Chapter 26 we will examine why potential output changes over periods of several years.)

Figure 24-1 shows real GDP being determined in the short run by the intersection of the AD and AS curves. Potential output is assumed to be constant, and it is shown by identical vertical lines in the two parts of the figure. In part (i), the AD and AS curves intersect to produce an equilibrium real GDP less than potential output. The result, as we saw in Chapter 19, is called a *recessionary gap* because recessions are often characterized as having GDP below potential output. In part (ii), the AD and AS

FIGURE 24-1   Output Gaps in the Short Run

(i) A recessionary gap

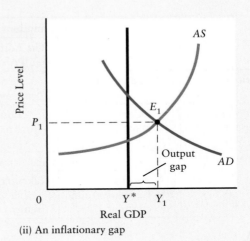
(ii) An inflationary gap

The output gap is the difference between potential GDP and actual GDP. Potential output is shown by the vertical line at Y^*. A recessionary gap, shown in panel (i), occurs when potential output is greater than real GDP. An inflationary gap, shown in panel (ii), occurs when real GDP is greater than potential output.

curves intersect to produce an equilibrium real GDP above potential output, resulting in what is called an *inflationary gap*. The way in which an inflationary output gap puts upward pressure on prices will become clear in the ensuing discussion.

Factor Prices and the Output Gap

When real GDP is above potential output, demand for factors will be high and there will be pressure on factor prices to rise. When real GDP is below potential output, demand for factors will be low and there will be pressure on factor prices to fall. This relationship is assumed to hold for all factors of production, including labour, land, and capital equipment.

Before we examine the detailed relationship between factor prices and output gaps, it is worth noting that even in the absence of an output gap, the presence of ongoing inflation influences factor prices, especially wages. Wage contracts often allow for changes in the price level that are expected to occur during the life of the contract. For the discussion in this chapter we make the simplifying assumption that the price level is expected to be constant (and therefore inflation is expected to be zero); hence changes in money wages are also expected to be changes in real wages. We will discuss inflation in considerable detail in Chapters 29 and 30.

Output Above Potential   Sometimes the *AD* and *AS* curves intersect where real GDP exceeds potential, as illustrated in part (ii) of Figure 24-1. Because firms are producing beyond their normal capacity output, there is an unusually large demand for all factor inputs, including labour. Labour shortages will emerge in some industries and among many groups of workers. Firms will try to bid workers away from other firms in order to maintain the high levels of output and sales made possible by the boom conditions.

As a result of these tight labour-market conditions, workers will find that they have considerable bargaining power with their employers, and they will put upward pressure on wages. Firms, recognizing that demand for their goods is strong, will be anxious to maintain a high level of output. To prevent their workers from either striking or quitting and moving to other employers, firms will be willing to accede to some of these upward pressures.

The boom that is associated with an inflationary gap generates a set of conditions—high profits for firms and unusually large demand for labour—that tends to cause wages (and other factor prices) to rise.

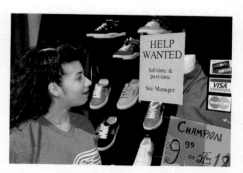

When output is above potential, the excess demand for labour tends to push up wages.

This increase in factor prices will increase firms' unit costs. As unit costs increase, firms will require higher prices in order to supply any given level of output, and the *AS* curve will therefore shift up. This shift has the effect of reducing equilibrium real GDP and raising the price level. Real GDP moves back toward potential and the inflationary gap begins to close.

In our model, factor prices are assumed to continue rising as long as some inflationary gap remains. In other words, they will continue rising until the *AS* curve shifts up to the point where the equilibrium level of GDP is equal to potential GDP. At this point, there is no more pressure for factor prices to rise, firms' costs are stable, and the *AS* curve stops shifting.

Output Below Potential   Sometimes the *AD* and *AS* curves intersect where real GDP is less than potential, as illustrated in part (i) of Figure 24-1. Because firms are producing below their normal-capacity output, there is an unusually low demand for all factor inputs, including labour. There will be labour surpluses in some industries and among some groups of workers. Firms will have below-normal sales and not only will resist upward pressures on wages but also may seek reductions in wages.

The slump that is associated with a recessionary gap generates a set of conditions—low profits for firms and low demand for labour—that tends to cause wages (and other factor prices) to fall.[1]

Whenever it does occur, this reduction in factor prices will reduce firms' unit costs. As unit costs fall, firms require a lower price in order to supply any given level of output, and the *AS* curve therefore shifts down. This shift has the effect of increasing equilibrium real GDP and reducing the price level. Real GDP moves back toward potential and the recessionary gap begins to close.

In our model, wages and other factor prices are assumed to fall as long as some recessionary gap remains. As factor prices fall, the *AS* curve shifts down, and this process continues until the equilibrium level of GDP is equal to potential output. At this point, there is no longer pressure for factor prices to fall, firms' unit costs are stable, and the *AS* curve stops shifting.

---

[1] Due to ongoing inflation and productivity growth, nominal wages rarely fall, even when there is a low demand for labour. But remember that in this chapter, to allow us to focus on the adjustment process, we are assuming that technology is constant and expected inflation is zero. Thus nominal (and real) wages and other factor prices are assumed to fall when real GDP is below potential output. With some ongoing inflation in our model, the assumption would be modified so that nominal wages rise less than prices, thus implying a reduction in real wages.

Potential output acts like an anchor for the level of real GDP. Following aggregate demand or supply shocks that push real GDP below or above potential, the adjustment of factor prices brings real GDP back to potential output.

Adjustment Asymmetry   At this stage, we encounter an important asymmetry in the economy's aggregate supply behaviour. Boom conditions (an inflationary gap), along with labour shortages, cause wages and unit costs to rise. The experience of many developed economies, however, suggests that the downward pressures on wages during slumps (recessionary gaps) often do not operate as strongly or as quickly as the upward pressures during booms. Even when wages do fall, they tend to fall more slowly than they would rise in an equally sized inflationary gap. This *wage stickiness* implies that the downward shift in the *AS* curve and the downward pressure on the price level are correspondingly slight.[2]

Both upward and downward adjustments to wages and unit costs do occur, but there are differences in the speed at which they typically operate. Booms can cause wages to rise rapidly; recessions usually cause wages to fall only slowly.

The Phillips Curve   The factor-price adjustment process that we have been discussing was explored many years ago in a famous study of wages and unemployment in the United Kingdom. A. W. Phillips observed that wages tend to fall in periods of high unemployment and rise in periods of low unemployment. The resulting negative relationship between unemployment and the rate of change in wages has been called the *Phillips* curve ever since. *Extensions in Theory 24-1* discusses the Phillips curve and its relationship to the aggregate supply (*AS*) curve.

Inflationary and Recessionary Gaps   Now it should be clear why the output gaps are named as they are. When real GDP exceeds potential GDP, there will normally be rising unit costs, and the *AS* curve will be shifting upward. This will in turn push the price level up and create temporary inflation. The larger the excess of real GDP over potential GDP, the greater the inflationary pressure. The term *inflationary gap* emphasizes this salient feature of the economy when output exceeds potential output.

When actual output is less than potential output, as we have seen, there will be unemployment of labour and other productive resources. Unit costs will tend to fall slowly, leading to a slow downward shift in the *AS* curve. Hence, the price level will be falling only slowly, so that *unemployment* will be the output gap's most obvious result. The term *recessionary gap* emphasizes this salient feature that high rates of unemployment occur when actual output falls short of potential output.

Potential Output as an "Anchor"

We have just argued that there is pressure on wages and other factor prices to change when output is above or below potential. When they occur, these changes in factor prices lead to changes in firms' unit costs that shift the *AS* curve and change the equilibrium level of GDP. Moreover, we assumed that this process of factor-price adjustment will continue as long as some output gap remains, coming to a halt only when the equilibrium level of GDP is equal to potential GDP, Y^*. This leads to an

---

2 This is the second asymmetry in aggregate supply that we have encountered. The first involves the changing slope of the *AS* curve, discussed in Chapter 23.

important prediction from our macroeconomic model regarding the distinction between the short-run and long-run effects of aggregate demand and supply shocks.

Following an aggregate demand or supply shock, the short-run equilibrium level of output may be different than potential output. Any output gap is assumed to cause wages and other factor prices to adjust, eventually bringing the equilibrium level of output back to potential. In this model, therefore, the level of potential output acts like an "anchor" for the economy.

We now go on to examine this factor-price adjustment process in greater detail, illustrating it for the cases of positive and negative shocks to aggregate demand and supply. We will also examine this factor-price adjustment process following changes in fiscal policy. The idea that Y^* acts as an "anchor" for the economy will become clear: Shocks of various kinds may cause output to rise above or fall below Y^* in the short run, but the adjustment of factor prices to output gaps ensures that output eventually returns to Y^*.

24.2 DEMAND AND SUPPLY SHOCKS

We can now study the consequences of aggregate demand and aggregate supply shocks in our model, distinguishing between the immediate effects of AD and AS shocks and the longer-term effects, after factor prices have adjusted fully. It is necessary to examine expansionary and contractionary shocks separately because the adjustment of factor prices is not symmetrical for the two cases. Let's begin with demand shocks.

Expansionary *AD* Shocks

Suppose the economy starts with a stable price level and real GDP equal to potential GDP as shown by the initial equilibrium in part (i) of Figure 24-2 on page 578. Now suppose this situation is disturbed by an increase in autonomous expenditure, perhaps caused by an upturn in business confidence and a resulting boom in investment spending. Figure 24-2(i) shows the effects of this aggregate demand shock in raising both the price level and real GDP. The AD curve shifts from AD_0 to AD_1, and real GDP rises above Y^*. An inflationary gap opens up.

We have assumed that an inflationary gap leads to increases in wages, which cause unit costs to rise. The AS curve shifts up as firms respond to the higher input costs by increasing their output prices. As seen in part (ii) of the figure, the upward shift of the AS curve causes a further rise in the price level, but this time the price rise is associated with a *fall* in output.

The cost increases (and the consequent upward shifts of the AS curve) continue until the inflationary gap has been removed—that is, until in part (ii) real GDP returns to Y^*. Only then is there no excess demand for labour, and only then do wages and unit costs, and hence the AS curve, stabilize.

The adjustment in wages and other factor prices eventually eliminates any boom caused by a demand shock; real GDP returns to its potential level.

Practise with Study Guide Chapter 24, Exercises 1 and 2.

EXTENSIONS IN THEORY 24-1

The Phillips Curve and the Adjustment Process

In the 1950s, Professor A. W. Phillips of the London School of Economics was conducting pioneering research on macroeconomic policy. In his early models, he related the rate of inflation to the difference between actual and potential output. Later he investigated the empirical underpinnings of this equation by studying the relationship between the rate of increase of wages and the level of unemployment. He studied these variables because unemployment data were available as far back as the mid-nineteenth century, whereas very few data on output gaps were available when he did his empirical work. In 1958, he reported that a stable relationship had existed between these two variables for 100 years in the United Kingdom. This relationship came to be known as the Phillips curve. The **Phillips curve** provided an explanation, rooted in empirical observation, of the speed with which wage changes shifted the *AS* curve by changing firms' unit costs.

In the form in which it became famous, the Phillips curve related wage changes to the level of unemployment. But we can express the same information in a slightly different way. Note that unemployment and output gaps are negatively related—a recessionary gap is associated with high unemployment, and an inflationary gap is associated with low unemployment. We can therefore create another Phillips curve that plots wage changes against output (rather than against unemployment). Both figures show the same information.

When output equals Y^* the corresponding unemployment rate is sometimes called the *natural rate of unemployment,* and is denoted U^*. Inflationary gaps (when $Y > Y^*$ and $U < U^*$) are associated with *increases*

in wages. Recessionary gaps (when $Y < Y^*$ and $U > U^*$) are associated with *decreases* in wages.* Thus, a Phillips curve that plots wage changes against real GDP is upward sloping, whereas a Phillips curve that plots wage changes against the unemployment rate is downward sloping. Both versions of the Phillips curve are shown in the accompanying figure.

When output is at potential, all factors are being used at their normal rates of utilization. There is neither upward nor downward pressure on wages (or other factor prices) because there is neither an excess demand nor an excess supply of labour. Hence, the Phillips curve cuts the horizontal axis at Y^* (and at U^*). This is how Phillips drew his original curve.

The Phillips curve is *not* the same as the *AS* curve. The *AS* curve has the *price level* on the vertical axis whereas the Phillips curve has the *rate of change of wages* on the vertical axis. How are the two curves related? The economy's location on the Phillips curve indicates how the *AS* curve is shifting as a result of the existing output gap.

For example, consider an economy that begins at point *A* in all three diagrams; there is no output gap and wages are therefore stable. Now, suppose a positive

---

* Recall that we are assuming productivity to be constant so that changes in wages imply changes in unit labour costs. When productivity is growing, however, recessionary output gaps cause unit labour costs to fall. This only requires wages to be growing more slowly than productivity, not to be actually falling.

Phillips curve Originally, a relationship between the unemployment rate and the rate of change of money wages. Now often drawn as a relationship between GDP and the rate of change of money wages.

Practise with Study Guide Chapter 24, Exercise 6.

Contractionary *AD* Shocks

Suppose again that the economy starts with stable prices and real GDP equal to potential, as shown in part (i) of Figure 24-3 on page 579. Now assume there is a *decline* in aggregate demand. This negative aggregate demand shock might be a reduction in investment expenditure, or perhaps a decline in the world demand for Canadian lumber or automobiles.

The first effects of the decline are a fall in output and some downward adjustment of prices, as shown in part (i) of the figure. As real GDP falls below potential, a recessionary gap is created, and unemployment rises. At this point we must analyze two separate cases. The first is where wages fall quickly in response to the excess supply of labour. The second is where wages fall only slowly.

aggregate demand shock causes real GDP to increase to Y_1 (and unemployment to fall to U_1) and thus produces an inflationary gap. The excess demand for labour puts upward pressure on wages and the economy moves along the Phillips curve to point B, where wages begin rising. The increase in wages increases unit costs and causes the AS curve to shift up. Thus, each point on the Phillips curve determines the rate at which the AS curve is shifting. To complete the example, note that as the AS curve shifts up, the level of GDP will fall back toward Y^* and the inflationary gap will begin to close. The economy moves back along the Phillips curve toward point A. When all adjustment is complete, the new equilibrium will be at point C in part (iii) of the figure, with output equal to Y^* and the price level and nominal wages higher than initially. On the Phillips curve, the economy will be back at point A, where real GDP equals Y^* and wages are constant (but at a higher level than before the demand shock occurred).

Note that the convex shape of the Phillips curve is not accidental—it reflects the adjustment asymmetry we mentioned in the text. The convexity of the Phillips curve implies that an inflationary gap of a given amount will lead to faster wage increases than an equally sized recessionary gap will lead to wage reductions. In other words, an inflationary gap will cause the AS curve to shift up more quickly than a recessionary gap will cause the AS curve to shift down.

Finally, you might be wondering what would happen if the Phillips curve were to shift. And what would cause such a shift? As we will see in Chapter 30 when we discuss the phenomenon of sustained inflation, an important cause of shifts of the Phillips curve is changes in firms' and households' *expectations* of future inflation. In this chapter, however, we have assumed that expected inflation is zero. But whether there is expected inflation or not, the Phillips curve embodies the factor-price adjustment process that is the focus of this chapter.

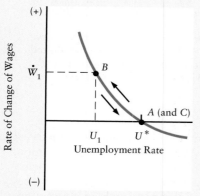

(i) Wage changes and unemployment

(ii) Wage changes and output

(iii) Aggregate demand and supply

Flexible Wages Suppose wages (and other factor prices) fell quickly in response to the recessionary gap. The AS curve would therefore shift quickly downward as the lower wages led to reduced unit costs.

As shown in part (ii) of Figure 24-3, the economy would move along the new AD curve, with falling prices and rising output, until real GDP was quickly restored to potential, Y^*. We conclude that if wages were to fall rapidly whenever there was unemployment, the resulting shift in the AS curve would quickly eliminate recessionary gaps.

Flexible wages that fall rapidly in the presence of a recessionary gap provide an automatic adjustment process that pushes the economy back toward potential output.

FIGURE 24-2 The Adjustment Process Following a Positive Aggregate Demand Shock

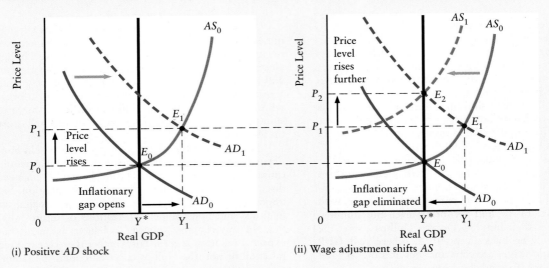

(i) Positive *AD* shock   (ii) Wage adjustment shifts *AS*

A positive *AD* shock first raises prices and output along the *AS* curve. It then induces a shift of the *AS* curve that further raises prices but lowers output along the new *AD* curve. In part (i), the economy is in equilibrium at E_0, at its level of potential output, Y^*, and price level P_0. The *AD* curve then shifts from AD_0 to AD_1. This moves equilibrium to E_1, with income Y_1 and price level P_1, and opens up an inflationary gap.

In part (ii), the inflationary gap results in an increase in wages and other factor prices, shifting the *AS* curve upward. As this happens, output falls and the price level rises along AD_1. Eventually, when the *AS* curve has shifted to AS_1, output is back to Y^* and the inflationary gap has been eliminated. However, the price level has risen to P_2. The long-run result of the aggregate demand shock is therefore a higher price level with no change in real GDP.

Sticky Wages As we noted earlier when we encountered the second asymmetry of aggregate supply, the experience of many economies, especially in the European Union, suggests that wages typically do not fall rapidly in response to even large recessionary gaps. It is sometimes said that wages are "sticky" in the downward direction. This does not mean that wages never fall, only that they tend to fall more slowly in a recessionary gap than they rise in an equally sized inflationary gap. When wages are sticky, the analysis is the same as when wages are flexible, and thus Figure 24-3 tells the right story. The only difference is that the *AS* curve shifts more slowly when wages are sticky and thus the recessionary gap remains open for longer. An important implication of sticky wages is that the high unemployment that comes with a recessionary gap may not be quickly eliminated. In extreme cases, as in some European countries, labour-market institutions may prevent wages from falling at all, in which case the economy can settle into a stable situation of heavy unemployment and a prolonged recessionary gap.

If wages are downwardly sticky, the economy's adjustment process is sluggish and thus recessionary gaps may not be eliminated quickly, if at all.[3]

---

[3] The causes of downward wage stickiness have been hotly debated among macroeconomists for years. We discuss several possible reasons in Chapter 31 when examining the causes of cyclical unemployment.

FIGURE 24-3 The Adjustment Process Following a Negative Aggregate Demand Shock

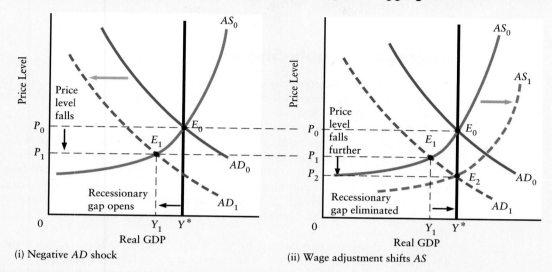

(i) Negative *AD* shock

(ii) Wage adjustment shifts *AS*

A negative *AD* shock first lowers the price level and GDP along the *AS* curve and then induces a (possibly slow) shift of the *AS* curve that further lowers prices but raises output along the new *AD* curve. In part (i), the economy is in equilibrium at E_0, at its level of potential output, Y^*, and price level P_0. The *AD* curve then shifts to AD_1, moving equilibrium to E_1, with income Y_1 and price level P_1, and opens up a recessionary gap.

Part (ii) shows the adjustment back to potential output that occurs from the supply side of the economy. The fall in wages shifts the *AS* curve downward. Real GDP rises, and the price level falls further along the new *AD* curve. Unless wages are completely rigid, the *AS* curve eventually reaches AS_1, with equilibrium at E_2. The price level stabilizes at P_2 when real GDP returns to Y^*, closing the recessionary gap.

The weakness of the adjustment process following a negative demand shock does not mean that recessionary gaps must always be prolonged. Rather, this weakness means that speedy recovery back to potential output must be generated mainly from the demand side. If wages are downwardly sticky and the economy is to avoid a persistent recessionary gap, a quick recovery requires a rightward shift of the *AD* curve. This sometimes happens when private-sector demand revives. But it also raises the possibility that government *stabilization policy* can be used to accomplish such a rightward shift in the *AD* curve. This is an important and contentious issue in macroeconomics, one to which we will return often throughout the remainder of this book.

The difference in the speed of adjustment of wages (and other factor prices) is the important asymmetry in the behaviour of aggregate supply that we noted earlier in this chapter. This asymmetry helps to explain two key facts about the Canadian economy. First, high unemployment can persist for quite long periods without causing decreases in wages and prices of sufficient magnitude to remove the unemployment. An example is the 1991–1995 period when unemployment was high and output was considerably below potential. Second, booms, along with labour shortages and production beyond normal capacity, do not

The slow adjustment of wages and prices when output is below potential means that the recessionary effects of negative shocks sometimes persist for long periods.

persist for long periods without causing increases in wages and the price level. The periods 1987–1990 and 1999–2001 both displayed output above potential and pressure on wages and prices to rise.

Aggregate Supply Shocks

We have discussed the economy's adjustment process that returns real GDP to Y^* following an aggregate demand shock. The same adjustment process operates following an aggregate supply shock.

Consider an economy that has a stable price level and real GDP at its potential level, as illustrated by point E_0 in part (i) of Figure 24-4. Suppose there is an increase in the world price of an important input, such as oil. An increase in the price increases unit costs for firms and causes the AS curve to shift upwards. Real GDP falls and the price level increases—a combination often called *stagflation*. The short-run equilibrium is at point E_1 in Figure 24-4. With the opening of a recessionary gap, the economy's adjustment process comes into play, though sticky wages may reduce the speed of this adjustment.

The recessionary gap caused by the negative supply shock causes firms to shut down and workers to be laid off. The excess supply of labour (and other factors) eventually pushes wages down and begins to reverse the initial increase in unit costs caused by the increase in the price of oil. This adjustment is shown in part (ii) of the figure. As wages fall, the AS curve shifts back toward its starting point, and real GDP rises back toward its potential level, Y^*. Eventually, the economy returns to its initial point, E_0.

FIGURE 24-4   The Adjustment Process Following a Negative Aggregate Supply Shock

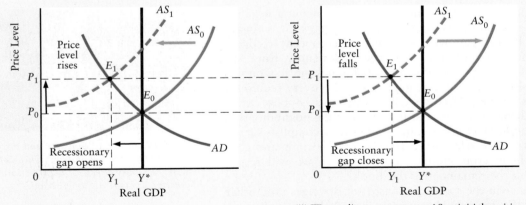

(i) Negative AS shock

(ii) Wage adjustment returns AS to initial position

A negative AS shock caused by an increase in input prices causes real GDP to fall and the price level to rise. The economy's adjustment process then reverses the AS shift and returns the economy to its starting point. The economy begins at point E_0 in part (i). The increase in the price of oil increases unit costs and causes the AS curve to shift up to AS_1. Real GDP falls to Y_1 and the price level rises to P_1. A recessionary gap is created. In part (ii), the excess supply of labour associated with the recessionary gap causes wages to fall, possibly slowly. As wages fall, unit costs fall and so the AS curve shifts back down to AS_0. The economy is finally in long-run equilibrium at Y^* and P_0, its starting point.

We leave it to the reader to analyze the adjustment process following a positive aggregate supply shock, such as the dramatic reduction in the world price of raw materials that occurred in 1997 and 1998. The logic of the analysis is exactly the same as illustrated in Figure 24-4, except that the initial shift in the AS curve is to the right, creating an inflationary gap.

Exogenous changes in input prices cause the AS curve to shift, creating an output gap. The adjustment process then reverses the initial AS shift and brings the economy back to potential output and the initial price level.

Long-Run Equilibrium

Following any AD or AS shocks, we have assumed that the adjustment process continues until real GDP returns to Y^*. The economy is said to be in a state of *long-run equilibrium* when factor prices are no longer adjusting to output gaps. As we have seen, wages and other factor prices are assumed to be stable only when the level of real GDP is equal to potential output, Y^*. Thus, in our model, the economy is in its long-run equilibrium when the intersection of the AD and AS curves occurs at Y^*.

The value of Y^* depends on real variables such as the labour force, capital stock, and the level of technology, but is independent of nominal variables such as the price level. In other words, the level of output that firms will produce in the long run is independent of the price level. The vertical line above Y^* that we have seen in our diagrams is therefore sometimes called a *long-run aggregate supply curve*—the relationship between the price level and the amount of output supplied by firms *after all factor prices have adjusted to output gaps*. This vertical line is also sometimes called a *Classical aggregate supply curve* because the Classical economists were mainly concerned with the behaviour of the economy in long-run equilibrium.[4]

Figure 24-5 shows an AD/AS diagram without the usual upward-sloping AS curve. It is useful to

FIGURE 24-5   Changes in Long-Run Equilibrium

(i) A rise in aggregate demand

(ii) A rise in potential output

Potential output determines the long-run equilibrium value of real GDP. Given Y^*, aggregate demand determines the long-run equilibrium value of the price level. In both parts of the figure, the initial long-run equilibrium is at E_0, so the price level is P_0 and real GDP is Y_0^*.

In part (i), a shift in the AD curve from AD_0 to AD_1 moves the long-run equilibrium from E_0 to E_1. This raises the price level from P_0 to P_1 but leaves real GDP unchanged at Y_0^* in the long run.

In part (ii), an increase in potential output from Y_0^* to Y_1^* moves the long-run equilibrium from E_0 to E_2. This raises real GDP from Y_0^* to Y_1^* and lowers the price level from P_0 to P_2.

---

4 The Classical school of economic thought began with Adam Smith (1723–1790) and was developed through the work of David Ricardo (1772–1823), Thomas Malthus (1766–1834) and John Stuart Mill (1806–1873). These economists emphasized the long-run behaviour of the economy. Beginning in the middle of the nineteenth century, Neoclassical economists devoted much time and effort to studying short-term fluctuations. *The General Theory of Employment, Interest and Money* (1936), written by John Maynard Keynes (1883–1946), was in a long tradition of the study of short-term fluctuations. Where Keynes differed from the Neoclassical economists was in approaching the issues from a macroeconomic perspective that emphasized fluctuations in expenditure. Each of the economists mentioned in this footnote, along with several others, is discussed in more detail in the timeline at the back of the book.

omit this curve if our focus is on the state of the economy *after* all factor prices have fully adjusted and output has returned to Y*. We can use this diagram to examine how shocks affect the economy's long-run equilibrium.

As shown in part (i) of Figure 24-5, any shift in the *AD* curve will cause a change in the price level in the long run, but will not affect the level of potential output, Y*. In our model, the only way that real GDP can change in the long run (*after* factor prices have fully adjusted) is for the level of Y* to change, as in part (ii) of the figure.

In the long run, real GDP is determined solely by Y*; the role of aggregate demand is only to determine the price level.

We will discuss the long-run behaviour of the economy in detail in Chapters 25 and 26. There we develop theories explaining why Y* grows over extended periods of time, and why this growth is important for determining our material living standards.

24.3 **FISCAL STABILIZATION POLICY**

In Chapter 22, we briefly considered the basic concepts of fiscal stabilization policy. In principle, this policy can be used to stabilize real GDP at or near potential output. In the remainder of this chapter, we look into taxing and spending as tools of fiscal stabilization policy. We will return to more advanced issues of fiscal policy in Chapter 32.

> **myeconlab**
>
> **Though macroeconomists tend to focus on fluctuations in real GDP when describing business cycles, there is no single "best" measure of the changes in economic activity. For a detailed description of several popular measures of changes in the level of economic activity—including *GDP growth, housing starts*, and *capacity utilization*—look for "Several Measures of Economic Fluctuations in Canada" in the *Additional Topics* section of this book's MyEconLab.**
>
> w w w . m y e c o n l a b . c o m

Because increases in government purchases (*G*) increase aggregate demand and increases in taxation (*T*) decrease aggregate demand, the *direction* of the required changes in spending and taxation is generally easy to determine once we know the direction of the desired change in real GDP. For example, if output is currently below potential, a fiscal policy designed to increase real GDP will include an increase in *G*, a decrease in *T*, or both. However, the *timing, magnitude,* and *mixture* of the changes are more difficult issues.

There is no doubt that the government can exert a major influence on real GDP. Prime examples are the massive increases in military spending during major wars. Canadian federal expenditure during the Second World War rose from 12.2 percent of GDP in 1939 to 41.8 percent in 1944. At the same time, the unemployment rate fell from 11.4 percent to 1.4 percent. Economists agree that the increase in government spending helped to bring about the rise in output and the associated fall in unemployment. More recently, the Canadian government increased spending and reduced taxes in the 2002–2006 period. Most economists agree that these expansionary fiscal policies contributed to the growth of Canadian real GDP during this period.

In the heyday of "activist" fiscal policy, from about 1945 to about 1970, many economists were convinced that the economy could be stabilized adequately just by varying the size of the government's taxes and expenditures. That day is past. Today, economists are more aware of the many limitations of fiscal policy.

The Basic Theory of Fiscal Stabilization

In our macroeconomic model, a reduction in tax rates or an increase in government purchases will shift the AD curve to the right, causing an increase in real GDP. An increase in tax rates or a cut in government expenditure will shift the AD curve to the left, causing a decrease in real GDP.

For information on the federal Department of Finance, the ministry in charge of fiscal policy, see: **www.fin.gc.ca**.

How Fiscal Stabilization Works   A more detailed look at how fiscal stabilization works will help to show some of the complications that arise when implementing fiscal policy.

Closing a Recessionary Gap.   A recessionary gap is shown in Figure 24-6; the economy's short-run equilibrium is at point E_0 with real GDP below Y^*. Such a recessionary gap can be closed in three ways, returning real GDP to Y^*. First, as often happens in practice, private-sector demand recovers and the AD curve shifts to the right, as shown in

Practise with Study Guide Chapter 24, Exercises 3 and 5, Extension Exercise E1.

FIGURE 24-6   The Closing of a Recessionary Gap

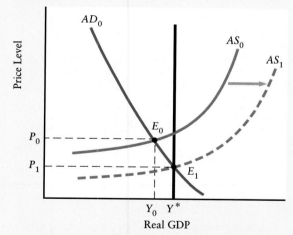

(i) A recessionary gap closed by falling wages and other factor prices

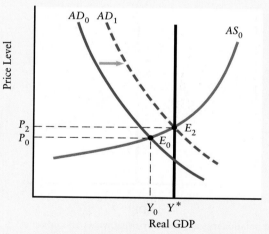

(ii) A recessionary gap closed by fiscal expansion or recovery of private-sector demand

A recessionary gap may be closed by a (slow) downward shift of the AS curve or an increase in aggregate demand. Initially, equilibrium is at E_0, with real GDP at Y_0 and the price level at P_0. There is a recessionary gap.

As shown in part (i), the gap might be removed by a shift in the AS curve to AS_1, as will eventually happen when wages and other factor prices fall in response to excess supply. The shift in the AS curve causes a movement down and to the right along AD_0 to a new equilibrium at E_1, achieving potential output Y^* and lowering the price level to P_1.

As shown in part (ii), the gap might also be removed by a shift of the AD curve to AD_1, caused by an expansionary fiscal policy or a recovery of private-sector spending. The shift in the AD curve causes a movement up and to the right along AS_0. This movement shifts the equilibrium to E_2, raising output to Y^* and the price level to P_2.

part (ii) of the figure. If such a recovery does not occur rapidly, the economy's adjustment process will come into play. The excess supply of factors at E_0 will eventually cause wages and other factor prices to fall, shifting the AS curve downward and restoring output to Y^*, as shown in part (i) of the figure. However, as we also discussed, because of the stickiness of wages this process may take a long time. Policymakers may not be prepared to wait the time necessary for the recessionary gap to correct itself. The government can instead use expansionary fiscal policy to shift the AD curve to the right and close the recessionary gap. It would do this by reducing tax rates or increasing the level of government purchases.

The advantage of using fiscal policy rather than allowing the economy's adjustment process to operate is that it may substantially shorten what might otherwise be a long recession. One disadvantage is that the use of fiscal policy may stimulate the economy just before private-sector spending recovers on its own. As a result, the economy may overshoot its potential output, and an inflationary gap may open up. In this case, fiscal policy that is intended to promote economic stability can actually cause instability.

Closing an Inflationary Gap. An inflationary gap is illustrated in Figure 24-7; the economy's short-run equilibrium is at point E_0, with real GDP above Y^*. There are three ways such an inflationary gap may be closed, returning real GDP to Y^*. First, private-sector demand may fall, thus shifting the AD curve to the left. If this does not occur

FIGURE 24-7   The Closing of an Inflationary Gap

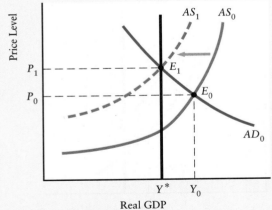

(i) An inflationary gap closed by rising wages and other factor prices

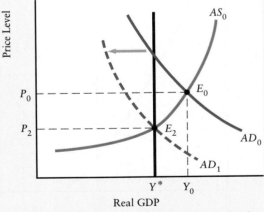

(ii) An inflationary gap closed by contractionary fiscal policy or a reduction in private-sector demand

An inflationary gap may be removed by an upward shift of the AS curve or by a leftward shift of the AD curve.
Initially, equilibrium is at E_0, with real GDP at Y_0 and the price level at P_0. There is an inflationary gap.

As shown in part (i), the gap might be removed by a shift in the AS curve to AS_1, as will happen when wages and other factor prices rise in response to the excess demand. The shift in the AS curve causes a movement up and to the left along AD_0. This movement establishes a new equilibrium at E_1, reducing output to its potential level Y^* and raising the price level to P_1.

As shown in part (ii), the gap might also be removed by a shift in the AD curve to AD_1 caused by, for example, a contractionary fiscal policy. The shift in the AD curve causes a movement down and to the left along AS_0. This movement shifts the equilibrium to E_2, lowering income to Y^* and the price level to P_2.

rapidly, the economy's adjustment process will come into play; excess demand for factors will cause wages and other factor prices to rise, shifting the AS curve upward and gradually restoring output to Y^*. Alternatively, the government can use a contractionary fiscal policy to shift the AD curve to the left and close the inflationary gap. The government would do this by increasing tax rates or reducing its level of purchases.

The advantage of using a contractionary fiscal policy to close the inflationary gap is that it avoids the inflationary increase in prices that would otherwise occur. One disadvantage is that if private-sector expenditures fall because of natural causes, real GDP may be pushed below potential, thus opening up a recessionary gap.

This discussion leads to a key proposition:

When the economy's adjustment process is slow to operate, or produces undesirable side effects such as rising prices, there is a potential stabilization role for fiscal policy.

The Paradox of Thrift   Suppose you have a good job but you are sufficiently unsure about your economic future that you decide to increase the fraction of disposable income that you save. Your increased saving today would not influence your current income but these funds would accumulate and be useful in the future if your economic situation changed for the worse. Most people would agree that a decision to increase your saving in these circumstances would be prudent.

But what would happen if *many people* did the same thing at the same time? In our macroeconomic model, an increase in national saving—caused by a reduction in household consumption (C), a reduction in government purchases (G), or an increase in tax revenues (T)—would shift the AD curve to the left and *reduce* the equilibrium level of real GDP in the short run. Thus, frugality on the part of individuals, which may seem to be prudent behaviour for each individual taken separately, ends up reducing short-run real GDP. This phenomenon is known as the *paradox of thrift*—the paradox being that what may be good for any individual when viewed in isolation ends up being undesirable for the economy as a whole.

The policy implication of this phenomenon is that a major and persistent recession can be battled by encouraging governments, firms, and households to reduce their saving and therefore increase their spending. In times of unemployment and recession, a greater desire to save will only make things worse. This result goes directly against the idea that we should "tighten our belts" when times are tough. The notion that it is not only possible but even *desirable* to spend one's way out of a recession touches a sensitive point with people raised on the belief that success is based on hard work and frugality; as a result, the idea often arouses great hostility.

As is discussed in *Lessons From History 24-1*, the implications of the paradox of thrift were not generally understood during the Great Depression of the 1930s. Most governments, faced with depression-induced reductions in tax revenues, reduced their expenditures to balance their budgets. As a result, many economists argue that the fiscal policies at the time actually made things worse. When Nobel Prize–winning economist Milton Friedman (many years later) said, "We are all Keynesians now," he was referring to the general acceptance of the view that the government's budget is much more than just the revenue and expenditure statement of a very large organization. Whether we like it or not, the sheer size of the government's budget inevitably makes it a powerful tool for influencing the economy.

The paradox of thrift applies to shifts in aggregate demand that have been caused by changes in saving (and hence spending) behaviour. That is why it applies only in the short run, when the AD curve plays an important role in the determination of real GDP.

LESSONS FROM HISTORY 24-1

Fiscal Policy in the Great Depression

The Great Depression, which is usually dated as beginning with the massive stock-market crash on October 29, 1929, was one of the most dramatic economic events of the twentieth century. As the accompanying figure shows, Canadian real GDP plummeted by almost 30 percent from its peak in 1929 to its low point in 1933. The price level actually *fell* beginning in 1930 and declined by about 20 percent over the next five years. The unemployment rate increased from 3 percent in 1929 to an unparalleled 19.3 percent four years later. To put these numbers in perspective, by today's standards a very serious recession (like the most recent one in 1990–1991) sees real GDP fall by 2 percent, the unemployment rate rise to 11 percent, and prices continue rising but perhaps at a slower rate. The economic events of the 1930s certainly deserve to be called the Great Depression!

The Great Depression was not just a catastrophic event that happened exogenously—its depth and duration were made worse by some fundamental mistakes in policy. Failure to understand the implication of the paradox of thrift led many countries to adopt disastrous fiscal policies during the Great Depression. In addition, failure to understand the role of automatic stabilizers has led many observers to conclude, erroneously, that fiscal expansion was tried in the Great Depression but failed. Let us see how these two misperceptions are related.

The Paradox of Thrift in Action

In 1932, Canadian Prime Minister R. B. Bennett said, "We are now faced with the real crisis in the history of Canada. To maintain our credit we must practise the most rigid economy and not spend a single cent." His government that year—at the deepest point in the recession—brought down a budget based on the principle of trying to balance revenues and expenditures, and it included *increases* in tax rates.

Data from Urquhart, M.C., and K.A.H. Buckley, ed. 1965. *Historical Statistics of Canada*. Toronto: Macmillan.

The paradox of thrift does not apply after factor prices have fully adjusted and the economy has achieved its new long-run equilibrium. Remember that in the long run, aggregate demand does not influence the level of real GDP—output is determined only by the level of potential output, Y^*. In the long run, the more people and government save, the larger is the supply of funds available for investment. As we will see in Chapter 26, this increase in the pool of available funds will reduce interest rates and encourage more investment by firms. The greater rate of investment leads to a higher rate of growth of potential output.

The paradox of thrift—the idea that an increase in saving reduces the level of real GDP—is only true in the short run. In the long run, the path of real GDP is determined by the path of potential output. The increase in saving has the long-run effect of increasing investment and therefore increasing potential output.

In the same year, Franklin Roosevelt was elected U.S. president on a platform of fighting the Great Depression with government policies. In his inaugural address he urged, "Our great primary task is to put people to work.... [This task] can be helped by insistence that the federal, state, and local governments act forthwith on the demand that their costs be drastically reduced...."

Across the Atlantic, King George V told the British House of Commons in 1931, "The present condition of the national finances, in the opinion of His Majesty's ministers, calls for the imposition of additional taxation and for the effecting of economies in public expenditure."

As the paradox of thrift predicts, these policies tended to worsen, rather than cure, the Depression.

Interpreting the Deficits in the 1930s

In general, governments can have a budget deficit for two different reasons. First, a government might increase its level of purchases without increasing its tax revenues. Such a *deficit-financed* increase in government spending represents an expansion in aggregate demand. Second, a government might leave its purchases unchanged but have lower tax revenues. If the lower tax revenues are caused by a policy decision to reduce tax *rates*, then this policy also represents an expansion in aggregate demand. But if the decline in tax revenues is caused by a fall in real GDP with unchanged tax rates, the existing budget deficit *does not* represent an expansion in aggregate demand. These distinctions are central to interpreting the budget deficits of the 1930s.

Government budget deficits did increase in the 1930s, but they were not the result of a program of deficit-financed public expenditure. Rather, they were the result of the fall in tax revenues, brought about by the fall in real GDP as the economy sank into depression. The various governments did not advocate programs of massive deficit-financed spending to shift the *AD* curve to the right. Instead, they hoped that a small amount of government spending in addition to numerous policies designed to stabilize prices and to restore confidence would lead to a recovery of private investment expenditure that would substantially shift the *AD* curve. To have expected a massive revival of private investment expenditure as a result of the puny increase in aggregate demand that was instituted by the federal government now seems hopelessly naive.

When we judge these policies from the viewpoint of modern theory, their failure is no mystery. Indeed, Professor E. Cary Brown of MIT, after a careful study for the United States, concluded, "Fiscal policy seems to have been an unsuccessful recovery device in the thirties—not because it did not work, but because it was not tried." Once the massive, war-geared expenditure of the 1940s began, output responded sharply and unemployment all but evaporated. A similar pattern occurred in Canada, as seen clearly in the figure.

The performance of the Canadian and U.S. economies from 1930 to 1945 is well explained by the macroeconomic theory that we have developed in the last few chapters. It is clear that the governments did not effectively use fiscal policy to stabilize their economies. War brought the Depression to an end because war demands made acceptable a level of government expenditure sufficient to remove the recessionary gap. Had the Canadian and American administrations been able to do the same in the early 1930s, it might have ended the waste of the Great Depression many years sooner.

Automatic Fiscal Stabilizers   The fiscal policies that we have been discussing are referred to as *discretionary* because the government uses its discretion in changing its purchases (G) or tax revenues (T) in an attempt to change the level of real GDP. However, even if the government makes no active decisions regarding changes in its purchases or taxation, the mere existence of the government's tax-and-transfer system will act as an *automatic stabilizer* for the economy. Let's see how this works.

When we first introduced government to our macro model in Chapter 22, we made the assumptions that government purchases (G) were autonomous with respect to national income but that government net tax revenues (T) were positively related to national income. Specifically, we assumed that

$$T = tY$$

where t is the net tax rate. This positive relationship between T and Y has an important implication for the stability of the economy in response to shocks to autonomous expenditure.

For example, consider a shock that increases the short-run level of real GDP. This could be either an aggregate demand or supply shock. As real GDP increases, tax revenues rise and, as there are fewer low-income households and unemployed persons requiring assistance, transfer payments fall. The rise in net tax revenues (taxes minus transfers) dampens the extent to which the rise in national income leads to induced increases in spending (and then, through the multiplier process, to an increase in real GDP). In other words, the tax-and-transfer system reduces the value of the multiplier and thus acts as an **automatic stabilizer** for the economy. In the absence of the tax-and-transfer system, the multiplier would be larger and a positive shock would lead to a larger increase in real GDP.

The same is true in the presence of a negative AD or AS shock. As real GDP declines in response to the shock, government's net tax revenues fall, thus dampening the extent to which the fall in Y leads to induced reductions in spending and output.

Even in the absence of discretionary fiscal stabilization policy, the presence of net taxes that vary with national income provides the economy with an automatic stabilizer.

At the end of Chapter 22 we argued that realistic Canadian values for our model's key parameters are as follows:

- marginal propensity to consume (MPC) = 0.8
- net tax rate (t) = 0.3
- marginal propensity to import (m) = 0.4

The implied value of z, the marginal propensity to spend on national income, is therefore

$$z = MPC(1 - t) - m$$
$$= (0.8)(0.7) - 0.4 = 0.16$$

As a result, a realistic value for the simple multiplier in Canada is

$$\text{Simple multiplier} = 1/(1 - z) = 1/0.84 = 1.19$$

The lower is the net tax rate, the larger is the simple multiplier and thus the less stable is real GDP in response to shocks to autonomous spending. For example, if the net tax rate were reduced to 20 percent ($t = 0.20$), the value of z would rise to 0.24 and the simple multiplier would rise to $1/(1 - 0.24) = 1/0.76 = 1.31$. The larger multiplier implies that a shock to autonomous expenditure would result in a larger total change in GDP—that is, the economy would be less stable. Therefore, whatever benefits might arise from a reduction in the net tax rate (and we will see later that lower tax rates may tend to increase the economy's long-run growth rate), one drawback is that the tax reduction would lead to the economy being less stable following shocks to autonomous expenditure.

The great advantage of automatic fiscal stabilizers is that they are "automatic." As long as the tax-and-transfer system is in place (and there is no sign of its imminent disappearance!) some stability is provided without anyone having to make active decisions about fiscal policy. As we see next, the sorts of decisions required for successful *discretionary* fiscal policy are not simple, and some attempts to provide stability through discretionary fiscal policy may actually reduce the stability of the economy.

---

automatic stabilizers
Elements of the tax-and-transfer system that reduce the responsiveness of real GDP to changes in autonomous expenditure.

Practical Limitations of Discretionary Fiscal Policy

According to our earlier discussion of fiscal stabilization policy, returning the economy to potential output would appear to be a simple matter of cutting taxes and raising government spending, in some combination. Why do so many economists believe that such policies would be "as likely to harm as help"? Part of the answer is that the practical use of discretionary fiscal policy is anything but simple.

Decision and Execution Lags To change fiscal policy requires making changes in taxes and government expenditures. The changes must be agreed on by the Cabinet and passed by Parliament. The political stakes in such changes are generally very large; taxes and spending are called "bread-and-butter issues" precisely because they affect the economic well-being of almost everyone. Thus, even if economists agreed that the economy would be helped by, say, a tax cut, politicians would likely spend a good deal of time debating *whose* taxes should be cut and by *how much*. The delay between the initial recognition of a recessionary or inflationary gap and the enactment of legislation to change fiscal policy, which may be several months long, is called a **decision lag**.

Once policy changes are agreed on, there is still an **execution lag**, adding time between the enactment of the legislation and the implementation of the policy action. Furthermore, once the new policies are in place, it will usually take still more time for their economic consequences to be felt. Because of these lags, it is quite possible that by the time a given policy decision has any impact on the economy, circumstances will have changed such that the policy is no longer appropriate.

Temporary Versus Permanent Tax Changes To make matters even more frustrating, tax measures that are known to be temporary are generally less effective than measures that are expected to be permanent. For example, if households know that an announced tax cut will last only a year, they may recognize that the effect on their long-run consumption possibilities is small and may choose to save their tax-cut-induced increase in disposable income rather than spend it. If so, the effect of the tax cut on aggregate demand will be nil. Thus, the more closely household consumption expenditure is related to *lifetime* income rather than to *current* income, the smaller will be the effects on current consumption of tax changes that are known to be of short duration. Or, to use the language that we used when introducing the consumption function in Chapter 21, the more forward-looking are households, the smaller will be the effects of what are perceived to be temporary changes in taxes.

The Role of Discretionary Fiscal Policy Attempts to use discretionary fiscal policy to "fine tune" the economy are thus fraught with difficulties. **Fine tuning** refers to the use of fiscal (and monetary) policy to offset virtually all fluctuations in private-sector spending so as to keep real GDP at or near its potential level. However, neither economic nor political science has yet advanced far enough to allow policymakers to undo the consequences of every aggregate demand or supply shock. Nevertheless, many economists still argue that when a recessionary gap is large enough and persists for long enough, *gross tuning* may be appropriate. **Gross tuning** refers to the use of fiscal and monetary policy to remove large and persistent output gaps. Other economists believe that fiscal policy should not be used for economic stabilization under any circumstances. Rather, they would argue, tax and spending behaviour should be the outcome of public choices regarding the long-term size and financing of the public sector and should not be altered for short-term considerations. We return to these debates in Chapter 32.

decision lag The period of time between perceiving some problem and reaching a decision on what to do about it.

execution lag The time that it takes to put policies in place after a decision has been made.

fine tuning The attempt to maintain output at its potential level by means of frequent changes in fiscal or monetary policy.

gross tuning The use of macroeconomic policy to stabilize the economy such that large deviations from potential output do not persist for extended periods of time.

Fiscal Policy and Growth

Fiscal policy has both short-run and long-run effects on the economy. Its short-run effects, which we have discussed in this chapter, are reflected by shifts in the *AD* curve and changes in the level of GDP. However, the theory presented here predicts that the adjustment of factor prices will eventually bring real GDP back to Y^*, so that the long-run effects of any given fiscal policy will depend on the policy's effects on Y^*. In both of the following examples, to highlight the difference between the short-run and long-run effects of the policies, we imagine starting in a macroeconomic equilibrium with real GDP equal to Y^*.

Increases in Government Purchases   A fiscal expansion created by an increase in government purchases (G) will shift the *AD* curve to the right and increase real GDP in the short run. As factor prices rise in response to the inflationary output gap, output will return back to Y^* but at a higher price level. As we will see in detail in later chapters, even though real GDP may return to Y^*, the *composition* of output will be altered. From the national-income accounting we saw in Chapter 20, we know that $Y = C_a + I_a + G_a + NX_a$, where the "a" subscripts denote the actual components of aggregate expenditure. If real GDP returns to Y^* after factor prices have fully adjusted, then the *rise* in G_a must be equal to the *fall* in $C_a + I_a + NX_a$. In this case we say that the increase in government purchases has "crowded out" private expenditures. Of particular concern is the possibility that private investment in plant and equipment will be reduced. If investment is crowded out, there will be a slower rate of accumulation of physical capital, and this will likely lead to a reduction in the future growth rate of potential output.[5]

Even though an increase in government purchases may have no effect on the *current level* of potential output, the crowding out of private investment implies that the *growth rate* of potential output may be lower than it would otherwise be.

In this situation, the short-run stimulative benefits of the fiscal expansion need to be weighed against the possible long-run costs of lower growth. If the economy is currently in a deep recession and the economy's adjustment process is slow, the gain in short-run economic activity may well outweigh the costs of slower growth. After all, part of Keynes' central message was that the state of the world at potential output is not very interesting to members of a society who are a long way from it.

Practise with Study Guide Chapter 24, Exercise 4.

Reductions in Taxes   A fiscal expansion created by a reduction in taxes is a little more complicated to analyze because there are likely to be longer-term, supply-side effects. The short-run demand-side effects are straightforward. A reduction in the GST rate or in the corporate or personal income-tax rates that are thought to be long-lasting will increase both investment and consumption spending and shift the *AD* curve to the right. The level of real GDP will rise in the short run. As wages and other factor prices increase, however, the level of output will gradually return to Y^*.

What is the long-run effect of lower taxes on the level of potential output? Lower corporate income-tax rates make investment more profitable to firms, and the stimulative effect on desired investment may offset the "crowding out" associated with the rightward shift of the *AD* curve and the rise in the price level. If the overall effect on investment is positive, there will tend to be a positive effect on the future growth rate

---

[5] Since some of the rise in G_a may be government investment in such things as roads or power plants, the overall effect on the path of Y^* depends on the productivity of the new public investment compared to that of the private investment that was crowded out.

of potential output. Lower GST rates and personal income-tax rates may have a similar effect. To the extent that high tax rates discourage work effort, reductions in tax rates will lead to increases in the labour force and consequent increases in the level of potential output.

Reductions in tax rates generate a short-run demand stimulus and may also generate a longer-run increase in the level and growth rate of potential output.

If reduced tax rates *do* lead to a higher growth rate of potential output, there would appear to be no clear tradeoff between the short-run and long-run effects of the fiscal expansion. The economy benefits in the short run from the increase in economic activity and in the long run from the increase in the growth rate. The absence of a tradeoff may, however, be illusory. Even though the growth rate of potential output is higher, the reduced tax revenues lead to fewer resources under the command of government. This means less public spending on many of the things citizens value, such as national parks, public education, and health care.

Another alleged but hotly debated possibility, however, is that the reduction in tax rates leads to such a significant increase in potential output that the government's tax revenues actually increase. (We saw this possibility in Chapter 18 with the Laffer curve, the relationship between tax rates and total tax revenues.) In this case, the tax reduction unleashes such a flood of investment and work effort that the increase in national income is sufficient to more than offset the reduction in tax rates, thus leaving the government able to fund more worthwhile public spending than before. This idea is central to what is often called "supply side" economics, as popularized during the early 1980s by advisors to U.S. President Ronald Reagan and British Prime Minister Margaret Thatcher. More recently, the central idea that tax reductions may significantly stimulate economic activity and growth played an important role in the policies of Alberta Premier Ralph Klein and former Ontario Premier Mike Harris, as well as in the tax cuts implemented in 2004 by U.S. President George W. Bush.

SUMMARY

24.1 **THE ADJUSTMENT PROCESS**   LO 1 2

- Potential output, Y^*, is the level of real GDP at which all factors of production are being used at their normal rates of utilization.
- The output gap is the difference between potential output and the actual level of real GDP, the latter determined by the intersection of the *AD* and *AS* curves.
- An inflationary gap means that Y is greater than Y^*, and hence there is excess demand in factor markets. As a result, wages and other factor prices rise, causing firms' unit costs to rise. The *AS* curve shifts upward, and the price level rises.

- A recessionary gap means that Y is less than Y^*, and hence there is excess supply in factor markets. Wages and other factor prices fall, but perhaps very slowly. As firms' unit costs fall, the *AS* curve gradually shifts downward, eventually returning output to potential.
- In our macro model, the level of potential output, Y^*, acts as an "anchor" for the economy. Given the short-run equilibrium as determined by the *AD* and *AS* curves, wages and other factor prices will adjust, shifting the *AS* curve, until output returns to Y^*.

24.2 **DEMAND AND SUPPLY SHOCKS**

- Beginning from a position of potential output, an expansionary demand shock creates an inflationary gap, causing wages and other factor prices to rise. Firms' unit costs rise, shifting the *AS* curve upward and bringing output back towards *Y**.
- Beginning from a position of potential output, a contractionary demand shock creates a recessionary gap. Because factor prices tend to be sticky downwards, the adjustment process tends to be slow, and a recessionary gap tends to persist for some time.
- Aggregate supply shocks, such as those caused by changes in the prices of inputs, lead the *AS* curve to shift, changing real GDP and the price level. But the economy's adjustment process reverses the shift in *AS*, tending eventually to bring the economy back to its initial level of output and prices.
- In the short run, macroeconomic equilibrium is determined by the intersection of the *AD* and *AS* curves. In the long run, the economy is in equilibrium only when real GDP is equal to potential output. In the long run, the price level is determined by the intersection of the *AD* curve and the vertical *Y** curve.
- Shocks to the *AD* or *AS* curves can change real GDP in the short run. Only changes in the level of potential output can change output in the long run.

24.3 **FISCAL STABILIZATION POLICY**

- In principle, fiscal policy can be used to stabilize output at *Y**. To remove a recessionary gap, governments can shift *AD* to the right by cutting taxes or increasing spending. To remove an inflationary gap, governments can pursue the opposite policies.
- In the short run, increases in desired saving on the part of firms, households, and governments lead to reductions in real GDP. This phenomenon is called the paradox of thrift. In the long run, the paradox of thrift does not apply, and increased saving will lead to increased investment and economic growth.
- Because government tax and transfer programs tend to reduce the size of the multiplier, they act as automatic stabilizers. When real GDP changes, disposable income changes by less because of taxes and transfers.
- Discretionary fiscal policy is subject to decision lags and execution lags that limit its ability to take effect quickly.

Some economists argue that these limitations are so severe that discretionary fiscal policy should never be used for stabilization because it will end up increasing instability. Others argue that the economy's adjustment process works so slowly that discretionary fiscal policy can play a useful role in stabilizing the economy.
- Fiscal policy has different effects in the short and long run. In the short run, a fiscal expansion created by an increase in government purchases (*G*) will increase real GDP. In the long run, the rise in *G* will "crowd out" private spending. If private investment is crowded out, the growth rate of potential output may be reduced.
- In the short run, a fiscal expansion created by a reduction in income taxes has a similar effect on real GDP. In the long run, if the tax reduction leads to more investment and work effort, there will be a positive effect on the level and growth rate of potential output.

KEY CONCEPTS

The output gap and factor prices
Inflationary and recessionary gaps
Asymmetry of wage adjustment: flexible and sticky wages
The Phillips curve

Potential output as an "anchor" for the economy
Short-run versus long-run effects of *AD* and *AS* shocks
Fiscal stabilization policy

The paradox of thrift
Decision lags and execution lags
Automatic stabilizers
Fine tuning and gross tuning

STUDY EXERCISES

1. Fill in the blanks to make the following statements correct.

   a. In our short-run macro model, it is assumed that factor prices are _exogenous_ and the level of potential output is _constant_. Changes in real GDP are caused by fluctuations in _AD_ and _AS_.

   b. During the adjustment process highlighted in this chapter, the central assumption is that factor prices are _flexible_ and responding to _output gaps_. Potential output is assumed to be _constant_, and acts as an _anchor_ for real GDP following *AD* or *AS* shocks.

2. Fill in the blanks to make the following statements correct.

   a. When actual GDP is higher than potential GDP, we say that there is a(n) _inflationary_ gap. When actual GDP is less than potential GDP we say there is a(n) _recessionary_ gap.

   b. An inflationary gap leads to excess demand for labour, which causes wages and thus _unit_ costs to rise. Firms require higher _prices_ in order to supply any level of output, and so the *AS* curve shifts _upward_.

   c. A recessionary gap leads to excess supply of labour, which causes wages and thus _unit_ costs to fall. Firms reduce _price_ for any level of output supplied, and so the *AS* curve shifts _downward_.

   d. The downward adjustment of wages in response to a recessionary gap is much _slower_ than the upward adjustment of wages in response to a(n) _inflationary_ gap. Economists refer to this phenomenon as _sticky wages_

3. Fill in the blanks to make the following statements correct.

   a. Beginning with output equal to potential, suppose there is a sudden increase in demand for Canadian exports. This is a(n) _Expansionary AD_ shock to the Canadian economy, which will result in the _AD_ curve shifting to the _right_ and the opening of a(n) _inflationary_ gap. Firms' unit costs will start to _increase_ and the _AS_ curve will shift _upward_. Long-run equilibrium will be restored at _potential_ output and _increased_ price level.

   b. Beginning with output equal to potential, suppose there is a drop in business confidence and investment falls. This is a(n) _contractionary AD_ shock to the Canadian economy, which shifts the _AD_ curve to the left and creates a(n) _recessionary_ gap.

   Unit costs will start to _decrease_ and the _AS_ curve will shift _downward_. Long-run equilibrium will (slowly) be restored at _potential_ output and _decreased_ price level.

   c. Beginning with output equal to potential, suppose there is a large and sudden increase in the price of electricity. This is a(n) _AS_ shock to the Canadian economy, which will result in the _AS_ curve shifting _upward_ and the opening of a(n) _recessionary_ gap. If wages are downwardly sticky the economy's _adjustment_ process could be very slow and the _recession_ will persist for a long time.

   d. Beginning with output equal to potential, suppose there is a large and sudden decrease in the price of electricity. This is a(n) _pos AS_ shock to the Canadian economy, which will result in the _AS_ curve shifting _downward_ and the opening of a(n) _inflationary_ gap. Unit costs will start to _increase_ and the _AD_ curve will shift _downward_, restoring equilibrium at _potential_ output and _decreased_ price level.

4. Fill in the blanks to make the following statements correct.

   a. In the long run, total output is determined only by _Potential output_. In the long run, aggregate demand determines the _price level_.

   b. Permanent increases in real GDP are possible only if _potential output_ is increasing.

   c. Suppose illiteracy in Canada were eliminated, and the school dropout rate were reduced to zero. The effect would be a permanent _increase_ in productivity and a(n) _increase_ in potential output.

   d. A reduction in corporate income tax is likely to make _investment_ more attractive and thus shift the _AD_ curve to the right. The result is a(n) _increase_ in the short-run level of real GDP. In the long run, the greater rate of _investment_ by firms will lead to a greater rate of growth of _potential output_.

5. ✕ **myeconlab** The following diagram shows two economies, A and B. Each are in short-run equilibrium at point *E*, where the *AD* and *AS* curves intersect.

   a. Explain why in Economy A wages and other factor prices will begin to rise, and why this will increase firms' unit costs.

   b. Following your answer in part (a), show the effect on the *AS* curve. Explain what happens to real GDP and the price level.

   c. Explain why in Economy B wages and other factor prices will begin to fall, and why this will decrease firms' unit costs.

Economy A

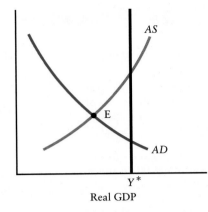

Economy B

d. Following your answer in part (c), show the effect on the *AS* curve. Explain what happens to real GDP and the price level.

6. ⓧ myeconlab The table shows several possible situations for the economy in terms of output gaps and the rate of change of wages. Real GDP is measured in billions of dollars. Assume that potential output is $800 billion.

Situation	Real GDP	Output Gap	Rate of Wage Change	Shift of AS Curve (+/0/−)
A	775	—	−2.0 %	—
B	785	—	−1.2 %	—
C	795	—	−0.2 %	—
D	800	—	0.0 %	—
E	805	—	1.0 %	—
F	815	—	2.4 %	—
G	825	—	4.0 %	—
H	835	—	5.8 %	—

a. Compute the output gap $(Y - Y^*)$ for each situation and fill in the table.
b. Explain why wages rise when output is greater than potential but fall when output is less than potential.
c. For each situation, explain whether the economy's *AS* curve is shifting up, shifting down, or is stationary. Fill in the table.
d. Plot the Phillips curve on a scale diagram for this economy. (See *Extensions in Theory 24-1* for a review of the Phillips curve.)

7. ⓧ myeconlab Consider an economy that is in equilibrium with output equal to Y^*. There is then a significant reduction in the world's demand for this country's goods.

a. Illustrate the initial equilibrium in a diagram.

b. What kind of shock occurred—aggregate demand or aggregate supply? Show the effects of the shock in your diagram.
c. Explain the process by which the economy will adjust back toward Y^* in the long run. Show this in your diagram.
d. Explain why policymakers may want to use a fiscal expansion to restore output back to Y^* rather than wait for the process you described in part (c). What role does downward wage stickiness play in the policymakers' thinking?

8. Consider an economy that is in equilibrium with output equal to Y^*. There is then a significant reduction in the world price of an important raw material, such as iron ore.

a. Illustrate the initial equilibrium in a diagram.
b. What kind of shock occurred—aggregate demand or aggregate supply? Show the effects of the shock in your diagram.
c. Explain the process by which the economy will adjust back toward Y^* in the long run. Show this in your diagram.
d. Is there a strong case for using a fiscal contraction to return output to Y^*? Explain why or why not.

9. In our discussion of fiscal stabilization policy, we explained how income taxes and transfers affected the size of the multiplier. The accompanying diagrams show the initial equilibrium of two hypothetical economies that are each about to experience a $10 billion increase in autonomous net exports. Economy A has high (net) tax rates whereas Economy B has low (net) tax rates. Both economies have the same *AS* curve.

a. Explain why Economy A has a lower simple multiplier than Economy B.
b. Explain why the lower simple multiplier in Economy A results in a steeper *AD* curve.

Economy A

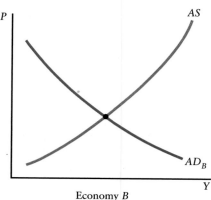

Economy B

c. Illustrate the shifts in the *AD* curves that result from the increases in net exports. (Hint: You may

want to review at this point the relationship between the *AD* curve and the *AE* curve, which we discussed in Chapter 23.)

10. The following diagram shows the *AD*, *AS*, and *Y** curves for an economy. Suppose the economy begins at point *A*. Then the government increases its level of purchases (*G*).

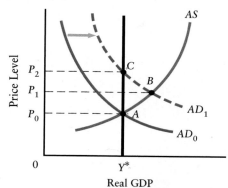

a. Describe the short-run effects of this fiscal expansion.
b. Describe the adjustment process, and the new long-run equilibrium for the economy.
c. Explain how the *composition* of real GDP has changed from the initial to the new long-run equilibrium.
d. Repeat (a), (b), and (c) for a fiscal expansion generated by a reduction in the net tax rate.

DISCUSSION QUESTIONS

1. Discuss the following two statements in terms of short-run versus long-run outcomes.

   a. "Starting from potential output, an increase in government spending can produce more output and employment at the cost of a once-and-for-all rise in the price level."
   b. "Increased government spending can never lead to a permanent increase in output."

2. Politicians are sometimes accused of adopting policies that bring "short-term gain at the cost of long-term pain," whereas statesmen offer "short-term pain to buy long-term gain." What policies that shift aggregate demand or aggregate supply curves might come under one or the other of these descriptions?

3. If downward flexibility of money wages would allow the economy's adjustment process to eliminate recessionary gaps quickly, why do workers usually resist wage cuts during times of economic slump?

4. Which of the following would be automatic stabilizers?

   a. Employment-insurance payments
   b. Cost-of-living escalators in government contracts and pensions
   c. Income taxes
   d. Free university tuition for unemployed workers after six months of unemployment, provided that they are under 30 years old and have had five or more years of full-time work experience since high school

5. During 1998 and 1999, the Canadian economy was experiencing a sufficiently high rate of growth of real GDP that many economists predicted an increase in inflation. Yet inflation declined slightly. At the same time, world commodity prices continued their decline that began in mid-1997. Explain the behaviour of the Canadian economy—high growth and falling

inflation—in terms of aggregate demand and aggregate supply curves. What role, if any, is played by the falling commodity prices? What role is played by the U.S. economy, which at this point was experiencing very strong growth?

6. In 2003, United States President George W. Bush announced a budget proposal to reduce income taxes. He argued that this policy would provide the necessary stimulus to the U.S. economy, which was growing very slowly at the time.

a. Does a reduction in personal income taxes produce a demand-side or a supply-side stimulus to the economy? Explain.

b. Discuss the likely time frame for each possible effect on the U.S. economy. Why did many economic commentators at the time argue that the proposal did not address the *immediate* needs of the U.S. economy?

CHAPTER 25

The Difference Between Short-Run and Long-Run Macroeconomics

⌾ LEARNING OBJECTIVES

In this chapter you will learn

① why economists think differently about short-run and long-run changes in macroeconomic variables.

② that any change in real GDP can be decomposed into changes in: factor supply, the utilization rate of factors, and productivity.

③ why short-run changes in GDP are mostly caused by changes in factor utilization, whereas long-run changes in GDP are mostly caused by changes in factor supplies and productivity.

④ that macroeconomic policies will only have a long-run effect on output if they influence factor supplies or productivity.

In Chapters 21, 22, and 23, we developed a model of the economy in the short run—a period of time over which technology and factor supplies are fixed, and wages and other factor prices are not changing in response to any existing output gap. In Chapter 24, we extended this model to show how the economy evolves, through a process of factor-price adjustment, from its short-run equilibrium to its long-run equilibrium. In the long run, wages and other factor prices have adjusted fully to excess demands or supplies that developed in the short run in response to inflationary or recessionary output gaps. There we saw how the level of potential output, Y^*, acts as an "anchor" for the economy. Aggregate demand or supply shocks can lead to short-run deviations of real GDP from Y^*, but the economy's adjustment process ensures that real GDP returns to Y^* in the long run. In the next chapter, we will examine why Y^* grows over periods of many years—a process that we call *long-run economic growth*.

In this chapter, we focus on the distinction between the short run and the long run in macroeconomics, ignoring the details of the adjustment process that gets the economy from one "run" to another. This distinction makes the study of macroeconomics more challenging but, at the same time, more interesting. The distinction becomes especially important when policymakers try to evaluate the effects of various policies. Different economists will sometimes use different time frames for the evaluation of any given policy. For example, one economist may say that a fiscal expansion is desirable because it will provide stimulus to an economy with unemployment and excess productive capacity; another economist may claim that it will have negative effects on the economy's long-run growth. These two views may be entirely consistent with one another (as we saw at the end of the previous chapter), but the observer is left confused because it is not clear in the debate whether the discussion is about the short-run or the long-run effects of the policy.

In this chapter, we seek to clarify the distinction between short-run GDP fluctuations and long-run GDP growth. With this distinction firmly in place, we will be ready for the detailed discussion of long-run economic growth in the next chapter.

25.1 TWO EXAMPLES

We begin with two examples of the difference between short-run and long-run macroeconomic relationships.

Inflation and Interest Rates in Canada

In the early 1990s, Canada's central bank (the Bank of Canada) embarked on a policy designed to reduce the rate of inflation. For reasons that we will see in detail in Chapters 28 and 29, the Bank's policy was controversial. When his term expired in 1994 the governor, John Crow, was replaced by his senior deputy governor, Gordon Thiessen. Though Thiessen was committed to following Crow's policy of reducing inflation, he was equally committed to explaining the policy to an often-skeptical public. As we will see, the explanation relies crucially on making the distinction between short-run and long-run macroeconomic relationships.

In April of 1995, Governor Thiessen was interviewed on CBC Radio. Thiessen was asked about the Bank's policy of reducing inflation, from about 6 percent a few years earlier, and maintaining it since then between 1 percent and 3 percent annually. Thiessen argued that the high nominal interest rates of the past were caused mostly by high inflation. The main reason for this connection between inflation and nominal interest rates is that inflation erodes the value of money. Lenders need to be compensated for the inflation-induced fall in the real value of their money between the time they lend it and the time that they are repaid. This requires charging a nominal interest rate high enough to cover the effects of inflation. Thus, higher inflation pushes up interest rates; lower inflation pushes them down.

At this point, the interviewer had no problem with Thiessen's line of argument, as he easily recalled the time back in 1981 when inflation was at an all-time high of 12 percent and mortgage rates at Canada's banks were an astounding 20 percent! In contrast, by 1995, the rate of inflation was down to just over 2 percent and mortgage rates were only 8 percent. So periods of high inflation did indeed appear to coincide with periods of high interest rates.

Thiessen then started the next part of his argument. He stated that in order to reduce the rate of inflation the Bank of Canada had to reduce the growth rate of the money supply. This action, he admitted, would tighten up credit-market conditions and push up interest rates. Understandably confused at this point, the interviewer asked the inevitable question: How can a policy that raises interest rates be a necessary part of a policy designed to *reduce* both inflation and interest rates?

Thiessen understood the apparent contradiction, but was ready with his answer. He stressed that the key to answering the question is to understand the different short-run and long-run effects of monetary policy. Recall that in macroeconomics the short run describes a time span over which technology is more or less constant, and wages and other factor prices have not yet adjusted to any output gaps. Thiessen argued that, in the short run, a policy by the Bank of Canada to reduce the growth rate of money will make credit more scarce (as we will see in detail in Chapter 28). This greater scarcity of credit causes both nominal and real interest rates to rise. Firms will reduce their investment in new factories, machines, and warehouses, and households will purchase fewer big-ticket items, such as cars, ski vacations, and furniture. Such reductions in expenditure will lead, through the multiplier process that we have already seen, to a reduction in national output. But as firms scale back their production and real GDP falls, workers get laid off and the unemployment rate increases—the economy enters a recession. In short, the Bank of Canada's contractionary monetary policy shifts the *AD* curve to the left and generates a reduction in GDP. When we examine the detailed workings of monetary policy in later chapters, we will see that a monetary policy designed to reduce inflation is usually effective precisely because *it creates a recession.*

So much for the short-run effects of the Bank's policy. What happens as wages and other factor prices adjust and the economy therefore starts to approach its new long-run equilibrium? As we saw in Chapter 24, the excess supply of labour that is a key part of the unemployment and recession puts downward pressure on wages. In other words, wages start to increase at a slower rate than before, and maybe even begin to fall. As wage growth declines the pressure on prices to rise also declines. That is, the rate of inflation falls. As inflation falls, and the rate of erosion of money's value falls with it, nominal interest rates will also fall. In the new long-run equilibrium, both inflation and nominal interest rates will be lower than before the policy was initiated. As Gordon Thiessen said in the interview, "The best way to get low interest rates is to get low inflation."

The details of monetary policy will be discussed in Chapters 28 and 29, and this argument will be repeated in considerable detail. At that time, we will more clearly see the difference between the short-run and long-run effects of monetary policy. Economists have a special term to reflect this difference. In the long run, economists say that *money is neutral*—meaning that changes in the money supply have no long-run effect on *real* variables such as GDP, employment, and investment but do have an effect on *nominal* variables such as the price level or the rate of inflation. This long-run neutrality of money is another way of stating that changes in the money supply do not change the level of potential output, Y^*. In the short run, however, economists say that *money is not neutral* because changes in the money supply affect real variables. In other words, monetary policy shifts the *AD* curve and generates short-run changes in real GDP. Understanding this difference is crucial to understanding most debates about monetary policy.

Saving and Growth in Japan

By early in 2006, the Japanese economy had been growing slowly, if at all, for over a decade. Japan's economy was stagnant. Many economists argued that an important part of the solution to Japan's economic malaise was for its firms and consumers to spend more. One problem with Japan, they argued, was that its firms and consumers saved "too much." On the other hand, many of these same economists acknowledged that Japan's remarkable economic success in the forty years following the Second World War—high growth rates of real GDP and low unemployment—was to a significant extent due to its high saving rate. But if "too much" saving is an important reason for Japan's economic slump during the 1990s and early 2000s, how can high

The high private saving rate in Japan is one reason that the Japanese economic recovery in the late 1990s was so slow.

saving also be a primary reason for Japan's remarkable economic success over four decades? How can both of these views be correct?

Once again, the key to understanding this apparent contradiction is to recognize that the short-run effect of saving is different from its long-run effect. We saw this distinction in Chapter 24 when we discussed the "paradox of thrift," but it is worth repeating. In the short run, with factor prices and technology more or less constant, an increase in households' desire to save, perhaps caused by some uncertainty about future economic events, implies a reduction in expenditure. Uncertainty leads firms to spend less on investment goods; households spend less on all sorts of consumer goods. This reduction in expenditure leads, through the usual multiplier process, to a reduction in output. In terms of our macro model, the *AD* curve shifts to the left and real GDP falls. Increased saving in the short run, therefore, can be one reason why an economy such as Japan's enters an economic slump.

But if an increase in firms' and households' saving can cause a recession, how can a high saving rate also explain Japan's many years of healthy economic growth? The answer is that in the long run, after wages and factor prices adjust to the recessionary gap, greater saving leads to a larger pool of financial capital. This larger pool of available funds drives down the price of credit—the interest rate—and makes firms' investment projects more profitable. More investment in factories, machines, and warehouses leads to a higher level of potential output, and it is to this higher level of potential output that the economy converges in the long run. This long-run relationship among saving, investment, and growth explains the striking correlation that we will see in the next chapter—countries with high long-run investment rates tend to be countries with high rates of long-run per capita GDP growth.

Economists have special terminology to describe this difference between the short run and the long run. Economists say that national income in the short run is largely *demand determined*, meaning that increases in demand will lead to increases in output. Thus, an increase in the desire to save, which is a reduction in the desire to spend, leads to less total spending and a reduction in national income. Even though aggregate supply (*AS*) shocks also affect output in the short run (as we saw in Chapters 23 and 24), the term *demand determined* reflects the fact that the position of the aggregate demand (*AD*) curve is important for determining the level of real GDP. In the long run, however, economists say that national income is *supply determined*, meaning that long-run increases in output will be possible only if the level of potential output increases; the position of the *AD* curve has no effect on real GDP in the long run. Increases in potential output require either more factors of production (like labour and capital) or technological change that improves productivity.

A Need to Think Differently

The two examples above suggest that a complete understanding of macroeconomics requires an understanding of both the short run and the long run. Such an understanding, in turn, requires us to think differently about short-run and long-run behaviour. It is one thing to say that macroeconomic variables behave differently over the short run than over the long run; it is quite another to understand *why* this is the case.

In this chapter, we emphasize the distinction between viewing short-run changes in GDP as deviations of output from potential, and long-run changes in GDP as changes in the level of potential output. We introduce a simple method of GDP accounting that clarifies this distinction, and also shows us the various sources of short-run and long-run changes in GDP.[1]

25.2 ACCOUNTING FOR CHANGES IN GDP

The simplest illustration of the distinction between short-run and long-run changes in economic activity is the behaviour of real GDP over time, as shown in Figure 25-1. The figure shows the path of Canadian real GDP and potential GDP, beginning from 1975. Actual GDP is measured by Statistics Canada. Potential GDP, as you may recall from Chapter 19, is the level of output that the economy produces when all factors of production are being utilized at their "normal" rates. But Statistics Canada can't tell us the value of potential GDP because it is not an observed variable—it must be estimated. The value of potential GDP is estimated by combining three pieces of information: the amounts of available factors of production (like the labour force and the capital stock); an estimate of these factors' "normal" rates of utilization; and an estimate of each factor's productivity.

Figure 25-1 shows two different types of changes in GDP. First, some changes involve departures of actual GDP from potential GDP. For example, notice that actual GDP is equal to potential GDP at point B in 1980. As the Canadian economy then entered a major recession, actual GDP dropped below potential GDP to point C in 1982. An economic recovery then took place, taking actual GDP back to potential GDP at point D in 1986. Such changes in GDP are what economists call short-run changes in GDP—they involve primarily the opening and then closing of an output gap.

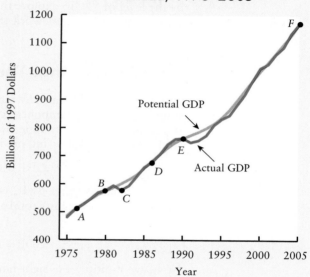

FIGURE 25-1 Actual and Potential GDP in Canada, 1975–2005

Long-run changes in GDP are reflected by changes in the level of potential GDP. Short-run changes in GDP are shown mostly by changes in the output gap.

(*Source:* Actual GDP: Statistics Canada CANSIM database, Series V3862685. Potential GDP: based on authors' calculations using data on the output gap from www.bankofcanada.ca.)

The second type of change in GDP involves changes in potential GDP, with little or no change in the output gap. For example, the change in actual GDP from point A in 1976 to point F in 2005 represents entirely a change in potential GDP. We know this

---

[1] It is worth emphasizing the different use of the terms "short run" and "long run" in macroeconomics and in microeconomics. In microeconomics, the short run for a firm or industry is the span of time during which the amount of physical capital is constant; the long run is the period of time during which firms are able to adjust their capital stock. In macroeconomics, however, the key distinction relates to whether wages and other factor prices have fully adjusted to excess demand or supply (the output gap) in the aggregate economy. Economists take wages and other factor prices to be given in the short run, but fully adjusted to the output gap in the long run.

because the output gap in both years is zero (that is, in both 1976 and 2005 GDP is equal to potential GDP). Such changes in GDP are what economists call long-run changes in GDP—they involve a change in potential GDP, with little or no change in the output gap.

When studying long-run trends in GDP, economists focus on the change in potential output. When studying short-run fluctuations, economists focus on the change in the output gap.

Practise with Study Guide Chapter 25, Exercise 1.

Figure 25-1 may make us wonder whether short-run changes in GDP have a different cause than long-run changes. In our macro model this is certainly the case; output is determined in the short run by the *AD* and *AS* curves, but in the long run only by the level of *Y**. To explore the different causes of changes in GDP, we turn to a very simple accounting framework that applies to *all* changes in GDP.

GDP Accounting: The Basic Principle

Suppose we could break down any change in GDP into its component parts. By understanding how each component changes, we can then gain some insights into how short-run changes differ from long-run changes. To break up GDP into the parts we want to study, we do the following obvious but useful things. First, we write

$$GDP = GDP$$

This is obviously true! Next, we multiply the right-hand side of the equation by F/F, where F is the economy's total available stock of factors, such as land, labour, and capital. This gives

$$GDP = F \times (GDP/F)$$

Next, we multiply the right-hand side by F_E/F_E, where F_E is the number of the economy's factors that are employed. This gives

$$GDP = F \times (F_E/F) \times (GDP/F_E) \tag{25-1}$$

It may seem like we have done nothing useful since we have simply twice multiplied the right-hand side of an obviously true equation by one. But, in fact, Equation 25-1 is very useful when thinking about the different sources of GDP changes.

First, however, note that Equation 25-1 is written as if we could add together units of labour and land and capital to get a meaningful number for the economy's "available factors", F. This is not actually possible since different factors are measured in different units. For example, we can't add together six workers and five machines and two hectares of land to get a total of 13 factors. In the next section, we will focus on a single factor to avoid this problem. For now, however, our point is simplified by thinking about the economy's total available factors, F, and the number of those factors that are employed, F_E.

To make the discussion less cumbersome, let's name the three components of Equation 25-1.

1. F is the economy's *factor supply;* it is the total amount of all factors of production that the economy currently possesses.

2. F_E/F is the *factor utilization rate;* it is the fraction of the total supply of factors that is actually used or employed at any time.

3. GDP/F_E is a simple measure of *productivity* because it shows the amount of output (GDP) per unit of input employed (F_E).

Note that Equation 25-1 does nothing more than separate any change in GDP into a change in one or more of the three components, F, F_E/F, or GDP/F_E. For example, Canadian GDP increased dramatically in the fifty years between 1950 and 2000. Also, Canadian GDP increased by a few percentage points from 2005 to 2007. In both cases, the increase in GDP can be attributed to changes in one or more of the three components—either the factor supply (F) increased, the factor utilization rate (F_E/F) increased, or the level of productivity (GDP/F_E) increased.

Any change in GDP can be decomposed into a change in factor supply, a change in factor utilization, and a change in productivity.

The usefulness of this accounting exercise becomes clear when we recognize that two of these components, factor supply and productivity, change mostly over long periods of time whereas the third component, factor utilization, changes mostly only over shorter periods. This points us toward a better understanding of the difference between short-run and long-run changes in GDP. We discuss each component in turn.

The Long Run: Factor Supply

Two main factors of production—labour and capital—account for most of the change in the economy's factor supply, F.

Labour. The economy's supply of labour can increase for two main reasons. First, population can increase. An increase in population can be caused, in turn, either by greater immigration, an increase in birth rates, or a decrease in the mortality rate. The second way to increase the economy's supply of labour is to increase the fraction of the population that chooses to seek employment. This fraction is called the *labour-force participation rate*. In Canada, the labour-force participation rate is currently about 66 percent. It has increased steadily from the 1960s, due mostly to the increase in the participation rate of married women and the coming-of-age of the baby-boom generation.

No matter how the economy's supply of labour increases, the important point for our purposes is that such changes are mostly *long-run changes*. Population growth, through whatever means, is a very gradual process. Changes in labour-force participation also tend to be gradual. As a result, the economy's supply of labour does not usually change significantly from year to year. Over a period of many years, however, the increase in the supply of labour can be very substantial.

Capital. The economy's supply of physical capital—machines, factories, and warehouses—increases for one reason. Firms that choose to purchase or build such investment goods today are accumulating physical capital that will be used to produce output in the future. Thus, today's flow of investment expenditure adds to the economy's stock of physical capital.[2]

As is the case for labour, the economy's stock of physical capital changes only very gradually. This is not to be confused with the very dramatic swings in investment that are often observed over the course of the business cycle. The difference is that investment is the *flow* that contributes to the *stock* of capital. But the economy's capital stock is so large compared to the annual flow of investment expenditure that even dramatic swings in the annual flow of investment generate almost imperceptible changes in the stock of capital.

Practise with Study Guide Chapter 25, Short-Answer Question 2.

---

[2] The part of investment that represents a change in inventories does not add to the economy's capital stock, but this component of investment is typically quite small (though volatile).

Changes in the economy's supply of labour and capital occur gradually, but over periods of many years their growth is considerable. As a result, changes in factor supply are important for explaining long-run changes in output, but relatively unimportant for explaining short-run changes.

Practise with Study Guide Chapter 25, Short-Answer Question 3.

The Long Run: Productivity   The economy's level of productivity (GDP/F_E) is a measure of the amount of output that is produced with a given level of input. In practice, there are several possible measures of productivity, each one measuring something slightly different. Although there is more than one measure of productivity, Equation 25-1 uses the concept of output per employed factor, GDP/F_E. An increase in productivity is called *productivity growth*. Productivity growth is an important source of long-term increases in per capita income and thus in rising living standards, and we will say much more about it in Chapter 26.

The economy's level of productivity changes only slowly over time. For example, the average rate of productivity growth in Canada over the past few decades has been about 1.5 percent per year. Such low growth rates do not lead to significant changes in GDP or living standards over short periods of time, but can generate huge improvements in living conditions over many years. For example, you may barely notice a 2 percent increase in your income from one year to the next, but you would surely notice the doubling that this annual growth rate would produce if it were sustained over 35 years. [31]

The economy's level of productivity changes only gradually from year to year, but grows substantially over periods of many years. As a result, productivity growth is very important for explaining long-run changes in output, but less important for explaining short-run changes.

The Short Run: Factor Utilization   In Chapters 21 to 23 we examined in detail the behaviour of the economy in the short run. Here we review some of these now-familiar concepts but express them in a way that helps us to understand our central equation decomposing the changes in real GDP.

The factor utilization rate (F_E/F) is the last remaining component from our equation. Recall that it is simply the fraction of the total supply of factors that is employed. An immediate question comes to mind: Why would firms ever use fewer factors than are available to them? The answer has to do with how firms respond to changes in the demand for their product. When a firm's sales start dropping off, it must make a choice. It can continue producing at the current rate and let its inventories build up. Or it can reduce its rate of production. For a firm that is interested in maximizing profits, there is a limit to the amount of costly inventories it will be prepared to accumulate. Eventually, a reduction in demand for its product leads the firm to reduce its output and, in turn, reduce its employment of factors. Workers are laid off and equipment and other physical capital is used less intensively, thus lowering the value of F_E/F for the economy.

Similarly, a firm that is faced with a sudden increase in demand for its product has two alternatives. It can continue with its previous rate of production and satisfy the increased demand by letting its inventories run down. Or it can increase its rate of production by hiring more available workers and machines. Since profit-maximizing firms do not want to miss an opportunity to make a profitable sale, as would happen if the stockpile of inventories gets fully depleted, eventually the increase in demand leads them to increase production and hire more factors. Extra workers are hired, existing workers work overtime, and machines and other physical capital are used more intensively, thus increasing F_E/F for the economy.

These responses by firms to changes in demand are only the firms' short-run responses. A low factor utilization rate describes *excess supply* in the factor markets. As we saw in Chapter 24, such a situation of excess supply typically causes some downward pressure on wages and other factor prices. This reduction of factor prices, in turn, reduces firms' costs, shifts the *AS* curve downward, and puts downward pressure on product prices. Similarly, in the case of the increase in demand, the situation of a high factor utilization rate describes *excess demand* in factor markets. Such excess demand causes upward pressure on wages and other factor prices. As factor prices rise, firms' costs increase, the *AS* curve shifts upward, and there is upward pressure on the price level. As we saw in Chapter 24, this process of factor-price adjustment in response to output gaps continues in our model until output returns to potential, at which point all factors of production are being used at their "normal" rates of utilization.

The factor utilization rate fluctuates in response to short-run changes in output caused by aggregate demand or aggregate supply shocks. Over time, however, excess supply or excess demand for factors causes an adjustment in factor prices that brings the factor utilization rate back to its "normal" level.

What do we mean by a "normal" factor utilization rate? In Chapter 19 we briefly discussed the fact that even when the economy is at potential output, some unemployment still exists. The rate of unemployment when real GDP is equal to potential output is often called the *natural rate of unemployment*. This "natural" or "normal" rate of unemployment is the rate of unemployment against which we compare the actual unemployment rate to judge whether the labour market has excess supply or excess demand. That is, if unemployment is above the natural rate, there is an excess supply of labour; if unemployment is below the natural rate, there is an excess demand for labour. For physical capital, the utilization rate is called the *capacity utilization rate* because the amount of physical capital largely determines the productive *capacity* of a given plant or factory. As with labour, so too is there a "natural" or "normal" capacity utilization rate for capital.

Changes in the factor utilization rate are important for explaining short-run changes in GDP. But after factor prices have fully adjusted, GDP returns to Y^* and the factor utilization rate returns to its "normal" level. As a result, changes in the factor utilization rate are not important for explaining long-run changes in GDP.

GDP Accounting: An Application

We made some strong statements in the previous section regarding the relative importance of short-run versus long-run changes in productivity, factor supplies, and factor utilization. Are these statements supported by the evidence? In this section, we apply the accounting concept contained in Equation 25-1 to Canadian GDP data to illustrate the basic arguments. Unfortunately, we cannot use *exactly* the same equation because, as we noted then, it is not possible to add units of labour together with units of physical capital and units of land. Using exactly the same intuition as earlier, however, we can express the GDP accounting equation in terms of a single factor of production—labour. Letting L be the labour force and E be the level of employment, the new equation is:[3]

$$GDP = L \times (E/L) \times (GDP/E) \qquad (25\text{-}2)$$

[3] We get this equation by beginning with GDP = GDP. We then multiply the right-hand side by E/E and then by L/L.

The basic interpretation of Equation 25-2 is the same as for Equation 25-1, except now the discussion relates only to labour. The labour force (L) is the supply of labour. The employment rate (E/L) is the fraction of the labour force actually employed (which is equal to one minus the unemployment rate). And the measure of productivity—in this case, labour productivity—is GDP/E.

Figure 25-2 shows the behaviour of these three components for Canada beginning in 1960. Each variable is expressed as an index number, with the value in 1960 set equal to 100. Expressing each variable in this way makes it easy to see each variable's percentage change over the four decades. Note that the vertical scale is different for each of the three variables. We do this intentionally so that we can see whatever trend and volatility exist for each variable separately. If we used the same vertical scale for graphing productivity and employment that we use for graphing the labour force, we would barely notice the fluctuations that do exist in these two variables.

FIGURE 25-2 Three Sources of Changes in GDP

(i) Labour force

(ii) Productivity

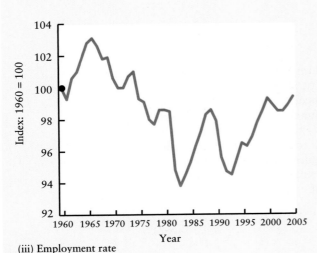

(iii) Employment rate

The sources of long-run changes in GDP differ from the sources of short-run changes in GDP. Panel (i) shows the upward trend in the Canadian labour force. Panel (ii) shows the upward trend in productivity, measured as GDP per worker. Both show substantial growth over the long run, but relatively small short-run fluctuations. Panel (iii) shows the employment rate, the fraction of the labour force that is employed. It shows almost no long-run trend but considerable short-run fluctuations.

(*Source:* All data for figures are authors' calculations using data from Statistics Canada CANSIM database. Labour force: Series V2091051. Employment: Series V2091072. Real GDP: Series V3862685.)

The first panel in the figure shows the growth of the Canadian labour force. From 1960 to 2005, the index number increased from 100 to 272, an increase of 172 percent. It is clear from the graph that any short-run fluctuations in the Canadian labour force are dwarfed in importance by the long-run upward trend.

Now look at the second panel, showing the growth of Canadian labour productivity. The level of GDP per person employed, expressed as an index number, increases from 100 in 1960 to 187 in 2005, an increase of 87 percent. Like the labour force, the level of labour productivity has its short-run fluctuations, but it is clear that the overriding change—the upward trend—takes place over many years.

Finally, consider the third panel, showing the Canadian employment rate—the utilization rate of labour. Compared to the other two variables graphed in Figure 25-2, the employment rate shows much more short-run volatility and much less long-run change. The employment rate (expressed as an index number) falls slightly from 100 in 1960 to over 99 in 2005, a long-run decrease of less than 1 percent. There is very little change over the long run, but considerable changes are occurring over shorter periods of time.

Summing Up

To summarize, we can decompose *any* change in GDP into changes in factor supply, the factor utilization rate, and productivity. But these three components typically contribute to GDP changes over different spans of time. In particular, factor supply and productivity typically change only gradually and hence are important for explaining long-run changes in GDP, but are not usually helpful in explaining short-run changes in GDP. In contrast, the factor utilization rate is quite volatile over short periods of time but returns to its normal level over several years. Thus, changes in the factor utilization rate are important for explaining short-run changes in GDP but are not of much importance for explaining long-run changes.

> ((X)) **myeconlab**
>
> **Canada and many other developed economies experienced a "productivity slowdown" in the early 1970s. And in recent years, many economists have expressed concern about Canada's slow rate of productivity growth compared to that of its major trading partners, especially the United States. For more information on Canada's recent productivity performance, and what can be done about it, look for "Understanding and Addressing Canada's Productivity Challenges" in the *Additional Topics* section of this book's MyEconLab.**
>
> w w w . m y e c o n l a b . c o m

25.3 POLICY IMPLICATIONS

Economists think differently about short-run and long-run macroeconomic relationships. When thinking about short-run fluctuations, economists focus on understanding why actual GDP deviates from potential GDP. As we have seen in previous chapters, such changes in real GDP are caused by aggregate demand and aggregate supply

Practise with Study Guide Chapter 25, Exercise 3.

shocks. When thinking about long-run changes in GDP, however, economists focus on understanding why potential GDP changes over time. As we said above, such long-run growth has its source in the growth of factor supplies and productivity. Thus, in understanding long-run growth, economists focus on what causes factor supplies and productivity to change.

When studying short-run fluctuations, economists focus on the deviations of actual output from potential output. When studying long-run changes, economists focus on changes in potential output.

Through the development of our macro model in the previous four chapters, we have a better understanding of what causes the *AD* and *AS* curves to shift, and thus a better understanding of the causes of short-run fluctuations in real GDP. Our picture of the short run will be more fully developed after we discuss monetary policy and interest rates in Chapters 27 and 28, and exchange rates and international trade in Chapter 35.

What we have not yet done, however, is to discuss in detail why potential output grows substantially over long periods of time, thereby improving average living standards from one generation to the next. In the next chapter we explore the issue of long-run economic growth, focusing on the importance of capital accumulation and technological change.

Before we do that, however, it is worth returning to a point that we raised at the beginning of this chapter—that the distinction between the short run and the long run has an important implication for the role and effectiveness of various macroeconomic policies.

We have discussed in this chapter how changes in demand may cause actual GDP to depart from potential GDP. For example, firms may feel optimistic about the future and increase their investment expenditure, thereby increasing the overall level of demand. Or the government may increase its purchases of goods and services, thus adding to demand. Or foreigners may decide to increase their demand for Canadian goods, thus adding to the overall demand for goods produced by Canadian firms. All of these changes would increase the overall level of demand in the economy and, in the short run, would lead actual GDP to rise above potential GDP. Conversely, any decrease in the demand for goods would, in the short run, cause actual GDP to fall below potential GDP.

In the long run, however, the economy has an adjustment process that tends to return the factor utilization rate to its "normal" level. As we saw in Chapter 24, when actual GDP is above potential GDP, there is an excess demand for factors. This causes factor prices to rise and thereby eliminates the excess demand, bringing actual GDP back to potential. Conversely, when actual GDP is less than potential GDP, there is an excess supply of factors. This tends to cause factor prices to fall and to eliminate the excess supply (though perhaps slowly), thereby bringing actual GDP back to potential.

This adjustment process that brings the economy back to the level of potential output in the long run implies a stark result regarding the effects of macroeconomic policy:

Fiscal and monetary policies affect the short-run level of GDP because they alter the level of demand, and thus the position of the *AD* curve. But unless they are able to affect the level of *potential* output, Y^*, they will have no long-run effect on GDP.

Looking Ahead

The discussion in this chapter has focused on one topic—the difference between the short run and the long run in macroeconomics. We have shown that short-run movements in GDP are mostly accounted for by changes in the factor utilization rate. For example, as economic events cause the *AD* or *AS* curves to shift, output will deviate from Y^* and the factor utilization rate will change. In contrast, long-run changes in GDP are mostly accounted for by changes in factor supplies and productivity which lead to increases in Y^*. This difference forces economists to think differently about macroeconomic relationships that exist over a few months as compared to those that exist over several years.

In the previous four chapters we examined in detail the behaviour of the economy in the short run, and the adjustment process that brings the economy from a short-run equilibrium to a long-run equilibrium. We are now ready to take the next step and examine the causes of long-run economic growth.

S U M M A R Y

25.1 **TWO EXAMPLES**

- Macroeconomic variables behave differently over the short run than over the long run. One example: a monetary policy designed to reduce inflation and nominal interest rates in the long run requires an *increase* in interest rates in the short run. Another example: An increase in households' or firms' saving rates will reduce

the level of output in the short run, but it will increase output in the long run.

- In the short run, there is some adjustment of output and employment, but little adjustment of wages and prices. In the long run, full adjustment of wages and prices is assumed to take place.

25.2 **ACCOUNTING FOR CHANGES IN GDP**

- All changes in GDP can be accounted for by changes in one or more of the following three variables:

    1. supply of factors
    2. factor utilization rates
    3. factor productivity

- Long-run changes in GDP are caused mostly by changes in factor supplies and factor productivity; the utilization rate of factors does not change significantly over the long run.
- Short-run changes in GDP are caused mostly by changes in the factor utilization rate; factor supplies and productivity have relatively minor short-run fluctuations.

25.3 **POLICY IMPLICATIONS**

- When studying short-run fluctuations, economists focus on changes in the output gap and tend to ignore changes in potential output. When studying long-run fluctuations, economists focus on changes in potential output and ignore changes in the output gap.

- Fiscal and monetary policies affect GDP in the short run because they affect the level of demand, and thus the position of the *AD* curve. Unless they are able to affect the level of *potential* output, they will have no long-run effect on GDP.

KEY CONCEPTS

Short-run fluctuations
Long-run trends

Changes in the output gap versus
  changes in potential output
Accounting for changes in GDP

Factor supplies
Factor utilization rates
Productivity

STUDY EXERCISES

1. Fill in the blanks to make the following statements correct.

   a. Short-run changes in real GDP are caused by _____ and _____ shocks, with little or no change in _____. In the short run, _____ prices and the level of _____ are assumed to be constant.

   b. Long-run trends in GDP involve changes in _____ output. Short-run fluctuations in GDP involve changes in the _____ with little or no change in _____.

   c. Any change in GDP is caused by changes in at least one of the following three component parts: _____, _____, and _____.

   d. Long-run changes in GDP are caused mainly by changes in _____ and _____. Short-run changes in GDP are caused mainly by changes in _____.

   e. The economy's adjustment process returns the _____ rate to its "normal" level in the long run.

   f. Fiscal and monetary policies alter the level of output in the short run by causing the _____ curve to shift. There will be a long-run effect on output only if _____ changes.

2. (myeconlab) Consider the data below for a hypothetical country.

Year	Real GDP (billions of constant dollars)	Labour Force (millions of people)	Employment (millions of people)
1960	100	1.5	1.4
1965	130	1.6	1.45
1970	175	1.75	1.55
1975	250	1.95	1.65
1980	230	2.15	1.85
1985	265	2.40	2.0
1990	300	2.70	2.2
1995	340	3.0	2.8
2000	375	3.3	3.05
2005	410	3.6	3.4

   a. Using the definitions in the chapter, compute the employment rate and the level of productivity (measured as GDP per worker) for each year.

   b. For each 5-year period, compute the percentage change in the labour force, the employment rate, and the level of productivity. Compute the same three things over the entire 45-year period.

   c. Compute the percentage change in real GDP over each 5-year period. Do it also for the entire 45-year period.

   d. Based on Equation 25-2, it can be shown that the percentage change in real GDP is approximately equal to the percentage change in the labour force *plus* the percentage change in the employment rate *plus* the percentage change in the level of productivity. Compare the sum of your answers from part (b) with your answers from part (c). Are they close?

   e. For each 5-year period, what fraction of the percentage change in GDP is accounted for by the change in the employment rate?

   f. Over the entire 45-year period, what fraction of the percentage change in GDP is accounted for by the change in the employment rate?

3. Go to Statistics Canada's website (www.statcan.ca) and look for data on capacity utilization rates in Canadian industries. The capacity utilization rate is the fraction of the capital stock that is utilized or employed. How has this variable changed over the past several decades? Contrast the short-run versus the long-run movements.

4. At the beginning of the chapter we discussed the short-run and long-run effects of an increase in desired saving (as applied to Japan's economy). Based on what you learned in Chapter 24 regarding the economy's adjustment process, use the *AD/AS* model to:

   a. Show the short-run effects of an increase in desired saving (assuming that the economy is initially in a long-run equilibrium with $Y = Y^*$).

   b. Describe the adjustment process that brings the economy to its new long-run equilibrium.

   c. Compare the initial and the new long-run equilibrium. What is the long-run effect of the increase in desired saving?

DISCUSSION QUESTIONS

1. Figure 25-1 shows the path of actual GDP as well as the path of potential GDP. The chapter mentioned that the economy has an adjustment mechanism that brings actual GDP back to potential.

   a. Describe this adjustment process, and how it relates to the concept of market-clearing.

   b. If, following the implementation of some policy, actual GDP eventually returns to potential GDP, does this mean that policy can have no long-run effect on GDP?

Long-Run Economic Growth

The Centre for the Study of Living Standards is an Ottawa-based research institute that studies the determinants of economic growth. Visit its website at **www.csls.ca**.

Most economists agree that economic growth is the single most powerful engine for generating long-term increases in material living standards. What happens to our living standards over time depends largely on the growth in real GDP in relation to the growth in population—that is, it depends on the growth of real per capita GDP. Growth in real per capita GDP does not necessarily make *everybody* in Canada better off. But it does mean that the *average* standard of living is higher.

What determines the long-run growth rate of per capita GDP in Canada? Is this something that is beyond our control, or are there some government policies that can stimulate economic growth? If there are, what are the costs of such policies, and are the benefits worth the costs?

In this chapter we examine this important issue of economic growth, beginning with some basic concepts and then moving on to explore the costs and benefits of growth. In the remainder of the chapter we consider various theories of economic growth, an area in which much new research is being done. Finally, we examine the idea that there may be *limits to growth* imposed by pollution and resource exhaustion.

26.1 THE NATURE OF ECONOMIC GROWTH

Figure 26-1 shows the paths of three variables in the Canadian economy since 1960, each of which relates to long-run economic growth. Each variable is expressed as an index number, which takes a value of 100 in 1960. The first is real GDP, which shows an overall growth from 1960 to 2005 of 407 percent, an average annual growth rate of 3.7 percent. Though real GDP is an accepted measure of the amount of annual economic activity, it is not a good measure of average material living standards because it does not take into account the growth in the population—more income is not necessarily better if more people have to share it. The second variable shown is the index of real *per capita* GDP. It shows an overall growth of 182 percent between 1960 and 2005, an annual average growth rate of 2.3 percent.

As we will see in this chapter, one of the most important reasons that both GDP and per capita GDP increase over many years is growth in *productivity*. The third variable provides one measure of productivity; it is an index of real GDP *per employed worker*. Its overall growth for 1960 to 2005 is 87 percent, an average annual growth rate of 1.4 percent. Therefore, the average Canadian worker produced 87 percent more in 2005 than in 1960.

The three variables in Figure 26-1 show different aspects of **economic growth**, a term that economists usually reserve for describing sustained or long-run increases in real GDP. This chapter will, at various points, discuss each of these three aspects of economic growth—real GDP, real per capita GDP, and productivity.

economic growth Sustained, long-run increases in the level of real GDP.

The average annual growth rates shown in Figure 26-1 may seem small, especially for the measure of productivity. It is important to realize, however, that these growth rates are sustained for periods of many years, and they can therefore have a profound influence on living standards from one generation to the next. Table 26-1 illustrates the cumulative effect of what appear to be very small differences in growth rates. Notice that if one country grows faster than another, the gap in their respective living standards will widen progressively. If, for example, Canada and France start from the same level of income but Canada grows at 3 percent per year while France grows at 2 percent per year, Canada's income will be twice France's in 72 years. **[31]** You may not think that it matters much whether the economy grows at 2 percent or 3 percent per year, but your children and grandchildren certainly will.

FIGURE 26-1   Three Aspects of Economic Growth

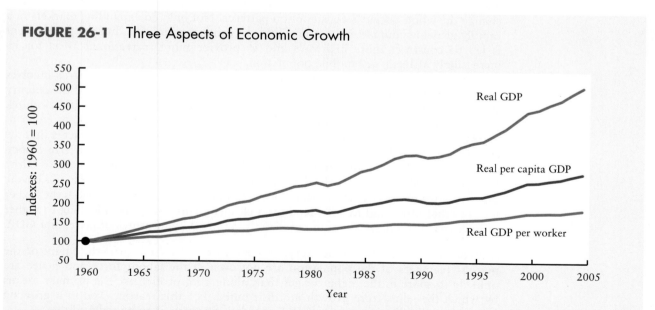

Real GDP, real per capita GDP, and productivity have all grown substantially over the past half-century. Each variable shown is an index number with 1960 = 100.

(*Source:* All data are from Statistics Canada, CANSIM database. Real GDP: Series V3862685. Employment: Series V2091072. Population: Series V2062809. Reprinted with permission of Statistics Canada.)

TABLE 26-1 The Cumulative Effect of Economic Growth

Year	Annual Growth Rate 1%	2%	3%	5%	7%
0	100	100	100	100	100
10	111	122	135	165	201
30	135	182	246	448	817
50	165	272	448	1 218	3 312
70	201	406	817	3 312	13 429
100	272	739	2 009	14 841	109 660

Small differences in income growth rates make enormous differences in levels of income over a few decades. Let income be 100 in year 0. At a growth rate of 3 percent per year, it will be 135 in 10 years, 448 after 50 years, and over 2000 in a century. Notice the difference between 2 percent and 3 percent growth—even small differences in growth rates make big differences in future income levels.

We now examine in more detail the benefits and costs of economic growth.

Benefits of Economic Growth

The benefits of economic growth—in particular, increases in income—may appear obvious. It certainly appears that way to the pro-growth author of the open letter in *Applying Economic Concepts 26-1*. But it is important to distinguish between the increases in average living standards that economic growth brings more or less automatically, and the reduction in poverty that economic growth makes possible but may still require active policy to make a reality.

Rising Average Material Living Standards
Economic growth is a powerful means of improving average material living standards. A family that is earning $35 000 today can expect an income of about $42 600 within 10 years (in constant dollars) if it experiences a 2 percent annual growth rate in its income. If it has a 4 percent growth rate, its income in 10 years will be $51 800.

A family often finds that an increase in its income can lead to changes in the pattern of its consumption—extra money buys important amenities of life and also allows more saving for the future. Similarly, economic growth that raises average income may change the whole society's consumption patterns. Not only do expanding markets in a rapidly growing country make it profitable to produce more cars, but the government is led to construct more highways and to provide more recreational areas for its increasingly affluent and mobile population.

Another example of how economic growth can improve living standards involves environmental protection. In developing countries, most of the resources of the country are devoted to providing basic requirements of life such as food, shelter, and clothing. These countries typically do not have the "luxury" of being concerned about environmental degradation. Some may consider this a short-sighted view, but the fact is that the concerns associated with hunger *today* are much more urgent than the concerns associated with *future* environmental problems. In contrast, richer countries are wealthy enough that they can easily afford to provide the basic requirements of life *and* devote significant resources to environmental protection. Economic growth provides the higher incomes that often lead to a demand for a cleaner environment, thus leading to higher average living standards that are not directly captured by measures of per capita GDP.

Alleviation of Poverty
Not everyone benefits equally from growth. Many of the poorest members of the population are not even in the labour force and hence are unlikely to share in the higher wages that, along with profits, are the primary means by which the gains from growth are distributed. For this reason, even in a growing economy, redistribution policies will be needed if poverty is to be reduced.

A rapid growth rate makes the alleviation of poverty easier politically. If existing income is to be redistributed, someone's standard of living will actually have to be lowered. However, when there is economic growth and when the *increment* in income is redistributed (through active government policy), it is possible to reduce income

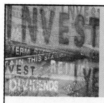

APPLYING ECONOMIC CONCEPTS 26-1

An Open Letter from a Supporter of the "Growth Is Good" School

Dear Ordinary Citizen:

You live in the world's first civilization that is devoted principally to satisfying *your* needs rather than those of a privileged minority. Past civilizations have always been based on leisure and high consumption for a tiny upper class, a reasonable living standard for a small middle class, and hard work with little more than subsistence consumption for the great mass of people.

The continuing Industrial Revolution that began two centuries ago is based on mass-produced goods for you, the ordinary citizen. It ushered in a period of sustained economic growth that has dramatically raised consumption standards of ordinary citizens. Consider a few examples: travel, live and recorded music, art, good food, universal literacy, inexpensive books, and a genuine chance to be educated. In addition, modern medical practices have eliminated a host of health scourges that killed and maimed vast numbers of your predecessors, resulting in a great increase in your life expectancy over that of your grandparents and great-grandparents. Finally, there is leisure to provide time and energy to enjoy the thousands of goods and services of the modern developed economy.

Would any ordinary family seriously prefer to go back to the world of 150 or 500 years ago in its same *relative* social and economic position? Surely the answer is no. However, for those with incomes in the top 1 or 2 percent of the income distribution, economic growth has destroyed much of their privileged consumption position. They must now vie with the masses when they visit the world's beauty spots and be annoyed, while lounging on the terrace of a palatial mansion, by the

sound of charter flights carrying ordinary people to inexpensive holidays in faraway places. Many of the rich complain bitterly about the loss of exclusive rights to luxury consumption, and it is not surprising that they find their intellectual apologists.

Whether they know it or not, the anti-growth economists are not the social revolutionaries they think they are. They say that growth has produced pollution and wasteful consumption of all kinds of frivolous products that add nothing to human happiness. However, the democratic solution to pollution is not to go back to the time when so few people consumed luxuries that pollution was trivial but rather to learn to control the pollution that mass consumption tends to create.

It is only through further growth that the average citizen will be able to enjoy consumption standards (of travel, culture, medical and health care, and so on) now available only to people in the top 25 percent of the income distribution—which includes the intellectuals who earn large royalties from the books they write in which they denounce growth. If you think that extra income confers little real benefit, just ask those in the top 25 percent to trade incomes with average citizens.

Ordinary citizens, do not be deceived by disguised elitist doctrines. Remember that the very rich and the elite have much to gain by stopping growth and even more by rolling it back, but you have everything to gain by letting it go forward.

Onward!

A. N. Optimist

inequalities without actually having to lower anyone's income. It is much easier for a rapidly growing economy to be generous toward its less fortunate citizens—or neighbours—than it is for a static economy.

Costs of Economic Growth

Applying Economic Concepts 26-2 contains an open letter from an anti-growth advocate who argues that we are caught up in a never-ending search for "more," and as a result are losing sight of the real values that guided our ancestors. You may or may not accept this particular line of argument, but it is important to recognize that economic growth does have some real costs. Let's see what they are.

Practise with Study Guide Chapter 26, Exercise 3.

The Opportunity Cost of Economic Growth In a world of scarcity, almost nothing is free. Growth requires heavy investment of resources in capital goods, as well as in activities such as education. Often these investments yield no immediate return in terms of goods and services for consumption; thus, they imply that sacrifices are being made by the current generation of consumers.

Economic growth, which promises more goods tomorrow, is achieved by consuming fewer goods today. For the economy as a whole, this sacrifice of current consumption is the primary cost of growth.

An example will suggest the importance of this cost. Suppose a hypothetical economy is operating at potential output and is experiencing growth in real GDP at the rate of 2 percent per year. Its citizens consume 85 percent of the GDP and invest 15 percent. But suppose that if they immediately decrease their consumption to 77 percent of GDP (and increase investment to 23 percent), they will produce more capital and thus shift at once to a 3 percent growth rate. The new growth rate can be maintained as long as they keep saving and investing 23 percent of real GDP. Should they do it?

Figure 26-2 illustrates the choice in terms of time paths of consumption. With the assumed figures, it takes 10 years for the actual amount of consumption to catch up to what it would have been had no reallocation been made. In the intervening 10 years, a good deal of consumption is lost, and the cumulative losses in consumption must be made up before society can really be said to have broken even. It takes an *additional* nine years before total consumption over the whole period is as large as it would have been if the economy had remained on the 2 percent path. [32] Over a longer period, however, the payoff from the growth policy becomes enormous. After thirty years, real GDP in the more rapidly growing economy is 21 percent higher than in the slower-growing economy. After fifty years, it is 48 percent higher.

FIGURE 26-2   The Opportunity Cost of Economic Growth

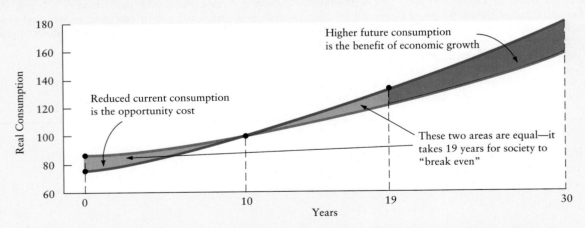

Transferring resources from consumption to investment lowers current consumption but raises future consumption. The example assumes that GDP in year 0 is 100 and that growth of 2 percent per year is possible when consumption equals 85 percent of GDP. The consumption path in this case is shown by the red line, starting at 85 and growing by 2 percent per year. It is further assumed that to achieve a 3 percent growth rate, consumption must fall to 77 percent of GDP. A shift from the red path to the blue path in year 0 decreases consumption for 10 years but increases it thereafter. By year 19 the gains in consumption have made up for the losses from the first 10 years. After 30 years, consumption is 21 percent higher than it would be on the original (red) path.

APPLYING ECONOMIC CONCEPTS 26-2

An Open Letter from a Supporter of the "Growth Is Bad" School

Dear Ordinary Citizen:

You live in a world that is being despoiled by a mindless search for ever-higher levels of material consumption at the cost of all other values. Once upon a time, men and women knew how to enjoy creative work and to derive satisfaction from simple activities. Today, the ordinary worker is a mindless cog in an assembly line that turns out more and more goods that the advertisers must work overtime to persuade the worker to consume.

Statisticians count the increasing flow of material output as a triumph of modern civilization. You wake to the hum of your air conditioner, watch the shopping channel while you dress for work, brew your chemically treated decaffeinated coffee, and eat your bread baked from superrefined flour; you climb into your car to sit in vast traffic jams on exhaust-polluted highways.

Television commercials tell you that by consuming more, you are happier, but happiness lies not in increasing consumption but in increasing the ratio of *satisfaction of wants* to *total wants*. Because the more you consume, the more the advertisers persuade you that you want to consume, you are almost certainly less happy than the average citizen in a small town in 1900, whom we can visualize sitting on the family porch, sipping lemonade, and enjoying the antics of the children as they jump rope using pieces of old clothesline.

Today, the landscape is dotted with endless factories that produce the plastic trivia of modern society. They drown you in a cloud of noise, air, and water pollution. The countryside is despoiled by strip mines, petroleum refineries, acid rain, and polluting power plants, producing energy that is devoured insatiably by modern factories and motor vehicles. And global warming, caused by our excessive consumption of fossil fuels, threatens to raise the sea level by so much over the next 50 years that anarchy will prevail as hundreds of millions of people are dispossessed of their coastal dwellings.

Now is the time to stop this madness. We must end this crazy rush to produce more and more output, reduce pollution, reverse global warming, and seek justice through a more equitable distribution of existing total income.

Many years ago, Thomas Malthus taught us that if we do not limit population voluntarily, nature will do it for us in a cruel and savage manner. Today, the same is true of output: If we do not halt its growth voluntarily, the halt will be imposed on us by a disastrous increase in pollution and a rapid exhaustion of natural resources.

Citizens, awake! Shake off the worship of growth, learn to enjoy the bounty that is yours already, and reject the endless, self-defeating search for increased happiness through ever-increasing consumption.

Upward!

I. Realvalues

If economic growth just means more of the truly "unnecessary" things in life, is it really worthwhile?

Social Costs of Economic Growth A growing economy is also a changing economy. Part of growth is accounted for by existing firms expanding and producing more output, hiring more workers, and using more equipment and intermediate goods. But another aspect of growth is that existing firms are overtaken and made obsolete by new firms, old products are made obsolete by new products, and existing skills are made obsolete by new skills.

The process of economic growth renders some machines obsolete and also leaves the skills of some workers partly obsolete.

No matter how well-trained workers are at age 25, in another 25 years many will find that their skills are at least partly obsolete. A high growth rate usually requires rapid adjustments in the labour force, which can cause much upset and misery to some of the people affected by it.

It is often argued that costs of this kind are a small price to pay for the great benefits that growth can bring. Even if this is true in the aggregate, these personal costs are borne very unevenly. Indeed, many of the people for whom growth is most costly (in terms of lost jobs or lowered incomes) share least in the fruits that growth brings.

Sources of Economic Growth

Most discussions of economic growth are based on the following four fundamental determinants:

1. *Growth in the labour force.* This may be caused by growth in population or by increases in the fraction of the population that chooses to participate in the labour force.

2. *Growth in human capital.* **Human capital** is the term economists use to refer to the set of skills that workers have. Human capital can increase through either formal education or on-the-job training. Human capital can be thought of as the *quality* of the labour force, but due to its importance we will treat it as a separate factor of production from labour.

human capital The set of skills workers acquire through formal education and on-the-job training.

3. *Growth in physical capital.* The stock of physical capital (such as factories, machines, and transportation and communications facilities) increases only through the process of investment. We include here improvements in the *quality* of the physical capital.

4. *Technological improvement.* This may be brought about by innovation that introduces new products, new ways of producing existing products, and new forms of organizing economic activity.

The various theories of economic growth that we explore in the remainder of this chapter can be viewed as theories of these different sources of growth. For example, some theories emphasize the role of increases in physical capital in explaining growth; others emphasize the role of increases in human capital; still others emphasize the importance of technological improvements. But all theories of economic growth take as a starting point these four fundamental determinants of growth.

26.2 ESTABLISHED THEORIES OF ECONOMIC GROWTH

In this section we discuss some of the theories of economic growth that have been used by economists for many years. Despite the appearance of some quite different theories in recent years (which we will see later), these established theories remain relevant and contain important insights about the growth process. Learning these established theories provides a solid basis for examining the newer theories in the next section. We begin with a detailed study of the relationship among saving, investment, and economic growth. We then examine the precise predictions of what economists call the Neoclassical growth theory. For simplicity, we assume in the following discussion that the economy is closed—there is no trade in goods or assets with the rest of the world.

Focus on the Long Run

In previous chapters we saw how shifts in the *AD* or *AS* curves led to changes in the short-run equilibrium level of real GDP. The discussion in this chapter focuses instead on the behaviour of the economy in the long run, and thus on the growth rate of potential output. We assume that all factor-price adjustment has occurred and thus real GDP equals Y^*.

The theory of economic growth is a long-run theory. It concentrates on the growth of potential output over long periods of time, not on short-run fluctuations of output around potential.

Though we will focus on the long-run behaviour of the economy, we can still use some of the insights we developed in the short-run version of our macro model. Remember back to Chapter 21 when we were building the simplest short-run macro model. The equilibrium level of real GDP in that model was such that real GDP was equal to desired aggregate expenditure, which in turn was equal to desired consumption plus desired investment:

$$Y = C + I$$

We can rearrange this equilibrium condition (as we did in the *Additional Topic* cited in Chapter 21) to get:

$$Y - C = I$$

or

$$S = I$$

which says that, in equilibrium, desired saving equals desired investment. This is just an alternative way to think about exactly the same equilibrium.

Recall also that in Chapter 21 we took the real interest rate as given, or *exogenous*. Thus, taking the real interest rate as given in our short-run model, the condition that desired saving equals desired investment determined the equilibrium level of real GDP.

We will now extend our model in a way that helps us to consider the long-run behaviour of the economy. In particular, we will allow the interest rate to be an *endogenous* variable—that is, a variable whose value is explained within the model. As you will soon see, when the interest rate is endogenous to the model, the sources of economic growth can be studied more clearly.

Fortunately, the logic of the equilibrium condition from the simple short-run model is just as true in the long run. In the long run, with real GDP equal to Y^*, we can use the saving/investment equilibrium condition by turning it "on its head." That is, we can take the level of output as given (at Y^*) and use the condition that desired saving equals desired investment to determine the equilibrium real interest rate. This long-run perspective of our model will tell us a great deal about the relationship among saving, investment, and economic growth—and the interest rate will play an important role.

Investment, Saving, and Growth

Recall that national saving is the sum of private saving and public (government) saving. Desired private saving is the difference between disposable income and desired consumption. With real GDP equal to Y^* in the long run, desired private saving is equal to:

$$Private\ saving = Y^* - T - C$$

Public saving is equal to the combined budget surpluses of the federal, provincial, and municipal governments:

$$Public\ saving = T - G$$

National saving is therefore equal to:

$$National\ saving = NS = Y^* - T - C + (T - G)$$

$$\Rightarrow NS = Y^* - C - G$$

In other words, for a given level of output in the long run, an increase in household consumption or government purchases must imply a reduction in national saving.[1]

Figure 26-3 shows the supply of national saving as a function of the real interest rate. We label the horizontal axis "Loanable Funds," which is measured in dollars. The real interest rate is shown on the vertical axis. The national saving (NS) curve is upward sloping because, as we first saw in Chapter 21, an increase in the interest rate leads households to reduce their current consumption, especially on big-ticket items and durable goods such as cars, furniture, and appliances that are often purchased on credit. Note also that the NS curve is quite steep, in keeping with empirical evidence suggesting that household consumption responds only modestly to changes in the real interest rate.

Figure 26-3 also shows a downward sloping investment demand curve, I. As we first saw in Chapter 21, all components of desired investment (plant and equipment, inventories, and residential investment) are negatively related to the real interest rate because, whether the investment is financed by borrowing or by using the firm's retained earnings, the real interest rate reflects the opportunity cost of using these funds.

Our long-run model of saving and investment is now complete. In the short-run model in Chapter 21, the economy is in equilibrium when desired saving

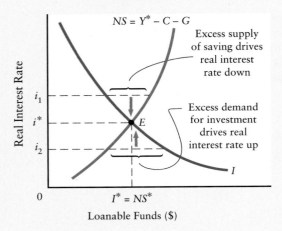

FIGURE 26-3 The Long-Run Connection Between Saving and Investment

In the long run, the condition that desired national saving equals desired investment determines the equilibrium real interest rate. Investment demand by firms is negatively related to the real interest rate. The supply of national (private plus public) saving is positively related to the real interest rate, since increases in the interest rate lead to a decline in desired consumption (C). Notice that real GDP in this figure is held constant at Y^* since the analysis applies to the long run.

At point E the market for loanable funds clears and the real interest rate is i^*. At this real interest rate, the amount of investment is I^*, which equals the amount of national saving, NS^*.

---

1 It appears in our NS equation that changes in taxes have no effect on the level of national saving, but this is misleading. Changes in T may affect national saving through an *indirect* effect on C. For example, as we saw at the end of Chapter 24, a reduction in taxes is likely to lead to an increase in consumption spending and therefore to a reduction in national saving (for given values of Y^* and G).

equals desired investment. We have modified that setting in only two ways. First, we have added government. Second, and more important, since we are examining the economy in the long run, we are holding real GDP constant at Y^* and letting the equilibrium condition determine the real interest rate in the market for loanable funds.

In the long-run version of our macro model, with real GDP equal to Y^*, the equilibrium interest rate is determined where desired national saving equals desired investment.

In Figure 26-3, equilibrium in the market for loanable funds occurs at interest rate i^* where $NS = I$. Imagine what would happen if the real interest rate were above i^* at i_1. At this high interest rate, the amount of desired saving exceeds the amount of desired investment, and this excess supply of loanable funds pushes down the price of credit—the real interest rate. Conversely, if the interest rate is below i^* at i_2, the quantity of desired investment exceeds the quantity of desired saving, and this excess demand for loanable funds pushes up the real interest rate. Only at point E is the economy in equilibrium, with the real interest rate equal to i^* and desired investment equal to desired saving.

Let's now see how changes in the supply of saving or investment demand lead to changes in the real interest rate, and what these changes imply for the economy's long-run economic growth.

An Increase in the Supply of National Saving
Suppose the supply of national saving increases, so that the NS curve shifts to the right, as shown in part (i) of Figure 26-4. This increase in the supply of national saving could happen either because household consumption (C) falls or because government purchases (G) fall. A decline in either C or G means that national saving rises *at any real interest rate* and so the NS curve shifts to the right.

The increase in the supply of national saving leads to an excess supply of loanable funds and thus to a decline in the real interest rate. As the interest rate falls, firms decide to undertake more investment projects and the economy moves from the initial equilibrium E_0 to the new equilibrium E_1. At the new equilibrium, more of the economy's resources are devoted to investment than before, and thus the country's capital stock is rising at a faster rate. The higher rate of investment therefore leads to a higher future growth rate of potential output.

In the long run, an increase in the supply of national saving reduces the real interest rate and encourages more investment. The higher rate of investment leads to a higher future growth rate of potential output.

An Increase in Investment Demand
Now suppose firms' demand for investment increases so that the I curve shifts to the right, as shown in part (ii) of Figure 26-4. The increase in desired investment might be caused by technological improvements that increase the productivity of investment goods or by a government tax incentive aimed at encouraging investment. Whatever its cause, the increase in investment demand creates an excess demand for loanable funds and therefore leads to a rise in the real interest rate. The rise in the interest rate encourages households to reduce their current consumption and increase their desired saving. At the new equilibrium, E_1, both the real interest rate and the amount of investment are higher than at the initial equilibrium. The greater investment means faster growth in the economy's capital stock and therefore a higher future rate of growth of potential output.

In the long run, an increase in the demand for investment pushes up the real interest rate and encourages more saving by households. The higher rate of saving (and investment) leads to a higher future growth rate of potential output.

FIGURE 26-4   Increases in Investment Demand and the Supply of National Saving

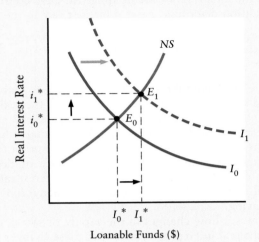

(i) Increase in the supply of saving

(ii) Increase in the demand for investment

Changes in the supply of national saving or the demand for investment will change the equilibrium real interest rate and the rate of growth of potential output. In part (i), the increase in the supply of national saving pushes down the real interest rate and encourages more investment. In part (ii), the increase in the demand for investment pushes up the real interest rate and encourages more saving. In both cases, there is an increase in the equilibrium amount of investment (and saving) and the economy moves from E_0 to E_1; this higher rate of capital accumulation leads to an increase in the economy's long-run rate of growth.

Summary   In our macro model, which we have now extended to enable us to determine the real interest rate in long-run equilibrium, there is a close relationship among saving, investment, and the rate of economic growth. We can see this relationship most clearly when studying the market for loanable funds. Let's summarize our results.

1. In long-run equilibrium, with $Y = Y^*$, the condition that desired national saving equals desired investment determines the equilibrium interest rate in the market for loanable funds. This equilibrium also determines the flows of investment and saving.

2. An increase in the supply of national saving will lead to a fall in the real interest rate and thus to an increase in the amount of investment. This is a shift of the NS curve and a movement along the I curve.

3. An increase in the demand for investment will lead to a rise in the real interest rate and thus to an increase in the amount of national saving. This is a shift of the I curve and a movement along the NS curve.

4. A shift in either the NS or the I curve will lead to a change in the equilibrium real interest rate and to a change in the amount of the economy's resources devoted to investment. An increase in the equilibrium amount of investment implies a greater growth rate of the capital stock and thus a higher future growth rate of potential output.

Investment and Growth in Industrialized Countries We said above that countries with high rates of investment are also countries with high rates of real GDP growth. To provide evidence in support of this claim, Figure 26-5 shows data from the most industrialized countries between 1970 and 1990. Each point in the figure corresponds to a single country and shows that country's annual average investment rate (as a percentage of GDP) plotted against the annual average growth rate in real per capita GDP. What is clear from the figure is a positive relationship between investment rates and growth rates, exactly as suggested by our discussion above.

myeconlab

We have been discussing the relationship between investment and saving in a model of a *closed* economy. In the reality of today's globalized financial markets, however, billions of dollars of financial capital flow across international boundaries every day. For more details about how our model can be modified for an open economy, look for "Investment and Saving in Globalized Financial Markets" in the *Additional Topics* section of this book's MyEconLab.

w w w . m y e c o n l a b . c o m

FIGURE 26-5 Cross-Country Investment and Growth Rates

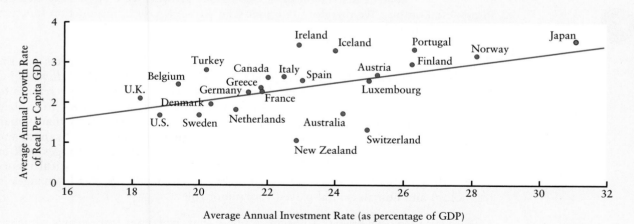

There is a positive relationship between a country's investment rate (as a percentage of GDP) and its growth rate of real per capita GDP. For each of the countries, the annual averages for investment rates and per capita GDP growth rates are computed between 1970 and 1990. Each point represents the average values of these variables for a single country over this 20-year period. The line is the "line of best fit" between the growth rates and the investment rates. Countries with high investment rates tend to be countries with high rates of economic growth.

(*Source:* © International Monetary Fund, www.imf.org. Reprinted with permission.)

Neoclassical Growth Theory

aggregate production function The relationship between the total amount of each factor of production employed in the nation and the nation's total GDP.

Recall the four fundamental sources of economic growth that we discussed at the beginning of this section. Much of what is referred to as *Neoclassical growth theory* is based on the idea that these four forces of economic growth can be connected by what is called the **aggregate production function**. This is an expression for the relationship between the total amounts of labour (L) and physical capital (K) employed, the quality of labour's human capital (H), the state of technology (T), and the nation's total level of output (GDP). The aggregate production function can be expressed as:

$$GDP = F_T (L, K, H)$$

It is an *aggregate* production function because it relates the economy's *total* output to the *total* amount of the factors that are used to produce that output.[2] (Those who have studied microeconomics will recall that a micro production function, such as is discussed in Chapters 7 and 8, relates the output of *one firm* to the factors of production employed by *that firm*.)

The production function above—indicated by F_T—tells us how much GDP will be produced for given amounts of labour and physical capital employed, given levels of human capital and a given state of technology. Using the notation F_T is a simple way of indicating that the function relating L, K, and H to GDP depends on the state of technology. For a given state of technology (T), changes in either L, K, or H will lead to changes in GDP. Similarly, for given values of L, K, and H, changes in T will lead to changes in GDP. **[33]**

Hong Kong is an example of an economy that has had very high rates of investment and also very high rates of real GDP growth.

When discussing long-run economic growth, we focus on the changes in potential output. We therefore interpret GDP in the aggregate production function as potential output.

Practise with Study Guide Chapter 26, Exercise 2.

Properties of the Aggregate Production Function The key aspects of the Neoclassical theory are that the aggregate production function displays *diminishing marginal returns* when either factor is increased on its own and *constant returns to scale* when all factors are increased together (and in the same proportion). To explain the meaning of these concepts more clearly, we will assume for simplicity that human capital and physical capital can be combined into a single variable called capital and that technology is held constant; we therefore focus on the effects of changes in K or L. This is an appropriate simplification when dealing with the Neoclassical theory since early versions of the theory focused on the importance of K and L; changes in technology and human capital played very minor roles.

law of diminishing marginal returns The hypothesis that if increasing quantities of a variable factor are applied to a given quantity of fixed factors, the marginal product of the variable factor will eventually decrease.

1. Diminishing Marginal Returns. To begin, suppose that the labour force grows while the stock of capital remains constant. More and more people go to work using a fixed quantity of capital. The amount that each new worker adds to total output is called labour's *marginal product*. The operation of the **law of diminishing marginal returns** tells us that the employment of additional workers (or hours of work) will eventually add less to total output than the previous worker. In other words, each additional worker will sooner or later produce a diminishing marginal product. A simple pro-

---

2 Natural resources (including land, forests, mineral deposits, etc.) are also important inputs to the production process. We leave them out of this discussion only for simplicity.

duction function is shown in Figure 26-6 and the law of diminishing marginal returns is illustrated.

The law of diminishing returns applies to any factor that is varied while the other factors are held constant. Hence, successive amounts of capital added to a fixed supply of labour will also eventually add less and less to GDP.

According to the law of diminishing marginal returns, whenever equal increases of one factor of production are combined with a fixed amount of another factor, the increment to total production will eventually decline.

FIGURE 26-6   The Aggregate Production Function and Diminishing Marginal Returns

Units of Labour (1)	Units of Output (GDP) (2)	Average Product of Labour (GDP/L) (3)	Marginal Product of Labour (ΔGDP/ΔL) (4)
1	12.0	12.0	
2	17.0	8.5	5.0
3	20.8	6.9	3.8
4	24.0	6.0	3.2
5	26.8	5.4	2.8
6	29.4	4.9	2.6
7	31.9	4.6	2.5
8	34.0	4.2	2.1
9	36.0	4.0	2.0
10	37.9	3.8	1.9

(i) Total output

(ii) Marginal and average product of labour

With one input held constant, the other input has a declining average and marginal product. We have assumed a hypothetical aggregate production function given by: GDP = $4\sqrt{KL}$; we have also assumed that K is constant and equal to 9. Column 2 shows total output as more of the variable factor, labour, is used with a fixed amount of capital. Total output is plotted in part (i) of the figure. Both the average product of labour and the marginal product of labour decline continuously. They are plotted in part (ii) of the figure.

constant returns to scale A situation in which output increases in proportion to the change in all inputs as the scale of production is increased.

Practise with Study Guide Chapter 26, Extension Exercise E1.

2. Constant Returns to Scale. The other main property of the Neoclassical aggregate production function is that it displays **constant returns to scale.** Remember that we are assuming for simplicity that labour and capital are the only two inputs. In that setting, the amounts of labour and capital are both changed in equal proportion; total output will also change by that proportion. For example, if L and K both increase by 10 percent, then GDP will also increase by 10 percent. [34]

Economic Growth in the Neoclassical Model   Now that we understand the properties of the aggregate production function, we can examine the predictions of the Neoclassical growth theory. Recall the four fundamental sources of growth:

1. Growth in labour force

2. Growth in human capital

3. Growth in physical capital

4. Technological improvement

What does the Neoclassical theory predict will happen when each of these elements changes? In this section, we focus on the effects of labour-force growth and the accumulation of physical and human capital, holding constant the level of technology. In the next section, we focus on technological change.

1. Labour-Force Growth. Over the long term, we can associate labour-force growth with population growth (although in the short term, the labour force can grow if participation rates rise even though the population remains constant). As more labour is used, more output will be produced. For a given stock of capital, however, the law of diminishing marginal returns tells us that sooner or later, each additional unit of labour employed will cause smaller and smaller additions to GDP. Once both the marginal product and average product of labour are falling (with each additional increment to labour), we get an interesting result. Although economic growth continues in the sense that total output is growing, material living standards are actually *falling* because average GDP *per person* is falling. If we are interested in growth in living standards, we are concerned with increasing real GDP per person.

In the Neoclassical growth model with diminishing marginal returns, increases in population (with a fixed stock of capital) lead to increases in GDP but an eventual decline in material living standards.

2. Physical and Human Capital Accumulation. Consider the accumulation of both physical and human capital. Growth in physical capital occurs whenever there is positive (net) investment in the economy. For example, if Canadian firms produce $100 billion of capital goods this year, and only $20 billion is for the replacement of old, worn-out equipment, then Canada's capital stock increases by $80 billion.

How does human capital accumulate? Human capital has several aspects. One involves improvements in the health and longevity of the population. Of course, these are desired as ends in themselves, but they also have consequences for both the size and the productivity of the labour force. There is no doubt that improvements in the health of workers have increased productivity per worker-hour by cutting down on illness, accidents, and absenteeism. A second aspect of human capital concerns technical training—from learning to operate a machine to learning how to be a scientist. This training depends on the current state of knowledge, and advances in knowledge allow us not only to build more productive physical capital but also to create more effective human capital. Also, the longer a person has been educated, the more adaptable and, hence, the more productive in the long run that person is in the face of new and changing challenges.

The accumulation of capital—either physical or human—affects GDP in a manner similar to population growth. The law of diminishing marginal returns implies that, eventually, each successive unit of capital will add less to total output than each previous unit of capital.

There is, however, a major contrast with the case of labour-force growth because it is output *per person* that determines living standards, not output per unit of capital. Thus, for a constant population, increases in the stock of physical or human capital *do* lead to increases in living standards because output *per person* increases. However, because the increases in capital are subject to diminishing marginal returns, successive additions to the economy's capital stock bring smaller and smaller increases in per capita output.

Increases in the amount and quality of physical capital lead to improvements in the productivity of labour. These productivity improvements lie at the heart of rising material living standards, as measured by real per capita GDP.

In the Neoclassical model, capital accumulation leads to improvements in living standards, but because of the law of diminishing marginal returns, these improvements become smaller with each additional increment of capital.

3. Balanced Growth with Constant Technology. Now consider what happens if labour and capital (both human and physical capital) grow at the same rate. This is what economists call "balanced" growth. In this case, the Neoclassical assumption of constant returns to scale means that GDP grows in proportion to the increases in inputs. For example, if capital and labour both increase by 2 percent per year, then GDP also increases by 2 percent per year. As a result, per capita output (GDP/L) remains constant. Thus, balanced growth in labour and capital leads to growth in total GDP but unchanged per capita GDP.

This balanced growth is not, however, the kind of growth that concerns people interested in explaining rising living standards. Since increases in living standards are determined largely by increases in *per capita* output, it is clear that balanced growth is unable to explain *rising* living standards.

If capital and labour grow at the same rate, GDP will increase. But in the Neoclassical growth model with constant returns to scale, such balanced growth will not lead to increases in per capita output and therefore will not generate improvements in living standards.

The Neoclassical growth theory predicts that growth in the labour force leads to declining per capita income, and capital accumulation leads to ever-diminishing growth rates of per capita income. Even increases in labour and capital together cannot explain increases in per capita income. What we observe in many countries around the world, however, is sustained growth in real per capita incomes. How does the Neoclassical theory explain this observation, if not through growth in labour or capital? The answer is technological change, to which we now turn.

The Importance of Technological Change

In Neoclassical growth theory, technological change is assumed to be exogenous—that is, it is *not* explained by the theory itself. This is an important weakness of the theory, however, because it means that the theory is unable to explain perhaps the most important determinant of long-run

Practise with Study Guide Chapter 26, Exercise 4.

improvements in living standards. For now we focus on the importance of technological change itself, and on how it might be measured. In the next section we move beyond Neoclassical growth theory and see some more modern theories designed to explain the sources of technological change.

New knowledge and inventions can contribute markedly to the growth of potential output, even without capital accumulation or labour-force growth. To illustrate this point, suppose the proportion of a society's resources devoted to the production of capital goods is just sufficient to replace capital as it wears out. If the old capital is merely replaced in the same form, the capital stock will be constant, and there will be no increase in the capacity to produce. However, if there is a growth of knowledge so that as old equipment wears out it is replaced by different and more productive equipment, then productive capacity will be growing.

embodied technical change
Technical change that is intrinsic to the particular capital goods in use.

The increase in productive capacity created by installing new and better capital goods is called **embodied technical change**. This term reflects the idea that technological improvements are contained in the new capital goods. Thus, even if the *quantity* of capital may be unchanged, improvements in its *quality* lead to increases in the economy's productive capacity. Embodied technical change has been enormously important through history and continues to be important today. Consider how improvements in the quality of airplanes have revolutionized transportation over the past 50 years, or how improvements in the quality of electronics have revolutionized communications over the same period. Indeed, once you start thinking about embodied technical change, you see many examples of it around you on a daily basis.

Less obvious but nonetheless important are technical changes that are embodied in *human* capital. These are changes that result from a better-educated, more experienced labour force; better management practices and techniques; improved design, marketing, and organization of business activities; and feedback from user experience leading to product improvement.

Many innovations are embodied in either physical or human capital. These innovations cause continual changes in the techniques of production and in the nature of what is produced. Embodied technical change leads to increases in potential output even if the amounts of labour and capital are held constant.

Not all technological change is embodied in capital. Examples of *disembodied* technical change include the development of new materials and production processes; both are examples in which technological improvement allows for more output to be produced from the same capital and labour. However, such disembodied technological changes often get quickly embodied in capital as machines or skills are modified to incorporate the latest developments. Thus, distinguishing precisely between embodied and disembodied technological change is often difficult.

We have been discussing the benefits of technological change in terms of raising overall living standards. Ever since the Industrial Revolution, however, some workers have feared the effects of technological change. Technological change, after all, is often responsible for workers losing their jobs as employers replace less efficient labour with more efficient equipment. *Lessons From History 26-1* examines the relationship between technological progress and changes in employment. The main lesson we learn is that technological change over the years has created far more jobs than it has destroyed.

Can We Measure Technological Change?   Technological change is obviously important. You need only look around you at the current products and production methods that did not exist a generation ago, or even a few years ago, to realize how the advance of technology changes our lives. But *how much* does technology change?

LESSONS FROM HISTORY 26-1
Should Workers Be Afraid of Technological Change?

From time immemorial people have observed that technological change destroys particular jobs and have worried that it will destroy jobs in general. Should they worry?

Technological change *does* destroy particular jobs. When water wheels were used to automate the production of cloth in twelfth-century Europe, there were riots and protests among the workers who lost their jobs. A century ago, 50 percent of the labour force in North America and Europe was required to produce the required food. Today, less than 5 percent of the labour force is needed in the high-income countries to feed all their citizens. In other words, out of every 100 jobs that existed in 1900, 50 were in agriculture and 45 of those were destroyed by technological progress over the course of the twentieth century.

Just as technological change destroys some jobs, it also creates many new jobs. The displaced agricultural workers did not join the ranks of the permanently unemployed—although some of the older ones may have, their children did not. Instead they, and their children, took jobs in manufacturing and service industries and helped to produce the mass of new goods and services—such as automobiles, refrigerators, computers, and foreign travel—that have raised living standards over the century.

Worries that technological change will cause general unemployment have been recorded for centuries but, so far at least, there is no sign that those displaced by technological change (or their children) are being forced into the ranks of the permanently unemployed. Over all of recorded history, technological change has created more jobs than it has destroyed.

But how about today? Aren't there good reasons to be more afraid of technological change now than in the past? Modern technologies have two aspects that worry some observers. First, they tend to be *knowledge intensive*. A fairly high degree of literacy and numeracy, as well as familiarity with computers, is needed to work with many of these new technologies. Second, through the process of globalization, unskilled workers in advanced countries have come into competition with unskilled workers everywhere in the world. Both of these forces are decreasing the relative demand for unskilled workers in developed countries and may lead to falling relative wages for unskilled workers in countries like Canada. If labour markets are insufficiently flexible, this change in relative demand may also lead to some structural unemployment.

For these reasons, some people blame the high unemployment rates in Europe (and to a lesser extent, in Canada) on the new technologies. This is hard to reconcile, however, with the fact that the lowest unemployment rates in the industrialized countries are currently being recorded in the United States, the most technologically dynamic of all countries. This suggests that the cause of high European unemployment rates may be not enough technological change and too much inflexibility in labour markets rather than too much technological change.

Unfortunately, technology is not something that is easily measured and so it is very difficult to know just how important it is to the process of economic growth.

In 1957, Robert Solow, an economist at MIT who was awarded the Nobel Prize 30 years later for his research on economic growth, attempted to measure the amount of technical change in the United States. He devised a way to infer from the data (under some assumptions about the aggregate production function) how much of the observed growth in real GDP was due to the growth in labour and capital, and how much was due to technical change. His method led to the creation of what is now called the "Solow residual." The Solow residual is the amount of growth in GDP that cannot be accounted for by growth in the labour force or by growth in the capital stock. Since Solow was thinking about changes in GDP as having only three possible sources—changes in capital, changes in labour, and changes in technology—the "residual" was naturally interpreted as a measure of technical change.

Today, economists do not view the Solow residual as a precise estimate of the amount of technical change. The main reason is that much technical change is known to be embodied in new physical and human capital. Thus, capital accumulation and technological change are inherently connected. For example, imagine a firm that adds to its stock of capital by purchasing two new computers. These new computers embody the latest technology, and are more productive than the firm's existing computers. In this case, there has been an increase in the capital stock but there has also been an increase—though unobserved—in the level of technology. Solow's method would attribute all of the change in (embodied) technology to the change in the capital stock even though we know that a technological change has taken place. Thus, in the presence of embodied technical change that gets measured as increases in capital, the Solow residual is, at best, an underestimate of the true amount of technological change.

Despite these problems, Solow's method of "growth accounting" and the Solow residual are still widely used by economists in universities and government. The Solow residual often goes by another name—the rate of growth of *total factor productivity (TFP)*.

---

myeconlab

Solow's method of growth accounting is sometimes used to decompose growth rates within a country and to compare these growth rates across countries. For an interesting application of his approach that compares the sources of growth in Hong Kong and Singapore, look for "A Growth Tale of Two Cities" in the *Additional Topics* section of this book's MyEconLab.

www.myeconlab.com

26.3 NEW GROWTH THEORIES

In recent years, economists have developed new theories of economic growth that go beyond the established Neoclassical theory based on diminishing marginal returns and exogenous technical change. Economic growth is an active area of research in which there is considerable debate over whether new theories are necessary, or whether the established theories do an adequate job of explaining the process of long-term economic growth.

In this section, we give a brief discussion of two strands of this new research— models that emphasize *endogenous technological change* and models based on *increasing marginal returns*.

Endogenous Technological Change

In Neoclassical growth theory, innovation increases the amount of output producible from a given level of factor inputs. But this innovation is itself unexplained. The Neoclassical model thus views technological change as *exogenous*. It has profound effects on economic variables but it is not itself influenced by economic causes. It just happens.

Yet research by many scholars has established that technological change is responsive to such economic signals as prices and profits; in other words, it is *endogenous* to the economic system. Though much of the earliest work on this issue was done in

Europe, the most influential overall single study was by an American, Nathan Rosenberg, whose trailblazing 1982 book *Inside the Black Box: Technology and Economics* argued this case in great detail.

Technological change stems from research and development and from innovating activities that put the results of R&D into practice. These are costly and highly risky activities, undertaken largely by firms and usually in pursuit of profit. It is not surprising, therefore, that these activities respond to economic incentives. If the price of some particular input such as petroleum or skilled labour goes up, R&D and innovating activities may be directed to altering the production function to economize on these inputs. This process is not simply a substitution of less expensive inputs for more expensive ones within the confines of known technologies; rather, it is the *development of new technologies* in response to changes in relative prices.

There are several important implications of this new understanding that, to a great extent, growth is achieved through costly, risky, innovative activity that often occurs in response to economic signals.

Learning by Doing The pioneering theorist of innovation, Joseph Schumpeter (1883–1950), developed a model in which innovation flowed in one direction, from a pure discovery "upstream," to more applied R&D, then to working machines, and finally to output "downstream."

In contrast, modern research shows that innovation involves a large amount of "learning by doing" at all of its stages. (We discuss this kind of learning in more detail in Chapter 33.) What is learned downstream then modifies what must be done upstream. The best innovation-managing systems encourage such "feedback" from the more applied steps to the purer researchers and from users to designers.

This interaction is illustrated, for example, by the differences that existed for many years between the Japanese automobile manufacturers and their North American competitors in the handling of new models. North American design was traditionally centralized: Design production teams developed the overall design and then instructed their production sections and asked for bids from parts manufacturers to produce according to specified blueprints. As a result, defects in the original design were often not discovered until production was underway, causing many costly delays and rejection of parts already supplied. In contrast, Japanese firms involved their design and production departments and their parts manufacturers in all stages of the design process. Parts manufacturers were not given specific blueprints for production; instead, they were given general specifications and asked to develop their own detailed designs. As they did so, they learned. They then fed information about the problems they were encountering back to the main designers while the general outlines of the new model were not yet finalized. As a result, the Japanese were able to design a new product faster, at less cost, and with far fewer problems than were the North American firms. In recent years, however, the North American automotive firms have adopted many of these Japanese design and production methods.

Knowledge Transfer The *diffusion* of technological knowledge from those who have it to those who want it is not costless (as it was assumed to be in Schumpeter's model). We often tend to think that once a production process is developed, it can easily be copied by others. In practice, however, the diffusion of new technological knowledge is not so simple. Firms need research capacity just to adopt the technologies developed by others. Some of the knowledge needed to use a new technology can be learned only through experience by plant managers, technicians, and operators.

For example, research has shown that most industrial technologies require technology-specific organizational skills that cannot be "embodied" in the machines themselves, instruction books, or blueprints. The needed knowledge is *tacit* in the sense that it cannot be taught through books and can only be acquired by experience—much like driving a car or playing a video game. Acquiring tacit knowledge requires a deliberate process of building up new skills, work practices, knowledge, and experience.

The fact that diffusion is a costly and time-consuming process explains why new technologies take considerable time to diffuse, first through the economy of the originating country and then through the rest of the world. If diffusion were simple and virtually costless, the puzzle would be why technological knowledge and best industrial practices did not diffuse very quickly. As it is, decades can pass before a new technological process is diffused everywhere that it could be employed.

Market Structure and Innovation   Because it is highly risky, innovation is encouraged by strong rivalry among firms and discouraged by monopoly practices. Competition among three or four large firms often produces much innovation, but a single firm, especially if it serves a secure home market protected by trade barriers, seems much less inclined to innovate. The reduction in trade barriers over the past several decades and the increasing globalization of markets as a result of falling transportation and communication costs have increased international competition. Whereas one firm in a national market might have had substantial monopoly power three or four decades ago, today it is more likely to be in intense competition with firms based in other countries. This greater international competition may lead to more innovation.

An important implication of this general idea is that policies that make firms more competitive—either by lowering protective tariffs or by reducing domestic regulations that hamper competition—are likely to have a positive effect on the amount of innovation and thus on an economy's rate of growth of productivity. This is a central conclusion in *The Power of Productivity*, a recent and influential book by William Lewis.

Shocks and Innovation   One interesting consequence of endogenous technical change is that shocks that would be unambiguously adverse to an economy operating with fixed technology can sometimes provide a spur to innovation that proves a blessing in disguise. A sharp rise in the price of one input can raise costs and lower the value of output per person for some time. But it may lead to a wave of innovations that reduce the need for this expensive input and, as a side effect, greatly raise productivity. One example is the development of fuel-efficient automobiles following large increases in the world price of oil in the 1970s.

Sometimes individual firms will respond differently to the same economic signal. Sometimes those that respond by altering technology will do better than those that concentrate their efforts on substituting within the confines of known technology. For example, in *The Competitive Advantage of Nations,* Harvard economist Michael Porter tells the story of the consumer electronics industry, in which U.S. firms moved their operations abroad to avoid high, rigid labour costs. They continued to use their existing technology and went where labour costs were low enough to make that technology pay. Their Japanese competitors, however, stayed at home. They innovated away most of their labour costs and then built factories in the United States to replace the factories of U.S. firms that had gone abroad!

Increasing Marginal Returns

We saw earlier that Neoclassical theories of economic growth assume that investment in capital is subject to diminishing marginal returns. New growth theories emphasize the possibility of *historical increasing returns*: As investment in some new area, product, or production technology proceeds through time, each new increment of investment is more productive than previous increments. Economists have noted a number of sources of increasing marginal returns. These fall under the two general categories of *market-development costs* and *knowledge.*

Market-Development Costs   For three reasons there may be important costs associated with the initial development of the market. These costs result in increasing marginal returns to investment.

1. Investment in the early stages of development of a country, province, or town may create new skills and attitudes in the workforce that are then available to all subsequent firms, whose costs are therefore lower than those encountered by the initial firms. (For those who have studied microeconomics, the early firms are conferring a positive *externality* on those who follow them, as described in Chapter 16.)

2. Each new firm may find the environment more and more favourable to its investment because of the physical infrastructure that has been created by those who came before.

3. The first investment in a new product will encounter countless production problems that, once overcome, cause fewer problems to subsequent investors.

In each of these examples, the returns to later investment are greater than the returns to the same investment made earlier for the simple reason that the economic environment becomes more fully developed over time. Early firms must incur costs in order to develop various aspects of the market, but some benefits of this development are then reaped by later firms that need not incur these costs. As a result, the investment returns for "followers" can be substantially greater than the investment returns for "pioneers." In short, doing something really new is difficult, whereas making further variations on an accepted and developed new idea becomes progressively easier over time.

Another important issue concerns the behaviour of customers. When a new product is developed, customers will often resist adopting it, both because they may be conservative and because they know that new products often experience "growing pains." Customers also need time to learn how best to use the new product—they need to do what is called "learning by using." And it may take time and "using experience" before producers get all the bugs out of the design of new products.

Slow acceptance of new products by customers is not necessarily irrational. When a sophisticated new product comes on the market, no one is sure if it will be a success, and the first customers to buy it take the risk that the product may subsequently turn out to be a failure. They also incur the costs of learning how to use it effectively. Many potential users take the not unreasonable attitude of letting others try a new product, following only after the product's success has been demonstrated. This makes the early stages of innovation especially costly and risky.

Successive increments of investment associated with an innovation often yield a range of increasing marginal returns as costs that are incurred in earlier investment expenditure provide publicly available knowledge and experience and as customer attitudes and abilities become more receptive to new products.

The implications of these ideas have been the subject of intense study and were first included in formal growth models by Paul Romer of Stanford University.[3]

---

[3] As with so many innovations, these new views have many historical antecedents, including a classic article in the 1960s by Nobel Prize winner Kenneth Arrow of Stanford University.

A computer is a private good because if I own it then you cannot also own it. But the knowledge required to build the computer is a public good. And knowledge, unlike traditional factors of production, is not necessarily subject to the law of diminishing returns.

Probably the most important contrast between these new theories and the Neoclassical theory concerns investment and income. In the Neoclassical model, diminishing marginal returns to investment imply a limit to the possible increase of per capita GDP. In the new models, investment alone can hold an economy on a "sustained growth path" in which per capita GDP increases without limit, provided that the investment embodies the results of continual advances in technological knowledge.

Knowledge An even more fundamental aspect of the new growth theories is the shift from the economics of goods to the economics of *ideas*. Physical goods, such as factories and machines, exist in one place at one time. This has two consequences. First, when physical goods are used by someone, they cannot be used by someone else. Second, if a given labour force is provided with more and more physical objects to use in production, sooner or later diminishing marginal returns will be encountered.

Ideas have different characteristics. Once someone develops an idea, it is available for use by everyone simultaneously. Ideas can be used by one person without reducing their use by others. For example, if one firm uses a truck, another firm cannot use it at the same time; but one firm's use of a revolutionary design for a new suspension system on a truck does not prevent other firms from using that design as well. Ideas are often not subject to the same use restrictions as goods. (For those who have studied microeconomics, some knowledge has aspects that make it a *public good,* as we discussed in Chapter 16.) Ideas are also not necessarily subject to diminishing marginal returns. As our knowledge increases, each increment of new knowledge does not inevitably add less to our productive ability than each previous increment.

New growth theories stress the importance of ideas in producing what is called *knowledge-driven growth.* New knowledge provides the input that allows investment to produce increasing rather than diminishing marginal returns. Because there are no practical limits to human knowledge, there need be no immediate boundaries to finding new ways to produce more output using less of all inputs.

Neoclassical growth theories gave economics the name "the dismal science" by emphasizing diminishing marginal returns under conditions of given technology. The new growth theories are more optimistic because they emphasize the unlimited potential of knowledge-driven technological change.

26.4 ARE THERE LIMITS TO GROWTH?

See the United Nations' website for international data on economic development: **www.un.org**. Click on "Economic and Social Development" and then go to "Statistics."

Many opponents of growth argue that sustained world growth is undesirable; some argue that it is impossible. The idea that economic growth is limited by nature is not new. In the early 1970s, a group called the "Club of Rome" published a book entitled *The Limits to Growth,* which focused on the limits to growth arising from the finite supply of natural resources. Extrapolating from the oil shortages caused by the OPEC cartel, the Club of Rome concluded that industrialized countries faced an imminent absolute limit to growth. Do such limits really exist? We discuss the two issues of resource exhaustion and pollution.

Resource Exhaustion

The years since the Second World War have seen a rapid acceleration in the consumption of the world's resources, particularly fossil fuels and basic minerals. World population has increased from under 2.5 billion to over 6 billion in that period; this increase alone has intensified the demand for the world's resources. Furthermore, as people attain higher incomes, they consume more resources. Thus, not only are there more people in the world, but many of those people are consuming increasing quantities of resources.

The resources available today could not possibly support all of the world's population at a standard of living equal to that of the average Canadian family—at least, not at the current level of technological development. Our current resources and our present capacity to cope with pollution and environmental degradation are insufficient to accomplish this rise in global living standards with present technology.

Most economists, however, agree that absolute limits to growth, based on the assumptions of constant technology and fixed resources, are not relevant. As emphasized by the new growth theories we discussed in the previous section, technology changes continually, as do the available stocks of resources. For example, 50 years ago, few would have thought that the world could produce enough food to feed its present population of 6 billion people, let alone the 10 billion at which the population is projected to stabilize sometime later this century. Yet significant advances in agricultural methods make this task now seem feasible. Further, while existing resources are being depleted, new ones are constantly being discovered or developed. One example is the development of the Alberta oil sands. In the early 1970s, this resource appeared to be far too expensive to develop and therefore an unlikely source of economical oil. Thirty-five years later, after considerable technological improvement, the oil sands now rank among the world's largest reserves of economical petroleum.

Another consideration relates to both resource use and technological progress. Along with advances in technological knowledge typically comes an increase in the economy's *resource efficiency*—a reduction in the amount of resources needed to produce one unit of output. In Canada, for example, an average dollar of real GDP is currently produced with 30 percent less energy than was the case in 1978, and if we focus just on petroleum use the improvement in efficiency is almost 50 percent. Such improvements in resource efficiency do not eliminate the concerns about resource exhaustion, but they do underline the importance of recognizing the role of technological change when considering limits to economic growth.

Technology is constantly advancing, and many things that seemed impossible a generation ago will be commonplace a generation from now. Such technological advance makes any absolute limits to economic growth less likely.

Yet there is surely cause for some concern. Although many barriers can be overcome by technological advances, such achievements are not instantaneous and are certainly not automatic. There is a critical problem of timing: How soon can we discover and put into practice the knowledge required to solve the problems that are made ever more imminent by the growth in the population, the affluence of the rich nations, and the aspirations of the billions who now live in poverty? There is no guarantee that a whole generation will not be caught in transition between technologies, with enormous social and political consequences.

A final point worth noting is that the extent of resource depletion is not something that "just happens." Since natural resources are typically owned by the public, government policy can be used to influence the rate of resource extraction if that objective is deemed to be appropriate. If we fail to protect some key natural resources, it will not be because we lacked the ability or the technology to do so, only that we lacked the political will to make contentious and difficult decisions—decisions that may nonetheless be in our long-run interests.

Pollution

A further problem is how to cope with pollution. Air, water, and soil are polluted by a variety of natural activities and, for billions of years, the environment has coped with them. The earth's natural processes had little trouble coping with the pollution generated by its 1 billion inhabitants in 1800. But the 6 billion people who now exist put such extreme demands on the earth's ecosystems that there are now legitimate concerns about "environmental sustainability." Smoke, sewage, chemical waste, hydrocarbon and greenhouse-gas emissions, spent nuclear fuel, and a host of other pollutants threaten to overwhelm the earth's natural regenerative processes.

Conscious management of pollution was unnecessary when the world's population was 1 billion people, but such management has now become a pressing matter.

Reducing the extent of environmental degradation, however, is different from advocating an "anti-growth" position. To put it differently, there is nothing inconsistent about an economy displaying *both* high rates of economic growth and active environmental protection. As students of microeconomics will recognize, an important part of a policy designed to reduce the extent of environmental degradation is to get polluters (firms or households) to face the full cost of their polluting activities—especially the external costs that their activities impose on society. This often involves levying some form of tax on polluters for every unit of pollution emitted. While such policies, if stringently enforced, will lead to output reductions in specific industries, they need not lead to reductions in the *overall* level of economic activity. And long-run economic growth is related to growth in the *overall* level of economic activity, not to the growth of specific industries.

Furthermore, many technological advances reduce the amount of pollution per unit of output, and also reduce the costs of dealing with whatever pollution remains. Rich, advanced economies such as Canada, the United States, and the European Union create less pollution per dollar of GDP and find it easier to bear the cost of pollution clean-up than do poorer, less technologically advanced economies.

Many of the insights about the determinants of economic growth that we explored in this chapter apply also to economic growth in the developing countries. But the developing countries also have some unique economic and institutional challenges, some which have plagued them for many years. For a detailed discussion, look for "Challenges Facing the Developing Countries" in the *Additional Topics* section of this book's MyEconLab.

www.myeconlab.com

None of this implies that environmental issues are not serious. It is possible that our management of these issues will be sufficiently inadequate that growth will be impaired and our living standards will suffer by significant amounts. If this happens,

it will probably *not* be because we lacked the technology or know-how to solve these problems once they were recognized. If we do create environmental disasters, more likely it will be because we failed to respond quickly enough (if at all) to the growing dangers as they were occurring.

Some scientists believe, for example, that we may already be too late to reverse the forces leading to global warming, and that dramatic changes in sea level are now a virtual certainty at some point in the not-too-distant future. Others argue that it is not too late to take significant actions that would reduce the extent of global warming. Concerted global actions and considerable political will in many countries must be part of the solution.

Conclusion

The world faces many problems. Starvation and poverty are the common lot of citizens in many countries and are not unknown even in countries such as Canada and the United States, where average living standards are very high. Growth has raised the average citizens of advanced countries from poverty to plenty in the course of two centuries—a short time in terms of human history. Further growth is needed if people in developing countries are to escape material poverty, and further growth would help advanced countries to deal with many of their pressing economic problems.

Rising population and rising per capita consumption, however, put pressure on the world's natural ecosystems, especially through the many forms of pollution. Further growth must be *sustainable* growth, which must in turn be based on knowledge-driven technological change. Past experience suggests that new technologies will use less of all resources per unit of output. But if they are to dramatically reduce the demands placed on the earth's ecosystems, price and policy incentives will be needed to direct technological change in more "environmentally friendly" ways. Just as present technologies are much less polluting than the technologies of a century ago, the technologies of the future must be made much less polluting than today's.

There is no guarantee that the world will solve the problems of sustainable growth, but there is nothing in modern growth theory and existing evidence to suggest that such an achievement is impossible.

S U M M A R Y

26.1 **THE NATURE OF ECONOMIC GROWTH**

- Sustained increases in real GDP are due mainly to economic growth, which continuously pushes the Y^* curve outward, thereby increasing potential output.
- Growth is frequently measured by using rates of change of potential real GDP per person. The cumulative effects of even small differences in growth rates become very large over periods of a decade or more.
- The most important benefit of growth lies in its contribution to the long-run struggle to raise living standards and to escape poverty. Growth also facilitates the redistribution of income among people.

- Growth, though often beneficial, is never costless. The opportunity cost of growth is the diversion of resources from current consumption to capital formation. For individuals who are left behind in a rapidly changing world, the costs are higher and more personal.
- There are four fundamental determinants of growth: increases in the labour force; increases in physical capital; increases in human capital; and improvements in technology.

26.2 **ESTABLISHED THEORIES OF ECONOMIC GROWTH**

- The long-run relationship among saving, investment, and economic growth is most easily observed in the market for loanable funds, in which the interest rate is determined by the equality of desired investment and desired national saving.
- Increases in the supply of national saving will reduce the interest rate and encourage more investment by firms, thus increasing the rate of growth of potential output.
- Increases in the demand for investment will increase the interest rate and encourage an increase in household saving. The higher saving (and investment) in equilibrium leads to a higher growth rate of potential output.
- Neoclassical growth theory assumes an aggregate production function that displays diminishing marginal returns (when one factor is changed in isolation) and constant returns to scale (when all factors are changed in equal proportions).

- In a balanced growth path, the quantity of labour, the quantity of capital, and real GDP all increase at a constant rate. But since per capita output is constant, living standards are not rising.
- Changes in output that cannot be accounted for by changes in the levels of physical and human capital and in the size of the labour force are attributed to changes in what is called total factor productivity (TFP). Although it is sometimes associated with technological change, TFP does not measure all of such change because much of it is embodied in new physical and human capital.
- In the Neoclassical growth model, technological change is assumed to be exogenous—unaffected by the size of the labour force, the size of the capital stock, or the level of economic activity.

26.3 **NEW GROWTH THEORIES**   (LO 4)

- Unlike the Neoclassical growth theory, new growth theories emphasize endogenous technological change that responds to market signals such as prices and profits. In particular, shocks that would be adverse in a setting of fixed technology may provide a spur to innovation and result in technological improvements.
- New growth theories also suggest that investment that embodies new technologies may be subject to *increasing* rather than diminishing marginal returns. Increasing

marginal returns can explain ongoing growth in per capita incomes due to capital accumulation—a phenomenon difficult to explain with the Neoclassical growth model.
- Knowledge is an important input to the production process and, because it is a public good that can be used simultaneously by many, may not be subject to diminishing marginal returns.

26.4 **ARE THERE LIMITS TO GROWTH?**   (LO 5)

- The critical importance of increasing knowledge and new technology to the goal of sustaining growth is highlighted by the great drain on existing natural resources that has resulted from the explosive growth of population and output in recent decades. Without continuing technological change, the present needs and aspirations of the world's population cannot come anywhere close to being met.
- Rising population and rising real incomes place pressure on resources. Technological improvements, however, lead to less resource use per unit of output produced,

and also to the discovery and development of new resources.
- The increase in population has similar effects on pollution: The earth's environment could cope naturally with much of human pollution 200 years ago, but the present population is so large that pollution has outstripped nature's coping mechanisms.
- Although problems associated with environmental degradation have been surmounted in the past, there is no guarantee that the ones now being encountered, such as the effects of global warming, will become objects of policy attention before the effects can be reversed.

KEY CONCEPTS

The cumulative nature of growth
Benefits and costs of growth
The market for loanable funds and the
  equilibrium interest rate
Saving, investment, and growth
Neoclassical growth theory

The aggregate production function
Diminishing marginal returns
Constant returns to scale
Balanced growth
Total factor productivity

Endogenous technical change
Increasing marginal returns to
  investment
The economics of goods and of ideas
Resource depletion and pollution

STUDY EXERCISES

1. Fill in the blanks to make the following statements correct.

   a. Long-run, sustained increases in real GDP are the result of increases in potential output, which we call _____.

   b. Increases in living standards are possible with increases in real _____.

   c. The primary cost of economic growth is the sacrifice of current _____ in exchange for investment that raises future _____.

   d. The four fundamental determinants of growth are
      • _____
      • _____
      • _____
      • _____

2. Fill in the blanks to make the following statements correct.

   a. An increase in the interest rate leads to a(n) _____ in the amount of national saving because households reduce their _____.

   b. An increase in the interest rate leads firms to _____ their amount of desired investment.

   c. In the long run, with output equal to potential, equilibrium in the market for loanable funds determines the interest rate as well as the amount of _____ and _____ in the economy.

   d. Following a shift in either the supply of national saving or the demand for investment, there will be a change in both the equilibrium _____ and the amount of _____ in the economy.

   e. An increase in the amount of the economy's resources devoted to _____ leads to an increase in the growth rate of _____.

3. Fill in the blanks to make the following statements correct.

   a. An important aspect of Neoclassical growth theory is that changes in the supply of one factor, all else held constant, imply eventually _____ marginal returns to that factor.

   b. In Neoclassical growth theory, an increase in the labour force _____ total output and _____ the level of per capita output.

   c. When a new harvesting machine replaces an old harvesting machine on a farm, and is more productive than the old one, we say there has been _____ technical change.

   d. Some new growth theories are based on the assumption that technological change is _____ to the economic system; others are based on the possibility that there are _____ marginal returns to investment.

   e. Neoclassical growth theories are pessimistic because they emphasize _____ returns with a given state of _____. Modern growth theories are more optimistic because they emphasize the unlimited potential of _____.

4. In the text we said that, over many years, small differences in growth rates can have large effects on the level of income. This question will help you understand this important point. Consider an initial value of real GDP equal to Y_0. If real GDP grows at a rate of g percent annually, after N years real GDP will equal $Y_0(1 + g)^N$. Now consider the following table. Let the initial level of GDP in all cases be 100.

	Real GDP With Alternative Growth Rates					
Year	1% (1)	1.5% (2)	2% (3)	2.5% (4)	3% (5)	3.5% (6)
0	100	100	100	100	100	100
1	—	—	—	—	—	—
3	—	—	—	—	—	—
5	—	—	—	—	—	—
10	—	—	—	—	—	—
20	—	—	—	—	—	—
30	—	—	—	—	—	—
50	—	—	—	—	—	—

a. Using the formula provided above, compute the level of real GDP in column 1 for each year. For example, in Year 1, real GDP will equal $100(1.01)^1 = 101$.

b. Now do the same for the rest of the columns.

c. In Year 20, how much larger (in percentage terms) is real GDP in the 3-percent growth case compared to the 1.5-percent growth case?

d. In Year 50, how much larger (in percentage terms) is real GDP in the 3-percent growth case compared to the 1.5-percent growth case?

5. The diagram below shows two paths for aggregate consumption. One grows at a rate of 3 percent per year; the other grows at 4 percent per year but begins at a lower level.

a. Suppose the economy jumps from Path 1 to Path 2 in Year 0 because its rate of capital accumulation increases. What is the opportunity cost in this economy for this increase in capital accumulation?

b. Suppose the economy jumps from Path 1 to Path 2 in Year 0 because its rate of R&D expenditures increases. The greater R&D leads to technological improvements that generate the higher growth rate. What is the opportunity cost to this economy for the increase in R&D expenditures?

c. Show in the figure the "breakeven" point for the economy after both of the changes described above. Explain.

6. Consider an economy in the long run with real GDP equal to the level of potential output, Y^*.

a. Draw the diagram of the market for loanable funds. Explain the shapes of the investment demand curve and the national saving curve.

b. Suppose the government pursued a fiscal contraction by reducing the level of government purchases. Explain what would happen to the equilibrium interest rate, the amount of investment in the economy, and the long-run growth rate.

c. Now suppose the fiscal contraction occurs by increasing taxes. Explain what effect this would have on the interest rate, investment, and long-run growth rate.

7. The Neoclassical growth theory is based on the existence of an aggregate production function—showing the relationship between labour (L), capital (K), technology (T), and real GDP (Y). The table below shows various values for L, K, and T. In all cases, the aggregate production function is assumed to take the following form:

$$Y = T \times \sqrt{KL}$$

Labour (L)	Capital (K)	Technology (T)	Real GDP (Y)
10	20	1	—
15	20	1	—
20	20	1	—
25	20	1	—
10	20	1	—
15	30	1	—
20	40	1	—
25	50	1	—
20	20	1	—
20	20	3	—
20	20	4	—
20	20	5	—

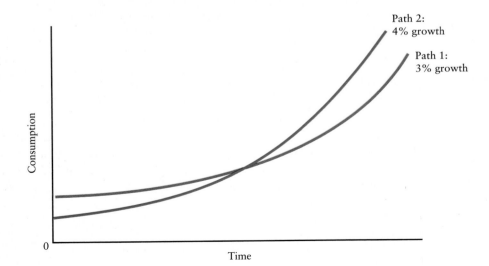

Path 2:
4% growth

Path 1:
3% growth

Consumption

0

Time

a. Compute real GDP for each case and complete the table.

b. In the first part of the table, capital is constant but labour is increasing. What property of the production function is displayed? Explain.

c. In the second part of the table, capital and labour are increasing by the same proportion. What property of the production function is displayed? Explain.

d. What type of growth is being shown in the third part of the table?

8. In the early 1970s the Club of Rome, extrapolating from the rates of resource use at the time, predicted that the supply of natural resources (especially oil) would be used up within a few decades. Subsequent events appear to have proven them wrong.

a. What is predicted to happen to the price of oil (and other natural resources) as population and per capita incomes rise?

b. Given your answer to part (a), what is the likely response by firms and consumers who use such resources?

c. Explain why resource exhaustion should, through the workings of the price system, lead to technological developments that reduce the use of the resource.

9. **myeconlab** Consider the market for loanable funds and the relationship between saving, investment, and the interest rate. In what follows, assume that the economy is in a long-run equilibrium with Y = Y*.

a. Suppose the government decides to encourage national saving. How could it do this, and what would be the effects of such a policy? Illustrate in a diagram.

b. Suppose instead that the government decides to encourage investment. How might this be accomplished, and what would be the effects? Illustrate in a diagram.

c. It is often heard in public debate that "high interest rates are bad for investment and growth." Is this true? Can you come up with a simple rule of thumb to describe the relationship between interest rates, investment, and growth?

DISCUSSION QUESTIONS

1. Economic growth is often studied in macroeconomic terms, but in a market economy, who makes the decisions that lead to growth? What kinds of decisions and what kinds of actions cause growth to occur? How might a detailed study of individual markets be relevant to understanding economic growth?

2. Discuss the following quote from a recent newspaper article: "Economics and the environment are not strange bedfellows. Environment-oriented tourism is one creative way to resolve the conflict between our desire for a higher standard of living and the realization that nature cannot absorb everything we throw at it. The growing demand for ecotourism has placed a premium on the remaining rain forests, undisturbed flora and fauna, and endangered species of the world."

3. "The case for economic growth is that it gives man greater control over his environment, and consequently increases his freedom." Explain why you agree or disagree with this statement by Nobel laureate W. Arthur Lewis.

4. Dr. David Suzuki, an opponent of further economic growth, has argued that despite the fact that "in the twentieth century the list of scientific and technological achievements has been absolutely dazzling, the costs of such progress are so large that negative economic growth may be right for the future." Policies to achieve this include "rigorous reduction of waste, a questioning and distrustful attitude toward technological progress, and braking demands on the globe's resources." Identify some of the benefits and costs of economic growth, and evaluate Suzuki's position. What government policies would be needed to achieve his ends?

5. In this chapter we discussed four fundamental determinants of growth in real output: increases in the labour force; increases in the stock of physical capital; increases in human capital; and improvements in technology. For each of the four, give an example of a government policy that is likely to increase growth. Discuss also the likely cost associated with each policy. Does one of your proposed policies appear better (in a cost–benefit sense) than the others?

6. The Solow residual has been called a "measure of our ignorance" of the causes of growth. Explain this viewpoint. Is the Solow residual a good measure of technical change?

7. This question is based on the MyEconLab item "Investment and Saving in Globalized Financial Markets." Consider the market for loanable funds and the long-run relationship among saving, investment and economic growth.

a. For a closed economy, if the government wants a higher long-run growth rate, explain why it can directly promote saving *or* investment.

b. For an open economy, explain why the amount of investment (and growth rate of output) is unlikely to be affected by a policy that encourages national saving.

c. If desired saving need not be equal to desired investment in an open economy, what accounts for the difference?

CHAPTER 27

Money and Banking

LEARNING OBJECTIVES

In this chapter you will learn

① about the various functions of money, and how money has evolved over time.

② that modern banking systems include both privately owned commercial banks and government-owned central banks.

③ how commercial banks create money through the process of taking deposits and making loans.

④ the various measures of the money supply.

In the next three chapters, we look at the role of money and monetary policy. The role of money may seem obvious—money is what people use to buy things. Yet as we shall see, increasing the amount of money circulating in Canada would not make the average Canadian better off in the long run. Although money allows those who have it to buy someone else's output, the total amount of goods and services available for everyone to buy depends on the total output produced, not on the total amount of money that people possess. In other words, an increase in the quantity of money is unlikely to increase the level of potential real GDP, Y^*, and thus unlikely to affect our long-run living standards. However, most economists agree that changes in the amount of money have important short-run effects on national income. A complete understanding of money's role in the economy requires that we recognize the distinction between the short run and the long run.

We begin by talking in detail about what money is and how it evolved over the centuries to its current form. We then examine the Canadian banking system, which includes a central bank (the Bank of Canada) and many commercial banks. Finally, we explain the process whereby commercial banks "create" money, seemingly out of thin air. This money creation process will play a central role in our discussion of how money influences the level of economic activity, a topic we begin in the next chapter.

27.1 THE NATURE OF MONEY

What exactly is money? In this section, we describe the functions of money and briefly outline its history.

What Is Money?

medium of exchange
Anything that is generally acceptable in return for goods and services sold.

In economics, *money* has usually been defined as any generally accepted medium of exchange. A **medium of exchange** is anything that will be widely accepted in a society in exchange for goods and services. Although its medium-of-exchange role is perhaps its most important one, money also acts as a *store of value* and as a *unit of account*. Different kinds of money vary in the degree of efficiency with which they fulfill these functions. As we shall see, the *money supply* is measured by using different definitions for different purposes.

Money as a Medium of Exchange   If there were no money, goods would have to be exchanged by barter. **Barter** is the system whereby goods and services are exchanged directly with each other. The major difficulty with barter is that each transaction requires a *double coincidence of wants:* anyone who specialized in producing one commodity would have to spend a great deal of time searching for satisfactory transactions. For example, the barber who needs his sink repaired would have to find a plumber who wants a haircut. In a world of many different goods and many different people, the effort required to make transactions would be extreme. The use of money as a medium of exchange solves this problem. People can sell their output for money and then use the money to buy what they wish from others.

barter A system in which goods and services are traded directly for other goods and services.

The double coincidence of wants is unnecessary when a medium of exchange is used.

By facilitating transactions, money makes possible the benefits of specialization and the division of labour, two concepts we first discussed in Chapter 1. As a result, money contributes to the efficiency of the economic system. It is not without justification that money has been called one of the great inventions contributing to human freedom and well-being.

To serve as an efficient medium of exchange, money must have a number of characteristics. It must be both easily recognizable and readily acceptable. It must have a high value relative to its weight (otherwise it would be a nuisance to carry around). It must be divisible, because money that comes only in large denominations is useless for transactions having only a small value. It must be reasonably durable (notice that Canadian paper money can easily survive several trips through a washing machine!). Finally, it must be difficult, if not impossible, to counterfeit.

Money as a Store of Value   Money is a convenient means of storing purchasing power; goods may be sold today for money and the money may then be stored until it is needed for some future purchase. To be a satisfactory store of value, however, money must have a relatively stable value. Recall from the beginning of Chapter 23 that a rise in the price level is also a decrease in the purchasing power of money. When the price level is stable, the purchasing power of a given sum of money is also stable; when the price level is highly variable, so is the purchasing power of money, and the usefulness of money as a store of value is undermined.

Between the early 1970s and the early 1990s, inflation in Canada was high enough and sufficiently variable to diminish money's usefulness as a store of value. Since 1992, however, inflation has been low and relatively stable, thus increasing money's role as a store of value. Even Canada's high-inflation experience, however, is very modest compared to that in some other countries, such as Chile in the mid-1970s, Bolivia in the mid-1980s, and Argentina, Romania, and Brazil in the early 1990s. Perhaps the most infamous experience of very high inflation—*hyperinflation*—comes from Germany in the early 1920s. This case is discussed in *Lessons From History 27-1.*

Practise with Study Guide Chapter 27, Exercise 1.

LESSONS FROM HISTORY 27-1

Hyperinflation and the Value of Money

Hyperinflation is generally defined as inflation that exceeds 50 percent per month. At this rate of inflation a chocolate bar that costs $1 on January 1 would cost $129.74 by December 31 of the same year. When prices are rising at such rapid rates, is it possible for money to maintain its usefulness as a medium of exchange or as a store of value? Several examples from history have allowed economists to study the role of money during hyperinflation. This historical record is not entirely reassuring. In a number of instances, prices rose at an ever-accelerating rate until a nation's money ceased to be a satisfactory store of value, even for the short period between receipt and expenditure, and hence ceased also to be useful as a medium of exchange.

The most spectacular example of hyperinflation is the experience of Germany in the period after the First World War. The price index in the accompanying table shows that a good purchased for one 100-mark note in July 1923 would cost *10 million* 100-mark notes only four months later! Although Germany had experienced substantial inflation during the First World War, averaging more than 30 percent per year, the immediate postwar years of 1920 and 1921 gave no sign of explosive inflation. Indeed, prices were relatively stable until 1922 and 1923 when they exploded. On November 15, 1923, the German mark was officially repudiated, its value wholly destroyed. How could such a dramatic increase in prices happen?

When inflation becomes so high that people lose confidence in the purchasing power of their currency, they rush to spend it. People who have goods become increasingly reluctant to accept the rapidly depreciating money in exchange. The rush to spend money accelerates the increase in prices until people finally become unwilling to accept money on any terms. What was once money ceases to be money. The price system can then be restored only by repudiation of the old monetary unit and its replacement by a new unit.

About a dozen hyperinflations in world history have been documented, among them the collapse of the continental during the American Revolution in 1776, the ruble during the Russian Revolution in 1917, the drachma during and after the German occupation of Greece in the Second World War, the pengö in Hungary in 1945 and 1946, the Chinese national currency from 1946 to 1948, the Bolivian peso in 1984–1985, the Argentinian peso in the early 1990s, and the Zimbabwean dollar in 2005–2006. Every one of these hyperinflations was accompanied by great increases in the money supply; new money was printed to give governments purchasing power that they could not or would not obtain by taxation. Further, every one occurred in the midst of a major political upheaval in which grave doubts existed about the stability and the future of the government itself.

Is hyperinflation likely in the absence of civil war, revolution, or collapse of the government? Most economists think not. Further, it is clear that high inflation rates over a period of time do not mean the inevitable or even likely onset of hyperinflation, however serious the distributive and social effects of such rates may be.

During hyperinflation money loses its value so quickly that people cease to accept it as a means of payment. At that point, money may as well be used for wallpaper.

Date	German Wholesale Price Index (1913 = 1)
January 1913	1
January 1920	13
January 1921	14
January 1922	37
July 1922	101
January 1923	2 785
July 1923	74 800
August 1923	944 000
September 1923	23 900 000
October 1923	7 096 000 000
November 1923	750 000 000 000

Money as a Unit of Account   Money may also be used purely for accounting purposes without having a physical existence of its own. For instance, a government store in a truly communist society might say that everyone had so many "dollars" to use each month. Goods could then be assigned prices and each consumer's purchases recorded, the consumer being allowed to buy until the allocated supply of dollars was exhausted. These dollars need have no existence other than as entries in the store's books, yet they would serve as a perfectly satisfactory unit of account.

Whether they could also serve as a medium of exchange between individuals depends on whether the store would agree to transfer dollar credits from one customer to another at the customer's request. Canadian banks transfer dollars credited to deposits in this way each time you make a purchase with your ATM card. Thus, a bank deposit can serve as both a unit of account and a medium of exchange. Notice that the use of *dollars* in this context suggests a further sense in which money is a unit of account. People think about values in terms of the monetary unit with which they are familiar.

The Origins of Money

The origins of money go far back in antiquity. Most primitive societies are known to have made some use of it.

Metallic Money   All sorts of commodities have been used as money at one time or another, but gold and silver proved to have great advantages. They were precious because their supplies were relatively limited, and they were in constant demand by the wealthy for ornament and decoration. Hence, these metals tended to have high and stable prices. Further, they were easily recognized, they were divisible into extremely small units, and they did not easily wear out. Thus, precious metals came to circulate as money and to be used in many transactions.

Before the invention of coins, it was necessary to carry the metals in bulk. When a purchase was made, the requisite quantity of the metal was carefully weighed on a scale. The invention of coinage eliminated the need to weigh the metal at each transaction, but it created an important role for an authority, usually a king or queen, who made the coins and affixed his or her seal, guaranteeing the amount of precious metal that the coin contained. This was clearly a great convenience, as long as traders knew that they could accept the coin at its "face value." The face value was nothing more than a statement that a certain weight of metal was contained therein.

However, coins often could not be taken at their face value. The practice of clipping a thin slice off the edge of the coin and keeping the valuable metal became common. This, of course, served to undermine the acceptability of coins, even if they were stamped. To get around this problem, the idea arose of minting the coins with a rough edge. The absence of the rough edge would immediately indicate that the coin had been clipped. This practice, called *milling*, survives on Canadian dimes, quarters, and two-dollar coins (but not pennies, nickels, or loonies!) as an interesting anachronism to remind us

Canadian quarters are intentionally produced with rough or bumpy edges. Such "milling" of coins is now unnecessary, but many decades ago when coins were made from precious metals, it was useful in preventing individuals from clipping the coins.

that there were days when the market value of the metal in the coin was equal to the face value of the coin.

Not to be outdone by the cunning of their subjects, some rulers were quick to seize the chance of getting something for nothing. The power to mint coins placed rulers in a position to work a very profitable fraud. They often used some suitable occasion—a marriage, an anniversary, an alliance—to remint the coinage. Subjects would be ordered to bring their coins in to the mint to be melted down and coined afresh with a new stamp. Between the melting down and the recoining, however, the rulers had only to toss some further inexpensive base metal in with the molten gold. This *debasing* of the coinage allowed the ruler to earn a handsome profit by minting more new coins than the number of old ones collected, and putting the extras in the royal vault. Through debasement, the amount of money in the economy (but not the amount of gold) had increased.

The result was inflation. The subjects had the same number of coins as before and hence could demand the same quantity of goods. When rulers paid their bills, however, the recipients of the extra coins could be expected to spend them. This caused a net increase in demand, which in turn bid up prices. Thus, increasing the money supply by debasing the coinage was a common cause of inflation.

Gresham's Law. The early experience of currency debasement led to the observation known as **Gresham's law**, after Sir Thomas Gresham (1519–1579), an adviser to the Elizabethan court, who coined the phrase "bad money drives out good."

When Queen Elizabeth I came to the chrone of England in the middle of the sixteenth century, the coinage had been severely debased. Seeking to help trade, Elizabeth minted new coins that contained their full face value in gold. However, as fast as she fed these new coins into circulation, they disappeared. Why?

Suppose you possessed one of these new coins and one of the old ones, each with the same face value, and had to make a purchase. What would you do? You would use the debased coin to make the purchase and keep the undebased one; you part with less gold that way. Suppose you wanted to obtain a certain amount of gold bullion by melting down the gold coins (as was frequently done). Which coins would you use? You would use new, undebased coins because you would part with less face value that way (it would take more of the debased coins than the new coins to get a given amount of gold bullion). The debased coins (bad money) would thus remain in circulation, and the undebased coins (good money) would disappear into peoples' private hoards—the "bad" money would drive out the "good" money.

Gresham's law predicts that when two types of money are used side by side, the one with the greater intrinsic value will be driven out of circulation.

Gresham's insights have proven helpful in explaining the experience of a number of modern high-inflation economies. For example, in the 1970s, inflation in Chile raised the value of the metallic content in coins above their face value. Coins quickly disappeared from circulation as private citizens sold them to entrepreneurs who melted them down for their metal. Only paper currency remained in circulation and was used even for tiny transactions such as purchasing a pack of matches. Gresham's law is one reason why modern coins, unlike their historical counterparts, are merely tokens that contain a metallic value that is only a small fraction of their face value.

Paper Money   The next important step in the history of money was the evolution of paper currency. Artisans who worked with gold required secure safes, and the public began to deposit gold with these goldsmiths for safekeeping. Goldsmiths would give their depositors receipts promising to return the gold on demand. When a depositor wished to make a large purchase, he could go to his goldsmith, reclaim some of his

Gresham's law The theory that "bad," or debased, money drives "good," or undebased, money out of circulation.

The development of paper money, such as this bank note issued by The Montreal Bank over a century ago, was an important step in the evolution of modern, fractional-reserve banking systems. Paper money allowed individuals to avoid the cumbersome transportation of gold when making their daily transactions.

gold, and pay it to the seller of the goods. If the seller had no immediate need for the gold, he would carry it back to the goldsmith for safekeeping.

If people knew the goldsmith to be reliable, there was no need to go through the cumbersome and risky business of physically transferring the gold. The buyer needed only to transfer the goldsmith's receipt to the seller, who would accept it as long as he was confident that the goldsmith would pay over the gold whenever it was needed. If the seller wished to buy a good from a third party, who also knew the goldsmith to be reliable, this transaction could also be effected by passing the goldsmith's receipt from the buyer to the seller. This transferring of paper receipts rather than gold was essentially the invention of paper money.

When it first came into being, paper money represented a promise to pay so much gold on demand. In this case, the promise was made first by goldsmiths and later by banks. Such paper money was *backed* by precious metal and was *convertible on demand* into this metal. In the nineteenth century, private banks commonly issued paper money, called **bank notes**, nominally convertible into gold. As with the goldsmiths, each bank issued its own notes, and these notes were convertible into gold at the issuing bank. Thus, in the nineteenth century, bank notes from many different banks circulated side by side, each of them being backed by gold at the bank that issued them.

bank notes Paper money issued by commercial banks.

Fractionally Backed Paper Money. Early on, many goldsmiths and banks discovered that it was not necessary to keep one ounce of gold in the vaults for every claim to one ounce circulating as paper money. At any one time, some of the bank's customers would be withdrawing gold, others would be depositing it, and most would be trading in the bank's paper notes without any need or desire to convert them into gold. As a result, the bank was able to issue more paper money redeemable in gold than the amount of gold that it held in its vaults. This was good business because the money could be invested profitably in interest-earning loans to households and firms. To this day, banks have many more claims outstanding against them than they actually have in reserves available to pay those claims. We say that the currency issued in such a situation is *fractionally backed* by the reserves.

The major problem with a fractionally backed convertible currency was maintaining its convertibility into the precious metal behind it. The imprudent bank that issued too much paper money would find itself unable to redeem its currency in gold when the demand for gold was even slightly higher than usual. It would then have to suspend payments, and all holders of its notes would suddenly find that the notes were worthless. The prudent bank that kept a reasonable relationship between its note issues and its gold reserves would find that it could meet a normal range of demand for gold without any trouble.

If, for whatever reason, the public lost confidence in the banks and demanded redemption of its currency *en masse,* the banks would be unable to honour their pledges. The history of nineteenth- and early-twentieth-century banking on both sides of the Atlantic is full of examples of banks that were ruined by "panics," or sudden runs on their gold reserves. When these happened, the banks' depositors and the holders of their notes would find themselves with worthless pieces of paper.

Fiat Money As time went on, currency (notes and coins) issued by private banks became less common, and central banks took control of issuing currency. In time, *only* central banks were permitted by law to issue currency. Originally, the central banks issued currency that was fully convertible into gold. In those days, gold would be brought to the central bank, which would issue currency in the form of "gold certificates" that asserted that the gold was available on demand. The reserves of gold thus set some upper limit on the amount of currency that could circulate in the economy. This practice of backing the currency with gold is known as a **gold standard.**

However, central banks, like private banks before them, could issue more currency than they had in gold because in normal times only a small fraction of the outstanding currency was presented for payment at any one time. Thus, even though the need to maintain convertibility into gold put an upper limit on note issuance, central banks had substantial discretionary control over the quantity of currency outstanding.

During the period between the World Wars (1919–1939), almost all of the countries of the world abandoned the gold standard; their currencies were thus no longer convertible into gold. Money that is not convertible by law into anything valuable derives its value from its acceptability in exchange. Such **fiat money** is widely acceptable because it is declared by government order, or *fiat*, to be legal tender. **Legal tender** is anything that by law must be accepted when offered either for the purchase of goods or services or to repay a debt.

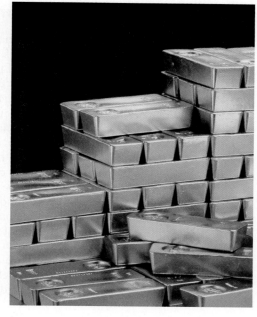

Paper money used to be backed by the value of gold—meaning that it was redeemable for gold. But now money is not redeemable for anything except itself—people hold it because they know that others will accept it as payment for goods and services.

Today, no country allows its currency to be converted into gold on demand. Gold backing for Canadian currency was eliminated in 1940, although note issues continued to carry the traditional statement "will pay to the bearer on demand" until 1954. Today's Bank of Canada notes simply say, "This note is legal tender." It is, in other words, fiat money pure and simple.[1]

If fiat money is generally acceptable, it is a medium of exchange. If its purchasing power remains stable, it is a satisfactory store of value. If both of these things are true, it serves as a satisfactory unit of account. Today, almost all currency is fiat money.

Many people are disturbed to learn that present-day paper money is neither backed by nor convertible into anything more valuable—that it consists of nothing but pieces of paper whose value derives from common acceptance and from confidence that it will continue to be accepted in the future. Many people believe that their money should be more "substantial" than this. Yet money is, in fact, nothing more than generally acceptable pieces of paper.

gold standard A currency standard whereby a country's currency is convertible into gold at a fixed rate of exchange.

fiat money Paper money or coinage that is neither backed by nor convertible into anything else but is decreed by the government to be accepted as legal tender.

legal tender Anything that by law must be accepted for the purchase of goods and services or the repayment of a debt.

---

[1] See *A History of the Canadian Dollar* (written by James Powell and published by the Bank of Canada) for a detailed and very readable discussion of the evolution of Canadian money.

Modern Money: Deposit Money

Early in the twentieth century, private banks lost the authority to issue bank notes, and this authority was reserved for central banks (which we discuss shortly). Yet, as we shall see, they did not lose the power to create *deposit money.*

Today's bank customers frequently deposit coins and paper money with the banks for safekeeping, just as in former times they deposited gold. Such a deposit is recorded as a credit to the customer's account. A customer who wishes to pay a debt may come to the bank and claim the money in dollars and then pay the money to other persons who may themselves redeposit the money in a bank.

deposit money Money held by the public in the form of deposits with commercial banks.

As with gold transfers, this is a tedious procedure. It is more convenient to have the bank transfer claims to money on deposit. As soon as cheques, which are written instructions to the bank to make a transfer, became widely accepted in payment for commodities and debts, bank deposits became a form of money called **deposit money**. Cheques, unlike bank notes, do not circulate freely from hand to hand; hence cheques themselves are not money. However, a balance in a bank account *is* money; the cheque transfers money from one person to another. Because cheques are easily drawn and deposited and are relatively safe from theft, they are widely used. In recent years, the development of debit cards has taken the place of cheques for many transactions. The use of a debit card instantly (electronically) transfers funds from the bank account of the purchaser to the bank account of the seller—it thus has the same effect as a cheque, only faster.

When commercial banks lost the right to issue notes of their own, the form of bank money changed, but the substance did not. Today, banks have money in their vaults (or on deposit with the central banks), just as they always did. Once it was gold; today it is the legal tender of the times, fiat money. It is true today, just as in the past, that most of the bank's customers are content to pay their bills by passing among themselves the bank's promises to pay money on demand. Only a small proportion of the transactions made by the bank's customers are made in cash.

Bank cards like this one are not money. They simply allow consumers to have convenient access to their bank deposits, which are money.

Bank deposits are money. Today, just as in the past, banks create money by issuing more promises to pay (deposits) than they have cash reserves available to pay out.

27.2 **THE CANADIAN BANKING SYSTEM**

Many types of institutions make up a modern banking system such as exists in Canada today. The **central bank** is the government-owned and government-operated institution that serves to control the banking system. Through it, the government's monetary policy is conducted. In Canada, the central bank is the Bank of Canada, often called just the Bank.

Financial intermediaries are privately owned institutions that serve the general public. They are called *intermediaries* because they stand between savers, from whom they accept deposits, and investors, to whom they make loans. For many years, government regulations created a sharp distinction among the various types of financial intermediaries by limiting the types of transactions in which each could engage. The past two decades have seen a sweeping deregulation of the financial system so that many of these traditional distinctions no longer apply. In this book, we use the term *commercial banks* to extend to all financial intermediaries that create deposit money, including chartered banks, trust companies, and credit unions.

central bank A bank that acts as banker to the commercial banking system and often to the government as well. Usually a government-owned institution that controls the banking system and is the sole money-issuing authority.

The Bank of Canada

All advanced free-market economies have, in addition to commercial banks, a central bank. Many of the world's early central banks were private, profit-making institutions that provided services to ordinary banks. Their importance, however, caused them to develop close ties with government. Central banks soon became instruments of the government, though not all of them were publicly owned. The Bank of England (the "Old Lady of Threadneedle Street"), one of the world's oldest and most famous central banks, began to operate as the central bank of England in the seventeenth century, but it was not formally taken over by the government until 1947.

The similarities in the functions performed and the tools used by the world's central banks are much more important than the differences in their organization. Although our attention is given to the operations of the Bank of Canada, its basic functions are similar to those of the Bank of England, the Federal Reserve System in the United States, or the European Central Bank (the sole issuer of the euro).

The European Central Bank's website is **www.ecb.org**.

Organization of the Bank of Canada   The Bank of Canada commenced operations on March 11, 1935. It is a publicly owned corporation; all profits accruing from its operations are remitted to the government of Canada. The responsibility for the Bank's affairs rests with a board of directors composed of the governor, the senior deputy governor, the deputy minister of finance, and 12 directors. The governor is appointed by the directors, with the approval of the federal cabinet, for a seven-year term. Since the Bank's inception, there have been seven governors:

- Graham Towers (1935–1954)
- James Coyne (1955–1961)
- Louis Rasminsky (1961–1973)
- Gerald Bouey (1973–1987)
- John Crow (1987–1994)
- Gordon Thiessen (1994–2001)
- David Dodge (2001–)

The offices of the Bank of Canada are located on Wellington Street in Ottawa, across the street from the Parliament Buildings.

For information on the Bank of
Canada, see its website:
www.bankofcanada.ca.

The organization of the Bank of Canada is designed to keep the operation of monetary policy free from day-to-day political influence. The Bank is not responsible to parliament for its day-to-day behaviour in the way that the department of finance is for the operation of fiscal policy. In this sense, the Bank of Canada has considerable autonomy in the way it carries out monetary policy. But the bank is not completely independent. The *ultimate* responsibility for the Bank's actions rests with the government, since it is the government that must answer to Parliament. This system is known as "joint responsibility," and it dates back to 1967.

Under the system of joint responsibility, the governor of the Bank and the minister of finance consult regularly. In the case of fundamental disagreement over monetary policy, the minister of finance has the option of issuing an explicit *directive* to the governor. In such a case (which has not happened since the inception of joint responsibility), the governor would simply carry out the minister's directive (or resign), and the responsibility for monetary policy would rest with the government. In the absence of such a directive, however, responsibility for monetary policy rests with the governor of the Bank.

The system of joint responsibility keeps the conduct of monetary policy free from day-to-day political influence while ensuring that the government retains ultimate responsibility for monetary policy.[2]

Basic Functions of the Bank   A central bank serves four main functions: as a banker for private banks, as a bank for the government, as the regulator of the nation's money supply, and as a supporter of financial markets. The first three functions are reflected in Table 27-1, which shows the balance sheet of the Bank of Canada.

TABLE 27-1   Assets and Liabilities of the Bank of Canada, December 2005 (millions of dollars)

Assets		Liabilities	
Government of Canada securities	46 411.0	Notes in circulation	46 077.9
Advances to commercial banks	0.0	Government of Canada deposits	911.1
Net foreign-currency assets	88.1	Deposits of commercial banks (reserves)	49.9
Other assets	1 821.2	Other liabilities and capital	1 281.4
Total	48 320.3	Total	48 320.3

The balance sheet of the Bank of Canada shows that it serves as banker to the commercial banks and to the Government of Canada, and as issuer of our currency; it also suggests the Bank's role as regulator of money markets and the money supply. The principal liabilities of the Bank are the basis of the money supply. Bank of Canada notes are currency, and the deposits of the commercial banks give them the reserves they need to create deposit money. The Bank's holdings of Government of Canada securities arise from its operations designed to regulate the money supply and financial markets.

(*Source:* From *Bank of Canada Review,* 2005. Copyright © 1995–2007, Bank of Canada.)

---

2 This system was motivated by the "Coyne Affair" in 1961, during the Progressive Conservative government of John Diefenbaker. James Coyne, then governor of the Bank of Canada, disagreed with the minister of finance, Donald Fleming, over the conduct of monetary policy and was eventually forced to resign. Louis Rasminsky then accepted the position as governor of the Bank on the condition that the *Bank of Canada Act* be modified to incorporate the idea of joint responsibility. The *Bank of Canada Act* was so amended in 1967. For a discussion of the early history of the Bank of Canada, see George Watts, *The Bank of Canada: Origins and Early History* (Carleton University Press, 1993).

Banker to the Commercial Banks. The central bank accepts deposits from commercial banks and will, on order, transfer them to the account of another bank. In this way, the central bank provides the commercial banks with the equivalent of a chequing account and with a means of settling debts to other banks. The deposits of the commercial banks with the Bank of Canada—also called *reserves*—appear in Table 27-1. In December 2005 the banks had just under $50 million on reserve at the Bank of Canada. Notice that the cash reserves of the commercial banks deposited with the central bank are liabilities of the central bank, because it promises to pay them on demand.

Historically, one of the earliest services provided by central banks was that of "lender of last resort" to the banking system. Central banks would lend money to private banks that had sound investments (such as government securities) but were in urgent need of cash. If such banks could not obtain ready cash, they might be forced into insolvency, because they could not meet the demands of their depositors, in spite of their being basically sound. Today's central banks continue to be lenders of last resort. Table 27-1 shows that as of December 2005 the Bank of Canada had *no* outstanding advances (loans) to the commercial banks.

Banker to the Federal Government. Governments, too, need to hold their funds in an account into which they can make deposits and on which they can write cheques. The government of Canada keeps some of its chequing deposits at the Bank of Canada. In December 2005, the federal government had $911 million in deposits at the Bank of Canada.

When the government requires more money than it collects in taxes, it needs to borrow, and it does so by issuing government securities (short-term Treasury bills or longer-term bonds). Most are sold directly to financial institutions and portfolio managers, but in most years the Bank of Canada buys some and credits the government's account with a deposit for the amount of the purchase. In December 2005, the Bank of Canada held $46.4 billion in government of Canada securities. These securities are an asset for the Bank of Canada but a liability for the government. (It is largely by earning interest on these securities that the Bank of Canada earns a profit every year—a profit that is eventually remitted to the government.)

Regulator of the Money Supply. One of the most important functions of a central bank is to regulate the *money supply.* Though we have not yet defined the money supply precisely—and there are several different definitions of the money supply that we will encounter—we will see that most measures of the money supply include currency plus deposits held at commercial banks. Table 27-1 shows that the overwhelming proportion of a central bank's liabilities (its promises to pay) are either currency or the reserves of the commercial banks.[3] These reserves, in turn, underlie the deposits of households and firms—in exactly the same way that the nineteenth-century goldsmith's holdings of gold underlay its issue of notes.

By changing its liabilities (currency plus reserves), the Bank of Canada can change the money supply. The Bank can change the levels of its assets and liabilities in many ways and, as its liabilities rise and fall, so does the money supply. In Chapter 29, we will explore in detail how this happens and how it is related to the Bank's decisions regarding monetary policy. At that point we will see that it is not a coincidence that the Bank's holdings of government securities (its largest asset) is very close to the value of notes in circulation (its largest liability).

---

[3] Currency is a liability for the central bank because holders of currency can take it back to the central bank and redeem it for...currency! In the days of the gold standard, currency was redeemable for gold. Today, it is just redeemable for itself.

Regulator and Supporter of Financial Markets. Central banks usually assume a major responsibility to support the country's financial system and to prevent serious disruption by wide-scale panic and resulting bank failures.

Various institutions—including commercial banks, credit unions, and trust companies—are in the business of borrowing on a short-term basis and lending on a long-term basis. Large, unanticipated increases in interest rates tend to squeeze these institutions. The average rate they earn on their investments rises only slowly as old contracts mature and new ones are made, but they must either pay higher rates to hold on to their deposits or accept wide-scale withdrawals that could easily bring about insolvency. Such dramatic events are relatively rare in the Canadian banking sector, though Canadian banks have failed in the past and it is possible that more may fail in the future.

Commercial Banks in Canada

commercial bank A privately owned, profit-seeking institution that provides a variety of financial services, such as accepting deposits from customers and making loans and other investments.

All Canadian banks owned in the private sector are referred to as **commercial banks**. The Canadian banking system is controlled by the provisions of the *Bank Act,* first passed in 1935 and revised several times since. Under the *Bank Act,* charters can be granted to financial institutions to operate as banks and, until 1980, there were only a few such *chartered banks,* most of which were very large and each of which operated under identical regulatory provisions. The 1980 revisions to the *Bank Act* allowed foreign banks to commence operations in Canada, although the Act severely limited the scale and scope of their activity. Subsequent revisions have removed some of these restrictions and made it easier to obtain new banking charters, but the revisions have maintained the distinction between these newer institutions and banks operating under what are essentially the pre-1980 provisions of the *Bank Act.*

Commercial banks have common attributes: they hold deposits for their customers; they permit certain deposits to be transferred by cheque from an individual account to other accounts held in any bank branch in the country; they make loans to households and firms; they invest in government securities.

For information and history of Canada's largest commercial bank, see the Royal Bank's website: **www.rbc.com**, and then click on "history."

Banks are not the only financial institutions in the country. Many other privately owned, profit-seeking institutions, such as trust companies and credit unions, accept deposits and grant loans for specific purposes. Finance companies make loans to households for practically any purpose—sometimes at very high interest rates. Department stores and credit-card companies will extend credit so that purchases can be made on a buy-now, pay-later basis.

The chartered banks are subject to federal regulations and until recently were required to hold reserves with the Bank of Canada against their deposit liabilities. Other institutions are subject to various federal and provincial regulations concerning ownership and control and the types of financial activities in which they are allowed to engage. Thus, there are differences among all types of financial institutions, not just between banks and others.

The Canadian chartered banks have historically been such a stable and dominant group that the terms *chartered banks* and the *Canadian banking system* have been considered virtually synonymous. However, events over the past three decades have broken this identification. Especially important have been sweeping changes in the structure and functioning of international financial markets; some of these developments are discussed further in *Applying Economic Concepts 27-1.*

Interbank Activities Commercial banks have a number of interbank cooperative relationships. For example, banks often share loans. Even the biggest bank cannot

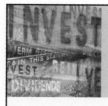

APPLYING ECONOMIC CONCEPTS 27-1

The Globalization of Financial Markets

Technological innovations in communication over the past three decades have led to a globalization of the financial service industry. Computers, satellite communication systems, reliable telephones with direct worldwide dialling, fax machines, and the widespread use of the Internet have put people in instantaneous contact anywhere in the world.

As a result of these new technologies, borrowers and lenders can learn about market conditions and then move their funds instantly in search of the best loan rates. Large firms need transaction balances only while banks in their area are open. Once banks close for the day in each centre, the firms will not need these balances until tomorrow's reopening; hence the funds can be moved to another market, where they are used until it closes. They are then moved to yet another market. Funds are thus free to move from London to New York to Tokyo and back to London on a daily rotation. This is a degree of global sophistication that was inconceivable before the advent of the computer, when international communication was much slower and costlier than it now is.

The increasing sophistication of information transfer has led to a breakdown of the high degree of specialization that characterized financial markets in earlier decades. When information was difficult to obtain and analyze, an efficient division of labour called for a host of specialist institutions, each with expertise in a narrow range of transactions. As a result of the new developments in communication technology, economies of large scale led to the integration of various financial operations within one firm. For example, in Canada and many other countries, banks will sell you securities (in mutual funds) and, similarly, the mutual-fund companies will now sell you banking services. As the scale of such integrated firms increases, these firms find it easier to extend their operations geographically as well as functionally.

Many economists believe that globalization has made the eventual consolidation (through mergers) of Canadian banks all but inevitable. Globalization, they argue, means that Canadian banks must increase in size if they are to avoid losing ground to fierce international competitors. Whether Canadian banks will merge, and to what extent the Canadian financial-services industry will be opened up to further international competition, is yet to be determined. But it is clear that the globalization of financial markets is real and is showing no signs of slowing down.

meet all the credit needs of a giant corporation, and often a group of banks will offer a "pool loan," agreeing on common terms and dividing the loan up into manageable segments. Another form of interbank cooperation is the bank credit card. Visa and MasterCard are the two most widely used credit cards, and each is operated by a group of banks.

Probably the most important form of interbank cooperation is cheque clearing and collection, including the clearing of electronic transfers through debit cards. Bank deposits are an effective medium of exchange only because banks accept each other's cheques and allow funds to be transferred electronically when purchases are made with debit cards. If a depositor in the Bank of Montreal writes a cheque to someone who deposits it in their account at CIBC, the Bank of Montreal now owes money to CIBC. This creates a need for the banks to present cheques to each other for payment. The same is true for transactions made with bank debit cards.

Millions of such transactions take place in the course of a day, and they result in an enormous sorting and bookkeeping job. Multibank systems make use of a **clearing house** where interbank debts are settled. At the end of the day, all the cheques drawn by the Bank of Montreal's customers and deposited in CIBC are totalled and set against the total of all the cheques drawn by CIBC's customers and deposited in the Bank of Montreal. It is necessary only to settle the difference between the two sums. The actual

clearing house An institution where interbank indebtedness, arising from the transfer of cheques between banks, is computed and offset and net amounts owing are calculated.

cheques are passed through the clearing house back to the bank on which they were drawn. Both banks are then able to adjust the individual accounts by a set of book entries. A flow of cash between banks is necessary only when there is a net transfer of cash from the customers of one bank to those of another. This flow of cash is accompanied by a daily transfer of deposits held by the commercial banks with the Bank of Canada.

Banks as Profit Seekers Banks are private firms that seek to make profits. A commercial bank provides a variety of services to its customers: the convenience of deposits that can be transferred by personal cheque or debit card, a safe and convenient place to earn a modest but guaranteed return on savings, and often financial advice and estate-management services.

Table 27-2 is the combined balance sheet of the chartered banks in Canada. The bulk of any bank's liabilities are deposits owed to its depositors. The principal assets of a bank are the *securities* it owns (including government bonds), which pay interest or dividends, and the interest-earning *loans* it makes to individuals and to businesses, both in Canada and abroad (which may be denominated in foreign currencies). A bank loan is a liability to the borrower (who must pay it back) but an asset to the bank.

Commercial banks attract deposits by paying interest to depositors and by providing them with services such as clearing cheques, automated teller machines, debit cards, and the provision of regular monthly statements. Banks earn profits by lending and investing money deposited with them for more than they pay their depositors in terms of interest and other services provided. They also earn profits through the wealth-management and investment services they provide to their customers.

Competition for deposits is active among commercial banks and between banks and other financial institutions. Interest paid on deposits, special high-interest certificates of deposit (CDs), advertising, personal solicitation of accounts, giveaway programs for new deposits to existing accounts, and improved services are all forms of competition for funds.

TABLE 27-2 Consolidated Balance Sheet of the Canadian Chartered Banks, March 2006 (millions of dollars)

Assets		Liabilities	
Reserves (including deposits with Bank of Canada)	4 253	Chequable deposits	153 358
Government of Canada securities	115 305	Savings deposits	428 515
Mortgage and nonmortgage loans	884 324	Time deposits	292 550
Canadian securities (corporate and provincial and municipal governments)	188 986	Government of Canada deposits	2 776
		Foreign-currency liabilities	837 838
Foreign-currency assets	806 762	Shareholders' equity	95 099
Other assets	145 910	Other liabilities	335 404
Total	2 145 540	Total	2 145 540

Reserves are only a tiny fraction of deposit liabilities. If all the chartered banks' customers who held chequable deposits tried to withdraw them in cash, the banks could not meet this demand without liquidating almost $150 billion of other assets. This would be impossible without assistance from the Bank of Canada.

(*Source:* From *Banking and Financial Statistics,* May 2006, Tables C3 and C4. Copyright © 1995–2007, Bank of Canada.)

Reserves

Commercial banks keep sufficient cash on hand to be able to meet depositors' day-to-day requirements for cash. However, just as the goldsmiths of long ago discovered that only a fraction of the gold they held was ever withdrawn at any given time, and just as banks of long ago discovered that only a small fraction of convertible bank notes was actually converted, so too do modern bankers know that only a small fraction of their deposits will be withdrawn in cash at any one time.

The reserves needed to ensure that depositors can withdraw their deposits on demand will normally be quite small.

Practise with Study Guide Chapter 27, Short-Answer Question 2.

In abnormal times, however, nothing short of 100 percent would do the job if the commercial banking system had to stand alone. If a major bank were to fail, it would probably cause a general loss of confidence in the ability of other banks to redeem their deposits. The results would then be devastating. Until relatively recently, such an event—or even the rumour of it—could lead to a **bank run** as depositors rushed to withdraw their money. Faced with such a panic, banks would have to close until either they had borrowed enough funds or sold enough assets to meet the demand, or the demand subsided. However, banks could not instantly turn their loans into cash because the borrowers would have the money tied up in such things as real estate or business enterprises. Neither could the banks obtain cash by selling their securities to the public because payments would be made by cheques, which would not provide cash to pay off depositors.

bank run A situation in which many depositors rush to withdraw their money, possibly leading to a bank's financial collapse.

The difficulty of providing sufficient reserves to meet abnormal situations is alleviated by the central bank, which can provide all the reserves that are needed to meet any abnormal situation. It can do this in two ways. First, it can lend reserves directly to commercial banks on the security of assets that are sound but not easy to liquidate quickly, such as interest-earning residential or commercial mortgages. Second, it can enter the open market and buy all the government securities that commercial banks need to sell. Once the public finds that deposits can be turned into cash, any panic would usually subside and any further drain of cash out of banks would cease.

The possibility of a bank run in Canada has been all but eliminated by the provision of deposit insurance by the Canada Deposit Insurance Corporation (CDIC), a federal Crown corporation. The CDIC guarantees that, in the unlikely event of a bank failure, depositors will get their money back, up to a limit of $100 000 per depositor. Most depositors will not rush to withdraw all of their money as long as they are certain they can get it when they need it.

The late Jimmy Stewart plays George Bailey in It's a Wonderful Life. *In this scene, Bailey, the owner of a small commercial bank, explains to his panicking customers why they can't all take their money out at the same time. It is a great illustration of the workings of a fractional-reserve banking system.*

myeconlab

Although deposit insurance provides benefits to depositors in the form of enhanced security, some economists argue that it encourages excessive risk-taking on the part of the banks themselves. For more details about the debate over deposit insurance, look for "The Costs and Benefits of Deposit Insurance" in the *Additional Topics* section of this book's MyEconLab.

w w w . m y e c o n l a b . c o m

Target and Excess Reserves   Canada's banks hold cash reserves against their deposit liabilities even though they are not required by law to do so. Banks hold reserves for the simple reason that they want to avoid situations where they cannot satisfy their depositors' demands for cash, and it is costly for them to borrow from other banks when they run short of reserves. Look again at Table 27-2. Notice that the chartered banks' cash reserves of just over $4 billion are less than one-half of one percent of its total liabilities of over $2 trillion. If the holders of even 5 percent of deposits demanded cash, the banks would be unable to meet the demand without outside help. Reserves can be as low as they are because the banks know that the Bank of Canada will help them out in time of temporary need. The Canadian banking system is thus a **fractional-reserve system**, with commercial banks holding reserves—either as cash or as deposits at the Bank of Canada—of much less than 100 percent of their deposits.

A bank's **reserve ratio** is the fraction of its deposits that it *actually* holds as reserves at any point in time, either as cash or as deposits with the Bank of Canada. A bank's **target reserve ratio** is the fraction of its deposits it would *ideally* like to hold as reserves. This target reserve ratio will generally not be constant over time. During holiday seasons, for example, banks may choose to hold more reserves because they know, based on past experience, that there will be heavy demands for cash.

At any given time, any commercial bank will probably not be exactly at its target level of reserves. Reserves may be slightly above or slightly below the target, but the commercial bank will take actions to restore its actual reserves toward its target level. Any reserves in excess of the target level are called **excess reserves**. As we will see next, a bank can expand or contract its portfolio of loans to adjust its actual reserves toward its target level. Understanding this process is the key to understanding the "creation" of deposit money.

fractional-reserve system A banking system in which commercial banks keep only a fraction of their deposits in cash or on deposit with the central bank.

reserve ratio The fraction of its deposits that a commercial bank holds as reserves in the form of cash or deposits with the central bank.

target reserve ratio The fraction of its deposits that a commercial bank wants to hold as reserves.

excess reserves Reserves held by a commercial bank in excess of its target reserves.

27.3 MONEY CREATION BY THE BANKING SYSTEM

We noted before that the *money supply* refers to both currency and deposits at commercial banks. The fractional-reserve system provides the leverage that permits commercial banks to create new deposits, and thus to create new money. The process is important, so it is worth examining in some detail.

Some Simplifying Assumptions

To focus on the essential aspects of how banks create money, suppose that banks can invest in only one kind of asset—loans—and that there is only one kind of deposit—a chequable deposit. Two other assumptions are provisional. When we have developed the basic ideas concerning the banks' creation of money, these assumptions will be relaxed.

1. *Fixed target reserve ratio.* We assume that all banks have the same target reserve ratio, which does not change. In our numerical illustration, we will assume that the target reserve ratio is 20 percent (0.20); that is, for every $5 of deposits the banks wish to hold $1 in cash reserves, investing the rest in new loans.

2. *No cash drain from the banking system.* We also assume that the public holds a fixed amount of the currency in circulation. In particular, we assume that the amount of currency held by the public is *not* a constant ratio of their bank deposits.

The Creation of Deposit Money

A hypothetical balance sheet, showing assets and liabilities, is shown for TD Canada Trust (TD) in Table 27-3. TD has assets of $200 of reserves, held partly as cash on hand and partly as deposits with the central bank, and $900 of loans outstanding to its customers. Its liabilities are $100 to investors who contributed capital to start the bank and $1000 to current depositors. The bank's ratio of reserves to deposits is 0.20 (200/1000), exactly equal to its target reserve ratio.

Practise with Study Guide Chapter 27, Exercise 4.

What Is a New Deposit?   In what follows, we are interested in knowing how the commercial banking system can "create money" when confronted with a new deposit. But what do we mean by a new deposit? By "new," we mean a deposit of cash that is new to the *commercial banking system*. There are three examples.

- First, an individual might immigrate to Canada and bring cash. When that cash is deposited into a commercial bank, it constitutes a new deposit to the (Canadian) banking system.
- Second, an individual who had some cash stashed under his bed (or in a safety deposit box) has now decided to deposit it into an account at a commercial bank.
- Third is the most interesting but also the most complicated example. If the Bank of Canada were to purchase a government security from an individual or from a firm, it would purchase that asset with a cheque drawn on the Bank of Canada. When the individual or firm deposits the cheque with a commercial bank, it would be a new deposit to the commercial banking system.

The important point to keep in mind here is that the *source* of the new deposit is irrelevant to the process of money creation by the commercial banks. In the discussion that follows, we use the example of the Bank of Canada buying government securities

TABLE 27-3 The Initial Balance Sheet of TD Canada Trust (TD)

Assets ($)		Liabilities ($)	
Reserves (cash and deposits with the central bank)	200	Deposits	1000
Loans	900	Capital	100
	1100		1100

TD Canada Trust has reserves equal to 20 percent of its deposit liabilities. The commercial bank earns profits by finding profitable investments for much of the money deposited with it. In this balance sheet, loans are its income-earning assets.

from firms or households as a way of generating a new deposit. But this is not crucial. We use this example because, as we shall see in Chapter 29, this is how the Bank of Canada would directly alter the level of reserves in the banking system if it chose to do so. But the general process of money creation we are about to describe applies to *any* new deposit, whatever its source.

The Expansion of Money from a Single New Deposit Suppose the Bank of Canada enters the open market and buys $100 worth of Government of Canada bonds from John Smith. The Bank issues a cheque to Smith, who then deposits the $100 cheque into his account at TD Canada Trust. This $100 is a wholly new deposit for the commercial bank, and it results in a revised balance sheet (Table 27-4). As a result of the new deposit, TD's cash assets and deposit liabilities have both increased by $100. More important, TD's ratio of reserves to deposits has increased from 0.20 to 0.27 (300/1100). The bank now has $80 in excess reserves; with $1100 in deposits, its target reserves are only $220.

TABLE 27-4 TD's Balance Sheet Immediately After a New Deposit of $100

Assets ($)		Liabilities ($)	
Reserves	300	Deposits	1100
Loans	900	Capital	100
	1200		1200

The new deposit raises liabilities and assets by the same amount. Because both cash and deposits rise by $100, the bank's actual reserve ratio, formerly 0.20, increases to 0.27. The bank now has excess reserves of $80.

TABLE 27-5 TD's Balance Sheet After Making a New Loan of $80

Assets ($)		Liabilities ($)	
Reserves	220	Deposits	1100
Loans	980	Capital	100
	1200		1200

TD lends its excess reserves and suffers a cash drain. The bank keeps $20 as a reserve against the initial new deposit of $100. It lends $80 to a customer, who writes a cheque to someone who deals with another bank. When the cheque is cleared, TD suffers an $80 cash drain. Comparing Tables 27-3 and 27-5 shows that the bank has increased its deposit liabilities by the $100 initially deposited and has increased its assets by $20 of cash reserves and $80 of new loans. It has also restored its target reserve ratio of 0.20.

TD can now lend the $80 in excess reserves that it is holding. As it lends the $80, it increases its loan portfolio by $80 but reduces its cash reserves by the same amount. We say that TD experiences a *cash drain*. Table 27-5 shows TD's balance sheet after this new loan and cash drain. Notice that TD has restored its reserve ratio to 20 percent, its target reserve ratio.

So far, of the $100 initial deposit at TD, $20 is held by TD as reserves against the deposit and $80 has been lent out in the system. As a result, other banks have received new deposits of $80 stemming from the loans made by TD; persons receiving payment from those who borrowed the $80 from TD will have deposited those payments in their own banks. Note that even though the *banking system* suffers no cash drain (our second simplifying assumption above), TD does suffer a cash drain because most of the $80 goes to other banks and is not redeposited at TD.

The banks that receive deposits from the proceeds of TD's loan are called second-round banks, third-round banks, and so on. In this case, the second-round banks receive new deposits of $80, and when the cheques clear, they have new reserves of $80. Because they desire to hold only $16 in additional reserves to support the new deposits, they have $64 of excess reserves. They now increase their loans by $64. After this money has been spent by the borrowers and has been deposited in other, third-round banks, the balance sheets of the second-round banks will have changed, as in Table 27-6.

The third-round banks now find themselves with $64 of new deposits. Against these they want to hold only $12.80 as reserves, so they have excess reserves of $51.20 that they can immediately lend out. Thus, there begins a long sequence of new deposits, new loans, new deposits, and new loans. These stages are shown in Table 27-7.

The new deposit of $100 to the banking system has led, through the banks' desire to lend their excess reserves, to the creation of new money. After the completion of the process depicted in Table 27-7, the total change in the combined balance sheets of the entire banking system is shown in Table 27-8.

If v is the target reserve ratio, a new deposit to the banking system will increase the total amount of deposits by $1/v$ times the new deposit. [35]

In our example, where $v = 0.2$ and the new deposit equals $100, total deposits in the banking system will eventually increase by (1/0.2) times $100—that is, by $500.

In our example in which there was an initial new deposit of $100, this $100 was also the amount by which reserves increased in the banking system as a whole. This is because the entire amount of new cash eventually ends up in reserves held against a much larger volume of new deposits. Identifying a new deposit as the change in reserves in the banking system permits us to state our central result slightly differently.

With no cash drain from the banking system, a banking system with a target reserve ratio of v can change its deposits by $1/v$ times any change in reserves.

Recalling that the Greek letter delta, Δ, means "the change in," we can express this result in a simple equation. We have

$$\Delta \text{ Deposits} = \frac{\Delta \text{ Reserves}}{v}$$

The "multiple expansion of deposits" that we have just described applies in reverse to a withdrawal of funds. Deposits of the banking system will fall by $1/v$ times the amount withdrawn from the banking system.

Excess Reserves and Cash Drains

The two simplifying assumptions that were made earlier can now be relaxed.

Excess Reserves If banks do not choose to lend their excess reserves, the multiple expansion that we discussed will not occur. Go back to Table 27-4. If TD Canada Trust had been content to hold 27 per-

TABLE 27-6 Changes in the Balance Sheets of Second-Round Banks

Assets ($)		Liabilities ($)	
Reserves	+16	Deposits	+80
Loans	+64		
	+80		+80

Second-round banks receive cash deposits and expand loans. The second-round banks gain new deposits of $80 as a result of the loan granted by TD. These banks keep 20 percent of the cash that they acquire as their reserve against the new deposit, and they can make new loans using the other 80 percent.

TABLE 27-7 The Sequence of Loans and Deposits After a Single New Deposit of $100

Bank	New Deposits	New Loans	Addition to Reserves
TD	100.00	80.00	20.00
2nd-round bank	80.00	64.00	16.00
3rd-round bank	64.00	51.20	12.80
4th-round bank	51.20	40.96	10.24
5th-round bank	40.96	32.77	8.19
6th-round bank	32.77	26.22	6.55
7th-round bank	26.22	20.98	5.24
8th-round bank	20.98	16.78	4.20
9th-round bank	16.78	13.42	3.36
10th-round bank	13.42	10.74	2.68
Total for first 10 rounds	446.33	357.07	89.26
All remaining rounds	53.67	42.93	10.74
Total for banking system	500.00	400.00	100.00

The banking system as a whole can create deposit money whenever it receives new deposits. The table shows the process of the creation of deposit money on the assumptions that all the loans made by one set of banks end up as deposits in another set of banks (the next-round banks), that the target reserve ratio (v) is 0.20, and that banks always lend out any excess reserves. Although each bank suffers a cash drain whenever it grants a new loan, the system as a whole does not, and in a series of steps it increases deposit money by $1/v$, which, in this example, is five times the amount of any increase in reserves that it obtains.

TABLE 27-8 Change in the Combined Balance Sheets of All the Banks in the System Following the Multiple Expansion of Deposits

Assets ($)		Liabilities ($)	
Reserves	+100	Deposits	+500
Loans	+400		
	+500		+500

The reserve ratio is returned to 0.20. The entire initial deposit of $100 ends up as additional reserves of the banking system. Therefore, deposits rise by (1/0.2) times the initial deposit—that is, by $500.

Practise with Study Guide Chapter 27, Exercises 5 and 7, Extension Exercise E1.

cent of its deposits in reserves, it would have done nothing more. Other things being equal, banks will choose to lend their excess reserves because of the profit motive, but there may be times when they believe that the risk is too great. It is one thing to be offered a good rate of interest on a loan, but if the borrower defaults on the payment of interest and principal, the bank will be the loser. Similarly, if the bank expects interest rates to rise in the future, it may hold off making loans now so that it will have reserves available to make more profitable loans after the interest rate has risen.

Deposit creation does not happen automatically; it depends on the decisions of bankers. If banks do not choose to lend their excess reserves, there will not be an expansion of deposits.

Recall that we have said that the money supply includes both currency and bank deposits. What we have just seen is that the behaviour of commercial banks is crucial to the process of deposit creation. It follows that the money supply is thus at least partly determined by the commercial banks—in response, for example, to changes in national income, interest rates, and expectations of future business conditions.

Cash Drain Until now, we have been assuming that the public holds a fixed amount of cash, so that when deposits were multiplying in the economy, there was no change in the amount of cash held by the public. But now suppose that instead of holding a fixed *number* of dollars people decide to hold an amount of cash equal to a fixed *fraction* of their bank deposits. An extra $100 that now gets injected into the banking system as a new cash deposit will not all stay in the banking system. As the amount of deposits multiplies, some fraction of that $100 will be added to the cash held by the public. In such a situation, any multiple expansion of bank deposits will be accompanied by what is called a *cash drain* to the public. This cash drain will reduce the maximum expansion of bank deposits, in exactly the same way that taxes and imports reduced the value of the simple multiplier in Chapter 22.

In the case of a cash drain, the relationship between the eventual change in deposits and an injection of cash into the banking system is slightly more complicated. If $X is injected into the system, reserves will ultimately increase by $X. But if c is the ratio of cash to deposits that people want to maintain, the final change in deposits will be given by: [36]

$$\Delta \text{Deposits} = \frac{\Delta \text{Reserves}}{c + v}$$

For example, suppose the Bank of Canada were to enter the open market and purchase $100 of government securities. As the previous bondholders deposit their $100 into their bank accounts, there is an injection of $100 into the banking system. If commercial banks' target reserve ratio is 20 percent and there is *no* cash drain, the eventual expansion of deposits will be $500 ($\Delta$Deposits = $100/0.20). But if there is a cash drain of 10 percent, the eventual expansion of deposits will only be $333.33 ($\Delta$Deposits = $100/(0.10 + 0.20)).

The larger is the cash drain from the banking system, the smaller will be the total expansion of deposits created by a change in reserves.

Realistic Expansion of Deposits So far we have explained the expansion of deposits in the banking system using reserve-deposit and cash-deposit ratios that are easy to work with but unrealistic for Canada. In particular, we have been assuming a reserve-deposit ratio (v) equal to 20 percent, whereas Table 27-2 shows that Canadian commercial banks hold reserves equal to *less than 1 percent* of their deposit liabilities. A realistic value for the cash-deposit ratio in Canada is also approximately 1 percent—indicating that firms and households hold cash outside the banks equal to 1 percent of the value of their bank deposits. Putting these more realistic values for v and c into our equation, we see that a $100 change in reserves generated by a new deposit to the banking system will eventually lead to a total change in deposits equal to $100/(c + v)$ = $100/(0.01 + 0.01) = $100/(0.02) = $5000. Therefore, small changes in the level of reserves can lead, through the commercial banks' process of deposit creation, to very large changes in the total level of deposits. Commercial banks really do create a lot of (deposit) money out of thin air!

27.4 THE MONEY SUPPLY

Several times in this chapter we have mentioned the *money supply* without ever defining it precisely. But now that you are familiar with the balance sheets of the Bank of Canada and the commercial banking system, and are comfortable with the idea of deposit creation by the commercial banks, we are ready to be more precise about what we mean by the money supply.

The total stock of money in the economy at any moment is called the **money supply** or the *supply of money*. Economists use several alternative definitions for the money supply, most of which are regularly reported in the *Bank of Canada Review*—a quarterly publication of the Bank of Canada. Each definition of the money supply includes the amount of currency in circulation *plus* some types of deposit liabilities of the financial institutions.

Money supply = Currency + Bank deposits

money supply The total quantity of money in an economy at a point in time. Also called the *supply of money*.

The different definitions vary only by which deposit liabilities are included. We begin by looking at the different kinds of deposits.

Kinds of Deposits

Over the past 20 years or so, banks have evolved a bewildering array of different types of deposits. From our point of view, the most important distinction is between deposits that can be transferred by cheque or debit card, called "chequable," and those that cannot, called "nonchequable." Chequable deposits are media of exchange; nonchequable deposits are not.

For many years, the distinction lay between *demand deposits*, which earned little or no interest but were chequable, and *savings deposits*, which earned a higher interest return but were nonchequable. Today, however, it is so easy to transfer funds from accounts that are technically nonchequable to other accounts that are chequable that the distinction becomes quite blurred. The deposit that is genuinely tied up for a period of time now takes the form of a **term deposit**, which has a specified withdrawal date, a minimum of 30 days into the future, and which pays a much reduced interest rate in

term deposit An interest-earning bank deposit, subject to notice before withdrawal.

the event of early withdrawal. Term and other nonchequable deposits pay significantly higher interest rates than do chequable deposits.

Nonbank financial institutions such as asset-management firms now offer *money market mutual funds* and *money market deposit accounts*. These accounts earn higher interest and are chequable, although some are subject to minimum withdrawal restrictions and others to prior notice of withdrawal.

The long-standing distinction between money and other highly liquid assets used to be that, narrowly defined, money was a medium of exchange that did not earn interest, whereas other liquid assets earned interest but were not media of exchange. Today, this distinction has almost completely broken down.

M1 Currency plus demand deposits.

M2 M1 plus savings deposits at the chartered banks.

M2+ M2 plus deposits held at institutions that are *not* chartered banks.

Definitions of the Money Supply

Different definitions of the money supply include different types of deposits. The narrowly defined money supply, called **M1**, includes currency and deposits that are themselves usable as media of exchange (such as chequable deposits). A broader definition, **M2**, includes M1 plus savings accounts at the chartered banks. A still broader measure, **M2+**, includes M2 plus the deposits held at the financial institutions that are *not* chartered banks, such as trust companies and credit unions.

M1 concentrates on the medium-of-exchange function of money. M2 and M2+ contain assets that serve the temporary store-of-value function and are in practice quickly convertible into a medium of exchange. Table 27-9 shows the principal elements in these definitions of the money supply. The details of the differences are not important at this stage; what matters is that, broadly defined, money comprises a spectrum of closely related financial assets that their holders regard as highly substitutable for each other.

TABLE 27-9 Three Measures of the Money Supply in Canada, April 2006 (millions of dollars)

Currency	45 002
+ Demand deposits	145 485
= **M1**	190 487
+ Personal saving deposits and nonpersonal notice deposits	492 629
= **M2**	683 116
+ Deposits at trust and mortgage loan companies, credit unions, and caisses populaires	168 160
+ Money market mutual funds and deposits at other institutions	90 285
= **M2+**	941 561

The three widely used measures of the money supply are M1, M2, and M2+. The narrowest definition, M1, concentrates on what can be used directly as media of exchange, and thus includes only currency and demand deposits. The broader definitions then add in deposits that serve the store-of-value function but can be readily converted to a medium of exchange. M2 is thus M1 plus saving deposits. M2+ is M2 plus deposits at the nonbank financial institutions.

(*Source:* From *Weekly Financial Statistics*, June 23, 2006. Copyright © 1995–2007, Bank of Canada.)

Near Money and Money Substitutes

Recall our early discussion of money as a medium of exchange and as a store of value. In arriving at empirical measures of money, we must consider some assets that do not perform one or both of these roles perfectly. This brings us to the concepts of *near money* and *money substitutes*.

Assets that adequately fulfill the store-of-value function and are readily converted into a medium of exchange but are not themselves a medium of exchange are sometimes called **near money**. Term deposits are a good example of near money. When you have a term deposit, you know exactly how much purchasing power you hold (at current prices), and, given modern banking practices, you can turn your deposit into a

near money Liquid assets that are easily convertible into money without risk of significant loss of value and can be used as short-term stores of value but are not themselves media of exchange.

medium of exchange—cash or a chequing deposit—at a moment's notice (though you may pay a penalty in the form of reduced interest if you withdraw the funds before the end of the specified term).

Why then does everybody not keep his or her money in such deposits instead of in demand deposits or currency? The answer is that the inconvenience of continually shifting money back and forth may outweigh the interest that can be earned. One week's interest on $100 (at 5 percent per year) is only about 10 cents, not enough to cover bus fare to the bank, the time spent going to an ATM, or perhaps even the time spent making an on-line transfer. For money that will be needed soon, it would hardly pay to shift it to a term deposit.

Things that serve as media of exchange but are not a store of value are sometimes called **money substitutes**. Credit cards are a prime example. With a credit card, many transactions can be made without either cash or a cheque. The evidence of credit, the credit slip you sign and hand over to the store, is not money, because it cannot be used to make other transactions. The credit card serves the short-run function of a medium of exchange by allowing you to make purchases, even though you have no cash or bank deposit currently in your possession. But this is only temporary; money remains the final medium of exchange for these transactions when the credit-card bill is paid.

Practise with Study Guide Chapter 27, Short-Answer Question 2.

money substitute Something that serves as a medium of exchange but is not a store of value.

Choosing a Measure

Since the eighteenth century, economists have known that the amount of money in circulation is an important economic variable. As theories became more carefully specified in the nineteenth and early twentieth centuries, they included a variable called the "money supply." But for theories to be useful (and especially for the predictions to be testable), we must be able to identify real-world counterparts of these theoretical variables.

The specifics of the definition of money have changed and will continue to change over time. New monetary assets are continually being developed to serve some, if not all, of the functions of money, and they are more or less readily convertible into money. There is no single, timeless definition of money and what is only near money or a money substitute. Indeed, as we have seen, the Bank of Canada uses several definitions of money.

The Role of the Bank of Canada

In this chapter, we have seen that the commercial banking system, when confronted with a new deposit, can create a multiple expansion of bank deposits. This shows how the reserves of the banking system are systematically related to the money supply. In Chapter 29 we will see the details of how the Bank of Canada conducts its monetary policy and how its actions influence the total amount of reserves in the banking system. At that point we will have a more complete picture of the connection between the Bank's monetary policy, reserves in the banking system, and the overall money supply.

Recall that in the previous chapter we examined how in the long run, with real GDP equal to Y^*, the real interest rate was determined by saving and investment. In the next chapter, we return to the short-run version of our macro model (in which Y is no longer assumed to equal Y^*) but add money to that model explicitly. There we will see how the interaction of money demand and money supply determines the equilibrium interest rate in the short run. We will also see how changes in the money market lead to changes in desired aggregate expenditure and real GDP. In Chapter 29 we examine the details of the Bank of Canada's monetary policy, with an emphasis on its current policy regime of *inflation targeting*.

S U M M A R Y

27.1 THE NATURE OF MONEY

- Money is anything that serves as a medium of exchange, a store of value, and a unit of account.
- Money arose because of the inconvenience of barter, and it developed in stages: from precious metal to metal coinage, to paper money convertible to precious metals, to token coinage and paper money fractionally backed by precious metals, to fiat money, and to deposit money.

27.2 THE CANADIAN BANKING SYSTEM

- The banking system in Canada consists of two main elements: the Bank of Canada (which is the central bank) and the commercial banks.
- The Bank of Canada is a government-owned corporation that is responsible for the day-to-day conduct of monetary policy. Though the Bank has considerable autonomy in its policy decisions, ultimate responsibility for monetary policy resides with the government.

- Commercial banks are profit-seeking institutions that allow their customers to transfer deposits from one bank to another by means of cheques or debit cards. They create money as a by-product of their commercial operations by making or liquidating loans and various other investments.

27.3 MONEY CREATION BY THE BANKING SYSTEM

- Because most customers are content to pay by cheque or debit card rather than with cash, banks need only small reserves to back their deposit liabilities. It is this *fractional-reserve* aspect of the banking system that enables commercial banks to create deposit money.

- When the banking system receives a new cash deposit, it can create new deposits equal to some multiple of this amount. For a target reserve ratio of v and a cash–deposit ratio of c, the total change in deposits following an injection of reserves is:

$$\Delta \text{Deposits} = \frac{\Delta \text{Reserves}}{c + v}$$

27.4 THE MONEY SUPPLY

- The money supply—the stock of money in an economy at a specific moment—can be defined in various ways. M1, the narrowest definition, includes currency and chequable deposits. M2 includes M1 plus savings deposits and smaller term deposits. M2+ includes M2 plus deposits at nonbank financial institutions and money-market mutual funds.

- Near money includes interest-earning assets that are convertible into money on a dollar-for-dollar basis but that are not currently a medium of exchange. Money substitutes are things such as credit cards that serve as a medium of exchange but are not money.

KEY CONCEPTS

Medium of exchange, store of value, and unit of account
Fully backed, fractionally backed, and fiat money

The banking system and the Bank of Canada
Target reserve ratio and excess reserves

The creation of deposit money
Demand and term deposits
The money supply
Near money and money substitutes

STUDY EXERCISES

1. Fill in the blanks to make the following statements correct.

   a. Money serves three functions: _____, _____ and _____.

   b. Suppose children at a summer camp are each given a credit of $20.00 at the snack shop, where purchases are recorded but no cash is exchanged. This is an example of money as a _____ and a _____.

   c. Paper money and coins that are not convertible into anything with intrinsic value, but are declared by the government to be legal tender, are known as _____.

   d. The Bank of Canada has four main functions in the Canadian economy. They are:
   - _____
   - _____
   - _____
   - _____

   e. Canada has a _____-reserve banking system, in which commercial banks keep only a fraction of their total deposits in reserves. A commercial bank has a _____ ratio that governs what it attempts to keep as reserves.

2. Fill in the blanks to make the following statements correct. Answer these questions in the sequence given.

   a. Suppose the Bank of Canada purchases a $1000 bond from Bob's Fishing Supplies, and Bob's deposits its cheque at the CIBC. This is a _____ deposit to the banking system and will allow the commercial banks to _____.

   b. If the CIBC has a target reserve ratio of 5 percent, it will keep _____ dollars as reserves and will lend _____ dollars.

   c. Assuming there is no cash drain from the banking system, the ultimate effect is a(n) _____ in deposits in the banking system of _____ × $1000 = _____.

   d. Suppose the Bank of Canada sells a $1000 bond to Bob's Fishing Supplies, and Bob's pays for that bond with a cheque drawn on its account at the CIBC. This is a _____ of funds from the banking system and will cause the commercial banks to _____.

   e. If the CIBC pays the $1000 from its reserves, its reserve ratio will then be _____ its target rate of 5 percent. If the CIBC keeps its reserves at the new level, its loans must fall by _____ to restore the 5-percent target reserve ratio.

3. Which of the following items can be considered money in the Canadian economy? Explain your answers by discussing the three functions of money—medium of exchange, store of value, and unit of account.

   a. A Canadian $100 bill
   b. A Visa credit card
   c. A well-known painting by Robert Bateman
   d. An interest-earning savings account
   e. A U.S. treasury bill payable in three months
   f. A share of Tim Hortons stock
   g. A $1 bill of Canadian Tire money

4. [myeconlab] The table below shows the balance sheet for the Regal Bank, a hypothetical commercial bank. Assume that the Regal Bank has achieved its target reserve ratio.

Balance Sheet: Regal Bank			
Assets		Liabilities	
Reserves	$ 200	Deposits	$4000
Loans	$4200	Capital	$ 400

   a. What is the Regal Bank's target reserve ratio?
   b. What is the value of the owners' investment in the bank?
   c. Suppose someone makes a new deposit to the Regal Bank of $100. Draw a new balance sheet showing the *immediate* effect of the new deposit. What is the Regal Bank's new reserve ratio?
   d. Suppose instead that someone *withdraws* $100 cash from the Regal Bank. Show the new balance sheet and the new reserve ratio.

5. **myeconlab** Consider a new deposit to the Canadian banking system of $1000. Suppose that all commercial banks have a target reserve ratio of 10 percent and there is no cash drain. The following table shows how deposits, reserves, and loans change as the new deposit permits the banks to "create" money.

Round	ΔDeposits	ΔReserves	ΔLoans
First	$1000	$100	$900
Second	—	—	—
Third	—	—	—
Fourth	—	—	—
Fifth	—	—	—

a. The first round has been completed in the table. Now, recalling that the new loans in the first round become the new deposits in the second round, complete the second round in the table.
b. Using the same approach, complete the entire table.
c. You have now completed the first five rounds of the deposit-creation process. What is the total change in deposits *so far* as a result of the single new deposit of $1000?
d. This deposit-creation process will go on forever, but it will have a *finite* sum. In the text, we showed that the eventual total change in deposits is equal to $1/v$ times the new deposit, where v is the target reserve ratio. What is the eventual total change in deposits in this case?
e. What is the eventual total change in reserves? What is the eventual change in loans?

6. **myeconlab** Consider a withdrawal of $5000 from the Canadian banking system. Suppose all commercial banks have a target reserve ratio of 8 percent and there is no cash drain.

a. Using a table like that shown in the previous question, show the change in deposits, reserves, and loans for the first three "rounds" of activity.
b. Compute the eventual total change in deposits, reserves, and loans.

7. Consider an individual who immigrates to Canada and deposits $3000 in Canadian currency into the Canadian banking system. Suppose all commercial banks have a target reserve ratio of 10 percent and individuals choose to hold cash equal to 10 percent of their bank deposits.

a. In the text, we showed that the eventual total change in deposits is equal to $1/(v+c)$ times the new deposit, where v is the target reserve ratio and c is the ratio of cash to deposits. What is the eventual total change in deposits in this case?
b. What is the eventual total change in reserves?
c. What is the eventual total change in loans?

8. Consider an individual who moves to Canada and brings with him $40 000 in Canadian currency, which he deposits in a Canadian bank. For each of the cases below, compute the overall change in deposits and reserves in the Canadian banking system as a result of this new deposit.

a. 10 percent target reserve ratio; no cash drain; no excess reserves
b. 10 percent target reserve ratio; 5 percent cash drain; no excess reserves
c. 10 percent target reserve ratio; 5 percent cash drain; 5 percent excess reserves

9. This question is intended to illustrate the similarity between the simple multiplier from Chapters 21 and 22 and the deposit multiplier that we examined in this chapter.

a. Recalling the macro model of Chapters 21 and 22, suppose the marginal propensity to spend out of GDP, z, is 0.6. If autonomous spending increases by $1000, fill in the table below.

Round	ΔAE	ΔY
First	$1000	$1000
Second	—	—
Third	—	—
Fourth	—	—
Fifth	—	—

b. The sum of the values in the third column should be:

$$\Delta Y = \$1000 + z\,\$1000 + z^2\,\$1000 + z^3\,\$1000 + \ldots$$

What is the total change in GDP?

c. Now consider the process of deposit creation from this chapter. Consider a new deposit of $1000 and a target reserve ratio, v, of 0.25 (with no cash drain). Fill in the following table:

Round	ΔDeposits	ΔReserves	ΔLoans
First	$1000	$250	$750
Second	—	—	—
Third	—	—	—
Fourth	—	—	—
Fifth	—	—	—

d. The sum of the values in the first column should be:

$$\Delta\text{Deposits} = \$1000 + (1-v)\$1000 + (1-v)^2\$1000 + (1-v)^3\$1000 + \ldots$$

What is the total change in deposits?

e. Explain why taxes and imports for the simple multiplier in Chapter 21 are similar to a reserve ratio for the deposit multiplier in this chapter.

DISCUSSION QUESTIONS

1. A Canadian who receives a U.S. coin has the option of spending it at face value or taking it to the bank and converting it to Canadian money at the going rate of exchange. When the rate of exchange was near par (in the early 1970s), so that $1 Canadian was within 3 cents of U.S.$1, U.S. and Canadian coins circulated side by side, exchanged at face value. Use Gresham's law to predict which coinage disappeared from circulation in Canada when the Canadian dollar fell to U.S.$0.67 in the late 1990s. Why did a 3-cent differential not produce this result?

2. During hyperinflations in several foreign countries after the Second World War, American cigarettes were sometimes used in place of money. What made them suitable?

3. Suppose that on January 1, 2005, a household had $100 000, which it wished to hold for use one year later. Calculate, using resources available on-line or in your university library, which of the following would have been the best store of value over that period. Will the best store of value over that period necessarily be the best over the next 24 months?

   a. The (Canadian) dollar
   b. Stocks whose prices moved with the Toronto Stock Exchange (S&P/TSX) index
   c. A Government of Canada 5.75 percent bond coming due in 2029
   d. Gold
   e. A house whose value changed with the average house price in Canada

4. If all depositors tried to turn their deposits into cash at once, they would find that there are not sufficient reserves in the system to allow all of them to do this at the same time. Why then do we not still have panicky runs on the banks? Would it be better for the Bank of Canada to impose a 100 percent reserve requirement? What effect would such a reserve requirement have on the banking system's ability to create money? Would it preclude any possibility of a panic?

5. Compared to a few years ago, credit and bank cards are used extensively today to facilitate purchase of goods and services all over the world. Does this distort the true measure of money in the economy? Should credit and bank cards be incorporated in the definitions of M1 or M2?

CHAPTER 28

Money, Interest Rates, and Economic Activity

LO LEARNING OBJECTIVES

In this chapter you will learn

1. why the price of a bond is inversely related to the market interest rate.
2. how the demand for money is related to the interest rate, the price level, and real GDP.
3. how monetary equilibrium determines the interest rate in the short run.
4. about the transmission mechanism of monetary policy.
5. the difference between the short-run and long-run effects of monetary policy.
6. when monetary policy is most effective in influencing real GDP in the short run.

In Chapter 27, we learned how the commercial banking system multiplies a given amount of reserves into deposit money and thus determines the nation's money supply. We also learned that because the Bank of Canada can influence the amount of reserves, it too has an influence on the money supply. What we have not yet discussed, however, is *how* the Bank influences the amount of reserves. We will leave that discussion until next chapter when we examine the details of Canadian monetary policy. For now, just think of the nation's money supply as being determined jointly by the actions of the Bank of Canada and the commercial banking system.

In this chapter, we focus on how money affects the economy. Understanding the role of money, however, requires an understanding of the interaction of money supply and money demand. To examine the nature of money demand, we begin by examining how households decide to divide their total holdings of assets between money and interest-earning assets (which here are called "bonds"). Once that is done, we put money supply and money demand together to examine *monetary equilibrium*. Only then can we ask how changes in the supply of money or in the demand for money affect the economy—interest rates, real GDP, and the price level. We begin with a discussion of the relationship between bond prices and interest rates.

28.1 UNDERSTANDING BONDS

At any moment, households have a stock of financial wealth that they hold in many forms. Some of it is money in the bank or in the wallet. Some may be in *treasury bills* and *bonds,* which are IOUs issued by the government or corporations. Some may be in *equity,* meaning ownership shares of a company.

To simplify our discussion, we will group financial wealth into just two categories, which we call "money" and "bonds." By money we mean all assets that serve as a medium of exchange—that is, paper money, coins, and deposits on which cheques can be drawn. By bonds we mean all other forms of wealth; this includes interest-earning financial assets and claims on real capital (equity). This simplification is useful because it emphasizes the important distinction between interest-earning and non-interest-earning assets. This distinction is central for understanding the demand for money.

Economists often simplify the analysis of financial assets by considering only two types of assets—non-interest-bearing "money" and interest-bearing "bonds."

Before discussing how individuals decide to divide their assets between money and bonds, we need to make sure we understand what bonds are, and how they are priced. This requires an understanding of *present value.*

myeconlab

For readers interested in learning more about the stock market, the market in which equities are traded, look for "A Beginner's Guide to the Stock Market" in the *Additional Topics* section of this book's MyEconLab.

w w w . m y e c o n l a b . c o m

Present Value and the Interest Rate

A bond is a financial asset that promises to make one or more specified payments at specified dates in the future. The **present value (*PV*)** of any asset refers to the value now of the future payments that the asset offers. Present value depends on the interest rate because when we calculate present value, the interest rate is used to *discount* the future payments. Let's consider two examples to illustrate the concept of present value.

present value (*PV*) The value now of one or more payments or receipts made in the future; often referred to as *discounted present value.*

A Single Payment One Year Hence
We start with the simplest case. What is the value *now* of a bond that will return a single payment of $100 in one year's time?

Suppose the interest rate is 5 percent. Now ask how much you would have to lend out at that interest rate today in order to have $100 a year from now. If we use *PV* to stand for this unknown amount, we can write $PV \times (1.05) = \$100$. Thus, $PV = \$100/1.05 = \$95.24$.[1] This tells us that the present value of $100 receivable in one year's time is $95.24; if you lend out $95.24 for one year at 5 percent interest you will get back the $95.24 plus $4.76 in interest, which makes $100.

We can generalize this relationship with a simple equation. If R_1 is the amount we receive one year from now and *i* is the annual interest rate, the present value of R_1 is:

$$PV = \frac{R_1}{1 + i}$$

---

[1] Notice that in this type of formula, the interest rate is expressed as a decimal fraction where, for example, 5 percent is expressed as 0.05, so $1 + i$ equals 1.05.

If the interest rate is 7 percent ($i = 0.07$) and the bond pays $100 in one year ($R_1 = \$100$), the present value of that bond is $PV = \$100/1.07 = \$93.46$. Notice that, when compared with the previous numerical example, the higher interest rate leads to a lower present value. The future payment of $100 gets discounted at a higher rate and so is worth less at the present time.

Practise with Study Guide Chapter 28, Exercise 1.

A Sequence of Future Payments   Now consider a more complicated case, but one that is actually more realistic. Many bonds promise to make "coupon" payments every year and then return the face value of the bond at the end of the term of the loan. For example, imagine a three-year bond that promises to repay the face value of $1000 in three years, but will also pay a 10 percent coupon payment of $100 at the end of each of the three years that the bond is held. How much is this bond worth now? We can compute the present value of this bond by adding together the present values of each of the payments. If the market interest rate is 7 percent, the present value of this bond is:

$$PV = \frac{\$100}{1.07} + \frac{\$100}{(1.07)^2} + \frac{\$1100}{(1.07)^3}$$

The first term is the value today of receiving $100 one year from now. The second term is the value today of receiving the second $100 payment two years from now. Note that we discount this second payment twice—once from Year 2 to Year 1, and once again from Year 1 to now—and thus the denominator shows an interest rate of 7 percent *compounded* for two years. Finally, the third term shows the value today of the $1100 repayment ($1000 of face value plus $100 of coupon payment) three years from now. The present value of this bond is:

$$PV = \$93.46 + \$87.34 + \$897.93$$
$$= \$1078.73$$

In general, any asset that promises to make a sequence of payments into the future of $R_1, R_2, \ldots$ and so on up to R_T has a present value given by:

$$PV = \frac{R_1}{1 + i} + \frac{R_2}{(1 + i)^2} + \cdots + \frac{R_T}{(1 + i)^T}$$

It is useful to try another example. Let's continue with the case in which the bond repays its face value of $1000 three years from now and makes three $100 coupon payments at the end of each year the bond is held. But this time we assume the market interest rate is 9 percent. In this case, the present value of the bond is:

$$PV = \frac{\$100}{1.09} + \frac{\$100}{(1.09)^2} + \frac{\$1100}{(1.09)^3}$$
$$= \$91.74 \quad + \quad \$84.17 \quad + \quad \$849.40$$
$$= \$1025.31$$

Notice that when the market interest rate is 9 percent, the present value of the bond is lower than the present value of the same bond when the market interest rate is 7 percent. The higher interest rate implies that any future payments are discounted at a higher rate and thus have a lower present value.

A General Relationship   There are many types of bonds. Some make no coupon payments but only a single payment (the "face value") at some point in the future. This is the case for short-term government bonds called *treasury bills*. Other bonds, typically longer-term government or corporate bonds, make regular coupon payments as well as a final payment of the bond's face value. Though there are many types of bonds, they all have one thing in common: They promise to make some payment or sequence of payments in the future. Because bonds make payments in the future, their present value is negatively related to the market interest rate.

The present value of any bond that promises a future payment or sequence of future payments is negatively related to the market interest rate.

Present Value and Market Price

Most bonds are bought and sold in financial markets in which there are large numbers of both buyers and sellers. The present value of a bond is important because it establishes the price at which a bond will be exchanged in the financial markets.

The present value of a bond is the most someone would be willing to pay now to own the bond's future stream of payments.

To understand this concept, let us return to our example of a bond that promises to pay $100 one year from now. When the interest rate is 5 percent, the present value of this bond is $95.24. To see why this is the maximum that anyone would pay for this bond, suppose that some sellers offer to sell the bond at some other price, say, $98. If, instead of paying this amount for the bond, a potential buyer lends $98 out at 5 percent interest, he or she would have at the end of one year more than the $100 that the bond will produce. (At 5 percent interest, $98 yields $4.90 in interest, which when added to the principal makes $102.90.) Clearly, no well-informed individual would pay $98—or, by the same reasoning, any sum in excess of $95.24—for the bond. Thus, at any price above the bond's present value, the lack of demand will cause the price to fall.

Now suppose the bond is offered for sale at a price less than $95.24, say, $90. A potential buyer could borrow $90 to buy the bond and would pay $4.50 in interest on the loan. At the end of the year, the bond yields $100. When this is used to repay the $90 loan and the $4.50 in interest, $5.50 is left as profit. Clearly, it would be worthwhile for someone to buy the bond at the price of $90 or, by the same argument, at any price less than $95.24. Thus, at any price below the bond's present value, the abundance of demand will cause the price to rise.

This discussion should make clear that the present value of an asset determines its equilibrium market price. If the market price of any asset is greater than the present value of its income stream, no one will want to buy it, and this excess supply will push down the market price. If the market price is below its present value, there will be a rush to buy it, and this excess demand will push up the market price. When the bond's market price is exactly equal to its present value, there is no pressure for the price to change.

The equilibrium market price of any bond will be the present value of the income stream that it produces.

Interest Rates, Market Prices, and Bond Yields

We now have two relationships that can be put together to tell us about the link between the market interest rate and bond prices. Let's restate these two relationships.

1. The present value of a bond is negatively related to the market interest rate.

2. A bond's equilibrium market price will be equal to its present value.

Putting these two relationships together, we come to a key relationship:

An increase in the market interest rate leads to a fall in the price of any given bond. A decrease in the market interest rate leads to an increase in the price of any given bond.

Remember that a bond is a financial investment for the purchaser. The cost of the investment is the price of the bond, and the return on the investment is the sequence of future payments. Thus, for a given sequence of future payments, a lower bond price implies a higher rate of return on the bond, or a higher *bond yield*.

To illustrate the yield on a bond, consider a simple example of a bond that promises to pay $1000 two years from now. If you purchase this bond for $857.34, your return on your investment will be 8 percent per year because $857.34 compounded for two years at 8 percent will yield $1000 in two years.

$$\$857.34 \, (1.08)^2 = \$1000$$

In other words, your yield on the bond will be 8 percent per year.

Notice that we are making a distinction between the concept of the *yield* on a bond and the *market interest rate*. The bond yield is a function of the sequence of payments and the bond price. The market interest rate is the rate at which you can borrow or lend money in the credit market.

Although they are logically distinct from each other, there is a close relationship between the market interest rate and bond yields. A rise in the market interest rate will lead to a decline in the present value of any bond and thus to a decline in its equilibrium price. As the bond price falls, its yield or rate of return rises. Thus, we see that market interest rates and bond yields tend to move in the same direction.

An increase in the market interest rate will reduce bond prices and increase bond yields. A reduction in the market interest rate will increase bond prices and reduce bond yields. Therefore, market interest rates and bond yields move together.

Because of this close relationship between bond yields and market interest rates, economists discussing the role of money in the macroeconomy typically refer to "the" interest rate—or perhaps to "interest rates" in general—rather than to any specific interest rate among the many different rates corresponding to the many different financial assets. Since these rates all tend to rise or fall together, it is a very useful simplification to refer only to "the" interest rate, meaning the rate of return that can be earned by holding interest-earning assets rather than money.

Bond Riskiness

Sometimes the yields on specific bonds rise or fall even when there is no change in the market interest rate. This occurs when there is a change in the perceived *riskiness* of the bond. If the bond purchasers (lenders) perceive that bond issuers (borrowers) are unlikely to be able to fulfill their future repayment obligations, the expected present value of the bond declines. A lower expected present value leads fewer buyers to be interested in purchasing that bond and, as a result, its equilibrium market price declines. As the market price falls, the yield on that bond rises. Bonds with high yields reflect high-risk investments.

An increase in the riskiness of any bond leads to a decline in its expected present value and thus to a decline in the bond's price. The lower bond price implies a higher bond yield.

It is rare in Canada that government bonds are perceived as risky, but many corporations are sometimes believed to be in precarious financial situations and thus their bonds are perceived to be risky assets. As a result, there are often very high yields (low bond prices) on specific corporate bonds. *Applying Economic Concepts 28-1* discusses the relationship among bond prices, bond yields, riskiness, and *term to maturity* of government and corporate bonds. It will help you understand some of those columns of confusing numbers that appear daily at the back of your favourite newspaper!

28.2 THE DEMAND FOR MONEY

The amount of money balances that everyone in the economy wishes to hold is called the **demand for money**. At any given time, households and firms have a specific stock of financial assets, and they must decide in which form to hold these assets. Remember that we make the simplifying assumption that there are only two types of assets—money and bonds. Therefore, if households and firms are choosing how to divide their given stock of assets between money and bonds, it follows that if we know the demand for money, we also know the demand for bonds. If people wish to hold $1 billion more of their assets in the form of money, they must also wish to hold $1 billion less of bonds.

demand for money The total amount of money balances that the public wishes to hold for all purposes.

Reasons for Holding Money

Why do firms and households hold money? There are three reasons. First, households and firms hold money in order to carry out *transactions*. Economists call this the *transactions demand* for money. You carry money in your pocket or keep it in a chequing account in order to have it readily available for your upcoming transactions; it would be very inconvenient to have to sell bonds or withdraw money from your savings account every time you wanted to spend. Similarly, firms are continually making expenditures on intermediate inputs and payments to labour and they keep money available in their chequing accounts to pay these expenses.

A second and related reason firms and households hold money is that they are uncertain about when some expenditures will be necessary, and they hold money as a precaution to avoid the problems associated with missing a transaction. This is referred to as the *precautionary demand* for money. For example, you might hold some cash because of the possibility that you might need to take an unplanned taxi ride during a rainstorm; a small business may hold cash because of the possibility that it might need the emergency services of a tradesman, such as a plumber or an electrician. In the days before the invention of ATMs, the precautionary demand for money was quite large since to be caught on a weekend or away from home without sufficient cash could be a serious matter. Today, this motive for holding money is less important.

The third reason for holding money applies more to large businesses and to professional money managers than to individuals because it involves *speculating* about how interest rates are likely to change in the future. Economists call this the *speculative demand* for money. To understand this reason for holding money, recall what we said earlier about the negative relationship between interest rates and bond prices. If interest rates are expected to rise in the future, bond prices will be expected to fall. Whenever bond prices fall, bondholders experience a decline in the value of their bond holdings. The expectation of increases in *future* interest rates will therefore lead to the

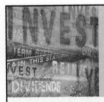

APPLYING ECONOMIC CONCEPTS 28-1

Understanding Bond Prices and Bond Yields

Look at the back of the business section of your newspaper and you will find several pages with columns of fine print that list prices for stocks, bonds, precious metals, and mutual funds. We focus here on how to read the section on bonds.

How to Read the Bond Tables

The accompanying table shows seven bond listings just as they appeared in the *Globe and Mail* on June 10, 2006. The five columns are as follows:

1. **Issuer.** This is the issuer of the bond—that is, the borrower of the money. The first five bonds shown are issued by the government of Canada. The last two are issued by firms whose names you surely recognize.

2. **Coupon.** This is the coupon rate—the annual rate of interest that the bond pays before it matures. For example, a 6 percent coupon rate means that the bondholder (the lender) will receive 6 percent of the face value of the bond every year until the bond matures.

3. **Maturity.** This is when the bond matures and the face value is repaid to the bondholder. All debt obligations are then fulfilled.

4. **Price.** This is the market price of the bond, expressed as the price per $100 of face value. For example, a price of $104.81 means that for every $100 of face value, the purchaser must pay $104.81. When the price is greater than $100, we say there is a *premium;* when the price is less than $100, we say the bond is selling at a *discount.*

5. **Yield.** This is the rate of return earned by the bondholder if the bond is bought at the *current* price and held to maturity, earning all regular coupon payments.

Bond Prices and Yields

Three general patterns can be seen in the accompanying table. First, for a given issuer and maturity, there is a positive relationship between the bond price and the coupon rate. Rows 1 and 2, for example, show two bonds, both issued by the government of Canada and both maturing on June 1, 2008. The common issuer suggests a common risk of non-repayment (in this case a very low risk). The first bond has a 6 percent coupon whereas the second has a 10 percent coupon. Not surprisingly, the higher coupon payments make the second bond a more attractive asset and thus its market price is higher—$110.94 as compared to $103.35. Note, how-

holding of more money (and fewer bonds) *now* as financial managers adjust their portfolios in order to preserve their values.

The Determinants of Money Demand

We have just seen three general reasons why firms and households hold money. We now want to examine which key macroeconomic variables affect the *amount* of money that is demanded in our macro model. We focus on three: the interest rate, the level of real GDP, and the price level.

The Interest Rate   No matter what benefits households or firms receive from holding money, there is also a cost. The cost of holding money is the income that *could have been earned* if that wealth were instead held in the form of interest-earning bonds. This is the *opportunity cost* of holding money. In our macro model, we assume that an increase in ever, that the implied yield on the two bonds is almost identical. If this weren't the case, demand would shift toward the high-yield (low-price) bond, driving down the yield (increasing the price) until the two yields were the same.

Second, for a given bond issuer, there is a positive relationship between the bond yield and the term to maturity. This is shown in the first five rows, as yields rise from 4.15 percent on bonds maturing in 24 months' time (from the date of the listing) to 4.45 percent on bonds maturing in 23 years' time. This positive relationship is often referred to as the *yield curve* or the *term structure of interest rates*. The higher yields on longer-term bonds reflect what is often called a *term premium*—the higher yield that bondholders must be paid in order to induce them to have their money tied up for longer periods of time.

Third, for a given term to maturity, there is a positive relationship between the bond yield and the perceived riskiness of the bond issuer. Compare rows 3 and 6, for example. Both bonds have very similar (but not identical) maturity dates in 2011, but one is issued by the government of Canada while the other is issued by the Bank of Montreal (BMO). Though it is almost impossible for the government of Canada to go bankrupt and almost inconceivable that it would default on its debt, it is at least possible for the Bank of Montreal to do so. This difference explains the 0.6-percentage-

point difference in yields. The same is true between rows 5 and 7 where the 1.3 percentage point yield difference is attributable to the higher likelihood of default by Loblaws than by the Canadian government.

If you run your eyes down the bond tables, you will easily see those corporations viewed by the market as being risky borrowers because the yields on their bonds will be higher—often dramatically so—than the yields on similar-maturity government bonds. For example, in 2003 when Air Canada was experiencing severe financial difficulties, its bonds were selling at such a discount that the implied annual yield was over 30 percent. Such high yields represent a great investment opportunity only if you are prepared to take the associated risk. Beware!

Issuer	Coupon	Maturity	Price	Yield
1. Canada	6.00	Jun 1, 2008	103.35	4.21
2. Canada	10.00	Jun 1, 2008	110.94	4.15
3. Canada	6.00	Jun 1, 2011	107.59	4.29
4. Canada	11.25	Jun 1, 2015	150.68	4.36
5. Canada	5.75	Jun 1, 2029	118.52	4.45
6. BMO	6.69	Dec 31, 2011	108.91	4.83
7. Loblaws Co.	6.45	Feb 9, 2028	107.03	5.87

the interest rate leads firms and households to reduce their desired money holdings. Conversely, a reduction in the interest rate means that holding money is less costly and so firms and households are assumed to increase their desired money holdings.

Other things being equal, the demand for money is assumed to be negatively related to the interest rate.[2]

This negative relationship between interest rates and desired money holdings is shown in Figure 28-1, and is drawn as the money demand (M_D) curve. Remember that the decision to hold money is also the decision *not* to hold bonds, and so movements

---

[2] The opportunity cost of holding money is the interest that could have been earned on bonds—this is the *nominal* interest rate. In the presence of expected inflation, we must distinguish between the *nominal* and *real* interest rates. In this chapter we assume, however, that expected inflation is zero, and so we simply speak of "the" interest rate. We discuss inflation in detail in Chapter 30.

FIGURE 28-1   Money Demand as a Function of the Interest Rate, Real GDP, and the Price Level

An increase in Y or P leads to an increase in money demand at any given interest rate

The quantity of money demanded is assumed to be negatively related to the interest rate and positively related to real GDP and the price level. The negative slope of the M_D curve comes from the choice between holding money or holding bonds. A fall in the interest rate from i_1 to i_0 lowers the opportunity cost of holding money because the rate of return on bonds declines. Thus the decision to hold more money (the movement from A to B as the interest rate falls) is the "flip side" of the decision to hold fewer bonds.

We show the initial money demand curve as M_D (Y, P), indicating that the curve is drawn for given values of Y and P. Increases in Y or P shift the M_D curve to the right; decreases in Y or P shift the M_D curve to the left.

along the M_D curve imply the substitution of assets between money and bonds. For example, as interest rates decline, bonds become a less attractive asset and money becomes more attractive, so firms and households substitute away from bonds and toward money.

Let's now see why changes in real GDP and the price level cause the M_D curve to shift.

Real GDP   An important reason for holding money is to make transactions. Not surprisingly, the amount of transactions that firms and households wish to make is positively related to the level of income and production in the economy—that is, to the level of real GDP. This positive relationship between real GDP and desired money holdings is shown in Figure 28-1 by a rightward shift of the M_D curve to M_D'. At any given interest rate, an increase in Y is assumed to generate more transactions and thus greater desired money holdings.

An increase in real GDP increases the volume of transactions in the economy and therefore leads to an increase in desired money holding.

The Price Level   An increase in the price level leads to an increase in the *dollar* value of transactions even if there is no change in the *real* value of transactions. That is, as P rises, households and firms will need to hold more money in order to carry out the same real value of transactions. This positive relationship between the price level and desired money holdings is also shown in Figure 28-1 as a rightward shift of the M_D curve to M_D'.

An increase in the price level is assumed to cause an increase in desired money holdings.

We can be more precise than just saying that there is a positive relationship between P and desired money holdings. Suppose, for example, that Y and i are constant but that all prices in the economy increase by 10 percent. Since Y is unchanged, the *real* value of desired transactions should also be unchanged. Furthermore, since i is unchanged, the opportunity cost of holding money is constant. Therefore, in order to make the same transactions as before, households and firms must not just hold more money than before—they must hold precisely 10 percent more. In other words, we assume that if real GDP and the interest rate are constant, the demand for money is *proportional* to the price level.

Money Demand: Summing Up

We have discussed why firms and households hold money and we have examined the relationship in our macroeconomic model between desired money holding and three macroeconomic variables. Since the demand for money reflects firms' and households' preference to hold wealth in the form of a *liquid* asset (money) rather than a less liquid asset (bonds), economists often refer to the money demand function as a *liquidity preference* function. We can summarize our assumptions regarding money demand with the following algebraic statement:

$$M_D = M_D \overset{- \; + \; +}{(i, \; Y, \; P)}$$

This equation says that the amount of money firms and households want to hold at any given time depends on three variables; the sign above each variable indicates whether that variable positively or negatively affects desired money holding. Our central assumptions are:

1. An increase in the interest rate increases the opportunity cost of holding money and leads to a reduction in the quantity of money demanded.

2. An increase in real GDP increases the volume of transactions and leads to an increase in the quantity of money demanded.

3. An increase in the price level increases the dollar value of a given volume of transactions and leads to an increase in the quantity of money demanded.

Remember that money demand is also related to bond demand. Firms and households must decide at any time how to divide their stock of assets between money and bonds. So our statements here about money demand apply in reverse to the demand for bonds. For example, in Figure 28-1, if the economy moves down the M_D curve from point A to point B as the interest rate falls, firms and households are deciding to hold more money and fewer bonds. The lower interest rate means a lower opportunity cost for holding money and so people choose to hold more; but the lower interest rate equally means that bonds are a less attractive asset and so they choose to hold fewer bonds. In other words, the movement from A to B involves a substitution away from holding bonds and toward holding money.

People hold money in order to make transactions. As real GDP rises, the volume of transactions also rises, and so people typically decide to hold more money.

28.3 **MONETARY EQUILIBRIUM AND NATIONAL INCOME**

So far, this chapter has been devoted to understanding bonds and how they relate to the demand for money. In the previous chapter we examined the supply of money. We are now ready to put these two sides of the money market together to develop a theory of how interest rates are determined. You may recall, however, that we already saw in Chapter 26 a theory of how interest rates are determined. But remember that Chapter 26 was a discussion of long-run economic growth, and real GDP was assumed to be equal to Y^* throughout that discussion. What we do in this chapter and the next

FIGURE 28-2   Monetary Equilibrium

The interest rate rises when there is an excess demand for money and falls when there is an excess supply of money. The fixed quantity of money M_0 is shown by the completely inelastic supply curve M_S. The demand for money is given by M_D; its negative slope indicates that a fall in the rate of interest causes the quantity of money demanded to increase. Monetary equilibrium is at E, with a rate of interest of i_0.

If the interest rate is i_1, there will be an excess demand for money of M_0M_1. Bonds will be offered for sale in an attempt to increase money holdings. This will force the rate of interest up to i_0 (the price of bonds falls), at which point the quantity of money demanded is equal to the fixed available quantity of M_0. If the interest rate is i_2, there will be an excess supply of money M_2M_0. Bonds will be demanded in return for excess money balances. This will force the rate of interest down to i_0 (the price of bonds rises), at which point the quantity of money demanded is equal to the fixed supply of M_0.

is to return to the short-run version of our macro model (in which Y is not assumed to equal Y^*), but make it more complete by adding money and interest rates explicitly. Here we will see how changes in the money market affect interest rates, aggregate expenditure, and the equilibrium level of real GDP in the short run.

We begin by examining the concept of *monetary equilibrium*—this shows how interest rates are determined by the interaction of money demand and money supply. We then explore what economists call the *monetary transmission mechanism*—the fairly involved chain of events that takes us from changes in the interest rate, through to changes in desired aggregate expenditure, to changes in the level of real GDP.

Monetary Equilibrium

Figure 28-2 illustrates the money market. The money supply (M_S) curve is vertical, indicating that it is assumed to be independent of the interest rate. The money supply increases (M_S shifts to the right) if the central bank increases reserves in the banking system or if the commercial banks decide to lend out a larger fraction of those reserves. The money supply decreases (M_S shifts to the left) if the central bank decreases reserves in the banking system or if the commercial banks decide to reduce lending. The money demand (M_D) curve is downward sloping, indicating that firms and households decide to hold more money when the interest rate falls.

Monetary equilibrium occurs when the quantity of money demanded equals the quantity of money supplied. In Chapter 4, we saw that in a competitive market for some commodity the price will adjust to establish equilibrium. In the market for money, the interest rate is that "price" that adjusts to bring about equilibrium. Let's see how this equilibrium is achieved.

monetary equilibrium A situation in which the demand for money equals the supply of money.

When a single household or firm finds that it is holding a smaller fraction of its wealth in money than it wishes, it can sell some bonds and add the proceeds to its money holdings. Such behaviour by an individual firm or household will have a negligible effect on the economy.

But what happens when *all* of the firms and households in the economy try to add to their money balances? They all try to sell bonds to add to their money balances, but what one person can do, all persons cannot do simultaneously. At any moment, the economy's total supply of money and bonds is fixed. Thus, as everyone tries to sell bonds, an excess supply of bonds develops. But since people are simply trying to switch between a given amount of bonds and money, the excess supply of bonds implies an excess demand for money, as shown at interest rate i_1 in Figure 28-2.

What happens when there is an excess supply of bonds? Like any other good or service, an excess supply causes a fall in the market price. As we saw earlier in the chapter, a fall in the price of bonds implies an increase in the interest rate. As the interest rate rises, people economize on money balances because the opportunity cost of holding such balances is rising. Eventually, the interest rate will rise enough that people will no longer be trying to add to their money balances by selling bonds. At that point, there is no longer an excess supply of bonds (or an excess demand for money), and the interest rate will stop rising. The demand for money again equals the supply, as at point E in Figure 28-2.

Suppose now there is more money than firms and households want to hold. That is, there is an excess supply of money, as at interest rate i_2 in Figure 28-2. The excess supply of money implies an excess demand for bonds—people are trying to "get rid of" their excess money balances by acquiring bonds. But when all households try to buy bonds, they bid up the price of bonds, and the interest rate falls. As the interest rate falls, households and firms become willing to hold larger quantities of money. The interest rate falls until firms and households stop trying to convert bonds into money. In other words, it continues until everyone is content to hold the existing supply of money and bonds, as at point E in Figure 28-2.

Monetary equilibrium occurs when the rate of interest is such that the quantity of money demanded equals the quantity of money supplied.

The theory of interest-rate determination depicted in Figure 28-2 is often called the *liquidity preference theory of interest*. This name reflects the fact that a demand to hold money (rather than bonds) is a demand for the more liquid of the two assets—a preference for liquidity.

The Monetary Transmission Mechanism

The connection between changes in the demand for and supply of money and the level of aggregate demand is called the **monetary transmission mechanism**. It operates in three stages:

1. Changes in the demand for money or the supply of money cause a change in the equilibrium interest rate;

2. The change in the interest rate leads to a change in desired investment and consumption expenditure;

3. The change in desired aggregate expenditure leads to a shift in the *AD* curve and thus to short-run changes in real GDP and the price level.

Let's examine these three stages in more detail.

1. Changes in the Interest Rate The interest rate will change if the equilibrium depicted in Figure 28-2 is disturbed by a change in either the supply of money or the demand for money. For example, as shown in part (i) of Figure 28-3, an increase in the supply of money, with an unchanged money demand curve, creates an excess supply of money at the original interest rate. As we have seen, an excess supply of money leads firms and households to buy bonds, thus driving up the price of bonds and pushing down the interest rate. The original increase in the supply of money could be caused by either the central bank increasing the reserves in the banking system or by the commercial banks lending out a higher fraction of their reserves.

Practise with Study Guide Chapter 28, Exercise 2 and Short-Answer Question 6.

monetary transmission mechanism The channels by which a change in the demand for or supply of money leads to a shift of the aggregate demand curve.

FIGURE 28-3   Changes in the Equilibrium Interest Rate

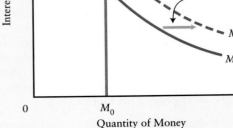

(i) An increase in the supply of money

(ii) An increase in the demand for money

Changes in the supply of money or in the demand for money cause the equilibrium interest rate to change. In both parts of the figure, the money supply is shown by the vertical curve M_S, and the demand for money is shown by the negatively sloped curve M_D. The initial monetary equilibrium is at E_0, with corresponding interest rate i_0. In part (i), an increase in the money supply causes M_S^0 to shift to M_S^1. The new equilibrium is at E_1, where the interest rate has fallen to i_1. In part (ii), an increase in the demand for money shifts M_D^0 to M_D^1. The new monetary equilibrium occurs at E_2, and the new equilibrium interest rate increases to i_2.

As shown in part (ii) of Figure 28-3, an increase in the demand for money, with an unchanged supply of money, creates an excess demand for money at the original interest rate. Firms and households try to acquire more money by selling their holdings of bonds, which drives down the price of bonds and pushes up the interest rate. The original increase in the demand for money could be caused by an increase in real GDP, an increase in the price level, or an increased preference to hold money rather than bonds, as would happen if there were an increase in the perceived riskiness of bonds.

Changes in either the demand for or the supply of money cause changes in the equilibrium interest rate.

Practise with Study Guide Chapter 28, Exercise 5.

2. Changes in Desired Investment and Consumption   The second link in the monetary transmission mechanism relates interest rates to desired investment and consumption expenditure. We saw in Chapter 21 that desired investment, which includes expenditure on inventory accumulation, residential construction, and business fixed investment, responds to changes in the interest rate. Other things being equal, a decrease in the interest rate reduces the opportunity cost of borrowing or using retained earnings for investment purposes. As a result, the lower interest rate leads to an increase in desired investment expenditure. We also saw that consumption expenditure, especially on big-ticket items like cars and furniture that are often purchased on credit, is negatively related to the interest rate. In Figure 28-4, this negative relationship between

FIGURE 28-4   The Effects of Changes in the Money Supply on Desired Investment Expenditure

(i) Money demand and supply

(ii) Investment demand

Increases in the money supply reduce the interest rate and increase desired investment expenditure. In part (i), equilibrium in the money market is at E_0, with a quantity of money of M_0 and an interest rate of i_0. The corresponding level of desired investment is I_0 (point A) in part (ii). An increase in the money supply to M_1 reduces the interest rate to i_1 and increases investment expenditure by ΔI to I_1 (point B).

desired expenditure and the interest rate is labelled I^D for investment demand, reflecting the fact that investment is the *most* interest-sensitive part of expenditure.

The first two links in the monetary transmission mechanism are shown in Figure 28-4.[3] Although the analysis in Figure 28-4 illustrates a change in the money supply, remember that the transmission mechanism can also be set in motion by a change in the demand for money. In part (i), we see that an increase in the money supply reduces the equilibrium interest rate. In part (ii), we see that a fall in the interest rate leads to an increase in desired investment expenditure.

3. Changes in Aggregate Demand   The third link in the monetary transmission mechanism is from changes in desired expenditure to shifts in the *AE* function and in the *AD* curve. This is familiar ground. In Chapter 23, we saw that a shift in the aggregate expenditure curve (caused by something *other than* a change in the price level) leads to a shift in the *AD* curve. This situation is shown again in Figure 28-5.

An increase in the money supply causes a reduction in the interest rate and an increase in desired investment; it therefore causes a rightward shift of the *AD* curve. A decrease in the money supply causes an increase in the interest rate and a decrease in desired investment; it therefore causes a leftward shift of the *AD* curve.

---

[3] In part (i) of Figure 28-4, it is the *nominal* interest rate—the rate of return on bonds—that affects money demand. In part (ii), however, it is the *real* interest rate that influences desired investment expenditure. It is therefore worth emphasizing that we are continuing with the assumption that inflation is expected to be zero and so the nominal and real interest rates are the same. This assumption allows us to use the same vertical axis in the two parts of the figure.

FIGURE 28-5 The Effects of Changes in the Money Supply on Aggregate Demand

(i) A shift in aggregate expenditure

(ii) A shift in aggregate demand

Changes in the money supply cause shifts in the *AE* and *AD* functions. In Figure 28-4, an increase in the money supply increased desired investment expenditure by ΔI. In part (i) of this figure, the *AE* function shifts up by ΔI. At the fixed price level P_0, equilibrium GDP rises from Y_0 to Y_1, as shown by the rightward shift in the curve *AD* in part (ii).

The entire monetary transmission mechanism is summarized in Figure 28-6 for the case of an expansionary monetary shock. An increase in money supply or a decrease in money demand reduces the interest rate, increases desired investment expenditure, and increases aggregate demand.

An Open-Economy Modification

So far, the emphasis in our discussion of the monetary transmission mechanism has been on the effect that a change in the interest rate has on desired investment. In an open economy, however, where financial capital flows easily across borders, the monetary transmission mechanism is a little more complex.

Financial capital is very mobile across international boundaries. Bondholders, either in Canada or abroad, are able to substitute among Canadian bonds, U.S. bonds, German bonds, or bonds from almost any country you can think of. Bonds from different countries are generally not *perfect* substitutes for each other because of varying amounts of political and economic instability, and thus different levels of *risk* associated with the different bonds. But bonds from similar countries—Canada and the United States, for example—are often viewed as very close substitutes.

The ability of bondholders to substitute easily between bonds from different countries implies that monetary disturbances which cause changes in interest rates often lead to international flows of financial capital, which in turn cause changes in exchange rates and changes in exports and imports.

To understand how capital mobility adds a second channel to the monetary transmission mechanism, consider an example. Suppose the Bank of Canada decides to increase the money supply. As shown in Figure 28-4, the increase in money supply reduces the interest rate and increases desired investment expenditure. This is the first channel of the monetary transmission mechanism. But the story does not end there.

The reduction in Canadian interest rates also makes Canadian bonds less attractive relative to foreign bonds. Canadian and foreign investors alike will sell some of their Canadian bonds and buy more of the high-return foreign bonds. But in order to buy foreign bonds, it is necessary first to exchange Canadian dollars for foreign currency. The increase in the demand for foreign currency causes the Canadian dollar to depreciate relative to other currencies.

An increase in the Canadian money supply reduces Canadian interest rates and leads to a capital outflow. This outflow of financial capital causes the Canadian dollar to depreciate.

As the Canadian dollar depreciates, however, Canadian goods and services become less expensive relative to those from other countries. As we first saw in Chapter 22, this change in international relative prices causes households and firms—both in Canada and abroad—to substitute away from foreign goods and toward Canadian goods. Imports fall and exports rise.

So the overall effect of the increase in the Canadian money supply is not just a fall in interest rates and an increase in investment. Because of the international mobility of financial capital, the low Canadian interest rates also lead to a capital outflow, a depreciation of the Canadian dollar, and an increase in Canadian net exports. This increase in net exports, of course, *strengthens* the positive effect on aggregate demand already coming from the increase in desired investment.

This complete open-economy monetary transmission mechanism is shown in Figure 28-7. This figure is based on Figure 28-6, but simply adds the second channel of the transmission mechanism that works through capital mobility, exchange rates, and net exports.

FIGURE 28-6 Summary of the Monetary Transmission Mechanism

In an open economy with capital mobility, an increase in the money supply results in an increase in aggregate demand for two reasons. First, the reduction in interest rates causes an increase in investment. Second, the lower interest rate causes a capital outflow, a currency depreciation, and a rise in net exports.

Our example has been that of a monetary expansion. A monetary contraction has the opposite effect, but the logic of the mechanism is the same. A reduction in the Canadian money supply raises Canadian interest rates and reduces desired investment expenditure. The higher Canadian interest rates attract foreign financial capital as bondholders sell low-return foreign bonds and purchase high-return Canadian bonds. This action increases the demand for Canadian dollars in the foreign-exchange market and thus causes the Canadian dollar to appreciate. Finally, the appreciation of the Canadian dollar increases Canadians' imports of foreign goods and reduces Canadian exports to other countries. Canadian net exports fall.

The Slope of the *AD* Curve

We can now use the monetary transmission mechanism to add to the explanation of the negative slope of the *AD* curve. In Chapter 23, we mentioned two reasons for the negative slope of the *AD* curve: the change in wealth, and the substitution between

FIGURE 28-7 The Open-Economy Monetary Transmission Mechanism

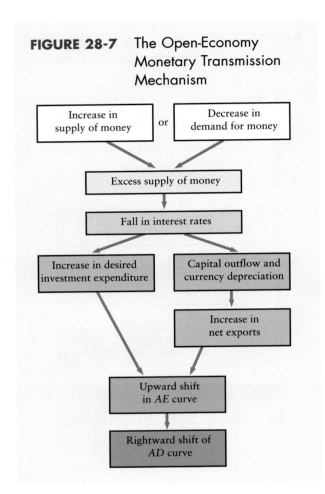

domestic and foreign goods, both of which occur when the price level changes. A third effect operates through interest rates. It works as follows. A rise in the price level raises the money value of transactions and thus leads to an increase in the demand for money. For a given vertical M^S curve, the increase in money demand means that the M^D curve shifts to the right, raising the equilibrium interest rate. The higher interest rate then leads to a reduction in desired investment expenditure. We therefore have a third reason why the price level and the level of aggregate demand are negatively related. This third reason for the negative slope of the AD curve is important because, empirically, the interest rate is the most important link between monetary factors and real expenditure flows.

myeconlab

For more details about how changes in the price level influence money demand, interest rates, and investment, and help explain the negative slope of the AD curve, look for "Interest Rates and the Slope of the AD Curve" in the *Additional Topics* section of this book's MyEconLab.

w w w . m y e c o n l a b . c o m

28.4 THE STRENGTH OF MONETARY FORCES

In the previous section we saw that a change in the money supply leads to a change in interest rates. The change in interest rates, in turn, leads to changes in investment and, through capital flows and changes in the exchange rate, to changes in net exports. Thus, a change in the money supply leads to a change in desired aggregate expenditure and therefore to a shift in the AD curve. From our analysis in Chapter 24, we know that a shift in the AD curve will lead to different effects in the short run and in the long run. It is in the long run that factor prices tend to fully adjust to excess demands or excess supplies, and output tends to return to the level of potential output, Y^*. Let's begin by examining the long-run effects of increases in the money supply, and then turn to an old debate about the strength of monetary forces in the short run.

money neutrality The idea that a change in the supply of money has no effect on any real variables but only affects the price level.

Long-Run Neutrality of Money

We saw in Chapter 24 that any shock—either to aggregate demand or aggregate supply—that creates an output gap sets in place an adjustment process that will eventually close that gap and return real GDP to its potential level, Y^*. The operation of this adjustment process following an increase in the money supply is illustrated in Figure 28-8, where we assume that Y^* is unaffected by changes in the money supply.

In the figure, the only long-run effect of a shift in the AD curve following a change in the money supply is a change in the price level. This result is often referred to as the *neutrality of money*.

In the eighteenth and nineteenth centuries, economists focused most of their attention on understanding the economy's long-run equilibrium and were less concerned with short-run fluctuations. These Classical economists believed that the "money" side of the economy was independent from the "real" side of the economy. This belief was referred to as the *Classical Dichotomy* and embodied the idea of **money neutrality**. The Classical view was that in the long run, relative prices, real GDP, employment, investment, and all other real variables in the economy were determined by real factors, such as the demands and supplies for various goods, which were in turn determined by firms' technologies and consumers' preferences.

The long-run effects of an expansion in the money supply, in their view, would be an increase in the price level but no change in the level of real GDP or any other real economic variables. In terms of Figure 28-8, the Classical economists were concerned with the movement from E_0 to E_2, a change caused by an increase in the money supply; real GDP would be unaffected but the price level would increase.

The Classical economists emphasized the economy's long-run equilibrium. In their view, changes in the supply of money had no effect on real GDP or other real variables; the only effect was to change the price level.

As compared to the eighteenth century, there is now more focus on the short-run effects of changes in monetary policy. Nevertheless, most modern economists recognize that the Classical view provides a good description of the economy's long-run equilibrium, after wages and other factor prices have fully adjusted and real GDP has returned to the level of potential output, Y^*. Modern economists' view that the neutrality of money holds in the long run leads them to stress the strong link between changes in the money supply and changes in the price level, at least over long periods of time. Figure 28-9 shows a scatter plot of inflation and money growth for 82 countries over the four decades following the Second

FIGURE 28-8   The Long-Run Neutrality of Money

(i) M_D and M_S

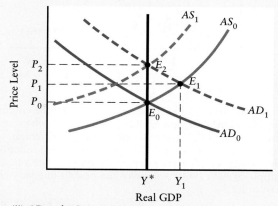

(ii) AD and AS

The long-run neutrality of money implies that the only long-run effect of an increase in the money supply is a higher price level. The economy is in long-run equilibrium at E_0 in both diagrams, with real GDP equal to Y^* and the price level equal to P_0. An increase in the money supply from M_S^0 to M_S^1 reduces interest rates immediately to i_1' and stimulates aggregate demand, thus shifting the aggregate demand curve from AD_0 to AD_1. As real GDP and the price level increase, the demand for money increases to M_D^1, thus pushing i_1' up to i_1. The point E_1 in part (i) therefore corresponds to E_1 in part (ii). Since real GDP is now above Y^*, wages and other factor prices start to increase, thus shifting the AS curve upward. The adjustment process continues until Y is back to Y^* and the price level has increased to P_2. In the new long-run equilibrium, the higher price level (with unchanged Y^*) has increased money demand to M_D^2, thus restoring the interest rate to its initial level, i_0.

FIGURE 28-9   Inflation and Money Growth Across Many Countries

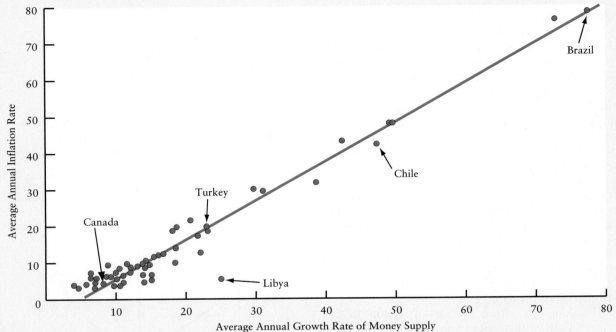

Countries with higher inflation rates tend to be countries with higher rates of growth of the money supply. This figure plots long-run data for many countries. Each point shows the average annual inflation rate and the average annual growth rate of the money supply for a specific country over the post-Second World War period (the precise years vary slightly across countries). For all countries, the inflation data refer to the rate of change of the Consumer Price Index; the money supply data refer to the growth rate of currency. The positive relationship between inflation and money supply growth (with a slope of the best-fit line very close to 1) is consistent with the proposition of long-run money neutrality.

(*Source:* The data are from the International Monetary Fund's *International Financial Statistics,* as compiled by R. J. Barro and R. F. Lucas, in *Macroeconomics,* Irwin, 1994.)

World War. Each point in the figure represents the rates of inflation and money supply growth for one country averaged over the 40-year period. The vertical axis measures each country's average annual inflation rate—that is, the average annual rate of increase of the price level. The horizontal axis measures each country's average annual rate of growth of the money supply. As is clear in the figure, there is a close positive relationship between money supply growth and inflation, as reflected by the tight bunching of points around the upward-sloping line, the "line of best fit" between money supply growth and inflation. The slope of the line of best fit is 0.97, indicating that two countries that differ in their money growth rates by 10 percent will, on average, differ in their inflation rates by 9.7 percent.

Many modern economists believe that money is neutral in the long run. Long-run neutrality implies that, in the absence of other shocks to the economy, changes in money and changes in the price level are closely linked over long periods of time.

Long-run money neutrality is debatable, however. Though most economists agree that the macroeconomic adjustment process will bring Y back to Y^* in the long run, some economists argue that the value of Y^* is itself influenced by the short-run path of real GDP. For example, a positive shock that raises Y may actually lead to an increase in Y^*; or a negative shock that reduces Y may also cause a decline in Y^*. The hypothesis that the path of real GDP may influence the value of Y^* is known as *hysteresis,* and there is some empirical support for it, especially in some Western European countries.

One possible explanation for hysteresis is the depreciation of human capital that often accompanies prolonged unemployment. Consider a negative shock that reduces real GDP and increases unemployment. If wages and other factor prices are slow to adjust, the unemployment will persist, and some individuals may experience long spells of unemployment. If prolonged lack of work leads these individuals' skills to depreciate, they may eventually become "unemployable," even after the aggregate economy recovers. In this case, the fall in the level of real GDP, if prolonged, will lead to a fall in the level of potential output. (Or equivalently, the rise in the unemployment rate will lead to a rise in the natural rate of unemployment.)

As we said earlier, there is some empirical support for hysteresis, but it is contentious. In Canada, the weight of the empirical evidence is against it, and in favour of the hypothesis that the long-run path of Y^* is independent of the short-run path of real GDP. In the macro model developed and analyzed in this book, it is assumed that Y^* is unaffected by the path of Y, and thus the model generates the prediction of long-run money neutrality. But it should be kept in mind that this particular behaviour of Y^* remains a debatable hypothesis, and should constantly be tested with data.

Short-Run Non-Neutrality of Money

There is less debate regarding the short-run effects of money: A change in the money supply affects the short-run equilibrium level of real GDP. For a given AS curve, the short-run effect of a change in the money supply on real GDP and the price level is determined by the extent of the shift of the AD curve.

How Effective Is Monetary Policy?
The AD curve shifts in response to an increase in the money supply. How much the AD curve shifts depends on the amount of investment expenditure that is stimulated. The change in investment expenditure in turn depends on the strength of two of the linkages that make up the monetary transmission mechanism: the link between money supply and interest rates, and the link between interest rates and investment. Let's look more closely at these separate parts of the monetary transmission mechanism.

First, consider how much interest rates fall in response to an increase in the money supply. If the M_D curve is steep, a given increase in the money supply will lead to a large reduction in the equilibrium interest rate. A steep M_D curve means that firms' and households' desired money holding is not very sensitive to changes in the interest rate, so interest rates have to fall a lot to get people to be content to hold a larger amount of money. The flatter is the M_D curve, the less interest rates will fall for any given increase in the supply of money.

Second, consider how much investment expenditure increases in response to a fall in interest rates. If the I^D curve is relatively flat, then any given reduction in interest rates will lead to a large increase in firms' desired investment. The steeper is the I^D curve, the less investment will increase for any given reduction in interest rates.

It follows that the size of the shift of the AD curve in response to a change in the money supply depends on the shapes of the M_D and I^D curves. The influence of the shapes of the two curves is shown in Figure 28-10 and can be summarized as follows:

1. The steeper the M_D curve, the more interest rates will change in response to a given change in the money supply.

2. The flatter the I^D curve, the more investment expenditure will change in response to a given change in the interest rate, and hence the larger will be the shift in the AD curve.

The combination that produces the largest shift in the AD curve for a given change in the money supply is a steep M_D curve and a flat I^D curve. This combination is illustrated in part (i) of Figure 28-10. It accords with the view that monetary policy is relatively effective as a means of influencing real GDP in the short run. The combination that produces the smallest shift in the AD curve is a flat M_D curve and a steep I^D curve. This combination is illustrated in part (ii) of Figure 28-10. It accords with the view that monetary policy is relatively ineffective in the short run.

The effectiveness of monetary policy in inducing short-run changes in real GDP depends on the slopes of the M_D and I^D curves. The steeper is the M_D curve, and the flatter is the I^D curve, the more effective is monetary policy.

Keynesians Versus Monetarists   Figure 28-10 characterizes a famous debate among economists that occurred in the three decades following the Second World War. Some economists, following the ideas of John Maynard Keynes, argued that changes in the money supply led to relatively small changes in interest rates and that investment was relatively insensitive to changes in the interest rate. These economists, who called themselves *Keynesians*, concluded that monetary policy was not a very effective method of stimulating aggregate demand—they therefore emphasized the value of using fiscal policy (as Keynes himself had argued during the Great Depression). Another group of economists, led by Milton Friedman, argued that changes in the money supply caused sharp changes in interest rates, which, in turn, led to significant changes in investment expenditure. These economists called themselves *Monetarists* and concluded that monetary policy was a very effective tool for stimulating aggregate demand.[4]

Today, this debate between Keynesians and Monetarists is all but over. A great deal of empirical research devoted to uncovering the relationship between interest rates and money demand suggests that money demand is relatively insensitive to changes in the interest rate. That is, the M_D curve is quite steep and, as a result, changes in the money supply cause relatively large changes in interest rates (as argued by the Monetarists). The evidence is much less clear, however, on the slope of the I^D curve. Though the evidence confirms that I^D is downward sloping, there is no consensus on

For brief descriptions of the contributions to economics of the Nobel laureates, go to **www.nobel.se/economics/laureates/**.

Practise with Study Guide Chapter 28, Exercise 4.

---

4 Monetarists argued that monetary policy was very effective for stimulating aggregate demand but they *did not* advocate an "activist" monetary policy. One of their concerns was that monetary forces were so strong that an activist monetary policy would destabilize the economy. We address these issues in Chapter 29.

FIGURE 28-10 Two Views on the Strength of Monetary Changes

(i) Changes in the money supply effective

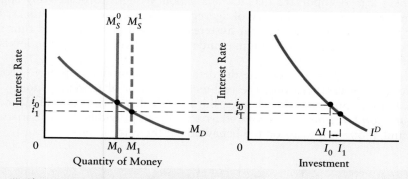

(ii) Changes in the money supply ineffective

The effect of a change in the money supply on aggregate demand depends on the slopes of the M_D and I^D curves. Initially, in parts (i) and (ii), the money supply is M_S^0, and the economy has an interest rate of i_0 and investment expenditure of I_0. The central bank then expands the money supply from M_S^0 to M_S^1. The rate of interest thus falls from i_0 to i_1, as shown in each of the left panels. This causes an increase in investment expenditure of ΔI, from I_0 to I_1, as shown in each of the right panels.

In part (i), the demand for money is insensitive to the interest rate, so the increase in the money supply leads to a large fall in the interest rate. Further, desired investment expenditure is highly interest sensitive, so the large fall in interest rates also leads to a large increase in investment expenditure. Hence, in this case, the change in the money supply will be very effective in stimulating aggregate demand.

In part (ii), the demand for money is more sensitive to the interest rate, so the increase in the money supply leads to only a small fall in the interest rate. Further, desired investment expenditure is much less sensitive to the interest rate, so the small fall in interest rates leads to only a small increase in investment expenditure. Hence, in this case, the change in the money supply will be less effective in stimulating aggregate demand.

whether the curve is steep or flat. Part of the problem facing researchers is that an important determinant of investment is not observable. Firms' expectations about the future—what Keynes famously called firms' "animal spirits"—have a significant effect on their investment decisions but this variable is not easily measured by researchers. The unobservability of this variable makes it very difficult to estimate precisely the relationship between interest rates and investment. Another problem is that the I^D curve is an aggregation of a number of different investment demands (plant, equipment, inventories, new housing, and durable consumer goods), each subject to different influences. While each type of investment is responsive to changes in the interest rate, their individual differences make it difficult to estimate the responsiveness of *aggregate* desired investment (I^D) to changes in the interest rate.

Though empirical research over the years has, to a large extent, filled the gaps in our knowledge and narrowed the differences between the Keynesian and Monetarist positions, there is still plenty of debate about the effectiveness and the appropriate objectives of monetary policy. Many economists argue that central bankers should be mindful of the long-run perspective of the Classical economists and expect a limited influence from monetary policy on the long-run level of real GDP. In this view, monetary policy should attempt to offset only the longest and most persistent of the shocks that hit the economy, while maintaining a long-run focus on the behaviour of the price level. Other economists argue that short-run fluctuations in income and employment are so important that monetary policy ought to be actively engaged in stabilizing the economy in the face of aggregate demand and supply shocks. Further, some of these economists argue that hysteresis is a real possibility and thus the central bank's actions in the short run may indeed have effects on long-run levels of real GDP and employment.

In the next chapter we examine the details of how monetary policy is conducted in Canada. For several reasons, the real-world practice of monetary policy is more complex than it appears in this chapter. But as we will see, the Bank of Canada's system of *inflation targeting* can be viewed as a means of providing both short-run stabilization and a long-run focus on the behaviour of the price level.

SUMMARY

28.1 UNDERSTANDING BONDS

- The present value of any bond that promises to pay some sequence of payments in the future is negatively related to the market interest rate. A bond's present value determines its market price. Thus, there is a negative relationship between the market interest rate and the price of a bond.
- The yield on a bond is the rate of return the bondholder receives, having bought the bond at its purchase price

and then receiving the stream of future payments the bond offers. For a given stream of future payments, a lower purchase price implies a higher bond yield.
- An increase in the perceived riskiness of bonds will lead to a reduction in bond prices and thus an increase in bond yields. These changes are associated with investors' adjustment of their portfolios out of bonds and toward money.

28.2 THE DEMAND FOR MONEY

- In our macro model, households and firms are assumed to divide their assets between interest-bearing "bonds" and non-interest-bearing "money." They hold money to facilitate both expected and unexpected transactions, and also to protect against the possibility of a decline in bond prices (a rise in interest rates).

- No matter why money is held, the cost of doing so is the interest that could have been earned if bonds were held instead. This is the opportunity cost of holding money.
- Households' and firms' desired money holdings are assumed to be influenced by three key macroeconomic variables:

1. Increases in the interest rate reduce desired money holdings;
2. Increases in real GDP increase desired money holdings;
3. Increases in the price level increase desired money holdings.

- These relationships are captured in the M_D curve, which is drawn as a negative relationship between interest rates (i) and desired money holding (M_D). Increases in real GDP (Y) or the price level (P) lead to a rightward shift of this M_D curve.

28.3 MONETARY EQUILIBRIUM AND NATIONAL INCOME

- In the short run, the interest rate is determined in the money market by the interaction of money supply and money demand. Monetary equilibrium is established when the interest rate is such that the quantity of money supplied is exactly equal to the quantity of money demanded.
- The first stage in the monetary transmission mechanism occurs when the equilibrium interest rate changes. A change in the money supply (coming from the central bank or the commercial banking system) or in the demand for money (coming from a change in Y or P) will lead to a change in the equilibrium interest rate.

- The second stage of the monetary transmission mechanism is that any change in the interest rate leads to a change in desired investment and consumption expenditure. In an open economy with capital mobility, the change in the interest rate leads to capital flows, changes in the exchange rate, and changes in net exports.
- The third stage of the monetary transmission mechanism is that any change in desired investment, consumption, or net exports leads to a shift in the aggregate demand (AD) curve, and thus to a change in real GDP and the price level.

28.4 THE STRENGTH OF MONETARY FORCES

- Changes in the money supply have different effects on the economy in the short run and in the long run.
- In the long run, after wages and other factor prices have fully adjusted to any output gaps, real GDP returns to potential output, Y^*. In our macro model it is assumed that the money supply does not influence Y^*, and so the only long-run effect of changes in the money supply is changes in the price level.

- Many modern economists believe that the neutrality of money is a property of the economy in the long run. There is a strong positive correlation between the rate of money growth and the rate of inflation across countries when viewed over the long run.
- In the short run, the effects of a change in the money supply depend on the shape of the M_D and I^D curves. The steeper is the M_D curve and the flatter is the I^D curve, the more effective changes in the money supply will be in causing short-run changes in real GDP.

KEY CONCEPTS

The interest rate and present value
Interest rates, bond prices, and bond yields
Reasons for holding money

The money demand (M_D) function
Monetary equilibrium
The monetary transmission mechanism
The investment demand (I^D) function

Effects of changes in the money supply
Long-run money neutrality
Debate between Keynesians and Monetarists

STUDY EXERCISES

1. Fill in the blanks to make the following statements correct.

   a. Monetary equilibrium occurs when the quantity of <u>money supplied</u> equals the quantity of <u>money demanded</u>. Monetary equilibrium determines the <u>interest rate</u>.

   b. When there is an excess supply of money, households and firms will attempt to <u>purchase</u> bonds. This action will cause the price of bonds to <u>rise</u> and the interest rate to <u>decrease</u>.

c. When there is an excess demand for money, households and firms will attempt to _sell_ bonds. This action will cause the price of bonds to _decrease_ and the interest rate to _increase_.

d. The _monetary_ _transmission_ _mechanism_ refers to the three stages that link the money market to aggregate demand. The first link is between monetary equilibrium and the _demand or supply of money_; the second link is between the _interest rate_ and desired _investment_; the third link is between desired _AE_ and _gross GDP and price level_.

e. Suppose the economy is in equilibrium and then the Bank of Canada increases the money supply. The first effect will be an excess _supply_ of/for money, which will then lead to a _decrease_ in the interest rate, which will in turn lead to a(n) _increase_ in desired investment.

f. Suppose the economy is in equilibrium and the Bank of Canada decreases the money supply. The first effect will be an excess _demand_ of/for money, which will lead to a _increase_ in the interest rate, which will in turn lead to a(n) _decrease_ in desired investment.

g. Through the monetary transmission mechanism, a rightward shift of the AD curve can be caused by a(n) _increase_ in the money supply; a leftward shift of the AD curve can be caused by a(n) _decrease_ in the money supply.

h. In an open economy with capital mobility, an increase in the money supply causes interest rates to _decrease_, which leads to a capital outflow. This causes a(n) _depreciation_ of the Canadian dollar and thus to a(n) _increase_ in net exports, which leads the AD curve to shift _to right_.

2. Fill in the blanks to make the following statements correct.

a. The theory of long-run neutrality of money predicts that changes in the money supply have no effect on _real GDP_ in the long run.

b. If the demand for money is not very sensitive to changes in the interest rate, then the M_D curve will be relatively _inelastic_. An increase in the money supply will lead to a _bigger_ reduction in the interest rate.

c. If the demand for money is very sensitive to changes in the interest rate, then the M_D curve will be relatively _elastic_. An increase in the money supply will lead to a _smaller_ reduction in the interest rate.

d. A relatively flat investment demand curve means that a change in the interest rate will have a _larger_ effect on _investment_, which leads to a relatively large shift in the _AD_ curve.

e. A relatively steep investment demand curve means that a change in the interest rate will have a

_____ effect on _____, which leads to a relatively small shift in the _____ curve.

f. Changes in the money supply will have the largest effect on the position of the AD curve when the M_D curve is _____ and the I^D curve is _____.

3. **myeconlab** The following table shows the stream of income produced by several different assets. In each case, P_1, P_2, and P_3 are the payments made by the asset in Years 1, 2, and 3.

Asset	Market Interest Rate (i)	P_1	P_2	P_3	Present Value
Treasury Bill	8%	$1000	$0	$0	—
Bond	7%	$0	$0	$5000	—
Bond	9%	$200	$200	$200	—
Stock	10%	$50	$40	$60	—

a. For each asset, compute the asset's present value. (Note that the market interest rate, i, is not the same in each situation.)

b. Explain why the market price for each asset will be the asset's present value.

4. **myeconlab** The table below provides information for six different bonds: current market price (P), the face value of the bond (FV), and the number of years before the bond matures (N).

Bond Number	Market Price (P)	Face Value (FV)	Years to Maturity (N)
1a	$926	$1000	1
1b	$850	$1000	1
2a	$1270	$2000	5
2b	$838	$2000	5
3a	$1760	$5000	10
3b	$684	$5000	10

a. In each case, compute the bond's yield, assuming that you buy the bond at its current market price and hold the bond until it matures. There are no coupons. If x is the bond's yield, then $P(1 + x)^N = FV$.

b. Suppose bonds 1a, 2a, and 3a are all issued by the same borrower. Can you offer an explanation for the relationship between the bond yields and the terms to maturity?

c. Suppose bonds 1b, 2b, and 3b are all issued by the same borrower. What can you conclude about the "a" borrower versus the "b" borrower? Explain.

d. Explain why knowledge of the market interest rate is unnecessary in order to compute a bond's yield, once you already know the bond's market price. What aspect of the bond does the market interest rate influence, if anything?

5. Imagine a bond that promises to make coupon payments of $100 one year from now and $100 two years from now, and to repay the principal of $1000 three years from now. Suppose also that the market interest rate is 8 percent per year, and that no perceived risk is associated with the bond.

 a. Compute the present value of this bond.
 b. Suppose the bond is being offered for $995. Would you buy the bond at that price? What is the implied yield on the bond at that price? What do you expect to happen to the bond price in the very near future?
 c. Suppose the bond is instead being offered at a price of $950. Would you buy the bond at that price? What is the implied bond yield at that price? Do you expect the bond price to change in the near future?
 d. If the price of the bond is equal to its computed present value from (a), what is the implied bond yield?
 e. Explain why bond yields and the market interest rate tend to move together so that economists can then sensibly speak about "the" interest rate.

6. **myeconlab** What motives for holding money—transactions, precautionary, or speculative—do you think explain the following holdings? Explain.

 a. Currency in the cash register of the local grocery store at the start of each working day.
 b. Money to meet Stelco's bi-weekly payroll deposited in the local bank.
 c. A household tries to keep a "buffer" of $1000 in its savings account.
 d. An investor sells bonds for cash, which she then deposits in a low-return bank account.
 e. You carry $20 in your pocket even though you have no planned expenditures.

7. The diagram below shows the demand for money and the supply of money.

a. Explain why the M_D function is downward sloping.
b. Suppose the interest rate is at i_A. Explain how firms and households attempt to satisfy their excess demand for money. What is the effect of their actions?
c. Suppose the interest rate is at i_B. Explain how firms and households attempt to dispose of their excess supply of money. What is the effect of their actions?
d. Now suppose there is an increase in the transactions demand for money (perhaps because of growth in real GDP). Beginning at i^*, explain what happens in the money market. How is this shown in the diagram?

8. The following diagrams show the determination of monetary equilibrium and the demand for investment. The economy begins with money supply M_S, money demand M_D, and investment demand I^D. The interest rate is i_0 and desired investment is I_0.

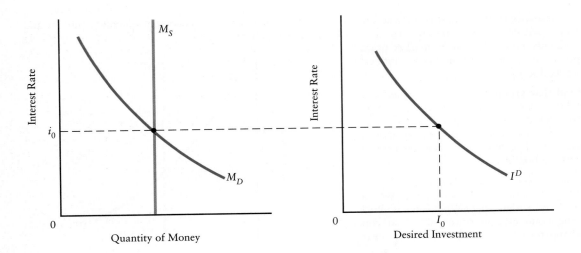

a. Beginning at the initial equilibrium, suppose the Bank of Canada increases the money supply. What happens in the money market and what happens to desired investment expenditure?

b. Beginning in the initial equilibrium, suppose there is a reduction in the demand for money (caused, perhaps, by bonds becoming more attractive to firms and households). What happens in the money market and what happens to desired investment expenditure?

c. Explain why an increase in money supply can have the same effects on desired investment expenditure as a reduction in money demand.

9. In the text we discussed why, in an open economy with international capital mobility, there is a second part to the monetary transmission mechanism. (It may be useful to review Figure 28-7 when answering this question.)

a. Explain why an increase in Canada's money supply makes Canadian bonds less attractive relative to foreign bonds.

b. Explain why Canada's bonds being less attractive leads to a depreciation of the Canadian dollar.

c. Why would such a depreciation of the Canadian dollar lead to an increase in Canada's net exports?

d. Now suppose that the Bank of Canada does not change its policy at all, but the Federal Reserve (the U.S. central bank) increases the U.S. money supply. What is the likely effect on Canada? Explain.

10. In the text we discussed the historical debate between Keynesians and Monetarists regarding the effectiveness of monetary policy in changing real GDP (see Figure 28-10 to review). Using the same sort of diagram, discuss two conditions in which a change in the money supply would have *no* effect on real GDP.

DISCUSSION QUESTIONS

1. Historically, construction of new houses has been one of the most interest-sensitive categories of aggregate expenditure. Recently, the financial press has carried a number of stories suggesting that because of financial deregulation and innovations in housing finance, this interest sensitivity has apparently decreased. If this is true, what are the implications for monetary policy?

2. Suppose you alone know that the Bank of Canada is going to engage in policies that will raise interest rates sharply, starting next month. How might you make profits by purchases or sales of bonds now, with the intention to sell in a few months' time?

3. In the late 1990s, central bankers in Canada and elsewhere (especially the United States) expressed concern about the dramatic increases in stock-market values. In December 1996, U.S. Federal Reserve chairman Alan Greenspan alarmed the markets by referring to investors' "irrational exuberance."

a. Explain why central bankers might be concerned about "excessive" increases in stock-market values.

b. Explain how a policy-induced increase in interest rates would affect the stock market.

c. Suppose prices in the stock market fell sharply for reasons unrelated to domestic interest rates. What would be the likely effect on aggregate demand?

4. In 2006, there was some concern that the U.S. economy would experience a significant slowing in its GDP growth.

   a. Explain the likely effects of a U.S. growth slow-down on the demand for Canadian exports. What would be the effect on Canadian aggregate demand?

   b. Suppose the Bank of Canada viewed its monetary policy as being appropriate (for keeping output close to potential) before any U.S. slowdown occurred. What would you then predict to be the Bank's response to the slowdown?

5. In the text we discussed how capital mobility in an open economy added a second part to the transmission mechanism. In this setting, discuss why changes in the Federal Reserve's policy in the United States are carefully watched—and often matched—by the Bank of Canada.

6. After the terrorist attacks of September 11, 2001, stock markets across the world, but especially in North America, fell dramatically. Central banks responded by increasing the money supply and therefore reducing interest rates.

   a. Explain why a sharp fall in stock-market values might be expected to lead to a recession.

   b. After 18 months of expansionary monetary policy, the U.S. economy was still showing no signs of recovery by the middle of 2003. Can you offer an explanation based on the slope of either the M_D or I^D curves?

   c. What else was going on in the world economy in 2003 that might explain why expansionary U.S. monetary policy seemed to be less effective than expected?

CHAPTER 29

Monetary Policy in Canada

🔵 LEARNING OBJECTIVES

In this chapter you will learn

1. why the Bank of Canada chooses to set interest rates rather than directly influence the money supply.
2. how changes in the Bank of Canada's target for the overnight interest rate affect longer-term interest rates.
3. why many central banks have adopted formal inflation targets.
4. how the Bank of Canada's policy of inflation targeting helps to stabilize the economy.
5. why monetary policy affects real GDP and the price level only after long time lags.
6. about the main economic challenges that the Bank of Canada has faced over the past three decades.

In the previous two chapters we encountered many details about money and why it is so important for the economy. In Chapter 27 we saw how commercial banks, through their activities of accepting deposits and extending loans, create deposit money. These bank deposits, together with the currency in circulation, make up the nation's money supply. In Chapter 28 we examined the variables that influence households' and firms' money demand. We then put money demand together with money supply to examine how interest rates are determined in monetary equilibrium. Finally, we examined the monetary transmission mechanism—the chain of cause-and-effect events describing how changes in money demand or supply lead to changes in interest rates, aggregate demand, real GDP, and the price level.

Chapters 27 and 28 presented a general view of the role of money in the economy. What is still missing is a detailed account of how the Bank of Canada conducts its monetary policy. We begin this chapter by describing some technical details about how the Bank influences the monetary equilibrium and thereby sets in motion the monetary transmission mechanism. We then discuss the Bank's current system of inflation targeting, and how this system helps to stabilize the economy. Finally, we discuss some limitations for monetary policy and some of the Bank's major challenges over the past 30 years.

29.1 HOW THE BANK OF CANADA IMPLEMENTS MONETARY POLICY

The monetary transmission mechanism describes how changes in the demand for or supply of money cause changes in the interest rate, which then lead to changes in aggregate demand, real GDP, and the price level. But how does the Bank of Canada influence the money market, and thereby implement its monetary policy?

Money Supply Versus the Interest Rate

In general, any central bank has two alternative approaches for implementing its monetary policy. These two approaches are illustrated in Figure 29-1, which shows money demand, money supply, and the equilibrium interest rate. But for any given M_D curve, the central bank must choose one approach or the other; it cannot set *both* the money supply and the interest rate independently. If it chooses to set the money supply, monetary equilibrium will determine the interest rate. Alternatively, if the central bank sets the interest rate, the money supply must adjust to accommodate the movement along the M_D curve.

FIGURE 29-1   Two Approaches to the Implementation of Monetary Policy

(i) Central bank sets the money supply   (ii) Central bank sets the interest rate

Monetary policy can be implemented either by influencing the money supply directly or by influencing the interest rate directly—but not both. In part (i), the Bank of Canada could attempt to shift the M_S curve directly, and thereby change the equilibrium interest rate. But because the Bank cannot directly control the money supply, and because the slope and position of the M_D curve is uncertain, this is an ineffective way to conduct monetary policy. The Bank's chosen method is illustrated in part (ii), whereby it influences the interest rate directly. It then accommodates the resulting change in money demand through its open-market operations.

Practise with Study Guide Chapter 29, Exercise 2.

In principle, monetary policy can be implemented either by setting the money supply or by setting the interest rate. But for a given M_D curve, both cannot be set independently.

Part (i) of Figure 29-1 shows how the Bank of Canada could attempt to shift the M_S curve directly, by changing the amount of currency in circulation in the economy. It could do this by buying or selling government securities in the financial markets—transactions called *open-market operations*. For example, by using currency to buy $100 000 of government bonds from a willing seller, the Bank of Canada would increase the amount of cash reserves in the banking system by $100 000. As we saw in Chapter 28, commercial banks would then be able to lend out these new reserves and would thereby increase the amount of deposit money in the economy. The combined effect of the new reserves and the new deposit money would be an increase in the money supply, a shift of the M_S curve to the right. For a given M_D curve, this increase in money supply would lead to a reduction in the equilibrium interest rate and, through the various parts of the transmission mechanism, to an eventual increase in aggregate demand.

The Bank of Canada does not implement its monetary policy in this way, for three reasons. First, while the Bank of Canada *can* control the amount of cash reserves in the banking system (through its open-market operations) it *cannot* control the process of deposit expansion carried out by the commercial banks. And since the money supply is the sum of currency and deposits, it follows that the Bank can influence the money supply but cannot *control* it. For example, if the Bank increased the amount of cash reserves in the system, the commercial banks might choose not to expand their lending, and as a result the overall increase in the money supply would be far smaller than the Bank initially intended.

The second reason the Bank does not try to influence the money supply directly is the uncertainty regarding the slope of the M_D curve. Even if the Bank had perfect control over the money supply (which it does not), it would be unsure about the change in the interest rate that would result from any given change in the supply of money. Since it is the change in the interest rate that ultimately determines the subsequent changes in aggregate demand, this uncertainty would make the conduct of monetary policy very difficult.

Finally, in addition to being uncertain about the *slope* of the M_D curve, the Bank is also unable to predict accurately the *position* of the M_D curve at any given time. Changes in both real GDP and the price level cause changes in money demand that the Bank can only approximate. Even more difficult to predict are the changes in money demand which occur as a result of innovations in the financial sector. During the late 1970s and early 1980s, for example, the creation of new types of bank deposits led to unprecedented and unpredicted changes in money demand, as people transferred funds between bank accounts of different types. Unpredictable changes in the demand for money make a monetary policy based on the direct control of the money supply difficult to implement.

The Bank of Canada cannot directly control the money supply, though it can influence it by changing the amount of cash reserves in the banking system. In addition, the slope and position of the M_D curve cannot be accurately predicted. As a result, the Bank of Canada chooses not to implement its monetary policy by attempting to control the money supply.

The alternative approach to implementing monetary policy is to influence the interest rate directly. This is the approach used by most central banks, including the Bank of Canada. As part (ii) of Figure 29-1 shows, if the Bank can directly change the interest rate, the result will be a change in the quantity of money demanded. In order for this new interest rate to be consistent with monetary equilibrium, the Bank must *accommodate* the change in the amount of money demanded—that is, it must alter the supply of money in order to satisfy the change in desired money holdings by firms and households (we will see shortly how this occurs).

Why does the Bank of Canada choose to implement its monetary policy in this manner? Let's consider the advantages. First, while the Bank cannot control the money supply for the reasons we have just discussed, it *is* able to control a particular market interest rate. (We will see shortly which rate it controls and how it does so.) Second, the Bank's uncertainty about the slope and position of the M_D curve is not a problem when the Bank chooses instead to set the interest rate directly. If the Bank ascertains that a lower interest rate is necessary in order to achieve its policy objectives, it can act directly to reduce the interest rate. Any uncertainty about the M_D curve then implies uncertainty about the ultimate change in the quantity of money, but it is the interest rate that matters, through the transmission mechanism, for determining the level of aggregate demand.

Finally, the Bank can more easily *communicate* its policy actions to the public by setting the interest rate than by setting the level of reserves in the banking system. Changes in the interest rate are more meaningful to firms and households than changes in the level of reserves or the money supply. For example, if we hear that mortgage-lending rates at commercial banks have just decreased by one percentage point, most people can readily assess what this means for their plans to buy a new house financed by a mortgage. In contrast, if we were to hear that the level of reserves in the banking system had just increased by $1 billion, it would not be clear to most people what this means, or that it would have any effect on interest rates, or by how much. Even the Bank itself might be uncertain about the magnitude of these effects.

By directly setting the interest rate, the Bank of Canada can avoid the problems associated with imperfect control over the money supply and uncertainty about the slope and position of the M_D curve.

The Bank of Canada and the Overnight Interest Rate

We have just explained why the Bank of Canada chooses to implement its monetary policy by setting the interest rate rather than by trying to influence the money supply directly. But *how* does the Bank do this, and *which* interest rate (among many) does it set?

As we discussed in Chapter 28, there are many interest rates in the Canadian economy. Commercial banks pay different rates to depositors on each of several different types of bank deposits. They also lend at different rates for different kinds of loans—home mortgages, small business loans, personal lines of credit, and car loans, to name just a few. In addition, government securities trade at different yields (interest rates) depending on the term to maturity. Economists refer to the overall pattern of interest rates corresponding to government securities of different maturities as the *term structure of interest rates*. Because bondholders generally require a higher rate of return in order to lend their funds for a longer period of time, yields on government securities generally increase as the term to maturity increases. At any given time, the yield on 90-day Treasury bills is usually less than that on 5-year government bonds which in turn is less than the yield on 30-year bonds. Furthermore, because these various assets are viewed as close substitutes by bondholders, the different rates tend to rise and fall together.

overnight interest rate The interest rate that commercial banks charge each other for overnight loans.

The interest rate corresponding to the shortest period of borrowing or lending is called the **overnight interest rate**, which is the interest rate that commercial banks charge each other for overnight loans. Banks that need cash because they have run short of reserves can borrow in the *overnight market* from banks that have excess reserves available. The overnight interest rate is a market-determined interest rate that fluctuates daily as the cash requirements of commercial banks change.

The Bank of Canada exercises considerable influence over the overnight interest rate. As this rate rises or falls, the other interest rates in the economy—from short-term lines of credit to longer-term home mortgages and government securities—tend to rise or fall as well. Thus, by influencing the overnight interest rate, the Bank of Canada also influences the longer-term interest rates that are more relevant for determining aggregate consumption and investment expenditure.

How does the Bank of Canada influence the overnight interest rate? The Bank's tool for conducting its monetary policy—what economists sometimes call the Bank's *policy instrument*—is a *target* that it sets for the overnight interest rate. This target is the midpoint of a 0.5 percentage point range within which the Bank would like to see the actual overnight interest rate. The Bank announces its target for the overnight interest rate eight times per year at pre-specified dates called *fixed announcement dates,* or FADs.

When the Bank sets its target for the overnight rate, it also sets two other rates: one at the top and one at the bottom of the 0.5 percentage point range. At the upper rate, called the **bank rate**, the Bank of Canada stands ready to lend to commercial banks any amount of cash they desire. At the lower rate, the Bank stands ready to accept any deposits from commercial banks and to pay them this interest rate. By changing its target for the overnight rate, and by changing the other two rates in lockstep, the Bank of Canada can more or less control the actual overnight interest rate. The 0.5 percentage point range is often referred to as the Bank's *target range* for the overnight interest rate.

bank rate The interest rate the Bank of Canada charges commercial banks for loans.

Consider an example that illustrates the Bank's control over the overnight interest rate. We begin by assuming that the Bank's announced target for the overnight interest rate is 4 percent. The Bank is then willing to lend to commercial banks at the bank rate, 4.25 percent. The Bank is also willing to pay 3.75 percent on any deposits it receives from commercial banks. In this case, what will be the *actual* overnight interest rate? Without knowing more details about commercial banks' demands and supplies for overnight funds, we cannot know exactly what the rate will be, but we can be sure that it will be within the Bank's target range—that is, *between* 3.75 percent and 4.25 percent. It will not be above 4.25 percent because any borrower would rather borrow from the Bank of Canada at 4.25 percent than at a higher rate from any commercial lender. Similarly, it will not be below 3.75 percent because any lender would rather lend to the Bank of Canada at 3.75 percent than accept a lower rate from any commercial borrower. Thus, the Bank can ensure that the actual overnight interest rate remains within its target range.

The Bank's policy instrument is its target for the overnight interest rate. By raising or lowering its target rate, the Bank affects the actual overnight interest rate. Changes in the overnight rate then lead to changes in other, longer-term, interest rates.

Figure 29-2 shows the path of the actual overnight interest rate and the Bank's target rate since 2000. It is almost impossible to tell the difference between the two lines in the figure, which shows the considerable influence that the Bank of Canada's actions have on the actual overnight interest rate.

FIGURE 29-2   The Overnight Interest Rate: Target and Actual

By setting a target for the overnight interest rate, the Bank of Canada exercises consider-able influence over the actual overnight interest rate. By establishing an upper lending rate (the Bank rate) and a lower borrowing rate, the Bank can ensure that the actual overnight interest rate remains within the Bank's target range. Since 2000, there have been only small differences between the actual overnight interest rate, the solid blue line, and the Bank's target for the overnight rate, the dashed red line.

(*Source:* All data are from the Bank of Canada: www.bankofcanada.ca. Overnight interest rate: Series V122514. Bank rate: Series V122530. The Bank's target rate is the bank rate minus 0.25 percentage points.)

The Money Supply Is Endogenous

When the Bank of Canada changes its target for the overnight rate, the change in the actual overnight rate happens almost instantly. Changes in other market interest rates, from home mortgage rates and the prime interest rate to the yields on short- and long-term government securities, also happen very quickly, usually within a day or two. As these rates adjust, firms and households begin to adjust their borrowing behaviour, but these changes take considerably longer to occur. For example, if the Bank of Canada lowered its target for the overnight rate by 25 basis points (0.25 percentage points), commercial banks might follow immediately by reducing the rate on home mortgages by the same amount. But individuals will not respond to this rate reduction by imme-diately increasing their demand for home mortgages. Usually such changes take a while to occur, as borrowers think carefully about how interest-rate changes affect their own economic situations, the affordability of a possible house purchase, or, in the case of firms, the profitability of a potential investment.

As the demand for new loans gradually adjusts to changes in interest rates, com-mercial banks often find themselves in need of more cash reserves with which to make

open-market operation The purchase and sale of government securities on the open market by the central bank.

new loans. When this occurs, banks can sell some of their government securities to the Bank of Canada for cash and then use this cash to extend new loans. By buying government securities with cash in such an **open-market operation**, the Bank of Canada increases the amount of currency in circulation in the economy. This new currency arrives at the commercial banks as cash reserves, which can then be loaned out to firms or households. As we saw in Chapter 27, this process of making loans results in an expansion in deposit money and thus an expansion of the money supply.

Through its open-market operations, the Bank of Canada changes the amount of currency in circulation. But the Bank does not initiate these transactions; it conducts them to accommodate the changing demand for currency by the commercial banks.

Economists often say that the amount of currency in circulation (and also the money supply) is *endogenous*. It is not directly controlled by the Bank of Canada, but instead is determined by the economic decisions of households, firms, and commercial banks. The Bank of Canada is *passive* in its decisions regarding the money supply; it conducts its open-market operations to accommodate the changing demand for currency coming from the commercial banks. *Applying Economic Concepts 29-1* discusses in more detail how the Bank of Canada conducts open-market operations in response to this changing demand.

Expansionary and Contractionary Monetary Policies

We can now clarify the meaning of a *contractionary* or an *expansionary* monetary policy. As we saw earlier, unpredictable shifts in the money demand curve imply that there is no clear relationship between changes in the interest rate and changes in the quantity of money in circulation. And since what matters for the monetary transmission mechanism is the change in interest rates, economists label a monetary-policy action as being expansionary or contractionary depending on how the policy affects interest rates, rather than how it affects the overall amount of money.

If the Bank of Canada wants to stimulate the level (or growth rate) of aggregate demand, it will reduce its target for the overnight interest rate, and the effect will soon be felt on longer-term market interest rates. Reducing the interest rate is an *expansionary* monetary policy because it leads to an expansion of aggregate demand. If the Bank instead wants to reduce aggregate demand (or its growth rate), it will increase its target for the overnight interest rate, and longer-term market interest rates will soon rise as a result. Increasing the interest rate is a *contractionary* monetary policy because it leads to a contraction (or slowing) of aggregate demand.

As the longer-term market interest rates change, the various steps in the monetary transmission mechanism come into play. As we saw in Chapter 28, in an open economy like Canada's there are two separate channels in this transmission mechanism. First, desired investment and consumption expenditure will begin to change. At the same time, international capital flows in response to changes in interest rates will cause the exchange rate to change which, in turn, causes net exports to change. Taken together, the total changes in aggregate expenditure lead to shifts in the *AD* curve, which then lead to changes in real GDP and the price level. The monetary transmission mechanism is reviewed in Figure 29-3.

APPLYING ECONOMIC CONCEPTS 29-1

What Determines the Amount of Currency in Circulation?

The Bank of Canada uses its *policy instrument*—its target for the overnight interest rate—to influence the money market and implement its monetary policy. A reduction in the Bank's target for the overnight rate will reduce market interest rates and lead to a greater demand for borrowing and hence spending by firms and households. In contrast, an increase in the Bank's target for the overnight rate will tend to raise market interest rates and reduce the demand for borrowing and spending by firms and households.

In response to these changes in the demand for loans, commercial banks may find themselves either with too few cash reserves with which to make new loans or with too many cash reserves for the amount of loans they wish to make. What happens in each case?

If Banks Need More Cash

Suppose that at the current market interest rates and level of economic activity, commercial banks are facing a growing demand for loans. If banks have excess reserves, these loans can be made easily. But once banks reach their target reserve ratio, they will be unable to extend new loans without increasing their cash reserves. Banks can increase their cash reserves by selling some of their government bonds to the Bank of Canada. In this case, the Bank of Canada is *purchasing* government bonds from the commercial banks. This transaction is called an *open-market purchase*.

Suppose a commercial bank wants to sell a $10 000 bond to the Bank of Canada. As the accompanying balance sheets show, this transaction does not change the total assets or liabilities for the commercial bank, although it changes the *form* of its assets. With more cash reserves (and fewer bonds), the commercial bank can now make more loans. For the Bank of Canada, however, there *is* a change in the level of assets and liabilities. Its holdings of bonds (assets) have increased and the amount of currency in circulation (liabilities) has also increased. Open-market purchases by the Bank of Canada are the means by which the amount of currency in the economy increases.

If Banks Have Excess Reserves

Now suppose that at the current market interest rates and level of economic activity the commercial banks cannot find enough suitable borrowers to whom they can lend their excess cash reserves. The commercial banks can reduce their excess cash reserves by using the cash to purchase government bonds from the Bank of Canada. In this case, the Bank of Canada is *selling* government bonds to the commercial banks. This transaction is called an *open-market sale*.

The changes in the balance sheets are the opposite to those shown in the accompanying table. The commercial bank now has less cash and more (interest-earning) bonds, but its total assets and liabilities are unchanged. The Bank of Canada now has fewer bonds and there is also less currency in circulation in the economy.

An Open-Market Purchase of Bonds from a Commercial Bank

Commercial Bank Balance Sheet

Assets		Liabilities
Bonds	– $10 000	No change
Cash Reserves	+ $10 000	

Bank of Canada Balance Sheet

Assets		Liabilities	
Bonds	+ $10 000	Currency in Circulation	+ $10 000

Currency in a Growing Economy

If you look at the Bank of Canada's balance sheets (like the one we showed in Chapter 27) over several years, you will notice that the amount of currency in circulation rarely (if ever) falls. In an economy where real GDP is steadily growing, the demand for loans by firms and households is also usually growing, as is the demand for currency by commercial banks. In some years, the demand for currency is growing very quickly, in which case the Bank of Canada has many open-market purchases. In other years, the demand for currency grows only slowly, in which case the Bank has fewer (or smaller) open-market purchases. In a typical year, however, the amount of currency in circulation increases by about 5 percent, which in 2006 represented about $2 billion. Thus, in a typical week, the Bank of Canada purchases about $40 million of government bonds in the open market.

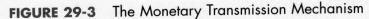

FIGURE 29-3   The Monetary Transmission Mechanism

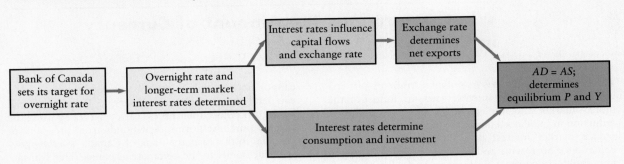

Monetary policy influences aggregate demand through the monetary transmission mechanism. The Bank of Canada sets a target for the overnight interest rate, which influences other market interest rates as well. The change in interest rates leads, via the monetary transmission mechanism, to changes in desired aggregate expenditure. Aggregate demand and aggregate supply then determine the price level and the level of real GDP.

29.2 INFLATION TARGETING

In the previous section we examined the technical details of how the Bank of Canada implements its monetary policy. In this section we examine the Bank's policy objectives and how it conducts its monetary policy to achieve those objectives. Our emphasis is on the Bank's policy of *inflation targeting*.

Why Target Inflation?

During the last few decades of the twentieth century, central banks the world over came to accept two economic propositions. The first proposition is that high inflation is damaging to the economy and is costly for firms and individuals. Among other things, inflation reduces the real purchasing power of those people whose incomes are stated in nominal (dollar) terms and insufficiently *indexed* to adjust for changes in the price level. For example, seniors whose pension incomes are not indexed to inflation suffer a reduction in their real incomes whenever inflation occurs.

The *uncertainty* generated by inflation is also damaging to the economy. When inflation is high, it tends to be quite volatile, and this volatility makes it difficult to predict. As a result, periods of high inflation are often characterized as having much *unexpected* inflation. As we first discussed in Chapter 19, unexpected inflation leads to reallocations of real income between workers and firms and borrowers and lenders that may be viewed as undesirable. Finally, high inflation undermines the ability of the price system to signal changes in relative scarcity through changes in relative prices. For example, if the prices of construction materials rise when inflation is high, consumers may be unable to discern whether the price is rising relative to other goods and services or whether it is rising only because of a widespread inflation. As a result, both producers and consumers will make mistakes regarding their own production and consumption decisions that they would not have made in the absence of high inflation.

High and uncertain inflation leads to arbitrary income redistributions and also under-mines the efficiency of the price system.

The second proposition that came to be accepted by most central banks is that the effects of monetary policy are different in the short run and in the long run. While in the short run monetary policy can have a profound influence on real economic vari-ables such as real GDP, employment, real wages, and investment, its long-run impact appears to fall mostly on nominal variables such as the price level and the inflation rate. Because of the economy's adjustment process that we examined in detail in Chapter 24, real GDP tends to return in the long run to its potential level, Y^*. As a result, monetary policy is unlikely to have a systematic and *sustained* influence on real economic variables. However, monetary policy does have a systematic and sustained influence on the rate of inflation.

A related proposition also came to be accepted by central banks. Various demand and supply shocks that are unrelated to monetary policy cause shifts in the *AD* and *AS* curves, and thus cause changes in the rate of inflation as the economy responds to these shocks. But over time it became clear that *sustained* inflation was not caused by such shocks—instead, *sustained* inflation appeared to only occur in those situations where monetary policy was allowing continual and rapid growth in the money supply. In other words, central banks came to recognize that *sustained* inflation was ultimately created by monetary policy.

Many economists and central bankers argue that monetary policy is the most impor-tant determinant of a country's long-run rate of inflation.

The first proposition is that high inflation is costly. The second proposition is that long-run inflation is ultimately determined by monetary policy, and that inflation is the only macroeconomic variable over which the central bank has such a sustained and systematic influence. Given these two propositions, which over the years have been increasingly supported by both theoretical reasoning and empirical evidence, it is not surprising that central banks have come to focus their attentions on the reduction and control of inflation.

In the early 1990s, many central banks around the world—the Bank of Canada being among the first—adopted formal systems of *inflation targeting*. The Bank of Canada first adopted its formal inflation targets in 1991 when the annual rate of infla-tion was almost 6 percent. The targets were expressed as a 2-percentage-point band, in recognition of the fact that modest fluctuations in the inflation rate are inevitable and thus it is unrealistic to expect the Bank to keep the inflation rate at a single, pre-cise value. Beginning in 1992, the Bank of Canada's target range for inflation was 3–5 percent, with the range falling to 2–4 percent by 1993 and to 1–3 percent by the end of 1995. The Bank's formal inflation targets were renewed in 1996 and again in 2001 and 2006. Today, the Bank of Canada conducts its monetary policy with the objective of keeping inflation at or near the 2-percent target.

The overall success of inflation targeting, in Canada and elsewhere, has led many central banks to adopt formal inflation targets. New Zealand was the first adopter, in 1990, and Canada was second, in 1991. Formal inflation targets were adopted soon thereafter in Israel, the United Kingdom, Australia, Finland, Spain, and Sweden. Since the mid-1990s, the list has grown to include Chile, Brazil, Colombia, Mexico, the Czech Republic, Poland, South Africa, Thailand, and others. The U.S. Federal Reserve has *not* yet adopted a formal inflation target, although its current Chairman, Ben Bernanke, has indicated that he would like the Federal Reserve to do so.

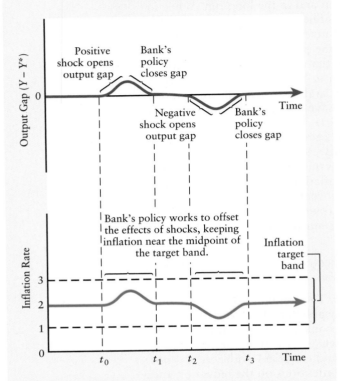

FIGURE 29-4 The Output Gap, Inflation, and Monetary Policy

The Bank of Canada closely monitors the output gap to determine the necessary policy for maintaining inflation near its target. The economy begins with no output gap and the inflation rate at 2 percent. At time t_0 a positive shock pushes real GDP above Y^* and increases inflationary pressure. The Bank can implement a contractionary monetary policy to close the output gap and reduce inflation back toward 2 percent. At time t_2 a negative shock reduces real GDP below Y^* and reduces inflationary pressure. The Bank can implement an expansionary monetary policy to close the output gap and increase inflation back toward 2 percent.

The Role of the Output Gap

The Bank of Canada recognizes that its monetary policy has real and important effects on the economy in the short run, even though its long-run influence is mainly limited to the price level and the inflation rate. The Bank also recognizes that the long-run effects of its policies only follow after the short-run effects on real GDP are experienced, after which the economy's adjustment process tends to return real GDP to the level of potential output. As a result, the Bank of Canada closely monitors the level of real GDP in the short run and also the gap between real GDP and Y^*—the output gap.

To understand why the Bank closely monitors the output gap in the short run, consider Figure 29-4, which shows hypothetical time paths for real GDP (Y) and potential output (Y^*) in part (i), and for the rate of inflation with the 1–3 percent target band in part (ii). Until time t_0, the economy is growing with Y equal to Y^* and inflation is more or less constant at the midpoint of the target band. At t_0, a positive shock pushes real GDP above Y^* and opens up an inflationary output gap. Labour and other factors of production are used intensively in order to increase output, and this generates excess demand in factor markets. Wages and other factor prices begin to rise, pushing up firms' costs, and adding to the inflationary pressure. The rate of inflation begins to rise above the midpoint of the target band.

At this point, the Bank of Canada must make a decision. It can choose to leave its policy unchanged, and let the economy's adjustment process operate. The AS curve will shift upward and eventually return real GDP to Y^* but only through more inflation. The other choice for the Bank is to attempt to close the output gap by "pulling" real GDP back toward Y^* with a contractionary monetary policy, shifting the AD curve to the left and bringing the rate of inflation back to its starting point near the midpoint of the target band.

The opposite situation can also occur, as shown in the figure at time t_2, when a negative shock pushes real GDP below Y^* and pushes inflation toward the bottom end of the target band. The Bank is again faced with a choice. It can do nothing and let real GDP return (perhaps slowly) to Y^*, but allow inflation to fall even further as the AS curve shifts down during the adjustment process. Or it can try to close the output gap by creating a monetary expansion to shift the AD curve to the right and "pull" real GDP back toward Y^*, raising the rate of inflation back toward the midpoint of the target band.

Output gaps create pressure for the rate of inflation to change. To keep the rate of inflation close to the 2-percent target, the Bank of Canada closely monitors real GDP in the short run and designs its policy to keep real GDP close to potential output.

Inflation Targeting as a Stabilizing Policy

Figure 29-4 also shows why an inflation-targeting policy helps to stabilize the economy. If the Bank of Canada is committed to keeping the rate of inflation near 2 percent, positive shocks to the economy that create an inflationary gap and threaten to increase the rate of inflation will be met by a contractionary monetary policy. The Bank will increase interest rates and shift the *AD* curve to the left. This policy will reduce the size of the output gap and push the rate of inflation back down toward 2 percent. Similarly, if a negative shock to the economy creates a recessionary gap and threatens to reduce the rate of inflation, a central bank committed to its inflation targets will respond with an expansionary monetary policy. In this situation, the Bank of Canada will reduce interest rates and shift the *AD* curve to the right. This policy will reduce the size of the output gap and push the inflation rate back toward the 2-percent target.

Inflation targeting is a stabilizing policy. Positive shocks will be met with a contractionary monetary policy; negative shocks will be met with an expansionary monetary policy.

Practise with Study Guide Chapter 29, Exercise 3.

Some economists go so far as to refer to a policy of inflation targeting as an "automatic" stabilizer. But this is an exaggeration, as we can see by recalling our discussion in Chapter 24 of automatic *fiscal* stabilizers, caused by taxes and transfers that vary with the level of national income. The automatic fiscal stabilizers we discussed in Chapter 24 were truly "automatic" in the sense that no group of policymakers had to actively adjust policy—the stabilizers were built right into the tax-and-transfer system. With inflation targeting, however, there must be an active policy decision to keep inflation close to its target rate, and only then will the Bank's policy adjustments work to stabilize the economy following either positive or negative shocks. But as long as the Bank wants to maintain its inflation target, and have it perceived as being *credible*, then it is committed to carrying out such policy adjustments.

Inflation targets are not as "automatic" a stabilizer as the fiscal stabilizers built into the tax-and-transfer system. But if the central bank is committed to maintaining the credibility of its inflation target, its policy adjustments will act to stabilize the economy.

Complications in Inflation Targeting

So far, our discussion of inflation targeting makes the conduct of monetary policy seem straightforward. But there are several details that complicate the task considerably. In this section we discuss two complications for the conduct of monetary policy, and in the next section we address a more general difficulty.

Volatile Food and Energy Prices
Sometimes the rate of inflation increases for reasons unrelated to a change in the output gap. For example, many commodities whose prices are included in the Consumer Price Index (CPI) are internationally traded goods and their prices are determined in world markets. Oil is an obvious example, as are many fruits and vegetables. When these prices rise suddenly, because of political

instability in the Middle East (oil) or because of poor crop conditions in tropical countries (fruits and vegetables), the measured rate of inflation of the Canadian CPI also
rises. Yet these price increases have little or nothing to do with the size of the output
gap in Canada and thus have little implication for what policy should be followed by
the Bank of Canada. By focusing exclusively on the rate of inflation of the CPI, the
Bank would be misled about the extent of inflationary pressures coming from excess
demand in Canada.

For this reason, the Bank of Canada pays attention to what is called the "core"
rate of inflation. This is the rate of growth of a special price index, one that is constructed by extracting food, energy, and the effects of indirect taxes (such as the GST
or excise taxes) from the Consumer Price Index. Figure 29-5 shows the paths of core
and CPI inflation since 1992. As is clear from the figure, even though the two measures of inflation move broadly together, core inflation is much less volatile than is CPI
inflation.

FIGURE 29-5   Canadian CPI and Core Inflation, 1992–2006

The CPI inflation rate is more volatile than the "core" inflation rate. The core rate of inflation in Canada is the rate
of change of a special price index constructed by removing food, energy, and the effects of indirect taxes from the overall Consumer Price Index. For both series shown here, the inflation rate is computed monthly, but is the rate of change
in the price index from 12 months earlier.

(*Source:* Statistics Canada, CANSIM database, Series V36397 and V735319. Reprinted with permission of Statistics Canada.)

Due to the volatility of food and energy prices that is often unrelated to the level of the output gap in Canada, the Bank of Canada closely monitors the rate of "core" inflation even though its formal target of 2 percent applies to the rate of CPI inflation. Changes in core inflation are a better indicator of Canadian excess demand than are changes in CPI inflation.

Note the sharp divergence between the two inflation rates in 1994. At that time, there were substantial decreases in the excise taxes on cigarettes, and those tax reductions led to a sharp decline in the CPI inflation rate. But this decline in CPI inflation was tax-created rather than caused by the opening of a recessionary output gap, and thus it would have been inappropriate for the Bank of Canada to respond to this decline in inflation by implementing an expansionary monetary policy. Instead, the Bank focused on the core inflation rate that excludes the effect of changes in indirect taxes. The core inflation rate in 1994 was relatively stable and close to the midpoint of the 1–3 percent target band, indicating no need for a change in monetary policy.

In the 2002–2006 period, the world price of oil rose sharply, thus driving up the price of gasoline and other energy-related products. The CPI rate of inflation during this period was substantially above the core rate of inflation (and consistently above the 2-percent target), even though the output gap in Canada was very close to zero. The Bank of Canada gradually tightened its monetary policy during 2005 and 2006, but more due to the signs of an emerging inflationary output gap than because of the high rate of CPI inflation.

The Exchange Rate and Monetary Policy

Given the large amount of trade that Canadian firms and households do with the rest of the world, it is not surprising that the Bank of Canada pays close attention to movements in the exchange rate, the Canadian-dollar price of one unit of foreign currency. However, because changes in the exchange rate can have several different causes, care must be taken when drawing inferences about the desired change in monetary policy resulting from changes in the exchange rate. As we will see, there is no simple "rule of thumb" for how the Bank should react to a change in the exchange rate. Recall that the Bank's objective is to keep the inflation rate near the midpoint of the 1–3 percent target band, and it does this by responding to changes in the output gap so as to offset changes in emerging inflationary pressure. The Bank's appropriate policy response to a change in the exchange rate depends crucially on the *cause* of the change.

Many economic events can lead to changes in the exchange rate. The cause of any change must be known before the appropriate monetary policy response can be determined.

We consider two different examples. In the first, an appreciation of the Canadian dollar leads the Bank to tighten its monetary policy by raising its target for the overnight interest rate. In the second example, an appreciation of the Canadian dollar leads the Bank to loosen its monetary policy by reducing its target for the overnight interest rate. In both cases, the Bank's actions are consistent with its objective of keeping the inflation rate near the midpoint of the 1–3 percent target band.

For the first example, suppose that the economies of Canada's trading partners are booming and thus demanding more Canadian exports. Foreigners' heightened demand for Canadian goods creates an increase in demand for the Canadian dollar in foreign-exchange markets. The Canadian dollar therefore appreciates. But the increase in demand for Canadian goods has added directly to Canadian aggregate demand. If this shock persists, it will eventually add to domestic inflationary pressures. In this case, if the Bank notes the appreciation of the dollar (and correctly determines its cause), it can take action to offset the positive demand shock by tightening monetary policy by raising its target for the overnight interest rate.

The second example involves an increase in demand for Canadian *assets* rather than Canadian goods, and has quite different implications from the first example. Suppose that investors, because of events happening elsewhere in the world, decide to liquidate some of their foreign assets and purchase more Canadian assets instead. In this case, the increase in demand for Canadian assets leads to an increase in demand for the Canadian dollar in foreign-exchange markets. This causes an appreciation of the Canadian dollar. As the dollar appreciates, however, Canadian exports become more expensive to foreigners. There will be a reduction in Canadian net exports and thus a reduction in Canadian aggregate demand. If this shock persists, it will eventually reduce inflationary pressure in Canada. In this case, if the Bank notes the appreciation of the dollar (and correctly determines its cause), it can take action to offset the negative demand shock by loosening monetary policy by reducing its target for the overnight interest rate.

Notice in both examples that the Canadian dollar appreciated as a result of the external shock, but the causes of the appreciation were different. In the first case, there was a positive demand shock to net exports, which then caused the appreciation, which in turn dampened the initial increase in net exports. But the overall effect on the demand for Canadian goods was positive. In the second case, there was a positive shock to the *asset* market, which then caused the appreciation, which in turn reduced the demand for net exports. The overall effect on the demand for Canadian goods was negative. Thus, in the first case, the appropriate response for monetary policy was contractionary, whereas in the second case the appropriate response for monetary policy was expansionary.

Changes in the exchange rate can signal the need for changes in the stance of monetary policy. Only once the cause of the exchange-rate change is determined, however, can the Bank of Canada design a policy response appropriate for keeping inflation close to its target.

ᚷ myeconlab

For a more detailed discussion of how movements in the exchange rate complicate the implementation of monetary policy, look for "Monetary Policy and the Exchange Rate in Canada" in the *Additional Topics* section of this book's MyEconLab.

w w w . m y e c o n l a b . c o m

29.3 LONG AND VARIABLE LAGS

In Chapter 28 we encountered a debate that was prominent between the 1950s and the early 1980s. *Monetarists* argued that monetary policy was potentially very powerful in the sense that a given change in the money supply would lead to a substantial change in aggregate demand, whereas *Keynesians* were associated with the view that monetary policy was much less powerful.

This debate had some of its roots in differing interpretations of the causes of the Great Depression, especially as it occurred in the United States amid a large number of commercial-bank failures. One interesting part of the debate is why Canada and the United Kingdom had collapses in economic activity similar in magnitude to that in the

United States even though they did not suffer the same banking crisis. *Lessons From History 29-1* provides a brief summary of this interesting debate and applies some of the lessons about monetary policy we have learned in the past two chapters.

The debate between the Monetarists and the Keynesians was about more than just the *effectiveness* of monetary policy. The debate sometimes also focused on the question of whether active use of monetary policy in an attempt to stabilize output and the price level was likely to be successful, or whether it would instead lead to an increase in fluctuations in those variables. This debate is as important today as it was then, and at its centre is the role of *lags*.

What Are the Lags in Monetary Policy?

Experience has shown that lags in the operation of policy can sometimes cause stabilization policy to be destabilizing. In Chapter 24, we discussed how decision and implementation lags might limit the extent to which active use of fiscal policy can be relied upon to stabilize the economy. Although both of these sources of lags are less relevant for monetary policy, the full effects of monetary policy nevertheless occur only after quite long time lags. There are two reasons why a change in monetary policy does not affect the economy instantly.

Changes in Expenditure Take Time When the Bank of Canada changes its target for the overnight interest rate, the actual overnight rate changes almost instantly. Other, longer-term market interest rates also change quickly, usually within a day or two. However, it takes more time before households and firms adjust their spending and borrowing plans in response to the change in interest rates. Consumers may respond relatively quickly and alter their plans for purchasing durable goods like cars and appliances. But it takes longer for firms to modify their investment plans and then put them into effect. It may take a year or more before the full increase in investment expenditure occurs in response to a fall in interest rates.

In an open economy like Canada's, the change in the interest rate also leads to capital flows and a change in the exchange rate. These changes occur very quickly. But the effect on net exports takes more time while purchasers of internationally traded goods and services switch to lower-cost suppliers.

The Multiplier Process Takes Time Changes in consumption, investment, and net export expenditures brought about by a change in monetary policy set off the multiplier process that increases national income. This process, too, takes some time to work out. Furthermore, although the end result is fairly predictable, the speed with which the entire expansionary or contractionary process works itself out can vary in ways that are hard to predict. Thus, though the effects of monetary policy might be reasonably straightforward to predict, the timing of those effects is difficult to predict.

Monetary policy is capable of exerting expansionary and contractionary forces on the economy, but it operates with a time lag that is long and variable.

Economists at the Bank of Canada estimate that it takes between 9 and 12 months for a change in monetary policy to have an effect on real GDP, and a further 9 to 12 months for the policy to have an effect on the price level (or the rate of inflation).

LESSONS FROM HISTORY 29-1

Two Views on the Role of Money in the Great Depression

In most people's minds, the Great Depression began with the stock market crash of October 1929. In the United States, Canada, and Europe, the decline in economic activity over the next four years was massive. From 1929 to 1933, real output fell by roughly 25 percent, one-quarter of the labour force was unemployed by 1933, the price level fell by over 25 percent, and businesses failed on a massive scale. In the seven decades that have followed, no recession has come close to the Great Depression in terms of reduced economic activity, business failures, or unemployment.

The Great Depression has naturally attracted the attention of economists and, especially in the United States, these few years of experience have served as a kind of "retrospective laboratory" in which they have tried to test their theories.

The Basic Facts

The stock market crash of 1929, and other factors associated with a moderate downswing in business activity during the late 1920s, caused U.S. firms and households to wish to hold more cash and fewer demand deposits. The banking system, however, could not meet this increased demand for liquidity (cash) without help from the Federal Reserve System (the U.S. central bank). As we saw in Chapter 27, because of the fractional-reserve banking system, commercial banks are never able to satisfy from their own reserves a large and sudden demand for cash—their reserves are always only a small fraction of total deposits.

The Federal Reserve had been set up to provide just such emergency assistance to commercial banks that were basically sound but were unable to meet sudden demands by depositors to withdraw cash. However, the Fed refused to extend the necessary help, and successive waves of bank failures followed as a direct result. During each wave, hundreds of banks failed, ruining many depositors and thereby worsening an already severe depression. In the second half of 1931, almost 2000 U.S. banks were forced to suspend operations. One consequence of these failures was a sharp drop in the money supply; by 1933, M2 was 33 percent lower than it had been in 1929.

Competing Explanations

After the Great Depression was over, economists were able to examine the data and construct explanations for these dramatic events. To Monetarists, the basic facts seem decisive: To them, the fall in the money supply was clearly the major *cause* of the fall in output and employment that occurred during the Great Depression. Monetarists see the Great Depression as perhaps the single best piece of evidence of the strength of monetary forces, and the single best lesson of the importance of monetary policy. In their view, the increased cash drain that led to the massive monetary contraction could have been prevented had the Federal Reserve quickly increased the level of cash reserves in the commercial banking system. In this case, the rise in cash reserves would have offset the increase in the cash drain, so that the money supply (currency plus bank deposits) could be maintained.

Keynesians argue that the fundamental cause of the Great Depression was a reduction in autonomous expenditure. They cite a large decline in housing construction (in response to a glut of housing), a decline in

Destabilizing Policy?

The fact that monetary-policy actions taken today will not affect output and inflation until 1–2 years in the future means that the Bank of Canada must design its policy for what *is expected* to occur in the future rather than what *has already been observed*. To see why a monetary policy guided only by past and current events may be destabilizing, consider the following simple example. Suppose that on January 1 the Bank observes $Y < Y^*$ and concludes that an expansionary monetary policy is appropriate. It can reduce its target for the overnight rate at the next fixed announcement date (FAD), typically within a few weeks. By early February, the overnight interest rate will automobile purchases (as most first-time buying was done and only replacement demand remained), and a reduction in consumption driven largely by pessimism caused by the stock market crash. Although Keynesians accept the argument that the Fed's behaviour was perverse, and exacerbated an already bad situation, they do not attribute a pivotal role to the Fed or to the money supply. Instead, they see the fall in the money supply as a *result* of the decline in economic activity (through a reduced demand for loans and thus reduced bank lending) rather than as its cause.

Lessons from Canada's Experience

Canada can be used as a "control" in this retrospective laboratory, for the simple reason that Canada had broadly the same magnitude of economic collapse as did the United States, but *did not* have the same magnitude of bank failures. Unfortunately, Canada's experience is not able to resolve the disagreement—both sides of the debate can offer explanations of the Canadian experience consistent with their central arguments.

Keynesians look to Canada's experience to support their view that money was not central to the cause of the economic collapse in the United States. They point out that in Canada, where the central bank came to the aid of the banking system, bank failures were much less common during the Great Depression, and as a consequence, the money supply did not shrink drastically as it did in the United States. Thus, their argument is that since Canada did not escape the Great Depression, but *did* escape the collapse in the money supply, money must not have been the central cause of the U.S. economic collapse.

Monetarists accept the point that Canada did not have a massive reduction in the money supply, but they argue that the economic contraction in the United States (which *was* caused by the collapse in the money supply) spilled over into Canada, largely through a dramatic reduction in demand for Canadian goods. This spillover implies a large decline in autonomous export expenditure for Canada, and thus a decline in Canadian national income. Thus, Monetarists essentially argue that money in the United States was an important contributor to the economic decline in Canada.

———

For a discussion of these two views, and some attempts to discriminate between them, see Peter Temin, *Did Monetary Forces Cause the Great Depression?* (New York: Norton, 1976).

During the Great Depression, bank failures were widespread in the United States, but relatively uncommon in Canada. This difference in experience can be used to test hypotheses regarding the causes of the Great Depression. But considerable disagreement still remains.

be reduced, as will the longer-term interest rates in the economy. The effects on aggregate demand, however, will not be felt in any significant way until October or November of that same year.

This policy action may turn out to be destabilizing, however. Some of the cyclical forces in the economy, unrelated to the Bank's actions, may have reversed since January, and by November there may be a substantial inflationary output gap. However, since the effects of the monetary expansion that was initiated nine months earlier are just beginning to be felt, an expansionary monetary stimulus is adding to the existing inflationary gap.

If the Bank now applies the monetary brakes by raising interest rates, the full effects of this policy reversal will not be felt for another 1–2 years. By that time, a contraction may have already set in because of the natural cyclical forces of the economy. Thus, the delayed effects of the monetary policy may turn a minor downturn into a major recession.

The long time lags in the effectiveness of monetary policy make monetary fine-tuning difficult; the policy may have a destabilizing effect.

The Bank of Canada recognizes the possibility that if it responds to every shock that influences real GDP, the overall effect of its policy may be to destabilize the economy rather than stabilize it. As a result, it is careful to assess the causes of the shocks that buffet the Canadian economy. It tries to avoid situations in which it responds to shocks that are believed to be short-lived and then must reverse its policy in the near future when the shocks disappear. In general, the Bank responds only to those shocks that are significant in magnitude and are expected to persist for several months or more.

Political Difficulties

Long lags in the workings of monetary policy also lead to some political criticism for the central bank.

Figure 29-6 shows a situation in which the current inflation rate is at the bottom of the Bank's 1–3 percent target band, but the expectation of future events suggests that inflation will be rising sharply. This situation is a typical one faced by the Bank anytime the economy is well into a healthy economic recovery, as was true in the spring of 1997 and also the spring of 2003. In the latter case, the Canadian economy had been growing much more quickly than the U.S. economy, and the future suggested more of the same. Core inflation at the time was still within the target band, but expectations of higher future growth threatened to push core inflation above 3 percent.

What is the political problem? Remember that because of the time lags involved, any policy change that occurs today has no effect on real GDP for roughly 9 months and the full effect on the price level (or the rate of inflation) does not occur for 18–24 months. If the economy is at point A in Figure 29-6, and inflation is expected to rise in the near future, then monetary policy must be changed *now* in order to counteract this future inflation. But this action could generate some criticism because the *current* inflation rate is low. The Bank finds itself in the awkward position of advocating a tightening of monetary policy, in order to fight the expectation of future inflation, at a time when the *current* inflation rate suggests no need for tightening. But if the goal is to keep inflation within the target range, such *preemptive* monetary policy is necessary because of the unavoidable time lags.

FIGURE 29-6   Forward-Looking Monetary Policy

Since monetary policy works only with a considerable time lag, central-bank actions to keep inflation within its target range must be taken in advance of expected future events. Suppose the economy is currently at point A with inflation at the lower bound of the target range. If events in the near future are expected to cause inflation to rise sharply, then monetary policy must be tightened immediately to keep inflation within the desired range.

Time lags in monetary policy require that decisions regarding a loosening or tightening of monetary policy be forward-looking. This often leads to criticism of monetary policy, especially by those who do not recognize the long time lags.

29.4 **30 YEARS OF CANADIAN MONETARY POLICY**

This section describes a few key episodes in recent Canadian monetary history. This is not done to teach history for its own sake, but because the lessons of past experience and past policy mistakes, interpreted through the filter of economic theory, provide our best hope for improving our policy performance in the future.

The OPEC oil-price shocks of 1973 and 1979–1980 led to reductions in GDP growth rates and increases in inflation in Canada—what came to be known as *stagflation*. At that time, the role of aggregate-supply shocks and their effect on macroeconomic equilibrium was not as well understood as it is today. The Bank of Canada's policy response involved considerable monetary expansion, and by 1980 the rate of inflation in Canada was over 12 percent.

The Bank of Canada (and also the U.S. Federal Reserve) then embarked on policies designed to reduce the growth rate of the money supply and eventually reduce the inflation rate. Unfortunately, at the same time innovations in the financial sector led to unexpected increases in the demand for money. The result was a much sharper increase in interest rates (see Figure 29-7) than was intended by the Bank of Canada, and the most serious recession since the 1930s. But the rate of inflation *did* fall, from over

FIGURE 29-7   Short-Term Interest Rates, Canada and the United States, 1975–2005

(*Source:* Bank of Canada. Canadian rate is Series V122495; U.S. rate is Series V122148. Both are quarterly averages of monthly data.)

12 percent in 1980 to about 4 percent in 1984. This experience taught the Bank two important lessons:

1. Monetary policy can be *very* effective in reducing inflation.
2. Due to unexpected changes in money demand, monetary policy should focus more on interest rates than on the money supply.

As we saw earlier in this chapter, this second lesson is an important reason why the Bank now implements its policy by setting the interest rate rather than by directly influencing the money supply.

Economic Recovery: 1983–1987

In early 1983, a sustained recovery began, and by mid-1987, real GDP had moved back toward potential. Much of the growth was centred in the export-oriented manufacturing industries in Ontario and Quebec. The first four years of the recovery saw cumulative output growth of 15.7 percent.

The main challenge for monetary policy in this period was to create sufficient liquidity to accommodate the recovery without triggering a return to the high inflation rates that prevailed at the start of the decade.

In other words, the Bank of Canada had to increase the money supply to *accommodate* the recovery-induced increase in money demand *without* increasing the money supply so much that it refuelled inflationary pressures.

In spite of much debate and uncertainty, the Bank handled this "re-entry" problem quite well. The Bank allowed a short but rapid burst of growth in the nominal money supply, thus generating the desired increase in real money balances. Once the new level of real balances was achieved, money growth was cut back to a rate consistent with low inflation, allowing for the underlying rate of growth in real income. The trick with this policy was that to avoid triggering expectations of renewed inflation, the Bank had to generate a one-shot increase in the *level* of the money supply without creating the impression that it was raising the long-term *rate of growth* of the money supply.

In late 1983 and early 1984, when growth in the money supply first started to surge, many voiced the fear that the Bank was being overly expansionary and was risking a return to higher inflation. As the re-entry problem came to be more widely understood and as inflationary pressures failed to re-emerge, these criticisms subsided, and the consensus appeared to be that the Bank had done a commendable job of handling the re-entry problem.

Rising Inflation: 1987–1990

By mid-1987, many observers began to worry that Canadian policymakers were too complacent in accepting the 4 percent range that Canadian inflation had settled into. Further, there was concern that inflationary pressures were starting to build—the money supply was growing quickly, real output growth was strong, unemployment was falling, and an inflationary gap was opening.

In 1987, many economists argued that if monetary policy was not tightened, Canada would experience gradually increasing inflation until once again a severe monetary restriction would be required to reduce the rate of inflation.

Inflation slowly crept upward. A monetary restriction designed to reduce inflation would obviously impose costs in the form of lower output and higher unemployment. Was the Bank prepared to inflict such costs, especially given that Canada had emerged from a deep recession only five years earlier?

In January 1988, Bank of Canada Governor John Crow announced that monetary policy would henceforth be guided less by short-term stabilization issues and more by the goal of long-term "price stability." Specifically, he said that "monetary policy should be conducted so as to achieve a pace of monetary expansion that promotes stability in the value of money. This means pursuing a policy aimed at achieving and maintaining stable prices."[1]

Disinflation: 1990–1992

This explicit adoption of price stability as the Bank's only target set off a heated debate about the appropriate stance for monetary policy. The debate was fuelled by Crow's decision to give a high profile to his policy by repeatedly articulating and defending it in speeches and public appearances. He believed that this was necessary because expectations of continuing inflation had become entrenched. In his view, until the public believed that the Bank was serious about controlling inflation, whatever the short-term consequences, inflation could not be reduced. Some critics said that price stability was unobtainable. Others said the costs of reaching it would be too large in terms of several years of recessionary gaps. Supporters said that the long-term gains from having a stable price level would exceed the costs of getting there.

Despite the Bank's explicit policy of "price stability," the actual inflation rate increased slightly in the years immediately following John Crow's policy announcement, from about 4 percent in 1987 to just over 5 percent in 1990.

The controversy reached new heights when in 1990 the country (and much of the world) entered a sustained recession. Maintaining a tight monetary policy with high interest rates (see Figure 29-7) seemed perverse to many when the economy was already suffering from too little aggregate demand to sustain potential output.

Furthermore, the high Canadian interest rates attracted foreign funds. Foreigners who wished to buy Canadian bonds needed Canadian dollars, and their demands led to an appreciation of the Canadian dollar. This increased the price of Canadian exports while reducing the price of Canadian imports, putting Canadian export and import-competing industries at a competitive disadvantage, and further increasing the unemployment that had been generated by the worldwide recession.

John Crow was the governor of the Bank of Canada from 1987 to 1994. In 1988 he announced that "price stability" would thenceforth be the Bank of Canada's objective.

1 John W. Crow, "The Work of Canadian Monetary Policy," speech given at the University of Alberta, January 18, 1988; reprinted in *Bank of Canada Review,* February 1988.

Inflation Targeting I: 1991–2000

In spite of heavy political pressure to lower interest rates, and of criticism from many economists who might have supported a move toward price stability in less depressed times, the Bank stood by its tight monetary policy. Indeed, in 1991, it formally announced *inflation-control targets* for the next several years. Beginning in 1992, inflation was to lie within the 3–5 percent range, with the range falling to 2–4 percent by 1993 and to 1–3 percent by the end of 1995.

As a result of the tight monetary policy of the Bank, the inflation rate fell sharply, from about 5 percent in 1990 to less than 2 percent in 1992. For 1993 and 1994, inflation hovered around 2 percent. Furthermore, short-term nominal interest rates fell from a high of about 13 percent in 1990 to about 6 percent by the end of 1993. Recall that the nominal interest rate is equal to the real interest rate plus the rate of inflation. So this decline in nominal interest rates was the eventual result of the tight monetary policy that reduced inflation.

The Bank had succeeded in coming close to its target of price stability. Controversy continued, however, on two issues. First, was the result worth the price of a deeper, possibly more prolonged recession than might have occurred if the Bank had been willing to accept 3–4 percent inflation? Second, would the low inflation rate be sustainable once the recovery took the economy back toward potential output? If the inflation rate were to rise to 4 percent during the post-1993 recovery, then the verdict might well be that the cost of temporarily reducing the rate to below 2 percent was not worth the transitory gains.

The debate over the Bank's emphasis on maintaining low inflation became centred on Governor John Crow, especially during the federal election campaign of 1993. Some called for the nonrenewal of Crow's term as governor (which would end in 1994), and his replacement with someone perceived to care more about the costs of fighting inflation. Others argued that the Bank's policy of "price stability" under Crow's stewardship was the right policy for the times, and that the long-run benefits of maintaining low inflation would be worth the costs required to achieve it.[2]

Gordon Thiessen became the governor of the Bank of Canada in 1994 after inflation had hovered around 2 percent for about two years.

In 1994, the minister of finance appointed Gordon Thiessen, the former senior deputy governor of the Bank, to be the new governor. With some irony, the minister of finance, whose party had been severe critics of Crow's policy while they were in opposition, affirmed the previous monetary policy of the Bank and urged the new governor to maintain the hard-won low inflation rate. The new governor agreed and extended the formal inflation target of 2 percent until 2001.

For the next three years, the rate of inflation continued to hover between 1 and 2 percent. The main challenge for the Bank in the next few years was to keep inflation low while at the same time encouraging the economy to progress through what was viewed as a fragile recovery. Excessive stimulation of the economy would lead to the rise of inflation which would sacrifice the hard-won gains achieved only a few years earlier. On the other hand, insufficient stimulation would itself be an obstacle to economic recovery.

---

2 For a very readable account of Canadian monetary policy from 1988 to 1993, see William Robson and David Laidler, *The Great Canadian Disinflation* (Toronto: C. D. Howe Institute, 1993).

Beginning in the summer of 1997, the economies of Thailand, Malaysia, Indonesia, and South Korea fell into serious recessions, thus beginning what is now known as the Asian Economic Crisis.[3] Since these countries are major importers of raw materials, their recessions led to a large decline in the world's demand for raw materials. As a result, the world price of raw materials fell by an average of about 30 percent in the subsequent year. Since Canada is a major producer and exporter of raw materials, this decline in the demand for raw materials was a negative aggregate demand shock for Canada. Working in the opposite direction, however, was the expansionary supply-side effect of lower raw materials prices for the many Canadian manufacturing firms that use raw materials as inputs. This positive supply shock was especially important for the United States, a major importer and user of raw materials. The impact of the Asian Crisis on the U.S. economy produced a third effect on Canada as the quickly growing U.S. economy increased its demand for Canadian goods and services.

In the spring of 1997, before the Asian Crisis had begun, the Canadian economy was growing and steadily closing a recessionary gap. The combination of forces created by the Asian Economic Crisis presented problems for the Bank of Canada and for the appropriate direction for monetary policy. Especially difficult was judging the relative strengths of the three separate effects. As it turned out, Canada's recessionary gap continued to shrink as the economy grew steadily. By 1999, the Asian economies were on their way to a healthy recovery.

Changes in stock-market values also created some challenges for the Bank of Canada in the 1990s. From 1994 through 1999, U.S. and Canadian stocks enjoyed unprecedented bull markets. The Dow Jones Industrial Average (an index of U.S. stock prices) increased from about 3500 in mid-1994 to about 11 000 in late 1999, an average annual increase of 26 percent. The Toronto Stock Exchange Index (now called the S&P/TSX), increased from roughly 4000 to 8000 over the same period, an average annual increase of 14 percent.

The concern for the Bank of Canada during this time was that the increase in wealth generated by these stock-market gains would stimulate consumption expenditures in what was already a steadily growing economy, thus increasing inflationary pressures. In December of 1996, the chairman of the U.S. Federal Reserve, Alan Greenspan, warned market participants about their "irrational exuberance." Bank of Canada Governor Gordon Thiessen made similar remarks in Canada. Both central bankers were trying to dampen expectations in the stock market so that the stock-market gains, and thus the increases in wealth-induced spending, would not significantly contribute to inflationary pressures. But they had to be careful not to have their comments create a "crash" in the market that would have even more dramatic effects in the opposite direction.

As it turned out, the crash happened anyway. In both the United States and Canada, the stock markets had reached such levels that many commentators said it was only a matter of time before participants realized that stock prices no longer reflected the underlying values of the companies, at which point there would be massive selling and an inevitable crash. From the fall of 2000 to the spring of 2001, the major Canadian stock-market indexes fell by roughly 40 percent, driven to a large extent by huge reductions in the stock prices of high-tech firms.

---

[3] An important part of the cause of these recessions was the sudden collapse of their currencies, which were previously pegged in value to the U.S. dollar. We examine fixed and flexible exchange rates in detail in Chapter 35.

Inflation Targeting II: 2001–Present

When the terrorist attacks in New York and Washington occurred on September 11, 2001, the stock markets took another dramatic plunge. By late in 2003, stock markets were still far below their pre-crash levels. The main challenge for monetary policy was to provide enough liquidity to the banking systems to prevent the economy from entering a recession. In both the United States and Canada, the central banks dramatically lowered their key interest rates over a period of several months.

Throughout 2002, 2003, and most of 2004, the Bank of Canada's target for the overnight interest rate was 3 percentage points below its level from the summer of 2000. During this period, two external forces on the Canadian economy became apparent, and presented a further challenge for the Bank of Canada. First, strong world economic growth, especially in China and India, contributed to a substantial increase in the world prices of oil and other raw materials. Given Canada's position as a major producer and exporter of these products, these price increases contributed to a substantial appreciation of the Canadian dollar, by over 40 percent from 2002 to 2005. Taken by itself, this external shock represented a persistent, positive shock to Canadian aggregate demand and created a justification for the Bank of Canada to tighten its monetary policy.

Working in the opposite direction was a second external shock, also contributing to an appreciation of the Canadian dollar. During the 2002–2005 period, partly in response to a large and growing U.S. current account deficit, the U.S. dollar was depreciating against the pound sterling and the euro. This "realignment" of the U.S. dollar also involved Canada, and explained some part of the Canadian dollar's appreciation during that period. These exchange-rate changes, which were not themselves being caused by changes in the demand for Canadian goods and services, nonetheless tended to reduce Canadian net exports and aggregate demand, thus providing some justification for a loosening of Canadian monetary policy.

The problem for the Bank of Canada during this period was to determine the *relative* strength of these opposing forces, and thus the appropriate *overall* direction for monetary policy. During the early part of this period, when Canadian real GDP was below potential, the Bank resisted its tightening policy, choosing instead to allow the commodity-price-driven expansion to close the existing output gap. By the summer of 2005, however, when the output gap appeared to be all but closed, the Bank began a series of increases in the target for the overnight interest rate, and by the summer of 2006 it had increased its target by two percentage points.

A related challenge for the Bank during this period involved regional and sectoral differences in economic performance within Canada. The strong growth in the prices of oil and raw materials naturally led to boom conditions in these sectors, which tend to be located in both Western and Atlantic Canada. However, these price increases harmed the profitability of many central Canadian manufacturing firms who used these products as important inputs. In addition, the appreciation of the Canadian dollar further challenged these firms, as foreign buyers reduced their demand for more expensive Canadian-made products.

Regional and sectoral differences highlight an inherent difficulty with monetary policy in a country as economically diverse as Canada. Because there must be a single monetary policy for the nation as a whole (as long as all parts of Canada continue to use the same currency!), policy must be guided by the *average* level of economic activity in order to keep the *average* rate of inflation close to its target. But significant differences in economic activity across regions and/or sectors means that many people will feel that monetary policy is being conducted inappropriately because economic activity in their specific region or sector is not the same as the national average.

With the success of many central banks in maintaining low and stable inflation, some economists have raised the concern that inflation may now be "too low," and that the economy may actually function more smoothly with slightly higher inflation. For more details about this contentious debate, look for "Can Inflation Be Too Low?" in the *Additional Topics* section of this book's MyEconLab.

www.myeconlab.com

S U M M A R Y

29.1 HOW THE BANK OF CANADA IMPLEMENTS MONETARY POLICY

- Monetary policy can be conducted either by setting the money supply or by setting the interest rate. But for a given negatively sloped M_D curve, both cannot be set independently.
- Because of its incomplete control over the money supply, as well as the uncertainty regarding both the slope and the position of the M_D curve, the Bank chooses to implement its policy by setting the interest rate.
- The Bank's policy instrument is the target it sets for the overnight interest rate. By offering to lend funds at a rate 25 basis points above this target (the bank rate) and to accept deposits on which it pays interest at 25 basis

points below the target, the Bank of Canada can control the actual overnight interest rate.
- Changes in the Bank's target for the overnight rate lead to changes in the actual overnight rate and also to changes in longer-term market interest rates. The various steps in the monetary transmission mechanism then come into play.
- The Bank of Canada conducts an expansionary monetary policy by reducing its target for the overnight interest rate. It conducts a contractionary monetary policy by raising its target for the overnight interest rate.

29.2 INFLATION TARGETING

- Many central banks have come to accept two propositions:

  1. High inflation is damaging to the economy.
  2. The long-run effects of monetary policy are mainly on the price level (or rate of inflation), and sustained inflation is ultimately generated by monetary policy.

  As a result, many central banks have adopted formal inflation targets.
- The Bank of Canada's formal inflation target is the rate of CPI inflation. It seeks to keep the annual inflation rate at 2 percent.

- In the short run, the Bank closely monitors the output gap. By tightening its policy during an inflationary gap (and loosening it during a recessionary gap), the Bank can keep the rate of inflation near 2 percent.
- The policy of inflation targeting helps to stabilize the economy. The Bank responds to positive shocks with a contractionary policy, and responds to negative shocks with an expansionary policy.
- Two technical issues complicate the conduct of monetary policy:

  1. Volatile food and energy prices
  2. Changes in the exchange rate

29.3 LONG AND VARIABLE LAGS   LO 5

- Though the Bank of Canada can change interest rates very quickly, it takes time for firms and households to change their expenditure. Even once those new plans are carried out, it takes time for the multiplier process to work its way through the economy, eventually increasing equilibrium national income.

- Long and variable lags in monetary policy lead many economists to argue that the Bank should not try to "fine-tune" the economy. Instead, it should respond only to shocks that are significant in size and persistent in duration.

29.4 30 YEARS OF CANADIAN MONETARY POLICY   LO 6

- In the early 1980s, the Bank of Canada embarked on a policy of tight money to reduce inflation. This policy contributed to the severity of the recession.
- A sustained economic recovery occurred from 1983 to 1987. The main challenge for monetary policy during this time was to create sufficient liquidity to accommodate the recovery without triggering a return to the high inflation rates that prevailed at the start of the decade.
- In 1988, when inflation was between 4 and 5 percent, the Bank of Canada announced that monetary policy would henceforth be guided by the long-term goal of "price stability." By 1992, the Bank's tight money policy had reduced inflation to below 2 percent.
- Controversy concerned two issues. First, was the cost in terms of lost output and heavy unemployment worth the benefits of lower inflation? Second, could the low inflation rate be sustained?

- This controversy was partly responsible for the 1994 change in the Bank of Canada's governor, from John Crow to Gordon Thiessen. Despite this administrative change, the stated policy of price stability continued. By 2000, the rate of inflation had been around 2 percent for about seven years.
- Following the stock-market declines in 2000–2001 and the terrorist attacks in the United States in September 2001, the Bank of Canada and the U.S. Federal Reserve dramatically reduced their policy interest rates in an attempt to prevent a recession.
- In the 2002–2005 period, the main challenges for the Bank involved determining the relative strength of the two different forces leading to a substantial appreciation of the Canadian dollar. By summer of 2006, the Bank had increased its target for the overnight interest rate by 2 percentage points, to a level still below its previous peak in the summer of 2000.

KEY CONCEPTS

Money supply vs. the interest rate
Overnight interest rate
The target overnight interest rate
The bank rate

Endogenous money supply
Open-market operations
Inflation targeting
CPI inflation vs. core inflation

The exchange rate and monetary policy
Lags in the effect of monetary policy

STUDY EXERCISES

1. Fill in the blanks to make the following statements correct.

   a. In general, there are two approaches to implementing monetary policy. The central bank can attempt to influence _____ directly or to influence _____ directly.

   b. The Bank of Canada chooses to implement its monetary policy by influencing the _____ directly. The Bank then uses _____ to accommodate the resulting change in money demand.

   c. The Bank of Canada does not try to influence the money supply directly because: (1) the Bank cannot control the process of _____ carried out by the commercial banks; (2) the Bank is unsure about the change in _____ that would result from a change in the money supply; (3) the Bank is unsure of the position of the _____ curve at any given time.

2. Fill in the blanks to make the following statements correct.

   a. The interest rate that commercial banks charge each other for overnight loans is called the _____.

   b. The bank rate is _____ points above the target overnight interest rate. At this rate, the Bank stands ready to _____ to commercial banks. At a rate _____ points below the target, the Bank stands ready to _____ from commercial banks (and pay that rate as interest).

   c. The Bank of Canada can change the amount of currency in circulation through _____. The Bank conducts these transactions to accommodate the changing demand for _____ by the commercial banks.

   d. An expansionary monetary policy is one where the Bank of Canada _____ its target for the overnight interest rate. A contractionary monetary policy is one where the Bank _____ its target for the overnight interest rate.

   e. If the Bank of Canada wants to stimulate aggregate demand it can implement a(n) _____ monetary policy by _____ its target for the overnight interest rate. If the Bank wants to dampen aggregate demand it can implement a(n) _____ monetary policy by _____ its target for the overnight interest rate.

3. Fill in the blanks to make the following statements correct.

   a. The long-run policy target for the Bank of Canada is the _____. The current target is to keep the inflation rate at _____ percent.

   b. In the short run, the Bank of Canada closely monitors the _____.

   c. It is not possible for the Bank of Canada to independently influence the following two variables: _____ and _____. The Bank of Canada conducts its policy by announcing a change in the _____. It then conducts the necessary _____ in order to make this rate an equilibrium in the money market.

   d. The conduct of monetary policy is made more difficult because of lags. Two reasons for these time lags are :

   • _____

   • _____

   e. Economists have estimated that a change in monetary policy has an effect on real GDP after a period of _____ months and an effect on the price level after a period of _____ months.

   f. Because of the long time lags involved in the execution of monetary policy, it is very possible that the policy may in fact have a _____ effect on the economy.

4. **myeconlab** Suppose a commercial bank has $100 000 of excess cash reserves and wishes to purchase a government security from the Bank of Canada, which then willingly sells the bond. The two balance sheets below are for the *changes* in assets and liabilities for the commercial bank and the Bank of Canada.

Commercial Bank		Bank of Canada	
Assets	Liabilities	Assets	Liabilities
Reserves	Deposits	Bonds	Commercial bank deposits —
—	—	—	

   a. What are the immediate effects on assets and liabilities for the commercial bank? Fill in the left-hand table.

   b. What are the changes for the Bank of Canada? Fill in the right-hand table.

   c. Explain what has happened to the amount of currency in circulation.

5. In the text we stated that the Bank of Canada's long-run policy target is the rate of inflation.

   a. How is this choice of a long-run policy target related to the proposition that high inflation is damaging to the economy?

   b. Is this choice also related to the idea of long-run money neutrality?

   c. If monetary policy had sustained and systematic effects on real economic variables, do you think the Bank might choose a different long-run policy target? Explain.

6. The diagram below shows the demand for money and the supply of money.

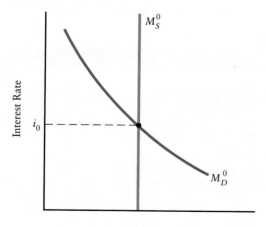

Quantity of Money

a. Explain (and show in the diagram) why the Bank of Canada cannot independently set the money supply and the interest rate.

b. Suppose the M_D curve is shifting in unpredictable ways. Explain, and show in the diagram, why a monetary policy that sets the interest rate is preferable to one that sets the money supply.

c. The Bank of Canada implements its monetary policy by setting the target for the overnight interest rate. If the Bank reduces its target, explain what happens to the amount of money in the economy. What is the role of open-market operations in the Bank's policy?

7. Milton Friedman was for many years a professor of economics at the University of Chicago, and was the most influential Monetarist of his generation. He was known for accusing the Federal Reserve (the U.S. central bank) of following "an unstable monetary policy," arguing that although the Fed "has given lip service to controlling the quantity of money...it has given its heart to controlling interest rates."

a. Explain why, if the M_D function were approximately stable, targeting the growth rate in the money supply would produce a "stable" monetary policy. Show this in a diagram.

b. Explain why, if the M_D function moves suddenly and in unpredictable ways, targeting the money supply produces an "unstable" monetary policy. Show this in a diagram.

c. The Bank of Canada conducts its policy by setting short-term interest rates. What is the implication for this policy of an "unstable" M_D function?

8. Suppose it is mid-2006 and the stock market has been growing rapidly for the past four years. Some economists argue that the stock market has become "overvalued" and thus a "crash" is imminent.

a. How does a rising stock market affect aggregate demand? Show this in an *AD/AS* diagram.

b. For a central bank that is trying to keep real GDP close to potential, explain what challenges are posed by a rapidly rising stock market.

c. Suppose the stock market "crashes," falling suddenly by 15 percent as it did in the summer of 2006. How does this affect aggregate demand? Show this in an *AD/AS* diagram.

9. [myeconlab] Consider the relationship between exchange-rate changes, aggregate demand, and monetary policy. Assume we begin in a situation with real GDP equal to Y^*.

a. Suppose the world price for raw materials rises, due to growing demand for these products. What is the likely effect on Canadian aggregate demand? Show this in an *AD/AS* diagram (assuming no change in the exchange rate).

b. Suppose instead that there is an increase in the demand by foreigners for Canadian financial assets such as government bonds. What is the direct effect on Canadian aggregate demand? Show this in an *AD/AS* diagram (assuming again no change in the exchange rate).

c. Both of the shocks described above are likely to cause an appreciation of the Canadian dollar on foreign-exchange markets. As the Canadian dollar appreciates, what are the effects on aggregate demand? Show these "secondary" effects in your diagram, and explain.

d. Given your answers to parts (a), (b), and (c), explain why the appropriate monetary policy response to a change in the exchange rate depends crucially on the *cause* of the exchange-rate change. What are the appropriate responses to each of the shocks (assuming they occur separately)?

DISCUSSION QUESTIONS

1. It is often said that an expansionary monetary policy is like "pushing on a string." What is meant by this statement? How does this contrast with a contractionary monetary policy?

2. In 1988, the Bank of Canada announced that it was committed to achieving "price stability," but it did not commit itself to a particular target growth rate for any monetary aggregate that would be consistent with achieving its price stability target. Why do you think it failed to make such a commitment?

3. In the last few years, the path of CPI inflation has deviated from the path of core inflation several times (see Figure 29-5). Why is core inflation less volatile

than CPI inflation, and why might the Bank focus more on core inflation during some periods?

4. Suppose the Canadian economy has real GDP equal to potential and that nothing significant is expected to change in the near future. Then the Canadian dollar suddenly depreciates—apparently permanently—by 5 percent against the U.S. dollar. Explain why the appropriate response of monetary policy depends on the *cause* of the depreciation. In particular, make a distinction between:

a. A depreciation caused by a reduction in demand for Canadian exports of raw materials; and

b. A depreciation caused by a reduction in demand for Canadian bonds that are now perceived as less attractive than U.S. bonds.

5. Consider a situation where the Bank decides to lower its target for the overnight interest (an expansionary monetary policy). But at the same time, there is an unpredicted reduction in the demand for money.

   a. Explain why the money supply is said to be endogenous when the Bank implements its policy by setting the interest rate.

   b. Following the Bank's expansionary policy, and the simultaneous reduction in money demand, what is the overall effect on the money supply? What does the answer depend on?

   c. If the money supply were to fall in this case, why would we still call this an expansionary monetary policy?

CHAPTER 30

Inflation and Disinflation

LO **LEARNING OBJECTIVES**

In this chapter you will learn

1. that wages change in response to both output gaps and inflation expectations.
2. how a constant rate of inflation is incorporated into the basic macroeconomic model.
3. how aggregate demand and supply shocks affect inflation and real GDP.
4. what happens when the Bank of Canada validates demand and supply shocks.
5. the three phases of a disinflation.
6. how the cost of disinflation is measured by the sacrifice ratio.

If you are a typical reader of this book, you were born in the mid-1980s. By the time you were old enough to notice some economic developments going on around you, it was well into the 1990s. By that time, the rate of inflation in Canada was about 2 percent per year. Thus, unless you are older than the typical student taking a course in introductory economics, or you have come to Canada recently from a high-inflation country, inflation has not been a significant phenomenon in your life. It was not so long ago, however, that inflation was considered to be a serious problem in Canada (and many other countries as well). Even though high inflation in Canada is no longer a "headline" issue, understanding the process of inflation, and how it can be reduced, is central to understanding why the Bank of Canada is so committed to keeping inflation low.

inflation A rise in the average level of all prices. Usually expressed as the annual percentage change in the Consumer Price Index.

Recall from Chapter 19 that **inflation** is a rise in the average level of prices—that is, a rise in the price level. Figure 30-1 shows the rate of CPI inflation in Canada since 1966, and shows what is often called the "twin peaks" of inflation. Rising from the mid-1960s, inflation peaked in 1974 at 11 percent, fell and then peaked again in 1981 at almost 13 percent, and then started its long but bumpy decline to its current level at around 2 percent, the midpoint of the Bank of Canada's official target band.

This bumpy path for the rate of inflation nicely illustrates one of the reasons that inflation is a problem for the economy. As we mentioned in Chapter 19, economists make the distinction between *anticipated* and *unanticipated* inflation, and we showed why unanticipated inflation is the more serious problem. If firms and workers have difficulty predicting what inflation will be, they have problems determining how wages and prices should be set. The result will be unexpected changes in real wages and relative prices as inflation ends up being different from what was expected. These inflation-induced changes in real wages and relative prices lead to changes in the allocation of resources. As you can imagine by looking at Figure 30-1, most of the changes in inflation between 1966 and 2006 were sudden and thus difficult to predict. To avoid

FIGURE 30-1   Canadian CPI Inflation, 1965–2006

(*Source:* Statistics Canada, CANSIM database, Series V735319. For each month, the inflation rate is computed as the percentage change from the CPI twelve months earlier. Reprinted with permission of Statistics Canada.)

this uncertainty in the economy, the Bank of Canada now strives to keep inflation both *low* and *stable,* near the official target of 2 percent. The result is an environment in which firms, workers, and households can more easily make plans for the future, secure in the knowledge that real wages, real interest rates, and relative prices will not be significantly different because of a volatile inflation rate.

What causes inflation? How can it be eliminated? And why are policies designed to reduce inflation so controversial? These are the central topics of this chapter.

To compute the total inflation from the day of your birth to today, check out the "Inflation Calculator" at the Bank of Canada's website: **www.bankofcanada.ca**. Click on "Monetary Policy" and then "Inflation."

High inflation is costly for several reasons. In addition to creating arbitrary redistributions of income, it undermines the efficiency of the price system by distorting the relative prices of goods and services. For more information, look for "The Costs of High Inflation" in the *Additional Topics* section of this book's MyEconLab.

w w w . m y e c o n l a b . c o m

30.1 **ADDING INFLATION TO THE MODEL**

In the previous several chapters we examined the effects of shocks to aggregate demand and aggregate supply. In our macroeconomic model, *AD* and *AS* shocks influenced the values of both real GDP and the price level. Following these shocks, the economy's adjustment process always pushed the economy back toward the potential level of real

GDP with a stable price level. In other words, any inflation that we have so far seen in our macroeconomic model was temporary—it only existed while the economy was adjusting toward its long-run equilibrium.

In this chapter we want to understand how a *sustained* inflation can exist, and how we modify our model to account for its presence. After all, even though inflation in Canada is very low, it still appears to be sustained at a rate of about 2 percent per year.

As we will soon see, one of the keys to understanding sustained inflation is to understand the role of *inflation expectations*. When combined with excess demand or excess supply, as reflected by the economy's output gap, such expectations give us a more complete understanding of why wages (and therefore prices) change. Let's begin our analysis by examining in more detail why wages change.

Why Wages Change

In Chapter 24, when we examined the economy's adjustment process, we saw that increases in wages led to increases in unit costs—because we maintained the assumption that technology (and thus productivity) was held constant. We continue with that assumption in this chapter. Thus, as wages and other factor prices rise, unit costs increase and the *AS* curve shifts up. Conversely, when wages and other factor prices fall, unit costs fall and the *AS* curve shifts down.

What are the forces that cause wages to change? Two of the main forces are the output gap and expectations of future inflation.[1] Much of what we discuss in the case of the output gap was first seen in Chapter 24, but the points are important enough to bear repeating.

Wages and the Output Gap In Chapter 24, we encountered three propositions about how changes in money wages were influenced by the output gap:

1. The excess demand for labour that is associated with an inflationary gap $(Y > Y^*)$ puts upward pressure on money wages.

2. The excess supply of labour associated with a recessionary gap $(Y < Y^*)$ puts downward pressure on money wages.

3. The absence of either an inflationary or a recessionary gap $(Y = Y^*)$ means that demand forces do not exert any pressure on money wages.[2]

When real GDP is equal to Y^*, the unemployment rate is said to be equal to the NAIRU, which stands for the *non-accelerating inflation rate of unemployment*. The use of this particular name will be explained later in this chapter. Another name sometimes used in place of NAIRU is the *natural rate of unemployment,* but NAIRU is now the more common usage. It is designated by the symbol U^*.

---

[1] Wages may be affected by other forces that are associated with neither output gaps nor expectations of inflation, such as government guidelines, union power, and employers' optimism. Because there are many such forces that tend to act independently of one another, they may be regarded as random shocks and must be analyzed as separate causes for shifts in the *AS* curve.

[2] As in Chapter 24, we are assuming that productivity is constant in our analysis in this chapter. Otherwise, output gaps would cause changes in wages *relative to productivity*.

The NAIRU is not zero. Instead, even when $Y = Y^*$, there may be a substantial amount of *frictional* and *structural* unemployment caused, for example, by the movement of people between jobs or between regions. When real output exceeds potential output ($Y > Y^*$), the unemployment rate will be less than the NAIRU ($U < U^*$). When real output is less than potential output ($Y < Y^*$), the unemployment rate will exceed the NAIRU ($U > U^*$).

We have assumed that wages react to various pressures of demand. These demand pressures can be stated either in terms of the relationship between actual and potential output or in terms of the relationship between the actual unemployment rate and the NAIRU. When $Y > Y^*$ (or $U < U^*$), there is an inflationary gap characterized by excess demand for labour, and wages are assumed to rise. Conversely, when $Y < Y^*$ (or $U > U^*$), there is a recessionary gap characterized by excess supply of labour, and wages are assumed to fall.

This relationship between the excess demand or supply of labour and the rate of change of money wages is represented by the Phillips curve, which we first discussed in Chapter 24.

Wages and Expected Inflation

A second force that can influence wages is *expectations* of future inflation. Suppose both employers and employees expect 3 percent inflation next year. Workers will start negotiations from a base of a 3 percent increase in money wages, which would hold their *real wages* constant. Firms will also be inclined to begin bargaining by conceding at least a 3 percent increase in money wages because they expect that the prices at which they sell their products will rise by 3 percent. Starting from that base, workers may attempt to obtain some desired increase in their real wages. At this point, such factors as profits and bargaining power become important.

The expectation of some specific inflation rate creates pressure for money wages to rise by that rate.

The key point is that money wages can be rising even if no inflationary gap is present. As long as people *expect* prices to rise, their behaviour will put upward pressure on money wages. Indeed, in every year since the Second World War, nominal wages have increased in Canada, even though in some years there were notable recessionary gaps. The reason is that in every year the price level was expected to increase (and did, in fact, increase). Clarifying the distinction between these two separate forces on wages is an important objective of this chapter.

The central role for the *expectations* of future inflation suggests the importance of examining how firms and workers *form* their expectations. This has been a very active area of research within macroeconomics. *Applying Economic Concepts 30-1* discusses the formation of expectations and explains the important difference between *backward-looking* and *forward-looking* expectations.

Practise with Study Guide Chapter 30, Extension Exercise E1.

Overall Effect on Wages

We can now think of changes in money wages as resulting from two different forces:

$$\text{Change in money wages} = \text{Output-gap effect} + \text{Expectational effect}$$

What happens to wages is the *net* effect of the two forces. Consider two examples. First, suppose both labour and management expect 3 percent inflation next year and are therefore willing to allow money wages to increase by 3 percent. Doing so would leave *real* wages unchanged. Suppose as well that there is a significant inflationary gap with an associated labour shortage. The excess demand for labour causes wages to rise by an additional 2 percentage points. The final outcome is that wages rise by 5 percent, the

APPLYING ECONOMIC CONCEPTS 30-1

How Do People Form Their Expectations?

The way in which firms and workers form their expectations about future inflation may have an important effect on that inflation. Generally, we can distinguish two main patterns: One is to look backward at past experience; the other is to look at current circumstances for a clue as to what may happen in the near future.

The first type of expectations are called *backward-looking*. People look at the past in order to predict what will happen in the future. The simplest possible form of such expectations is to expect the past to be repeated in the future. According to this view, if inflation has been 5 percent over the past year, people will expect it to be 5 percent next year. This expectation, however, is quite naive. Everyone knows that the inflation rate does change, and therefore the past cannot be a perfectly accurate guide to the future.

A less naive version has people revise their expectations in light of the mistakes that they made in estimating inflation in the past. For example, if you thought that this year's inflation rate was going to be 5 percent but it turned out to be only 3 percent, you might revise your estimate of next year's rate down somewhat from 5 percent.

Backward-looking expectations tend to change slowly because some time must pass before a change in the actual rate of inflation provides enough past experience to cause expectations to adjust.

The second main type of expectations are those that look to current economic conditions to estimate what is likely to happen in the future. One version of this type assumes that people look to the government's current macroeconomic policy to form their expectations of future inflation. They are assumed to understand how the economy works, and they form their expectations by predicting the outcome of the policies

now being followed. In an obvious sense, such expectations are *forward-looking*.

A strong version of forward-looking expectations is called **rational expectations**. Rational expectations are not necessarily always correct; rather, the *rational expectations hypothesis* assumes that people make the best possible use of all the available information. One implication is that they will not continue to make persistent, systematic errors when forming their expectations. Thus, if the economic system about which they are forming expectations remains stable, their expectations will be correct *on average*. Sometimes next year's inflation rate will turn out to be above what people expected it to be; at other times, it will turn out to be below what people expected it to be. On average over many years, however, the actual rate will not, according to the rational expectations theory, be consistently under- or overestimated.

Forward-looking expectations can adjust quickly to changes in events. Instead of being based on past inflation rates, expected inflation is based on expected economic conditions and government policies.

Assuming that expectations are solely backward-looking seems overly naive. People do look ahead and assess future possibilities rather than just blindly reacting to what has gone before. Yet the assumption of "fully rational" forward-looking expectations requires workers and firms to have a degree of understanding of the economy that few economists would claim to have. The actual process of wage setting probably combines forward-looking behaviour with expectations based on the experience of the recent past. Depending on the circumstances, expectations will sometimes tend to rely more on past experience and at other times more on present events whose effects are expected to influence the future.

rational expectations The theory that people understand how the economy works and learn quickly from their mistakes so that even though random errors may be made, systematic and persistent errors are not.

net effect of a 3 percent increase due to expected inflation and a 2 percent increase due to the excess demand for labour when $Y > Y^*$.

For the second example, assume again that expected inflation is 3 percent, but this time there is a recessionary gap. The associated heavy unemployment represents an excess supply of labour which exerts downward pressure on wage bargains. Hence, the output-gap effect now works to dampen wage increases, say, to the extent of 2 percentage points. Wages therefore rise by 1 percent, the net effect of a 3 percent increase due to expected inflation and a 2 percent decrease due to the excess supply of labour when $Y < Y^*$.

From Wages to Prices

We saw in Chapters 23 and 24 that shifts in the *AS* curve depend on what happens to factor prices. We have just seen that inflationary output gaps and expectations of future inflation put pressure on wages to rise and hence cause the *AS* curve to shift upward. Recessionary output gaps and expectations of future deflation put pressure on wages to fall and hence cause the *AS* curve to shift downward.

The net effect of the two forces acting on wages—output gaps and inflation expectations—determines what happens to the *AS* curve.

If the net effect of the output-gap effect and the expectational effect is to raise wages, then the *AS* curve will shift up. This shift will cause the price level to rise—that is, the forces pushing up wages will be *inflationary*. On the other hand, if the net effect of the output-gap effect and the expectational effect is to reduce wages, the *AS* curve will shift down—the forces reducing wages will be *deflationary*.

Since anything that leads to higher wages will shift the *AS* curve up and lead to higher prices, we can decompose inflation due to wage increases into two component parts: *output-gap inflation* and *expected inflation*. But because the *AS* curve can also shift for reasons unrelated to changes in wages, we must add a third element. Specifically, we must consider the effect of non-wage supply shocks on the *AS* curve and thus on the price level. The best example of a non-wage supply shock is a change in the prices of raw materials. We can then decompose actual inflation into its three component parts:

$$\text{Actual inflation} = \text{Output-gap inflation} + \text{Expected inflation} + \text{Supply-shock inflation}$$

For example, consider an economy that begins with real GDP equal to potential GDP and expectations of inflation are zero. In this case, the first two terms on the right-hand side are zero. But if an adverse supply shock then occurs, such as a significant increase in the price of imported raw materials, the *AS* curve shifts up and the price level rises. Actual inflation will be positive. As we will see later in the chapter, such supply shocks are not uncommon, and they generate challenges for the Bank of Canada in its attempt to maintain low inflation.

Having discussed the component parts of inflation, we are now in a position to see how constant inflation can be included in our macroeconomic model.

Constant Inflation

Suppose the inflation rate is 2 percent per year and has been 2 percent for several years. This is what we mean by a *constant* inflation. In such a setting, people with backward-looking expectations about inflation will expect the actual level to continue into the future. Furthermore, in the absence of any announcements that the central bank will be attempting to alter its monetary policy, people with forward-looking expectations will expect the actual inflation rate to continue. Thus, for the economy as a whole, the expected rate of inflation will equal the actual rate of inflation.

If inflation and monetary policy have been constant for several years, the expected rate of inflation will tend to equal the actual rate of inflation.

Suppose there are no supply shocks (we address these later in the chapter). Since actual inflation equals expected inflation, it immediately follows from the equation

The Conference Board of Canada conducts a regular survey about people's expectations about inflation. See its website at:
www.conferenceboard.ca.

FIGURE 30-2   Constant Inflation with No Supply Shocks

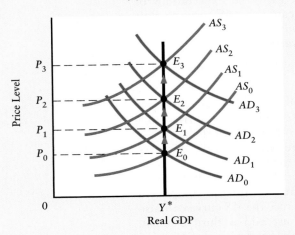

In the *AD/AS* model with no supply shocks, constant inflation is only possible when $Y = Y^*$. Expectations of a constant rate of inflation cause wages and thus the *AS* curve to shift upward at a uniform rate from AS_0 to AS_1 to AS_2. Monetary validation is causing the *AD* curve to shift upward at the same time from AD_0 to AD_1 to AD_2. As a result, real GDP remains at Y^* as the economy moves from equilibrium E_0 to E_1 to E_2 and so on. The constant inflation rate takes the price level from P_0 to P_1 to P_2. Wage costs are rising due to expectations of inflation, and these expectations are being fulfilled.

above that actual and expected inflation can only be equal if there is *no* output gap—real GDP must equal its potential level, Y^*.

In the absence of supply shocks, if expected inflation equals actual inflation, real GDP must be equal to potential GDP.

Figure 30-2 shows a constant inflation in the *AD/AS* diagram. What is causing this inflation? As we will see, such a constant inflation requires both the *expectations* of inflation (which shift the *AS* curve) and the continuing expansion of the money supply by the central bank (which shifts the *AD* curve). Let's see how this works.

Suppose both workers and employers expect 2 percent inflation over the coming years and that employers are therefore prepared to increase wages by 2 percent per year. As wages rise by 2 percent, the *AS* curve shifts up by that amount. But, in order for 2 percent to be the *actual* rate of inflation, the intersection of the *AS* and *AD* curves must be shifting up at the rate of 2 percent. This requires the *AD* curve to be shifting up at the same 2 percent rate—this *AD* shift is caused by the growth of the money supply. So in this case there is no output-gap inflation ($Y = Y^*$), and actual and expected inflation are equal. When the central bank increases the money supply at such a rate that the expectations of inflation end up being correct, it is said to be *validating* the expectations.

Constant inflation with $Y = Y^*$ occurs when the rate of monetary growth, the rate of wage increase, and the expected rate of inflation are all consistent with the actual inflation rate.

The key point about constant inflation in our macro model is that there is no output-gap effect operating on wages. Wages rise at the expected rate of inflation. Expansions of the money supply validate those expectations.

Note that in this constant-inflation equilibrium, monetary policy is not "expansionary" in the sense that we defined it in Chapter 29—that is, the central bank is not *reducing* its policy interest rate. Instead, interest rates are stable but the central bank is accommodating the growing demand for money (which is growing due to the rising price level) by steadily increasing the supply of money. As we will see later in this chapter, in order to *reduce* the rate of inflation, the central bank would have to implement a contractionary monetary policy—by raising interest rates (which would normally lead to a reduction in the growth rate of the money supply).

30.2 SHOCKS AND POLICY RESPONSES

A constant rate of inflation is a special case in our macroeconomic model because the rising price level is not caused by an inflationary output gap. In many cases of inflation, however, inflationary pressure is initially created by an aggregate demand or sup-ply shock. In this section we examine how AS and AD shocks affect inflation and the subsequent effects of the policy responses chosen by the central bank.

Before we do so, however, recall an assumption we made in Chapter 28 when we discussed the long-run effects of monetary policy. In that chapter we assumed the level of potential output to be independent of the path of real GDP. Thus, shocks that led to shifts in the AD or AS curves, and thus led to short-run changes in the level of real GDP, were assumed to have no influence on the level of potential output, Y^*.

We continue with that assumption in this chapter, but note that we can alterna-tively state the assumption in terms of the NAIRU, U^*. Specifically, we assume that the path of the actual unemployment rate does not affect the value of U^*, which is instead determined by various policy and institutional factors that we explore in detail in the next chapter. As in Chapter 28, the implication of this assumption is that, following AD or AS shocks, the economy's adjustment process eventually returns real GDP and unemployment to their unchanged levels of Y^* and U^*, respectively. As we first noted in Chapter 28, this assumption is controversial. In Western European countries, in par-ticular, there is some empirical evidence to the contrary. But in Canada and the United States the weight of evidence supports the assumption made in this book that Y^* and U^* are independent of the paths of Y and U.

Practise with Study Guide Chapter 30, Short-Answer Question 2.

Demand Shocks

Any rightward shift in the AD curve that creates an inflationary output gap also cre-ates what is called **demand inflation**. The shift in the AD curve could have been caused by a reduction in taxes, by an increase in such autonomous expenditure items as invest-ment, government, and net exports, or by an expansionary monetary policy.

Major demand-shock inflations occurred in Canada during and after the First and Second World Wars. In these cases, large increases in government expenditure without fully offsetting increases in taxes led to general excess demand ($Y > Y^*$). More gener-ally, demand inflation sometimes occurs at the end of a strong upswing, as rising out-put causes excess demand to develop simultaneously in the markets for labour, intermediate goods, and final output. Demand inflation of this type occurred in Canada in 1989–1990 and to a lesser extent in 2002–2003.

To begin our study of demand inflation, we make some simplifying assumptions. First, we assume that Y^* is constant. Second, we assume that there is no ongoing infla-tion. These two assumptions imply that our starting point is a stable long-run equilib-rium, with constant real GDP and price level, rather than the long-run equilibrium with constant inflation as shown in Figure 30-2. We then suppose that this long-run equilib-rium is disturbed by a rightward shift in the AD curve. This shift causes the price level and output to rise. It is important next to distinguish between the case in which the Bank of Canada validates the demand shock and the case in which it does not.

No Monetary Validation Because the initial rise in AD takes output above poten-tial, an inflationary gap opens up. The pressure of excess demand soon causes wages to rise, shifting the AS curve upward as shown in Figure 30-3. As long as the Bank of Canada holds the money supply constant, the rise in the price level moves the economy upward and to the left along the new AD curve, reducing the inflationary gap. Eventually, the gap is eliminated, and equilibrium is established at a higher but stable price level, with output at its potential level. In this case, the initial period of inflation is followed by further inflation that lasts only until the new equilibrium is reached.

demand inflation Inflation aris-ing from an inflationary output gap caused, in turn, by a positive AD shock.

FIGURE 30-3   A Demand Shock with No Validation

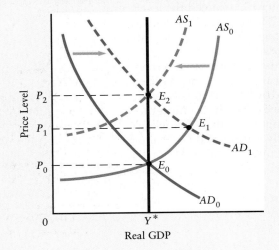

A demand shock that is not validated produces temporary inflation, but the economy's adjustment process eventually restores potential GDP and stable prices. The initial long-run equilibrium is at P_0 and Y^*. A positive demand shock shifts AD_0 to AD_1, generating an inflationary gap. The excess demand puts upward pressure on wages, thus shifting AS_0 to AS_1. There is inflation as the economy moves from E_0 to E_1 to E_2, but at E_2 the price level is stable.

supply inflation Inflation arising from a negative AS shock that is not the result of excess demand in the domestic markets for factors of production.

Monetary Validation   Suppose that after the demand shock has created an inflationary gap, the Bank of Canada validates the demand shock by reducing interest rates and allowing the money supply to increase. We illustrate this situation in Figure 30-4.

Two forces are now brought into play. Spurred by the inflationary gap, the increase in wages causes the AS curve to shift upward. Fuelled by the expansionary monetary policy, however, the AD curve shifts further to the right. As a result of both of these shifts, the price level rises, but real GDP remains above Y^*. Indeed, if the shift in the AD curve *exactly* offsets the shift in the AS curve, real GDP and the inflationary gap will remain constant.

Continued validation of a demand shock turns what would have been transitory inflation into sustained inflation fuelled by monetary expansion.

Supply Shocks

Any leftward shift in the AS curve that is *not* caused by excess demand in the markets for factors of production creates what is called **supply inflation.**

An example of a supply shock is a rise in the costs of imported raw materials. Another is a rise in domestic wages not due to excess demand in the labour market. The rise in wages may occur, as we saw earlier, because of generally held expectations of future inflation. If both employers and employees expect inflation, money wages are likely to rise in anticipation of that inflation. These shocks cause the AS curve to shift upward.[3]

The initial effects of any negative supply shock are that the equilibrium price level rises while equilibrium output falls, as shown in Figure 30-5. As with the case of a demand shock, what happens next depends on how the Bank of Canada reacts. If the Bank allows the money supply to increase, it validates the supply shock; if it holds the money supply constant, the shock is not validated.

No Monetary Validation   The upward shift in the AS curve in Figure 30-5 causes the price level to rise and pushes output below its potential level, opening up a recessionary gap. Pressure mounts for money wages and other factor prices to fall. As wages and other factor prices fall, unit costs will fall. Consequently, the AS curve shifts down, increasing equilibrium output while reducing the price level. The AS curve will continue to shift, perhaps slowly, stopping only when real GDP is returned to its potential level and the price level is returned to its initial value of P_0. Thus, the period of inflation accompanying the original supply shock is eventually reversed until the initial long-run equilibrium is re-established.

---

3 Recall our discussion in Chapter 24 of how some shocks affect *both* the AD and AS curves. A rise in the price of oil is one example; since Canada is a producer and exporter of oil, a rise in the price of oil does represent a positive AD shock for Canada. In this discussion we confine ourselves to the effect of the AS shift.

A major concern in this case is the speed of the adjustment, which in earlier chapters was referred to as the second asymmetry of aggregate supply. If wages do not fall rapidly in the face of excess supply in the labour market, the adjustment back to potential output can take a long time. For example, suppose the original shock raised firms' costs by 6 percent. To reverse this shock, firms' costs must fall by 6 percent. If money wages fell by only 2 percent per year it would take three years to complete the adjustment.[4]

Whenever wages and other factor prices fall only slowly in the face of excess supply, the recovery to potential output after a non-validated negative supply shock will take a long time.

Concern that such a lengthy adjustment will occur is the motive that often lies behind the strong pressure on the Bank of Canada to validate negative supply shocks.

Monetary Validation What happens if the Bank of Canada responds to the negative supply shock by lowering interest rates and allowing the money supply to increase, thus *validating* the shock? The monetary validation shifts the AD curve to the right and causes both the price level and output to rise. As the recessionary gap is eliminated, the price level rises further, rather than falling back to its original value as it did when the supply shock was not validated. These effects are also illustrated in Figure 30-5.

Monetary validation of a negative supply shock causes the initial rise in the price level to be followed by a further rise, resulting in a higher price level than would occur if the recessionary gap were relied on to reduce factor prices.

The most dramatic example of a supply-shock inflation came in the wake of the first OPEC oil-price shock. In 1974, the countries who were members of the Organization of Petroleum Exporting Countries (OPEC) agreed to restrict output. Their action caused a dramatic increase in the prices of petroleum and many petroleum-related products such as fertilizer and chemicals. The resulting increase in industrial costs shifted AS curves upward in all industrial countries. At this time, the Bank of Canada validated the supply shock with large increases in the money supply, whereas the Fed (the U.S. central bank) did not. As the theory predicts, Canada experienced a large increase in its price level but almost no recession, and the United States

FIGURE 30-4 A Demand Shock with Validation

Monetary validation of a positive demand shock causes the *AD* curve to shift further to the right, offsetting the upward shift in the *AS* curve and thereby leaving an inflationary gap despite the ever-rising price level. An initial demand shock moves the economy along the path of arrow ①, taking output to Y_1 and the price level to P_1. The resulting inflationary gap then causes the *AS* curve to shift upward. This time, however, the Bank of Canada validates the demand shock by increasing the money supply. As the money supply is increased, the *AD* curve shifts to the right. By the time the aggregate supply curve has reached AS_1, the aggregate demand curve has reached AD_2. The new equilibrium is at E_2. Output remains constant at Y_1 leaving the inflationary gap constant while the price level rises to P_2.

The persistent inflationary gap continues to push the *AS* curve upward, while the continued monetary validation continues to push the *AD* curve to the right. As long as this monetary validation continues, the economy moves along the vertical path of arrow ②.

For information on OPEC, see its website: **www.opec.org**.

---

[4] Nominal wages rarely fall because there is ongoing productivity growth that offsets the effect on wages of excess supply. But in this chapter we are holding productivity (and thus Y*) constant so we can focus on the causes and consequences of inflation.

FIGURE 30-5   A Supply Shock With and Without Validation

Adverse supply shocks initially raise prices while lowering output. An adverse supply shock causes the AS curve to shift upward from AS_0 to AS_1, as shown by arrow ①. Equilibrium is established at E_1. If there is no monetary validation, the reduction in factor prices makes the AS curve shift slowly back down to AS_0. If there is monetary validation, the AD curve shifts from AD_0 to AD_1, as shown by arrow ②. Equilibrium is re-established at E_2 with output equal to potential output but with a higher price level, P_2.

A contract settlement that raises wages for a large number of workers will increase firms' costs and shift the AS curve upward, thus tending to reduce real GDP and raise the price level.

experienced a much smaller increase in its price level but a severe recession.

Is Monetary Validation of Supply Shocks Desirable?

Suppose the Bank of Canada were to validate a negative supply shock and thus prevent what could otherwise be a protracted recession. Expressed in this way, monetary validation sounds like a good policy. Unfortunately, however, there is also a possible cost associated with this policy. The effect of the monetary validation is to extend the period of inflation. If this inflation leads firms and workers to expect *further* inflation, then point E_2 in Figure 30-5 will not be the end of the story. As expectations for further inflation develop, the AS curve will continue to shift upward. But if the Bank continues its policy of validation, then the AD curve will also continue to shift upward. It may not take long before the economy is in a *wage–price spiral*.

Once started, a wage–price spiral can be halted only if the Bank of Canada stops validating the supply shocks that are causing the inflation. But the longer it waits to do so, the more firmly held will be the *expectations* that it will continue its policy of validating the shocks. These entrenched expectations may cause wages to continue rising even after validation has ceased. Because employers expect prices to rise, they go on granting wage increases. If expectations are entrenched firmly enough, the wage push can continue for quite some time, in spite of the downward pressure caused by the high unemployment associated with the recessionary gap.

Because of this possibility, many economists argue that the wage–price spiral should not be allowed to begin. One way to ensure that it does not begin is to refuse to validate any supply shock whatsoever.

To some economists, caution dictates that negative supply shocks should never be validated, in order to avoid a wage–price spiral. Other economists are willing to risk validation in order to avoid the significant, though transitory, recessions that otherwise accompany the supply shock.

Accelerating Inflation

Consider a situation where a demand or supply shock increases real GDP above Y^*. For example, a booming U.S. economy may lead to an increase in demand for Canadian goods, thus shifting Canada's AD curve to the right. Or, a reduction in the world price of raw materials may reduce firms' costs and shift the Canadian *AS* curve downward. In both cases, the effect in Canada would be to increase real GDP above Y^*—unemployment is low, businesses are booming, and most people would describe this situation as "good economic times." It may be natural for the Bank of Canada to contemplate sustaining these "good times" by validating the shock. What would be the result of this policy on the rate of inflation?

What happens to the rate of inflation is predicted by the **acceleration hypothesis**, which says that when the central bank conducts its policy to hold the inflationary gap constant, the actual inflation rate will *accelerate*. The Bank of Canada may start by validating 2 percent inflation, but soon 2 percent will become 3 percent and, if the Bank insists on validating 3 percent, the rate will become 4 percent, and so on without limit. The process will only end when the Bank ends its policy of validation. Avoiding this possibility of gradually increasing inflation is one important reason why the Bank has adopted a formal (and unchanging) inflation target of 2 percent.

There are several steps in the reasoning behind the acceleration hypothesis. The first concerns the development of inflationary expectations.

acceleration hypothesis The hypothesis that when real GDP is held above potential, the persistent inflationary gap will cause inflation to accelerate.

Expectational Effects
Recall our earlier discussion in this chapter about how actual inflation has three separate causes: output gaps, expectations, and non-wage supply shocks. It is restated here:

$$\text{Actual inflation} = \text{Output-gap inflation} + \text{Expected inflation} + \text{Supply-shock inflation}$$

To illustrate the importance of expectations in accelerating inflation, suppose the inflationary output gap creates sufficient excess demand to push up wages by 2 percent per year. As a result, the *AS* curve will also tend to be shifting upward at 2 percent per year.

When inflation has persisted for some time, however, people will likely come to expect that the inflation will continue. The expectation of 2 percent inflation will tend to push up wages by that amount *in addition to* the demand pressure. As the output-gap effect on wages is augmented by the expectational effect, the *AS* curve will begin to shift upward more rapidly. When expectations are for a 2 percent inflation and demand pressure is also pushing wages up by 2 percent, the overall effect will be a 4 percent increase in wages. Sooner or later, however, 4 percent inflation will come to be expected, and the expectational effect will rise to 4 percent. This new expectational component of 4 percent, when added to the output-gap component, will create an inflation rate of 6 percent. And so this cycle will go on. As long as there is excess demand arising from an inflationary output gap, and as long as actual inflation is equal to the output-gap effect plus the expectational effect, the inflation rate cannot stay constant because expectations will always be revised upward toward the actual inflation rate.

More Rapid Monetary Validation Required
The second step in the argument is that if the Bank of Canada still wishes to hold the level of output constant above Y^*, it must implement an expansionary monetary policy and allow the growth rate of the money supply to rise. This action is necessary because to hold real GDP constant, the *AD* curve must be shifted at an increasingly rapid pace to offset the increasingly rapid shifts in the *AS* curve, which are driven by the continually rising rate of expected inflation.

An Increasing Rate of Inflation
The third step in the argument is that the rate of inflation must now be increasing because of the increasingly rapid upward shifts in both the *AD* and *AS* curves. The rise in the actual inflation rate will in turn cause an increase in the expected inflation rate. This will then cause the actual inflation rate to increase, which will in turn increase the expected inflation rate, and so on. The net result is a *continually increasing rate of inflation*. Now we see the reason for the name

NAIRU. At any level of unemployment less than the NAIRU, real GDP is above Y^*, and the inflation rate tends to accelerate. Thus, the NAIRU is the lowest level of sustained unemployment consistent with a *non-accelerating* rate of inflation.

According to the acceleration hypothesis, as long as an inflationary output gap persists, expectations of inflation will be rising, which will lead to increases in the actual rate of inflation.

The tendency for inflation to accelerate is discussed further in *Extensions in Theory 30-1*, which examines how expected inflation affects the position of the Phillips curve.

Inflation as a Monetary Phenomenon

For many years, a debate among economists concerned the extent to which inflation is a monetary phenomenon. Does it have purely monetary causes—changes in the demand or the supply of money? Does it have purely monetary consequences—only

EXTENSIONS IN THEORY 30-1

The Phillips Curve and Accelerating Inflation

As we first saw in Chapter 24, the Phillips curve describes the relationship between unemployment (or output) and the rate of change of wages. The Phillips curve was born in 1958 when Professor A. W. Phillips from the London School of Economics noted a relationship between unemployment and the rate of change of wages over a period of 100 years in the United Kingdom. Phillips was interested in studying the short-run behaviour of an economy subjected to cyclical fluctuations. In the years following Phillips's study, however, some economists treated the Phillips curve as establishing a long-term tradeoff between inflation and unemployment.

Suppose the government stabilizes output at Y_1 (and hence the unemployment rate at U_1), as shown by points A in the accompanying figures. To do this, it must validate the ensuing wage inflation, which is indicated by $\dot{W}_1$ in the figures. The government thus *appears*

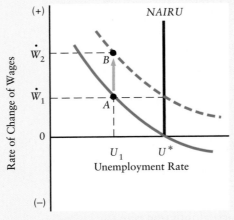

(i) Wage changes and unemployment

There is no stable tradeoff between inflation and output. To maintain $Y > Y^*$, inflation must be steadily rising.

(ii) Wage changes and output

the price level is affected? One slogan that states an extreme position on this issue was popularized many years ago by the late Milton Friedman: "Inflation is *everywhere* and *always* a monetary phenomenon." To consider these issues, let us summarize what we have learned already. First, look at the *causes* of inflation:

- *Cause 1:* On the demand side, anything that shifts the AD curve to the right will cause the price level to rise (demand inflation).
- *Cause 2:* On the supply side, anything that shifts the AS curve upward will cause the price level to rise (supply inflation).
- *Cause 3:* Unless continual monetary validation occurs, the increases in the price level must eventually come to a halt.

The first two points tell us that a temporary burst of inflation need not be a monetary phenomenon. It need not have monetary causes, and it need not be accompanied by monetary expansion. The third point tells us that *sustained* inflation *must* be a monetary phenomenon. If a rise in prices is to continue indefinitely, it *must* be accompanied

expectations-augmented Phillips curve The relationship between unemployment and the rate of increase of money wages that arises when the output-gap and expectations components of inflation are combined.

to be able to choose among particular combinations of inflation and unemployment, in which lower levels of unemployment are attained at the cost of higher rates of inflation.

In the 1960s, Phillips curves were fitted to the data for many countries, and governments made decisions about where they wished to be on the tradeoff between inflation and unemployment. Then, in the late 1960s, in country after country, the rate of wage and price inflation associated with any given level of unemployment began to rise. Instead of being stable, the Phillips curves began to shift upward. The explanation lay primarily in the rise of inflation expectations.

It was gradually understood that the original Phillips curve concerned only the influence of the output gap and left out inflationary expectations. This omission proved important and unfortunate. An increase in expected inflation shows up as an upward shift in the original Phillips curve that was drawn in Chapter 24. The importance of expectations can be shown by drawing what is called an **expectations-augmented Phillips curve**, as shown by the dashed Phillips curve here. The height of the Phillips curves above the axis at Y^* and at U^* show the expected inflation rate. These distances represent the amount that wages will rise even when $Y = Y^*$ (or $U = U^*$) and there is neither excess demand nor supply in labour markets. The actual wage increase is shown by the augmented (dashed) curve, with the increase in wages exceeding expected inflation whenever $Y > Y^*$ ($U < U^*$) and falling short of expected inflation whenever $Y < Y^*$ ($U > U^*$).

Now we can see what was wrong with the idea of a stable inflation–unemployment tradeoff. Targeting a particular output Y_1 or unemployment U_1 in the figures is fine only if no inflation is expected. But getting to Y_1 or U_1 itself requires some inflation $\dot{W}_1$. And once this rate of inflation comes to be expected, people will demand that much just to hold their own. The Phillips curve will then shift upward to the position shown in the figures and the economy will be at points B. Now there is inflation $\dot{W}_2$ because of the combined effects of expectations and excess demand. However, this higher rate is above the expected rate ($\dot{W}_1$). Once this higher rate comes to be expected, the Phillips curve will shift upward once again.

As a result of the combination of output-gap inflation and expectational inflation, the inflation rate associated with any given positive output gap ($Y > Y^*$ or $U < U^*$) rises over time. This is the phenomenon of accelerating inflation that we discussed in the text.

The shifts in the Phillips curve are such that most economists agree that in the long run, when inflationary expectations have fully adjusted to actual inflation, there is no tradeoff between inflation and unemployment. That is, they believe that the only long-run *equilibrium* is where expected inflation and actual inflation are equal, which occurs only when unemployment is equal to the NAIRU and real GDP is equal to Y^*. In other words, the long-run Phillips curve is a vertical line above U^* (or Y^*).

by a monetary policy that allows the money supply to continually increase. This is true regardless of the cause that set the inflation in motion.

Now, let us summarize the *consequences* of inflation, assuming that real GDP was initially at its potential level.

- *Consequence 1:* In the short run, demand inflation tends to be accompanied by an *increase* in real GDP above its potential level.
- *Consequence 2:* In the short run, supply inflation tends to be accompanied by a *decrease* in real GDP below its potential level.
- *Consequence 3:* When all costs and prices are adjusted *fully* (so that real GDP has returned to Y^*), shifts in either the *AD* or *AS* curve leave real GDP unchanged and affect only the price level.

The first two points tell us that inflation is not, in the short run, a purely monetary phenomenon. The third point tells us that inflation is a purely monetary phenomenon from the point of view of long-run equilibrium. There is still plenty of room for debate, however, on how long the short run will last. Most economists believe that the short run can be long enough for inflation to have major real effects on important economic variables such as the distribution of wealth (which partly explains why most economists believe that keeping inflation low is desirable).

We have now reached three important conclusions:

- *Conclusion 1:* Without monetary validation, positive demand shocks cause inflationary output gaps and a temporary burst of inflation. The gaps are removed as rising factor prices push the *AS* curve upward, returning real GDP to its potential level, but at a higher price level.
- *Conclusion 2:* Without monetary validation, negative supply shocks cause recessionary output gaps and a temporary burst of inflation. The gaps are eventually removed as factor prices fall, restoring real GDP to its potential and the price level to its initial level.
- *Conclusion 3:* Only with continuing monetary validation can inflation initiated by either supply or demand shocks continue indefinitely.

To put these conclusions differently, we can modify Friedman's statement slightly to represent the causes of inflation more accurately. While *AD* and *AS* shocks may lead to temporary inflation even in the absence of any actions by the central bank, *sustained* inflation can only occur if there is continual monetary validation by the central bank.

Sustained inflation is everywhere and always a monetary phenomenon.

30.3 REDUCING INFLATION

Suppose an economy has had a sustained rate of inflation for several years. What must the central bank do to reduce the rate of inflation? What are the costs involved in doing so?

The Process of Disinflation

disinflation A reduction in the rate of inflation.

Disinflation means a reduction in the rate of inflation. In recent years, Canada has had two notable periods of disinflation—in 1981–1982 when inflation fell from 12 percent to 4 percent, and in 1990–1992 when inflation fell from 5 percent to below 2 percent.

Reducing the rate of inflation takes time and involves major costs. The process begins when the Bank of Canada stops validating the ongoing inflation. It does this by raising its target for the overnight interest rate which, in turn, raises longer-term market interest rates (and reduces the growth rate of the money supply). This action lowers real aggregate demand, reducing any existing inflationary gap. We will soon see, however, that it is usually necessary for the Bank to go further, creating a substantial recessionary gap that persists until the inflation is eliminated.

The process involves many costs. The recessionary gap hurts all who suffer in recessions, including the unemployed workers and the owners of firms who lose profits and risk bankruptcy. Unemployed resources means lower output than would otherwise be produced. The temporary rise in interest rates hurts borrowers, including people with mortgages and firms with large loans. Among these groups who are most exposed and risk losing their wealth are young households with large mortgages and small firms that have taken on large debts to finance expansions.

Disinflation is thus a classic example of a policy that brings short-term pain for long-term gain. Inevitably, the question arises: Are the future benefits of lower inflation worth the immediate costs of reduced output and higher unemployment?

Reducing sustained inflation quickly incurs high costs for a short period of time; reducing it slowly incurs lower costs but for a longer period of time.

The process of reducing sustained inflation can be divided into three phases. In the first phase, the monetary validation is stopped and any inflationary gap is eliminated. In the second phase, the economy still suffers from declining output and rising prices—*stagflation*. In the final phase, the economy experiences both increasing output and increasing prices, but the inflation then comes to an end. We now examine these three phases in detail.

The starting point for our analysis is an economy with an inflationary gap $(Y > Y^*)$ and rising inflation.[5]

Practise with Study Guide Chapter 30, Exercise 1.

Phase 1: Removing Monetary Validation

The first phase consists of tightening monetary policy by raising interest rates and thus reducing the growth rate of the money supply. This policy action slows the rate at which the AD curve is shifting upward. An extreme case of monetary tightening in this setting is one where the Bank of Canada adopts a "cold-turkey approach"; interest rates are increased so much that the growth rate of the money supply is reduced to zero and the upward shift of the AD curve is halted abruptly.

At this point, a controversy often breaks out—as it did in the early 1980s and early 1990s—over the effects that the increase in interest rates has on inflation. One group will point out that the rise in the interest rate increases business costs and that passing on the extra costs through higher prices adds to inflation. They will condemn the Bank's tight monetary policy as inflationary. A second group will argue that rising interest rates are a necessary part of the disinflation policy.

The first group is correct in pointing out that the rise in interest rates may cause a one-time increase in the price level. The rise in interest costs may shift the AS curve upward, just as a rise in wage costs does. This rise in interest costs, however, has only a *one-time effect* on the price level. The first group is wrong, therefore, in asserting that the Bank's policy of driving up interest rates is contributing to a long-term increase in the rate of inflation. The second group is correct in saying that the rise in the interest

---

[5] In the simpler case where the economy begins with $Y = Y^*$ and constant inflation, only the second and third phases are relevant.

rate is a necessary part of an anti-inflationary policy. As long as the price level continues to rise, the rise in the interest rate reduces desired aggregate expenditure, thus reducing equilibrium real GDP by moving leftward along a fixed *AD* curve.

Now suppose the Bank resists the pleas to hold down interest rates. It continues with its no-validation policy. The *AD* curve stops shifting, but under the combined influence of the present inflationary gap and expectations of continued inflation, wages continue to rise. Hence, the *AS* curve continues to shift upward. Eventually, the inflationary gap will be removed, as shown in part (i) of Figure 30-6.

If the excess demand from the inflationary output gap were the only influence on wages, the story would be ended. At $Y = Y^*$, there would be no upward demand pres-

FIGURE 30-6   Eliminating a Sustained Inflation

(i) Phase 1: Removing the inflationary gap

(ii) Phase 2: Stagflation

(iii) Phase 3: Recovery

(i) Phase 1: The elimination of a sustained inflation begins with a monetary tightening to remove the inflationary gap. The initial position is one where fully validated inflation is taking the economy along the path shown by arrow ①. When the curves reach AS_1 and AD_1, the central bank adopts a tight monetary policy which halts the growth of the money supply, thus stabilizing aggregate demand at AD_1. Because of inflation expectations, wages continue to rise, taking the *AS* curve leftward. The economy moves along arrow ②, with output falling and the price level rising. When aggregate supply reaches AS_2, the inflationary gap is removed, output is Y^*, and the price level is P_2.

(ii) Phase 2: Expectations and wage momentum lead to stagflation, with falling output and continuing inflation. The economy moves along the path shown by arrow ③. The driving force is now the *AS* curve, which continues to shift because inflation expectations cause wages to continue rising. The recessionary gap grows as output falls. Inflation continues, but at a diminishing rate. If wages stop rising when output has reached Y_3 and the price level has reached P_3, the stagflation phase is over, with equilibrium at E_3.

(iii) Phase 3: After expectations are reversed, recovery takes output to Y^*, and the price level is stabilized. There are two possible scenarios for recovery. In the first, the recessionary gap causes wages to fall (slowly), taking the *AS* curve back to AS_2 (slowly), as shown by arrow ④. The economy retraces the path originally followed in part (ii) back to E_2. In the second scenario, the central bank increases the money supply sufficiently to shift the *AD* curve to AD_2. The economy then moves along the path shown by arrow ⑤. This restores output to potential at the cost of further temporary inflation that takes the price level to P_4. Potential output and a stable price level are now achieved.

sure on wages and other factor prices. The *AS* curve would be stabilized, and real GDP would remain at Y^*. But it is usually not so simple.

Phase 2: Stagflation

Wages depend not only on current excess demand but also on inflation expectations. Once inflation expectations have been established, it is not always easy to get people to revise them downward, even in the face of announced changes in monetary policies. Hence, the *AS* curve continues to shift upward, causing the price level to continue to rise and output to fall. The combination of increased inflation and a reduction in output (or its growth rate) is called **stagflation**. This is phase 2, shown in part (ii) of Figure 30-6.

Expectations can cause inflation to persist even after its original causes have been removed. What was initially a demand and expectational inflation due to an inflationary gap becomes a pure expectational inflation.

The ease with which the Bank of Canada can end such an inflation depends on how easy it is to change these expectations of continued inflation. This change is more difficult to the extent that expectations are backward-looking and easier to the extent that expectations are forward-looking.

To the extent that people look mainly to past inflation rates to determine their expectations of the future, they will be slow to change their expectations. As the actual inflation rate falls below the expected rate, a long time will be required for the downward adjustment to take place. The longer a given rate has persisted, the more firmly will people expect that rate to persist.

To the extent that expectations are forward-looking, people will take notice of the Bank's announced changes in policy and revise their expectations of future inflation downward in the light of the new policy. If people fully understand the Bank's policies as soon as they are implemented, if they have full confidence that the Bank will stick to its policies, if they know exactly how much time will be required for the Bank's policies to have effect, and if they adjust their expectations exactly in line with this knowledge, there is little need for any recessionary gap to develop. Once the inflationary gap has been removed, expectations will immediately be revised downward, so there will then be no pressure on wages to rise because of either demand or expectational forces. In Figure 30-6, Y would not fall below Y^* because the *AS* curve would stop shifting upward at AS_2. The inflation would be eliminated at almost no cost.

How long inflation persists after the inflationary gap has been removed depends on how quickly expectations of continued inflation are revised downward.

The importance of expectations explains why the Bank of Canada and other central banks emphasize their precise objectives in their many public speeches. In 1990–1991, the Bank's governor, John Crow, gave many speeches in an effort to convince the public that the Bank would stick to its newly adopted inflation target. This communications strategy was an attempt to reduce inflationary expectations and thus slow the upward shift of Canada's *AS* curve.

If the *AS* curve does continue to shift upward, causing Y to fall below Y^*, the emerging recessionary gap has two effects. First, unemployment rises and the output-gap effect begins to put downward pressure on wages. Second, the continuing expectations of inflation tend to raise wages further. The overall effect on wages and thus the *AS* curve is a combination of the output-gap effect and the expectational effect. When the recessionary gap is still new, the expectational effect is likely to outweigh the output-gap effect; wages will continue rising and the *AS* curve will continue to shift upward. But as the extent of excess supply deepens, and inflation itself begins to moderate, the output-gap effect will eventually come to offset the expectational effect;

stagflation The simultaneous increase in inflation and reduction in output (or its growth rate) that is caused by an upward shift of the *AS* curve.

The main cost of disinflation is the reduction in economic activity that is a necessary part of the process. Increases in unemployment and plant closures are typical.

wages will stop rising and the *AS* curve will stop shifting upward. At this point the stagflation phase is over. Inflation has come to a halt, but a large recessionary gap now exists.

Phase 3: Recovery   The final phase is the return to potential output. When the economy comes to rest at the end of the stagflation, the situation is exactly the same as when the economy is hit by a negative supply shock. The move back to potential output can be accomplished in either of two ways. First, the recessionary gap can be relied on to reduce factor prices, thereby shifting the *AS* curve downward, reducing prices but increasing real GDP. Second, an expansionary monetary policy can shift the *AD* curve upward, increasing both prices and real GDP. These two possibilities are illustrated in part (iii) of Figure 30-6.

Some economists worry about relying on the *AS* curve to shift downward to return the economy to potential output. Their concern is primarily that it will take too long for wages to fall sufficiently to shift the *AS* curve—though output will eventually return to potential, the long adjustment period will be characterized by high unemployment. These economists have a preference for a monetary expansion to get output back to potential.

Other economists worry about a temporary burst of monetary expansion because they fear that expectations of inflation may be rekindled when the Bank's monetary expansion shifts the *AD* curve to the right. And, if inflationary expectations *are* revived, the Bank will then be faced with a tough decision—either it must let another recession develop to break these new inflation expectations, or it must validate the inflation to reduce unemployment. In the latter case, the Bank is back where it started, with validated inflation on its hands—and diminished credibility.

The Cost of Disinflation

The foregoing discussion of the process of disinflation makes the cost of disinflation pretty clear:

The cost of disinflation is the loss of output that is generated in the process.

As we said earlier, the size and duration of the recession depends to a large extent on how quickly inflation expectations are revised downward as the disinflation continues. If expectations are backward looking and thus slow to adjust to the changes in policy, the recession will be deep and protracted. Conversely, if expectations are forward looking and quick to adjust to changes in policy, the recession may be mild and of short duration.

But *how costly* is the process of disinflation? Economists have derived a simple measure of the cost of disinflation based on the depth and length of the recession and on the amount of disinflation. This measure is called the **sacrifice ratio**, and is defined to be the cumulative loss of real GDP due to a given disinflation (expressed as a percentage of potential GDP) divided by the number of percentage points by which inflation has fallen. For example, the 1990–1992 disinflation in Canada reduced inflation by roughly four percentage points. Suppose the cumulative loss of real GDP due to that disinflation was equal to $80 billion and that potential GDP at the time was equal to $800 billion. The cumulative loss of output would then be 10 percent of potential output. The sacrifice ratio would therefore have been 10/4 = 2.5. The interpretation of this number is that it "costs" 2.5 percent of real GDP for each percentage point of inflation that is reduced.

sacrifice ratio The cumulative loss in real GDP, expressed as a percentage of potential output, divided by the percentage-point reduction in the rate of inflation.

The numbers in the above example are hypothetical, but typical estimates of the sacrifice ratio for many developed countries range between 2 and 4. Figure 30-7 illustrates the time paths of real GDP and inflation following a disinflation and shows how to compute the sacrifice ratio. Note an important assumption that is implicit whenever measuring the sacrifice ratio in this way. The assumption is that all changes in the path of real GDP are *caused by* the disinflation.

Conclusion

Throughout the history of economics, inflation has been recognized as a harmful phenomenon. The high inflation rates that Canada experienced in the 1970s and early 1980s (see Figure 30-1) were also experienced in many developed countries. In the past 30 years these countries have learned much about the causes of inflation, the policies required to reduce it, and the costs associated with doing so.

In recent years, some commentators have argued that the dangers of inflation have been eliminated, that inflation is now "dead." Central to these arguments is the view that greater international competition through the process of globalization means that the economy is now subject to different rules, specifically that greater competitive forces will keep inflationary pressures at bay. *Applying Economic Concepts 30-2* discusses the alleged death of inflation and argues that one central macroeconomic rule is still present: Sustained inflation is still a monetary phenomenon, and therefore inflation can only ever be as dead as central bankers' commitment to maintaining low inflation is alive.

FIGURE 30-7   The Cost of Disinflation: The Sacrifice Ratio

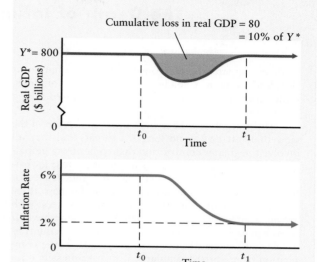

The sacrifice ratio is larger the deeper the recession and the longer it takes real GDP to return to potential. In this example, the economy begins with $Y = Y^*$ and inflation of 6 percent. At t_0, the disinflation begins. A recessionary gap opens up and inflation falls only slowly. By t_1, real GDP has returned to Y^* and inflation has been reduced by 4 percentage points. In this figure, the cumulative loss of real GDP is 10 percent of Y^* and inflation has fallen by 4 percentage points. The sacrifice ratio is therefore 10/4 = 2.5, indicating that it costs 2.5 percent of GDP to reduce inflation by one percentage point.

APPLYING ECONOMIC CONCEPTS 30-2

The Death of Inflation?

With the apparent success in maintaining inflation at very low levels, in Canada and many other countries, some economists and policymakers have started asking an inevitable question: Is inflation dead?

Many arguments have been made in defence of the view that inflation is no longer a threat, and they all involve the greater competition that comes from globalization. As we have noted earlier in this book, globalization—the sharp reductions in the cost of transportation and communication in the past three decades—presents domestic firms and workers with greater competition than they would otherwise have. If firms can easily ship their products to various countries quickly and efficiently, domestic firms face greater competition from abroad. Similarly, if firms can easily relocate their factories to produce in lower-cost countries, domestic workers face greater competition from abroad. As a result, domestic firms are less likely to raise prices and domestic workers are less likely to push for wage increases. In short, globalization increases the competitive pressures in the economy, thus reducing the economy's inflationary forces.

Most economists, however, reject this view that the ongoing process of globalization spells an end to inflation. Instead, they are more likely to argue that the greater competitive forces brought by globalization make it less likely that any particular shock will cause prices or wages to increase, thus making it less likely that a wage–price spiral will be initiated. In this sense, the forces of globalization may well help central banks maintain low inflation.

These same economists, however, continue to view *sustained* inflation as a monetary phenomenon. They believe that sustained inflation is only possible when there is continual growth in the money supply. Thus, while globalization may make it easier to sustain low inflation, an economy's long-run rate of inflation is ultimately determined by monetary policy.

In this view, inflation is dead only if central banks maintain their current commitment to keeping inflation at very low levels. Any future shocks, followed by monetary validation, could easily tip any individual country—or group of countries—back into an inflationary wage–price spiral.

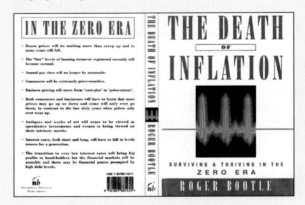

This book by Roger Bootle argues that the forces of globalization spell the death of inflation. Most central banks disagree.

S U M M A R Y

30.1 ADDING INFLATION TO THE MODEL   (LO) ❶ ❷

- Sustained price inflation will be accompanied by closely related growth in wages and other factor prices such that the *AS* curve is shifting upward. Factors that influence shifts in the *AS* curve can be divided into two main components: output gaps and expectations. Random supply-side shocks will also exert an influence.
- Inflationary output gaps tend to cause wages to rise; recessionary output gaps tend to cause wages to fall.
- Expectations of inflation tend to cause wage increases equal to the expected price-level increases. Expectations can be backward-looking, forward-looking, or some combination of the two.
- With a constant rate of inflation and no supply shocks, expected inflation will eventually come to equal actual inflation. This implies that there is no output-gap effect on inflation—that is, real GDP equals its potential level.
- Constant inflation of 2 percent per year is shown graphically in the macroeconomic model by the *AD* and *AS* curves shifting up by 2 percent per year, keeping real GDP equal to Y^*.

30.2 SHOCKS AND POLICY RESPONSES   (LO) ❸ ❹

- The initial effects of positive demand shocks are a rise in the price level and a rise in real GDP. If the inflation is unvalidated, output tends to return to its potential level while the price level rises further (as the *AS* curve shifts upward). Monetary validation allows demand inflation to proceed without reducing the inflationary gap (*AD* curve continues to shift upward).
- The initial effects of negative supply shocks are a rise in the price level and a fall in real GDP. If inflation is unvalidated, output will slowly move back to its potential level as the price level slowly falls to its preshock level (*AS* curve slowly shifts down). Monetary valida-

tion allows supply inflation to continue in spite of a persistent recessionary gap (*AD* curve shifts up with monetary validation).
- If the Bank of Canada tries to keep real GDP constant at some level above Y^*, the actual inflation rate will eventually accelerate. In our macro model, in the absence of supply shocks, constant inflation is only possible when there are no demand pressures on inflation—that is, when $Y = Y^*$.
- Aggregate demand and supply shocks have temporary effects on inflation. But *sustained* inflation is a monetary phenomenon.

30.3 REDUCING INFLATION   (LO) ❺ ❻

- The process of ending a sustained inflation can be divided into three phases.
  1. Phase 1 consists of ending monetary validation and allowing the upward shift in the *AS* curve to remove any inflationary gap that does exist.
  2. In Phase 2, a recessionary gap develops as expectations of further inflation cause the *AS* curve to continue to shift upward even after the inflationary gap is removed.
  3. In Phase 3, the economy returns to potential output, sometimes aided by a one-time monetary expansion that raises the *AD* curve to the level consistent with potential output.
- The cost of disinflation is the recession (output loss) that is created in the process. The sacrifice ratio is a measure of this cost and is calculated as the cumulative loss in real GDP (expressed as a percentage of Y^*) divided by the reduction in inflation.

K E Y   C O N C E P T S

Temporary and sustained inflation
The NAIRU
Forward-looking and backward-looking expectations

Expectational, output-gap, and supply-shock pressures on inflation
Monetary validation of demand and supply shocks

Expectations-augmented Phillips curve
Accelerating inflation
Disinflation
Sacrifice ratio

STUDY EXERCISES

1. Fill in the blanks to make the following statements correct.

   a. The term NAIRU stands for the _____.
   b. Unemployment is said to be equal to the NAIRU when GDP is equal to _____.
   c. Changes in money wages result from two different effects: the _____ effect and the _____ effect. Both of these effects cause the _____ curve to shift.
   d. The *AS* curve shifts up when money wages _____ and also shifts up with a negative _____ shock.
   e. Actual inflation can come from any of its three component parts. They are _____, _____, and _____.
   f. If the rate of inflation is constant at 6 percent and actual GDP equals potential GDP, then we can say that the central bank is _____ inflation expectations. That is, the central bank is permitting a(n) _____ in the money supply such that the expected and actual inflation rates are equal at _____ percent.

2. Fill in the blanks to make the following statements correct.

   a. Suppose the economy is initially at potential GDP (Y*) and then there is a sudden increase in the demand for Canadian exports. The *AD* curve shifts to the _____ and opens a(n) _____ gap.
   b. With an inflationary gap, the economy is operating where GDP is above _____. In an effort to maintain the output gap, the Bank of Canada may choose to validate the inflation by _____ the interest rate and allowing the money supply to _____. The actual inflation rate will _____.
   c. The alternative policy response to an inflationary gap is to not validate the inflation. The _____ curve stops shifting upward. The _____ curve shifts upward due to rising wages caused by _____. Real GDP eventually returns to _____ at a higher _____.
   d. Economists say that sustained inflation is a _____ phenomenon.
   e. Reducing a sustained inflation requires that monetary _____ be stopped. Inflation will persist, however, until _____ of continued inflation are revised downward.
   f. The cost of disinflation is the cost of the _____ that is generated in the process.

3. **myeconlab** The table below shows several macro-economic situations, each with a given amount of excess demand (or supply) for labour and a level of inflation expectations. Both are expressed in percent per year. For example, in Case A excess demand for labour is pushing wages up by 4 percent per year, and expected inflation is pushing wages up by 3 percent per year.

Case	Excess Demand	Inflation Expectations	Total Wage Change	AS Shift
A	+4	+3	—	—
B	+4	0	—	—
C	0	+3	—	—
D	−3	0	—	—
E	−3	+4	—	—

   a. For each case, identify whether there is an inflationary or a recessionary output gap.
   b. For each case, what is the total effect on nominal wages? Fill in the third column.
   c. For each case, in which direction is the *AS* curve shifting (up or down)? Fill in the last column.

4. **myeconlab** This exercise requires you to compute inflationary expectations based on a simple formula, and it will help you to understand why backward-looking expectations adjust slowly to changes in economic events. Suppose that the *actual* inflation rate in year t is denoted Π_t. *Expected* inflation for year $t+1$ is denoted Π^e_{t+1}. Now, suppose that workers and firms form their expectations according to:

   $$\Pi^e_{t+1} = \theta\Pi^T + (1-\theta)\Pi_t \qquad \text{(with } 0 < \theta < 1\text{)}$$

   where Π^T is the central bank's announced *inflation target*. This simple equation says that people's expectations for inflation at $t + 1$ are a weighted average of last year's actual inflation rate and the central bank's currently announced target. We will use this equation to see how the size of θ determines the extent to which expectations are backward looking. Consider the table below, which shows the data for a reduction in actual inflation from 10 percent to 2 percent.

Year (t)	Π_t	Π^T	Π^e_{t+1}
1	10	2	—
2	9	2	—
3	6	2	—
4	3	2	—
5	2	2	—
6	2	2	—
7	2	2	—
8	2	2	—

a. Assume that θ is equal to 0.1. Compute expected inflation for each year and fill in the table.
b. On a scale diagram, plot the time path of actual inflation, expected inflation, and the inflation target.
c. Now assume that θ equals 0.9. Repeat parts (a) and (b).
d. Which value of θ corresponds to more backward-looking expectations? Explain.
e. Given the different speed of adjustment of inflationary expectations, predict which disinflation is more costly in terms of lost output—the one with θ = 0.1 or with θ = 0.9. Explain.

5. The diagram below shows an AD/AS diagram. The economy is in long-run equilibrium with real GDP equal to Y* and the price level is stable at P_0.

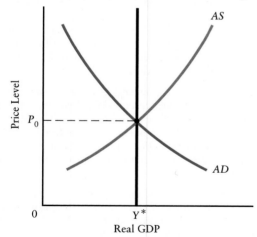

a. Suppose the central bank announces that it will implement an expansionary monetary policy that will shift the AD curve up by 5 percent. Show the likely effect of this announcement on the AS curve.
b. Why does the shift of the AS curve in part (a) depend on whether workers and firms believe the central bank's announcement?
c. In a new AD/AS diagram, show how a sustained and constant inflation of 5 percent is represented.

d. In the absence of any supply shocks, explain why a constant inflation is only possible when real GDP is equal to Y*.

6. The diagram below shows an AD/AS diagram. Suppose the economy is hit by some positive aggregate demand shock—say an increase in the demand for Canada's exports. This increases real GDP to Y_1.

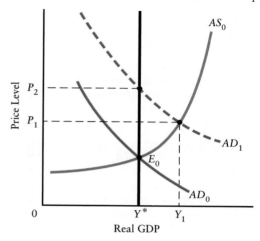

a. Explain what happens if the Bank of Canada does not react to the shock. Show this in the diagram.
b. Now suppose the Bank decides to maintain real GDP at Y_1—that is, it decides to validate the shock. Explain how this is possible, and show it in a diagram.
c. What is the effect on inflation from the policy in part (b)? Is inflation constant or is it rising? Explain.

7. The diagram below shows an AD/AS diagram. Suppose the economy is hit by some negative aggregate supply shock—say an increase in wages driven by a major union settlement. This reduces real GDP to Y_1.

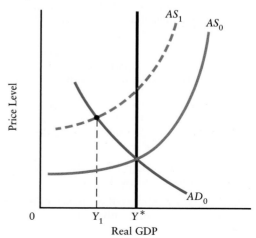

a. Explain what happens if the Bank of Canada does not react to the shock. Show this in the diagram.

b. Now suppose the Bank decides to offset the shock's effect on real GDP—that is, it validates the shock. Explain how this is possible, and show it in a diagram.

c. What danger do many economists see in validating such supply shocks? What is the alternative?

8. **myeconlab** The table below shows some data on various disinflations. In each case, assume that potential GDP is equal to $900 billion.

a. In each case, compute the sacrifice ratio.

b. Explain why the sacrifice ratio can be expected to be smaller when expectations are more forward looking.

c. Explain why the sacrifice ratio can be expected to be smaller when central-bank announcements are more credible.

Case	Inflation Reduction	Cumulative GDP Loss	Sacrifice Ratio
A	5 percentage points	$100 billion	—
B	2	30	—
C	6	60	—
D	8	80	—

DISCUSSION QUESTIONS

1. Why might the cost of disinflation vary from one inflationary period to another? Are there reasons to think the cost might be higher the longer inflation has persisted? What might the Bank of Canada do to reduce the cost?

2. What sources of inflation are suggested by each of the following quotations?

   a. A newspaper editorial in Manchester, England: "If American unions were as strong as those in Britain, America's inflationary experience would have been as disastrous as Britain's."

   b. An article in *The Economist*: "Oil price collapse will reduce inflation."

   c. A Canadian newspaper article in June 2006: "Tensions in Iran fuel an oil-driven inflation."

   d. A newspaper headline in October 2005: "Bank's fast growth of money will spur inflation."

3. Discuss the apparent conflict between the following views. Can you suggest how they might be reconciled using aggregate demand and aggregate supply analysis?

   a. "A rise in interest rates is deflationary, because ending entrenched inflation with a tight monetary policy usually requires that interest rates rise steeply."

   b. "A rise in interest rates is inflationary, because interest is a major business cost and, as with other costs, a rise in interest will be passed on by firms in the form of higher prices."

4. What is the relationship between the sacrifice ratio and the central bank's credibility?

   a. Explain why a more credible policy of disinflation reduces the costs of disinflation.

   b. Explain how you think the Bank of Canada might be able to make its disinflation policy more credible.

   c. Can the Bank's policy responses to negative supply shocks influence the credibility it is likely to have when trying to end a sustained inflation? Explain.

5. Suppose you are the governor of the Bank of Canada and that inflation has been high and roughly constant for a number of years. You have two policy choices: You can continue to validate the ongoing inflation; or you can attempt to eliminate the sustained inflation. Outline the issues involved when making this choice. List and explain the costs of ongoing inflation, and also the costs of a potential disinflation. Explain how you make your policy decision.

6. In January 1991, the federal government introduced the Goods and Services Tax (GST). If you were to suppose that the GST was a *new* tax (in fact, it replaced an existing tax), what would be the effect on the *AS* curve? Is the introduction of the GST (or an increase in its rate) inflationary? Does it increase inflation permanently?

7. In the summer of 2006, a time when U.S. inflation was rising and output was above potential, a story in *The Globe and Mail* reported that the release of strong employment-growth data for the United States led to a plunge in prices on the U.S. stock market.

   a. Explain why high employment growth would lead people to expect the U.S. central bank to tighten its monetary policy.

   b. Explain why higher U.S. interest rates would lead to lower prices of U.S. stocks.

   c. How would you expect this announcement to affect Canada?

CHAPTER 31

Unemployment Fluctuations and the NAIRU

LO LEARNING OBJECTIVES

In this chapter you will learn

1. how employment and unemployment change over the short and long runs.
2. the difference between the New Classical and New Keynesian views of unemployment fluctuations.
3. the causes of frictional and structural unemployment.
4. the various forces that cause the NAIRU to change.
5. about policies that might be used to reduce unemployment.

When the level of economic activity changes, so do the levels of employment and unemployment. When real GDP increases in the short run, employment usually rises and unemployment falls. Conversely, when real GDP falls in the short run, employment falls and unemployment rises. Figure 31-1 shows the course of the unemployment rate in Canada over the past few decades. Recall from Chapter 19 that the unemployment rate is the percentage of the labour force that is unemployed. It is clear that the unemployment rate has followed a cyclical path, rising during the recessions of 1981–1982 and 1991–1992, and falling during the expansions of the late 1980s and late 1990s. In this chapter we examine theories designed to explain these short-run fluctuations.

In addition to examining short-run fluctuations in the unemployment rate, economists also study the NAIRU—the rate of unemployment that exists when real GDP is equal to potential output, Y^*. At points A, B, C, and D in Figure 31-1, real GDP was approximately equal to potential output, and thus the unemployment rates then were approximately equal to the NAIRU. We will see in this chapter several reasons why the NAIRU might change over time, and thus offer some explanations for the gradual decline in the NAIRU apparent in the figure, from about 8 percent in 1977 (point A) to a little over 6 percent in 2005 (point D).

We begin by examining some basic facts about employment and unemployment.

FIGURE 31-1   Canadian Unemployment Rate, 1976–2006

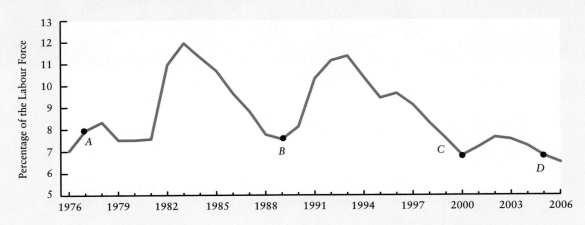

(*Source:* Data from Statistics Canada, CANSIM database, annual average of monthly series V2091977. Reprinted with permission of Statistics Canada.)

31.1 **EMPLOYMENT AND UNEMPLOYMENT**

Look back at Figure 19-3 in Chapter 19, which shows the path of employment and the labour force in Canada since 1960. The most striking feature of part (i) of the figure is that, when viewed over the long term, the growth in employment has approximately matched the growth in the labour force. Also notice in part (ii) of Figure 19-3, and also in Figure 31-1, that the unemployment rate displays considerable short-run fluctuations. These two characteristics of the labour force—long-term growth in employment but short-term fluctuations in the unemployment rate—are common to most developed countries.

Over the span of many years, increases in the labour force are more or less matched by increases in employment. Over the short term, however, the unemployment rate fluctuates considerably because changes in the labour force are not exactly matched by changes in employment.

Changes in Employment

The level of employment in Canada has increased dramatically over the past few decades. In 1959, there were approximately 5 million employed Canadians. By 2006, total employment was 16.7 million. The actual level of employment, of course, is determined both by the demand for labour and by the supply of labour. How have the two "sides" of the Canadian labour market been changing?

On the supply side, the labour force has expanded virtually every year since the end of the Second World War. The causes have included a rising population, which boosts entry into the labour force of people born 15 to 25 years previously; increased labour force participation by various groups, especially women; and net immigration of working-age persons.

On the demand side, many existing jobs are eliminated every year, and many new jobs are created. Economic growth causes some sectors of the economy to decline and others to expand. Jobs are lost in the sectors that are contracting and created in sectors that are expanding. Furthermore, even in relatively stable industries, many firms disappear and many new ones are set up. The net increase in employment is the difference between all the jobs that are lost and all those that are created.

In most years, enough new jobs are created both to replace old jobs that have been eliminated and to provide jobs for the growing labour force. The result is a net increase in employment in most years.

In a typical year in Canada, the level of employment increases by about 230 000 workers, an annual growth rate of roughly 1.3 percent.

Changes in Unemployment

In the early 1980s, worldwide unemployment rose to high levels. The unemployment rate remained high in many advanced industrial countries and only began to fall, and even then very slowly, during the latter half of the decade. Canadian experience reflected these international developments rather closely. From a high of over 12 percent in 1983, the Canadian unemployment rate fell to 7.5 percent in 1989, a point that many economists at the time thought was close to the Canadian NAIRU (see point *B* in Figure 31-1).

With the onset of another recession in the early 1990s, the unemployment rate then rose through 1990 and 1991, reaching 11.3 percent by 1992. During the next few years, the unemployment rate fell only slowly as the Canadian recovery was weak; by early 1994 the unemployment rate was still above 10 percent. But the speed of the Canadian recovery quickened and unemployment began to drop. By early 2000, after five years of healthy economic recovery, the unemployment rate was 6.8 percent. Following the large stock-market decline in late 2000, together with the decline in confidence associated with the 2001 terrorist attacks in New York and Washington, the Canadian and U.S. economies slowed, and unemployment increased. Recovery was rapid, however, and by the summer of 2006 Canadian real GDP was at or above its potential, and the unemployment rate had declined to 6.1 percent, the lowest it had been in over 30 years.

During periods of rapid economic growth, the unemployment rate usually falls. During recessions or periods of slow growth, the unemployment rate usually rises.

Flows in the Labour Market

As we have observed above, many existing jobs are eliminated every year, as industries contract and firms either shrink or close down altogether. Similarly, new jobs are continually being created, as other industries expand and new firms are born. The focus on the labour market, however, tends to be on the overall level of employment and unemployment rather than on the amount of *job creation* and *job destruction*. This focus can often lead us to the conclusion that few changes are occurring in the labour market when in fact the truth is exactly the opposite.

For example, the Canadian unemployment rate was roughly constant at 7.5 percent from 2002 to 2003. Does this mean no jobs were created during the year? Or that the Canadian labour market was stagnant during this period? No. In fact, workers

For data on current employment and unemployment in Canada, see Statistics Canada's website: **www.statcan.ca**. Click on "Canadian Statistics" and then type in "unemployment."

were finding jobs at the rate of roughly 400 000 *per month*. At the same time, however, other workers were leaving jobs or entering the labour force at roughly the same rate. This tremendous number of flows *out of unemployment* was being approximately matched by the number of flows *into unemployment*. The net result was that total unemployment changed only slightly.

The level of activity in the labour market is better reflected by the flows into and out of unemployment than by the overall unemployment rate.

By looking at the *gross flows* in the labour market, we are able to see economic activity that is hidden when we just look at the overall level of employment and unemployment (which is determined by *net* flows). Indeed, these gross flows are typically so large that they dwarf the net flows. See *Applying Economic Concepts 31-1* for more discussion of the gross flows in the Canadian labour market, and how these gross-flows data can be used to compute the average length of unemployment spells.

Practise with Study Guide Chapter 31,
Additional Multiple-Choice
Questions 1–8.

A number of problems are associated with the measurement of unemployment, some of which relate to how "actively" people currently not working are searching for a job. For a detailed discussion of some of these problems, as well as an illustration of why they are important for understanding the gap between U.S. and Canadian unemployment rates, look for "Understanding the Canada–U.S. Unemployment Gap" in the *Additional Topics* section of this book's MyEconLab.

w w w . m y e c o n l a b . c o m

Consequences of Unemployment

Economists view unemployment as a social "bad" just as they view output as a social "good." But this does not mean *all* unemployment is bad, just as we know that all output—such as noise or air pollution—is not good. Indeed, we will see later in this chapter that some unemployment is socially desirable as it reflects the necessary time spent searching to make appropriate matches between firms and workers.

We examine two costs of unemployment. The first is reflected by the loss in output. The second is the harm done to the individuals who are unemployed.

Lost Output   Every person counted as unemployed is willing and able to work but has yet to find a job. Hence, the unemployed are valuable resources who are currently not producing output. The output that is not produced, but potentially could be, is a loss for society. Once an unemployed person regains employment, however, output rises again and this loss goes away. But nothing makes up for the *past* loss that existed while the worker was unemployed. In other words, the loss of output that accompanies unemployment is lost forever. In a world of scarcity with many unsatisfied wants, this loss represents a serious waste of resources.

Personal Costs   For the typical Canadian worker, being unemployed for long periods of time is very unusual, and even when it does occur it is not the disaster it once was. Most spells of unemployment are short; in 2004, the OECD estimated that only 17.7 percent of Canadian unemployment spells lasted six months or longer. In other words, the vast majority of unemployed workers find new jobs in just a few months.

Moreover, many workers experiencing temporary unemployment have access to the employment insurance program that provides some income during their spell of unemployment.

But this does not mean there are no problems associated with unemployment, especially for those relatively few workers who are unemployed for long periods of time. The effects of long-term unemployment, in terms of the disillusioned who have given up trying to make it within the system and who contribute to social unrest, should be a matter of serious concern to the "haves" as well as the "have-nots." The loss of self-esteem and the dislocation of families that often result from situations of prolonged unemployment are genuine tragedies.

The general case for concern about high unemployment has been eloquently put by Princeton economist Alan Blinder:

> *A high-pressure economy provides opportunities, facilitates structural change, encourages inventiveness and innovation, and opens doors for society's under-dogs.... All these promote the social cohesion and economic progress that make democratic mixed capitalism such a wonderful system when it works well. A low-pressure economy slams the doors shut, breeds a bunker mental-ity that resists change, stifles productivity growth, and fosters both inequality and mean-spirited public policy. All this makes reducing high unemployment a political, economic, and moral challenge of the highest order.[1]*

31.2 **UNEMPLOYMENT FLUCTUATIONS**

It is clear from Figure 31-1 that the unemployment rate fluctuates considerably over relatively short periods of time. Over the years, economists have debated the sources of these fluctuations. One group of economists, who are often referred to as *New Keynesians,* emphasize the distinction between the unemployment that exists when real GDP is equal to Y^*, and unemployment that is due to deviations of real GDP from Y^*. The former, as we saw in Chapter 19, is called the NAIRU, and is made up of frictional and structural unemployment. The latter is often called **cyclical unemployment**, which falls (or rises) as real GDP rises above (or falls below) Y^*. As we will soon see, New Keynesians argue that such cyclical unemployment exists because real wages do not quickly adjust to clear labour markets in response to shocks of various kinds.

The second group, often called *New Classical* economists, has a different view of short-run fluctuations in unemployment. In their models, real wages adjust very quickly to clear labour markets and as a result real GDP is always equal to Y^*. (As we saw in Chapter 24, if the economy's adjustment process operates very quickly, real GDP returns to Y^* very soon after any *AD* or *AS* shock.) In the New Classical perspective, the unemployment rate does fluctuate, but only because of changes in the amount of frictional or structural unemployment. For the New Classical economists, there is no cyclical unemployment whatsoever.

A central difference between the two schools of thought regards the *nature* of unemployment. For New Keynesians, workers who are suffering cyclical unemployment are normally presumed to be *involuntarily* unemployed—they are willing to work

cyclical unemployment
Unemployment not due to fric-tional or structural factors; it is due to deviations of GDP from Y^*.

---

[1] A. S. Blinder, "The Challenge of High Unemployment," *American Economic Review* 78 (1988), 2:1.

APPLYING ECONOMIC CONCEPTS 31-1

Stocks and Flows in the Canadian Labour Market

In most reports about changes in unemployment, both in Canada and abroad, emphasis is typically on the changes in the *stock* of unemployment—that is, on the number of people who are unemployed at a particular point in time. But as we said in the text, the focus on the stock of unemployment can often hide much activity in the labour market, activity that is revealed by looking at *gross flows* in the labour market.

What Are Labour-Market Flows?

The first figure in this box shows the difference between stocks and flows in the labour market. The blue circles represent the number of individuals at the end of each month (the *stocks*) in each possible "state"—employment (*E*), unemployment (*U*), and *not* in the labour force (*N*). The six red arrows represent the monthly *flows* of individuals between the various states. For example, arrow 1 shows the monthly flow of individuals from *E* to *U*. These individuals begin the month in *E* (employed), leave their jobs sometime during the month, and end the month as unemployed individuals, in *U*. Arrow 3 shows the flow from *N* to *U*—these individuals are new entrants to the labour force during the month and begin their labour-force experience as unemployed individuals.

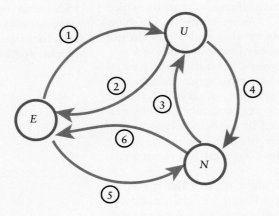

In the second figure, three series of data are shown for Canada from 1976 to 2003—a period that includes the major recessions of 1981 and 1991. The top line is the stock of unemployment—the actual *number* of people unemployed at a specific point in time. During the severe recession of the early 1980s, unemployment peaked at approximately 1.7 million people, and then fell during the recovery until 1989. With the onset of the next recession in 1990–1991, unemployment rose again, reaching nearly 1.8 million in 1992.

The two lower lines show *gross flows* in the labour market. (These flows data are not available for 1997 and 1998, which explains the break in the lines at that point.) The orange line shows the monthly flow into unemployment, corresponding to the sum of the flows in arrows 1 and 3 in the first figure. This flow into unemployment represents either:

- workers losing jobs through layoffs or plant closure; or
- workers quitting jobs to search for a different job; or
- new entrants to the labour force searching for a job.

The monthly flow into unemployment varies between approximately 300 000 and 500 000 *per month*.

The green line shows the monthly flow out of unemployment, corresponding to the sum of the flows in arrows 2 and 4 in the first figure. This outflow represents either:

- unemployed individuals finding new jobs; or
- unemployed individuals becoming discouraged and leaving the labour force.

The monthly flow out of unemployment is roughly the same size as the monthly inflow (300 000–500 000 per month).

What is the connection between the flows and the stocks in the labour market? Whenever the flows into unemployment exceed the flows out of unemployment, the stock of unemployment rises. Conversely, whenever the flows out of unemployment exceed the flows into unemployment, the stock of unemployment falls.

Using Flows Data

There are two reasons why looking at flows can be very useful when we think about the labour market. First, they show the tremendous amount of activity in the labour market even though the stock of unemployment may not be changing significantly. For example, between 1991 and 1992 the stock of unemployment in Canada varied between 1.4 million and 1.6 million persons. But during that two-year period, roughly 400 000 persons *per month* either became unemployed or ceased being unemployed. This number reflects the massive amount of regular turnover that exists in the Canadian labour market—turnover that is the essence of what economists call *frictional unemployment*.

The second reason why looking at flows is useful is that the relationship between the flows and the stock can tell us something about the amount of time the average unemployed person spends unemployed. If U_S is the stock of unemployment, and U_O is the monthly outflow from unemployment, then one simple estimate of the average duration of an unemployment spell is

$$\text{Average duration of unemployment spell} = \frac{U_S}{U_O}$$

Consider the situation in 1999, at the peak of the business cycle. At that time, the stock of unemployment was approximately 1 million people and the outflow from unemployment was at a rate of approximately 400 000 persons per month. Thus, the average unemployed person in 1999 could expect to leave unemployment in about 2½ months (1 000 000 people/400 000 people per month = 2.5 months). In contrast, in 1992, at the depth of the previous recession, the expected duration of an unemployment spell was over 3½ months (1 600 000/450 000 = 3.6).

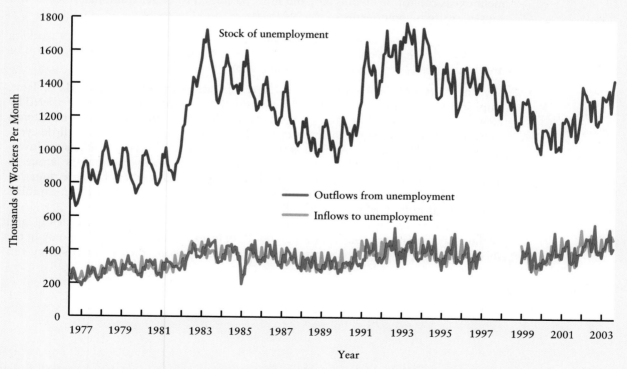

(*Source:* Statistics Canada, Labour Force Survey, available at www.statcan.ca. Reprinted with permission of Statistics Canada.)

at the going wage but are unable to find appropriate jobs. In contrast, for New Classical economists, all unemployment is deemed to be *voluntary*—workers are only unemployed because they choose not to work or not to accept available job offers.

We now explore in more detail the New Classical and New Keynesian theories of unemployment fluctuations.

New Classical Theories[2]

Two major characteristics of New Classical models are that agents continuously optimize and markets continuously clear. In such models, there can be no involuntary unemployment. These theories then seek to explain unemployment as the outcome of voluntary decisions made by individuals who are choosing to do what they do, including spending some time out of employment.

The New Classical theory explains fluctuations in employment and real wages as having one of two causes. First, as shown in part (i) of Figure 31-2, changes in technology that affect the *marginal product* of labour will lead to changes in the demand for labour, and thus to fluctuations in the level of employment and real wages. Second, as shown in part (ii) of Figure 31-2, changes in the willingness of individuals to work will lead to changes in the supply of labour and thus to fluctuations in the level of employment and real wages. In both cases, however, note that the flexibility of real wages results in a *clearing* of the labour market. In this setting, whatever unemployment exists cannot be involuntary and must be caused by either frictional or structural causes, the two components of the NAIRU.

New Classical theory assumes that labour markets clear. People who are not working are assumed to have voluntarily withdrawn from the labour market for one reason or another. There is no involuntary unemployment.

There are two problems with this New Classical view of labour markets. First, empirical observation is not consistent with the fluctuations in real wages predicted by New Classical theory. In Canada and other developed economies, employment tends to be quite volatile over the business cycle whereas real wages tend to show little cyclical variation. The second problem is that the New Classical theory predicts *no* involuntary unemployment whatsoever, a prediction that many economists argue is unsupported by empirical observation. (Many unemployed workers who are nonetheless actively searching for a job would be shocked to find out that some economists view them as *voluntarily* unemployed!)

Extensions in Theory 31-1 examines New Classical theory in more detail, and explains why many economists, though rejecting its explanations of the economy in the short run, believe that it contains valuable insights about the economy's long-run behaviour.

---

2 The label "New Classical" is used because many of the arguments put forward by this group of economists are essentially more detailed and precise versions of arguments that would have been very familiar to the Classical economists, from Adam Smith and David Ricardo to Alfred Marshall.

FIGURE 31-2   Employment and Wages in a New Classical Labour Market

(i) Demand shifts

(ii) Supply shifts

In a New Classical labour market, there is no involuntary unemployment. The figure shows a perfectly competitive market for one type of labour. In part (i), the demand curves D_1, D_0, and D_2 are the demands for this market corresponding to low, medium, and high values for the marginal product of labour. As demand rises from D_1 to D_0 to D_2, real wages rise from w_1 to w_0 to w_2, and employment rises from L_1 to L_0 to L_2. In part (ii), the supply of labour fluctuates from S_1 to S_0 to S_2, and wages fluctuate from w_1 to w_0 to w_2. In both parts, the labour market always clears and there is no involuntary unemployment.

New Keynesian Theories[3]

Many of the economists who reject the New Classical approach argue that people, despite reading market signals correctly, nonetheless react in ways that do not cause markets to clear at all times. These economists—many of whom refer to themselves as New Keynesians—believe that many people are involuntarily unemployed in the sense that *they would accept an offer of work in jobs for which they are trained, at the going wage rate, if such an offer were made.* These economists concentrate their efforts on explaining why wages do not quickly adjust to eliminate involuntary unemployment. If wages do not respond quickly to shifts in supply and demand in the labour market, quantity supplied and quantity demanded may *not* be equated for extended periods of time. Labour markets will then display unemployment during recessions and excess demand during booms, as shown in Figure 31-3.

---

[3] The label "New Keynesian" is used because many of the arguments put forward by these economists are closely related to ideas famously argued by John Maynard Keynes in *The General Theory of Employment, Interest and Money* (1936).

EXTENSIONS IN THEORY 31-1

A Closer Look at New Classical Theory

New Classical theory attempts to explain cyclical fluctuations in the context of models in which wages and prices adjust very quickly to shocks. These models contrast sharply with the models we have discussed in this book in which fluctuations in output arise largely because wages and prices adjust only gradually to shocks. If wages and prices were able to adjust instantly to all shocks, output would always be equal to potential output—there would never be inflationary or recessionary gaps. The full flexibility of wages and prices is therefore a distinguishing feature of New Classical macro theory.

Key Propositions and Criticisms

The view of the business cycle found in New Classical models is that short-run fluctuations in real GDP are caused by fluctuations in potential output, Y^*. In this view, unemployment is always equal to the NAIRU, and it is the NAIRU itself that fluctuates. Thus, the explanation of cyclical fluctuations that arises in New Classical models is based on the role of supply shocks originating from sources such as oil price changes, technical progress, and changes in tastes. Monetary factors typically play no role in these models.

The New Classical approach is controversial. The major claims in its favour include:

1. It has been able to explain the recent behaviour of the economy quite well statistically, while downplaying the role for aggregate demand fluctuations in the business cycle.

2. It suggests that an integrated approach to understanding cycles and growth may be appropriate, as both reflect forces that affect the level of potential output. The distinction it makes is that some shocks are temporary (and hence have cyclical effects) whereas others are permanent (and therefore affect the economy's long-term growth).

3. It provides valuable insights into how shocks, regardless of their origin, spread over time to the different sectors of the economy.

Critics of the New Classical approach express concern about its assumptions of individuals' behaviour. They are also skeptical about an approach that ignores monetary issues. For example, they point out that New Classical models are unable to provide insights into the short-term correlation between money and output that is at the heart of the traditional macro model and for which a considerable amount of empirical evidence exists, in Canada as well as many other countries.

Policy Implications

Because the New Classical approach gives no role to aggregate demand in influencing business cycles, it provides no role for stabilization operating through monetary and fiscal policies. Indeed, the models predict that the use of such demand-management policies can be *harmful*.

The basis for this prediction is the proposition that cycles represent *efficient* responses to the shocks that are hitting the economy. Policymakers may mistakenly interpret cyclical fluctuations as deviations from potential output caused by shifts in either the *AD* or *AS* curves. The policymakers may try to stabilize output and thereby distort the maximizing decisions made by households and firms. This distortion will in turn cause the responses to the real shocks (as opposed to nominal, monetary shocks) to be inefficient.

Economists disagree about how well New Classical models explain short-run fluctuations. However, since the New Classical approach emphasizes the importance of markets always clearing in response to changes in technology or other shocks, many economists who view New Classical models as a poor description of the economy in the short run believe that many of the New Classical insights are important when thinking about the behaviour of the economy in the long run.

New Keynesian theories start with the observation that wages do not change every time demand or supply shifts. When unemployed workers are looking for jobs, they do not knock on employers' doors and offer to work at lower wages than are being paid to current workers; instead, they answer help-wanted ads and hope to get the jobs offered but are often disappointed. Nor do employers, seeing an excess of applicants for the few jobs that are available, go to the current workers and reduce their wages until there is no one who is looking for a job; instead, they pick and choose until they fill their needs and then hang a sign saying "No Help Wanted."

There are several possible reasons why wages do not quickly adjust to all shocks in the labour market.

Long-Term Employment Relationships

One set of theories is based on the advantages to both workers and employers of relatively long-term and stable employment relationships. Workers want job security in the face of fluctuating demand. Employers want workers who understand the firm's organization, production, and marketing plans. Under these circumstances, both parties care about things in addition to the wage rate, and wages are somewhat insensitive to fluctuations in current economic conditions. Wages are, in effect, regular payments to workers over an extended employment relationship rather than a device for fine-tuning the current supplies of and demands for labour. Given this situation, the tendency is for employers to "smooth" the income of employees by paying a steady wage and letting profits and employment fluctuate to absorb the effects of temporary increases and decreases in demand for the firm's product.

A number of labour-market institutions work to achieve these results. For example, many long-term contracts provide for a schedule of wages over a period of several years. Similarly, employee benefits, such as pensions and supplementary health insurance, tend to bind workers to particular employers. Another example is pay that rises with years of service. This helps to bind the employee to the company, whereas seniority rules for layoffs bind the employer to the long-term worker.

In labour markets in which long-term relationships are important (as is the case in many labour markets), the wage rate does not fluctuate to clear the market continuously.

Menu Costs and Wage Contracts

A typical large firm sells dozens of differentiated products and employs many different types of labour. Changing prices and wages in response to every minor fluctuation in demand is a costly and time-consuming activity. Many firms therefore find it optimal to keep their price lists (*menus*) constant for significant periods of time. Since large firms are often operating in imperfectly

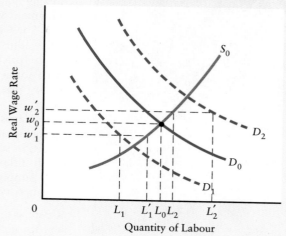

FIGURE 31-3 Unemployment and Sticky Wages in a New Keynesian Labour Market

When the wage rate does not change enough to equate quantity demanded with quantity supplied, there will be unemployment in slumps and labour shortages in booms. When demand is at its normal level D_0, the market is cleared with wage rate w_0, employment is L_0, and there is no involuntary unemployment. In a recession, demand falls to D_1, but the wage only falls to w_1'. As a result, L_1 of labour is demanded and L_1' is supplied. Employment is determined by the quantity demanded at L_1. The remainder of the supply for which there is no demand, L_1L_1', is involuntarily unemployed. In a boom, demand rises to D_2, but the wage rate rises only to w_2'. As a result, the quantity demanded is L_2', whereas only L_2 is supplied. Employment rises to L_2, which is the amount supplied. The rest of the demand cannot be satisfied, making excess demand for labour of L_2L_2'.

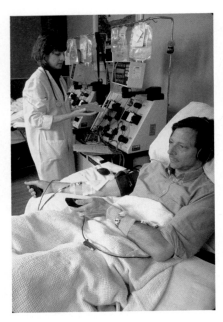

The quick adjustment of wages to excess demands and supplies is not a characteristic of labour markets in which employees and firms have long-term relationships, such as in the health-care sector.

competitive markets, they have some discretion over price. Hence, firms often react to small changes in demand by holding prices constant and responding with changes in output and employment. If many firms behave this way, output and employment will respond to changes in aggregate demand. In other words, the amount of involuntary unemployment will fluctuate over the business cycle.

The Canadian evidence is consistent with the existence of sluggish price adjustment by firms, especially those in manufacturing industries. Such "price stickiness" was a central feature of Keynesian economics; today, much of the New Keynesian perspective is based on the idea that sticky prices are a result of firms' optimal responses to adjustment costs.

Wages tend to be inflexible in the short term because wage rates are generally set only occasionally. Wages are often set on an annual basis; in some unionized contracts wages are set for up to three years. Such inflexibility of wages implies that changes in aggregate demand and supply will tend to cause changes in the amount of involuntary unemployment.

Costs associated with changing prices and wages lead firms and workers to make such changes only infrequently. As a result, many prices and wages are slow in adjusting to shocks.

Efficiency Wages The idea of *efficiency wages* forms the core of another strand of New Keynesian thinking about why wages do not quickly adjust to clear labour markets. For any of a number of reasons, employers may find that they get more output per dollar of wages paid—that is, a more efficient workforce—when they pay labour somewhat more than the minimum amount that would induce workers to work for them.

Suppose it is costly for employers to monitor workers' performance on the job, so that some workers will be able to shirk duties with a low probability of being caught. Given prevailing labour-market institutions, it is generally impossible for employers to levy fines on employees for shirking on the job since the employees could just leave their jobs rather than pay the fines. So firms may instead choose to pay a wage premium—an efficiency wage—to the workers, in excess of the wage that the workers will get elsewhere in the labour market. With such a wage premium, workers will be reluctant to shirk because, if they get caught and laid off, they will then lose this wage premium.

How does this relate to involuntary unemployment? The wage premium paid to prevent workers from shirking means that the quantity of labour supplied may exceed the quantity demanded by firms, thereby creating involuntary unemployment. Wages do not fall to clear the labour market because firms would rather pay a high wage to motivated workers than a lower wage to workers who would then shirk their duties. The result is involuntary unemployment for some workers.

Efficiency-wage theory predicts that firms may find it profitable to pay high enough wages so that working is a clearly superior alternative to being laid off. Involuntary unemployment results.

Union Bargaining The final New Keynesian theory to be considered assumes that those already employed ("insiders") have more say in wage bargaining than those currently not employed ("outsiders"). Employed workers are often represented by a union, which negotiates the wage rate with firms. The union will generally represent the interests of the insiders but will not necessarily reflect the interests of the outsiders.

Insiders will naturally wish to bid up wages even though to do so will harm the employment prospects of the outsiders. Hence, this theory generates an outcome to the bargaining process between firms and unions in which the wage is set higher than the market-clearing level, just as with efficiency wages. The consequence is some involuntary unemployment.

In addition to explaining the existence of involuntary unemployment, this theory adds one important insight regarding international differences in unemployment. In some countries, unions bargain at the level of the firm; in others they bargain at the level of the whole industry or the whole economy. Where bargaining is decentralized, as in Canada and the United States, the union can push for higher wages for the insiders without worrying about the effects on outsiders or on the rest of the economy. However, where bargaining is more centralized, as in much of Western Europe, the effects on the rest of the economy become partially internalized into the bargaining process, because union negotiators are bargaining on behalf of a larger group of workers, rather than just those currently employed.

This theory leads to the following predictions. Decentralized bargaining with strong unions will lead to higher than market-clearing wages, and higher unemployment as the outsiders are excluded from jobs. In contrast, more centralized bargaining will produce an outcome closer to the market-clearing outcome, so unemployment will be lower. In situations where unionization is low or unions are weak, the outcome will be close to the market-clearing outcome. This analysis may partly explain why unemployment is relatively high in EU countries (where unions are strong and bargaining is decentralized), lower in Scandinavia (where unions are also strong but bargaining is centralized), and even lower in Canada and the United States (where the extent of unionization is much lower and thus even decentralized wage bargaining affects only a small portion of the economy).

In labour markets with powerful unions, wages are set in a bargaining process. If unions act in the interests of the current "insiders," wages will be high and involuntary unemployment will exist. If unions act in the interests of all workers, wages and involuntary unemployment will both be lower.

Convergence of Theories?

We have examined two classes of theories of unemployment fluctuations. In the New Classical theories, wages and prices adjust instantly to clear markets and so real GDP is always equal to potential GDP. Unemployment fluctuates, but it is always equal to the NAIRU, U^*. Using the terminology we introduced earlier, there is no *cyclical* unemployment in New Classical models; all unemployment is either frictional or structural. In contrast, New Keynesian models emphasize the gradual adjustment of wages and prices and thus the existence of periods in which real GDP is either above or below potential GDP. In these models, unemployment fluctuates around the value of U^*—that is, U does not always equal U^*. Cyclical unemployment fluctuates over the business cycle. Table 31-1 provides a summary of the key assumptions and predictions of these two classes of theories.

Note, however, that the sharp contrast between New Classical and New Keynesian models applies only to the short-run behaviour of the economy. It is in the short run that the extent of wage and price flexibility distinguishes these two classes of models. In the long run, even the staunchest New Keynesians accept the proposition that wages and prices tend to adjust to eliminate output gaps and thus return real GDP to its potential level and the unemployment rate to the NAIRU (U^*).

TABLE 31-1 Summary of New Classical and New Keynesian Theories

	New Classical Theory	New Keynesian Theory
Key Assumptions		
Market clearing	Wages and price are perfectly flexible; all markets are continuously clearing.	Wages and prices are slow to adjust; markets are not continuously clearing.
Key Predictions		
Unemployment	U is always equal to NAIRU. There is no cyclical or involuntary unemployment; all unemployment is voluntary.	U often deviates from NAIRU. Unemployment has both voluntary and involuntary components.
Role of *AD* shocks	*AD* shocks do not cause changes in output because the *AS* curve adjusts instantly to bring Y back to Y^*.	*AD* shocks cause changes in output because the *AS* curve adjusts only gradually to bring Y back to Y^*.
Changes in Y^* and NAIRU	Shocks to technology and preferences lead to changes in both Y^* and NAIRU.	Shocks to technology and preferences lead to changes in both Y^* and NAIRU.

Both New Classical economists and New Keynesians agree that in the long run wage and price flexibility tends to bring the unemployment rate back to U^*.

Let's restate the difference between New Keynesian and New Classical models another way. In New Keynesian models there is a meaningful difference between the short run and the long run that is determined by the degree of wage and price flexibility. In New Classical models, however, wages and prices adjust instantly, so there is no similar distinction between the short run and the long run. But, since *both* classes of models agree that wages and prices are flexible in the long run, they have the same predictions regarding the long-run effects of policy.

For example, New Keynesians argue that a monetary expansion will raise real GDP above Y^* and reduce U below U^*. In the long run, however, output will tend to return to Y^*, U will return to U^*, and the main long-run effect of the monetary expansion will be a higher price level. New Classical economists agree on this predicted long-run effect, but they argue that the short-run real effects on output and unemployment will either be absent or of much shorter duration since wages and prices adjust very quickly.

New Keynesians and New Classical economists agree that the actual unemployment rate will tend toward the NAIRU in the long run. Our next job is to understand why the NAIRU changes. We turn to this topic now.

31.3 WHAT DETERMINES THE NAIRU?

The NAIRU is composed of frictional and structural unemployment. Our interest is in why the NAIRU changes over time and in the extent that economic policy can affect it.

Frictional Unemployment

As we saw in Chapter 19, **frictional unemployment** results from the normal turnover of labour. One source of frictional unemployment is young people who enter the labour force and look for jobs. Another source is people who leave their jobs. Some may quit because they are dissatisfied with the type of work or their working conditions; others may be fired or laid off because their employers go out of business. Whatever the reason, they must search for new jobs, which takes time. Persons who are unemployed while searching for jobs are said to be frictionally unemployed or in *search unemployment.*

The normal turnover of labour causes frictional unemployment to persist, even if the economy is at potential output.

How "voluntary" is frictional unemployment? Some of it is clearly voluntary. For example, a worker may know of an available job but may not accept it so she can search for a better one. Some of it is also involuntary, as when a worker gets laid off and cannot find *any* job offer for a period of weeks, even though he may be actively searching. *Extensions in Theory 31-2* shows that the distinction between voluntary and involuntary unemployment is not always as clear as it might at first seem.

frictional unemployment
Unemployment that results from the turnover in the labour market as workers move between jobs.

Structural Unemployment

Structural adjustments in the economy can cause unemployment. When the pattern of demand for goods changes, the pattern of the demand for labour changes. Until labour adjusts fully, structural unemployment develops. **Structural unemployment** is caused by a mismatch between the structure of the labour force—in terms of skills, occupations, industries, or geographical locations—and the structure of the demand for labour.

structural unemployment
Unemployment due to a mismatch in skills, industry, or location between available jobs and unemployed workers.

Natural Causes Changes that accompany economic growth shift the structure of the demand for labour. Demand rises in such expanding areas as British Columbia's Lower Mainland or Ontario's Ottawa Valley and falls in declining areas such as southern Manitoba and parts of Quebec. Demand rises for workers with certain skills, such as computer programming and electronics engineering, and falls for workers with other skills, such as stenography, assembly line work, and middle management. To meet changing demands, the structure of the labour force must change. Some existing workers can retrain and some new entrants can acquire fresh skills, but the transition is often difficult, especially for already experienced workers whose skills become economically obsolete.

Increases in international competition can also cause structural unemployment. As the geographical distribution of world production changes, so does the composition of production and of labour demand in any one country. Labour adapts to such shifts by changing jobs, skills, and locations, but until the transition is complete, structural unemployment exists.

Increases in the world price of oil between 2002 and 2006 led to a reduction in manufacturing activity in Central Canada and economic expansions in oil-producing regions of the country, such as the Alberta oil sands shown here. Structural unemployment was created until workers could move from Eastern and Central Canada to Alberta.

EXTENSIONS IN THEORY 31-2

Voluntary Versus Involuntary Unemployment

Frictional unemployment is *involuntary* if the job seeker has not yet found a job for which his or her training and experience are suitable. Frictional unemployment is *voluntary* if the unemployed person is aware of available jobs for which he or she is suited but is searching for better options. But how should we classify an unemployed person who refuses to accept a job at a lower skill level than the one for which she is qualified? What if she turns down a job for which she is trained because she hopes to get a higher wage offer for a similar job from another employer?

In one sense, people in search unemployment are voluntarily unemployed because they could almost always find *some* job, no matter how poorly paid or inappropriate to their training; in another sense, they are involuntarily unemployed because they have not yet succeeded in finding the job for which they feel they are suited at a rate of pay that they believe is attainable.

Workers do not have perfect knowledge of all available jobs and rates of pay, and they may be able to gain information only by searching the labour market. Facing this uncertainty, they may find it sensible to refuse a first job offer, for the offer may prove to be a poor one in light of further market information. But too much search—for example, holding off while being supported by others in the hope of finding a job better than a job for which one is really suited—is an economic waste. Thus, search unemployment is a grey area: Some of it is useful, but too much can be wasteful.

Some search unemployment is desirable because it gives unemployed people time to find an available job that makes the best use of their skills. How long it pays for people to remain in search unemployment depends on the economic costs of being unemployed. By lowering the costs of being unemployed, employment insurance tends to increase the amount of search unemployment. This may or may not increase economic efficiency, depending on whether or not it induces people to search beyond the point at which they acquire new and valuable information about the labour market.

Structural unemployment will increase if there is either an increase in the pace at which the structure of the demand for labour is changing or a decrease in the pace at which labour is adapting to these changes.

Following the Canada–U.S. Free Trade Agreement in 1989 and the North American Free Trade Agreement (NAFTA) in 1994, there were significant shifts of economic activity within Canada. For example, the textiles industry, much of which was located in Quebec, contracted; at the same time there was an expansion of the high-tech industry, much of which was located in the Ottawa Valley. The types of workers released from the textiles industry, however, were not exactly what was required in the expanding high-tech industry. This type of mismatch in skills and locations contributed to structural unemployment during the early 1990s.

Policy Causes Government policies can influence the speed with which labour markets adapt to changes. Some countries, including Canada, have adopted policies that *discourage* movement among regions, industries, and occupations. These policies (which may be desirable for other reasons) tend to reduce the rate at which unemployed workers are matched with vacant jobs, and thus tend to raise the amount of structural unemployment.

For two related reasons, the employment-insurance (EI) program also contributes to structural unemployment. First, the Canadian EI system ties workers' benefits to the regional unemployment rate in such a way that unemployed workers can collect EI benefits for more weeks in regions where unemployment is high than where it is low. The EI system therefore encourages unemployed workers to remain in high-unemployment regions rather than encouraging them to move to regions where employment prospects are more favourable. Second, workers are only eligible for employment insurance if they have worked for a given number of weeks in the previous year—this is known as the *entrance requirement*. In some cases, however, these entrance requirements are very low and thus seasonal workers are encouraged to work for a few months and then collect employment insurance and wait for the next season, rather than finding other jobs during the off season.

Finally, labour-market policies that make it difficult or costly for firms to fire workers also make employers more reluctant to hire workers in the first place. Such policies, which are very common in the European Union, reduce the amount of turnover in the labour market and are believed to be an important contributor to the amount of long-term unemployment in those countries. In Germany, Italy, and Belgium, for example, the labour laws impose significant costs on firms whenever workers are laid off. In those countries, approximately 50 percent of all unemployment spells last for *longer* than 12 months.

The Frictional–Structural Distinction

As with many distinctions, the one between frictional and structural unemployment is not precise. In a sense, structural unemployment is really long-term frictional unemployment. Consider, for example, what would happen if there were an increase in world demand for Canadian-made car parts but at the same time a decline in world demand for Canadian-assembled cars. This change would require labour to move from one sector (the car-assembly sector) to another (the car-parts manufacturing sector). If the reallocation were to occur quickly, we call the unemployment *frictional*; if the reallocation were to occur slowly, we call the unemployment *structural*.

In practice, structural and frictional unemployment cannot be separated. But the two of them, taken together, *can* be separated from cyclical unemployment. Specifically, when real GDP is at its potential level, the *only* unemployment (by definition) is the NAIRU, which comprises frictional and structural unemployment. For example, real GDP in Canada was approximately equal to potential GDP in early 2006. At that time, the unemployment rate was 6.3 percent, and thus the NAIRU was approximately 6.3 percent. In contrast, three years earlier in 2003, the unemployment rate was 7.5 percent. To the extent that the underlying frictions and structural change in the economy were unchanged over those three years, we can conclude that in 2003, 1.2 percentage points of the actual unemployment rate was due to cyclical factors and the rest was due to frictional and structural factors.

Why Does the NAIRU Change?

In general, the NAIRU can rise for two reasons. First, the economy may be subjected to *more* shocks requiring an adjustment of the labour force between sectors or regions. Second, the *ability* of the labour force to adjust to any given shock may decline. In either case, the amount of frictional or structural unemployment will rise, and NAIRU will therefore increase.

We now examine several specific causes of changes in the NAIRU.

Demographic Shifts   Because young people usually try several jobs before settling into one for a longer period of time, young or inexperienced workers have higher unemployment rates than experienced workers. The proportion of inexperienced

For information on Canada's Employment Insurance program, see the website for Human Resources and Social Development Canada: **www.hrsdc.gc.ca**.

*Young workers have higher employ-
ment rates than do older workers. As
the share of younger workers in the
labour force decreases, so will the economy's NAIRU.*

workers in the labour force rose significantly as the baby-boom generation of the 1950s entered the labour force in the 1970s and 1980s. This
trend had the effect of increasing the NAIRU during the 1970s and
1980s. But as the baby-boom generation aged, and the fraction of young
workers in the labour force declined in the late 1990s and early 2000s,
the opposite effect was observed, and tended to reduce the NAIRU.

A second demographic trend relates to the labour-force participation of women. During the 1960s and 1970s women tended to have
higher unemployment rates than men. Since this was true at all points
of the business cycle, the higher unemployment was higher frictional
and structural unemployment. Thus, when female labour-force participation rates increased dramatically in the 1960s and 1970s, the NAIRU
naturally increased. In recent years, however, female unemployment
rates have dropped below the rates for men, and so continued increases
in female participation will, if anything, tend to decrease the NAIRU.

Greater labour-force participation by groups with high unemployment
rates increases the NAIRU.

See Figure 31-4 for Canadian unemployment rates for various demographic
groups in 2005. Notice especially the significantly higher unemployment rates for
youth of both sexes. These data form the basis for the often-heard view that while

FIGURE 31-4   Canadian Unemployment Rates by Demographic Groups, 2005

Unemployment is unevenly spread among different groups in the labour force. In 2005, when the overall unemployment rate was 6.8 percent, the unemployment rates for youths (of both sexes) were considerably higher.

(*Source:* These data are available on Statistics Canada's website, www.statcan.ca, by searching for "labour force." Then
select "labour force characteristics by age and sex.")

overall unemployment may be at acceptable levels, youth unemployment may be a serious problem.

Hysteresis

Some models of unemployment show that the NAIRU can be influenced by the current rate of unemployment. Such models get their name from the Greek word *hysteresis,* meaning "lagged effect."

One mechanism that can lead to hysteresis arises from the importance of experience and on-the-job training. Suppose a recession causes a significant group of new entrants to the labour force to encounter unusual difficulty obtaining their first jobs. As a result, this unlucky group will be slow to acquire the important skills that workers generally learn in their first jobs. When demand increases again, this group of workers will be at a disadvantage relative to workers with normal histories of experience, and the unlucky group may take longer to find jobs and thus have unemployment rates that will be higher than average. Hence, the NAIRU will be higher than it would have been had there been no recession.

Another force that can cause such effects is emphasized by commentators in the European Union, which has a more heavily unionized labour force than does either Canada or the United States. In times of high unemployment, people who are currently employed ("insiders") may use their bargaining power to ensure that their own status is maintained and prevent new entrants to the labour force ("outsiders") from competing effectively. For this reason, high unemployment—whatever its initial cause—will tend to become "locked in." If outsiders are denied access to the labour market, their unemployment will fail to exert downward pressure on wages, and the NAIRU will tend to rise.

Globalization and Structural Change

Many economists believe that the ongoing process of globalization, especially since the mid-1970s, has increased the rate at which labour is being reallocated across regions and sectors in the Canadian economy. While most economists argue that the growing integration of Canada in the global economy generates net benefits for Canada, they also recognize a downside. One less fortunate consequence is that Canadian labour markets are increasingly affected by changes in demand and supply conditions elsewhere in the world. As it becomes more necessary for Canadian labour markets to adjust to economic events occurring in other parts of the world, the NAIRU will tend to increase.

Policy and Labour-Market Flexibility

We mentioned briefly above how policies can affect structural unemployment. It is worthwhile emphasizing again the important role that government policy can have on the NAIRU.

One important cause of unemployment is *inflexibility* in the labour market. If wages are inflexible, shocks to labour demand or supply can cause unemployment. If workers are unable or unwilling to move between regions or between industries, changes in the structure of the economy can cause unemployment. If it is costly for firms to hire workers, firms will find other ways of increasing output (such as switching to more capital-intensive methods of production). In general, since the economy is always being buffetted by shocks of one sort or another, the less flexible is the labour market, the higher structural unemployment will be.

Any government policy that reduces labour-market flexibility is likely to increase the NAIRU.

Consider employment insurance (EI) as an example of a policy that reduces labour-market flexibility. EI provides income support to eligible unemployed workers and thus reduces the costs to the worker of being unemployed. This income support will typically lead the worker to search longer for a new job and thus increase frictional unemployment. This longer search may be desirable since by reducing the cost of unemployment the worker is able to conduct a thorough search for a job that is an appropriate match for his or her specific skills. On the other hand, if the EI system is so generous that workers have little incentive to accept reasonable jobs—instead holding out for the "perfect" job—then the increase in unemployment generated by the EI system will be undesirable.

In general, however, the basic message should be clear. The more generous is the employment insurance system, the less motivated unemployed workers will be to accept a new job quickly. This reduction in labour-market flexibility will increase the NAIRU.

A second example concerns policies designed to increase job security for workers. In most Western European countries, firms cannot lay off workers without showing cause, which can lead to costly delays and even litigation. When they do lay them off they are required either to give several months' notice before doing so or, in lieu of such notice, are required to make severance payments equal to several months' worth of pay. In Italy, for example, a worker who has been with the firm for 10 years is guaranteed either 20 months' notice before termination or a severance payment equal to 20 months' worth of pay.

Such job-security provisions greatly reduce the flexibility of firms. But this inflexibility on the part of the firms is passed on to workers. Any policy that forces the firm to incur large costs for laying off workers is likely to lead the same firm to be very hesitant about hiring workers in the first place. Given this reduction in labour-market flexibility, such policies are likely to increase the NAIRU.

Such mandated job security is relatively rare in Canada and the United States. Its rarity contributes to the general belief among economists that North American labour markets are much more flexible than those in Europe. Many economists see this as the most important explanation for why unemployment rates in Canada and the United States are significantly below the unemployment rates in Europe, and have been for over two decades.

31.4 REDUCING UNEMPLOYMENT

Practise with Study Guide Chapter 31, Exercise 2.

In the remainder of this chapter we briefly examine what can be done to reduce unemployment. Other things being equal, all governments would like to reduce unemployment. The questions are "Can it be done?" and "If so, at what cost?"

Cyclical Unemployment

We do not need to say much more about cyclical unemployment because its control is the subject of stabilization policy, which we have studied in several earlier chapters. A major recession that occurs because of natural causes can be countered by monetary and fiscal policies to reduce cyclical unemployment.

There is room for debate, however, about *how much* the government can and should do in this respect. Advocates of stabilization policy call for expansionary fiscal and monetary policies to reduce cyclical unemployment (and increase output) during recessionary gaps, at least when they last for sustained periods of time. Advocates of a hands-off approach say that normal market adjustments can be relied on to remove recessionary gaps and that government policy, no matter how well intentioned, will only make things worse. They call for setting simple rules for monetary and fiscal policy that would make discretionary stabilization policy impossible.

Whatever may be argued in principle, however, policymakers have not yet agreed to abandon stabilization measures in practice.

Frictional Unemployment

The turnover in the labour market that causes frictional unemployment is an inevitable part of the functioning of the economy. Some frictional unemployment is a natural part of the learning process for young workers. New entrants to the labour force (many of whom are young) have to try several jobs to see which is most suitable, and this leads to a high turnover rate among the young and hence high frictional unemployment.

Employment insurance is one method of helping people cope with unemployment. It has reduced significantly the human costs of the bouts with unemployment that are inevitable in a changing society. Nothing, however, is without cost. Although employment insurance alleviates the suffering caused by some kinds of unemployment, it also contributes to search unemployment, as we have already observed. As with any policy, a rational assessment of the value of employment insurance requires a balancing of its undoubted benefits against its undoubted costs. Many Canadians believe that when this calculation is made, the benefits greatly exceed the costs, although many also recognize the scope for reform of certain aspects of the program.

Many provisions have been added over the years to the employment insurance scheme to focus it more on people in general need and to reduce its effect of raising the unemployment rate. For example, workers must be actively seeking employment in order to be eligible for EI. Also, workers who voluntarily quit their jobs (without cause) are not eligible to collect EI. In recent years, the benefits received by eligible unemployed workers have been reduced, thus decreasing the likelihood that job seekers will reject early job offers. These changes have contributed to a decline in the amount of frictional unemployment.

For two of the most widely used job-match websites, go to **www.monster.ca** or **www.workopolis.ca**.

Structural Unemployment

The reallocation of labour among occupations, industries, skill categories, and regions that gives rise to structural unemployment is an inevitable part of a market economy. Much of this required reallocation is driven by technological change, which occurs in different ways and at different paces in various parts of the economy. Ever since the beginning of the Industrial Revolution in the late eighteenth century, workers have resisted the introduction of new techniques that replace the older techniques at which they were skilled. Such resistance is understandable. New techniques often destroy the value of the knowledge and experience of workers skilled in the displaced techniques. Older workers may not even get a chance to start over with the new technique. Employers may prefer to hire younger persons who will learn the new skills faster than older workers who are set in their ways of thinking. From society's point of view, new techniques are beneficial because they are a major source of economic growth. From the point of view of the workers they displace, however, new techniques can be an unmitigated disaster.

There are two basic approaches to reducing structural unemployment: Try to resist the changes that the economy experiences or accept the changes and try to assist the necessary adjustments. Throughout history, both approaches have been tried.

Resisting Change   Over the long term, policies aimed at maintaining employment levels in declining industries run into increasing difficulties. Agreements to hire unneeded workers raise costs and can hasten the decline of an industry threatened by competitive products. An industry that is declining because of economic change becomes an increasingly large burden on the public purse as economic forces become less and less favourable to its success. Sooner or later, public support is withdrawn, followed by a precipitous decline.

As we assess these remedies for structural unemployment, it is important to realize that although they are not viable in the long run for the entire economy, they may be the best alternatives for the affected workers during their lifetimes.

There is often a genuine conflict between the private interest of workers threatened by structural unemployment, whose interests lie in preserving existing jobs, and the social interest served by reallocating resources to where they are most valuable.

Assisting Adjustment   A second general approach to dealing with structural change is to accept the decline of specific industries and the loss of specific jobs that go with them and to try to reduce the cost of adjustment for the workers affected. A number of policies have been introduced in Canada to ease the adjustment to changing economic conditions.

One such policy is publicly subsidized education and retraining schemes. The public involvement is motivated largely by imperfections in capital markets that make it difficult for workers to borrow funds for education, training, or retraining. A major component of labour-market policies is a system of loans and subsidies for higher education.

Another policy is motivated by the difficulty in obtaining good information about current and future job prospects. In recent years, the development of the Internet has greatly improved the flow of this type of information. Human Resources and Social Development Canada (HRSDC), for example, operates an Internet-based service to speed up and improve the quality of matches between firms and workers. The HRSDC Job Bank allows firms (or workers) to specify certain characteristics and skills and then match these characteristics with workers (or firms) on the "other side" of the labour market.

Policies to increase retraining and to improve the flow of labour-market information will tend to reduce the amount of structural unemployment.

To learn more about the National Job Bank, go to HRSDC's website: **www.hrsdc.gc.ca** and click on "jobs."

Conclusion

Over the years, unemployment has been regarded in many different ways. Harsh critics see it as proof that the market system is badly flawed. Reformers regard it as a necessary evil of the market system and a suitable object for government policy to reduce its incidence and its harmful effects. Others see it as overblown in importance and believe that it does not reflect any real inability of workers to obtain jobs if they really want to work.

Most government policy has followed a middle route. Fiscal and monetary policies have sought to reduce at least the most persistent of recessionary gaps, and a host of labour-market policies have sought to reduce frictional and structural unemployment. Such social policies as employment insurance have sought to reduce the sting of unemployment for the many who were thought to suffer from it for reasons beyond their control.

As global economic competition becomes more intense and as new knowledge-driven methods of production spread, the ability to adjust to economic change will become increasingly important. Countries that succeed in the global marketplace, while also managing to maintain humane social welfare systems, will be those that best learn how to cooperate with change. This will mean avoiding economic policies that inhibit change while adopting social policies that reduce the human cost of adjusting to change. This is an enormous challenge for future Canadian economic and social policies.

SUMMARY

31.1 EMPLOYMENT AND UNEMPLOYMENT

- Canadian employment and the Canadian labour force increased along a strong upward trend throughout the twentieth century. The unemployment rate fluctuates significantly over the course of the business cycle.
- Looking only at the level of employment or unemployment misses a tremendous amount of activity in the labour market as individuals flow from unemployment to employment or from employment to unemployment. In recent years in Canada, approximately 400 000 people *per month* flowed between employment and unemployment. This level of gross flows reflects the turnover that is a normal part of any labour market.

- It is useful to distinguish among several types of unemployment: cyclical unemployment, which is associated with output gaps; frictional unemployment, which is a result of normal labour-market turnover; and structural unemployment, which is caused by the need to reallocate resources among occupations, regions, and industries as the structure of demand and supply changes.
- Together, frictional unemployment and structural unemployment make up the NAIRU. The actual unemployment rate is equal to the NAIRU when real GDP is equal to Y^*.

31.2 UNEMPLOYMENT FLUCTUATIONS

- There is a long-standing debate among economists regarding the causes of unemployment fluctuations.
- New Classical theories look to explanations that allow the labour market to be cleared continuously by perfectly flexible wages and prices. Such theories can explain cyclical variations in employment but predict no involuntary unemployment.
- New Keynesian theories have focused on the long-term nature of employer–worker relationships in which wages tend to respond only a little, and employment

tends to respond a lot, to changes in the demand and supply of labour. More recent New Keynesian theories have examined the possibility that it may be efficient for employers to pay wages that are above the level that would clear the labour market (efficiency wages).
- This debate only applies to the short-run behaviour of the economy. Both classes of models, for example, predict that in the long run, monetary expansions or contractions have few effects on output, employment, or unemployment.

31.3 WHAT DETERMINES THE NAIRU?

- The NAIRU will always be positive because it takes time for labour to move between jobs both in normal turnover (frictional unemployment) and in response to changes in the structure of the demand for labour (structural unemployment).
- Because different workers have different sets of skills and because different firms require workers with different sets of skills, some unemployment—resulting from workers searching for appropriate job matches with employers—is socially desirable.

- Anything that increases the rate of turnover in the labour market, or the pace of structural change in the economy, will likely increase the NAIRU.
- Employment insurance also increases the NAIRU by encouraging workers to continue searching for an appropriate job. Policies that mandate job security increase the costs to firms of laying off workers. This makes them reluctant to hire workers in the first place and may increase the NAIRU.

31.4 **REDUCING UNEMPLOYMENT**

- Cyclical unemployment can be reduced by using monetary or fiscal policies to close recessionary gaps.
- Frictional and structural unemployment can be reduced by making it easier to move between jobs and by raising the cost of staying unemployed (e.g., by reducing employment insurance benefits).

- In a growing, changing economy populated by people who wish to change jobs for many reasons, it is neither possible nor desirable to reduce unemployment to zero.
- Policies that assist workers in retraining and in moving between jobs, regions, or industries may be the most effective way to deal with the various shocks that buffet the economy.

KEY CONCEPTS

Gross flows in the labour market
Cyclical, frictional, and structural unemployment
New Classical and New Keynesian theories of unemployment

Long-term employment relationships
Efficiency wages
Hysteresis
The components of the NAIRU

Determinants of the NAIRU
Policies to reduce the NAIRU
Labour-market flexibility

STUDY EXERCISES

1. Fill in the blanks to make the following statements correct.

   a. The overall unemployment rate in Canada is not a good indicator of the level of *activity* in the labour market because _____.

   b. *Gross* flows in the labour market are much _____ than *net* flows in the labour market.

   c. In a typical month in Canada, _____ workers flow in each direction between unemployment and employment.

   d. Cyclical unemployment exists when real GDP is _____ than potential GDP. When real GDP is equal to potential GDP, then all unemployment is either _____ or _____.

   e. New Classical theories assume that the labour market always _____ with flexible _____ and that any unemployment that does exist is _____.

   f. New Keynesian theories assume that wages do not instantly _____ to clear the market. A recessionary gap can persist and result in unemployment that is _____.

   g. The New Classical and New Keynesian theories both assume that, in the long run, wages and prices _____ and the unemployment rate will revert to the _____, as any _____ gap is closed.

2. Fill in the blanks to make the following statements correct.

   a. The NAIRU is composed of _____ unemployment and _____ unemployment. The NAIRU is always _____ than zero.

   b. If there are 1000 loggers in British Columbia who are unemployed, and 1000 vacant positions for call-centre operators in New Brunswick, we say that this unemployment is _____.

   c. Suppose the NAIRU in June 2003 was 6.5 percent. If the actual unemployment rate was 7.6 percent, we can conclude that _____ percentage points are due to _____ factors and the remaining _____ percentage points are due to _____ and _____ factors.

   d. Suppose the government increased the number of weeks that an unemployed worker can collect employment-insurance benefits from 12 weeks to 16 weeks. The NAIRU is likely to _____ because of an increase in the amount of _____ unemployment.

   e. Countries with greater labour-market flexibility are likely to have _____ unemployment rates than countries in which policies inhibit flexibility.

   f. Cyclical unemployment can be reduced by closing a(n) _____ gap using _____ and _____ policies.

3. **myeconlab** The following table shows the pattern of real GDP, potential GDP, and the unemployment rate for several years in Cycleland.

Year	Real GDP (billions of dollars)	Potential GDP (billions of dollars)	Unemployment Rate (%)
1998	790	740	6.3
1999	800	760	6.5
2000	780	780	6.8
2001	750	800	8.2
2002	765	810	8.4
2003	790	830	8.4
2004	815	850	8.0
2005	845	870	7.5
2006	875	890	7.2
2007	900	900	6.8
2008	930	920	6.7

a. On a scale diagram, draw the path of real GDP and potential GDP (with time on the horizontal axis).
b. On a separate diagram (below the first one) show the path of the unemployment rate.
c. For which years is it possible to determine the value of NAIRU?
d. Does the NAIRU change over the 10-year period? Provide one reason why the NAIRU could increase.

4. The diagram below shows a simple *AD/AS* diagram. The economy begins in long-run equilibrium at E_0 with real GDP equal to Y^*.

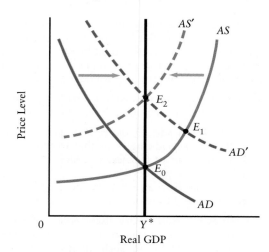

a. At E_0, the unemployment rate is 8 percent. What type of unemployment is this?
b. A positive aggregate demand shock now shifts the *AD* curve to *AD'*. At E_1 the unemployment rate is only 6.5 percent. Is there cyclical unemployment at E_1?

c. Describe the economy's adjustment process to E_2.
d. What is the unemployment rate at E_2? What kind of unemployment exists at E_2?

5. The diagram below shows a simple *AD/AS* diagram. The economy begins in long-run equilibrium at E_0 with real GDP equal to Y^*.

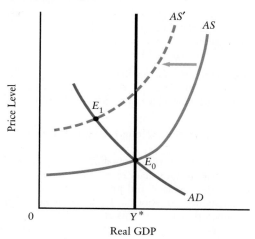

a. At E_0, the unemployment rate is 6 percent. What type of unemployment is this?
b. A negative aggregate supply shock now shifts the *AS* curve to *AS'*. At E_1 the unemployment rate is 7.5 percent. Is there cyclical unemployment at E_1? How much?
c. If monetary and fiscal policy do not react to the shock, describe the economy's adjustment process to its new long-run equilibrium.
d. What is the unemployment rate at the economy's new long-run equilibrium? What kind of unemployment exists there? Explain.

6. The diagram below shows a perfectly competitive labour market. The initial equilibrium is with wage w^* and employment L^*.

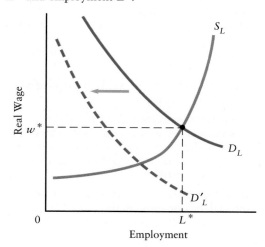

a. Suppose the demand for labour decreases to D'_L. If wages are perfectly flexible, what is the effect on wages and employment? Show this in the diagram.

b. Is there any involuntary unemployment in part (a) after the shock?

c. Now suppose wages can only adjust half as much as in part (a)—that is, wages are sticky. What is the effect on wages and employment in this case? Show this in the diagram.

d. Is there any involuntary unemployment in part (c) after the shock? How much?

7. Consider an economy that begins with real GDP equal to potential. There is then a sudden increase in the prices of raw materials, which shifts the AS curve upwards.

a. Draw the initial long-run equilibrium in an AD/AS diagram.

b. Now show the immediate effect of the supply shock in your diagram.

c. Suppose wages and prices in this economy adjust instantly to shocks. Describe what happens to unemployment in this economy. Explain.

d. If wages and prices adjust only slowly to shocks, what happens to unemployment? Explain.

e. Explain why a key difference between New Keynesian and New Classical theories of unemployment involves the degree of wage and price flexibility.

8. **myeconlab** The table below shows the percentage of the labour force accounted for by youths (15–24 years old) and older workers (25 years and older) over several years. Suppose that, due to their lower skills and greater turnover, youths have a higher unemployment rate than older workers (see Figure 31-4).

Year	Percentage of Labour Force	
	Youths	Older Workers
1	20	80
2	21	79
3	22	78
4	23	77
5	25	75
6	27	73
7	29	71
8	31	69

a. Suppose that in Year 1 real GDP is equal to potential GDP, and the unemployment rate among older workers is 6 percent but is 14 percent among youths. What is the economy's NAIRU?

b. Now suppose that for the next eight years real GDP remains equal to potential. Compute the value of NAIRU for each year.

c. Explain why NAIRU rises even though output is always equal to potential.

DISCUSSION QUESTIONS

1. Interpret the following statements from newspapers in terms of types of unemployment.

a. "Recession hits local factory; 2000 laid off."

b. "Of course, I could take a job as a dishwasher, but I'm trying to find something that makes use of my high school education," says a local teenager in our survey of the unemployed.

c. "Retraining is the best reaction to the increased use of robots."

d. "Uneven growth: Alberta booms while Ontario sputters."

2. Discuss the following views. Is it possible that both views are right? Explain.

a. "Canadian workers should resist the automation that is destroying their jobs," says a labour leader.

b. "Given the fierce foreign competition faced by Canadian firms, it's a case of automate or die," says an industrialist.

3. "No one needs to be out of work if he or she really wants a job; just look at the Help Wanted signs in many fast-food businesses and retail shops." Does the existence of the unfilled vacancies suggested in the quotation imply that there need be no cyclical unemployment as long as workers are not excessively fussy about the kinds of jobs they will take?

4. What differences in approach toward the problem of unemployment are suggested by the following facts?

a. In the 1960s and 1970s, Britain spent billions of dollars on subsidizing firms that would otherwise have gone out of business in order to protect the jobs of the employees.

b. Sweden has been a pioneer in spending large sums to retrain and to relocate displaced workers.

5. Advocates of discretionary fiscal policy often argue that the government can reduce unemployment by increasing spending on such things as highways, bridges, sewer systems, and so on. What do you think of such a policy to "create jobs"? Is such a policy equally likely to create jobs during a recession as when the economy is already operating at potential output? Explain.

6. Consider two hypothetical countries. In Country A, 20 percent of the labour force is unemployed for half the year and employed for the other half; the remaining 80 percent of the labour force is never unemployed. In Country B, 100 percent of the labour force is unemployed for 10 percent of the year and employed for the other 90 percent of the year. Note that both countries have an overall unemployment rate of 10 percent. Discuss which of these countries seems to have the more serious unemployment problem, and explain why.

7. There is a great deal of debate over the appropriate level of generosity for Canada's employment insurance program.

   a. Explain what problem can be caused by having an EI system that is too generous.
   b. Explain what problem can be caused by having an EI system that is not generous enough.
   c. If EI generosity were reduced and the NAIRU declined as a result, is this necessarily a desirable outcome?

Government Debt and Deficits

LEARNING OBJECTIVES

In this chapter you will learn

1. how the government's annual budget deficit (or surplus) is related to its stock of debt.
2. about the cyclically adjusted deficit and how it can be used to measure the stance of fiscal policy.
3. how budget deficits may crowd out investment and net exports.
4. why a high stock of debt may hamper the conduct of monetary and fiscal policies.
5. why legislation requiring balanced budgets may be undesirable.

Until the late 1990s, no single measure associated with the government was the focus of more attention and controversy than the size of the government's annual budget deficit and its accumulated level of debt. Some people argued that the debt was an economic time bomb, waiting to explode and cause serious harm to our living standards. Others argued that the only real danger posed by debt was from the dramatic policy changes proposed to reduce it. By 2006, after two decades of debate about debt and deficits, the focus had shifted to what the governments—federal and provincial— should do with their actual and projected budget surpluses. Just as debates once raged over the harmful effects of high government budget deficits, debates currently rage about whether governments that are facing budget surpluses should increase spending, reduce taxes, or use the surpluses to reduce the outstanding stock of government debt.

In this chapter, we examine various issues surrounding government debt, deficits, and surpluses. We begin by considering the simple arithmetic of government budgets. This tells us how the deficit or surplus in any given year is related to the outstanding stock of debt. We then explore why deficits and debt matter for the performance of the economy—as well as what changes we can expect over the near future if Canadian governments are successful in maintaining either balanced budgets or budget surpluses.

32.1 **FACTS AND DEFINITIONS**

There is a simple relationship between the government's expenditures, its tax revenues, and its borrowing. This relationship is summarized in what economists call the government's *budget constraint*.

The Government's Budget Constraint

As is true for any individual's expenditures, government expenditures must be financed either by income or by borrowing. The difference between individuals and governments, however, is that governments typically do not earn income by selling products or labour services; instead, they earn income by levying taxes. Thus, all government expenditure must be financed either by tax revenues or by borrowing. This point is illustrated by the following simple equation, which is called the government's *budget constraint:*

$$\text{Government expenditure} = \text{Tax revenue} + \text{Borrowing}$$

We divide government expenditure into two categories. The first is purchases of goods and services, G. The second is the interest payments on the outstanding stock of debt; this is referred to as **debt-service payments** and is denoted $i \times D$, where i is the interest rate and D is the stock of government debt (which has accumulated over time from the government's past borrowing). A third category of government spending is *transfers* to individuals and firms (such as employment-insurance benefits and industrial subsidies) but, as we did in earlier chapters, we include transfers as part of T, which is the government's *net tax revenue* (tax revenue minus transfers). The government's budget constraint can therefore be rewritten as

$$G + i \times D = T + \text{Borrowing}$$

or, subtracting T from both sides,

$$(G + i \times D) - T = \text{Borrowing}$$

This equation simply says that any excess of total government spending over net tax revenues must be financed by government borrowing.

The government's annual **budget deficit** is the excess of government expenditure over tax revenues in a given year. From the budget constraint above, this annual deficit is exactly the same as the amount borrowed by the government during the year. Since the government borrows by issuing bonds and selling them to lenders, borrowing by the government increases the government's outstanding stock of debt. Since D is the outstanding stock of government debt, ΔD is the *change* in the stock of debt during the course of the year. The budget deficit can therefore be written as

$$\text{Budget deficit} = \Delta D = (G + i \times D) - T$$

The government's annual budget deficit is the excess of expenditure over tax revenues in a given year. It is also equal to the change in the stock of government debt during the year.

Notice two points about budget deficits. First, a change in the size of the deficit requires a change in the level of expenditures *relative* to the level of tax revenues. For a given level of tax revenues, a smaller deficit can come about only through a reduction in government expenditures; conversely, for a given level of expenditures, a smaller deficit requires an increase in tax revenues. Second, since the budget deficit is equal to the amount of new government borrowing, the stock of **government debt** will rise whenever the budget deficit is positive. Even a drastic reduction in the size of the annual budget deficit is therefore not sufficient to reduce the outstanding stock of government debt; the stock of debt will fall only if the budget deficit becomes *negative*. In this case, there is said to be a **budget surplus.**

debt-service payments Payments that represent the interest owed on a current stock of debt.

budget deficit Any shortfall of current revenue below current expenditure.

government debt The outstanding stock of financial liabilities for the government, equal to the accumulation of past budget deficits.

budget surplus Any excess of current revenue over current expenditure.

A budget deficit increases the stock of debt; a budget surplus reduces it.

The Primary Budget Deficit   Government expenditure comprises purchases of goods and services (G), and debt-service payments ($i \times D$). Since at any point in time the outstanding stock of government debt—determined by *past* government borrowing—cannot be influenced by current government policy, the debt-service component of total expenditures is beyond the control of the government. In contrast, the other components of the government's budget are said to be *discretionary* because the government can choose to change the levels of G or T. To capture the part of the budget deficit that is attributable to discretionary expenditures and revenues, the government's **primary budget deficit** is defined as the difference between government purchases and net tax revenues:

$$\text{Primary budget deficit} = G - T$$

The government's primary budget deficit shows the extent to which tax revenues are able to finance the *discretionary* part of total expenditure. Another name for discretionary expenditure is the government's *program spending*.

Because of the need to make debt-service payments, there are often large differences between the government's overall budget deficit (or surplus) and its primary budget deficit (or surplus). In the 2005–2006 fiscal year, for example, the Canadian government had about $221 billion in tax revenues and only $213 billion in expenditures. The overall surplus in that year was therefore $8 billion. But of the $213 billion in expenditures, $179 billion were discretionary or program expenditures and $34 billion were debt-service payments. Thus, while tax revenues exceeded total expenditures by $8 billion (the overall budget surplus), they exceeded *discretionary* expenditures by $42 billion ($221B – $179B). The primary budget surplus was therefore $42 billion.

In recent years, the federal government has had a significant primary budget surplus, indicating that tax revenues have been more than sufficient to cover program spending.

Deficits and Debt in Canada

Federal Government   In a growing economy, many macroeconomic variables such as the levels of government expenditure and tax revenue tend also to grow. As a result, rather than looking at the absolute size of the government deficit or debt, economists focus on government debt and deficits in relation to the overall size of the economy. Some budget deficits that would be unmanageable in a small country like New Zealand might be quite acceptable for a larger country like Canada, and trivial for a huge economy like the United States. Similarly, a government budget deficit that seemed crushing in Canada in 1907 might appear trivial in 2007 because the size of the Canadian economy is many times larger now than it was then.

The path of federal budget deficits since 1962 is shown in Figure 32-1. The top panel shows total federal spending and total federal tax revenues as percentages of GDP. The bottom panel shows the total federal budget deficit as a percentage of GDP. Large and persistent budget deficits began in the mid-1970s. Throughout the 1980s and early 1990s, the average budget deficit was over 5 percent of GDP. In the mid-1990s, the federal government embarked on a successful policy of deficit reduction and by 1998 reported its first budget surplus in almost twenty years. Ever since 1998, the federal budget has been in surplus.

primary budget deficit The difference between the government's overall budget deficit and its debt-service payments.

For the most recent federal budget forecasts, see the website for the Department of Finance: **www.fin.gc.ca**.

As we saw in the previous section, a deficit implies that the stock of government debt is rising. Thus, the persistent deficits that began in the 1970s have their counterpart in a steadily rising stock of government debt. Figure 32-2 shows the path of Canadian federal government debt since 1940. At the beginning of the Second World War, the stock of federal debt was equal to about 45 percent of GDP. The enormous increase in the debt-to-GDP ratio over the next five years reflects wartime borrowing used to finance military expenditures. From 1946 to 1974, however, there was a continual decline in the debt-to-GDP ratio. The economy was growing quickly during this period. But equally important was that the federal government in the post-war years typically ran significant budget surpluses. These two factors explain the dramatic decline in the debt-to-GDP ratio between 1946 and 1974.

By 1974 the federal debt was only 14 percent of GDP. The large and persistent budget deficits beginning in the mid-1970s, however, along with a general slowdown in the rate of economic growth, led to a significant upward trend in the debt-to-GDP ratio. The ratio climbed steadily from 1979 to 1996 when it peaked at over 69 percent of GDP. Then, with the significant reductions in the deficit beginning in 1996, the debt-to-GDP ratio began to fall. By 2006 the federal government's stock of debt was just below 38 percent of GDP, and was projected to fall to 25 percent by 2010.

Provincial Governments Canadian provincial governments are responsible for a significant fraction of total government revenues and expenditures. In many countries, sizable regional governments either do not exist, as in New Zealand, or are often required to run balanced budgets, as is the case for about two-thirds of the 50 states in the United States. In contrast, the size of Canadian provincial governments—measured by their spending and taxing powers relative to that of the federal government—means that an examination of government debt and deficits in Canada would not be complete without paying attention to the provincial governments' fiscal positions.

For example, in the 2005–2006 fiscal year, the federal government had $230 billion of tax revenues, representing 16.8 percent of GDP. In the same year, the combined provincial and territorial governments had more tax revenues—a total of $272 billion, or 19.8 percent of GDP.

FIGURE 32-1 Federal Government Expenditures, Revenues, and Deficit, 1962–2005

(i) Revenues and expenditures

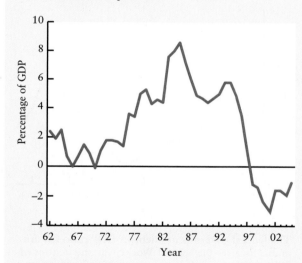

(ii) The budget deficit

The federal budget was in deficit every year between 1971 and 1997, but since 1998 there have been budget surpluses. Part (i) shows revenues and expenditures as a percentage of GDP. Part (ii) shows the budget deficit (or surplus) as a percentage of GDP.

(*Source:* Data from Department of Finance: www.fin.gc. ca. © Public Works and Government Services Canada.)

When examining the size and effects of budget deficits or surpluses, it is important to consider all levels of government—federal, provincial, territorial, and municipal.

The Canadian government ran very large budget deficits to finance Canada's participation in the Second World War. As a result, Canada's debt increased to 110 percent of GDP by 1946.

FIGURE 32-2   Federal Government Net Debt as Percentage of GDP, 1940–2005

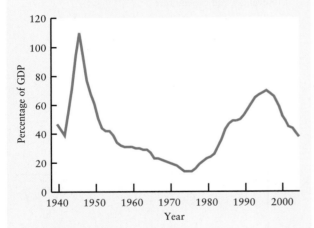

The federal government's debt-to-GDP ratio fell dramatically after the Second World War and continued falling until 1975. It then increased markedly for the next two decades. In the late 1990s when government deficits were reduced and the economy was in a healthy recovery, the debt-to-GDP ratio began to fall.

(*Source:* Statistics Canada, CANSIM database, Series V151548, and authors' calculations. Reprinted with permission of Statistics Canada.)

For macroeconomic data that are comparable across countries, see the OECD's website: **www.oecd.org**.

During the 1970s, the provincial governments were running budget deficits and so the stock of provincial government debt was increasing. But the deficits were small enough for the debt not to be growing relative to GDP. During the 1980s and early 1990s, however, provincial deficits grew dramatically. The provincial debt grew from roughly 4 percent of GDP in 1980 to 25 percent in 1998. Since then, most provincial governments have eliminated their deficits, and some are operating surpluses. By 2005–2006, the combined surplus for the provinces and territories was $9 billion, and their debt was 21 percent of GDP.

32.2 TWO ANALYTICAL ISSUES

Before we can discuss some of the macroeconomic effects of budget deficits and surpluses, we must examine two analytical issues: deficits and the stance of fiscal policy; and changes in the debt-to-GDP ratio.

The Stance of Fiscal Policy

In Chapters 22 and 24 we examined *fiscal policy*, which is the use of government spending and tax policies. We noted there that changes in expenditure and taxation normally lead to changes in the government's budget deficit or surplus. Thus, it is tempting to view changes in the government's budget deficit as reflecting changes in fiscal policy. For example, we could interpret a decrease in the deficit as indicating a contractionary fiscal policy, since the fall in the deficit is associated with either a reduction in government expenditures or an increase in tax revenue (or both). Was the dramatic fall in the Canadian federal budget deficit between 1995 and 1999 *purely* the result of fiscal policy?

No. In general, only some changes in the budget deficit are due to discretionary changes in the government's expenditure or taxation policies. Other changes have nothing to do with explicit changes in policy, but instead are the result of changes in the level of economic activity that are outside the influence of government policy. If our goal is to judge the stance of fiscal policy, however, it is only the changes in the deficit *caused by changes in policy* that are relevant.

The Budget Deficit Function   To see why the budget deficit can rise or fall even when there is no change in fiscal policy, recall the equation defining the government's budget deficit.

$$\text{Budget deficit} = (G + i \times D) - T$$

As we first discussed in Chapter 22, the level of net tax revenues typically depends on the level of national income, even with unchanged policy. For example, as income rises the level of revenue raised through income taxation also rises. Furthermore, as income rises there are typically fewer transfers (such as welfare or employment insurance) made to the private sector. Thus, net taxes, T, increase when national income increases. In contrast, the level of government purchases and debt-service payments can be viewed as more or less independent of the level of national income, at least over short periods of time. Thus, with no changes in expenditure or taxation policies, the budget deficit will tend to increase in recessions and fall in booms. That is, there is a negative relationship between national income and the government's budget deficit.

For a given set of expenditure and taxation policies, the budget deficit rises as real GDP falls, and falls as real GDP rises.

Figure 32-3 plots this basic relationship, which is called the **budget deficit function**. When the government determines its expenditure and taxation polices, it determines the *position* of the budget deficit function. A more expansionary fiscal policy shifts the budget deficit function up. A more contractionary fiscal policy shifts the budget deficit function down. In contrast, a change in the level of real GDP in the absence of any policy change will represent a *movement along* the budget deficit function. Thus, for a given set of policies, the budget deficit will decrease when Y rises and increase when Y falls.

Fiscal policy determines the position of the budget deficit function. Changes in real GDP lead to movements along a given budget deficit function.

The Cyclically Adjusted Deficit   We have said that a more expansionary fiscal policy will shift the budget deficit function up, whereas a more contractionary policy will shift it down. Therefore, *if we could hold real GDP constant*, an increase in the deficit would reveal a fiscal expansion, whereas a decrease in the deficit would reveal a fiscal contraction. While we cannot actually hold GDP constant in practice, we can accomplish the same thing by measuring what the budget deficit would be at a specific level of GDP. The **cyclically adjusted deficit (CAD)** does just this; it measures the deficit as if real GDP were equal to Y^*. Changes in the CAD then reveal changes in the stance of fiscal policy, as illustrated in Figure 32-4.

budget deficit function A relationship that plots, for a given fiscal policy, the government's budget deficit as a function of the level of real GDP.

cyclically adjusted deficit (CAD) An estimate of what the government budget deficit would be if real GDP were equal to Y^*.

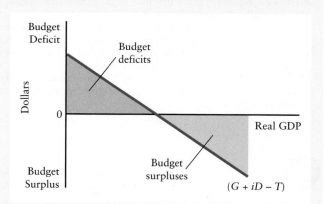

FIGURE 32-3   The Budget Deficit Function

For given government purchases and debt-service payments, there is a negative relationship between real GDP and the government budget deficit. G and iD are assumed to be independent of the level of real GDP. In contrast, a rise in real GDP leads to higher tax revenues and lower transfers, and thus to higher net tax revenue, T. Thus, the budget deficit falls as real GDP increases. Therefore, even with unchanged fiscal policies, changes in real GDP will lead to changes in the budget deficit.

A more expansionary fiscal policy implies an increase in spending or a reduction in taxes *at any level of real GDP*, and thus an upward shift of the budget deficit function. A more contractionary fiscal policy shifts the budget deficit function down.

FIGURE 32-4   The Cyclically Adjusted Deficit and Changes in Fiscal Policy

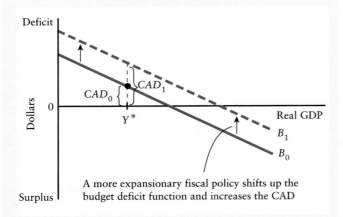

A more expansionary fiscal policy shifts up the budget deficit function and increases the CAD

A more expansionary fiscal policy increases the cyclically adjusted deficit; a more contractionary fiscal policy reduces it. Initially, fiscal policy gives rise to the budget deficit function B_0. Changes in real GDP will change the actual budget deficit, but the CAD is the deficit that would exist if real GDP were equal to Y^*. With the budget deficit function B_0, the cyclically adjusted deficit is CAD_0. Now suppose that fiscal policy becomes more expansionary because of greater spending or a reduction in taxes. The budget deficit function shifts upward to B_1 and the cyclically adjusted deficit rises to CAD_1. The increase in the CAD reveals the expansionary change in fiscal policy. Conversely, a more contractionary fiscal policy would shift the budget deficit function down and reduce the CAD.

Practise with Study Guide Chapter 32, Exercise 2.

An expansionary change in fiscal policy increases the cyclically adjusted deficit; a contractionary change in fiscal policy reduces the cyclically adjusted deficit.

Figure 32-5 shows the cyclically adjusted deficit in Canada, and plots it together with the actual budget deficit. Both are expressed as percentages of GDP and represent the combined budget deficits of all levels of government. Unlike the actual budget deficit, which can be precisely measured, the cyclically adjusted deficit can only be estimated. The reason is that its value depends on the value of potential GDP, Y^*, which itself is not directly observable and hence must be estimated. Note from Figure 32-5 that the actual deficit is larger than the cyclically adjusted deficit during times of recessionary gaps such as 1981–1985 and 1990–1998. This relationship reflects the fact that during these periods actual GDP is less than potential GDP and thus actual tax revenues are *less than they would be if output were equal to potential.* Conversely, the actual budget deficit is less than the cyclically adjusted deficit during periods of inflationary gaps, such as 1986–1989 and 2000, reflecting the fact that during these periods actual GDP is greater than potential and thus tax revenues are *greater than they would be if output were equal to potential.* In years where the actual deficit is approximately equal to the cyclically adjusted deficit, such as 1985, 1990, and 1999, real GDP is approximately equal to potential.

Changes in the expansionary or contractionary stance of fiscal policy are shown by the *changes* in the cyclically adjusted deficit. For example, the dramatic rise in Canada's cyclically adjusted deficit from 1982 to 1985 reveals a considerable fiscal expansion; the more gradual decline from 1985 to 1994 reveals a moderate fiscal contraction. From 1994 to 2000, the very substantial fiscal contraction, at both federal and provincial levels, led to the sharp decline in the cyclically adjusted deficit. Since 2000, the combined government sector has had an actual and cyclically adjusted budget surplus of about 1 percent of GDP, and the stance of fiscal policy has not changed markedly.

Changes in the Debt-to-GDP Ratio

In order to gauge the importance of government deficits and debt they should be considered relative to the size of the economy. This is why economists often discuss the federal government's debt-to-GDP ratio rather than the absolute amount of government debt. Here we examine the link between the overall budget deficit, the primary budget deficit, and changes in the debt-to-GDP ratio.

With a little algebra, it is possible to write a simple expression that relates the government's primary budget deficit to the change in the debt-to-GDP ratio. (To see the complete derivation of this equation, see *Extensions in Theory 32-1*.) The equation is:

$$\Delta d = x + (r - g) \times d$$

where d is the debt-to-GDP ratio, x is the government's primary budget deficit as a percentage of GDP, r is the real interest rate on government bonds, g is the growth rate of real GDP, and Δd is the *change* in the debt-to-GDP ratio.

This simple equation shows two separate forces, each of which tend to increase the debt-to-GDP ratio. First, if the real interest rate exceeds the growth rate of real GDP (if r exceeds g), the debt-to-GDP ratio will rise, for the simple reason that the debt accumulates at a faster rate than GDP grows. Second, if the government has a *primary* budget deficit (if x is positive), the debt-to-GDP ratio will rise because the government is incurring new debt to finance its program spending.

Let's use some recent numbers for Canada to interpret this equation. In the 2005–2006 fiscal year, the federal government had a primary budget surplus of 3 percent of GDP, so x was −0.03. The real interest rate on government bonds, r, was about 2.5 percent, or 0.025, while the growth rate of real GDP was about 3 percent, 0.03. Finally, the government's

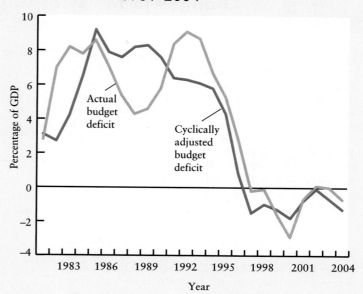

FIGURE 32-5 The Actual and Cyclically Adjusted Deficit, Combined Government, 1981–2004

The difference between the actual budget deficit and the cyclically adjusted budget deficit reveals the level of output compared to potential. The changes in the cyclically adjusted deficit show changes in the stance of fiscal policy. The actual budget deficit is above the cyclically adjusted budget deficit when output is below potential; the actual deficit is less than the cyclically adjusted deficit when output is above potential. An increase in the cyclically adjusted deficit reveals a fiscal expansion; a decrease reveals a fiscal contraction.

(*Source:* Data from Department of Finance: www.fin.gc.ca. © Public Works and Government Services Canada.)

outstanding stock of debt at the start of the fiscal year was about 38 percent of GDP, 0.38. Putting this information together, we see that Δd was

$$\Delta d = -0.03 + (0.025 - 0.03) \times (0.38)$$
$$= -0.032$$

which means that the government's debt-to-GDP ratio fell by over 3 percentage points during that fiscal year.

In the 2006 federal budget, the government announced its goal of further reducing the debt-to-GDP ratio to 25 percent by 2010. What is necessary for this objective to be met? First, continuing primary budget surpluses are helpful. Second, a real interest rate that is less than the growth rate of real GDP is helpful. If both of these occur, then the debt ratio will definitely fall; if only one of these two occurs, then the overall effect on the debt ratio will depend on the relative size of the two effects.

Practise with Study Guide Chapter 32, Exercise 3.

EXTENSIONS IN THEORY 32-1

Changes in the Debt-to-GDP Ratio

This box derives the simple equation in the text describing the change in the debt-to-GDP ratio. Let d be the debt-to-GDP ratio and let Δd be the amount by which d changes annually. Since d is a ratio, its change over time depends on the change in the numerator relative to the change in the denominator. That is, the debt-to-GDP ratio will increase if the stock of debt grows more quickly than GDP; it will decrease if the stock of debt grows less quickly than GDP. Representing the *percentage change* in d as $\Delta d/d$, we have*

$$\frac{\Delta d}{d} = \frac{\Delta D}{D} - \frac{\Delta\text{GDP}}{\text{GDP}}$$

Think about each of these terms separately. As you will recall from the first section of this chapter, the change in the stock of debt, ΔD, is equal to the amount of new government borrowing—that is, it is equal to the budget deficit. From the government's budget constraint, the deficit is equal to $(G - T + i \times D)$. The second term in the equation above is the growth rate of nominal GDP. Note that the growth rate of nominal GDP depends on both the rate of growth of real output and the rate of inflation. If we let g be the rate of growth of *real* GDP and π be the rate of inflation, then $g + \pi$ is the growth rate of nominal GDP.

_____

* For any variable X that is equal to the ratio of two other variables, Y/Z, the percentage change in X is closely approximated by the percentage change in Y *minus* the percentage change in Z. The lower are the rates of change of Y and Z, the better is this approximation.

We therefore rewrite the previous expression to get

$$\frac{\Delta d}{d} = \frac{G - T + i \times D}{D} - (g + \pi)$$

Now we multiply both sides by d to get an expression for the absolute change in the debt-to-GDP ratio:

$$\Delta d = \frac{G - T + i \times D}{D} \times d - (g + \pi) \times d$$

Since d is equal to D/GDP, our equation can be simplified:

$$\Delta d = \frac{G - T + i \times D}{\text{GDP}} - (g + \pi) \times d$$

Now recall that $(G - T)$ is the primary budget deficit. Let x be this primary budget deficit *as a percentage of GDP* and express the debt-service payments also as a percentage of GDP. This gives

$$\Delta d = x + i \times d - (g + \pi) \times d$$

Finally, recall that the real interest rate is equal to the nominal interest rate minus the rate of inflation,

$$r = i - \pi$$

We now combine terms to get

$$\Delta d = x + (r - g) \times d$$

which is the equation shown in the text.

If the real interest rate on government debt is approximately equal to the growth rate of real GDP, reductions in the debt-to-GDP ratio require the government to run primary budget surpluses.

This simple equation can be used to identify the various causes of the accumulation of Canada's federal debt, and also to illustrate some useful policy lessons regarding debt reduction. For more details, look for "What Caused the Build-Up of Canada's Public Debt?" in the *Additional Topics* section of this book's MyEconLab.

32.3 THE EFFECTS OF GOVERNMENT DEBT AND DEFICITS

Let's now examine why we should care about the size of the government deficit or surplus. We begin with the important idea that deficits *crowd out* private-sector activity and thereby may harm future generations. The opposite idea is equally important—that budget surpluses *crowd in* private-sector activity and therefore may be beneficial to future generations. In this section, we pose the issue as the effects of budget deficits. At the end of the section we review the arguments by discussing the effects of budget surpluses, which are currently more relevant in Canada.

Before beginning our analysis, we must be clear about an assumption in our macro model. As we saw earlier in this chapter, when the government increases its budget deficit, it necessarily increases its borrowing. This increase in borrowing is a reduction in the government's saving. In our model, we make the assumption that any reduction in the government's saving has only small effects on the amount of saving by the private sector—with the result that *national* saving falls along with government saving. Thus, we assume in our model that an increase in the government's budget deficit leads to a reduction in national saving. We make this assumption because it is consistent with the bulk of empirical evidence on this issue.

In our model, we assume that an increase in the government's budget deficit leads to a decrease in national saving. Alternatively, a reduction in the budget deficit leads to an increase in national saving.

The relationship between the government's budget deficit and national saving has been actively debated for many years. Central to this debate is the extent to which consumers and taxpayers are forward looking, and care about *future* tax changes. For more details on this debate, look for "Budget Deficits and National Saving" in the *Additional Topics* section of this book's MyEconLab.

w w w . m y e c o n l a b . c o m

Do Deficits Crowd Out Private Activity?

It is useful to make the distinction between closed and open economies. We consider the two cases separately.

Investment in Closed Economies We know from Chapter 26, in which we examined the relationship between saving and investment, that in a closed economy saving must exactly equal investment. The only way that a closed economy can save is to accumulate physical capital. Suppose in a closed economy there is an increase in the budget deficit, and thus a reduction in government saving, brought about either by an increase in government spending or a reduction in taxes. This reduction in government saving is assumed to lead to a similar reduction in national saving. As we saw in Chapter 26, the decrease in the supply of national saving will lead to an excess demand for loanable funds and thus to an increase in the interest rate. As the real interest rate increases, those components of aggregate demand that are sensitive to the interest

Practise with Study Guide Chapter 32, Extension Exercise E1.

crowding out The offsetting reduction in private expenditure caused by the rise in interest rates that follows an expansionary fiscal policy.

rate—investment in particular—will fall. The result is what is called the **crowding out** of domestic investment and other interest-sensitive expenditures; it is shown in Figure 32-6.

If a government budget deficit leads to a reduction in national saving, real interest rates will rise and private investment will be crowded out.

Net Exports in Open Economies   There is a second effect in an open economy when financial capital is internationally mobile. Consider once again the possibility that the Canadian government increases its budget deficit either by increasing spending or reducing taxes. What is the effect of the reduction in national saving in an open economy like Canada's?

As real interest rates rise in Canada, foreigners are attracted to the higher-yield Canadian assets and thus foreign financial capital flows into Canada. But since Canadian dollars are required in order to buy Canadian interest-earning assets, this capital inflow increases the demand for Canadian dollars and thus leads to an appreciation of the Canadian dollar.

This appreciation makes Canadian goods more expensive relative to foreign goods, inducing an increase in imports and a reduction in exports, thereby reducing Canada's net exports. In an open economy like Canada's, therefore, a rise in the government deficit leads to an appreciation of the currency and to a crowding out of net exports.

In an open economy, the government budget deficit attracts foreign financial capital and appreciates the domestic currency. The result is a crowding out of net exports.

Do Deficits Harm Future Generations?

In a closed economy, a rise in the government deficit pushes up interest rates and crowds out domestic investment. In an open economy a rise in the government deficit also appreciates the currency and crowds out net exports. In both cases, there may be a cost to future generations. Economists call this cost the *long-term burden of government debt*. Such a burden will be present if the private expenditure that is crowded out would have added more to the economy's productive capacity than what is added by the government's expenditure financed by the budget deficit. In this case, the economy's reduced productive capacity implies a lower future growth rate of potential GDP.

Budget deficits used to finance investment projects may not harm future generations because the future generations will benefit from the investment.

The previous paragraph suggests that whether government budget deficits harm future generations depends on the nature of the government goods and services being financed by the deficit. At one extreme, the government borrowing may finance a project that generates a substantial return to future generations, and thus the future generations may not be made worse off by today's budget deficit. An example might be the government's financing of long-term medical research projects that generate a return in the distant future. Another example is the government's financing of a new highway. At the other extreme, the government deficit may finance some government program that benefits mainly the current generation, and thus future generations may be harmed. An example might be the government's financing of cultural or sporting events that benefit the current generation but produce little or no benefits for future generations.

The concern that deficits may be inappropriately placing a burden on future generations has led some economists to advocate the idea of *cap-*

ital budgeting by the government. Under this scheme, the government would essentially classify each of its expenditures as either consumption or investment; the former would be spending that mostly benefits the current generation while the latter would be spending that mostly benefits future generations.

With capital budgeting, government deficits could be used to minimize the undesirable redistributions of income between generations. For example, the government might be committed to borrowing no more in any given year than the expenditures classified as investments. In this way, future generations would receive benefits from current government spending that are approximately equivalent to the future taxes they will pay.

Government budget deficits represent taxes that must be paid by future generations. Whether these future generations are harmed by the current budget deficit depends to a large extent on the nature of the government spending financed by the deficit.

Does Government Debt Hamper Economic Policy?

The costs imposed on future generations by government debt are very real. Unfortunately, the fact that these costs sometimes occur in the very distant future often leads us to ignore their importance. But other problems associated with the presence of government debt are more immediately apparent. In particular, government debt may make the conduct of monetary and fiscal policy more difficult.

Monetary Policy To see how a large stock of government debt can hamper the conduct of monetary policy, consider a country that has a high debt-to-GDP ratio and that has a real interest rate above the growth rate of GDP. As we saw previously, the debt-to-GDP ratio will continue to grow in this situation unless the government starts running significant primary budget *surpluses*. But such primary surpluses require either increases in taxation or reductions in program spending, both of which are politically unpopular. If such primary surpluses look unlikely to be achieved in the near future, both foreign and domestic creditors may come to expect the government to put pressure on the central bank to purchase—or *monetize*—an

FIGURE 32-6 The Crowding Out of Investment

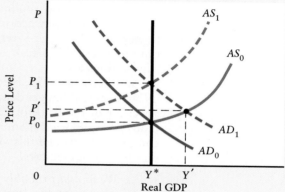

(i) Aggregate demand and supply

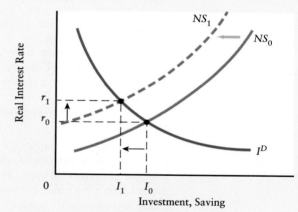

(ii) Saving and investment $(Y = Y^*)$

For a closed economy whose real GDP equals potential, an increase in the budget deficit will cause a reduction in national saving, an increase in the interest rate, and a reduction in investment. Consider a closed economy that is in long-run equilibrium at Y^* and P_0 in part (i). Suppose the government increases its spending or reduces its taxes, thus increasing the budget deficit. Either policy raises aggregate demand and shifts AD_0 to AD_1. The new short-run equilibrium is at Y' and P', but the adjustment process will then cause factor prices to rise, shifting the AS curve from AS_0 to AS_1. The new long-run equilibrium will be at Y^* and P_1.

The effect of this change on saving and investment can be seen in part (ii), which shows the market for loanable funds in the long run, with real GDP equal to Y^*. The increase in the government's budget deficit reduces national saving and shifts NS_0 to NS_1. The equilibrium real interest rate rises and the amount of investment falls from I_0 to I_1.

increasing portion of its deficit. Such monetization means that the money supply is increasing and will eventually be reflected in higher inflation. Any ensuing inflation would thus erode the real value of the bonds held by creditors. Such fears of future debt monetization will lead to expectations of future inflation and thus will put upward pressure on nominal interest rates and on some prices and wages. Thus, even in the absence of any actions by the central bank to increase the rate of growth of the money supply, a large government debt may lead to the *expectation* of future inflation, thus hampering the task of the central bank in keeping inflation and inflationary expectations low.

In December 1995, before the federal government had been successful in reducing its large annual budget deficits and thus slowing the rise of the debt-to-GDP ratio, the governor of the Bank of Canada at the time, Gordon Thiessen, appeared before the House of Commons Standing Committee on Public Accounts. His comments to that committee expressed this view that high levels of government debt generate concerns on the part of creditors.

> *... We would probably all agree... that our society needs to sort out its views about acceptable levels of taxation and the size of government, and those views can influence the amount of debt our society can afford to carry. However, when you reach a high debt-to-GDP ratio, what is sustainable is also very much influenced by the willingness of investors in financial markets to hold your debt.*
>
> *I do not mean to imply that financial markets might suddenly decide to stop lending to Canadian governments. What happens, as recent experience has shown, is that at very high levels of debt, there may be an increasing nervousness among lenders so that they would only continue to hold Canadian government debt at much higher interest rates.*[1]

Fiscal Policy In Chapter 22 we saw that fiscal policy could potentially be used to stabilize aggregate demand and thereby stabilize real GDP. For example, during a recession the government might reduce tax rates or increase spending to stimulate aggregate demand; in a booming economy, the government might reduce spending or increase tax rates to reduce inflationary pressures. Having cyclically-adjusted budget deficits in recessions and cyclically-adjusted budget surpluses in booms is one way of implementing *counter-cyclical fiscal policy*.

How does the presence of government debt affect the government's ability to conduct such counter-cyclical fiscal policy? Perhaps the easiest way to answer this question is to recall the equation that describes the change in the debt-to-GDP ratio:

$$\Delta d = x + (r - g) \times d$$

This equation shows that the *change* in the debt-to-GDP ratio (Δd) depends on the *level* of the debt-to-GDP ratio (d). For example, if the real interest rate exceeds the growth rate of real GDP, so that $r - g$ is positive, the increase in the debt-to-GDP ratio (Δd) will be higher if d is already high than if it is low (for any given value of x).

With this relationship in mind, consider the dilemma faced during a recession by a government that is considering an expansionary fiscal policy. Such an expansionary fiscal policy would increase the primary budget deficit and therefore increase x. On the one hand, the short-run benefits of a fiscal expansion in terms of raising the level of

---

1 Comments by Gordon Thiessen in the *Bank of Canada Review*, Winter 1995–1996.

real GDP seem clear; on the other hand, the same government may be wary of taking actions that lead to large increases in the debt-to-GDP ratio.

If the stock of outstanding government debt is small relative to the size of the economy, the government has a great deal of flexibility in conducting counter-cyclical fiscal policy. The small value of d implies that d will be rising only slowly in the absence of a primary deficit. Thus, the government may be able to increase the primary deficit—either by increasing program spending or by reducing tax rates—without generating a large increase in the debt-to-GDP ratio. But the government has significantly less flexibility if the stock of outstanding government debt is already very large. In this case, the high value of d means that even in the absence of a primary budget deficit, d will be increasing quickly. Thus, any increase in the primary deficit brought about by the counter-cyclical fiscal policy runs the danger of generating increases in the debt-to-GDP ratio that may be viewed by creditors as unsustainable. As the previous quote from Gordon Thiessen suggests, such perceptions of unsustainability may lead to an increase in the real interest rate on government debt, which exacerbates the problem by driving d up even faster.

The idea that a large and rising stock of government debt could "tie the hands" of the government in times when it would otherwise want to conduct counter-cyclical fiscal policy was brought to the fore of Canadian economic policy by the late Douglas Purvis of Queen's University (and a co-author on this textbook for many years). Purvis argued in the mid-1980s that Canadian government deficits must be brought under control quickly so that the debt would not accumulate to the point where the government would have no room left for fiscal stabilization policy. These warnings were not heeded. By the onset of the next recession in 1990, the federal government had added roughly $200 billion to the stock of debt and, predictably, the government felt unable to use discretionary fiscal policy to reduce some of the effects of the recession.

Notice that during our analysis of the effects of government deficits and debt, we never mentioned *who* buys the bonds issued by the government. In particular, we have made no distinction between government bonds held by Canadians and those held by foreign residents. However, we often hear the claim that foreign-held debt is a serious problem, because the government's debt-service payments leave the country, whereas government debt held by domestic residents is not a problem because it is just money "we owe to ourselves." *Applying Economic Concepts 32-1* investigates this issue, and explains why it may be irrelevant *who* holds the government debt.

Current Budget Surpluses

We have been discussing the effects of government debt and deficits on the economy. As we saw earlier, government deficits were an important part of the Canadian economic environment for over 20 years from the early 1970s to the mid-1990s. But by 1998, after several years of devoted deficit fighting, the federal government had its first surplus in over 20 years, and most of the provinces had also eliminated their budget deficits. For the next several years, the federal government had modest budget surpluses. This period was also one of rapid economic growth. The combination of the surpluses and the fast-growing economy led to a dramatic decline in the debt-to-GDP ratio. From its peak of almost 70 percent in 1996, the debt-to-GDP ratio fell below 50 percent in 2001, fell below 40 percent by 2005, and is now projected to reach 25 percent by 2010.

To analyze the economic effects of budget surpluses, we need only to reverse the arguments that we have developed in this chapter. After all, an increase in the budget

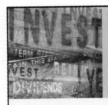

APPLYING ECONOMIC CONCEPTS 32-1

Is Foreign-Held Debt a Problem?

In 2006 about one-quarter of the federal government's debt was held outside Canada. Thus, of the $33 billion in interest payments made on the government debt in 2006, roughly $8 billion was paid to foreigners. This fact has led many commentators in the popular press to suggest that Canada "reclaim" its national debt and keep these "lost" interest payments. These observers seem to believe that if more of the Canadian government debt were held within Canada, then Canada would be a richer country.

How do we "reclaim" the debt? The federal government simply has to issue new debt to Canadians and use the proceeds of this borrowing to redeem existing debt held by foreigners. By so doing, the fraction of government debt held by Canadians would be increased and the fraction held by foreigners decreased. Advocates of this proposal argue that the result would be higher Canadian income in the long run as fewer interest payments are sent to foreign creditors.

Proponents of this view fail to recognize the importance of an *integrated* world capital market and the fact that government bonds are only one type of asset held by creditors. Suppose the federal government issued $1 billion of new "Canadians-only" bonds to Canadians and used the proceeds to redeem an equal amount of existing foreign-held federal government debt. Two questions must be addressed: (1) What would make Canadians buy such bonds? and (2) What would happen to Canada's net foreign indebtedness as a result? We deal with these two issues in turn.

In order to convince Canadians to buy $1 billion worth of these new bonds, these same Canadians must somehow be convinced to divert $1 billion from some other use. For example, they could give up $1 billion worth of consumption to buy these bonds or they could sell $1 billion worth of their holdings of private corporate bonds to buy these new government bonds. In the first case, the reduction in consumption implies an increase in private saving. But it is difficult to see why Canadians would be prepared to increase their private saving simply in response to a change in the ownership of the federal government debt. What might convince them to increase their saving is if these new bonds offered a rate of return greater than that of other assets available on the market. But, in this case, it is hard to see how the federal government could improve its fiscal position by issuing new high-interest-rate bonds to raise funds used to redeem existing lower-interest-rate bonds.

Suppose, then, that these new "Canadians-only" bonds are *not* successful in increasing the amount of total private saving. Instead, the issuance of these bonds simply leads some Canadians to sell $1 billion of their holdings of private corporate debt so they can purchase the new bonds. The government then takes the $1 billion raised by the selling of the new bonds and redeems $1 billion worth of foreign-held debt. The total amount of government debt is unchanged, but less of the government debt is held by foreigners. The story does not end there, however. Recall that Canadians were able to buy these new government bonds only by selling off some of their current holdings of private corporate debt. But with an unchanged pool of Canadian savings, these corporate bonds *must* then be bought by foreigners. Thus, total private corporate debt is unchanged, but *more* of it is held by foreigners. While it is true that the federal government has $1 billion less foreign-held debt, the private sector has $1 billion *more* foreign-held debt. And, though the government will now be making fewer interest payments to foreign creditors, the Canadian economy as a whole—the private plus public sectors—will be making the same interest payments to foreigners as before. Thus, the issuing of "Canadians-only" bonds, and the reduction in foreign-held government debt, has no effect on the stream of income available to domestic residents.

Is there some way for the Canadian economy to reduce its foreign indebtedness? Yes, but with a highly integrated global capital market like the one that exists today, schemes like Canadians-only bonds will not work. The only way that the Canadian economy can reduce its indebtedness to foreign creditors is to increase its national saving rate. This requires either an increase in private saving or an increase in public saving (that is, an increase in the government's budget surplus), or both. Thus, if the Canadian budget surpluses continue over the next few years, we should observe a gradual decline in Canadian foreign indebtedness.

surplus is just the same as a reduction in the budget deficit. But it will be useful to review and summarize these arguments. If the Canadian federal and provincial governments succeed in running budget surpluses over the next few years, our economic theory tells us we should start to see the following things:

- The rise in the government budget surplus will raise the level of national saving.
- The rise in national saving will create an excess supply of loanable funds, thus putting downward pressure on interest rates. The result will be a "crowding in" of investment.
- The budget surplus should also lead to a "crowding in" of net exports.
- As the surpluses continue, the stock of government debt will be falling. Combined with a growing economy, this will make the debt-to-GDP ratio fall relatively sharply.
- The lower debt-to-GDP ratio will reduce bondholders' fears of future monetization and thus reduce interest rates on government debt.
- The lower debt-to-GDP ratio will restore the government's flexibility to use counter-cyclical fiscal policy if the economy enters another recession.

Paul Martin was the federal finance minister from 1993 to 2002. During this period, the federal government's budget improved from a deficit of 6 percent of GDP to a surplus of 1 percent of GDP.

32.4 **FORMAL FISCAL RULES?**

After more than two decades of persistent budget deficits in Canada, and then several years of budget surpluses, the nature of political debate about fiscal policy has shifted. Whereas during the mid-1980s there was active political debate about whether deficits were a problem, and what costs would be involved in reducing them, all major political parties in Canada now stress the importance of avoiding budget deficits. In some quarters, there is support for the idea that legislation should be amended to make balanced budgets a legal requirement. Would such legislation be desirable? We examine two related but slightly different proposals.

Annually Balanced Budgets?

Balancing the budget on an annual basis would be extremely difficult to achieve. The reason is that a significant portion of the government budget is beyond the short-term control of the government, and a further large amount is hard to change quickly. For example, the entire debt-service component of government expenditures is determined by past borrowing and thus cannot be altered by the current government. In addition, as we saw in our discussion of the cyclically adjusted deficit, changes in real GDP that are beyond the control of the government lead to significant changes in tax revenues (and transfer payments) and thus generate significant changes in the budget deficit.

Even if it were possible for the government to control its path of spending and revenues perfectly on a year-to-year basis, it would probably be *undesirable* to balance the budget every year. We saw above that government tax revenues (net of transfers) tend to fall in recessions and rise in booms. In contrast, the level of government purchases is more or less independent of the level of real GDP. As a result, fiscal policy contains

Practise with Study Guide Chapter 32, Extension Exercise E2.

a built-in stabilizer as we first saw in Chapter 24; in recessions, the increase in the budget deficit stimulates aggregate demand whereas in booms the budget surplus reduces aggregate demand.

But things would be very different with an annually balanced budget. With a balanced budget, government expenditures would be *forced* to adjust to the changing level of tax revenues. In a recession, when tax revenues naturally decline, a balanced budget would require either a *reduction* in government expenditures or an *increase* in tax rates, thus generating a major *destabilizing* force on real GDP. Similarly, as tax revenues naturally rise in an economic boom, the balanced budget would require either an increase in government expenditures or a reduction in taxes, thus risking an overheating of the economy.

An annually balanced budget would accentuate the swings in real GDP, and thus undermine other stabilization policies being followed.

Cyclically Balanced Budgets?

One alternative to the extreme policy of requiring an annually balanced budget is to require that the government budget be balanced over the course of a full economic cycle. Budget deficits would be permitted in recessions as long as they were matched by surpluses in booms. In this way, the built-in stabilizers could still perform their important role, but there would be no persistent build-up of government debt. In principle, this is a desirable treatment of the tradeoff between the short-run benefits of deficits and the long-run costs of debt.

Despite its appeal, the idea of cyclically balanced budgets has its problems as well. Perhaps the most important problem with a cyclically balanced budget is an operational one. In order to have a law that requires the budget to be balanced over the business cycle, it is necessary to be able to *define* the cycle precisely. But there will always be disagreement about what stage of the cycle the economy is currently in, and thus there will be disagreement as to whether the current government should be increasing or reducing its deficit. Compounding this problem is the fact that politicians will have a stake in the identification of the cycle. Those who favour increased deficits will argue that this year is an unusually bad year and thus an increase in the deficit is justified; deficit "hawks," in contrast, will always tend to find this year to be unusually good, and thus a time to run budget surpluses.

Though a budget balanced over the course of the business cycle is in principle a desirable means of reconciling short-term stabilization with long-term fiscal prudence, the business cycle may not be well enough defined to make a formal policy of this type operational.

A second problem is largely political. Suppose one government runs large deficits for a few years and then gets replaced in an election. Would the succeeding government then be bound to run budget surpluses? What one government commits itself to in one year does not necessarily restrict what it (or its successor) does in the next year. This problem leads many in the United States to suggest a Constitutional Amendment to deal with deficits; once the Constitution is altered, any government is bound by it until, through a very lengthy process, it is changed again.

For some forecasts and analysis of the government's fiscal options, see the Royal Bank's website: **www.royalbank.ca**. Go to "corporate information" and then "economics."

Allowing for Growth

A further problem with any policy that requires a balanced budget—whether over one year or over the business cycle—is that the emphasis is naturally on the overall budget deficit. But, as we saw earlier in this chapter, what determines the change in the debt-to-GDP ratio is the growth of the debt *relative* to the growth of the economy. With a growing economy, it is possible to have positive overall budget deficits—and thus a growing debt—and still have a falling debt-to-GDP ratio. Thus, to the extent that the debt-to-GDP ratio is the relevant gauge of a country's debt problem, focus should be placed on the debt-to-GDP ratio rather than on the budget deficit itself.

Some economists view a stable (or falling) debt-to-GDP ratio as the appropriate indicator of fiscal prudence. Their view permits a budget deficit such that the stock of debt grows no faster than GDP.

By this standard, the budgets of the last several years have been "prudent" because they have led to a growth rate in the stock of debt smaller than the growth rate of real GDP, and thus a reduction in the debt-to-GDP ratio. For example, in 1996, the debt-to-GDP ratio reached its recent maximum of 70 percent. Significant fiscal contractions, combined with healthy economic growth, led to a decline in the debt-to-GDP ratio to 50 percent by 2001, and below 40 percent by 2005. If the current projections of modest budget surpluses for the next few years are realized, the government will achieve its target debt-to-GDP ratio of 25 percent by 2010.

S U M M A R Y

32.1 FACTS AND DEFINITIONS

- The government's budget deficit is equal to total government expenditure minus total government revenue. Since the government must borrow to finance any shortfall in its revenues, the annual deficit is equal to the annual increase in the stock of government debt. Whenever the deficit is positive, the stock of government debt is growing.

- The primary budget deficit is equal to the excess of the government's program spending over total tax revenues.
- Large and persistent budget deficits beginning in the 1970s increased the stock of debt so that by 1996 the federal government net debt was equal to 70 percent of GDP. By 2006, after several years of fiscal contraction, the federal debt-to-GDP ratio was 36 percent.

32.2 TWO ANALYTICAL ISSUES

- Since taxes (net of transfers) tend to rise when real GDP rises, the overall budget deficit tends to rise during recessions and fall during booms. This tendency makes the budget deficit a poor measure of the stance of fiscal policy.
- The cyclically adjusted deficit is the budget deficit that would exist with the current set of fiscal policies if real GDP were equal to potential GDP. Changes in the cyclically adjusted deficit reflect changes in the stance of fiscal policy.

- The change in the debt-to-GDP ratio from one year to the next is given by

$$\Delta d = x + (r - g) \times d$$

where d is the debt-to-GDP ratio, x is the primary deficit as a percentage of GDP, r is the real interest rate on government bonds, and g is the growth rate of real GDP.

32.3 THE EFFECTS OF GOVERNMENT DEBT AND DEFICITS LO 3 4

- In a closed economy, an increase in the budget deficit leads to a reduction in national saving and a rise in real interest rates. This increase in interest rates reduces the amount of investment and leads to a reduction in the growth rate of potential output.
- In an open economy, an increase in the budget deficit also pushes up interest rates and attracts foreign financial capital. This leads to a currency appreciation and a reduction in net exports.
- In either open or closed economies, the long-term burden of government debt is a redistribution of resources away from future generations and toward current generations.

- A large debt-to-GDP ratio may lead creditors to expect increases in inflation, as the government attempts to finance deficits through the creation of money. Such increases in inflationary expectations hamper the conduct of monetary policy.
- A large debt-to-GDP ratio also limits the extent to which the government can conduct counter-cyclical fiscal policy without risking large increases in the debt-to-GDP ratio that may be viewed by creditors as unsustainable.

32.4 FORMAL FISCAL RULES? LO 5

- Since tax revenues (net of transfers) naturally rise as real GDP increases, legislation requiring an annually balanced budget forces either expenditures to rise or tax rates to fall during booms. This produces destabilizing fiscal policy.
- Cyclically balanced budgets, in principle, permit the short-run benefits of deficits to be realized without incurring the long-run costs of debt accumulation. Implementation of this policy is difficult, however, since the precise identification of the business cycle is very controversial.
- In a growing economy, it is more sensible to focus on changes in the debt-to-GDP ratio than on balancing the budget over some specific horizon.

KEY CONCEPTS

Government's budget constraint
Primary budget deficit
The relationship between deficits and the national debt

Debt-service payments
Debt-to-GDP ratio
Crowding out of investment
Crowding out of net exports

Long-term burden of the debt
Annually balanced budget
Cyclically balanced budget

STUDY EXERCISES

1. Fill in the blanks to make the following statements correct.

   a. The government's budget constraint shows that government expenditures must be equal to the sum of _____ and _____.

   b. The government's annual budget deficit is the excess of total _____ over total _____ in a given year.

   c. If the government's total budget deficit is $20 billion and its debt-service payments are $18 billion, then its _____ is $2 billion. If the total budget deficit is $20 billion and its debt-service payments are $26 billion, then its _____ is $6 billion.

   d. In recent years, Canada has had a series of _____ and the debt-to-GDP ratio has been _____.

2. Fill in the blanks to make the following statements correct.

   a. When there is no change in the government's fiscal policy it is still possible for the budget deficit to fall because _____.

   b. For a given set of fiscal policies, the budget deficit _____ as real GDP rises and _____ as real GDP falls.

   c. The cyclically adjusted deficit is the budget deficit that would exist if real GDP equalled _____ and the government's _____ were at their current levels.

d. Suppose the real interest rate is 2 percent and the growth rate of real GDP is 1.5 percent. If the government wants to stabilize the debt-to-GDP ratio, then it is necessary to have a _____.

3. Fill in the blanks to make the following statements correct.

   a. In a closed economy, when the government borrows to finance the deficit, interest rates will _____ and some private investment will be _____.

   b. In an open economy, when the government borrows to finance the deficit, interest rates will _____, the Canadian dollar will _____, and net exports will _____.

   c. The long-term burden of government debt is the reduced _____ for future generations.

   d. Suppose a law was passed that required the government to balance its budget each year. Fiscal policy would then have a _____ effect.

   e. A cyclically balanced budget is difficult to implement because it is difficult to identify the _____.

4. **myeconlab** The table below shows government spending data over eight years in Debtland. All figures are in billions of dollars. The symbols used are as defined in the text.

Year	G (1)	T (2)	iD (3)	Budget Deficit (4)	Primary Budget Deficit (5)	Stock of Debt (6)
2002	175	175	25	—	—	—
2003	180	180	26	—	—	—
2004	185	185	27	—	—	—
2005	188	190	26	—	—	—
2006	185	195	25	—	—	—
2007	185	200	24	—	—	—
2008	180	205	23	—	—	—
2009	175	210	22	—	—	—

   a. Compute Debtland's budget deficit in each year and complete column 4 in the table. (Since we are computing the deficit, a negative number indicates a surplus.)

   b. Compute Debtland's primary budget deficit in each year and complete column 5 in the table.

   c. Suppose the initial stock of debt (in 2001) was $400 billion. Noting that the deficit in 2002 adds to the existing stock of debt, what is the stock of debt by the end of 2002?

   d. Compute the stock of debt for each year and complete column 6 in the table.

   e. Suppose you know that Debtland's debt-to-GDP ratio was the same in 2009 as in 2001. By what percentage did GDP grow between 2001 and 2009?

5. **myeconlab** The figure below shows the budget deficit function for a country.

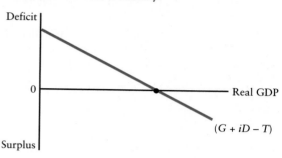

   a. Explain why the budget deficit function is downward sloping.

   b. If the government increases its level of purchases (G), what happens to the budget deficit at any level of real GDP? Show this in the diagram.

   c. If the government increases its level of net tax revenues (T), what happens to the deficit at any level of real GDP? Show this in the diagram.

   d. Explain why a rise in the actual budget deficit does not necessarily reflect a change in fiscal policy. How would a fiscal expansion appear in the diagram? A fiscal contraction?

6. **myeconlab** In the late 1990s, the U.S. government was slightly ahead of the Canadian government in reducing its budget deficit. The following table shows the actual budget deficit and the cyclically adjusted deficit (both as a percentage of GDP) for the United States from 1989 to 1997.

Year	Actual Deficit	CAD
1989	2.8	2.9
1990	3.9	3.2
1991	4.6	3.4
1992	4.7	3.7
1993	3.9	3.7
1994	3.0	2.8
1995	2.3	2.6
1996	1.4	1.6
1997	0.3	1.0

a. On a scale diagram (with the year on the horizontal axis) graph the actual deficit and the cyclically adjusted deficit.
b. Identify the periods when U.S. fiscal policy was expansionary.
c. Identify the periods when U.S. fiscal policy was contractionary.
d. Look back at Figure 32-5. How does the stance of U.S. fiscal policy over this period compare with Canada's?

7. The following table shows hypothetical data from 1999 to 2005 that can be used to compute the change in the debt-to-GDP ratio. The symbols used are as defined in the text.

Year	x (1)	r (2)	g (3)	d (4)	Δd (5)
1999	0.03	0.045	0.025	0.70	—
2000	0.02	0.04	0.025	—	—
2001	0.01	0.035	0.025	—	—
2002	0.00	0.035	0.025	—	—
2003	−0.01	0.03	0.025	—	—
2004	−0.02	0.03	0.025	—	—
2005	−0.03	0.025	0.025	—	—

a. Remember from the text that the change in the debt-to-GDP ratio (Δd) during a year is given by $\Delta d = x + (r - g)d$. Compute Δd for 1999.
b. Column 4 is the debt-to-GDP ratio. Note that d in 2000 is equal to d from 1999 plus Δd in 1999. Compute d in 2000.
c. Using the same method, compute d and Δd for each year, and complete columns 4 and 5.
d. Plot d in a scale diagram with the year on the horizontal axis. What discretionary variable was most responsible for the observed decline in d?
e. Note that as the primary deficit (x) falls between 1999 and 2005, there is also a downward trend in the real interest rate. Can you offer an explanation for this?

8. The diagram below shows an AD/AS diagram. The economy begins at E_0 with output equal to Y^*. Suppose the government in this closed economy increases G and finances it by running a deficit (borrowing). The AD curve shifts to the right.

a. How does the interest rate at E_1 compare with that at E_0? Explain.
b. Given your answer to part (a), how does investment at E_1 compare to investment at E_0?
c. Explain the economy's adjustment toward E_2. What happens to the interest rate and investment?
d. What is the long-run effect of the fiscal expansion? How would this be reflected in the diagram?

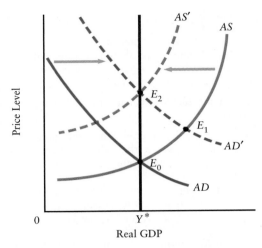

9. The diagram below shows an AD/AS diagram. The economy begins at E_0 with output equal to Y^*. Suppose the government in this closed economy decreases its budget deficit by increasing T (and keeping G unchanged), thus causing the AD curve to shift to the left.

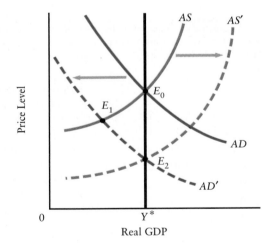

a. How does the interest rate at E_1 compare with that at E_0? Explain.
b. Given your answer to part (a), how does investment at E_1 compare to investment at E_0?
c. Explain the economy's adjustment toward E_2. What happens to the interest rate and investment?
d. What is the long-run effect of the government deficit? How would this be reflected in the diagram?
e. Comparing the short-run and the long-run effects of this policy, what dilemma does the government face in reducing its deficit?

DISCUSSION QUESTIONS

1. Evaluate each of the following proposals to "control the deficit" in order to avoid the long-run burden of the debt.

   a. Maintain a zero cyclically adjusted deficit.
   b. Keep the debt-to-GDP ratio constant.
   c. Limit government borrowing in each year to some fixed percentage of national income in that year.

2. Judith Maxwell, a noted Canadian economist, has warned that "when interest rates are higher than the economic growth rate, the ratio of debt to GDP acquires dangerous upward momentum." Discuss why this is so. How does the primary deficit enter the analysis?

3. In a recent federal budget, the minister of finance announced that expenditures would rise, yet he still predicted that the budget surplus would increase. Explain how these statements should be interpreted.

4. Paul Martin was the federal minister of finance from 1993 to 2002 and is credited with reducing Canada's budget deficit during that period. He stressed the importance of using very conservative forecasts for economic growth. Explain the role of forecasts, and why Martin chose to use conservative ones.

5. In the text we discussed the effects of government budget deficits. In the past 15 years, however, the Canadian federal deficit has fallen markedly, from 5 percent of GDP in 1989 (the peak of the business cycle) to a *surplus* of 0.5 percent of GDP in 2006 (a peak in the business cycle). Discuss the likely short-term and long-term effects that you would expect to follow such a sustained *reduction* in the deficit.

6. A government official recently exclaimed, "The prime minister's policies are working! Lower interest rates combined with staunch fiscal policy have reduced the deficit significantly." What do interest rates have to do with government spending and taxes when it comes to deficit management?

7. In recent years, the U.S. federal budget deficit increased enormously—from a small surplus in 1998 to a deficit of roughly 5 percent of GDP by 2006. Over this period, government spending increased markedly and income taxes were reduced. What would our macro model predict for the path of U.S. net exports? Has that prediction been supported by the evidence?

CHAPTER 33

The Gains from International Trade

LO LEARNING OBJECTIVES

In this chapter you will learn

1. why the gains from trade depend on the pattern of comparative advantage.
2. how factor endowments and climate can influence a country's comparative advantage.
3. about the law of one price.
4. why countries export some goods and import others.

Canadian consumers buy cars from Germany, Germans take holidays in Italy, Italians buy spices from Africa, Africans import oil from Kuwait, Kuwaitis buy Japanese cameras, and the Japanese buy Canadian lumber. *International trade* refers to the exchange of goods and services that takes place across international boundaries.

The founders of modern economics were concerned with foreign trade problems. The great eighteenth-century British philosopher and economist David Hume (1711–1776), one of the first to work out the theory of the price system, developed his concepts mainly in terms of prices in foreign trade. Adam Smith (1723–1790), in *The Wealth of Nations,* attacked government restriction of international trade. David Ricardo (1772–1823) developed the basic theory of the gains from trade that is studied in this chapter. The repeal of the Corn Laws—tariffs on the importation of grains into the United Kingdom—and the transformation of that country during the nineteenth century from a country of high tariffs to one of complete free trade were to some extent the result of agitation by economists whose theories of the gains from international trade led them to condemn tariffs.

International trade is becoming increasingly important, not just for Canada but for the world as a whole. As Figure 33-1 shows, the volume of world trade has grown much faster than has world real GDP over the past half-century. Since 1950, the world's real GDP has increased by over six times, an average annual growth rate of 3.7 percent. Over the same period, however, the volume of world trade has increased by over 24 times, an average annual growth rate of 6.1 percent.

Figure 33-2 shows some data for Canadian trade in 2005. The figure shows the value of Canadian exports and imports of goods in several broad industry groupings. There are three important points to note from the figure. First, international trade is very important for Canada. In 2005, Canada exported $453 billion and imported over $388 billion in goods—if we added trade in services, the values would be higher by about $70 billion; each flow (exports and imports) amounts to over 40 percent of GDP. Second, exports and imports are roughly the same size, so that the *volume* of trade is

FIGURE 33-1   The Growth in World Trade, 1950–2004

The volume of world trade has grown much faster than world GDP over the past 50 years. The figure shows the growth of real GDP and the volume of trade since 1950. Both are expressed as index numbers, set equal to 100 in 1950. Real world GDP has increased over six times since 1950; world trade volume has increased 24 times.

(*Source:* International Trade Statistics 2005, Chart 11.1, available at the World Trade Organization website: www.wto.org. Go to "Resources" and select "Trade Statistics." Then click on "International Trade Statistics, 2005" and go to "Selected Long-Term Trends." Choose Table 11.1. © World Trade Organization (WTO) 2007.)

FIGURE 33-2   Canadian Exports and Imports of Goods by Industry, 2005

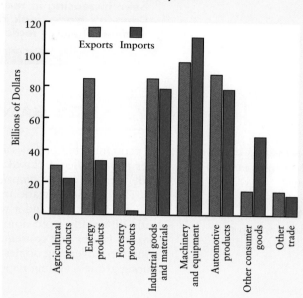

Canada exports and imports large volumes of goods in most industries. The data show the value of goods exported and imported by industry in 2005 (trade in services is not shown). The total value of goods exported was $453 billion; the total value of goods imported was $388 billion.

(*Source:* These data are available on Statistics Canada's website: www.statcan.ca. Search for "International trade." Reprinted with permission of Statistics Canada.)

much larger than the *balance* of trade—the value of exports minus the value of imports. Third, in most of the industry groupings there are significant amounts of both imports and exports. Such *intra-industry trade* will be discussed later in the chapter. Canada does not just export resource products and import manufactured goods; it also imports many resource products and exports many manufactured goods.

In this chapter, we inquire into the gains to living standards that result from international trade. We find that the source of the gains from trade lies in differing cost conditions among geographical regions. World income is maximized when countries specialize in the products in which they have the lowest opportunity costs of production. These costs are partly determined by natural endowments (geographical and climatic conditions), partly by public policy, and partly by historical accident.

For information on world trade, see the World Trade Organization's website: **www.wto.org**.

myeconlab

Canada trades with many countries, but most of our trade is with the United States, and the fraction of our total trade with the United States has been increasing in recent years. For more information on the location of Canada's trade, look for "Who Are Canada's Trading Partners?" in the *Additional Topics* section of this book's MyEconLab.

www.myeconlab.com

33.1 THE GAINS FROM TRADE

open economy An economy that engages in international trade.

closed economy An economy that has no foreign trade.

An economy that engages in international trade is called an **open economy**; one that does not is called a **closed economy**. A situation in which a country does no foreign trade is called one of *autarky*.

The benefits of trade are easiest to visualize by considering the differences between a world with trade and a world without it. Although politicians often regard foreign trade differently from domestic trade, economists from Adam Smith on have argued that the causes and consequences of international trade are simply an extension of the principles governing domestic trade. What are the benefits of trade among individuals, among groups, among regions, or among countries?

Interpersonal, Interregional, and International Trade

To begin, consider trade among individuals. Without trade, each person would have to be self-sufficient: Each would have to produce all the food, clothing, shelter, medical services, entertainment, and luxuries that he or she consumed. A world of individual self-sufficiency would be a world with extremely low living standards.

Trade among individuals allows people to specialize in activities they can do well and to buy from others the goods and services they cannot easily produce. A good doctor who is a bad carpenter can provide medical services not only for her own family but also for an excellent carpenter without the training or the ability to practise medicine. Thus, trade and specialization are intimately connected.

Without trade, everyone must be self-sufficient; with trade, people can specialize in what they do well and satisfy other needs by trading.

The same principle applies to regions. Without interregional trade, each region would be forced to be self-sufficient. With trade, each region can specialize in producing products for which it has some natural or acquired advantage. Prairie regions can specialize in growing grain, mountain regions in mining and forest products, and regions with abundant power can specialize in manufacturing. Cool regions can produce wheat and other crops that thrive in temperate climates, and hot regions can grow such tropical crops as bananas, sugarcane, and coffee. The living standards of the inhabitants of all regions will be higher when each region specializes in products in which it has some natural or acquired advantage and obtains other products by trade than when all regions seek to be self-sufficient.

This same basic principle also applies to nations. A national boundary is a political invention and rarely delimits an area that is naturally self-sufficient. Nations, like regions and individuals, can gain from specialization. More of some goods are produced domestically than residents wish to consume, while residents would like to consume more of other goods than is produced domestically. International trade is necessary to achieve the gains that international specialization makes possible.

With trade, each individual, region, or nation is able to concentrate on producing goods and services that it produces efficiently while trading to obtain goods and services that it does not produce efficiently.

Specialization and trade go hand in hand because there is no incentive to achieve the gains from specialization without being able to trade the goods produced for goods desired. Economists use the term **gains from trade** to embrace the results of both.

gains from trade The increased output due to the specialization according to comparative advantage that is made possible by trade.

Illustrating the Gains from Trade

Our discussion of individuals, regions, and countries emphasized the *differences* in their abilities to produce various products. In what follows we focus on trade between countries and, in order to focus on the differences across countries, we assume that within each country the average cost of production of any good is independent of *how much* of that good gets produced. That is, we are making the assumption of *constant costs*. Our example below involves only two countries and two products, but the general principles apply as well as to the case of many countries and many products.

Absolute Advantage   One region is said to have an **absolute advantage** over another in the production of good X when an equal quantity of resources can produce more X in the first region than in the second. Or, to put it differently, one country has an absolute advantage in the production of good X if it takes fewer resources to produce one unit of good X there than in another country. Table 33-1 shows an example. The two "countries" are Canada and the European Union (EU) and the two goods are wheat and cloth. The table shows the *absolute cost* of producing one unit of wheat and one unit of cloth in each country. The absolute cost is the dollar cost of the labour, capital, and other resources required to produce the goods. Thus, the country that can produce a specific good with fewer resources can produce it at a lower absolute cost.

absolute advantage The situation that exists when one country can produce some commodity at lower absolute cost than another country.

In Table 33-1, the absolute resource cost for both wheat and cloth is less in Canada than in the EU. Canada is therefore said to have an *absolute advantage* over the EU in the production of both wheat and cloth. Canada has an absolute advantage over the EU in producing these goods because it is a more efficient producer—it takes less labour and other resources to produce the goods in Canada than in the EU.

The situation in Table 33-1 is hypothetical, but it is encountered often in the real world. Some countries, because they have access to cheap natural resources or better-trained workers or more sophisticated capital equipment, are low-cost producers for a wide range of products. Does this mean that high-cost countries stand no chance of being successful producers in a globalized world of international trade? Will the low-cost countries produce everything, leaving nothing to be done by high-cost countries? The

TABLE 33-1   Absolute Costs and Absolute Advantage

	Wheat (kilograms)	Cloth (metres)
Canada	$1 per kilogram	$5 per metre
EU	$3 per kilogram	$6 per metre

Absolute advantage reflects the differences in absolute costs of producing goods between countries. The numbers show the dollar cost of the total amount of resources necessary for producing wheat and cloth in Canada and the EU. Note that Canada is a lower-cost producer than the EU for both wheat and cloth. Canada is therefore said to have an absolute advantage in the production of both goods.

Practise with Study Guide Chapter 33, Exercise 1.

comparative advantage The situation that exists when a country can produce a good with less forgone output of other goods than can another country.

answer is no. As we will see immediately, the gains from international trade do *not* depend on the pattern of absolute advantage.

Comparative Advantage   The great English economist David Ricardo (1722–1823) was the first to provide an explanation of the pattern of international trade in a world in which countries had different costs. His theory of *comparative advantage* is still accepted by economists as a valid statement of one of the major sources of the gains from international trade. A country is said to have a **comparative advantage** in the production of good X if the cost of producing X *in terms of forgone output of other goods* is lower in that country than in another. Thus, the pattern of comparative advantage is based on *opportunity costs* rather than absolute costs. Table 33-2 illustrates the pattern of comparative advantage in the Canada–EU example. The opportunity cost in Canada for one kilogram of wheat is computed by determining how much cloth must be given up in Canada in order to produce an additional kilogram of wheat. From Table 33-1, the absolute costs of wheat and cloth were $1 per kilogram and $5 per metre, respectively. Thus, in order to produce one extra kilogram of wheat, Canada must use resources that could have produced one-fifth of a metre of cloth. So the opportunity cost of one kilogram of wheat is 0.2 metres of cloth. By exactly the same reasoning, the opportunity cost of one metre of cloth in Canada is 5.0 kilograms of wheat. These opportunity costs are shown in Table 33-2.

Even though a country may have an absolute advantage in all goods (as Canada does in Table 33-1), it *cannot* have a comparative advantage in all goods. Similarly, even though a country may be inefficient in absolute terms and thus have no absolute advantage in any goods (as is the case for the EU in Table 33-1) it *must* have a comparative advantage in some good. In Table 33-2, Canada has a comparative advantage in the production of wheat because Canada must give up less cloth to produce one kilogram of wheat than must be given up in the EU. Similarly, the EU has a comparative advantage in the production of cloth because the EU must give up less wheat in order to produce one metre of cloth than must be given up in Canada.

The gains from specialization and trade depend on the pattern of comparative, not absolute, advantage.

TABLE 33-2   Opportunity Costs and Comparative Advantage

	Wheat (kilograms)	Cloth (metres)
Canada	0.2 m of cloth	5.0 kg of wheat
EU	0.5 m of cloth	2.0 kg of wheat

Comparative advantages reflect opportunity costs that differ between countries. The first column shows the opportunity cost of a kilogram of wheat in terms of the amount of cloth that must be given up. The second column shows the opportunity cost of a metre of cloth in terms of the amount of wheat that must be given up. Canada has a comparative advantage in wheat production because it has a lower opportunity cost for wheat than does the EU. The EU has a comparative advantage in cloth because its opportunity cost for cloth is lower than that in Canada.

In our example, total world wheat production can be increased if Canada devotes more resources to the production of wheat and fewer resources to the production of cloth—that is, if it *specializes* in wheat production. Similarly, total world cloth production can be increased if the EU devotes more resources to the production of cloth and fewer to wheat—if it specializes in cloth production. Such reallocations of resources increase total world output because each country is specializing in the production of the good in which it has the lowest opportunity cost. The gains from specialization along the lines of comparative advantage are shown in Table 33-3.

World output increases if countries specialize in the production of the goods in which they have a comparative advantage.

Not *any* pattern of specialization, however, is beneficial for the world. In our example, if Canada were to specialize in cloth and the EU in wheat, total world output would *fall*. To see this, note that in order to produce one extra metre of cloth in Canada, 5.0 kilograms of wheat must be sacrificed (see Table 33-2). Similarly, in order to produce four extra kilograms of wheat in the EU, two metres of cloth must be sacrificed. Thus, if each country produced these additional units of the "wrong" good, total world output of wheat would fall by one kilogram and total output of cloth would fall by one metre.

Specialization of production *against* the pattern of comparative advantage leads to a decline in total world output.

We have discussed comparative advantage in terms of opportunity costs. We can also illustrate it by considering the two countries' production possibilities boundaries. Recall the connection between a country's production possibilities boundary and the opportunity costs of production. The slope of the production possibilities boundary indicates the opportunity costs. The existence of different opportunity costs across countries implies comparative advantages that can lead to gains from trade. Figure 33-3 illustrates how two countries can both gain from trade when they have different opportunity costs in production and those opportunity costs are independent of the level of production. An alternative diagrammatic illustration of the gains from trade appears in *Extensions in Theory 33-1* where the production possibilities boundary is concave (which means that the opportunity cost for each good is higher when more of that good is being produced).

The conclusions about the gains from trade arising from international differences in opportunity costs are summarized below.

1. Country *A* has a comparative advantage over Country *B* in producing a product when the opportunity cost of production in Country *A* is lower. This implies, however, that it has a comparative *dis*advantage in some other product(s).

2. The opportunity cost of product *X* is the amount of output of other products that must be sacrificed in order to increase the output of *X* by one unit.

3. When opportunity costs for all products are the same in all countries, there is no comparative advantage and there is no possibility of gains from specialization and trade.

4. When opportunity costs differ in any two countries and both countries are producing both products, it is always possible to increase production of both products by a suitable reallocation of resources within each country.

TABLE 33-3 The Gains from Specialization

	Changes from each country producing more units of the product in which it has the lower opportunity cost	
	Wheat (kilograms)	Cloth (metres)
Canada	+5.0	−1.0
EU	−4.0	+2.0
Total	+1.0	+1.0

Whenever opportunity costs differ between countries, specialization can increase the production of both products. These calculations show that there are gains from specialization given the opportunity costs of Table 33-2. To produce five more kilograms of wheat, Canada must sacrifice 1.0 m of cloth. To produce two more metres of cloth, the EU must sacrifice 4.0 kg of wheat. Making both changes increases world production of both wheat and cloth.

Practise with Study Guide Chapter 33, Exercise 4.

Practise with Study Guide Chapter 33, Extension Exercise E1.

The Gains from Trade with Variable Costs

So far, we have assumed that opportunity costs are the same whatever the scale of output, and we have seen that there are gains from specialization and trade as long as there are interregional differences in opportunity costs. If costs vary with the level of output, or as experience is acquired via specialization, *additional* gains are possible.

FIGURE 33-3 The Gains from Trade with Constant Opportunity Costs

(i) Canada

(ii) European Union

International trade leads to specialization in production and increased consumption possibilities. The purple lines in parts (i) and (ii) represent the production possibilities boundaries for Canada and the EU, respectively. In the absence of any international trade these also represent each country's consumption possibilities.

The difference in the slopes of the production possibilities boundaries reflects differences in comparative advantage, as shown in Table 33-2. In each part the opportunity cost of increasing production of wheat by the same amount (measured by the distance *ba*) is the amount by which the production of cloth must be reduced (measured by the distance *bc*). The relatively steep production possibilities boundary for Canada thus indicates that the opportunity cost of producing wheat in Canada is less than that in the European Union.

If trade is possible at some relative prices between the two countries' opportunity costs of production, each country will specialize in the production of the good in which it has a comparative advantage. In each part of the figure, the slope of the green line shows the relative prices at which trade takes place. Production occurs in each country at *S* (for specialization); Canada produces only wheat, and the EU produces only cloth.

Consumption possibilities for each country are now given by the green line that passes through *S*. Consumption possibilities are increased in both countries; consumption may occur at some point such as *d* that involves a combination of wheat and cloth that was not obtainable in the absence of trade.

Economies of Scale In many industries, production costs fall as the scale of output increases. The larger the scale of operations, the more efficiently large-scale machinery can be used and the more a detailed division of tasks among workers is possible. Small countries (such as Switzerland, Belgium, and Israel) whose domestic markets are not large enough to exploit economies of scale would find it prohibitively expensive to become self-sufficient by producing a little bit of everything at very high cost.

One of the important lessons learned from patterns of world trade since the Second World War has concerned imperfect competition and product differentiation. Virtually all of today's manufactured consumer goods are produced in a vast array of differentiated product lines. In some industries, many firms produce this array; in others, only a few firms produce the entire array. In either case, they do not exhaust all available economies of scale. Thus, an increase in the size of the market, even in a large economy, may allow the exploitation of some previously unexploited scale economies in individual product lines.

These possibilities were first dramatically illustrated when the European Common Market (now known as the European Union) was set up in the late 1950s. Economists had expected that specialization would occur according to the theory of comparative advantage, with one country specializing in cars, another in refrigerators, another in fashion and clothing, another in shoes, and so on. This is not the way it worked out. Instead, much of the vast growth of trade was in *intra-industry* trade—that is, trade of goods or services within the same broad industry. Today, one can buy French, English, Italian, and German fashion goods, cars, shoes, appliances, and a host of other products in London, Paris, Berlin, and Rome. Ships loaded with Swedish furniture bound for London pass ships loaded with English furniture bound for Stockholm, and so on.

The same increase in intra-industry trade happened with Canada–U.S. trade over successive rounds of tariff cuts that were negotiated after the Second World War, the most recent being those associated with the 1989 Canada–U.S. Free Trade Agreement, and its 1994 expansion into the North American Free Trade Agreement (NAFTA) which included Mexico. In several broad industrial groups, including automotive products, machinery, textiles, and forestry products, both imports and exports increased in each country. What free trade in Europe and North America did was to allow a proliferation of differentiated products, with different countries each specializing in different subproduct lines. Consumers have shown by their expenditures that they value this enormous increase in the range of choice among differentiated products.

Wine is a good example of an industry in which there is much intra-industry trade. Canada, for example, imports wine from many countries but also exports Canadian-made wine to the same countries.

In industries with significant scale economies, small countries that do not trade will have low levels of output and therefore high costs. With international trade, however, small countries can produce for the large global market and thus produce at lower costs. International trade therefore allows small countries to reap the benefits of scale economies.

Learning by Doing

Learning by Doing   The discussion so far has assumed that costs vary with the *level* of output. But they may also vary with the *accumulated experience* in producing a product over time.

Early economists placed great importance on a concept that is now called **learning by doing**. They believed that as countries gained experience in particular tasks, workers and managers would become more efficient in performing them. As people acquire expertise, costs tend to fall. There is substantial evidence that such learning by doing does occur. It is particularly important in many of today's knowledge-intensive high-tech industries. The distinction between this phenomenon and economies of scale is illustrated in Figure 33-4. It is one more example of the difference between a movement along a curve and a shift of the curve.

The opportunity for learning by doing has an important implication: Policymakers need not accept *current* comparative advantages as given. Through such means as education and tax incentives, they can seek to develop new comparative advantages. Moreover, countries cannot complacently assume that their existing comparative advantages will persist. Misguided education policies, the wrong tax incentives, or policies that discourage risk taking can lead to the rapid erosion of a country's comparative advantage in particular products and industries.

learning by doing The reduction in unit costs that often results as workers learn through repeatedly performing the same tasks. It causes a downward shift in the average cost curve.

Sources of Comparative Advantage

David Ricardo's analysis taught us that the gains from trade arise from the pattern of comparative advantage. However, his analysis did not explain the *source* of a country's

EXTENSIONS IN THEORY 33-1

The Gains From Trade More Generally

Examining the gains from trade is relatively easy in the case where each country's production possibilities boundary is a straight line. What happens in the more realistic case where the production possibilities boundary is concave? As this box shows, the same basic principles of the gains from trade apply to this more complex case.

International trade leads to an expansion of the set of goods that can be consumed in the economy in two ways:

1. By allowing the bundle of goods consumed to differ from the bundle produced; and,

2. By permitting a profitable change in the pattern of production.

Without international trade, the bundle of goods produced is the bundle consumed. With international trade, the consumption and production bundles can be altered independently to reflect the relative values placed on goods by international markets.

Fixed Production

In each part of the figure, the purple curve is the economy's production possibilities boundary. In the absence of international trade, the economy must consume the same bundle of goods that it produces. Thus, the production possibilities boundary is also the consumption possibilities boundary. Suppose the economy produces and consumes at point a, with x_1 of good X and y_1 of good Y, as in part (i) of the figure.

Next suppose that with production point a, good Y can be exchanged for good X internationally. The consumption possibilities are now shown by the line tt drawn through point a. The slope of tt indicates the quantity of Y that exchanges for a unit of X on the international market—that is, the relative price of X in terms of Y.

Although production is fixed at point a, consumption can now be anywhere on the line tt. For example, the consumption point could be at b. This could be achieved by exporting y_2y_1 units of Y and importing x_1x_2 units of X. Because point b (and all others on line tt to the right of a) lies outside the production possibilities boundary, there are potential gains from trade. Consumers are no longer limited by their own country's production possibilities. Let us suppose that they prefer point b to point a. They have achieved a gain from trade by being allowed to exchange some of their production of good Y for some quantity of good X and thus to consume more of good X than is produced at home.

comparative advantage. Why do comparative advantages exist? Since a country's comparative advantage depends on its opportunity costs, we could also ask: Why do different countries have different opportunity costs?

Different Factor Endowments The traditional answer to this question was provided early in the twentieth century by two Swedish economists, Eli Heckscher and Bertil Ohlin. Ohlin was subsequently awarded the Nobel Prize in economics for his work in the theory of international trade. Their explanation for international differences in opportunity costs is now incorporated in the Heckscher-Ohlin model. According to their theory, the international cost differences that form the basis for comparative advantage arise because factor endowments differ across countries. This is often called the *factor endowment theory of comparative advantage.*

To see how this theory works, consider the prices for various types of goods in countries *in the absence of trade.* A country that is well endowed with fertile land but has a small population (like Canada) will find that land is cheap but labour is expensive. It will therefore produce land-intensive agricultural goods cheaply and labour-intensive goods, such as machine tools, only at high cost. The reverse will be true for

Variable Production

There is a further opportunity for the expansion of the country's consumption possibilities: With trade, production may be altered in response to international prices. The country may produce the bundle of goods that is most valuable in world markets. That is represented by the bundle *d* in part (ii). The consumption possibilities boundary is shifted to the line *t'*t' by changing production from *a* to *d* and thereby increasing the country's degree of specialization in good *Y*. For every point on the original consumption possibilities boundary *tt*, there are points on the new boundary *t'*t' that

allow more consumption of both goods—for example, compare points *b* and *f*. Notice also that, except at the zero-trade point *d*, the new consumption possibilities boundary lies *everywhere above the production possibilities curve*.

The benefits of moving from a no-trade position, such as point *a*, to a trading position, such as points *b* or *f*, are the *gains from trade* to the country. When the production of good *Y* is increased and the production of good *X* decreased, the country is able to move to a point such as *f* by producing more of good *Y*, in which the country has a comparative advantage, and trading the additional production for good *X*.

(i) Fixed production

(ii) Variable production

a second country that is small in size but possesses abundant and efficient labour (like Japan). As a result, the first country will have a comparative advantage in agricultural production and the second in goods that use much labour and little land.

According to the Heckscher-Ohlin theory, countries have comparative advantages in the production of goods that use intensively the factors of production with which they are abundantly endowed.

For example, Canada is abundantly endowed with forests relative to most other countries. According to the Hecksher-Ohlin theory, Canada has a comparative advantage in goods that use forest products intensively, such as newsprint, paper, raw lumber, and wooden furniture. In contrast, relative to most other countries, Canada is sparsely endowed with labour. Thus, Canada has a comparative disadvantage in goods that use labour intensively, such as cotton or many other textile products.

Canada is extremely well endowed with forests. It is no surprise, therefore, that it has a comparative advantage in a whole range of forestry products.

FIGURE 33-4 Economies of Scale vs. Learning by Doing

Specialization may lead to gains from trade through scale economies, learning by doing, or both. Consider a country that wishes to consume the quantity Q_0. Suppose it can produce that quantity at an average cost per unit of c_0. Suppose further that the country has a comparative advantage in producing this product and can export the quantity Q_0Q_1 if it produces Q_1. This may lead to cost savings in two ways.

First, the increased level of production of Q_1 compared to Q_0 permits it to *move along* its cost curve from a to b, thereby reducing costs per unit to c_1. This is an economy of scale.

Second, as workers and management become more experienced, they may be able to produce at lower costs. This is learning by doing and it shifts the cost curve from $LRAC$ to $LRAC'$. At output Q_1, costs per unit fall to c_2. The movement from a to b' incorporates both economies of scale and learning by doing.

Different Climates The factor endowment theory has considerable power to explain comparative advantage but it does not provide the whole explanation. One additional influence comes from all those natural factors that can be called *climate* in the broadest sense. If you combine land, labour, and capital in the same way in Nicaragua and in Iceland, you will not get the same output of most agricultural goods. Sunshine, rainfall, and average temperature also matter. If you seek to work with wool or cotton in dry climates, you will get different results than when you work in damp climates. (You can, of course, artificially create any climate you wish in a factory, but it costs money to create what is freely provided elsewhere.)

Climate affects comparative advantage.

Of course, if we consider "warm weather" a factor of production, then we could simply say that countries like Nicaragua are better endowed with that factor than countries like Iceland. In this sense, explanations of comparative advantage based on different climates are really just a special case of explanations based on factor endowments.

Acquired Comparative Advantage Today it is clear that many comparative advantages are *acquired*. Further, they can change. Thus, comparative advantage should be viewed as being *dynamic* rather than static. Many new industries are seen to depend more on human capital than on fixed physical capital or natural resources. The skills of a computer designer, a videogame programmer, or a sound mix technician are acquired by education and on-the-job training. Natural endowments of energy and raw materials cannot account for Silicon Valley's leadership in computer technology, for Canada's prominence in communications technology, for Taiwan's excellence in electronics, or for Switzerland's prominence in private banking.

If comparative advantage can be acquired, it can also be *lost*. If firms within one country fail to innovate and adopt the latest technologies available in their industry, but competing firms in other countries are aggressively innovating and reducing their production costs, the first country will eventually lose whatever comparative advantage it once had in that industry. In recent years, for example, pulp and paper mills in Canada have been closing, driven out of the industry by Scandinavian firms that more aggressively pursue improvements in productivity.

With today's growing international competition, no country's comparative advantages are secure unless its firms innovate and keep up with their foreign competitors.

myeconlab

The "race" between firms for innovation and productivity improvements is often used as an illustration for how countries also "compete" against each other in terms of international trade. Many observers appear to adopt this view when they argue that productivity growth in the developing world harms living standards in the developed countries. Is this argument correct? Look for "Does Third-World Growth Harm First-World Prosperity?" in the *Additional Topics* section of this book's MyEconLab.

w w w . m y e c o n l a b . c o m

Contrasting Views? This modern view is in sharp contrast with the traditional assumption that cost structures based largely on a country's natural endowments lead to a given pattern of international comparative advantage. The traditional view suggests that a government interested in maximizing its citizens' material standard of living should encourage specialization of production in goods for which it *currently* has a comparative advantage. If all countries follow this advice, each will be specialized in a relatively narrow range of distinct products. The British will produce engineering products, Canadians will be producers of resource-based primary products, Americans will be farmers and factory workers, Central Americans will be banana and coffee growers, and so on.

There are surely elements of truth in both extreme views. It would be unwise to neglect resource endowments, climate, culture, social patterns, and institutional arrangements. But it would also be unwise to assume that all advantages are innate and immutable.

To some extent, these views are reconciled by the theory of human capital, which is a topic we discussed in Chapter 14. Comparative advantages that depend on human capital are consistent with traditional Heckscher-Ohlin theory. The difference is that this type of capital is acquired through conscious decisions relating to such matters as education and technical training.

33.2 **THE DETERMINATION OF TRADE PATTERNS**

Comparative advantage has been the central concept in our discussion about the gains from trade. If Canada has a comparative advantage in lumber and Italy has a comparative advantage in shoes, then the total output of lumber and shoes can be increased if Canada specializes in the production of lumber and Italy specializes in the production of shoes. With such patterns of specialization, Canada will naturally export lumber to Italy and Italy will export shoes to Canada.

It is one thing to discuss the potential gains from trade if countries specialized in the production of particular goods and exported these to other countries. But do *actual* trade patterns occur along the lines of comparative advantage? In this section of the chapter we use a simple demand-and-supply model to examine why Canada exports some products and imports others. We will see that comparative advantage, whether natural or acquired, plays a central role in determining actual trade patterns.

For data on Canadian trade by industry and by country, go to Statistics Canada's website at **www.statcan.ca** and search for "trade."

There are some products, such as coffee and mangoes, that Canada does not produce (and will probably never produce). Any domestic consumption of these products must therefore be satisfied by imports from other countries. At the other extreme, there are some products, such as nickel or potash, of which Canada is one of the world's major suppliers, and demand in the rest of the world must be satisfied partly by exports from Canada. There are also some products, such as houses, that are so expensive to transport that every country produces approximately what it consumes.

Our interest in this section is with the vast number of intermediate cases in which Canada is only one of many producers of an internationally traded product, as with beef, oil, copper, wheat, lumber, and newsprint. Will Canada be an exporter or an importer of such products? And what is the role played by comparative advantage?

The Law of One Price

Whether Canada imports or exports a product for which it is only one of many producers depends to a great extent on the product's price. This brings us to what economists call the *law of one price*.

The law of one price states that when a product is traded throughout the entire world, the prices in various countries will differ by no more than the cost of transporting the product between countries. Aside from differences due to these transport costs, there is a single world price.

Many basic products—such as copper wire, steel pipe, iron ore, and computer RAM chips—fall within this category. The world price for each good is the price that equates the quantity demanded worldwide with the quantity supplied worldwide. The world price of an internationally traded product may be influenced greatly, or only slightly, by the demand and supply coming from any one country. The extent of one country's influence will depend on how important its quantities demanded and supplied are in relation to the worldwide totals.

The simplest case for us to study arises when the country, which we will take to be Canada, accounts for only a small part of the total worldwide demand and supply. In this case, Canada does not itself produce enough to influence the world price significantly. Similarly, Canadian purchases are too small a proportion of worldwide demand to affect the world price in any significant way. Producers and consumers in Canada thus face a world price that they cannot influence by their own actions.

In this case, the price that rules in the Canadian market must be the world price (adjusted for the exchange rate between the Canadian dollar and the foreign currency). The law of one price says that this must be so. What would happen if the Canadian domestic price diverged from the world price? If the Canadian price were below the world price, no supplier would sell in the Canadian market because more money could be made by selling abroad. The absence of supply to the Canadian market would thus drive up the Canadian price. Conversely, if the Canadian domestic price were above the worldwide price, no buyer would buy from a Canadian seller because money could be saved by buying abroad. The absence of demand on the Canadian market would thus drive down the Canadian price.

The Pattern of Foreign Trade

Let us now see what determines the pattern of international trade in such circumstances.

An Exported Product To determine the pattern of Canadian trade, we first show the Canadian domestic demand and supply curves for some product, say, lumber. This is done in Figure 33-5. The intersection of these two curves tells us what the price and quantity would be *if there were no foreign trade.* Now compare this no-trade price with the world price of that product.[1] If the world price is higher, the actual price in Canada will exceed the no-trade price. In this situation there will be an excess of Canadian supply over Canadian demand. Domestic producers want to sell Q_2 units of lumber but domestic consumers want to buy only Q_1 units. If Canada were a closed economy, such excess supply would drive the price down to p_d. But in an open economy with a world price of p_w, this excess supply gets exported to Canada's trading partners.

Countries export products whose world price exceeds the price that would exist domestically if there were no foreign trade.

What is the role of comparative advantage in this analysis? We have said that Canada will export lumber if the world price exceeds Canada's no-trade price. Note that in a competitive market the price of the product reflects the product's marginal cost, which in turn reflects the opportunity cost of producing the product. That Canada's no-trade price for lumber is lower than the world price reflects the fact that the opportunity cost of producing lumber in Canada is less than the opportunity cost of producing it in the rest of the world. Thus, by exporting goods that have a low no-trade price, Canada is exporting the goods for which it has a comparative advantage.

Countries export the goods for which they are low-cost producers. That is, they export goods for which they have a comparative advantage.

An Imported Product Now consider some other product—for example, computer RAM chips. Once again, look first at the domestic demand and supply curves, shown this time in Figure 33-6. The intersection of these curves determines the no-trade price that would rule if there were no foreign trade. The world price of RAM chips is below the Canadian no-trade price so that, at the price ruling in Canada, domestic demand is larger and domestic supply is smaller than if the no-trade price had ruled. The excess of domestic demand over domestic supply is met by imports.

Practise with Study Guide Chapter 33, Exercise 5.

Export Development Canada is a Crown corporation devoted to improving Canada's export prospects. For information about Canada's exports, check out its website: **www.edc.ca**.

FIGURE 33-5   An Exported Good

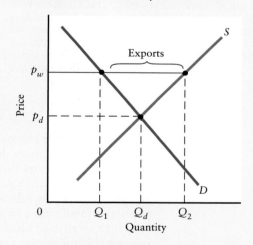

Exports occur whenever there is excess supply domestically at the world price. The domestic demand and supply curves are D and S, respectively. The domestic price in the absence of foreign trade is p_d, with Q_d produced and consumed domestically. The world price of p_w is higher than p_d. At p_w, Q_1 is demanded while Q_2 is supplied domestically. The excess of the domestic supply over the domestic demand is exported.

---

[1] If the world price is stated in terms of some foreign currency (as it often is), the price must be converted into Canadian dollars using the current exchange rate between the foreign currency and Canadian dollars.

FIGURE 33-6   An Imported Good

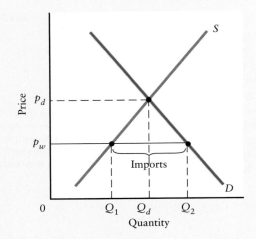

Imports occur whenever there is excess demand domestically at the world price. The domestic demand and supply curves are D and S, respectively. The domestic price in the absence of foreign trade is p_d, with Q_d produced and consumed domestically. The world price of p_w is less than p_d. At the world price Q_2 is demanded, whereas Q_1 is supplied domestically. The excess of domestic demand over domestic supply is satisfied through imports.

Countries import products whose world price is less than the price that would exist domestically if there were no foreign trade.

Again, this analysis can be restated in terms of comparative advantage. The high Canadian no-trade price of RAM chips reflects the fact that RAM chips have a higher opportunity cost in Canada than elsewhere in the world. This high cost means that Canada has a comparative disadvantage in RAM chips. So Canada imports goods for which it has a comparative disadvantage.

Countries import the goods for which they are high-cost producers. That is, they import goods for which they have a comparative disadvantage.

Is Comparative Advantage Obsolete?

In the debate preceding the signing of both the Canada–U.S. Free Trade Agreement and the North American Free Trade Agreement (NAFTA), some opponents argued that the agreements relied on an outdated view of the gains from trade based on comparative advantage. The theory of comparative advantage was said to be obsolete.

Contrary to such assertions, comparative advantage remains an important economic concept. At any one time—because comparative advantage is reflected in international relative prices, and these relative prices determine what goods a country will import and what it will export—the operation of the price system will result in trade that follows the current pattern of comparative advantage. For example, if Canadian costs of producing steel are particularly low relative to other Canadian costs, steel will be a Canadian export at international prices (which it is). If Canada's costs of producing textiles are particularly high relative to other Canadian costs, Canada will import textiles at international prices (which it does). Thus, there is no reason to change the view that Ricardo long ago expounded: *Current comparative advantage is a major determinant of trade under free-market conditions.*

What has changed, however, is economists' views about the *determinants* of comparative advantage. It now seems that current comparative advantage may be more open to change by private entrepreneurial activities and by government policy than used to be thought. Thus, what is obsolete is the belief that a country's current pattern of comparative advantage, and hence its current pattern of imports and exports, must be accepted as given and unchangeable.

The theory that comparative advantage determines trade flows is not obsolete, but the theory that comparative advantage is completely determined by forces beyond the reach of decisions made by private firms and by public policy has been discredited.

One caveat should be noted. It is one thing to observe that it is *possible* for governments to influence a country's pattern of comparative advantage. It is quite another to conclude that it is *advisable* for them to try. The case in support of a specific government intervention requires that (1) there is scope for governments to improve on the results achieved by the free market, (2) the costs of the intervention be less than the value of the improvement to be achieved, and (3) governments will actually be able to carry out the required interventionist policies (without, for example, being sidetracked by considerations of electoral advantage).

The Terms of Trade

We have seen that world production can be increased when countries specialize in the production of the goods for which they have a comparative advantage and then trade with one another. We now ask: How will these gains from specialization and trade be shared among countries? The division of the gain depends on what is called the **terms of trade**, which relate to the quantity of imported goods that can be obtained per unit of goods exported. The terms of trade are measured by the ratio of the price of exports to the price of imports.

terms of trade The ratio of the average price of a country's exports to the average price of its imports.

A rise in the price of imported goods, with the price of exports unchanged, indicates a *fall in the terms of trade*; it will now take more exports to buy the same quantity of imports. Similarly, a rise in the price of exported goods, with the price of imports unchanged, indicates a *rise in the terms of trade*; it will now take fewer exports to buy the same quantity of imports. Thus, the ratio of these prices measures the amount of imports that can be obtained per unit of goods exported.

The terms of trade can be illustrated along with the country's production possibilities boundary, as shown in Figure 33-7. The figure shows the hypothetical case in which Canada can produce only wheat and cloth. As we saw earlier, the slope of Canada's production possibilities boundary shows the relative opportunity costs of producing the two goods in Canada. A steep production possibilities boundary indicates that only a small amount of cloth must be given up to get more wheat; thus cloth is relatively costly and wheat is relatively cheap. A flatter production possibilities boundary indicates that a larger amount of cloth must be given up to get more wheat; thus cloth is relatively cheap and wheat is relatively expensive. Thus, the slope of the production possibilities boundary in Figure 33-7 shows the relative price of cloth (in terms of wheat) that Canada faces in the absence of international trade.

If, through international trade, Canada has access to different relative prices, Canada will be led to specialize in the production of one good or the other. In Figure 33-7, we show a case in which the

FIGURE 33-7   A Change in the Terms of Trade

A rise in the relative price of exports leads to a terms-of-trade improvement

Changes in the terms of trade lead to changes in a country's consumption possibilities. The hypothetical production possibilities boundary is shown for Canada. With international trade at relative prices T_0, Canada specializes in the production of wheat, producing at point S, but is able to consume at a point like A. It pays for its imports of cloth with its exports of wheat. If the price of wheat rises relative to the price of cloth, production remains at S but the line T_1 shows Canada's new consumption possibilities. Consumption can now take place at a point like B where consumption of both wheat and cloth has increased. The increase in the terms of trade makes Canada better off because of the increase in consumption possibilities.

Practise with Study Guide Chapter 33, Exercise 3.

world relative price of cloth is lower than the relative price Canada would have if it did not trade. Faced with a lower relative price of cloth, Canada ends up specializing in the production of the relatively high-priced product (wheat), and importing the relatively low-priced product (cloth). This point of specialization is point S in Figure 33-7.

The *green* lines in the figure show alternative values of the world relative prices— that is, alternative values for Canada's terms of trade. A rise in the terms of trade indicates a fall in the relative price of cloth (or a rise in the relative price of wheat). This increase in the terms of trade is shown as an upward rotation of the green line from T_0 to T_1. A reduction in the terms of trade is shown as a downward rotation in the green line, from T_1 to T_0.

It should be clear from Figure 33-7 why changes in the terms of trade are important. Suppose the international relative prices are initially given by T_0. Canada specializes in the production of wheat (point S) but consumes at some point like A where it finances imports of cloth with exports of wheat. Now suppose there is a shift in world demand toward wheat and away from cloth, and this leads to an increase in the relative price of wheat. The terms of trade increase to T_1 and, with unchanged production at point S, Canada can now afford to consume at a point like B where consumption of both wheat and cloth has increased.

A rise in a country's terms of trade is beneficial because it expands the country's consumption possibilities.

Conversely, a reduction in the price of a country's exports (relative to the price of its imports) is harmful for a country. In Figure 33-7, this is shown as a change of the terms of trade from T_1 to T_0. Even though production may remain unchanged, the range of goods available to be consumed falls, and this reduction in consumption possibilities leads to an overall loss of welfare.

How do we measure the terms of trade in real economies? Because international trade involves many countries and many products, we cannot use the simple ratio of the prices of two goods as in Figure 33-7. The basic principle, however, is the same. A country's terms of trade are computed as an index number:

$$\text{Terms of trade} = \frac{\text{Index of export prices}}{\text{Index of import prices}} \times 100$$

A rise in the index is referred to as a *favourable* change in a country's terms of trade (sometimes called a terms of trade *improvement*). A decrease in the index of the terms of trade is called an *unfavourable* change (or a terms of trade *deterioration*). For example, the sharp rise in oil prices in the 1970s led to large unfavourable shifts in the terms of trade of oil-importing countries. When oil prices fell sharply in the mid-1980s, the terms of trade of oil-importing countries changed favourably. The converse was true for oil-exporting countries.

Canada's terms of trade since 1961 are shown in Figure 33-8. As is clear, the terms of trade are quite variable, reflecting frequent changes in the relative prices of different products. Note the dramatic increase (improvement) in Canada's terms of trade in the early 1970s, reflecting the large increase in oil prices caused by OPEC's output restrictions. Since Canada is a net exporter of oil, its terms of trade improve when the price of oil increases. An even larger increase occurred in the 2002–2005 period, when the world prices of most commodities, especially energy-related commodities, increased sharply.

FIGURE 33-8   Canada's Terms of Trade, 1961–2005

Canada's terms of trade have been quite variable over the past 40 years. The data shown are Canada's terms of trade—the ratio of an index of Canadian export prices to an index of Canadian import prices. As the relative prices of lumber, oil, wheat, electronic equipment, textiles, fruit, and other products change, the terms of trade naturally change.

(*Source:* Statistics Canada, CANSIM database, Series V1997754 and V1997751 and authors' calculations. Reprinted with permission of Statistics Canada.)

S U M M A R Y

33.1 **THE GAINS FROM TRADE**

- Country A has an absolute advantage over Country B in the production of a specific product when the absolute resource cost of the product is less in Country A than in Country B.
- Country A has a comparative advantage over Country B in the production of a specific good if the forgone output of other goods is less in Country A than in Country B.
- Comparative advantage occurs whenever countries have different opportunity costs of producing particular goods. World production of all products can be increased if each country transfers resources into the production of the products for which it has a comparative advantage.
- Trade allows all countries to obtain the goods for which they do not have a comparative advantage at a lower

opportunity cost than they would face if they were to produce all products for themselves; specialization and trade therefore allow all countries to have more of all products than they could have if they tried to be self-sufficient.

- A nation that engages in trade and specialization may also realize the benefits of economies of large-scale production and of learning by doing.
- Classical theory regarded comparative advantage as largely determined by natural resource endowments that are difficult to change. Economists now believe that some comparative advantages can be acquired and consequently can be changed. A country may, in this view, influence its role in world production and trade.

33.2 THE DETERMINATION OF TRADE PATTERNS

- The law of one price says that the national prices of goods must differ by no more than the costs of transporting these goods between countries. After accounting for these transport costs, there is a single world price.
- Countries will export a good when the world price exceeds the price that would exist in the country if there were no trade. The low no-trade price reflects a low opportunity cost and thus a comparative advantage in that good. Thus, countries export goods for which they have a comparative advantage.
- Countries will import a good when the world price is less than the price that would exist in the country if there were no trade. The high no-trade price reflects a high opportunity cost and thus a comparative disadvantage in that good. Thus, countries import goods for which they have a comparative disadvantage.
- The terms of trade refer to the ratio of the prices of goods exported to the prices of those imported. The terms of trade determine the quantity of imports that can be obtained per unit of exports.
- A favourable change in the terms of trade—a rise in export prices relative to import prices—is beneficial for a country because it expands its consumption possibilities.

KEY CONCEPTS

Interpersonal, interregional, and international specialization
Absolute advantage and comparative advantage

Opportunity cost and comparative advantage
The gains from trade: specialization, scale economies, and learning by doing

The sources of comparative advantage
Factor endowments
Acquired comparative advantage
The law of one price
The terms of trade

STUDY EXERCISES

1. Fill in the blanks to make the following statements correct.

    a. A nation that engages in international trade is able to specialize in producing goods that it produces _____ and trade to obtain goods that it does not produce _____.
    b. The "gains from trade" refers to the increased _____ due to specialization and trade.
    c. Suppose Argentina can produce one kilogram of beef for $2.50 and Brazil can produce one kilogram of beef for $2.90. Argentina is said to have a(n) _____ in beef production over Brazil. The gains from trade do *not* depend on _____.
    d. Comparative advantage is based on _____ rather than absolute costs.
    e. It is possible for a country to have a comparative advantage in some good and a(n) _____ in none.
    f. If all countries specialize in the production of goods for which they have a comparative advantage, then world output will _____.
    g. If opportunity costs are the same in all countries, there is no _____ and no possibility of _____.

2. Fill in the blanks to make the following statements correct.

    a. A product such as coffee beans is cheaply transported and is traded around the world. The law of _____ tells us that it will tend to have _____ worldwide price.
    b. If the domestic price of copper wire in Canada (in the absence of trade) is $20 per unit and the world price is $24 per unit, then Canada will have an excess _____ which it will then _____. The opportunity cost of producing copper wire in Canada is _____ than the opportunity cost of producing it in the rest of the world.
    c. Canada will import goods for which it has an excess _____ at the world price. In the absence of trade, the _____ price of these goods would be less than the _____ price.
    d. A rise in Canada's terms of trade means that the average price of Canada's _____ has risen compared to the average price of Canada's _____. This change is referred to as a terms of trade _____.

e. The terms of trade determine the quantity of _____ that can be obtained per unit of _____ .

3. The following diagram shows the production possibilities boundary for Arcticland, a country that produces only two goods, ice and fish. Labour is the only factor of production.

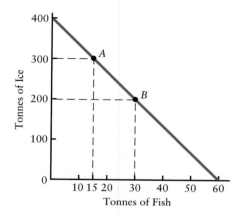

a. Beginning at any point on Arcticland's production possibilities boundary, what is the opportunity cost of producing 10 more tonnes of fish?

b. Beginning at any point on Arcticland's production possibilities boundary, what is the opportunity cost of producing 100 more tonnes of ice?

4. **myeconlab** The following table shows the production of wheat and corn in Brazil and Mexico. Assume that both countries have one million acres of arable land.

	Brazil	Mexico
Wheat	90 bushels per acre	50 bushels per acre
Corn	30 bushels per acre	20 bushels per acre

a. Which country has the absolute advantage in wheat? In corn? Explain.

b. Which country has the comparative advantage in wheat? In corn? Explain.

c. Explain why one country can have an absolute advantage in both goods but cannot have a comparative advantage in both goods.

d. On a scale diagram with wheat on the horizontal axis and corn on the vertical axis, draw each country's production possibilities boundary.

e. What is shown by the slope of each country's production possibilities boundary? Be as precise as possible.

5. **myeconlab** The following diagrams show the production possibilities boundaries for Canada and France, both of which produce only two goods, wine and lumber.

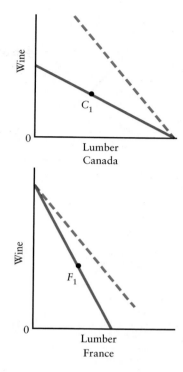

a. Which country has the comparative advantage in lumber? Explain.

b. Which country has the comparative advantage in wine? Explain.

c. Suppose Canada and France are initially not trading with each other and are producing at points C_1 and F_1, respectively. Suppose when trade is introduced, the free-trade relative prices are shown by the slope of the dashed line. Which combination of goods will each country now produce?

d. In this case, what will be the pattern of trade for each country?

6. The diagrams on the next page show the Canadian markets for newsprint and machinery, which we assume to be competitive.

a. Suppose there is no international trade. What would be the equilibrium price and quantity in the Canadian newsprint and machinery markets?

b. Now suppose Canada is open to trade with the rest of the world. If the world price of newsprint is higher than the price of newsprint from part (a), what will happen to the levels of domestic production and consumption? Explain.

c. If the world price of machinery is lower than the price of machinery from part (a), what happens to the levels of domestic consumption and production? Explain.

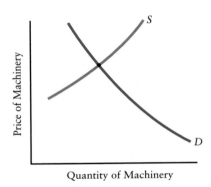

7. **myeconlab** The table below shows indexes for the prices of imports and exports over several years for a hypothetical country.

Year	Import Prices	Export Prices	Terms of Trade
2002	90	110	—
2003	95	87	—
2004	98	83	—
2005	100	100	—
2006	102	105	—
2007	100	112	—
2008	103	118	—

a. Compute the terms of trade in each year for this country and fill in the table.
b. In which years do the terms of trade improve?
c. In which years do the terms of trade deteriorate?
d. Explain why a terms of trade "improvement" is good for the country.

8. For each of the following events, explain the likely effect on Canada's terms of trade. Your existing knowledge of Canada's imports and exports should be adequate to answer this question.

a. A hurricane damages much of Brazil's coffee crop.
b. OPEC countries succeed in significantly restricting the world supply of oil.
c. Several new large copper mines come into production in Chile.
d. A major recession in Southeast Asia reduces the world demand for pork.

DISCUSSION QUESTIONS

1. Adam Smith saw a close connection between the wealth of a nation and its willingness "freely to engage" in foreign trade. What is the connection?

2. One critic of the North American Free Trade Agreement argued that "it can't be in our interest to sign this deal; Mexico gains too much from it." What does the theory of the gains from trade have to say about that criticism?

3. One product innovation that appears imminent is the electric car. However, development costs are high and economies of scale and learning by doing are both likely to be operative. As a result, there will be a substantial competitive advantage for those who develop a marketable product early. What implications might this have for government policies toward North American automobile manufacturers' activities in this area? Should the Canadian or U.S. governments encourage joint efforts by Chrysler, Ford, and GM, even if this appears to lessen competition among them?

4. Studies of Canadian trade patterns have shown that industries with high wages are among the largest and fastest-growing export sectors. One example is the computer software industry. Does this finding contradict the principle of comparative advantage?

5. Predict what each of the following events would do to the terms of trade of the importing country and the exporting country, other things being equal.

a. A blight destroys a large part of the coffee beans produced in the world.
b. The Koreans cut the price of the steel they sell to Canada.
c. General inflation of 4 percent occurs around the world.
d. Violation of OPEC output quotas leads to a sharp fall in the price of oil.

6. Are there always benefits to specialization and trade? When are the benefits greatest? Under what situations are there *no* benefits from specialization and trade?

CHAPTER 34

Trade Policy

LO LEARNING OBJECTIVES

In this chapter you will learn

1. the various situations in which a country may rationally choose to protect some industries.
2. the most common fallacious arguments in favour of protection.
3. the effects of a tariff or quota on imported goods.
4. why trade-remedy laws are sometimes just thinly disguised protection.
5. the distinction between trade creation and trade diversion.
6. the main features of the North American Free Trade Agreement.

trade policy A government's policy involving restrictions placed on international trade.

protectionism Any government policy that interferes with free trade in order to protect domestic firms and workers from foreign competition.

Conducting business in a foreign country is not always easy. Differences in language, in local laws and customs, and in currency often complicate transactions. Our concern in this chapter, however, is not with these complications but with government policy toward international trade, which is called **trade policy**. At one extreme is a policy of free trade—that is, an absence of any form of government interference with the free flow of international trade. Any departure from free trade designed to protect domestic industries from foreign competition is called **protectionism.**

We begin by briefly restating the case for free trade and then go on to examine various valid and invalid arguments that are commonly advanced for some degree of protection. We then explore some of the methods commonly used to restrict trade, such as tariffs and quotas. Finally, we examine the many modern institutions designed to foster freer trade on either a global or a regional basis. In particular, we discuss the North American Free Trade Agreement (NAFTA) and the World Trade Organization.

34.1 FREE TRADE OR PROTECTION?

tariff A tax applied on imports of goods or services.

nontariff barriers (NTBs) Restrictions other than tariffs designed to reduce imports.

Today, most governments accept the proposition that a relatively free flow of international trade is desirable for the health of their individual economies. But heated debates still occur over trade policy. Should a country permit the completely free flow of international trade, or should it sometimes seek to protect its local producers from foreign competition? If some protection is desired, should it be achieved by tariffs or by nontariff barriers? **Tariffs** are taxes designed to raise the price of imported goods. **Nontariff barriers (NTBs)** are devices other than tariffs designed to reduce the flow of imports; examples are import quotas and customs procedures that are deliberately more cumbersome than necessary.

The Case for Free Trade

The case for free trade was presented in Chapter 33. Comparative advantages arise whenever countries have different opportunity costs. Free trade encourages all countries to specialize in producing products in which they have a comparative advantage. This pattern of specialization maximizes world production and hence maximizes average world living standards (as measured by the world's per capita GDP).

Free trade does not necessarily make *everyone* better off than they would be in its absence. For example, reducing an existing tariff often results in individual groups receiving a smaller share of a larger world output so that they lose even though the average person gains. If we ask whether it is *possible* for free trade to improve everyone's living standards, the answer is yes because the larger total value of output that free trade generates could, at least in principle, be divided up in such a way that every individual is better off. If we ask whether free trade always does so in practice, however, the answer is, not necessarily.

Free trade makes the country as a whole better off, even though it may not make every individual in the country better off.

In today's world, a country's products must stand up to international competition if they are to survive. Over even so short a period as a few years, firms that do not develop new products and new production methods fall seriously behind their foreign competitors. If one country protects its domestic firms by imposing a tariff, those firms are likely to become complacent about the need to adopt new technologies, and over time they will become less competitive in international markets. As the technology gap between domestic and foreign firms widens, the tariff wall will provide less and less protection. Eventually, the domestic firms will succumb to foreign competition. Meanwhile, domestic living standards will fall relative to foreign ones.

Given that any country can be better off by specializing in those goods in which it has a comparative advantage, one might wonder why most countries of the world continue in some way to restrict the flow of trade. Why do tariffs and other barriers to trade continue to exist two centuries after Adam Smith and David Ricardo stated the case for free trade? Is there a valid case for some protection?

The Case for Protection

Two kinds of arguments for protection are commonly heard. The first concerns objectives *other than* maximizing national income; the second concerns the desire to increase one country's national income, possibly at the expense of the national incomes of other countries.

Objectives Other Than Maximizing National Income
A country's national income may be maximized with free trade and yet it may still be rational to oppose free trade because of other policy objectives.

Advantages of Diversification. For a very small country, specializing in the production of only a few products—though dictated by comparative advantage—might involve risks that the country does not wish to take. One such risk is that technological advances may render its basic product obsolete. Another risk, especially for countries specialized in producing a small range of agricultural products, is that swings in world prices lead to large swings in national income. Everyone understands these risks, but there is debate about what governments can do about it. The pro-tariff argument is that the government can encourage a more diversified economy by protecting industries that otherwise could not compete. Opponents argue that governments, being naturally influenced by political motives, are poor judges of which industries can be protected in order to produce diversification at a reasonable cost.

Protection of Specific Groups. Although specialization according to comparative advantage will maximize *average* per capita GDP, some specific groups may have higher incomes under protection than under free trade. Of particular interest in Canada and the United States has been the effect that greater international trade has on the incomes of unskilled workers.

Countries whose economies are based on the production of only a few goods face risks from fluctuations in world prices. For this reason, protection to promote diversification may be viewed as desirable.

Consider the ratio of skilled workers to unskilled workers. There are plenty of both types throughout the world. Compared to much of the rest of the world, however, Canada has more skilled and fewer unskilled people. When trade is expanded because of a reduction in tariffs, Canada will tend to export goods made by its abundant skilled workers and import goods made by unskilled workers. (This is the basic prediction of the *factor endowment theory* of comparative advantage that we discussed in Chapter 33.) Because Canada is now exporting more goods made by skilled labour, the domestic demand for such labour rises. Because Canada is now importing more goods made by unskilled labour, the domestic demand for such labour falls. This specialization according to comparative advantage raises average Canadian living standards, but it will also tend to raise the wages of skilled Canadian workers relative to the wages of unskilled Canadian workers.

If increasing trade has these effects, then reducing trade by erecting protectionist trade barriers can have the opposite effects. Protectionist policies may raise the incomes of unskilled Canadian workers, giving them a larger share of a smaller total GDP. The conclusion is that trade restrictions can improve the earnings of one group whenever the restrictions increase the demand for that group's services. This is done, however, at the expense of a reduction in *overall* national income and hence the country's average living standards.

This analysis is important because it reveals both the grain of truth and the dangers that lie behind the resistance to trade liberalization (i.e., freer trade) on the part of some labour groups and some organizations whose main concern is with the poor.

Social and distributional concerns may lead to the rational adoption of protectionist policies. But the cost of such protection is a reduction in the country's average living standards.

Economists cannot say that it is irrational for a society to sacrifice average living standards in order to protect specific groups. But economists can do three things when presented with such arguments for adopting protectionist measures. First, they can ask if the proposed measures really do achieve the ends suggested. Second, they can calculate the cost of the measures in terms of lowered average living standards. Third, they can see if there are alternative means of achieving the stated goals at lower cost in terms of lost national income.

Maximizing National Income   Next we consider several arguments for the use of tariffs when the stated objective is to maximize a country's national income.

To Improve the Terms of Trade. Tariffs can be used to change the terms of trade in favour of a country that makes up a large fraction of the world demand for some product that it imports. By restricting its demand for that product through a tariff, it can force down

Practise with Study Guide Chapter 34, Extension Exercise E1.

the price that foreign exporters receive for that product. The price paid by domestic consumers will probably rise but as long as the increase is less than the tariff, foreign suppliers will receive less per unit. For example, a 20 percent U.S. tariff on the import of Canadian softwood lumber might raise the price paid by U.S. consumers by 12 percent and lower the price received by Canadian suppliers by 8 percent (the difference between the two prices being received by the U.S. treasury). This reduction in the price received by the Canadian suppliers of a U.S. import is a terms-of-trade improvement for the United States (and a terms-of-trade deterioration for Canada).

Note that not all countries can improve their terms of trade by levying tariffs on imported goods. A *necessary* condition is that the importing country has *market power,* in other words, that it is a large importer of the good in question, so that its restrictive trade policies lead to a decline in the world price of its imports. Small countries, like Canada, are not large enough importers of any good to have a significant effect on world prices. For small countries, therefore, tariffs cannot improve their terms of trade.

Large countries can sometimes improve their terms of trade by levying tariffs on some imported goods; small countries cannot.

To Protect Infant Industries. The oldest valid arguments for protection as a means of raising living standards concern economies of scale or learning by doing. It is usually called the **infant industry argument.** An infant industry is nothing more than a new, small industry. If such an industry has large economies of scale or the scope for learning by doing, costs will be high when the industry is small but will fall as the industry grows. In such industries, the country to first enter the field has a tremendous advantage. A developing country may find that in the early stages of development, its industries are unable to compete with established foreign rivals. A trade restriction may protect these industries from foreign competition while they grow up. When they are large enough, they will be able to produce as cheaply as foreign rivals and thus be able to compete without protection.

Most of the now industrialized countries developed their industries initially under quite heavy tariff protection. (In Canada's case, the National Policy of 1876 established a high tariff wall behind which many Canadian industries developed and thrived for many years.) Once the industrial sector was well developed, these countries moved to reduce their levels of protection, thus moving a long way toward freer trade. Electronics in Taiwan, automobiles in Japan, commercial aircraft in Europe (specifically the consortium of European governments that created Airbus), and shipbuilding in South Korea are all examples in which protection of infant industries was successful. In each case, the national industry, protected by its home government, developed into a major player in the global marketplace.

One practical problem with this argument for protection is that some infants "never grow up." Once the young firm gets used to operating in a protected environment, it may resist having that protection disappear, even though all economies of scale may have been achieved. This is as much a political problem as an economic one. Political leaders must therefore be careful before offering protection to infant industries because they must recognize the political difficulties involved in removing that protection in the future. The countries that were most successful in having their protected industries eventually grow up and succeed in fierce international competition were those, such as Taiwan and South Korea, that ruthlessly withdrew support from unsuccessful infants within a specified time period.

To Earn Economic Profits in Foreign Markets. Another argument for protectionist policies is to help create an advantage in producing or marketing some product that is expected

---

infant industry argument The argument that new domestic industries with potential for economies of scale or learning by doing need to be protected from competition from established, low-cost foreign producers so that they can grow large enough to achieve costs as low as those of foreign producers.

to generate economic profits through its sales to foreign consumers. If protection of the domestic market, which might include subsidizing domestic firms, can increase the chance that one of the domestic firms will become established and thus earn high profits, the protection may pay off. The economic profits earned in foreign markets may exceed the cost to domestic taxpayers of the protection. This is the general idea behind the concept of *strategic trade policy*.

Opponents of strategic trade policy argue that it is nothing more than a modern version of age-old and faulty justifications for tariff protection. Once all countries try to be strategic, they will all waste vast sums trying to break into industries in which there is no room for most of them. Domestic consumers would benefit most, they say, if their governments let other countries engage in this game. Consumers could then buy the cheap, subsidized foreign products and export traditional nonsubsidized products in return. The opponents of strategic trade policy also

For many years, Canada and Brazil have been in a trade dispute centred around each country's alleged support of aerospace manufacturers. Canada's Bombardier and Brazil's Embraer both receive considerable financial assistance from their respective federal governments. Taxpayers in each country foot the bill.

argue that democratic governments that enter the game of picking and backing winners are likely to make more bad choices than good ones. One bad choice, with all of its massive development costs written off, would require that many good choices also be made in order to make the equivalent in profits that would allow taxpayers to break even overall.

An ongoing dispute between Canada and Brazil illustrates how strategic trade policy is often difficult to distinguish from pure protection. The world's two major producers of regional jets are Bombardier, based in Montreal, and Embraer SA, based in Brazil. For several years, each company has accused its competitor's government of using illegal subsidies to help the domestic company sell jets in world markets. Brazil's Pro-Ex program provides Embraer's customers with low-interest loans with which to purchase Embraer's jets. Export Development Canada (EDC) provides similar loans to Bombardier's customers. In addition, the Canadian government's Technology Partnerships program subsidizes research and development activities in high-tech aerospace and defence companies. As the leading Canadian aerospace company, Bombardier benefits significantly from this program.

In 1999, the World Trade Organization (WTO) ruled that both the Brazilian and Canadian governments were using illegal subsidy programs to support their aerospace firms. Both countries, however, naturally view their respective programs as necessary responses to the other country's subsidization. Many economists believe that an agreement to eliminate both programs would leave a "level playing field" while saving Brazilian and Canadian taxpayers a considerable amount of money. As of 2006, however, both countries continue to support their respective aerospace firms and both sets of taxpayers continue to foot the bill.

For a list and discussion of many ongoing trade disputes, see the WTO's website: **www.wto.org**.

Fallacious Arguments for Protection

We have seen that free trade is generally beneficial for a country overall even though it does not necessarily make every person better off. We have also seen that there are some situations in which there are valid arguments for restricting trade. For every valid argument, however, there are many fallacious arguments—many of these are based, directly or indirectly, on the misconception that in every transaction there is a winner and a loser. Here we review a few arguments that are frequently heard in political debates concerning international trade.

Keep the Money at Home   This argument says that if I buy a foreign good, I have the good and the foreigner has the money, whereas if I buy the same good locally, I have the good and our country has the money, too. This argument is based on a common misconception. It assumes that domestic money actually goes abroad physically when imports are purchased and that trade flows only in one direction. But when Canadian importers purchase Japanese goods, they do not send dollars abroad. They (or their financial agents) buy Japanese yen and use them to pay the Japanese manufacturers. They purchase the yen on the foreign-exchange market by giving up dollars to someone who wishes to use them for expenditure in Canada. Even if the money did go abroad physically—that is, if a Japanese firm accepted a bunch of Canadian $100 bills—it would be because that firm (or someone to whom it could sell the dollars) wanted them to spend in the only country where they are legal tender—Canada.

Canadian currency ultimately does no one any good except as purchasing power in Canada. It would be miraculous if Canadian money could be exported in return for real goods. After all, the Bank of Canada has the power to create as much new Canadian money as it wishes (at almost zero direct cost). It is only because Canadian money can buy Canadian products and Canadian assets that others want it.

Protect Against Low-Wage Foreign Labour   This argument says that the products of low-wage countries will drive Canadian products from the market, and the high Canadian standard of living will be dragged down to that of its poorer trading partners. For example, if Canada imports cotton shirts from China, higher-cost Canadian textile firms may go out of business and Canadian workers may be laid off. Arguments of this sort have swayed many voters over the years.

As a prelude to considering this argument, think what the argument would imply if taken out of the international context and put into a local one, where the same principles govern the gains from trade. Is it really impossible for a rich person to gain by trading with a poor person? Would the local millionaire be better off if she did all her own typing, gardening, and cooking? No one believes that a rich person gains nothing by trading with those who are less rich.

Why, then, must a rich group of people lose when they trade with a poor group? "Well," some may say, "the poor group will price its goods too cheaply." Does anyone believe that consumers lose from buying in discount stores or supermarkets just because the prices are lower there than at the old-fashioned corner store? Consumers gain when they can buy the same goods at a lower price. If Chinese, Mexican, or Malaysian workers earn low wages and the goods they produce are sold at low prices, Canadians will gain by obtaining imports at a low cost in terms of the goods that must be exported in return. The cheaper our imports are, the better off we are in terms of the goods and services available for domestic consumption.

As we said earlier in this chapter, *some* Canadians may be better off if Canada places high tariffs on the import of Chinese goods. In particular, if the Chinese goods compete with goods made by unskilled Canadian workers, then those unskilled workers will be better off if a Canadian tariff protects their firms and thus their jobs. But Canadian income overall—that is, average per capita real income—will be higher when there is free trade.

Exports Are Good; Imports Are Bad   Exports create domestic income; imports create income for foreigners. Thus, other things being equal, exports tend to increase our total GDP, and imports tend to reduce it. Surely, then, it is desirable to encourage exports by subsidizing them and to discourage imports by taxing them. This is an appealing argument, but it is incorrect.

Exports raise GDP by adding to the value of domestic output and income, but they do not add to the value of domestic consumption. The standard of living in a country depends on the level of consumption, not on the level of income. In other words, income is not of much use except that it provides the means for consumption.

If exports really were "good" and imports really were "bad," then a fully employed economy that managed to increase exports without a corresponding increase in imports ought to be better off. Such a change, however, would result in a reduction in current standards of living because when more goods are sent abroad but no more are brought in from abroad, the total goods available for domestic consumption must fall.

The living standards of a country depend on the goods and services consumed in that country. The importance of exports is that they provide the resources required to purchase imports, either now or in the future.

Create Domestic Jobs   It is sometimes said that an economy with substantial unemployment, such as Canada during much of the 1990s, provides an exception to the case for freer trade. Suppose tariffs or import quotas reduce the imports of Japanese cars, Korean textiles, German kitchen equipment, and Polish vodka. Surely, the argument goes, this will create more employment in Canadian industries producing similar products. This may be true but it will also *reduce* employment in other industries.

The Japanese, Koreans, Germans, and Poles can buy from Canada only if they earn Canadian dollars by selling their domestically produced goods and services to Canada (or by borrowing dollars from Canada).[1] The decline in their sales of cars, textiles, kitchen equipment, and vodka will decrease their purchases of Canadian lumber, cars, software, banking services, and holidays. Jobs will be lost in Canadian export industries and gained in industries that formerly faced competition from imports. The major long-term effect is that the same amount of total employment in Canada will merely be redistributed among industries. In the process, living standards will be reduced because employment expands in inefficient import-competing industries and contracts in efficient exporting industries.

A country that imposes tariffs in an attempt to create domestic jobs risks starting a "trade war" with its trading partners. Such a trade war can easily leave every country worse off, as world output (and thus income) falls significantly. An income-reducing trade war followed the onset of the Great Depression in 1929 as many countries increased tariffs to protect their domestic industries in an attempt to stimulate domestic production and employment. Most economists agree that this trade war made the Great Depression worse than it otherwise would have been.

34.2 **METHODS OF PROTECTION**

We now go on to explore some specific protectionist policies. Two types of protectionist policy are illustrated in Figure 34-1. Both cause the price of the imported good to rise and the quantity demanded by domestic consumers to fall. They differ, however, in how they achieve these results.

---

[1] They can also get dollars by selling to other countries and then using their currencies to buy Canadian dollars. But this intermediate step only complicates the transaction; it does not change its fundamental nature. Other countries must have earned the dollars by selling goods to Canada or borrowing from Canada.

FIGURE 34-1   The Deadweight Loss of a Tariff

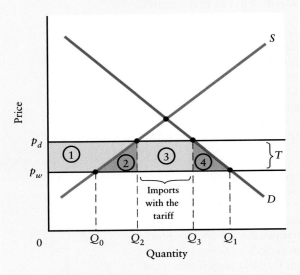

A tariff imposes a deadweight loss for the importing country. Before the tariff, the price in the domestic economy is the world price, p_w. Imports are Q_0Q_1. With a tariff of $\$T$ per unit, the domestic price rises to p_d. Domestic consumption falls to Q_3, and consumer surplus falls by areas ① + ② + ③ + ④. Domestic production rises to Q_2 and producer surplus increases by area ①. Imports fall to Q_2Q_3 and the government collects tariff revenue equal to area ③. The sum of areas ② and ④ represents the deadweight loss of the tariff.

Practise with Study Guide Chapter 34, Exercise 1.

Tariffs

A tariff, also called an *import duty,* is a tax on imported goods. For example, consider a Canadian firm that wants to import cotton T-shirts from India at $5 per shirt. If the Canadian government levies a 20 percent tariff on imported cotton shirts, the Canadian firm pays $5 to the Indian exporter *plus* $1 (20 percent of $5) in import duties to the Canada Revenue Agency. The immediate effect of a tariff is therefore to increase the domestic price of the T-shirt to $6. This price increase has important implications for domestic consumers as well as domestic producers. The effect of a tariff is shown in Figure 34-1.

The initial effect of the tariff is to raise the domestic price of the imported product above its world price by the amount of the tariff. Imports fall. As a result, foreign producers sell less and must transfer resources to other lines of production. The price received on domestically produced units rises, as does the quantity produced domestically. On both counts, domestic producers earn more. However, the cost of producing the extra production at home exceeds the price at which it could be purchased on the world market. Thus, the benefit to domestic producers comes at the expense of domestic consumers. Indeed, domestic consumers lose on two counts: First, they consume less of the product because its price rises, and second, they pay a higher price for the amount that they do consume. This extra spending ends up in two places: The extra that is paid on all units produced at home goes to domestic producers, and the extra that is paid on units still imported goes to the government as tariff revenue.

The overall loss to the domestic economy from levying a tariff is best seen in terms of the changes in consumer and producer surplus. Before the tariff, consumer surplus was equal to the entire area below the demand curve and above the price line at p_w. After the tariff, the price increase leads to less consumption and less consumer surplus. The loss of consumer surplus is the sum of the areas ①, ②, ③, and ④ in Figure 34-1. As domestic producers respond to the higher domestic price by increasing their production and sales, they earn more producer surplus, equal to area ①. Finally, the taxpayers gain the tariff revenue equal to area ③. This is simply a redistribution of surplus away from consumers toward taxpayers. In summary:

Loss of consumer surplus	= ① + ② + ③ + ④
Gain of producer surplus	= ①
Gain of tariff revenue	= ③
Net loss in surplus	= ② + ④

The overall effect of the tariff is therefore to create a deadweight loss to the domestic economy equal to areas ② plus ④. Domestic consumers are worse off, while domestic firms and taxpayers are better off. But the net effect is a loss of surplus for the economy as a whole. This is the overall cost of levying a tariff.

A tariff imposes costs on domestic consumers, generates benefits for domestic producers, and generates revenue for the government. But the overall net effect is negative; a tariff generates a deadweight loss for the economy.

Quotas and Voluntary Export Restrictions (VERs)

The second type of protectionist policy directly restricts the quantity of an imported product. A common example is the **import quota,** by which the importing country sets a maximum quantity of some product that may be imported each year. Another measure is the **voluntary export restriction (VER),** an agreement by an exporting country to limit the amount of a product that it sells to the importing country.

Figure 34-2 shows that a quantity restriction and a tariff have similar effects on domestic consumers and producers—they both raise domestic prices, increase domestic production, and reduce domestic consumption. But a direct quantity restriction is actually *worse* than a tariff for the importing country because the effect of the quantity restriction is to raise the price received by the foreign suppliers of the good. In contrast, a tariff leaves the foreign suppliers' price unchanged and instead generates tariff revenue for the government of the importing country.

Import quotas and voluntary export restrictions (VERs) impose larger deadweight losses on the importing country than do tariffs that lead to the same level of imports.

Canada, the United States, and the European Union have used VERs extensively, and the EU makes frequent use of import quotas. Japan has been pressured into negotiating several VERs with Canada, the United States, and the EU in order to limit sales of some of the Japanese goods that have had the most success in international competition. For example, in 1983, the United States and Canada negotiated VERs whereby the Japanese government agreed to restrict total sales of Japanese cars to these two countries for three years. When the agreements ran out in 1986, the Japanese continued to restrict their automobile sales by unilateral voluntary action. Japan's readiness to restrict its exports to North America partly reflects the high profits that Japanese automobile producers were making under the system of VERs, as explained in Figure 34-2. In recent years, such VERs have become less important because Japan's major automobile producers, Honda and Toyota, both have established manufacturing plants in Canada.

Tariffs Versus Quotas?

The dispute that raged for several years between Canada and the United States over Canadian softwood lumber exports illustrates an important distinction between tariffs and quotas. The United States protected its softwood lumber industry in two ways:

- by imposing tariffs on imports of Canadian softwood lumber
- by pressuring Canadian governments to place export quotas on Canadian softwood lumber shipments to the United States.

Analysis of Figures 34-1 and 34-2 reveals that the choice between tariffs and quotas matters greatly for Canadian producers.

In the case of a U.S. tariff on imported Canadian softwood lumber, Figure 34-1 illustrates the U.S. market. An import tariff raises the domestic price for U.S. lumber users and also increases the profits of U.S. lumber producers. Canadian lumber pro-

import quota A limit set on the quantity of a foreign commodity that may be imported in a given time period.

voluntary export restriction (VER) An agreement by an exporting country to limit the amount of a good exported to another country.

Practise with Study Guide Chapter 34, Exercise 2.

FIGURE 34-2 The Deadweight Loss of an Import Quota

An import quota drives up the domestic price and imposes a deadweight loss on the importing country. With free trade, the domestic price is the world price, p_w. Imports are Q_0Q_1. If imports are restricted to only Q_2Q_3 (either through quotas or VERs), the domestic price must rise to the point where the restricted level of imports just satisfies the domestic excess demand. The rise in price and reduction in consumption reduces consumer surplus by areas ① + ② + ③ + ④. Domestic producers increase their output as the domestic price rises, and producer surplus increases by area ①. Area ③ does *not* accrue to the domestic economy; instead this area represents extra producer surplus for the *foreign* firms that export their product to this country. The net effect of the quota or VER is a deadweight loss for the importing country of areas ② + ③ + ④. Import quotas are therefore worse than tariffs for the importing country.

ducers are harmed because there is less demand for their product at the unchanged world price. Area ③ in the figure represents U.S. tariff revenue collected on the imports of Canadian lumber—revenue that accrues to the United States.

Figure 34-2 illustrates the U.S. market for softwood lumber when a quota is placed on the level of Canadian exports (U.S. imports). As with the tariff, the restricted supply of Canadian lumber to the U.S. market drives up the price to U.S. users and also raises profits for U.S. producers. But with a quota there is an important difference: The higher price in the U.S. market is received by the Canadian lumber producers, as shown by area ③ in the figure.

While a tariff and quota may lead to the same reduced volume of exports, the tariff permits some surplus to be captured by the importing country whereas the quota allows some surplus to be captured by the exporting country (area ③ in both cases). In the U.S.–Canadian softwood lumber dispute, both tariffs and quotas were used. And while both systems were to be preferred *overall* by a system of free trade, Canada had an interest in imposing quotas on Canadian lumber exporters rather than having the same export reduction accomplished by a U.S. tariff.

myeconlab

The trade dispute regarding Canada's softwood-lumber exports to the United States raged for almost 20 years. By 2006, a new agreement had been approved by the Canadian and U.S. governments. For details about the history, politics, and economics of this trade dispute, look for "The Continuing Saga of Softwood Lumber" in the *Additional Topics* section of this book's MyEconLab.

www.myeconlab.com

Trade-Remedy Laws and Nontariff Barriers

As tariffs in many countries were lowered over the years since the Second World War, countries that wished to protect domestic industries began using, and often abusing, a series of trade restrictions that came to be known as nontariff barriers (NTBs). The original purpose of some of these barriers was to remedy certain legitimate problems that arise in international trade and, for this reason, they are often called *trade-remedy laws*. All too often, however, such laws are misused to become potent means of simple protection.

Dumping Selling a product in a foreign country at a lower price than in the domestic market is known as **dumping**. For example, if U.S.-made cars are sold for less in Canada than they are sold for in the United States, the U.S. automobile firms are said to be *dumping*. Dumping is a form of price discrimination studied in the theory of monopoly. Most governments have antidumping duties designed to protect their own industries against what is viewed as unfair foreign pricing practices.

Dumping, if it lasts indefinitely, can be a gift to the receiving country. Its consumers get goods from abroad at lower prices than they otherwise would.

Dumping is more often a temporary measure, designed to get rid of unwanted surpluses, or a predatory attempt to drive competitors out of business. In either case, domestic producers complain about unfair foreign competition. In both cases, it is accepted international practice to levy *antidumping duties* on foreign imports. These duties are designed to eliminate the discriminatory elements in their prices.

Unfortunately, antidumping laws have been evolving over the past three decades in ways that allow antidumping duties to become barriers to trade and competition rather than to provide redress for unfair trading practices.

Several features of the antidumping system that is now in place in many countries make it highly protectionist. First, any price discrimination between national markets is classified as dumping and is subject to penalties. Thus, prices in the producer's domestic market become, in effect, minimum prices below which no sales can be made in foreign markets, whatever the nature of demand in the domestic and foreign markets. Second, many countries' laws calculate the "margin of dumping" as the difference between the price that is charged in that country's market and the foreign producer's average cost. Thus, when there is a global slump in some industry so that the profit-maximizing price for all producers is below average cost, foreign producers can be convicted of dumping. This gives domestic producers enormous protection whenever the market price falls temporarily below average cost. Third, law in the United States (but not in all other countries) places the onus of proof on the accused. Facing a charge of dumping, a foreign producer must prove that the charge is unfounded. Fourth, U.S. antidumping duties are imposed with no time limit, so they often persist long after foreign firms have altered the prices that gave rise to them.

Antidumping laws were first designed to permit countries to respond to predatory pricing by foreign firms. More recently, they have been used to protect domestic firms against any foreign competition.

Countervailing Duties Countervailing duties, which are commonly used by the U.S. government but much less so elsewhere, provide another case in which a trade-remedy law can become a covert method of protection. The countervailing duty is designed to act as a means of creating a "level playing field" on which fair international competition can take place. Privately owned domestic firms rightly complain that they cannot compete against the seemingly bottomless purses of foreign governments. Subsidized foreign exports can be sold indefinitely at prices that would produce losses in the absence of the subsidy. The original object of countervailing duties was to counteract the effect on price of the presence of such foreign subsidies.

If a domestic firm suspects the existence of such a subsidy and registers a complaint, its government is required to make an investigation. For a countervailing duty to be levied, the investigation must determine, first, that the foreign subsidy to the specific industry in question does exist and, second, that it is large enough to cause significant injury to competing domestic firms.

dumping The practice of selling a commodity at a lower price in the export market than in the domestic market for reasons unrelated to differences in costs of servicing the two markets.

Softwood lumber (spruce, pine, and fir) is extensively used in North America for the framing of houses and small buildings. For many years, the United States levied countervailing duties on Canadian softwood lumber exports, alleging that Canadian provinces unfairly subsidized production. In 2006, the Canadian and U.S. governments reached an agreement to end the dispute.

There is no doubt that countervailing duties have sometimes been used to counteract the effects of foreign subsidies. Many governments complain, however, that countervailing duties are often used as thinly disguised protection. At the early stages of the development of countervailing duties, only subsidies whose prime effect was to distort trade were possible objects of countervailing duties. Even then, however, the existence of equivalent domestic subsidies was not taken into account when decisions were made to put countervailing duties on subsidized imports. Thus, the United States levies some countervailing duties against foreign goods even though the foreign subsidy is less than the domestic subsidy. This does not create a level playing field.

Over time, the type of subsidy that is subject to countervailing duties has evolved until almost any government program that affects industry now risks becoming the object of a countervailing duty. Because all governments, including most U.S. state governments, have programs that provide direct or indirect assistance to industry, the potential for the use of countervailing duties as thinly disguised trade barriers is enormous.

The most well-known example in Canada of a U.S. countervailing duty is the 27-percent duty imposed between 2001 and 2005 on U.S. imports of Canadian softwood lumber. The U.S. justification for the duty was that Canadian provincial governments allegedly provided a subsidy to domestic lumber producers by charging artificially low *stumpage fees*—the fees paid by the companies to cut trees on Crown land. In 2006, the U.S. government agreed to eliminate the countervailing duty but only if restrictions were placed on Canadian lumber exports. Thus, a tariff was replaced by a combination of an export quota and an export tax.

34.3 CURRENT TRADE POLICY

In the remainder of the chapter, we discuss trade policy in practice. We start with the many international agreements that govern current trade policies and then look in a little more detail at the NAFTA.

Before 1947, any country was free to impose tariffs on its imports. However, when one country increased its tariffs, the action often triggered retaliatory actions by its trading partners. The 1930s saw a high-water mark of world protectionism as each country sought to raise its employment and output by raising its tariffs. The end result was lowered efficiency, less trade, but no more employment or income. Since the end of the Second World War, much effort has been devoted to reducing tariff barriers, both on a multilateral and on a regional basis.

The GATT and the WTO

One of the most notable achievements of the post-Second World War era was the creation of the General Agreement on Tariffs and Trade (GATT) in 1947. The GATT has since been replaced by the World Trade Organization (WTO). The principle of the GATT was that each member country agreed not to make unilateral tariff increases. This prevented the outbreak of "tariff wars" in which countries raised tariffs to protect particular domestic industries and to retaliate against other countries' tariff increases.

The Uruguay Round The Uruguay Round—the final round of trade agreements under GATT—was completed in 1994 after years of negotiations. It reduced world tariffs by about 40 percent. A significant failure of these negotiations was the absence of an agreement to liberalize trade in agricultural goods. The European Union and Canada both resisted an agreement in this area. The EU's Common Agricultural Policy (CAP) provides general support for most of its agricultural products, many of which are exported. The EU's position as a subsidized exporter causes major harm to agricultural producers in developing countries whose governments are too poor to compete with the EU in a subsidy war. Canada, which has free trade in many agricultural commodities, was concerned about maintaining its "supply management" over a number of industries including poultry, eggs, and dairy products. These schemes are administered by the provinces, who restrict domestic production and thus push domestic prices well above world levels. The federal government made such high domestic prices possible by imposing quotas on imports of these products at the national level.

Canada, the EU, and a number of other countries that lavishly protect some or all of their domestic agricultural producers were finally forced to agree to a plan to end all import quotas on agricultural products. In a process called "tariffication," these quotas were replaced by "tariff equivalents"—tariffs that restrict trade by the same amount as the quotas did. For example, a quota that restricted imports of some products to no more than 100 000 units per month and resulted in an increase in the domestic price by 20 percent was replaced by a tariff on that imported product of 20 percent. In the case of the Canadian poultry, egg, and dairy industries, some of the tariff equivalents were as high as several hundred percent, which illustrates the restrictiveness of the Canadian policy. The hope among countries that are pushing for freer trade in agricultural commodities is that pressure will build to reduce these very high tariffs over the next few decades.

Despite the failure to achieve free trade in agricultural products, the Uruguay Round is generally viewed as a success. Perhaps its most significant achievement was the creation of the World Trade Organization (WTO) to replace the GATT. An important part of the WTO is its formal dispute-settlement mechanism. This mechanism allows countries to take cases of alleged trade violations—such as illegal subsidies or tariffs—to the WTO for a formal ruling, and also obliges member countries to follow the ruling. The WTO's dispute-settlement mechanism is thus a significant step toward a "rules based" global trading system.

The Doha Round Agriculture also plays a central role in the current round of trade negotiations, which began in Doha, Qatar, in 2000. Many issues were discussed and negotiated in the period before the 2006 deadline, ranging from competition policy to antidumping and from environmental policies to electronic commerce. But one of the most contentious issues is agriculture. The WTO member governments claim to be committed to reducing export subsidies and other forms of government support to agriculture. Movements in this direction will naturally cause political friction within the developed economies that currently protect and support their agricultural producers, especially the United States and the European Union, which provide (by far) the most support to their

International trade negotiations sometimes generate considerable grass-roots opposition. There is some opposition to the reduction of tariffs in developed countries, and some controversy regarding the appropriate way to address the concerns of developing countries.

farmers. A failure to reduce agricultural support in the developed countries, however, will increase the political frictions that already exist between developed and developing nations. For the many developing countries who have natural comparative advantages in agricultural products and who cannot afford to compete in a "subsidy war" with the developed countries, the liberalization of trade in agricultural products is crucial. They see the Doha round as central to their economic development.

At a set of WTO meetings in Cancún, Mexico, in September 2003, the developed countries began to backtrack on their commitment to reduce agricultural subsidies. In addition, the major developing countries, led by China, Brazil, and India, for the first time presented a united front and refused to back down on their position that further access to their own markets would not occur without significant cuts to agricultural subsidies by the rich countries. The Cancún meetings ended in a stalemate and many observers wondered how the Doha round would get back on track.

Late in 2005, another meeting in Hong Kong provided more positive results. Agreement was reached in principle to end all subsidies of agricultural exports by 2013, but the difficult bargaining over the all-important details was postponed. As this book went to press in the fall of 2006, there was still plenty of reason to be skeptical that a binding agreement to reduce agricultural subsidies would be reached.

myeconlab

Many countries, including Canada, provide generous financial support to their farmers and livestock producers. For some international comparisons of the generosity of agricultural subsidies, and for how these policies affect the ongoing WTO negotiations, look for "Farm Subsidies and the World Trade Organization" in the Additional Topics section of this book's MyEconLab.

www.myeconlab.com

Protests About the WTO Despite the successes of the WTO, it has its critics. In December 1999, trade ministers from the WTO member countries met in Seattle to set the agenda for what would become the Doha Round of trade negotiations. The Seattle meetings were delayed and interrupted by massive protests from environmental and labour groups, among others, who argued that the WTO's process of negotiating trade agreements pays insufficient attention to environmental and labour standards, especially in the developing countries. Many WTO officials and trade ministers, including those from the developing countries, recognized the importance of environmental and labour issues but questioned the wisdom of formally including these concerns in trade agreements. Reaching agreement on trade issues among the 155 (and growing) member countries of the WTO is difficult enough—it would be almost impossible if the issues were bundled with the even more contentious environmental and labour issues. The result would be an overall agreement that achieved very little in terms of either trade liberalization, environmental protection, or establishing labour standards. Instead, many trade officials argued that the existing International Labour Organization should be strengthened and a separate international organization like the WTO should be created to promote environmental issues. These organizations could then push ahead to achieve in their respective domains the same success that the GATT achieved over 50 years of negotiations.

Some of the protesters against the WTO process argue that paying greater attention to environmental and labour issues will improve the living standards in developing countries, where such standards typically fall far behind those in developed economies. One of the interesting ironies of the negotiations, however, is that the governments of the developing countries are among the strongest *opponents* of including environmental and labour issues in trade negotiations. They feel that developed countries would use stringent environmental and labour standards as a means of preventing imports from developing countries, thus protecting their own industries.

As it turned out, the work programme for the Doha Round includes very little on environmental issues and nothing on labour standards. Apparently, the view of the Doha negotiators was that many trade issues could usefully be discussed without getting embroiled in the very contentious but important environmental and labour issues. Perhaps the *next* round of WTO talks will include these broader issues.

In any event, it seems a safe bet that these tensions between trade policy and environmental/labour policies will continue. At some point, further progress on trade liberalization will require that environmental and labour issues be addressed. Either domestic political pressures will push individual member countries to insist that these issues be included within the WTO negotiations, or other organizations like the WTO will be developed and/or strengthened to address the concerns. Whatever approach is followed, it appears that these will surely continue to be hot policy issues in the twenty-first century.

Applying Economic Concepts 34-1 addresses some of the often-heard criticisms of the WTO and argues that, as imperfect as the institution may be, it holds out much promise for continued progress in trade liberalization.

For more information on the WTO, see its website at **www.wto.org**.

Regional Trade Agreements

Regional agreements seek to liberalize trade over a much smaller group of countries than the WTO membership. Three standard forms of regional trade-liberalizing agreements are *free trade areas, customs unions,* and *common markets.*

A **free trade area (FTA)** is the least comprehensive of the three. It allows for tariff-free trade among the member countries, but it leaves each member free to levy its own trade policy with respect to other countries. As a result, members must maintain customs points at their common borders to make sure that imports into the free trade area do not all enter through the member that is levying the lowest tariff on each item. They must also agree on *rules of origin* to establish when a good is made in a member country and hence is able to pass tariff-free across their borders, and when it is imported from outside the FTA and hence is subject to tariffs when it crosses borders within the FTA. The three countries in North America formed a free-trade area when they created the NAFTA in 1994. In 1997, Canada signed a bilateral FTA with Chile, and in 2001 negotiated an FTA with Costa Rica. It is currently in negotiations with Singapore.

free trade area (FTA) An agreement among two or more countries to abolish tariffs on trade among themselves while each remains free to set its own tariffs against other countries.

A **customs union** is a free trade area in which the member countries agree to establish a common trade policy with the rest of the world. Because they have a common trade policy, the members need neither customs controls on goods moving among themselves nor rules of origin. Once a good has entered any member country it has met the common rules and regulations and paid the common tariff and so it may henceforth be treated the same as a good that is produced within the union. An example of a customs union is Mercosur, an agreement linking Argentina, Brazil, Paraguay, and Uruguay.

customs union A group of countries who agree to have free trade among themselves and a common set of barriers against imports from the rest of the world.

A **common market** is a customs union that also has free movement of labour and capital among its members. The European Union is by far the most successful example of a common market. Indeed, the EU is now moving toward a full *economic union* in which all economic policies in the member countries are harmonized. The adoption of the euro as the EU's common currency in 1999 was a significant step in this direction.

common market A customs union with the added provision that labour and capital can move freely among the members.

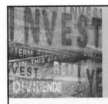

APPLYING ECONOMIC CONCEPTS 34-1

Should the WTO Be Abolished?

Globalization protesters often direct their wrath at the World Trade Organization. Extremists argue that all institutions supporting globalization should be abolished. Other critics admit that globalization is inevitable, but the WTO is so faulty in providing a rules-based system that it does more harm than good.

Supporters of the WTO argue that it is the best hope for poor countries who would be most oppressed in a lawless world where rich countries, particularly the United States and members of the European Union, could behave as they wished. Rather than allowing the poorer countries to flounder in a lawless world, the WTO provides a rules-based regime and has a dispute-settlement function that has heard more than 300 cases. Even if the rich countries do exert undue power over the negotiations, at least the WTO meetings provide a forum for poor nations to speak out and broker alliances. The alternative—no voice in a no-rules system—would be much worse.

Critics may respond that while the existence of the dispute-settlement mechanism may be beneficial, the enforcement of those settlements is undermined by disparities in economic power. Nations with large economies can use trade sanctions against small nations, but the small nation that attempts the same often inflicts the most harm on its own economy. Supporters of the WTO agree that this *is* a major defect, but the dispute-settlement mechanism has accomplished much, and to discard it because of imperfect enforcement would be a great loss. What is needed is *reform*—with larger economies agreeing to graduated enforcement mechanisms, including stiffer penalties for themselves.

Critics also claim that the WTO is a failure because it does not permit the imposition of trade sanctions against countries which pollute their own environments or exploit their own workers. But the poorest countries, many of whom are strong WTO supporters, fear that advanced countries would use environmental and labour standards written into the body of trade agreements as disguised non-tariff barriers. To the poorer countries it would be "policy imperialism" to argue that they should be forced to accept the standards of environmental and labour protection that the rich countries can only now afford.

Critics also complain that the WTO is undemocratic. In response, supporters point out that it is representatives of sovereign nations, usually elected ones, who conduct the negotiations, and that any agreements must be ratified by respective national parliaments before they come into effect. It is unlikely that any organization able to achieve agreement among 155 member-country governments could be any more democratic while still being effective.

Finally, some critics claim that the WTO is simply a tool for those who advocate a doctrinaire form of *laissez-faire* capitalism. It is true that some WTO supporters believe that unfettered free markets can meet all social requirements. A far larger number of supporters, however, believe that the market system needs government involvement if it is to meet societal needs for justice and growth. The vast majority of supporters agree that most, if not all, trade restrictions are harmful and that the WTO, with its mission of continued trade liberalization, can create significant benefits to rich and poor countries alike.

Trade Creation and Trade Diversion   A major effect of regional trade liberalization is to reallocate resources. Economists divide these effects into two categories: *trade creation* and *trade diversion*. These concepts were first developed by Jacob Viner, a Canadian-born economist who taught at the University of Chicago and Princeton University and was a leading economic theorist in the first half of the twentieth century.

Trade creation occurs when producers in one member country find that they can export to another member country as a result of the elimination of the tariffs. For example, when the North American Free Trade Agreement (NAFTA) eliminated most cross-border tariffs among Mexico, Canada, and the United States, some U.S. firms found that they could undersell their Canadian competitors in some product lines, and some Canadian firms found that they could undersell their U.S. competitors in other

trade creation A consequence of reduced trade barriers among a set of countries whereby trade within the group is increased and trade with the rest of the world remains roughly constant.

product lines. As a result, specialization occurred, and new international trade developed.

Trade creation represents efficient specialization according to comparative advantage.

Trade diversion occurs when exporters in one member country *replace* foreign exporters as suppliers to another member country. For example, trade diversion occurs when U.S. firms find that they can undersell competitors from the rest of the world in the Canadian market, not because they are the cheapest source of supply, but because their tariff-free prices under NAFTA are lower than the tariff-burdened prices of imports from other countries. This effect is a gain to U.S. firms and Canadian consumers of the product. U.S. firms get new business and therefore they clearly gain. Canadian consumers buy the product at a lower tariff-free price from the U.S. producer than they used to pay to the third-country producer (with a tariff), and so they are also better off. But Canada as a whole is worse off as a result of the trade diversion. Canada is now buying the product from a U.S. producer at a higher price with no tariff. Previous to the agreement, it was buying from a third-country producer at a lower price (and collecting tariff revenue).

> **trade diversion** A consequence of reduced trade barriers among a set of countries whereby trade within the group replaces trade that used to take place with countries outside the group.

From the global perspective, trade diversion represents an inefficient use of resources.

One argument *against* regional trade agreements is that the costs of trade diversion may outweigh the benefits of trade creation. While recognizing this possibility, many economists believe that regional agreements, especially among only a few countries, are much easier to negotiate than multilateral agreements through the WTO. In addition, regional agreements may represent effective incremental progress in what is a very lengthy process of achieving global free trade.

The North American Free Trade Agreement

The NAFTA dates from 1994 and is an extension of the 1989 Canada–U.S. Free Trade Agreement (FTA). It is a free trade area and not a customs union; each country retains its own external trade policy, and rules of origin are needed to determine when a good is made within the NAFTA and thus allowed to move freely among the members.

National Treatment The fundamental principle that guides the NAFTA is the principle of *national treatment*. The principle of national treatment is that individual countries are free to establish any laws they wish, with the sole proviso that these laws must not discriminate on the basis of nationality. For example, Canada can have tough environmental laws, but it must enforce these laws equally on *all* firms located in Canada, independent of their nationality. In addition, Canada can have strict product standards, but it must enforce these equally on domestically produced and imported goods. The idea of national treatment is to allow a maximum of policy independence while preventing national policies from being used as trade barriers.

Other Major Provisions There are several other major provisions in NAFTA. First, all tariffs on trade between the United States and Canada were eliminated by 1999. Canada–Mexico and Mexico–U.S. tariffs are to be phased out by 2010. Also, a number of nontariff barriers are eliminated or restricted.

Second, the agreement guarantees national treatment to foreign investment once it enters a country while permitting each country to screen a substantial amount of inbound foreign investment before it enters.

Third, all existing measures that restrict trade and investment that are not explicitly removed by the agreement are "grandfathered," a term referring to the continuation of a practice that predates the agreement and would have been prohibited by the terms of the agreement were it not specifically exempted. This is probably the single most important departure from free trade under the NAFTA. Under it, a large collection of restrictive measures in each of the three countries are given indefinite life. An alternative would have been to "sunset" all of these provisions by negotiating dates at which each would be eliminated. From the point of view of long-term trade liberalization, even a 50-year extension would have been preferable to an indefinite exemption. In Canada, the main examples are supply-managed agricultural products and the cultural industries (both of which may be liberalized over time as a result of WTO negotiations).

Fourth, trade in most nongovernmental services is liberalized by giving service firms the right of establishment in all member countries and the privilege of national treatment. There is also a limited opening of the markets in financial services to entry from firms based in the NAFTA countries.

Finally, a significant minority of government procurement is opened to cross-border bids.

Dispute Settlement   From Canada's point of view, by far the biggest setback in the negotiations for the Canada–U.S. FTA was the failure to obtain agreement on a common regime for countervailing and antidumping duties. In view of that failure, no significant attempt was made to deal with this issue in the subsequent NAFTA negotiations. The U.S. Congress had been unwilling to abandon the unilateral use of these powerful weapons.

In the absence of such a multilateral regime, a NAFTA dispute-settlement mechanism was created. Under it, the justifications required for the levying of antidumping and countervailing duties are subject to review by a panel of Canadians, Americans, and Mexicans. This international review replaces appeal through the domestic courts. The panel has the power to suspend any duties until it is satisfied that the domestic laws have been correctly and fairly applied.

The establishment of the dispute-settlement mechanism in NAFTA was pathbreaking: For the first time in its history, the United States agreed to submit the administration of its domestic laws to *binding* scrutiny by an international panel that often contains a majority of foreigners.

Results   The Canada–U.S. FTA aroused a great debate in Canada. Indeed, the Canadian federal election of 1988 was fought almost entirely on the issue of free trade. Supporters looked for major increases in the security of existing trade from U.S. protectionist attacks and for a growth of new trade. Detractors predicted a flight of firms to the United States, the loss of many Canadian jobs, and even the demise of Canada's political independence.

By and large, however, both the Canada–U.S. FTA and NAFTA agreements worked out just about as expected by their supporters. Industry restructured in the direction of greater export orientation in all three countries, and trade creation occurred. The flow of trade among the three countries increased markedly, but especially so between Canada and the United States. As the theory of trade predicts, specialization occurred in many areas, resulting in more U.S. imports of some product lines from Canada and more U.S. exports of other goods to Canada. In 1988, before the Canada–U.S. FTA took effect, Canada exported $85 billion in goods to the United States, and imported $74 billion from the United States. By 2005, the value of Canada–U.S. trade had more than quadrupled—Canadian exports of goods to the United States had increased to $369 billion and imports from the United States had

For information about NAFTA, go to the website for the NAFTA Secretariat: **www.nafta-sec-alena.org**.

APPLYING ECONOMIC CONCEPTS 34-2

Canadian Wine: A Free-Trade Success Story

Before the Canada–U.S. FTA was signed in 1989, great fears were expressed over the fate of the Canadian wine industry, located mainly in Ontario and British Columbia. It was heavily tariff protected and, with a few notable exceptions, concentrated mainly on cheap, low-quality products. Contrary to most people's expectations, rather than being decimated, the industry now produces a wide variety of high-quality products, some of which have won international competitions.

The nature of the pre-FTA protection largely explains the dramatic turnaround of the Canadian wine industry once the FTA took effect. First, Canadian wine producers were protected by high tariffs on imported wine, but were at the same time required by law to produce wine using only domestically grown grapes. The domestic grape growers, however, produced varieties of grapes not conducive to the production of high-quality wines, and with a captive domestic market, they had little incentive to change their behaviour. Thus, Canadian wine producers concentrated their efforts on "hiding" the attributes of poor-quality grapes rather than enhancing the attributes of high-quality grapes. The result was low-quality wine.

The second important aspect of the protection was that the high Canadian tariff was levied on a per unit rather than on an *ad valorem* basis. For example, the tariff was expressed as so many dollars per litre rather than as a specific percentage of the price. Charging a tariff by the litre gave most protection to the low quality wines with low value per litre. The higher the per-litre value of the wine, the lower the percentage tariff protection. For example, a $5-per-litre tariff would have the following effects. A low-quality imported wine valued at $5 per litre would have its price raised to $10, a 100 percent increase in price, whereas a higher quality imported wine valued at $25 per litre would have its price increased to $30, only a 20 percent increase in price.

Responding to these incentives, the Canadian industry concentrated on low-quality wines. The market for these wines was protected by the nearly prohibitive tariffs on competing low-quality imports, and also by the high prices charged for high-quality imports. In addition, protection was provided by many hidden charges that the various provincial governments' liquor monopolies levied in order to protect local producers.

When the tariff was removed under the FTA, the incentives were to move up-market, producing much more value per acre of land. Fortunately, much of the Canadian wine-growing land in the Okanagan Valley in B.C. and the Niagara Peninsula in Ontario is well-suited for growing the grapes required for good wines. Within a very few years, and with some government assistance to grape growers to make the transition from low-quality to high-quality grapes, Canadian wines were competing effectively with imported products in the medium-quality range. B.C. and Ontario wines do not yet reach the quality of major French wines in the $50–$70 (per bottle) range but they compete very effectively in quality with wines in the $15–$25 range, and sometimes even higher up the quality scale.

The success of the wine industry is a fine example of how tariffs can distort incentives and push an industry into a structure that makes it dependent on the tariff. Looking at the pre-FTA industry, very few people suspected that it would be able to survive, let alone produce a world-class product.

Prior to the FTA, the nature of protection encouraged the production of low-quality grapes and wine in Canada. The reduction in tariffs brought about by the FTA led to a successful restructuring of the Canadian wine industry.

increased to $260 billion. (Note that these figures exclude trade in services; with services included, the increase in Canada–U.S. trade between 1988 and 2005 would be even larger.)

It is hard to say how much trade diversion there has been and will be in the future. The greatest potential for trade diversion is with Mexico, which competes in the U.S. and Canadian markets with a large number of products produced in other low-wage countries. Southeast Asian exporters to the United States and Canada have been worried that Mexico would capture some of their markets by virtue of having tariff-free access denied to their goods. Most estimates predict, however, that trade creation will dominate over trade diversion.

Most transitional difficulties were initially felt in each country's import-competing industries, just as theory predicts. An agreement such as the NAFTA brings its advantages by encouraging a movement of resources out of protected but inefficient import-competing industries, which decline, and into efficient export industries, which expand because they have better access to the markets of other member countries. Southern Ontario and parts of Quebec had difficulties as some traditional exports fell and labour and capital were shifting to sectors where trade was expanding. By the late 1990s, however, Southern Ontario was booming again and its most profitable sectors were those that exported to the United States.

There were also some pleasant surprises resulting from free trade. Two Canadian industries that many economists expected to suffer from the FTA and NAFTA were winemaking and textiles. Yet both of these industries prospered as Canadian firms improved quality, productivity, and benefited from increased access to the huge U.S. market. *Applying Economic Concepts 34-2* discusses the success of the Canadian wine industry after the tariffs on wine were eliminated.

Finally, the dispute-settlement mechanism seems to have worked well. A large number of disputes have arisen and have been referred to panels. (Interested readers can read updated accounts of settled and ongoing disputes on the website for the Department of Foreign Affairs and International Trade at **www.dfait.gc.ca**.) Panel members have usually reacted as professionals rather than as nationals. Most cases have been decided on their merits; allegations that decisions were reached on national rather than professional grounds have been rare.

S U M M A R Y

34.1 **FREE TRADE OR PROTECTION?**

- The case for free trade is that world output of all products can be higher under free trade than when protectionism restricts regional specialization.
- Trade protection may be advocated to promote economic diversification or to provide protection for specific groups. The cost of such protection is lower average living standards.
- Protection can also be urged on the grounds that it may lead to higher living standards for the protectionist country than would a policy of free trade. Such a result might come about by using a monopoly position to influence the terms of trade or by developing a dynamic

comparative advantage by allowing inexperienced or uneconomically small industries to become efficient enough to compete with foreign industries.

- Some fallacious protectionist arguments are that (a) mutually advantageous trade is impossible because one trader's gain must always be the other's loss; (b) buying abroad sends our money abroad, while buying at home keeps our money at home; (c) our high-paid workers must be protected against the competition from low-paid foreign workers; and (d) imports are to be discouraged because they reduce national income and cause unemployment.

34.2 **METHODS OF PROTECTION**

- A tariff raises the domestic price of the imported product and leads to a reduction in the level of imports. Domestic consumers lose and domestic producers gain. The overall effect of a tariff is a deadweight loss for the importing country.
- A quota (or voluntary export restriction) restricts the amount of imports and thus drives up the domestic price of the good. Domestic consumers lose and domes-

tic producers gain. The overall effect is a *larger* deadweight loss than with a tariff because, rather than the importing country collecting tariff revenue, foreign producers benefit from a higher price.
- Antidumping and countervailing duties, although providing legitimate restraints on unfair trading practices, are often used as serious barriers to trade.

34.3 **CURRENT TRADE POLICY**

- The General Agreement on Tariffs and Trade (GATT), under which countries agreed to reduce trade barriers through multilateral negotiations and not to raise them unilaterally, has greatly reduced world tariffs since its inception in 1947.
- The World Trade Organization (WTO) was created in 1995 as the successor to GATT. It has 155 member countries and contains a formal dispute-settlement mechanism.
- Regional trade-liberalizing agreements such as free trade areas and common markets bring efficiency gains

through trade creation and efficiency losses through trade diversion.
- The North American Free Trade Agreement (NAFTA) is the world's largest and most successful free trade area, and the European Union is the world's largest and most successful common market.
- NAFTA is based on the principle of "national treatment." This allows Canada, the United States, and Mexico to implement whatever social, economic, or environmental policies they choose providing that such policies treat foreign and domestic firms (and their products) equally.

KEY CONCEPTS

Free trade and protectionism
Tariffs and import quotas
Voluntary export restrictions (VERs)
Countervailing and antidumping
 duties

The General Agreement on Tariffs and
 Trade (GATT)
The World Trade Organization (WTO)
Common markets, customs unions,
 and free trade areas

Trade creation and trade diversion
Nontariff barriers
The North American Free Trade
 Agreement (NAFTA)

STUDY EXERCISES

1. Fill in the blanks to make the following statements correct.

   a. The _____ argument provided the rationale for Canada's National Policy of 1876. A high tariff wall allowed many Canadian industries to develop where they may not have been able to compete otherwise.
   b. Advertisements that encourage us to "buy Canadian" are promoting a(n) _____ argument for protection. The reason is that money spent on imported goods must ultimately be spent on _____ goods and services anyway.

   c. Fallacious arguments for protection usually come from a misunderstanding of the gains from _____ or from the misbelief that protection can increase total _____.

2. Fill in the blanks to make the following statements correct.

   a. A tariff imposed on the import of leather shoes will cause a(n) _____ in the domestic price. Total quantity of leather shoes sold in Canada will _____. Domestic (Canadian) production of leather shoes will _____ and the quantity of shoes imported will _____.

b. The beneficiaries of the tariff described above are _____ because they receive a higher price for the same good and _____ because they receive tariff revenue. The parties that are clearly worse off are _____ because they now pay a higher price for the same good, and _____ because they sell less in the Canadian market.

c. The overall effect of a tariff on the importing country is a(n) _____ in welfare. The tariff creates a(n) _____ loss for the economy.

d. Suppose an import quota restricted the import of leather shoes into Canada to 20 000 pairs per year when the free trade imported amount was 40 000 pairs. The domestic price will _____, total quantity sold in Canada will _____, and domestic production will _____.

e. The beneficiaries of the quota described above are _____ and _____ because they both receive a higher price in the Canadian market. The party that is clearly worse off is _____ because they are now paying a higher price.

f. The overall effect of an import quota on the importing country is a(n) _____ in welfare. The quota imposes a(n) _____ loss for the economy.

3. Fill in the blanks to make the following statements correct.

a. A regional trade agreement such as NAFTA, or a common market such as the European Union, allows for _____, whereby trade within the group of member countries is increased.

b. A regional trade agreement such as NAFTA, or a common market such as the European Union, also results in _____, whereby trade within the group of member countries replaces trade previously done with other _____.

c. The fundamental principle that guides NAFTA is the principle of _____, which means that any member country can implement the policies of its choosing, as long as _____ and _____ firms are treated equally.

4. Canada produces steel domestically and also imports it from abroad. Assume that the world market for steel is competitive and that Canada is a small producer, unable to affect the world price. Since Canada imports steel, we know that in the absence of trade, the Canadian equilibrium price would exceed the world price.

a. Draw a diagram showing the Canadian market for steel, with imports at the world price.

b. Explain why the imposition of a tariff on imported steel will increase the price of steel in Canada.

c. Who benefits and who is harmed by such a tariff? Show these effects in your diagram.

5. **myeconlab** The diagram below shows the Canadian market for leather shoes, which we assume to be competitive. The world price is p_w. If the Canadian government imposes a tariff of t dollars per unit, the domestic price then rises to $p_w + t$.

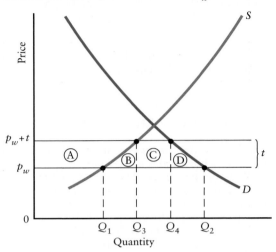

a. What quantity of leather shoes is imported before the tariff is imposed? After the tariff?

b. What is the effect of the tariff on the Canadian production of shoes? Which areas in the diagram show the increase in domestic producer surplus?

c. Which areas in the diagram show the reduction in domestic consumer surplus as a result of the higher Canadian price?

d. The Canadian government earns tariff revenue on the imported shoes. Which area in the diagram shows this tariff revenue?

6. Use the diagram from Question 5 to analyze the effects of imposing an import quota instead of a tariff to protect domestic shoe producers. Draw the diagram as in Question 5 and answer the following questions.

a. Explain why an import quota of Q_3Q_4 raises the domestic price to $p_w + t$.

b. With import quotas, the Canadian government earns no tariff revenue. Who gets this money now?

c. Is the import quota better or worse than the tariff for Canada as a whole? Explain.

7. Under pressure from the Canadian and U.S. governments in the early 1980s, Japanese automobile producers agreed to restrict their exports to the North American market. After the formal agreement ended, the Japanese producers decided unilaterally to continue restricting their exports. Carefully review Figure 34-2 and then answer the following questions.

a. Explain why such Voluntary Export Restrictions (VERs) are "voluntary."

b. Explain why an agreement to export only 100 000 cars to North America is better for the Japanese producers than a North American tariff that results in the same volume of Japanese exports.

c. Who is paying for these benefits to the Japanese producers?

8. Go to Statistics Canada's website: **www.statcan.ca**. Go to "Canadian Statistics," type in "international trade," and answer the following questions.

   a. For the most recent year shown, what was the value of Canada's exports to the United States? To the European Union?

   b. For the same year, what was the value of Canada's imports from the United States? From the European Union?

   c. Compute what economists call the "volume of trade" (the sum of exports and imports) between Canada and the United States. How has the volume of trade grown over the past five years? Has trade grown faster than national income?

9. **myeconlab** The table below shows the prices *in Canada* of cotton towels produced in the United States, Canada, and Malaysia. Suppose cotton towels are identical.

Producing Country	Canadian Price (in $) Without Tariff	Canadian Price (in $) With 20% Tariff
Canada	4.75	4.75
United States	4.50	5.40
Malaysia	4.00	4.80

a. Suppose Canada imposes a 20 percent tariff on imported towels from any country. Assuming that Canadians purchase only the lowest-price towels, from which country will Canada buy its towels?

b. Now suppose Canada eliminates tariffs on towels from all countries. Which towels will Canada now buy?

c. Canada and the United States now negotiate a free-trade agreement that eliminates all tariffs between the two countries, but Canada maintains the 20 percent tariff on other countries. Which towels now get imported into Canada?

d. Which of the situations described above is called trade creation and which is called trade diversion?

DISCUSSION QUESTIONS

1. Some Canadians opposed Canada's entry into NAFTA on the grounds that Canadian firms could not compete with the goods produced by cheap Mexican labour. Comment on the following points in relation to the above worries:

   a. "Mexicans are the most expensive cheap labour I have ever encountered"—statement by the owner of a Canadian firm that is moving back to Canada from Mexico.

   b. The theory of the gains from trade says that a high-productivity, high-wage country can gain from trading with a low-wage, low-productivity country.

   c. Technological change is rapidly reducing labour costs as a proportion of total costs in many products; in many industries that use high-tech production methods this proportion is already well below 20 percent.

2. Should Canada and the United States trade with countries with poor human rights records? If trade with China is severely restricted because of its lack of respect for human rights, who will be the gainers and who the losers? Argue the cases that this policy will help, and that it will hinder, human rights progress in China.

3. Import quotas and voluntary export restrictions are often used instead of tariffs. What real difference, if any, is there between quotas, voluntary export restrictions (VERs), and tariffs? Explain why lobbyists for some import-competing industries (cheese, milk, shoes) support import quotas while lobbyists for others (pizza manufacturers, soft drink manufacturers, retail stores) oppose them. Would you expect labour unions to support or oppose quotas?

4. Over the past several years, many foreign automobile producers have built production and assembly facilities in Canada. What are some advantages and disadvantages associated with shifting production from, for example, Japan to Canada? Will these cars still be considered "imports"? What is beginning to happen to the definitions of "foreign made" and "domestic made"?

5. Consider a mythical country called Forestland, which exports a large amount of lumber to a nearby country called Houseland. The lumber industry in Houseland has convinced its federal government that it is being harmed by the low prices being charged by the lumber producers in Forestland. You are an advisor to the government in Forestland. Explain who gains and who loses from each of the following policies.

a. Houseland imposes a tariff on lumber imports from Forestland

b. Forestland imposes a tax on each unit of lumber exported to Houseland

c. Forestland agrees to restrict its exports of lumber to Houseland

d. Which policy is likely to garner the most political support in Houseland? In Forestland?

6. In March 1999, the Canadian government imposed antidumping duties of up to 43 percent on hot-rolled steel imports from France, Russia, Slovakia, and Romania. The allegation was that these countries were dumping steel into the Canadian market.

a. Who benefits from such alleged dumping? Who is harmed?

b. Who benefits from the imposition of the antidumping duties? Who is harmed?

c. Is Canada as a whole made better off by the imposition of the duties? Explain.

Exchange Rates and the Balance of Payments

LO LEARNING OBJECTIVES

In this chapter you will learn

1. the components of Canada's balance of payments and why the balance of payments must always balance.
2. about the demand for and supply of foreign currency.
3. the various factors that cause fluctuations in the exchange rate.
4. why a current account deficit is not necessarily undesirable.
5. the theory of purchasing power parity (PPP) and its limitations.
6. how flexible exchange rates can dampen the effects of external shocks.

In 1973, it cost only 96 Canadian cents to purchase one U.S. dollar. Almost thirty years later, in 2001, the Canadian dollar had depreciated so much that it then cost over $1.55 Canadian to purchase one U.S. dollar. This 30-year depreciation of the Canadian dollar was neither smooth nor steady. During the late 1980s, the Canadian dollar appreciated by over 10 percent; during the late 1990s, it depreciated just as much. Then, between 2002 and 2006, the Canadian dollar appreciated sharply against the U.S. dollar; the price of a U.S. dollar fell from $1.55 Canadian to $1.11 Canadian. What explains these dramatic movements in the exchange rate?

In this chapter we examine what determines the exchange rate, why it changes, and the effects these changes have on the economy. The discussion will bring together material on three topics studied elsewhere in this book: the theory of supply and demand (Chapter 3), the nature of money (Chapter 27), and international trade (Chapter 33).

We begin by examining a country's balance of payments—the record of transactions in goods, services, and assets with the rest of the world. After introducing terms, we see why the balance of payments is defined in such a way that it *always* balances.

35.1 THE BALANCE OF PAYMENTS

balance of payments accounts A summary record of a country's transactions with the rest of the world, including the buying and selling of goods, services, and assets.

Statistics Canada documents transactions between Canada and the rest of the world. The record of such transactions is made in the **balance of payments accounts**. For computing Canada's balance of payments, each transaction, such as the exports or imports of goods, or the international purchase or sales of assets, is classified according to whether the transaction generates a *payment* or a *receipt* for Canada.

Table 35-1 shows the major items in the Canadian balance of payments accounts for 2005. Transactions that represent a receipt for Canada, such as the sale of a product or asset to foreigners, are recorded in the balance of payments accounts as a *credit* item. Transactions that represent a payment for Canada, such as the purchase of a product or asset from foreigners, are recorded as a *debit* item.

There are two main categories to the balance of payments: the *current account* and the *capital account*. We examine each account in turn.

The Current Account

current account The part of the balance of payments accounts that records payments and receipts arising from trade in goods and services and from interest and dividends that are earned by capital owned in one country and invested in another.

The **current account** records transactions arising from trade in goods and services. It also includes net investment income earned from foreign asset holdings. The current account is divided into two main sections.

The first section, called the **trade account**, records payments and receipts arising from the import and export of goods, such as computers and cars, and services, such as legal or architectural services. (Tourism constitutes a large part of the trade in services.) Canadian imports of goods and services require a payment to foreigners and thus are entered as debit items on the trade account; Canadian exports of goods and services generate a receipt to Canada and thus are recorded as credit items.

trade account In the balance of payments, this account records exports and imports of goods and services.

The second section, called the **capital-service account**, records the payments and receipts that represent income on assets. When a firm located in Canada, for example, pays dividends to foreign owners, the payments to foreigners are a debit item in Canada's balance of payments. In contrast, when Canadians earn income from their foreign-located investments, these receipts for Canada are recorded as credit items.

capital-service account In the balance of payments, this account records the payments and receipts that represent income on assets (such as interest and dividends).

As shown in Table 35-1, Canadian exports of goods and services were $518 billion in 2005, and Canadian imports of goods and services were $467 billion. The trade account had a surplus of $51 billion—in other words, in 2005 Canada sold $51 billion more worth of goods and services to the world than it bought from the world. But in terms of the capital-service account, things were the other way around. The table shows that Canadians paid $19 billion more to foreigners in investment income than they received from foreigners. The current account balance (the sum of the trade and capital-service accounts) had a surplus of $31.9 billion.

The Capital Account

capital account The part of the balance of payments accounts that records payments and receipts arising from the import and export of long-term and short-term financial capital.

The **capital account** records international transactions in assets, including bonds, shares of companies, real estate, and factories. The purchase of foreign assets by Canadians is treated just like the purchase of foreign goods. Since purchasing a foreign asset requires a payment from Canadians to foreigners, it is entered as a debit item in the Canadian capital account. Note that when Canadians purchase foreign assets, financial capital is leaving Canada and going abroad, and so this is called a *capital outflow*. In contrast, the sale of Canadian assets to foreigners generates a receipt for Canada, and thus is entered as a credit item in the Canadian capital account. When Canadians sell assets to foreigners, financial capital is entering Canada from abroad, and so this is called a *capital inflow*.

As shown in Table 35-1, in 2005, Canadians increased their holdings of assets abroad by $114.2 billion, resulting in a capital outflow of that amount. At the same time, foreigners increased their holdings of assets in Canada by $86.6 billion, resulting in a capital inflow of that amount. Though not shown in the table, the capital account distinguishes between *direct investment* and *portfolio investment*. The former involves the purchase or sale of assets that alter the legal control of those assets, such as when a controlling interest of a company is purchased. The latter involves transactions in assets that do not alter the legal control of the assets, such as when a minority of a company's shares is purchased.

One part of the capital account shows the government's transactions in its official foreign-exchange reserves. This *official financing account* is included as part of the capital account because official reserves are *assets* rather than goods or services. If the government increases its reserves, it does so by purchasing foreign-currency assets, and this is recorded as a debit item in the official financing account. If the government instead reduces its reserves, it sells some foreign-currency assets, and this transaction would be recorded as a credit item in the official financing account. In 2005, the Government of Canada increased its official reserves by $1.7 billion.

In 2005, the overall capital account had a deficit of $29.3 billion, meaning that there was a net capital outflow of this amount from Canada to the rest of the world. In other words, Canadian households, firms, and governments, taken together, increased their net holdings of foreign assets by $29.3 billion in 2005.

The Balance of Payments Must Balance

The current account balance represents the difference between the payments and receipts from international transactions in goods and services. The capital account balance is the difference between payments and receipts from international transactions in assets. The balance of payments is the sum of current account and capital account balances. In any given period (usually a year) the *current account plus the capital account must equal zero*. In other words, the balance of payments is always equal to zero. In algebraic terms, we can write

$$\text{Balance of Payments} = CA + KA = 0$$

where *CA* is the current account balance and *KA* is the capital account balance. Note that this is an *identity*—the accounting system used for the balance of payments defines transactions in such a way that *CA* + *KA* = 0. But this accounting system is based on

TABLE 35-1 Canadian Balance of Payments, 2005 (billions of dollars)

CURRENT ACCOUNT	
Trade Account	
Merchandise exports	+453.1
Service exports	+65.0
Merchandise imports	−388.2
Service imports	−78.7
Trade balance	+51.2
Capital-Service Account	
Net investment income (including unilateral transfers)	−19.3
Current Account balance	+31.9
CAPITAL ACCOUNT	
Net change in Canadian investments abroad [capital outflow (−)]	−114.2
Net change in foreign investments in Canada [capital inflow (+)]	+86.6
Official Financing Account	
Changes in international reserves [increases (−)]	−1.7
Capital Account Balance	−29.3
Statistical Discrepancy	−2.6
Balance of Payments	0.0

The overall balance of payments always balances, but the individual components do not have to. In 2005, Canada had an overall trade surplus (including trade in goods and services) of $51.2 billion. There was a deficit of $19.3 billion on the capital-service account. There was thus a $31.9 billion surplus on the current account. There was a deficit on the capital account of $29.3 billion because the trading of assets internationally resulted in a net outflow of capital. The statistical discrepancy entry of $2.6 billion compensates for the inability to measure some items accurately. The current account plus the capital account (plus the statistical discrepancy) is equal to the balance of payments—which is always zero.

(*Source:* Statistics Canada webpage: www.statcan.ca. Search for "balance of payments.")

some economic logic. Let's consider an example that illustrates the logical connection between the current and capital accounts.

Consider a year in which Canadian households, firms, and governments, taken together, purchase $100 billion in goods and services from the rest of the world. During the same year, Canadians sell $150 billion of goods and services to the rest of the world. Exports are $150 billion and imports are $100 billion, so Canada has a current account surplus of $50 billion, CA = $50 billion. (We suppose for simplicity that the capital-service account is zero.) The meaning of this $50 billion surplus is that Canadians now have claims on foreigners equal to $50 billion—that is, foreigners owe Canadians $50 billion. What does Canada do with these claims?

There are *only* two possibilities. The first is that Canadians use these $50 billion in claims to purchase $50 billion in additional goods and services from the rest of the world. In this case, Canada's imports rise to $150 billion and the current account is now in balance (CA = 0). Since there have been no transactions in assets, the capital account is also in balance (KA = 0). It is clear now that $CA + KA = 0$.

The only other possibility is that Canadians use these $50 billion in claims to purchase assets from foreigners—a capital outflow from Canada. They could purchase land, bonds, corporate shares, or factories. But whatever they purchase, the capital account will now be in deficit by $50 billion ($KA$ = –$50 billion). In this case, the current account surplus of $50 billion is exactly offset by the capital account deficit of $50 billion. Once again we have $CA + KA = 0$.

Any surplus on the current account must be matched by an equal deficit on the capital account. A current account surplus thus implies a capital outflow. The balance of payments is always zero.

Notice that the opposite situation is also possible, and that the balance of payments again sums to zero. Suppose Canadians purchase $75 billion more in goods and services from the rest of the world than they sell—so Canada has a current account deficit of $75 billion, CA = –$75 billion. (We continue to assume that the capital-service account is zero.) The rest of the world now has claims of this amount on Canadians, claims which must be used either to purchase more Canadian goods and services or more Canadian assets. If foreigners purchase $75 billion in additional Canadian goods and services, Canada's current account is balanced (CA = 0) and we again have $CA + KA = 0$. If foreigners choose instead to purchase $75 billion in Canadian assets, then Canada's capital account will be in surplus by $75 billion—a capital inflow. In this case, the current account will be in deficit (CA = –$75 billion) and the capital account will be in surplus (KA = $75 billion), but again we see that $CA + KA = 0$.

Any deficit in the current account must be matched by an equal surplus in the capital account. A current-account deficit thus implies a net capital inflow. The balance of payments is always zero.

Let's go back and review the actual numbers from Table 35-1. In 2005, Canada had a current account surplus of $31.9 billion. From these net exports of goods and services, Canadian firms and households therefore accumulated $31.9 billion in new claims on foreigners in that year. With these claims, Canadians then purchased the same amount (aside from the statistical discrepancy) in foreign assets, and so there was a capital outflow, or a capital account deficit. The balance of payments, as always, was in balance.

That the balance of payments always sums to zero is important. This result is not based on assumptions about behaviour or any other theoretical reasoning—it is an *accounting identity*. Many people nonetheless find balance of payments accounting

For balance of payments statistics for many countries, see the IMF's website: **www.imf.org**.

confusing. *Applying Economic Concepts 35-1* discusses an individual student's balance of payments with the rest of the world, and illustrates why an individual's balance of payments must always balance.

A Balance of Payments Deficit?

The term "balance of payments deficit" does not make sense since the balance of payments must always balance. But such a term is nonetheless often used in the press and even by some economists. What does this mean? Most often the term is used carelessly—a balance of payments deficit is mentioned when what is actually meant is a current account deficit.

There are also occasions when people speak of a country as having a balance of payments deficit or surplus when they are actually referring to the balance of all accounts *excluding* the official financing account. In other words, they are referring to the combined balance on current and capital accounts, *excluding* the changes in the government's foreign-currency reserves. For example, consider a year in which the Government of Canada sells $5 billion of its foreign-currency reserves. This transaction is a credit item in the official financing account (part of Canada's capital account). It must be the case that *all other* items in the current and capital accounts *combined* must sum to an overall deficit. In this case, some people might say that Canada's balance of payments "deficit" is being financed by the government's sale of foreign-currency reserves. But when we use the terms properly, we know that Canada's balance of payments, as always, is balanced.

A "balance of payments deficit" refers to a situation in which the government is selling official foreign-currency reserves. A "balance of payments surplus" refers to a situation in which the government is buying official foreign-currency reserves. In both cases, as always, the balance of payments is actually in balance.

Summary

This brings us to the end of our discussion of the balance of payments. Keep in mind that this is just an exercise in accounting. Though at times you may find it difficult to keep the various credits and debits in the various accounts straight in your mind, remember that the structure of the accounting system is quite simple. Here is a brief review:

Practise with Study Guide Chapter 35, Short-Answer Question 1.

1. The current account shows all transactions in goods and services between Canada and the rest of the world (including investment income and transfers).

2. The capital account shows all transactions in assets between Canada and the rest of the world. Part of the capital account shows the change in the government's holding of foreign-currency reserves.

3. All transactions involving a payment from Canada appear as debit items. All transactions involving a receipt to Canada appear as credit items.

4. The balance of payments—the sum of the current account and the capital account—must, by definition, always be zero.

APPLYING ECONOMIC CONCEPTS 35-1

A Student's Balance of Payments with the Rest of the World

Many students find a country's balance of payments confusing, especially the idea that the balance of payments *must always* balance. Why, they often ask, can't Canada export more goods and services to the world than it imports, and at the same time have a net sale of assets to the rest of the world? The connection between the current-account transactions and the capital-account transactions is not always obvious.

Perhaps the easiest way to see this connection is to consider an individual's "balance of payments" with the rest of the world. Of course, most individuals would not normally compute their balance of payments, but by doing so we can recognize the everyday concepts involved and also see the necessary connection between any individual's "current account" and "capital account." The reason why Canada's balance of payments must always balance is exactly the same reason why an individual's balance of payments must always balance.

The table shows the balance of payments for Stefan, a university student. Stefan is fortunate in several respects. First, his parents are able to provide some of the funds needed to finance his education. Second, he has a summer job that pays well. Third, he was given some Canada Savings Bonds when he was born that provide him with some interest income every year.

Stefan's Balance of Payments

Current Account (Income and Expenditure)	
Labour income ("exports")	+$10 000
Purchase of goods and services ("imports")	−$17 000
Interest income	+$ 500
Transfers (from his parents)	+$10 000
Current Account Balance	+ $3 500

Capital Account (Changes in Assets) (− denotes an increase)	
Financial Assets	
Purchase of Canada Savings Bonds	−$1 500
Increase in Savings Account Deposits	−$2 000
Capital Account Balance	−$3 500
BALANCE OF PAYMENTS	$0

We now go on to explore how exchange rates are determined in the foreign-exchange market. We will see that a knowledge of the various categories in the balance of payments will help in our understanding of why changes in exchange rates occur.

35.2 THE FOREIGN-EXCHANGE MARKET

Money is vital in any sophisticated economy that relies on specialization and trade. Yet money as we know it is a *national* matter. If you live in Argentina, you earn pesos and spend pesos; if you operate a business in Austria, you borrow euros and pay your workers in euros. The currency of a country is acceptable within the border of that country, but usually it will not be accepted by firms and households in another country. Just try buying your next pair of jeans in Canada with British pounds sterling or Japanese yen.

The top part of the table shows Stefan's income and expenditures for a single year. This is his current account. The bottom part shows the change in Stefan's assets over the same year. This is his capital account. (Note that, for Stefan as well as for any country, the capital account does not show the overall stock of assets—it only shows the *changes* in the stock of assets during the year.)

Let's begin with his current account. Stefan has a good summer job that earns him $10 000 after taxes. This $10 000 represents Stefan's "exports" to the rest of the world—he earns this income by selling his labour services to a tree-planting company. Over the year, however, he spends $17 000 on tuition, books, clothes, beer, pizza, photocopying, and other goods and services. These are Stefan's "imports" from the rest of the world. Stefan clearly has a "trade deficit" equal to $7000—he "imports" more than he "exports."

There are two other sources of income shown in Stefan's current account. First, he earns $500 in interest income. Second, his parents give him $10 000 to help pay for his education—a *transfer* in the terminology of balance of payments accounting. The interest income and transfer together make up Stefan's "capital-service account"—Stefan has a surplus of $10 500.

Stefan's overall current account shows a surplus of $3500. This means he receives $3500 more than he spends on goods and services. But where does this $3500 go?

Now let's consider Stefan's capital account, the bottom part of the table. The $3500 surplus on current account *must* end up as increases in Stefan's assets. He increases his holdings of Canada Savings Bonds by $1500 and increases his savings-account deposits by $2000. In both cases he is purchasing assets—he buys a bond and he also "buys" a bank deposit. Since Stefan must make a payment to purchase these assets, each appears as a debit item in his capital account. Stefan's capital account balance is a deficit of $3500.

Finally, note that Stefan's current account and capital account *must* sum to zero. There is no way around this. Any surplus of income over expenditures (on current account) must show up as an increase in his assets (or a decrease in his debts) on capital account. Conversely, any excess of expenditures over income must be financed by reducing his assets (or by increasing his debts). Stefan's balance of payments *must* balance.

What is true for Stefan is true for any individual and also true for any accounting unit you choose to consider. Saskatoon's balance of payments with the rest of the world must balance. Saskatchewan's balance of payments with the rest of the world must balance. Western Canada's balance of payments with the rest of the world must balance. And so must Canada's, and any other country's.

Trade between countries normally requires the exchange of the currency of one country for that of another.

The exchange of one currency for another is called a *foreign-exchange transaction*. The **exchange rate** is the rate at which one currency exchanges for another. In Canada's case, the exchange rate is the Canadian-dollar price of one unit of foreign currency. For example, in July 2006, the price of one U.S. dollar was 1.11 Canadian dollars. Thus, the Canada–U.S. exchange rate was 1.11.

Note that in newspapers or radio reports the exchange rate is usually expressed in the opposite way—as the number of U.S. dollars that it takes to buy one Canadian dollar. So instead of reporting that the Canadian–U.S. exchange rate in July 2006 was 1.11, the press would say that the Canadian dollar was "worth" 90.1 U.S. cents (1/1.11 = 0.901).

We can choose to define the Canada–U.S. exchange rate either way: as the Canadian-dollar price of one U.S. dollar or as the U.S.-dollar price of one Canadian dollar. But we must choose one method and stick to it, otherwise our discussions will quickly become very confusing. In this book we *always* define the exchange rate in the

exchange rate The number of units of domestic currency required to purchase one unit of foreign currency.

way Canadian economists usually do—as the Canadian-dollar price of one unit of foreign currency. This definition makes it clear that foreign currency, like any good or service, has a price expressed in Canadian dollars. In this case, the price of the "good" has a special name—the exchange rate.

An **appreciation** of the Canadian dollar means that the Canadian dollar has become more valuable so that it takes fewer Canadian dollars to purchase one unit of foreign currency. For example, if the Canadian dollar appreciates against the U.S. dollar from 1.11 to 1.04, it takes 7 fewer Canadian cents to purchase one U.S. dollar. Thus, an appreciation of the Canadian dollar implies a *fall* in the exchange rate. Conversely, a **depreciation** of the Canadian dollar means that the Canadian dollar has become less valuable so that it takes more Canadian dollars to purchase one unit of foreign currency. Thus, a depreciation of the Canadian dollar means a *rise* in the exchange rate.

An appreciation of the Canadian dollar is a fall in the exchange rate; a depreciation of the Canadian dollar is a rise in the exchange rate.

We now go on to build a simple model of the foreign-exchange market. This will allow us to analyze the determinants of the exchange rate. To keep things simple, we use an example involving trade between Canada and Europe, and thus we examine the determination of the exchange rate between the two currencies, the Canadian dollar and the euro. But, in this example, Europe is just a shorthand for "the rest of the world" and the euro is just a shorthand for "all other currencies." (It would be more natural to think in terms of Canada–U.S. trade since 80 percent of Canadian trade is with the United States, but this quickly becomes confusing because both countries' currencies are called the dollar.)

Because Canadian dollars are traded for euros in the foreign-exchange market, it follows that a demand for euros implies a supply of Canadian dollars and that a supply of euros implies a demand for Canadian dollars.

For this reason, a theory of the exchange rate between dollars and euros can deal either with the demand and supply of dollars or with the demand and supply of euros; both need not be considered. We will concentrate on the demand, supply, and price of euros. Thus, the market we will be considering (in general terms) is the foreign-exchange market—the "product" is foreign exchange (euros in our case) and the "price" is the exchange rate (the Canadian-dollar price of euros).

We develop our example in terms of the demand and supply analysis first encountered in Chapter 3. To do so, we need only to recall that in the market for foreign exchange, transactions that generate a receipt for Canada in its balance of payments represent a *supply* of foreign exchange. Foreign exchange is being supplied by the foreigners who purchase Canadian goods or assets. Conversely, transactions that are a payment from Canada in the balance of payments represent a *demand* for foreign exchange. Foreign exchange is being demanded by the Canadians who are purchasing foreign goods or assets. In what follows we make the (realistic) assumption that the Bank of Canada makes no transactions in the foreign-exchange market. Later we discuss the role of central bank transactions.

The Supply of Foreign Exchange

Whenever foreigners purchase Canadian goods, services, or assets, they supply foreign currency to the foreign-exchange market and demand, in return, Canadian dollars with which to pay for their purchases. Thus, the supply of foreign exchange (and the asso-

---

appreciation A fall in the exchange rate—the domestic currency has become more valuable so that it takes fewer units of domestic currency to purchase one unit of foreign currency.

depreciation A rise in the exchange rate—the domestic currency has become less valuable so that it takes more units of domestic currency to purchase one unit of foreign currency.

ciated demand for Canadian dollars) arises from Canada's sales of goods, services, and assets to the rest of the world.

Canadian Exports   One important source of supply of foreign exchange is foreigners who wish to buy Canadian-made goods and services. A Japanese importer of lumber is such a purchaser; an Austrian couple planning a vacation in Canada is another; the Russian government seeking to buy Canadian engineering services is a third. All are sources of supply of foreign exchange, arising out of international trade. Each potential buyer wants to sell its own currency in exchange for Canadian dollars that it can then use to purchase Canadian goods and services.

Asset Sales: Capital Inflows   A second source of supply of foreign exchange comes from foreigners who wish to purchase Canadian assets, such as government or corporate bonds, real estate, or shares in a Canadian firm. To buy Canadian assets, holders of foreign currencies must first sell their foreign currency and buy Canadian dollars. As we saw earlier in the chapter, when Canadians sell assets to foreigners, we say there is a *capital inflow* to Canada.

Reserve Currency   Firms, banks, and governments often accumulate and hold foreign-exchange reserves, just as individuals maintain savings accounts. These reserves may be in several different currencies. For example, the government of Nigeria may decide to increase its reserve holdings of Canadian dollars and reduce its reserve holdings of euros; if it does so, it will be a supplier of euros (and a demander of Canadian dollars) in foreign-exchange markets.

Trade between countries that use different currencies requires that currencies also be exchanged; this takes place in foreign-exchange markets where exchange rates—the price of one currency in terms of another—are determined.

The Total Supply of Foreign Exchange   The supply of foreign exchange (or the demand for Canadian dollars) by holders of foreign currencies is the sum of the supplies for all of the purposes just discussed—for purchases of Canadian exports, for capital inflow to Canada, and for the purchase of Canadian dollars to add to currency reserves.

Furthermore, because people, firms, and governments in all countries purchase goods and assets from many other countries, the demand for any one currency will be the aggregate demand of individuals, firms, and governments in a number of different countries. Thus, the total supply of foreign exchange (or the demand for Canadian dollars) may include Germans who are offering euros, Japanese who are offering yen, Argentinians who are offering pesos, and so on. For simplicity, however, we go back to our two-country example and use only Canada and Europe.

The Supply Curve for Foreign Exchange   The supply of foreign exchange on the foreign-exchange market is represented by a positively sloped curve, such as the one shown in Figure 35-1. This figure plots the Canadian-dollar price of euros (the exchange rate) on the vertical axis and the quantity of euros on the horizontal axis. Moving up the vertical scale, more dollars are needed to purchase one euro—the dollar is depreciating. Moving down the vertical scale, fewer dollars are needed to purchase one euro—the dollar is appreciating.

FIGURE 35-1   The Foreign-Exchange Market

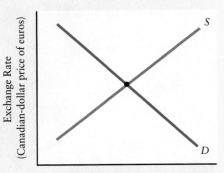

The demand for foreign exchange is negatively sloped, and the supply of foreign exchange is positively sloped, when plotted against the exchange rate, measured as the Canadian-dollar price of one unit of foreign currency. The demand for foreign exchange is given by the negatively sloped blue line *D*. It represents the sum of transactions on both current and capital accounts that require payments to foreigners.

The supply of foreign exchange is given by the positively sloped red line *S*. It represents the sum of transactions on both current and capital accounts that represent receipts from foreigners.

Why is the supply curve for foreign exchange positively sloped? Consider the supply of foreign exchange derived from foreign purchases of Canadian exports. If the Canadian dollar depreciates, it takes fewer euros to purchase one Canadian dollar. Thus, for a given Canadian-dollar price of the product the euro price has fallen. European consumers will therefore buy more of the cheaper Canadian goods and will thus supply more foreign exchange for this purpose. In the opposite case, when the dollar appreciates, the euro price of Canadian exports rises. European consumers will buy fewer Canadian goods and thus supply less foreign exchange.[1]

Similar considerations affect other sources of supply of foreign exchange. When the Canadian dollar depreciates (a higher exchange rate), Canadian securities and other assets become attractive purchases, and the quantity purchased will rise. With this rise, the amount of foreign exchange supplied to pay for the purchases will increase.

The supply curve for foreign exchange is positively sloped when it is plotted against the exchange rate; a depreciation of the Canadian dollar (a rise in the exchange rate) increases the quantity of foreign exchange supplied.

The Demand for Foreign Exchange

The demand for foreign exchange arises from all international transactions that represent a payment in Canada's balance of payments. What sorts of international transactions generate a demand for foreign exchange (and a supply of Canadian dollars)? Canadians seeking to purchase foreign products will be supplying Canadian dollars and demanding foreign exchange for this purpose. Canadians may also seek to purchase foreign assets. If they do, they will supply Canadian dollars and demand foreign exchange. Similarly, a country with reserves of Canadian dollars may decide to sell them in order to demand some other currency.

The Demand Curve for Foreign Exchange When the Canadian dollar depreciates against the euro, the Canadian-dollar price of European goods rises. Because it takes more dollars to buy the same European good, Canadians will buy fewer of the now more expensive European goods. The amount of foreign exchange being demanded by

---

1 We have assumed here that the foreign price elasticity of demand for Canadian exports is greater than 1, so that a price change leads to a proportionately larger change in quantity demanded. This is a common assumption in the analysis of international trade. In the case of Canada (and other small countries) it is common to go further and make the "small open economy" assumption—that the country faces *given world prices* for both its exports and imports. In this case, the foreign price elasticity of demand for exports is infinite.

Canadians in order to pay for imported European goods will fall.[2] In the opposite case, when the Canadian dollar appreciates, European goods become cheaper, more are sold, and more dollars are spent on them. Thus, more foreign exchange will be demanded to pay for the extra imports. This same argument applies in exactly the same way to the purchases of foreign assets. Figure 35-1 shows the demand curve for foreign exchange.

The demand curve for foreign exchange is negatively sloped when it is plotted against the exchange rate; an appreciation of the Canadian dollar (a fall in the exchange rate) increases the quantity of foreign exchange demanded.

35.3 THE DETERMINATION OF EXCHANGE RATES

The demand and supply curves in Figure 35-1 do not include official financing transactions (the demands for or supplies of foreign exchange by the Bank of Canada). To complete our analysis, we must incorporate the role of official financing transactions. We need to consider three important cases:

1. When the central bank makes no transactions in the foreign-exchange market, there is said to be a purely **flexible exchange rate.**

2. When the central bank intervenes in the foreign-exchange market to "fix" the exchange rate at a particular value, there is said to be a **fixed exchange rate** or *pegged exchange rate.*

3. Between these two "pure" systems is a variety of possible intermediate cases, including the *adjustable peg* and the *managed float.* In the **adjustable peg system,** central banks fix specific values for their exchange rates, but they explicitly recognize that circumstances may arise in which they will change that value. In a **managed float,** the central bank seeks to have some stabilizing influence on the exchange rate but does not try to fix it at some publicly announced value.

Most industrialized countries today operate a mostly flexible exchange rate. It is mostly market determined but the central bank sometimes intervenes to offset short-run fluctuations. The countries of the European Union (EU) had a system of fixed exchange rates (relative to each other's currencies) between 1979 and 1999. In 1999 the EU introduced a common currency—the euro—that was adopted by most of the EU member countries (an important exception being the United Kingdom). Thus, they now have no exchange rates for national currencies within the EU but the single common currency has a flexible exchange rate relative to countries outside the EU. The United States, Japan, the United Kingdom, Australia, and most other major industrialized countries have flexible exchange rates with relatively small amounts of foreign-exchange intervention by their central banks.

flexible exchange rate An exchange rate that is left free to be determined by the forces of demand and supply on the free market, with no intervention by central banks.

fixed exchange rate An exchange rate that is maintained within a small range around its publicly stated par value by the intervention in the foreign-exchange market by a country's central bank.

adjustable peg system A system in which exchange rates are fixed in the short term but are occasionally changed in response to changes in economic events.

managed float A situation in which the central bank intervenes in the foreign-exchange market to smooth out some of the large, short-term fluctuations in a country's exchange rate, while still leaving the market to determine the exchange rate in the longer term.

---

[2] As long as the price elasticity of demand for imports is greater than 1, the fall in the volume of imports will exceed the rise in price, and hence fewer dollars will be spent on them. This condition (and the one in the previous footnote) is related to a famous long-standing issue in international economics, called the *Marshall-Lerner condition.* In what follows, we take the standard approach of assuming that both the price elasticity of demand for imports and the price elasticity of the demand for Canadian exports exceeds 1. This guarantees that the slopes of the curves are as shown in Figure 35-1.

Canada alternated between a system of fixed exchange rates and flexible exchange rates (with limited intervention) throughout most of the period following the Second World War. In contrast, most other countries pegged their currencies to the U.S. dollar under the Bretton Woods system. Canada has had a flexible exchange rate since 1970. Later in the chapter we examine the issues involved in choosing between a flexible and fixed exchange-rate system. For now, let's explore how the various systems operate.

Flexible Exchange Rates

We begin with an exchange rate that is set in a freely competitive market, with no intervention by the central bank. Like any competitive price, the exchange rate fluctuates as the conditions of demand and supply change.

Suppose the current exchange rate is so high (say, e_1 in Figure 35-2) that the quantity of foreign exchange supplied exceeds the quantity demanded. There is thus an abundance of foreign exchange and a shortage of Canadian dollars. This excess supply of foreign exchange, just as in our analysis in Chapter 3, will cause the price of foreign exchange (the exchange rate) to fall. As the exchange rate falls—an appreciation of the Canadian dollar—the euro price of Canadian goods rises, and this leads to a reduction in the quantity of foreign exchange supplied. Also, as the exchange rate falls, the Canadian-dollar price of European goods falls, and this fall leads to an increase in the quantity of foreign exchange demanded. Thus, the excess supply of foreign exchange leads to a fall in the exchange rate, which in turn reduces the amount of excess supply. Where the two curves intersect, quantity demanded equals quantity supplied, and the exchange rate is at its equilibrium value.

What happens when the exchange rate is below its equilibrium value, such as at e_2 in Figure 35-2? The quantity of foreign exchange demanded will exceed the quantity supplied. With foreign exchange in excess demand, its price will naturally rise, and as it does the amount of excess demand will be reduced until equilibrium is re-established.

A foreign-exchange market is like other competitive markets in that the forces of demand and supply lead to an equilibrium price at which quantity demanded equals quantity supplied.

Recall that we have been assuming that there is no official financing by the central bank. We now consider a system of fixed exchange rates in which official financing plays a central role in the analysis.

In 1999, 11 countries of the European Union adopted a common currency— the euro. Late in 2006, the price of one euro was 1.41 Canadian dollars.

Fixed Exchange Rates

If the central bank chooses to fix the exchange rate at a particular value, its official financing transactions must offset the excess demand or supply of foreign exchange that arises at that exchange rate. These transactions are described in Figure 35-2.

The gold standard that operated for much of the nineteenth century and the early part of the twentieth century was a fixed exchange-rate system. The Bretton Woods system, established by international agreement in 1944 and operated until the early 1970s, was a fixed exchange-rate system that provided for circumstances under which exchange rates could be adjusted. It was thus an adjustable peg system; the International Monetary Fund (IMF) has its origins in the Bretton Woods system, and one of its principal tasks was approving and monitoring exchange-rate changes. The European Exchange Rate Mechanism (ERM), which existed from 1979 to 1999, was also a fixed exchange-rate system for the countries in the European Union; their exchange rates were fixed to each other but floated as a block against the U.S. dollar and other currencies. As mentioned earlier, this system of separate currencies with fixed exchange rates was replaced in 1999 when most of the countries of the EU adopted a common currency—the euro.

Applying Economic Concepts 35-2 examines how a fixed exchange-rate system operates. It shows why a central bank that chooses to fix its exchange rate must give up some control of its foreign-exchange reserves. We now go on to study the workings of a flexible exchange-rate system, the system used in Canada and most industrialized countries.

Changes in Flexible Exchange Rates

What causes exchange rates to vary? The simplest answer to this question is changes in demand or supply in the foreign-exchange market. Anything that shifts the demand curve for foreign exchange to the right or the supply curve for foreign exchange to the left leads to a rise in the exchange rate—a depreciation of the Canadian dollar. Conversely, anything that shifts the demand curve for foreign exchange to the left or the supply curve for foreign exchange to the right leads to a fall in the exchange rate—an appreciation of the Canadian dollar. These points are nothing more than a restatement of the laws of supply and demand, applied now to the market for foreign exchange; they are illustrated in Figure 35-3.

What causes the shifts in demand and supply that lead to changes in exchange rates? There are many causes, some transitory and some persistent. Let's look at several of the most important ones.

A Supply-Side Increase in the Domestic Price of Exports
Suppose some event on the supply side of the paper market results in an increase in the Canadian-dollar price of Canadian paper. For example, the government may impose a new pollution tax on paper producers. What this will do to the supply of foreign exchange depends on the price elasticity of foreign demand for the Canadian product. If foreign demand for Canadian paper is elastic, perhaps because other countries supply the same product in world markets, the total amount spent on Canadian paper will decrease and hence less foreign exchange will be supplied to purchase Canadian paper. Thus, the supply curve for

FIGURE 35-2 Fixed and Flexible Exchanges Rates

Quantity of Foreign Currency (euros)

In the absence of central bank intervention, the exchange rate adjusts to clear the foreign-exchange market. The demand for and supply of foreign exchange are as in Figure 35-1. If official financing is zero, there is a purely flexible exchange rate. It will adjust to equate the demand and supply of foreign exchange; this occurs at E with an exchange rate of e_0.

If the exchange rate is higher than that, say at e_1, the supply of foreign exchange will exceed the demand. The exchange rate will fall (the dollar will appreciate) until it reaches e_0, where balance is achieved at E. If the exchange rate is below e_0, say at e_2, the demand for foreign exchange will exceed the supply. The exchange rate will rise (the dollar will depreciate) until it reaches e_0, where balance is achieved at E.

In the case of a fixed exchange rate, the central bank uses its official financing transactions to meet the excess demands or supplies that arise at the fixed value of the exchange rate. For example, if it chooses to fix the exchange rate at e_1, there will be an excess supply of foreign exchange. The central bank will purchase foreign exchange (and sell dollars) to meet the excess supply. Alternatively, if the central bank chooses to fix the exchange rate at e_2, there will be an excess demand for foreign exchange. The central bank will sell foreign exchange (and buy dollars) to meet the excess demand.

For information on the European Central Bank, see its website: **www.ecb.int**.

FIGURE 35-3 Changes in Exchange Rates

(i) Demand shifts

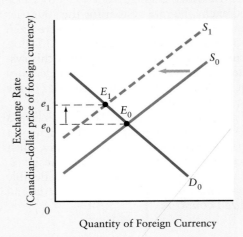

(ii) Supply shifts

An increase in the demand for foreign exchange or a decrease in the supply will cause the dollar to depreciate (the exchange rate to rise); a decrease in the demand or an increase in supply will cause the dollar to appreciate (the exchange rate to fall). The initial demand and supply curves are D_0 and S_0. Equilibrium is at E_0 with an exchange rate of e_0. An increase in the demand for foreign exchange from D_0 to D_1 in part (i), or a decrease in the supply of foreign exchange from S_0 to S_1 in part (ii), will cause the dollar to depreciate. In both parts, the new equilibrium is at E_1, and the dollar depreciation is shown by the rise in the exchange rate from e_0 to e_1. Conversely, a decrease in the demand for foreign exchange or an increase in the supply of foreign exchange will cause the dollar to appreciate.

Practise with Study Guide Chapter 35, Exercise 2.

foreign exchange will shift to the left and the Canadian dollar will depreciate. This is illustrated in part (ii) of Figure 35-3. If the demand is inelastic (say, because Canada is the only country that produces this particular kind of paper), then more will be spent, the supply of foreign exchange to pay the bigger bill will shift the supply curve to the right, and the Canadian dollar will appreciate.

A Rise in the Foreign Price of Imports Suppose the euro price of European automobiles increases sharply. Suppose also that Canadian consumers have an elastic demand for European cars because they can easily switch to Canadian-made substitutes. Consequently, they spend fewer euros for European automobiles than they did before and hence demand less foreign exchange. The demand curve for foreign exchange shifts to the left, and the Canadian dollar will appreciate. If the demand for European cars were inelastic, total spending on them would rise, and the demand for foreign exchange would shift to the right, leading to a depreciation of the Canadian dollar. This is illustrated in part (i) of Figure 35-3.

Changes in Overall Price Levels Suppose that instead of a change in the price of a specific product, such as cars or paper, there is a change in *all* prices because of general inflation. We consider separate cases, each corresponding to a different pattern of Canadian inflation relative to foreign inflation.

Equal Inflation in Both Countries. Suppose inflation is running at 5 percent in both Canada and Europe. In this case, the euro prices of European goods and the dollar prices of

Canadian goods both rise by 5 percent. At the *existing* exchange rate, the dollar prices of European goods and the euro prices of Canadian goods will each rise by 5 percent, and hence the relative prices of imports and domestically produced goods will be unchanged in both countries. Since there is no reason to expect a change in either country's demand for imports at the original exchange rate, the inflation in the two countries leaves the equilibrium exchange rate unchanged.

Inflation in Only One Country. What will happen if there is inflation in Canada while the price level remains stable in Europe? The dollar price of Canadian goods will rise, and they will become more expensive in Europe. This increase will cause the quantity of Canadian exports, and therefore the amount of foreign exchange supplied by European importers, to decrease. Thus, the supply curve for foreign exchange shifts to the left.

At the same time, European goods in Canada will have an unchanged Canadian-dollar price, while the price of Canadian goods sold in Canada will increase because of the inflation. Thus, European goods will be more attractive compared with Canadian goods (because they have become relatively cheaper), and thus more European goods will be bought in Canada. At any exchange rate, the amount of foreign exchange demanded to purchase imports will rise. Thus, the demand curve for foreign exchange shifts to the right.

Canadian inflation that is unmatched in Europe will therefore cause the supply curve for foreign exchange to shift to the left and the demand curve for foreign exchange to shift to the right. As a result, the equilibrium exchange rate *must* rise—there is a depreciation of the Canadian dollar relative to the euro.

Inflation at Unequal Rates. The two foregoing examples are, of course, just limiting cases of a more general situation in which the rate of inflation is different in the two countries. The arguments can readily be extended when we realize that it is the *relative* inflation in two countries that determines whether home goods or foreign goods look more or less attractive. If country A's inflation rate is higher than country B's, country A's exports are becoming relatively expensive in B's markets while imports from B are becoming relatively cheap in A's markets. This causes A's currency to depreciate relative to B's.

Other things being equal, if Canada has higher inflation than other countries, the Canadian dollar will be depreciating relative to other currencies. If Canada has lower inflation than other countries, the Canadian dollar will be appreciating.

Capital Movements

Capital flows can exert strong influences on exchange rates. For example, an increased desire by Canadians to purchase European assets (a capital outflow from Canada) will shift the demand curve for foreign exchange to the right, and the dollar will depreciate. In contrast, a desire by foreigners to increase their holdings of Canadian assets will shift the supply curve for foreign currency to the right and cause the Canadian dollar to appreciate.

Short-Term Capital Movements. An important motive for short-term capital flows is a change in interest rates. International traders hold transaction balances just as do domestic traders. These balances are often lent out on a short-term basis rather than being left idle. Naturally, the holders of these balances will tend to lend them, other things being equal, in markets where interest rates are highest. Thus, if one country's short-term interest rate rises above the rates in other countries (say, because that country undertakes a contractionary monetary policy), there will tend to be a large inflow of short-term capital into that country in an effort to take advantage of the high rate. This

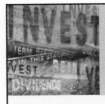

APPLYING ECONOMIC CONCEPTS 35-2

Managing Fixed Exchange Rates

This box provides some details on how a central bank operates a regime of fixed exchange rates. Though Canada has a flexible exchange rate (with very rare foreign-exchange intervention by the Bank of Canada), we will imagine a situation in which the Bank of Canada pegs the Canadian–U.S. exchange rate. The accompanying figure shows the *monthly* demand for and supply of foreign exchange (U.S. dollars).

Suppose the Bank of Canada fixed the exchange rate between the narrow limits of, say, C$1.10 to C$1.15 to the U.S. dollar. The Bank then stabilizes the exchange rate in the face of seasonal, cyclical, and other fluctuations in demand and supply, entering the market to prevent the rate from going outside the permitted band. At the price of $1.10, the Bank offers to buy any amount of U.S. dollars; at the price of $1.15, the Bank offers to sell any amount of U.S. dollars. When the Bank buys U.S. dollars, its foreign-exchange reserves rise; when it sells U.S. dollars, its foreign-exchange reserves fall.

We make the following observations:

1. If the demand curve cuts the supply curve in the range 1.10 to 1.15, as D_0 does in the accompanying figure, the Bank need not intervene in the market.

2. If the demand curve shifts to D_1, the Bank must sell U.S. dollars from its reserves to the extent of Q_4Q_1 per month in order to prevent the price of U.S. dollars from rising above 1.15.

3. If the demand curve shifts to D_2, the Bank must buy U.S. dollars to the extent of Q_2Q_3 per month in order to prevent the price of U.S. dollars from falling below 1.10.

If, on average, the demand and supply curves intersect in the range 1.10 to 1.15, the Bank's foreign-exchange reserves will be relatively stable, with the Bank buying U.S. dollars when the demand is abnormally low and selling them when the demand is abnormally high. Over a long period, however, the average level of reserves will be fairly stable.

If conditions change, the Bank's foreign-exchange reserves will rise or fall more or less continuously. For example, suppose the average level of demand becomes D_1, with fluctuations on either side of this level. The average drain on the Bank's foreign-exchange reserves will then be Q_4Q_1 *per month*. But this situation cannot continue indefinitely because the Bank only has a limited amount of foreign-exchange reserves. In this situa-

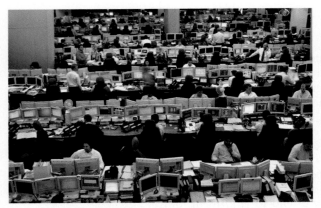

Currencies are traded and exchange rates are determined in sophisticated foreign-exchange markets in which thousands of currency traders all over the world transact with one another. Economic and political events influence their buying and selling decisions, and thus influence exchange rates.

inflow of financial capital will increase the demand for the domestic currency and cause it to appreciate. If the short-term interest rate should fall in one country (say, because of a monetary expansion in that country), there will tend to be a shift of financial capital away from that country and its currency will tend to depreciate. We saw this basic relationship between interest rates, capital flows, and the exchange rate in Chapter 28 when we discussed the monetary transmission mechanism in an open economy.

Changes in Canadian monetary policy lead to changes in interest rates and thus to international flows of financial capital. A contractionary monetary policy in Canada will lead to a rise in Canadian interest rates, a capital inflow, and an appreciation of the Canadian dollar. An expansionary monetary policy tion, the Bank has two alternatives: It can change the fixed exchange rate so that the band of permissible prices straddles the new equilibrium price, or it can try to shift the curves so that the intersection is in the band 1.10 to 1.15. To accomplish this goal, it must restrict demand for foreign exchange: It can impose import quotas and foreign-travel restrictions, or it can seek to increase the supply of U.S. dollars by encouraging Canadian exports.

Quantity of Foreign Exchange
(U.S. dollars)

Thailand in 1997 provides an example of an exchange rate fixed at a level that led to a persistent excess demand for foreign exchange. Thailand's central bank had fixed the value of its currency, the baht, to the U.S. dollar. When an excess demand for foreign currency developed in Thailand, the central bank began to deplete its stock of foreign-exchange reserves as it purchased the baht in an attempt to support its external value. By July of 1997, however, the central bank's stock of foreign-exchange reserves had been depleted to such an extent that it could no longer fix the exchange rate. With an excess demand for foreign exchange and a central bank that could no longer fix the exchange rate, depreciation was the natural result. The baht depreciated dramatically and Thailand then moved away from a fixed exchange-rate system.

China currently fixes its exchange rate at a level which results in a persistent excess supply of foreign exchange (and excess demand for Chinese currency). The Chinese yuan is permitted to fluctuate in a very narrow band around 8 yuan to the U.S. dollar. This exchange rate is well above what would otherwise be the free-market equilibrium, and as a result there is a significant excess supply of foreign currency. To prevent the yuan from appreciating, the Chinese central bank purchases foreign-exchange reserves every month. In recent years, these purchases have led to an enormous accumulation of foreign-exchange reserves in China.

in Canada will lead to a reduction in Canadian interest rates, a capital outflow, and a depreciation of the Canadian dollar.

A second motive for short-term capital movements is speculation about the *future value* of a country's exchange rate. If foreigners expect the Canadian dollar to appreciate in the near future, they will rush to buy assets that pay off in Canadian dollars, such as Canadian stocks or bonds; if they expect the Canadian dollar to depreciate in the near future, they will be reluctant to buy or to hold Canadian securities.

Long-Term Capital Movements. Long-term capital movements are largely influenced by long-term expectations about another country's profit opportunities and the long-run value of its currency. A French firm would be more willing to purchase a Canadian factory if it expected that the dollar profits would buy more euros in future years than the profits from investment in a French factory. This could happen if the Canadian firm earned greater profits than the French firm, with exchange rates remaining unchanged. It could also happen if the profits were the same but the French firm expected the Canadian dollar to appreciate relative to the euro.

Structural Changes

An economy can undergo structural changes that alter the equilibrium exchange rate. *Structural change* is an all-purpose term for a change in cost structures, the invention of new products, changes in preferences between products, or anything else that affects the pattern of comparative advantage. Consider three examples.

Suppose the reluctance of firms in one country to adopt technological innovations results in that country's products not improving as rapidly as those produced in other countries. Consumers' demand (at fixed prices) will shift slowly away from the first country's products and toward those of its foreign competitors. This shift will cause a gradual depreciation in the first country's currency because fewer people want to buy that country's goods and thus fewer people want to buy that country's currency. For this reason, a country with faster productivity growth than other countries tends to experience an appreciation of its currency.

A second example relates to the discovery of valuable mineral resources. Prominent examples are the development of natural gas in the Netherlands in the early 1960s, the development of North Sea oil in the United Kingdom in the 1970s, and the recent discovery of large diamond mines in the Northwest Territories. If firms in one country make such a discovery and begin selling these resources to the rest of the world, the foreign purchasers must supply their foreign currency in order to purchase the currency of the exporting country. The result is an appreciation of the currency of the exporting country.

Anything that leads to changes in the pattern of trade, such as changes in costs or changes in demand, will generally lead to changes in exchange rates.

A final example of particular relevance to Canada relates to changes in demand for a country's exports. For many countries, including Canada, the prices of the goods that it sells to other countries are determined in world markets. Examples include commodities such as oil, copper, pulp, lumber, wheat, coffee, cocoa, zinc, tin, aluminum, and gold. Changes in the world demand for or supply of these commodities typically have significant effects on exchange rates. For example, if there is a reduction in the world demand for these products there will be an accompanying reduction in demand for the currencies of those countries that export these products. Their currencies will depreciate. Similarly, increases in the world price of these commodities will lead to appreciations of the currencies in countries that export them. For this reason, the Canadian dollar is often referred to as a "commodity currency" because there is a strong correlation between changes in world commodity prices and changes in the Canadian exchange rate. In the 2002–2006 period, large increases in the world prices of energy and other raw materials were an important factor in the sharp appreciation of the Canadian dollar.

The Volatility of Exchange Rates

We have discussed several variables that can lead to changes in the exchange rate, including changes in relative prices, changes in interest rates, and changes in the pattern of trade. Since these variables are changing at different times by different amounts and often in different directions, it should not be surprising that exchange rates are constantly changing. Indeed, exchange rates are one of the most volatile of all macroeconomic variables. One reason for this volatility that we have not yet discussed is that foreign-exchange traders, when they are deciding whether to buy or sell foreign currency, respond to all sorts of "news" that they think will influence economic conditions, both currently and in the future. Since such news is constantly becoming available, the exchange rate is continuously changing as this new information leads traders to change their demand and supply decisions. *Applying Economic Concepts 35-3* discusses in more detail how news affects the volatility of exchange rates.

> ## myeconlab
>
> **Economists have long noticed that exchange rates tend to be more volatile than any of the variables we have been discussing. For a brief discussion of a famous theory in which the expectations of future exchange-rate changes play a central role, look for "Expectations and Exchange-Rate Overshooting" in the *Additional Topics* section of this book's MyEconLab.**
>
> w w w . m y e c o n l a b . c o m

35.4 THREE POLICY ISSUES

This chapter has so far explained how the balance of payments accounts are constructed and how exchange rates are determined. It is now time to use this knowledge to explore some important policy issues. We examine three issues commonly discussed in the popular press. As we will see, these press discussions are not always as well-informed as they could be. We pose the three policy issues as questions:

1. Is a current account deficit "bad," and a surplus "good"?

2. Is there a "correct" value for the Canadian dollar?

3. Should Canada fix its exchange rate with the U.S. dollar?

Current Account Deficits and Surpluses

Figure 35-4 shows the path of Canada's current account balance (as a percentage of GDP) since 1961. In most years, Canada has a significant trade surplus since it exports more goods and services to the world than it imports. But because it makes more investment payments (both interest and dividends) to foreigners than it receives from foreigners, it has a deficit on the capital-service portion of the current account. During most of the 1960–1995 period, Canada had an overall current account deficit of 2 or 3 percent of GDP. In the past few years, however, Canada's trade surplus has increased by more than the capital-service deficit, and the result has been a significant turnaround in the current account balance. In 2005, Canada had a current account surplus of over 2 percent of GDP.

As we have learned, Canada's balance of payments must always balance, so during the 1960–1995 period the current account deficits were matched by capital account surpluses of the same size. During these years, Canada was selling more assets to the rest of the world—both bonds and equity—than it was buying from the rest of the world. Similarly, the recent current account surpluses are matched by capital account deficits, meaning that in recent years Canada has been buying more assets from foreigners than we have been selling to foreigners.

APPLYING ECONOMIC CONCEPTS 35-3

News and the Exchange Rate

Foreign-exchange markets are different from markets for consumer goods in that the vast bulk of trading takes place between professional foreign-exchange traders working for banks, mutual-fund companies, and pension funds. These traders do not meet each other face to face. Rather, they do their transactions over the telephone or the computer, and the other party to the transaction could be anywhere in the world. The structure of this market has one interesting implication: Exchange rates respond to news. Let's see why this is and what this means.

Deals done by the professional traders are all on a large scale, typically involving sums no smaller than $1 million and often very much larger. Each trader tends to specialize in trades between a small number of currencies, say the Canadian and the U.S. dollars, or the U.S. dollar and the Japanese yen. But the traders for all currencies for each bank sit close together in a trading room so they can hear what is going on in the other markets. When a big news event breaks, anywhere in the world, this will be shouted out simultaneously to all traders in the room.

Each trader is also faced with several computer screens and many buttons that connect him or her quickly by telephone to other traders. Speed of transaction can be very important if you are dealing with large amounts of money in a market that is continuously changing the prices quoted. The most recent price quotes from around the world appear on the screens. However, contracts are agreed over the telephone (and are recorded in case of a disagreement) and the paperwork follows within two days.

As exchange rates are closely related to expectations and to interest rates, the foreign-exchange traders have to keep an eye on all major news events affecting the economic environment. Since all the players in the foreign-exchange markets are professionals, they are well-informed, not just about what has happened but also about forecasts of what is likely to happen. Accordingly, the exchange rate at any point in time reflects not just history but also current expectations of future events.

As soon as some future event comes to be expected—such as the central bank's plans to tighten monetary policy—it will be reflected in the current exchange rate. Events expected to happen soon will be given more weight than those events expected to happen in the more distant future. The fact that expectations of future events get incorporated quickly into the exchange rate has an interesting implication: The only component in today's news that will cause the exchange rate to change is what was *not expected* to happen. Economists attribute the unforecastable component of news to a random error. It is random in the sense that it has no detectable pattern and it is unrelated to the information available before it happened.

Some events are clearly unforecastable, like an earthquake in Japan or a head of state having a heart attack. Others are the production of economic statistics for which forecasts have generally been published. In the latter case it is the deviation of announced figures from their forecast value that tends to move exchange rates.

Exchange rates are therefore moved by news. And since news is random and unpredictable, changes in exchange rates will tend to be random. Some people, observing the volatility of exchange rates, conclude that foreign-exchange markets are inefficient. However, with well-informed professional traders who have forward-looking expectations, new information is rapidly transmitted into prices. The volatility of exchange rates, therefore, largely reflects the volatility of relevant, but unexpected, events around the world.

Current news events, the announcements made by public officials, and the expectation of future events play a large role in determining whether currency traders decide to buy or sell foreign exchange. The frequency and randomness of news releases partly explain why exchange rates tend to be so volatile.

FIGURE 35-4   Canada's Current Account Balance, 1961–2005

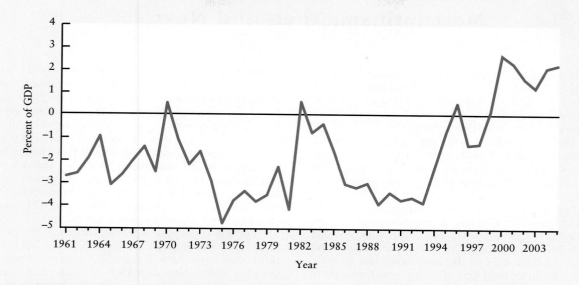

(*Source:* Statistics Canada, CANSIM database, Series V113713 expressed as a percentage of nominal GDP, Series V646937. Reprinted with permission of Statistics Canada.)

It is common for TV anchors to report negatively upon a rise in the current account deficit and positively upon its decline. But are current account deficits really a problem? Should we be celebrating Canada's recent current account surpluses? We address this issue in three parts.

Mercantilism Many people argue that a current account deficit is undesirable because it means that Canada is buying more goods and services from the world than it is selling to the world. Central to this view is the belief that exports are "good" and imports are "bad." We discussed this belief, and argued why it was incorrect, in Chapter 34 when we explored some of the fallacious arguments for trade protection.

As a carryover from a long-discredited eighteenth-century doctrine called *mercantilism,* a current account surplus is sometimes called a "favourable balance," and a current account deficit is sometimes called an "unfavourable balance." Mercantilists, both ancient and modern, believe that a country's gains from trade arise only from having a "favourable" balance of trade—that is, by exporting more goods and services than it imports. But this belief misses the central point of comparative advantage that we explored in Chapter 33—that countries gain from trade because trade allows each country to specialize in the production of those products in which its opportunity costs are low. The gains from trade have *nothing* to do with whether there is a trade deficit or a trade surplus.

Lessons From History 35-1 discusses the doctrine of mercantilism. The lesson to be learned is that the gains from trade depend on the *volume* of trade (imports plus exports) rather than the *balance* of trade. There is nothing inherently bad about having a current account deficit and nothing inherently good about having a current account surplus.

LESSONS FROM HISTORY 35-1

Mercantilism, Then and Now

Media commentators, politicians, and much of the general public often appear to believe that a nation should secure a current account surplus. They appear to believe that the benefits derived from international trade are measured by the size of that surplus.

This view is related to the *exploitation doctrine* of international trade: One country's surplus is another country's deficit. Hence, one country's gain, judged by its surplus, must be another country's loss, judged by its deficit.

People who hold such views today are echoing an ancient economic doctrine called *mercantilism*. The mercantilists were a group of economists who preceded Adam Smith. They judged the success of trade by the size of the trade balance. In many cases, this doctrine made sense in terms of their objective, which was to use international trade as a means of building up the political and military power of the state, rather than as a means of raising the living standards of its citizens. A current account surplus allowed the nation (then and now) to acquire assets. (In those days, the assets took the form of gold. Today, they are mostly claims on the currencies of other countries.) These assets could then be used to pay armies, to purchase weapons from abroad, and to finance colonial expansions.

If the objective is to promote the welfare and living standards of ordinary citizens, however, the mercantilist focus on the balance of trade makes no sense. The principle of comparative advantage shows that average living standards are maximized by having individuals, regions, and countries specialize in the things they produce comparatively best and then trading to obtain the things they produce comparatively worst. The more specialization there is, the more trade occurs.

For the country as a whole, therefore, the gains from trade are to be judged by the *volume* of trade rather than by the *balance* of trade. A situation in which there is a large volume of trade even though each country has a zero balance of trade can thus be regarded as satisfactory. Furthermore, a change in policy that results in an equal increase in both exports and imports will generate gains because it allows for specialization according to comparative advantage, even though it causes no change in either country's trade balance.

International Borrowing   If Canada has a current account deficit, it also has a capital account surplus. It is a net seller of assets to the rest of the world. These assets are either bonds, in which case Canadians are borrowing from foreigners, or they are shares in firms (equities), in which case Canadians are selling their capital stock to foreigners.

It follows that the question "Should Canada have a current account deficit?" is the same as the question "Should Canadians be net sellers of assets to foreigners?" It is not immediately clear that the answer to this question should be no. It is true that by selling bonds to foreigners, Canadians increase their indebtedness to foreigners and will eventually have to redeem the bonds as well as pay interest. And by selling income-earning equities to foreigners, Canadians give up a stream of income that they would otherwise have. But, in both cases, they get a lump sum of funds that can be used for any type of consumption or investment. Is it obviously "better" to have a lower debt or a higher future income stream than to have a lump sum of funds right now? If it were better, no family would ever borrow money to buy a house or a car, and no firm would ever borrow money to build a factory.

A country that has a current account deficit is either borrowing from the rest of the world or selling its ownership of some of its capital assets to the rest of the world. This is not necessarily undesirable.

To argue that it is undesirable for Canada to have a current account deficit is to argue that Canadians as a whole should not borrow from (or sell assets to) the rest of the world. But surely the wisdom of borrowing depends on *why* Canadians are borrowing. It is therefore important to know *why* there is a current account deficit.

Causes of Current Account Deficits   There are several possible causes of a current account deficit. This can be seen most clearly by recalling some national-income accounting from Chapter 20. Recall that GDP is equal to the sum of actual consumption, investment, government purchases, and net exports,

$$GDP = C_a + I_a + G_a + NX_a$$

where the subscript "*a*" denotes *actual* expenditure rather than desired expenditure. Next, note that GNP is equal to GDP plus the net investment income received from abroad, which we call R.

$$GNP = GDP + R = C_a + I_a + G_a + NX_a + R$$

Note that the current account balance is simply the trade balance, NX_a, plus the net investment income, R. We denote the actual current account balance CA_a. If CA_a is positive, there is a current account surplus; if CA_a is negative, there is a current account deficit. The equation now becomes

$$GNP = C_a + I_a + G_a + CA_a \qquad (35\text{-}1)$$

Now consider how a given amount of GNP that accrues to households can be spent. There are only three ways to dispose of income. It can be consumed, saved, or paid in taxes. That is,

$$GNP = C_a + S_a + T_a \qquad (35\text{-}2)$$

By equating Equations 35-1 and 35-2, and by omitting the "*a*" subscripts for simplicity, we derive an interesting relationship among national saving, investment, and the current account balance:

$$C + I + G + CA = C + S + T$$

$$\Rightarrow CA = S + (T - G) - I$$

This last equation says that the current account balance in any year is exactly equal to the excess of national saving, $S + (T - G)$, over domestic investment I. If Canadians (and their governments) decide to save more than is needed to finance the amount of domestic investment, where do the excess funds go? They are used to acquire foreign assets, and thus Canada has a current account surplus ($CA > 0$). In contrast, if Canadians do not save enough to finance the amount of domestic investment, the balance must be financed by foreign funds. Thus, Canada has a current account deficit ($CA < 0$). Finally, we can re-arrange this equation very slightly to get

$$CA = (S - I) + (T - G) \qquad (35\text{-}3)$$

which says that the current account balance is equal to the excess of private saving over investment plus the government budget surplus.

Equation 35-3 shows three separate reasons for any given increase in the current account deficit (a fall in *CA*). First, a reduction in private saving, other things being equal, will lead to a rise in the current account deficit. Second, a rise in domestic investment, other things being equal, will increase the current account deficit. Finally, other things being equal, a rise in the government's budget deficit (a fall in the budget surplus) will raise the current account deficit. This third case is often referred to as a situation of

A boom in domestic investment, other things being equal, will lead to an increase in the current account deficit. But there is little that is undesirable about this situation!

twin deficits. That is, a rise in the government's budget deficit will also have the effect (if *S* and *I* remain constant) of increasing the current account deficit.

An increase in the level of investment, a decrease in the level of saving, and an increase in the government's budget deficit are all possible causes of an increase in a country's current account deficit.

In the end, it makes little sense to discuss the desirability of a change in the current account deficit without first knowing the *cause* of the change. Knowing the cause is crucial to knowing whether the change in the current account deficit is undesirable. The following two examples illustrate this important point.

First, suppose business opportunities in Canada are very promising and, as a result, there is an increase in the level of private-sector investment. Most people would consider such an investment boom desirable because it would increase current output and employment and, by increasing the country's capital stock, it would also increase the level of potential output in the future. But as is clear from Equation 35-3, other things being equal, the immediate effect of the rise in Canadian investment is an increase in the Canadian current account deficit. The current account deficit increases because, in the absence of increased domestic saving, the increase in domestic investment can only take place if it is financed by a capital inflow from other countries. This capital inflow represents a rise in Canada's current account deficit (or capital account surplus). In this case, however, it would be difficult to argue that the increase in Canada's current account deficit is undesirable as it simply reflects a boom in domestic business opportunities.

For a second example, suppose the domestic economy begins to slow and households and firms become pessimistic about the future. In such a situation, we expect households to increase their saving and firms to reduce their investment, thus increasing the value of (*S* − *I*). As the economy slows we would also expect the government's net tax revenues to fall, thus decreasing the value of (*T* − *G*). But it is possible that the first effect dominates the second effect, thus leading to an increase in the current account surplus. Is the increase in Canada's current account surplus desirable? Most people would probably agree that the onset of a recession as described above is surely undesirable, involving a loss of output and employment.

A country's current account deficit can increase for a number of reasons. Whether the rise in the current account deficit is desirable depends on its underlying cause. A rise in the current account deficit may reflect a positive economic development; a decline in the current account deficit may reflect a negative economic development.

Is There a "Correct" Value for the Canadian Dollar?

From the summer of 1997 to the end of 1999, the external value of the Canadian dollar fell from about 72 to 65 U.S. cents. It was common to hear financial commentators discuss how the Canadian dollar was "undervalued." Opposite statements were heard a few years later in 2005 when, as a result of high world prices for raw materials, the Canadian dollar appreciated enormously. At that time some financial commentators argued that the Canadian dollar was "overvalued." In both cases, the observers appeared to believe that there was some "correct" value for the Canadian dollar. Is there?

As we saw in the previous section, a country that chooses to use a flexible exchange rate has its exchange rate determined by competitive forces in the foreign-exchange market. In Canada, and other countries as well, fluctuations in exchange rates have many causes. Some changes may be good for Canada, such as a worldwide shortage of wheat that drives up the world price of wheat, a major Canadian export. Others may be bad for Canada, such as the discovery of new copper mines in Chile that drives down the price of copper, also a major Canadian export. But the various supply and demand forces are coming together in the foreign-exchange market to determine the equilibrium value of the exchange rate. Changes in this value may reflect positive or negative events for Canada, but it makes little sense to think of this equilibrium value as being either too high or too low.

With a flexible exchange rate, the market determines the value of the exchange rate. With respect to the forces of demand and supply, the equilibrium exchange rate is the "correct" exchange rate.

Saying that the current equilibrium exchange rate is the "correct" rate in no way suggests that this "correct" rate is constant. Indeed, foreign-exchange markets are so large, with so many participants in so many countries, each responding to a slightly different set of events and expectations, that the equilibrium exchange rate is constantly changing. In other words, as various forces lead to frequent changes in the demand for and supply of the Canadian dollar in foreign-exchange markets, the "correct" value of the Canadian exchange rate is constantly changing.

Some economists accept that the current exchange rate, as determined by the foreign-exchange market, is indeed the correct rate, but they make a distinction between the immediate value of the exchange rate and its long-run value. These economists argue that, whereas various shocks may cause the exchange rate to rise or fall in the short run, there does exist some "fundamental" level to which it will return. This brings us to the theory of *purchasing power parity*.

Purchasing Power Parity   The theory of **purchasing power parity (PPP)** holds that over the long term, the value of the exchange rate between two currencies depends on the two currencies' relative purchasing power. The theory holds that a currency will tend to have the same purchasing power when it is spent in its home country as it would have if it were converted to foreign exchange and spent in the foreign country. Another way to say the same thing is that the price of *identical baskets of goods* should be the same in the two countries when the price is expressed in the same currency. If we let P_C and P_E be the price levels in Canada and Europe, respectively, and let e be the price of euros in terms of Canadian dollars (the exchange rate), then the theory of purchasing power parity predicts the following equality in the long run:

$$P_C = e \times P_E \tag{35-4}$$

This equation simply says that if a basket of goods costs 1000 euros in Europe and the exchange rate is 1.4 (that is, 1.4 Canadian dollars per euro), then that same basket of goods should cost 1400 dollars in Canada (1.4 × 1000 = 1400).

According to the theory of purchasing power parity, the exchange rate between two countries' currencies is determined by the relative price levels in the two countries.

The idea behind PPP is a simple one. Suppose that Equation 35-4 did *not* hold—specifically, suppose that P_C was greater than $e \times P_E$, so that Canadian-dollar prices in Canada exceeded the Canadian-dollar prices of the same goods in Europe. In this case, people would increase their purchases of European goods and reduce their purchases of

purchasing power parity (PPP) The theory that over the long term, the exchange rate between two currencies adjusts to reflect relative price levels (relative purchasing power).

For *The Economist*'s Big Mac Index, which uses the idea of PPP, see its website: **www.economist.com**.

Practise with Study Guide Chapter 35, Exercise 4.

Canadian goods. These actions would have the effect of depreciating the Canadian dollar (a rise in e); this depreciation would continue until the equality was re-established.

The *PPP exchange rate* is the value of the exchange rate that makes Equation 35-4 hold. That is, the PPP exchange rate (between the Canadian dollar and the euro) is defined to be

$$e^{PPP} \equiv P_C/P_E \qquad (35\text{-}5)$$

Note that the PPP exchange rate is itself not constant. If inflation is higher in Canada than in Europe, for example, P_C will be rising faster than P_E and so the PPP exchange rate will be rising. Conversely, if inflation is lower in Canada than in Europe, P_C will be rising more slowly than P_E and the PPP exchange rate will be falling.[3]

A Caveat About PPP   Should we expect the *actual* exchange rate to equal the PPP exchange rate? The theory of purchasing power parity predicts that if the actual exchange rate (e) does not equal the PPP exchange rate (e^{PPP}), then demands and supplies of Canadian and European goods will change until $e = e^{PPP}$. Thus, the theory of PPP predicts that the actual exchange rate will eventually equal the PPP exchange rate.

Figure 35-5 shows the path of the actual Canadian–U.S. exchange rate and the PPP exchange rate over the past 25 years. It is clear from the figure that there are long periods of time over which the actual exchange rate deviates significantly from the PPP exchange rate. Why is this the case? Is there something wrong with the theory of purchasing power parity?

Recall from Equation 35-4 that P_C and P_E were defined as the prices of *identical baskets of goods* in Canada and Europe, respectively. Given that the goods are the same, the argument that the prices should (eventually) be equated across the two countries is sensible—if the prices are not equated across the two countries, there would be an incentive to purchase in the cheaper country rather than in the more expensive country, and this would lead to changes in the exchange rate until Equation 35-4 *did* hold.

One problem, however, when we apply the theory of purchasing power parity to *national price indices,* such as the Consumer Price Index or the Implicit GDP Deflator, is that the two baskets of goods are typically *not* the same—for two reasons.

Different Countries Produce Different Goods. Suppose we apply the theory of PPP to the Canada–Europe exchange rate and we use the GDP deflators from the two countries as the measures of prices. Recall from Chapter 20 that the GDP deflator is an index of prices of the goods *produced within the country.* But Canada and Europe clearly produce very different goods. The price of forest products will have a large weight in the Canadian GDP deflator, but less weight in the European GDP deflator; in contrast, the price of wine will have a much larger weight in the European GDP deflator than in the Canadian GDP deflator.

The implication of these differences for the theory of PPP is important. As long as changes in the *relative* prices of goods occur, such as a change in the price of forest products relative to wine, then P_C (the Canadian GDP deflator) will change relative to P_E (the European GDP deflator) *even though the prices of individual goods might be equated across the two countries.* Thus, differences in the structure of the price indices between two countries mean that using a PPP exchange rate computed on the basis of Equation 35-5 will be misleading. In other words, in the presence of changing relative

---

3 For a very readable review of the PPP theory and its empirical testing, see R. Lafrance and L. Schembri, "Purchasing Power Parity: Definitions, Measurement, and Interpretation," *Bank of Canada Review,* Autumn, 2002.

FIGURE 35-5   Actual and PPP Exchange Rates, 1981–2005

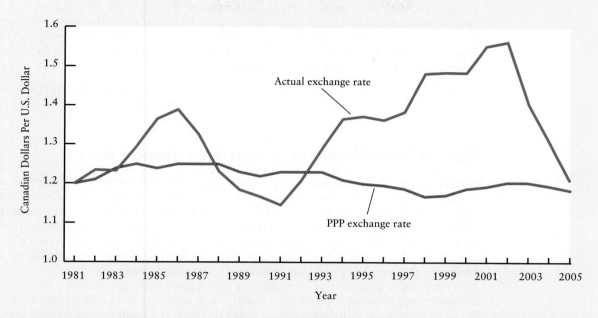

The actual exchange rate deviates from the PPP exchange rate for extended periods. The Canada–U.S. PPP exchange rate is the ratio of Canadian to U.S. price indices. Since these two price indices have moved closely together since 1981 (similar paths for inflation), the PPP exchange rate has not changed significantly. In contrast, the actual Canada–U.S. exchange rate has fluctuated dramatically and shows little or no tendency to track the PPP exchange rate.

(*Source:* Canadian CPI is from the Bank of Canada, Series PCPISA, annual average. U.S. CPI is from U.S. Bureau of Labor Statistics: www.bls.org. Exchange rate is from Statistics Canada, CANSIM database, Series V37432, annual average.)

prices, there is no reason to expect the actual exchange rate to equal the PPP exchange rate as defined in Equation 35-5.

Nontraded Goods Are Important. The previous discussion emphasized that the *baskets* of goods across two countries might differ even though the products in the baskets were the same. But even if Canada and Europe produced exactly the same range of goods, so that the various weights in the GDP deflators were the same, there is another reason why the basket of goods in Canada differs from the basket of goods in Europe. Some of the goods produced in Canada are *nontraded goods,* such as haircuts and restaurant meals. Nontraded goods are also produced in Europe. But, since nontraded goods cannot be traded (by definition), there is nothing that will force their prices to be equal across the two countries. If haircuts are more expensive in Paris than in Toronto (as they are), we do not expect people to shift their consumption of haircuts away from Paris toward Toronto, and thus we should not expect the actual exchange rate to move to make Equation 35-4 hold.

The conclusion of this discussion is that we must be very careful in selecting the price indices we use when we apply the theory of purchasing power parity. We know that countries have different patterns of production and thus have different structures to their national price indices. Thus, in the presence of changes in relative prices of various products, the national price indices can change in ways that will not lead to changes in the exchange rate. Similarly, the presence of nontraded goods implies that some differences in prices across countries will not lead to changes in the location of demand and thus changes in the exchange rate.

Changes in relative prices and the presence of nontraded goods imply that purchasing power parity need not hold—not even as a long-run proposition.

Should Canada Have a Fixed Exchange Rate?

In recent years, some economists have suggested that Canada peg the value of its currency to the U.S. dollar. Advocates of a fixed Canadian exchange rate see this policy as a means of avoiding the significant fluctuations in the Canadian exchange rate that would otherwise occur—fluctuations such as the 10 percent depreciation that occurred between 1997 and 1998 and the 40 percent appreciation that occurred between 2002 and 2006. They argue that exchange-rate fluctuations generate uncertainty for importers and exporters and thus increase the costs associated with trade.

Others have gone further in suggesting that Canada actually abandon its currency altogether and simply adopt the U.S. dollar. They point to the European Union, which introduced the euro as its common currency in 1999. If a common currency is acceptable to most of Europe, why should Canada and the United States be any different?

These are contentious suggestions that have attracted a great deal of public attention in recent years. We examine this issue by comparing the main benefits of flexible and fixed exchange rates. Whereas flexible exchange rates dampen the effects on output and employment from external shocks to the economy, fixed exchange rates reduce the uncertainty faced by traders. The benefits and costs of having a common currency between two regions is examined in *Extensions in Theory 35-1,* which explains the theory of "optimal currency areas."

Flexible Exchange Rates as "Shock Absorbers"   For most of the years following the Second World War, Canada has used a flexible exchange rate. Even when most other major countries chose to peg the value of their currencies to the U.S. dollar (and to gold) under the Bretton Woods system, Canada usually chose a flexible exchange rate (there were a few short periods in which Canada fixed its exchange rate). For all of its history Canada's economy has been dependent on the export of resource-based products, the prices of which are determined in world markets and are often highly variable from year to year. Changes in these prices constitute changes in Canada's terms of trade and, as we saw earlier in this chapter, changes in a country's terms of trade are an important reason why exchange rates are so variable.

That the exchange rate adjusts in response to shocks is actually the main advantage of a flexible (rather than fixed) exchange rate. A flexible exchange rate acts as a "shock absorber," dampening the effects on the country's output and employment from external shocks. To understand how this happens, consider a simple example.

Suppose a reduction in world demand leads to a reduction in the world prices of raw materials, which are major Canadian exports. When world demand for raw materials declines, there is a reduction in demand for Canadian exports and an accompanying reduction in demand for Canadian dollars (or a reduction in the supply of foreign exchange) in the foreign-exchange market. The effect on Canadian real GDP is shown in part (ii) of Figure 35-6 by the leftward shift of the AD curve. The effect in the foreign-exchange market is shown in part (i) by the leftward shift of the supply curve for foreign exchange. Consider the effect of this shock in two different situations. In the first, the Bank of Canada maintains a fixed exchange rate; in the second, the Bank of Canada allows the exchange rate to be freely determined by demand and supply.

If the Bank of Canada fixes the exchange rate at e_0, the reduction in the supply of foreign exchange from S_0 to S_1 leads to an excess demand for foreign currency. To keep the exchange rate fixed at e_0, the Bank must sell sufficient foreign-exchange reserves to satisfy the excess demand. But the negative shock to aggregate demand still occurs and thus output and employment in Canada fall, as shown in part (ii) of Figure 35-6. Canadian wages will eventually fall and the AS curve will eventually shift downward, returning real GDP to the level of potential output. But the closing of the recessionary gap may be slow and painful.

If Canada instead has a flexible exchange rate, the reduction in the world prices of raw materials will lead to a reduction in the supply of foreign exchange and thus to a depreciation of the Canadian dollar. The exchange rate will increase from e_0 to e_1. The AD curve will shift to the left, reducing Canada's GDP, just as in the fixed-exchange-rate case. The sectors of the Canadian economy producing raw materials will still be

FIGURE 35-6   Flexible Exchange Rates as a Shock Absorber

(i) Foreign-exchange market   (ii) AD and AS

Flexible exchange rates adjust to terms of trade shocks and thus dampen the effect on output and employment. The economy begins with the exchange rate equal to e_0 in part (i) and GDP equal to Y^* in part (ii). A reduction in the world's demand for Canadian exports causes a reduction in the supply of foreign exchange, shifting S_0 to S_1 in part (i).

With a fixed exchange rate, the Bank of Canada maintains the exchange rate at e_0, satisfying the excess demand for foreign exchange by selling its foreign-currency reserves. The reduction in the demand for Canada's exports is a negative aggregate demand shock. AD_0 shifts to the left to AD_1 in part (ii), causing GDP to fall to Y_1. The recessionary gap eventually pushes wages down, the AS curve shifts downward over time, and the economy moves along AD_1 to Y^*. The adjustment, however, may be protracted.

With a flexible exchange rate, the Bank of Canada allows the Canadian dollar to depreciate. The exchange rate rises to e_1 in part (i). The reduction in demand for Canadian exports still causes the AD curve to shift to the left in part (ii), but the shift is dampened by the depreciation of the dollar, which makes Canadian products more competitive in world markets. The AD curve shifts only to AD_2 and so GDP falls only to Y_2. There is still a recession, but smaller than in the case with a fixed exchange rate.

EXTENSIONS IN THEORY 35-1

Optimal Currency Areas

In 1961, Canadian economist Robert Mundell, now at Columbia University, developed the theory of "optimal currency areas." In 1999 he was awarded the Nobel Prize in economics, partly for this work. He examined the conditions under which it is optimal for two countries to have a common currency, and the conditions under which the countries would be better off maintaining separate currencies with a flexible exchange rate. Mundell's conclusions can be summarized as follows.

1. Other things being equal, the more the two countries trade with one another, the larger are the benefits from having a common currency (and the lower are the benefits from having separate currencies with a flexible exchange rate).

2. Other things being equal, the less correlated are the two countries' terms of trade, the smaller are the benefits from having a common currency (and the larger are the benefits from having separate currencies with a flexible exchange rate).

The Basic Theory

The accompanying diagram illustrates the situation that Mundell describes. Our example is that of Canada and the United States. The green arrows represent the trade of goods, services, and assets between the two countries. The red arrows represent the various shocks to each country's terms of trade. Mundell's central result is that, other things being equal, the more important the green arrows are, the better it is to have a common currency. On the other hand, the "less similar" each country's red arrows are, the worse it is to have a common currency. By "less similar" we mean that the changes in one country's terms of trade are different, or occur at different times, than the changes in the other country's terms of trade.

To understand Mundell's arguments, we must understand how the green and red arrows relate to the costs and benefits of having a common currency (rather than separate currencies with a flexible exchange rate).

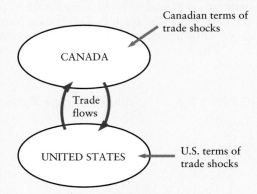

The main benefit of having a common currency is that importers and exporters in each country can save on the costs associated with having a flexible (and perhaps volatile) exchange rate. There are two types of costs. The first is the *uncertainty* that is generated by having a volatile exchange rate. The more uncertainty there is surrounding the price of foreign currency, the less likely are firms to enter contracts that involve foreign exchange. This reduction in trade leads to a reduction in the gains from trade. The second cost is the *transaction cost* of converting one currency into another. With separate currencies someone (either the importer or the exporter) must spend the time and resources necessary to convert currencies for every

in recession, for there has been a reduction in demand for these products. But the overall Canadian downturn will be dampened by the depreciation of the Canadian dollar. Other exporting sectors of the Canadian economy will actually *expand* as a result of the depreciation because their products are now more competitive in world markets. Thus, as shown in part (ii) of Figure 35-6, the leftward shift of the *AD* curve will not be as large as in the case of the fixed exchange rate. The overall result is that, with a flexible exchange rate, the deterioration in Canada's terms of trade leads to a less severe Canadian recession than if Canada had a fixed exchange rate.

transaction between the two countries. Given that such costs are incurred every time goods are traded, it follows that the greater is the volume of trade between the two regions, the greater are the benefits (that is, the costs avoided) from having a common currency.

The main benefit from each country's maintaining a separate currency with a flexible exchange rate is that the exchange rate can act as a "shock absorber," dampening the effects on the country's output and employment from shocks to its terms of trade. For example, consider what would happen if there were a reduction in the world price of copper. Copper is a major Canadian export but a U.S. import. When the price of copper falls due to a reduction in world copper demand, Canada's terms of trade deteriorate but the U.S. terms of trade improve. The fall in the price of copper leads to a contraction in the Canadian copper industry. If Canada shares a common currency with the United States, the result of the shock will simply be a reduction in output and employment in Canada's copper industry. The contraction in that sector will eventually reduce wages, and the economy will eventually return to potential output. But the adjustment may be long and painful.

In contrast, if Canada and the United States have separate currencies, the reduction in the world price of copper will tend to depreciate the Canadian dollar relative to the U.S. dollar. The Canadian copper industry will still be in recession, for there has been a reduction in demand for its products, but the overall Canadian downturn will be dampened by the depreciation of the Canadian dollar. In other words, even though the copper industry is in recession, other sectors of the Canadian economy will actually *expand* as a result of the currency depreciation because their products are now more competitive in world markets. The overall result is that, with a separate currency and flexible exchange rate, the deterioration in Canada's terms of trade leads to a less severe Canadian recession than if Canada shared a currency with the United States.

Mundell said that two countries constitute an *optimal currency area* if by adopting a common currency the two countries together save more in uncertainty and transaction costs than they incur by sacrificing the output-dampening effects of a flexible exchange rate.

What Is the Optimal Currency Area?

Some economists have recently advocated that Canada adopt the U.S. dollar as its currency. Do they believe that Canada and the United States constitute an optimal currency area? Probably not, but that is also not quite the right policy question. The provinces and territories of Canada already use a common currency even though they may not satisfy Mundell's condition for being an optimal currency area. Similarly, the U.S. states use a common currency and may not constitute an optimal currency area. Thus, the relevant policy question from Canada's perspective is whether Canada and the United States together form a *better* currency area than Canada by itself.

Some economists think this is probably true. They point to the massive and growing volume of trade between the two countries as the best reason for Canada and the United States to share a currency. Other economists stress the importance of exchange rates as shock absorbers. They point to the 1997–1998 decline in world commodity prices as an ideal example of a situation in which Canada benefited from having a flexible exchange rate. Canada's resource sector contracted sharply in response to this shock. Especially hard hit was British Columbia's forestry industry. But the depreciation of the Canadian dollar (by roughly 10 percent against the U.S. dollar) led to expansions in manufacturing industries in Ontario and Quebec that significantly reduced the overall effect of the shock.

One of the advantages of flexible exchange rates is that, in response to shocks to the terms of trade, the exchange rate can act as a shock absorber, dampening the effects of the shock on output and employment.

The Asian Crisis of 1997–1998 provides an excellent example of how Canada's flexible exchange rate dampened the effects of a negative external shock. When the Asian countries of Malaysia, Indonesia, Thailand, and South Korea experienced their large recessions in 1997 and 1998, their demand for many raw materials declined sharply. As they are major users of raw materials, the effect was felt on world markets.

The average prices of raw materials fell by roughly 30 percent from the summer of 1997 to the end of 1998. Many of these raw materials, of course, are important exports for Canada, and so the decline in their world prices implied a terms-of-trade deterioration for Canada.

Especially hard hit was British Columbia's forestry sector, in which output fell dramatically in many paper and lumber mills due to the lack of sales in Asia. As expected, there was also a significant depreciation of the Canadian dollar, just as described in Figure 35-6. But as the Canadian dollar depreciated, the Canadian manufacturing sector, concentrated mainly in Ontario and Quebec, was given a large boost. The 10 percent depreciation of the Canadian dollar meant that Canadian machinery, furniture, telecommunications equipment, and a whole range of other products were now more competitive in world markets. Thus, the boom in the Central Canadian manufacturing sector offset to some extent the significant recession that was going on in British Columbia. If Canada had had a fixed exchange rate, the 10 percent depreciation would not have occurred. But the initial shock from the Asian Crisis would still have taken place. The net result would have been lower output and higher unemployment than actually occurred.

A few years later, between 2002 and 2005, the opposite forces were at work, and once again Canada's flexible exchange rate acted as a shock absorber. Due to strong global economic growth, especially in China and India, world prices for energy and other raw materials increased significantly. This was a positive shock to Canadian aggregate demand, and the price increase caused an improvement in Canada's terms of trade and an appreciation of the Canadian dollar by approximately 40 percent. During this period the energy and commodity-producing sectors of the Canadian economy were booming. At the same time, however, the appreciation of the Canadian dollar tended to reduce activity in the manufacturing sector, thus dampening the overall effect of the positive shock on the Canadian economy.

Note that having a fixed exchange rate does not prevent a country from being subjected to shocks from the rest of the world. Many advocates of fixed exchange rates seem to think that by fixing the value of a country's currency, the country is shielding itself from undesirable fluctuations. But shocks to a country's terms of trade will always occur. As long as there are changes in the demand for and supply of various products around the world, there will also be changes in a country's terms of trade. What Figure 35-6 shows, however, is that by fixing the exchange rate and thus avoiding the fluctuations in the value of the currency, the effects of the shock merely show up as increased volatility in output and employment.

A country will always experience shocks in its terms of trade. A flexible exchange rate absorbs some of the shock, reducing the effect on output and employment. A fixed exchange rate simply redistributes the effect of the shock—the exchange rate is smoother but output and employment are more volatile.

Trade, Transaction Costs, and Uncertainty

Despite the benefits of international trade, there are costs involved in exporting and importing goods and services. The *transaction costs* of international trade involve the costs associated with converting one currency to another, as must be done either by the importer or the exporter of the product that is traded. For example, if you have an import–export business in Canada and want to import some bicycles from Japan, you will probably have to purchase Japanese yen at a bank or foreign-exchange dealer and, with those yen, pay the Japanese seller for the bicycles. Even if the Japanese seller accepts Canadian dollars for the bicycles, and this often is the case, he will be required to convert those Canadian dollars into yen before he can use that money in Japan to pay his workers or pay for other costs of production.

Practise with Study Guide Chapter 35, Extension Exercise E1.

The greater is the volume of trade between two countries, the higher are the aggregate transaction costs associated with international trade.

Such transaction costs exist even if trade takes place between two countries with fixed exchange rates. For example, if the Bank of Canada pegged the value of the Canadian dollar to the U.S. dollar, any trade between the two countries would still require the costly conversion of one currency to the other. Thus, the existence of transaction costs cannot be used as an argument in favour of fixed exchange rates and against flexible exchange rates. As long as there are two currencies, the transaction costs must be borne by one party or the other. These transaction costs could only be avoided if the two countries shared a common currency. *Extensions in Theory 35-1* examines the theory of "optimal currency areas" in which these transactions costs play a central role.

Many economists believe, however, that the volatility of flexible exchange rates generates another type of cost for importers and exporters. Specifically, the unpredictability of the exchange rate leads to *uncertainty* about the profitability of any specific international transaction. Such uncertainty, given risk-averse firms, can be expected to lead to a smaller volume of international trade and thus to fewer benefits from such trade.

For example, suppose a Canadian appliance manufacturer enters into a contract to purchase a specified amount of steel from a Japanese producer for a specified yen price in one year's time. In this case, the Japanese producer bears no *foreign-exchange risk* because the price is specified in yen. But the Canadian appliance manufacturer bears considerable risk. If the yen depreciates relative to the dollar over the coming year, fewer Canadian dollars will be required to pay for the steel. But if the yen appreciates relative to the dollar over the coming year, more Canadian dollars will be required to pay for the steel. The Canadian buyer therefore faces a risk in terms of the Canadian-dollar cost of the steel. If the firm is *risk averse,* meaning simply that it would be prepared to pay a cost to avoid the risk, the presence of the risk may lead to fewer international transactions of this type. Perhaps to avoid the foreign-exchange risk, the Canadian buyer will decide instead to buy Canadian-made steel, even though it may be slightly more expensive or not quite the right type that is needed.

If the presence of foreign-exchange risk leads to less international trade, there will be a reduction in the gains from trade.

Many of the people who advocate Canada's move to a fixed exchange rate point to the avoidance of this foreign-exchange risk as the main benefit. They argue that if the Canadian dollar were pegged in value to the U.S. dollar, both importers and exporters would face less uncertainty on the most important part of their trade—that between Canada and the United States. With the greater certainty, they argue, would come greater trade flows and thus an increase in the overall gains from trade.

But many economists disagree. While accepting the basic argument regarding the risks created by flexible (and volatile) exchange rates, they note that importers and exporters already have the means to avoid this uncertainty. In particular, traders can participate in *forward markets* in which they can buy or sell foreign exchange *in the future* at prices specified today. For example, the Canadian appliance manufacturer could enter into a contract to purchase the required amount of yen in one year's time at a price of 100 yen per Canadian dollar. In this case, no matter what happened to the yen–dollar exchange rate in the intervening year, the uncertainty regarding the Canadian-dollar price of the steel would be entirely eliminated.

Monetary Policy   One final point should be noted about the choice between flexible and fixed exchange rates. If the Bank of Canada chooses to allow the exchange rate to fluctuate in response to shocks, it can focus its monetary policy on the control of inflation. In other words, it can adjust its monetary policy—sometimes tightening and other times loosening—to keep inflation close to the stated 2-percent target. But if the Bank chooses instead to fix the exchange rate, it is not *also* able to control inflation.

As we saw in Chapter 29, the Bank of Canada has only one policy instrument, its target for the overnight interest rate. If the Bank must intervene in the foreign-exchange market to keep the exchange rate fixed—sometimes buying foreign exchange and other times selling it—these transactions will influence the Canadian money supply directly, and thus influence Canadian interest rates. But these changes in interest rates may not be consistent with the Bank's policy objective of keeping inflation close to the 2-percent target.

If the Bank of Canada chooses to fix the exchange rate, it cannot also conduct its policy to keep inflation at 2 percent. The Bank of Canada has only one policy instrument.

Summing Up

So, should Canada give up its flexible exchange rate and instead peg the value of the Canadian dollar to the U.S. dollar? Advocates of this policy emphasize the foreign-exchange risk faced by importers and exporters, and the gains from increased trade that would result from a fixed exchange rate. Opponents to the policy emphasize the shock-absorption benefits from a flexible exchange rate, and the benefits of having monetary policy directed at controlling inflation.

This debate will surely go on for a while, partly because it is difficult to quantify the costs and benefits of a flexible exchange rate. Economists on both sides of the debate understand and accept the logic of the arguments from the other side. But researchers have so far been unable to determine how much of a shock is absorbed by a flexible exchange rate, and thus to estimate how much more volatile output and employment would be with a fixed exchange rate. Similarly, it is very difficult to estimate just how much more trade would take place if the foreign-exchange risk faced by traders were eliminated by means of a fixed exchange rate. Without convincing empirical evidence supporting the move to a fixed exchange rate, however, the status quo will probably remain. It is probably safe to assume that Canada will continue to have a flexible exchange rate, at least for the next several years.

S U M M A R Y

35.1 **THE BALANCE OF PAYMENTS**

- Actual transactions among Canadian firms, households, and governments and those in the rest of the world are reported in the balance of payments accounts. In these accounts, any transaction that represents a receipt for Canada (Canadians sell goods or assets to foreigners) is recorded as a credit item. Any transaction that represents a payment from Canada (Canadians purchase goods or assets from foreigners) is recorded as a debit item.

- Categories in the balance of payments accounts are the trade account, the capital-service account, the current account (which is equal to the trade account plus the capital-service account), and the capital account (which includes the official financing account).

- If all transactions are recorded in the balance of payments, the sum of all credit items necessarily equals the sum of all debit items. Thus, the balance of payments must always balance.

- A country with a current account deficit must also have a capital inflow—a capital account surplus. A country with a current account surplus must also have a capital outflow—a capital account deficit.

35.2 **THE FOREIGN-EXCHANGE MARKET**

- The exchange rate between the Canadian dollar and some foreign currency is defined to be the number of Canadian dollars required to purchase one unit of the foreign currency. A rise in the exchange rate is a depreciation of the Canadian dollar; a fall in the exchange rate is an appreciation of the Canadian dollar.
- The supply of foreign exchange (or the demand for Canadian dollars) arises from Canadian exports of goods and services, capital flows into Canada, and the desire of foreign banks, firms, and governments to use Canadian dollars as part of their reserves.
- The demand for foreign exchange (or the supply of Canadian dollars to purchase foreign currencies) arises from Canadian imports of goods and services, capital

flows from Canada, and the desire of holders of Canadian dollars to decrease the size of their holdings.
- A depreciation of the Canadian dollar lowers the foreign price of Canadian exports and increases the amount of foreign exchange supplied (to purchase Canadian exports). Thus, the supply curve for foreign exchange is positively sloped when plotted against the exchange rate.
- A depreciation of the Canadian dollar raises the dollar price of imports from abroad and hence lowers the amount of foreign exchange demanded to purchase foreign goods. Thus, the demand curve for foreign exchange is negatively sloped when plotted against the exchange rate.

35.3 **THE DETERMINATION OF EXCHANGE RATES**

- When the central bank does not intervene in the foreign exchange market, there is a purely flexible exchange rate. Under fixed exchange rates, the central bank intervenes in the foreign-exchange market to maintain the exchange rate at an announced value. To do this, the central bank must hold sufficient stocks of foreign-exchange reserves.
- Under a flexible, or floating, exchange rate, the exchange rate is determined by supply of and demand for the currency.

- The Canadian dollar will appreciate in foreign-exchange markets if there is an increase in the supply of foreign exchange (an increase in the demand for Canadian dollars) or if there is a reduction in the demand for foreign exchange (a reduction in the supply of Canadian dollars). The opposite changes will lead to a depreciation of the Canadian dollar.
- Changes in the exchange rate are caused by changes in such things as the rate of inflation in different countries, capital movements, structural conditions, and expectations about the future exchange rate.

35.4 **THREE POLICY ISSUES**

- The view that current account deficits are undesirable is usually based on the mercantilist notion that exports are "good" and imports are "bad." But the gains from trade have nothing to do with the balance of trade—they depend on the volume of trade.
- From national income accounting, the current account balance is given by

$$CA = (S - I) + (T - G)$$

- An increase in investment, a decrease in saving, and an increase in the government budget deficit can each be the cause of a rise in the current account deficit.
- With a flexible exchange rate, supply and demand in the foreign-exchange market determine the "correct" value

of the exchange rate. But this "correct" value is constantly changing as market conditions vary.
- The theory of purchasing power parity (PPP) predicts that exchange rates will adjust so that the purchasing power of a given currency is the same in different countries. That is, the prices of identical baskets of goods will be equated in different countries (when expressed in the same currency).
- If price indices from different countries are used as the basis for computing the PPP exchange rate, differences in the structure of price indices across countries, together with the presence of nontraded goods, can be responsible for persistent deviations of the actual exchange rate from this measure of the PPP exchange rate.

- An important benefit of a flexible exchange rate is that it acts as a shock absorber, dampening the effects on output and employment from shocks to a country's terms of trade.

- An important benefit of fixed exchange rates is that it reduces transaction costs and foreign-exchange risk faced by importers and exporters.

KEY CONCEPTS

Balance of payments accounts
Current and capital accounts
Changes in official reserves
Foreign exchange and exchange rates
Appreciation and depreciation
Sources of the demand for and supply of foreign exchange

Fixed and flexible exchange rates
Mercantilist views on the balance of trade and volume of trade
Purchasing power parity
PPP exchange rate

Flexible exchange rates as shock absorbers
Foreign-exchange risk
Optimal currency areas

STUDY EXERCISES

1. Fill in the blanks to make the following statements correct.

   a. If a wine shop in Alberta buys a case of wine from Chile, the transaction is recorded as a(n) _____ in the _____ account, which is a subsection of the _____ account.

   b. If a Canadian receives dividend payments from a firm in Britain, the transaction is recorded as a(n) _____ in the _____ account, which is a subsection of the _____ account.

   c. If a German pension-fund manager purchases a B.C. Hydro bond, the transaction is recorded as a(n) _____ in the _____ account. If a Canadian sells her ownership stake in a newspaper chain to an American, the transaction is recorded as a(n) _____ in the _____ account.

   d. The sum of the current account and the capital account is known as the _____ and must *always* equal _____.

2. Fill in the blanks to make the following statements correct.

   a. A depreciation of the Canadian dollar means that it takes _____ Canadian dollars to purchase one unit of foreign currency, and there has been a(n) _____ in the exchange rate. An appreciation of the Canadian dollar means that it takes _____ Canadian dollars to purchase one unit of foreign currency, and there has been a(n) _____ in the exchange rate.

   b. Suppose a newscaster tells us that the Canadian dollar is valued at 89.6 U.S. cents. In this case, we say the Canadian–U.S. exchange rate is _____, meaning that it takes _____ Canadian dollars to buy one U.S. dollar.

   c. The exchange rate is determined at the intersection of the _____ curve for foreign exchange and the _____ curve for foreign exchange. An exchange rate above this level means an excess _____ foreign exchange, which is also an excess _____ Canadian dollars. The exchange rate will _____ and the Canadian dollar will _____.

   d. If there is a rise in foreign GDP, and foreign demand for Canadian goods increases, there will be a(n) _____ in supply of foreign currency. The Canadian dollar will _____.

   e. An increase in Canadian prices relative to foreign prices will cause a(n) _____ in the demand for foreign exchange, and a(n) _____ in the supply of foreign exchange. The exchange rate will _____ and the Canadian dollar will therefore _____.

3. Fill in the blanks to make the following statements correct.

   a. If the exchange rate is determined by the equality of supply and demand for foreign exchange and the central bank makes no foreign-exchange transactions, we say there is a(n) _____ exchange rate.

   b. If the central bank buys and sells foreign exchange in an effort to maintain the exchange rate at a specific value, we say we have a(n) _____ exchange rate.

   c. If the central bank pegs the exchange rate above its free-market equilibrium level, there will be a(n) _____ foreign exchange and the central bank will _____ foreign currency.

d. If the central bank pegs the exchange rate below its free-market equilibrium level, there will be a(n) _____ foreign exchange and the central bank will _____ foreign currency.

4. **myeconlab** The table below shows Tess's financial details for 2007. Answer the following questions about her "balance of payments."

Tess's Financial Details, 2007	
Income from babysitting	$2500
Income from newspaper route	3500
Gift from grandparents	1000
Interest from bank deposits	150
Expenditure on coffee and pastry	1000
Expenditure on tuition	3500
Purchase of mutual funds	1200
Bank balance at end of year	3500
Increase in bank balance during the year	1450

a. What is Tess's "trade balance"? Explain.
b. What is Tess's overall current account balance? Explain.
c. What is Tess's capital account balance? Explain.
d. There is one (and only one) piece of information shown above that is not needed to compute Tess's balance of payments. What is it? Explain why it is not needed.

5. The diagram below shows the demand for foreign currency (the supply of Canadian dollars) and the supply of foreign currency (the demand for Canadian dollars). The equilibrium exchange rate is e^*. Assume that Canada has a purely flexible exchange rate.

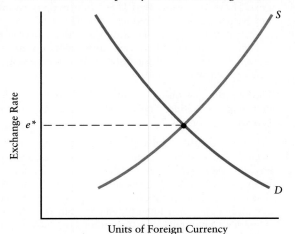

a. Show in the diagram the effect of a general inflation in Canada (when there is no inflation in the rest of the world). Explain.

b. Show what happens to the exchange rate if there is a large increase in foreign demand for Canadian telecommunications equipment. Explain.
c. Show the effect of an increase in Canadian investors' demand for Japanese government bonds. Explain.

6. **myeconlab** The diagram below shows the demand for foreign currency (the supply of Canadian dollars) and the supply of foreign currency (the demand for Canadian dollars). The equilibrium exchange rate is e^*.

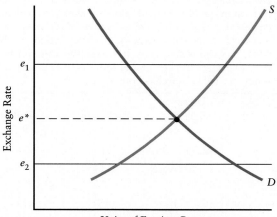

a. Suppose the Bank of Canada decides to fix the exchange rate at e_1. What must the Bank do to accomplish its goal?
b. In part (a), explain why some people would call this a "a balance of payments surplus" even though the balance of payments is in balance.
c. Now suppose the Bank of Canada decides to fix the exchange rate at e_2. What must the Bank do to accomplish this goal?
d. With the exchange rate fixed at e_2, explain why some people would call this a "balance of payments deficit" even though the balance of payments is in balance.

7. Suppose the Canadian economy is at potential output with a stable price level. There is then an upturn in the world demand for construction materials, especially lumber.

a. Draw a diagram of the foreign-exchange market. Assuming that Canada has a flexible exchange rate, show the likely effect on Canada's exchange rate.
b. Explain the Bank of Canada's participation in the foreign-exchange market if Canada has a fixed exchange rate.
c. Now draw an *AD/AS* diagram for the Canadian economy. What is the likely effect of the shock on Canadian GDP under the conditions in part (a)?

d. What would be the effect of the shock on Canadian GDP under the conditions of part (b)?

e. Explain how a flexible exchange rate acts as a shock absorber, insulating the economy from both positive and negative shocks.

8. **myeconlab** Every few months, *The Economist* publishes its "Big Mac Index." Using the current exchange rates, it compares the U.S.-dollar price of Big Macs in several countries. It then concludes that countries in which the Big Mac is cheaper (in U.S. dollars) than in the United States have "undervalued" currencies. Similarly, countries with Big Macs more expensive than in the United States have "overvalued" currencies. The table below shows data from July 2006. It shows the domestic-currency prices of Big Macs in various countries. It also shows the exchange rate, expressed as the number of units of domestic currency needed to purchase one U.S. dollar.

Country	Domestic Currency Price	Exchange Rate	U.S. Dollar Price
Canada	$2.75 (Cdn.)	1.11	$ —
Australia	$3.50 (Aus.)	1.34	$ —
U.S.A.	$2.25	1.00	$ —
Japan	375 yen	115	$ —
France	3.6 euros	0.78	$ —
U.K.	1.50 pounds	0.55	$ —

a. For each country, use the exchange rate provided to convert the domestic-currency price to the U.S.-dollar price.

b. By the logic used in *The Economist*, which currencies are overvalued and which are undervalued relative to the U.S. dollar?

c. Are Big Macs traded goods? If not, does this present a problem for *The Economist*? Explain.

d. Which of the following goods do you think would be a better candidate for this exercise? Explain your choice.
   (i) cement
   (ii) diamonds
   (iii) fresh fruit
   (iv) computer RAM chips

9. A former Canadian prime minister once suggested that Canada should try to have balanced trade, industry by industry.

a. Do you think this makes sense? Explain.

b. How about the idea of balanced trade, country by country? Explain whether this makes sense.

DISCUSSION QUESTIONS

1. What is the probable effect of each of the following on the exchange rate of a country, other things being equal?

a. The quantity of oil imports is greatly decreased, but the value of imported oil is higher due to price increases.

b. The country's inflation rate falls well below that of its trading partners.

c. Rising labour costs of the country's manufacturers lead to a worsening ability to compete in world markets.

d. The government greatly expands its gifts of food and machinery to developing countries.

e. A major boom occurs with rising employment.

f. The central bank raises interest rates sharply.

g. More domestic oil is discovered and developed.

2. Canada's trade surplus with the United States (or the U.S. trade deficit with Canada) is the cause of considerable concern to some U.S. politicians. Many economists, however, argue that U.S. policymakers should not be concerned with reducing the U.S. trade deficit with Canada primarily because there is no reason to expect a balance between any two countries. Comment on the need for policies to address the U.S. trade deficit with Canada.

3. Outline the reasoning behind the following recent newspaper headline: "Loonie strengthens as Bank of Canada raises rates."

4. "Under a flexible exchange rate system, no country need suffer unemployment, for if its prices are low enough, there will be more than enough demand to keep its factories and farms fully occupied." The evidence suggests that flexible exchange rates have not generally eliminated unemployment. Can you explain why? Can changing exchange rates ever cure unemployment?

5. A recent letter to *The Globe and Mail* said that "the economy of this once wonderful country is in the

sewer and the politicians keep on tinkering, not knowing how to fix it." The letter proposed a 20 percent depreciation of the Canadian dollar, and argued that the immediate effects would be (among other things):

- a dramatic rise in exports
- a dramatic fall in imports
- a large net inflow of new foreign investment

What do you think of the proposal? What would the Bank of Canada have to do to achieve a 20 percent depreciation of the Canadian dollar? If such a depreciation were to take place, is it possible for it to have the effects claimed by the author of the letter? Explain.

6. Many commentators are perplexed when they observe a depreciation of the Canadian dollar but not a reduction in the Canadian current account deficit. Explain why there is not a precise relationship between the value of the dollar and the current account balance. Give one example of an event that would give rise to each of the following:

a. Appreciation of the Canadian dollar and a fall in Canada's current account surplus.
b. Depreciation of the Canadian dollar and a fall in Canada's current account surplus.

Challenges Facing the Developing Countries

myeconlab

The chapter Challenges Facing the Developing Countries can be found on the MyEconLab.

www.myeconlab.com

Mathematical Notes

1. Because one cannot divide by zero, the ratio $\Delta Y / \Delta X$ cannot be evaluated when $\Delta X = 0$. However, as ΔX *approaches* zero, the ratio $\Delta Y / \Delta X$ increases without limit:

$$\lim_{\Delta X \to 0} \frac{\Delta Y}{\Delta X} = \infty$$

Therefore, we say that the slope of a vertical line (when $\Delta X = 0$ for any ΔY) is equal to infinity. (p. 39)

2. Many variables affect the quantity demanded. Using functional notation, the argument of the next several pages of the text can be anticipated. Let Q^D represent the quantity of a commodity demanded and

$$T, \overline{Y}, N, \hat{Y}, p, p_j$$

represent, respectively, tastes, average household income, population, income distribution, the commodity's own price, and the price of the jth other commodity.

The demand function is

$$Q^D = D(T, \overline{Y}, N, \hat{Y}, p, p_j), \qquad j = 1, 2, \ldots, n$$

The demand schedule or curve is given by

$$Q^D = d(p) \Big|_{T, \overline{Y}, N, \hat{Y}, p_j}$$

where the notation means that the variables to the right of the vertical line are held constant.

This function is correctly described as the demand function with respect to price, all other variables being held constant. This function, often written concisely as $Q^D = d(p)$, shifts in response to changes in other variables. Consider average income: if, as is usually hypothesized, $\partial Q^D / \partial \overline{Y} > 0$, then increases in average income shift $Q^D = d(p)$ rightward and decreases in average income shift $Q^D = d(p)$ leftward. Changes in other variables likewise shift this function in the direction implied by the relationship of that variable to the quantity demanded. (p. 48)

3. Quantity demanded is a simple and straightforward but frequently misunderstood concept in everyday use, but it has a clear mathematical meaning. It refers to the dependent variable in the demand function from note 2:

$$Q^D = D(T, \overline{Y}, N, \hat{Y}, p, p_j)$$

It takes on a specific value whenever a specific value is assigned to each of the independent variables. The value of Q^D changes whenever the value of any independent variable is changed. Q^D could change, for example, as a result of a change in any one price, in average income, in the distribution of income, in tastes, or in population. It could also change as a result of the net effect of changes in all of the independent variables occurring at once.

Some textbooks reserve the term *change in quantity demanded* for a movement along a demand curve, that is, a change in Q^D as a result *only* of a change in p. They then use other words for a change in Q^D caused by a change in the other variables in the demand function. This usage is potentially confusing because it gives the single variable Q^D more than one name.

Our usage, which corresponds to that in more advanced treatments, avoids this confusion. We call Q^D quantity demanded and refer to any change in Q^D as a *change in quantity demanded*. In this usage it is correct to say that a movement along a demand curve is a change in quantity demanded, but it is incorrect to say that a change in quantity demanded can occur *only because of* a movement along a demand curve (because Q^D can change for other reasons, for example, a *ceteris paribus* change in average household income). (p. 55)

4. Similar to the way we treated quantity demanded in note 2, let Q^S represent the quantity of a commodity supplied and

$$C, X, p, w_i$$

represent, respectively, producers' goals, technology, the product's price, and the price of the ith input.

The supply function is

$$Q^S = S(C, X, p, w_i), \qquad i = 1, 2, \ldots, m$$

The supply schedule or curve is given by

$$Q^S = s(p) \Big|_{C, X, w_i}$$

This is the supply function with respect to price, all other variables being held constant. This function, often written concisely as $Q^S = s(p)$, shifts in response to changes in other variables. (p. 56)

5. Equilibrium occurs where $Q^D = Q^S$. For *specified values of all other variables,* this requires that

$$d(p) = s(p) \qquad [5.1]$$

Equation 5.1 defines an equilibrium value of p; hence, although p is an *independent* or *exogenous* variable in each of the supply and demand functions, it is an *endogenous* variable in the economic model that imposes the equilibrium condition expressed in Equation 5.1. Price is endogenous because it is assumed to adjust to bring about equality between quantity demanded and quantity supplied. Equilibrium quantity, also an endogenous variable, is determined by substituting the equilibrium price into either $d(p)$ or $s(p)$.

Graphically, Equation 5.1 is satisfied only at the point where the demand and supply curves intersect. Thus, supply and demand curves are said to determine the equilibrium values of the endogenous variables, price and quantity. A shift in any of the independent variables held constant in the d and s functions will shift the demand or supply curves and lead to different equilibrium values for price and quantity. (p. 62)

6. The axis reversal arose in the following way. Alfred Marshall (1842–1924) theorized in terms of "demand price" and "supply price," these being the prices that would lead to a given quantity being demanded or supplied. Thus,

$$p^D = d(Q) \qquad [6.1]$$
$$p^S = s(Q) \qquad [6.2]$$

and the condition of equilibrium is

$$d(Q) = s(Q)$$

When graphing the behavioural relationships expressed in Equations 6.1 and 6.2, Marshall naturally put the independent variable, Q, on the horizontal axis.

Leon Walras (1834–1910), whose formulation of the working of a competitive market has become the accepted one, focused on quantity demanded and quantity supplied *at a given price.* Thus,

$$Q^D = d(p)$$
$$Q^S = s(p)$$

and the condition of equilibrium is

$$d(p) = s(p)$$

Walras did not use graphical representation. Had he done so, he would surely have placed p (his independent variable) on the horizontal axis.

Marshall, among his other influences on later generations of economists, was the great popularizer of graphical analysis in economics. Today, we use his graphs, even for Walras's analysis. The axis reversal is thus one of those historical accidents that seem odd to people who did not live through the "perfectly natural" sequence of steps that produced it. (p. 62)

7. The definition in the text uses finite changes and is called *arc elasticity.* The parallel definition using derivatives is

$$\eta = \frac{dQ}{dp} \cdot \frac{p}{Q}$$

and is called *point elasticity.* Further discussion appears in the Appendix to Chapter 4. (p. 76)

8. The propositions in the text are proved as follows. Letting *TE* stand for total expenditure, we can write

$$TE = p \cdot Q$$

It follows that the change in total expenditure is

$$dTE = Q \cdot dp + p \cdot dQ \qquad [8.1]$$

Multiplying and dividing both terms on the right-hand side of Equation 8.1 by $p \cdot Q$ yields

$$dTE = \left[\frac{dp}{p} + \frac{dQ}{Q} \right] \cdot (p \cdot Q)$$

Because dp and dQ are opposite in sign as we move along the demand curve, dTE will have the same sign as the term in brackets on the right-hand side that dominates—that is, on which percentage change is largest.

A second way of arranging Equation 8.1 is to divide both sides by dp to get

$$\frac{dTE}{dp} = Q + p \cdot \frac{dQ}{dp} \qquad [8.2]$$

From the definition of point elasticity in note 7, however,

$$Q \cdot \eta = p \cdot \frac{dQ}{dp} \qquad [8.3]$$

which we can substitute into Equation 8.1 to obtain

$$\frac{dTE}{dp} = Q + Q \cdot \eta = Q \cdot (1 + \eta) \qquad [8.4]$$

Because η is a negative number, the sign of the right-hand side of Equation 8.4 is negative if the absolute value of η exceeds unity (elastic demand) and positive if it is less than unity (inelastic demand).

Total expenditure is maximized when dTE/dp is equal to zero. As can be seen from Equation 8.4, this occurs when elasticity is equal to -1. (p. 80)

9. The distinction made between an incremental change and a marginal change is the distinction for the function $Y = Y(X)$ between $\Delta Y/\Delta X$ and the derivative dY/dX. The latter is the limit of the former as ΔX approaches zero. We shall meet this distinction repeatedly—in this chapter in reference to marginal and incremental *utility* and in later chapters with respect to such concepts as marginal and incremental *product, cost,* and *revenue.* Where Y is a function of more than one variable—for example, $Y = f(X,Z)$—the marginal relationship between Y and X is the partial derivative $\partial Y/\partial X$ rather than the total derivative, dY/dX. (p. 117)

10. The hypothesis of diminishing marginal utility requires that we can measure utility of consumption by a function

$$U = U(X_1, X_2, \ldots, X_n)$$

where $X_1, \ldots, X_n$ are quantities of the n goods consumed by a household. It really embodies two utility hypotheses: first,

$$\partial U/\partial X_i > 0$$

which says that the consumer can get more utility by increasing consumption of the commodity; second,

$$\partial^2 U/\partial X_i^2 < 0$$

which says that the utility of *additional* consumption of some good declines as the amount of that good consumed increases. (p. 118)

11. Because the slope of the indifference curve is negative, it is the absolute value of the slope that declines as one moves downward to the right along the curve. The algebraic value, of course, increases. The phrase *diminishing marginal rate of substitution* thus refers to the absolute, not the algebraic, value of the slope. (p. 136)

12. The relationship between the slope of the budget line and relative prices can be seen as follows. In the two-good example, a change in expenditure (ΔE) is given by the equation

$$\Delta E = p_C \cdot \Delta C + p_F \cdot \Delta F \qquad [12.1]$$

Expenditure is constant for all combinations of F and C that lie on the same budget line. Thus, along such a line we have $\Delta E = 0$. This implies

$$p_C \cdot \Delta C + p_F \cdot \Delta F = 0 \qquad [12.2]$$

and thus

$$\Delta C/\Delta F = -p_F/p_C \qquad [12.3]$$

The ratio $\Delta C/\Delta F$ is the slope of the budget line. It is negative because, with a fixed budget, one must consume less C in order to consume more F. In other words, Equation 12.3 says that the negative of the slope of the budget line is the ratio of the absolute prices (i.e., the relative price). Although prices do not show directly in Figure 6A-3, they are implicit in the budget line: Its slope depends solely on the relative price, while its position, given a fixed money income, depends on the absolute prices of the two goods. (p. 138)

13. *Marginal product,* as defined in the text, is really *incremental* product. More advanced treatments distinguish between this notion and marginal product as the limit of the ratio as ΔL approaches zero. Marginal product thus measures the rate at which total product is changing as one factor is varied and

is the partial derivative of the total product with respect to the variable factor. In symbols,

$$MP = \frac{\partial TP}{\partial L}$$

(p. 156)

14. We have referred specifically both to diminishing *marginal* product and to diminishing *average* product. In most cases, eventually diminishing marginal product implies eventually diminishing average product. This is, however, not necessary, as the accompanying figure shows.

    In this case, marginal product diminishes after v units of the variable factor are employed. Because marginal product falls toward, but never quite reaches, a value of m, average product rises continually toward, but never quite reaches, the same value. (p. 157)

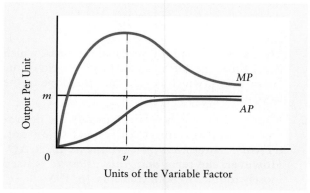

15. Let Q be the quantity of output and L the quantity of the variable factor. In the short run,

$$TP = Q = f(L) \qquad [15.1]$$

We now define

$$AP = \frac{Q}{L} = \frac{f(L)}{L} \qquad [15.2]$$

$$MP = \frac{dQ}{dL} \qquad [15.3]$$

We are concerned with the relationship between AP and MP. Where average product is rising, at a maximum, or falling is determined by its derivative with respect to L:

$$\frac{d(Q/L)}{dL} = \frac{L \cdot (dQ/dL) - Q}{L^2} \qquad [15.4]$$

This may be rewritten

$$\frac{1}{L} \cdot \left[\frac{dQ}{dL} - \frac{Q}{L} \right] = \frac{1}{L} \cdot (MP - AP) \qquad [15.5]$$

Clearly, when MP is greater than AP, the expression in Equation 15.5 is positive and thus AP is rising. When MP is less than AP, AP is falling. When they are equal, AP is neither rising nor falling. (p. 158)

16. The text defines *incremental cost*. Strictly, marginal cost is the rate of change of total cost with respect to output, Q. Thus,

$$MC = \frac{dTC}{dQ}$$

From the definitions, $TC = TFC + TVC$. Fixed costs are not a function of output. Thus, we may write $TC = Z + f(Q)$, where $f(Q)$ is total variable costs and Z is a constant. From this we see that $MC = df(Q)/dQ$. MC is thus independent of the size of the fixed costs. (p. 160)

17. This point is easily seen if a little algebra is used:

$$AVC = \frac{TVC}{Q}$$

but note that $TVC = L \cdot w$ and $Q = AP \cdot L$, where L is the quantity of the variable factor used and w is its cost per unit. Therefore,

$$AVC = \frac{L \cdot w}{AP \cdot L} = \frac{w}{AP}$$

Because w is a constant, it follows that AVC and AP vary inversely with each other, and when AP is at its maximum value, AVC must be at its minimum value. (p. 162)

18. A little elementary calculus will prove the point:

$$MC = \frac{dTC}{dQ} = \frac{dTVC}{dQ} = \frac{d(L \cdot w)}{dQ}$$

If w does not vary with output,

$$MC = \frac{dL}{dQ} \cdot w$$

However, referring to note 15 (Equation 15.3), we see that

$$\frac{dL}{dQ} = \frac{1}{MP}$$

Thus,

$$MC = \frac{w}{MP}$$

Because w is fixed, MC varies negatively with MP. When MP is at a maximum, MC is at a minimum. (p. 163)

19. Strictly speaking, the marginal rate of substitution refers to the slope of the tangent to the isoquant at a particular point, whereas the calculations in Table 8A-1 refer to the average rate of substitution between two distinct points on the isoquant. Assume a production function

$$Q = Q(K, L) \qquad [19.1]$$

Isoquants are given by the function

$$K = I(L, \overline{Q}) \qquad [19.2]$$

derived from Equation 19.1 by expressing K as an explicit function of L and Q. A single isoquant relates to a particular level of output, $\overline{Q}$. Define Q_K and Q_L as an alternative, more compact notation for $\partial Q/\partial K$ and $\partial Q/\partial L$, the marginal products of capital and labour. Also, let Q_{KK} and Q_{LL} stand for $\partial^2 Q/\partial K^2$ and $\partial^2 Q/\partial L^2$, respectively. To obtain the slope of the isoquant, totally differentiate Equation 19.1 to obtain

$$dQ = Q_K \cdot dK + Q_L \cdot dL$$

Then, because we are moving along a single isoquant, set $dQ = 0$ to obtain

$$\frac{dK}{dL} = -\frac{Q_L}{Q_K} = MRS$$

Diminishing marginal productivity implies $Q_{LL} < 0$ and $Q_{KK} < 0$, and hence, as we move down the isoquant of Figure 8A-1, Q_K is rising and Q_L is falling, so the absolute value of MRS is diminishing. This is called the *hypothesis of a diminishing marginal rate of substitution*. (p. 186)

20. Formally, the problem is to choose K and L in order to maximize

$$Q = Q(K, L)$$

subject to the constraint

$$p_K \cdot K + p_L \cdot L = C$$

To do this, form the Lagrangean,

$$\mathcal{L} = Q(K, L) - \lambda(p_K \cdot K + p_L \cdot L - C)$$

where λ is called the Lagrange multiplier.

The first-order conditions for this maximization problem are

$$Q_K = \lambda \cdot p_K \qquad [20.1]$$
$$Q_L = \lambda \cdot p_L \qquad [20.2]$$
$$p_K \cdot K + p_L \cdot L = C \qquad [20.3]$$

Dividing Equation 20.1 by Equation 20.2 yields

$$\frac{Q_K}{Q_L} = \frac{p_K}{p_L}$$

That is, the ratio of the marginal products, which is -1 times the MRS, is equal to the ratio of the factor prices, which is -1 times the slope of the isocost line. (p. 188)

21. Marginal revenue is mathematically the derivative of total revenue with respect to output, dTR/dQ. Incremental revenue is $\Delta TR/\Delta Q$. However, the term *marginal revenue* is used loosely to refer to both concepts. (p. 195)

22. For notes 22 through 24, it is helpful first to define some terms. Let

$$\pi_n = TR_n - TC_n$$

where π_n is the profit when Q_n units are sold.

If the firm is maximizing its profits by producing Q_n units, it is necessary that its profits be at least as large as the profits at output zero. That is,

$$\pi_n \geq \pi_0 \qquad [22.1]$$

The condition says that profits from producing must be greater than profits from not producing. Condition 22.1 can be rewritten as

$$TR_n - TVC_n - TFC_n \\ \geq TR_0 - TVC_0 - TFC_0 \qquad [22.2]$$

However, note that by definition

$$TR_0 = 0 \qquad [22.3]$$

$$TVC_0 = 0 \qquad [22.4]$$

$$TFC_n = TFC_0 = Z \qquad [22.5]$$

where Z is a constant. By substituting Equations 22.3, 22.4, and 22.5 into Condition 22.2, we get

$$TR_n - TVC_n \geq 0$$

from which we obtain

$$TR_n \geq TVC_n$$

This proves Rule 1.

On a per-unit basis, it becomes

$$\frac{TR_n}{Q_n} \geq \frac{TVC_n}{Q_n} \qquad [22.6]$$

where Q_n is the number of units produced.

Because $TR_n = Q_n \cdot p_n$, where p_n is the price when n units are sold, Condition 22.6 may be rewritten as

$$p_n \geq AVC_n$$

(p. 198)

23. Using elementary calculus, we may prove Rule 2.

$$\pi_n = TR_n - TC_n$$

each of which is a function of output Q. To maximize π, it is necessary that

$$\frac{d\pi}{dQ} = 0 \qquad [23.1]$$

and that

$$\frac{d^2\pi}{dQ^2} < 0 \qquad [23.2]$$

From the definitions,

$$\frac{d\pi}{dQ} = \frac{dTR}{dQ} - \frac{dTC}{dQ} = MR - MC \quad [23.3]$$

From Equations 23.1 and 23.3, a necessary condition for attaining maximum π is $MR - MC = 0$, or $MR = MC$, as is required by Rule 2. (p. 199)

24. To prove that for a negatively sloped demand curve, marginal revenue is less than price, let $p = p(Q)$. Then

$$TR = p \cdot Q = p(Q) \cdot Q$$

$$MR = \frac{dTR}{dQ} = Q \cdot \frac{dp}{dQ} + p$$

For a negatively sloped demand curve, dp/dQ is negative, and thus MR is less than price for positive values of Q. (p. 219)

25. The equation for a downward-sloping straight-line demand curve with price on the vertical axis is

$$p = a - b \cdot Q$$

where $-b$ is the slope of the demand curve. Total revenue is price times quantity:

$$TR = p \cdot Q = a \cdot Q - b \cdot Q^2$$

Marginal revenue is

$$MR = \frac{dTR}{dQ} = a - 2 \cdot b \cdot Q$$

Thus, the MR curve and the demand curve are both straight lines, and the (absolute value of the) slope of the MR curve ($2b$) is twice that of the demand curve (b). (p. 220)

26. The marginal revenue produced by the factor involves two elements: first, the additional output that an extra unit of the factor produces and, second, the change in price of the product that the extra output causes. Let Q be output, R revenue, and L the number of units of the variable factor hired. The contribution to revenue of additional labour is $\partial R / \partial L$. This, in turn, depends on the contribution of the extra labour to output $\partial Q / \partial L$ (the marginal product of the factor) and $\partial R / \partial Q$ (the firm's marginal revenue from the extra output). Thus,

$$\frac{\partial R}{\partial L} = \frac{\partial Q}{\partial L} \cdot \frac{\partial R}{\partial Q}$$

We define the left-hand side as marginal revenue product, MRP. Thus,

$$MRP = MP \cdot MR$$

(p. 301)

27. The proposition that the marginal labour cost is above the average labour cost when the average is rising is essentially the same proposition proved in note 15. Nevertheless, let us do it again, using elementary calculus.

The quantity of labour supplied depends on the wage rate: $L^s = f(w)$. Total labour cost along the supply curve is $w \cdot L^s$. The average cost of labour is $(w \cdot L^s) / L^s = w$. The marginal cost of labour is

$$\frac{d(w \cdot L^s)}{dL^s} = w + L^s \cdot \frac{dw}{dL^s}$$

Rewrite this as

$$MC = AC + L^s \cdot \frac{dw}{dL^s}$$

As long as the supply curve slopes upward, $dw/dL^s > 0$; therefore, $MC > AC$. (p. 332)

28. In the text, we define MPC as an incremental ratio. For mathematical treatment, it is sometimes convenient to define all marginal concepts as derivatives: $MPC = dC/dY_D$, $MPS = dS/dY_D$, and so on. (p. 502)

29. The basic relationship is

$$Y_D = C + S$$

Dividing through by Y_D yields

$$\frac{Y_D}{Y_D} = \frac{C}{Y_D} + \frac{S}{Y_D}$$

and thus

$$1 = APC + APS$$

Next, take the first difference of the basic relationship to get

$$\Delta Y_D = \Delta C + \Delta S$$

Dividing through by ΔY_D gives

$$\frac{\Delta Y_D}{\Delta Y_D} = \frac{\Delta C}{\Delta Y_D} + \frac{\Delta S}{\Delta Y_D}$$

and thus

$$1 = MPC + MPS$$

(p. 504)

30. The total expenditure over all rounds is the sum of an infinite series. If we let A stand for autonomous expenditure and z for the marginal propensity to spend, the change in autonomous expenditure is ΔA in the first round, $z \cdot \Delta A$ in the second, $z^2 \cdot \Delta A$ in the third, and so on. This can be written as

$$\Delta A \cdot (1 + z + z^2 + \ldots + z^n)$$

If z is less than 1, the series in parentheses converges to $1/(1 - z)$ as n approaches infinity. The total change in expenditure is thus $\Delta A/(1 - z)$. In the example in the box, $z = 0.80$; therefore, the change in total expenditure is

$$\frac{\Delta A}{1 - z} = \frac{\Delta A}{0.2} = 5 \cdot \Delta A$$

(p. 516)

31. This is based on what is called the "rule of 72." Any sum growing at the rate of X percent per year will double in approximately $72/X$ years. For two sums growing at the rates of X percent and Y percent per year, the *difference* between the two sums will double in approximately $72/(X - Y)$ years. (pp. 604, 613)

32. The time taken to break even is a function of the *difference* in growth rates, not their *levels*. Thus, if 4 percent and 5 percent or 5 percent and 6 percent had been used in the example, it still would have taken the same number of years. To see this quickly, recognize that we are interested in the ratio of two exponential growth paths:

$$\frac{e^{r_1 t}}{e^{r_2 t}} = e^{(r_1 - r_2)t}$$

(p. 616)

33. A simple example of a production function is $GDP = z(LK)^{1/2}$. This equation says that to find the amount of GDP produced, multiply the amount of labour by the amount of capital, take the square root, and multiply the result by the constant z. This production function has positive but diminishing marginal returns to either factor. This can be seen by evaluating the first and second partial derivatives and showing the first derivatives to be positive and the second derivatives to be negative.

For example,

$$\frac{\partial GDP}{\partial K} = \frac{z \cdot L^{1/2}}{2 \cdot K^{1/2}} > 0$$

and

$$\frac{\partial^2 GDP}{\partial K^2} = -\frac{z \cdot L^{1/2}}{4 \cdot K^{3/2}} < 0$$

(p. 624)

34. The production function GDP $= z(LK)^{1/2}$ displays contant returns to scale. To see this, multiply both L and K by the same constant, θ, and see that this multiplies the whole value of GDP by θ:

$$z(\theta L \cdot \theta K)^{1/2} = z(\theta^2 \cdot LK)^{1/2} = \theta z(LK)^{1/2} = \theta \cdot \text{GDP}$$

(p. 626)

35. This is easily proved. The banking system wants sufficient deposits (D) to establish the target ratio (v) of deposits to reserves (R). This gives $R/D = v$. Any change in D of size ΔD has to be accompanied by a change in R of ΔR of sufficient size to restore v. Thus, $\Delta R/\Delta D = v$, so $\Delta D = \Delta R/v$ and $\Delta D/\Delta R = 1/v$. This can be shown also in terms of the deposits created by the sequence in Table 27-7. Let v be the reserve ratio and $e = 1 - v$ be the excess reserves per dollar of new deposits. If X dollars are initially deposited in the system, the successive rounds of new deposits will be X, eX, e^2X, e^3X,.... The series

$$X + eX + e^2X + e^3X + \ldots$$
$$= X \cdot [1 + e + e^2 + e^3 + \ldots]$$

has a limit of $X \cdot \dfrac{1}{1 - e}$

$$= X \cdot \frac{1}{1 - (1 - v)} = \frac{X}{v}$$

This is the total new deposits created by an injection of X of new reserves into the banking system. For example, when $v = 0.20$, an injection of $100 into the system will lead to an overall increase in deposits of $500. (p. 661)

36. Suppose that the public wishes to hold a fraction, c, of deposits in cash, C. Now suppose that X dollars are injected into the system. Ultimately, this money will be held either as reserves by the banking system or as cash by the public. Thus, we have

$$\Delta C + \Delta R = X$$

From the banking system's reserve behaviour, we have $\Delta R = v \cdot \Delta D$, and from the public's cash behaviour, we have $\Delta C = c \cdot \Delta D$. Substituting into the above equation, we get the result that

$$\Delta D = \frac{X}{v + c}$$

From this we can also relate the change in reserves and the change in cash holdings to the initial injection:

$$\Delta R = \frac{v}{v + c} \cdot X$$

$$\Delta C = \frac{c}{v + c} \cdot X$$

For example, when $v = 0.20$ and $c = 0.05$, an injection of $100 will lead to an increase in reserves of $80, an increase in cash in the hands of the public of $20, and an increase in deposits of $400. (p. 662)

Timeline
of Great
Economists

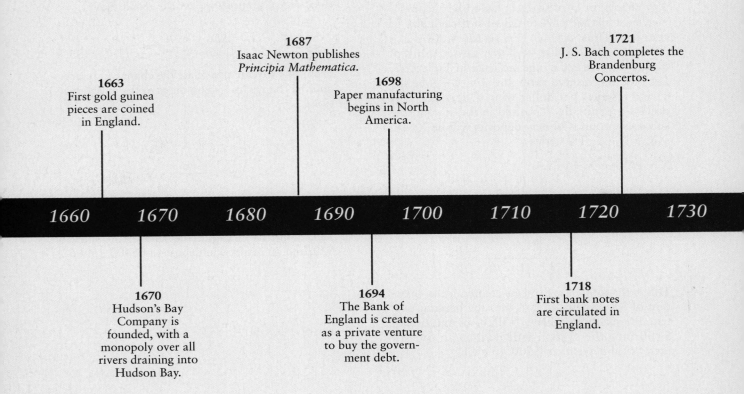

1687
Isaac Newton publishes
Principia Mathematica.

1721
J. S. Bach completes the
Brandenburg
Concertos.

1663
First gold guinea
pieces are coined
in England.

1698
Paper manufacturing
begins in North
America.

1660   1670   1680   1690   1700   1710   1720   1730

1670
Hudson's Bay
Company is
founded, with a
monopoly over all
rivers draining into
Hudson Bay.

1694
The Bank of
England is created
as a private venture
to buy the govern-
ment debt.

1718
First bank notes
are circulated in
England.

ADAM SMITH (1723–1790)

Adam Smith was born in 1723 in the small Scottish town of Kirkcaldy. He is perhaps the single most influential figure in the development of modern economics, and even those who have never studied economics know of his most famous work, *The Wealth of Nations,* and of the terms *laissez-faire* and the *invisible hand,* both attributable to Smith. He was able to describe the workings of the capitalist market economy, the division of labour in production, the role of money, free trade, and the nature of economic growth. Even today, the breadth of his scholarship is considered astounding.

Smith was raised by his mother, as his father had died before his birth. His intellectual promise was discovered early, and at age 14 Smith was sent to study at Glasgow and then at Oxford. He then returned to an appointment as professor of moral philosophy at University of Glasgow, where he became one of the leading philosophers of his day. He lectured on natural theology, ethics, jurisprudence, and political economy to students who travelled from as far away as Russia to hear his lectures.

In 1759, Smith published *The Theory of Moral Sentiments,* in which he attempted to identify the origins of moral judgment. In this early work, Smith writes of the motivation of self-interest and of the morality that keeps it in check. After its publication, Smith left his post at the University of Glasgow to embark on a European tour as the tutor to a young aristocrat, the Duke of Buccleuch, with whom he travelled for two years. In exchange for this assignment Smith was provided with a salary for the remainder of his life. He returned to the small town of his birth and spent the next 10 years alone, writing his most famous work.

An Inquiry into the Nature and Causes of the Wealth of Nations was published in 1776. His contributions in this book (generally known as *The Wealth of Nations*) were revolutionary, and the text became the foundation of much of modern economics. It continues to be reprinted today. Smith rejected the notion that a country's supply of gold and silver was the measure of its wealth—rather, it was the real incomes of the people that determined national wealth. Growth in the real incomes of the country's citizens—that is, economic growth—would result from specialization in production, the division of labour, and the use of money to facilitate trade. Smith provided a framework for analyzing the questions of income growth, value, and distribution.

Smith's work marked the beginning of what is called the Classical period in economic thought, which continued for the next 75 years. This school of thought was centred on the principles of natural liberty (laissez-faire) and the importance of economic growth as a means of bettering the conditions of human existence.

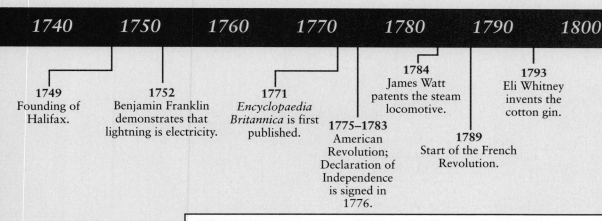

1740   *1750*   *1760*   *1770*   *1780*   *1790*   *1800*

1749
Founding of
Halifax.

1752
Benjamin Franklin
demonstrates that
lightning is electricity.

1771
*Encyclopaedia
Britannica* is first
published.

1775–1783
American
Revolution;
Declaration of
Independence
is signed in
1776.

1784
James Watt
patents the steam
locomotive.

1789
Start of the French
Revolution.

1793
Eli Whitney
invents the
cotton gin.

THOMAS MALTHUS (1766–1834)

Thomas Malthus was born into a reasonably well-to-do English family. He was educated at Cambridge and from 1805 until his death he held the first British professorship of political economy in the East India Company's college at Haileybury. In 1798 he published *An Essay on the Principle of Population as It Affects the Future Improvement of Society,* which was revised many times in subsequent years until finally he published *A Summary View of the Principle of Population* in 1830.

It is these essays on population for which Malthus is best known. His first proposition was that population, when unchecked, would increase in a geometric progression such that the population would double every 25 years. His second proposition was that the means of subsistence (i.e. the food supply) cannot possibly increase faster than in arithmetic progression (increasing by a given number of units every year). The result would be population growth eventually outstripping food production, and thus abject poverty and suffering for the majority of people in every society.

Malthus's population theory had tremendous intellectual influence at the time and became an integral part of the Classical theory of income distribution. However, it is no longer taken as a good description of current or past trends.

DAVID RICARDO (1772–1823)

David Ricardo was born in London to parents who had immigrated from the Netherlands. Ricardo's father was very successful in money markets, and Ricardo himself had earned enough money on the stock exchange that he was very wealthy before he was 30. He had little formal education, but after reading Adam Smith's *The Wealth of Nations* in 1799, he chose to divide his time between studying and writing about political economy and increasing his own personal wealth.

Ricardo's place in the history of economics was assured by his achievement in constructing an abstract model of how capitalism worked. He built an analytic "system" using deductive reasoning that characterizes economic theorizing to the present day. The three critical principles in Ricardo's system were (1) the theory of rent, (2) Thomas Malthus's population principle, and (3) the wages-fund doctrine. Ricardo published *The Principles of Political Economy and Taxation* in 1817, which dominated Classical economics for the following half-century.

Ricardo also contributed the concept of comparative advantage to the study of international trade. Ricardo's theories regarding the gains from trade had some influence on the repeal of the British Corn Laws in 1846—tariffs on the importation of grains into Great Britain—and the subsequent transformation of that country during the nineteenth century from a country of high tariffs to one of completely free trade.

1837
Victoria becomes
Queen of England
(until 1901).
Rebellions in
Upper and Lower
Canada.

1814
British forces burn
Washington, D.C., in the
War of 1812.

1831
The first horse-
drawn buses
appear in
New York.

1800   **1810**   **1820**   **1830**

1805
Admiral Horatio
Nelson's victory
(and death)
at Trafalgar.

1815
Napoleon
defeated at Waterloo
and exiled to
St. Helena;
Corn Laws passed
in Britain.

1822
First textile
mills are built
in Lowell,
Massachusetts.

JOHN STUART MILL (1806–1873)

John Stuart Mill, born in London, was the son of James Mill, a prominent British historian, economist, and philosopher. By age 12 he was acquainted with the major economics works of the day, and at 13 he was correcting the proofs of his father's book, *Elements of Political Economy*. J. S. Mill spent most of his life working at the East India Company—his extraordinarily prolific writing career was conducted entirely as an aside. In 1848 he published his *Principles of Political Economy*, which updated the principles found in Adam Smith's *The Wealth of Nations* and which remained the basic textbook for students of economics until the end of the nineteenth century. In *Principles*, Mill made an important contribution to the economics discipline by distinguishing between the economics of production and of distribution. He pointed out that economic laws had nothing to do with the distribution of wealth, which was a societal matter, but had everything to do with production.

Previous to Mill's *Principles* was his *System of Logic* (1843), which was the century's most influential text on logic and the theory of knowledge. His essays on ethics, contemporary culture, and freedom of speech, such as *Utilitarianism* and *On Liberty,* are still widely studied today.

KARL MARX *(1818–1883)*

Karl Marx was born in Trier, Germany (then part of Prussia), and studied law, history, and philosophy at the universities of Bonn, Berlin, and Jena. Marx travelled between Prussia, Paris, and Brussels, working at various jobs until finally settling in London in 1849, where he lived the remainder of his life. Most of his time was spent in the mainly unpaid pursuits of writing and studying economics in the library of the British Museum. Marx's contributions to economics are intricately bound to his views of history and society. *The Communist Manifesto* was published with Friedrich Engels in 1848, his *Critique of Political Economy* in 1859, and in 1867 the first volume of *Das Kapital*. (The remaining volumes, edited by Engels, were published after Marx's death.)

For Marx, capitalism was a stage in an evolutionary process from a primitive agricultural economy toward an inevitable elimination of private property and the class structure. Marx's "labour theory of value," whereby the quantity of labour used in the manufacture of a product determined its value, held the central place in his economic thought. He believed that the worker provided "surplus value" to the capitalist. The capitalist would then use the profit arising from this surplus value to reinvest in plant and machinery. Through time, more would be spent for plant and machinery than for wages, which would lead to lower profits (since profits arose only from the surplus value from labour) and a resulting squeeze in the real income of workers. Marx believed that in the capitalists' effort to maintain profits in this unstable system, there would emerge a "reserve army of the unemployed." The resulting class conflict would become increasingly acute until revolution by the workers would overthrow capitalism.

1859
Charles Darwin publishes *On the Origin of Species*.

1846
Britain repeals the Corn Laws.

1867
British North America Act establishes the Dominion of Canada. Alfred Nobel invents dynamite.

1840   *1850*   *1860*   *1870*

1844
Electric telegraph opens between Washington and Baltimore.

1861–1865
The U.S. Civil War; Abraham Lincoln is assassinated in 1865.

1869
Opening of the Suez Canal.

1840
Act of Union unites Upper and Lower Canada.

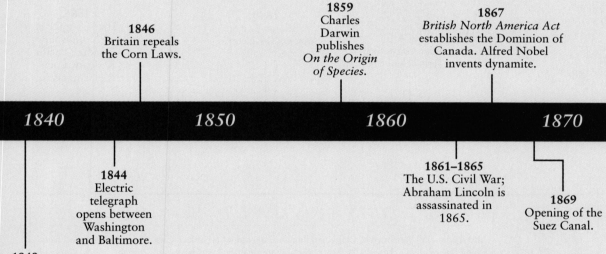

LEON WALRAS *(1834–1910)*

Leon Walras was born in France, the son of an economist. After being trained inauspiciously in engineering and performing poorly in mathematics, Walras spent some time pursuing other endeavours, such as novel writing and working for the railway. Eventually he promised his father he would study economics, and by 1870 he was given a professorship in economics in the Faculty of Law at the University of Lausanne in Switzerland. Once there, Walras began the feverish activity that eventually led to his important contributions to economic theory.

In the 1870s, Walras was one of three economists to put forward the marginal utility theory of value (simultaneously with William Stanley Jevons of England and Carl Menger of Austria). Further, he constructed a mathematical model of general equilibrium using a system of simultaneous equations that he used to argue that equilibrium prices and quantities are uniquely determined. Central to general equilibrium analysis is the notion that the prices and quantities of all commodities are determined simultaneously because the whole system is interdependent. Walras's most important work was *Elements of Pure Economics*, published in 1874. In addition to all of Walras's other accomplishments in economics (and despite his early poor performance in mathematics!), we today regard him as the founder of mathematical economics.

Leon Walras and Alfred Marshall are regarded by many economists to be the two most important economic theorists who ever lived. Much of the framework of economic theory studied today is either Walrasian or Marshallian in character.

CARL MENGER (1840–1921)

Carl Menger was born in Galicia (then part of Austria), and he came from a family of Austrian civil servants and army officers. After studying law in Prague and Vienna, he turned to economics and in 1871 published *Grundsatze der Volkswirtschaftslehre* (translated as *Principles of Economics*), for which he became famous. He held a professorship at the University of Vienna until 1903. Menger was the founder of a school of thought known as the "Austrian School," which effectively displaced the German historical method on the continent and which survives today as an alternative to mainstream Neoclassical economics.

Menger was one of three economists in the 1870s who independently put forward a theory of value based on marginal utility. Prior to what economists now call the "marginal revolution," value was thought to be derived solely from the inputs of labour and capital. Menger developed the marginal utility theory of value, in which the value of any good is determined by individuals' subjective evaluations of that good. According to Menger, a good has some value if it has the ability to satisfy some human want or desire, and *utility* is the capacity of the good to do so. Menger went on to develop the idea that the individual will maximize total utility at the point where the last unit of each good consumed provides equal utility—that is, where marginal utilities are equal.

Menger's emphasis on the marginal utility theory of value led him to focus on consumption rather than production as the determinant of price. Menger focused only on the demand for goods and largely ignored the supply. It would remain for Alfred Marshall and Leon Walras to combine demand and supply for a more complete picture of price determination.

1871
The Great Fire destroys much of Chicago.

1876
Alexander Graham Bell founds Bell Telephone Co.

1880
Thomas Edison invents the electric light bulb.

1885
The last spike is driven on the Canadian Pacific Railway. Louis Riel is hanged.

1870   *1875*   *1880*   *1885*

ALFRED MARSHALL (1842–1924)

Alfred Marshall was born in Clapham, England, the son of a bank cashier, and was descended from a long line of clerics. Marshall's father, despite intense effort, was unable to steer the young Marshall into the church. Instead, Marshall followed his passion for mathematics at Cambridge and chose economics as a field of study after reading J. S. Mill's *Principles of Political Economy*. His career was then spent mainly at Cambridge, where he taught economics to John Maynard Keynes, Arthur Pigou, Joan Robinson, and countless other British theorists in the "Cambridge tradition." His *Principles of Economics*, published in 1890, replaced Mill's *Principles* as the dominant economics textbook of English-speaking universities.

Marshall institutionalized modern marginal analysis, the basic concepts of supply and demand, and perhaps most importantly the notion of economic equilibrium resulting from the interaction of supply and demand. He also pioneered partial equilibrium analysis—examining the forces of supply and demand in a particular market provided that all other influences can be excluded, *ceteris paribus*.

Although many of the ideas had been put forward by previous writers, Marshall was able to synthesize the previous analyses of utility and cost and present a thorough and complete statement of the laws of demand and supply. Marshall refined and developed microeconomic theory to such a degree that much of what he wrote would be familiar to students of this textbook today.

It is also interesting to note that although Alfred Marshall and Leon Walras were simultaneously expanding the frontiers of economic theory, there was almost no communication between the two men. Though Marshall chose partial equilibrium analysis as the appropriate method for dealing with selected markets in a complex world, he did acknowledge the correctness of Walras's general equilibrium system. Walras, on the other hand, was adamant (and sometimes rude) in his opposition to the methods that Marshall was putting forward. History has shown that both the partial and the general equilibrium approaches to economic analysis are required for understanding the functioning of the economy.

THORSTEIN VEBLEN (1857–1929)

Thorstein Veblen was born on a farm in Wisconsin to Norwegian parents. He received his Ph.D. in philosophy from Yale University, after which he returned to his father's farm because he was unable to secure an academic position. For seven years he remained there, reading voraciously on economics and other social sciences. Eventually, he took academic positions at the University of Chicago, Stanford University, the University of Missouri, and the New School for Social Research (in New York). Veblen was the founder of "institutional economics," the only uniquely North American school of economic thought.

In 1899, Veblen published *The Theory of the Leisure Class,* in which he sought to apply Charles Darwin's evolutionism to the study of modern economic life. He examined problems in the social institutions of the day, and savagely criticized Classical and Neoclassical economic analysis. Although Veblen failed to shift the path of mainstream economic analysis, he did contribute the idea of the importance of long-run institutional studies as a useful complement to short-run price theory analysis. He also reminded the profession that economics is a *social* science, and not merely a branch of mathematics.

Veblen remains most famous today for his idea of "conspicuous consumption." He observed that some commodities were consumed not for their intrinsic qualities but because they carried snob appeal. He suggested that the more expensive such a commodity became, the greater might be its ability to confer status on its purchaser.

1896
First modern Olympic Games are held in Athens. Klondike Gold Rush begins.

1900
J. P. Morgan buys out Andrew Carnegie, forming the biggest business in the world, U.S. Steel.

1890   1895   1900   1905

1889
Gustave Eiffel designs the Eiffel Tower for the Paris World Exposition.

1898
Spanish-American War.

1903
The Wright Brothers' first successful flight.

VILFREDO PARETO (1848–1923)

Vilfredo Pareto was an Italian, born in Paris, and was trained to be an engineer. Though he actually practised as an engineer, he would later succeed Leon Walras to the Chair of Economics in the Faculty of Law at the University of Lausanne.

Pareto built upon the system of general equilibrium that Walras had developed. In his *Cours d'économie politique* (1897) and his *Manuel d'économie politique* (1906) Pareto set forth the foundations of modern welfare economics. He showed that theories of consumer behaviour and exchange could be constructed on assumptions of ordinal utility, rather than cardinal utility, eliminating the need to compare one person's utility with another's. Using the indifference curve analysis developed by F. Y. Edgeworth, Pareto was able to demonstrate that total welfare could be increased by an exchange if one person could be made better off without anyone else becoming worse off. Pareto applied this analysis to consumption and exchange, as well as to production. Pareto's contributions in this area are remembered in economists' references to *Pareto optimality* and *Pareto efficiency*.

JOSEPH SCHUMPETER *(1883–1950)*

Joseph Schumpeter was born in Triesch, Moravia (now in the Czech Republic). He was a university professor and later a Minister of Finance in Austria. In 1932, he emigrated to the United States to avoid the rise to power of Adolf Hitler. He spent his remaining years at Harvard University.

Schumpeter, a pioneering theorist of innovation, emphasized the role of the entrepreneur in economic development. The existence of the entrepreneur meant continuous innovation and waves of adaptation to changing technology. He is best known for his theory of "creative destruction," where the prospect of monopoly profits provides owners the incentive to finance inventions and innovations. One monopoly can replace another with superior technology or a superior product, thereby circumventing the entry barriers of a monopolized industry. He criticized mainstream economists for emphasizing the static (allocative) efficiency of perfect competition—a market structure that would, if it could ever be achieved, retard technological change and economic growth.

Schumpeter's best known works are *The Theory of Economic Development* (1911), *Business Cycles* (1939), and *Capitalism, Socialism and Democracy* (1943).

1908
Henry Ford introduces
the Model T.

1912
Titanic sinks on her
maiden voyage, killing
1513 people.

1914
Opening of the
Panama Canal.
First World War
begins.

1917
Bolshevik Revolution
in Russia brings
V. I. Lenin to power.

1918
Treaty of Versailles ends
First World War.

1905   *1910*   *1915*   *1920*

JOHN MAYNARD KEYNES *(1883–1946)*

John Maynard Keynes was born in Cambridge, England. His parents were both intellectuals, and his father, John Neville Keynes, was a famous logician and writer on economic methodology. The young Keynes was educated at Eton and then at Kings College, Cambridge, where he was a student of Alfred Marshall and Arthur Pigou. His career included appointments to the Treasury in Britain during both World Wars, a leading role in the establishment of the International Monetary Fund (through discussions at Bretton Woods, New Hampshire, in 1944), and editorship of the *Economic Journal* from 1911 to 1945, all in addition to his academic position at Kings College.

Keynes published extensively during his life but his most influential work, *The General Theory of Employment, Interest, and Money,* appeared in 1936. This book was published in the midst of the Great Depression when the output of goods and services had fallen drastically, unemployment was intolerably high, and it had become clear to many that the market would not self-adjust to achieve potential output within an acceptable period of time. Fluctuations in economic activity were familiar at this point, but the failure of the economy to recover rapidly from this depression was unprecedented. Neoclassical economists held that during a downturn both wages and the interest rate would fall low enough to induce investment and employment and cause an expansion. They believed that the persistent unemployment during the 1930s was caused by inflexible wages and they recommended that workers be convinced to accept wage cuts.

Keynes believed that this policy, though perhaps correct for a single industry, was not correct for the entire economy. Widespread wage cuts would reduce the consumption portion of aggregate demand, which would offset any increase in employment. Keynes argued that unemployment could be cured only by manipulating aggregate demand, whereby increased demand (through government expenditure) would increase the price level, reduce real wages, and thereby stimulate employment.

Keynes's views found acceptance after the publication of his *General Theory* and had a profound effect on government policy around the world, particularly in the 1940s, 1950s, and 1960s. As we know from this textbook, Keynes's name is attached to much of macroeconomics, from much of the basic theory to the Keynesian short-run aggregate supply curve and the Keynesian consumption function. His contributions to economics go well beyond what can be mentioned in a few paragraphs—for, in effect, he laid the foundations for modern macroeconomics.

EDWARD CHAMBERLIN *(1899–1967)*

Edward Chamberlin was born in La Conner, Washington, and received his Ph.D. from Harvard University in 1927. He became a full professor at Harvard in 1937 and stayed there until his retirement in 1966. He published *The Theory of Monopolistic Competition* in 1933.

Before Chamberlin's book (which appeared more or less simultaneously with Joan Robinson's *The Economics of Imperfect Competition*), the models of perfect competition and monopoly had been fairly well worked out. Though economists were aware of a middle ground between these two market structures and some analysis of duopoly (two sellers) had been presented, it was Chamberlin and Robinson who closely examined this problem of imperfect markets.

Chamberlin's main contribution was explaining the importance of product differentiation for firms in market structures between perfect competition and monopoly. Chamberlin saw that though there may be a large number of firms in the market (the competitive element), each firm created for itself a unique product or advantage that gave it some control over price (the monopoly element). Specifically, he identified items such as copyrights, trademarks, brand names, and location as monopoly elements behind a product. Though Alfred Marshall regarded price as the only variable in question, Chamberlin saw both price and the product itself as variables under control of the firm in monopolistically competitive markets.

1927	**1929**	**1933**	**1939**	**1940**
Charles Lindbergh flies *Spirit of St. Louis* nonstop from New York to Paris.	Stock market crashes (October 29). Beginning of Great Depression.	Adolf Hitler becomes German Chancellor.	Germany invades Poland; Second World War begins.	Unemployment Insurance begins as national program in Canada.

1925   **1930**   **1935**   **1940**

1922
The Soviet Union is formed; Joseph Stalin named Secretary General of the Communist Party.

FRIEDRICH AUGUST VON HAYEK *(1899–1992)*

Friedrich von Hayek was born in Vienna and studied at the University of Vienna, where he was trained in the Austrian tradition of economics (a school of thought originating with Carl Menger). He held academic positions at the London School of Economics and the University of Chicago. He returned to Europe in 1962 to the University of Freiburg in what was then West Germany and the University of Salzburg in Austria. He was awarded the Nobel Prize in Economics in 1974.

Hayek contributed new ideas and theories in many different areas of economics, but he is perhaps best known for his general conception of economics as a "coordination problem." His observation of market economies suggested that the relative prices determined in free markets provided the signals that allowed the actions of all decision makers to mesh—even though there was no formal planning taking place to coordinate these actions. He emphasized this "spontaneous order" at work in the economy as the subject matter for economics. The role of knowledge and information in the market process became central to Hayek, an idea that has grown in importance to the economics profession over the years.

Hayek's theory of business cycles provided an example of the breakdown of this coordination. A monetary disturbance (e.g., an increase in the money supply) would distort the signals (relative prices) by artificially raising the return to certain types of economic activity. When the disturbance disappeared, the boom caused by these distorted signals would be followed by a slump. Although Hayek's business-cycle theory was eclipsed by the Keynesian revolution, his emphasis on economics as a coordination problem has had a major influence on contemporary economic thought.

Hayek was also prominent in advocating the virtues of free markets as contributing to human freedom in the broad sense as well as to economic efficiency in the narrow sense. His *The Road to Serfdom* (1944) sounded an alarm about the political and economic implications of the then-growing belief in the virtues of central planning. His *Constitution of Liberty* (1960) is a much deeper philosophical analysis of the forces, economic and otherwise, that contribute to the liberty of the individual.

MILTON FRIEDMAN (b. 1912–2006)

Milton Friedman completed graduate studies in economics at the University of Chicago and at Columbia University, where he received his Ph.D. in 1946. Most of Friedman's academic career was spent as a professor at the University of Chicago, and after retiring in 1977 he was a senior research fellow at the Hoover Institution at Stanford University. Friedman is best known as one of the leading proponents of Monetarism and for his belief in the power of free markets. His work greatly influenced modern macroeconomics.

Friedman made his first significant mark on the profession with the publication of *The Theory of the Consumption Function* in 1957. There he developed the permanent income hypothesis, and argued that consumption depends on long-run average income rather than current disposable income, as it does in Keynesian analysis. This was an early example of a macroeconomic theory that emphasized the importance of forward-looking consumers. In 1963, he co-authored with Anna Schwartz his most influential book, *A Monetary History of the United States, 1867–1960*, where they presented evidence in support of the monetarist view that changes in the supply of money can cause dramatic fluctuations in the level of economic activity. Although this view was seriously challenged by subsequent research, Friedman helped the profession to understand the power of and the limitations of monetary policy. He also introduced (along with Edmund Phelps) the idea that in the long run the Phillips curve is vertical at the natural rate of unemployment. He argued that a tradeoff between inflation and unemployment exists *only* in the short run and that any attempt to maintain unemployment below this natural rate will lead to accelerating inflation.

Capitalism and Freedom (1962) and *Free to Choose* (1980), the latter co-written with his wife, Rose Friedman, are part of Friedman's attempts to communicate his ideas about economics and, in particular, the power of the free market, to a mass audience of non-economists. Both books became international bestsellers, and these books, in addition to his writing for newspapers and magazines, made Milton Friedman one of the most famous modern economists. He was awarded the Nobel Prize in Economics in 1976.

1941
United States enters war after the attack on Pearl Harbor (December 7).

1944
Bretton Woods Conference. IMF and World Bank are created.

1945
United States drops atomic bomb on Japan; Second World War ends.

1949
Mao Tse-tung's communists gain control of China.

1957
Treaty of Rome establishes the European Common Market.

1940   *1945*   *1950*   *1955*

JOHN KENNETH GALBRAITH (1908–2006)

John Kenneth Galbraith was born on a farm in Southeastern Ontario, to a family of Scottish-Canadian farmers. He began his undergraduate education at the Ontario Agricultural College in Guelph in 1926 where he studied agricultural economics and animal husbandry. He moved to California to study at the University of California at Berkeley and completed a Ph.D. in agricultural economics in 1934. Galbraith was hired by Harvard University in 1934 and, aside from his government and diplomatic postings, remained on staff there until his death.

Galbraith was heavily influenced by the ideas of John Maynard Keynes, Thorstein Veblen, and the "institutional" school of economics. He rejected the technical and mathematical approach of Neoclassical economics. Instead he emphasized the interplay of economics, politics, culture, and tradition, a combination that does not lend itself well to mathematical modelling. He was much more of a "political economist" in the style of the nineteenth century than a theoretical economist of the late twentieth century.

One of his earliest books was *American Capitalism: The Concept of Countervailing Power* (1952), in which he argued that the competitive model was not a good description of reality in the United States economy, nor was it an ideal to strive for. Rather, he described the U.S. economy as one where big corporations and big unions exert pressure on each other (countervailing power) and, along with an activist government, keep the nation's economy prosperous and stable. His most famous book was *The Affluent Society* (1958), where he argued that the United States had become obsessed with overproducing consumer goods and instead should be making large public investments in highways, education, and other public services. His expression "private opulence and public squalor" became well known, and many would agree is even more relevant today than it was when he wrote the words over 50 years ago. In a later book, *The New Industrial State* (1967), Galbraith argued that very few U.S. industries fit economists' model of perfect competition, and that the economy was dominated by large, powerful firms. In general, Galbraith continued to write about topics that he believed the economics profession had neglected—topics such as advertising, the separation of corporate ownership and management, oligopoly, and government and military spending.

Because of Galbraith's desire to focus on the interplay of economics, politics, and society, he was often criticized (or ignored) by mainstream economists. But he was undeterred. And while many economists disagreed with his approach and some of his political views, he was widely recognized as a gifted and insightful writer and speaker.

KENNETH ARROW (b. 1921)

Kenneth Arrow was born and educated in New York City. He began graduate work at Columbia University and received an M.A. in mathematics in 1941. Over the following ten years, after Arrow had completed his Ph.D. course work, he served in the U.S. Army Air Corps during the Second World War and held various research jobs while searching for a dissertation topic. His dissertation, which earned him his Ph.D. from Columbia in 1951, subsequently became a classic in economics, *Social Choice and Individual Values* (1951). Kenneth Arrow is currently Professor, Emeritus, at Stanford University.

In his 1951 book Arrow presented his "Impossibility Theorem," which we encounter in Chapter 16 of this book. His conclusion that it is not possible to construct a set of voting rules for making public choices that is simultaneously democratic and efficient has led to decades of work by economists, philosophers, and political scientists in the field of social choice theory.

Arrow also made significant contributions in other areas of economics. In 1954 (with Gerard Debreu) he constructed a mathematical model of an economy with many individual, inter-related markets, and proved the existence of a general market-clearing equilibrium. While his model was based on many unrealistic assumptions, including the presence of forward markets in all goods and services (that is, one can pay today to obtain a good or service in the future), many believe that Arrow's proof gave economists valuable insights into the workings of multi-market systems.

Arrow's work in the economics of uncertainty was also a major contribution. In *Essays in the Theory of Risk-Bearing* (1971), he introduced the concepts of moral hazard and adverse selection (among other ideas about risk), which we also encounter in Chapter 16 of this book. Arrow was one of the first economists to develop the idea of "learning by doing"; as producers increase their cumulative output of a product, they gain experience and are then able to produce that product at lower average costs. This idea has played an important role in modern theories of economic growth.

Arrow was awarded the Nobel Prize in 1972 (jointly with British economist John Hicks) and in 2004 was awarded the National Medal of Science, the United States' highest scientific honour.

| 1960 | 1965 | 1970 | 1975 |

1959
St. Lawrence Seaway officially opens.

1962
Cuban Missile Crisis.

1963
U.S. President John F. Kennedy assassinated.

1967
Canada celebrates its Centennial; Montreal hosts Expo '67.

1969
Neil Armstrong is first person to walk on the moon.

1973
First OPEC oil shock.

1975
Bill Gates and Paul Allen found Microsoft Corporation.

PAUL SAMUELSON (b. 1915)

Paul Samuelson was born in Gary, Indiana, the son of a drugstore owner. He received his Ph.D. in economics in 1941 from Harvard University and spent his academic career at the Massachusetts Institute of Technology (MIT), where he is currently Institute Professor of Economics, Emeritus.

Samuelson is generally regarded as one of the greatest economic theorists of the twentieth century. While still a graduate student at Harvard, Samuelson wrote most of *Foundations of Economic Analysis* (1947), which was path-breaking at the time and used mathematical analysis and constrained optimization techniques to shed insight into economic behaviour. He systematized economic theory into a more rigorous mathematical discipline, which has had enormous effects on the way economics is studied today.

Though Samuelson has made major contributions to many branches of economics, three are particularly notable. First, he showed how the central predictions of demand theory could be tested using the "revealed preferences" of consumers from observed market behaviour. Second, in international trade theory, he made important contributions in the analysis of the gains from trade and the effects of tariff protection on the distribution of income. Third, most familiar to readers of this book, he is credited with introducing the 45°-line model of short-run national income determination. This diagram, encountered throughout Chapters 21 and 22 of this book, has become the standard tool for teaching the Keynesian theory of national-income determination in the short run. Samuelson's work has also provided valuable insights in other areas of economics, including government taxation and expenditure, capital theory, and theories of economic growth.

Samuelson is also well known for his famous introductory economics textbook, *Economics,* first published in 1948, which provided a systematic treatment of both micro- and macroeconomics in a way that had not been presented before. In general, he is credited with raising the level of scientific and mathematical analysis in economics. Samuelson was awarded the Nobel Prize in Economics in 1970, and was the first American scholar to receive this honour.

Photo Credits

Index

Key terms and their page references are in boldface. *f* denotes a figure, *t* denotes a table, and *n* denotes a footnote.

A

ability-to-pay principle, 432–433
absolute advantage, 805, 805*t*
absolute costs, 805*t*
absolute price, 68
accelerating inflation, 738–741
acceleration hypothesis, 739
accounting profit, 151–152, 430–431
acquired comparative advantage, 812
acquired differences, 314
adjustable peg system, 857
adjustment asymmetry, 574
adjustment process
  assumptions of, 570
  factor prices and output gap, 572–574
  following negative aggregate demand shock, 579*f*
  following negative aggregate supply shock, 580*f*
  following positive aggregate demand shock, 578*f*
  long-run policy implications, 608
  Phillips curve, 576–577
  potential output and output gap, 571–572
  potential output as "anchor," 574–575
administered price, 248
administrative efficiency, 439
adverse selection, 388
advertising, 249, 262–263
aggregate demand *(AD)*
  flat range, 558
  increases in, 559*f*
  intermediate range, 558
  monetary transmission mechanism, 683–684
  money supply, 684*f*
  steep range, 558
aggregate demand *(AD)* curve, 550

and aggregate expenditure *(AE)* curve, 550
  derivation of, 551*f*
  described, 550
  and monetary equilibrium, 685–686
  shifts in, 551–552
  simple multiplier, 552, 552*f*
  slope of, 550–551, 685–686
aggregate demand shocks, 552
  adjustment process following, 578*f*, 579*f*
  and *AE* curve, 559
  contractionary, 576
  AS curve, shape of, 558–559
  described, 557, 557*f*
  expansionary, 575
  increases in aggregate demand, 559*f*
  long-run equilibrium, 581–582, 581*f*
  multiplier, when price level varies, 557–558, 558*f*
aggregate expenditure *(AE)*
  aggregate expenditure *(AE)* function, 509–511
  curve, 550, 559
  desired aggregate expenditure *(AE)*. *See* desired aggregate expenditure *(AE)*
aggregate expenditure *(AE)* function, 509–510
  described, 510*f*, 532*f*
  downward shifts, 514–515
  government purchases, 531–532
  marginal propensity to spend, 510–511
  net exports, 531–532
  shifts in, 513–515, 514*f*
  slope of, and size of simple multiplier, 516
  upward shifts, 513–514
aggregate production function, 624
  and constant returns to scale, 626
  described, 624
  and diminishing marginal returns, 624–625, 625*f*

  properties of, 624–626
aggregate supply *(AS)*, 554
aggregate supply *(AS)* curve, 553
  costs and output, 553
  increasing slope of, 554
  input prices, changes in, 555
  Keynesian aggregate supply curve, 560
  long-run aggregate supply curve, 581
  positive slope of, 553–554, 554*f*
  prices and output, 553–554
  productivity, changes in, 555
  shape of, 558–559
  shifts in, 554–555, 555*f*
aggregate supply shocks, 554, 560–561, 580–581, 580*f*, 581–582
Akerlof, George, 387, 389
algebra
  of market equilibrium, 64–65
  of simple multiplier, 519
  of simple short-run macro model, 545–546
  of tax incidence, 87
allocative efficiency, 274
  see also market efficiency
  competition policy, 282
  economic regulations, 282
  and externalities, 382*f*
  imperfect competition, 277–278
  as market efficiency, 275*n*
  market failure, 280–281
  monopolistic competition, 278
  monopoly, 277, 280
  oligopoly, 278
  Pareto efficient, 274
  perfect competition, 277, 279–280, 279*f*
  and production possibilities boundary, 275, 276*f*
  and total surplus, 278–280
and illegal activities, 491–492
anti-globalization activists, 13
anticipated inflation, 466, 728
antidumping laws, 833

appreciation, **469**–470, **854**
arbitrage, 233, 235
Arrow, Kenneth, 401, 633*n*
Arrow theorem, 401
artisans, 11–12
Asian crisis, 563, 721, 877–878
asset sales, 855
Association of Coffee Producing Countries (ACPC), 231
assumptions
  conditions of application, 26
  described, 26
  direction of causation, 26
  motives, 26
  physical relations, 26
asymmetric adjustment, 574
asymmetric information, 387
  adverse selection, 388
  importance of, 387
  moral hazard, 387
attitude surveys, 130–131
automated teller machines (ATMs), 181
automatic coordination, 378
automatic fiscal stabilizers, 587–588
autonomous consumption, 501
autonomous expenditures, 498, 509, 509*f*
average cost, 159
average-cost pricing, 283–284
average fixed cost *(AFC)*, 159
average fixed cost *(AFC)* curve, 161, 162*f*
average income, 53
average-marginal relationship, 157–158
average price, 76
average product *(AP)*, 155, 155*f*
average propensity to consume *(APC)*, 502
average propensity to save *(APS)*, 504
average quantity, 76
average revenue *(AR)*, 195, 219
average tax rate, 427, 428
average total cost *(ATC)*, 159